MAGICAL BOOK SERIES

ANALYTICAL REASONING

AN IMPORTANT NOTE

The subject of **Analytical Reasoning** is also given the name of **Logical Reasoning** or **Critical Reasoning**. The author sticks to the title of **Analytical Reasoning** because it includes questions of logic as well as purely analytical questions (such as 'Problem-Solving') in its realm.

MAGICAL BOOK
SERIES

ANALYTICAL REASONING

For Bank PO, Reserve Bank Officers Grades A and B, RRBs, CAT, MAT, GRE, GMAT, XLRI, FMS, LLB Entrance and other competitive exams

MK PANDEY

Dedicated to
Shri Sheo Govind Pandey
(my father)

BSC PUBLISHING CO. PVT. LTD.

SEEKOSITY BOOKS

LDS Marketing
Daryaganj, N.Delhi-2

BSC PUBLISHING CO. PVT. LTD.

First Edition — 1996
Fifth Editon — 2022
Reprint Edition- 2026

ISBN: 978-93-65901-76-4

Price: Rs 495.00

Distributed by

Lov Dev & Sons

96, Chapter House, Daryaganj, N.Delhi-2
Mob.: 9355100299

Printed at

Rama Printers
F-7/B Okhla Phase-1 New Delhi-110020

Contents

Part I: Reasoning based on Logic

Part II: Reasoning based on Rules

Foreword

"To argue well is the end of logic." In an age of material prosperity one would hardly care for logic if it could not take one "beyond this end. We have moved centuries away from Descartes' "I think, therefore I am." In the global village, what others think is equally "important. What I assume may not be what others assume. If this be the case, it becomes imperative for me to know what is wrong with the way I think. Because to argue well is only the means. The end for which we argue or reason is making policy decisions — bureaucratic, "business, diplomatic or domestic — that fetch results.

In order to excel in today's world, it has therefore become necessary to have a sound reasoning. Exams like those for banking and management entrance consider your faculty of reasoning as the prerequisite for success. And for this you need not be a born genius. Not if you read *Analytical Reasoning*, the book in your hand, properly.

The book provides a systematic study and can therefore be read even by the uninitiated. The writer has a pragmatic approach "in mind. And a fine balance has been struck between theory and practice. The writer introduces you to a problem, analyses it in detail in all "its hues and variations, guides you through solved examples and offers you plenty of practice questions. And in case there is any confusion still felt, the answers are provided with explanations at the end of every chapter.

I concur with the writer on what he suggests you on page 12: "Take this book as a journey and if you take this journey as a dedicated, faithful tourist who follows his guide keenly, you will emerge as a master of analytical reasoning." What I would like to add is this: this book is in keeping with the concept of a *modern* journey.

Time was when journeys were inherently arduous. The traveller "had to be up before daybreak. He would get ready, pack his lunch in a *potli* (briefcases were unheard of) and set out at sunrise to make most of the daytime. He would walk and walk, hunger gnawing at his "entrails (the contents of the *potli* had to be sparingly used) and thirst goading him on towards mirages. The journey had to be ended at sunset if he loved life. And how much had he travelled? Thirty to forty miles if he had a robust physique. Similarly, earlier "books" on Reasoning showed little achievement even for an intelligent person. "Besides, the reader had to undergo the travails of travel.

The book in your hand may be compared to hi-tech travel. Bombay to New York is only a matter of hours even for a person of frail physique. And that too comfortably in an airbus with smiling hostesses catering to your needs. The sun does not scorch the traveller. What is it that has made journey so easy? The understanding of the "basics — laws of nature — and their application — technology. In other words, for the reader of this book, concepts and practice exercises.

The book can help anyone and everyone because at every step in life, one has to make up one's mind. For example, see why any reader would recommend the book to others.

Premise: The book has helped me solve questions on Analytical Reasoning correctly.

Assumptions: Like me (before reading the book), others too have more or less the same difficulties.

Inference: The book must help others too to solve questions on Analytical Reasoning correctly.

If a recommendation is based on such a solid inference, it would never go wrong. Once again, an assumption is being made: that the latter reader would be as devoted as the one who recommends. Well, it's time I stopped making assumptions. I *assume* I'll make none (punchline?!).

Foreword to Second Edition

Patterns change with the course of time. And good reasoning must keep in touch with the changing trends. The author has done a wonderful job in updating the book.

Chetananand Singh
Editor, *Banking Services Chronicle*

Author's Preface

Analytical Reasoning is increasingly moving centrestage in today's competitive exams. Whether you plan to join the banking or the management sector, as an officer you will be expected to take decisions. You cannot take a proper course of action unless you can reason analytically. It is this faculty of yours that is judged through the paper of Analytical Reasoning. To score well then means a solid preparation in the paper. It is high time that a book solely devoted to Analytical Reasoning was published. The book, therefore, is intended to fill a long-felt void.

Although humility may not permit so, I would say that there are certain features of this book that make it unique and I would like to mention these features for the benefit of the readers.

First of all, I would like to complain that Reasoning has always been treated as a step-child of the publishing industry. Very few books treat Reasoning as a *subject*. There never was any attempt to familiarise the students with the theoretical aspects of Reasoning. This despite the fact that Logic is a subject offered in the curricula of many Indian universities!! This book seeks to rectify this error.

Secondly, very few authors recognise that the competitive exams of today demand *speed* as strongly as *accuracy*. Hence, an emphasis is needed to provide quicker techniques, wherever possible. This book places due emphasis on this aspect by providing quicker methods wherever possible. However, between *speed* and *conceptual clarity*, the latter has been given the priority.

Without claiming to be exhaustive, the following points make a list of certain special features of this book:

- Conceptual clarity for logical reasoning.
- A new, much quicker analytical method for Syllogism in addition to the method of Venn diagrams.
- Quicker methods for Analytical Decision-Making and Problem-"Solving.
- A complete chapter each on two recently-introduced topics: `Punchlines' and 'Strengthening and Weakening Arguments'.

I sincerely hope that this book will prove immensely beneficial for students appearing in all types of competitive examinations.

Finally, I would like to add that an effort of more than three years has gone into the preparation of this book. Since my articles started appearing in *Banking Services Chronicle* three years ago, many readers have written to me offering some valuable suggestions. Every new suggestion proves to be an asset to the writer and thereby to the readers of the book he writes. I would like to offer my sincerest gratitude to them all. I would also like to thank Mr Manoj Kumar, publisher, Mr Nagendra K. Sinha and Mr Niranjan Bharti, members, Research Team, and Mr Chetananand Singh, editor, *Banking Services Chronicle*, for some valuable suggestions and help in the preparation of the manuscript. And special thanks to Mr Ashok Kumar for helping me with the computer.

Preface to Second Edition

Over the years new topics have been introduced in the exams. There is always a speedier and better way to solve the problem if you look for it. I have made efforts to revise the old topics and simplify the new ones. Hope you continue to be benefited like the earlier readers. Rather, more benefited.

P.S.: No work is perfect. I would be obliged to those who point out the errors of this book. Advices and suggestions for the improvement of the book will be gratefully received.

Preface to the Fourth Edition

When I first wrote this book it was more than 20 years ago. Internet had just arrived in India. Majority of population was still writing handwritten letters to their loved ones.

This book was well received then and has continued to be received well. It became very popular in a very short span of time. After that I have done only one honest sincere revision of the book. Even that is old news as that revision took place around 15 years ago.

Since then, the publishers have continuously requested me to revise the book and I kept on resisting. Because I believe that classics are never to be retold. There are some books in chemistry, medical science, physics, trigonometry, elementary physics etc which were written more than 100 years ago and are considered Bibles in their own field even today.

By the way, is it correct to say that this book is some kind of classic on Analytical Reasoning? As an author I might be biased but there is some merit in the argument. This book was the first to attempt to "teach" the concept of Reasoning before jumping on to solve exercises. Every topic here has been covered using a general technique and a shortcut method as far as possible. This is the first and the only book in which complicated problems of syllogism have been attempted to be solved by four simple formulas.

Well, then why did I agree to revise this book? There are two strong reasons for this. First, looking at the recent pattern of questions, a little bit of focus reallocation was required. This time I agreed with the publisher.

Secondly, there is some merit in the argument that good and clear concepts are a good thing but a little extra practice will never do any harm. So two major changes are there in this edition. Firstly, two new chapters have been added—one chapter builds the foundation of coding technique while the other deals with a special type of coding. Secondly, a lot of practice exercises have been added. The biggest volume has been added to the chapter on problem solving in which more than a hundred new problems have been added along with their detailed solutions.

On a personal level I do not like big, voluminous books. Brevity being the soul of wit, I have tried to maintain and preserve the soul of this classic without adding too much bulk and yet giving sufficient concept elucidation followed by a great deal of practice .

Hope the readers will bless this effort with their continued love and patronage.

Part I
Reasoning Based on Logic

Chapter One

The Basics of Logic

(A Study of Argumentation)

1.1: Introduction

This chapter is a study of argumentation. Argumentation is fundamental to all logic. In logic, we advocate a certain point of view with the help of some evidences and certain assumptions. The whole thing may be called "arguing", or simply "argumentation". As you will see, arguments are the backbone of analytical reasoning and it is very important to understand the way they work. Almost all possible types of questions are in some way related to argumentation: "What is the inference of this argument?", "What are the assumptions of this argument?", "What are the strengthening points of this argument?", "Whether this argument is weak or strong." etc. Hence, I would advise you to go through this chapter very carefully before you move on to the deeper aspects of reasoning.

1.2: What is an argument?

An *argument* is a sequence of two or more phrases, clauses, sentences or statements which includes a claim or a conclusion. This conclusion is arrived at with the help of one or more than one statement which may be called *premise* or *proposition*. In addition, the argument also takes the help of some hidden premises which may be called *assumptions*. The following two examples will illustrate the concept.

Ex 1: The ground was slippery, it must have been raining.

Comments: In the foregoing example, the argument proposes a conclusion that "it must have been raining". This conclusion is arrived at with the help of the supporting evidence or premise that "The ground was slippery". The conclusion and the premise are connected by the assumption (which is not explicitly stated, it is hidden) that "The ground becomes slippery only when it rains."

Thus, a careful postmortem leads to the following break-up of its constituent parts.

Premise: The ground was slippery.

Assumption (hidden premise): The ground becomes slippery only when it rains.

Conclusion: It must have rained.

The foregoing example brings before us the basic characteristics of argumentation. It also leaves some doubts. For example, is the number of premises necessarily one? Is the assumption always present? The answer to both these questions is: NO. In an argument, the number of premises can be more than one as explained in Ex 2. Further, it is not necessary that every argument have an assumption. Remember, an assumption is the hidden premise — a missing link in the chain of logic — and if an argument is complete in itself and does not have missing links, it will not have any assumptions. For example, the following argument has no hidden assumptions:

"The ground was slippery. The ground cannot have become slippery without rains. So, it must have rained."

Ex 2: If Sudha eats rice, Ram also eats rice. If Ram eats rice, Shyam also eats rice. If Shyam eats rice. Manju also eats rice. If Manju eats rice, Madan also eats rice.

Sudha eats rice.

So, Madan also eats rice.

Comments: Here, the first five sentences provide premises. The last sentence provides the conclusion. Obviously, here, there is no hidden assumption as there are no missing links in the argument.

The following diagram clearly states how an argument works.

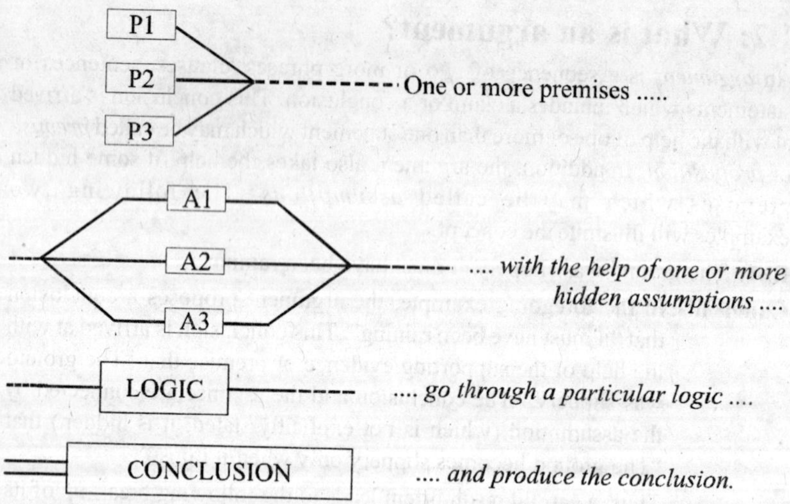

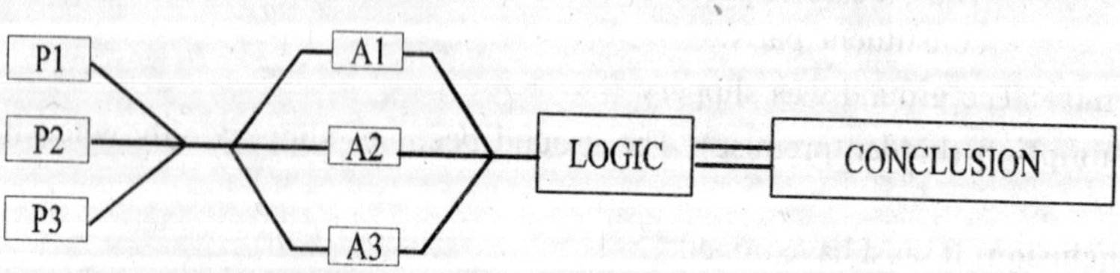

The complete process of argumentation

Thus, it is obvious that in order to gain mastery of argumentation-based reasoning, you will need to

- *differentiate between the premises and the conclusion*
- *identify the assumptions made*
- *understand the logic of the arguments*

Let us look at these aspects one by one.

1.2.1: Identifying the conclusion

A typical passage usually places its conclusion at the end. But this may not be true in many cases. Depending upon the style of the author, the conclusion can be found in the middle or even in the very beginning of the passage. This is illustrated by the following example.

Ex 3:

Format 1. A daily programme of Yoga is believed to increase the average life expectancy and reduce stress of a common individual. Yet, people who want to make Yoga a part of their lives are hampered by lack of adequate information about Yoga training centres. Therefore, Doordarshan should give a priority-based, concessional advertisement for Yoga training centres.

Format 2. Doordarshan should give a priority-based, concessional advertisement for Yoga training centres. A daily programme of yoga is believed to increase the average life expectancy and reduce stress of a common individual. Yet, people who want to make Yoga a part of their lives are hampered by lack of adequate information about Yoga training centres.

Format 3. A daily programme of Yoga is believed to increase the average life expectancy and reduce stress of a common individual. Doordarshan should give a priority-based, concessional advertisement for Yoga training centres. People who want to make Yoga a part of their lives are hampered by lack of adequate information about Yoga training centres.

This example illustrates how the same thing could be rewritten in different ways. If you go by the thumb-rule that a conclusion always appears at the end of a passage you will get different conclusions from the different formats of the same passage. In Format 1, the conclusion appears at the end. The first two lines provide a premise — a case is made out therein for the need for publicity of Yoga training centres. Then is placed the conclusion which says that Doordarshan should provide a concessional and priority-based advertisement for Yoga training centres. But in Format 2, the conclusion appears first and the supporting premises appear later. In Format 3, the conclusion appears in the middle.

This example, therefore, states that in a passage the conclusion can appear anywhere. How can we then identify a conclusion? How do we differentiate a conclusion from a premise?

This is mostly a matter of skill and experience. If you go through passages regularly, your mind develops the ability to identify the conclusion without putting any conscious effort. However, to begin with, you can take the help of the following test:

"What is the author trying to prove here?" If you ask yourself this question, your answer will invariably point towards that portion of the paragraph which is the conclusion. For example, in the preceding example, if you ask yourself this question, what answer will you get? Obviously, what the author wants to prove (say) is that Doordarshan should give concessional advertising for Yoga-training centres. The other two sentences are only facts used by the author to support his conclusion.

There is also another way of testing as to which part of a given passage forms a conclusion. Because the conclusion of the argument can appear anywhere, the authors usually include signals for the reader. Here is a list of words and phrases that are often used to signal a conclusion.

therefore
thus
so
hence
consequently
as a result
it follows that
it can be inferred that
which shows that
which suggests that
which proves that
which means that

If you find one of these signal-words/phrases before any sentence, you can be sure that the sentence is the conclusion. At times, if the signal-words are absent, you can ask yourself this question: **"Before which of these sentences can I put one of these signal-words/phrases?"** The answer will be your conclusion. (Try this method on Ex 3.)

Let us take an example to understand the point.

Ex 4: It is immoral to take something that one has not earned. Gambling winnings are not earned, so gambling is immoral. Therefore, a state government that operates a lottery is acting immorally.

Comments: This argument consists of four propositions.

1. It is immoral to take something that one has not earned.
2. Gambling winnings are not earned.
3. Gambling is immoral.
4. State governments that operate lotteries are acting immorally.

If we try to identify the conclusion of this argument by the first method, i.e., by asking ourselves the question: "What is the author trying to prove here?", what answer do we get? The ultimate conclusion to be proved here is statement 4. Statement 3 is a premise of the conclusion. (However, statement 3 also functions as the conclusion of a sub-argument, of which statement 1 and 2 are the premises). If we attempt to draw a diagram of this argument it would look like this

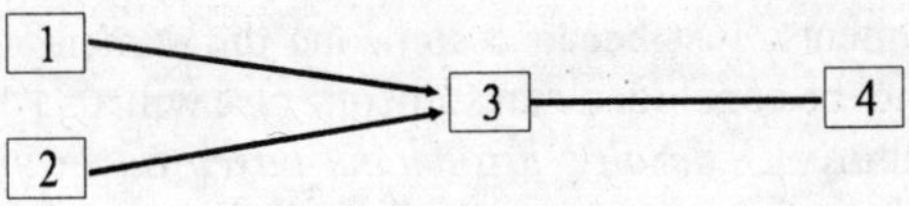

However, if we apply the second method of identifying the conclusion of an argument, i.e., looking for a signal-word, we would readily find that statement 4 is the conclusion because it is preceded by the signal-word *'therefore'*.

1.2.2: Identifying the assumptions

An assumption, as we have already defined it, is the hidden premise - the missing link [see the method of identifying the assumptions in an argument more clearly and more comprehensively in a separate chapter.] (See Chapter 3.)

1.2.3: Understanding the logic: Standard ways of arguing

An argument is usually made to make a point or to strengthen a point or in an effort to convince someone about something. Different people may resort to different techniques while arguing. Some of the commoner ways of arguing are presented below:

(i) Argument by Example

In certain instances, an author or speaker tries to come to a conclusion by citing some example(s) as his premise(s). This is an illustration of arguing by example. The following arguments illustrate the concept:

Ex:- The Indian Union should declare a war on Pakistan because even the United States did so when Libya had resorted to international terrorism.

Ex:- We should follow the policy of non-violence because Gandhiji used to preach and practise it.

Ex:- Bradman was out for a duck in his last Test while Gavaskar scored four in his last one-day international. Therefore, Tendulkar too should be expected to put a dismal score in his last cricket match.

In the three examples mentioned above, three conclusions have been reached. These three conclusions are: "India should declare a war on Pakistan",

"We should follow the policy of non-violence" and "Tendulkar will probably put a dismal score in his last test match". These three conclusions have been arrived at by using certain examples as premises. Thus, "India should declare war on Pakistan" has been inferred by taking the example of the United States, non-violence has been advised by citing Gandhi as an example, while Tendulkar's low score has been predicted by taking the examples of Don Bradman and Sunil Gavaskar.

Comments: You may yourself conclude that examples do not make strong arguments. Just because someone did something in the past, it cannot be concluded that someone else will also do a similar thing in future. *Generally, arguments based on examples are either weak or fallacious.*

(ii) Argument by Analogy

We often use the method of analogy to put forth our argument. Loosely speaking, **analogy is an inference from a resemblance between particular things, events or occasions (that are known) to a further (un known) resemblance.** For example, if we find a fat man jovial and later meet another fat man, we expect him to be jovial too. If we find males more interested in mathematics than females are and if we find males more interested in Physics than females then we expect that males are more interested in astronomy than females. By noting certain resemblance between two or two sets of things we infer that they must resemble in other respects also. Schematically, where a, b, c and d are any entities and P, Q, R are any attributes, an analogical argument may be represented by the form

> a, b, c, d all have the attributes P and Q
> a, b, c have the attribute R
> So, d probably has the attribute R

Ex.A: Congress Party is in favour of privatisation of the economy and so is the BJP. Similarly, the Congress Party favours more autonomy for the States and so does the BJP. The Congress oppose Ram Temple constructed at disputed site. So, BJP will also oppose construction of Ram Temple at the site.

Ex. B: Pakistan and Bangladesh have both lost to India in cricket and kabaddi. So, India should defeat them in hockey also.

Ex. C: Shores of pharmaceutical industries had shot up last year when special package was announced for the pharmaceutical sector. This year special packages have been announced for the software sector. So, software shares should shoot.

In the above three example, a conclusion has been arrived at because of one (or more) similar things have taken place before. Thus, Congress and

BJP are expected to have a similar stance on one more issue because they had identical stances on two previous issues, India is expected to do in Hockey what it did in Kabaddi and Cricket and software shores are expected to do.

(iii) Causal Argument

Causal arguments are one of the commonest ways of arguing. This type of argument tries to relate a cause with a result. It may have many forms. For example, it can have the form: " X is the cause of Y. X has occurred. So Y will occur." or " X is the only cause of Y. Y has occurred. So X must have occurred." or any other such variety of it.

Ex:- The city has been facing the problem of water-logging for ten days. An outbreak of cholera is being feared.

Ex:- The BJP should win the elections because it has an organised cadre.

Ex:- The cricket match has been abandoned. It must have rained.

In the foregoing examples, some effects have been related with some causes. For example, the effects "outbreak of cholera" and "victory in elections" are being expected because their causes, "water-logging" and "organised cadre", exist. In the last example, it is argued that since the effect (*abandoning of match*) has taken place, the cause (*rains*) must have occurred.

Comments: Arguments that are causal in nature may be strong arguments or weak arguments or fallacious arguments. This will depend solely on the degree of certainty that the cause-effect relationship (made in that argument) holds. In the three examples above, the first two are reasonably good arguments; the third one is fallacious. In the first two, it is seen that the cause does usually lead to the effect. In the last example, cause is being predicted because effect has occurred. But the point is that the effect may occur (a match may bc abandoned) because of other reasons as well.

Note: Also see the chapter **"Cause and Effect"**.

(iv) Salesman's Argument

How does a salesman argue? Once a salesman was selling combs on a street. He wanted to convince every interested observer how strong was the stuff which the comb was made of. In his enthusiasm he ventured to demonstrate the unbreakability of the comb by bending it sharply. And then the impossible happened. The comb cracked into two pieces. The salesman looked at the comb for a couple of seconds and then hastily readdressed his audience "And now gentlemen! I would like you to see for yourself how strong and solid the comb is, **even from inside**".

So, that is how salesmen argue. They would speak of the advantages, the benefits of their stand. Hence, a salesman's argument is one where a conclusion is arrived at because of the advantages, positive points and the benefits that it leads to. Such arguments are the commonest in everyday life.

Ex:- Sports will help the students to keep in good health. So, it should be made compulsory for colleges.

Ex:- Religion and politics should be kept apart since religious inclinations will be violative of democratic principles.

Ex:- Strikes disrupt the normal life of the common man. There should be a ban on strikes.

In the above-mentioned examples, some conclusion (or course of action) is advised (or prohibited) because of the advantages (or disadvantages) of pursuing that course of action. Thus, sports are to be made compulsory because it carries the advantage that it will help the students keep in good health. Strikes are being prohibited because they have the negative feature that they disrupt the normal life of the common man.

Comments: Arguments of this nature can be both weak or strong. It depends upon many factors such as:

(i) Is the advantage (disadvantage) being talked about actually true?

(ii) Even if it is true, does the suggested course of action look a practically possible and reasonable policy to follow?

We would look at such arguments in greater detail when we discuss the forcefulness of arguments exclusively. Presently, I would only state that the first example is a weak argument while the remaining two are strong arguments.

(v) Argument based on Chronology

Sometimes a conclusion is arrived at solely on the basis of the chronological order of some events. Some examples are:

Ex:- "I arrived at the house at 10:30 AM. I rang the call-bell and waited. The door opened. A lady welcomed me inside and made me sit on a sofa, taking off my hat and overcoat. I looked at my watch, it was 10:33. I read the newspaper for the next 15 minutes or so. And then I went inside to see if the lady had forgotten about me. It would be around 10:50 when I entered the room."

The murder was committed at about 10:55. Therefore, this man (whose statement is quoted above) must have either committed the murder or seen the act of murder.

Ex:- Television was invented many years after radio. Therefore, a television has a technology superior to that of a radio.

Ex:- The song "Tamma Tamma Loge" was released two months earlier than "Jumma Chumma". So, the former could not be a copy of the latter.

In all the foregoing examples, the order of some events (their chronology) is made the basis of predicting something. Thus, I entered the room at 10:50, where a murder was committed at 10:55; so I must have been a part of the crime. Or, since TV came after radio, TV should be technologically advanced compared to the radio. Similarly, because the release of a song X preceded that of another song Y, X could not have been a copy of Y.

Comments: Unless elaborately detailed and minutely justified, arguments of this type are usually unconvincing and weak. All the three arguments above are weak. The second argument could have been strong if it had been added that technology always develops towards more complex objects.

For example, in the first example above, it is assumed that if the man entered the room at 10:50 and if the murder took place at 10:55, then he must have some vital information about the murder. But, what about the possibility that he entered the room at 10:50, left at 10:52, came back to the drawing room and was sitting in the drawing room at 10:55 when the murder took place in the lady's room? Similarly, in example 2, it is assumed that a technologically superior object **always** comes **after** an inferior object. This may be true 99% of the times, but not always. So, the inference could be questioned here. In the last example, the dates of release of two songs is made the basis of the conclusion that one could not have been the copy of the other. But what about the date of recording? It might have happened that "Jumma Chumma" was recorded earlier although released later than the number "Tamma Tamma". In this case, a possibility of copying cannot be ruled out.

The above, then, is a detailed study of the standard ways of argumentation. Although, there are many more ways in which arguments are made, these are one of the commonest types of arguments. [Some other ways of argumentation include **argument by negation, argument by force, argument using trapping questions** etc. All these are fallacious ways of arguing and should be discussed for fun and nothing more. There must be some friends of yours who prefer these ways of argumentation during discussions. Look at some examples:

Argument by negation: He is not guilty because this is impossible.

Argument by force: He is not guilty. Accept it or I will break your head. (!!)

Argument using trapping questions: Suppose I tell you that I always lie, will you accept this as true or false? Therefore, believe me if I told you that he is not guilty.

Arguments by challenge: He is not guilty. Accept it or prove that he is guilty.

Thus, in this chapter we have seen how an argument works. We have seen that there are three essential constituents of an argument: premises, assumptions and conclusion; and these three are related in a particular fashion or logic. **Questions on analytical reasoning seek to test your understanding of all these aspects. Thus, some common questions are worded as:**

Type I: Is this conclusion true or false? (Is this conclusion probably or definitely true/probably or definitely false?)

Type II: Is this an assumption of the argument?

Type III: Is it a strong (forceful) argument?

Type IV: Does this premise strengthen (or weaken) the main argument?

We shall study each of these problems separately in subsequent chapters. The realms of analytical reasoning are very wide and very interesting: take this book as a journey and if you take this journey as a dedicated, faithful tourist who follows his guide keenly, you will emerge as a master of analytical reasoning. The journey - by the way - has *already begun.*

Summary

- Arguments are the fundamental units of logic.
- An argument contains two explicit constituents: supporting **premises** and **conclusion**. There is also an implicit (hidden) constituent called **assumption**.
- It is important that you are able to identify each of these constituents. Further, it is also important that you understand the logic with which the conclusion is reached.
- To identify a conclusion you can follow either of the two methods. In the first method, you should ask yourself this question: **"What is the author trying to prove?"** In the second method, you should look for certain signal-words/phrases such as

  therefore
  thus
  so
  hence
  consequently
  as a result
  if follows that
  it can be inferred that
  which shows that
  which suggests that
  which proves that
  which means that

  If there are no signal-words, you may ask yourself this question: **"Before which of the sentences can I put one of these signal-words?"**.
- In order to identify an assumption you must identify the missing link in the logical chain. These methods are comprehensively covered in Chapter 3.
- There are many ways of arguing. Some of these include: argument by example, argument by analogy, argument by causal relationships, argument by chronology, argument by blind advocacy (salesman's arguments), etc.

Chapter Two

Some Informal Tips

2.1: Introduction

Questions on reasoning are not very difficult. In fact, they are very easy. Usually, the examiner tries to frame questions which are difficult - this is true. But remember that the examiner must take that answer as correct which looks obvious. **When the examiner is framing choices, he knows that he has to frame one correct choice and all the other three (or four) choices must be wrong.** Therefore, he has to face the responsibility of ensuring that the wrong choices are not very close to the correct choice. This means that it will be very difficult for him to frame a very difficult question which has very close choices. This makes the examiner look for some other tactics. **These tactics include saying something obliquely, highlighting some unimportant information, underplaying a vital information, using complicated language** etc.

We can have a look at some of these tactics by looking at some of the following examples:

(i) "Raman is the most intelligent person of the class." may be said as "No one in the class has as much intelligence as Raman." (Here, the matter is told obliquely.)

(ii) "He over-ate" can be said as "He partook of more food than what could be considered wholesome for his constitution". (Here, complicated language tries to confuse you.)

(iii) "Madan is Sohan's father" may be told as "Madan is the only son of Soni's mother's father-in-law". (Here, again, complicated language tries to confuse you.)

You must pardon the examiner for taking to such tactics because, as I have already pointed out, it is very difficult for him to frame questions where the wrong answers can be differentiated from the correct ones but still they be very close.

2.2: Strategy

In this chapter, we will see some of these tactics. We shall also see how to defeat the purpose of the examiner, i.e., how not to be misled. The last chapter gave you a solid concept of argumentation - something that could work as a foundation for you in later chapters. In this chapter, we will look at some informal aspects of the same.

1. Read like a detective

As I have already pointed out, the examiner - in his desperate attempt to frame a tough problem - uses evasive language. **He will use a language that**

would create one impression but would have another meaning. In order to defeat this tactic, you should think of yourself as Sherlock Holmes, the greatest detective. Try to develop a "mental magnifying glass" and just as a detective studies the scene of crime in minute details with the help of a magnifying glass, you should also develop the ability to read a question (or a passage) like a detective. Read carefully, read in the most minute details, read with a smile on your face, read while telling yourself:

Dear examiner, you cannot fool me.

The following few examples will illustrate how a careful reading can give a different meaning to a passage that gives a different impression on the first reading.

Ex. 1: "Eat only Brand X low-sugar chocolates. Four out of five doctors surveyed recommend Brand X low-sugar chocolates for their patients who eat chocolates." — an advertisement

Comments: This is an advertisement and you may have seen a similar advertisement somewhere or the other. This is a classic example of how words can be used to highlight the non-significant aspects, underplay the important information and, overall, create a wrong impression.

On a first and casual reading: On a first and casual reading the advertisement may give the impression that 80 per cent of all doctors recommend that people eat Brand X sugarless chocolates.

On a careful, microscopic reading: On a closer examination, however, it will be revealed that the claim is much less ambitious. There are many shortcomings in the advertisement. These are:

1. *Why only Brand X?*: First of all, the advertisement says that you should eat *only* Brand X chocolates. But the subsequent premise does not say that the doctors do not recommend any other brand of sugarless chocolates. They do recommend Brand X, but it is not said that they recommend only Brand X.
2. **Recommendation only for those who eat chocolates:** Second, the advertisement does not claim that the doctors recommend that people should eat chocolates. They recommend Brand X sugarless chocolates but only to *those who eat chocolates*. The claim is that the doctors recommend that patients who eat chocolates should eat sugarless chocolates. Actually, the doctors surveyed might be universally opposed to all chocolate-eating but regard the eating of sugarless chocolates as the lesser of the two evils.
3. **Recommendation only by a section of (and not all) doctors:** Finally, the advertisement does not make a claim about all doctors. Notice that the advertisement takes the support of four out of five doctors *surveyed*. The ad does not state how many doctors were in the survey. Was their number large enough to reach an unbiased conclusion? It may happen that only five doctors were surveyed and by some stroke of luck, four of them recom-

mended brand X. Naturally, a small sample of doctors cannot be said to represent the "true opinion of doctors" in general.

Thus, you may see how clever words can create one impression and mean something else. Once you understand the clever way in which the claim in the example above is qualified, you can see that the claim does not provide any really good reason for eating Brand X sugarless chocolates. Let us look at another example to understand why you should - as I have already pointed out - *read like a detective.*

Ex 2: "Only Good-fight mosquito repellants can give you twenty-four-hour protection from mosquitoes and that special Good-fight scent" — an advertisement

Comments: On a first casual reading, this advertisement gives an impression that only Good-fight mosquito repellant can give 24-hour protection against mosquitoes. It also means that only Good-fight mosquito-repellants can give that special Good-fight scent. But, in standard terms, there is a vast difference between 'and' and 'or'. Notice the "and" in the advertisement. See how this "and" gives it a different meaning from what an "or" would have given it. Because of this "and" the meaning of the advertisement can be broken up as:

(1) twenty-four hour protection from mosquitoes,

(2) the special Good-fight s*cent.*

Only a Good-fight mosquito repellant can give **both**(1) **and** (2).

But, this is hardly surprising because no other brand can give the scent of the Good-fight brand. So, other brands can give 24-hour protection from mosqitoes but cannot provide the Good-fight scent. So, the advertisement uses this fact (which is not false) and words it in a language that gives a meaning that only Good-fight brand can provide 24-hour protection against mosquitoes.

2. Keep the question at the back of your mind

This is a book of analytical reasoning and it omits the general intelligence-testing questions. In this book, those questions are covered that come in a set of five or may be ten. Usually, before you begin to tackle each of the questions independently, you will come across certain directions. These directions will tell you what to do. It would be a good thing if you keep the question for each set at the back of your mind. Whenever you read the direction prepare your mind accordingly for what you are going to do. For example, if you come across a set of questions on assumptions, tell your mind - *"These are questions on assumptions; assumptions are statements taken for granted or assumed; and therefore, I am going to read each statement carefully and wherever I find anything presupposed or taken for granted I am immediately going to notice that."*

This kind of approach prepares you with just the right kind of mindset and you will be more likely to solve a question correctly.

3. Learn to identify key words

In the first tip, I asked you to "read like a detective". This is a reaffirmation of the same advice. Key words or signal-words are very important and they play a decisive role in logical reasoning. Some frequently used key words are

all
always
at least
at most
but can be
cannot be
consecutive
directly
each
every
exactly
except
if
immediately
impossible
must be
never
no fewer than
no more than
none
only once
perfectly
possible
certain
sure
probably
same
some
the least
the most
unless
in spite of
despite
because of

Thus, you can see how the following pairs of sentences create different meanings.

Ex 3: **I.** *All* history teachers have been guided by archaeological evidences.

II. *Some* history teachers have been guided by archaeological evidences.

Ex 4: **I.** The history lecture should be held *immediately before* the Physics lecture.

II. The history lecture should be held *before* the Physics lecture.

Ex 5: **I.** *Although* Indian army was trained in USA, it lost.

II. *Because* the Indian army was trained in USA, it lost.

Ex 6: **I.** With the rising prices and cuts in subsidies, the small farmers are *certain* to overthrow the ruling party.

II. With the rising prices and cuts in subsidies, the small farmers are *likely* to overthrow the ruling party.

Ex 7: **I.** Indian political pundits do not have the moral conviction to take such a strong decision; *at most*, they *can* agree on a national government.

II. Indian political pundits do not have the moral conviction to take such a strong decision, *yet* they *will* agree on a national government.

4. Do not make unwarranted assumptions

Sometimes, a student misreads some facts or information and this makes him solve the entire problem incorrectly. For example, consider the following illustration.

Ex.8: In an office, there are five persons A, B, C, D, E - one a peon, one a clerk, one a head clerk, one a manager and one a chief manager. The peon is 18 years old and he is 12 years younger than B, the manager. The clerk is four years younger than the head clerk. The chief manager is 53 years old.

Comments: In the above example, which is a question (I have given an incomplete question because only this much will serve our purpose) of problem-solving, there are two dimensions to the problem. One is the ages of various persons and the other is their designations (ranks). Now, you may notice that wherever both age and rank are given, the person of a lower rank is usually the younger person. This may create an impression in your mind that the clerk and the head clerk are both younger than the manager. But, do the facts point to any such case? No. It may happen that the clerk is 53 years old and the head clerk is 57.

Similarly, some students tend to read too much into an information. Consider the following examples.

Ex 9: If the government is able to contain inflation, the fiscal deficit will also come down.... History stands witness to how the government brought down fiscal deficit in the seventies....

Inference: The government had succeeded in containing inflation in the seventies.

Comments: You may take the inference to be true which may not be correct. Or, if such an inference is not given, you may form the same opinion in your mind. This would again be a case of making an unwarranted assumption. The statement says that containing inflation is a way of cutting down fiscal deficit. But, it does not say that it works in the reverse as well, i.e., if fiscal deficit is brought down, inflation must have been contained. This would have been true if the statement had said that containing inflation is the *only* way of bringing down fiscal deficit. The inference given is, at best, 'probably true' but not 'definitely true'.

Note I:

In logical terms, this is a case of what is called **hypothetical reasoning**. The general format is

Case I :

> **If p then q.**
> **p.**
> **Therefore, q.**
> (correct inference)

Ex (i): If inflation is controlled, fiscal deficit will be controlled.
Inflation is controlled.

Inference: Fiscal deficit will be controlled.

Remark: Correct inference.

Some other variations are:

Case II :

> **If p then q.**
> **Not p.**
> **Therefore, not q.**
> (incorrect inference)

Ex (ii): If inflation is controlled, fiscal deficit will be brought down.
Inflation is not controlled.

Inference: Fiscal deficit will not be controlled.

Remark: Incorrect inference. At best, it is *probably true*.

Case III :

> **If p then q.**
> **q.**
> **Therefore, p.**
> (incorrect inference)

Ex (iii): If inflation is controlled, fiscal deficit will be controlled.
Fiscal deficit is controlled.

Inference: Inflation must have been controlled.

Remark: Incorrect inference. At best, it is *probably true*.

Case IV :

If p then q.
Not q.
Therefore, not p.
(correct inference)

Ex (iv): If inflation is controlled, fiscal deficit will be controlled.
Fiscal deficit is not controlled.

Inference: Inflation was not controlled.

Remark: Correct inference.

- You must understand that Ex 8 was an example of Case III above.

Note II:

It would be prudent to mention another class of arguments called **disjunctive arguments**. Their formats are:

Case I:

Either p or q.
Not p.
Therefore, q.
(correct inference)

Ex. (v): Either the government should accept the workers' demands or it should take steps to tackle the strike.
The government has decided not to accept the workers' demands.

Inference: The government should take steps to tackle the strike.

Remark: Correct inference.

Case II:

Either p or q.
p.
Therefore, not q.
(incorrect inference)

Ex. (vi): Either the government should accept the workers' demands or it should take steps to tackle the strike.
The government has accepted the workers' demands.

Inference: The government need not take any steps to tackle the strike.

Remark: Incorrect inference.

Case III:

Either p or q.
q.
Therefore, not p.
(incorrect inference)

Ex. (vii): Either I will go or she will come.
She has come.

Inference: *I will not go.*

Remark: Incorrect inference.

Case IV:

Either p or q.
Not q.
Therefore p.
(correct inference)

Ex. (viii): Either I'll go or she will come. She has not come.
Inference: I'll go.

Remark: Correct inference.

Ex 10: A is 200 m from B and B is 300 m from C. Therefore, A is 500 m from C.
Comments: This is a very easy fact to tackle but students get misled in it. They make an unwarranted assumption that A, B and C lie on a straight line and that B lies between A and C. And, thus, they conclude that A is 500 m from C. But, this will be wrong if A was not in a straight line with B and C or if A and C were both on the same side of B.

Summary

- Usually examiners try to put some difficulty in a question by using tactics such as highlighting unimportant facts, downplaying the important facts, using evasive language etc.
- To beat these tactics you should
  (1) read as if you were a detective, i.e., read the facts very carefully.
  (2) keep the question-type at the back of your mind.
  (3) learn to identify key words.
  (4) not make any unwarranted assumptions.

Chapter Three

Assumptions

3.1: Introduction

We have seen in chapter 1 that an assumption is the hidden part of an argument. In many examinations we come across questions wherein the candidate is asked to identify an assumption. In this chapter, we will see how to identify an assumption. Let us begin by looking at the common format of the question. (There are other formats too of asking the question as seen in Exercises 3B and 3C.)

3. 2: Format of the problem (What is the problem like?)

Directions: In each question below a statement (or a passage) is followed by two assumptions numbered I and II. An assumption is something supposed or taken for granted. You have to consider the statement and the following assumptions and then decide which of the assumptions is implicit in the statement. Give answer:

1) if only assumption I is implicit.
2) if only assumption II is implicit.
3) if either assumption I or assumption II is implicit.
4) if neither of the assumptions is implicit.
5) if both the assumptions are implicit.

Statement: "Take our reasoning-improvement courses and brighten your chances of success." — an advertisement

Assumptions: **I.** Good reasoning ability will help to succeed.
II. The courses offered are of good quality.

3.3: Theoretical discussion

The above is a sample of such problems. The given statement may be a passage, a single line, an advertisement, a notice, an appeal or any such thing. These days, more advertisements/appeals/advices/notices are seen than simple statements/passages. Anyway, first of all, we should see: what does an assumption mean and how can it be detected?

3.3.1: What is an assumption?

An assumption is something which is assumed, supposed and taken for granted. When somebody says something he does not put every thing, every aspect of his idea into words. There is a lot which he leaves unsaid. *That which he leaves unsaid, that which he takes for granted, may be defined as an assumption.* Do you remember your childhood days when you used to describe every detail, every subsequent step, not omitting even the rough work, when you used to solve your arithmetic questions? You still solve many such questions (for your Quantitative Aptitude paper), don't you? But do you incorporate every step even now? No. Now you jump over the easier steps (addition, substraction, etc., for example). This is because you assume that the one who reads your solution will know these elementary operations, that he will also assume that you know these operations. This is an example of assumption. Take another example from your everyday life. Suppose an exciting one-day international cricket match is going on. The other country has piled up a good total and India, in reply, have lost two quick wickets. Now, Tendulkar comes to bat. You are a die-hard fan of Tendulkar and, despite the odds, you are so excited that you can't help exclaiming - "Tendulkar is a fine batsman. India shall win this match." Now, in this statement of yours, you co-relate two facts: one, that Tendulkar is a fine batsman and, two, that India shall win. How do you relate the two? Obviously, by assuming that a fine batsman may help his team win a match. This is, therefore, another example of assumption.

Ideal way of arguing	Actual way of arguing
1. Tendulkar is a fine batsman. 2. A fine batsman is likely to help his team win the match. [This statement is left unsaid because it is taken for granted. Hence it is an assumption.] 3. So, India may win the match.	1. Tendulkar is a fine batsman. 2. So, India should win the match.

3.4: Some simple cases of assumption

Let us solve a few examples now to develop a better idea of the subject matter.

Ex.1

Statement: "According to me, you should get your child examined by a specialist doctor."

Assumption: Specialist doctors are able to diagnose better than ordinary doctors.

Explanation: The assumption is valid. One is advising (perhaps his friend) to get his child examined by a specialist doctor. Obviously, he must be assuming that specialist doctors diagnose better than ordinary ones, otherwise he would not have advised thus.

Ex. 2

Statement: The book is intended to guide the layman to study yoga in the absence of a teacher.

Assumptions: I. A teacher of yoga may not be available to everyone.

II. Yoga can be learnt with the help of a book.

Explanation: Both assumptions are correct. The book is intended to teach yoga in the absence of a teacher. This means that the absence of teachers is a possibility: hence I is valid. That the book intends to teach yoga implies that II is also valid.

Ex. 3

Statement: The next meeting of the Governing Body of the institute will be held after one year.

Assumption: The institute will remain in function after one year.

Explanation: The assumption is valid. The common practice is to hold meetings of only those bodies that are functional. So, if it is being announced that the next meeting will be held after one year, the announcers must be assuming that the institute will remain functional after one year.

Ex. 4

Statement: The girl is too clever to fail in the examination.

Assumption: Very clever girls do not fail in the examination.

Explanation: The assumption is correct. The statement says that the girl won't fail (effect) because she is very clever (cause). Obviously, it is assumed that very clever girls do not fail.

Ex. 5

Statement : Of all the TV sets manufactured in India, X brand has the largest sale.

Assumption: The sale of all the TV sets manufactured in India is known.

Explanation: The assumption is valid. Here, it is claimed that *of all* the TV sets manufactured, X brand has the largest sale. No such claim could be made if the sale figures *of all* brands was not known. Hence, it must have been implicitly assumed in the statement that the sale figures of all brands is known.

3.5: More on Assumptions

The difference that a single word/phrase can make

(i) Definitive Words

The task of determining the validity of an assumption, as the foregoing examples suggest, is not very difficult. Yet, it is delicate enough to demand an alert and cautious approach on your part. You must, therefore, develop an awareness of the difference that can be created by the use of different words.

There are some words that lend a greater degree of emphasis — more weight — on the sentence than some others. These words impart a kind of exclusiveness to the sentence and, thereby, reduce the range or scope of the sentence. Some of these key words are: '**only**', '**best**', '**strongest**', '**all**', '**definitely**', '**certainly**' etc. All these words have some kind of certainty associated with them and you should be able to understand it. Consider the following examples.

Ex. 6

Statement: The BoP crisis has worsened and the government should make every effort to boost exports.

Assumptions: **I.** Exports are the best solution to avert the BoP crisis.

II. Exports are a reasonably good solution to the BoP crisis.

III. Exports are the only solution to overcome the BoP crisis.

IV. The BoP crisis will definitely be averted by boosting exports.

V. The BoP crisis will probably be averted by boosting exports.

Explanation: In the above example, II and V are valid assumptions while I, III and IV are not. The reason is that I, III and IV use definitive words such as 'best', 'only' and 'definitely'. The statement in the question mentions a fact that the BoP crisis has worsened and then makes a suggestion that exports should be boosted. Undoubtedly, the author of the advice is assuming that exports should help the country overcome the BoP crisis or that exports are a good (or, say, 'reasonably good') solution to BoP crisis. But there is no hint whatsoever that exports are the **only** solution or the **best** solution or a **definitely** effective solution.

The above example illustrates how the use of definitive words may lend a different '*tone*' to a sentence and how one should be careful about them.

(ii) Conjunctions

When a statement consists of two clauses and the clauses are connected by a conjunction, the nature of the conjunction used goes a long way in detecting the assumption that the author must have made. Some significant conjunctions are: 'because', 'so', 'therefore', 'despite', 'in spite of', 'even after', 'although', 'as', 'as a result of'. When one clause of the sentence mentions an event / fact / suggestion called **A** (let us say) and the other clause of the sentence mentions another event/fact/suggestion called **B,** then, depending upon the conjunction, the following assumptions can be concluded.

(a) A (because / as a result of) B $\Rightarrow$ It is assumed that B leads to A.

Ex. 7

Statement: The literacy scenario will improve after the national awareness drive.

Valid Assumption: National awareness drive on literacy is a good means of improving the literacy rate.

(b) A (therefore / hence) B ⇒ It is assumed that A leads to B.

Ex. 8

Statement: The record has been broken by an Indian, therefore all Indians must be feeling very proud.

Valid Assumption: Breaking of a record by a fellow countryman makes other citizens proud.

(c) A (even after / in spite of / despite) B ⇒ It is assumed that usually A does not occur when B occurs.

Ex. 9

Statement: There was a murder last night even after the police had arranged for maximum security around the area.

Valid Assumption: Arrangement of maximum security is usually sufficient to prevent murders.

(d) not A (even after/in spite of/despite) B ⇒ It is assumed that usually A occurs when B does.

Ex. 10

Statement: There was no outbreak of cholera this year in spite of the continuous deposition of rain water for four days.

Valid Assumption: Deposition of rain water usually leads to cholera.

(iii) Connotive phrases

Sometimes it so happens that an author would say what he wants to say but you may miss that he has said any such thing because the words that the author uses to say it are slightly indirect, slightly unconventional. We shall call these *connotative* or *connotive phrases*. For example, "It is true that ..." can be written as

(a) It would be correct to say that...

(b) Even the most sceptic of men would agree that...

(c) It can be claimed with reasonable degree of truth that...

Similarly, "It is false" can be written as:

(a) It would be highly misleading to say that ...

(b) Nothing could be farther from truth than....

(c) It is baseless to say that ....

Although, the role of connotative phrases in the type of questions that are asked these days is very limited, they have been mentioned so they do not escape your eyes whenever you come across them.

3.6 : Some standard categories of assumptions

In the section titled 'some simple cases of assumption' we have seen diverse examples of statements and evaluated their assumptions. Although, it is not very difficult to detect or evaluate an assumption, it would be better if we categorise the statements into some standard types so that a deeper understanding of the subject-matter could be achieved. Some of these standard categories are:

(a) Existence / Non-existence of the subject

This category makes a very simple assumption that what is being talked about must be existing. Similarly, if its absence is being talked about, it must not be existing.

Ex. 11

Statement: Love marriages mostly end in divorce.

Valid Assumptions: **I.** Love marriages do take place.

II. There are cases of divorce.

Note: Above was an example where we assume existence of what is being talked about.

Ex. 12

Statement: The company will not go into profit unless a foreign-trained manager is brought.

Valid Assumption: At present, there are no foreign-trained managers in the company.

Note: Above was an example where we assume non-existence of something whose absence is being discussed.

(b) Adjectives

We know that an adjective is something which denotes a quality of the subject. Naturally then, if an adjective is attached (unconditionally) to any subject, it must be assumed that "the subject does have the quality as denoted by the adjective". For example:

Ex. 13

Statement: The social nature of man leads to cooperation and coordination within the society.

Valid Assumption: Man is social.

Ex 14

Statement: The bright-red sky looked beautiful enough to bring out the poet in him.

Valid Assumption: The sky appears bright-red sometimes.

(c) Cause-effect

Some statements mention a cause-and-effect relationship. The conjunctions between the clauses are usually 'therefore', 'as', 'hence', 'thus' etc. In all such cases it would be a valid assumption to say that " this cause leads to this effect". There may be different versions of the question: sometimes the cause-effect relationship may be explicitly stated (see Ex 15), sometimes it may be in the form of "because no cause, hence no effect"(see Ex 16) and sometimes in the form of " Although cause, yet no effect" (see Ex 17).

Ex 15

Statement: It rained last night. The grounds must have become wet.

Valid Assumption: When it rains, grounds become wet.

Ex 16

Statement: As you do not have the expertise, you cannot be selected.

Valid Assumption: Expertise is essential for selectiion.

Ex 17

Statement: Although the city was under knee-deep water for four days in this monsoon, there was no outbreak of cholera.

Valid Assumption: Water-logging usually leads to cholera.

(d) Course of action

Sometimes a fact / report / observation/ study / data is given followed by a suggested course of action. Let us call the given fact / data etc. X and the suggested course of action Y. Then, either some negative aspect of X is mentioned and a course of action Y is suggested or some positive aspect of X is mentioned and a course of action Y is suggested. In the former case, i.e., when some negative aspect of X is mentioned, the following assumptions will be valid:

(i) X needs improvement. (see Asmp I, Ex 18) [Asmp stands for Assumption)

(ii) The negative aspects of X (if mentioned) are undesirable/harmful. (see Asmp. II, Ex 18)

(iii) Y will improve X. (see Asmp III, Ex 18)

(iv) The advantages of adopting Y far outweigh the disadvantages (if any) of not adopting it.(see Asmp IV, Ex 18)

Ex 18

Statement: The working atmosphere in our public sector units can only be described as indisciplined and uncoordinated. Therefore, some harsh disciplinary actions need to be taken.

Valid Assumptions: **I.** The working atmosphere of our public sector units is not ideal / needs improvement.

II. Indiscipline and lack of coordination are undesirable in any industry.

III. Taking harsh disciplinary action would improve the working atmosphere of our public sectors.

IV. The benefits outweigh the disadvantages (if any) of taking harsh disciplinary actions.

Similarly, you may contemplate and evaluate the assumptions if any positive aspect of X is mentioned and a course of action Y is suggested. The logic will be exactly on the same lines.

(e) Analogy

In some cases it is concluded that, because a cause leads to some effect in one type of objects, it will also lead to the same effect in another type of objects. This is an example of reasoning by analogy. In such cases, it is assumed that " The effect of the cause on both the species is similar".

Ex 19

Statement: Properly-fed and starved monkeys were made to run through a maze (puzzle). It was seen that starved monkeys could not make their way fast. This proves that the lower intelligence of people in poor countries is the result of malnutrition.

Valid Assumption: The effect of malnutrition on the intelligence of the monkeys is parallel to those on human beings.

(f) Advertisements/notices/appeals

In the examinations of today, the statements are usually in the form of an advertisement or an official notice or a notice issued in public interest or an appeal.

I assume that you can appreciate that advertisements (see Ex 20) are usually given by firms / companies, official notices (see Ex 21) within an office, appeals (see Ex 22) by governments or voluntary organisations and public interest notices by government or government bodies (see Ex 23). In all these cases the following assumptions will be considered valid:

(i) An advertisement / appeal / notice does have some effect (see Asmp I, Ex 20, 21, 22, 23).

(ii) In case of an advertisement, that which is being highlighted is looked for and expected by the people (see Asmp II, Ex 20).

(iii) In case of a public-interest notice, it is the duty of those who issue it, to issue such notices (see Asmp II, Ex 23).

(iv) In case of a public-interest notice, what is being advised must be beneficial for people and its non-practice harmful in some way (see Asmp III, IV, Ex 23).

(v) In case of an appeal, the reason for issuing it exists (you can determine the reason using your common sense) (see Asmp II, Ex 22).

(vi) In case of an official notice, the effect of its implementation will be beneficial for the organisation (see Asmp II, Ex 21).

Ex. 20

Statement: Banking Services Chronicle - the only magazine that gives exclusive articles on reasoning and quicker mathematics. - an advertisement.

Valid Assumptions: I. The advertisement will have some effect on those who read it.

II. People look forward to exclusive articles on reasoning and quicker mathematics.

Ex. 21

Statement: From next month onwards, it has been made compulsory for every worker to submit a daily report. - a notice issued by a company.

Valid Assumptions: I. The notice will be read by the workers.
II. The daily submission of reports by workers will prove beneficial for the company.

Ex. 22
Statement: Donate money for the earthquake victims. - an appeal
Valid Assumptions: I. The appeal will have some effect on people.
II. There has been an earthquake and the condition of the earthquake victims is pitiable.

Ex. 23
Statement: Please do not lean out of the running train. - a notice in the railway compartment
Valid Assumptions: I. The people are likely to pay attention to this notice.
II. It is the duty of the Railways to issue such notices.
III. Leaning out of running trains is dangerous.
IV. Not leaning out of running trains ensures safety.

3.7 : When is an assumption invalid?

In the foregoing discussion, we have elaborately discussed the validity of a given assumption. By virtue of this discussion we are now in a position to say with certainty whether a given assumption is valid. But this is only half of the actual task. We should also see the cases and reasons wherein an assumption becomes invalid or incorrect. Broadly, there may be two categories of invalid assumptions: one, where the assumption is outrightly incorrect, and two, where the given assumption does not *look* outrightly incorrect but a close look shows that it is invalid. Let us look at these categories.

(i) When an assumption can be outrightly rejected

These assumptions are very easy to be shown incorrect because they are either just contrary to what the given statement says or they seem to have simply no connection with what the given statement says. Only a look at them will be enough to declare that they are not valid assumptions for the given statement.

Ex 24
Statement: "Use aluminium - the versatile metal - for packing" - an advertisement
Invalid Assumption: Aluminium is the only metal used for packing.

It is obvious by the statement that aluminium is a versatile metal for packaging. These may be many more but not all would be versatile. Where does one get any hint that aluminium is the **only** metal possible for packaging?

Ex 25
Statement: "Get your child examined by a specialist doctor" - A tells B.
Invalid Assumption: B will not heed to A's advice.

Generally, one advises somebody with an assumption that the advice would be listened to. (See Q. 27, Ex. 3A and its answer). How could we conclude that B will not heed to A's advice?

Ex 26

Statement: The government has increased the price of bread.

Invalid Assumption: The price of bread was very low.

Generally, prices are increased not beause they are low but because these are compulsions to raise it. The Government is not a cruel and mean agency that goes around raising prices of everything that is cheap. In fact, all Govts try their best to keep inflation under control (that is, to keep the prices low.) They raise prices only because they are not left with any choice and they need revenue. Yes, when they raise prices they do try to raise prices of only those goods in particular whose prices are lower than what could be tolerated. But, even then, the word **"Very low"** in the given assumption is definitely questionable.

(ii) When an assumption cannot be outrightly rejected

These are circumstances where the given assumption is likely to force you to think. Some important categories of such assumptions are:

(a) Restatement

An assumption will be invalid if it is a mere restatement—putting it in different words of the given statement. The following examples illustrate this point:

Ex 27

Statement: Since certain sections of the society are going to be unhappy whenever reforms are implemented, there is little that can be done to prevent it except abandoning it.

Invalid Assumption: Some people would not like the implementation of reforms.

Ex 28

Statement: Of all the TV sets manufactured in India, brand X has the largest sale.

Invalid Assumption: No other brand of TV sets has as high a sale as brand X.

(b) Obversion

Obversion is a slightly different case of restating the same fact. In it, two of the trio (subject, verb, predicate) are changed into negative which changes the appearance of the sentence without changing its meaning. An obverted form of the statement is an invalid assumption.

Ex 29

Statement: Friendship is beneficial.

Invalid Assumptions: **I.** Enmity is harmful.
II. Enmity is not beneficial.
III. Frendship is not harmful.

Ex. 30

Statement: "Smoking is injurious to health." - a notice

Invalid Assumption: Non-smoking promotes health.

(c) Conversion

In our lesson on syllogism, we have mentioned conversion as a method of immediate inference. In brief, there are three standard cases of conversion (for details see chapter 10):

All X are Y → Some Y are X;

Some X are Y → Some Y are X;

No X are Y → No Y are X.

The given assumption will be invalid if it is only a converted form of the given statement.

Ex.31

Statement: Some / many historians harm the society by distorting facts.

Invalid Assumption: Some of those who distort facts and harm society are historians.

Ex.32

Statement: No unexperienced fellow could be employed.

Invalid Assumption: No one who could be employed should lack in experience.

(d) Inference

The given assumption is invalid if it is an inference derivable from the given statement. An assumption is something on which the statement is based and not something which itself is based upon (an inference of a statement is based upon the statement) the statement.

Ex.33

Statement: Ram went to Gaya on 27th July. Shyam went two days after him.

Invalid assumption: Shyam went to Gaya on 29th July.

Ex.34

Statement: Religion is based primarily and mainly upon fear; it is partly the fear of the unknown and partly the wish to feel that one has a saviour who will stand by in times of despair and defeat.

Invalid Assumption: Man's fear of the unknown and defeat makes him religious.

(e) Long-drawn conclusion

An assumption will be invalid if it makes too far-fetched reasoning or long-drawn conclusion, even if it appears to be probably correct.

The following examples illustrate the point:

Ex.35

Statement: Religious instruction leads to a curiosity for knowledge. So, all teaching should be done in religious spirit.

Invalid Assumption: Curious persons are good persons.

Ex.36

Statement: The Central Excise Collectorate has begun the exercise of smooth transition from licence system to simplified registration system for all the manufacturers. - a news item

Invalid Assumptions: I. The Central Excise Collectorate had carefully reviewed the licence system.

In Ex. 35, it is too long-drawn to conclude that religious instructions lead to curiosity and religious people are generally good and therefore curious persons must be good. It is too far-fetched. Again, in Ex. 36, it is likely that the Central Excise System had indeed reviewed the licensing system, but there is nothing in the statement given which make us think so with any degree of certainty. It is only probable but not certain. It would be a bit far-fetched if we assume that a review was also done, without these being any hint whatsoever in the given statement.

What Pharmaceutical shares did when special packages were announced?

Comments: It should be clear to you that agreement based on analogy is never certain. It only denotes some probability. The better the analogy, the higher are the chances of it coming true in the unknown attribute also and the stronger is the argument. Otherwise, the argument is weak.

How do we know if an argument based on analogy is a strong one or not? For this, we should ask ourselves this question: **How *similar* is the unknown attribute to the known attributed?** If the attributes in which the given entities have exhibited likeness is not very different from the attribute in question, then we should take it as a strong argument. Otherwise, it is a weak argument.

For example, in the above three examples

(i) Privatisation and autonomy are very different from Ram Temple. So, this is a weak argument.

(ii) Cricket and kabaddi are very different from hockey. So, Ex. B is a weak argument.

(iii) Pharmaceutical and software shares are not similar. But both have the essential identical property, both are speculative instruments of business. So, Ex. C is a strong argument.

Note: The above rule of appraising an analogy-based argument is merely a tip, a guideline. A detailed discussion is not within the scope of this book. We are, however, giving some hints on how do we weigh analogy-based arguments:

(i) The more similar the unknown attribute is, to the given known attributes of the entities, the stronger is the argument. (Ex. already discussed)

(ii) The more the number of known attributes in which the given entities exhibit likeness, the stronger is the analogy.

(Ex.: If Congress and BJP have shown identical stands on only two issues before then the chances of their showing identical stand on another new issue is lesser than if they had exhibited identical stands on hundreds of issues before).

(iii) The more moderate the claim, the stronger is the argument.

(Ex. If I have bought Hero Puch from Rama Motors and it gives me 100 km per litre then if my friend also purchases a Hero Puch from Rama Motors then if he expects his bike to give *at least 80 km* per litre, his argument is more probable than if he expected it to be at least 99 km per litre.]

3.8: Difference between implications and assumptions

Sometimes, implications are also treated as assumptions. Implication means something which is implied. It is slightly different from assumption. Implication means the "hidden *meaning*" of the statement. Consider the following example to appreciate the difference :

"I am not going to call off the strike unless the government announces free education to every child in the area. Education is a basic right of every child and it is impossible for me to keep a blind eye when this right is being violated." - X, a political leader.

In the passage above, Mr. X

(i) defines education as a basic right of every child,

(ii) claims that this right is being violated and

(iii) threatens to carry on the strike until the government announces free education.

Using (i) and (ii), we can conclude that "many children fail to get education". This is **implied** by Mr. X's claim that the basic right (of getting education) is being violated. Finally in (iii), Mr. X **assumes** that the "threat of continuation of strike may lead to the government's acceptance of his demands". Thus, one thing is **implied** here while the other is **assumed.**

To summarise, an assumption is something **on which** the statement is based, while an implication is something which is derived from and therefore, **based upon** the statement.

Summary

- Assumption is the missing link of the logical structure of an argument. It is left unsaid and therefore, *assumed*.
- There are some standard categories of statements that have standard ways of assuming certain things. These have been elaborately discussed.
- We have also discussed some usual cases that make an assumption invalid.
- In judging the validity of a given assumption, special note should be taken of some **keywords**.

Some tips for Quick Answers

(i) No either

An argument may have more than one assumption. But they are almost never exclusive of each other. It implies that if both assumptions look true to you, choose the choice "both are implicit" and not "either of them is implicit." **The answer-choice "either of them is implicit" is very rarely correct for assumption questions.** You can take this as a thumb-rule.

(ii) Eliminate with the help of the certain

Usually, we are unsure of only one or two of the assumptions and we are sure of some other assumptions. We can take the help of these sure ones to eliminate some choices. For example, suppose that a question has three assumptions - I, II and III. When you read these suggested assumptions you may find that you are certain that I **is** an assumption and that III **is not** an assumption. But, you are not sure about II. So, you can look for those choices that include I and exclude III. This will reduce your number of answer choices from 5 to 2 or may be 1.

(iii) Remember some examples

Many of the questions form a usual standard pattern. In such cases, it helps to keep a similar example at the back of your mind. It would be immensely beneficial for you if you remember Ex 11 to Ex 23 and follow these examples as rules.

Practice Exercises

Type I: Exercise 3A

Directions : In each question below is given a statement followed by two assumptions numbered I and II. An assumption is something supposed or taken for granted. You have to consider the statement and the following assumptions and decide which of the assumptions is implicit in the statement.

Give answer (a) if only assumption I is implicit; (b) if only assumption II is implicit; (c) if either I or II is implicit; (d) if neither I nor II is implicit; and (e) if both I and II are implicit.

1. **Statement:** The boy is too honest not to speak the truth.
   Assumptions: **I.** Very honest boys also tell lies.
   II. Dishonest boys also speak the truth.
2. **Statement:** "X air-conditioner - the largest-selling name with the largest range" - an advertisement
   Assumptions: **I.** X air-conditioner is the only one with wide variations.
   II. There is a demand for air-conditioners in the market.
3. **Statement:** "To buy a TV X, contact Y, the sole agent of X TV." - an advertisement
   Assumptions: **I.** People generally prefer to buy TV through sole agent.
   II. The TV-producing companies do not sell their products directly.
4. **Statement:** Opening a library in Rambli will be a wastage.
   Assumptions: **I.** Inhabitants of Rambli are illiterate.
   II. Inhabitants of Rambli are not interested in reading.
5. **Statement:** It is through participative management policy alone that indiscipline in our industries can be contained and a quality of life ensured to the worker.
   Assumptions: **I.** Quality of life in our industry is better.
   II. Indiscipline results in a poor quality of life.

6. **Statement:** Please consult me before making any decision on exports from the company.
Assumptions: I. You may take a wrong decision if you don't consult me.
II. It is important to take a right decision.

7. **Statement:** Warning : Cigarette smoking is injurious to health.
Assumptions: I. Non-smoking promotes health.
II. Really, this warning is not necessary.

8. **Statement:** Children are influenced more by their teachers nowadays.
Assumptions: I. Children consider teachers as their models.
II. A large amount of children's time is spent at school.

9. **Statement:** Apart from the entertainment value of television, its educational value cannot be ignored.
Assumptions: I. People take television to be a means of entertainment only.
II. The educational value of television in not realised properly.

10. **Statement:** " If you trouble me, I will slap you." - A mother warns her child.
Assumptions: I. With the warning, the child may stop troubling her.
II. All children are basically naughty.

11. **Statement:** "A car is required on rent." - an advertisement
Assumptions: I. All types of vehicles are available on rent.
II. People will respond to the advertisement.

12. **Statement:** "Buy pure butter of company A." - an advertisement in a magazine
Assumptions: I. No other company supplies pure butter.
II. People read advertisements.

13. **Statement:** Of all the radio sets manufactured in India, 'X' brand has the largest sale.
Assumptions: I. The sale of all the radio sets manufactured in India is known.
II. The manufacturing of no other radio set in India is as large as 'X' brand radio.

14. **Statement:** A's advice to B - "Go to Jammu via Amritsar - the shortest route."
Assumptions: I. B wishes to go to Jammu.
II. A gives advice to everybody.

15. **Statement:** Films have become indispensable for the entertainment of people.
Assumptions: I. Films are the only medium of entertainment.
II. People enjoy films.

16. **Statement:** "Do not lean out of the door of the bus." - a warning in a school bus
Assumptions: I. Leaning out of a running bus is dangerous.
II. Children do not pay any heed to such warnings.

17. **Statement:** "If you are a mechanical engineer, we want you as our supervisor." - an advertisement by company X

Assumptions: **I.** Mechanical engineers are expected to be better performers by company X.

II. The company X needs supervisors.

18. **Statement:** Be humble even after being victorious.

Assumptions: **I.** Many people are humble after being victorious.

II. Generally, people are not humble.

19. **Statement:** A sentence in the letter to the candidates called for written examinations — 'You have to bear your expenses on travel etc.'

Assumptions: **I.** If not clarified, all the candidates may claim reimbursement of expenses.

II. Many organisations reimburse expenses on travel to candidates called for written examinations.

20. **Statement:** One of the opposition leaders said that the time had come for like-minded opposition parties to unite and dislodge the corrupt government.

Assumptions: **I.** Like-minded opposition parties should unite only when they have to dislodge a corrupt government.

II. Opposition parties are not corrupt.

21. **Statement:** Postal rates have been increased to meet the deficit.

Assumptions: **I.** The present rates are very low.

II. If the rates are not increased, the deficit cannot be met.

22. **Statement:** If degrees are delinked from jobs, boys will think twice before joining college.

Assumptions: **I.** Boys join college education to get jobs.

II. A degree is of no use in getting a job.

23. **Statement:** "Present-day education is in a shambles and the country is going to the dogs."

Assumptions: **I.** A good education system is essential for the well-being of a nation.

II. A good education alone is sufficient for the well-being of a nation.

24. **Statement:** The next meeting of the Governing Board of the Institute will be held after one year.

Assumptions: **I.** The Institute will remain in function after one year.

II. The Governing Board will be dissolved after one year.

25. **Statement:** "Computer education should start at school level itself."

Assumptions: **I.** Learning computers is easy.

II. Computer education fetches jobs easily.

26. **Statement:** The new education policy envisages major modifications in the education system.

Assumptions: I. Present education system is inconsistent with national needs.

II. Present education system needs change.

27. **Statement:** A's advice to B - "If you want to study Accounts, join Institute Y."

Assumptions: I. Institute Y provides good Accounts education.

II. B listens to A's advice.

28. **Statement:** "Drop this letter in the letter-box on your way to school." - A mother to her son.

Assumptions: I. The child knows the address of the person to whom the letter is being sent.

II. The child will comply with the orders of his mother.

29. **Statement:** Everybody loves reading adventure stories.

Assumptions: I. Adventure stories are the only reading material.

II. Nobody loves reading any other material.

30. **Statement:** Read this notice before entering the club.

Assumptions: I. People coming to the club are literate.

II. No blind person comes to the club.

31. **Statement:** Equality of income throughout a community is the essential condition for maximising the total utility which the total income available could confer on the members of that community.

Assumptions: I. If extra income were taken from the rich and given to the poor, the total utility experienced by the community would increase.

II. Equal pay for equal work.

32. **Statement:** "If you are beautiful, we will catch your beauty. If you are not, we will make you beautiful." - an advertisement of a photo studio.

Assumptions: I. How to look beautiful is a problem of youngsters.

II. Nobody desires to be beautiful.

33. **Statement:** "If you are beautiful, we will catch your beauty. If you are not, we wll make you beautiful." - an advertisement of a photo studio.

Assumptions: I. A photograph can be beautiful even if a person is not.

II. People like to be considered beautiful.

34. **Statement:** A line in an advertisement in a newspaper - "You really get your money's worth when you buy from our shop."

Assumptions: I. Other shops price goods above their worth.

II. People want full value for their money.

35. **Statement:** The integrated steel plants in India would no longer have to depend on imports for continuous casting refractories.

Assumptions: I. India needs continuous casting refractories.

II. There are steel plants in India.

36. **Statement:** "Buy pure and natural honey of company X." - an advertisement in a newspaper

Assumptions: **I.** Artificial honey can be prepared.

II. People do not mind paying more for pure and natural honey.

37. **Statement:** Detergents should be used to clean clothes.

Assumptions: **I.** Detergents form more lather.

II. Detergents help to dislodge grease and dirt.

38. **Statement:** "We must appoint more clerks in our office staff." - The manager said to the chairman.

Assumptions: **I.** Clerks are available.

II. The present office staff is inefficient.

39. **Statement:** "If I am not well, you will have to go for the meeting." - A manager tells his subordinate.

Assumptions: **I.** It is not necessary that only manager-level personnel attend the meeting.

II. If the manager is well, he would himself like to go for the meeting.

40. **Statement:** To pass the examination, you have to practice very hard.

Assumptions: **I.** Passing the examination is desirable.

II. Hard practice leads to success.

41. **Statement:** "In case you cannot return from the office by 8 p.m., inform us on phone at home." - The parents tell their son.

Assumptions: **I.** The son never informs about his late-coming.

II. Unless specified, the son may not inform his parents.

42. **Statement:** "Use aluminium - the versatile metal for packaging" - an advertisement.

Assumptions: **I.** Aluminium is the only versatile metal.

II. Some companies use metallic packing.

43. **Statement:** The President assured the people that elections will be held here every five years.

Assumptions: **I.** People are afraid that the elections may not be held at all.

II. People are afraid that elections may not be held after five years.

44. **Statement:** These apples are too cheap to be good.

Assumptions: **I.** When the apple crop is abundant, the prices go down.

II. The lower the selling price, the inferior the qualiity of the commodity.

45. **Statement:** If it is easy to become an engineer, I don't want to be an engineer.

Assumptions: **I.** An individual aspires to be a professional.

II. One desires to achieve a thing which is hard-earned.

46. **Statement:** This book is so prepared that even a layman can study science in the absence of a teacher.

Assumptions: I. A layman wishes to study science without a teacher.
II. This book is a good substitute for a teacher.

47. **Statement:** If you have any problems, bring them to me.
Assumptions: I. You have some problems.
II. I can solve any problem.

48. **Statement:** Over 1.4 lakh quintals of cotton has been procured in the state under Cotton Procurement Scheme, a press note said.
Assumptions: I. Cotton procurement scheme is successful.
II. No cotton procurement should be done now.

49. **Statement:** More commuters now travel by this route, but there is no public demand for more buses.
Assumptions: I. The number of buses depends upon the number of passengers.
II. Usually people do not tolerate inconvenience.

50. **Statement:** You know that your suit is excellent when people ask about your tailor who tailored the suit.
Assumptions: I. People do not ask about your tailor if your suit is not good.
II. People want to know the criterion of an excellent suit.

51. **Statement:** All existing inequalities can be reduced, if not utterly eradicated, by action of governments or by revolutionary change of governments.
Assumptions: I. Inequality is a man-made phenomenon.
II. No person would voluntarily part with what he possesses.

52. **Statement:** Neither fascism nor communism has any chance of succeeding in America.
Assumptions: I. American people are strongly in favour of preserving the rights of the individual.
II. American have so far not suffered any pangs of poverty or deprivation.

53. **Statement:** "In order to bring punctuality in our office, we must provide conveyance allowance to our employees." - The incharge of a company tells the Personnel Manager.
Assumptions: I. Conveyance allowance will not help in bringing punctuality.
II. Discipline and reward should always go hand in hand.

54. **Statement:** A warning in a train compartment - "To stop train, pull the chain. Penalty for misuse: Rs. 500."
Assumptions: I. Some people misuse the alarm chain.
II. On certain occasions, people may want to stop a running train.

55. **Statement:** If you are a classical singer, we have a challenging job for you.
Assumptions: **I.** We need a classical singer.
II. You are a classical singer.

56. **Statement:** The successful man has the ability to judge himself correctly.
Assumptions: **I.** To judge others is of no use to a successful man.
II. The successful man cannot make a wrong judgement.

57. **Statement:** "You should not grant him leave in this week because of exigency of work." - A supervisor advises the administrative office.
Assumptions: **I.** Request for leave can even be turned down.
II. The supervisor has reviewed the work required to be done during the said period.

58. **Statement:** "The function will start at 3 p.m. You are requested to take your seats before 3 p.m." - last sentence in an invitation card.
Assumptions: **I.** If the invitee is not in his seat before 3 p.m., the function will not start.
II. The function will start as scheduled.

59. **Statement:** Use PVC pipes which have life years longer than any other.
Assumptions: **I.** People prefer those pipes which are durable.
II. Other pipes are not durable.

60. **Statement:** "You are hereby appointed as a programmer with a probation period of one year and your performance will be reviewed at the end of the period for confirmation." - a line in an appointment letter
Assumptions: **I.** The performance of an individual is generally not known at the time of appointment offer.
II. Generally, an individual tries to prove his worth in the probation period.

61. **Statement:** Lock your valuables in a cupboard and call everybody a gentleman.
Assumptions: **I.** Valuables locked in a cupboard cannot be stolen.
II. Stealing is a crime.

62. **Statement:** "Ensure a good night's sleep for your family with safe and effective X mosquito coil." - an advertisement
Assumptions: **I.** X mosquito coil is better than any other mosquito coil.
II. A good night's sleep is desirable.

63. **Statement:** Lack of stimulation in the first four or five years of life can have adverse consequences.
Assumptions: **I.** A great part of the development of observed intelligence occurs in the earliest years of life.
II. 50 per cent of the measurable intelligence at age 17 is predictable by the age of four.

64. **Statement:** The present examination system needs thorough overhauling.
Assumptions: **I.** The present examination system is obsolete.
II. Overhauling results in improvement.

65. **Statement:** The improvement in the quality of TV programmes will lead to increase in the sales of TV.
Assumptions: **I.** TV is a good entertainment medium.
II. The quality of TV programmes has improved recently.

66. **Statement:** "Banking services are fine-tuned to meet growing business needs." - an advertisement
Assumptions: **I.** Banking is a part of business activity.
II. Industrialists prefer better banking services.

67. **Statement:** Vitamin E tablets keep your complexion in a glowing condition by improving circulation.
Assumptions: **I.** People like a glowing complexion.
II. Complexion becomes dull in the absence of circulation.

68. **Statement:** "We offer the best training in the field of computers." — an advertisement
Assumptions: **I.** People are interested in getting training in computers.
II. People want the best training.

69. **Statement:** "Please put more people on the job but make up for the delay."
Assumptions: **I.** Delay is inevitable in most jobs.
II. The output will increase with more number of people on the job.

70. **Statement:** An advertisement in a newspaper - "Wanted unmarried, presentable matriculate girls between 18 and 21, able to speak fluently in English, to be hired as models."
Assumptions: **I.** Fluency in English is a prerequisite for good preformance as a model.
II. Height does not matter in performing as a model.

71. **Statement:** Like a mad man, I decided to follow him.
Assumptions: **I.** I am not a mad man.
II. I am a mad man.

72. **Statement:** What a fool I am to rely on a trickster like Shaleen!
Assumptions: **I.** Shaleen is unreliable.
II. I am a fool.

73. **Statement:** The taste of food contributes to the intake of nourishment which is essential for the survival of human beings.
Assumptions: **I.** Human beings take food for the enjoyment of its taste.
II. Human beings experience the taste of food.

74. **Statement:** All the workers are hereby instructed to reach the factory by 8.30 a.m.
Assumptions: **I.** Some of the workers do not arrive at the factory in time.
II. Workers will follow the strict warning given in the notice.

75. **Statement:** "Join X coaching classes - we guarantee you success." - an advertisement

Assumptions: **I.** Such coaching classes are well-equipped.

II. Students joining coaching classes expect success.

76. **Statement:** If parking space is not available in office, park your vehicles in the mall and walk to the office.

Assumptions: **I.** The mall is at a walkable distance from the office.

II. The office does not allow visitors' vehicles in its premises.

77. **Statement:** Farmers must immediately switch over to organic fertilizers from chemical fertilizers for better yield.

Assumptions: **I.** All the farmers use only chemical fertilizers.

II. Organic fertilizers are readily available to the farmers.

78. **Statement:** An advertisement by bank X — 'Our interest rates for education loans are lower than those of any other bank.'

Assumptions: **I.** Some other banks also provide education loans.

II. Interest rates charged on education loans are different for different banks.

79. **Statement:** For any kind of problem with your mobile phone, contact our helpdesk immediately.

Assumptions: **I.** Helpdesk has a solution to all kinds of problems related to mobile phones or will guide accordingly.

II. Unless the problem is reported immediately, it cannot be solved.

80. **Statement:** Use our medicine to fight the problem of obesity.

Assumptions: **I.** Other slimming medicines available in the market do not reduce weight.

II. Obesity cannot be controlled without medicines.

81. **Statement:** The driver of the huge truck pulled the emergency brakes to avoid hitting the auto rickshaw which suddenly came in front of the truck.

Assumptions: **I.** The auto rickshaw driver may be able to steer his vehicle away from the oncoming truck.

II. The truck driver may be able to stop the truck before it hits the auto rickshaw.

82. **Statement:** The doctor warned the patient against any further consumption of alcohol if he desired to get cured from the ailment and live a longer life.

Assumptions: **I.** The patient may follow the doctor's advice and stop consuming alcohol.

II. The doctor may be able to cure the patient from the ailment if the patient stops consuming alcohol.

83. **Statement:** The Chairman of the company urged all the employees to refrain from making long personal calls during working hours in order to boost productivity.

Assumptions : I. Majority of the employees may respond positively to the Chairman's appeal.

II. Most of the employees may continue to make long personal calls during working hours.

84. **Statement:** The local cultural club decided to organise a musical event to raise money for the construction of the club building.

Assumptions: I. The local residents may not allow the club to organise the musical event in the locality.

II. The money collected by organising the musical event may be substantial enough for the club to start construction.

85. **Statement:** The largest domestic airlines corporation has announced new summer schedules in which more number of flights in trunk routes are introduced.

Assumptions: I. More number of passengers may travel by this airlines corporation during summer months in trunk routes.

II. Other airlines companies may also increase the number of flights in all the sectors.

86. **Statement:** The chairman of the company decided to hold a grand function to celebrate silver jubilee during the next weekend and invited a large number of guests.

Assumptions: I. The company officials may be able to make all the necessary preparations for the silver jubilee celebration.

II. Majority of the guests invited by the chairman may attend the function.

87. **Statement:** The largest computer manufacturing company slashed the prices of most of the desktop models by about 15 per cent with immediate effect.

Assumptions: I. The company may incur heavy losses due to reduction in prices of the desktop.

II. The sales of desktop manufactured by the company may increase substantially in the near future.

88. **Statement:** The school authority decided to rent out the school premises during weekends and holidays for organising various functions to augment its resources to meet the growing needs of the school.

Assumptions: I. The parents of the school students may protest against the decision of the school authority.

II. There may not be enough demand for hiring the school premises for organising functions.

89. **Statement:** The local civic body has urged all the residents to voluntarily reduce consumption of potable water by about 30 per cent to tide over the water crisis.

Assumptions: I. Many residents may reduce consumption of potable water.

II. Many activists may welcome the civic body's move and spread awareness among residents.

90. **Statement:** A very large number of people stood in the queue for buying tickets for the one-day international cricket match scheduled to be played in the city on the next day.

Assumptions: I. No other one-day international cricket match may be played in the city for the next six months.

II. Majority of those who stood in the queue may be able to get ticket for the one-day international cricket match.

91. **Statement:** The highway police authority put up large boards at regular intervals indicating the speed limit and dangers of over-speeding on the highways.

Assumptions: I. Most of the motorists may drive their vehicles within the speed limit on the highways.

II. Motorists generally ignore such cautions and over-speed on the highways.

92. **Statement:** The employees'association urged its members to stay away from the annual function as many of their demands were not met by the management.

Assumptions: I. Majority of the members of the association may not attend the function.

II. The management may cancel the annual function.

93. **Statement:** The *sarpanch* of the village called a meeting of all the heads of the families to discuss the problem of acute shortage of drinking water in the village.

Assumptions: I. The sarpanch had earlier called such meetings to discuss about various problems.

II. Most of the heads of families may attend the meeting called by the sarpanch

94. **Statement:** The municipal corporation advised all the people living in the shanties along the beaches to move to higher places during monsoon.

Assumptions: I. Many people living in the shanties may leave the city and relocate themselves elsewhere in the state.

II. Majority of the people living in the shanties along the beach may try to relocate to higher places during monsoon.

95. **Statement:** Please send an official letter rather than semiofficial on this subject this time.

Assumptions : I. The format and emphasis of different types of letters is different.

II. We can send different types of letters on the same subject.

96. **Statement:** Please check the availability of two tickets from Delhi to Lucknow.

Assumptions: I. The person checking knows the desired mode of travel.

II. The person checking knows the details of the person travelling.

97. **Statement:** If you want to increase your writing speed, use 0.7 pen.

Assumptions: I. There are different types of pen available.

II. The person being told understands what is 0.7 pen.

98. **Statement:** In order to build more space, extra FSI needs to be bought.

Assumptions: I. The person being told does not know the meaning of FSI.

II. More space will reduce the construction cost.

99. **Statement:** Let there be a signboard also indicating the directions and instructions.

Assumptions: I. Signboard can be prepared without using any language.

II. Signboard is the only effective tool to indicate directions.

100. **Statement:** Banks should always check financial status before lending money to a client.

Assumptions: I. Checking before lending would give a true picture of the client's financial status.

II. Clients sometimes may not present the correct picture of their ability to repay loan amount to the bank.

101. **Statement:** The government has decided to run all commercial vehicles on bio-fuels in order to save the depleting fossil fuel reserves.

Assumptions: I. It is possible to switch over from fossil fuels to bio-fuels for vehicles.

II. Sufficient amount of bio-fuel can be produced in the country to run all commercial vehicles.

102. **Statement:** To save the environment enforce total ban on illegal mining throughout the country.

Assumptions: I. Mining which is done legally does not cause any harm to the environment.

II. Mining is one of the factors responsible for environmental degradation.

103. **Statement:** Give adequate job-related training to the employees before assigning them full-fledged work.

Assumptions: I. Training helps in boosting the performance of employees.

II. Employees have no skill sets before training is provided to them.

104. **Statement:** Take a ferry or a boat instead of a bus to reach the Kravi islands faster.

Assumptions: I. The islands being in remote location are not easily accessible.

II. Ferries and boats are available to travel to Kravi islands.

105. **Statement:** A leading university has begun a practice of displaying results only on the Internet rather than on the main notice boards.

Assumptions: I. All the students enrolled with the university have access to Internet at home.

II. Most of the students referred to the results displayed on both the internet as well as the notice boards earlier.

106. **Statement:** In order to replenish the nutrients in the soil, it is important to grow different types of crops every alternate season.

Assumptions: I. A crop can never be grown for the second time in the same field.

II. If a different crop is grown in the successive season, no additional nutrients such as fertilizers are required to be added to the soil.

107. **Statement:** If farmers want to improve their yield, they must use organic fertilizers in place of chemical fertilizers.

Assumptions: I. Chemical fertilizers have certain ill effects on health.

II. Chemical fertilizers do not produce as much yield as the organic fertilizers.

108. **Statement:** Store eatables in the deep freeze in order to preserve these for a long time.

Assumptions: I. Food material remains eatable even after deep freezing for a long time.

II. It is not possible to store any eatable at room temperature even for a shorter period of time.

109. **Statement:** A leading NGO decided to open a library containing books and newspapers of all major publishers in a remote village.

Assumptions: I. All other nearby villages already have similar libraries.

II. There is adequate number of literate people in the village.

Type II : Exercise 3B

Directions: A statement is given followed by several assumptions. An assumption is something assumed or taken for granted. Read the statement carefully and decide which of the assumptions are implicit in the statement.

1. "If he does not mend his ways, I will call the police".
   Assumptions: I. He may mend his ways.
   II. The police may help me.
   III. He has been making hoax calls to me.
   1) I and II are implicit 2) II and III are implicit 3) I and III are implicit
   4) All are implicit 5) Only II is implicit
2. **Statement:** "Do not touch stray objects. They may be bombs." - a notice by the City Police
   Assumptions: I. Stray objects are harmless.
   II. Stray objects may be touched by people.
   III. People will take notice of the warning.
   1) I and II are implicit 2) I and III are implicit 3) II and III are implicit
   4) I and either II or III are implicit
   5) At least one of the above is implicit
3. **Statement:** "I think that she has gone mad. Last night, I saw her barking like a dog." - A tells B about Madhu.
   Assumptions: I. Madhu is a friend of A.
   II. B knows Madhu.
   III. Some people do not bark like dogs.
   1) I and II are implicit 2) II and III are implicit 3) I and III are implicit
   4) All are implicit 5) Either I or II and III are implicit
4. **Statement:** "The prices should fall after May. By that time the demand of foodgrains starts dropping." - an economist
   Assumptions: I. Price will not fall before May.
   II. The economist is in link with farmers of the country.
   III. A drop in demand (of foodgrains) will result in a drop in supply (of foodgrains).
   1) Only I is implicit 2) Only II is implicit 3) Only III is implicit
   4) II and III are implicit 5) None is implicit
5. **Statement:** "The Finance Commission must grant more funds to our state. After all, we are the biggest suppliers of ores to the rest of India." - the CM of a state
   Assumptions: I. The Finance Commission is not in a mood to grant more funds to the state.
   II. More funds should be given to states that supply ores.
   III. The Chief Minister has already written to the Finance Commission asking for more funds.

1) I and II are implicit 2) II and III are implicit 3) I and III are implicit
4) Only III is implicit 5) Only II is implicit

6. **Statement:** "I do not like to give consumer goods as a wedding gift. I prefer to give cash." - A tells B.

Assumptions: **I.** A is invited at weddings.
II. Some people give consumer goods as wedding gifts.
III. Some people give useless things as wedding gifts.

1) I and II are implicit 2) II and III are implicit 3) I and III are implicit
4) All are implicit 5) None is implicit

7. **Statement:** "The Prime Minister is expected to announce an expansion in his ministry shortly." - a newspaper report

Assumptions: **I.** The newspaper has quoted authentic sources.
II. The newspaper has reliable sources for the news.
III. The Prime Minister has the power to expand his cabinet.

1) I and II are implicit 2) II and III are implicit 3) I and III are implicit
4) All are implicit 5) Only I is implicit

8. **Statement:** "You cannot solve such questions without consulting a diagram. Difficult questions need diagrams for solving." - A teacher tells his students.

Assumptions: **I.** The students are not intelligent.
II. The problem cannot be solved.
III. Such questions are difficult.

1) I and II are implicit 2) II and III are implicit 3) Only II is implicit
4) Only III is implicit 5) None is implicit

9. **Statement:** "You should not drink whisky. You must take care of your health." - A tells his friend.

Assumptions: **I.** A knows about the ill-effects of whisky.
II. Whisky is intoxicating.
III. Whisky is not good for health.

1) Only III is implicit 2) I and II are implicit 3) II and III are implicit
4) I and III are implicit 5) All are implicit

10. **Statement:** "I have decided to cut down on coffee. People tell me that caffeine is not good for health." - A tells B.

Assumptions: **I.** Coffee contains caffeine.
II. People are correct in their views about coffee.
III. B may also cut down on coffee.

1) I and II are implicit 2) All are implicit 3) Only I is implicit
4) Only II is implicit 5) Only III is implicit

11. **Statement:** "We buy used imported items. Contact us at the earliest." - an advertisement

Assumptions: **I.** Used imported items may not be useless.
II. There are people who are willing to sell used imported items.

III. The advertisement will be read by people who may sell such items.

1) I and II are implicit 2) II and III are implicit 3) I and III are implicit
4) All are implicit 5) Only II is implicit

12. **Statement:** "If he proves a single charge against me, I vow that I will quit politics for ever.", said a politician in a speech

Assumptions: **I.** The charges levelled against the politician are false.
II. The charges levelled against the politician are beyond proof even if true.
III. The politician is fed up of politics.

1) Only I is implicit 2) Only II is implicit 3) Only III is implicit
4) I and III are implicit 5) II and III are implicit

13. **Statement:** "History will not forgive them. They have tried to silence the voice of peace. Violence can never silence peace." - A leader while expressing grief over the assassination of Israeli leader Yitzak Rabin.

Assumptions: **I.** Mr. Rabin was a follower of history.
II. Mr. Rabin was a champion of peace.
III. Mr. Rabin was killed by Jew fundamentalists.

1) I and II are implicit 2) II and III are implicit 3) I and III are implicit
4) Only I is implicit 5) Only II is implicit

14. **Statement:** "Clearly, the judiciary cannot provide all answers. But it seems the public, weary of an inactive executive, is turning to the Supreme Court as a last resort." - an article

Assumptions: **I.** The Supreme Court is above the executive.
II. The Supreme Court is more active than the executive.
III. The executive does not have sufficient powers.

1) I and II are implicit 2) II and III are implicit 3) I and III are implicit
4) Only I is implicit 5) Only II is implicit

15. **Statement:** "No democracy has paid a heavier price of adult franchise than India. Illiterate people, after being given the power to vote, have ushered in a kind of functional anarchy." - Excerpts from a speech

Assumptions: **I.** Adult franchise is not a healthy thing for a democracy.
II. Only literate people should be given the right to vote.
III. There is functional anarchy in India.

1) Only I is implicit 2) Only II is implicit 3) Only III is implicit
4) I and III are implicit 5) II and III are implicit

16. **Statement:** "You won't get sweets at any cost. I will not let you eat things that are not good for your teeth." - A mother tells her child.

Assumptions: **I.** The mother cares for her child.
II. Sweets are not good for health.
III. The mother has the authority to decide what her child is to eat.

1) I and II are implicit 2) II and III are implicit 3) I and III are implicit
4) All are implicit 5) None of these

17. **Statement:** "Washing powder: Safed. For a washing that is brightest and cleanest. And cheap too." - an advertisement

Assumptions: **I.** Safed is a good washing powder

II. People want cheap washing.

III. People accord price a secondary importance.

1) I and II are implicit 2) II and III are implicit 3) I and III are implicit
4) All are implicit 5) None of these

18. **Statement:** "There is so much noise out here. How can a sincere student study here?" - a mother of a student tells her husband.

Assumptions: **I.** Noise is not very conducive to children.

II. Noise may hamper study.

III. The mother cares for her child's health.

1) Only II is implicit 2) I and II are implicit 3) II and III are implicit
4) Only III is implicit 5) All are implicit

19. **Statement:** "I think we will win. We have got the most talented scorers on our side." - The national hockey coach in an interview

Assumptions: **I.** Talented scorers are crucial for any team's victory.

II. Hockey is different from other sports.

III. Chances of victory are different from actual occurrences of victory.

1) Only I is implicit 2) Only II is implicit 3) Only III is implicit
4) I and II are implicit 5) I and III are implicit

20. **Statement:** "This is a gun in my hand. So you better behave like a good boy and bring out all your valuables without calling the police." - A thief tells a housekeeper.

Assumptions: **I.** When people see a gun they behave like good boys.

II. Fear brings a sense of surrender.

III. The police should not be called when people are afraid.

1) I and II are implicit 2) II and III are implicit 3) I and III are implicit
4) Only II is implicit 5) Only I is implicit

21. **Statement:** Unless we give sufficient autonomy to them, these units will not be profitable.

Assumptions: **I.** These units are not profitable.

II. These units can become profitable.

III. Autonomy is a necessary condition for profitability.

1) I and II are implicit 2) II and III are implicit 3) I and III are implicit
4) All are implicit 5) None is implicit

22. **Statement:** "I do not really understand why people discourage us from drinking beer. Beer is good for health, a mood elevator. Obesity is a small price to pay for such a good thing." - A tells B.

Assumptions: **I.** Beer is not good for health.

II. Beer is good for health.

III. Apart from obesity, there are no disadvantages of drinking beer.

1) I and III are implicit 2) II and III are implicit 3) I and II are implicit
4) Either I or II and III are implicit 5) None is implicit

23. **Statement:** "I cannot get my daughter married to him. He drinks, gambles and even visits brothels." - A tells B.

Assumptions: **I.** My daughter will agree to my decision.

II. Drinking is not a desirable quality of a husband.

III. B is interested in marrying A's daughter.

1) Only I is implicit 2) Only II is implicit 3) I and II are implicit
4) II and III are implicit 5) Only III is implicit

24. **Statement:** "They shall be punished. I gave them several warnings but they did not stop wearing pleated skirts in school." - The principal tells a teacher.

Assumptions: **I.** The Principal has the authority to punish them.

II. A punishment must always follow some warnings.

III. Pleated skirts are not allowed in the school.

1) I and II are implicit 2) II and III are implicit 3) I and III are implicit
4) I, II and III are implciit 5) Only III is implicit

25. **Statement:** "The Red Line buses must be banned. They have killed so many people on the roads." - A passenger tells a colleague.

Assumptions: **I.** The passenger has the authority to ban them.

II. Buses that kill must be banned.

III. The colleague may agree with the passenger's view.

1) Only I is implicit 2) Only II is implicit 3) Only III is implicit
4) II and III are implicit 5) All are implicit

26. **Statement:** "The death of the convict in the police custody was a result of excessive torture. His autopsy proves it." - A lawyer in the court

Assumptions: **I.** The convict died in police custody.

II. Autopsy can be used to find the reason of death.

III. The lawyer is an expert on autopsy.

1) Only I is implicit 2) Only II is implicit 3) Only III is implicit
4) I and II are implicit 5) I and III are implicit

27. **Statement:** "The Bombay Stock Exchange Index has collapsed. Perhaps the brokers were panicked rumours of at the finance minister's resignation." - a newspaper report

Assumptions: **I.** The cause of the collapse is not definitely known.

II. The finance minister is important in the eyes of the brokers.

III. The rumours of the finance minister's resignation were baseless.

1) Only I is implicit 2) Only II is implicit 3) Only III is implicit
4) I and II are implicit 5) II and III are implicit

28. **Statement:** "Nathuram Godse was prepared to kill anybody who came between him and his dream of a 'Hindu Rashtra'. He had his reasons to kill Gandhiji." - a book of history

Assumptions: **I.** The author knows the character of Nathuram Godse well.

II. Godse thought that Gandhiji was an obstruction in the way to a 'Hindu Rashtra'.

III. Godse might be a fanatic but he was not irrational.

1) Only I is implicit 2) Only II is implicit 3) I and II are implicit
4) All are implicit 5) II and III are implicit

29. **Statement:** "There is disagreement on many questions. But the conflict with Chechnya can still be resolved by peaceful means." - Russian defence minister

Assumptions: **I.** Disagreement can be resolved by peaceful means.

II. Chechnya may be persuaded.

III. Chechnya may not be persuaded.

1) Only I is implicit 2) I and II are implicit 3) I and III are implicit
4) Either II or III is implicit 5) I and either II or III are implicit

30. **Statement:** "The court here plays so fast that it really helps my game. Yzaga was at a disadvantage." - Sampras after beating Yzaga in a tennis match.

Assumptions: **I.** Tennis courts should be fast and not slow.

II. Tennis courts should be slow and not fast.

III. Yzaga is a better player at slower courts.

1) I and III are implicit 2) II and III are implicit 3) Either I or II is implicit
4) III and either I or II are implicit 5) Only III is implicit

31. **Statement:** "The success of a film does not change me or my behaviour. Why should it? I don't think I have become arrogant after *Baazigar's* success." - Shah Rukh Khan in an interview

Assumptions: **I.** Some stars do change after a successful film.

II. *Baazigar* is a successful film.

III. There is no reason why a star should change after a successful film.

1) Only I is implicit 2) Only II is implicit 3) Only III is implicit
4) I and II are implicit 5) All are implicit.

32. **Statement:** "We cannot prevent the shock waves but we do compensate for them. Insure with Oriental Insurance — the company that offers most comprehensive insurance against earthquakes." - an advertisement

Assumptions: **I.** Earthquakes carry shock waves with them.

II. Oriental Insurance is not the only company that insures against earthquakes.

III. Earthquakes are natural phenomena.

1) I and II are implicit 2) I and III are implicit 3) II and III are implicit
4) Only I is implicit 5) All are implicit

33. **Statement:** "Please do not preach us non-violence. It was not your wife they raped. It was not your son they killed." - A group of irate Sikhs to Gandhi in 1947.

Assumptions: **I.** People wanted to use violence.
II. In 1947, some women were raped.
III. The pain of a tragedy is the greatest when it happens to one's own folks.

1) I and II are implicit 2) II and III are implicit 3) III and I are implicit
4) All are implicit 5) Only III is implicit

34. **Statement:** "Yes, it was my wife, it was my son. Because your women are my women and your sons, my sons. And still, I shall preach non-violence." - Gandhi replying to the same mob.

Assumptions: **I.** Gandhi believed that non-violence is the best answer to all conflicts.
II. Gandhi did suffer in the sufferings of the Sikhs.
III. People could be transformed by showing to them the rational way.

1) Only I is implicit 2) Only II is implicit 3) I and II are implicit
4) II and III are implicit 5) All are implicit.

35. **Statement:** "The tickets have been sold out. Poor fellow, he came all the way from Maya Nagar and now, he has to return disappointed." - A man about a stranger outside a cinema hall.

Assumptions: **I.** Maya Nagar is far off from the cinema hall.
II. The man himself got his tickets.
III. The movie is a super hit.

1) Only I is implicit 2) Only II is implicit 3) Only III is implicit
4) I and II are implicit 5) I and III are implicit

36. **Statement:** "A short man was seen around the shop at seven o'clock. This does not mean that he was Khashogi. Khashogi is five feet eight." - A lawyer in the court.

Assumptions: **I.** Khashogi is the man whom the lawyer is defending.
II. There is truth in the statement that a short man was seen around the shop at seven.
III. Five-feet-eight-inch-tall men are not 'short'.

1) I and II are implicit 2) II and III are implicit 3) I and III are implicit
4) All are implicit. 5) Only I is implicit

37. **Statement:** "There is very heavy traffic on the road between 5 to 7 p.m. We need to have a flyover in this area." - A planning engineer in a meeting.

Assumptions: **I.** Heavy traffic is sought to be maintained.

II. Previous planning engineers did not do much about heavy traffic.

III. A flyover is likely to solve the problem of heavy traffic.

1) Only II is implicit 2) Only III is implicit 3) I and II are implicit
4) II and III are implicit 5) I and III are implicit

38. **Statement:** "There were red spots all over his body. Among other things, he could be suffering from measles." - A doctor in his patient's report.

Assumptions: **I.** One symptom of measles is appearance of red spots over the body.

II. Very few diseases have the appearance of red spots as a symptom.

III. Quite many diseases have the appearance of red spots as a symptom.

1) Only I is implicit 2) I and II are implicit
3) I and III are implicit 4) I and either II or III are implicit
5) None of the above

39. **Statement:** "People of all castes, religion and locality were swayed. Who can deny the power of a good orator?" - an excerpt from a politician's diary

Assumptions: **I.** A speech was made by the politician.

II. The politician does not believe in caste.

III. Only powerful oratory has the power to transcend the barrier of caste and religion.

1) Only I is implicit 2) Only II is implicit 3) Only III is implicit
4) All are implicit 5) None are implicit

40. **Statement:** "Corruption needs to be fought at all costs. We are paying a heavy price for corruption." - A minister in his speech.

Assumptions: **I.** The minister is not corrupt.

II. There exists corruption in our system.

III. Politicians suffer the most as a result of corruption.

1) I and II are implicit 2) II and III are implicit
3) I and III are implicit 4) I, II and III are implicit
5) Only II is implicit

41. **Statement:** "There is a nasty wind blowing fom the north. We must reach an island before the storm reaches us." - A captain to his crew.

Assumptions: **I.** The wind is blowing very fast.

II. It is dangerous to sail during a strom.

III. There is an island somewhere near the ship.

1) Only I is implicit 2) Only II is implicit 3) Only III is implicit
4) II and III are implicit 5) I and II are implicit

42. **Statement:** "She looked so pale. It immediately struck me that she might be suffering from a dreaded disease." - A man tells his friend.

Assumptions: **I.** The friend knows about the woman being talked about.
II. Looking pale is a likely symptom of a dreaded disease.
III. The disease had cast a terror in that area during these times.

1) Only I is implicit 2) Only II is implicit 3) Only III is implicit
4) I and II are implicit 5) II and III are implicit

43. **Statement:** "The workers have decided to go on strike. God! What will happen to our supply orders!" - a manufacturer

Assumptions: **I.** It is not moral for workers to go on strike.
II. Supply is likely to be disturbed as a result of the strike.
III. Praying to God may help one in a critical situation.

1) Only I is implicit 2) Only II is implicit 3) I and II are implicit
4) I and III are implicit 5) II and III are implicit

44. **Statement:** "God! If my intentions have been pure and if my efforts sincere, I pray that, by Your majestic grace, I emerge successful. Amen!" - a woman in a church

Assumptions: **I.** God helps only those who pray to Him.
II. God helps only those whose intentions are pure.
III. Prayers do help people.

1) I and II are implicit 2) II and III are implicit 3) Only II is implicit
4) Only III is implicit 5) All are implicit

45. **Statement:** "To err is human. Every man makes mistakes. But to learn from those mistakes is what makes men great. And this is why there are so few of great men around us." - A philosopher in his speech.

Assumptions: **I.** Mistakes do not make significant issues.
II. There are very few persons who learn from mistakes.
III. If a man learns from mistakes, he is a great man.

1) Only I is implicit 2) Only II is implicit 3) Only III is implicit
4) I and II are implicit 5) I, II and III are implicit

46. **Statement:** "In our report, published last week, the name of the author was misspelt. We regret the error." - a magazine editor

Assumptions: **I.** The name of the author was not easy to spell.
II. Publishing correct names of authors is not as important as the quality of the article.
III. Publishing correct names of authors is desirable.

1) Only I is implicit 2) Only II is implicit 3) Only III is implicit
4) I and III are implicit 5) II and III are implicit

47. **Statement:** "Why should we not protest? When we ask for drinking water they give us Pepsi and Coca-Cola." - A politician in an interview.

Assumptions: **I.** Only drinking water is good for people's health.

II. Providing people with drinking water is more important than providing Pepsi and Coca-Cola.

III. Pepsi and Coca-Cola do not contain healthy drinking water.

1) I and II are implicit 2) Only I is implicit 3) II and III are implicit
4) Only II is implicit 5) Either II or III is implicit

48. **Statement:** "If obscene songs have become popular, the masses are responsible for it. Why do they listen to these songs or buy these cassettes?" - A writer in his speech on today's society.

Assumptions: I. Buying cassettes of a song is an indication of its popularity.

II. Obscene songs were not recorded earlier.

III. The masses have no taste for good music.

1) Only I is implicit 2) I and II are implicit 3) II and III are implicit
4) I and III are implicit 5) Can't say

49. **Statement:** "The involvement of our senior scientists in the ISRO case is really shocking. It is regrettable that they put money before national interest." - an editorial

Assumptions: I. The ISRO case involves the active hand of our scientists in supplying secret documents to another country.

II. Our scientists were not expected to do such a thing.

III. National interest should command a higher priority than money.

1) I and II are implicit 2) II and III are implicit 3) I and III are implicit
4) All are implicit 5) Only III is implicit

50. **Statement:** "I don't care if the world calls me conservative. But my wife won't work in films after she marries me." - An actor in an interview.

Assumptions: I. The actor is not much bothered about what the world think of him.

II. The actor is unmarried.

III. Not allowing the wife to work in films may be taken as a sign of conservatism.

1) I and II are implicit 2) II and III are implicit 3) I and III are implicit
4) All are implicit 5) Only II is implicit

51. **Statement:** "Persons with strong political connections are being posted as judges. It is no surprise that the judiciary is coming in the shadow of corruption." - A person in a debate.

Assumptions: I. A person with strong political connections is likely to be corrupt.

II. A person with strong political connections may or may not be corrupt.

III. Politics and judiciary have hopelessly mingled these days.

1) Only I is implicit
2) Only II is implicit
3) I and III are implicit
4) Either I or II is implicit
5) All are implicit

52. **Statement:** Hungry stomachs do not understand high values and economic ethics. They will vote a man who gives them rice." - A political analyst on why a particular party won the election.

Assumptions: I. A lot of people are hungry.

II. Rice was not available previously.

III. Rice was available only in limited quantity.

1) Only I is implicit
2) I and II are implicit
3) I and III are implicit
4) Either II or III is implicit
5) All are implicit

53. **Statement:** "The Samba spying case has blown away the myth that the Indian army is disciplined and impartial." - an editorial

Assumptions: I. Samba is the name of the file that was smuggled to another country.

II. It was believed that Indian army is disciplined.

III. Spying scandals are not welcome in an army.

1) Only II is implicit
2) I and II are implicit
3) II and III are implicit
4) Only III is implicit
5) All are implicit

54. **Statement:** "Nokia introduces the world's easiest-to-use cellular phone. Small in size, huge in performance." - an advertisement

Assumptions: I. People want convenience while using a cellular phone.

II. People want small-sized cellular phones.

III. Cellular phones were not available before.

1) Only I is implicit
2) Only II is implicit
3) Only III is implicit
4) I and II are implicit
5) All are implicit

55. **Statement:** "A majority of our population is still suspicious of our stock markets. We need to have greater transparency in trading." - a stockbroker.

Assumptions: I. Greater transparency in trading is a desirable feature of the stock markets.

II. Stock market operations are not transparent these days.

III. Lack of adequate transparency is one of the main reasons behind people's suspicion of our stock markets.

1) Only I is implicit
2) Only II is implicit
3) II and III are implicit
4) I and II are implicit
5) I and III are implicit.

Type III : Exercise 3C

Directions: Each of the following items asks you to pick up the hidden premises (assumptions) of an argument. Mark the best answer.

1. Edward was just elected president of the Student Senate, so he must be a senior.

   The statement above makes which of the following assumptions?

   I. Only seniors can be members of the Student Senate.
   II. Only seniors can be president of the Student Senate.
   III. Only members of the Student Senate can be seniors.

   A) I only B) II only C) III only
   D) I and III only E) I, II and III

2. If these cabinets were built after 1975, they were not made of oak plywood.

   The statement above depends upon which of the following assumptions?

   A) All cabinets made after 1975 were made of oak plywood.
   B) All cabinets made in 1975 or earlier were made of oak plywood.
   C) Only cabinets made of oak plywood were built in 1975 or earlier.
   D) No cabinets made in 1975 or earlier were made of oak plywood.
   E) No cabinets made after 1975 were made of oak plywood.

3. Max: "Every painting done by Picasso is a masterpiece."

   Ernst: "That's not true. Several masterpieces by David and Delacroix hang in the Louvre in Paris."

   Ernst apparently assumes that Max said that

   A) only masterpieces were painted by Picasso.
   B) all masterpieces were painted by either David or Delacroix.
   C) only masterpieces by Picasso hang in the Louvre.
   D) only masterpieces by David and Delacroix hang in the Louvre.
   E) some of Picasso's masterpieces do not hang in the Louvre.

4. Students at Duns Scotus High must get a better education than students at Erasmus High because the grade point average of students at Duns Scotus High is higher than that of students at Erasmus High.

   The claim above depends upon which of the following assumptions?

   I. The average grade earned by students is a good measure of the quality of education that a student receives.
   II. Extracurricular activities at Duns Scotus High are given more emphasis than at Erasmus High.
   III. The grading standards at the two high schools are roughly the same.

   A) I only B) III only C) I and III only
   D) II and III only E) I, II and III

5. A government survey released today shows that 80 per cent of the people who fly are satisfied with the service they receive from the airlines in this country. Three interviewers stood outside a major airport and asked people

leaving the terminal, "Do you have any complaints about the flight you just got off?" Only 20 per cent responded "yes!"

Which of the following, if true, would most undermine the conclusion of the argument above?

A) Sixty per cent of the people coming out of the airline terminal were not people who had just gotten off a flight.

B) One per cent of the people approached by the interviewers refused to respond to their inquiries.

C) The interviewers began their inquiry just after passengers were discharged from a flight that was 40 minutes late.

D) The interviewers were able to speak to only 70 per cent of the people leaving the terminal, but those people were selected at random.

E) For six months following the day of the interviews, no official complaints were filed by any passenger with the Federal agency that regulated the airlines.

6. Colonel Mustard did not commit the murder in the dining room with the candlestick. Therefore, Mrs. Peacock committed the murder in the conservatory with the knife.

The argument above depends upon which of the following assumptions?

I. The murder was committed either with the candlestick or with the knife.

II. The murder was committed either in the dining room or in the conservatory.

III. The murder was committed either by Colonel Mustard or by Mrs Peacock.

IV. The murder was either committed by Colonel Mustard in the dining room with the candlestick or by Mrs Peacock in the conservatory with the knife.

A) I only B) IV only C) I and III only
D) I, II and III only E) I, II, III and IV

7. An efficiency expert made the following suggestion to the manager of a shirt factory: "Purchase larger spools of sewing thread. With more thread to a spool, your operators will not need to stop production as often to change spools. This will reduce your labour cost."

The efficiency expert apparently assumes that

A) thread wound on larger spools is not as strong as thread wound on smaller spools.

B) sewing machines do not break down and do not require routine maintenance.

C) workers in the factory are paid by the hour rather than on a piecework basis.

D) machine operators are not allowed to leave their machines during the work period.

E) speeding up production will improve the quality of shirts made at the factory.

8. A major insurance company reported that approximately 80 per cent of all traffic accidents never result in an insurance claim. So, we can conclude that about 80 per cent of all losses due to theft also go unreported.

The argument above assumes that

I. Statistics of automobile insurance claims are applicable to claims for theft losses.

II. Traffic accidents represent a more serious danger to the individual than do thefts.

III. The average dollar value of a traffic accident claim is equal to the average dollar value of a thefts claim.

A) I only B) II only C) III only
D) I and II only E) I and III only

9. The continuing and increasing reliance on computers represents a serious threat to the privacy of the individual. Recently, we have seen numerous examples of teenage and other 'hackers' breaking the security codes of stores and banks and obtaining sensitive financial information of customers.

The argument above depends upon which of the following assumptions?

I. People who obtain sensitive financial information about others will not share it.

II. It is not possible to develop a security system for a computer that cannot be broken.

III. Computers are not more efficient than other systems of recordkeeping.

A) I only B) II only C) III only
D) I and II only E) II and III only

10. The need for drug and sex counselling for teenagers has been overemphasised. Instead, we should channel the money spent on those programmes into marriage counselling and other programmes designed to hold the family together. Lower the rate of family dissolution and you will reduce the incidence of teen drug abuse and pregnancies.

The author makes which of the following assumptions?

I. Marriage counselling and other programmes are effective in maintaining the unity of the family.

II. Family dissolution contributes to problems of teen drugs and sex.

III. People presently working in teen-counselling programmes can be re-employed as marriage counsellor.

A) I only B) II only C) I and II only
D) II and III only E) I, II and III

11. Archaeologists have uncovered evidence that human beings, even as early as in palaeolithic times, had a belief in an afterlife. Burial sites located close to ancient settlements have been found in which the dead were buried along with some of the tools, clothing, and other artifacts they might have used while alive. This is the earliest known evidence of a belief in life after death.
Which of the following is an assumption underlying the argument above?
A) The placement of burial sites near ancient settlements indicates a feeling of piety towards the dead.
B) Belief in life after death is a central tenet of most religious faiths.
C) The remains of tools and clothing found in the burial sites had belonged to those buried nearby.
D) Religious belief is a characteristic of the most civilised societies.
E) Only those people who believe in life after death would bury artifacts with the dead.

12. Some of the most popular television advertisements are those employing humour. But as an advertising technique, humour has its drawbacks. Studies have shown that while many viewers of humorous advertisements vividly recall the commercials, far fewer recall the name of the product being promoted. This casts doubt on the ability of humorous commercials, no matter how funny or enjoyable, to increase product sales.
Which of the following is implied by the passage above?
A) Humorous commercials tend to reduce the credibility of products in the eyes of viewers.
B) Though enjoyable, humorous commercials are often less memorable than serious commercials.
C) The most important criterion of a successful advertisement is its ability to increase product sales.
D) Humorous commercials may alienate almost as many viewers as they entertain.
E) The ultimate goal of advertising is to increase the name recognition of the product being promoted.

13. Religious leaders in our country were once expected to express and articulate lasting moral values. This is no longer the case. Today, we see spokespersons for major religious denominations entering into debate over mere political matters formerly reserved for members of the secular community.
The logical structure of the passage above depends upon the author's assumption that the expression of lasting moral values is

A) a strictly religious function
B) no longer deeply valued
C) essentially nonpolitical
D) reserved for secular society
E) the most important role of a religion

14. For the purposes of this study, ten qualities of a liveable city were chosen, including low crime rate, cleanliness, cultural attractions, and other amenities. For each city in the study, scores from 1 (lowest) to 10 (highest) were assigned for each of the ten qualities. The ten scores for each city were then summed, yielding a total liveability score for each city. We hope the resulting ratings will help you in choosing your next place of residence.

The passage above makes which of the following assumptions?

I. It is possible to assign an accurate numerical score to each of the city's amenities.

II. Each of the ten qualities of a liveable city is equally important.

III. Most people enjoy some degree of personal choice in where they reside.

A) I only
B) II only
C) III only
D) I and II only
E) II and III only

15. Superficially, today's problems with the abuse of illegal drugs such as heroin and cocaine resemble the abuse of alcohol during the 1920s, when many people kept drinking in spite of prohibition. There is, however, a significant difference. The abuse of drugs such as heroin and cocaine has never been a widespread, socially-accepted practice among most middle-class, otherwise law-abiding Americans.

An underlying assumption of the passage is that

A) during prohibition, drinking of alcohol was commonly accepted among most Americans.

B) as long as drugs are available, they will be abused despite laws for the contrary.

C) most Americans consider heroin and cocaine to be in the same category as alcohol.

D) in a democracy, laws must be based on the fundamental beliefs and values of majority of citizens.

E) American popular opinion has always been moulded primarily by the values of the middle class.

16. Philosophy should be taught to students at a very early age. It will instil in them a healthy skepticism towards values that they might otherwise accept without question.

The argument above makes which of the following assumptions?

I. Unless students are exposed to philosophy at an early age, they will accept every idea.

II. Even at an early age, students are able to understand some philosophical concepts.

III. It is a good idea for students to question traditional values.

A) II only B) III only C) I and II only
D) II and III only E) I, II and III

17. In an extensive study of reading habits of magazine readers, it was found that an average of four to five people actually read each copy of the most popular weekly news magazine. On this basis, we estimate that the 12,000 copies of *Poets and Poetry* that are sold each month are actually read by 48,000 to 60,000 people.

The estimate above assumes that

A) individual magazine readers generally enjoy more than one type of magazine.
B) most of the readers of *Poets and Poetry* subscribe to magazine.
C) the ratio of readers to copies is the same for *Poets and Poetry* as for the weekly news magazine.
D) the number of readers of the weekly news magazine is similar to the number of readers of *Poets and Poetry*.
E) most of the readers enjoy sharing copies of their favourite magazines with friends and family members.

18. It is a truism of military science that "Generals always prepare for the last war." In the same way, public officials generally spend their efforts on problems that were resolved - one way or another - years before. By the time a public issue reaches the consciousness of enough of the citizenry to become a high priority of our elected leaders, the problem is usually past the point at which government efforts can significantly affect it.

All of the following are assumed in the argument above EXCEPT

A) Most of the public problems tend to evolve towards a point at which the government can do little to control them.
B) Political and military leaders are both prone to react tardily to changes in their fields.
C) Issues attain importance for public officials when large number of citizens are concerned about them.
D) Planning policies, solely based on past experiences are likely to be ineffective.
E) The government officials can generally do little to influence directly the course of public policy.

Questions (19-20): Government spending in support of pure research is often treated as somehow wasteful, as though only immediate technological application can justify any scientific endeavour. Yet, unless the well of basic knowledge is continually replenished through pure research, the flow of beneficial technology will soon dry up. Today's pure research may appear to be of little use; but no one can tell what good it may yield someday. One might just as well ask: "Of what use is a newborn baby?"

19. *The argument above depends on which of the following assumptions?*
    I. There is a time lag between the discovery of a new phenomenon and the discovery of a practical application for it.
    II. Pure research is more costly and time-consuming than the attempt to develop new technologies.
    III. Most of the pure researchs will eventually benefit future generations but will not be of any advantage to people currently alive.
    A) I only B) II only C) I and II only
    D) I and III only E) I, II and III
20. *To which of the following would the author compare the "newborn baby" mentioned in the last sentence of the passage?*
    A) A technological breakthrough based on pure research
    B) Government funding in support of scientific endeavour
    C) Public support for spending on pure research
    D) The flow of public benefits from new technological developments
    E) A scientific discovery with no immediate apparent application
21. One major obligation of the social psychologist is to provide his own discipline, the other social sciences, and interested laymen with conceptual tools that will increase the range and the reliability of their understanding of social phenomena. Beyond that, responsible government officials are today turning more frequently to social scientists for insights into the nature and solution of problems with which they are confronted.
    The above argument assumes that
    A) Social psychologists must have a strong background in other sciences as well as their own.
    B) A study of social psychology should be a part of the curriculum of government officials.
    C) The social scientist has an obligation to provide the means by which social phenomena may be understood by others.
    D) Social phenomena are little understood by those outside the field of social psychology.
    E) A good social psychologist is obligated principally by the need to solve interdisciplinary problems.
22. New problems require new solutions. And new problems arise with new populations and new technologies. The solutions of these problems require new institutions as well as new political, economic, and social mechanisms. Yet, institutions and political and economic arrangements grow slowly and die slowly. Because old institutions die slowly, new institutions should be given every chance of success.
    The writer of the above passage makes which of the following assumptions?
    A) New institutions are needed because old institutions are inefficient.
    B) New institutions are created in order to solve existing problems.
    C) As old institutions are phased out, new ones take their place.

D) If there were no growth, old institutions would die more slowly.
E) Socio-technological change requires new forms of institutional arrangements.

23. A political analyst wrote the following: "I realise there are some shortcomings in the questionnaire method. However, since I send a copy of the questionnaire to every home in the district, I believe the results are quite representative. I think the numbers received are so large that it is quite accurate even though the survey is not done scientifically."
The writer of the above statement makes which of the following assumptions?
A) Most people who received the questionnaire have replied.
B) Most people in the district live in homes.
C) The questionnaire method of data collection is not scientific.
D) The large number of replies means a high proportion of those surveyed have replied.
E) A large and absolute number of replies is synonymous with accuracy.

24. Donors are almost never offended by being asked for too much (in fact, they are usually flattered). And if you ask for too much, your donor can always suggest a smaller amount. On the other hand, donors are frequently offended by being asked for too little. A common reaction is, "So, that's all they think I'm worth".
The above statement assumes that:
A) Donors are usually never asked for enough.
B) A good fund-raiser will value the worth of the donor.
C) It is worth the gamble to ask for large donations.
D) Fund-raisers often think that donors are incapable of giving much.
E) Donors are seldom offended by fund-raisers.

25. A recent communique noted that China's foreign minister told officials in Italy that Beijing intends to maintain and extend its open-door policy to the West. The minister also said that China would continue with its programme of political and economic changes despite a recent campaign against Western ideas and foreign aids.
The writer of the communique above makes which of the following assumptions?
A) China's foreign minister asserts that internal change is a matter for only the Chinese to decide.
B) Internal political and economic changes will not be tolerated.
C) China's external relations with the West will continue despite turmoil at home.
D) Internal changes in China will not follow Western models although foreign trade between them may continue.

E) China's foreign minister does not realise that an open-door policy and rejection of Western ideas are mutually exclusive.

26. Once a company has established an extensive sales network in a foreign market and therefore has achieved substantial sales, it seems that these markets should be treated in a fashion very similar to those in one's own country. It is, therefore, those countries where only initial sales and representation have been developed where marketing methods will have to differ from domestic activities.

The above statement assumes that:

A) Sales networks can be the same in both foreign and domestic markets.
B) Extensive sales networks are preferable to less developed ones.
C) Some countries develop economically faster than the others.
D) Larger markets abroad are more adaptable to domestic marketing methods.
E) A study of marketing should consider the adaptability of advertising campaigns in different countries.

27. The principal monetary policy objective is to reduce substantially the import surplus of the coming years while resuming economic growth. Realisation of this goal entails a market structural change of the economy, which can be brought about by freezing the standard of living (per capita private consumption plus public services) and restricting investments that do not further exports.

The writer of the above policy assumes that

A) Economic growth will result in a structural change of the economy.
B) Only if people consume less can the economy grow.
C) The import surplus can be reduced if investment is restricted.
D) Only a structural change in the economy can substantially increase imports.
E) People will have to be persuaded to give up consumption for the national good.

Answers and Explanations

Exercise 3A

1. d; None of them is implicit. The statement only implies that if a boy is very honest, it would not be possible for him to lie. But, I is just the opposite of it. Assumption II is not implicit because the statement does not talk about "dishonest" boys.
2. b; X air-conditioner has the largest range. But, this does not mean that it is *the only brand to have a wide range*. So, I is not implicit. But II is. If airconditoners are being advertised, a demand for them must be existing.
3. a; "Sole agent" is the highlight of the advertisement. So I is implicit. But II is not.

4. d; None is implicit. The statement only says that opening a library in Rambli would be a wastage. But it does not say why? I and II are only guesses. Maybe, opening a library in Rambli is a wastage because there is already a library there. (It is an example of a long-drawn conclusion.)

5. d; I is just the opposite of what the statement is saying. Even II is not implicit. Indiscipline in industry and poor quality of life for workers — these are the two problems that participatory management is said to be able to solve. But this does not mean that out of these two, one is a cause of another.

6. e; Both are implicit. The author asks him to consult 'me' before taking any decision. Obviously, he is worried that a decision without his consultation may not be correct. So, I is implicit. Further, he wouldn't have said so unless he thought that taking a correct decision was important. Hence, II is implicit

7. d; None is implicit. Assumption I is a mere twisted form of the given statement. Smoking is injurious. It means that non-smoking is not injurious. And that's it. It doesn't mean that non-smoking *promotes* health. II obviously is just the opposite of what is true. Public warnings are given only when they are assumed to be necessary.

8. a; Children must be considering their teachers as role models. otherwise there is no reason why they would be influenced by them. Hence, I is implicit. II is not directly stated. It may or may not be true.

9. e; Both are implicit. The statement recognises the entertainment value of television and, at the same time, it asserts that its educational value "cannot be ignored". The tone of the passage is slightly lamenting which implies that what the author wants to happen, is not happening presently. This means that both I and II are implicit.

10. a; When mother gives warning to the child, she must be assuming that her warning would be successful. II is not relevant to the statement made by the mother.

11. b; The statement says that *a car* is required on rent. It does not say that *any vehicle* is required. So, the statement cannot be said to have assumed that *any vehicle* is available for rent. But II is obviously implicit; whenever an advertisement is made it is assumed that people will respond to it.

12. b; I is definitely not mentioned in the advertisement. II is implicit, otherwise Company A wouldn't have given the advertisements.

13. a; Unless the sale of all radio sets manufactured in India was known, the statement could not have been made. Hence, I is implicit. II is not implicit because we do not know about manufacturing; we know only about sales. X brand has the largest sale but it may not be the largest manufacturer of radio sets. Maybe company Y manufactures more sets than X does but it exports all its sets. In that case, Y is a bigger

manufacturer but its sale in India would be lesser than that of X.

14. a; Unless B would be going to Jammu, A would not have advised him this. Hence, I is implicit. But it is not certain that A gives advice to *everybody*. Maybe A is giving advice to B because B is A's friend.

15. b; Films have become indispensable but it does not imply that they are the *only* medium of entertainment. But it is certain that people enjoy films. Hence, II is implicit.

16. a; Leaning out of a running bus must be dangerous, otherwise the warning would not have been there. Hence, I is implicit. But II is not implicit. If the authorities would have assumed that children do not pay any heed to such warnings, they would not have put it up there.

17. b; I is not implicit. The company wants mechanical engineers. One reason could be that the company expects mechanical engineers to be good performers, as I suggests. But there could be another reason: for example, the company's supervisory job could be such that only a mechanical engineer could perform it. But one thing is certain, the advertisement was for supervisors; this means supervisors are needed. Hence, II is implicit.

18. d; The statement asks a man to be humble *even after* being victorious. This implies that people are usually not humble after victory. I is just the opposite of it. II is not implicit because it generalises the statement. Generally, people may be humble; the point is if they are humble or not *after victory*.

19. e; If the letter mentions expenses to be borne by candidates, those who sent the letter must have assumed that candidates may demand for reimbursement if the point is not clarified to them. Also, the candidates would not demand reimbursement if it was not a prevalent practice. So, I and II both are implicit.

20. d; To dislodge a corrupt government has been mentioned as the *present purpose* for the call of unity. But this does not mean that this is the *only purpose*. So, I is not implicit. Further, the leader asks *like-minded* parties to unite against the government and *not the entire oppositon*. So, we cannot generalise that (all) opposition parties are non-corrupt. Hence, II is not implicit.

21. b; Postal rates have been increased the cause being to meet the deficit. This never means that the present rates are low. If the price of goods increases, it is not necessary that the earlier price was low. But the tone of the statement clearly implies that postal rates have been increased out of compulsion. So, II is implicit.

22. a; The statement says that if degrees are delinked from jobs, boys will not join colleges. This implies that jobs are a major reason for them to join college. So, I is implicit. Now, if I is implicit, II is not because II is just the opposite of I.

23. a; The statement uses a tone that implies that *if* education is in a shambles, *then* the country deteriorates. This means that a good education is needed for the well-being of a nation. But this does not mean that a good education *alone* is sufficient for it. So, I is implicit but II is not.

24. a; Obviously, the author assumes that the Board will be functioning after one year, otherwise he would not have fixed the date of the meeting one year later. But there is no hint that the Board will be dissolved after that. So I is implicit, II is not.

25. a; If one says that computers should be taught at schools, he must have assumed that it is an easy subject, because schools are a place of elementary education; tougher things are taught at colleges. But the statement does not say anything about jobs. So, I is implied, II is not.

26. e; If major modifications are being envisaged, it must have been assumed that the present educational system is inconsistent with what the nation needs. So, I is implicit. Again, if I is implicit, II also is, because II says the same thing as I.

27. e; If A advises B to join a particular institute, A must have assumed that the particular institute was a good institute. So, I is implicit. While advising B, A must also have thought that B would listen to A's advice; so II is implicit.

28. b; The mother only asks her son to drop the letter. I would have been implicit if she had asked her son to drop the letter and write the address also. But II is implicit. Had the mother not assumed that her son would comply, she wouldn't have asked him to do the job.

29. d; People love reading adventure stories but this does not mean that they have nothing else to read. Nor does it mean that they do not like to read anything else. So, both I and II are not implicit.

30. e; When someone says "read this notice" he must have assumed that the other person *can* read. This would be possible only if the person is literate and not blind. So, both I and II are implicit.

31. a; If extra income were taken from the rich and given to the poor, what would happen? Obviously, it would result in equality of income. But the statement says that equality of income is necessary for maximising the utility. So, I is implicit. But II is not. It is a different kind of thing. "Equal pay for equal work" allows, in a way, for "unequal pay if unequal work". But the statement highlights equality of income (whether equal work or unequal).

32. d; The statement does not mention youngsters. So, I is not implicit. II is just the opposite of what the statement assumes. So, II is also not implicit.

33. e; If a photographer claims to make a person beautiful, even if he is not, he means that he would create a beautiful photograph of that person. What else can a photographer do? Had he been a plastic surgeon, the

statement might have meant that he would really face-lift the person, but for a photographer the meaning is only that he would create a beautiful photograph of a person even if he is not beautiful. Hence, I is implicit. II is obvious, otherwise why would the photograph "lure" people to make them beautiful?

34. b; The statement only highlights the quality of one shop; it does not talk about *others*. So, I is not implicit. But II is, otherwise why would they have highlighted "you get your money's worth" in their advertisement? What is advertised and highlighted must be desirable.

35. e; I is implicit. Otherwise, why would India *import* for the continuous casting refractories? II is obvious.

36. a; The advertisement highlights the fact that the honey is *natural*. This means that non-natural honey is also possible. So, I is implicit. But the advertisement never touches the cost aspect of honey. So, II is not implicit.

37. b; Detergents are being recommended *to clean* clothes. This implies that they must be having the *ability to clean*. Now, ability to clean means the ability to dislodge grease and dirt, it does not mean the ability to form more lather. So, I is not implicit, but II is.

38. a; When the manager stresses the need to appoint more clerks, it must be because more clerks are needed. This means that the present staff is *not sufficient*. But this does not mean that the present staff is *inefficient*. So, II is not implicit. Obviously, more clerks are available, otherwise the question of appointing more clerks would not have arisen.

39. e; The manager asks his subordinate to go for the meeting *if* he is not well. This implies that if he is well, the manager would like to attend the meeting himself. So, II is implicit. Also, since, according to the manager, his subordinate can attend that meeting, it is obvious that the meeting can be attended by personnel having a lower rank than managers. So I is implicit.

40. e; The advice is given on the behaviour that should be followed to pass the exam. This shows that passing exams is necessary. So, assumption I is implicit. Passing the examination is a form of success. And, according to the statement, it may be achieved by hard work, so assumption II is implicit.

41. b; It is not necessary that the son does not inform about his late-coming. The parents may only be afraid that, unless specified, he may not come.

42. b; Aluminium is described as a versatile metal but it is not necessarily the *only* versatile metal. But II is implicit: if no company would be using aluminium for packaging, there would have been no advertisement.

43. b; If the President has assured people something, we may assume that that 'something' was making people apprehensive. But we cannot add anything of our own. The President has assured people of elections in five years. This means that people were apprehensive about no elections

being held *every five years*. We cannot conclude that people were apprehensive that elections would not be held after all.

44. b; I is not hinted in the statement. II is. The author says that apples cannot be good because they are *"too cheap*: this means that he thinks that cheap things are usually not good.

45. b; The word 'professional' has not come anywhere in the statement. But the way the author says that he doesn't want to become an engineer because it is "easy" implies that one wants to become something which is hard-earned.

46. b; The phrase "even a layman can study" is not used to mean that a "layman" necessarily wants to study science: it only means that he can study it *if* he wants. The statement is only meant to highlight the good qualities of the book, which II states.

47. d; None of them is implicit. The author asks the listener to bring his problems *if* he has some. He may be having problems or he may not be having problems: I may be false. Similarly, the tone of the statement implies that the author *would try to solve* the problem. It does not necessarily imply that the author can solve *any* problem.

48. d; None of them is implicit. We cannot declare that the scheme is successful unless we know how much procurement is targeted. If 1.4 lakh was the target, it's succesful, but if 100 lakh was the target, it's a gross failure. So, we are not sure. Similarly, we cannot say with certainty that no procurement should be done now because we do not know whether the procurement has been successful or short of target.

49. e; Both are implicit. Firstly, the author expresses *surprise* that despite more commuters being there, more buses are not being demanded: this implies that the author believes that the number of buses in a line depends upon the number of commuters. Secondly, the author's tone of surprise also implies that under normal conditions, people would have demanded more buses. This means that people do not usually tolerate inconvenience.

[**Note:** Refer to Section 3.5 (ii)(c); Ex. 9.]

50. a; The statement says that if people ask about your tailor, it indicates a good suit. This automatically means that if you are not wearing a good suit, they will not ask about your tailor. II is not implicit. The statement talks about a criterion of a good suit. It does not talk about people's *desire to know about this criterion.*

51. a; Since inequality can be reduced by man's actions, it must be a man-made phenomenon. But the eradication of inequality does not necessarily mean forcing anybody to part with what he possesses. We may reduce inequality by making the poor rich as well.

52. d; I is not implicit becuase that would mean that fascim or communism have just one meaning and that is: denying the rights of the individual. Similarly,

II is not implicit because that would mean that fascism and communism succeed only where people have suffered from poverty and deprivation. This may not be true.

53. b; If I was assumed by the incharge, he would not recommend conveyance allowance for employees. He wants to give reward (of conveyance allowance) in order to bring in discipline (punctuality). This means II is implicit.

54. e; Since penalty has been provided for, it means that there must be some misuse of alarm chain, so I is implicit. Since the alarm chain has not been taken off despite its misuse, it means that people may genuinely want to stop a train on some occasions. Hence, II is implicit.

55. a; I is definitely implicit because otherwise there wouldn't have been the advertisement. But II is not necessarily implied. The reader may or may not be a classical singer. Otherwise, they would not have used the word 'if' in the statement; they would simply have said: "We have a challenging job for you."

56. d; The successful man has the ability to judge himself correctly. But this does not mean that the ability to judge himself correctly is the *only* cause of his success. This means that the ability to judge *others* may not be useless for him. Hence, I is not implicit. Similarly, II is also doubtful for similar reasons.

57. e; I is implicit because had this not been so, the supervisor couldn't have thought of asking the officer not to grant leave. II is implicit because had this not been so, the supervisor wouldn't have been in a position to say that there was some "exigency of work".

58. b; Since the card says that the invitee should take his seat *before* 3:00 p.m., it implies that the function will start as scheduled. It is the invitee who will have to see that he reaches before 3:00 p.m.

59. a; **Remember the rule:** *In an advertisement, what is being highlighted must be desired by people*. This makes I implicit. The statement does not say that other pipes are not durable. It only says that they are less durable. So, II is not implicit.

60. a; Since the job is not "confirmed" without the review of the performace *at the end* of the probation period, it implies that *at the beginning* the performance may not be known. So, I is implicit. II may be true. It is clear by the way the sentence relates "confirmation" with "performance".

61. d; Even valuables locked in a cupboard can be stolen, but they would be more difficult to steal. It implies extra safety and not perfect safety, so I is not implicit. Whether stealing is a crime or not is not discussed in the statement.

62. b; The statement only says that X mosquito coils are good, but it does not say that it is "better than any other". So, I is not implicit. However, since

the advertisement promises a "good night's sleep", it must be a desirable thing. So, II is implicit.

63. d; What the statement says has no direct correlation with either of the statements. They may be true but they may be false as well. The statement does not make any mention of the word "intelligence".

64. e; Anything which needs overhauling must be obsolete. Also, overhauling must improve the situation, otherwise why would the author have recommended it? So, both are implicit.

65. d; The statement has not remarked about the *quality of TV itself* as an entertainment medium; it only talks about the *quality of TV programmes*. We may improve the quality of village-*nautankis* but that does not mean that these *nauntankis* are a good entertainment medium. So, assumption I is not implicit. Assumption II is not implicit because it is a restatement.

66. e; Banking services meet business needs. This means banking is a part of business activity. So, I is implicit. If we allow for the assumption that "business needs" includes "industrial needs", assumption II is also implicit.

67. a; The statement tells us about an effect produced by Vitamin E. If it is a good effect we may call the effect desirable, if it is not, we may call the effect undesired. How do we know? Structurally, there is not much difference between "Vitamin E makes your complexion glowing" and "Snake venom makes your senses dull." How can we say if the mentioned effect of Vitamin E is positive?

Here, the keyword is "*improving* your circulation". Improvement is a positive thing, so the effect of improvement of circulation, i.e. a glowing complexion, must also be a positive thing. So, I is implicit. Hence, I is implicit. But II is not. If vitamin E is present, we can have improved circulation and hence good complexion. But this does not mean that the converse is also true, i.e., if we do not have an improved circulation, we have dull complexion. Further, if we take the language of the question, II reads: "Complexion becomes dull in the absence of circulation." In the *absence of circulation*? If circulation itself is absent, man will die! There is no question of a dull or glowing complexion, then!

68. e; Since an advertisement offers "best training" in the field of "computers", it must have been assumed by the advertisers that people want "computer" training and that they want the "best training". So, both are implicit.

69. b; The statement says nothing about the inevitability or non-inevitability of delay. So, I is not implicit. However, since the statement talks of "more people" as a solution for the "delay", it must have assumed that with more people output will increase.

70. a; Since the advertisement wants girls "able to speak fluently in English", it must have assumed that fluency in English is a requirement for a good

model. So, I is implicit. Good height is not mentioned as a requirement. But we should not jump to the conclusion that height does not matter in modelling. Note that the statement wants *presentable* girls. It can be assumed that very short girls would not be as presentable as the taller ones. So, II is not implicit

71. a; When I say that I did something madly, I mean that I was out of senses while doing that act but otherwise, I am not mad, I am fine. Mad men do not say that "I chased him like a mad man." And, more importantly, even when they say such a thing, *they assume* that they are sane. Only I is implicit.

72. a; If relying on Shaleen was foolish, it obviously follows that Shaleen is unreliable. Again, II is not implicit in this case for the same reasons as those in the previous question. Remember, an assumption is something assumed. Now, it must be assumed *by* the one who makes a statement. When I say that "I did something foolishly", I actually want to say that I am wise, I know what doing something foolishly means, I can see the difference, and there I did a mistake and in that case I acted foolishly. Hence, II is not implicit.

73. b; Since taste "contributes" to the intake of food, one reason why people eat is the taste of food. But this is only one of possibly many more reasons. But the given assumption I is a too definitive. It makes it look as if taste is the **only** reason why people eat. The statement does not go **so far** in its support for taste. So, I is not implicit. Obviously, human beings must be experiencing food, otherwise there would have been no question of its enjoyment. Hence, II is also implicit.

74. b; If a notice is given, it must have been assumed that it will have its desired effect. Hence, II is implicit. But I is doubtful. We do not know that 8:30 a.m. is the required arrival time. The notice might be for an urgent meeting scheduled at 8:30 am.

75. b; The advertisers must have assumed that they were well-equipped while declaring that they guarantee "success". But we cannot generalise this assumption. "*Such* classes are well-equipped" is a generalised statement which means that "all classes are well-equipped" and this may not be true. But II is obviously implicit.

76. a; I is implicit because only then does the direction to walk make sense. II is not implicit as the statement makes no distinction between the members of the office and the visitors.

77. b; I is not implicit because of the word "all". II is implicit because only then does the appeal to switch over make sense.

78. e; The comparison is possible only when I is assumed. Same for II.

79. a; I is implicit because of the use of "any" in the statement. II is not implicit.

It is possible that the problem can be solved even later. The instruction to contact "immediately" is only for the sake of convenience of the customer.

80. d; I would be implicit if the statement said "Use *only* our medicine ...". Again, the instruction to use is only of an advisory nature, not mandatory. Hence II is not implicit.
81. b; The driver does not have control on what the auto driver will do. Hence I is not implicit. But II is implicit as one assumes the outcome while taking an action.
82. e; I is implicit in the very giving of the advice. II is implicit in the condition attached.
83. a; I is implicit: when you urge someone to do something, you assume a positive response. For the same reason, II is not implicit.
84. b; If I were implicit, such a decision would not be taken. II is implicit in the purpose of fund-raising that has been mentioned in the statement.
85. a; Without passengers, the increase would make no sense. Hence I is implicit. II may be a probable reason but not a necessary one for the increase.
86. e; I is implicit: you don't hold a function without being ready for the preparations. II is also positive: when you invite someone, you assume that he will come.
87. b; Price have been slashed with the assumption that sales will increase, thus leading to profit.
88. d; Both of these assumptions are negative.
89. a; A request is made to the people with the assumption that they would comply. Hence I is implicit. II talks of activists and is hence beyond the scope of the statement.
90. b; I is not implicit: Even if other matches are played in the near future, people may like to see this match. II is implicit: When you stand in the queue, you hope to get ticket.
91. a; The boards have been put with the assumption that they may have a positive impact.
92. a; Only I is implicit. II may not be there in the association's mind. It may only be assuming that a reduced attendance may drive home the employees' point.
93. b; There is no indication of an earlier meeting. Hence I is not implicit. II is implicit in the calling of the meeting.
94. b; I is not implicit because the corporation has not advised the people to leave the city
95. e; I is implicit from the need of different types of letters on different occasions. II is implicit from "official" and "semi-official".

96. a; I is implicit because only then the person checking can check the availability. But II is not implicit. Personal details are generally required at the time of booking tickets.

97. e; Obviously, 0.7 is one of the types. Hence I is implicit. II is also implicit or else the statement would make no sense.

98. d; When we mention something to someone, we assume they know its meaning. Hence I is implicit. But II is not implicit as the details cannot be assumed.

99. d; The statement does not give any clue to the use of language. Hence I is not implicit. II is not implicit because of *only*.

100. a; I is implicit in the norm prescribed in the sentence. This is why checking is being advised. Again, what would the banks check? Obviously, what the clients reveal. Banks would assume the revelation to be true. Hence II is not implicit. However, II is vague. If *cross-checking* is what the speaker has in mind, II would become implicit.

101. a; If the govt has taken the decision, it must have assumed that its implementation would be possible. II would not be implicit because of "produced in the country". It is possible that the govt has import on its mind for the said purpose.

102. b; It is not implied that legal mining does not harm and illegal mining does all harm. It is only implied that illegal mining is more harmful for the environment. This happens because norms are flouted with impunity in illegal mining.

103. a; I is implicit in the need for training. But II takes things to an extreme with the phrase "no skill sets".

104. b; I is not an assumption because there may be several reasons for the preference being stated. II is implicit because you ask someone to employ a means only when you assume that the means is available

105. d; The assumption is that students have access to the Internet. But it is not necessary that they have this access *at home.* Hence I is not implicit. Again, past practice may not have been borne in mind while switching over to Internet-only display. Hence II is not implicit.

106. d; I is rather contrary to the assumption. The need to grow *different* types of crops is talked about precisely because there is a likelihood of farmers growing the same crop again and again unless instructed. Again, growing different type of crops is important but not sufficient. Hence II is not implicit.

107. b; I is not implicit because health is not the focus of the statement. II is implicit in the very need for substitution.

108. a; I is implicit because only then does the storage make sense. II is not implicit as the statement has nothing to do with "a shorter period of time."

109. b; I is not implicit as the action of the NGO need not be based on comparison. II is implicit as literacy is necessary to make the library successful.

Exercise 3B

1. 1; The word 'if' implies that both are equally probable: he may mind his ways and he may not mind his ways. Also, the person is depending upon police (if needed), so he must be assuming that the police will help. III is not certain: it is not told as to exactly how he harasses the speaker.
2. 3; I is just the opposite of what the notice intends to say. Of course, the City Police must have assumed - while giving such a notice - that (i) people tend to touch stray objects and that (ii) they would hesitate in doing so after reading the notice. [*Whenever a notice is issued it is assumed that the notice will have the desired effect* : ***Remember this rule***]
3. 2; Since A is telling B about Madhu in a matter-of-fact tone, this much may be assumed that both of them know Madhu. But it is not certain whether this acquaintance is to the extent of *friendship*. Hence, I is not implicit while II is. III, of course, is the whole logic on the basis of which A reaches his conclusion (that Madhu has gone mad.)
4. 1; When the economist says that prices should fall after May because then demand **starts** dropping, it appears as if demand remains heavy till then and, as if, therefore, prices might not drop before May. So, I is implicit. II again may or may not be true. And, moreover, it has nothing to do with the statement. Similarly, III has nothing to do with the statement, although it may be true.
5. 5; II is of course the basis on which the CM is demanding more funds. I may or may not be true: enough indications are not given in the CM's statement. The same is true of III as well.
6. 1; I is implicit because A cannot give wedding gifts without being invited to weddings. II is implicit because A wouldn't have raised the point of "consumer goods" as wedding gifts. III is not implicit because A never mentions consumer goods as `useless' gifts.
7. 2; The newspaper must have had authentic and reliable sources to publish such news but it is nowhere mentioned that it has *quoted* such sources. Hence I is not implicit but II is. III is obvious.
8. 4; The teacher does not mean that the students are not intelligent. He only says that questions are difficult and need additional strategy. Hence, I is not implicit but III is. II is not implicit: in fact, the teacher says that the problem *can be solved* if you have drawn suitable diagrams.
9. 4; I and III are obvious. But "intoxicating effect" of whisky has never been mentioned.

10. 1; I is obvious by the way the two sentences have been put together. II is obvious: had A thought that people's view about coffee (that it was bad for health) was not correct, why would he decide to cut down on it? But B may or may not act on A's line of action: III may or may not follow. It is not sure whether B drinks coffee at all.

11. 4; I is obvious from the very fact that there are some persons who want to buy used imported items. II is obvious because had there been no such people willing to sell such items, the advertisers wouldn't have placed the ad. For the same reason, III is also implicit. [*Whenever something is advertised, it is assumed that it will be read by the people for whom it is meant* : **Remember this rule**]

12. 1; To get the assumptions, try to find what the politician *wants us to think*. He wants us to think that the charges are false (and not true, although beyond proof). Hence, I is implicit while II is not. The politician is not fed up of *politics*, he seems fed up of the *charges* levelled against him.

13. 5; I is obviously rubbish; the statement uses the term 'History' not in the sense of a subject but in its general sense. II is obvious by the second sentence. III is never hinted at in the statement.

14. 5; People are turning to Supreme Court because they are weary of an *inactive executive*. Hence, it implies that the Supreme Court is *more active* than the executive. But it is never implied that the Supreme Court is more powerful or that the executive does not have sufficient powers. The question of *power* has never been touched in the statement.

15. 5; The author is not against adult franchise in general. He is against adult franchise if it is practised by illiterate people. In other words, he is against **universal** adult franchise. Hence, I is not implicit. II is obviously implied. III, again, is an assumption for obvious reasons. (See, Section 3.6, (a); Ex. 11.)

16. 4; I is obvious: in fact, it is taken as a universal truth. II is obvious because the mother forbids sweets as they are not "good for teeth". III is obvious by the tone of the author's language.

17. 4; I is obvious in the advertisement. II is obvious. [*Whenever an advertisement highlights any aspect of a product, it is assumed that people expect that aspect*: **Remember this rule.**] The ad does assume that price is of secondary importance to people because otherwise they would have highlighted the cheapness of the product and not its quality. So, III is implicit.

18. 1; The mother is concerned because the noise may hamper her son's study. Hence II is implicit. But there is nothing which can suggest that noise is not conducive to children in general. All that we can infer from the statement is that noise is not conducive to their study; that's all. Also, we may not be able to conclude from the statement that the mother cares

for her child's health: in the statement the mother has shown concern not for her child's health, but for her study.

19. 1; I is obvious. But there is nothing to suggest that hockey is a different game or that chances of victory are different from actual victories. So, II and III are not implied.

20. 4; The thief uses the gun to arouse fear. This fear brings a sense of command or compulsion. Hence II is implicit. But I is not. The thief uses the phrase "behave like a good boy" in a tone of sarcasm only: we should not take it in a literal sense. Similarly, III is also not implicit.

21. 4; The word "unless" implies that presently there is neither autonomy nor profit in the units. Hence, I is implicit. II and III are obvious.

22. 5; The statement clearly says that "Beer is good for health". Hence, I is not true while II is a mere restatement. Remember that an assumption is something *assumed and not something explicitly stated*. III may or may not be true. The statement mentions obesity but does not say that it is the *only* disadvantage of beer.

23. 2; The question of the daughter's agreement has not been touched. Maybe, A will marry his daughter even without her agreement. II is obvious by the statement. III is not clear.

24. 3; I is obvious by the way the Principal says that those students *shall* be punished. It implies that he *can* punish them. III is obvious. II may not be correct. It should have been: a punishment may follow warnings *only* if there is no effect of those warnings.

25. 2; The passenger is merely uttering complaint; obviously, he has no authority to ban them. II is obvious. III may or may not be assumed by the passenger. He may think that his colleague may disagree.

26. 2; I is not an assumption; it is merely a restatement. II is implicit: if the lawyer cites autopsy to prove that the cause of death was torture, he must be assuming that autopsy can help in determining the cause of death. III is not implicit: it is not told that the lawyer performed the autopsy himself.

27. 4; I is implicit: the use of the word 'probably' indicates that the cause of the collapse is probably the rumour of the FM's resignation but it is not definitely known. II is implicit: if the rumour of the FM's resignation can be a probable cause of the collapse, then the FM must be important to the brokers. III is not implicit: the rumours may or may not be baseless.

28. 3; Since the author describes the thoughts of Godse, he must be assuming that he knows the character of Godse well. Since Godse intended to kill anybody who came in the way of Hindu Rashtra and since he killed Gandhi for these reasons, it is obvious that he thought Gandhi to be an obstruction before Hindu Rashtra. III is not implicit: it is not the meaning of the given sentence. He might have had his reasons but these reasons

themselves could be very irrational.

29. 2; I is obviously implicit: that disagreement exists and that it can be resolved through peaceful means implies that disagreement can be resolved through peaceful means. For the same reasons, II is also implicit.

30. 5; Sampras does not make any comment about how a tennis court should be. He only observes what it was. Hence, neither I nor II is implicit. III is implicit: the court played fast and, in this situation, Yzaga was at a disadvantage. It implies that Yzaga is a better player at slower courts.

31. 5; All are implicit. Since the star gives emphasis on the fact that he has not changed, it means that some people do change after success; and hence I is implcit. Since the star quotes *Baazigar* while saying that success has not changed him it implies that *Baazigar* is a successful film. Hence, II is implicit. Finally, the statement "Why should it?" implies III.

32. 1; The first line promises to insure against shock waves. The second line promises to insure against earthquakes. Hence, it is implicit that earthquakes and shock waves are almost synonymous. Hence I is implicit. II is implicit because of the word 'most' in the second sentence. Because of this word the meaning of this sentence becomes: there are many companies offering insurance against earthquakes but Oriental Insurance offers the most comprehensive insurance. III is not implicit. Although it is a well-known fact that earthquakes are a natural phenomenon, the given statement never mentions nature.

33. 4; That the people were being persuaded to follow non-violence is implied by the first sentence. It, in turn, implies that they were planning to use violence; hence I is implicit. II is obviously implicit in the second sentence. III is also implicit: the Sikhs wanted to say that Gandhi could easily preach non-violence because his own folk were not affected by violence. This implies III.

34. 5; Gandhi accepts that tragedy occurred for the Sikhs and yet he advocates non-violence. It means that he thought non-violence to be the best method. This implies I. By admitting that the women and the sons of Sikhs were like his own, Gandhi shares their sorrow and hence II is implicit. Also, Gandhi was persuading the Sikhs because he thought that his persuasion may work, that his rational approach may transform the Sikhs. Hence III is also implicit.

35. 1; The use of the phrase 'all the way' implies that Maya Nagar is far off. There is no hint, however, that the man making the statement got his ticket. Similarly, it cannot be declared that the movie is a superhit. There are many films which flop despite running house-full for a first few days.

36. 2; I may or may not be true. Since the lawyer does not contradict the statement that a short man was seen, it implies that he assumes it to be true. Hence, II is implicit. Also, the short man should not be Khashogi

because the latter is five-feet-eight, which implies that III is implicit.

37. 2; I is just the opposite of truth. II is not implicit by the engineer's statement. He makes no hints at previous planning engineers, etc. III is obviously valid.

38. 1; I is obviously implicit. Either II or III must be true and you may be tempted to choose 4 as your answer choice. But the question is about assumption. The doctor's statement does not assume either II or III. Although, any one of these two must be true but they are not assumptions. See **"Some tips for Quick Answers" at the end of the lesson, before the Exercises.**

39. 5; I is invalid: the speech may have been made by anybody. II is not implicit: the politician says that people of all castes were swayed; this makes no hint about *his* belief in casteism. He may believe in casteism or he may not. III is invalid because of the word 'only'. There could be other means also, of transcending the barriers of caste and religion.

40. 1; II is obviously implicit: if corruption is being talked about it must be existing. I is implicit. It is slightly tricky. The politician may or may not be corrupt. As a fact, I may be true or false, but this is a question of assumption. For this we need to consider who is making the statement. Please note carefully that the politician himself is making this statement against corruption. While making this statement he obviously assumes that he himself is honest because this is the image that he wants to project. Hence I is valid. It is implicit in the statement.

41. 2; I is a restatement. II must be assumed otherwise why would the captain want to stop sailing? III is again not certain, an island may or may not be near.

42. 2; Since a pale look implies the possibility of the disease, assumption II is valid. Others are not necessarily true.

43. 2; The tone of the statement implies II. I is not mentioned: 'morality' is not the theme. III is invalid because the statement is just an exclamation, not a prayer.

44. 4; The woman asks God to help her *if* her intentions have been pure. But this does not imply that God would not have helped her if her intentions were not pure. Hence, I is invalid. Similarly, II is also invalid. III is a valid assumption - when somebody prays, she must be assuming (taking for granted) that God answers prayers.

45. 4; The theme of the passage is that learning from mistakes is important; mistakes themselves are not important. Hence, I is implicit. Again, the second sentence says that learning from mistakes makes great men, while the third sentence says that because of it, there are very few great men. This naturally implies that very few learn from mistakes. Hence, II is implicit. III is not an assumption, it is a restatement.

46. 3; It is only said that the name was misspelt and that it is regretted. It would not be proper to draw conclusions such as I or II. Only III is implicit. If it were not desirable, the name would be spelt correctly.
47. 4; The anger of the politician is for the fact that the government is talking of soft drinks when drinking water is not available. This justifies assumption II. I and III relate the politician's comment to health considerations. But this is not true. The politician never talks of health.
48. 1; The first sentence mentions 'popularity' of some songs; the second mentions people 'buying these cassettes'. The way these two are related in the statement, it becomes obvious that the writer assumes that buying cassettes is a sign of their popularity. Hence, I is implicit. II may or may not be true: no such hint is given. III is a long-drawn conclusion. It assumes that obscene songs do not have good music. Not all people could agree to II. Obscene songs may have obscene language and *double entendre* but their music is not necessarily bad. (In fact, some people offer excuses in everyday life such as: "I listen to "*Choli ke Peechhe*" because it has good music!")
49. 2; I talks of some details. But the statement has not given these details. How do we know what exactly was there in ISRO case, on the basis of the given statement alone? So, I is not implicit. II is implicit; it is clear from the use of the word 'shocking'. If it was not unexpected, it could not have shocked. III is obviously implicit.
50. 2; I is a restatement II and III are obvious.
51. 3; The tone of the statement implies that I and III are both implicit in the statement. The person links political connections - blindly, so to say - with corruption. Therefore, I and III are implicit. II is not implicit. It may be true in general; but, in the person's statement, it is never implied.
52. 3; The analyst talks of hungry stomachs, so people with hungry stomachs must be existing. It means that I is implicit. II is NOT implicit although it looks otherwise. *Some* rice must have been available because *all* people could not have been hungry. But rice would have been available only in limited amount (otherwise people wouldn't have been hungry). Hence, III is implicit.
53. 3; I is not implicit; no clue is given about the exact identity of Samba. II is implicit; it is clear from the use of the word 'myth'. The statement says that Indian army's discipline was believed in, although, it was not true and that it was a 'myth'. Myth or otherwise, such belief did exist. III is implicit in the tone of the statement: look at the way the statement links 'spying case' with non-existence of 'discipline'. It is a derogatory fashion in which these two are linked. This implies III.
54. 1; The way the phrase 'easiest-to-use' is highlighted in the advertisement, it is apparent that people look for convenience in a cellular phone. Hence,

I is implicit. But it is not clear whether the size of the phone is also highlighted. It may be of the tone: "Small in size, but huge in performance" or it may be like "Not only small in size, but also huge in performance." In case one, the advertiser is apologetic about the size; in the other, he is boastful of it. So it could be either of these situations and hence II is not implicit. III is not hinted in the statement.

55. 5; I is obviously implicit: What is being suggested must be desirable. II may not be true. The brother talks of 'greater' transparency. It means that some degree of transparency was already there and 'greater' transparency is needed. Hence II is doubtful. III is implicit; it is obvious by the way people's suspicion of the stock markets is related with the need of greater transparency.

Exercise 3C

1. B; If Edward is President must mean that he is senior, II automatically follows. I and III don't.

2. E; Obvious.

3. C; What Ernst says means something like this: "Max, you are wrong. Because, even masterpieces by David and Delacsoix hang in the Lauvre. So, if you say that all paintings by Picasso are masterpieces, don't forget the ones by David and Delacsoix". Obviously, he assumes that only Picasso masterpieces hang in Louvre, is what Max meant.

4. C; The conclusion about better education at Duns is made by comparing the grades. But grades in the two schools are awarded separately. Hence the conclusion couldn't be valid unless it was assumed that the grading systems of the two schools were alike. Hence III is implicit. Now, if better grading means better education, I is implicit. II is not because nothing is mentioned of extra curricular activities.

5. A; The question was put to people who were *coming out of the terminal* about the services *aboard the flight*. If it was shown that a majority of people coming out of the terminal were not passengers, then the conclusion would really be jeopardised. A does just that.

6. B; **To understand this reasoning better, bindly refer to *disjunctive arguments* Note II, Case I, at the end of Chapter II.**

7. C; The expert suggests that labour costs will be reduced if the workers stop less often while working. This means that when they stop more often to change spools; that part of time which they waste in changing the spools is also paid-time. (And this makes it costlier if they stop more often.) This means that they are paid by the hours and not by the work done. If they were paid by the work done, the wasted time in changing the spools would have been unpaid-time.

8. A; **To understand this reasoning better, kindly refer to *argument by analogy*, Section 1.2.3, chapter 1.**

9. B; Since the argument straightaway declares that increasing reliance on computers threatens individual privacy without pausing to think that there would be no such threat if an unbreakable security system could be developed, II follows. I just do not follow. III also do not because the author does not reject computers as a system for record keeping *per se*, it only warns against increasing reliance on them.

10. C; I and II are obviously implicit. III is never suggested.

11. E; This is a question that asks you to identify a hidden assumption of the argument. (E) does this. The conclusion of the argument is that early humans believed in a life after death. The evidence for this conclusion is the discovery of certain articles buried with the dead. For this evidence to support the conclusion, the argument must implicitly presuppose that such articles would be buried with the dead only by people who had such beliefs.

(A) is incorrect, for what is needed for this argument is a connection between the articles buried and a belief in afterlife, not a feeling of piety towards the dead. After all, one might venerate one's ancestors, even though one does not hold a belief in afterlife. As for (B), this goes beyond the scope of the argument. The author's conclusion, as delimited by the wording of the passage, is that certain early humans held a belief in afterlife, not that such beliefs are widespread. (C) is incorrect because the ownership of the articles is not important, only that the articles were placed there for use by the deceased. Finally, (D) makes essentially the same error as (B) does; it goes beyond the scope of the argument.

12. C; This question, too, asks about a hidden assumption of the argument. The conclusion of the argument is that humorous ads are not effective. Supporting this conclusion is a sub-argument: such ads do not promote sales because consumers remember the humour but not the product name. This assumes that the effectiveness of an ad is determined by the sales it generates, which is pointed out by (C).

As for (A), this goes beyond the scope of the argument. The speaker merely says that such ads are not effective, not that they are damaging as well. As for (B), the author never states that viewers don't remember the ad, only that they don't remember the product. (D) makes the same error made by (A). The author does not say that the ads are damaging, only that they are ineffective in promoting the product.

(E) is perhaps the most attractive of the distractors here. But, a careful reading of the argument will show that (E) is incorrect. The conclusion of the argument is that humorous ads do not *increase sales*. We should infer, therefore, that the ultimate objective of advertising is to increase sales and that name recognition is merely a *means* to that *end*.

13. C; This item asks you to identify a hidden assumption of the argument. The speaker argues that religion is creeping into the political sphere. Critical to this argument is the assumption that there are two distinct and separate spheres, religion and politics. (C) correctly points out that this is an assumption of the argument.

14. D;This item asks you to identify hidden assumptions in the argument. Test each statement. Statement I is an assumption of the argument, for the author states that he has assigned numerical values for the various aspects - and that assumes that some sort of quantitative measure is possible. II is also an assumption, for the author treats each variable as a separete, independent measure. Finally, however, III is not necessarily an assumption of the argument. The author does address those who do have flexibility in their living plans (otherwise he would not have prepared the study), but this does not commit him to the assumption that most of the people, in general, enjoy such flexibility.

15. A;This item asks for an underlying assumption. The author claims that the situation with heroin and cocaine use is unlike that which existed with respect to alcohol during prohibition. What is the difference? According to the author, heroin and cocaine are not preferred by the middle-class. Thus, we can infer (though the author never specifically says so), that alcohol, even during prohibition, was preferred by the middle-class.

16. D; This item asks you to identify hidden assumptions in the argument. Test each statement. I is not an assumption of the argument, for the author need not commit himself to the view that children accept every idea. It is just that they would be more critical of ideas if given philosophical training. The author is, however, committed to II. If children were not able to grasp philosophical concepts, then it would make no sense trying to teach them the concepts. Also, the author is committed to III. Implicit in the argument is the premise that it is a good idea to have students question ideas - otherwise, the author would be content to let them absorb the ideas without question.

17. C; This argument is, in fact, a kind of generalisation. It assumes that what is true of one magazine is true of other magazines as well. (C) points out that the argument is implicitly committed to this idea.

18. E; Here, you are looking for the one idea that is not assumed by the speaker, and this is articulated by (E). The paragraph is really an argument for the position that government leaders should act more quickly to address problems. So, the author is committed to the idea that public policy is

under the control of the government. It just hasn't been effectively used in the past.

19. A; Test each statement. I is an assumption of the argument. If there were no such time lag, then the distinction between pure research and application would be nonexistent. It is the lag that creates the distinction. Statement II, however, is not an assumption of the argument. The author assumes only that pure research seems "pure" because its applications are not immediately obvious, but he is not necessarily commited to the idea that it is more expensive than any other kind of research. Finally, III is not an assumption of the speaker. Although, the time lag creates the distinction between the types of research, the author doesn't say how long the time period that separates the types, is.
20. E; Once you understand the main point of the passage, you also understand the answer to this question. The author is arguing that seemingly "pure" research with no obvious, immediate applications, is still valuable - like a baby, it has potential.
21. C; The statement refers to the social psychologist's obligation to provide a wide range of people - those in his own discipline, other social scientists, laymen, and government officials - with the tools to understand social phenomena. Alternative (E) might be a correct assumption if it was not linked to inter-disciplinary problems. Alternatives (A), (B) and (D) are incorrect assumptions.
22. E; New technologies and populations represent problems related to socio-technological changes and require new mechanisms. The other alternatives are incorrect assumptions.
23. E; The politician assumes that a large, absolute number of replies means that the survey results are representative of the population (total homes in the district), even though a proportionately small number of replies may have resulted. Alternatives (A), (B) and (D) cannot be assumed from the statement. Alternative (C) is incorrect.
24. C; The assumption is that potential donors will be flattered by requests for large donations and frequently offended by requests for smaller amounts. Therefore, it is worth the gamble to start high. At worse, the potential donor may decrease his gift. Alternatives (A), (B) and (D) are not assumptions made in the statement. Alternative (E) is partially correct: donors are seldom offended if they are asked *too much by* fund-raisers.
25. D; While (A) may be inferred, (D) better summarises the minister's assertion. In this case, "open-door policy" may signify increased trade since ideas and foreign aid are ruled out. There is no proof for (E) while (B) and (C) may not be inferred from the communique.
26. D; The assumption is that domestic marketing techniques may be transfer-

able to only those markets that have substantial sales volume. The words "marketing methods" in the last sentence refer to the word "treated" in the first sentence.

27. E; If the principal monetary policy is to be attained - reducing the import surplus while resuming economic growth - per capita consumption will have to be frozen. Thus, consumers will have to be persuaded to give up consumption to further national economic goals. The assumption is that people will be willing to put a halt to growth in their standard of living.

Chapter Four

Forcefulness of Arguments

4.1: Introduction

In chapter one we have seen how some premises give support to reach a conclusion. Some of these make strong arguments while some make weak arguments. In some exams, questions are asked wherein a candidate is required to evaluate the forcefulness of the proposed arguments.

4.2: Format of the question

In making decisions about important questions, it is desirable to be able to distinguish between "Strong" arguments and "Weak" arguments in sofar as they relate to the question. "Strong" arguments are those which are both important and directly related to the question. "Weak" arguments are those which are of minor importance and also may not be directly related to the question or may be related to a trivial aspect of the question.

Instructions: Each question below is followed by two arguments numbered I and II. You have to decide which of the arguments is a strong argument and which is a weak argument. Give answer

1) if only argument I is strong
2) if only argument II is strong
3) if either I or II is strong
4) if neither I nor II is strong
5) if both I and II are strong

1. **Statement:** Should primary education be made a fundamental right in India?

   Arguments: I. No, what is the use? Have we fulfilled our duties regarding other fundamental rights?

   II. Yes, this is what all the developed countries have done.

2. **Statement:** Should lotteries be completely banned in India?

   Arguments: I. No, many state governments will have to stop some of their developmental activities which they fund from the surplus generated by their lottery scheme.

   II. No, many unemployed youth who sell lottery tickets to earn their livelihood will face hardship.

3. **Statement:** Should dependents of India's freedom fighters be given benefits of reservation in jobs?

Arguments: I. Yes. We should keep the dependents happy as the freedom fighters have fought for a noble cause.

II. No. We already have too many reservations; let us not add more to it.

4. **Statement:** Should e-commerce be encouraged in our country?

Arguments: I. Yes, when we are in the age of computers, why should trade be left out of this realm?

II. No, people in our country are more interested in trading only when they come across eachother physically.

Questions of this type are frequently asked in various P.O. examinations, including IBPS, UTI Officers', Income Tax, MBA entrance examinations etc.

4.3: An Analysis

How do we answer such questions? To get an idea of this we should begin by having an insight into the problem. What is it that the problem seeks to know?

Well, let us, therefore, scrutinise the question. We see that the question consists of a statement. The statement is (usually) in the form of a suggested course of action. Followed by the statement are two arguments. One argument advocates the suggested course of action by pointing at the positive features or positive results of that action and the other argues against the suggested course of action by pointing at the negative features or harmful results of that action.

Now, what is our job?

Our job is to determine whether a given argument is forceful or not. Naturally, an argument will be forceful only if it is 100% perfect. This 100% perfectness of an argument can be checked in three stages - one, you should check whether the positive (or negative) results of the given course of action indeed follow, as stated in the argument; two, you should check that the positive (or negative) results are really desirable (or harmful, in case of negative arguments); and three, you should check whether the suggested course of action is directly related to the argument or not.

But before making this deep-down analysis of the arguments, you should subject them to a preliminary screening - a 'first-look test'- where you could reject an argument on the basis of preliminary observations. For example, an argument can be rejected if it is ambiguous or if it is 'half-hearted' or if it is too simple to be acceptable or if it is in the form of a question. We shall see details of these later on.

To conclude, we have analysed our problem and devised a four-step action plan to solve it. The diagram given below presents a picture of this:

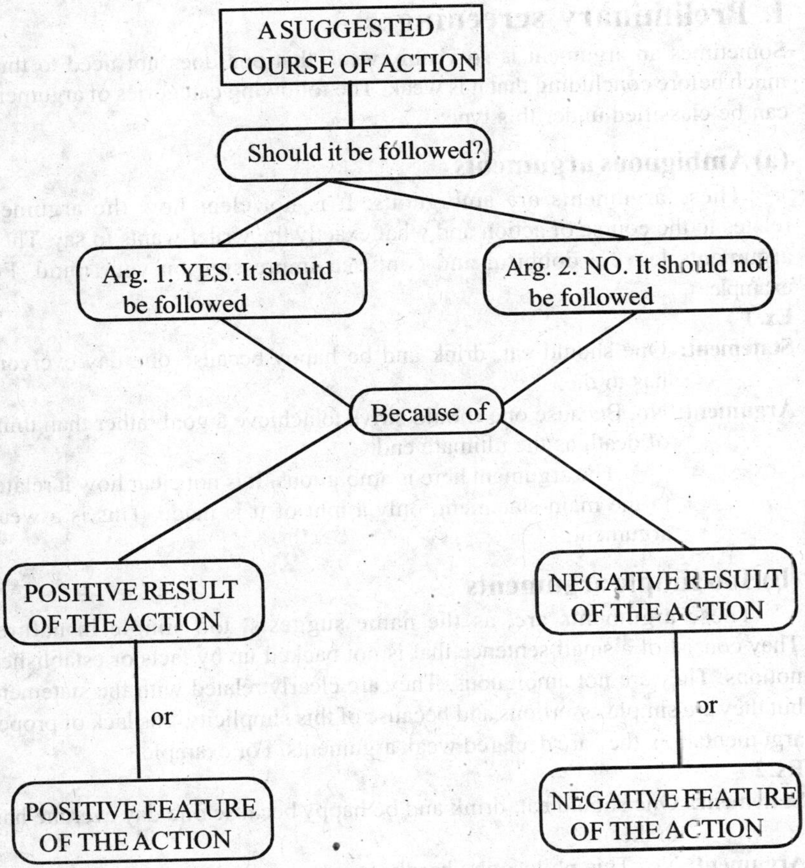

Fig.: An Analysis of the Problem

4.4: A Four-step Plan of Solution

- **I. Preliminary Screening**
- **II. Will the result really follow?**
- **III. Is the result really desirable?** (or **harmful**, in case of negative arguments)
- **IV. Are the argument and the suggested course of action properly related?**

Thus, we have seen that we have broken up our solution into four stages. Now, the solution of a problem would consist of a simple act: **read the question; subject the argument to these four tests; if it passes all the four tests, it is a strong argument, otherwise it is a weak argument**. Let us now see in greater detail the four steps of our solution:

I. Preliminary screening

Sometimes an argument is so visibly weak that one does not need to think much before concluding that it is weak. The following categories of arguments can be classified under this type:

(a) Ambiguous arguments

These arguments are ambiguous. It is not clear how the argument relates to the course of action and what exactly the writer wants to say. These arguments leave a doubtful and confused impression on your mind. For example:

Ex. 1

Statement: One should eat, drink and be happy because one day everyone has to die.

Argument: No. Because one should strive to achieve a goal rather than think of death as the ultimate end.

The argument here is ambiguous. It is not clear how it relates to the main statement, only a hint of it is made. This is a weak argument.

(b) Too simple arguments

These arguments are, as the name suggests, too simple in nature. They consist of a small sentence that is not backed up by facts or established notions. They are not ambiguous. They are clearly related with the statement but they are simple assertions and because of this simplicity, this lack of proper argumentation, they are declared weak arguments. For example,

Ex. 2

Statement: One should eat, drink and be happy because one day everone has to die.

Argument: No. This philosophy hardly enables us to do anything.

This argument is a simple assertion. There is no substance in it and hence it is a weak argument.

(c) Superfluous arguments

These arguments are superfluous. They only 'glance' at the theme and do not make an 'in-depth' analysis of it. The following two examples illustrate the point:

Ex. 3

Statement: Traditional culture should be preferred to modern culture.

Argument: No. Both have their good as well as bad points.

Ex. 4

Statement: Import of foreign books should be banned.

Argument: Yes. Importing foreign books is of no use.

Both the above arguments are superfluous. They do not delve into the core of the topic. Hence, these are weak arguments.

(d) Question-back

These arguments consist of a question thrown back by the arguer. The questions are without any substance, without any technique of argumentation and, consequently, such arguments are weak. For example;

Ex. 5

Statement: Should India be declared a Hindu Rashtra?

Argument: Yes. Why not?

Ex. 6

Statement: Should India be declared a Hindu Rashtra?

Argument: No. Would this be a wise thing to do?

Besides these, there can be other types of arguments too, which can be rejected in first look. Such arguments are always very easy to evaluate and, therefore, we move over to the other three main steps of argument-evaluation.

II. Will the result really follow?

After having a preliminary screening of the given argument, you have to subject them to three tests. The first of these is to determine whether the result, as indicated in the argument, will really follow. How can we judge this? Usually, an intuitive idea and some commonsense would be sufficient for this judgement. However, we are presenting below specific cases to have a proper understanding of this point.

(i) Will follow

The result WILL FOLLOW in the following cases:

(a) Established fact

A result will follow a course of action if it is an established fact that such a result does usually follow such a course of action. An established fact may be scientifically established or it may be universally acknowledged. See the following examples:

Ex. 7

Statement: Should vegetarianism be preferred to non-vegetarianism?

Argument: Yes. it contributes to better health.

Ex. 8

Statement: Should vegetarianism be preferred to non-vegetarianism?

Argument: No. Non-vegetarian diet is richer in protein.

Ex. 9

Statement: There should be no disparity in pay scales of different jobs requiring equivalent qualifications.

Argument: No. Because the nature of work is different from one job to the other.

Ex. 10

Statement: One should not bother about what is happening in other parts of the world.

Argument: No. Because whatever happens in one part of the world may have its repercussions on other parts of the world.

Ex. 11

Statement: Nuclear families should be preferred to joint families.

Argument: Yes. Nuclear families ensure greater freedom.

In all the foregoing examples, whatever has been predicted in the arguments can be expected to follow because it is an established fact. It is an established fact that vegetarianism contributes to better health, that non- vegetarian diet is richer in protein, that nuclear families ensure greater freedom, etc. Therefore, all the arguments presented above can be said to pass this test.

[**Note:** Please note that we have not yet determined whether the arguments above are forceful or not. We have only determined that these arguments have passed step II. Whether they are really strong would depend upon whether they pass the next two steps III and IV, or not].

(b) Experiences predict that the result will follow

In this category are results which can be expected to follow because experiences indicate this. This category is very much similar to the previous category of established facts. The difference is that here we are talking of experiences that are not yet so universally acknowledged as to be treated as established facts. The following examples illustrate the point:

Ex. 12

Statement: Should there be internal assessment in colleges?

Argument: No. It would encourage favouritism among teachers.

Ex. 13

Statement: Should one follow a more or less rigid programme daily?

Argument: Yes. It would lead to better discipline.

Ex. 14

Statement: Should there be free trade between countries?

Argument: No. The poor countries are likely to be exploited by the rich ones.

In all the examples above, the results or the consequences that have been predicted can be taken as probable because our experiences have been like that only. For example, it has been an 'experience' that internal assessment may lead to favouritism, that following a rigid programme leads to better discipline.

(c) Logically, the result is probable

In this case, we deal with arguments that talk of a result that is probable, *logically speaking*. The emphasis here is on logic instead of experience or established fact. In practice, no such case could have occurred. This leads us to a lack of experience for such a case. But if we 'think' over such a scenario then, with proper logic, we come to the conclusion that such a result may indeed follow. For example, an argument may say that "internal assessment will enable the teachers to have a better control over the students". This is something which we can agree with if we think over it. Similarly, "Complete disarmament will lead to a control of wars" is also a probable consequence because of the simple logic that if there are no arms, there will be no wars.

Some more examples are being presented below:

Ex. 15

Statement: Should there be internal assessment in the colleges?

Argument: Yes. It will enable the teachers to have a better control over the students.

Ex. 16

Statement: Should there be compulsory military training for all?

Argument: Yes. This will give us a reserve force for the protection of the country.

Ex. 17

Statement: Should all sectarian religions be replaced by one common religion?

Argument: Yes. It will lead to a better integration of people.

Ex. 18

Statement: Should there be one government for the whole world?

Argument: Yes. It would lead to a better control on wars in the world.

Ex. 19

Statement: Should all property belong to the state concerned?

Argument: Yes. It will ensure equal distribution of wealth to all.

All the arguments mentioned above are consequences that look logically convincing. For example, if all property belongs to the state, it logically follows that it will ensure equal distribution of wealth to all. Similarly, in other examples too, the consequences look logically probable. The reader should carefully go through each of them and check whether he understands this point or not.

(d) Prevailing notions of truth

There are certain things or ideas that are universally accepted and acknowledged by the society and they are treated as unquestionable notions of truth. In many ways, they are similar to 'established facts'.

If an argument consists of this type of ideas or notions, it can be accepted. The following examples illustrate this point.

Ex. 20

Statement: Simple living and high thinking should be our motto

Argument: Yes. These virtues make a person great.

Ex. 21

Statement: Should brother-sister marriage be allowed?
Argument: No. Incest is a sin.

Ex. 22

Statement: Should capitation fee in private professional colleges be abolished?
Argument: Yes. Money should not be the criterion in the selection of students but merit should be.

(i) Will not follow

Let us now turn our attention to cases where the result mentioned in the argument does not follow. This can be studied under various categories. The result WILL NOT FOLLOW in the following cases:

(a) Established fact

If it is an established fact that such a result would not follow such an action. See the following example:

Ex. 23

Statement: Should one be using mosquito-repelling coils or mats?
Argument: No. The fumes emanating from these devices are harmful to health.

The argument is incorrect because it is an established fact that the fumes emanating from these devices are almost completely harmless to human beings.

(b) Experiences predict that the result will not follow

This is exactly the opposite of the point (b) made earlier. See the following example:

Ex. 24

Statement: Should the Government hold competitive examinations for all public-sector jobs?
Argument: Yes. The system of competitive examinations is free from corruption and hence deserving candidates will be selected.

This argument says that competitive exams are free from corruption but our experiences tell us that some degree of corruption does exist in competitive exams. [Remember the question-papers leakage of UPSC Civil Services Exam in 1991?] Hence, this argument can be rejected.

(c) Logically, the result is not probable

This is exactly the opposite of point (c) made earlier. See the following example:

Ex. 25

Statement: Should the culprits behind the Bofors scandal be punished?
Argument: No. It would create a political vacuum.

Logic says that punishing culprits behind the Bofors scandal would please the public and improve the image of the government. How can it create a political vacuum? This argument is logically faulty and hence it can be rejected.

(d) Prevailing notions of truth

An argument can be rejected if it violates the prevailing notions of truth. See the following example:

Ex. 26

Statement: Should brother-sister marriage be allowed?

Argument: Yes. If both are mature and willing then they cannot be prohibited from doing it.

This argument promotes incest and can, therefore, be rejected.

(e) Assumptions/Individual perceptions

Sometimes an argument promotes or prohibits an action on the basis of consequences which are not universally accepted and which are not given proper logical back-up either. They can only be described as the assumptions or the individual perceptions of the author. Such arguments can be rejected. See the following examples:

Ex. 27

Statement: Should all sectarian religions be replaced by one common religion?

Argument: No. It would lead to chaos.

Ex. 28

Statement: Should one follow a more or less rigid programme daily?

Argument: No. It will kill creativity in individuals.

Ex. 29

Statement: The mind can be sound if the body is sound.

Argument: Yes. A sound body always has a sound mind.

Ex. 30

Statement: Should all property belong to the state concerned?

Argument: No. In that case, people will not be serious to work hard.

Ex. 31

Statement: Should the specialists administer their departments and not the generalists?

Argument: No. Because the specialists are generally poor administrators.

In all the examples above, the argument makes some assertions. These assertions may or may not follow in actual practice and if the author of the argument insists upon these (assertions), it is *his individual perception* or assumption. For these reasons, these arguments can be rejected as weak arguments. [For example, it might be the author's view that right to property is as important as right to live. One may or may not agree with the assumption.]

(f) Examples/Analogies

Sometimes an argument predicts something on the basis of a precedent or an example. An example or an analogy is usually bad argumentation. Just because somebody did something in the past, the same cannot be declared as pursuable. See the following illustrations:

Ex. 32

Statement: Should we follow the policy of non-violence?

Argument: Yes. Gandhiji preached non-violence.

Ex. 33

Statement: Should we be optimistic in life?

Argument: Yes. Napoleon was optimistic and see how famous he became!

Note: The above was an exhaustive study of our second step of the solution, viz. "Will the result really follow?" If the argument passes this step, i.e., if it does follow, then you should take the third and the fourth steps. If the argument does not pass this step, you may declare it as weak. For example, in the examples considered till now, Example 7 to Example 22 have passed the second step and they need to be subjected to the third and fourth steps while Example 23 to Example 33 have failed the test and can straightaway be declared as weak arguments. [Example 1 to Example 6 have been rejected in preliminary screening itself.]

Let us now see the easy third step where we decide the desirability of a prediction made in an argument. (or the non- desirability, in case of a negative argument.)

III. Is the result DESIRABLE? (or HARMFUL, in case of negative results)

If an argument has passed the first two tests, i.e., if it has looked okay in the preliminary screening and, further, the predictions made in it have appeared probable and possible, then we subject the argument to this third question. The idea behind this question is very simple: a course of action is suggested, and an argument is made either favouring or protesting against the suggested course of action. The support of protest made in the argument is in the form of predicting consequences usually in the way of : " Yes. Do it. It will bring such and such benefits." or "No. Don't do it. It will bring such and such harms." So, first of all, we check whether the arguer is right in saying that the course of action will bring "such and such benefits" (or "such and such harms"). This was done in step II. Next, we check whether "such and such benefits" are really beneficial (or whether "such and such harms" are really harmful).

Consider these for example:

Ex. 34

Statement: Should Yoga be made compulsory in schools?

Argument: Yes. It will increase the number of teachers by introducing a Yoga teacher.

Ex. 35

Statement: Should English magazines be made costlier?

Argument: No. It would increase the readership of magazines in Hindi and other regional languages.

Do you find anything striking in the two examples above? Both the arguments are fit enough to pass the preliminary screening. Both will pass step II as well: if yoga is made compulsory, a yoga teacher will have to be there and the number of teachers will increase as a result. Similarly, if English magazines are made costlier, a simple logical extension of price-demand law states that people would shift a little towards the magazines in other languages. Thus, logically both these results are probable.

What, then, is wrong with these two arguments? The problem with them is that what they are based upon, what they are harping on, what they are boasting of, is not really desirable (or harmful). For example, the first argument gives a strong 'Yes-Yes' signal to the course of action that makes yoga compulsory in schools. Why? Because the number of teachers will increase. By no means the number of teachers in a school is an important factor and by no means an increase in this number is desirable. Similarly, the second argument makes a strong 'No-No' signal for the course of action that proposes a price hike of English magazines. Why? Because this will increase the demand for magazines in other languages. But why not? Where is the harm? It might be the author's perception that an increase in the demand for other magazines is a harmful consequence but few people would agree with it. (Hence, both are weak arguments.)

[**Note:** How do we judge if a predicted consequence in a recommending argument is really desirable and one in a prohibiting argument is really harmful? Well, you need not think too deep over this matter. It is a matter of pure common sense. Go by your common sense and general norms of society. For example, consider Ex. 7. Isn't it plainly obvious that "better health" is desirable? Or consider Ex. 12. Do you really need any logical calculations to see that "favouritism among teachers" is a harmful consequence?]

IV. Are the argument and the suggested course of action properly related?

We have seen that we can reject an argument solely on the basis that what the argument says seems to have no connection with the suggested course of action. This was a case of complete *non-relation*. Now, in this fourth and final step, we shall consider the case of *'proper relation'* between the argument and the suggested course of action.

What do we mean by '*proper relation*' between the statement and the argument? A statement and an argument are said to be properly related if the argument pin-points on the main issue involved (it should not emphasise any irrelevant, insignificant or minor issues) on one hand, and the course of action seems a balanced option to pursue (it should neither look like a needle trying to kill an elephant nor should it look like a sword trying to kill a mosquito) on the other. Let us see a few examples.

Ex. 36

Statement: Should there be compulsory military training for all?

Argument: Yes. It will bring a sense of discipline in people.

Ex. 37

Statement: Should the number of compulsory working-hours per week be decreased?

Argument: Yes. It would increase the average life expectancy of people.

Ex 36 above is an example of killing a mosquito with a sword. A sense of discipline will be generated and it is a desirable thing too, but compulsory military training is too big an action to be taken for this objective.

Just contrary to this, Ex 37 is a case of trying to kill an elephant with a needle. If the number of working-hours get reduced, the strain on those who work will be reduced. Consequently, the amount of tension and tension-oriented diseases will get reduced and, hence, the life expectancy will increase. Thus, we see that the proposed course of action will contribute towards the predicted consequence and, also, that the consequence is desirable. But if one wanted to improve the life expectancy of society, one would try to improve the living conditions, the health facilities, the treatment techniques etc.

Reducing the number of working hours will be the last thing on his agenda. Thus, because of the reason that the argument talks of an objective for which the proposed course of action would prove too little, the argument is weak.

Summary

- The forcefulness of an argument can be determined in four simple and quick steps.
- In the first step, you have to make a preliminary screening of the given argument: just read the argument and you will have an intuitive feeling whether to accept it or reject it. (Some cases where the arguments can be rejected under this category of preliminary screening have been discussed earlier.)
- After that you are left with three steps. These three steps consist of three simple questions: "Will the predicted consequence really follow?", " Is the predicted consequence really desirable (or harmful)?" and "Are the argument and the statement properly related?". An argument that answers 'Yes' when tested with all the three questions, would be called a strong argument, otherwise it would be called a weak argument.

[**A final note:** Some questions (see Ex. 9, Ex. 10, Ex. 20, Ex. 21, Ex. 22) are in the format of "Suggested Course of Action" $\xrightarrow[\text{no}]{\text{yes}}$ "Positive or negative features" instead of the usual format "Suggested Course of Action" $\xrightarrow[\text{no}]{\text{yes}}$ "Positive or negative consequences". In such cases, step III should be ignored while step II should be altered to " Is the positive (or negative) feature mentioned here true?" instead of "will the result really follow?". The remaining strategies will remain the same.]

Practice Exercise

Directions: Each question given below is followed by two arguments numbered I and II. You have to decide which of the arguments is a 'strong' argument and which is a 'weak' argument.

Give answer (A) if only argument I is strong; (B) if only argument II is strong; (C) if either I or II is strong; (D) if neither I nor II is strong; and (E) if both I and II strong.

1. **Statement:** Should a total ban be put on trapping wild animals?
   Arguments: I. Yes. Trappers are making a lot of money.
   II. No. Bans on hunting and trapping are not effective.
2. **Statement:** Should military service be made compulsory in our country?
   Arguments: I. No. It is against the policy of non-violence.
   II. Yes. Every citizen should protect his country.
3. **Statement:** Should all the remote parts of a country be connected by road?
   Arguments: I. No. It will disturb peaceful simple life of the villagers.
   II. Yes. It must be done immediately.
4. **Statement:** Should government jobs in rural areas be given more incentives?
   Arguments: I. Yes. Incentives are essential for attracting government servants there.
   II. No. Rural areas are already cheaper, healthier and less complex than big towns. So, why offer extra incentives!
5. **Statement:** Should religion be taught in our schools?
   Arguments: I. No. Ours is a secular state.
   II. Yes. Teaching religion helps inculcate moral values among children.
6. **Statement:** Should non-vegetarian food be totally banned in our country?
   Arguments: I. Yes. It is expensive and, therefore, beyond the reach of most of the people in our country.
   II. No. Nothing should be banned in a democratic country.

7. **Statement:** Should films be included in the Concurrent List?
Arguments: I. Yes. It will give respect to the views of the states.
II. No. It will deteriorate the standard of films.

8. **Statement:** Should there be only one university throughout India?
Arguments: I. Yes. This is the only way to bring about uniformity in educational standards.
II. No. This is administratively impossible.

9. **Statement:** Should mercy death be legalised?
Arguments: I. Yes. Patients undergoing terrible suffering and having absolutely no chance of recovery should be liberated from suffering through mercy death.
II. No. Even mercy death is a sort of killing and killing can never be legalised.

10. **Statement:** Should there be a single government in the world?
Arguments: I. Yes. It will help in eliminating tensions among the nations.
II. No. Because then, only the developed countries will dominate in the government.

11. **Statement:** Should the institution of marriages be abolished?
Arguments: I. Yes. It is already showing cracks.
II. No. It is necessary for the survival of society.

12. **Statement:** Should healthcare service be nationalised?
Arguments: I. Yes. It has been done elsewhere also.
II. No. The quality of healthcare service will deteriorate.

13. **Statement:** Should telecasting feature films be stopped?
Arguments: I. Yes. Young children are misguided by feature films.
II. No. This is the only way to educate the masses.

14. **Statement:** Should agriculture in rural India be mechanised?
Arguments: I. Yes. It would lead to higher production.
II. No. It would lead to rural unemployment.

15. **Statement:** Should the illiterate be debarred from voting?
Arguments: I. Yes. They are easily misguided.
II. No. It is their constitutional right.

16. **Statement:** Should luxury hotels be banned in India?
Arguments: I. Yes. They are places from where international criminals operate.
II. No. Affluent foreign tourists will have no place to stay.

17. **Statement:** Can pollution be controlled?
Arguments: I. Yes. If every one realizes the hazard it may pose and cooperates to get rid of it, pollution may be controlled.
II. No. The crowded highways, factories and industries and an ever-growing population eager to acquire more and more land for constructing houses are beyond control.

18. **Statement:** Is Governorship better than Chief Ministership?
Arguments: I. Yes. It is the highest post in a state.
II. No. The Chief Minister commands more power.

19. **Statement:** Should there be no place for interview in selection procedures?
Arguments: I. Yes. It is very subjective in assessment.
II. No. It is the only instrument to judge the candidates' motives and personality.

20. **Statement:** Should higher education be completely stopped for some time?
Arguments: I. No. It will hamper the country's progress.
II. Yes. It will reduce educated unemployment.

21. **Statement:** Should all the news be controlled by the government in a democracy?
Arguments: I. Yes. Variety of news only confuses people.
II. No. Controlled news loses credibility.

22. **Statement:** Should private companies be allowed to operate air services in India?
Arguments: I. Yes. Indian private managements usually give better services.
II. No. We should not ape the western countries.

23. **Statement:** Should there be students' union in college/university?
Arguments: I. No. This will create a political atmosphere in the campus.
II. Yes. It is very necessary. Students are the future political leaders.

24. **Statement:** Should new big industries be started in Bombay?
Arguments: I. Yes. It will create new job opportunities.
II. No. It will further add to the pollution of the city.

25. **Statement:** Should India manufacture atom bombs?
Arguments: I. Yes. It is imperative to protect the sovereignty and integrity of the country.
II. No. This will create imbalance in the power of nations in this region.

26. **Statement:** Should computers be used in all possible sectors in India?
Arguments: I. Yes. It will bring efficiency and accuracy in the work.
II. No. It will be an injustice to the monumental human resources which are at present underutilised.

27. **Statement:** Is paying ransom or agreeing to the conditions of kidnappers of political figures a proper course of action?
Arguments: I. Yes. Victims must be saved at any cost.
II. No. It encourages the kidnappers to continue with their sinister activities.

28. **Statement:** Should India go in for computerisation in industry?

Arguments: **I.** No. Computerisation demands a lot of money. We should not waste money on it.

II. Yes. When advanced countries are introducing computers in various areas, how can we afford to lag behind?

29. **Statement:** Is monarchy better than democracy?

Arguments: **I.** Yes. If the chair has one confirmed ruler, there are no ambitious aspirants fighting for it.

II. No. People are more contented and happy in a democracy.

30. **Statement:** Should Doordarshan be given autonomous status?

Arguments: **I.** Yes. It will help Doordarshan to have fair and impartial coverage of all important events.

II. No. The coverage of the events will be decided by a few who may not have a healthy outlook.

31. **Statement:** Should colleges be given the status of a university in India?

Arguments: **I.** Yes. Colleges are in a better position to assess the students' performance and, therefore, the degrees will be more valid.

II. No. It is utopian to think that there will not be nepotism and corruption in degrees being awarded by colleges.

32. **Statement:** Should private sector be permitted to operate telephone services?

Arguments: **I.** Yes. They are operated in advanced western countries.

II. No. It is risky to put them in private hands.

33. **Statement:** Should so much money be spent on games and sports?

Arguments: **I.** Yes. We are a rich nation and can easily spare any amount of money for games and sports.

II. No. Our teams are unable to put up a good show in international competitions.

34. **Statement:** Should workers be allowed to participate in the management of factories in India?

Arguments: **I.** Yes. It is the present management theory.

II. No. Many workers are illiterate and, so, their contributions will not be of any value.

35. **Statement:** Are educational institutions responsible for unrest among the youth?

Arguments: **I.** Yes. There is no discipline in educational institutions.

II. No. There is no disciplinary problem in educational institutions.

36. **Statement:** Should political parties be banned?

Arguments: **I.** Yes. It is necessary to teach a lesson to the politicians.

II. No. It will lead to the end of democracy.

37. **Statement:** Should jobs be delinked from academic degrees and diplomas?

Arguments: I. No. A very large number of persons with hardly any academic qualifications will apply.

II. No. Importance of higher education will be diminished.

38. **Statement:** Should coal engines be replaced by electric engines in trains?

Arguments: I. Yes. Coal engines cause a lot of pollution.

II. No. India does not produce enough electricity to fulfil even the domestic needs.

39. **Statement:** Should women be provided more job opportunities?

Arguments: I. No. They are entrusted with household jobs.

II. Yes. They should also go into the outside world.

40. **Statement:** Should personal tax be abolished in India?

Arguments: I. Yes. It will motivate people to earn more.

II. No. Individuals must learn to share their wealth with other people.

41. **Statement:** Should smoking be prohibited?

Arguments: I. Yes. It is wrong to smoke away millions of money.

II. No. It will throw thousands of workers in the tobacco industry out of employment.

42. **Statement:** Should high chimneys be installed in industries?

Arguments: I. Yes. It reduces pollution at ground level.

II. No. It increases pollution in upper atmosphere.

43. **Statement:** Should we take care of the ozone layer?

Arguments: I. Yes. It protects us from the harmful ultraviolet rays.

II. No. There is no harm from it.

44. **Statement:** Should shifting agriculture be practiced?

Arguments: I. No. It is a wasteful practice.

II. Yes. Modern methods of farming are too expensive.

45. **Statement:** Should loyalty be the only criterion for promotion in any organisation?

Arguments: I. Yes. No organisation can function without loyal men.

II. No. It leads to hypocrisy and partiality.

46. **Statement:** Should untouchability be banned in India?

Arguments: I. No. Menial people worsen the living standard of society.

II. Yes. All people should be treated equally in a democratic country like India.

47. **Statement:** Should India encourage exports when most things are insufficient for internal use itself?

Arguments: I. Yes. We have to earn foreign exchange to pay for our imports.

II. No. Even selective encouragement would lead to shortages.

48. **Statement:** Should India make efforts to harness solar energy to fulfil its energy requirements?

Arguments: **I.** Yes. Most of the energy sources used at present are exhaustible.

II. No. Harnessing solar energy requires a lot of capital which India lacks.

49. **Statement:** Should education be made compulsory for all children upto the age of 14?

Arguments: **I.** Yes. This will help to eradicate the system of forced employment of these children.

II. Yes. This would improve the standard of living.

50. **Statement:** Should judiciary be independent of the executive?

Arguments: **I.** Yes. This would help curb the unlawful activities of the executive.

II. No. The executive would not be able to take bold measures.

51. **Statement:** Should all refugees who have made an unauthorized entry into a country, be forced to go back to their homeland?

Arguments: **I.** Yes. They make their colonies and occupy a lot of land.

II. No. They leave their homes because of hunger or some terror and, on human grounds, should not be forced to go back.

52. **Statement:** Should the system of Lok Adalats and mobile courts be encouraged in India?

Arguments: **I.** Yes. It helps to grant speedy justice to the masses.

II. No. These courts are usually partial in granting justice.

53. **Statement:** Should India give away Kashmir to Pakistan?

Arguments: **I.** No. Kashmir is a beautiful state. It earns a lot of foreign exchange for India.

II. Yes. This would help settle conflicts.

54. **Statement:** Should India have no military force at all?

Arguments: **I.** No. Other countries in the world do not believe in non-violence.

II. Yes. Many Indians believe in non-violence.

55. **Statement:** Should religion be banned?

Arguments: **I.** Yes. It develops fanaticism in people.

II. No. Religion binds people together.

56. **Statement:** Should so much money be spent on advertisements?

Arguments: **I.** Yes. It is an essential feature of a capitalist economy.

II. No. It leads to a wastage of resources.

57. **Statement:** Should there be a complete ban on strikes by government employees in India?

Arguments: **I.** Yes. This is the only way to teach discipline to the employees.

II. No. This deprives the citizens of their democratic rights.

58. **Statement:** Should state lotteries be banned?

Arguments: **I.** Yes. The government should not promote gambling.

II. No. The government will lose a large amount of revenue.

59. **Statement:** Should cottage industries be encouraged in rural areas?

Arguments: **I.** Yes. Rural people are creative.

II. Yes. This would help in solving the problem of unemployment to some extent.

60. **Statement:** Should income tax be evaded by people?

Arguments: **I.** Yes. Taxes are excessively high.

II. No. It is anti-national to do so.

61. **Statement:** Should dams be built on rivers?

Arguments: **I.** No. Some dam projects have proved to be unsuccessful in recent years.

II. Yes. They are beneficial in checking floods and conserving soil.

62. **Statement:** Should taxes on colour television be increased further?

Arguments: **I.** Yes. Colour television is a luxury item and only rich people buy it.

II. No. Televisions are bought by the poor too.

63. **Statement:** Should officers accepting bribe be punished?

Arguments: **I.** No. Certain circumstances may have compelled them to take bribe.

II. Yes. They should do the job they are entrusted with honestly.

64. **Statement:** Are nuclear families better than joint families?

Arguments: **I.** No. Joint families ensure security and also reduce the burden of work.

II. Yes. Nuclear families ensure greater freedom.

65. **Statement:** Should there be reservation of seats and posts on communal basis?

Arguments: **I.** Yes. It will check most of the inter-communal biases.

II. No. Ours is a secular state.

66. **Statement:** Should correspondence courses at university level be discontinued?

Arguments: **I.** No. Such courses are there in advanced countries like USA.

II. Yes. It will substantially lessen the burden of the postal department.

67. **Statement:** Should higher education be reserved for the deserving few?

Arguments: **I.** No. It will increase unemployment.

II. Yes. It will minimise wastage in higher education.

68. **Statement:** Should those who receive dowry, despite the law prohibiting it, be punished?

Arguments: **I.** Yes. Those who violate the law must be punished.

II. No. Dowry system is firmly rooted in the society since time immemorial.

Answers and Explanations

1. D; None is strong. If trappers make money, they should not be stopped solely on this ground. And if bans are not effective, then care should be taken to enforce them strictly instead of not banning at all.
2. D; If non-violence is that strong a principle then we should not have any army either! Second argument lacks proper relation (see step IV). None is strong.
3. D; None is strong. I is rejected because it may not happen (will not follow). II is rejected because it is too simple and does not have argumentative substance.
4. E; Both are strong. Incentives do lure people. Second is also an established fact.
5. B; Second is strong. First is not very clear. If the state is secular, it means it is against religious bias but not against religion as such. Second is in consonance with the prevailing notions of truth.
6. D; Both are weak. It is for the people to decide whether they want to eat expensive food. A ban should not be enforced upon them. Second is weak because it is not an acceptable truth. Nobody has said that "democratic country" means a country where nothing could be banned, however harmful it was.
7. D; Both are weak. First is weak as it is not sure that including films in concurrent list would give respect to people's views. Second will not follow (it seems), hence it is weak.
8. B; Second is strong. First is weak because it is not correct. (Is it the only way?) Second is perhaps correct, on logical thinking.
9. E; Both are strong. They mention a positive and a negative feature of mercy death; both these features are desirable/harmful respectively and both are related with important aspects of the topic of mercy death.
10. E; Both are strong. On logical thinking, both look probable, both are desirable (harmful in the case of second) and both touch significant aspects of the issue.
11. B; Second is strong. First is weak as you cannot abolish a system simply because it is showing cracks. Second is an accepted truth.
12. D; None is strong. First is weak as it is based upon example. Second is weak as it is debatable.
13. A; First is strong. First is an acceptable piece of truth backed by evidence. Second is weak as it is not true.

14. E; Both are strong. Both are true (both will follow). The first is really desirable while the second is really harmful.
15. B; Second is strong. First talks of a negative feature which does exist but is not sufficient enough to go for such a drastic action as disallowing for vote. Second is an established fact.
16. B; Second is strong. Affluent foreign tourists tend to prefer luxury hotels. First is debatable and, even if it is true, then what is the guarantee that criminals would not operate from other places?
17. E; Both are strong. Although both arguments contradict each other, yet both are based upon sound assumptions or facts and hence, independently, both are strong.
18. E; Both are strong. Same explanation as in previous question.
19. E; I is strong as a subjective mode of selection is not desirable. II is of course, right.
20. D; None is strong. Temporary stopping of higher education will not hamper the nation's progress. It will reduce educated unemployment but so what? It will, then, increase uneducated unemployment.
21. B; Second is strong. First argument is debatable while the second is an established fact.
22. A; First is strong as it is based upon an established fact. Second is based upon example; hence it is a weak argument.
23. E; I is true as it is based on experiences. And political atmosphere in the campus is not really desirable as the campus is a place of learning, not politics. II is also true because tomorrow's leaders will come from today's students and it is good that they get some political training early.
24. E; Both are correct and strong arguments.
25. A; I is strong as it is true that atomic power works as deterrent to possible invades that thus enhances sovereignity. II is not a strong argument as the imbalance would only be in India's favour and that won't be an undesirable thing.
26. E; Both are strong. Using computer does have the positive feature as mentioned in I but the negative feature is also there as mentioned in II.
27. E; Both are strong. Explanation same as in Q. 26.
28. D; None is strong. We do not 'waste' money if we invest in computers. The second is based upon example.
29. E; I talks of a positive feature of "absence of fight for power" in monarchy and this absence of fight is indeed, a desirable thing. II is a strong argument in the sense that it is in confirmity with today's prevailing notions of truth.
30. E; Both are strong arguments.
31. E; Both are strong arguments.
32. D; None is strong. First is based on example while second is rejected in preliminary screening; it has no reasoning.

33. D;None is strong. It is not true that we are a rich nation. Similarly, the reasons mentioned in the second are not sufficient to put a stop on spending money (lack of proper relation).
34. D;None is strong. First is based upon example. Second says that many workers are illiterate. What about the remaining ones who are illiterate and whose suggestions will be of some value?
35. D;None is strong. First is ambiguous while second is simply not true.
36. B; Second is strong. First is rejected in preliminary screening.
37. B; Second is strong as diminished importance of higher education won't be a good thing really. One is not strong. Although, it is true that a phenomenally large number of people might apply for jobs, we should not think of it as a problem. It is almost cruel to decide that more unemployed persons knocking on your doors for jobs should mean headache.
38. E; Both arguments are strong as both mention correct facts.
39. B; Second is strong. First is not because it is not a sufficient reason to withhold them from going out.
40. A;First is strong. Logically thinking, it looks probable. Second is irrelevant and a little too ideological.
41. E; First is a piece of truth. Second is a logical consequence of ban over smoking and does have some merit.
42. C; This is one of the rarest types of question on forcefulness of arguments where the choice 'either of the two is strong' follows. Either increase of pollution at upper level is favourable or that at ground level. So, one of the two should be desirable. Hence the choice.
43. A;Argument one is strong. Argument two has no substance, rejectable in preliminary screening.
44. A; First is strong in the sense that it is an established fact that a lot of resources are wasted in shifting agriculture. Second is not a strong argument as it is, to begin with, debatable if other methods are really more expensive in the long run than the resource - crippling shifting agriculture.
45. B; Second is strong as it does look probable on thinking logically. First is true but this is not reason enough to make loyalty the sole criterion for promotion (lack of proper relation).
46. B; Second is strong. First statement is objectionable and debatable.
47. E; Both are strong. First is simple and straightforward. It is also true. Second is also correct, specially when seen in the light of the fact that the question itself states that there are shortages for 'internal use itself'.
48. A;First is strong. Currently, we use exhaustible sources of energy while solar energy is not exhaustible. The second is not correct. In fact, solar energy is cheap.
49. D;None is strong. First lacks proper relation. Eradication of forced employment is not the goal of education. Also, it is not clear how

compulsory education can help to eradicate forced employment. The second is ambiguous.

50. B; Second is strong. Curbing unlawful activities of the executive is not so big a problem as would demand so strict a solution as delinking executive and judiciary. Second is however correct.

51. E; Both arguments are strong.

52. A; First is strong. Second is debatable.

53. D; None is strong. The subject of giving away a state is too sensitive a topic to be determined by or to get influenced by beauty or foreign exchange or by the fact that it may settle conflicts. Suppose Kashmir was not beautiful and it did not earn any foreign exchange. Would we then have given it away?

54. D; None is strong. Non-violence as such is too ideological and not practical.

55. B; Second is strong as it is taken as universal truth. The first is a debatable point.

56. D; None is strong because of indirect assertions. The first may be true but why is it essential? The second says it is a wastage of resources but it also generates resources: as a result of advertisement business picks up.

57. B; Second is strong as it is factually correct. First is debatable. It is certainly not the 'only' way to teach discipline to employees.

58. E; Both are strong. It is true that the government should not promote gambling habits which it does through its lotteries. It is also true that the government would lose a major source of revenue if lotteries were stopped.

59. B; First may or may not be true. Second is definitely correct.

60. B; Only second is strong. Tax rates are decided by democratically elected ministers and they are not excessively high.

61. B; Only second is strong. Some dam projects may have failed but we should see the reasons of failure instead of abandoning it fully.

62. D; None is strong. First is debatable. Colour T.V. may or may not be a luxury item. The second argument does not talk about colour television.

63. B; Only second is strong.

64. E; Both are strong. Both talk of certain features of joint families and nuclear families respectively and both the features are desirable in themselves.

65. B; Second is strong. First is debatable: it may rather increase the inter-communal bias.

66. D; None is strong. First is based on example while second lacks proper relation. Correspondence courses are not given with the postal department in mind. So lessening of burden on postal department is not a good reason to stop correspondence courses.

67. B; Second is strong. First is weak because it is not clear how it may lead to unemployment.

68. A; Only first is strong. Second is weak. Even if dowry system is deep-rooted, it is still illegal and hence punishable.

Chapter Five

Evaluating Inferences

5.1: Introduction

It has become a regular trend of almost all competitive examinations to ask questions of this type. A passage is given which is usually a part of a report or an economic essay or any other similar thought-provoking subject. Some inferences are given followed by the passage (there are usually five inferences). The candidate is asked to decide whether a given inference follows or not in the light of the given passage. The complete format is presented below for the reader's convenience:

5.2: Format of the question

Directions: Given below is a passage followed by several inferences based upon it. You have to examine the passage carefully and then decide the validity of each of the inferences. Mark answer,

A) if the inference is definitely true;

B) if the inference is probably true;

C) if the data are inadequate, i.e., in the light of the given passage, you cannot say whether the inference is likely to be true or false;

D) if the inference is probably false; and

E) if the inference is definitely false.

Now, read the passage and the inferences and choose your answers.

Sample Passage 0

The theory of Odgen and Williams is being taken seriously by the scientific community ever since photovoltaic cells with thirty per cent efficiency were produced under experimental conditions. Companies like Siemens are spending millions of dollars to produce more efficient solar cells. The American Department of Energy is confident that it will be able to produce 22-per cent-efficient solar cells by the turn of the century. But anyway, to fulfil the needs of a country the size of America, an area equal to the state of Michigan would have to be blanketed by solar cells.

Inferences

1) Odgen and Williams were respectable scientists of the late 19th century.
2) The theory of Odgen and Williams proposes that solar energy can be produced at a higher rate of efficiency than normally expected by following certain rules and norms.
3) In America, research on solar power is undertaken by private as well as government enterprise.

4) The current efficiency of photovoltaic cells in America is far below 30%.
5) In terms of area, America is not very big.

5.3: An analysis

First of all, let us see what these questions seek to test. Examiners put these questions because they test your ability to derive correct inference and your reasoning ability is thus evaluated. Also, here the examiner can 'grade' the choices closely. Thus, there are two positive choices instead of one: "probably true" and "definitely true" and two negative choices instead of one: "probably false" and "definitely false". This requires slightly deeper thinking. Further, syllogistic reasoning has a very set pattern; there are a fixed combination of four fixed types of propositions (A, E, I or O) in inferences. Also, in those questions, the given statements are hypothetical in nature - like "All boys are toys" or "Some cows are elephants". In this respect, passage-based inferences are different from syllogism-based inferences because in the former, passages are from a practical world, cover everyday-life situations and are not hypothetical. Thus, it gives the examiner a wider scope to examine your intelligence.

Having discussed the purpose of these questions (which was not of much use practically), let us come to something really important: let us examine what the difficult aspects of such questions are; or, in other words, what may make such questions difficult.

The most sensitive aspect of this question is its *gradedness*. Some of the inferences can be easily and quickly judged because they can be easily compared with the facts given in the passage. But, in some cases, an inference is indirect. Here, it may lead to confusion. You may vacillate between 'Definitely true' and 'probably true' or between 'probably true' and 'data inadequate' or between 'data inadequate' and 'probably false' or between 'probably false' and 'definitely false'. For example, look at inference (3) of the sample passage given above. This is straightforward and you shouldn't have any difficulty in seeing that the correct answer is 'definitely true', because the passage clearly mentions the involvement of a 'company' (Siemens) and a government body (Department of Energy). But now, look at inferences (2) and (5). In (2), one may vacillate between 'data inadequate' and 'probably true'. 'Data inadequate' will look correct because no mention has been made of what exactly is proposed in the theory of Odgen and Williams. 'Probably true' looks correct because the passage says that the theory of Odgen and Williams began to be taken seriously after photovoltaic cells with higher efficiency were made. This means that there was something in the theory which got support from higher-efficiency photovoltaic cells. Thus, it 'looks' true that the theory had proposed that higher-efficiency cells could be created, etc. On the other hand, in (5), you may vacillate between 'data inadequate' and 'probably false'. 'Data inadequate' may appear correct because no information is presented about the 'comparative' size of America, whether it is big or small. 'Probably false' may appear correct because the 'tone' of the sentence - "..... of a country the size of America ...." - is such as if America were a big country.

The conclusion of our analysis, therefore, is that the main areas of difficulty in solving such questions is the possibility of a confusion between two similar choices. These possibilities are depicted pictorially in the figure below.

In this lesson, we shall have special emphasis upon these 'confusion areas' which will follow an overall study of the technique of solving such questions.

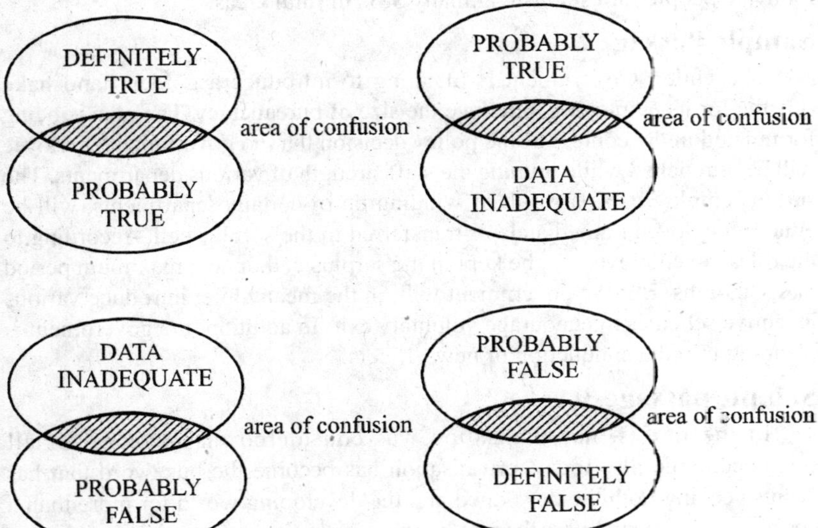

5.4: Technique

The best technique of evaluating a given inference is to subject it to a three-pronged, graded test. This test consists of three steps:

(i) Directly follows from the passage.
(ii) Can be inferred from the passage.
(iii) Can be inferred with the help of some key words.

In the first category lie the easy questions where an inference is more or less a restatement of something already stated in the passage. In the second category, we check if the inference can be derived from the facts mentioned in the passage. And finally in the third category, we see if some key words justify the given inference. Let us study each of these cases one by one. In this study of ours we shall make use of the sample passages given below.

Sample Passages

Sample passage 1

The Government of India has announced extremely attractive incentives to promote the small scale industries (SSIs) in rural areas for the current year 1992-93. The support amount has been raised and fixed at Rs 30 lacs in comparison to Rs 25 lacs in the year 1991-92 and Rs 20 lacs in 1990-91. This decision is perceived by many as a very timely incentive in the right direction to motivate people for establishing many SSIs in rural areas.

Sample Passage 2

The Union Government is planning to introduce a golden handshake scheme for its employees to reduce the size of bureaucracy. The plan is being formulated in the context of the policy decision that no government employee will be retrenched while pruning the staff strength of various departments. The surplus employees as a result of winding up of certain departments, will be either redeployed immediately or transferred to the surplus cell. According to the rules, an employee can be kept in the surplus cell up to a maximum period of six months. But the government will, in the meanwhile, introduce various incentive schemes to encourage voluntary exit. In addition, the government is planning to reduce induction of new officers.

Sample passage 3

In the forties, nationalisation was considered the panacea for all socio-economic ills. Today, privatisation has become the buzzword that has been sweeping both the developed and the developing world for more than a decade now. Even in India, the idea has been gathering momentum. But, before the idea is transplanted in India, there are several aspects of privatisation that need to be understood. It would be worth while, in this context, to look at the experiences of other countries.

Sample Passage 4

Even "mild" and "moderate" degrees of malnutrition could impair muscular efficiency and intellectual development of children. This was revealed in a study made by the nutrition section of the department of paediatrics of Banaras University for the Nutrition Foundation of India. The study covered 1, 136 children aged between six and eight years in 22 schools in the Kashi Vidyapeeth block of Varanasi. They were investigated with a view to determining the relationship between their nutritional status and functional competence.

Sample passage 5

One of the important facts of the history of science is that majority of discoveries have been made by the youth. It proves that the most important requirement for success in scientific research is the freshness of outlook associated with youth, and not the maturity of knowledge associated with age and experience. Conservatism is a hindering factor in scientific achievement, but it is useful so far as it puts brakes on wilder flights of youthful imagination.

Sample passage 6

In India, only Tamil Nadu has a fairly extensive mid-day meal scheme for school children. A mid-day meal scheme is not a perfect solution to the nutrition problem but has the added advantage of providing an incentive to parents to send their kids to school.

Sample passage 7

The serious accident in which a person was run down by a car yesterday has again focussed attention on the most unsatisfactory state of street lighting. No one expects side roads to be provided with the same standard of lighting as a main road but unless the council is prepared to make good its promise as regards road lighting, it will only be a question of time before there are further, and perhaps more fatal, accidents.

I. Directly follows from the passage

This is a relatively easy job. All we have to check in this case is whether a given inference is a direct consequence of something given in the passage. **If it is so, the inference will be 'definitely true'.** Just opposite to it could be the case of *does not follow from the passage*. In this case, the given inference could be just the opposite of something clearly mentioned in the passage. **If it is so, the inference will be 'definitely false'**. The following examples illustrate this point.

Ex 1: Refer to sample passage 2.

Inference: Many employees would be retrenched as a result of golden handshake scheme.

Explanation: The passage clearly mentions that the government is reducing the size of its staff while seeing to it that no government employee would be retrenched. The given inference is simply opposite to it. Hence, it is definitely false.

Ex 2: Refer to sample passage 3.

Inference: India is also thinking of privatisation.

Explanation: The sentence "Even in India .... momentum." clearly and directly implies that India is also thinking of privatisation. Hence, the given inference is definitely true.

Ex 3: Refer to sample passage 4.

Inference: 1136 boys of 22 schools were taught by Banaras University.

Explanation: It is an exact restatement of one of the sentences of the passage. Hence, it is definitely true.

Ex 4: Refer to sample passage 5.

Inferences: I. All the scientific discoveries have been made by old scientists.

II. For success in scientific research, freshness of outlook is necessary.

III. Maturity due to age and experience is not an important requirement for success in scientific research.

Explanation: The first inference says that all the scientific discoveries have been made by old scientists. This is exactly opposite of the statement made in the passage that majority of discoveries have been made by the youth. Hence, the inference is definitely false.

The second inference is a restatement of the second sentence of the passage. Hence, it is definitely true.

The same sentence goes on to say that the "most important requirement" for success in scientific research is not the maturity of knowledge associated with age and experience. The third inference is more or less a restatement of the same. Hence, it is definitely true.

II. Can be inferred from the passage

The first category of inferences that we saw just now was relatively easy to judge as in this case the inferences were very direct. They were more or less a restatement of a fact already mentioned (or they were exactly opposite).

In the second, category comes the case of inferences that are not so direct. They will require the application of some logic on your part. To test these inferences, you will have to make certain assumptions; and using these assumptions together with a fact mentioned in the passage, the inference may be evaluated.

For example consider the following.

Ex 5:

Statement: All countries having a large population are giving priority to family planning.

Inference: Family planning is given priority in India.

Explanation: You can notice that, here, the inference is very indirectly related to the given statement. The statement does not even mention India. Hence, to evaluate this inference you will have to apply some logic. You can safely make an assumption that 'India has a large population'. Now, this assumption, together with the given statement leads to the given inference. Hence, the given inference is definitely true.

Thus, we see that in the case of inferences that do not directly follow from the passage, we need to make certain assumptions. These assumptions will play the crucial role in determining the correctness of your answers. Hence, for your benefit, we are enlisting certain standard assumptions that can be made while analysing a passage. (Please note this is not a complete list and, depending upon a particular passage, different cases may arise. However, by studying these assumptions you can easily learn the essence of the concept.)

Some standard assumptions for some standard cases

(a) Action-Motive

(i) "If an action is being undertaken, and if such an action is ***always*** *taken with a particular type of motive, then such a motive must exist."*

Ex 6: Refer to sample passage 1.

Inference: The Government is keen to develop rural areas.

Explanation: The action is that the Government has announced several incentives to promote the SSIs. What is the motive? Obviously, for such incentives by governments, the only possible motive could be a keenness to develop the related area. Therefore, assuming this, the given inference is definitely true.

(ii) "If an action is being undertaken, and if such an action is ***never*** *taken with a particular type of motive, then it is definitely false that such a motive exists."*

Ex 7: Refer to sample passage 2.

Inference: The government wants to increase unemployment.

Explanation: We may safely assume that no government 'wants' to increase unemployment. This makes the inference definitely false.

(iii) "If an action is being undertaken, and if such an action is ***usually*** *taken with a particular type of motive, then it is probably true that such a motive exists."*

Ex 8: Refer to sample passage 2.

Inference: The government is trying to reduce its non-plan expenditure.

Explanation: The government is trying to cut down the size of its bureaucracy. An effort to cut down on the non-plan expenditure could be the motive. However, this is only probable but not certain. Hence, it is probably true.

*(iv) "If an action is being undertaken, and if such an action is **usually not** taken with a particular type of motive, then it is probably false that such a motive exists."*

Ex 9: Passage: There was not much to be looked about beside the body. The murder might have occurred anytime during midnight. There was no evidence of any document or valuables missing. Incidentally, the TV was switched on with its volume very loud.

Inference: The murderer killed the owner of the TV as a result of a quarrel, because the latter was not ready to reduce the volume.

Explanation: We cannot discard this inference as definitely false because anything is possible in this world. But, we may safely assume that murders are *usually not* committed on such small issues as the volume of a TV. Hence we take the inference as probably false.

(b) Cause-Effect

*(i) "If an action is being undertaken and if such an action **always** leads to a particular type of effect, then it is definitely true that such an effect would take place."*

Ex 10: Refer to sample passage 1.

Inference: The government step would generate more employment opportunities.

Explanation: It can be safely assumed that if more and more 'attractive' incentives for the SSIs of rural sector are announced, this would attract more and more people to open SSIs and this in turn would generate more employment. Hence, the inference is definitely true.

*(ii) "If an action is being undertaken and if such an action **never** leads to a particular type of effect, it is definitely false that such an effect would occur."*

Ex 11: Refer to sample passage 1.

Inference: The small scale industries' organisations would protest against the action.

Explanation: It can be safely assumed that nobody can protest against an action which is beneficial to him. Hence, "the action" of providing incentives to the SSIs can not have the `effect' of protests from the SSIs. The inference is definitely false.

*(iii) "If an action is being undertaken and if such an action **usually** leads to a particular type of effect, it is probably true that such an effect would occur."*

Ex 12: Refer to sample passage 6.

Inference: Mid-day meal scheme will improve the school attendance of children.

Explanation: We can safely assume that free food usually attracts people. Under this assumption we may consider it likely that more parents would send their children to school. Hence, the school attendance will improve. However, this effect is not definite to happen. Maybe, the parents would find it better to send their children to work than to eat a free meal. Hence, the inference is probably true but not definitely true.

*(iv) "If an action is being undertaken and if such an action **usually does not** lead to a particular type of effect, then it is probably false that such an effect would occur."*

Ex 13: Refer to sample passage 2.

Inference: There will be a violent revolution against the government's plans.

Explanation: People may not like the idea of reducing the size of bureaucracy but history suggests that mildly harsh decisions do not bring Indian people on the verge of revolution. Under this assumption, therefore, the conclusion appears false. But, it cannot be declared definitely false; after all, anything may happen. Hence, it is probably false.

(c) Analogy (similarity)

*(i) "If a group (of objects or persons etc.) shows some kind of property and if another group is similar (analogous) to the former group in **all relevant aspects**, then it is definitely true that the second group will also show the same property."*

Ex 14: Refer to sample passage 4.

Inference: Many children from poor families are likely to have less muscular efficiency and intellectual development.

Explanation: The passage states that children having 'malnutrition' form one group that shows the 'property' of muscular inefficiency and less intellectual development. Now, children from poor families are an exactly similar group because they live under the constant condition of malnutrition because of poverty. Hence, they too will exhibit the same property. Thus, the given inference is definitely true.

*(ii) "If a group (of objects or persons etc.) shows some kind of property and if another group is **exactly** similar in nature to that group, then it is definitely false that the second group will not show that property."*

Ex 15: Refer to sample passage 6.

Inference: In Bihar, the mid-day meal scheme won't work because here the parents won't be lured by the incentive of mid-day meals.

Explanation: There is no reason why Bihar and Tamil Nadu will show variations in response to similar conditions. We can safely assume that Bihar and Tamil Nadu form an identical (similar) pair of states. Hence, it would be definitely false that the property exhibited in Tamil Nadu will not be exhibited in Bihar.

(iii) "If a group (of objects or persons etc.) shows some kind of property and if another group is similar to this group in ***some (but not all)*** *aspects, then it is probably true that the same property is exhibited by the second group.*

Ex 16: Refer to sample passage 4.

Inference: A person who goes on a diet control (weight reduction programme) for a long period, will also develop muscular inefficiency.

Explanation: We have seen that children who suffer from malnutrition develop muscular inefficiency. Now, a person on diet control deliberately starves himself of food and hence he is also - in some way - similar to a malnutritioned man. But, his is not *exactly* a case of malnutrition; there are some differences. Thus, this group is similar but not *exactly* similar to the first group. Hence, it is probably true that he will also develop muscular inefficiency.

(iv) "If a group (of objects or persons etc.) shows some kind of property and if another group is similar to the former group in ***some (not all)*** *aspects, then it is probably false that the second group does not exhibit that property."*

Ex 17: Passage: "India has pursued the policy of non-alignment since Independence. Though a little inclined towards the former USSR, it has been able to establish a graceful position as a neutral nation. Consequently, it has been able to achieve the much-needed foreign aids without much difficulty."

Inference: Sri Lanka would have a lot of difficulty in getting foreign aids.

Explanation: India and Sri Lanka are both part of the Non-Aligned Movement and hence they can be said to be similar in this aspect. But they are not exactly similar because other conditions (that influence foreign aid) might be different. Now, India has been shown to get foreign aid without much hassles and it has been linked with its non-aligned status. Hence, it would be probably false that a similar (non-aligned) nation should have a lot of difficulty in getting aids. But it can't be declared definitely false because India and Sri Lanka can't be assumed to be *exactly similar*.

(d) Miscellaneous Cases

We have seen that in evaluating some indirectly derived inferences, we should use our commonsense and logic. We can evaluate the inference by making some general and unobjectionable assumptions and using this and the passage we can come to the given inferences. Some very common cases and common assumptions were also discussed under the head of action-motive, cause-effect, analogy. However, although these constitute a good percentage of commonly given inferences, we may be given cases which do not fall under any of these categories. But, you can easily evaluate them, once you have understood the concept. Some miscellaneous cases are being given below for illustration.

Ex 18: Refer to sample passage 5.

Inference: Progressivism is a helping hand in scientific research.

Explanation: The given passage says that "conservatism is a hindering factor in scientific achievement". If we make a general (and unobjectionable) assumption that progressivism is exactly the opposite of conservatism, we can see that the given inference follows at once. Hence, it is definitely true.

Ex 19: Refer to sample passage 6.

Inference: Schoolchildren in Tamil Nadu need no further nutrition.

Explanation: We can safely assume that one meal in a day (mid-day meal) is not sufficient for nutrition. Hence, the given inference must be definitely false.

Ex 20: Refer to sample passage 7.

Inference: The accident that occurred was fatal.

Explanation: The passage says that the man was run down by a car. We can assume that when a man is run down by a car, he is extremely likely to die. Hence, the inference is probably true. It is not definitely true because the man may have escaped death in spite of being run down. [There are always miraculous escapes from death.]

Ex 21: Refer to sample passage 3.

Inference: Some countries which have adopted privatisation are considering to change over to nationalisation now.

Explanation: The passage says that privatisation has become the 'buzzword' today. Hence, it is unlikely that any country would be swimming against the tide and thinking of nationalisation. Hence, the inference is probably false. However, it is not definitely false because there are always exceptions. [A good example of the same could be Nepal, where - in today's world of falling Communism - the Communist Party still dominates.]

III. A study of key words

One of the most important aspects of evaluating a given inference is a proper understanding of some words, which we may call key words. They are called key words because they offer the 'key' to the problem. These words may alter, emphasise or substantiate the meaning of a sentence. The most important use of key words is in differentiating between definitely true-probably true and definitely false-probably false statements.

What are these key words, after all? We can categorise them into two different types:

(i) Standard key words. (ii) Contextual key words.

(i) Standard key words

These are adjectives, conjunctions, verbs or adverbs that give an idea about the quantity as well as the quality of a statement. Some examples are: *all, some, none, never, always, sometimes, must be, may be, might be, will be, would be, although, nevertheless, despite, in spite of, because of,* etc.

For example, look at 'all', 'some' and 'none'. All of these are used to denote the quantity of the subject. While 'all' denotes the whole, 'some' only a part. 'None' denotes nothing. Therefore, there is a substantial difference between "All girls are beautiful", "Some girls are beautiful" and "No girl is beautiful". [Can you not easily see that the first of these statements can be declared "definitely false", the second "definitely true" and the third, "definitely false"?]

As another example, consider the words 'need' and 'desperate need'. These two words denote the quality of the state of misery. Thus, there is a good deal of difference between "I am in need of some money" and "I am in desperate need of some money". An inference such as "I think I'll have to pawn my wife's jewellery" is uncertain in the first case but it can be declared "probably true" in the second case. [In the above, 'desperate' is the key word making the difference between the two sentences, by putting emphasis on 'need'.]

Given below are some more examples of how the key words play an important role in inference.

Ex 22: Passage: All those who have pride for their country and love for their motherland will not tolerate the remarks of the journalist.

1st Inference: Some people will find the remarks of the journalist intolerable.

Explanation: We may safely assume that **some** (may be not **all**) people do love their country and motherland. Now, **all** such people will not tolerate the remarks of the journalist. Hence, it can be inferred that the inference is definitely true.

2nd Inference: Everyone will find the remarks of the journalist intolerable.

Explanation: This inference would have been definitely true, provided it could be assumed that everyone has pride for their country and love for their motherland. But, this is not the case. Although this point is debatable, we may assume that there are some who have no feelings for their motherland. In this light, the given inference is definitely false.

Ex 23: Passage: Although the government has raised taxes, the tax revenue has dropped.

1st inference: A raise in taxes **usually** results in a rise in tax revenue.

Explanation: The use of the word 'although' implies that tax revenue was expected to rise after the raise in taxes. This means that it was assumed that usually tax raise implies a rise in tax revenue. This means that the given inference is definitely true.

2nd inference: A raise in taxes **always** results in a rise in tax revenue.

Explanation: By its very background this inference has to be definitely false. The given passage itself, where the taxes were raised and yet the revenue dropped, contradicts it.

3rd Inference: Sometimes, the collections drop when taxes are raised.

Explanation: By its very background this inference has to be definitely true as the given passage itself provides supporting evidence.

4th Inference: The collections **always** drop when taxes are raised.

Explanation: Although the given passage gives supporting evidence by giving one case where collections dropped when taxes were raised, we cannot take this inference to be true. The reason is the use of the word 'although' in the passage. This key word implies that it was assumed that usually a raise in taxes results in a rise in revenue. The inference is definitely false.

Ex 24: Passage: Because the government raised taxes, the collections improved.

1st inference: Usually, when taxes are raised, collections improve.

Explanation: Definitely true.

2nd inference: Sometimes, collections drop when taxes are raised.

Explanation: Uncertain or Data Inadequate. The passage says that collections improved because taxes were raised. But there is no hint about its certainty, that is, no hint is given that the collections always improve when taxes are raised. They may (or may not) drop. Hence, data inadequate.

Ex 25: Passage: The collections **had to** improve **as** the taxes were raised.

Inference: Sometimes, collections drop when taxes are raised.

Explanation: Definitely false. This case is slightly different from the previous one. Here, the use of the emphatic words 'had to' implies that tax raise 'has to' result in a rise in collections: it is an absolute must. Hence, the given inference is definitely false.

Ex 26: Passage: The collections **may** improve **only if** the government raises taxes.

Inference: I. **Whenever** the taxes are raised, the collections improve.

II. The collections **never** improve when taxes are raised.

III. The collections **will not** improve if the taxes are **not** raised.

Explanation: The use of the word 'only if' implies that the condition that the taxes be raised is 'necessary' but the use of the word 'may' implies that it is not 'sufficient' for the collections to improve. In other words, the sentence implies that collections are not going to improve without tax raise, while if taxes were indeed raised, it may or may not improve. Consequent to this, the evaluation of the three inferences are:

I. data inadequate

II. definitely false

III. definitely true

(ii) Contextual key words

In the preceding pages, we have studied some standard key words and the roles they play. Their meanings and importance are fixed in nature.

But the scope for key words is not limited to these. Sometimes, some general, common words play the role of key words because of the context in which they are used. And consequently, they give an inference a definite degree of truth (or falsity).

Let us see some examples to understand these.

Ex 27: Passage: Refer to sample passage 3.

Inference: Privatisation has been practiced in the USA since long.

Explanation: The passage says that privatisation has been sweeping both the '**developed**' and the developing countries for **more than a decade.** Now, 'developed' and 'more than a decade' are key words here because the context in which they have been used will prove useful in evaluating the given inference. We know that 'USA' is a 'developed' nation and we may further assume that a period of 'more than a decade' may be treated as 'since long'. Hence, the given inference is probably true. It is not definitely true because concrete evidence is not available.

Ex 28: Passage: Refer to sample passage 7.

Inference: There will **not be a single** accident on roads if they are satisfactorily illuminated.

Explanation: The passage talks of accidents and holds the poor state of street-lighting responsible for this state. Naturally, then, we would expect that an inference will be true if it says that proper illumination will reduce the number of accidents. But the inference given above makes an overstatement. It says 'not a single' accident will occur. This is very unlikely. If lights were the only solution, then not a single accident would occur during day time. The inference is probably false.

[**Note:** You may argue that the inference should be declared definitely false. But you should remember that accidents are 'accidents'. They are not normal phenomena. They are exceptions. Theoretically, it is always possible that no accidents would occur if sufficient precautions were taken, although it may be very very unlikely in practice.]

Ex 29: Passage: Refer to sample passage 7.

Inference: Several accidents have so far taken place because of unsatisfactory lighting.

Explanation: See the sentence: "The serious accident .... has *again* focussed our ...... street lighting." The keyword here, is 'again'. Its use implies that many accidents have preceded the accident of last night. Hence the inference is probably true, but not definitely true.

Why is the inference not definitely true? Because the use of the word 'again' here implies that the serious accident has again focussed the attention on street-lighting conditions. It does not explicitly state that the *accident* has 'again' occurred. It only states that attention has 'again' been drawn to street-lighting conditions and that the reason for it this time was an accident. It is likely that attention on street lighting was drawn earlier because of people's demonstrations against the bad state of street lighting and that the accident of last night is only the first accident of its kind. These possibilities cannot be ruled out. Hence, the given inference cannot be taken as definitely true. It must be taken as probably true.

5.5: How to avoid confusion while deriving inferences

We have seen that a given inference can, sometimes, be very easily evaluated because it is almost explicitly stated in the passage. At other times, we may have to apply a little logic while evaluating a given inference because the inference may be only indirectly related to the passage. While doing this, we need to pay some special attention to some key words because they may provide the key to the answer.

But we are likely to get confused sometimes, specially if the questions are tough. As already stated there are four main possibilities of confusion. We are giving some tips so that you overcome the confusion easily.

I. Definitely True or Probably True?

This confusion may arise if the given inference is not directly stated in the passage and yet appears 'almost' definitely true to you. But since it is not directly or explicitly stated you hesitate and think that even 'probably true' could be correct.

To avoid this confusion recheck your reasoning. If the inference is not mentioned directly in the passage, then you must have assumed something 'extra' to come to this conclusion. Now ask yourself this question: "Is this extra assumption universally true?" or "Can it never be false?" If you get 'yes' for the first question and 'no, never' for the second, accept is as definitely true. Otherwise, choose 'probably true'.

[For instance, look at Ex 29. If you think that the inference is definitely true then you will have to make an extra assumption: "Earlier too, attention has been focussed on street-lighting because of accidents." Now, can it never be false? In other words, can it never be true that in many of the previous cases the reason for attention-focussing was not an accident? You can immediately see that it is improbable but not impossible.]

II. Definitely False or Probably False?

This confusion may arise if the given inference is not directly stated in the passage and yet appears 'almost' definitely false to you. But since the related thing is not explicitly mentioned, you hesitate and think that even 'probably false' may be correct.

To avoid this confusion recheck your reasoning. If the opposite of the inference is not mentioned directly in the passage, then you must have assumed something 'extra' to come to this conclusion. Now ask yourself this question: "Is this assumption universally true?" or "Can it never be false?" If you get 'yes' for the first question and 'no, never' for the second, then choose definitely false as your answer. Otherwise, pick probably false.

[For instance, look at Ex 28. The passage states that the poor state of street lighting is responsible for accidents. But it is almost impossible, nevertheless, that "not a single" accident would occur if streets were properly illuminated. Hence, it appears definitely false. But it can be definitely false only if it were theoretically impossible for accidents to occur in proper illumination. Now, is this assumption universally true? No. Hence, the given inference is likely to be false but not certain to be false.]

III. Data Inadequate or Probably True?

This confusion arises when an inference is drawn indirectly from the passage. Since it is not explicitly mentioned, you think that the data are inadequate, and that sufficient information has not been provided to come to the conclusion. However, the inference appears to you in tune with the general 'tone' of the passage and, hence, you are tempted to opt for probably true.

To avoid this confusion, recheck your reasoning. You can declare an inference probably true, if with the help of the given passage and some extra assumption, the inference appears likely to be true. Thus, you can somehow convince yourself that the inference is likely to be true. On the other hand, you can declare that data are inadequate if no definite conclusion seems to be coming from the passage even with the help of some extra assumption. Thus, in this case, you cannot convince yourself that the inference is likely to be true or false.

[For instance, consider Q 2 of sample passage 0. The passage never explicitly mentions what exactly the theories of Odgen and Williams were. Hence, you may choose 'data inadequate'. But the whole passage is about the possibilities of high-efficiency photovoltaic cells and the names of Odgen and Williams have been mentioned in the beginning. Thus, the two scientists appear to be associated with the theory of high efficiency of photovoltaic cells. Hence, the inference looks probably true.

On a closer look, the inference is probably true. We can make a reasonable assumption that the mentioning of the names of the two scientists is not without reason, that it is not irrelevant. If this be assumed, then the inference is likely to be true. Data inadequate would not be a correct choice.]

IV. Data Inadequate or Probably False?

This confusion arises when the inference is drawn indirectly from the passage. Since it is not explicitly stated, you think that the data are inadequate, that insufficient information has been provided to come to a definite conclusion. However, the inference appears to you in contradiction with the general 'tone' of the passage and, hence, you are tempted to choose 'probably false' as your answer.

To avoid this confusion, recheck your reasoning. You can declare an inference probably false only if you can find a reasonable assumption, combining which with what is stated in the passage the inference appears likely to be false. Thus, you can somehow convince yourself that the inference is likely to be false. On the other hand, you should choose the choice 'data are inadequate' only if you cannot find any acceptable assumption which, combined with what is stated in the passage, may lead to some definite conclusion. In this case, you cannot convince yourself whether the inference is likely to be true or false.

[For instance, consider Ex 9. Here, the reason for the murder has not been provided and, hence, you may choose data inadequate. But common sense tells that the occurrence of murder on such a small issue as a quarrel over the volume of a TV set is very unlikely. This is a reasonable assumption and if we make this assumption, the inference is probably false.].

Summary

- In order to evaluate an inference, first of all check whether it can be evaluated with the help of the passage directly. Check if this inference is directly supported (or contradicted) by something in the passage.
- If an inference cannot be directly related with the passage, check if you can justify or contradict it with the help of an additional assumption. The only condition is that the assumption you make should be justifiable and universally acceptable. (Refer to section 5.4 for some examples.)
- You can also evaluate an inference with the help of some key words used in the passage.

- To avoid confusion between the choices "definitely true" and "probably true", you should check if the extra assumption you have made to evaluate the inference is universally true. The same strategy can be employed to avoid confusion between the choices "definitely false" and "probably false".
- To avoid confusion between the choices "probably true" and "data inadequate", check if it is possible to make an extra assumption to take the inference as "probably true". If you *can* make a reasonable extra assumption, the answer would be "probably true". The same strategy could be used to avoid confusion between the choices "probably false" and "data inadequate".

Practice Exercises

Special Note: In the preceding study-material, we have discussed deriving inference from the given passage. *A passage, as you know, is nothing but a set of statements*. Therefore, a simpler version of the question could be one when we derive inferences from a single statement. Again, in our study material, we have discussed not only those inferences that definitely follow from the statements (i.e. definitely true) but also those that follow with slightly lesser probability (i.e., probably true). A simpler version of the question could be one when you only had to evaluate if a given infgerence was definitely true or not.

Thus, an overall simpler version of the type of questions discussed in the chapter version would be one where you had only one single statement and you only had to worry about *definitely* true inferences. Such type of questions are there in Ex. 5A. The other type of questions are in Ex. 5B, Ex. 5C etc.

Therefore, in this exercise, you must note that "a conclusion follows" means "a conclusion is *definitely* true". In this exercise, a *probably* true conclusion has no place and you should treat that as "does not follow." Of course, "definitely false" and "probably false" and "data inadequate" would also come in the category of "does not follow".

Type I: Exercise 5A

Directions: In each of the following questions, a statement or two are followed by two conclusions. Give answer (a) if conclusion I follows; (b) if conclusion II follows; (c) if both I and II follow; (d) if either I or II follows; and (e) if neither I nor II follows.

1. **Statement:** Ten persons who were on the waiting list could finally get berth reservation in the Frontier Mail.

   Conclusions: **I.** Wait-listed passengers generally find it difficult to get berth reservation in the Frontier Mail.

   II. The number of berths available in the Frontier Mail is less.

2. **Statement:** Parents are prepared to pay any price for elite education of their children.

Conclusions: **I.** All parents, these days, are very well-off.

II. Parents have an obsessive passion for a perfect development of their children through good schooling.

3. **Statements:** **I.** Mud houses are cooler in summers than stone-and-brick houses.

II. Mud houses are occupied by the poor only.

Conclusions: **I.** Poor people are more comfortable in summers than the rich.

II. Stone-and-brick houses are more sophisticated than mud houses.

4. **Statement:** Patients with minor ailments usually do not go to eminent doctors.

Conclusions: **I.** Eminent doctors remain too busy with patients suffering from serious complications.

II. Their charges are rather high.

5. **Statement:** The use of non-conventional sources of energy will eliminate the energy crisis in the world.

Conclusions: **I.** Modern technology is gradually replacing the conventional sources of energy.

II. The excessive exploitation of environment has led to depletion of conventional sources of energy.

6. **Statement:** The increase in adult literacy will lead to the country's development and progress.

Conclusions: **I.** Educated persons offer less resistance to new innovations.

II. This country's population is totally illiterate.

7. **Statement:** In a one-day cricket match, the total runs made by a team were 200. Out of these, 160 runs were made by spinners.

Conclusions: **I.** 80% of the team consists of spinners.

II. The opening batsmen were spinners.

8. **Statement:** The doctors nurse only those bleeding wounds which are caused by bullets. A patient X was bleeding profusely.

Conclusions: **I.** X was nursed by the doctors.

II. The doctors did not nurse X.

9. **Statement:** Apart from the educational value of newspapers, their entertainment value should also be realised.

Conclusions: **I.** People take newspapers as a means of education.

II. The entertainment value of newspapers is realised properly.

10. **Statement:** These apples are too expensive to be bad.

Conclusions: **I.** When apples are in short supply, the prices go up.

II. The higher the selling price, the superior is the quality of the commodity.

11. **Statement:** In deserts, camels are indispensable for people to travel from one place to another.

Conclusions: **I.** Camels are the only cheapest mode of transportation available in deserts.

II. There are plenty of camels in deserts.

12. **Statement:** Of all the television sets manufactured in India, the 'solar' brand has the largest sale.

Conclusions: **I.** The volume of sales of all the brands of television sets manufactured in India is known.

II. The production of no other television set in India is as large as that of 'solar'.

13. **Statements:** **I.** The TV programmes telecasted specially for women are packed with a variety of recipes and household hints.

II. A major portion of magazines for women also contains the items mentioned above.

Conclusions: **I.** Women are not interested in other things.

II. An average woman's primary interest lies in home, specially in the kitchen.

14. **Statement:** Cases of bride-burning for dowry are not uncommon.

Conclusions: **I.** Inspite of anti-dowry laws, the ill practice continues.

II. The punishment inflicted on the party concerned is not sufficient.

15. **Statement:** Players who break various records in a fair way get special prizes. Player X broke the world record but was found to be under the influence of a prohibited drug.

Conclusions: **I.** X will get the special prize.

II. X will not get the special prize.

16. **Statement:** Inspite of the claim of the government that terrorism is under check, killing continues.

Conclusions: **I.** The terrorists have not come to an understanding with the government.

II. The government has been constantly telling a lie.

17. **Statement:** National Aluminium Company has moved India from a position of shortage to self-sufficiency in the metal.

Conclusions: **I.** Previously, India had to import aluminum.

II. With this speed, it can soon become a foreign exchange earner.

18. **Statement:** Smoking is one of those human weaknesses which tends to test the will-power of the smoker to the edge.

Conclusions: **I.** It is very difficult for the smokers to give up smoking even if they want to do so.

II. Human beings have other weaknesses as well.

19. **Statement:** No country is absolutely self-dependent these days.

Conclusions: **I.** It is impossible to grow and produce all that a country needs.

II. Countrymen in general have become lazy.

20. **Statement:** Video libraries are flourishing very much these days.

Conclusions: **I.** People, in general, have got a video craze.

II. It is much cheaper to see as many movies as one likes on videos rather than in the cinema hall.

21. **Statement:** About 50 per cent of animal by-products — hair, skin, horns etc. — is edible protein. American chemists have developed a method of isolating 45 per cent of this protein. They use an enzyme developed in Japan to break down Soya protein.

Conclusions: **I.** Americans have not been able to develop enzymes.

II. Animal by-products' protein has the same composition as Soya protein.

22. **Statement:** Domestic demand has been increasing faster than the production of indigenous crude oil.

Conclusions: **I.** Crude oil must be imported.

II. Domestic demand should be reduced.

23. **Statement:** He stressed the need to stop the present examination system and replace it by other methods which would measure the real merit of the students.

Conclusions: **I.** Examinations should be abolished.

II. The present examination system does not measure the real merit of the student.

24. **Statement:** The oceans are a storehouse of practically every mineral, including uranium. But, like most other minerals, it is found in extremely low concentrations - about three grams for 1000 tonnes of water.

Conclusions: **I.** Sea water contains gold.

II. The oceans harbour radiation hazards.

25. **Statement:** I know nothing except the fact of my ignorance.

Conclusions: **I.** The writer's knowledge is very poor.

II. The world of knowledge is too vast to be explored by a single person.

26. **Statement:** The devil can cite scripture for his purpose.

Conclusions: **I.** Even an unscrupulous person has some principles.

II. The real wisdom is to be found in scriptures.

27. **Statements:** **I.** Reading makes a full man, conference a ready man, and writing an exact man.
II. Extensive reading makes a man complete.
Conclusions: **I.** Pointed and precise expression comes only through extensive writing.
II. Extensive reading makes a man complete.

28. **Statement:** Fashion is a form of ugliness so intolerable that we have to alter it every six months.
Conclusions: **I.** Fashion designers do not understand people's mind very well.
II. People, by and large, are highly susceptible to novelty.

29. **Statement:** Old order changeth yielding place to new.
Conclusions: **I.** Change is the law of nature.
II. Discard old ideas because they are old.

30. **Statement:** All those political prisoners were released on bail who had gone to jail for reasons other than political dharnas. Bail was not granted to persons involved in murders.
Conclusions: **I.** No political prisoner had committed murder.
II. Some politicians were not arrested.

31. **Statement:** Crime is a function of the criminal's biological make-up and his family relations.
Conclusions: **I.** The incidence of crime is higher in identical twins than in fraternal twins.
II. Families in which parents lack in warmth and affection fail to build a moral conscience in the children.

32. **Statement:** The percentage of the national income shared by top 10 per cent of households in India is 35.
Conclusions: **I.** When an economy grows fast, concentration of wealth in certain packets of population takes place.
II. The national income is unevenly distributed in India.

33. **Statement:** Good is the enemy of the best.
Conclusions: **I.** You should be good to your best enemy.
II. The best do not like the good.

34. **Statement:** The essence of one-day cricket is the ability to score runs fast and to bowl with a mixture of control and aggression which, handled adroitly, can tie the opponents hand and foot.
Conclusions: **I.** Kapil Dev, when he won the Prudential Cup for India in 1983, had all the above qualities.
II. The other teams which participated in the Prudential tournament did not have these abilities.

35. **Statement:** The best way to escape from a problem is to solve it.
Conclusions: **I.** Your life will be dull if you don't face a problem.
II. To escape from problems, you should always have some solutions with you.

36. **Statement:** In a highly centralised power structure, in which even senior cabinet ministers are prepared to reduce themselves to pathetic yes-men airing views that are primarily intended to anticipate or reflect the Prime Minister's own performances, there can be no place for any consensus that is quite different from real or contrived unanimity of opinion, expressed through a well-orchestrated endorsement of the leader's actions.

Conclusions: **I.** The ministers play safe by not giving anti-government views.

II. The Prime Minister does not encourage his colleagues to render their own views.

Type II: Exercise 5B

Directions: In each question below is given a passage followed by several inferences. You have to examine each inference separately in the context of the passage and decide upon its degree of truth or falsity.

Mark answer (1) if you think the inference is 'definitely true'; (2) if you think the inference is 'probably true' though not definitely true in the light of the facts given; (3) if you think the 'data are inadequate', i.e., from the facts given you cannot say whether the inference is likely to be true or false; (4) if you think the inference is 'probably false' though not definitely false in the light of the facts given; and (5) if you think the inference is 'definitely false', i.e. it contradicts the given facts.

Note: The above directions do not apply to Q. 76-80.

Passage

India and other developing countries, while expressing their commitment to the upgradation of labour standards, have been resisting the move to link international trade, not only with labour standards, but also with environmental concerns and human rights. The move was set afoot on the successful conclusion of the Uruguay Round of trade negotiations with a proposal for the inclusion of a social clause in the World Trade Organisation (WTO), which succeeds GATT. Later, on stiff opposition to the move on the ground that the matter did not fall in the area of trade, a proposal was mooted for the inclusion of a social clause in ILO.

1. India has been sidelined on the issue of linking international trade with labour.
2. The efforts of linking international trade with labour are being carried out by developed countries.
3. All countries appear committed to the cause of upgradation of labour standards.
4. The Uruguay Round concluded successfully.
5. India claims that environmental issue and trade are uncorrelated.

Passage

India has signed two separate agreements with the USA and the EC. This brings to a satisfactory conclusion the Market Access Conciliations in textiles which had been in progress for some time. These discussions were held with a view to facilitating trade in textile products between India and the USA and EU countries. At present, more than two-thirds of India's total textile exports go to these countries. These agreements which came into force from Dec. 31, 1994, prior to the establishment of the WTO, provide very significant additional market access in these two major markets (USA and EU) for Indian textile products. In particular, the agreements are expected to provide a fillip to handloom and powerloom production and exports which are of high priority because of their direct linkage with employment generation.

6. India has been treated with bias in the two agreements mentioned.
7. Textiles are an important constituent of India's exports.
8. The WTO was established on 1 Jan, 1995.
9. The agreements may help India in solving its employment problem.
10. India will have to abide by certain quality standards to continue getting export orders from these countries.

Passage

The Fifth Conference of Labour Ministers of Non-Aligned and other developing countries, which concluded in New Delhi on January 23, was not just another conference held under the auspices of International Labour Organisation to discuss labour welfare. For one, it was in the run-up to the World Summit on Social Development that the conference was held, and for another, it was under the shadow of the demand by the industrialised countries to link labour standards to international trade through a social clause. The Conference covered a large part of the agenda to be discussed at the Summit to be held at Copenhagen in March, i.e., employment creation, poverty reduction and eradication and social integration.

11. The Fourth Conference of Labour Ministers was not held at New Delhi.
12. International Labour Organisation took an active part in a Conference of Labour Ministers for the first time.
13. Linking labour standards to international trade would benefit the industrial countries.
14. The Copenhagen Summit did not discuss questions on poverty.
15. India sent no representative to the Conference.

Passage

The country has taken a major initiative by introducing convertibility of the Rupee on the current account. It has also been declared that the ultimate goal is to make the Rupee fully convertible. These are signs of the country's achieving economic maturity. India is now ready to welcome foreign capital. It is preparing to reduce import tariffs to levels which are currently the norm in other developing countries. All these measures show that India is today mature and strong enough to face international competition and to integrate itself successfully with the global economy. The country is ready to shed its ideological inhibitions and ready to evaluate the international economic environment in a pragmatic spirit.

16. Convertibility has not been introduced on the capital account.
17. Current account convertibility means full convertibility.
18. An economically immature country does not have any convertibility of currency.
19. Import tariffs in India are lower than those in other developing countries.
20. Socialistic ideals prevented India from evaluating the international economic environment in a pragmatic spirit.

Passage

The economic reforms programme is going to affect not only the private industrial sector but also the public sector. Many people associate the economic restructuring programme with privatisation. This is one area of economic reforms where India has chosen to tread cautiously. The process of privatisation has been set in motion by the disinvestment campaign in the public sector. Public sector industries in India have been characterised by inefficiency, and many of them have been incurring losses over long periods while their counterparts in the private sector are making profits. The economic reforms programme in India will be incomplete without a restructuring of the public sector undertakings.

21. The greater emphasis of reforms is on the private sector.
22. India's approach towards reforms is cautious.
23. The reforms have not intended to restructure the public sector units.
24. Economic restructuring programme means privatisation.
25. Disinvestment of public sector is a part of economic restructuring.

Passage

The rights of the child in broad parameters is not a new concept in the country as it was enshrined in our Constitution in its directive principles. But a chasm lies agape between practice and precept. The government adopted a National Policy For Children in 1974 and started the ambitious Integrated Child Development Services (ICDS) scheme the next year but the progress was slow. However, the situation is now poised for a big take-off with the political will backing it up with enhanced funds.

26. The directive principles are not a new concept in the country.
27. Since Independence, there has been enormous progress in the realisation of the rights of children.
28. Dr. Rajendra Prasad and Dr. Ambedkar were not in favour of giving too much emphasis on children's rights.
29. The ICDS was started in May, 1975.
30. The political will to realise the children's rights was lacking initially.

Passage

The happiest situation would be to provide employment assurance of say 100 days in a year to all the households which are below poverty line. Assuming that all the persons would not offer themselves for casual manual work, let us say only 30 million persons would come for such works. As the average cost of generation of one man-day under the Jawahar Rozgar Yojana and also under the Employment Assurance Scheme is Rs 45/-, the total requirement would be about Rs. 13500 crore per year. This requirement will also build up gradually as it is dependent on monsoons, wage levels and cost of material, etc. The current allocations under various wage employment programmes are, however, far less than required for such an employment assurance scenario.

31. There are, actually, less than 30 million persons below the poverty line.
32. The Jawahar Rozgar Yojana is backed with adequate funds and political will.
33. In the year 2000 AD the cost of generation of one man-day under the EAS would be more than Rs 45.
34. Weather conditions have some role to play in the fund allocation of employment schemes.
35. The Jawahar Rozgar Yojana and the EAS would provide employment to as many persons as needed.

Passage

The Product Certification Marks Scheme (PCMS) was introduced in 1956. It provides the consumer an assurance of quality conforming to national standards. It is a voluntary scheme in general wherein producers claiming conformity to standards apply for licence. The scheme is, however, compulsory for items of mass consumption which affect the safety and health of consumers. To date, over 11,750 licences are in operation covering 1438 products, out of which about 129 are under compulsory certification.

36. Before 1956, there was no certification scheme in India.
37. The Product Certification Marks Scheme gives an assurance of quality conforming to national standards.
38. There are more items of mass consumption affecting safety and health of public than others.
39. A publisher of books must send his products to the PCMS for quality assurance.
40. The PCMS also tries to give assurance of international standards on selected items.

Passage

The reforms are aimed at having an impact over a wide cross-section of the economy. With improvements and greater efficiency in mobilising and allocating resources, the basis will become stronger for promoting economic growth and development. The reforms aim at increasing efficiency of the financial sector and the range of financial services available within the economy. The introduction of bank capital adequacy and accounting standards, together with improvement in the regulation and supervision of financial institutions and capital market, is aimed at installing greater public confidence, ensuring safety and soundness of the financial system, bringing about greater transparency and accountability in operations and encouraging overall increased resources mobilisation within the economy.

41. Economic reforms are pro-rich.
42. Bank capital adequacy was not in operation before reforms.
43. Prior to reforms, the banking sector was running inefficiently although resource allocation was efficient.
44. Public confidence has some connection with resource mobilisation.
45. The economic reforms have aimed only at the financial sector.

Passage

In a fast-moving world, the attitude towards children has undergone a sea-change from the draconian "spare the rod and spoil the child" to a growing awareness of the rights of the child. In our society, even fifty years back, the elders would have frowned at any mention of the rights of the child and would have dismissed it as an absurd proposition and a futile intellectual aberration. But times have changed and people have come to realise that if due attention and proper thought are not given to the children of today to ensure their healthy growth, we are bound to invite doom for our citizens of tomorrow. And who can deny that improvement in the condition of children is the primary concern of a nation?

46. The maxim of "spare the rod and spoil and child" was very irrational and brutal.
47. There has been a sea-change in the attitude towards children since the 1920s.
48. Rights of the children is an intellectual aberration.
49. A child that shows unhealthy growth could have been treated cruelly.
50. The world has shown very little change in attitude in areas other than that of children's rights.

Passage

A distinct feature of the Indian financial system is the dominance by public sector institutions, be in the area of banking or term-lending or insurance. Motivated by socio-economic considerations, the system has also been subject to a high degree of regulation. Both entry and expansion have remained subject to control. There has also been a mandatory allocation of credit for specific sectors, including government, with varying degrees of concessionality in interest rates. Superimposed on all this is an administered structure of interest rates under which interest rates on deposits and credits has been specified in great detail. Of course, all of these are undergoing changes.

51. Dominance by public sector institutions in the financial system is rare in other countries.
52. Public sector institutions are supposed to serve socio-economic purposes better than private sector.

53. Interest rates are graded in India.
54. The dominance of public sector institutions has been increasing.
55. Administered rates on deposits is a common phenomenon in developing countries.

Passage

Independent testing of certified products is an essential feature of the BIS Certification Marks Scheme. For this purpose, BIS has a network of eight laboratories in the country, which are in a position to issue around 42000 test reports in a year. These laboratories are being constantly expanded and their testing facilities augmented and modernised. BIS has also recognised around 280 laboratories belonging to public and private sectors for testing products under its certification scheme.

56. The BIS Scheme does not test uncertified products.
57. Every laboratory of the BIS can issue more than 4000 test reports in a year.
58. The BIS has no dynamism in its workings.
59. The BIS is an autonomous body.
60. Certification is a process that needs to be constantly modernised.

Passage

One of the avowed goals of elementary education is improving learner achievement, apart from access and retention. This is a crucial area of concern to planners and educationists as investment in elementary education has not been giving commensurate returns. The scenario with regard to learner achievement has been pretty bleak over the decades. Two national surveys of achievement of primary school children conducted by NCERT are a case in point. The survey on achievement in mathematics was conducted in 1965-66. The second on attainment in language and mathematics was conducted in 1990. Both surveys have indicated low levels of learner achievement.

61. Retention is not an avowed goal of elementary education.
62. Elementary education is an investment as well as a duty of the government.
63. Planners have not paid due attention to learner achievement while planning elementary education schemes.
64. NCERT is the only body related with the schemes of elementary education.
65. The rate of learner achievement has improved very marginally after 1990.

Passage

Although studies have shown that India's performance in health (level as well as speed) is poor (UNDP, 1992), the health status, in general, has improved. Life expectancy and infant survival conditions are better than what is predicted for a country with India's level of income. Between 1951 and 1992, life expectancy at birth (LEB) increased from 32.1 years to 60.3 years, the death rate fell from 27.4 to 10 per thousand and IMR fell from 139 per thousand live births in 1972 to 79 in 1992. But, the improvement has not been even across regions and between genders.

An attempt is made here to look at the inter-regional disparities in health development.

66. Performance in speed of health has no bearing on health status.
67. Infant survival conditions are not good in India.
68. There is regional disparity in health improvement in India.
69. Reports of UNDP are the only reliable reports in matters of health.
70. India has surpassed many countries in forms of health improvement from 1951 to 1992.

Passage

While liberalisation essentially involves dismantling the barriers to entry and exit and the lifting of controls, it does not automatically imply no regulation at all. In fact, regulation assumes its own level of sophistication in terms of letting the system operate without unnecessarily restraining it, while at the same time protecting the financial system from its own excesses. In the banking sector, for instance, while liberalisation can bring about a removal of barriers on the entry of new banks and credit restrictions, it is accompanied by a more stringent set of prudential, supervisory and regulatory structure. Similarly, in the area of capital market, while liberalisation could mean the opening up of markets to new products and new participants, regulation is put in place to protect investors' interests and to prevent excessive speculation.

71. Liberalisation is synonymous with deregulation.
72. Regulation must be done sensibly.
73. The financial system needs to have some regulation even in a free-market economy.
74. Excessive speculation was unheard of in the pre-liberalisation stock markets.
75. The author of the piece is an economist of good standards.

Passage

The finance minister's promise of a structural adjustment programme with a human face remains a pipedream. When the reforms started, he had assured that priorities of public spending will focus more sharply on welfare programmes, once the fiscal imbalances were controlled. This assurance is yet to be materialised. Recently, he said that "only when the growth momentum picks up, the resources needed for these programmes can be mobilised." Such excessive emphasis on economic growth will hamper social welfare and indefinitely postpone the promise of a reform with a human face thus leaving out in the cold a substantial section of the society.

76. A major chunk of our society is in desperate need of social welfare programmes.

1) Probably true 2) Definitely true 3) Probably false
4) Definitely false 5) Data inadequate

77. The finance minister is not consistent in his thought.
    1) Probably true 2) Definitely true 3) Probably false
    4) Definitely false 5) Data inadequate
78. The fiscal imbalances have not been controlled yet.
    1) Probably true 2) Definitely true 3) Probably false
    4) Definitely false 5) Data inadequate
79. Economic growth is being given greater priority over social welfare by the government.
    1) Probably true 2) Definitely true 3) Probably false
    4) Definitely false 5) Data inadequate
80. Economic growth will pick up momentum quickly.
    1) Probably true 2) Definitely true 3) Probably false
    4) Definitely false 5) Data inadequate

Passage

When a mixed economy with a dominant public sector and extensive domestic and external controls begins to liberalise at a rapid pace, it imposes a special responsibility on the private sector. It is no longer subject to control on its activities but at the same time it no longer benefits from protection from internal and external competitions. For the private sector in India, therefore, the rules of the game have changed dramatically. In the new environment, private enterprise is required to think globally. This implies not only that the market for Indian manufacturers and traders is now global, but also that the Indian market is now part of a global market and, therefore, open to manufacturers and traders from all over the world. Technological changes can no longer be ignored.

81. The public sector used to play a dominant role in India.
82. Private enterprise in India used to be quick to adopt technological changes.
83. In the new environment, many private sector industries may suffer.
84. Among private sector industries, those catering to domestic demand are at a comparative disadvantage when compared to those in export business.
85. Foreign-made consumer durables will not be accepted by the Indian masses.

Passage

The complexion of the world economy has changed beyond recognition. A few years ago, the Soviet Union and its friends used to accuse the World Bank, IMF and other international institutions as the promoters of economic imperialism of USA and its allies and in the same breath as the bloodsuckers of the poorer member-countries. GATT, for them, was a rich man's club. In their views, transnational corporations were worse than the dreaded buccaneers. These corporations worked exclusively for the benefit of parent countries and exploited the host countries thoroughly. Economic relations of communist countries remained chiefly confined within the four walls of communism. However, it crossed over to some third world countries as well.

86. The Soviet Union was not a member of GATT.
87. The IMF is not accused of being a promoter of economic imperialism of USA anymore.
88. Soviet Union had economic relations with the USA.
89. The world's economic scenario has changed rapidly because of a change in the stance of the Communist nations.
90. GATT has stopped exploiting its host countries.

Passage

The South Asian region has its own regional identity. The common issues or themes shared by the South Asian nations are colonial rule, underdevelopment, unemployment, illiteracy, poverty, gender inequality and relatively unstable political system, as compared to the developed nations. All these countries have been ruled by Western powers for quite some time. The economy is still in a developing stage. Almost half of the population is illiterate and mass unemployment has resulted in immense poverty. There have been frequent changes in governments. Women in most of South Asian countries are an object of physical and mental oppression.

91. Pakistan has seen more governments than India.
92. 30 million Indians are illiterate.
93. The situation of women is better in the developed nations than in South Asian countries.
94. The Gross Domestic Product of most of the South Asian countries is below the world average.
95. The number of female entrepreneurs is more in South Asian nations than that of male ones.

Passage

Even after allowing for the inclusion of the unavoidable chillies, on the whole the Indian diet seems to be more protective than carcinogenic. The per capita fat intake is only 14-20 g daily, far below even the per capita consumption of 35 g daily recommended by the Indian Council of Medical Research. In practice, most of the population is essentially vegetarian, as even the so-called non-vegetarians eat meat only once or twice a week, meat being expensive. The incidence of cancer in India, with the age standardised rate of 115 per 100,000, is one of the lowest in Asia; and is only about one-third the incidence in the West. The Indian diet may be one of the factors responsible.

96. Chillies make a diet carcinogenic.
97. Indians are likely to be more overweight than others.
98. Consumption of meat would go up if meat becomes cheaper.
99. The percentage of people suffering from cancer is the lowest in the case of India.
100. Indian diet is the main reason behind the low incidence of cancer.

Passage

The Election Commission has imposed controls on three types of expenses — deployment of vehicles, publicity and payment to the voters — by activating the People's Representative Act and evolving a code of conduct for parties and candidates. First, the ceiling on election expenses (fixed in 1984) was raised by three times to make it realistic in the light of the huge costs involved to conduct campaigns in a larger constituency. (The ceiling of Rs. 50,000, which was fixed in 1984, was found to be too low to conduct a campaign in a constituency which has a population between 75,000 and seven lakhs spread over 200-500 sq km). This has helped many candidates stick to the ceiling and also present realistic accounts.

101. The ceiling on election expenses now stands at Rs 1.5 lakh.
102. Candidates are required to present accounts of their spending in an election.
103. Some candidates have been paying to the voters in order to get votes.
104. People's Representative Act was passed in 1984.
105. Almost no candidate has been sticking to the ceiling on expenses fixed by the Election Commission.

Passage

Then come the Tehri Dam evacuees. The Forest Department recently decided to acquire about 46 hectares of land in the Patri division of Haridwar district and rehabilitate these 33 families there. Besides, as compensation for uprooting them once more, the department is willing to distribute Rs 26 lakh among them. In addition, the department also plans to acquire 63 hectares from the Raiwallah cantonment, including the army ammunition dump. The lure of the army to move is the 220 hectares of land and the fact that the tab of building a new ammunition dump will be picked up. "These proposals are being pursued by us," says M. Ahsan, chief conservator of Rajaji National Park.

106. Tehri Dam evacuees have not been compensated.
107. The 33 families in Patri division will not shift easily.
108. The amount of Rs 26 lakh to be given as compensation by the forest department is adequate.
109. The army may not agree to shift Raiwallah cantonment.
110. Mr M Ahsan has introduced a set of forestry reforms in India.

Passage

How far a seismic facility can eavesdrop does not depend on the distance from the test but on the seismic characteristics of its location, as faultlines which run for thousands of kilometres are effective conveyors of sound. For example, the Indian seismic sniffer at Gauribidanoor near Bangalore keeps its ear right to the ground for sounds of nuclear activity from as far as Lop Nor in China. The US may have extracted a major concession from Pakistan on the promise that the seismic test facility could serve as an excuse to get around Pressler Act by convincing the US Congress that this will be a foolproof way of monitoring the Pakistani promise of freezing its nuclear programme. US officials, however, assert that there is nothing new in it.

111. Seismic tests can be conducted on another country's activities, too.
112. Gauribidanoor is not an ideal location for a seismic sniffer.
113. The US has set up a seismic test centre in Pakistan.
114. Pressler Act supports the nuclear programme of Pakistan.
115. Pakistan was less than willing to set up the seismic facility.

Passage

There has been considerable debate in India regarding the privatisation of higher education. In this debate, there is generally an implicit assumption that privatisation is essentially the same as corporatisation, ie private investment comes due to the potential of returns. In the higher education field, privatisation and corporatisation are actually quite different. Privatisation is regarding who controls the educational institute and the role of government in the management and funding of the institute, while corporatisation is about making profits. In India, there is no doubt that private not-for-profit universities need to be encouraged to increase education opportunities, and for the fact that there is no other alternative as the government simply cannot create enough public universities to satisfy the demand. However, guidelines for private not-for-profit universities should be made clear, simple and transparent to ensure that they are truly not for profit and offer a level playing field to all those who might want to set up a private university.

116. Privatisation of higher education has yet to take proper shape in India.
117. Expansion of higher education opportunities in India is needed to meet the increasing demand.
118. Corporatisation of higher education has benefited the students in the developed countries.
119. Privatisation of higher education will lead to commercialisation of education in India.
120. India does not have any extant guidelines for setting up higher educational institutions by private entities.

Passage

Aviation is important, both as an industry in its own right and as a facilitator for the success and competitiveness of other industries. The success of the aviation industry is also integral to national competitiveness, economic development and social progress. More importantly, aviation supports those new economic sectors on which India's future prosperity relies, like Information Technology, Biotechnology, Finance and Electronics. That India's air transport industry is on the rise is an undisputable fact. However, the Indian economy will only achieve its true potential if we are able to compete in the industries of the future. We need to be strong in the areas with potential to grow and the role of India's aviation sector is critical in this regard.

121. India needs to make massive investments in infrastructural development.
122. Growth in India's aviation sector is important to its economic development.
123. India has made substantial development in the Biotechnology sector.
124. India has tremendous potential to grow in the emerging industries.
125. Aviation sector in India has not fulfilled its role in the past in its economic development.

Passage

Asia has become the growth centre of the world economy in recent years. Within the region, India and South Korea are the third and fourth largest economies after China and Japan. Though the Asian growth stories mainly revolve around India and China, South Korea has remained a key player for these countries as one of their major trading and investment partners. South Korea adopted outward-oriented economic policies with the beginning of its first five-year economic development plan in 1962, which resulted in high growth and the integration of the Korean economy with the rest of the world. Subsequently, high and consistent economic growth made South Korea one of the high-income economies in Asia. Korea is still growing at a faster rate compared to other developed economies. India on the other hand adopted an import substitution policy since its Independence until the early 1990s. Since then India has introduced wide-ranging economic policy reforms and is moving towards market-driven economy. This has resulted in consistent high economic growth over the last one-and-a-half decades.

126. Only Korean economy is considered as robust by the international community.
127. Japan's economic growth over the last decade is the highest in Asia.
128. The Korean economy is traditionally different than the Indian economy in its approach.
129. The economic growth of India prior to 1990s was much higher than the present growth rate.
130. India and China together are considered to be the driving force of the Asian economy.

Passage

Investors today have more investment options than were available just a few years ago. Choice in any decision making is good in so far it provides variety differentiation and bench- marking. It could also, however, at times lead to clutter and "noise" if the options are mostly similar and undifferentiated. To make sense of this choice conundrum, it is imperative for an investor to define the objective — both returns and digestible risk and then identify the possible options. The investor also needs to select the mix and regularly monitor that objectives and investment outcomes remain aligned. Sounds simple, but can present the most confounding situations which multiplies with the quantum of wealth.

131. Investment of higher amount is relatively simpler than smaller amounts.
132. Investors need to critically evaluate the risk of each investment option.
133. Present-day investors need to use their judgement more critically before investing.
134. Multiple investment options of similar type help in making better investment decisions.
135. In the past, investors were generally guided by the fund managers.

Passage

The first time I saw *The Wizard of Oz,* the story bewitched me. The second time I saw *The Wizard of Oz,* the special effects amazed me. The third time I saw *The Wizard of Oz,* the photography dazzled me. Have you ever seen a movie twice, three times? You notice subtleties and hear sounds you completely missed the first time around.

It's the same on the phone. Because your business conversations are more consequential than movies, you should listen to them two, maybe three times, Often, we have no clear idea of what *really* happened in our phone conversation until we hear it again. You'll find shadings more significant than the colour of Toto's collar- and more scarecrows than you imagined who 'haven't got a brain!'

How do you listen to your important business conversa- tions again? Simply legally and ethically tape-record them. I call the technique of recording and analysing your business conversations for subtleties *Instant Replay.*

(Note: Although directions remain the same please note that in these 5 questions, Each of the five questions has only one distinct answer, ie no two questions can have the same answer. If you get same answer for more than one question, consider both again and decide which one of the two would more definitely be that answer and same way review the other also.)

136. The movie *'The Wizard of Oz'* will help improve business conversation.
137. For most, if they watch a movie more than once, different aspects in different order, like special effects, photography, story, music etc would impress in a better way.
138. The tips are given for understanding business conversation.
139. The advice is being given to the sales team.
140. The author watches most movies more than twice.

Type III: Exercise 5C

Directions: Each of the following questions tests your ability to derive conclusions from complex situations. Read each question carefully and answer the questions that follow.

1. Those in the business community who decry government regulation claim that it increases the costs of doing business and reduces beneficial competition, ultimately harming both business and the community as a whole. They point to industries such as trucking, airlines, and telecommunications, in which deregulation has apparently brought greater economic efficiency. These commentators ignore the industries, such as financial services, in which government regulation is essential; indeed, without government intervention in the 1930s, some whole segments of that industry might have permanently collapsed.

   The author's point is made primarily by

   A) offering a counter-example to rebut his opponents' argument
   B) calling into question the motives of his opponents
   C) pointing out an inconsistency in his opponents' use of terms
   D) drawing a distinction between valid and invalid methods of argument
   E) underscoring the subjectivity of his opponents' basic assumptions

2. The cleaning and restoration of Michelangelo's frescoes on the ceiling of the Sistine Chapel were undertaken by some of the world's finest art restorers under the close supervision of an international team of art experts and historians. Nonetheless, the results have produced a storm of controversy. Most modern viewers, it seems, had become accustomed to seeing the frescoes with their colours dulled by layers of yellowing glue and varnish and with the contours of the figures obscured by centuries' accumulation of grime.

   The passage implies that Michelangelo's frescoes

   A) have been the subject of intense controversy over their artistic merit
   B) suffered until recently from centuries of obscurity and neglect
   C) should not have been cleaned and restored without more careful planning
   D) have been obscured by dirt during the recent process of restoration
   E) were originally much brighter and more vivid than most modern viewers realize

3. Young people who imagine that the life of the writer is one of glamour, riches or fame soon discover not only the difficulties of the craft but the long odds against achieving any measure of recognition or financial security. Upon being asked, "Aren't most editors failed writers?", T.S. Eliot is said to have remarked, "Yes, but so are most writers."

   Th[illegible]tatement by T.S. Eliot conveys which of the following ideas?

A) The profession of editing can be just as creative and challenging as writing.
B) Few writers are fortunate enough to attain real success in their profession.
C) For a writer, success is measured more by influence exerted than by material gain achieved.
D) Many writers find that a stint at editorial work is a beneficial apprenticeship in their craft.
E) There are no clear-cut standards of success and failure for writers, but there are such standards for editors.

4. Between 1960 and 1970, ivory poachers in the African nation of Zinbaku killed over 6,500 elephants. During that period, the total elephant population in Zinbaku fell from about 35,000 to just under 30,000. In 1970, new anti-poaching measures were implemented in Zinbaku and between 1970 and 1980, over 800 poachers were arrested and expelled from the country. Nevertheless, by 1980, the elephant population in Zinbaku had fallen to about 21,000.
Which of the following, if true, would best help to explain the apparent paradox presented above?
A) The poachers arrested in Zinbaku between 1970 and 1980 were rarely sentenced to long prison terms.
B) Because of highly publicised campaigns against the slaughter of elephants, demand for ivory fell between 1970 and 1980.
C) The elephant population in neighbouring Mombasa rose slightly between 1970 and 1980.
D) Before 1970, the anti-poaching laws passed by the parliament in Zinbaku were rarely enforced.
E) In Zinbaku, between 1970 and 1980, thousands of acres of forest, the elephant's natural habitat, were cleared for farming.

5. If the wind is strong, kites are flown.
If the sky is not clear, kites are not flown.
If the temperature is high, kites are flown.
Assume the statements above to be true. If kites are flown, which of the following statements must be true?
I. The wind is strong.
II. The sky is clear.
III. The temperature is not high.
A) I only B) II only C) III only
D) I and III only E) II and III only

6. Last year, the number of cases of rape reported by women in this city increased by twenty per cent. Ironically, these statistics have been cited with approval by advocates of women's rights.

Which of the following, if true, would logically explain the seemingly paradoxical approval of the women's rights advocates?

A) A new city policy of encouraging women to report cases of rape has sharply diminished the number of unreported cases.

B) The rate of convictions in rape cases in the city has increased steadily over the past three years.

C) Rape prevention has long been a high priority for leaders of women's rights organisations.

D) Most of the increase in reported cases of rape occurred in three particularly dangerous neighbourhoods of the city.

E) Local judges have begun to deal more harshly with those found guilty of committing rape.

7. In reaction against the heavy, ornate designs favoured by the neoclassical architects of the Victorian era, architectural critics and historians in the first half of this century went to the opposite extreme, declaring that only what was stripped-down, light, and free of decoration could be beautiful. Today, an overdue revaluation of this aesthetic is under way, as exemplified by the current exhibition of designs from the Beaux Arts school of the nineteenth century.

It can be inferred from the passage above that the present movement among architectural critics is towards

A) a renewed appreciation of the use of decorative motifs in building designs

B) a rejection of neoclassical standards of beauty in architectural design

C) a greater admiration of the light, simple designs characteristic of the early twentieth century

D) the adaptation of Victorian styles in the work of today's younger architects

E) a deeper understanding of the aesthetic values of underlying neoclassical theory

8. In national surveys taken between 1970 and 1985, the percentage of respondents who reported that they usually attended weekly religious services rose from 28 per cent to 34 per cent. However, statistics compiled during the same period by the nation's major religious denominations showed a gradual decline in attendance at weekly services.

Each of the following, if true, could help explain the apparent contradiction in the statements above EXCEPT

A) There was a sharp drop in the number of persons who attended religious services on an occasional basis.

B) Attendance statistics compiled by the religious denominations are often highly inaccurate.

C) As older churchgoers died, they were not replaced by an equal number of younger churchgoers.

D) There was no significant increase in attendance among religious groups outside the major denominations.

E) Those responding to the surveys were not representative of the population as a whole.

9. Stronger patent laws are needed to protect inventions from being pirated. With that protection manufacturers would be encouraged to invest in the development of new products and technologies. Such investment frequently results in an increase in manufacturer's productivity.

Which of the following conclusions can most properly be drawn from the information above?

A) Stronger patent laws tend to benefit financial institutions as well as manufacturers.

B) Increased productivity in manufacturing is likely to be accompanied by the creation of more manufacturing jobs.

C) Manufacturers will decrease investment in the development of new products and technologies unless there are stronger patent laws.

D) The weakness of current patent laws has been a cause of economic recession.

E) Stronger patent laws would stimulate improvements in productivity for many manufacturers.

10. Partly because of bad weather, but also partly because some major pepper growers have switched to high-priced cocoa, world production of pepper has been running well below worldwide sales for three years. Pepper is consequently in relatively short supply. The price of pepper has soared in response: it now equals that of cocoa.

Which of the following can be inferred from the passage?

A) Pepper is a profitable crop only if it is grown on a large scale.

B) World consumption of pepper has been unusually high for three years.

C) World production of pepper will return to previous levels once normal weather returns.

D) Surplus stocks of pepper have been reduced in the last three years.

E) The profits that the growers of pepper have made in the past three years have been unprecedented.

11. Technological education is worsening. People between eighteen and twenty-four, who are just emerging from their formal education, are more likely to be technologically illiterate than somewhat older adults. And yet, issues for public referenda will increasingly involve aspects of technology.

Which of the following conclusions can be properly drawn from the statements above?

A) If all young people are to make informed decisions on public reference, many of them must learn more about technology.

B) Thorough studies of technological issues and innovations should be made a required part of the public and private school curriculum.

C) It should be suggested that prospective voters attend applied science courses in order to acquire a minimal competency in technical matters.

D) If young people are not to be overly influenced by famous technocrats, they must increase their knowledge of pure science.

E) On public referenda issues, young people tend to confuse real or probable technologies with impossible ideals.

12. In a political system with only two major parties, the entrance of a third-party candidate into an election race damages the chances of only one of the two major candidates. The third- party candidate always attracts some of the voters who might otherwise have voted for one of the two major candidates, but not voters who support the other candidate. Since a third-party candidacy affects the two major candidates unequally, for reasons neither of them has any control over, the practice is unfair and should not be allowed.

If the factual information in the passage above is true, which of the following can be most reliably inferred from it?

A) If the political platform of the third party is a compromise position between that of the two major parties, the third party will draw its voters equally from the two major parties.

B) If, before the emergence of a third party, voters were divided equally between the two major parties, neither of the major parties is likely to capture much more than one-half of the votes.

C) A third-party candidate will not capture the votes of new voters who have never voted for candidates of either of the two major parties.

D) The political stance of a third party will be more radical than that of either of the two major parties.

E) The founders of a third party are likely to be a coalition consisting of former leaders of two major parties.

13. Thirty years after African colonies began emerging as nations, modern loyalties still often go first to the tribe. From Angola to Ethiopia, ethnic hatred has forced hundreds of thousands of people to flee their homes, making Africa the continent with the world's largest number of refugees.

Which of the following statements best summarises the above?

A) Africa is best characterised by ethnic fractionalisation.

B) Angola and Ethiopia have the worst record of inter-ethnic strife in Africa.

C) Continued warfare has made Africa a nation of refugees.

D) Africa is best characterised as a federation of many states.

E) Africa is best characterised as a continent without loyalties.

14. Average family income is right where it was 20 years ago, even though, in most families these days, husbands and wives are working.

The above statement implies all of the following EXCEPT:

A) Even though nominal family income may have increased, inflation has risen at an equal rate.

B) More husbands and wives are working today than 20 years ago.

C) It was more prevalent for one spouse to work 20 years ago than today.

D) Wives earn more than husbands today.

E) The price level was lower 20 years ago.

15. In 1980, global service exports totalled about $370 billion, approximately 20 per cent of world trade. Still, no coherent system of rules, principles and procedures exists to govern trade in services.

Which of the following best summarises the argument?

A) Regulatory systems lag behind reality.

B) A regulatory system ought to reflect the importance of services exports.

C) World trade totalled $1850 billion in 1980.

D) Service trade legislation is a veritable wasteland.

E) While trade legislation exists, it is uncoordinated.

16. Every town with a pool hall has its share of unsavoury characters. This is because the pool hall attracts gamblers and all gamblers are unsavoury.

Which of the following, if true, cannot be inferred from the above?

A) All gamblers are unsavoury.

B) All pool halls attract gamblers.

C) Every town has unsavoury characters.

D) All gamblers are attracted by pool halls.

E) An explanation of what attracts gamblers.

17. Team sports like baseball display strong socialist tendencies in their requirement of individual subordination to the authority of coaches and managers.

Which of the following conclusions may not be inferred from the above information?

A) All team sports are authoritarian.

B) All team players are subordinate to their coaches.

C) Without employee subordination to managerial authority, production for profit would not be possible.

D) All team sports have socialist tendencies.

E) Individual subordination to authority is an aspect of socialism.

18. In the human body, platelets promote blood clotting by clumping together. Aspirin has been found to prevent clotting by making platelets less sticky. Research has now shown that heart attacks and strokes caused by blood clots could be avoided by taking one aspirin a day. Statistics show that the incidence of second heart attacks has been reduced by 21% and overall mortality rates by 15% as a result of taking aspirin.

Unfortunately, the drug has several unpleasant side-effects, including nausea, gastric bleeding, and, in severe cases, shock. In children, it has been linked to Reye's syndrome, a rare, but occasionally fatal, childhood illness.

On balance, however, for men aged 40 and over, an aspirin a day may present an excellent prophylactic measure for a disease that affects 1.5 million American yearly and claims the lives of about 540,000.

Which of the following conclusions can most properly be drawn from the information above?

A) All people should take an aspirin a day to prevent heart attacks.

B) Painkillers prevent heart attacks.

C) Smokers can safely continue smoking, provided they take at least one aspirin a day.

D) The majority of people suffering second subsequent cardiac arrests could have been saved by taking an aspirin a day.

E) Aspirin can be used to reduce mortality rates in patients who have already suffered heart attacks.

19. More and more organisations in the world today are prepared to carry out criminal acts that involve the taking of innocent people as hostages. One of the most urgent problems on the agenda of most Western European governments is terrorism and how to deal with it. In handling the situations that arise, all agree that swift and effective action must be taken to combat the terrorist, but, for some reason, when terrorism arrives on their doorstep in the form of hijacked airplanes, for example, some governments give in all too quickly to the demands of the terrorist. It is understandable that governments must act to safeguard the welfare of their citizens and other innocent people caught up in the criminal act. However, what the governments seem to ignore is that if you give in to the terrorist once, he or she will play upon your weakness and therefore be encouraged to indulge in terrorist acts on future occasions.

Which of the following conclusions best describes the views of the writer of the above passage?

A) There is a subtle but certain difference between state terrorism and terrorist acts carried out by individuals or members of illegal terrorist groups.

B) One man's terrorist is another man's freedom fighter!

C) Governments make no distinction between terrorism carried out for financial gain and that carried out in the name of a political organisation.

D) Surrender to blackmail and you invite more blackmail!

E) There seems to be no solution to the problem of terrorist incidents occurring in Western European countries and other democracies.

20. The function of a food technologist in a large marketing chain of food stores is to ensure that all foodstuffs which are offered for sale in the various retail outlets meet certain standard criteria for nonperishability, freshness, and fitness for human consumption.

It is the technologist's job to visit the premises of suppliers and food producers (factory or farm), inspect the facilities and report thereon. His responsibility also includes receiving new products from local and foreign suppliers and performing exhaustive quality control testing on them. Finally, he should carry out surprise spot checks on goods in the marketing chain's own workhouses and stores.

What conclusion can best be drawn from the preceding paragraph?

A) A university degree in food technology is a necessary and sufficient condition for becoming a food technologist.

B) Imported products, as well as home-produced goods, must be rigorously tested.

C) The food technologist stands between the unhygienic producer and the unsuspecting consumer.

D) Home-produced foodstuffs are safer to eat than goods imported from abroad because they are subject to more regular and closer inspection procedures.

E) Random checking of the quality of goods stored on the shelves in a foodstore is the best way of ensuring that foodstuffs of an inferior quality are not purchased by the general public.

21. There are three main factors that control the risks of becoming dependent on drugs. These factors are the type of drug, the personality of the individual, and the circumstances in which the drug is taken. Indeed, it could be said that the majority of the adult population have taken alcohol, yet few have become dependent on it. Also, many strong drugs that have been used for medical purposes have not caused the patient to become addicted.

However, it can be demonstrated that people who have taken drugs for fun are more likely to become dependent on the drug. The dependence is not always physiological but may remain psychological, although the effects are still essentially the same. Those at greatest risk appear to be personalities that are psychopathic, immature, or otherwise unstable.

Psychological dependence is very strong with heroin, morphine, cocaine, and amphetamines. Physiological dependence is great with heroin and morphine, but less with amphetamines, barbiturates, and alcohol.

Which of the following conclusions can be drawn from the text?

A) One cannot become addicted to certain drugs if one has a strong personality.

B) Taking drugs for "kicks" increases the possibility of becoming dependent on drugs.

C) Psychological dependence is the greatest with heroin.

D) Alcohol is a safe drug since very few people become dependent on it.

E) Long-term use of certain drugs for medical purposes does not cause addiction.

22. Sally overslept. Therefore, she did not eat breakfast. She realized that she was late for school, so she ran as fast as she could and did not see a hole in the ground which was in her path. She tripped and broke her ankle. She was then taken to the hospital and while lying in bed was visited by her friend, who wanted to know why she had got up so late.

Which of the following conclusions can be made from the above passage?

A) Because Sally did not eat her breakfast, she broke her ankle.

B) Sally's friend visited her in the hospital because she wanted to know why she was late for school.

C) Sally did not notice the hole because she overslept.

D) Sally broke her ankle because she went to bed late the previous night.

E) Sally's broken ankle meant she did not go to school that day.

23. The owners of a local supermarket have decided to make use of three now-redundant check-out counters. They believe that they will attract those customers who have lately been put off by the long check-out lines during the mid-morning and evening rush hours. The owners have concluded that in order to be successful, the increased revenue from existing and added counters will have to be more than the increase in maintenance costs for the added counters.

The underlying goal of the owners can be summarised thus:

A) To improve services to all customers

B) To attract people who have never been to the store

C) To make use of the redundant counters

D) To keep maintenance costs on the added counters as low as possible.

E) To increase monthly profits

24. Pioneers of the motor-car industry realised that if they were going to meet the growing demand for their product, they had to adapt the labour force used in the productive process. Instead of many men working to complete all the stages of one car at a time, they assigned defined tasks to each man which they would repeat on every car.

Which of the following can be concluded from the passage?

A) Early motor-car manufacturers intended to increase productivity by applying the principle of division of labour.

B) The car workers became disgruntled because they were assigned monotonous, repetitive tasks on the assembly line.

C) Economies of scale enabled early motor companies to expand.

D) A bad worker would perform the same task badly on each car leading to many more rejects.

E) The new production process enabled certain car workers to become specialists in the part of the process to which they were assigned.

25. In 1989, Japanese economic growth is expected to increase 50 times more than that of the United States.

Japanese economic policy ensures that faster growth is caused by greater investment in modern industrial plants. The initial investment leads to lower production costs, increased competitiveness, higher living standards, and low inflation.

The United States, on the other hand, is more concerned with curbing inflation and is pursuing a policy of slow growth, thus preventing investment in the modernisation of American industry.

Which of the following conclusions can be drawn from the above?

A) Slow growth prevents inflation.

B) Slow-growth policies reduce inflation, but also decrease the efficiency and competitiveness of industry.

C) Investment in industry causes inflation.

D) Inflation can be reduced by increasing productivity.

E) The US must curb inflation before it can modernise and streamline its industry.

26. A pill that can induce abortions in pregnant women has become available in France. The drug, RU486, has proved more than 95% effective in tests conducted by a scientific team in Paris. The drug is an antiphormone which disrupts pregnancy by blocking the implantation of a fertilised egg in the wall of the uterus. In France, the pill will be available to women who are 49 days late in their menstrual cycle. The company that manufactures the pill, Roussel Uclaf, states, however, that the pill is not a "morning after" pill for use as a contraceptive.

Which of the following statements can be correctly deduced from the text above?

A) The drug RU486 is a new type of contraceptive.

B) The drug RU486 blocks egg production.

C) The drug RU486 can be used to terminate pregnancy.

D) The drug RU486 will replace conventional abortion techniques.

E) The drug RU486 will only be available in France.

27. Jane and Bella are both successful women and also members of a minority group. Jane believes in positive discrimination. She believes that if

positions of power and honour are offered principally to minority groups, then these groups will begin to play a more significant role in society today.

Bella, on the other hand, feels that she has succeeded in her chosen field of work on her own merits. She thinks that positive discrimination will lower standards and decrease competition between similarly qualified personnel, who will expect to achieve positions because of their minority status rather than their suitability for the particular position.

Which of the following best sums up Jane's argument?

A) Positive discrimination will encourage more people to apply for jobs, previously unavailable to them.

B) Positive discrimination will give extra opportunities to minority groups.

C) Quality and professionalism will improve because of the greater number of positions held by members of minority groups.

D) Positive discrimination will ensure that each position is filled by the most suitably qualified candidate.

E) Positive discrimination will eradicate prejudice from the work arena.

28. In order to boost sales of toys at times other than the peak sale time — Christmas — manufacturers use many techniques. Character toys from movies or TV series are promoted, and all sets are 'collectible' by their young purchasers. Collections, however, never appear to be complete, because as soon as all the characters are acquired, the child then requires the 'car', the 'phone', the 'mobile home', and even the 'airplane' to ensure a happy environment for the toys. Ultimately, the elusive final piece of the series is attained just as the manufacturer and promoter release the next series of 'collectibles'.

The prime aim of the manufacturer and promoter is to ensure that

A) all children should be happy and no child can be happy without a complete series of toys.

B) as soon as one set is complete or almost complete, then the next one arrives on the scene.

C) children should be encouraged to complete their collections of toys.

D) Christmas must be the peak selling period for toys.

E) sales need to be bolstered throughout the year.

Answers and Explanations

Exercise 5A

1. a; The use of 'could' implies a difficulty in obtaining reservation. Hence, conclusion I is valid. Conclusion II is not certain.
2. b; Since all parents are not very well off it must mean that all of them are driven by a desire as mentioned in conclusion II.
3. e; Since the poor live in mud houses and mud houses are cooler in summer, it means that poor people would have been more comfortable in summer, had everything else remained the same. But what about the coolers and air-conditioners that rich people have?
   Conclusion II is irrelevant to the given statement.
4. d; Only one of the two reasons mentioned could stop patients from going to eminent doctors.
5. b; The statement says that the user of non-conventional energy sources *will* replace (eliminate) the energy crisis. It does not say that the replacement is already on. Hence, the first conclusion is invalid. The second is valid because there *is* an energy crisis.
6. e; The given conclusions are far-fatched and not certain.
7. e; Neither of the conclusions is certain. May be only one spinner made 150 runs.
8. d; Although no certain conclusion can be derived because it is not given whether X was hit by a bullet or not, yet one of the two conclusions must be true.
9. a; The first does follow because the tone of the statement is that educational value of newspapers is given due importance while its entertainment value is not. Clearly, the second conclusion is invalid.
10. b; The first conclusion is irrelevant. The second is the meaning of the given statement. 'Too expensive to be bad' means that it can't be bad because it is expensive.
11. e; The statement merely says that camels are very useful for deserts. It does not state whether they are cheap or available in large number.
12. a; The first conclusion is obviously true; otherwise how could one know that the brand has the largest sale? The second speaks of 'production' and not 'sale', and hence it is not certain.
13. b; From the two facts given, the second conclusion seems valid. But the first conclusion is fallacious as it declares that women are not interested in anything else.
14. a; The first conclusion is obviously valid as it is a restatement of the given sentence. The second may or may not be true.
15. d; What happens to players who broke records with the help of drugs is not given. Hence, either the player will receive the prize or he will not.

[Although we do know that such players are commonly not given the prize, here we have to concentrate only on the given sentence.]

16. c; Both conclusions are correct. Killing continues, means the first conclusion is valid. Killing continues while the government says that terrorists are in check, means that the second is valid.

17. c; Both conclusions are correct. Shortage means that imports must have been made since aluminium is a metal which can't be done without. If a movement from shortage to self-sufficiency can be achieved and 'this rate' is also continued, then soon surplus could be reached. Hence, the second conclusion is also valid.

18. c; The first conclusion is obviously correct. The second is also correct because the statement talks of human 'weaknesses' and not just a single weakness.

19. a; The first conclusion is correct since this is a fact. The second is an irrational inference.

20. a; The first is a direct consequence of the given statement. The second is *probably* true. But we can't be sure.

21. e; Both conclusions are invalid. Americans have not been able to develop a particular enzyme. It does not mean that they have not developed any enzymes. Similarly, the second conclusion is also invalid. Just because an analogous effect of the enzyme was observed on the two types of proteins, it can not be certainly said that both the proteins have the same composition.

22. e; Both conclusions are invalid. Maybe, although the demand is increasing at a faster rate, yet its actual value is less than the production. [For example, India's population is increasing at a faster rate than China's although its population is less than that of China.] In this case, there may be a surplus and hence no need to import. Similarly, instead of reducing demand we may try for a boost in production.

23. b; The first conclusion is too severe. The second is directly implied by the statement.

24. e; Neither of the conclusions can be said to definitely follow. 'Practically every mineral' does not mean 'every mineral' and hence gold may or may not be there. Similarly, a uranium content of 3 grams per 1000 tonnes of water may or may not harbour radiation hazard.

25. b; The author's tone implies that he knows some things but does not know so many more; that he is practically ignorant of everything. This means conclusion II is valid.

26. e

27. b; Conclusion I is vague, nothing has been mentioned about "expressions". II is obvious.

28. e; None of the conclusions is in any way related to the given statement.

29. a; The first conclusion is the meaning of the statement. The second is not implied in the statement.

30. e; None of the conclusions can be definitely asserted in the light of the given statement.
31. e; None of the conclusions can be definitely established since the statement itself is rather vague.
32. b; The second conclusion is a direct consequence of the given statement. The first is irrelevant.
33. e; None is directly related to the statement.
34. e; None of the conclusions is certain. Kapil might not have had these qualities and yet, because of the fact that the others were also lacking these qualities, he won. Or maybe, he won because of luck. Or maybe, he did have all these qualities, after all. Nothing can be certainly established.
35. b; The first conclusion is invalid; it is not directly related with the statement. The second is valid. To escape from a problem one should solve it: it means that one should have some solutions.
36. a; Although the passage does say that the ministers reduce themselves to yesmen, it never hints that the prime minister too does not want them to speak openly.

Exercise 5B

1. 5; Definitely false. The first sentence says that India has been resisting the issue *alongwith "other developing countries"*. Hence, it is not true that India is sidelined.
2. 2; Probably true. The efforts are being resisted by India and other *developing countries*. So, it is likely that these efforts are being carried out by *developed countries*.
3. 2; Probably true. The first sentence says that India and other developing countries are committed to upgradation of labour standards. So, there does not seem to be any dispute over this. Hence, the inference appears to be true. However, the inference may not be *definitely true* because it is not certain that *all* countries are committed to the cause.
4. 1; Definitely true. See the passage carefully. ("Successful conclusion of Uruguay Round ..." etc.)
5. 2; Probably true. The last sentence says that there was stiff opposition to the efforts on the ground that the matter did not fall in the area of trade. The first sentence says that India is opposing the efforts. So, it is likely that Indian ground of resistance is also the same (i.e., the issues such as labour standards, environmental concerns, human rights etc. are not related with trade).
6. 5; Definitely false. The passage says that the consultations have been brought to a *satisfactory* conclusion. Had India been treated with bias, the word *satisfactory* would not have been used.
7. 2; Probably true. This appears likely from the fact that India held discussions for a single product.

8. 3; Data Inadequate. It is clear that WTO came into being after 31-12-94. But the exact date cannot be established.
9. 2; Probably true. The passage says that these agreements *are expected to* boost handloom and powerloom sectors. It further says that these two sectors are important for employment generation. So, the inference looks likely to be true. It is not definitely true because the passage uses an uncertain phrase *expected to* instead of a definite phrase such as *will* or *will certainly* etc.
10. 2; Probably true. There has been no mention of any such conditions. But common sense tells us that this must be true.
11. 3; Data inadequate. No information is given about the Fourth Conference. It may be argued that two consecutive Conferences are usually not held in the same country but this is only a convention and not a rule.
12. 2; Probably true. The passage gives a special importance to the role of ILO by giving it a special mention. Had the involvement of ILO been a routine affair, it would not have been given a special mention. Hence, the given inference appears true.
13. 2; Probably true. This looks true; otherwise why would the industrial nations be making such demands?
14. 4; Probably false. The passage does not give any information about what happened in the Copenhagen Summit. It talks of Copenhagen Summit in future tense. It says that "poverty allocation" was one of the items on the agenda *to be* discussed in this Summit. Since this is an uncontroversial topic, it is unlikely that this topic would not have been actually discussed when the Summit took place in March.
15. 4; Probably false. It is very unlikely that India would not send a representative to a Conference that is being held in New Delhi.
16. 1; Definitely true. The second sentence says: the aim is to make Rupee fully convertible. *Conclusion*: Rupee is still not fully convertible. *We know:* full convertibility means convertibility on capital account as well. *Conclusion*: convertibility on capital account has not materalised.
17. 5; Definitely false. The first sentence says: Rupee has been made convertible on current account. The second sentence *means* full convertibility is still due. *Conclusion*: Current account convertibility does not mean full convertibility.
18. 2; Probably true. The passage says that steps towards convertibility are signs of growing economic maturity. In the wake of this, the given inference appears likely to be true.
19. 5; Definitely false. The passage says that India is preparing to *lower* its import tariffs to levels existing in other developing countries. It means that, presently, the tariffs are *actually more* than those in developing countries.
20. 2; Probably true. The last sentence says: India is ready to shed its *ideological* inhibitions and evaluate the international economic

environment in a pragmatic spirit. We know that before the age of convertibility India was governed by socialistic ideals. So, it is likely that the ideological inhibitions referred to in the passage mean the socialistic ideals. Hence, the given inference appears likely to be true.

21. 2; Probably true. The tone of the first sentence is such that it means that reforms affect mainly private sector and also, to some extent, public sector.
22. 1; Definitely true. See the third sentence ("This is ... *continuously*.").
23. 5; Definitely false. Although the last sentence may give an impression that the inference is true, you must also see the first sentence as well as the **fact** that disinvestment in public sector has already taken place.
24. 5; Definitely false. The second sentence says that many people treat reforms as a synonym of privatisation. But the first sentence disputes this belief by claiming that reforms have affected the public sector too.
25. 1; Definitely true. It is obvious.
26. 1; Definitely true. The directive principles are a part of the Constitution. So, they are at least as old as the Constitution.
27. 5; Definitely false. See the second sentence ("But a chasm .....").
28. 4; Probably false. Both these persons were involved in the process of preparing the Constitution. It is likely to be false that they disapproved of something which they incorporated as an important part (directive principles) of the Constitution.
29. 3; Data inadequate. NPFC started in 1974. ICDS was started next year. Hence, ICDS was started in 1975. But was it May? We cannot be sure.
30. 2; Probably true. The last sentence says that the situation is likely to improve now *because now there is a backup of "political will"* with enhanced funds. If the presence of political will arouses hopes of improvement, it is very likely that, earlier, lack of political will was the reason for lack of improvement.
31. 5; Definitely false. It is assumed that *only* 30 million people will come from amongst those living below poverty line. Actually many *more* are living below poverty line.
32. 5; Definitely false. The passage has, in fact, proved that the JRY is *short* of funds.
33. 2; Probably true. By the year 2000 A.D., inflation, monsoon etc. would have some effect on the level of Rs 45 and are likely to push it upwards.
34. 1; Definitely true. See the fourth sentence ("This requirement will also build up ... dependent on *monsoons* ... etc.").
35. 5; Definitely false. See explanation to Q. 32.
36. 3; Data inadequate. There is no hint about the state of affairs before 1956.
37. 1; Definitely true.
38. 4; Probably false. The last sentence says that out of 1438 products, only 129 are under compulsory certification. Hence, it appears false that there are more items of mass consumption than others.

39. 5; Definitely false. Books are not items of mass consumption; so the certification would be voluntary and not compulsory.
40. 3; Data inadequate. There is no mention of *international* standards.
41. 4; Probably false. The first sentence says that the reforms are aimed at "a wide cross-section" of the economy. So, it is unlikely that it is to benefit only the rich. But it is not mentioned that the "wide cross-section" is to be taken on the basis of "income"; so we cannot say that the inference is definitely false.
42. 1; Definitely true. The passage says that after reforms there has been an *introduction* of capital adequacy norms. Introduction means that it has come for the first time.
43. 5; Definitely false. The resource allocation was also inefficient. See the second sentence.
44. 1; Definitely true. The last sentence talks of "greater public confidence" which will "ensure" safety ... and "bring about" transparency ... and *"encourage" resource mobilisation*. So, it is seen that public confidence is not entirely irrelevant to resource mobilisation.
45. 3; Data inadequate. The passage neither supports nor denies that the reforms are aimed *only* at the financial sector.
46. 1; Definitely true. The passage gives the adjective "draconian" to the maxim "spare the rod ... child".
47. 5; Definitely false. "Even fifty years back" the attitude had not changed. It means that the attitude changed only after the 1940s.
48. 5; Definitely false. Rights of the children was *thought to be* an intellectual aberration but this attitude has *now* undergone a *sea-change*.
49. 2; Probably true. Cruel treatment is one of the likely reasons for the unhealthy growth of a child. But it is not definitely true because there can be other reasons too.
50. 4; Probably false. The first line says that today we have a "fast-changing world". The inference looks likely to be false in the context of a fast-changing world. But there is no definite information in the passage about whether there is any change in attitude in any other area as well. Hence, we can't say that it is definitely false.
51. 2; Probably true. The first sentence says that "dominance by public sector" is "a *distinct* feature of the Indian financial system". The word *distinct* implies that such a thing is uncommon.
52. 2; Probably true. The first sentence says that there is dominance of public sector. The second sentence says that this was motivated by socio-economic considerations. So, it must have been assumed that public sector would serve socio-economic purpose better than private sector.
53. 1; Definitely true. (There are "*varying* degrees of concessionality" in interest rates.)

54. 5; Definitely false. (See last sentence.)
55. 3; Data inadequate. There is no mention of other countries.
56. 3; Data inadequate. The first sentence says that the BIS scheme tests certified products but no information is given about products that are uncertified.
57. 2; Probably true. Logically, if 8 laboratories can issue 42000 test reports, then, on an average, one laboratory can issue about 5250 test reports in a year. So, the inference looks true. But we cannot be *definite* (sure) because it has not been clearly stated that all laboratories have equal capacity.
58. 5; Definitely false. Read the third sentence. It says that these laboratories are being "constantly expanded ... and modernised."
59. 2; Probably true. The first sentence says that the BIS does *independent* testing. So, it is likely that the body is autonomous.
60. 1; Definitely true. Had it not been so, why would BIS "constantly" expand and modernise its laboratories?
61. 5; Definitely false. The first sentence mentions three avowed goals of elementary education: learner achievement *apart from* access and retention. Note that *apart from* means *in addition to*.
62. 1; Definitely true. Elementary education is, of course, a duty of the government. But the second sentence mentions "investment in elementary education". This means that elementary education is a type of investment too.
63. 2; Probably true. The failure implies that the planners *probably* did not pay due attention to this aspect.
64. 4; Probably false. The passage neither claims nor contradicts that NCERT is the *only* such body. But our commonsense tells us that this is more likely to be false.
65. 3; Data inadequate. There has not been any mention of any improvement after 1990.
66. 1; Definitely true. The first sentence says that India's health is poor but health status has improved. This means that the given inference is true.
67. 2; Probably true. Infant survival conditions have improved but read the first sentence that says that health status has improved, but is still poor. Most likely, the improvement has been from 'very bad' to 'so so'.
68. 1; Definitely true. See the last sentence ("inter-regional disparities").
69. 4; Probably false. Although the passage neither claims nor denies that reports of UNDP are the *only* authentic reports, our commonsense tells us that such a conclusion is most likely to be false.
70. 3; Data inadequate. No doubt India has improved vastly from 1951 to 1992. Yet we must also know the performance of other countries to reach any definite conclusion.
71. 5; Definitely false. The first sentence clearly says that liberalisation does not imply "no regulation at all".

72. 1; Definitely true. The whole passage is on this very theme: that regulation should not be excessive but there must be *some* regulation and that must be done sensibly.
73. 1; Definitely true. Otherwise the financial system will display "its own excesses".
74. 3; Data inadequate. The passage mentions the chances of excessive speculation in the capital markets (i.e., stock markets) in the age of liberalisation but no information is presented about what used to happen in the pre-liberalisation age.
75. 2; Probably true. Although there is no definite information yet the meritorious views put forth indicate that the author knows economics very well.
76. 1; The last line says that if excessive emphasis is laid on economic growth it will postpone social welfare and leave 'in the cold a substantial section of the society.' This and the overall tone of the passage indicate that a major chunk of our society does need social welfare programmes. But still, the inference is 'probably true' and not 'definitely true'. The reason is the word *desperate*. It is not explicitly stated that people 'desperately' need social welfare programmes.
77. 2; At one time the FM said that welfare programmes would start once the fiscal imbalances were controlled. He now says that these programmes would start only after growth gathers momentum. It is clear that he is not consistent in his thought.
78. 4; The author complains that the FM has not fulfilled his promise of starting welfare programmes after fiscal imbalances were controlled. His complaint obviously implies that fiscal imbalances have been controlled and yet welfare programmes have not been started. Also, the FM now says that welfare programmes would start after growth gains momentum. But economic growth cannot be possible in a state of fiscal imbalance. So, fiscal imbalances must have cleared up by now.
79. 2; Obvious.
80. 3; The author says that the FM promises to start welfare programmes once growth gathers momentum. This, he says, may 'postpone indefinitely' the promise of a reform with a human face. The use of the word 'indefinitely' here indicates that the process of growth gaining momentum may not be quick. However, it is not explicitly stated that this process is time-taking. Hence, the inference is probably false but not definitely false.
81. 1; The first line talks about a country having a dominant public sector while, in the same breath, another line mentions that private sector in India should, therefore, change. It is obvious that the passage is talking about India. Hence the inference is definitely true.
82. 5; Definitely false. The last line implies just the opposite: that private sector used to ignore technological changes.

83. 2; Probably true. The passage clearly mentions that the Indian market is now subject to global producers too. This will definitely put pressure on private sector and many private industries may suffer as a result of this increased competition. But the inference can not be declared as definitely true because it is a type of forecast and nobody can predict the future with certainty.
84. 1; Definitely true. Those who are into exports have already been competing with foreign companies and hence, for them, there is no change in the prospects. Those who are catering to domestic demand are now open to global competition and hence subject to new pressures.
85. 3; Data inadequate. No hint of such nature is made anywhere in the passage.
86. 2; It is likely that the Soviet Union could not have been the member of a body which it so vehemently opposed.
87. 2; The second sentence of the passage says that the IMF was accused of being a promoter of economic imperialism. But this sentence is preceded by the first sentence, which says that things have changed. Most probably, this change is in the opinion of such countries about IMF.
88. 5; Definitely false. The last two sentences clearly indicate that a communist country used to have economic relations only with another communist country or a third-world country. USA belongs to neither of these categories.
89. 3; Both the facts are true: one, that the world economic scenario has changed and, two, that the communist countries have changed their stance. But it is not clearly stated anywhere in the passage whether the latter is a cause and the former is an effect.
90. 3; It is not mentioned clearly in the passage whether GATT indeed exploited its host countries, let alone stopping this exploitation.
91. 3; There is no information to compare Pakistan and India both of which are South Asian nations.
92. 2; The passage says that in South Asia *almost* half of the population is illiterate. Now, India is in South Asia. So, even in India, *almost* half of the population is *probably* illiterate. (Probably and not definitely so, because the passage talks about South Asian region in general and there may be intra-regional variations.) Now, if we add to our knowledge that India has roughly 100 million people, the conclusion is: *almost* 50 million people are probably illiterate. So, given inference is probably true. Not definitely true because we can't say if the figure is exact.
93. 1; Definitely true. The second sentence clearly says that South Asian countries face "gender inequality .... as compared to developed nations."
94. 2; Probably true. The passage clearly says that South Asian nations are poor. But poverty and GDP are not the same thing. Poverty has more to do with per capita income. Thus, a country of 1 million people with

$10000 million GDP is richer than a country of 100 million people with $100,000 million GDP because the per capita income in the former is $10000 while in the second it is $1000 per man, although the farmer has less GDP. Hence, the inference is probably true but not definitely true.

95. 4; Probably false. It is extremely unlikely in a region of "gender inequality" and of women being objects of "mental oppression".

96. 2; The first sentence of the passage hints at it. But no clear-cut statement is made. Hence, probably true but not definitely true.

97. 4; If they eat less fat they are not likely to be overweight. Hence, the inference is likely to be false. But it is not definitely false in the light of the given facts. Hence, probably false.

98. 1

99. 3; Sufficient data is not given. It is 'one of the lowest' in Asia. But this neither supports nor contradicts the inference that it is 'the lowest'.

100. 2; The last sentence of the passage says the same thing. But that sentence itself is not sure: it uses the phrase 'may be'. Hence, the given inference is 'probably true' but not 'definitely true'.

101. 1; It was 50000. It has now been raised by three times.

102. 2; The last sentence mentions that the raising of ceiling has helped candidates present realistic accounts. It means that candidates do present their accounts. In the light of these facts, the inference is likely to be true. But, the passage never gives a clear-cut hint. Hence, the inference is not definitely true. It is probably true.

103. 2; The Election Commission has tried to reform three areas, one of which is 'payment to the voters'. In this light, the inference must be true. But the passage does not clearly say that payments used to be made to the voters. It only says that the EC is seeking to control these areas. Hence, the inference can only be taken as probably true but not definitely true.

104. 3; No such information is there in the passage. Read carefully if you are getting confused.

105. 5; This inference is just the opposite of the last sentence of the passage which says that many candidates have sticked to the ceiling.

(Q.106-110): The choices 'data inadequate' is applicable to all the questions except Q. 109 where probably false should be chosen. The reason is that neither supporting nor contradicting data is present in the case of these inferences [except Q. 109]. No hint is given in the passage, for example, whether Tehri Dam evacuees were compensated or not. How do we know whether the 33 families of Patri will shift easily or offer resistance? How do we know if Rs 26 lakh is adequate? How can we check if Mr Ahsan indeed introduced some forestry reforms? But we can say that the army is less likely to decline the proposal to shift its Raiwallah cantonment. It is because they are being offered 220 hectares of land (in place of existing 63) and they will not have to spend any amount on building a new ammunition dump. We cannot really assert whether the army will accept or reject this proposal. But, according to the given passage, it is a tempting offer because the author uses the word *lure* for it. This means that, in the eyes of the author, the offer is unlikely to be declined by the army. Hence, it is probably false that the army will not agree to shift Raiwallah cantonment.

106. 3 107. 3 108. 3 109. 4 110. 3

111. 1; Definitely true. Indian seismic sniffer at Gauribidanoor can also 'sniff' nuclear sounds of China.

112. 4; The passage says that the Gauribidanoor sniffer can detect nuclear sound from *as far as* Lop Nor in China. The use of the phrase *as far as* indicates that the Gauribidanoor sniffer has a good range. Now, the first sentence of the passage states that any seismic centre with a good range must have a good location. Thus, Gauribidanoor must have a good location. In view of this, the given inference is probably false.

(Q. 113-115): *The second-last sentence of the passage can be broken as:*

(i) The US made a promise to Pakistan.

(ii) The promise was that the seismic facility would help the US to get around the Pressler Act.

(iii) The Pressler Act could be gotten around because the Congress could be convinced that

(iv) the seismic facility would help monitor Pakistan's nuclear non-involvement.

(v) The US has extracted a major concession from Pakistan.

Now, look at (iv). It says that the seismic facility could help in monitoring the nuclear activity of Pakistan. It means that the seismic facility was to be set up either in Pakistan or some place not very far from Pakistan. But if the facility were to be set up in some other country, why would the US make any promise to Pakistan? And why would it be called a 'concession' from Pakistan? This means that the seismic test centre is to be probably set up in Pakistan itself. This makes the inference of Q. 113 'probably true'. (It is not definitely true because we can not be sure.) Now, look at (iii) and (iv). Together, these two imply that Pressler Act comes into force if the US Congress is not convinced about any country's non-involvement in nuclear activities. Hence, Pressler Act is probably an anti-nuclear act. This makes the inference of Q. 114 probably false (but not definitely false). Now, look at (v). If this agreement is called a 'major concession' from Pakistan, it means that Pakistan has lost more than it has gained in the deal. This means that it was probably less than willing for the agreement. This makes the inference of Q. 115 probably true.

113. 2 114. 4 115. 2

116. 1; That's what the entire passage is about.

117. 1; The passage says: "... the government simply cannot create enough public universities to satisfy the demand."
118. 3; There is no information about developed countries.
119. 4; Probably not if private not-for-profit universities are encouraged.
120. 5; The passage says that "guidelines ... should be made clear, ..." Which means the guidelines are there.
121. 2; Aviation is an example of infrastructure.
122. 1; The last two sentences clearly state this.
123. 3; Not clear from the passage.
124. 1; That we are talking of achieving true potential implies that the potential exists.
125. 3; Nothing can be said about the past.
126. 5; China, Japan and India also have robust economies.
127. 4; India and China seem to be in that position.
128. 1; South Korea adopted "outward- oriented economic policies" while India continued with "import substitution policy".
129. 5; Clear from the last sentence of the passage.
130. 2; The Asian growth stories mainly revolve around India and China.
131. 5; The confounding multiplies with the quantum of wealth.
132. 1; Read the fourth sentence.
133. 2; Because there are more investment options at present.
134. 4; Remember the "clutter and noise".
135. 3; No information about fund managers.
136. 5; The movie has been used just as an example of how repeated interactions acquaint us with a fuller meaning.
137. 2; Could even have been 'definitely true'. Except that Q 138 below is a sure shot.
138. 1
139. 3; It could be given to any individual or any business team.
140. 4; Note the tone in "Have you *ever* seen ... ?"

Exercise 5C

1. A; This item asks you to describe the logical structure of the argument. The author cites the position of those who oppose government regulations and mentions some of the reasons they give for their position. Then the author introduces an example in which regulation was essential and successful. (A) best describes this tack.

As for (B), when you attack the motives of an opponent, as opposed to the argument of the opponent, you make what is called an *ad hominem* attack, but the speaker here doesn't make such an attack. As for (C), though the author does attack the position he cites, he does so by counter-example, not by pointing to any contradiction. As for (D), the author never raises the issue of what constitutes a proper mode of argumentation. Without any such theoretical justification, he simply launches his attack by counter-example. Finally, as for (E), the author never suggests that any of the terms of judgments involved are based on anything but objective, economic facts.

2. E; This item asks you to determine what is implied by the argument, that is, what is implicit in the argument. (E) is the correct choice. The speaker states that modern viewers, accustomed to the dull colours, were startled and even offended by the result of the restoration. We may infer from this that the cleaning restored the original, brighter colours.

As for (A), the passage deals with the restoration, not with the artistic merit of the work itself. (B) and (D) both represent misreadings of the paragraph. The author implies that the damage was the result of the natural process of the passing of centuries. Finally, as for (C), the author is not critical of the restoration. He even notes that it was conducted under the supervision of a team of experts. If anything, the author implies criticism of those who did not like the result of the restoration.

3. B; The main point of the passage is that most writers don't fare well. This is why the author quotes T.S. Eliot, who, somewhat ironically, points out that even most people who claim to be writers aren't really *successful* writers.

4. E; This question asks you to look for an alternative causal linkage. The passage implies that, given the legal actions to stop poaching, the elephant population should not have declined, but it did. What would explain that? (E) gives a very good explanation - another cause was working at the same time.

5. B; This is a problem involving deductive arguments. Assume that the initial statements are true. Then test each choice. I is not necessarily true. For example, even though it is true that when it is raining, there are clouds in the sky, you cannot conclude from the fact that there are clouds in the sky that it is raining. III makes the same error. II, however, is inferable. It's like reasoning as follows: When there are no clouds in the sky, it is not raining. It is raining, therefore, there are clouds in the sky.

6. A; Again, you are looking for an alternative causal explanation. The explanation for the paradoxical result is that there was not an increase in the *incidence* of rape, but an increase in the number of cases reported.

7. A; This item requires that you draw a further inference from the material given. The speaker claims that for years architects were not interested in ornamentation. They wanted simple, light lines. Then, the author states that we are seeing a re-evaluation of this attitude - as exemplified by a current exhibition. We may infer from this that the re-examination is prompting a renewed appreciation of the function of ornamentation.

8. D; This is one of those items that ask you to find alternative causal explanations. Here, you are asked to find the one choice that does not provide an alternative explanation that would help eliminate the paradox.

Every choice but (D) suggests a way of eliminating the paradox. *(D), however, if anything, strengthens the paradox by eliminating a possible way of explaining away the paradox.*

9. E; Stronger patent laws increase protection; protection encourages investment; investment often raises productivity. Thus, stronger patent laws initiate a chain of events that often culminates in improved productivity. Choice E expresses that and is, therefore, the best answer.

Choice A is inappropriate because the role, if any, that financial institutions would play in investments is left open. The increased productivity mentioned in B may mean fewer hours of labour for a given level of output, and may, thus, threaten jobs. Investments of the sort described in C may already be at the lowest possible level. The passage gives no indication that there has been an economic recession as D suggests; hence, there is no attempt to isolate the causes of economic recessions.

10. D; If more pepper was sold than produced, some sales must have come from surplus stocks, and those stocks must have dropped during the three-year period in question. Therefore, D is the best answer.

Choice A is inappropriate because the information in the passage is consistent with pepper being a profitable crop if grown on a modest scale. The passage provides no figures on which to base estimates of the world consumption of pepper, such as those made in B. Choice C is inconsistent with the information in the passage that states that world production will not return to previous levels unless either the pepper acreage lost to cocoa is replaced or the reduced remaining acreage is made more productive. No clear inferences can be made about the grower's profits in the last three, or any earlier years. So, E is inappropriate.

11. A; The technologically illiterate among the young people cannot make informed decisions about technological issues that are increasingly a part of the referenda. Informed decisions require knowledge. Therefore, choice A can be inferred and is the best answer.

Choices B, C and D are inappropriate because while the passage presents a problem and allows the general outlines of a solution to be inferred, specific solutions such as those presented in B and C go beyond what can be inferred, as do recommendations like D that address potential problems that are not touched on in the passage. Choice E is too specific. The passage supports the conclusion that some young people will be unable to make informed decisions, but it suggests nothing about the kinds of errors young people might make.

12. B; If, as the stimulus states, the electorate is split evenly between two parties and then a third-party candidate attracts votes from only one of the two parties, even the party that loses no votes to the third party is

unlikely to capture more than one-half of the votes. Therefore, B is the best answer.

Choice A is inappropriate because it contradicts information given in the passage, while C goes beyond the passage, which does not exclude new voters from those "who might otherwise have voted for one of the two major candidates". The information given in the passage is not specific enough to make the inferences about the politics, or the founding, of the third party, as suggested in D and E.

13. A; Ethno-fractionalisation is characteristic of a continent with many tribes that are ethnically different. Statement (B) is flawed: Angola and Ethiopia are not given as worst-case examples. Alternatives (D) and (E) are not true. Alternative (C) is the second best summarisation, even though warfare is at most inferred.

14. D; Alternative (D) cannot be implied from the statement. There is no information in the statement that implies that wives earn more than husbands. Alternative (A) may be implied because as wives contributed to the household nominal income, if prices increased at the same rate as the income, real income would stay the same. Alternatives (B) and (C) are implicit in the statement.

If the added income contribution of wives leaves average family income at the level it was 20 years ago, then the reason must be that the price level was lower 20 years ago. So, (E) is implied.

15. B; Choice (A) is vague, while (D) equates services trade with legislation. Choice (C) is irrelevant to the argument. (E) comes close to summarising the argument but it is incomplete. *Un-coordinated* is not an antonym for *coherent*.

16. C; The statement's conclusion is that all towns have unsavoury characters. This conclusion is false. According to the passage, only towns with pool halls have unsavoury characters and since we cannot infer that all towns have pool halls, conclusion (C) is wrong. Alternatives (A) and (B) are stated in the passage, while alternatives (D) and (E) can be deduced.

17. C; The sentence does not contain cue words which could help the reader identify premises and a conclusion. However, two sets of arguments may be identified:

1. All team sports have socialist tendencies.
2. Baseball is a team sport.
3. Baseball has socialist tendencies.

and

1. Individual subordination to authority is a form of socialism.
2. All players in team sports are subordinate to their coaches.

18. E; According to the passage, all people cannot take aspirin without undesirable side effects and, in some cases, the danger caused by aspirin

itself outweighs its benefits. The passage, by saying "On balance, however, for men aged 40 and over, an aspirin a day may present ....", also implies that not all, but only some people (men over 40) should take an aspirin a day. Clearly, alternative (A) cannot be concluded from the passage. Answer alternative (B) is also inappropriate. No painkiller other than aspirin is mentioned in the passage, and it cannot be inferred that all painkillers reduce the "stickiness" of platelets. (C) is incorrect. Smoking is not mentioned in the passage and, since studies of the effects of smoking and aspirin have not been reported, no conclusions can be drawn. (D) is wrong because the statistics given in the passage say that 15% of second heart attack victims were saved from death by taking aspirin, and 15% does not constitute a majority. (E) is the correct choice since it simply states that mortality rates can be reduced in patients who have already suffered a heart attack (as stated in the passage), without giving any specific statistics.

19. D; The writer has strong views on terrorist acts and on the policies adopted by Western European governments in handling them. The writer's main premise is that these governments are wrong when they concede to any of the demands of a hijacker or other terrorist - or any other criminal for that matter - because then they are conveying an impression of weakness and the perpetrator will feel that he or she will be able to win concessions and achieve his or her aims on subsequent occasions. Therefore, (D) is the correct answer. The statements in alternatives (A), (B) and (C) may all be statements on which the writer may concur, but they cannot be concluded with certainty from the text. Statement (E), on the other hand, is a statement with which the writer would probably not agree but, in any case, it cannot be inferred or concluded from the paragraph.

20. C; The paragraph demonstrates from beginning to end that the function of the food technologist is to prevent unfit foodstuffs from being marketed by the stores and passed on to the consumer, who relies on the store's control procedures. (C), therefore, is the most appropriate answer. Answer alternative (A) is inappropriate because it cannot be inferred from the text (even if it were true). Answer (B), and possibly, answer (D) are factually correct, but these conclusions cannot be drawn from the text itself. (E) is not a correct interpretation of the facts; random checking is not the best way, since below-standard goods are caught in the net only by chance.

21. B; Although a strong personality might have some resistance to the psychological dependence factors of drug use, it cannot be stated with any certainty that a strong personality can prevent physiological dependence. In this way, (A) is not a reasonable conclusion.

Psychological dependence on heroin is greater than that on alcohol and marijuana, but it is not stated to be the 'greatest' since psychological dependence is also great on cocaine and amphitamines. There is no conclusive evidence in the text to support this view. (C) is not, therefore, a reasonable conclusion.

A safe drug implies no danger of addiction and since it cannot be shown that there is no danger of addiction to alcohol, statement (D) is also not valid.

Although short-term use of certain drugs for medical purposes rarely produces dependence, long-term use of certain drugs often causes physiological dependence; in this respect (E) is not a valid assumption.

(B) is the only conclusion that can probably be true. Statistics show that many hard-drug addicts and regular users started their habit by taking drugs for 'kicks. Also, the search for drugs to be used for 'kicks' almost inevitably causes exposure to localities where harder and more addictive drugs are available, thus increasing the chances of attempting more addictive drugs for 'kicks'. The passage states that the circumstances in which the drug is taken is one of the factors controlling the risk of becoming dependent and also that it can be demonstrated that people who have taken drugs for fun are more likely to become dependent on the drug.

22. C; Here, we have a chain of events when the conclusion of one argument becomes the premise for another. Only (C) can be concluded from the facts given in the passage - that is, because Sally overslept, she ran towards school, and because she ran, she did not notice the hole. Choice (A) is inappropriate because the chain of events is not linked by the fact that Sally did not eat her breakfast. The passage does not include a consequence emanating from that fact. Choice (B) is not appropriate because there is no way to link Sally's friend to the events in the passage. Similarly, facts not included preclude (D) from being the appropriate answer. Finally, (E) cannot be inferred, as we do not know what Sally did later that day; she may have been released from the hospital and gone to school.

23. E; Services will be improved, it is hoped, for a certain segment of customers — those that shop during the rush hours — but not for all customers. This fact makes choice (A) inappropriate. To attract new customers is not stated in the passage as an objective, so (B) is inappropriate. The utilisation of excess capacity, as in (C), is a useful by-product of the new system, but it is not the main goal. If maintenance costs are kept low it will probably make the achievement of the main goal that much easier, but this is not the major objective; so choice (D) is not appropriate. The principal purpose of the owners is to make more money from the change by increasing income by an amount worth more than the added costs. Therefore, (E) is the appropriate answer.

24. A; Choice (A) sums up the conclusion of the passage and is thus the appropriate answer. It combines the intention of the car manufacturers - to produce more cars - with the chosen method, dividing labour into component tasks. Choice (B) may have been a further outcome of implementing this policy, but the passage does not comment on this; therefore, (B) is not appropriate. Choice (C) mentions another direction in which the car manufacturers may have moved, i.e., opening larger plants, etc. and this process may have been assisted by what is discussed in the passage, but again this cannot be concluded from the passage. So, (C) is also inappropriate.

Choices (D) and (E) are both concomitant with the division of labour process - (D), a disadvantage, and (E), an advantage - but neither of them can be inferred from the passage and therefore are inappropriate.

25. B; The statement in choice (A) cannot be inferred or concluded. We may conclude that slow growth may reduce inflation since the United States is pursuing such a policy as part of a concern to curb inflation, but we may not infer or conclude that slow growth can prevent inflation. According to the passage, investment in industry in Japan has been shown to lead to low, not high, inflation; so, choice (C) is not appropriate. The statement in choice (D) is partially correct since increased productivity has lowered the rate of inflation in Japan. However, this has been coupled with lowering of production costs. Statement (D) is insufficient by itself, and so is not the correct choice. The statement in (E) is a correct interpretation of the US economic policy, but it is not a proven statement, and it cannot be concluded on the basis of the paragraph provided. The text does not state that the United States must curb inflation before improving industry; it merely states that this is the current policy and understanding. Choice (B) is the correct choice. Since modernisation lowers costs of production, this increases competitiveness and business activity. This has been demonstrated by Japan's high productivity, export record, and low inflation. Slow growth in the United States has had the opposite effect on industry, causing a decrease in efficiency and production. Therefore, (B) is the only conclusion that can be drawn.

26. C; Statement (A) cannot be deduced from the text. It is an untrue statement: a contraceptive is something that can prevent conception and the drug discussed here does not prevent conception. Therefore, (A) is an incorrect choice. Statement (B) is also an untrue statement. The drug is reported to block egg implantation, not egg production. There is nothing in the paragraph concerning the drug's effectiveness, side-effects, benefits, or dangers as compared to other abortion techniques, so there is no basis on which the reader can deduce or infer that the new drug will

replace conventional abortion techniques. So, (D) is not appropriate. Although the drug has been manufactured and tested in France, there is no indication that its use will be limited to that country alone, so statement (E) is not valid. The statement in (C) is the only limited statement that can be deduced from the text - that the drug RU486 can be used to induce abortion, thus terminating pregnancy.

27. B; Improvement in quality and professionalism can only be ensured if the most suitable candidates are chosen. Since positive discrimination does not guarantee this, statement (C) is not valid. Similarly, statement (D) only ensures that the most suitably qualified candidate from a minority group will fill the position and he or she might be less well-suited than a candidate from a non-minority group. Therefore, (D) is an incorrect choice. Positive discrimination cannot be shown to be capable of eradicating prejudice, as claimed in (E): this is a totally separate issue and is not covered within the realm of the text. Statement (A) is probably a correct statement of fact, but it is not the basis of Jane's argument. Jane's argument is that, for better or worse, positive discrimination is a tool to be used to enable minority groups to play a more significant role in society. Because applicants from minority groups will receive more favourable consideration with a policy of positive discrimination, it can be assumed that they will receive opportunities. These opportunities are Jane's immediate and long-term objectives. Statement (B), which states all the above in one sentence, is, therefore, the best summary of Jane's position and the correct answer.

28. E; Sentence (A) is a sublime idea, but it cannot be proven to be the intention of the manufacturer. Similarly, sentence (C) is true, but, again, it cannot be proven to be the prime motive of the manufacturer. Sentence (B) is a tactical move, not a motive or aim. Sentence (D) is untrue and so cannot be the prime aim of the manufacturer. Sentence (E) is the only statement that can be obtained from the paragraph and thus the appropriate answer.

Chapter Six

Evaluating Given Courses of Action

6.1: Introduction

In many of the competitive examinations, this type of questions has become a regular feature. In such questions, a situation is presented and some courses of action are suggested in the context of that situation. The candidate is asked to determine which of them should be followed.

6.2: Format of the problem

Usually, the question is asked in the following format:

Directions: In the following questions, a fact-situation is given followed by two suggested courses of action. A course of action is a step of administrative decision taken for improvement or follow-up action. Read the situation and then decide which of the given courses of action follow(s).

Mark answer:

A) if only course of action I follows;

B) if only course of action II follows;

C) if both the courses of action follow;

D) if neither follows; and

E) if the data given is inadequate, i.e., if in the light of the given information, it cannot be asserted with certainty whether a course of action follows or not.

Example:

Q. The plague epidemic has spread to many parts of the country.

Courses of action: I. Doctors should be asked to perform their duty religiously.

II. The government should take up a cleanliness drive across the country.

6.3: Technique

You should know why these questions are asked in the first place. Such questions are asked to test your ability to judge a problem correctly, to determine the root cause of the problem and then to prescribe a suitable course of action. As responsible officers, you will have to face many administrative challenges when the ability to decide on correct course of action will prove very important. Therefore, these questions are asked to test this very ability in you.

Let us come to the technique now. On the basis of the experience of coming across a large number of such questions, I can foretell you that basically there will be two broad types of patterns in such questions:

i) **one**, where the presented situation talks of a *problem* and the suggested courses of action talk of a *solution*;

and

ii) **two**, where the presented situation talks of a simple *fact* (not a problem, just a situation) and the suggested courses of action suggest ways of *improvement*.

Therefore, in solving questions of this type your utmost care should go to the first step. You must have understood the first step by now. It is:

First step: *Decide quickly whether the problem involves a problem-solution relationship or a fact-improvement relationship.*

Now that you have decided the type of the problem, you can go through the logical steps for each one of these as outlined below.

Type I: Problem-Solution Relationship

As already stated, in this type of questions, the suggestion involves a solution while the given fact is a type of problem. It is easy to see when a suggested course of action, in these cases, is suitable, and when it is not. **In the case of a problem-solution relationship, the suggested course of action will be declared suitable if:**

i) it does solve or reduce or minimise the problem;

and

ii) if it is a practical solution.

Now, by your everyday experiences, your common sense and your general knowledge you can easily judge whether a suggested course of action solves (or reduces or minimises) a problem. That is not difficult to guess. Next comes the problem of practicality. Here, you should check if the solution is applicable in everyday life, if it would be practical and wise to follow it, etc.

If you have not understood these points clearly, let us go over them in detail, one by one.

A. How to determine whether a suggested action reduces or solves a problem

If you are having problems in determining whether a suggested action reduces or solves a problem, then you can follow the following rules:

i) *Established fact*
ii) *Experiences predict so*
iii) *Logic predicts so*
iv) *Prevailing notion of truth*

i) Established fact: In certain cases, it may be an established fact that this problem is solved or reduced by this solution. The type of this established fact may be social, biological or sociological or anything. But it is universally acknowledged as a solution to the mentioned type of problem.

For example, it is a biologically established fact that malaria can be prevented by using safeguards against mosquitoes; it is a socially established fact that child criminals should not be treated as punishable wretches but they should be made to mend their ways, etc. Now, compare these with the following.

Ex 1: Statement: Malaria has been spreading rapidly in northern Rajasthan.

Course of action: Anti-mosquito liquids should be sprayed in northern Rajasthan. (√)

Ex 2: Statement: A child was caught in a train while attempting to steal the jewellery of a respectable lady.

Courses of action: **I.** The child should be severely beaten. (×)

II. The child should be handed over to child welfare society. (√)

[The inappropriate course of action has been attached a (×) mark while the appropriate one a (√) mark.]

ii) Experiences predict so: In some cases, the problem that is talked about may be relatively a new one. It will not be completely new but it will not be very old either. And, therefore, the solution cannot be declared as a universal fact. However, based on previous experiences, in the same or similar type of situations, it can be easily ascertained that the problem is indeed solved by this particular action.

For example, past experiences tell us that India has fallen victim to foreign powers only when it has not remained united. Past experiences also tell us that the dowry problem has not been solved despite several legislations being made against it. [Note that we are talking of experience and not established fact. It is not an established fact that whenever India develops lack of unity, foreign powers will come to rule us; nor is it an established fact that legislations cannot control the dowry problem; maybe a tougher legislation will; but till now, our experiences have proved otherwise.] Now, compare these with the following:

Ex 3: Statement: India is gravely endangered by several expansionist foreign powers.

Course of action: Efforts should be made that the Indians remain united for any eventuality. (√)

Ex 4: Statement: Casteism has become an integral part of our life, to an alarming extent.

Course of action: Strict legislation should be passed promoting inter-caste marriages. (×)

Explanation: Experiences tell that legislation could do nothing in the case of dowry. Casteism is equally deep rooted in our minds as dowry is. So, if legislation failed in the case of dowry, how could it be expected to succeed in the case of inter-caste marriages?

iii) **Logic predicts so:** In some cases, the presented problem may be almost new and hardly any experience of any kind on this type of problems may be available. In such cases, you will have to use your own logic and reasoning to see whether a particular problem is reduced or solved by a particular solution.

For example, we know that a balance-of-payments (BoP) crisis emerges when a country is short of foreign exchange, i.e., when its inflow of foreign currency is less than the outflow. In such cases, it is a mater of simple logic, that if exports were sought to be increased and imports reduced, then a reverse situation will occur and hence the BoP crisis will be averted. Similarly, it is a matter of simple logic of diplomacy that, if a hostile nation is trying to bring disharmony within our country, we should bring this act of interference before the international bodies so that the hostile nation stands at a disadvantage. Now, compare these with the following:

Ex 5: Statement: It appears that within two to three years India will again face a severe BoP crisis.

Courses of action: I. India should offer special incentives to its export-oriented industries. (√)

II. Custom duties on imports should be hiked. (√)

Explanation: This step would make imports costlier. Hence, imports will be reduced.

Ex 6: Statement: The terrorists are rising again in Punjab and Kashmir and Pakistan's hand behind these developments is obvious.

Course of action: India should knock at the doors of international bodies, asking them to declare Pakistan a terrorist state by furnishing proof of its involvement in terrorism in Punjab and Kashmir. (√)

iv) **Prevailing notion of truth:** In some cases, the presented solution would be considered a good solution as per the prevailing notions of truth or as per societal norms. For example, in Vedic culture of varna-hierarchy, it would not be considered a good idea to give martial training to a Brahmin boy even if he was very agile and well-built. It was not in conformity with the prevailing notions of truth, **then**. But today it is not so. As another illustration, imagine a pupil who is not very disciplined. One hundred years ago, it would have been a good idea to get that child caned by his teacher (remember the saying: spare the rod and spoil the child?). But today, the notions of truth have changed. Today it is universally acknowledged that beating a child is not a good way to discipline him.

Ex. 7: Statement: Most of our power-producing companies are running in losses.

Courses of action: I. Prospects of privatisation of these companies should be explored. (√)

II. Chances of inviting foreign capital into these companies should be explored. (√)

Ex. 8: Statement: Manvir got angry and beat his wife mercilessly.

Course of action: I. Manvir should be publicly caned. (×)

Comment: Even ten-twenty years ago, when Nehruvian model of socialist economy was dominant, suggestions of privatisation and foreign capital were taboo. But today we would accept both suggestions in Ex. 7 as correct. Again, in Ex. 8, caning is prescribed which would be an accepted punishment for medieval times but today public-beating is not considered a good punishment for even the most serious of offences.

B. How to determine whether a suggested solution is practical or not

So far we have focussed our attention on the first part of our approach: to determine whether a suggested action really solves or reduces a problem or not. But an important second part also remains to be checked: whether it is a practical solution. A suggested course of action may indeed solve a problem but in practical life it may not be advisable. If it were so, it would be useless. So this point, too, needs sound checking. Let us try to understand this point by way of a few examples:

(i) ***Are you killing a mosquito with a sword or, conversely, an elephant with a needle?***

The problem and the solution should be well-matched and should be in proportion. Too simple solutions are useless for too severe problems and, conversely, too severe solutions are not advisable for too simple problems.

For example, we know that indiscipline in our daily life is the problem of an average Indian and, therefore, it is desirable to have discipline. Suppose someone suggests that to solve this problem, military training should be made compulsory. Now, by general experience, it can be confidently said that military training would be a solution for indiscipline. Still, this is not a practical solution. It is too severe solution for a relatively small problem. It is like trying to kill a mosquito with a sword.

Again, let us take the problem of the declining life expectancy of the average Indian. Someone may suggest that to solve this problem children should not be allowed to shout. Now, logic may show us that this solution may at least reduce the problem to some extent, in this way: less noise → less blood pressure (B.P.) → less deaths due to B.P.-related problems → increased life expectancy. But can the solution be declared a practical solution? No. It would be too far-fetched, too simple a solution for a serious problem. It would be like killing an elephant with a needle.

Now, compare these with the following cases:

Ex 9: Statement: Reports show that a good reason for low productivity in India is lack of discipline.

Course of action: Military training should be made compulsory for all citizens. (×)

Ex 10: Statement: Reports show that the life expectancy of an average Indian is declining continuously.

Course of action: Efforts should be made to prevent children from making noises. (×)

(ii) ***Are you solving the problem or are you creating a new problem?***

A course of action may sometimes appear to be an obvious solution to the problem and you may be tempted to accept it. But a slightly deeper second look will quickly reveal that the problem will actually not be solved but, in fact, become worse.

As an example, we may consider the case of tax evasion in India. We know that many of the rich people show less income than they actually earn and thus they pay less taxes than what is due. This is called tax evasion and this generates black money. [It may be of interest to you to know that the total black money of India, deposited in foreign banks, is estimated to be somewhere between 5,000 and 10,000 crore rupees!] Now, it is the headache of all governments to try to stop this habit of tax evasion. One right step in this direction is to reduce the tax rate. For example, if the tax rate is 50%, then somebody will pay 2 lakhs as income tax if he shows his income as 4 lakhs. But if tax rate was reduced to 20%, then he would have no problem in showing his income 10 lakhs because he will have to pay only 2 lakhs as income-tax because of lower tax rate. The benefit of the latter option is that in this case he will show up more income and thus he will not try to 'hide' money. He will try to invest it somewhere which will ultimately help the country.

Now, suppose somebody suggests that the best solution is to abolish taxes altogether! If you look at this course of action, *prima facie* you may quickly accept it because it is definitely true that it will solve the problem of tax evasion. When there is no tax, why will anybody 'hide' money? But if you give it a second thought, it would be easy to see that this course of action is unacceptable. Taxes are levied so that the government has money to invest in welfare and development activities. If there are no taxes, there will be no money with the government and consequently no welfare and development activities.

The lesson of this example is that a solution should solve the given problem but it should not create new problems. In the above example, one has to have a suitable balance between the two options. A suggestion of 'lowering the tax rate' may be accepted but one of 'abolishing the taxes altogether' is not acceptable. Now, compare with the following examples:

Ex. 11

Statement: The problem of tax evasion has reached an alarming level in recent years.

Courses of action: **I.** The tax rate should be lowered. (×)

[Explanation: It has not been mentioned, by how much the tax rate should be lowered.]

II. The tax rate should be lowered in such a way that the benefits of non-evasion outweigh the disadvantage of a drop in tax collection. (√)

III. Taxes should be abolished. (×)

C. Some final tips

Generally, when you are to evaluate a suggested course of action you should **never** allow your individual perception to come into play. Many candidates get influenced by their own perceptions and thus choose wrong answers. You should give due weightage to the way in which public bodies and systems function and you should accept them even if you may not trust them. Think of yourself as the officer-in-charge concerned, who has to take the decision impartially and impersonally. This will help you choose the correct answer.

For example, consider the situation presented in Ex 11. In this case, a suggestion may come that an enquiry committee should be formed to find out the basic reasons for tax evasion and the possible ways to stop them. Now, you may not like this suggestion. It may appear too time-taking and slightly useless to you. But, remember, this is your personal and individual opinion. In our system of functioning enquiry committees do play an important role. [You must have noticed how, after any major scandal or upheaval, an enquiry committee is immediately formed.] It is a part of the bureaucratic process and you should give due respect to it. Now, compare with the following examples.

Ex 12:

Statement: The problem of tax-evasion has reached an alarming high in recent years.

Course of action: An enquiry committee should be set up to analyse the causes of tax-evasion and to suggest measures to stop it. (√)

Ex. 13

Statement: In the last Olympic Games, Indian squad fared badly and returned with only a bronze medal.

Course of action: An enquiry committee should be set up to analyse the causes of the debacle and to suggest measures for improvement. (√)

Type II: Fact: Follow-up Action Relationship

As already mentioned, the given statement and the suggested courses of action may have either a 'problem-solution relationship' or a 'fact-follow-up action' relationship between them. We have seen how to attempt questions of the first type.

The second type does not require any new skills. It is to be solved exactly on the pattern of the first type. Thus, you have to solve this problem in two steps: in the first step, determine whether the suggested action will help in an improvement of the situation and, in the second step, determine whether the two are properly balanced.

Ex 9 can be said to belong to this category. You may look at Ex 9 once more to reassure yourself about this second type.

Summary

To solve questions on 'course of action' first of all, decide whether it is a 'problem-solution' or 'fact-follow-up action' type.

If it is 'problem-solution', then accept the suggested course of action if
(i) you are convinced that the action would indeed solve or reduce the problem; and
(ii) the solution is a practical solution.

- In case you are having difficulty in deciding whether a suggested course of action will really solve a problem or not, ask yourself these questions.
  Is it an established fact?
  Do experiences predict so?
  Does logic predict so?
  Is it in conformity with the prevailing notions of truth?
- And, if you are having difficulty in deciding whether a solution is practical or not, ask yourself these questions:
  Are the problem and the solution properly balanced? (It shouldn't be 'too simple a problem, too severe a solution' or 'too severe a problem, too simple a solution'.)
  Will the solution not create another problem?

If it is a 'fact-follow-up action' type question, then accept the suggested course of action if
(i) you are convinced that the action would result in an improvement of the situation; and
(ii) the course of action is a practical suggestion.

- In case you are having difficulty in deciding whether a suggested course of action will really improve a situation, ask yourself these questions.
  Is it an established fact?
  Do experiences predict so?
  Does logic predict so?
- And if you are having difficulty in deciding whether a suggested course of action is practical or not, ask yourself these questions:
  Are the given situation and the suggested course of action properly related? (It shouldn't be 'too simple an action for a severe situation' or 'too severe an action for a simple situation'.)
  Will the suggested course of action create any new problems?

Some tips for quick answers

- **No either**
  In some cases, depending upon the situation, more than one course of action could be suggested. But they are almost never exclusive of each other. Thus, if both courses of action look correct to you, you should choose the choice "both follow" and not "either of them follows". **The choice** ***"either of them follows"*** **is very rarely correct** in practical life. **You can take this as a thumb-rule.**
- **Eliminate with the help of the certain**
  Usually, we are not sure about only one or two of the suggested courses of action. About the rest, we are sure whether they are to be accepted or rejected. For example, suppose a question gives you three courses of action: I, II and III. Suppose you find that I is surely to be rejected and III is surely to be accepted, but you are not sure about II. So, you can look for those choices that include III and exclude I. This will reduce your possible number of answer choices from 5 to 2 or may be even 1.
- **Remember some examples**
  Many of the questions in this chapter follow a usual, standard pattern. In such cases, it helps to keep some similar examples at the back of your mind. It would be immensely beneficial for you if you remembered the solved examples of this chapter in a rough manner.

Practice Exercises

Type-I: Exercise 6A

Directions: In each question below is given a statement followed by two courses of action numbered I and II. A course of action is a step or administrative decision to be taken for improvement, follow-up, or further action in regard to the problem, policy etc. on the basis of the information given in the statement. You have to assume everything in the statement to be true then decide which of the two given suggested courses of action logically follows for pursuing.

Give answer (a) if only I follows; (b) if only II follows; (c) if either I or II follows; (d) if neither I nor II follows; and (e) if both I and II follow.

1. **Statement:** The State Government has decided to declare "Kala Azar" as a notifiable disease under the Epidemics Act, 1987. Family members or neighbours of the patient are liable to be punished in case they do not inform the State authorities.

   Courses of action: I. Efforts should be made to effectively implement the Act.

   II. The cases of punishment should be propagated through mass media so that more people become aware of the stern action.

2. **Statement:** A group of school students was reported to be enjoying at a picnic spot during school hours.

   Courses of action: **I.** The Principal should contact the parents of those students and tell them about the incident with a real warning for the future.

   II. Some disciplinary action must be taken against those students and all other students should be made aware of it.

3. **Statement:** India's performance in the recent Olympic Games was very poor. Not even a single medal could be bagged by the players. The Government had spent Rs 5 crores in training and deputing a team of players to participate in the Olympic Games.

   Courses of action: **I.** India should stop sending players to the future Olympic Games.

   II. The Government should immediately set up an enquiry commission to find out the reason for India's dismal performance.

4. **Statement:** Every year, at the beginning or at the end of the monsoons, we have some cases of conjunctivitis, but this year it seems to be a major epidemic witnessed after nearly four years.

   Courses of action: **I.** Precautionary measures should be taken after every four years to check this epidemic.

   II. People should be advised to drink boiled water during winter season.

5. **Statement:** Footpaths of a busy road are crowded with vendors selling cheap items.

   Courses of action: **I.** The help of police should be sought to drive them away.

   II. Some space should be provided to them where they can earn their bread without blocking footpaths.

6. **Statement:** Since its launching in 1981, Vayudoot has so far accumulated losses amounting to Rs. 153 crore during the last ten years.

   Courses of action: **I.** Vayudoot should be directed to reduce wasteful expenditure and to increase passenger fare.

   II. An amount of about Rs. 300 crore should be provided to Vayudoot to make the airline economically viable.

7. **Statement:** The Indian electronic component industry venturing into the West European markets faces tough competition from the Japanese.

   Courses of action: **I.** India should search for other international markets for its products.

   II. India should improve the quality of the electronic components to compete with the Japanese in capturing these markets.

8. **Statement:** A recent study shows that children below five die in the cities of the developing countries mainly of diarrhoea and parasitic intestinal worms.

Courses of action: I. Governments of the developing countries should take adequate measures to improve the hygienic conditions in the cities.

II. Children below five years in the cities of the developing countries need to be brought under constant medication.

9. **Statement:** The sale of a particular product has gone down considerably, causing great concern to the company.

Courses of action: I. The company should make a proper study of rival products in the market.

II. The price of the product should be reduced and the quality improved.

10. **Statement:** The police department has come under a cloud with recent revelations that at least two senior police officials are suspected to have been involved in illegal sale of a large quantity of weapons from the state police armoury.

Courses of action: I. A thorough investigation should be ordered by the State Government to bring out all those who are involved in the illegal sale of arms.

II. State police armoury should be kept under the Central Government's control.

11. **Statement:** One of the problems the food-processing industry is facing is the irregular supply of raw material. The producers of raw material are not getting a reasonable price.

Courses of action: I. The government should regulate the supply of raw material to other industries also.

II. The government should announce an attractive package to ensure regular supply of raw material for the food-processing industry.

12. **Statement:** A leading US multinational engineering and construction firm is keen to invest in India in a variety of sectors ranging from power to land management.

Courses of action: I. Such multinational companies should not be allowed to operate in India.

II. India should encourage multinational companies from other developed countries to invest in power sectors to bring in a competitive climate

13. **Statement:** Mr X, an active member of the union, often insults his superiors in the office with his rude behaviour.

Courses of action: **I.** He should be transferred to some other department.

II. The matter should be referred to the union.

14. **Statement:** The Government should consider the possibility of increasing the software budget from the current Rs 20 crore to Rs 100 crore in the Eighth Plan, provided there are concrete suggestions for the utilisation of the funds.

Courses of action: **I.** The Government should consult the trade unions in this regard.

II. Software companies should submit detailed proposals to the Government.

15. **Statement:** Most of the development plans develop on paper only.

Courses of action: **I.** The incharges should be instructed to supervise the field-work regularly.

II. The supply of paper to such departments should be cut short.

16. **Statement:** Some serious blunders were detected in the Accounts Section of a factory.

Courses of action: **I.** An efficient team of auditors should be appointed to check the accounts.

II. A show-cause notice should be issued to all the employees involved in the irregularity.

17. **Statement:** The Government will slap legally enforceable penalties on coal companies defaulting on quality and quantity of coal supplies to bulk consumers, especially to the thermal power stations.

Courses of action: **I.** The requirement of coal for thermal power stations should be assessed realistically.

II. The coal companies should introduce welfare measures for their employees.

18. **Statement:** The officer incharge of a company had a hunch that some money was missing from the safe.

Courses of action: **I.** He should get it recounted with the help of the staff and check it with the balance-sheet.

II. He should inform the police.

19. **Statement:** Doordarshan is concerned about the quality of its programmes particularly in view of the stiff competition it is facing from Star and other satellite TV channels and is contemplating various measures to attract talent for its programmes.

Courses of action: **I.** In an effort to attract talent, Doordarshan has decided to revise its fee structure for the artists.

II. The fee structure should not be revised until other electronic media also revise it.

20. Statement: Youngsters are often found staring at obscene posters.

Courses of action: I. Children should be punished and penalised if they are found doing so.

II. Any display of such materials should be banned.

21. Statement: In spite of the Principal's repeated warnings, a child was caught exploding crackers secretly in the school.

Courses of action: I. All the crackers should be taken away from the child and he should be threatened not to do it again.

II. The child should be severely punished for his wrong act.

22. Statement: A train was derailed near a station while moving over a bridge and fell into the river.

Courses of action: I. The Railway authorities should clarify the reason of the accident to the Government.

II. The Government should allocate funds to compensate for the destruction caused.

23. Statement: Most of the children in India are not able to get education because they get employed to earn livelihood in their childhood only.

Courses of action: I. Education should be made compulsory for all children upto the age of 14.

II. Employment of children below the age of 14 years should be banned.

24. Statement: The Central Bureau of Investigation receives the complaint of an officer taking bribe to do the duty he is supposed to.

Courses of action: I. CBI should try to catch the officer red-handed and then take a strict action against him.

II. CBI should wait for some more complaints about the officer to be sure about the matter.

25. Statement: Courts take too long in deciding important disputes of various departments.

Courses of action: I. Courts should be ordered to speed up matters.

II. Special powers should be granted to officers to settle disputes concerning their department.

26. Statement: The Committee has criticised the Institute for its failure to implement a dozen of regular programmes despite an increase in the staff strength and not drawing up a firm action plan for studies and research.

Courses of action: I. The broad objectives of the Institute should be redefined to implement a practical action plan.

II. The Institute should give a report on reasons for not having implemented the planned programmes.

27. **Statement:** Financial stringency prevented the State Government from paying salaries to its employees for the last three months.

Courses of action: **I.** The State Government should reduce wasteful expenditure and arrange to pay the salaries of its employees.

II. The State Government should immediately curtail the staff strength.

28. **Statement:** The Finance Minister submits his resignation a month before the new budget is to be presented in the Parliament.

Courses of action: **I.** The resignation should be accepted and another person should be appointed as the Finance Minister.

II. The resignation should not be accepted.

29. **Statement:** The Librarian finds some cases in which the pages from certain books issued from the library are torn.

Courses of action: **I.** The Librarian should keep a record of books issued by each student and if the pages are found torn, strict measures should be taken against the child who had been issued that book.

II. Some funds should be collected from the children collectively to renovate the library.

30. **Statement:** The killer enteric fever has so far claimed 100 lives in some tribal villages in M.P. during the past three weeks.

Courses of action: **I.** The residents of these villages should immediately be shifted to a non-infected area.

II. The Government should immediately send a medical squad to this area to restrict spread of the killer disease.

31. **Statement:** Many pilgrims died in a stampede while boarding a private ferry to the holy place on the first day of the ten-day-long festival.

Courses of action: **I.** The Govt should immediately cancel the licences of all the private ferry operators with immediate effect.

II. The Govt should deploy an adequate number of its personnel to guide pilgrims on their journey to the holy place.

32. **Statement:** Some students of the local college were caught travelling in the train without purchasing valid tickets.

Courses of action: **I.** The parents of these students should be informed about the incident and requested to counsel their wards.

II. These students should be put behind bars for travelling without bona fide credentials..

33. Statement: A large part of the locality was flooded as the main pipe supplying drinking water burst while the workers of a utility company were laying cables in the area.

Courses of action: I. The civic authority should immediately arrange to repair the damage and stop loss of water.

II. The civic authority should seek an explanation and compensation from the utility company for the damage caused by them.

34. Statement: Millions of pilgrims are expected to take a dip in the Ganges at the holy place during the next fortnight.

Courses of action: I. The Govt should restrict the number of pilgrims who can take dip each day during the fortnight.

II. The Govt should deploy an adequate number of security personnel to maintain law and order during the next fortnight at the holy place.

35. Statement: The rate of inflation has reached its highest in last twenty years and there is no sign of it softening in the coming months.

Courses of action: I. The Govt should initiate steps like reducing Govt taxes on essential commodities with immediate effect.

II. Farmers should be asked by the Govt to sell their produce at lower prices.

36. Statement: There have been sporadic cases of stone throwing and damaging vehicles in the locality during the day following altercation between two local youth clubs last night.

Courses of action: I. The local police administration should arrest all those who are caught committing these acts.

II. The local police administration should call a meeting of office bearers of both the clubs of the locality to bring the situation under control.

37. Statement: A huge truck overturned on the middle of the main road and blocked most part of the road, causing a huge traffic jam.

Courses of action: I. The traffic department should immediately deploy its personnel to divert traffic through other roads.

II. The traffic department should immediately send men and equipment to move the truck and clear the road.

38. Statement: Some workers of the company making diamond jewellery were caught while there were leaving the premises as they were trying to smuggle small pieces of diamonds hidden in their purses.

Courses of action: I. The management of the company should immediately put on hold all activities in the premises till a fool-proof security system is in place.

II. The belongings of all the workers should thoroughly be searched before they leave the premises of the company.

39. **Statement:** A huge tidal wave swept away many fishing boats and hutments of the fishermen living along the coastline.

Courses of action: I. The fishermen should henceforth be restrainedfromconstructingtheirhutsalongthecoastline.

II. The local administration should send a team of officials to assess the extent of damage and suggest remedial measures.

40. **Statement:** A large number of invitees who attended the marriage function fell ill due to food poisoning and were rushed to various hospitals located in the area.

Courses of action: I. The government should ban such marriage functions till further notice.

II. The local hospitals should be advised by the government to provide best services to the affected people.

41. **Statement:** An increasing number of farmers prefer to avail loans from local moneylenders instead of the banks owing to complicated paperwork involved in banks.

Courses of action: I. Local moneylenders who charge interest rates lower than the banks should be punished.

II. Banks should simplify the procedure to avail of loans so as to suit the farmers.

42. **Statement:** A major river in the city was reduced to a polluted and dirty canal after tonnes of sewage made way into it over the years.

Courses of action: I. All those who dumped garbage and sewage into the river should be penalized.

II. The government should modify the sewage system and find an alternate way to dump the city's waste.

43. **Statement:** Water table in most parts of the State has gone down to such a level that its extraction for irrigation purposes is not economical any more.

Courses of action: I. Extraction of ground water for any purpose in the State should be banned for some time in order to replenish the water table.

II. The Government should make provisions for alternative methods of irrigation so that the farmers are not compelled to use ground water.

44. **Statement:** A university librarian reported increased cases of theft of books from the library.

Courses of action: I. Stricter security arrangements should be put in place in order to prevent such incidents.

II. All the students in the university should be made to pay a hefty fine in order to replace the lost books.

45. **Statement:** Indigenous tribes living near Amazon forests are cutting down trees to cover their basic needs, thus severely affecting the ecological balance in the area.

Courses of action: I. All the tribes living near theAmazon rain forests should be forced to shift to urban areas of the country.

II. The tribes should be allowed to continue doing so as they cut down trees for their basic needs and not for commercial purposes.

46. **Statement:** According to latest statistics, the number of rhinos killed by tigers was much more than the number of rhinos killed by poachers in a wildlife sanctuary.

Courses of action: I. Stricter regulations should be framed in order to punish the poachers.

II. As done in some sanctuaries, the areas where tigers hunt and the areas with dominant rhino population should be artificially separated.

47. **Statement:** A mid-air collision was narrowly avoided when the pilot of one of the aircrafts neglected the air traffic controller's instructions.

Courses of action: I. Pilots of both of the aircrafts should be immediately reprimanded by revoking their licenses.

II. The training of air traffic controllers should be improved and made more comprehensive in order to avoid such incidents in future.

48. **Statement:** Oil spill from the oil carrier of one of the biggest oil companies has severely affected the marine life in a large area near the Gulf region.

Courses of action: I. The oil company should be penalised for the negligence and the harm caused to the environment.

II. Efforts should be made to shift as many marine animals in the area as possible to safer habitats.

49. **Statement:** Many private schools have been reportedly denying admission to students from poor families while preferring those with sound financial background regardless of their merit.

Courses of action: I. Poor students should be encouraged to take admissions only in Government-run schools where such discrimination does not exist.

II. The government should enforce a certain percentage of seats for students from poor families in every school.

50. Statement: The number of malaria cases has been rising significantly in the city for the last few months.

Courses of action: **I.** The municipal authorities should take immediate steps to destroy the breeding places of mosquitoes and improve hygiene in the area.

II. A campaign to educate people about the ways to prevent the disease should be started using local media and social workers.

Type II: Exercise 6B

Directions: A statement is given followed by three courses of action. A course of action is taken for improvement, follow-up etc. Read the statement carefully and pick the correct answer choice.

1. Statement: Although advancement in medical sciences has raised life expectancy, the rate of child mortality remains high in India.

Courses of action: **I.** Efforts should be made to lower life expectancy.

II. Medical scientists should be asked to give up their jobs.

III. Efforts should be made to decrease the rate of child mortality.

1) I and II follow 2) II and III follow 3) I and II follow
4) Only I follows 5) Only III follows

2. Statement: A new case of fraud and misappropriation of Government fund has been detected in a certain state.

Courses of action: **I.** The case should be fully investigated.

II. The government should reconsider the mode of appropriation of its funds.

III. Officials concerned with the fraud should be punished.

1) I and II follow 2) II and III follow 3) I and III follow
4) All follow 5) Only II follows

3. Statement: Rapid growth of urban population has led to a severe shortage of living space resulting in a drop in living conditions.

Courses of action: **I.** The Government should draw plans for urban replanning and development.

II. All village-to-town migrations should be stopped.

III. The Government should demolish the five-star hotels and build people's cottages there.

1) Only I follows 2) Only III follows 3) I and III follow
4) I and II follow 5) All follow

4. **Statement:** The police has failed to protect the elderly citizens of the society. Only last week three old persons were killed at three different places.

Courses of action: **I.** The police should be asked to take special care of women and children.

II. The Government should bring a legislation against the killing of elderly people.

III. Criminals who are accused of killing elderly people should be prosecuted by the state.

1) Only I follows 2) Only II follows 3) Only III follows
4) III and II follow 5) None follows

5. **Statement:** Passengers travelling by the Indian Railways face a lot of hardships and inconveniences.

Courses of action: **I.** Efforts should be made to stop overcrowding in trains.

II. Facilities for safe and pure drinking water should be provided.

III. The railway stations and platforms should be made more clean and hygienic.

1) I and II follow 2) II and III follow 3) I and III follow
4) All follow 5) None of these

6. **Statement:** The problem of female infanticide has still not disappeared from our society.

Courses of action: **I.** Severe punishment should be given to those who indulge in female infanticide.

II. Efforts should be made to eradicate illiteracy.

III. Child labour should be banned.

1) Only I follows 2) I and II follow 3) II and III follow
4) I and III follow 5) All follow

7. **Statement:** Inflation is rising again.

Courses of action: **I.** Efforts should be made to find out the cause of this.

II. Fiscal deficit should be controlled.

III. Special efforts should be made towards drip-irrigation technology.

1) Only I follows 2) I and II follow 3) Only II follows
4) None follows 5) All follow

8. **Statement:** It is rumoured that there is a bomb in the Rashtrapati Bhawan.

Courses of action: **I.** The President should be escorted to a safe area.

II. A proper search of bomb should be carried out.

III. No attention should be paid to such baseless rumours.

1) Only III follows 2) Only I follows 3) Only II follows
4) Either II or III follows 5) I and II follow

9. Statement: Except cricket, our sportsmen have fared badly in international events.

Courses of action: **I.** All sportsmen (except those associated with cricket) should be stopped from getting any incentives.

II. Special promotion drive should be made to encourage sports.

III. International coaching and technology should be made available to our sportsmen.

1) Only I follows 2) Only II follows 3) Only III follows
4) II and III follow 5) Either I or II and III follow

10. Statement: There have been incessant rains in the north-eastern parts of our country. Chances of heavy floods are not being ruled out.

Courses of action: **I.** The Army should be given a notice to be on the alert.

II. Precautionary measures should be taken.

III. North-eastern parts of our country should be disconnected from the rest of India.

1) Only I follows 2) I and II follow 3) II and III follow
4) I and III follow 5) None follows

11. Statement: Indian space research is valuable not only because of its importance in defence and communication but also because it has value as a potential forex earner too.

Courses of action: **I.** India should step up its space research programme.

II. India should explore the commercial possibilities of its space research programme.

III. The defence aspect of Indian space research should be given secondary treatment.

1) Only I follows 2) Only II follows 3) I and II follow
4) II and III follow 5) All follow

12. Statement: India has been facing the problem of child labour despite several legislations.

Courses of action: **I.** India should treat child labour as a trivial issue.

II. Child labour should be declared civil offence.

III. Children indulging in such activities should be punished.

1) Only I follows 2) Only II follows 3) Only III follows
4) Either II or III follows 5) None of these

13. Statement: After the success of films such as *Hum Aapke Hain Kaun* and *Dilwale Dulhaniya Le Jayenge* good music and clean entertainment are back again.

Courses of action: I. Movies having good music and clean entertainment should be promoted.

II. The two movies mentioned above should be awarded for their clean entertainment.

III. The government should ban movies that are not like these two films.

1) Only I follows 2) Only II follows 3) I and II follow
4) I and III follow 5) II and III follow

14. Statement: Although launched with great fanfare, private mutual funds have performed badly.

Courses of action: I. Private mutual funds should be banned.

II. Operations of mutual funds should be controlled by the government.

III. Mutual funds should be given the government's protection.

1) Only I follows 2) Only II follows 3) Only III follow
4) II and III follow 5) None follows

15. Statement: Despite several efforts, AIDS appears to be spreading rapidly in India.

Courses of action: I. The government should confine people suffering from AIDS in a separate cell.

II. An awareness drive should be launched to increase awareness about AIDS.

III. Sexual promiscuity should be discouraged.

1) I and II follow 2) II and III follow 3) I and III follow
4) Only II follows 5) All follow

16. Statement: Some politicians have expressed apprehension over the government's proposal not to allow a wage hike for the loss-making PSUs. They think that this not justified.

Courses of action: I. The government should abandon its proposal.

II. The government should ignore the apprehension of these politicians and enact its proposals.

III. The government should consult the employees of the loss-making PSUs and listen to their point of view.

1) Either I or II follow 2) Only III follows 3) I and III follow
4) II and III follow 5) III and either I or II follow

17. Statement: The economic scenario of the country is improving rapidly. But some states like Bihar seem to be going from bad to worse.

Courses of action: I. President rule should be imposed in Bihar.

II. Heavy privatisation should be pursued in such states.

III. The governments of such states should be asked to re- evaluate their economic planning.

1) Only II follows 2) I and II follow 3) II and III follow
4) Only III follows 5) Either II or III follows

18. Statement: As a result of the efforts of some Pakistani spies and the collusion of some Indian scientists, vital secrets of ISRO are feared to have been leaked to Pakistan.

Courses of action: I. The security arrangement around the ISRO network should be tightened.

II. The Indian scientists involved in the scandal should be brought to court.

III. India should approach Pakistan and diplomatically ask her to return the secrets.

1) I and II follow 2) II and III follow 3) I and III follow
4) All of them follow 5) None of these

19. Statement: Indian press is sceptic about the government's plans to open Indian newsmarket to international competition. It is feared that Western press will pump biased opinion into Indian mind.

Courses of action: I. Indian Press should be convinced that its apprehensions are baseless.

II. Western press should not be allowed to come to India.

III. The government should set up a censor board for Western press.

1) Only I follows 2) Only II follows 3) Only III follows
4) II and III follow 5) I and III follow

20. Statement: Despite its various measures, the SEBI has not had much success in controlling the stock market. The brokers continue to flaunt rules making use of the loopholes therein.

Courses of action: I. The SEBI should be wound up.

II. The rules should be reviewed so that there are no loopholes in them.

III. The SEBI should be given more powers so that it could deal sternly with the erring brokers.

1) I and II follow 2) II and III follow 3) I and III follow
4) All of them follow 5) Only III follows

21. Statement: An IAS officer has been killed in Bihar by irate mobs. It is being suspected that the police played a deliberately inert role during the incident.

Courses of action: **I.** All IAS officers in Bihar should be given tight security.

II. The police officials concerned should be suspended.

III. The Chief Minister of Bihar should resign on moral grounds.

1) Only I follows 2) Only II follows 3) I and II follow
4) I and III follow 5) All follow

22. Statement: The new wave of the parallel cinema has become a sick industry. Plagued by lack of funds and willing talent, it has lost its appeal, which is an unfortunate development.

Courses of action: **I.** The government should provide financial aid to parallel cinema.

II. The parallel cinema should change itself to have commercial appeal.

III. People should be persuaded to watch parallel cinema.

1) Only I follows 2) I and II follow 3) Only II follows
4) II and III follow 5) I and either II or III follow

23. Statement: The pollution level in some parts of Delhi has reached an alarming level. Already, one day in Delhi means an involuntary smoking of 12 cigarettes.

Courses of action: **I.** Automobiles exceeding the pollution limit should be dealt with severely.

II. The government should close down some of the high-pollution industries in Delhi.

III. Cigarettes should be rationed in Delhi.

1) Only I follows 2) Only II follows 3) I and II follow
4) I and III follow 5) II and III follow

24. Statement: The salaries of private sector employees has nearly doubled in the past two years.

Courses of action: **I.** Higher income tax rate should be imposed on private sector employees.

II. The wages of public sector employees should also be doubled.

III. A further rise should not be allowed.

1) Only I follows 2) Only II follows 3) Either I or II follows
4) None follows 5) At least one of the above follows

25. Statement: Some bottles of cold drinks have been found to contain dead insects, flies and even lizards.

Courses of action: **I.** People should be told about these incidents.

II. Cold drink manufacturers should be punished and imprisoned for selling hazardous products.

III. The sale of cold drinks should be banned.

1) Only I follows 2) I and II follow 3) Only II follows
4) II and III follow 5) Only III follows

26. Statement: There has been a record jump in Kharif crop this year as a result of timely monsoon.

Courses of action: I. An enquiry commission should be set up to analyse the technical reasons of the jump.

II. Efforts should be made to maintain the growth rate of the crops.

III. The country should take adequate steps for food-storing facilities.

1) Only II follows 2) Only III follows 3) II and III follow
4) I, II and III follow 5) Either II or III follows

27. Statement: The economic policies of the government are being criticised by some economists as being opposed to the concept of social equality.

Courses of action: I. Since capitalism and social equality can't go together, the government need not bother about such criticisms.

II. The government should evaluate such criticisms for any possible merit.

III. The economic policies should be changed in such a way that social equality is included in its objectives.

1) Either I or II follows 2) I and III follow 3) Only II follows
4) II and III follow 5) All of them follow

28. Statement: There has been a spate of kidnapping in Delhi over the recent months.

Courses of action: I. The law and order situation should be tightened.

II. An anti-kidnapping squad should be formed within the police.

III. People should not be allowed to travel alone and unprotected during night hours.

1) Only I follows 2) I and II follow 3) I, II and III follow
4) II and III follows 5) Either I and II, or III follows

29. Statement: According to weather experts, heavy winds and storms are likely to occur in the coastal areas of Andhra Pradesh and Kerala.

Course of action: I. The weather experts should be awarded for their timely warning.

II. The fishermen of these areas should be forewarned not to venture into the sea.

III. The government should not air such reports because they disturb the people unnecessarily.

1) I and II follow 2) II and III follow 3) Only II follows
4) I and III follow 5) All of them follow

30. Statement: Despite the provision of legal punishments, the system of dowry remains prevalent in our society.

Courses of action: I. Focus should be diverted to proper execution of the legal provisions.

II. Stricter laws should be enforced by the Parliament against dowry.

III. The youth should be persuaded to rebel against their parents and indulge in no-dowry marriages.

1) Only I follows 2) I and II follow 3) II and III follow
4) All follow 5) I and III follow

31. Statement: The elections have become expensive and complicated. One of the reasons is that anybody can stand for election; this sometimes results in an extremely large number of candidates and awfully large ballot papers.

Courses of action: I. Not more than five people should be allowed to contest from one constituency.

II. A commission should be set up to suggest how to get over this problem without hurting the democratic nature of our elections.

III. Since, in a democracy, any citizen should be given the right to contest, we should accept the situation as inevitable.

1) I or II follows 2) II or III follows 3) I or III follows
4) I or II or III follows 5) None of the above

32. Statement: Recently, in an unfortunate development, more than 100 people were killed when the police resorted to lathicharge on a mob.

Courses of action: I. An enquiry commission should be set up to examine any avoidable reasons of the incident.

II. The police officer on duty should immediately be suspended.

III. The police trainees should be given a course on mob behaviour and group psychology.

1) I and II follow 2) II and III follow 3) I and III follow
4) I, II and III follow 5) I and either II or III follow

33. Statement: The fiscal deficit of the country is not likely to be contained within the 6.5% limit as prescribed by the IMF.

Courses of action: **I.** Efforts should be made to reduce the fiscal deficit.

II. Efforts should be made not to let the fiscal deficit grow anymore.

III. Efforts should be made not to allow IMF to interfere in our internal economic matters.

1) Only I follows 2) I and II follow 3) Only II follows
4) II and III follow 5) I, II and III follow

34. Statement: It has been observed that out of every 10 students who drop out of school before class X, eight are female students.

Courses of action: **I.** Efforts should be made to reduce the aggregate number of drop-outs at school level.

II. An awareness programme should be undertaken to tell people about the importance of female education.

III. Female education should be made legally compulsory with punishable violations.

1) Only I follows 2) Only II follows 3) Either II or III follows
4) Only III follows 5) I and either II or III follow

35. Statement: An official of the sports committee has been accused of corruption and favouritism.

Courses of action: **I.** The committee should sack the official immediately.

II. The committee should dismiss the allegation as mischievous talk.

III. The committee should suspend the official for the time being.

1) None follows 2) Only III follows 3) Either I or III follows
4) Either II or III follows 5) Any one of I, II or III follows

36. Statement: It has now been proved that most of the cases of leprosy are not infectious and that they are curable.

Courses of action: **I.** An awareness drive should be launched among people regarding this fact.

II. People should be encouraged not to boycott leprosy patients from the society.

III. Leprosy should be declared a risk-free disease by the government.

1) Only I follows 2) I and II follow 3) I and III follow
4) II and III follow 5) All follow

37. Statement: The demand for automobiles has slumped indicating a possible recession in the automobile sector.

Courses of action: **I.** The government should announce tax reliefs to the automobile sector.

II. The automobile sector should reduce the prices of the products.
III. The industrialists should look for some better business ventures than automobiles.

1) I and II follow 2) II and III follow 3) I and III follow
4) Only I follows 5) Only II follows

38. Statement: The neighbours suspect that the murderer could be one of the relatives of the deceased.

Courses of action: **I.** The relatives of the deceased should be interrogated.
II. The neighbours should be prosecuted for defamation.
III. The relatives of the deceased should be punished.

1) Only I follows 2) Only II follows 3) Either II or III follows
4) I and II follow 5) I and III follow

39. Statement: The red-tapism in our official work has become a nuisance.

Courses of action: **I.** The government should try to minimise the paper work.
II. The officials should be directed not to sit on files without justifiable reasons.
III. The official staff should be asked to remove red-tapism within the next ten days.

1) Only I follows 2) Only II follows 3) I and II follow
4) I and III follow 5) All follow

40. Statement: The demand for Indian garments in the foreign countries has registered a sharp growth.

Courses of action: **I.** An enquiry commission should be set up to examine the causes of this growth.
II. Garment manufacturing industries should follow strict quality control programmes.
III. Export of Indian garments should be banned.

1) I and III follow 2) Either I or II follows 3) Either II or III follows
4) Only II follows 5) Either II or I and III follow

41. Statement: According to one report, the cases of kidnapping have risen exponentially over the last couple of years.

Courses of action: **I.** Stricter laws should be enacted against kidnapping.
II. A separate monitoring cell should be created within the police department to monitor cases of kidnapping.
III. Children should be taught self-defence skills such as judo to keep kidnappers away.

1) Only I follows 2) I and II follow 3) I and III follow
4) All follow 5) Can't say

42. Statement: In a calamity, over 62 persons were frozen to death in Kashmir as a result of avalanches and landslides.

Courses of action: **I.** The government should give compensation to the kith and kin of the deceased.

II. The government should evacuate the affected areas immediately.

III. The government should come down heavily on terrorists.

1) Only I follows 2) Only II follows 3) I and II follow
4) I and III follow 5) All follow

43. Statement: The National Human Rights Commission has been set up for the purpose of evaluating the human rights scenario of the country and ensuring that gross violations of human rights do not occur.

Courses of action: **I.** The Government should conduct elections so that the NHRC (National Human Rights Commission) could be a democratic body.

II. The Government should extend all possible help to NHRC for its smooth functioning.

III. The NHRC should be given adequate powers to be able to handle the cases of human rights violations.

1) Only I follows 2) I and II follow 3) Only II follows
4) II and III follow 5) All follow

44. Statement: It is suspected that one of the main reasons behind the Jammu bomb explosion on this Republic Day could be the compliance of some government officials.

Courses of action: **I.** The Government should ask all government officials to go on leave until the truth is finally out.

II. The Government should set up an enquiry commission to look into the matter.

III. Security arrangements should be tightened in and around the area.

1) Only II follows 2) Only III follows 3) I and II follow
4) II and III follow 5) All follow

45. Statement: Crores of rupees are spent each year for the purpose of removing illiteracy, but the plan has failed to deliver.

Courses of action: **I.** The spending should be permanently abandoned.

II. The spending should be temporarily halted.

III. The government should employ funds in some more rewarding areas.

1) Only I follows 2) Either I or II follows 3) Only II follows
4) Only III follows 5) None of these

46. Statement: The film industry has been on the downslide because of the invasion of unauthorised videos.

Courses of action: **I.** Persons making unauthorised videos should be sentenced to life imprisonment.

II. The film industry should make commercially lucrative films.

III. The government should waive entertainment tax levied upon films.

1) Only I follows 2) I and II follow 3) II and III follow
4) I and III follow 5) None follows

47. Statement: As a result of communal tensions in the city, everyday activity has come to a halt.

Courses of action: **I.** The government should employ additional security.

II. Care should be taken to stop rumours from spreading.

III. Extremist religious leaders of both the communities should be jailed.

1) I and II follow 2) II and III follow 3) I and III follow
4) All follow 5) Only II follows

48. Statement: According to one survey, noise pollution in the metros is likely to make at least ten thousand people deaf in the next five years.

Courses of action: **I.** Noise pollution should be declared as the most sensitive issue by the ministry of health.

II. Fines should be imposed on vehicles, factories etc. that emit sound at a higher level than permitted.

III. People should be made aware of this prospect.

1) Only II follows 2) I and II follow 3) I and III follow
4) II and III follow 5) All follow

49. Statement: Because of heavy rains for the last three days, the water level of the river has crossed the danger mark.

Courses of action: **I.** The government should employ para-military personnel to meet any eventuality.

II. The health officials should gear up to face the onset of any disease.

III. Relief operations should be planned in advance.

1) I and II follow 2) II and III follow 3) I and III follow
4) I and either II or III follow 5) All follow

50. Statement: Some newspapers have alleged that some of our eminent sportsmen offered bribe to their adversary team to ensure victory.

Courses of action: I. The concerned sportsmen should be suspended from all active participation in sports.

II. The concerned sportsmen should file a defamation suit against the newspapers.

III. Proper enquiry should be done regarding the matter.

1) Only I follows 2) Only II follows 3) I and III follow
4) Only III follows 5) Either I or II and III follow

51. Statement: The Disciplinary Action Committee of the school has recommended that stern action be taken against students indulging in anti-social acts.

Courses of action: I. Students should be expelled if they still indulge in anti-social activities.

II. Students should be informed of the recommendations of the Disciplinary Action Committee.

III. The Disciplinary Action Committee should be asked to give a guarantee for the success of its recommendations.

1) Only I follows 2) Only II follows 3) Only III follows
4) I and II follow 5) II and III follow

52. Statement: Violence on an unprecedented scale is being feared in the next general elections.

Courses of action: I. Para-military forces should be employed in adequate number.

II. The Election Commission should be given emergency powers.

III. The elections should be postponed.

1) Only I follows 2) Either I or III follows 3) Either II or III follows
4) I and II follow 5) Only II follows

53. Statement: The office working committee has suggested that in view of the poor production in the company, efforts should be made to improve the work culture.

Courses of action: I. Performance-based incentives should be announced.

II. The workers should be informed of the committee's suggestions.

III. Those indulging in indiscipline should be fired.

1) I and II follow 2) II and III follow 3) I and III follow
4) Either I or III follows 5) Either I or II follows

54. Statement: It is feared that the food which the delegates have just consumed could be poisonous.

Courses of action: **I.** The delegates should be given treatment for food-poisoning.

II. The delegates should be rushed to a hospital.

III. Medical help should immediately be sought.

1) I and III follow 2) II and III follow 3) Only I follows
4) Either I or III follows 5) Either II or III follows

55. Statement: Indian books are not read in foreign countries. Lack of quality paper and less emphasis on fiction is said to be its main causes.

Courses of action: **I.** Non-fiction writers should be discouraged.

II. Fiction writers should be encouraged.

III. Indian paper industry should be given tax exemptions.

1) Only III follows 2) Only II follows 3) I and II follow
4) II and III follow 5) All follow

56. Statement: A heavy unseasonal downpour during the last two days has paralysed the normal life in the state in which five persons were killed but this has provided a huge relief to the problem of acute water crisis in the state.

Courses of action: **I.** The state government should set up a committee to review the alarming situation.

II. The state government should immediately remove all the restrictions on use of potable water in all the major cities in the state.

III. The state government should send relief supplies to all the affected areas in the state.

1) None 2) Only I 3) Only II and III
4) Only III 5) All I, II, III

57. Statement: A large private bank has decided to retrench one-third of its employees in view of the huge losses incurred by it during the past three quarters.

Courses of action: **I.** The Govt should issue a notification to general public to immediately stop all transactions with the bank.

II. The Govt should direct the bank to refrain from retrenching its employees.

III. The Govt should ask the central bank of the country to initiate an enquiry into the bank's activities and submit its report.

1) None 2) Only I 3) Only II
4) Only III 5) Only I and III

58. **Statement:** Many political activists have decided to stage demonstrations and block traffic movement in the city during peak hours to protest against the steep rise in prices of essential commodities.

Courses of action: **I.** The Govt should immediately ban all forms of agitations in the country.

II. The police authority of the city should deploy additional forces all over the city to help traffic movement in the city.

III. The state administration should carry out preventive arrests of the known criminals staying in the city.

1) Only I 2) Only II 3) Only III
4) Only I and II 5) None of these

59. **Statement:** The school dropout rate in many districts in the state has increased sharply during the last few years as the parents of these children make them work in the fields owned by others to earn enough for them to get at least one meal a day.

Courses of action: **I.** The Govt should put up a mechanism to provide foodgrains to the poor people in these districts through public distribution system to encourage the parents to send their wards to school.

II. The Govt should close down some of these schools in the district and deploy the teachers of these schools to nearby schools and also ask remaining students to join these schools.

III. Govt should issue arrest warrants for all the parents who force their children to work in fields instead of attending classes.

1) Only I 2) Only II 3) Only III
4) Only I and II 5) None of these

60. **Statement:** One aspirant was killed due to stampede while participating in a recruitment drive of police constables.

Courses of action: **I.** The officials in charge of the recruitment process should immediately be suspended.

II. A team of officials should be asked to find out the circumstances which led to the death of the aspirant and submit its report within a week.

III. The Govt should ask the home department to stagger the number of aspirants over more number of days to avoid such incidents in future.

1) Only I 2) Only II 3) Only III
4) Only II and III 5) None of these

Answers and Explanations

Exercise 6A

1. e; When the Government takes such an action it is necessary that people are made aware of the consequences they would face if they do not obey the directives. Hence, II follows. I is obvious.
2. e; If students are out of the school during school hours, it is a case of sheer indiscipline. Both I and II will tend to solve the problem. Also, both are suitable courses of action and not extreme actions. Both warning and some punishment are necessary: both follow.
3. b; I will not solve the problem: the problem is not *wastage of money*; it is *poor performance*. Also, it is an extreme action. Hence, I does not follow. II will be a positive action. The first step towards a cure is to know the disease. Hence, II follows.
4. b; Against an epidemic, precautionary measures should be taken *every year* and *not every four years*. Hence, I does not follow. But II is, of course, a positive step. It is a preventive action and it should be followed. Hence, I does not follow while II does.
5. e; Vendors are not meant for footpaths. So, they should be driven away from there. This is what I suggests. But will it not be an extreme action? Yes, it will be. The vendors earn their livelihood from that place and this action would snatch away their livelihood. This is what II suggests. But will it not be an incomplete action? Yes, it will be. How can we be sure that the vendors would leave the footpaths if they are given alternative means of livelihood? Therefore, the best action would be to provide alternative livelihood so that they earn their bread and to use force to drive them away so that footpaths are cleaned. Hence, both I and II follow.
6. a; The problem is: loss-making by Vayudoot. Will I solve the problem? Yes. Reducing wasteful expenditure and increasing fare would definitely reduce the losses. Will II solve the problem? Yes (it is obvious). Are I and II suitable actions? Yes, I is; but II isn't. To reduce wasteful expenditure is a welcome and harmless step. But it is not a wise thing to invest money in a loss-making unit. Vayudoot should be made to stand on its own feet and not to walk on others' legs. Hence, I follows but II does not.
7. e; First, if Indian companies face stiff competition, it would be advisable that they improve their quality to international standards, so that Japanese goods look "no better" to a buyer. Secondly, there is nothing wrong in searching for other markets as well. This would be a practical approach. In case Japanese companies drive them out of West European markets, Indian companies may fall back on these *alternative* markets. Hence, I and II both follow.
8. a; To improve the unhygienic condition is always a welcome step and in

view of the statement, it becomes even more necessary. Hence, I unquestionably follows. But II does not follow. We should not *medicate* any child unless he has actually contracted the disease. Prevention is all right but curing should begin only *after* the disease has been contracted.

9. a; If sale has gone down there must be some solid reasons. The company must know these reasons. Since I suggests a similar thing, it follows. But II does not follow. *The company should first know if price was a factor* behind the drop in sales. Without knowing this, reducing price may turn out to be a harmful action.

10. a; If such a serious allegation has been levelled, it must be thoroughly examined. So, I follows. But II is an arbitrary action. If officials of the state police can be corrupt, so can be the officials of the Central government. The issue is corruption and mere transfer of control will not solve this problem.

11. b; I is an absurd suggestion: when one industry is facing trouble because of regulations, it talks of regulating the supply of other industrial raw materials too! II is a better action because it would tend to solve the problem.

12. b; Such questions can only be answered in the context of contemporary values. In the age of Nehru, choice I would have been correct, II would have been blasphemy. But today, in the age of liberalisation, in the India of the nineties, I is not a correct action while II is.

13. b; If Mr. X insults his superiors in one department, he may insult them in another department too. Transferring him will not help; so I does not follow. Since Mr. X is an active member of the union, it would be advisable that the union be asked to pressurise him. Hence, II follows.

14. b; I is absurd; what do trade unions have to do with software budgets? II is a proper course of action. The statement says that it would consider the possibility of raising the software budget allocation **if** it receives concrete suggestions about how these funds be utilised. So, software companies should come forward and present their cases.

15. a; The statement mentions a problem that most of the development plans develop on paper only. They are not materialised in reality. This problem could be solved if field-work was supervised properly. Hence I follows. But II is an absurd suggestion. The issue is: *lack of actual field-work* and not *misuse of paper*.

16. e; First of all, if some blunders have been found, they should be rectified and rechecked. Hence, I follows. Further, it should also be known if the blunders were *errors* or *deliberate manipulations*. Hence, II should also follow.

17. a; If the government has decided that the coal companies would have to pay penalties if they fail to supply enough coal to thermal power stations, then it is also the government's duty to see that the thermal power

stations don't make unrealistic demands. Otherwise the coal companies will have an unfair treatment. Hence I follows. But II is irrelevant: welfare measures for employees is not the issue here.

18. a; If the officer thinks that some money is missing the best thing for him to do is to check it. Thus, I follows. Informing police is not necessary at this stage. The police should be informed *only if it is confirmed* that the money is missing.

19. a; The problem is being faced by the Doordarshan and therefore it is Doordarshan which has to solve it. If revising the fee structure is the solution, Doordarshan should do it and not wait till **others** do it. Hence, I follows; II doesn't.

20. b; Children stare at obscene posters out of curiosity. Curiosity is not a bad quality. Therefore, the suggestion of *punishing* children, if they look at obscene posters, is absurd. But on the other hand, this also is a fact that obscene posters create unhealthy imprints on the impressionable fragile minds of children. Therefore, it is necessary to ensure that the display of obscene posters itself is banned so that children keep away from this evil. Hence, I doesn't follow but II does.

21. b; I says that the child should be *threatened not to do it again*. This means yet another warning. But the statement has already mentioned that the child has done it *after repeated warnings*. So, course of action I does not follow. It would be better to punish the child because when repeated warnings fail some action must be taken. Hence, II follows.

22. e; If a train has been derailed, the Government must obtain necessary information as to what caused the accident. This would enable the Government to take necessary preventive measures. Hence, course of action I follows. Further, the derailment of the train is the government's responsibility and, consequently, the government must pay compensation to the men affected. Hence II follows.

23. e; We do not even need to think twice for this question. Both courses of action I and II are *Constitutional obligations. II, in fact, is a fundamental right*! So, there is no doubt that these choices are correct.

24. a; When the CBI receives even a single complaint against an officer, it is a serious matter. The CBI should try to do something and not wait for some more complaints. Should the CBI leave a person, who is hopelessly corrupt, untouched simply because there is just one complaint against him? The CBI should investigate the matter and, if possible, try to catch the officer red-handed if he is corrupt. Hence, I follows and II does not.

25. e; The problem here is: delay in justice. Both the suggested courses of action will solve the problem. I will solve it because if courts speed up, justice would not be delayed. II will solve it because it would create other forums for settlement of disputes and this will automatically mean faster

rate of dispensing of justice. Also, neither of the suggested actions is objectionable in any way. Hence, both of them follow.

26. b; The Institute has failed to implement many of the regular programmes. Nor has it drawn a firm action plan for studies and research. And this has happened despite an increased staff strength! What should be done now? Well, the first step is to ask: *why*? The Institute should be asked why it failed in fulfilling its task. Hence, II follows. But I doesn't. *We should not change the very objectives* of the Institute. The *Institute should try to achieve its objectives* and not to change them.

27. a; The problem is non-payment to employees. The cause: financial stringency. Will I solve it? Yes. To reduce wasteful expenditure would definitely be a right step towards solution. Will II solve the problem? Yes. If we reduce the number of employees, the question of paying them salaries does not arise. But is II a proper action? No. To curtail staff strength would mean to leave many people jobless: this is an extreme action and should not be taken without sufficient reason.

28. c; Why has the FM submitted his resignation, it is not sure. So, we can't give a certain advice. If he has resigned because it has been proved that he took bribe, couse I definitely follows. But if he has resigned because he was hurt by some adverse comments by some opposition leaders, course II is a better choice: at least, the resignation should not be accepted just one month before budget.

But we don't have any information about the circumstances behind his resignation and in such a case we can only take "either follows" as our answer.

[**Note:** This is a rare case where "either of the two follows" is the correct choice.]

29. a; The problem: some students tear the pages off the books issued to them. Will I solve the problem? Yes, obviously. Hence, I follows. But II doesn't. The renovation of library is not the issue.

30. e; It is obvious that both the actions are necessary steps and hence both follow.

31. b; I is an insensible action. But II will be helpful in preventing such accidents.

32. a; We should remember that the culprits are mere students. Going for II instead of I would make sense only if it is a repeated act.

33. e; I is advisable in the short term and II in the long term.

34. b; I is a sensitive issue and not feasible. II will help take care of the rush.

35. d; Going for I and II would create other problems.

36. b; II would suffice; hence no need to go for I.

37. c; Both of these are solutions to traffic jam but both together may not be feasible or necessary.

38. b; I is an extreme step but II should bring things under control.

39. b; I is not practical. II is necessary.

40. b; Again, I is not practical.
41. b; I is simply absurd. II follows as a solution to the complicated paperwork.
42. b; I is easier said than done. Even I makes sense only when the govt goes for II.
43. b; I is impractical. Water is essential for life to go on. II is sensible, especially when using ground water is proving to be uneconomical.
44. a; I is the obvious course of action. But II is absurd: punishment for thieves is understandable. But how can you punish "all the students"?
45. d; I is simply absurd. But even II is not the solution.
46. b; Obviously, the problem focuses on the killing of rhinos by tigers. Hence I is beside the point. II hits the problem right on its head.
47. d; I does not follow because the pilot of the second aircraft is not at fault. Neither does II follow, because the air traffic controller has done his job.
48. e; Obviously, the oil company needs to shoulder the responsibility. Hence I follows. II is also a step that would protect marine life.
49. b; Going for I would be running away from the problem. II is likely to bring some relief to students from poor families.
50. e; Both the steps will help keep a check on the rising number of malaria cases.

Exercise 6B

1. 5; I is an absurd suggestion. II is an extreme action not required in the present circumstances. III is indisputably a proper course of action.
2. 4; Since misappropriation has occurred, the government should analyse the loopholes in its mode of appropriation. Hence, II follows. Of course, the case should be investigated and the guilty officials should be punished.
3. 1; I is a positive step towards the solution of the problem. II is rather harsh and undemocratic. III too is an extreme action. Both II and III would violate the Fundamental Rights of the Indian Constitution.
4. 5; *This question is slightly tricky*. I does not follow because the problem mentions elderly people and *not* women and children. II and III are proper courses of action, *yet they do not follow* because such provisions are already there. Killing elderly people is a punishable offense under Sec. 300 and 302 of the Indian Penal Code while murderers as a rule are prosecuted by the State. II and III are not new suggestions. They are already in practice.
5. 4; All the recommendations would be positive steps towards a solution of the problem, i.e., hardships and inconvenience to passengers. Hence, all follow.
6. 2; I is obviously a proper course of action. Also, it is an established fact that there is a direct correlation between female infanticide and illiteracy.

Hence, II follows. But there is no obvious relation between child labour and female infanticide. Hence, III does not follow.

7. 2; Whenever a problem arises, it is always a sensible course of action to find out the causes. Hence, I follows. Fiscal deficit is almost always a cause of inflation. Hence, II follows. But drip irrigation has a very remote link with inflation. Hence, III does not follow.

8. 5; We cannot treat such rumours as involve the President's life as baseless. Hence III, does not follow and, instead, I and II follow.

9. 4; I is an extreme action. II and III are better because they are more likely to improve the situation than I.

10. 2; Precautions must be taken in case of chances of a crisis. Hence, I and II follow. But III is an extreme action.

11. 3; I and II are proper courses of action. But we cannot give defence a secondary treatment; hence, III does not follow.

12. 5. I is of course rubbish: it talks of escaping from a problem. II is not proper: civil offence means that we are making it lighter because it is a criminal offence presently. III is also not proper. To stop child labour we must stop and punish those who employ children. To punish the innocent children themselves would be inhuman.

13. 3; I and II are proper courses of action. Good things must be (i) promoted and (ii) rewarded. III is not proper: we cannot ban a movie only because it is not similar to a particular movie. [On these grounds, even a *Pather Panchali* would be banned!!]

14. 5; I is an extreme action. II and III are not proper; they are biased actions. III has a positive bias as it suggests unfair protection by the government; II has a negative bias as it suggests unfair control by the government. The best thing would be to let the mutual funds determine their own future. Again, here we have the idea of prevailing notions of truth. Today, privatisation and non-interference is the buzzward. Some years ago, we were advocating either licensing and control (as in II) or safeguarding from competition (as in III). But today we call these license-raj and protectionism, respectively.

15. 2; I is an extreme and inhuman action. Both II and III are necessary steps towards prevention of AIDS.

16. 2; Both I and II are extreme and irrational actions. A good government should be willing to listen to criticism, on one hand, and should not abandon its plans just because of some criticism, on the other. III is proper: the PSU employees must be given an opportunity to put forward their pleas before a decision - so ruthless towards them - is implemented.

17. 4; Both I and II are questionable. I is not acceptable; it is an extreme action and some efforts to redress the situation under the popularly elected government must precede it. II appears without any explanation; why

should one take privatisation to be the cure of all evils? III is proper; the governments concerned must be asked to re-evaluate their system and correct the faults.

18. 1; I and II are obvious and do not need any explanation. III does not follow: it is ridiculous and, in fact, laughable. Pakistan may simply return the copies after getting them xeroxed.

19. 3; I does not follow: why start convincing Indian press that its apprehensions are baseless? What if they are not (baseless)? II does not follow: it is an extreme action. III is a proper course of action. A censor board may filter the views that the Western press may publish and this will take care of the apprehensions as mentioned.

20. 2; I is an extreme action. Instead of winding up SEBI, II and III should be followed, i.e. the rules should be reviewed and loopholes plugged so that it becomes difficult for the brokers to circumvent them on the one hand; and on the other, the SEBI should be given more powers so that it could punish the brokers adequately if they still flouted the norms.

21. 1; That IAS officers should be given more security is obvious. Police officials should be suspended only if their guilt is proved. Currently, it is only suspected. The Chief Minister may or may not resign and it is an individual decision; however, it must be understood that a Chief Minister is very remotely responsible for such incidents and hence his resignation is not a must.

22. 1; The parallel cinema has become sick because of lack of funds. Also, it is an undesirable development since it is 'unfortunate'. Naturally, the government should try to save it by giving financial aid. II does not follow: by incorporating commercial appeal such as (songs, dances and stunts) the very soul of art cinema will be killed. III is ridiculous: you cannot 'request' people to buy tickets; they will buy it if they like it.

23. 1; I is obvious: all those violating the pollution norms should be severely dealt with. II is an extreme action: before closing down a unit, the government should check if its pollution level can be brought down. III is ridiculous: if pollution is equivalent to cigarettes, it is not a fault of cigarettes.

24. 4; None follows. Why higher income tax rate? If they are earning more, they will automatically pay more taxes because taxes are proportional to income. Similarly, wages of public sector employees can't be doubled: there are many differences between a private sector employee and a public sector employee. The latter enjoys many hidden perks such as free medical facilities, free house, gratuity, etc. His working conditions may not be as tough as those of a private sector employee. Also, he has a greater security of job. Before raising his salary, these factors should also be borne in mind. III also does not follow because it is an irrational action

and no causes have been given.

25. 1; Obviously, people should be made aware of these possibilities so that they are not under the impression that cold drinks are always safe; they must know the correct picture. II does not follow: you cannot subject anyone to imprisonment for a fault which may, after all, be an accident. It is for the judiciary to decide. III is an extreme action; a better action would be to take cleanliness measures and to ensure that no such incidents occur in the future.

26. 3; I does not follow: inquiries are not made for positive development; they are made in case of scandals, accidents, scams etc. II is obviously a logical course of action. A bumper crop may lead to problem of storage and lack of storage space, etc; hence III follows.

27. 3; I is not valid: any government should always be willing to listen to criticisms. II follows for this very reason. III does not follow because it assumes beforehand that the objective of social equality is indeed ignored in the current policies.

28. 2; I and II are obvious. III is an extreme action; it puts a check on people's privacy.

29. 3; I does not follow because it is the job of the weather experts to provide forecasts. They have only carried out their normal job and for carrying out an assigned job, awards cannot be given. III is rubbish.

30. 2; If legal provisions have proved inadequate, will it means either or both will follow: one, that the provisions are not adequate (hence I follows) and two, that they are not being sincerely executed (hence II follows). III could have been accepted but it carries the objectionable advice of rebelling against the parents.

31. 5; II follows. I does not follow; there may be six good candidates. III asks us to accept a problem as inevitable. This is a negative approach.

32. 3; II is an extreme action. Suspension should be carried out only if the official has been proved guilty.

33. 2; No hint is made that IMF is interfering in our affairs. Hence, III does not follow.

34. 2; The statement focuses on girl dropouts and not total dropouts. Hence, I does not follow. III is an extreme action.

35. 1; None of the actions is rational enough. I advocates sacking the official on mere accusation and without enquiry. II suggests ignoring the accusation without enquiry. III has the same flow as I has. None of the three actions are recommendable without at least a *prima facie* evidence.

36. 2; People should know the truth about *any* disease. Further, they boycott leprosy patients which is not justified, particularly if leprosy is not contagious. So, I and II are justified courses of action but III is not. It seeks to declare leprosy as a risk-free disease. But only some, not all,

forms of leprosy are non-contagious. Some of them are contagious and hence it can't be declared risk-free.

37. 1; I and II are proper courses of action because both of these are time-tested 'treatments' for recession. III does not follow because it promotes escapism. Recession is an integral part of business and all businesses are cyclic in nature. It makes no sense to abandon a business simply because its demand has slumped.

38. 1; Anybody suspected of murder must be interrogated; hence I follows. Neither II nor III is a proper course of action. II would not be correct if the relatives were indeed guilty and III would be incorrect if they were not.

39. 3; Both I and II follow because these steps will reduce red-tapism. III is an extreme action. Red-tapism cannot possibly be removed in ten days.

40. 4; I and III are ridiculous courses of action. Enquiry commissions are not established to find out the causes for positive developments; they are established to find out the causes for scam etc.

41. 4; I and II follow because both of these will help in checking cases of kidnapping. III is also a good suggestion considering that today even 7-8 year old rids are getting black-belt in martial arts: such kids would definitely be a deterrant for kidnappers.

42.3; I follows because compensation must be given to those who have suffered. II is also practical. III is rubbish: terrorists have nothing to do with the case.

43. 4; II and III follow because these actions will ensure that NHRC serves the purpose for which it was framed. I does not follow: NHRC is not a political body.

44. 4; II and III are logical steps. I is an over-reaction: You cannot suspend all the officials only because some of them are being suspected. Moreover, asking all the officials to go on leave would mean a total breakdown in the government machinery.

45. 5; None follows. All the suggested courses of action suggest that spending money on illiteracy is almost a wastage. This attitude is wrong.

46. 5; None of these could solve the problem in a practical manner. Life imprisonment would be a little too harsh for video piracy. Making more lucrative films will not solve the problem; equally lucrative unauthorised video-copy will be prepared instantly. III is slightly impractical. Waiving the tax altogether may mean great loss of revenue, which the government may not forgo easily.

47. 1; I and II are advisable actions as they will tend to reduce the problem. III may, in fact, worsen the situation; hence it is not advisable.

48. 4; II and III are proper courses of action as they would tend to reduce the problem. I may not be advisable; 'noise pollution' is not such a major issue. It is not as sensitive as AIDS.

49. 5; All the actions are advisable as they would reduce the chances of any epidemic etc.
50. 4; The statement does not say whether the allegations are true or false. If they are true, II will not follow; if they are false, I will not follow. As per the information given at present, only III follows unquestionably.
51. 2; Expelling may not be a welcome step and some may take it as too harsh. II definitely follows because students must be informed of the development. III is rubbish: nobody can give a guarantee of the success of such a thing.
52. 1; Adequate safety arrangements are a must, so I follows. II does not follow: what exactly is meant by the emergency powers of the EC? III does not follow because it is escapism. Unless I has been tried, III can't be employed.
53. 1; I involves the enactment of the suggestion: incentives may improve work culture. So, I follows. II is a must: workers must be informed about a committee's report. III is an extreme action. It may not be welcome by all.
54. 5; I is misleading. If you have chosen I as your answer check your English and not Reasoning. Food-poisoning actually refers to a state of stomach disorder which starts with digestive failure. It does not mean poisoning of food in the literal sense. Because of this (literal) reason, I does not follow. Now, if delegates are feared to have consumed poison, they must be given medical attention immediately. Either II or III fulfils this purpose.
55. 4; II and III seek to rectify the causes that have been mentioned as the reasons behind failure of Indian books. So, both of them follow. But I does not follow because of its negative approach. If demand for fiction exists, it does not mean that non-fiction writing should be discouraged.
56. 4; The alarming situation is pretty *obvious*. So a review committee is not required, rather action is required. Hence I does not follow. Water crisis is not the concern of the statement. Hence II does not follow. III is a logical response of any administration.
57. 4; I would be an extreme step. II is not within the govt's purview. III is advisable when there is retrenchment on such a large scale.
58. 2; I is not feasible in a democracy. III does not follow because the problem is not concerned with "criminals". II is the only course the authorities can resort to.
59. 1; I would be a step in the right direction .it would ensure that hunger does not deprive the children of education.
60. 4;I does not make sense unless it be known that these officials are the culprits. II is necessary to prevent such incidents in the future. So is III.

Chapter Seven

Data Sufficiency

7.1: Introduction

In the reasoning section of various competitive exams, some questions are asked on 'data sufficiency'. This is a new trend because earlier 'data sufficiency' used to be a part of mathematics section only. Questions on data sufficiency in Reasoning are very typical. If you go through the previous questions of some PO exams you will feel that there are not more than 5 or 6 types of questions. Let us see what is the best method of tackling such questions.

7.2: Format of the problem

Let us begin by looking at the format of the problem:

Directions: The questions below consist of a question followed by two statements labelled as (1) and (2). You have to decide if these statements are sufficient to conclusively answer the question. Give answer

- **(A) if statement (1) alone is sufficient to answer the question but statement (2) alone is not sufficient to answer the question.**
- **(B) if statement (2) alone is sufficient to answer the question but statement (1) alone is not sufficient to answer the question.**
- **(C) if you can get the answer from (1) and (2) together although neither statement by itself suffices.**
- **(D) if statement (1) alone is sufficient and statement (2) alone is sufficient.**
- **(E) if you cannot get the answer from statements (1) and (2) together but still more data are needed.**

Ex. 1. What is the relation of X and Y?

(1) Y is the mother of Z.

(2) Z is the brother of A.

(Answer to this question is presented later on. First, let us carry out our analysis of how to solve these questions.)

7.3: Analysis and suggested steps

You should note that data sufficiency questions are not new topics in themselves. All you have to do is to analyse the given data and see if you can get the answer to the question using the given data.

When you are attempting a question of data sufficiency you should follow a systematic approach as laid down below. This approach being a systematic one, will save your time. Also, in case you get stuck at any point, it will help your chances of guessing a correct answer because it narrows down the possible answers from five to three or two.

By looking at this format of the question, we would suggest you to try the first statement [labelled (1)] and see if this statement is sufficient. There are two possible outcomes: either the statement will be sufficient or it will not be sufficient. If the former is true, then either A or D is the correct answer and if the latter be true, then either B or C or E is the correct answer. Thus, we have narrowed down the number of possible answers from five to two or three. Similarly, this procedure can be continued with the second statement. The complete step-by-step approach is explained by the following diagram.

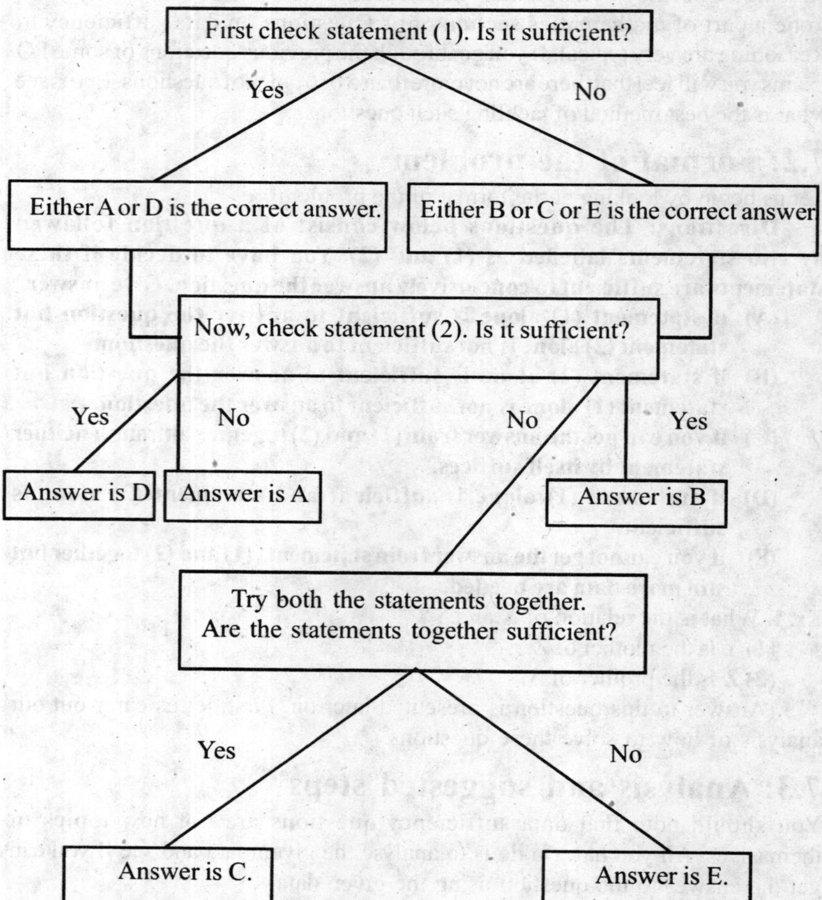

The step-by-step approach outlined here will be sufficient for you to lead to correct answers quickly. However, there are some additional facts which you should keep in mind to have a still quicker approach. These points are discussed below in the following section.

7.3.1: Some Important Additional Points

If a question involves two unknowns then (i) *two* (ii) *distinct* equations are required for it. If this condition is fulfilled then C is the answer, or else E is the answer. No other answers are possible. See the following examples:-

Ex. 2 : What is the value of x?

1) $x+y=15$

2) $3x-y=1$

Soln : Since two unknowns are there and two distinct equations are given, the correct answer is C.

7.4: More on Data Sufficiency: Some typical cases

In the foregoing analysis, we presented a general method for solving such questions. This method is a systematic one and you should apply this 'orderly' approach while solving questions on data sufficiency.

Now that we have seen the method of solving such a question, we should turn our attention to some typical questions as asked in exams. The questions can be broadly divided into the following categories:

1) Relationships 2) Dates
3) Comparison 4) Critical analysis
5) Age 6) Miscellaneous

Let us look at these types one by one:

1. Relationships

This is a typical question in the exam. The wording goes like this: "How is x related to y?" In these questions, one very prominent source of confusion is the fact that **students tend to conclude about the relationship without knowing about the sex of the person involved.** For example, consider the following:

Ex. 3: "How is P related to Q" ?

1) Q is the father of P.

2) S is the brother of P.

Soln: We see that statement (1) says that Q is the father of P. **Is it enough to conclude how P is related to Q?** No. P could be a son or may as well be a daughter of Q. Hence, to establish exactly how P is related to Q, **we must also know the sex of P, i.e., whether P is a male or a female.** This information can be given directly in the wording "P is a male/female" or indirectly in the wording (such as):

a. P is a brother/sister of (say) X.

b. P is the father/mother of (say) X.

c. P is an uncle/aunt of (say) X.

Note that the above three statements are indirect ways of saying that P is a male/female.

Coming back to Ex. 3, it is obvious that the two statements taken together are not sufficient (it is not sure whether P is a son or a daughter of Q). Hence, E is the answer. But the answer would be C if statement (2) of Example 3 is replaced by any of the statements (a), (b) or (c), as above.

Let us consider another example.

Ex. 4: X is the brother of Y and X is the brother of Z. How are Y and Z related?

1) Sex of Z
2) Sex of Y

Soln: Since X is the brother of both Y and Z, it means that Y and Z are also brothers or sisters. So, we must know their sex to know who is the brother and who is the sister or both are brothers or both sisters. Hence, 'C' is the answer.

2. Dates

Another very typical question is asked on 'dates'. The wording of the question goes like this: "On which day of the week did X reach (say) Agra?" or "What is the date of birth of X?" In such questions, you have to determine 'a day' or 'a date'. Usually, the data will provide you with some knowledge of some previous 'day' or 'date' and from this you can work out the required day or date. Hence, you should note that **a day or a date can exactly be established if and only if**

A. *The 'day' or the 'date' of some earlier incident is mentioned*; and

B. *The number of days between that incident and the required day is given.*

If any of the above information is not given, data will be insufficient. If both are given, data will be sufficient. Consider these examples:

Ex. 5: "On which day of the week did Atul reach Bombay?"

(1) Atul's brother reached Bombay one day earlier than Atul.

(2) Atul's mother reached Bombay on Thursday which was two days later than the arrival of his brother.

Soln: Statement (1) satisfies condition (B) above because here the number of days between an earlier incident (Atul's brother's reaching Bombay) and the required day has been given. Now, we need to know the day when that earlier incident took place [as in (A)]. In other words, we need to know on which day Atul's brother reached Bombay. For this, we turn to the second statement. It says that Atul's mother reached Bombay on Thursday, which was two days later than the arrival of his brother. Here, the number of days between 'Atul's mother's reaching Bombay' and 'Atul's brother's reaching Bombay' are given. Also, the exact day of 'Atul's mother's reaching Bombay' is given. Hence, both the data — type (A) and (B) — are given. Thus, we can find out the day of 'Atul's brother's reaching Bombay'.

Therefore, both the statements together are sufficient because the first statement supplies the gap between the required incident and an earlier incident and the second statement supplies the day of the earlier incident. 'C' is the answer.

Ex. 6: What is the date of birth of Ratna? (Assume that the memories of Vani and Sapna are correct.)

1) Vani remembers that Ratna's date of birth is between 17th June and 21st June.
2) Sapna says that Ratna's date of birth is after 19th June but before 23rd June.

Soln: From statement (1), we conclude that the possible answers are 18th June, 19th June and 20th June. From statement (2), we conclude that 18th June and 19th June are ruled out. So, 20th June must be the answer. Hence, the question can be answered using both the statements and, therefore, the answer is C.

3. Comparison

This is another typical question on data sufficiency. The wording of the question is: "Who is the tallest among X, Y and Z?" or "Who is the heaviest among A, B and C?" or "Who is sitting to the left of A when A, B and C are sitting together?" etc. In all these questions, you have to write the names of various persons in ascending or descending order of heights (or weights etc) or write their seating arrangement (from left to right or right to left etc). In other words, you have to make 'comparisons' of the respective places of some persons in a fixed pattern or order.

To solve such questions, it is best to write the data given in the two statements in the form of inequalities and then see if the two can be combined into one single inequality to get the answer. [**Note:** An inequality means "not equal to". Here, I mean statements like "A > B" which may imply "A is heavier than B" or "A is taller than B" or "A is sitting to the left of B" etc.]

Let us see some examples.

Ex. 7: Among four friends, A, B, C and D, who is the heaviest?

1) B is heavier than A, but lighter than D.
2) C is lighter than B.

Soln: Write statement (1) as:

$D > B > A$ ['>' means heavier than]

Write statement (2) as:

$$B > C$$

Now, the two inequalities can be combined as

$D > B > C > A$ or $D > B > A > C$; but in either case 'D' is the heaviest.

So, 'C' is the answer.

[If the question were "who is the lightest among them", the answer would have been E because the two possible combinations do not give a unique answer about the lightest person.]

Ex. 8: A, B, C, D and E are sitting in a row. B is sitting between A and E. Who is sitting in the middle?

1) A is sitting left of B but right of D.

2) C is sitting on the extreme right.

Soln: The question itself says that B is between A and E. Write it as:

A > B > E ['>' means 'is to the left of']

Now, (1) implies:

D > A > B

And, (2) implies:

all > C

Obviously, these can be combined into one single inequality:

D > A > B > E > C.

Hence, 'B' is in the middle and the two statements together are sufficient to answer it. Hence, 'C' is the answer.

4. Critical Analysis

Sometimes, questions asked in the exam are qualitative in nature, wherein you have to apply your value-judgement in order to reach a conclusion. Here, you have to 'think deeply' in order to reach the conclusion. To tackle these types of problems, you should revise your general background of argumentation techniques, assumptions of arguments and inference-making. No general method can be delineated to tackle these problems, but this does not mean that these are very difficult questions. On the contrary, they are very easy; only, you need to have a clear mind and its unhesitant application.

Let us see some more examples to understand the approach.

Ex. 9: Many Indian experts think that India has very meagre oil reserves. Is that correct?

(1) India imports about 1.5 crore tonnes of crude every year.

(2) When foreign companies were recently invited to participate in oil exploration and production activity in India, nearly 67 companies took up the offer.

Soln: The fact that India imports a huge quantity of crude oil does not prove that India has very meagre oil reserves. The imports may be due to large consumption or small production. That 67 companies rushed to India for oil exploration also does not imply that India has large oil reserves. They might have rushed taking other points of advantage like cheap labour and favourable economic and political conditions. Thus, our answer is E.

Ex. 10: Is running good for health?

(1) Running within proper limits in an open area is good for heart and lungs.

(2) Knee, ankle and foot-bone problems are not uncommon as a result of protracted running.

Soln: Both the statements independently give answer. Statement (1) gives affirmative answer whereas statement (2) gives negative answer.

Ex. 11: Should I invite him to my wedding anniversary?

(1) This is my first wedding anniversary.

(2) He is the only person who has helped me in bad days.

Soln: Invitation totally depends on personal relationship. The first statement doesn't give the answer. Statement (2) gives an affirmative answer. Hence, our answer is B.

Ex. 12: Is environmental control harmful for the good of the industry?

(1) As industrial nations have come to face increasing economic difficulties, governments have been under pressure to relax environmental controls.

(2) Increase of carbon content in the air by the burning of coal has to be tolerated because we have to use coal in order to reduce pressure on oil supplies.

Soln: Statement (1) says that governments have been under pressure to relax environmental controls. This implies that environmental controls are harmful for industrial development. Nothing is mentioned about environmental control and industry in statement (2). Thus, answer is A.

Ex. 13: Is India a developing country?

(1) The per capita income of Indians has been increasing.

(2) In spite of a large population, very few Indians die of hunger.

Soln: The per capita income increases in developed as well as in backward countries. Thus, increase in per capita income can't be a criterion for a developing country. Similarly, statement (2) also cannot be a criterion for deciding the developing condition of any country. So, our answer is E.

5. Age

In some questions of data sufficiency, problems are concerned with age. Here, some data are given and the question generally asks you to find a particular person's age. You have to decide whether the given data are sufficient to reach the answer to the question.

Again, **we must emphasise that the question does not ask you to *actually* calculate the age of the person.** It only wants you to tell whether the given statements are sufficient (or not) to calculate the age of that person. Many students tackle such questions by actually solving the question. They try to find out the age and, if they succeed, they conclude that the data are sufficient, and if they do not, they conclude insufficiency. This is unnecessary and time-consuming. Instead of finding the actual age you should only determine the sufficiency. This will be a better and quicker approach. How? Let us see.

Usually one information or one statement provides one equation. **You must remember this: one information = one equation.**

Again, usually, one person's name means one unknown. You must remember this: **one person = one unknown.**

Now, the approach to such problems is easy. If the number of equations is equal to the number of unknowns, the data are sufficient; otherwise they are not. How do you find the number of equations? For this, you should see the number of informations. How do you find the number of unknowns? For this, you should see the number of persons mentioned.

(If you have no problems with algebra, it is better to use 'x', 'y' etc and to form equations. This is better because in certain cases there is a repetition of information and you can easily detect it if you use 'x', 'y' symbols. Otherwise, you can use the 'number of equations' ⇔ 'number of unknowns' approach.)

Let us see some examples in order to understand it.

Ex. 14: Is my son 12 years old?

Statements: **I.** Four years later, he will be twenty years younger than me.

II. Now, I am twenty years older than him.

Soln: This is a deceptive problem. You should notice that there are two unknowns in this case: 'Father' and 'Son'. But how many informations are there? Two? No. There is only one information. Both statements I and II only state that the father is older than the son by 20 years (although the language of I and II are different). So, here, we have repetition of data. Since there is one information (one equation) for two unknowns, data are insufficient and the answer is E.

Ex. 15: What is the age of Shubham?

Statements: **I.** Shubham is twelve years older than Shyam.

II. Four years later, Shyam will be twelve years younger than Shubham.

Soln: No. of unknowns = 2 (Shubham, Shyam)

No. of information = 1 (A similar deception as in the above example.)

Hence, data are insufficient. Answer is E.

Ex. 16: What is the age of Shubham?

Statements: **I.** Twice the age of Shubham, when added to Shyam's age, gives 72 years.

II. 10 years later, Shubham will be 38 years old.

Soln: Take statement I. Here, No. of unknowns = 2 (Shubham, Shyam) and No. of informations = one. In statement II, however, there is only one unknown (Shubham) and one information. Therefore, statement II alone is sufficient although statement I is not sufficient. Answer is B.

Ex. 17: What is the age of Shubham?

Statements: **I.** Shubham is 10 years older than Richa.

II. Richa is 14 years younger than Shyam.

Soln: In statement I, we have two unknowns but one equation. Hence, statement I alone is insufficient. Similarly, statement II alone is insufficient. Taking the two statements together, there are three unknowns (Shubham, Richa, Shyam) and only two informations. Hence, even together the data are insufficient. Answer is E.

An Important Note: When we talk of information in a statement, we mean **definite information**. It should not be an indefinite information. What do we mean by definite information and indefinite information? A *definite information* is one that gives us an exact relation. For example, "Suresh's age will be equal to 16 years after four years" is a definite information while "Suresh will be less than 20 years old after 4 years" is not. Similarly, "Suresh is 12 years younger than Mohan" is a definite information while "Suresh is much younger than Mohan" is not a definite information. The reader should clearly understand this point. (See Ex 18 below.)

Ex. 18: What is the age of Shubham ?

Statements: **I.** Richa is 10 years younger than Shubham.

II. 9 years later, Richa's age will be more than half of Shubham's.

Soln: E. Data insufficient because there are two unknowns and only one information. II is not an information because it is not definite. It is not definite because it uses the word *more than*.

Note: If we replace the words 'more than' with 'equal to' in II, the answer will be C. Then, data are sufficient.

6. Miscellaneous

Although the five categories mentioned above are standard categories and most of the questions asked will be from these five categories, there are certain types which do not belong to any of them. We may call them miscellaneous questions. Let us see some of them.

Ex. 19: Are some books chocolates?

Statements: **I.** All books are ducks.

II. All ducks are chocolates.

Soln: I and II together make a syllogistic problem. We have, A + A = A (see "Syllogism" chapter). Hence, the two statements together imply "All books are chocolates". Hence, "Some books are chocolates" follows, using both the statement together. Hence, conclusion is 'C'.

Ex. 20: How many children in a room are boys?

Statements: **I.** 50% of the children are in white dress.

II. Only boys are in white dress.

Soln: E. Together they are not sufficient. Exact strength of the class is not known.

Ex. 21: Is x greater than y?

Statements: I. x is two times y.

II. y is less than z which is more than x.

Soln: E. The statements are not sufficient. Statement I is not sufficient (!!) because, though x > y when the numbers are positive, the opposite would happen if the numbers are negative. (Consider x = 10, y = 5 as one case and x = -20, y = -10 as another). Also, it is easy to see that even II is not sufficient.

Practice Exercises

Type I: Exercise 7A

Directions (Q. 1-50): Below is given a question followed by two statements numbered I and II. The question may or may not be answered with the help of these statements. You have to decide if these statements are sufficient to answer the question. Give answer

1) if only statement I is sufficient to answer the question but statement II is not;

2) if only statement II is sufficient to answer the question but statement I is not;

3) if both statements I and II are together sufficient to answer the question although neither statement suffices by itself;

4) if statement I and statement II are sufficient to answer the question independently and separately; and

5) if the two statements are not sufficient but still more data is needed to answer the question.

1. What is the age of A?

   Statements: I. The age of B is 24 years.

   II. A is older than B.

2. What is the age of B?

   Statements: I. The age of A is 18 years.

   II. B is 5 years younger than A.

3. Is Shyam the brother of Mohan?

   Statements: I. Mohan is the son of Ram.

   II. Shyam is the son of Ram.

4. Is X the brother of Y?

   Statemetns: I. X is the son of Z.

   II. Y is the daughter of Z.

5. Is X the brother of Y?

   Statements: I. Z is the father of X.

   II. Z is the father of Y.

6. Is X the brother of Y?
 Statements: **I.** X is the daughter of Z.
 II. Y is the daughter of Z.
7. Is Shyam the brother of Mohan?
 Statements: **I.** Ram is the father of Shyam.
 II. Ram is the father of Mohan.
8. Is Minu the mother of Shanu?
 Statements: **I.** Shanu is the mother of Sonu.
 II. Sonu is the grandson of Minu.
9. How far is Patna from Shimla?
 Statements: **I.** Patna is 200 km from Delhi.
 II. Delhi is 500 km from Shimla.
10. How far is Patna from Shimla?
 Statements: **I.** Patna is 200 km from Delhi.
 II. Delhi is 500 km from Shimla and is between Patna and Shimla.
11. On which day did Radha reach Shimla?
 Statements: **I.** Sunday is a holiday.
 II. Radha travels only on a holiday.
12. On which day did Radha reach Shimla?
 Statements: **I.** Only Sunday is a holiday.
 II. Radha travels only on a holiday.
13. On what day did Radha reach Shimla?
 Statements: **I.** Only Sunday is a holiday.
 II. Radha was in Shimla on a holiday.
14. On what date is Anju's birthday?
 Statements: **I.** Anju's birthday comes only in a leap year.
 II. Anju's birthday is the same as that of Morarji Desai.
15. On what date is Anju's birthday?
 Statements: **I.** Her birthday falls on the Independence Day of a country.
 II. That country has a flag made of three colours.
16. On what date is Anju's birthday?
 Statements: **I.** Minu says that her birthday falls before 28th March, 1974.
 II. Sonu says that her birthday falls after 28th March, 1974.
17. On what date is Anju's birthday?
 Statements: **I.** Ram says that her birthday falls before 27th March, 1974.
 II. Shyam says that her birthday falls after 25th March, 1974.
18. On what date is Anju's birthday?
 Statements: **I.** Paro says that her birthday falls sometime in February, 1976.
 II. Charu says that her birthday falls after 27th of the month.

19. On what date is Anju's birthday?
Statements: **I.** X says that her birthday falls sometime in February, 1974.
II. Charu says that her birthday falls after 27th of the month.
20. On what date in Anju's birthday?
Statements: **I.** Anju's zodiac sign is Aries.
II. She was born on the first date of a month.
21. What is the age of Shyam?
Statements: **I.** 5 years ago, Shyam was 20.
II. Shyam is 15 years older than Ram.
22. What is the age of Shyam?
Statements: **I.** Shyam is half as old as Madan.
II. Shyam is twice as old as Sonu, who is 10.
23. What is the age of Shyam?
Statements: **I.** When India got independence Shyam was nine years old.
II. Shyam has just reached the retirement age for public sector employees.
24. Among three friends A, B and C, who is the tallest?
Statements: **I.** A is taller than B.
II. A is taller than C.
25. Among three friends A, B and C, who is the tallest?
Statements: **I.** A is shorter than B.
II. A is shorter than C.
26. Among three friends A, B and C, who is the shortest?
Statements: **I.** A is taller than B.
II. A is taller than C.
27. Among three friends A, B and C, who is the shortest?
Statements: **I.** A is shorter than B.
II. A is shorter than C.
28. Among three friends A, B and C, who is not the tallest?
Statements: **I.** A is taller than B.
II. A is taller than C.
29. Among three friends A, B and C, who are not the tallest?
Statements: **I.** A is taller than B.
II. A is taller than C.
30. Are some Indians hot-blooded?
Statements: **I.** All hot-blooded men are Indians.
II. Some hot-blooded men are Asians.
31. Are some pens pencils?
Statements: **I.** Some pencils are flowers.
II. All pencils are pens.
32. Are all pens flowers?
Statements: **I.** All pens are potatoes.
II. All flowers are potatoes.

33. Are some papers not flowers?
Statements: **I.** Some papers are potatoes.
II. No potatoes are flowers.

34. Are some papers flowers?
Statements: **I.** Some papers are potatoes.
II. No potatoes are flowers.

35. Are all papers flowers?
Statements: **I.** Some papers are bags.
II. No bags are flowers.

36. Are some Indians chairs?
Statements: **I.** All chairs are Asians.
II. No chair is an Indian.

37. Are no Indians honest?
Statements: **I.** Some Indians are businessmen.
II. All businessman are honest.

38. Are no Indians honest?
Statements: **I.** Some Indians are businessmen.
II. No businessman is honest.

39. Are some baskets glasses?
Statements: **I.** All glasses are baskets.
II. Only glasses are baskets.

40. Are some players not sincere?
Statements: **I.** All players are books.
II. Some books are sincere.

41. On a table are sitting four people: A, B, C and D. Who is sitting opposite to A?
Statements: **I.** B is sitting opposite to D.
II. A is sitting between B and D.

42. Around a circular table are sitting six persons: A, B, C, D, E and F. Who is on the immediate left of A?
Statements: **I.** B is opposite to C and D is opposite to E.
II. F is on the immediate left of B.

43. Around a circular table are sitting six persons: A, B, C, D, E and F. Who is on the immediate right of A?
Statements: **I.** B is opposite to C and D is opposite to E.
II. F is on the immediate left of B.

44. Is Ram taller than Shyam?
Statements: **I.** Madan is shorter than Shyam.
II. Shyam is shorter than Ram.

45. Is Rohit heavier than Anju?
Statements: **I.** Anju is lighter than Sonu.
II. Sonu is heavier than Rohit.

46. Is my son 24 years old?

Statements: **I.** Four years later, he will be twenty years younger than me.

II. At present, I am twenty years older than him.

47. Are some books chocolates?

Statements: **I.** All books are ducks.

II. All ducks are chocolates.

48. Is A the mother of B?

Statements: **I.** B is the son of A.

II. A is older than B.

49. What is the speed of train A?

Statements: **I.** It crosses a bridge in 5 seconds.

II. The train is 200 m long.

50. What is the speed of train A?

Statements: **I.** It crosses a pole in 5 seconds.

II. The train is 200 m long.

Type II: Exercise 7B

Directions: The questions below consist of a question followed by two statements labelled I and II. You have to decide if these statements are sufficient to answer the question. Give answer

1) if statement I alone is sufficient to answer the question but statement II alone is not sufficient to answer the question;

2) if statement II alone is sufficient to answer the question but statement I alone is not sufficient to answer the question;

3) if you can get the answer from I and II together although neither statement suffices by itself;

4) if statement I alone is sufficient and statement II alone is sufficient; and

5) if you cannot get the answer from statements I and II together but still more data are needed.

1. Is A the father of B?

Statements: **I.** A is the father of X.

II. X is the mother of B.

2. Is A the father of B?

Statements: **I.** A is the father of C.

II. C is the brother of B.

3. Who is the tallest among A, B and C?

Statements: **I.** A is taller than B.

II. A is taller than C.

4. Who is the shortest among A, B and C?
Statements: **I.** A is taller than B.
II. A is taller than C.

5. What is the age of the mother ?
Statements: **I.** The son is 10 years old.
II. The mother is thrice as old as the son.

6. What is the age of Mona?
Statements: **I.** Mona's mother is 30 years old.
II. Mona is much younger than her mother.

7. Where is the capital of India?
Statements: **I.** The capital of India is not Lucknow.
II. The capital of India is in U.P.

8. What is the value of the coins in my pocket?
Statements: **I.** There are 20 coins in my pocket.
II. 15 of them are 10-paise coins.

9. How many legs are there in a group of animals?
Statements: **I.** There are 20 heads.
II. Half of the animals are birds while half are cows.

10. Is Sonu the father of Guddi?
Statements: **I.** Guddi is the daughter of Sonu.
II. Sonu's father is the grandfather of Guddi.

11. Is Monu the brother of Sonu?
Statements: **I.** Anju is the mother of Sonu.
II. Mahendru is the husband of Anju.

12. How far is Patiala from Delhi?
Statements: **I.** Delhi is 200 km from Patiala.
II. Patiala is 400 km from Chandigarh.

13. On which day did Sudha reach Bombay? (Sudha and Manju reach Bombay on different days.) Assume that they travelled by flight.
Statements: **I.** Manju reached Bombay on Thursday and earlier than Sudha in the same week.
II. No flight reached Bombay on Saturday or Sunday.

14. What is the age of Madan?
Statements: **I.** Madan is 20 years younger than his father.
II. 5 years later, their ages will be in the ratio 1 : 2.

15. Are some Indians Asians?
Statements: **I.** Some Africans are Indians.
II. No Africans are Asians.

16. Is Manju the mother of Sanju?
Statements: **I.** Sanju is the daughter of Manju.
II. Sanju is the mother of Pinki.

17. How far is Delhi from Rohtak?
    Statements: I. Delhi is 200 km from Hisar.
    II. Hisar is 300 km from Rohtak.
18. What is the area of a circle?
    Statements: I. The radius of the circle is 7 cm.
    II. The circumference of the circle is 44 cm.
19. Is Madan the brother of Sohan?
    Statements: I. Anju is the mother of both.
    II. Minu is the sister of both.
20. Is tomorrow a Tuesday?
    Statements: I. Tommorrow is 20th March, 1876.
    II. 17th June, 1885 was a Monday.
21. Is X the brother of Y?
    Statements: I. Y is the brother of X.
    II. A is the mother of both X and Y.
22. What is the age of Mohan?
    Statements: I. Mohan's father is 62 years old.
    II. Mohan's father is 30 years older than Mohan.
23. Will Tendulkar hit a century today?
    Statements: I. Tendulkar is the best batsman in the world.
    II. The pitch is suitable for strokeplay.
24. Did the murder occur on the 14th?
    Statements: I. The murderer was caught on the 18th.
    II. The police took four days to detect who the murderer was.
25. What is the perimeter of a square?
    Statements: I. If the side is doubled, the perimeter also doubles.
    II. If the perimeter triples, the area becomes nine times.
26. Is Mohan taller than Sudha?
    Statements: I. Sudha is not the tallest.
    II. Vandana is not the tallest.
27. Is Mohan taller than Sudha?
    Statements: I. Sudha is not the tallest.
    II. The group consists of two people.
28. Is the price of a pen Rs 18?
    Statements: I. The two pens Sudhir bought cost him Rs 34.
    II. The price of a pen is a number which is prime.
29. What is the charge for making a phone call, given that it is a whole number (in rupees)?
    Statements: I. Sudha has five rupees in her pocket and she can make at most two calls.
    II. Raman has one rupee in his pocket and he can't make a call.

30. Has democracy suffered after the recent poll violence?
Statements: I. Poll violences are not a good thing.
II. India's image as a vibrant democracy has taken a beating.
31. How is X related to Y?
Statements: I. Y is the brother of X.
II. X is the mother of Z.
32. Is Z the mother of Y?
Statements: I. Y is the son of Z.
II. X is the son of Y.
33. Are mangoes sweet?
Statements: I. All vegetables are sweet.
II. Mango is a vegetable.
34. Is $\sqrt{16} = 6$?
Statements: I. Square of 6 is not equal to 16.
II. Square root of 6 is not equal to square of 16.
35. Will it be a Sunday tomorrow?
Statements: I. It is not a Saturday today.
II. It was Wednesday the day before yesterday.
36. Is Manju older than Minu?
Statements: I. Manju was born after Radhu.
II. Radhu was born after Minu.
37. Is it going to rain tomorrow?
Statements: I. Tomorrow is Tuesday.
II. Sometimes, it rains on Tuesdays.
38. What is the diameter of the circle?
Statements: I. Its circumference is 44 cm.
II. Its area is 154 sq. cm.
39. What is the age of a student?
Statements: I. 10 years ago the student was half as old as his father.
II. 5 years from now his father will be 1.5 times as old as he.
40. Is A the father of B?
Statements: I. C is the grandson of A.
II. C is the son of B.
41. Are merchants greedy?
Statements: I. Some merchants are money-minded.
II. All money-minded are greedy.
42. How much did Ajay score in the exam?
Statements: I. His score was a prime number between 40 and 50.
II. He scored more than 45.
43. Does smoking lead to ill-health?
Statements: I. According to a survey, out of 1000 people suffering from lung cancer, 876 are smokers.
II. Cancer is a sign of ill-health.

44. What is the number of sides of a regular polygon?
Statements: **I.** The sum of all its internal angles is 540°.
II. The angles subtended by all the side at its centre are equal to 72°.

45. What is the colour of his eye?
Statements: **I.** The colour of his eye is the same as the colour of my shirt.
II. I am not wearing a blue shirt.

46. Is it going to be Monday tomorrow?
Statements: **I.** It was Tuesday on 1st January, 1971.
II. Today is 2nd April, 1995.

47. Does he go to office everyday?
Statements: **I.** He is never fined for absence.
II. He is never at his home during office hours.

48. Are all footballs basketballs?
Statements: **I.** All animals are footballs.
II. All basketballs are animals.

49. Are some Indians sportsmen?
Statements: **I.** All those who love sports watch television.
II. Many Indians watch television.

50. Did Tendulkar hit a century yesterday?
Statements: **I.** After yesterday's innings, his average increased from 50 to 52 in a total of 80 innings.
II. Tendulkar scored more than Manjrekar who missed his century by just one run.

Directions (Q. 51-55): Each of the questions below consists of a question and two statements numbered I and II given below it. You have to decide whether the data provided in the statements are sufficient to answer the question. Give answer

1) if the data in statement I alone are sufficient to answer the question, while the data in statement II alone are not sufficient to answer the question.

2) if the data in statement II alone are sufficient to answer the question, while the data in statement I alone are not sufficient to answer the question.

3) if the data either in statement I alone or in statement II alone are sufficient to answer the question.

4) if the data given in both the statements I & II together are not sufficient to answer the question.

5) if the data in both the statements I & II together are necessary to answer the question.

51. Among M, P, T, R and W, each of a different age, who is the youngest?
   I. T is younger than only P and W.
   II. M is younger than T and older than R.
52. How is 'gone' written in a code language?
   I. 'you will be gone' is written as 'ka pa ni sa' in that code language.
   II. 'he will be there' is written as 'ja da ka ni' in that code language.
53. On which day of the week (starting from Monday and ending on Sunday of the same week) did Sushant visit Chennai.
   I. Sushant visited Chennai two days after his brother visited Chennai.
   II. Sushant did not visit Chennai either on Wednesday or on Friday.
54. Towards which direction is P with respect to the starting point?
   I. P walked 20 metres, took a right turn and walked 30 metres, again took a right turn and walked 20 metres towards West.
   II. P walked 30 metres, took a left turn and walked 20 metres, again tock a left turn and walked 30 metres towards East.
55. How is K related to Z?
   I. Z and P are the only sisters of D.
   II. D's mother is the wife of K's father.

Directions (Q. 56-60): Each of the questions below consists of a question and three statements numbered I, II and III given below it. You have to decide whether the data provided in the statements are sufficient to answer the question. Read all the three statements and Give answer

1) if the data in Statement I and II are sufficient to answer the question, while the data in Statement III are not required to answer the question.

2) if the data in Statement I and III are sufficient to answer the question, while the data in Statement II are not required to answer the question.

3) if the data in Statement II and III are sufficient to answer the question, while the data in Statement I are not required to answer the question.

4) if the data in Statement I alone or in Statement II alone or in Statement III alone are sufficient to answer the question.

5) if the data in all the Statements I, II and III together are necessary to answer the question.

56. Among six people P, Q, R, S, T and V, each lives on a different floor of a six-storey building having its six floors numbered one to six (the ground floor is numbered 1, the floor above it, number 2, and so on, and the topmost floor is numbered 6. Who lives on the topmost floor?
   I. There is cnly one floor between the floors on which R and Q live. P lives on an even-numbered floor.
   II. T does not live on an even-numbered floor. Q lives on an even-numbered floor. Q does not live on the topmost floor.

III. S lives on an odd-numbered floor. There are two floors between the floors on which S and P live. T lives on a floor immediately above R's floor.

57. There are six letters W, A, R, S, N and E. Is 'ANSWER' the word formed after performing the following operations using these six letters only?
   I. E is placed fourth to the right of A. S is not placed immediately next to either A or E.
   II. R is placed immediately next (either left or right) to E. W is placed immediately next (either left or right) to S.
   I. Both N and W are placed immediately next to S. The word does not begin with R. A is not placed immediately next to W.

58. Point D is in which direction with respect to Point B?
   I. Point A is to the west of Point B. Point C is to the north of Point B. Point D is to the south of Point C.
   II. Point G is to the south of Point D. Point G is 4m from Point B. Point D is 9m from Point B.
   I. Point A is to the west of Point B. Point B is exactly midway between Point A and E. Point F is to the south of Point E. Point D is to the west of Point F.

59. How is 'one' coded in a code language?
   I. 'one of its kind, is coded as 'zo pi ko fe' and 'in kind and cash' is coded as 'ga to ru ko'.
   II. 'its point for origin' is coded as 'ba le fe mi' and 'make a point clear' is coded as 'yu si mi de'.
   I. 'make money and cash' is coded as 'to mi ru hy' and 'money of various kind' is coded as 'qu ko zo hy'.

60. Are all the four friends, viz A, B, C and D, who are sitting around a circular table, facing the centre?
   I. B sits second to the right of D. D faces the centre. C sits on the immediate right of both B and D.
   II. A sits on the immediate left of B. C is not an immediate neighbour of A. C sits on the immediate right of D.
   I. D is an immediate neighbour of both A and C. B sits on the immediate left of A. C sits on the immediate right of B.

Directions (61-110): Each of the following questions below consists of a question and two statements numbered I and II given below it. You have to decide whether the data provided in the statements are sufficient to answer the question. Read both the statements and give answer

1) **if the data in statement I alone are sufficient to answer the question, while the data in statement II alone are not sufficient in answer the question.**

2) if the data in statement II alone are sufficient to answer the question, while the data in statement I alone are not sufficient to answer the question.

3) if the data in either in statement I alone or in statement II alone are sufficient to answer the question.

4) if the data in both the statements I and II together are not sufficient to answer the question.

5) if the data in both the statements I and II are together necessary to answer the question.

61. Who amongst P, Q, R, S and T is the tallest?
    I. P is taller than Q. T is not the tallest.
    II. R is taller than P. S is not the tallest.

62. In which direction is point E, with reference to point S?
    I. Point D is to the east of point E. Point E is to the south of point F.
    II. Point F is to the north-west to point S. Point D is to the north of point S.

63. In which month of the year did Rahul go abroad for a vacation?
    I. Rahul correctly remembers that he went for a vacation in the first half of the year.
    II. Rahul's son correctly remembers that they went for a vacation after 31st March but before 1st May.

64. On which day of the same week is Ramesh's exam scheduled (Monday being the first day of the week)?
    I. Ramesh correctly remembers that his exam is scheduled on a day after Tuesday, but before Thursday of the same week.
    II. Ramesh's father correctly remembers that Ramesh's exam is scheduled on the third day of the week.

65. How many marks has Suman scored in the test ? (Maximum marks 20)
    I. Suman scored two-digit marks. Her marks were not in decimals.
    II. Suman scored more than 9 marks in the test.

66. On which day was Yasir born? (His date of birth is February 29.)
    I. He was born between year 2005 and 2011.
    II. He will complete 4 years on February 29, 2012.

67. Out of 64 students, 38 play both chess and cricket. How many students play only chess?
    I. Out of 64 students, 22 students don't play any game. 4 students play only cricket.
    II. Out of 64 students, 20 are girls and 10 of them don't play any game.

68. What is the total number of students in the school?
    I. The ratio of girls to boys is 2 : 3.
    II. The number of students has grown by 5% this year as compared to 4% last year from the number 2000, which it was year before last.

69. Who among the six of them is the tallest if Geetha is taller than Shilpa and Deepa is taller than Meeta? (Sunita and Sadhana are the other two).
    I. Sadhana is taller than Sunita.
    II. Sadhana is taller than Shilpa and Meeta as well as Deepa.
70. On which date is Amit's birthday in September 2010?
    I. Last year his birthday was on the last Thursday of the month in September 2009.
    II. This year his birthday will be on the last Friday of the month in September 2010.
71. Is S, T's aunt?
    I. K is the father of two children P and T.
    II. T is S's niece
72. Who among S, T, U and V is the tallest?
    I. U is shorter than only T.
    II. V is taller than only S.
73. Out of three friends L, M and N, each one likes Chocolates, Ice-cream or Chips (not necessarily in the same order). Who, out of the three, likes Chips? Statements:
    I. L does not like Chocolates.
    II. N likes Ice-cream.
74. What is today's date (not taking into account the month and the year)?
    I. Exactly four weeks ago, the date was 24th.
    II. The previous month was one of the longest months in terms of number of days.
75. How will 'WATCH' be coded in the code language?
    I. In that code language 'PERIL' is coded as 'QFQJM'.
    II. In that code language 'FOSTERS' is coded as 'GPTSFST'.
76. How is 'never' written in a code language?
    I. 'never ever go there' is written as 'na ja ni ho' in that code language.
    II. 'go there and come back' is written as 'ma ho sa ni da' in that code language.
77. Among M, P, K, J, T and W, who is lighter than only the heaviest?
    I. P is heavier than M and T.
    II. W is heavier than P but lighter than J who is not the heaviest.
78. What does '$' mean in a code language?
    I. '5 $ # 3' means 'flowers are really good'.
    II. '7 # 3 5' means 'good flowers are available'.
79. How is P related to J?
    I. M is the brother of P and T is the sister of P.
    II. P's mother is married to J's husband who has one son and two daughters.
80. How many students are there between Suresh and Mohan in a row of fifty students?

I. Suresh is twelfth from the left end and Mohan is seventeenth from the right end.

II. Suresh is six places away from Jayesh, who is twentieth from the left end.

81. Who amongst L, M, N, O and P is the shortest?

I. O is shorter than P but taller than N.

II. M is not as tall as L.

82. Are all the five friends, viz, Leena, Amit, Arun, Ali and Ken, who are seated around a circular table, facing the centre?

I. Leena sits second to the left of Amit. Amit faces the centre. Arun sits second to the right of Leena.

II. Ali sits third to the left of Ken. Ken faces the centre. Amit sits on the immediate left of Ali but Ken is not an immediate neighbour of Amit.

83. Is T grandmother of Q?

I. P is the mother of Q. Q is the son of R. R is the son of T.

II. L is father of N and N is daughter of T.

84. Point A is towards which direction from point B?

I. If a person walks 4m towards the north from point A, and takes two consecutive right turns each after walking 4m, he would reach point C, which is 8 m away from point B.

II. Point D is 2m towards the east of point A and 4m towards the west of point B.

85. How many brothers does Bharat have?

I. Shiela, the mother of Bharat, has only three children.

II. Meena, the grandmother of Bharat, has only one granddaughter.

86. How is 'letter' written in a code language?

I. 'please write a letter' is written as **'7218'** ' and received a Greek letter' is written as **'7513'**.

II. 'write in English please' is written as **'2084'** and 'a letter in Greek' is written as **'5714'**.

87. Among A, B, C, D and E, seated in a straight line, facing North, who sits exactly in the middle of the line?

I. A sits third to the left of D. B sits on the immediate right of C.

II. B sits second to the right of A. E is not an immediate neighbour of D.

88. A six-storey building consisting of an unoccupied ground floor and five floors on top of the ground floor numbered 1, 2, 3, 4 and 5 houses five different persons, viz A, B, C, D and E. Who lives on the third floor?

I. C lives on an even-numbered floor. A lives immediately above D. B lives immediately above A.

II. D lives on an odd-numbered floor. A and B are immediate neighbours. Similarly, C and E are immediate neighbours. C does not live on an odd-numbered floor.

89. Are all the four friends, Abhay, Kavita, Prashant and Yasir, who are sitting around a circular table, facing the centre?

I. Kavita sits second to the left of Abhay. Abhay faces the centre. Yasir sits on the immediate right of Abhay as well as Kavita.

II. Prashant sits third to the right of Kavita. Abhay sits on the immediate right of Prashant as well as Yasir.

90. Is R the grand-daughter of C?

I. The only sister of A is the mother of R's brother B.

II. C, the mother of A, has only one grandson

91. How many students are there between S and M in a row of 50 students ?

I. S is twelfth from the left end and Mohan is seventeenth from the right end.

II. S is six places away from J, who is twentieth from the left end.

92. What does '$' mean in a code language?

I. '5 $ # 3' means 'flowers are really good'.

II. '7 # 3 5' means 'good flowers are available'.

93. How is P related to J?

I. M is the brother of P and T is the sister of P.

II. P's mother is married to J's husband, who has one son and two daughters.

94. How is 'never' written in a code language ?

I. 'never ever go there' is written as 'na ja ni ho' in that code language.

II. 'go there and come back' is written as 'ma ho sa ni da' in that code language.

95. Among M, P, K, J, T and W, who is lighter than only the heaviest ?

I. P is heavier than M and T.

II. W is heavier than P but lighter than J, who is not the heaviest.

96. Who amongst A, B, C, D and E is the tallest?

I. A is taller than B but shorter than C. D is not the tallest.

II. Two people are taller than C.

97. Which direction is Ali facing?

I. If Ken, who is currently facing East, turns 90° towards his right, he would face a direction exactly opposite to the direction which Ali is facing.

II. If Priya who, is currently facing South, turns left, walks 1m and then takes a left turn again, she would face the same direction as Ali.

98. Did 300 candidates appear for the written examination for admission into College X?

I. The principal of the college correctly mentions that the number of candidates who had appeared for the examination was more than 200.

II. According to a statistical report, only 175 candidates could qualify the examination.

99. How far is Point P from Point Q? (All the points lie on a straight line.)
    I. Point T is exactly midway between Points P and Q. Point T is 5 km towards west of Point R.
    II. Point Q is 2 km towards the east of Point R.
100. How many brothers does A have?
    I. A, who is B's brother, has two siblings.
    II. D is brother of A and is youngest in the family.
101. How is J related to K?
    I. J's father P is the brother of N. N is K's wife.
    II. J is the son of P. P is the brother of N. N is K's wife.
102. On which floor of the building does G stay? (The building has five floors 1, 2, 3, 4, 5.)
    I. Only the even-numbered floors are occupied and G does not stay on the second floor.
    II. G does not stay on an odd-numbered floor.
103. How many days did Raju take to complete his assignment?
    I. Mohit correctly remembers that Raju took more than 3 days but less than 9 days to complete his assignment.
    II. Mina correctly remembers that Raju took more than 7 days but less than 11 days to complete his; assignment.
104. How is the word 'GATES' coded in the code language?
    I. 'BRICK' is coded as 'LDJSC' and 'PIN' is coded as 'OJQ'.
    II. 'WATER' is coded as 'SFUBX' and 'DISH' is coded as 'ITJE'.
105. Among A, B, C and D, which school has the highest number of students?
    I. School A has fewer students than school D.
    II. School C has fewer students than school D.
106. Which bag amongst P, Q, R, S and T is the heaviest?
    I. Bag Q is heavier than R and S. Bag T is heavier than only bag P.
    II. Only three bags are lighter than R. The weight of bag Q is 50 kg, which is 2 kg more than bag R.
107. Are all the five friends – A, B, C, D and E – who are seated around a circular table facing the centre ?
    I. A sits to the left of B. B faces the centre. D and E are immediate neighbours of each other. C sits second to the right of E.
    II. D sits second to right of C. C faces the centre. Both E and A are immediate neighbours of D. B sits second to the right of A.
108. In a college, five different subjects, viz Physics, Chemistry, Botany, Zoology and Mathematics, are taught on five different days of the same week, starting from Monday and ending on Friday. Is Chemistry taught on Wednesday?
    I. Two subjects are taught between Zoology and Mathematics. Mathematics is taught before Zoology. Chemistry is taught on the day

immediately next to the day when Physics is taught. Botany is not taught on Friday.

II. Three lectures are scheduled between the lectures of Botany and Zoology. Mathematics is taught immediately before Physics.

109. Is it 9 o'clock now?

I. After half an hour, the minute and the hour hands of the clock will make an angle of exactly 90° with each other.

II. Exactly 15 minutes ago, the hour and the minute hands of the clock coincided with each other.

110. Is F granddaughter of B?

I. B is the father of M. M is the sister of T. T is the mother of F.

II. S is the son of F. V is the daughter of F. R is the brother of T.

Directions (Q. 111-115): Each of the questions below consists of a question and three statements numbered I, II and III given below it. You have to decide whether the data provided in the statements are sufficient to answer the question.

111. How many daughters does W have?

I. B and D are the sisters of M.

II. M's father T is the husband of W.

III. Out of the three children which T has, only one is a boy.

1) Only I and III are sufficient to answer the question.
2) All I, II and III are required to answer the question.
3) Only II and III are sufficient to answer the question.
4) Question cannot be answered even with all I, II and III.
5) Only I and II are sufficient to answer the question.

112. Who among A, B, C, D, E and F, each having a different height, is the tallest?

I. B is taller than A but shorter than E.

II. Only two of them are shorter than C.

III. D is taller than only F.

1) Only I and II are sufficient to answer the question.
2) Only I and III are sufficient to answer the question.
3) Only II and III are sufficient to answer the question.
4) All I, II and III are required to answer the question.
5) All I, II and III even together are not sufficient to answer the question.

113. Towards which direction is Village J from Village W?

I. Village R is to the west of Village W and to the north of Village T.

II. Village Z is to the east of Village J and to the south of Village T.

III. Village M is to the north-east of Village J and to the north of Village Z.

1) Only III is sufficient to answer the question.
2) Only II and III sufficient to answer the question.
3) All I, II and III are required to answer the question.

4) Question cannot be answered even with all I, II and III.
5) None of these

114. On which day of the week did Suresh visit Chennai? (Assume that the week starts from Monday.)
I. Suresh took a leave on Wednesday.
II. Suresh visited Chennai the day after his mother's visit to his house.
III. Suresh's mother visited Suresh's house on neither Monday nor Thursday.
1) Only II and III are sufficient to answer the question.
2) Only I and II are sufficient to answer the question.
3) Only I and III are sufficient to answer the question.
4) All I, II and III are required to answer the question.
5) Question cannot be answered even with all I, II and III.

115. How is 'go' written in a code language?
I. 'now or never again' is written as 'torn ka na sa' in that code language.
II. 'you come again now' is written as 'ja ka ta sa' in that code language.
III. 'again go now or never' is written as 'na ho ka sa torn' in that code language.
1) Only I and III are sufficient to answer the question.
2) Only II and III are sufficient to answer the question.
3) Only I and II are sufficient to answer the question.
4) All I, II and III are required to answer the question.
5) None of these

Answers and Explanations

Exercise 7A

1. 5; The information is not suficient. A can be of any age greater than 24 years.
2. 3; There are **two informations** and **two unknowns** (A's age, B's age); so both the unknowns can be found.
3. 3; Since both have the same father, they must be brothers.
4. 3; Since both have the same father and since X is a male (a son), X must be the brother of Y.
5. 5; It is clear that X and Y are siblings but we cannot be sure that X is a brother unless we know that he is a male. X may also be a sister of Y.
6. 1; From the first statement itself we find that X cannot be a brother (a male) because she is, in fact, a daughter (a female) of Z.
7. 3; From the two statements together we find that Shyam and Mohan are siblings. **We assume that Shyam must be the name of a male.** Then we can conclude that Shyam is a brother of Mohan. (Compare this with Q. 5.

There, we could not answer the question because we could not assume that X is a male.)

8. 5; We cannot be sure that Minu is a mother. She may as well be the mother-in-law of Shanu.

9. 5; The two statements are not sufficient. We would also need to know if Delhi is between Patna and Shimla or Patna is between Delhi and Shimla.

10. 5; The two statements are not sufficient. We would also need to know if the three points representing Patna, Delhi and Shimla fall on a straight line on the map or they form a triangle. The answer would be different in the two cases.

11. 5; The two statements are not sufficient: the information they provide is slightly ambiguous. Firstly, Radha may have started the travel on a Sunday but may have reached Shimla on a Monday. Secondly, the statement says that Sunday is a holiday. But it does not say that no other day was a holiday. So, we cannot restrict our answers to Sundays alone.

12. 5; From the two statements, we can be sure that Radha travelled for Shimla on a Sunday but we still cannot be sure that she **reached** Shimla on Sunday.

13. 5; From the two statements, we can be sure that Radha was in Shimla on Sunday but the question is not about the day when Radha **was** in Shimla; it is about the day when Radha **reached** Shimla.

14. 4; We can get the answer (29 February) from I alone because 29 February is the only date that comes *only in a leap year*. From the second statement alone, we can also find the answer.

15. 5; There are many countries whose flags have three colours. Hence, the data are insufficient to point out the exact date of her birthday.

16. 5; From the two statements, we cannot pinpoint the exact date of birth. It may be 26th March, 1974 or 27th March, 1974.

17. 3; From the two statements together, we can find the correct answer. It can only be 26th March, 1974.

18. 5; Since 1976 was a leap year we get two possible dates of birth: 28th Feb, 1976, and 29th Feb, 1976. Hence, the data are insufficient.

19. 3; 28th Feb, 1974 can be the only possible date of birth.

20. 3; For any zodiac sign the 1st date of a month comes only once. For Aries the zodiac dates are 21st March to 20th April. So, Anju must have been born on the 1st April.

21. 1; From the first statement alone, we can conclude that Shyam is 25. The second statement alone is not sufficient.

22. 2; From the second statement alone, we can conclude that Shyam is 20 years old. The first statement alone is not sufficient.

23. 4; The two statements are independently sufficient to answer the question. From the first statement we find that Shyam was 9 years old in 1947. From

this, his present age can be found. From the second statement, we can easily find that Shyam has just completed 58 years of age.

24. 3; From the two statements, we find that A is taller than both B and C. So, A must be the tallest.

25. 5; From the two statements, we cannot find out who is the tallest. For this, we will need a comparison of the heights of B and C, which is not given.

26. 5; From the two statements we cannot find who is the shortest. This could be either B or C and we will need a comparison between the heights of B and C, which is not given.

27. 3; From the two statements we find that A is shorter than both B and C. So, A must be the shortest person.

28. 4; The two statements are independently sufficient to answer the question. Notice that you are asked to find a person who is not the tallest. From the first, we find that B is one such person. From the second, we find that C is one such person.

29. 3; The two statements together are sufficient to answer the question. Notice that you are asked to find the persons who are not the tallest. From the first, we find that B is one such person. From the second, we find that C is one such person. Combining the two informations we can conclude that B and C are the persons who are not the tallest.

[**Note:** Note carefully the difference between the languages of Q. 28 and Q. 29. In Q. 28, you have to find **one** person who **is** not the tallest. In Q. 29, you have to find **persons** who **are** not the tallest. Because of this you get different answers.]

30. 1; If you *convert* statement I, you will find that its immediate inference is "some Indians are hotblooded". But statement II alone is not sufficient. [**Note:** For Q. 30 to Q. 40 you are advised to go through the chapter on **Syllogism**.]

31. 2; On converting, statement II gives the immediate inference: "Some pens are pencils." But we do not get any answer from the first statement.

32. 5; Since the two statements have the same predicate we will first have to align them for getting an inference. For this, convert the second sentence to "Some potatoes are flowers." Now, we have A + I = no conclusion. Hence, we get no conclusion.

33. 3; We use the rule I + E = O. Hence, the two statements together give the conclusion: Some papers are not flowers. This answers the question.

34. 5; We use the rule I + E = O. Hence, the two statements together give the conclusion : Some papers are not flowers. But this does not answer the question fully. Some papers are not flowers but the remaining papers may or may not be flowers. Hence, data insufficient.

35. 3; We use the rule I + E = O. Hence, the two statements together give the conclusion that "Some papers are not flowers." This answers the question

in negative. Since some papers are not flowers, the conclusion "All papers are flowers" must be false. So, we do get an answer and the answer is 'No'.

36. 2; We do not get an answer to our question from statement I. But from statement II we get a negative answer. Since "No chair is an Indian", the conclusion that "Some Indians are chairs" must be false. This does answer the question and the answer is 'No'.

37. 3; Using the two statements together we can conclude that "Some Indians are honest." [Rule: I + A = I]. Since "Some Indians are honest" implies that it is false that "No Indian is honest", we may conclude that we do get an answer to the above question and the answer is 'No'.

38. 5; Using the two statements together we can conclude that "Some Indians are not honest." [Rule: I + E = O]. Since "Some Indians are not honest" does not provide complete information, we may conclude that data is insufficient. From "Some Indians are not honest" we do not know whether the remaining Indians are also honest or not. If the remaining Indians are also dishonest the answer would be 'Yes', otherwise it would be 'No'.

39. 4; From I we conclude by immediate inference that "Some baskets are glasses". From II, we conclude by converting that "All baskets are glasses", which implies automatically that "Some baskets are glasses." Hence, both the statements are independently sufficient to answer the question.

40. 5; We cannot get an answer to our question from the two statements. By the rules of syllogism, we find that A + I = no conclusion.

41. 4; Both the statements are individually sufficient to answer the question. Since there are only four persons, from I we find that if B is opposite D, the remaining two, viz. A and C, must be facing each other. Again, from II we find that since A is between B and D, C must be opposite A. Hence, both the statements are independently sufficient to answer the question.

42. 5; We cannot get a concrete answer from the two statements. From statement I we find that B is opposite C and D is opposite E. This implies that the remaining two, viz. F and A must be opposite each other. Now, F is on the immediate left of B. This can be pictorially represented as

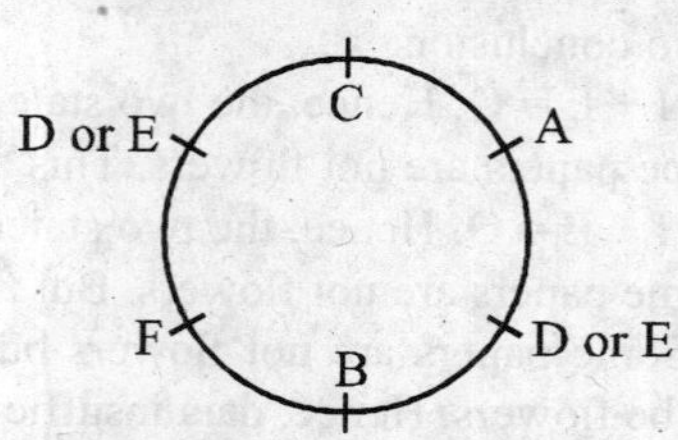

From the figure, it is clear that on the immediate left of A we can have either D or E and hence, the information is insufficient.

43. 3; We **can** get a correct answer from the information provided. From statement I, we find that B is opposite C, and D is opposite E. This implies that the remaining two, viz. F and A, are opposite each other. Now, F is on the immediate left of B. This can be pictorially represented as

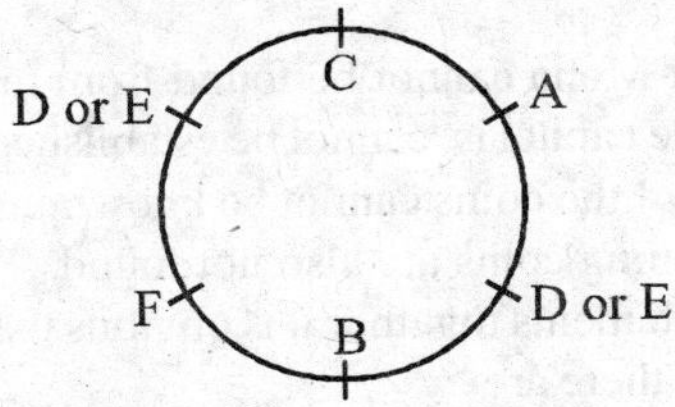

From the figure, it is obvious that C is on the immediate right of A.

44. 2; Our answer is obtainable from statement II alone but not from statement I alone.

45. 5; Data are inadequate to come to a definite conclusion.
I implies Anju < Sonu
II implies Rohit < Sonu
We can't compare Anju and Rohit with the help of this data.

46. 5; If the father is 20 years older than his son, he will always remain 20 years older than him. Both the statements say the same thing.

47. 3; Since A + A = A, we can get a conclusion "All books are chocolates." This automatically implies that Some books are chocolates.

48. 5; The two statements are not sufficient to come to a definite conclusion. It is obvious that B is the son of A but we do not know if A is the mother or father of B.

49. 5; We cannot find the speed of the train from the given data. To find an answer to this question we will also need to know the length of the bridge. When a train crosses a bridge it covers a distance which is equal to the sum of the length of the train and that of the bridge. Since the length of the bridge is not given, the information is incomplete.

50. 3; From the two statements together, we can find that the answer to the question is 200 ÷ 5 = 40 m per second. We can safely assume that a pole has no length and, hence, in passing a pole a train only covers a distance which is equal to its own length.

Exercise 7B

1. 3; From the two statements together we can immediately see that A is the grandfather of B. Hence the answer to the question can be found. [The answer is: No.]

2. 3; From the two statements together we can immediately see that A is the father of B. Hence, the answer to the question can be found. [The answer is: Yes.]

3\. 3; From the two statements together we see that A is the tallest because A is taller than both B and C.

4\. 5; Either B or C may be the shortest.

5\. 3; From the two statements together it can be seen that the mother is 30 years old.

6\. 5; The exact age of Mona cannot be found from the two statements.

7\. 5; Exactly where the capital is, cannot be established by the two statements.

8\. 5; The exact value of the coins cannot be known unless the denominations of the five remaining coins are also not found.

9\. 3; From the two statements together it is obvious that there are 10 birds and 10 cows. Hence, there are
$10 \times 2 + 10 \times 4 = 60$ legs.

10\. 5; In I Guddi is the daughter of Sonu but Sonu may be the father or mother of Guddi. So we must also know the sex of Sonu. In II also the sex of Sonu is not given; hence, whether Sonu is the father or mother of Guddi cannot be established.

However, if you have chosen your answer as 4; assuming that Sonu is always a male name, this approach is also correct. Ideally, the answer should be 5. But we can, in such cases, assume that Sonu is a male name. For this question then, the answer becomes 4.

11\. 5; Even together, the two statements are not sufficient.

12\. 1

13\. 3; Using the two statements we can easily see that the answer is Friday.

14\. 3; There are two variables in the statements: Madan and Madan's father. Since there are two informations, we can solve it mathematically to get the answer.

15\. 5; We may write I as 'Some Indians are Africans'. Now, Some Indians are Africans + No Africans are Asians = I + E = O = Some Indians are not Asians. Hence, it is established that there are some Indians who are not Asians. But are there some Indians who are Asians? We do not know. Hence, data inadequate.

16\. 5; From I, it is not clear whether Manju is the father or mother of Sanju. II does not help in this aspect.

Again, like in Q. 10, if we assume that Manju is always a female name, the correct answer would be 1.

17\. 5; There may be two possibilities leading to two answers:

← 300 km →
← 200 km →
I. Hisar Delhi Rohtak

← 200 km → ← 300 km →
II. Delhi Hisar Rohtak

18. 4; From both the statements area can be found independently.

$$\text{Area} = \pi \times (\text{radius})^2$$

or

$$\text{Area} = \frac{(\text{circumference})^2}{4\pi}$$

19. 4

20. 3; If the day of any date in history is given, the day of any other date can be found. [See *Magical Book on Quicker Maths* published by BSC Publications for the method.]

21. 5; Even together these statements are not sufficient: it never becomes clear whether X is the brother or sister of Y.

22. 3; From the two statements taken together, the age can be found out. It is equal to 62 - 30 = 32 years.

23. 5; The statements do not provide **solid** reasons why it should be believed that Tendulkar **will** hit a century today. Even the best of batsmen can fail on even the most suitable of pitches.

24. 5; The two statements do not provide complete evidence about the exact date of murder. The police took 4 days to detect who the murderer was. But how may extra days did it take to **nab** the murderer? For example, if the police took 4 days to *detect* and 13 days to *chase and catch* the murderer then the murder could have occured on 18 - (4 + 13) = 1st. Hence, the data given in the question are not sufficient to answer the question.

25. 5; The two statements are not sufficient to answer the question. In fact, **for any square**, whatever be its size, the two statements I and II are always true. Thus, in fact, no additional data is given. [If you cannot imagine how the two statements I and II will always be true for *any* square, refer to *Magical Book on Quicker Maths*.]

26. 5

27. 3; If the group is of two people only and if Sudha is not the tallest, then the other person, i.e. Mohan, must be the tallest. Hence, the two statements, taken together, are sufficient to answer the question.

28. 4; Both the statements are separately sufficient to answer the question. From I, it is obvious that price of one pen = Rs 17. From II, it is obvious that price of one pen ≠ Rs 18, because 18 is not a prime number. Hence, the answer can be obtained (the answer is 'No') from both the statements separately.

29. 1; Think keenly. You can get the answer from I alone but not from II alone. Let us see how.

Statement I. If Sudha has five rupees in her pocket and if she can make two calls at most, it implies that the rate per call is Rs 2. Because (i) it can't be Re 1/call as it could have enabled her to make 5 calls and (ii) it can't be Rs 3/ call as it could not have enabled her to make 2 calls. So, the charge per call must be between Re 1 and Rs 3. Also, it is given that it is a whole number. So, it must be Rs 2.

Statement II. Raman can't make a call with one rupee. This statement is sufficient only as far as it enables one to know that the charge per call is more than one rupee. But it can be Rs 2 or 3 or maybe Rs 100. The statement is not sufficient to find out the actual charge per call.

30. 5; Neither is sufficient. Statement II is tempting but note that it only says that **the image** (of India as a vibrant democracy) **has suffered**; it does not say that democracy itself has suffered.
31. 3; Both needed. I tells us that X could be either the brother or sister of Y. II tells us that X is a female. So, she must be a sister.
32. 5; Data not sufficient. I tells us that Z could be either father or mother. II does not give any further hint.
33. 3; Use syllogism.
34. 1
35. 4; Both statements are independently sufficient to come to the conclusion that it will not be a Sunday tomorrow.
36. 3; Together, from the two statements we see that Minu > Radhu > Manju which means Minu > Manju. This answers the question in the negative.
37. 5; It rains *sometimes* on Tuesdays. It may or may not rain.
38. 4; Both the statements are sufficient in themselves.
39. 3; From the two statements together we can draw the conclusion.
40. 5; The question is not fully answered. A could be either the mother or father of B.
41. 5; Using syllogistic reasoning (I + A = I), we infer that "Some merchants are greedy". But the question is "Are merchants greedy?". It takes the whole class of merchants in its fold. If answered `Yes', it would mean that "All merchants are greedy" and if answered `No', it would mean that "No merchant is greedy". But all we can conclude from the two given statements is that "Some merchants are greedy". We cannot talk about the **whole** class from these statements. So, still more clues are needed.
42. 3; There is only one prime number greater than 45 and less than 50. It is 47. So the answer can be found from the two statements taken together.
43. 5; I *may be just a coincidence*. Examples can not make laws. Concrete evidence is not given in the two statements that smoking indeed promotes ill-health. [*You should note the lesson of this example carefully*.]

44. 4; From statement I, n, the number of sides, can be found by using the formula:

Sum of angles = 540° = 90° × (2n - 4)

From Statement II, n, the number of sides, can be found by using the formula:

$$n = \frac{360°}{\text{angle subtended by anyone side}}$$

45. 5; From the two statements, all that can be inferred is that the colour of his eye is not blue. But the actual colour can't be found.

46. 3; Together, the two statements are sufficient to get an answer. We know that we can find the day of any date if we know the day of any other date. So, the day falling on 2nd April, 1995, can be found by using statement I. Then, the day falling on 3rd April can be found out.

Note: You must note that this is a question of data sufficiency. All you have to do here is to state whether the question can be answered from the given data. You are not supposed **to find** the answer. For example, in the preceding question, it is a matter of 5 seconds to say that the two data are sufficient to answer the question while it may take upto 5 minutes to find out the actual date of 3rd April, 1995.

You **must**, therefore, understand that data-sufficiency questions ask you whether the data are sufficient for finding an answer. *They do not ask you to **find** the answer.*

47. 5; The two statements are not sufficient to guarantee that he never misses his office. A possibility remains that he goes to some third place and is never fined for absence because of the simple fact that there is no provision of fine for absence in his office (!). Who knows!

48. 5; Using syllogistic reasoning (Rule: A + A = A), we find "All basketballs are footballs." But "All footballs are basketballs" is neither proved nor disproved.

49. 5; Using syllogistic reasoning, we get A + I = no conclusion. Further, statement I talks about 'sports lovers' not 'sportsmen'.

50. 4; Both the statements are independently sufficient. From statement I, Tendulkar's score is (80 × 52 - 79 × 50) which is definitely more than 100. (You do not need to find out the actual answer. See, the note after the answer to Q. 46.) From II, Manjrekar scored 99. Tendulkar scored more; so, he must have hit a century.

51. 5; **From I.** P, W > T

II. T > M > R

From I and II; P, W > T > M > R

52. 4; From I and II, we can deduce the code for 'will be'. But that still leaves us with two words.

53. 4

54. 3; **From I:**

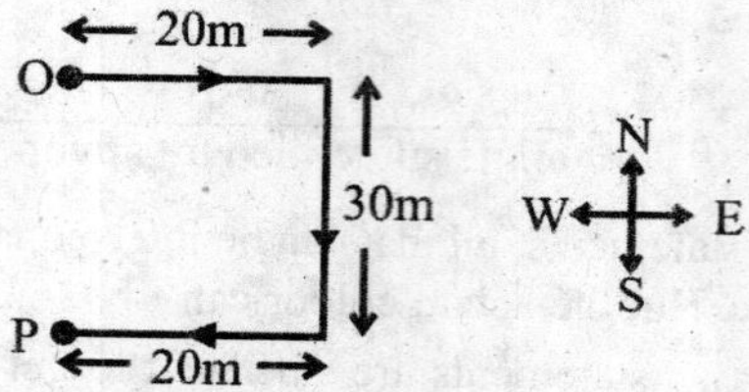

P is to the South of O (starting point).

From II:

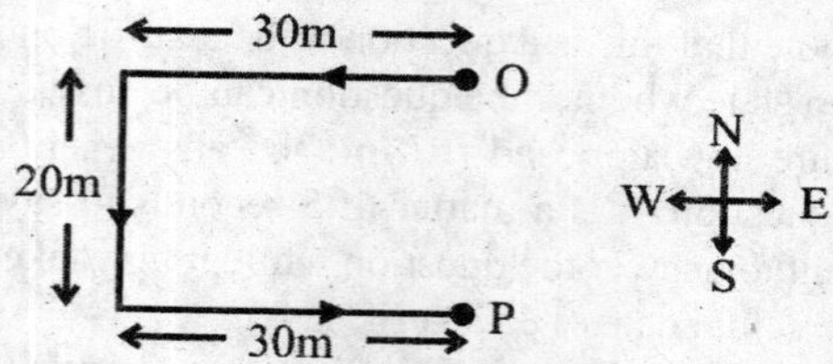

Again, P is to the South of O.

55. 4; **From I and II:**

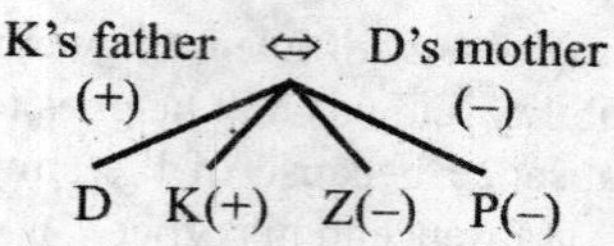

Hence K is Z's brother.

Note: Since Z and P are D's only sister, any other siblings of D will be a brother.

56. 3; **From II and III:** T lives on an odd-numbered floor. Also, T lives immediately above R. So, R lives on an even-numbered floor which is not the topmost. Again, II says Q lives on an even numbered floor which is not the topmost. Thus R and Q occupy floor 2 and 4.

Now, S lives on an odd-numbered floor. And there are two floors between S and P. So, P lives on an even-numbered floor and this must be floor 6 (the topmost)

57. 2; **From I:** _A_S_E or A_S_E

From II: RE or ER; WS or SW

From III: NSW or WSN...(a) R not at the beginning ... (b) neither AW nor WA ... (c)

From I and III (a): RANSWE (ruled out by III b)
RAWSNE (ruled out by III b and c)
ANSWER (possible)
AWSNER (ruled out by III c)
Hence, ANSWER is the word.

58. 2
59. 5
60. 4
61. 5; **From I:** P > Q, but T is not the tallest.
From II: R > P, but S is not the tallest.
From I and II: R > P > Q. Neither S nor T can be the tallest. Hence R is the tallest.
62. 5; **From I:**

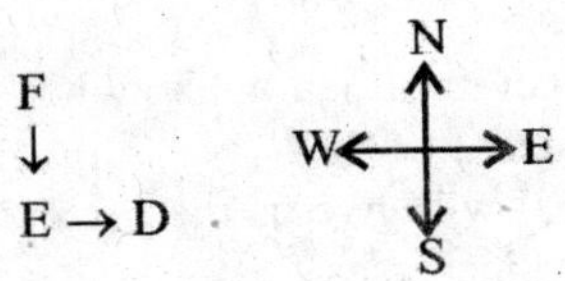

From II:

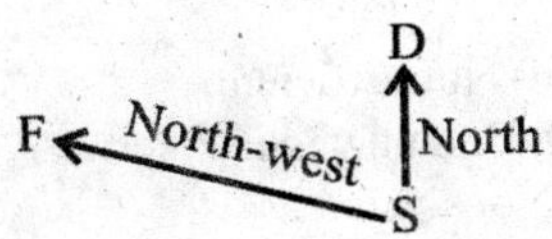

From I and II:

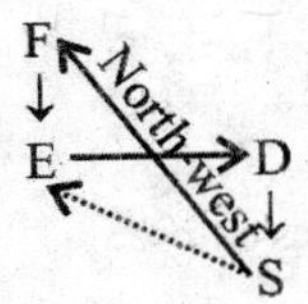

Point E is to the north-west of Point S.
63. 2; **From I:** Possible months: January, February, March, April, May or June.
From II: Rahul's son correctly remembers that his father went on vacation after 31st March but before 1st May.
So his father went on vacation in the month of April.
Hence only II is sufficient.
64. 3; **From I:** The possible day of exam is Wednesday.
From II: The third day of the week is Wednesday.
Hence, either statement I alone or statement II alone is sufficient.
65. 4; **From I:** Two-digit marks is less than or equal to 20.
Possible marks: 10, 11, 12, 13, 14, 15, 16, 17, 18, 19 and 20.

From II: Suman scored more than 9 marks.
Possible marks: 10, 11, 12, 13, 14, 15, 16, 17, 18, 19 and 20.
Hence statement I and II together are not sufficient.

66. 3; Feb 29 can occur only in a leap year. 2008 happens to be the the only leap year between 2005 and 2011. Hence Yasir was born on Feb 29, 2008. Using Calendar Method, we can find out the day. Hence I is sufficient. From II, Yasir was born on Feb 29, 2008. (2012 - 4 = 2008). Hence II is also sufficient.

67. 1; **From I:** 22 students don't play any game. Which means 64 - 22 = 42 play either chess or cricket.
Now, either chess or cricket = Only chess + Only cricket + Chess and Cricket
or 42 = Only chess + 4 + 38
or Only chess = 0
From II: We don't get information about boys.
Hence II is not sufficient.

68. 2; I leads us nowhere. II will give us the present strength as we have the base and percentage increases.

69. 4; **From the question:**
G > Sh; D > M ... (i)
From I: Sa > Su ... (ii) Not sufficient.
From II: Sa > Sh, M, D. But who is taller between Sa and G? Not sufficient.

70. 3; The calendar method is helpful in either case.

71. 4; The sex of S is not clear.

72. 1; **From I:** If U is shorter than only T, obviously T is the tallest.
From II: Either T or U is the tallest.

73. 5; **From I:** It alone leads us nowhere.
From II: Either L or M likes chips.
From I and II:

Person	Liking
L	Chips
M	Chocolates
N	Ice-cream

74. 5; From II, we get that last month had 31 days.
Now, use I and we get:
Today = 24 + 4 weeks
= 24 + 28 = (24 + 28 - 31) of next month
= 21st of next month

75. 3; Either of the codes can work.

76. 4; Only two words are common between I and II.

77. 5; **From I:** P > M, T
From II: J > W > P
Combining, we get K > J > W > P > M, T
Hence, K is the heaviest and J lighter than only the heaviest.

78. 5; **From I:** 5$#3 = flowers are really good ... (i)
From II: 7#35 = good flowers are available ... (ii)
From I and II: 5#3 = flowers are good ... (iii)
Putting (iii) in (i), we get: $ = really

79. 5; **From I:** M(+)—P—T(-)

From II:

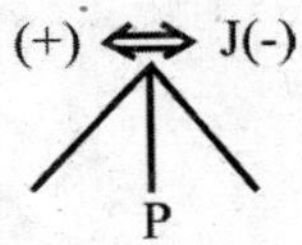

Combining, we get

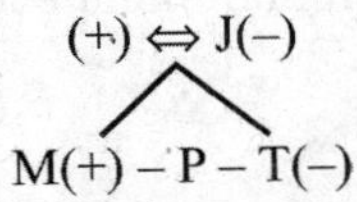

But II also says J's husband has one son and two daughters. Hence P must be daughter of J.

80. 1; **From I:**
Suresh = 12th from left
Mohan = 17th from right = (50 - 17 + 1 =) 34th from left
∴ No. of students between them = 34 - 12 - 1 = 21
From II: No data about Mohan.

81. 4; **From I:** P > O > N
From II: L > M
From I and II, either M or N is the shortest. We can't determine who is shorter between the two of them.

82. 3; **From I:** If all of them face the centre, it means if A sits second to the left of B, then B should sit second to the right of A. But here Amit and Arun are different persons. Hence all of them do not face the centre.
From II: Again, suppose all of them face the centre like Ken. Ali sits third to the left of Ken. Now, if Amit sits on the left of Ali, obviously Ken should be his neighbour. But the statement says otherwise. Hence our assumption is disproved. All of them do not face the centre.

83. 5; In I, the sex of T is not known. In II, Q does not figure. Hence we need both the statements to establish the relationship.

84. 2; **From I:** We don't know whether B is to the west or east of C. In fact, it could be in any other direction.

From II:

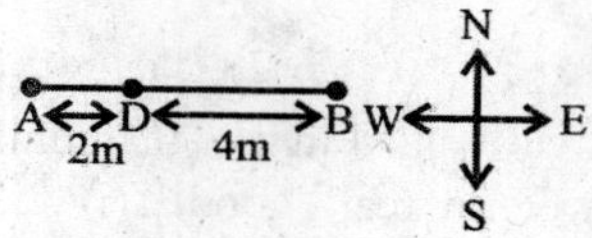

Obviously, A is west of B.

85. 4; **From I:** Bharat has two siblings but we don't know their sex.
From II: This granddaughter may be Bharat's sister or cousin.

86. 4; **Using Statement I:**
a letter → '71'
Using statement II:
'in' → '4'
Using both:
'Greek' → '5' and 'receired' → '3'
Code for, 'letter', cannot be found even by using both statements together.

87. 5; **Using Statement I:**
A C B D
Position of E cannot be found: it can be left of A or right of D.
Using Statement II:
Many seating arrangements are possible.
Using both:
E A C B D is the unique arrangement that is possible and C sits in the middle.

88. 4; **Using Statement I:**
We get two arrangements, ie

5→B		E
4→A		C
3→D	or	B
2→C		A
1→E		D

Using Statement II:
Many arrangements are possible.

89. 3; **Using Statement I:**
From the line "Yasir sits on the immediate right of Abhay as well as Kavita" we can conclude that one of Abhay and Kavita is facing towards the centre and the other outside. So, all friends are NOT facing the centre.
Using Statement II:
From the line "Abhay sits on the immediate right of Prashant as well as Yasir" we can conclude that one of Prashant and Yasir is facing towards the centre and the other outside. So, all friends are NOT facing the centre.

90. 5; **Using Statement I:**

C is not in the statement. So using I only we can never find the relation between R and C.

Using Statement II:

R is not in the statement. So using II only we can never find the relation between R and C.

Using both:

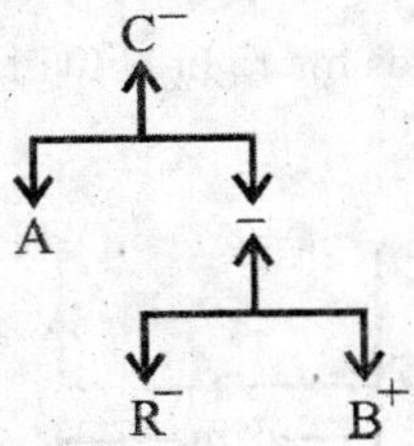

We can conclude that R is the granddaughter of C.

91. 1; See answer to Q 80 above

92. 5; Using either of the statements alone we cannot find the code for $, but using both the statements together we can find that '#53' is 'good flowers are'. So, the code for $ is 'really'.

93. 5; **Using statement I:**

We cannot find the relation using this statement as J's name is not even mentioned in it.

Using statement II:

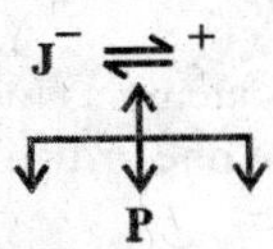

We can say that J is the mother of P but cannot decide whether P is the son or daughter of J.

Using both statements together:

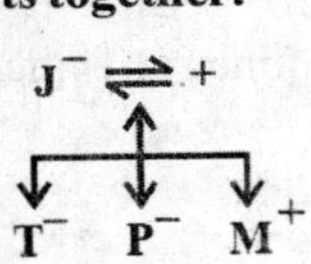

P is the daughter of J.

94. 4; Using either of the statements alone we cannot find the code, and even by using both the statements together we can only find that 'never ever' is coded as 'na ja' the code for 'never' cannot be uniquely determined even by using both the statements together.

95. 5; Using either of the statements alone we cannot find the answer, but when we use both the statements together we can find the relation in terms of weight, ie

$$K > J > W > P > M, T$$

96. 5; **From I:** $C > A > B$ and $- > D$.

From II: $- > - > C$.

Combining, we get $E > D > C > A > B$.

97. 3; **Using Statement I:**

If Ken turns 90° towards his right he will face South. So Ali is facing North.

Using Statement II:

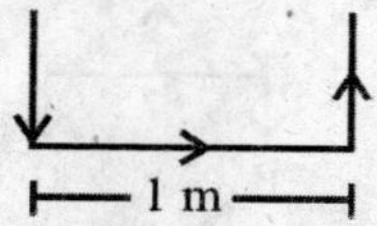

In the end Priya faces North. So Ali also faces North.

98. 4; Even by using both the statements together we can only determine that number of candidates appeared was more than 200.

99. 5; **Using I:**

T —5— R and T is midway between P and Q

Using II:

R —2— Q

Using Both:

P —7— T —5— R —2— Q

100. 4; Even by using both the statements together we cannot determine the gender of B. So A can have one or two brothers.

101. 2; **I.**

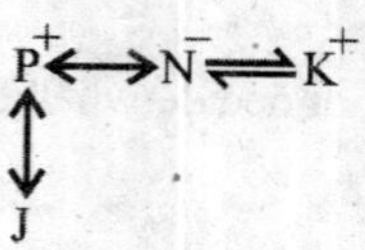

Using I only, we cannot determine if J is the nephew or niece of K.

II.

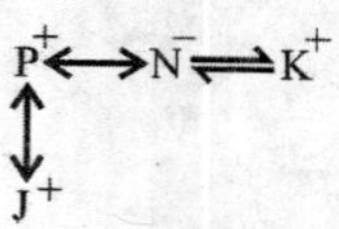

J is the nephew of K.

102. 1; **I.** Using I only we can determine that G stays on 4th floor.

II. Using II alone, we cannot determine if G stays on 2nd or 4th floor.

103. 5; **I.** Raju can take 4 to 8 days to complete the work.

II. Raju can take 8 to 10 days to complete the work.

Using both the statements together, we can determine that Raju took 8 days to complete the work.

104. 3

105. 4; Even by using both the statements together we cannot determine whether B has higher number of students or D.

106. 3; **Using statement I:**

Q > R, S > T > P

Q is the heaviest.

Using statement II:

Q > R > S, T, P

Q is the heaviest.

107. 2; **Using statement I:**

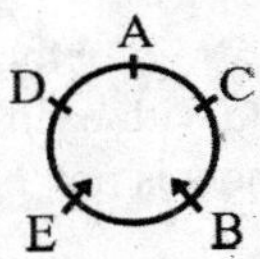

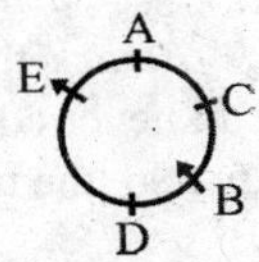

We cannot determine if all the friends are facing the centre.

Using statement II:

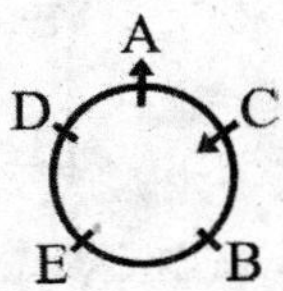

A is facing outside and C is facing the centre of circle. So, all friends are not facing the centre.

108. 3; **Using statement I:**

Monday	Botany
Tuesday	Mathematics
Wednesday	Physics
Thursday	Chemistry
Friday	Zoology

Chemistry is not taught on Wednesday.

Using statement II:

Monday	Botany/Zoology
Tuesday	Mathematics
Wednesday	Physics
Thursday	Chemistry
Friday	Zoology/Botany

OR

Monday	Botany/Zoology
Tuesday	Chemistry
Wednesday	Mathematics
Thursday	Physics
Friday	Zoology/Botany

Chemistry is not taught on Wednesday.

109. 3; **Using statement I:**

If the time is 9 o'clock now then after 30 minutes ie at 9:30 the angle between the minute hand and hour hand cannot be 90°. So, now the time is not 9 o'clock.

Using statement II:

If the time now is 9 o'clock then 15 min before the hour and minutes hand of the clock can never coincide with each other. Instead they will have an angle of 7.5°. So, the time now is not 9 o'clock.

110. 4; **Using statement I:**

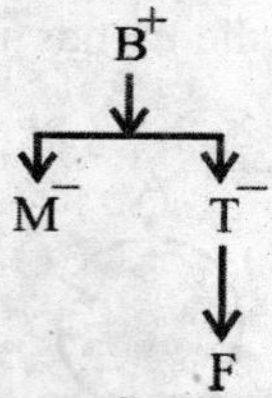

The gender of F is not known. So, we cannot say if F is granddaughter or grandson of B.

Using statement II:

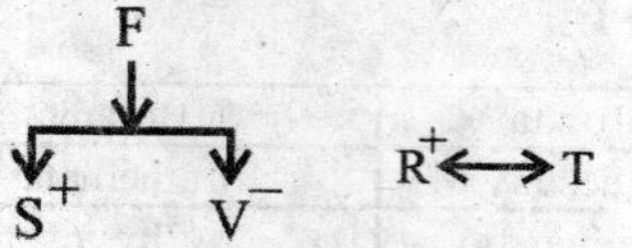

The name of B has not even been mentioned.

Using both statements together:

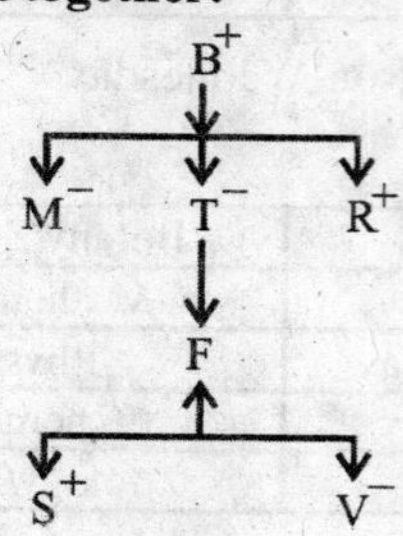

Still, the gender of F cannot be determined. So, we cannot determine if F is grandson or granddaughter of B.

111. 3; **From the statements II and III:**

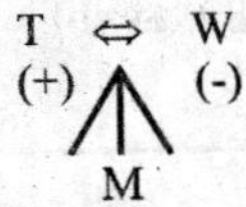

Though, sex of M is not known, it is given in statement III, that T has three children and only one of them is boy. Therefore, we may conclude that W has two daughters.

112. 4; **From statement I:**

E>B>A

From statement II:

—>—>—>C>—>—

From statement III:

Now combining all the above statements, we have

E>B>A>C>D>F

113. 5; **From statement II:**

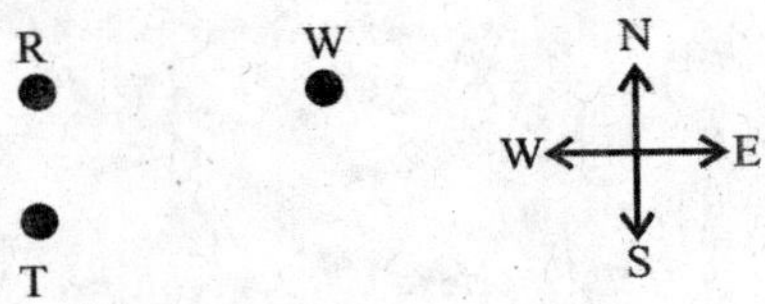

From statement III:

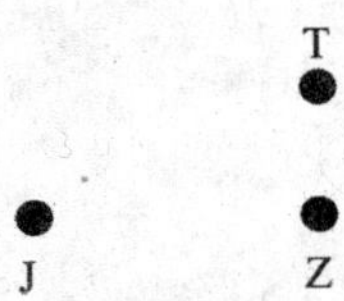

Now combining statements I and II:

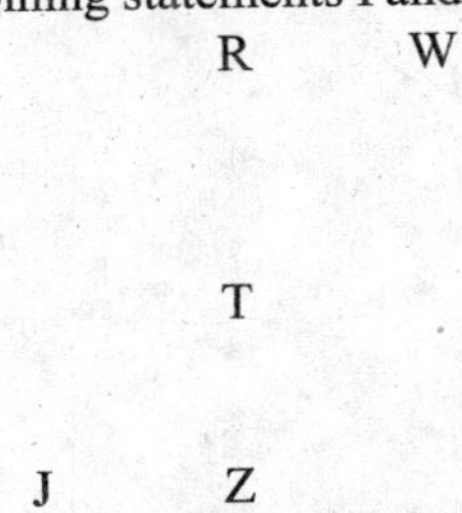

J is in south-west direction from W.

114. 5; Even by combining all the statements, we cannot find the day of the week on which Suresh's mother visited Suresh's house.

115. 1; **From statements I and III:**

now or never again ⇒ torn ka na sa ...(i)

again go now or never ⇒ na ho ka sa torn ...(ii)

From (i) and (ii), code for 'go' is 'ho'.

Chapter Eight

Punchline

8.1: Introduction

Let us begin our study with a short story. Agatha Christie, the famous author of many detective stories, was once invited to a conference where she was to deliver an address. When she arrived, she found that there was a long queue of 'distinguished' persons, each one giving his speech furiously. And the audience was getting bored to death. Agatha sensed the mood of the audience immediately. So, when the convenor of the conference finally announced before a restless audience: "Gentlemen, the famous author Agatha Christie will now give you her address.", Agatha rose, stood for a second and then announced: "Ladies and gentlemen, my address: 37, Chelmsford Street, London." Saying this, she sat down. Naturally, the audience laughed. They also gave her the biggest applause.

What did Agatha do? She twisted the meaning of the word *address*, deliberately used the meaning which was not intended, and thus, created a funny situation. *Address* means speech. It also means the place where a person lives. When the convenor invited her "to give an address", he meant a speech. And this is what the audience expected. But Agatha used the other meaning of the word *address* and gave them her residential address. The audience was definitely not expecting this. So, this had *an element of surprise, a sudden twist*. And *this sudden twist made the incident funny*.

This, friends, is a classic example of a punchline. A punchline is characterised by a surprising, sudden twist at the end of a statement so that the whole thing becomes very funny.

We will go deeper into punchlines after having a look at the format in which the questions are put.

8.2: Format of the problem

Directions: We come across many funny incidents related to different walks of life. One of the funny incidents is the punchline or a climax - which gives the incident a sudden transformation or twist (into something not expected). It is this punchline which makes the incident funny.

In each of the following questions an incident is described but the punchline is missing - indicated by a blank. After the incident, two statements numbered I and II are given. Considering the incident, you have to decide which of the two statements fits best as a punchline.

Give answer '**Only I**' if you think only statement I fits; Give answer '**Only II**' if you think only statement II fits; Give answer '**Both with contrasting ideas**' if you think both I and II fit but the idea or wavelength of approach in both the statements is different and contrasting; Give answer '**Both with same idea**' if you think both I and II fit and the wavelength of approach in both the statements is also more or less the same; and Give answer '**Neither**' if you think neither of the statement fits.

Ex 1: Seeing a boy crying the teacher asked, "Why are you crying?" The boy replied, "_______".

I. I cry whenever I don't laugh.

II. I am crying because I have nothing else to do.

a) Only II b) Both with same idea c) Neither
d) Only I e) Both with contrasting ideas

8.3: An analysis

By the foregoing format it is clear that you have to find the answer to two questions simultaneously. These two questions are:

A. *Does the suggested statement qualify as a punchline?*

B. *If yes, what is the idea behind it? Is it similar to or different from the other one?*

Thus, you will work out your answers if you can get an answer to both the questions. So, let us divide our study into two parts. In the first part, we will learn how to find an answer to the first question. This will be necessary for all the choices. In the second part, we will learn how to find an answer for the second question. This will be necessary if you will have to choose between choices "both fit with same idea" and "both fit with contrasting ideas".

A. Does a suggested statement qualify as a punchline?

To get an answer to this question, we should analyse the directions as given in the question. If you look at the directions of the sample example given earlier, you will notice certain key words, giving vital clues about a punchline. Look at the first sentence: it talks about *funny* incidents. So, the incident must be funny. Another key word is *climax* which means that it should be the last part of a statement or conversation. The third key word is *sudden twist (into something not expected)*. This means that a suggested statement would qualify as a punchline only if it has an element of surprise.

To conclude, we can say that:

A given statement would fit as a punchline if it passes the following three tests:

I. It must be a climax.

II. It must be funny.

III. It must bring in sudden twist.

A. I. It must be a climax

In order to be a valid punchline, a given statement must be the concluding part of a statement or a conversation. In other words, it should be a "twist in the *tail*". A statement would not qualify as a punchline if the funny part is hidden in its opening portion itself.

Note: However, the BSRBs (and other examining bodies) set the questions in such a way that the suggested punchline always appears at the end. This means that this criterion is fulfilled by all suggested punchlines. As such, for all practical purposes, it can be said that the reader should not bother about this test and may skip it. This test may become relevant at a later date when the format of the questions changes.

A. II. It must be funny

A suggested punchline may not fit if it is not funny. It may be a climax and it may give the incident a sudden transformation or twist into something not expected; still it would fail to qualify as a punchline if it is not funny. This brings us to the following question:

What is funny?

An incident is funny if it makes an average human being laugh - or at least smile. It should be humorous. You see many horses on the roads. How would you feel if you see a horse running sideways? You would feel 'funny'. Perhaps you have seen some movies of Charlie Chaplin. How do you feel when you see him walk at a rapid pace with flowing trousers and oversized boots? You feel 'funny'. In short, it can be said that:

An incident is funny if it has a tendency to make a man smile or laugh.

The following examples would illustrate what is funny and what is not:

(i) *Sometimes an incident may be funny because the answer is given after misinterpreting the question.*

Ex 2: A visitor asked the guide during an art exhibition - "Why did they hang that picture?"

The guide replied: "________"

I. They couldn't find the artist.

II. I don't know; I have nothing to do with their business.

Explanation: In the above example, you will find that answer I is funny but II is not. The visitor asks why the picture was hung. He probably doubled the merit of the picture and its eligibility for being displayed. But answer I makes the displeasure with the painting to extremes and means that the picture was hung because the artist was not there. That is, *had the artist been there he would've been hanged*. This makes I funny. II, of course, is a plain answer and has no humour.

Ex 3: The guest asked the little boy: "Do you say a prayer before you eat?"

The little boy replied: ....

I. "No sir, my mother is a good cook."

II. "No sir, it is not a custom in my family."

Explanation: Here too, reply I is funny because this twists the question's meaning. The guest casually asked the boy whether he prayed before eating. All he wanted to know was about the good habits of the boy. But the boy interpreted the question wrongly. *He thought that the guest wanted to know if the food served in the house was so bad that one needed to pray before eating it.* Reply I is based on this interpretation and this is what makes the incident funny. Reply II is straightforward and has no humour in it; it's not funny.

(ii) *Sometimes the way of saying a thing can lead to a funny incident.*

Ex 4: "Did you get my cheque?" enquired Shyam of Parveen.

I. "Yes, twice," replied Parveen. "Once from you and once from the bank."

II. "Yes, but it bounced."

Explanation: This is a good example of how the way of saying something can make the same incident funny in one case and plain in the other. The situation is simple: Shyam gave a cheque to Parveen and the cheque was not cleared. But in reply I, Parveen says it obliquely by saying that he got the cheque not once but twice. *This way of saying makes the incident funny.* In reply II, he makes a plain statement. It is simply a report of what happened and there is no humour in it.

(iii) *Sometimes a statement is funny because it has an element of extreme surprise - something that may never have occurred to you.*

Ex 5: Rich people miss one of life's greatest pleasures. For example,

I. Paying the last instalment.

II. Helping a poor friend.

Explanation: Here, reply I is funny. The idea is that those who are rich have so much money that they never have to buy goods on instalments. On the other hand, people with limited income often buy goods on instalments and when they pay the last instalment they experience the exhilaration of owning the good 'at long last'. This statement is probably true as well, but it may never have occurred to a common man in his daily life. *The idea of comparing the paying of the last instalment with the greatest pleasures of life is unique and, of course, funny.* II, on the other hand, is not funny. It assumes that rich people do not help a poor friend. This may not even be true, in the first place.

Ex 6: "It's raining outside."

I. "Have you ever seen it raining inside?"

II. "Draw the curtains lest it may become wet inside."

Explanation: Here, too, I makes an unexpected reply. When somebody says that "it's raining outside", we normally tend to say "Oh, really?

So unexpected!" or may be "Damn this rainy season!". But a witty person may say something like "it never rains inside". This is, of course, a fact. But this usually does not occur to us when we say "it's raining outside" instead of "it's raining." So, I is funny. II, of course, is not because it is a simple, mechanical response to the news of raining.

(iv) *Sometimes an incident may be funny because of the use of a similar-sounding word.*

Ex 7: Ireland should be the richest country in the world. ...

I. Her capital has been Dublin for years.

II. There are so many markets in this country.

Explanation: Reply I is funny because *Dublin* has been used in the sense of *doubling*. The *capital* (economic meaning!) of Ireland is doubling! And it has been doubling for years!! So, it must be the richest country in the world. This idea is certainly funny. II is not funny. Some people may take a large number of markets to be an indicator of richness and there is nothing humorous in it.

Ex 8: Why are the mediaeval centuries called the "Dark Ages"? ...

I. Because it was the knight time.

II. Because it was a period of ignorance.

Explanation: Reply I is funny as it uses the word *knight* in the sense of *night*. The mediaeval centuries were *dark* because it was the time of *night*! Isn't it funny? Reply II, of course, is not funny as it has taken the question straight and answered it straight.

(v) *Sometimes a funny incident may arise because of a tit-for-tat situation. The reply may have an element of "one-upmanship" (synonymous to* Nahle pe Dahla *in Hindi), making it funny.*

Ex 9: He: "Your meals are not like my mother used to make." ...

I. She: " Well, your salary is not like my father used to make."

II. She: "Why don't you go back to your mother then?"

Explanation: Here, reply I is funny. A husband snaps at his wife by saying that her cooking is inferior to that of his mother. To this the wife replies witfully that his salary is inferior to that of her father. The ready wit with which she shoots back at her husband makes the reply very funny. Reply II is not. It is the most common reply an irritated wife gives to a complaining husband.

Ex 10: A to B: "I am sorry, old man, my hen got loose and ran havoc with your garden."

B to A: ....

I. "That's all right, my dog ate your hen."

II. "You'll have to pay for it, you rascal."

Explanation: Here, A apologises to B that his hen destroyed B's gardens. B readily answers in I that it was all right because his dog had eaten the hen. B says it as if there were an issue and it were settled with the hen being eaten up. This is funny if we try to imagine A's face when he hears the answer. Reply II is not funny as it is the most common reponse to such a news.

(vi) *Sometimes an incident may be funny because of a twisted use of a word into a different meaning.*

Ex 11: "That guy is one of the greatest half-backs that ever lived. He ...

I. always pays back half of what he borrows."

II. was an asset for his club team."

Explanation: I is funny as it twists the meaning of the word *half-back.* Usually, *half-back* is a term associated with football. But here it is used in the sense of "one who pays back half of what he borrows". This twisted use makes it funny. II, of course, is not funny as it is in the tone of the mood of respect that the opening part of the sentence creates.

Conclusion: There are many ways in which an incident can be funny. In the foregoing pages, we have tried to enlist some of them. But we cannot produce a list of all the possible cases because their number is infinite. But it won't be too difficult for you to detect a funny incident if you learn to appreciate the basic idea. Instead of doing a full-fledged post-mortem, I would suggest a simple method: *Read the thing: if it makes you smile, it is funny; if it doesn't, chances are it is not.*

A. III: It must have a *sudden twist* and the twist should be into something not expected

The third and final criterion for a suggested statement to fit as a punchline is that it must have a sudden twist so that it brings about something not expected. The keyword here is *twist into something not expected.* So, there must be an element of surprise in it.

Now, detecting whether a given statement has a sudden twist or not, is a very easy job. If there is a sudden twist, you will automatically notice it. When there is an element of surprise, you will automatically be surprised.

The following few examples show how a surprising twist is brought about in statements.

Ex. 12: When a man talks enthusiastically about hard work, the chances are ...

I. that he is an employer.

II. that he is just another loudmouth.

Explanation: I, here, has a twist because the incomplete sentence that precedes it, creates the impression that the quality of the man is going to be discussed. Being enthusiastic about hard work is a quality and this quality may arise from "loud-mouthedness", as II suggests. So, II does not bring any surprise as it compares quality with quality. But I relates quality to profession. An emplcyer is the one who would be enthusiastic about hard work as he would want his employees to be hardworking. This is both funny and unexpected.

Ex. 13: A: "That article was so boring it sent me to sleep."

B: "What did it discuss?"

A: "..........."

I. Insomnia.

II. Drug abuse and its psychosomatic after-effects.

Explanation: Reply I has an element of surprise in it. Insomnia is a disease which means a lack of sleep. Now, A has already mentioned that he was bored to sleep by reading the article. It was completely unexpected that an article which puts him to sleep, would be talking about *insomnia!* Therefore, I passes as a punchline. But II does not. When we read "Drug abuse and its psychosomatic after-effects", we feel neither funny nor surprised.

Ex. 14: A: "When I stand on my head, the blood rushes to it. Why doesn't it rush to my feet now?"

B: "......."

I. Because your feet aren't empty.

II. You should get yourself examined by a doctor.

Explanation: Here, reply I has a sudden twist into an unexpected answer. A makes a query which looks a normal example of human curiosity. But B twists A's statement. When he says "Because your feet aren't empty", it implies that A's head is empty. This is an unexpected twist. Reply II has no such twist; most people would say a similar thing in such circumstances.

Ex. 15: Doctor: "You'll be pleased to hear that the operation you had for deafness has been a complete success."

Patient: ....

I. "I beg your pardon?"

II. "Let us see if I am equally pleased to hear about the bill."

Explanation: In this question, both reply I and reply II have that sudden twist. When the doctor breaks the news of successful operation, we normally expect people to say things like "Oh, thank you, Doctor!" or "That's great. I can hear now." But both the replies here are unexpected. Reply I implies that *the patient has still not been cured* because he cannot hear the doctor's voice. Reply II is also unexpected in that the patient expresses "apprehension of the doctor's bills" while we'd expect him to express "joy over a successful operation".

B. If a given statement fits as a punchline, what is its idea or wavelength?

When you examine the two suggested statements and find that both of them fit as punchlines, you will have to further find whether both of them have the same idea (the same wavelength of approach) or contrasting ideas (contrasting wavelengths of approach). You will be able to answer this question if you learn to identify the idea or logic behind a punchline.

This is an easy job and can be accomplished quickly if you ask yourself one question: What makes it funny? This will automatically lead you to the logic of the punchline.

For example, consider Ex 12 to Ex 15 above. What makes reply I of Ex 12 funny? It is the indirect way in which the nature of employers has been criticised, which makes it funny. What about Ex 13? It is the juxtaposition of 'insomnia' and 'going to sleep while reading about it' which makes it funny. What about reply I of Ex 14? It is funny because B takes a dig at A's stupidity and indirectly says that A's head is empty. Finally, we come to Ex 15. Here both the statements fit as punchlines. How? Reply I fits because it implies that the patient is still deaf and reply II fits because it implies that the patient is more worried about his bills than about his deafness.

The Complete Method of Solving a Punchline Problem

We have discussed how to detect whether a given statement fits as punchline and how to detect the logic behind it. So far, we have seen the problem in parts only. Let us now piece together all these parts into one and draw a complete step-by-step approach.

A punchline problem can be solved in the following steps.

Step I: Consider statement I and statement II. See if they fit as punchline. If only I fits, your answer is (a); if only II fits your answer is (b); if neither fits your answer is (e).

Step II: If both statements fit as punchlines, find out the idea behind them. If the two match, your answer is (c); if they do not match, your answer is (d).

This method has been outlined in the following diagram below.

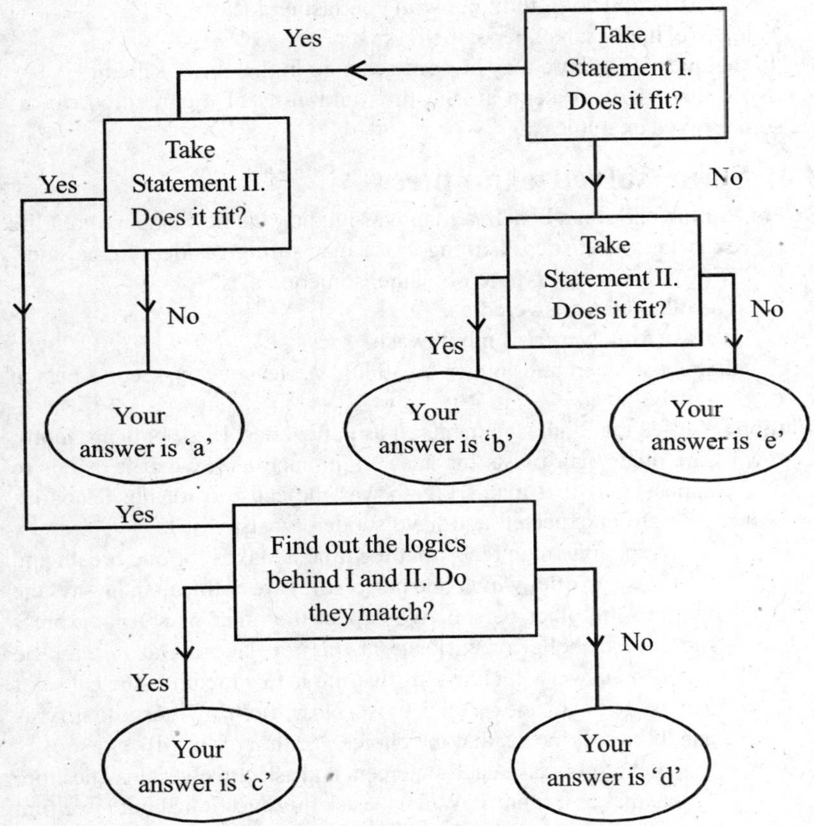

Fig. 1

Note:

(i) To test if a given statement fits as a punchline ask yourself two questions:

I. Is it funny?

II. Does it contain a sudden twist into something not expected?

If the answer to both the questions is yes, the statement fits as a punchline, otherwise not.

(ii) To find the logic behind a punchline, ask yourself one question: "What makes it funny?" The answer would automatically give you the required logic.

(iii) In the diagram we have assumed that:

Choice (a) implies: Only I fits

Choice (b) implies: Only II fits

Choice (c) implies: Both fit with same idea

Choice (d) implies: Both fit but with contrasting ideas

Choice (e) implies: Neither of them fits

In the questions, there may be some change in the above scheme.

Now that we have seen all the pros and cons of our method, let us see some solved examples.

8.4: Some solved examples

Ex. 16: "In the park on a bench, a man was reading the newspaper about life expectancy statistics. Turning to the man sitting beside him, he said," Do you know: everytime I breathe, someone dies?"

The other man answered, "...."

I. Have you ever tried mouthwash?

II. Practise deep and longer breathing. At least every second person will be saved.

Solution: We see that both statements fit as punchlines. First, both are funny. The other man twists his answers in such a way that it begins to appear as if that man's breath was the cause of death. Secondly, both are unexpected and have sudden twists.

When the man reads that the time he takes for one breath and the time gap after which one person dies are both equal, he says the same to the other person. We expect the other person to express shock or disbelief or curiosity at this revelation. But instead, he gives an answer which means that the man's breath is the cause of deaths. It is an unexpected twist. Now, both of these qualify as punchlines. It means that the choice is either (c) or (d).

Let us now take each statement and ask ourselves this question: "What makes it funny?" When we ask this question about I, we find that the other man's implying that the first person's breath was the cause of death, makes it funny. We see that the same logic works behind II as well. It means that both of them fit with the same idea. The correct answer is (c).

Ex. 17: The cleaning lady of a bank gave notice saying: "You do not trust me." The branch manager replied: "How can you say that? I even leave the keys of the safe lying around."

Said the cleaning lady, ...

I. "That is true, but there is no cash in the safe."

II. "Yes, but none of them fits."

Solution: Here, statement I and II both fit as punchlines. Both are funny because the lady first raises objection to her being mistrusted and then adds that no cash is present in the safe or that the keys of the safe do not fit. It is unexpected because we do not expect a woman who is showing indignation over her master's mistrust to reveal that she had seen no cash in the safe or that she had not seen the keys fit the safe. Again, both of them have the same idea. In both the cases it is implied that the lady has, in fact, tried to steal and failed. Hence, the correct answer is (c).

Ex. 18: One afternoon, a customer came into the shop and hurriedly said, "A mousetrap, please. But quickly, I have to catch the next bus."
The shopkeeper replied : ....
I. "But there are no mice in the bus."
II. "Sorry. We don't have that big a mousetrap."

Solution: Here, statement I does not fit as a punchline. It is **not** funny. It is certainly an unexpected answer but it does not make us laugh. There is nothing in the customer's statement which leaves room for cutting such a joke. He does leave room for cutting a joke like II because he says that he has to "catch the next bus." The shopkeeper may misinterpret it and say that he does not have mousetraps big enough to catch buses. So II fits as a punchline. But I does not. Hence, correct answer is (b).

Ex. 19: Two boys came to a doctor. "I've swallowed a marble," said one boy. "Oh, I see," replied the doctor, "and is this your brother with you?" "No", said the other boy, ...
I. "I own the marble."
II. "I saw him swallow it."

Solution: Here, I fits as a punchline. It is funny and unexpected because what it effectively states is that *the other child has accompanied the first child only to reclaim his marble!* But II does not fit. It is not funny. The boy saw him swallow a marble and the two have come together: it is a plain fact and there can be no humour in it. Correct answer: (a).

Ex. 20: My wife and I always take decisions with consensus; ....
I. ... she proposes and I agree.
II. ... she beats me if we don't agree.

Solution: Both fit as punchlines. The opening part of the statement merely mentions a husband describing an aspect of marital relationship. And we expect the sentence to be completed as something like: "... both of us understand each other so well". But as it turns out in both the cases, the meaning of consensus is forced agreement in which the wife's will dominates. This is funny. And both of them have two same idea. Correct answer is (c).

Note: Ex. 16, 17, 18, 19, 20 have actually appeared in a PO exam.

A Final Note: This article has now given you a complete method of solving the punchline problem. A step-by-step approach has been outlined and this should make you a master of punchline problems. However, as the first step of testing whether a statement fits as a punchline is the most crucial step. Let us take another look at this step.

We have seen that there are two tests for this step. First, the incident must be funny and, second, it must have an element of surprise.

[There is a third test that it should be a climax - a concluding part - but this is irrelevant because the current format of questions fulfils this criterion automatically.]

We have seen how the first criterion is fulfilled; we have then seen how the second criterion is fulfilled; then, we have seen how some statements fit as punchlines because both the criteria are fulfilled; but we have not seen how a statement fails to be a punchline because of satisfying one criterion but failing in another. Let us see a few of them.

Case I: When a statement is funny but has no element of surprise

Ex. 21: A: "I saw a very funny thing today. There was a man walking around in the campus and ....

I. his trousers were unbuttoned."

Comments: In this example, we hear of a person who was walking around with his trousers unbuttoned. Without doubt, this is a funny situation because we would laugh when we see such a man. But the statement has no element of surprise. In the opening part of the statement itself, A says that he saw a "funny thing". This prepares us to hear something funny. After we have been prepared to hear something funny, the element of surprise is gone. So, this statement fulfils the first criterion but fails to fulfil the second and, as such, will not fit as a punchline.

Case II: When a statement has an element of surprise but is not funny

Ex. 22: Mayor: "Mr. Tinkertrain would not be able to attend today's meeting. Unfortunately, ...

I. he had a severe stroke yesterday night and he passed away the following morning".

Comments: This statement does have a sudden, unexpected twist. When we hear that Mr. Tinkertrain will not be able to attend the meeting, we expect to hear something like "He is ill", or "He is out of station" or "He has some other appointments". So, the news that he has passed away comes as a surprise. However, the statement is not funny. There is a person who had to attend a meeting but died before the date. There is no humour in it. So, this statement fulfils the second criterion but fails to fulfil the first and, as such, will not fit as a punchline.

Note: Compare Ex 22 with the following:

Ex. 23: A: Has your wife stopped fighting with you?

B: ....

I. "Yes. She died."

Comments: This does fit as a punchline. First, there is definitely an element of surprise as in Ex 22. Next, the idea that she stopped fighting only because she is no more is funny. This creates an impression that apart from her death there could be no other factor that could stop her from fighting with her husband. So, it does fit as a punchline.

8.5: Conclusion

We have seen that the punchline problem can be solved in two simple steps. In step I, we apply two tests to detect if a statement fits as a punchline. If both the statements fit as punchlines, we apply step II (See Fig 1). This is all there is about the **concept** of punchlines. Next, we come to the no-less- important aspect of **practice.**

Practice Exercises

Exercise 8A

Directions : We come across many funny incidents related to different walks of life. One of the funny incidents is the punchline or a climax - which gives the incident a sudden transformation or twist (into something not expected). It is this punchline which makes the incident funny.

In each of the following questions, an incident is described but the punchline is missing - indicated by a blank. After the incident, two statements numbered I and II are given. Considering the incident, you have to decide which of the two statements fits as a punchline.

Give answer 'Only I' if you think only statement I fits; 'Only II' if you think only statement II fits; 'both with contrasting ideas' if you think both I and II fit but the ideas or wavelengths of approach in both the statements are different and contrasting; 'Both with same idea' if you think both I and II fit and the wavelengths of approach in both the statements are also more or less the same; and 'Neither' if you think neither of the statements fits.

1. A: "Do you believe in free speech?"
B: "Sure."
A: "........"
I. Good. Would you mind if I use your telephone?
II. Good. Will you give a speech in our school - free of cost, of course?
1) Only I 2) Only II 3) Both with same idea
4) Both with contrasting ideas 5) Neither

2. Judge : "Order! Order !!"
Convict : ....
I. "But I am not making any noise, Sir."
II. "One cup of coffee, please!"
1) Only I 2) Both with same idea 3) Only II
4) Both with contrasting ideas 5) Neither

3. A : "I prefer springs for bath."
B : ....
I. "I prefer the beaches."
II. "But what do you do in other seasons?"
1) Only I 2) Only II 3) Neither
4) Both with same idea 5) Both with contrasting ideas

4. Passenger : "Which end of the bus do I get off?"
Conductor : "......."
I. Either. It stops at both ends.
II. Either. You are a free man, aren't you?
1) Only I 2) Only II 3) Neither
4) Both with same idea 5) Both with contrasting ideas

5. A child says to his mother : "I liked the circus a lot but I don't think highly of the man who was throwing knives at the woman." "Why, son?", the mother asked. The child replied, ...
I. "He missed everytime, didn't he?"
II. "I don't like people who show violence towards ladies."
1) Only I 2) Only II 3) Both with same idea
4) Neither 5) Both with contrasting ideas

6. Foreman : "Has the mechanic told you what to do?"
Apprentice : ......
I. "Yes, sir, he told me to wake him up when I heard you coming."
II. "No, sir, he said that you wouldn't be coming here for inspection."
1) Only I 2) Neither 3) Only II
4) Both with same idea 5) Both with contrasting ideas

7. A friend asked Pramod - "Don't you ever take your wife out with you in the car?"
Pramod retorted, "........."
I. No, I just don't feel like it.
II. No, I can't contend with both of them together.
1) Only I 2) Neither 3) Only II
4) Both with same idea 5) Both with contrasting ideas

8. "Do you believe that moonlight makes people silly, Raj?" asked the sweet young bride. Raj replied : ....
I. "Yes, I had proposed to you in the moonlight".
II. "No. Moonlight makes animals silly."
1) Only I 2) Only II 3) Both with same idea
4) Both with contrasting ideas 5) Neither

9. "Well, Tinku, what does your sister think of the engagement ring I gave her?" Tinku replied : ....
I. "She says that the other two are costlier."
II. "She says that the police will find it soon."

1) Only I 2) Only II 3) Both with same idea
4) Both with contrasting ideas 5) Neither

10. The doctor asked: "Do you permit your wife to have her own way?"
The man replied : ....
I. "No, sir, she has it without my permission."
II. "Yes, but only if there is enough petrol in the tank."
1) Neither 2) Only I 3) Both with same idea
4) Only II 5) Both with contrasting ideas

11. Actress : "Darling, we'll have to postpone our marriage for a short while."
Actor : "But why? Don't you love me?"
Actress : "Certainly I do, darling, ..."
I. but Dilip Khanna had proposed to me earlier.
II. but I just married another man.
1) Only I 2) Only II 3) Neither
4) Both with same idea 5) Both with contrasting ideas

12. Husband : "Drinking makes you look extraordinarily beautiful."
Wife : "But I've not been drinking."
Husband : ......
I. "Why? Did you quit drinking?"
II. "No. But I have."
1) Only I 2) Only II 3) Neither
4) Both with same idea 5) Both with contrasting ideas

13. They say that the way to a man's heart goes through his stomach. If I knew that, I would ......
I. have never married any man.
II. have tried to be a good cook.
1) Only I 2) Only II 3) Neither
4) Both with same idea 5) Both with contrasting ideas

14. The commander was shouting at the cadet: "The cook told me that you were so much drunk last night that you kept on rolling an empty barrel in the basement for three hours."
The cadet replied: .....
I. "But it wasn't empty, sir. You were inside the barrel."
II. "No, sir, I rolled it for only ten minutes."
1) Only I 2) Only II 3) Neither
4) Both with same idea 5) Both with contrasting ideas

15. A : "Has your wife stopped fighting with you?"
B : "....."
I. Yes. She died.
II. No. She is still alive.
1) Only I 2) Neither 3) Only II
4) Both with contrasting ideas 5) Both with same idea

16. A heavy altercation developed between Uma and Ravi, a bachelor. "What do you bachelors know about women, anyway?"
Ravi replied, ...
I. "And what do you know about bachelors, for that matter?"
II. "Plenty. That's why we are still unmarried."
1) Neither 2) Only I 3) Both with same idea
4) Both with contrasting ideas 5) Only II

17. "I wish to marry your daughter, Sir". "Er, do you drink, young man?", asked the girl's father in a stern voice.
The young man replied : ....
I. "Yes. But only on special occasions, sir."
II. "Yes. But I don't drink like a drum, sir."
1) Only I 2) Neither 3) Only II
4) Both with same idea 5) Both with contrasting ideas

18. "Our life has become a picnic ....
I. ever since we started using paper plates."
II. ever since we started using the psychiatrist's advice."
1) Only I 2) Neither 3) Both with same idea
4) Only II 5) Both with contrasting ideas

19. "Do you know a man with one eye named Jackie?" "I am not sure. .....
I. What's the name of his other eye?"
II. I don't go and ask a guy his name without any reason."
1) Only I 2) Only II 3) Both with same idea
4) Both with contrasting ideas 5) Neither

20. "You are such a jovial man, sir. You always seem to have a reason for laughter." — said the young man. The old man replied:
I. "Not always son. You visit me only occasionally."
II. "I had read many jokes when I was young."
1) Only I 2) Only II 3) Neither
4) Both with same idea 5) Both with contrasting ideas

21. A gentleman: "Does your watch tell the time?"
Another gentleman : "......."
I. No sir. You have to look at it.
II. No sir. It tells us stories.
1) Only I 2) Only II 3) Both with same idea
4) Both with contrasting ideas 5) Neither

22. She has a dog that growls, a parrot that swears, a fireplace that smokes and a cat that stays out all night. .....
I. Why should she want a husband, then?
II. It's a man's world she lives in.
1) Only I 2) Only II 3) Both with same idea
4) Both with contrasting ideas 5) Neither

23. Sita: "I wonder why a woman has never been the President of our country?"
Suresh : ....
I. "Because a President has to be at least 35 years old."
II. "Well, why don't you go and change this convention?"
1) Only I 2) Only II 3) Neither
4) Both with same idea 5) Both with contrasting ideas

24. A: "There's nothing like cheerfulness. I admire those who can sing while they work."
B: .....
I. "Do you also admire professional singers?"
II. "Do you also admire mosquitoes?"
1) Only I 2) Only II 3) Both with same idea
4) Both with contrasting ideas 5) Neither

25. A: "Ireland should be the richest country in the world"
B: "How is that?"
A: "....."
I. Her capital has been Dublin for years.
II. Because its name starts with an 'I'.
1) Only I 2) Only II 3) Neither
4) Both with same idea 5) Both with contrasting ideas

26. A worker says to his colleague: "I am caught in a power struggle with my boss. I ....."
I. have to supply candles to his house whenever there is a power failure.
II. have the struggle and he has the power.
1) Only I 2) Only II 3) Neither
4) Both with same idea 5) Both with contrasting ideas

27. Wife: "Why are you making such a scene if my mom just threw one of your suits out of the window?" Husband: ....
I. "But I was inside the suit"
II. "But your father was standing just outside the window at the time."
1) Only I 2) Only II 3) Neither
4) Both with same idea 5) Both with contrasting ideas

28. Son: "Do you believe in heredity, father?"
Father: "No son, ...
I. even my father didn't."
II. not if you continue to get 'D' in all your exams."
1) Only I 2) Only II 3) Neither
4) Both with contrasting ideas 5) Both with same idea

29. Lady teacher: "Tell me, Rinku, what tense is *I am beautiful*?"
Rinku: .....
I. "For me it is future tense, ma'am "
II. "For you it is past tense, ma'am."
1) Only I 2) Only II 3) Both with same idea
4) Both with contrasting ideas 5) Neither

30. Judge: "You have committed the most heinous crime of murdering both your parents."
Convict: "Yes sir. But I hope ....."
I. that the jury would look with pity into the case of an orphan.
II. that the jury would not order the last surviving member of my family to be killed.
1) Only I 2) Only II 3) Both with same idea
4) Both with contrasting ideas 5) Neither

31. The teacher scolded a pupil thus: "When George Washington was your age, he had become a working surveyor."
Pupil: ......
I. "But I don't want to become the President of USA, sir."
II. "And when he was your age, he had become the President of USA."
1) Only I 2) Only II 3) Neither
4) Both with same idea 5) Both with contrasting ideas

32. The economics teacher asked: "Give me an example of indirect taxation."
Student: ......
I. "Income tax, sir. It acts as an income of the Government."
II. "House tax, sir. We pay tax for living in our own houses."
1) Only I 2) Neither 3) Only II
4) Both with same idea 5) Both with contrasting ideas

33. "My youngest boy has trouble with eczema", the woman said. The neighbour asked, "Goodness! How did he get it?"
The woman replied: ......
I. "I don't know. Otherwise I would've cured it."
II. "He hasn't got it; he just can't spell it."
1) Only I 2) Only II 3) Neither
4) Both with same idea 5) Both with contrasting ideas

34. Judge: "So, you admit that you drove over the victim in a loaded truck."
Defendant: "I do, Your Honour. But ......"
I. I did not intend to kill him.
II. I swear I had no idea that the truck was loaded.
1) Only I 2) Only II 3) Neither
4) Both with same idea 5) Both with contrasting ideas

35. Judge: "Are you guilty?"
Prisoner: ....
I. "I haven't heard the evidence yet."
II. "Who is not, Your Honour?"
1) Only I 2) Only II 3) Neither
4) Both with same idea 5) Both with contrasting ideas

36. A young boy was taking an examination for a job. The question was: "What is the distance between the sun and the earth?"
He answered: .....

I. "It must be farther from earth than moon."
II. "At least twice the distance between the sun and the moon."
1) Only I 2) Only II 3) Neither
4) Both with same idea 5) Both with contrasting ideas

37. "I remember having been seeing you in this very court for the last twenty years," said the Judge to the accused. "Yes, Your Honour," said the accused, ...
I. "your promotion is due for such a long period."
II. "even practice has not made me perfect."
1) Only I 2) Only II 3) Both with same idea
4) Neither 5) Both with contrasting ideas

38. I wish I were Adam. For then, ...
I. If I cracked a joke, nobody would say, "I've heard that before."
II. I would've seen the best of both the worlds.
1) Only I 2) Only II 3) Both with same idea
4) Both with contrasting ideas 5) Neither

39. A political orator finished his speech thus, "I'm sorry I have spoken so long. You see, I haven't got my watch with me."
To this a voice rose from the audience, ...
I. "But there was a calendar behind you."
II. "Next time you must bring your watch with you."
1) Only I 2) Only II 3) Neither
4) Both with same idea 5) Both with contrasting ideas

40. The Manager reported to the Chief Manager, "Sir, Abdul has completely lost his hearing. What do we do with him?"
The Chief manager replied: ......
I. "Fire him. We cannot have deaf accountants in our office."
II. "Do as you please with him; I am partially deaf myself."
1) Only I 2) Only II 3) Neither
4) Both with same idea 5) Both with contrasting ideas

Exercise 8B

Directions : We come across many funny incidents related to different walks of life. One of the funny incidents is the punchline or a climax - which gives the incident a sudden transformation or twist (into something not expected). It is this punchline which makes the incident funny.

In each of the following questions, an incident is described but the punchline is missing, indicated by a blank. After the incident, two statements numbered I and II are given. Considering the incident, you have to decide which of the two statements fits as a punchline.

Give answer

1) if you think only statement I fits;

2) if you think only statement II fits;

3) if you think both I and II fit and the wavelengths of approach in both the statements are also more or less the same;

4) if you think both I and II fit but the ideas or wavelengths of approach in both the statements are different and contrasting;

5) if you think neither of the statements fits.

1. Judge: "Well, we have thirty witnesses who saw you steal the automobile."
Prisoner: "Sir, ..."
I. I can give you sixty witnesses who did not see me stealing it.
II. may be all of them are liars.

2. Wife: The cleaning woman seems to have stolen two of our new towels.
Husband: Which towels?
Wife : ....
I. "The ones we had been gifted on our anniversary."
II. "The ones we brought back from the hotel in Bombay."

3. A hunter was talking of his adventures : "Once I was taking a nap in the jungle and suddenly I felt a lion's breath on the back of my neck.
So, ...
I. I turned back and requested the lion not to disturb me".
II. I turned up my collars".

4. The father was vexed with his son's careless attitude towards life. So, he said: "Monty, you ought to mend your ways. If I died suddenly where would you be?"
The son replied: "......."
I. Here. The question is, where will you be?
II. Oh, come on, dad; you are not going to die so soon.

5. "Excuse me, but I'm in a hurry. You have been holding that phone for twenty minutes and not said a word." said the woman.
The man replied, ...
I. "I am talking to my wife, madam."
II. "That is because I am in no hurry, madam."

6. I've been feeding my dog garlic. Now, ...
I. his bark is worse than his bite.
II. he may be needing onions, maybe.

7. A quack was selling an elixir which he said was the reason why he was so hale and hearty despite being 300 years old! A man passing by stopped and asked his assistant: "Is he really as old as that?".
The assistant replied: "I don't know. ....."
I. I have been working with him for the last 100 years only."
II. Even Lord Clive had taken him to be a cheat."

8. Servant: "The doctor is here, Professor."
Professor: "I don't want to see him. ......"
I. Tell him I'm ill.
II. Tell him I'm alright.

9. A doctor warned his patient: "You must stop smoking, otherwise you might ...."
I. set fire to my couch.
II. not be able to pay my bills.

10. Patient: "I have a pain in my right leg." The doctor examined the leg carefully and declared : "It's nothing. Just because of old age."
Patient: ....
I. "Then cure me of senility, doctor!"
II. "Strange! So far as I know both legs are of the same age."

11. The psychiatrist was assuring the husband: "Don't worry about your wife. You'll have a different woman when she gets back from hospital."
Husband: ....
I. "And what if she finds out?"
II. "No sir, I love my wife."

12. Boarder: "When I left my last boarding-house, the landlady actualy wept."
Landlady: "Well, I shan't. ....
I. I always collect payment in advance."
II. I am a woman with tough interiors."

13. The errant son reported to his father: "Dad, the car has developed some trouble. There is water in its carburettor." When the father asked how it happened, he replied: ".........."
I. Oh, I was checking the carburettor when, suddenly, it began to rain.
II. Oh, I was driving the car when the bridge collapsed suddenly and fell into the river.

14. The electrician came to repair the socket. He asked: "Does the bulb work when this plug is switched on?"
The houseowner replied: ....
I. "I don't know, I do not have a bulb."
II. "I can't say. I do not have a plug."

15. A asked his friend B how the latter had amassed so much wealth in such a short time. B said: "I joined hands with a rich man. He had the money and I had the experience." He added: ....
I. "Now he has the experience and I the money."
II. "When experience joins money, it creates miracles."

16. A asked B: "Have you forgotten that you owe me five hundred rupees?"
B replied: ....
I. "No. I tried but I still remember it."
II. "Yes, I have."

17. A husband was breathing forth his grievances: "It's all right if a woman wants her husband to be a bread-winner. But ......

I. it's not fair if she wants him to be a bakery."

II. it's not fair if she wants him to be a bread-maker too."

18. Clerk: "My wife told me to ask you for a raise, Sir."

Manager: ....

I. "All right, I'll ask my wife if I can give you one."

II. "Doesn't she also tell you to do some hard work, Sinha?"

19. Srivastava: "I applied for the post of secretary and the manager asked me if my punctuation was good. I immediately told him that throughout my career I had never ....

I. been late for work."

II. been bad at grammar."

20. The conductor asked the commuter for the ticket. The commuter produced the ticket which the conductor examined carefully and then said : ....

I. "I asked you for a season ticket, not a seasoned ticket."

II. "You have travelled farther than your ticket could take you, sir."

21. A husband was saying: "My wife has not come back yet. She's either been kidnapped, hit by a motor car or is shopping. ....

I. I hope she's not been kidnapped."

II. I hope she's not shopping."

22. The speed of a jet flight is truly staggering. You can have breakfast in London, lunch in New York and ....

I. dine with the airhostess in a Korean hotel.

II. indigestion in Tokyo.

23. Mansi asked her elder sister Manjul, "Why does a traffic light turn red, sister?"

Manjul replied : ....

I. "Why not? You'd blush too if you had to change in the middle of the street?"

II. "Maybe it warns us of a possible accident by showing the colour of blood."

24. When the daughter was about to leave for the cocktail, her mother told her: "Have a good time at the party, daughter; and be a good girl."

The daughter replied : ......

I. "Make up your mind, Mother!"

II. "Okay, I would be a good girl after the party, I promise."

25. Gopu: "If you sell your watches at cost price, how can you make any profit?"

Dipu: ....

I. "We make our profit by repairing them."

II. "Ours is a long-term business strategy."

26. Son: "When will I be old enough to do as I please, Dad?"
Daddy: ....
I. "When you become as old as myself, son."
II. "Nobody lives that long, son."

27. It's not wise to argue with a fool because ......
I. the bystanders might not know who is who.
II. it is foolish not to argue with a wise man.

28. The patient was grumbling about the fee. "Twenty five rupees for pulling out a tooth!", she exclaimed, "and it's only a minute's work."
The dentist said: "Well, ...
I. I can give you 50% discount if you got all your teeth pulled out."
II. I will pull it out slowly, if you wish."

29. Doctor: "Congratulation, Awasthi jee, you are going to have triplets".
Awasthi jee: ....
I. "Well, find out from her who are the other two guys."
II. "So I will have to buy three `Your-Baby's-future-policies' instead of one?"

30. A: "Do you know, reports reveal that infants do not like their periods of infancy?"
B: ....
I. "Yes. When they become adults they can indulge in adultery."
II. "Gosh. How good it'd be if we were born adults!"

31. A: "What kind of a doctor do you consult - allopath, homoeopath or osteopath?"
B: ....
I. "How does it matter? All paths lead but to the grave."
II. "That depends upon the kind of fee they charge."

32. A doctor was boasting: "I do not believe in unnecessary surgery. ......
I. My patients have seams only on their purses."
II. I never operate unless I really need the money."

33. It is hard to lose all your relatives ......
I. and impossible if you are a financier.
II. with none of them having left you any money.

34. An advertisement went thus: "If you'd like a job which requires you to just stand around, keep looking at beautiful heavenly bodies, ...
I. you may join us as an astronomer."
II. we are sorry; but we do have an opening for a sincere swimming coach."

35. Patient: "Doctor, I need something to stir me up to charge my senses. Have you put anything like that in this prescription?"

Doctor: ......

I. "No. I don't think you need any kind of stirring up."

II. "No. But you'll find something like that in the bill."

Answers with Explanations

Exercise 8A

1. 4; Both are funny because the meaning of the term 'free speech' has been twisted in both of them in a funny way. But the ideas are contrasting. In I, 'free speech' means 'free use of telephone'; in II it means 'delivering a speech free of cost'.

2. 3; I is not funny because it's a normal response. II is funny because it twists the meaning of 'order'; as if the person were a waiter instead of a judge.

3. 2; I is not funny: it is a normal reply. II is funny. It twists the meaning of 'springs' from 'streams' to 'the season of spring'.

4. 1; Only I is funny. The way the conductor tells him that the bus stops at both ends, makes the passenger look like a fool. But II is not funny; there is no element of humour in it.

5. 5; Both are funny with contrasting ideas. The child notices that the man "missed every time"; he doesn't realise that he was supposed to miss. Similarly, in II, the child accuses the man of trying to injure the lady. So, the basic idea is the same in both the punchlines, which is the innocence of the child. But there is a difference: in I, the child is almost supporting violence; in II, he is condemning it.

6. 4; Both are funny with the same idea. The foreman simply wants to know whether a job has been assigned to the apprentice. In both the answers, we find that the mechanic works only when the foreman is nearby. So, we have a similar idea in both of them.

7. 3; I is not funny: it is a straightforward answer. II is funny: it twists the meaning, implying that the wife and the car are both headaches for Pramod.

8. 1; Only I is funny. It twists the conversation and implies that marrying her was a silly act. II is not funny: it is only an unexpected answer which the husband may have given out of ignorance or out of bad temper but certainly not out of humour.

9. 4; Both are funny. In I, we find the meaning that Tinku's sister received engagement rings from three persons; in II we find that she has lost the ring. Both are funny but the idea is different in each of them.

10. 5; I is funny because here the man highlights the word 'permit' in the doctor's sentence and says that she does it without his 'permission'! In II, the man highlights the word 'her own way' and says that only if there is 'enough petrol'. Thus, both are funny but the ideas are contrasting.

11. 4; Both are funny because the notion that actresses marry and divorce too many persons, has been highlighted here in a funny way. In both of them, the same idea has made the climax funny: the actress' willingness to marry another man.

12. 2; Only II is funny. The conversation initially creates an impression that 'drinking' is like a medicine for the wife which makes her look beautiful. But in the climax we find that she looks beautiful when *he* drinks!

13. 3; I is certainly not funny; it is a simple plain expression of an inner feeling. In II, there is some element of humour but the *twist* is not there: usually we find a sudden 'jerk' in punchlines — an unexpected twist — but here it is missing. If a lady repents about the fact that a man's stomach is *en route* his heart, the most obvious way is to repent the fact of not being a good cook. There is nothing surprising here.

14. 1; Only I is funny: in the climax we find that the commander was more drunk; he was inside the barrel that was being rolled about. In II, there is no humour; it's the most usual response in such situations.

15. 5; Both are funny. In I, we find that the wife has stopped fighting because she is no more! In II, we find that she hasn't stopped fighting because she is still alive! So, the basic idea is the same in both the cases : *the wife is not going to stop fighting as long as she is alive.*

16. 5; I is not funny: it is a plain shooting-back, a retort. II is funny as it implies that those who know women are wise enough not to marry them!

17. 2; Neither of them is funny. I is a very plain answer. In II, there is an element of humour when he says that he doesn't drink "like a drum"; but it has no *punch*, no *sudden twist.*

18. 1; I is funny. We use paper plates in picnics. So, if we use paper plates in everyday life, our life becomes a picnic! This is the idea in I. In II, there is a plain fact that life has improved after psychiatric advices. There is no humour in it.

19. 1; I is funny. It creates an impression that Jackie is, in fact, the name of the eye! But II is a plain answer.

20. 5; Both are funny. I is funny becaust it implies that the young man is the 'reason for laughter' of the old man. So, the old man declares the young fellow to be an object of laughter in a subtle, twisted way. II is funny as it implies that the old man laughs at jokes which he read during his youth! It implies that he understands the jokes *now*. So, both are funny, but with contrasting ideas. In I, the young man is made an idiot; in II, the old man.

21. 3; To ask if a watch tells the time may be an irritating question. The other gentleman gives irritated but funny answers in both the cases. In I, he says that his watch doesn't **tell** the time, one has to **look** at it. In II, he wonders if a watch tells stories, if not the time. So, the basic idea is the same in both the cases: *"Yes, my watch tells the time, that is why I am wearing it"* - this is what seems to be going on inside the mind of the man.

22. 3; Both are funny because, in the climax, we find a sudden twist with the message that growling, swearing, smoking and staying out all night are characteristic qualities of males. The central idea (or as the questions put it: "the wavelength of approach") is similar in both the cases and it is: *men growl, swear, smoke and stay out all night; it's their habit.*
23. 1; I is funny as it implies that women rarely tell their correct age: to admit that she is over 35 may be difficult for any lady! II is funny only in that Suresh exhorts her to "change the convention". But there is no unexpected twist, no punch in this answer.
24. 4; Both are funny with contrasting ideas. I is funny in that B raises the point of professional singers: professional singers do not sing *while* they work; *their work itself is singing*. So, A's logic would imply that all professional singers are cheerful and worth admiring. II, of course, is funny in that it reminds A that mosquitoes also *sing* while they *work*!
25. 1; I is funny because here 'Dublin' has been used in the sense of 'doubling'. II is not funny: it is not even clear what it wants to say.
26. 5; I is funny as the 'struggle' of the worker in supplying candles to his boss in times of 'power' failures has been called 'power struggle'. II is funny as the word 'power struggle' has been dichotomised with the boss having the power and the clerk having the struggle! The ideas are contrasting. In I, *power* implies *electricity*; in II, it implies *official superiority*.
27. 1; I is funny because in the climax we find unexpectedly that the man was *inside* the suit which was thrown out of the window. In II, the message is not clear. It creates an impression that the wife's father was waiting outside to grab the suit. If it were true, II would have been very funny but the language of II is not clear enough.
28. 4; I is funny because he says that he does not believe in heredity, and that even his father did not believe in heredity. This creates a paradox-like situation that *not believing in heredity was hereditary in his family*! In II, he says that he would not like to believe in heredity if his son got 'D' grades because that would imply that poor grades was hereditary in the family. Thus, both are funny in separate ways.
29. 3; Both are funny and the wavelengths of approach are more or less the same in both of them. "I am beautiful" has been used in the literal sense in both of them.
30. 3; Both are funny with the same idea. The convict has killed his parents and now seeks pity because he is an orphan/he is the last survivor of his family! Thus, he seeks mercy in both the cases on those grounds only which are the results of his actions.
31. 5; I is funny. The pupil brushes aside the example of Washington because he does not want to become the President. II is funny in a different way. Here, the pupil throws the ball back into the teacher's court by reminding him that Washington had become President at the teacher's age.

32. 2; Neither is funny.

33. 2; Only II is funny. I is a plain answer, just what we'd expect. II is an unexpected answer. In this climax, we find that the 'trouble' was not of *suffering* from eczema, the disease, but it was one of *misspelling* eczema, the word!

34. 2; II is funny. I is not; it is a plain, expected clarification. In II, he implies that *the man wouldn't have died if the truck was not loaded!* This makes II funny.

35. 1; I is funny. The prisoner shoots back at the judge that *he'd tell* whether he is guilty after hearing the evidence! But II is not humorous. We can definitely admit that it is a twisted answer, rather unexpected, but still it's not a punchline because it's not funny; it's philosophical.

36. 3; Neither is funny. Both are stupid-looking answers but there is nothing in them to make us laugh.

37. 5; I is funny because there the convict twists the conversation into the direction of concluding that the judge has been sitting in the same court for 25 years, *without promotion*! II is funny because here the convict changes the course of conversation into the direction of repenting that despite 25 years of practice, *he's still not perfect and gets caught*. Of course, the ideas are contrasting.

38. 4; Both are funny because in both of them, there are funny reasons for wishing to be Adam. In I, Adam's primitiveness is highlighted: since he was the first man, no one could say that he was telling second-hand jokes. In II, Adam's unique experience of having lived both in heaven and on earth, is highlighted: since he had been in both the places, he'd seen the best of both the worlds. Remember, "to see the best of both the worlds" is a proverb in English. In Hindi, a close synonym is: *"Dono hath mein laddu"*.

39. 1; II is not funny; it is a simple, angry answer. I is funny: it implies that the speaker has been speaking for days and not hours! (We count hours on a watch and days on a calendar.)

40. 3; Neither fits. There is no element of humour in either of them.

Exercise 8B

1. 1; Only I fits. *Witness* means one who has seen someone *doing* something. But in I, the meaning has been twisted to one who has seen someone *not doing that thing*! But, II is not funny; it is a straightforward answer.

2. 2; I is not funny; there is no surprise in it. But in II, we find that the couple themselves had stolen the towels from a hotel! So, II is funny.

3. 2; I is funny only in the sense that it looks like a funny exaggeration. *When we read it we do not feel like laughing*, we feel like disbelieving. But II is funny. It highlights the fact that there was some breath on his neck, so he turned up his collars, and *underplays the fact that the breath was coming from the nostrils of a lion!*

4. 1; II is not funny; it is a simple, expected response. But I is. The father wants to know where would his son be if he dies. He means that his son would have trouble making ends meet. But the son misinterprets the question. He says that he'd be there (on earth) only but the question was where would the father be after dying! This is humorous.
5. 1; I is funny. In I, the idea is that he is holding the phone without talking for twenty minutes, because he is talking to his wife (*and the wife has been doing all the talking*). In II, the idea is that he is talking for so long because he is in "no hurry". This is not very humorous.
6. 1; I is definitely funny because it twists the popular saying "bark worse than a bite", with the help of garlics! (The dog's bark will now have the smell of garlics.) II has no humour, it does not make us laugh.
7. 3; Both are funny. When the man asks his assistant whether the quack was really 300 years old, we expect the assistant to say 'Yes' or 'No'. But in I, he says that he doesn't know because he has seen him only for 100 years. In II, he declares the quack to be a contemporary of Lord Clive. So, in both the answers there is a 'punch', which is funny. Also the basic idea is the same in both: in both of them, the quack's claim has been supported indirectly, in similar ways.
8. 4; Both are funny. I is funny because *illness is being feigned to avoid meeting a man whose job is to cure illness*. II is funny because here an impression is created *as if the doctor had come not to meet him but to cure him*. Thus, both are funny in different ways.
9. 4; The lines are funny because in the climax it turns out that the *doctor wants the patient to stop smoking not for health reasons but due to the fear that (in I) he may set fire to the doctor's couch (or in II) that he may overspend on cigarettes and have no money to pay the bills!* But the two, obviously, are using contrasting ideas.
10. 4; Old age or senility is a natural development and not a disease. But, in I, the patient asks the doctor to 'cure' him of it. This makes I funny. In II, the patient misinterprets the doctor's statement in such a way *as if his right leg were older than the left leg*. So, II is also funny. But, of course, the basic ideas are different.
11. 3; When the doctor says that "you'll have a different woman", he wants to say that his wife would be transformed. But the husband misinterprets it and takes it quite literally. He thinks *that the doctor would give him a different woman*.This is the basic idea in both the punchlines.
12. 1; I is funny. The boarder wanted to mean that he was such a nice fellow that when he was leaving, his previous landlady wept. But the new landlady misinterprets him. She takes him to mean that *he'd not paid up fully and that's why the earlier landlady had to weep*. This misinterpretation makes I funny. II is obviously not funny.
13. 1; I is not funny because there is no twist in it. But II is twisted. When we hear that there is some water in the carburettor we anticipate that some

water may have leaked into it. But we do not guess that the reason would be the falling down of *the whole car in a river!* This makes II funny.

14. 5; Neither is funny. Both are simple, everyday answers and there is no punch in them.

15. 1; I is funny. It indirectly says that B amassed this wealth by *cheating a rich man*. This is why he says that the rich man has the '*experience*' now and he the money. But II is not funny. It is a straightforward answer.

16. 4; I is funny as here he regrets that *he has tried* but still not *forgotten* that he owed 500 rupees. II is funny by virtue of its very language. If a person would really forget about taking money, his response to the question would be "Which money? When did I take it" and not "Yes. I have forgotten".

17. 4; I is funny: husbands are conventionally called bread-winners, so husbands of demanding wives are here being called bakery. II is funny in a different way: here what is implied is that husbands have *not only to earn* money *but also to cook* for the family!

18. 1; I is funny: the clerk uses his wife as an excuse for asking for the raise and, in a gesture of one-upmanship, the officer uses *his wife* as an excuse to avoid the question. But II is not funny. It is the usual, scolding remark that officers often make.

19. 1; II is a straightforward answer. But I is funny. He has taken 'punctuation' as a synonym for 'punctuality' which has made him give a funny answer.

20. 1; II is the most common way in which an angry but cultured conductor would tell a commuter that he has over-travelled. But I is a funny way of telling a commuter that his ticket is outdated. Here, the juxtaposition of 'season ticket' and 'seasoned' is funny.

21. 2; I is not funny because there is nothing unusual in it. But II is funny as it gives the impression that a wife who is shopping is less acceptable to the husband than a wife who's been kidnapped or run over. (Here, husbands' fear of overspending wives has been highlighted.)

22. 4; I is funny as it presupposes that when you travel on a jet plane, you would win over the air hostess before you reach Korea. II is funny in a different way: the use of the word 'indigestion' is quite unexpected.

23. 1; I is very humorous. The traffic lights *change* in the middle of the street. Also, when we change our dresses, we call it - in short - to *change*. It is this latter meaning that she has used in I. II is not funny.

24. 3; The mother wants the daughter to have a good time **and** to be a good girl. In both the answers, the daughter however implies that these two are not possible to *co-exist*. She means that good girls do not have a good time. In both the answers the same twist exists.

25. 1; I is funny. They sell watches at cost prices, and the watches are so bad that they make profits by repairing them! But II is not funny. It is a plain-looking statement.

26. 2; I is not funny. In II, the father implies that nobody is able to do as he wishes in his lifetime. This makes II funny.
27. 1; I is funny as it indirectly implies that only fools argue with fools. But II is a vague statement: the meaning in not clear.
28. 4; Nobody would like his healthy teeth pulled out just to avail of discount. This makes I funny. Further, in II, the dentist offers to pull out the teeth *slowly*, so that the patient does not feel that she paid 25 rupees for *a minute's job*! This makes II funny. Of course, the basic idea is different in the two.
29. 4; Mr. Awasthi thinks that if his wife gave birth to triplets there must be *three different fathers!* This makes I funny. Hearing the news of triplets makes Mr. Awasthi think of insurance-policies *at just place*. This makes II funny. It is obvious that both of them have contrasting ideas.
30. 4; Infancy means the period of being an infant. But adultery has a different meaning. It does not mean the period of being an adult. It means sexual promiscuity. This makes I funny. In II, we find a solution to the problem: let us all be born adults. Of course, it is a funny idea.
31. 4; I is funny because of the twist it has given to the suffix 'path' and II is funny because of the way it has correlated the preference with money.
32. 3; Both are funny and both have the same idea. In both of them, the doctor has been shown to be greedy while pretending otherwise.
33. 4; Everyone wants to *relate* somehow with a financier. This is the basic idea of I. Everyone wishes that some relative of his would leave him a fortune when he dies. This is the basic idea of II. Of course, both I and II fit as punchlines because they are both funny and both turn along quite unexpected lines.
34. 4; I is funny because in the climax we find that the "beautiful heavenly bodies" are actually stars of the sky. In II, the twist is different. Initially, the advertisement creates an impression that it *wants* people who stand around and look at beautiful bodies but it actually declares that it doesn't. This makes II funny.
35. 2; I is not funny; it's a plain answer to a plain question. In II, the doctor hints at his exorbitant fee in a funny manner. So, II fits as a punchline.

Chapter Nine

Strengthening and Weakening Arguments

9.1: Introduction

Besides the numerous types of problems discussed in the preceding chapters, there is another without the study of which our study of analytical reasoning would be incomplete. This is the problem of deciding whether a given seondary argument strengthens or weakens the main or central arguments. [See **"A study of argumentation"**]

These questions are a regular feature of the Reasoning paper of various MBA entrance examinations including the CAT. With the way the PO papers are being upgraded it would hardly be long before they are asked in PO exams as well.

9.2: Format of the problem

The most common way of putting up the question is like this:

Ex. 1: Direction: Read the passage below and then answer the questions that follow.

In a laboratory study, 160 rabbits in an experimental group were injected with Serum D, while 160 rabbits in a control group were injected with a harmless sugar solution. Within two weeks, 39% of the experimental group rabbits had contracted jungle fever, a highly contagious and usually fatal disease. Therefore, jungle fever must be caused by some substance similar to the substances found in Serum D.

Q.1. The above argument would be most greatly strengthened if it were shown that

(A) the normal rate of jungle fever among rabbits is less than 0.01%.

(B) 40% of the rabbits in the control group had also contracted jungle fever within two weeks.

(C) Serum D contains substances extracted from the root of a poisonous jungle wildflower.

(D) the blood of jungle fever victims invariably contains a high level of certain toxic substance also found in Serum D.

(E) nearly all the rabbits which contracted jungle fever died within two days of the appearance of the first symptoms.

Q. 2. The above argument would be most seriously weakened if it were shown that

(A) none of the substances in Serum D occurs naturally in the habitats of most species of the rabbit.

(B) the rabbits in an experimental group had been kept strictly isolated from one another.

(C) jungle fever is usually found only among victims of the bite of the South American Lesser Hooded Viper.

(D) the scientists administering the injections were unaware of the contents of the solutions they were using.

(E) one of the rabbits in the experimental group had jungle fever prior to the start of the experiment.

9.3: An analysis

In the chapter **"A study of argumentation"**, you have seen how arguments work. You must recall that arguments are based on (1) certain **premises**; these premises act as a support and further, the argument makes (2) certain **assumptions**; these assumptions are implicit, they are not stated and they also provide support and, using the support of these two, the argument reaches (3) a certain **conclusion.** This can be shown diagrammatically as in the figure below:

Premises [support]	+	Hidden Assumptions [hidden support]	=	Conclusion

Fig I: This is how an argument works

This is a general sketch of argumentation. Further, you must recall from that chapter: the arguments can have different types depending upon how they take the support of the premises. For example, we can have: **Arguments by example** (here, the supporting premise is an example), **arguments by analogy** (here, the supporting premise is an analogy between two objects), **arguments by cause-and-effect strategy** (here, the supporting premise is a cause, the conclusion is an effect, and it is assumed that the cause leads to the effect), **arguments by chronology** (here, the supporting premise is a chronological study of facts and the conclusion is based on this).

[It would be advisable that the reader go through the chapter "A study of argumentation" before going any further]

Now, we have seen the general working of arguments and their major types. We are now in a position to derive a strategy for solving the questions.

9.4: Suggested Method:

We have seen that a standard argument consists of the following three stages:

(a) the stated premises
(b) the hidden assumptions
(c) the conclusion

This means that

(i) an argument would be strengthened if

(a) the stated premises are supported by some more facts of the same nature,

or

(b) the hidden assumptions are supported by a fact of the same nature,

or

(c) the conclusion itself is supported by a fact of the same nature.

AND

(ii) an argument would be weakened if

(a) the stated premises are contradicted by some contradicting facts,

or

(b) the hidden assumptions are attacked by some contradicting facts,

or

(c) the conclusion itself is directly contradicted by some contradicting facts.

This means that if we have an argument by example, this argument would be strengthened (weakened) if

(a) we prove that the example itself is totally correct (incorrect),

or

(b) we support (contradict) the assumption,

or

(c) we support (contradict) the conclusion directly or by some other means.

This would be clear from the following examples.

Ex 2: *We must follow the policy of non-violence because Gandhiji used to practise it.*

Analysis: Let us first make a complete post-mortem of this argument:

Type: *Argument by example.*

Premise (support): Gandhiji used to practise non-violence.

Hidden assumption: What Gandhiji did must be correct.

Conclusion: We must follow the policy of non-violence.

Now, we can easily see that statements I, II and III (if they were true) would strengthen the argument while statements IV, V and VI would weaken it.

I (supports the premise): Even Lord Buddha advocated non-violence.

II (supports the assumption): We must follow our great leaders' example.

III (supports the conclusion): Non-violence is our Constitutional obligation.

IV (contradicts the premise): At certain stages, Gandhiji also advocated violence.

V (contradicts the assumption): It is not necessary that whatever Gandhiji did must be correct.

VI (contradicts the conclusion): Non-violence has been declared to be an unconstitutional policy.

[**Note:** We have clearly said that the statements above would strengthen or weaken the arguments only if they were true. As such, IV and VI are not true. We have used them only to make you understand the logic: we are studying logic and not history or polity, remember.]

Let us take another example. We have presented the argument first and then enlisted its break-up and possible strengthening or weakening arguments in a tabular fashion below.

Ex 3: *Pakistan and Bangladesh have suffered defeats at the hands of the Indian cricket team. So, India must defeat them in tennis as well.*

Analysis:

Type: *Argument by analogy*

Argument	Break-up	Strengthening Statement	Weakening Statement
Premise (Support)	India has defeated both countries in cricket.	In fact, India has been defeating them for the past ten years.	But India has been losing to them also.
Hidden Assumption	What happens in cricket also happens in tennis.	Cricket and tennis are very similar games.	It is not necessary that what happens in cricket also happens in tennis.
Conclusion	India will defeat both countries in tennis also.		

[Above, we could not have any statement that strengthened or weakened the conclusion directly because the conclusion is in future tense and we cannot support or contradict the future.]

Let us see one more example:

Ex 4: *The government has announced a devaluation of the rupee against the dollar by at least 20%. Economists have criticised the step saying that it would bring inflation into the economy.*

Analysis:

Type: *Argument by cause-and-effect relationship.*

Argument	Break-up	Strengthening Statement	Weakening Statement
Premise (Support or cause)	Economists have criticised the devaluation of rupee by 20%.	Devaluation of rupee could be avoided by taking some other measures.	Devaluation was long overdue in the economy.
Hidden Assumptions	(i) Economists are correct.	Economists must have some merit in their criticism.	It's not necessary that what economists say is correct.
	(ii) **Devaluation is a cause and inflation is its effect.**	Whenever there is devaluation inflation follows.	Devaluation may not always result in inflation.
	(iii) Inflation is not desirable.	Inflation is not good for the health of the economy.	Inflation is not very harmful for the economy.
Conclusion (effect)	There will be inflation in the economy.		

Explanation:

(i) As in Ex 3, we have no strengthening or weakening statements related with the conclusion because it is in future tense and we cannot support or contradict the future.

(ii) When the argument says that "economists have criticised" the move because it will "bring inflation" it becomes apparent that the argument assumes

(a) that *the economists are correct.* Otherwise, it would not have quoted the economists to reach its conclusion.

(b) that *inflation is undesirable.* Otherwise, it would not have "criticised" the government's move.

But all these are secondary assumptions. The argument is based on cause-and-effect relationship and in such cases the major assumption is this: *the cause leads to the effect.* In the context of the passage, the cause is devaluation and the effect is inflation. So, the assumption is

(c) *devaluation leads to inflation.* This is the major assumption made by the argument.

The question of *most* strengthening and *most* weakening statements

In the foregoing examples, we have seen how an argument can be strengthened (or weakened) by statements that support (or contradict) its various constituent parts. This was good from the point of view of understanding the concept but this would give us *many* strengthening (or weakening) statements, while in the examination, we'd have to choose just one. Usually we have to choose - as the language of the question says - the *most* strengthening (or weakening) statement. How do we choose the *most* strengthening (or weakening) statement. Well, this is easy. The idea is :

(1) Out of several statements, all of which seem to support or strengthen an argument, the one that supports the basic assumption of the argument would be the *most* strengthening.

Analogously we have:

(2) Out of several statements, all of which seem to contradict or weaken an argument, the one that contradicts the basic assumption of the argument would be the *most* weakening.

Thus, in Ex 2, out of the six statements, statement II is the most strengthening while statement IV is the most weakening because statement II supports the assumption while IV contradicts the assumption. Similarly, in Ex 3, the most strengthening statement is: "Cricket and tennis are very similar games" and the most weakening statement is: "It is not necessary that what happens in cricket also happens in tennis".

What about Ex 4? Here, the assumption itself has three parts. Does this mean that we'll have three most strengthening and three most weakening statements? No.

In such cases, we have to look at the statement that supports (contradicts) the most "basic" assumption. Hence, in Ex 4, the most strengthening statement is "Whenever there is devaluation, inflation follows." and the most weakening statement is "Devaluation may not always result in inflation."

Solution to Ex 1

Let us now turn our attention to Ex 1. This argument can be broken up as:

Type: *Argument by analogy.*

Premise: 39% of rabbits injected with Serum D developed jungle fever.

Hidden Assumptions: (i) In the other group, a much less percentage of rabbits developed jungle fever.

(ii) Apart from the fact that one group was given Serum D and the other wasn't the two groups were under similar conditions in all aspects. [*Analogous*]

Conclusion: Serum D must have some substances that cause jungle fever.

Let us now take the choices of Ex 1.

Q. 1. D; Choice A *strengthens* the argument because it gives weight to the supporting premise: if the normal rate is .01% then 39% is surely an alarming number. Choice B *weakens* the argument by contradicting the premise: if 39% was developed by the first group, so what? 40% was developed by the second. This shakes the very support of the conclusion. Choice C is irrelevant: does jungle wildflower have anything to do with jungle fever? Choice D *strengthens* the argument by providing an additional supporting evidence or a supporting premise. Choice E is irrelevant: all it proves is that jungle fever is a fatal disease but that is not in controversy here.

So, our choices narrow down to A and D. Which one do we choose? A little insight would show that choice A is irrelevant in the sense that it only gives credence to the fact that the experimental group contracted jungle fever at a higher rate than expected but it does not relate to the *cause* of jungle fever. **The conclusion that some substance found in Serum D causes jungle fever would be greatly strengthened if the substance and the fever were invariably found together, as stated in choice D.**

Q.2: E; Choice A is irrelevant, since we have no idea whether rabbits or any particular species of rabbits are frequent victims of jungle fever in the first place. Choice B supports the assumption [See hidden assumption (ii)] and hence *strengthens* the statement instead of weakening it. Choice C is irrelevant: what does a viper have to do with our argument? Choice D is also irrelevant: the question is not which constituent of the solution caused jungle fever; the question is whether the solution causes jungle fever at all. Choice E *weakens* the argument by defeating the assumption: if there was an infected rabbit initially in the experimental group, this coupled with the fact that jungle fever is "highly contagious", leads us to conclude that the two groups were not under identical conditions. This defeats our basic assumption. Hence, the answer is choice (E).

We shall close this topic with the study of two more examples.

Ex 5: Read the passage below and then answer the question that follows:

The current trend towards specialisation in nearly all occupational groups is exactly the opposite of what is needed. World problems today are so diverse, complex, and interrelated that only the generalist stands a chance of understanding the broad picture. Unless our schools stress a truly broad, liberal education, the world will crumble around us as each of us expertly performs our own narrow functions.

Each of the following, if true, would weaken the conclusion drawn above EXCEPT

(A) Many of the world's problems can be solved only by highly specialised experts working on specific problems.

(B) Relatively few generalists are needed to coordinate the work of the many specialists.

(C) Specialisation does not necessarily entail losing the ability to see the broad picture.

(D) Increasingly complex problems require a growing level of technical expertise which can only be acquired through specialisation.

(E) Even the traditional liberal education is becoming more highly specialised today.

Answer: E

Solution: We can break up the argument in the following way:

Premise (i): Today's problems are complex and interrelated.

Assumption (i): These interrelated problems require an understanding of the broad picture and not of merely a narrow aspect, for solution.

Premise (ii): Only a generalist can understand this broad picture.

Assumption: (ii): Truly broad and liberal education prepares generalists.

Conclusions (i): The current trend towards specialisation should be checked and reversed.

(ii): Schools should stress a truly broad and liberal education.

Now, we can easily see that choices (A) and (B) contradict assumption (i), choice (C) contradicts premise (ii), and choice (D) again contradicts assumption (i). But choice E does not contradict the logic of the argument anywhere.

Ex 6: Read the passage below and answer the question that follows:

Strict gun control laws cause a decrease in violent crime; in the six months since the city council passed a gun control law, armed robberies in Bombay have dropped by 18 per cent.

Q. Which of the following, if true, would strengthen the argument above?

I. Before the law was passed, the number of armed robberies had been steadily increasing.

II. The more severe the punishment mandated for a crime, the less likely that the crime is to occur.

III. Three-fourths of all violent crimes involve the use of a gun.

A) I only B) III only C) I and II only

D) II and III only E) I, II and III

Answer: E

Solution: We can break up the argument as following:

Premise: In the six months since the passing of a gun control law, armed robberies have dropped by 18%.

Hidden Assumptions: (i) Apart from the gun control law, there is no other apparent cause for the armed robberies to drop.

(ii) Decrease in armed robberies means a decrease in violent crime.

Conclusion: Strict gun control laws cause a decrease in violent crime.

Now, we may see that statement (I) indirectly supports assumption (i), statement (II) supports the conclusion, while statement (III) indirectly supports assumption (ii). Hence, all of these strengthen the argument in their own way. Correct choice: E.

[Which one is the *most* strengthening statement? It is statement I because it supports the basic assumption.].

Summary

In order to decide whether a statement strengthens (or weakens) an argument, follow these steps:

Step I: Break up the argument mentally. See what is the supporting premise, what is the assumption and what is the conclusion.

Step II: If a suggested statement supports any of the three, it would be a strengthening statement; if it contradicts any of the three, it would be a weakening statement.

In order to decide which statement strengthens (or weakens) an argument the most, follow an additional step:

Step III: If a suggested statement supports (or weakens) the basic assumption of an argument, it would be the most strengthening (weakening) argument.

OR

If a suggested statement provides a very strong proof (or contradictory proof) in favour of (or in contradiction to) the conclusion of the argument, it would be the most strengthening (or weakening) statement.

Practice Exercise

Exercise 9

Directions : Do as directed in each of the following questions.

1. Landmark preservation laws unfairly impinge on the freedom of owners to develop their own property as they see fit. In some cases, owners of hotels and office buildings designated as landmarks have been forbidden to make changes in the original facades or interiors, even though they reasonably believe that the changes would enhance the structures and make them more valuable.

   Which of the following statements, if true, seriously weakens the author's argument?

   A) Altering the appearance of a historic structure sometimes does not enhance its beauty or value.

   B) In traditional legal doctrine, ownership of a property implies the right to alter it at will.

   C) Only buildings over 75 years old are normally affected by landmark preservation laws.

   D) Landmark designations must be approved by a local regulatory body before taking effect.

   E) Historic buildings represent a cultural heritage which the community has a legitimate stake in preserving.

2. The existence of flying saucers, unidentified flying objects supposedly piloted by extraterrestrial beings, has been shown to be illusory. Skeptical researchers have demonstrated that a number of photographs purportedly showing flying saucers are either crude forgeries or misinterpreted images of such earthly objects as weather baloons or small private planes.
If the photographs mentioned above are accurately explained in the passage, which of the following is the best argument AGAINST the conclusion drawn?
   A) Not all unidentified flying objects can be conclusively shown to be man-made objects.
   B) The fact that a number of photographs of flying saucers are fake does not generally disprove the phenomenon.
   C) Some of those who claim to have witnessed flying saucers have no apparent motive for lying.
   D) Given the size and complexity of the universe, it seems unreasonable to assume that life exist only on Earth.
   E) Researchers who are skeptical about flying saucers inevitably bring their own biases and preconceptions to their work.

3. All the members of the Student Rights Coalition signed the petition calling for a meeting with the university trustees. Philip must be a member of the Student Rights Coalition since his signature appears on the petition.
Which of the following best states the central flaw in the reasoning above?
   A) Some members of the Student Rights Coalition may not support all of the organisation's positions.
   B) It is possible that Philip's signature on the petition was forged by a member of the Student Rights Coalition.
   C) Any member of the student body is eligible to sign a petition dealing with university affairs.
   D) Philip may have resigned from the Student Rights Coalition after signing the petition.
   E) Some of those who signed the petition may not be members of the Student Rights Coalition.

Questions 4-5: Pollution control can no longer be viewed as a national problem to be addressed by individual countries on the basis of national sovereignty. As the international effects of the Chernobyl nuclear accident make clear, pollutants do not respect political boundaries; thus every nation has a legitimate stake in the environmental practices and policies of its neighbours.

4. *Which of the following would be the most logical continuation of the argument above?*
   A) So, growth of the nuclear power industry should be halted until more rigorous safety procedures have been developed.
   B) Hence, attempts made by one nation to impose its environmental policies on another should be resisted - if necessary, by force.

C) Consequently, issues of pollution should be handled by an international commission with the authority to set policies for all nations.

D) Thus, every nation should pledge itself to environmental policies that will minimise the danger to its neighbours.

E) As a result, only the ultimate emergence of a sovereign world government will resolve today's most pressing environmental dilemmas.

5. *Which of the following, if true, most strongly supports the view expressed in the passage?*

A) Acid rain from factories in the midwestern United States pollutes lakes in Canada.

B) Soviet leaders refused western reporters' access to safety records after the Chernobyl accident.

C) Neighbouring states within the United States are often unable to agree on joint pollution control efforts.

D) Existing international bodies have no authority to impose pollution control regulations on member-nations.

E) Fishers form Japanese fleets have increasingly depleted fish supplies in United States' territorial waters.

6. Foreign-made electronics products gained populartiy in the United States during the 1970s primarily because of their low cost. In recent years, changes in the exchange rates of currencies have increased the prices of imported electronic products relative to those produced in the United States. However, sales of imported electronics products have not declined in recent years.

Which of the following, if true, would best explain why sales of imported electronics products remain high?

A) Trade ministries in foreign nations have pursued policies that prevented prices of electronics products from rising even faster.

B) The cost of manufacturing electronics products abroad is still lower than it is in the United States.

C) A coming shortage in consumer credit in the United States is expected to depress sales of imported products during the next two years.

D) American consumers now perceive the quality of imports as being high enough to justify the increased prices.

E) United States manufacturers have tried to convince Americans to buy United States-made products for patriotic reasons.

7. The percentage of family income spent on entertainment has remained almost the same over the past twenty years - about twelve per cent. When new forms of entertainment become popular, they do not expand this percentage; instead, they take consumer spending away from other forms of entertainment. Therefore, film producers have observed the video boom with concern, knowing that every dollar spent on rental of videos means a dollar less spent on movie theatre admissions.

Which of the following, if true, most forcefully undermines the argument of the passage above?

A) The cost of renting a video is generally substantially less than the price of a movie theatre admission.

B) Most film producers receive a portion of the income from the sale of video rights to their movies.

C) Fears of some film producers that videos would completely supersede movies have not come to pass.

D) Since the start of the video boom, money spent on forms of entertainment other than videos and movies has dropped.

E) Some movies that were unprofitable when shown in theatres have become successful when released in video form.

8. The use of petroleum products in the manufacture of plastics should be regulated and limited by law. Our country's need for petroleum for energy production is more vital than our need for plastics, and our growing dependence on foreign sources of petroleum could have serious consequences if, for example, a war cut off our access to those imports. By reducing our use of petroleum products in making plastics, we can take a major step towards national energy independence and so enhance our country's security.

Which of the following, if true, would most greatly weaken the argument above?

A) Only a small fraction of petroleum products consumed in this country is used in making plastics.

B) New methods of plastics manufacture can somewhat reduce the amount of petroleum needed.

C) The development of atomic energy as an alternative to petroleum-based energy has been slowed by legitimate concerns over safety.

D) In times of war, combatant nations would be seriously tempted to sieze forcibly the territories of petroleum-producing nations.

E) Some plastic products, such as aircraft and motor vehicles' parts, play vital roles in our nation's defence.

9. Some scientists believe that, in certain species of birds, actual particles of metal within the brain react to the Earth's magnetic field in the same way as the needle in a compass. It is this mechanism that is thought to underlie the birds' amazing ability to navigate accurately over distances of thousands of miles by day and night during migration. To test this theory, researchers surgically removed the metal particles from the heads of some birds and then released them, alongwith a number of untreated birds, at the usual time and place of their annual winter migration.

W   of the following results would most seriously weaken the theory
l   sted?

A) The untreated birds were confused by the erratic flight patterns of the surgically treated birds and failed to migrate successfully.
B) The surgically treated birds were able to follow their usual flight patterns successfully by day, but not by night.
C) The surgically treated birds were able to migrate about as accurately as the untreated birds.
D) The surgically treated birds were able to migrate successfully only when closely following a group of untreated birds.
E) In addition to being impaired in their migration ability, the surgically treated birds suffered a variety of other disabling effects.

10. For our nation to compete successfully in the high-technology enterprises of the future, workers with skills in maths and science will be needed. But it is doubtful that they will be available, since there is a shortage of high school maths and science teachers that shows no signs of improving. Industry can help alleviate this problem by funding scholarship grants and aid to college students who graduate in maths and science with the hope of pursuing teaching careers.
Which of the following, if true, would most probably prevent the proposed plan from achieving its intended effect?
A) After graduation from college, most maths and science graduates opt for jobs in industry rather than in teaching.
B) Many high schools have been forced to lower their standards in hiring maths and science teachers.
C) More scholarship money is already available for students of maths and science than is available for those in any other field.
D) Population statistics show that the number of high school students is expected to decline over the next ten years.
E) Many experts say that business of the future will require relatively few highly trained workers, along with many semi-skilled and purely technical employees.

11. Secondary school graduates in Japan score significantly higher on tests of science and mathematics than do students at the same level in the United States. Some educational reformers in the United States attribute this difference to the more rigid and rigorous Japanese secondary school programme, which emphasises required courses, long hours of study and homework, and memorisation to a far greater degree than do American schools.
Which of the following, if true, would most seriously weaken the conclusion drawn by the educational reformers cited?
A) The Japanese elementary school programme is far less rigid and structured than the elementary school programmes in most United States schools.

B) Many Japanese parents and educators decry the Japanese educational system, saying that it stifles independent thinking on the part of students.

C) United States schools, in which creativity and flexible student schedules are emphasised, usually produce students with science and maths scores equal to those of the best Japanese students.

D) On an average, Japanese students score lower than United States students on tests of logical thinking, language arts, and communications skills.

E) A higher percentage of American students go for higher education than in Japan.

12. Archaeologists seeking the location of a legendary siege and destruction of city are excavating in several possible places, including a middle and a lower layer of a large mound. The bottom of the middle layer contains some pieces of pottery of type 3, known to be from a later period than the time of the destruction of the city, but lower layer does not.

Which of the following hypotheses is best supported by the evidence above?

A) The lower layer contains the remains of the city where the siege took place.

B) The legend confuses stories from two different historical periods.

C) The middle layer does not represent the period of the siege.

D) The siege lasted for a long time before the city was destroyed.

E) The pottery of type 3 was imported to the city by traders.

13. *The force of the evidence cited above is most seriously weakened if which of the following is true ?*

A) Gerbils, small animals long native to the area, dig large burrows into which objects can fall when the burrows collapse.

B) Pottery of types 1 and 2, found in the lower level, was used in the cities from which, according to the legend, the besieging forces came.

C) Several pieces of stone from a lower-layer well have been found incorporated into the remains of a building in the middle layer.

D) Both the middle and lower layers show evidence of large-scale destruction of habitations by fire.

E) Bronze axeheads of a type used at the time of the siege were found in the lower level of excavation.

14. There are far fewer children available for adoption than there are people who want to adopt. Two million couples are currently waiting to adopt. But in 1982, the last year for which figures exist, there were only some 50,000 adoptions.

Which of the following statements, if true, most strengthens the author's claim that there are far fewer children available for adoption than there are people who want to adopt ?

A) The number of couples waiting to adopt has increased significantly in the last decade.

B) The number of adoptions in the current year is greater than the number of adoptions in any preceding year.

C) The number of adoptions in a year is approximately equal to the number of children available for adoption in that period.

D) People who seek to adopt children often go through a long process of interviews and investigation by adoption agencies.

E) People who seek to adopt children generally make very good parents.

15. Federal agricultural programmes aimed at benefiting one group whose livelihood depends on farming often end up harming another such group.

Which of the following statements provides support for the claim above ?

I. An effort to help food-grain producers resulted in higher prices for their crops, but the higher prices decreased the profits of livestock producers.

II. In order to reduce crop surpluses and increase prices, growers of certain crops were paid to leave a portion of their land idle, but the reduction was not achieved because improvements in efficiency resulted in higher production on the land in use.

III. Many farm workers were put out of work when a programme meant to raise the price of grain provided grain-growers with an incentive to reduce production by giving them surplus grain from government reserves.

A) I, but not II and III
B) II, but not I and III
C) I and III, but not II
D) II and III, but not I
E) I, II and III

16. Companies considering new cost-cutting manufacturing processes often compare the projected results of making the investment against the alternative of not making the investment with costs, selling prices, and share of market remaining constant.

Which of the following, assuming that each is a realistic possibility, constitutes the most serious disadvantage for companies using the above method for evaluating financial benefit of new manufacturing processes?

A) The costs of materials required by the new process might not be known with certainty.

B) In several years interest rates might go down, reducing the interest costs of borrowing money to pay for the investment.

C) Some cost-cutting processes might require such expensive investments that there would be no net gain for many years, until the investment was paid for by savings in the manufacturing process.

D) Competitors that do invest in a new process might reduce their selling prices and, thus, take market share away from companies that do not.

E) The period of year chosen for averaging the cost of the investment might be somewhat longer or shorter, thus affecting the result.

17. Using computer techniques, researchers analyse layers of paint that lie buried beneath the surface layers of old paintings. They claim, for example, that additional mountainous scenery once appeared in Leonardo da Vinci's *Mona Lisa*, which was later painted over. Skeptics reply to these claims, however, that X-ray examinations of the *Mona Lisa* do not show hidden mountains.

Which of the following, if true, would tend most to weaken the force of the skeptics' objections?

A) There is no written or anecdotal record that Leonardo da Vinci ever painted over major areas of his *Mona Lisa*.

B) Painters of da Vinci's time commonly created images of mountainous scenery in the backgrounds of portraits like the *Mona Lisa*.

C) No one knows for certain what parts of the *Mona Lisa* may have been painted by da Vinci's assistants rather than by da Vinci himself.

D) Infrared photography of the *Mona Lisa* has revealed no trace of hidden mountainous scenery.

E) Analysis relying on X-rays only has the capacity to detect lead-based white pigments in layers of paint beneath a painting's surface layers.

18. While Governor Verdant has been in office, the state's budget has increased by an aveage of 6 per cent each year. While the previous governor was in office, the state's budget increased by an average of 11.5 per cent each year. Obviously, the austere budgets during Governor Verdant's term have caused the slowdown in the growth in state spending.

Which of the following, if true, would most seriously weaken the conclusion drawn above?

A) The rate of inflation in the state averaged 10 per cent each year during the previous governor's term in office and 3 per cent each year during Verdant's term.

B) Both federal and state income tax rates have been lowered considerably during Verdant's term in office.

C) In each year of Verdant's term in office, the state's budget has shown some increase in spending over the previous year.

D) During Verdant's term in office, the state has either discontinued or begun to charge private citizens for numerous services that the state offered free to citizens during the previous governor's term.

E) During the previous governor's term in office, the state introduced several so called " austerity" budgets intended to reduce the growth in state spending.

19. Psychological research indicates that college hockey and football players are more quickly moved to hostility and aggression than are college athletes not in contact sports such as swimming. But the researchers' conclusion — that contact sports encourage and teach participants to be hostile and

aggressive — is untenable. The football and hockey players were probably more hostile and aggressive to start with than the swimmers.

Which of the following, if true, would most strengthen the conclusion drawn by the psychological researchers?

A) The football and hockey players became more hostile and aggressive during the season and remained so during the offseason, whereas there was no increase in aggressiveness among the swimmers.

B) The football and hockey players, but not the swimmers, were aware at the start of the experiment that they were being tested for aggressiveness.

C) The same psychological research indicated that the football and hockey players had a great respect for cooperation and team play, whereas the swimmers were more concerned with excelling as individual competitors.

D) The research studies were designed to include no college athletes who participated in both contact and noncontact sports.

E) Throughout the United States, more incidents of fan violence occur at baseball games than at hockey or football games.

20. Contrary to the charges made by some of its opponents, the provisions of the new deficit reduction law for indiscriminate cuts in the federal budget are justified. Opponents should remember that the New Deal pulled this country out of economic troubles even though some of its provisions were slightly unconstitutional.

The opponents could effectively defend their position against the author's strategy by pointing out that

A) the expertise of those opposing the law is outstanding.

B) the lack of justification for the new law does not imply that those who drew it up were either inept or immoral.

C) the practical application of the new law will not entail indiscriminate budget cuts.

D) economic troubles present at the time of the New Deal were equal in severity to those that have led to the present law.

E) the fact that certain flawed programmes or laws have improved the economy does not prove that every such programme can do so.

21. In the past, to run for one's country in the Olympics was the ultimate achievement for any athlete. Nowadays an athlete's motives are more and more influenced by financial gain, and consequently we do not see our best athletes in the Olympics, which is still only for amateurs.

Which of the following will most weaken the above conclusion?

A) The publicity and fame that can be achieved by competing in the Olympics makes athletes more "marketable" by agents and potential sponsors, while allowing the athletes to retain their amateur status.

B) The winning of a race is not as important as participating.

C) There is a widely-held belief that our best Olympic athletes already receive enough in terms of promotion and sponsorship.

D) It has been suggested that professional athletes should be allowed to compete in the games.

E) Athletics as an entertainment is like any other entertainment job and deserves a financial reward.

22. Unless new reserves are found soon, the world's supply of coal is being depleted in such a way that with demand continuing to grow at present rates, reserves will be exhausted by the year 2050.

Which of the following, if true, would most weaken the above argument?

A) There has been a slowdown in the rate of increase in world demand for coal over the last 5 years from 10% to 5%.

B) It has been known for many years that there are vast stocks of coal under Antarctica which are yet to be economically exploited.

C) Oil is being used increasingly in place of coal for many industrial and domestic uses.

D) As coal resources are depleted more marginal supplies, which are more costly to produce and less efficient in use, are being mined.

E) None of the above

23. In accordance with their powers, many state authorities are introducing fluoridation of drinking water. This follows the conclusion of 10 years of research that the process ensures that children and adults receive the required intake of fluoride that will strengthen teeth. The maximum level has been set at one part per million. However, there are many who object, claiming that fluoridation removes freedom of choice.

Which of the following will weaken the claim of the proponents of fluoridation?

A) Fluoridation over a certain prescribed level has been shown to lead to a general weakening of teeth.

B) There is no record of the long-term effects of drinking fluoridated water.

C) The people to be affected by fluoridation claim that they have not had sufficient opportunity to voice their views.

D) Fluoridation is only one part of general dental health.

E) Water already contains natural fluoride.

24. The burning of coal, oil and other combustible energy sources produces carbon dioxide, a natural constituent of the atmosphere. Elevated levels of carbon dioxide are thought to be responsible for half the greenhouse effect. Enough carbon dioxide has been sent into the atmosphere already to cause a significant temperature increase. Growth in industrial production must be slowed, or production processes must be changed.

Which of the following, if true, would tend to weaken the strength of the above conclusion?

A) Many areas of the world are cold anyway, so a small rise in temperature would be welcome.

B) Carbon dioxide is bad for health.

C) Most carbon dioxide is emitted by automobiles.

D) Industry is switching over to synthetic liquid fuel extracted from coal.

E) A shift to other energy sources would be too costly.

25. In August 1980, according to a *New York Times* / CBS news poll, 36 per cent of the voters called themselves Republican or said they were independents leaning towards being Republicans. In November 1984, the Republican figure rose to 47 per cent. But in the latest *Time* / CBS survey, the Republicans were down to 38 per cent. Therefore, the Democrats are likely to win the next election.

Which of the following, if true, would most seriously weaken the above conclusion?

A) Republicans were a minority in 1984, but a Republican President was elected.

B) People tend to switch their votes at the last minute.

C) People vote for the best candidate, not for a political party.

D) No one can predict how people will vote.

E) It has been shown that 85 per cent of Republicans vote in an election, compared to 50 per cent of the Democrats.

26. The states of New York, Ohio, Pennsylvania and California provide extensive free higher education to their residents. These states are representative of different geographic areas of the United States. There is little reason why most states cannot provide the same service to their residents.

Which of the following, if true, would weaken the above argument?

A) Free education is not guaranteed by the Constitution.

B) New York, Ohio, Pennsylvania and California have more qualified high school graduates than other states.

C) Most other states do not have the tax base that New York, Ohio, Pennsylvania and California have.

D) Other states do not have as many high school graduates.

E) Quality education cannot be free; it must be paid for.

27. Prompted by a proposal to convert a shipyard into a complex of condominiums with a full-service marina and boat repair centre and by concern about the proposal from local residents, baymen, and environmentalists, the town is considering a one-year building moratorium for the waterfront area.

Which of the following, if true, would most seriously weaken opposition to the complex?

A) Condominiums would sell for $350,000 each.
B) There is a large demand for boat repair services.
C) A growing population results in the closure of shellfish.
D) There are already 1200 moorings on the waterfront.
E) The shipyard may be sold for another commercial use.

28. Before the arrival of Joe, a new partner, sales output in Bill's company, Midas in Reverse Ltd., had been rising by 10% per year on average. Innovations by Joe included computerisation of technical processes and reductions in the work force, but annual sales output has only risen by 5% per year. It appears that Joe's innovations have caused the reduction in the annual growth rate.

Which of the following, if true, would most seriously weaken the conclusion above?

A) The investment in new machinery entails a provision for depreciation of the cost of the fixed assets, which causes a reduction in profit.
B) Midas in Reverse Ltd. does not base increase in the selling price of its products with costs.
C) Joe's innovations were intended as long-term investment and not made for short-term profit growth.
D) General demand for the product manufactured by the company has declined.
E) Workers laid off by Midas in Reverse Ltd. have been hired by a competitor who is taking an increasing share of the market.

Answers and Explanations

1.E; This question asks you to weaken an argument. *Often, the correct answer to such a question states that a key hidden assumption of the argument is false.* In this case, the conclusion of the argument is that landmark preservation laws deprive landlords of their right to use their own property. This argument presupposes a clear distinction between public and private property and, further, that the building owned by a landlord is purely private property in which the community has no legitimate interest. (E) comes to grips with this assumption by noting that a landmark building may not be purely private property and that some part of building (the heritage) may belong to the community at large.

(A) is perhaps the second best response. It does seem to attack the landlord's judgment that his actions in altering a historical structure will be valuable. The difficulty with (A) is that it represents only a partial attack on the argument. It questions whether this or that alteration would be useful or valuable but seems to grant the main philosophical point that the community, in some cases, should be able to substitute its judgment for that of the landlord.

As for (B), this seems to strengthen the speaker's claim that landmark preservation laws represent an unwarranted interference with the rights of the landlord. (C) fails to come to grips with the issue here - even if the building is over 75 years old, doesn't it still belong to the owner and not to the community? Finally, (D) makes the same kind of error. Even if we grant that landmark status must be approved by a public body, that doesn't explain why a public body should be allowed to substitute its judgment for that of the building's owner in the first place.

2. B; The logical structure of this argument is an attempt to conclude from the failure to prove "A", that "Not A" is true. It says in essence: "No one has proved that flying saucers exist, therefore, they do not exist." (B) correctly notes this logical structure.

3. E; This argument has the following logical structure:

All S are P.
F is a P.
Therefore, F is an S.

The argument is fatally flawed. It's like arguing:

All soft drinks are liquid.
Water is a liquid.
Therefore, water is a soft drink.

(E) correctly notes this logical flaw.

4. C; This question asks that you draw a further conclusion from the premises given. The argument is leading up to a call for some sort of international agency to control pollution, which, as the author claims, is an international problem. Thus, (C) is the best response. As for (A), the author would consider the Chernobyl incident merely one example of the problem he is addressing; and, in fact, he may or may not oppose nuclear power *per se*. (B) and (D) are in tension with the paragraph, for the author is skeptical of the ability of a nation as an individual nation to solve the problems of pollution. Finally, however, (E) overstates the case. The author is concerned with a specific subject area - not world government in general.

5. A; The author cites one example of international pollution, so another example would help strengthen his claim. (A) provides such an example. As for (B), the fact that journalists were not given access to the Chernobyl plant does not show that the incident had international repercussions. As for (C), this is a problem within a nation state, but the author is addressing the problem of international pollution. As for (D), the fact that there does not yet exist an international agency to control pollution neither strengthens nor weakens the author's claim that there ought to be some such authority. Finally, as for (E), this too is a problem that can be handled completely within the jurisdiction of a single nation: stop the fishers from fishing in the territorial waters.

6. D; This question asks you to examine a causal linkage. Ordinarily, we would expect higher prices to result in less demand for a product. Yet, according to the speaker, in the face of higher prices for imported electronics, demand has not weakened. What alternative causal explanation could account for this? (D) gives a good one. Here, (B) is perhaps the second-best answer. If (B) is true, then we would expect some consumers to prefer imports over domestically produced items; but the argument doesn't just claim that there has been less weakening in the demand for imports than might be expected, but no weakening at all.

7. D; This is one of those questions that are answered by finding an alternative causal explanation. The author argues for the following connection: videos take money away from movies. What choice (D) asserts, in effect, is that the money spent on videos came from some other source. So, the projected cause-effect sequence was incorrect.

8. A; This item asks you to find a hidden assumption of the argument. The speaker claims that in order to ensure that we have sufficient energy, we should quit using petroleum (an energy source) to manufacture plastics. If we do, so he claims, we will have made a significant step towards energy independence. This arugument, however, assumes that we use a lot of petroleum in the manufacture of plastic - an assumption questioned by (A).

9. C; The question stem here asks for the evidence that would most weaken the theory that the metal particles are important to the bird's navigational mechanism. The best refutation of the theory would be a finding that when the particles are removed, the birds continue to migrate as effectively as before. (C) is tantamount to saying that this was the case.

10. A; The correct response to this question is a statement that focuses upon an unforeseen causal outcome. What (A) asserts is that you can pour the money into the system, and you can train students in maths and science, but they will not go into teaching. Thus, your plan will not achieve the desired result.

11. C; Focus on the claim that you are asked to assess. The reformers claim that the critical difference between the maths and science scores of Japanese and American children is the discipline of the Japanese educational system. (C) directly contradicts this claim. It says, in essence, that this cannot be the proper causal explanation because American students, in highly flexible environments, actually outscore the Japanese students in their rigid environments.

12. C; If the city was destroyed before any pottery of type 3 was made, the hypothesis that the middle layer represents a period later than that of the siege is strongly supported. The major assumptions on which this hypothesis rests are only that lower layers represent earlier time periods and that objects from a later period did not become embedded in some unusual way in layers present in earlier periods. Hypothesis A is not strongly supported since the large mound may just be the wrong place

to look in. The evidence as described reveals nothing about any particular siege or episode of destruction; so neither hypothesis B nor D is supported. Hypothesis E is not supported because the city of the legend is known to have been destroyed before type 3 pottery was first made. On balance, then, the best answer is C.

13. A; Choice A provides a way for an object from a higher, thus more recent, layer to get into a lower, older layer. If the lower layer is dated by such an object, that layer's age will be underestimated. Choice A suggests that it is possible that the type 3 pottery ended up in an older layer than is chronologically appropriate. The evidence cited leaves open what B and E suggest: that the lower layer represents the period of the siege. B and E are, thus, not contrary to the evidence cited. Choice C shows that materials from an earlier period may be reused in a later period. The question raised by the evidence cited, however, is whether materials from a later period can end up in a layer that dates from an earlier period. D is an additional evidence of a neutral kind. Therefore, A is the best answer.

14. C; The evidence the author presents is weak because it is unclear how the number of adoptions in a year is related to the number of children available for adoption. Choice C settles the question in a way that strengthens the author's claim. The only remaining point of uncertainty is whether the 1982 figures are representative. Choices A, B and D are all compatible with a situation in which there are as many children available for adoption as there are people wanting to adopt, but only a small fraction of the children available get adopted in any given year. The quality of parenting mentioned in E is irrelevant to any of the numbers cited. Thus, C is the only choice that clearly strengthens the author's claim and is, therefore, the best answer.

15. C; Any specific agricultural programme that is designed to benefit one group whose livelihood depends on farming but also harms another such group, provides support for the claim made here. Statement I describes such a case: food-grain producers were intended to benefit, but livestock producers' interests were hurt. Statement III also describes such a case: grain growers were meant to benefit, but farm workers were adversely affected. Statement II does not describe a relevantly similar case: growers of certain crops were meant to benefit, but the hoped-for benefit did not materialise; yet there is no indication of any harm coming to another group making its living from farming. Therefore, C is the best answer.

16. D; The method of evaluation described assumes that D will not happen. If D did happen, the method would systematically tend to value the non-investment option too highly. Since D is said to be entirely possible, it represents a disadvantage of the method described. Therefore, D is the best answer.

Since the cost mentioned in A has to be estimate, no matter what method of evaluation is chosen, A cannot be a disadvantage of one method relative to another. The factor mentioned in B may affect the timing of the investment but the method described can accommodate alternative investment dates. The payback of the investment is a feature that the method described can presumably accommodate and, thus, C is not appropriate. Evaluating the investment option inevitably involves uncertainty, but this is not a function of the method used, as E suggests it is.

17. E; Even assuming that lead-based white pigments were, in fact, used in painting the *Mona Lisa*, it is not clear, without further argument, that mountainous scenery, if it had been painted, would contain white pigments in such a configuration that the presence of mountainous scenery could be deduced. Thus, the skeptics' evidence might have no force. Therefore, E is the best answer.

The fact cited in A does not bear on whether mountainous scenery was ever present; it merely suggests that, if someone painted over any mountainous scenery, it was not *da Vinci*. The skeptics base their case on a physical examination of the *Mona Lisa*. Unless it is shown that their method yields inconclusive results, counter-evidence derived from general artistic conventions, such as that mentioned in B, has no force. The information in C does not help to determine what was in the painting. The statement in D strengthens the skeptics' case, or is irrelevant if infra-red photography does not reveal deeper layers of paint.

18. A; Choice B deals with the courses of government income, not with government spending. The accuracy of the six-per cent figure given in the argument and on which the argument rests is not called into question; so, C does not weaken, the conclusion. Choice D tends to strengthen, rather than weaken, the position that Verdant's budgets have been austere. Choice E is inappropriate because the conclusion is based on actual figures, not descriptive phrases and avowed goals.

19. A; Choice A strengthens the psychologist's conclusion by citing facts that their conclusion can help account for while the opposing view cannot. Therefore, A is the best answer.

The differential awareness among experimental subjects suggested in B is a serious design flaw that tends to invalidate the experimental results and any conclusions drawn from them. The additional finding reported in C has no apparent bearing on the conclusion being examined. Choice D is an element of good experimental design that increases the likelihood that the experimental data were sound but not the likelihood that the correct conclusion was drawn from them. Choice E makes a statement about spectators that has no direct relevance to the psychological states of athletes participating in the games.

20. E; Choice E is an instance of a basic defence against any loose argument by analogy: the mere fact that two situations share one set of characteristics - here, an economic goal and the use of controversial means to achieve that goal - does not mean that they will automatically

share other characteristics - here, effectiveness in reaching the objective. Therefore, E is the best answer.

Choices A and B suggest that the disagreement between author and opponents deserves to be taken seriously, but neither addresses the specific merits of the author's argument. Both C and D seem to favour the author's, not the opponent's, side of the argument - C by suggesting judicious implementation of the new law and D by suggesting that the circumstances that engendered New Deal programmes are analogous and thus New Deal programmes are an appropriate precedent

21. A; It is a fact that athletes can attract sponsorship and make money and that participation in the Olympics can aid this process. On the basis that it is true that athletes are more and more attracted by the profit motive, the conclusion that the best athletes do not compete in the Olympics is weakened. Therefore, A is the appropriate answer. Alternative (B) is an oft-stated maxim, but in this case, it is not relevant to the argument. The fact that people believe that amateur athletes are receiving adequate alternative remuneration does not bear on the argument for allowing genuine professional athletes into the games. So, (C) is inappropriate. Choice (D) comes close to weakening the argument, because if professional (as well as amateur) athletes were allowed to compete, presuming the participants were selected on merit, then the best athletes would be seen. However, it has only been a suggestion, perhaps in the past (in which case it was not adopted) or in the future (in which case its adoption is not certain). Choice (E) represents an opinion that might or might not be held by the writer, but, whether or not the author agrees, it does not weaken the argument: therefore (E) is inappropriate

22. E; Even if the rate of increase in demand has slowed from 10% per annum to 5% per annum over the last five years, that means that demand is still increasing at 5% per annum. If, as the passage states, demand continues to grow at the present rate - that is, by 5% per annum - the world's resources will be used up by the year 2050. Therefore, the argument is not weakened by the statement in answer alternative (A). Choice (B) introduces the matter of supply, but apparently the reserves in Antarctica have not been discovered recently, and this, therefore, does not affect the argument that stocks will be depleted unless new reserves are found. Choice (C) informs us that there is an alternative to coal which is being used increasingly. However, the questions of the supply of and the rate of growth of demand for oil do not affect the argument in the paragraph. Choice (D) states an economic fact of life that would have to be faced if the statements in the paragraph are true. It may lead to a search for alternative fuels and consequent decrease in demand for coal, but this is uncertain and cannot be inferred. So, neither (A), (B), (C) nor (D) is appropriate. Choice (E) is, therefore, the correct answer.

23. B; Choice (A) contains an important point which would have been considered in setting the maximum treatment level. So, it does not weaken the argument of the authorities and is inappropriate. Choice (C) is incorrect as the passage states that the authorities are carrying out this policy in accordance with their powers. Choice (D) is a fact that would be acknowledged by both sides and weakens neither's case. Choice (E) is also a well-known fact, which, like the fact in (A), would have been taken into consideration by the researchers; so it is also not appropriate. The fact that the authorities have no record of the long-term good or damage of fluoridation (B) is a significant weakness in their case.
24. C; Choice (C) would weaken the conclusion the most. If most carbon dioxide is emitted by automobiles, then cutting industrial production or changing production processes would only solve a small part of the problem. Alternative (A) weakens the conclusion, but not as much. It does not attach the basic premise of the passage - namely, that industrial production is responsible for elevated carbon-dioxide levels. It also disregards the effect of a temperature increase even in cold areas. Alternative (B) adds to the conclusion. Alternative (D) would not change the conclusion because liquid fuel may also produce carbon dioxide (in actuality, it produces quite a bit). Alternative (E) does not weaken the conclusion because even if a shift to other energy sources were too costly, this does not mean that a slowing of or changes in production would be too costly.
25. E; 85 per cent of 38 per cent is 32 per cent, while 50 per cent of 62 per cent is 31 per cent; therefore, it can be expected that more Republicans will vote. Alternative (A) shows that even though 47 per cent of the voters called themselves Republicans, the Republican Party won the election. In the latest poll, the proportion of Republicans declined to 38 per cent. (A) weakens the conclusion but not as strongly as (E). Alternatives (B) and (C) hold equally for both Repubicans and Democrats. Alternative (D) weakens the conclusion but not as much as (E); the fact that no one can predict how people will vote does not imply that results cannot be forecast with a high probability.
26. C; It can be argued that New York, Ohio, Pennsylvania and California have large populations and extensive industry and, thus, a wide tax base from which to finance higher education. Most other states (there may be some exceptions) do not have such an extensive tax base. The argument in the statement is a fallacy of analogy, incorrectly making an analogy between the four states mentioned and most other states.
27. E; If the shipyard is not converted into the proposed complex, it might be sold for another use, which could be more detrimental to the opposition's interests than the current plan.
28. D; In order to shift the blame for the reduction in the annual rate of growth of sales output away from Joe's new regime, we must find another reason for the lack of sales. (D) provides us with this alternative.

Chapter Ten

Cause and Effect

10.1: Introduction

These types of question are beginning to be fairly frequently asked these days. Usually in such questions the candidates are asked to determine whether a given event is the cause or the effect of some other event. The idea behind putting these questions is to ascertain the analytical and logical reasoning ability of the aspirants. Let us first have a quick look at a sample problem.

10.2: Format of the problem

Directions (Q. 1-5): Given below are pairs of events 'A' and 'B'. You have to read both the events 'A' and 'B' and decide their nature of relationship. You have to assume that the information given in 'A' and 'B' is true and you will not assume anything beyond the given information in deciding the answer. Mark answer

1) If 'A' is the effect and 'B' is its immediate and principal cause
2) If 'A' is the immediate and principal cause and 'B' is its effect
3) If 'A' is an effect but 'B' is not its immediate and principal cause
4) If 'B' is an effect but 'A' is not its immediate and principal cause
5) None of these

1. **Event: (A)** Prices of gold have gone up in the local market.
   Event: (B) India has won several prizes in design of gold ornaments.
2. **Event: (A)** Today, the Prime Ministers of country 'P' and 'Q' have decided to take steps to improve the bilateral relations.
   Event: (B) Next week, the Foreign Ministers of country 'P' and 'Q' will work out further steps to improve the relationship.
3. **Event: (A)** The prices of the personal computers (PCs) have come down.
   Event: (B) Some school children are showing keen interest in learning computers.
4. **Event: (A)** This year, Bank 'M' has celebrated its silver jubilee.
   Event: (B) Customers are getting attracted to market branch of Bank M.
5. **Event: (A)** Recently, the traffic jams on MG Road of city 'Z' have not only been reduced but the traffic has also become manageable.
   Event: (B) The flyover on MG Road of city'Z' has been recently made operational and the no. of traffic police personnel have been increased.

10.3: Cause and effect: a theoretical discussion

It is a fundamental property of nature that events do not just happen; they happen because there was a *cause* behind them. These causes are the **conditions** under which these *events* (or *results* or *effects*) happen. As we shall see later, something can be said to be a cause of another event only if it is a *necessary as well as sufficient condition* for that effect to take place. But before that, we must distinguish between the commonsense view of cause and the scientific view of cause.

You must have heard your grandmother exclaim that you fell down from your bicycle because a black cat had crossed your path. In other words, she is saying that your falling down from the bicycle was the effect and a black cat crossing your path was the cause. Well, your grandmother has a right to her own views but most other people would consider this unscientific and mere superstition. On the other hand, if a person dies because of respiratory failure, here death is a scientific effect of respiratory failure, the cause.

However, not all the time can a cause be so scientifically accurate and precise. In our day-to-day life we may come across situations which are more subjective and require an intuitive skill. For example, reduction of fiscal deficit may result in upgradation of our country's credit rating. But can we be so sure of the reduction of fiscal deficit being the only cause for the said effect (upgradation of our credit rating) as we are of respiratory failure being the cause of death? Of course not. Because the former is not as scientifically and precisely proven by experiments as the latter, yet it wouldn't be wrong to say that reduction of fiscal deficit leads to an upgradation of a country's credit rating. Here, it wouldn't be wrong to say this because it is *logical*. If somebody hits me hard then it is *logical* to expect that I will be angry at him, although scientists have not proved it by experiments that when somebody hits me, I get angry.

Therefore, a scientific view of cause is one where

> It must be a *scientifically proven fact* that the cause leads to the said effect.
>
> Or
>
> The said effect should be a *logical consequence* of the said cause.

Coming back to our assertion about cause being a necessary as well as sufficient condition, let us first understand what is meant by a necessary condition and what by a sufficient coundition. **A necessary condition for the occurrence of a specified event is a circumstance in whose absence the event cannot occur**. For example, the presence of oxygen is a necessary condition for any fire. No fire can take place without oxygen being present. But, although it is a necessary condition, the presence of oxygen is not a sufficient condition for fire to occur. **A sufficient condition for the occurrence of an event is a circumstance in whose presence the event *must* occur**. The presence of oxygen is not a sufficient condition for fire because it is not so that wherever there is oxygen, there follows a fire. Fire takes place only if the substance is (a) combustible, (b) the substance reaches a minimum temperature and (c) there is oxygen present. Thus here (a), (b) and (c) make a sufficient condition and together they make the cause for the effect of fire. Note that each of the three makes a necessary condition for fire to take place and when they are combined they make a sufficient condition. *Thus, there may be several necessary conditions for the occurrence of an event and that they must all be included in the sufficient condition.*

Immediate cause

Sometimes we use the word cause in the sense of merely a necessary condition and sometimes in the sense of a sufficient condition. But most of the times the word cause is used in the sense of **proximity**. The following illustrations will explain this.

An insurance company might send its investigations to determine the cause of a mysterious fire. If the investigators report that the fire was caused because of oxygen present in the atmosphere, they would surely be dismissed from the jobs. And yet they are not really wrong- the fire can't take place without oxygen. So, here is an example where a necessary condition (the presence of oxygen) is not really the cause that we are looking for.

Again, the investigation may report that the fire was caused by an extremely combustible substance lit up at 300° C in presence of oxygen, they are giving a sufficient condition and yet they are not giving the answer actually sought. So, this is an example of a sufficient condition not really being the cause that we are looking for.

But if the investigators report that the fire was caused by deliberate ignition by the policy-holder who used kerosene oil and a matchbox to ignite the fire; they would be giving the *correct* cause (or the cause that was sought.) Because what the company wanted to find out was the incident or action that, in the presence of those conditions that usually prevail (presence of oxygen for example), made the difference between the occurrence or non-occurrence of the event.

This leads us to our third interpretation of the word cause: **remote** vs. **proximate** cause. When there is casual sequence or chain of several events, A causing B, B causing C, C causing D, and D causing E; we can regard E as effect of any or all of the preceding events. Here, it won't be wrong to say that "E was caused by A". And yet, it may look ridiculous to say that. For example, in the previous case, we may have the following chain of events:

Event A: oil glut in the Middle East
Event B: sharp drop in prices of oil, internationally
Event C: losses to those who invested in oil companies
Event D: need for money to cover losses
Event E: policy-holder lighting the fire.

In the above sequence, Event A leads to B, B leads to C, C leads to D and D to E. And yet if we say that the "fire was caused by oil glut in the Middle East" it looks so ridiculous.

The oil glut may be the remote cause of fire but in our practical sense, we mean the **immediate and the proximate** cause. Here, the immediate and proximate cause of fire is the policy-holder igniting it and this is the cause we are interested in.

Principal cause:

We have seen that an effect takes place because of several necessary conditions being fulfilled. Out of these several necessary conditions, one may be glaring because it makes the difference between the occurrence and the non-occurrence of the event. In our example of the policy-holder igniting the fire; the oxygen was always there in the atmosphere and kerosene oil and matchbox were always available in the market. What made the big difference was the fact that the policyholder sprayed the kerosene and ignited the fire. Therefore, here, the **principal** cause for the fire was the policy-holder igniting the fire. As another example, imagine that India and Pakistan sign a peace treaty of mutual non-interference and non-abetment to cross- border terrorism. As a result, very few incidents of militants crossing over from the border take place. Now, here, the fact that very few militants are crossing over may also be caused by factors such as extremely ruthless winter, vigilant patrolling, dying support for militancy etc. But these reasons were always there. What perhaps made the difference was the treaty of non-abetment of cross-border terrorism and, therefore, this should be considered the **principal** cause. As another example, imagine that Sudha has very *keen interest* in learning computers. This effect may be caused by several things. For example, one reason could be that *computers are cheap.* So, Sudha bought a computer easily. Another reason could be that Sudha is being taught by a very *good teacher*. And then, another reason could be that Sudha has a *natural aptitude for computers*. Now, here, had Sudha not had a natural aptitude for computers a cheap computer or a good teacher wouldn't have made much difference. Thus, although the latter are also causes in their own right, the principal cause is her own aptitude in computers because this is the reason that makes the difference between her interest and non-interest.

Note 1: Difference between immediate and principal cause

Although they sound similar there is a difference between immediate causes and principal causes. Immediate causes are the most proximate in time, to the effect. The principal cause is the main and the most important reason for the effect. If you have read Indian history you may appreciate that the *principal* cause for the mutiny of 1857 was the Doctrine of Lapse and other repressive policies of Lord Dalhousie but the *immediate* cause was the fact that the sepoys were made to bite cartridges that had fat of sacred animals such as cows.

[Note 2: In our examinations, however, we are asked to find out if a cause is immediate as well as principal. Roughly, it means that the said cause must be the principal reason of the given effect and it should also be fairly proximate in time to the said effect.]

10.4: A Quick Check

We are now in a position to evolve our strategy for our solution. Before giving the actual strategy for picking up the correct choice, I would suggest the following "Quick-check" to eliminate obviously wrong choices.

Quick Check: Cause always antecedent

Naturally the cause will always occur *before* the effect. Hence, if two events are given then the effect that is chronologically antecedent to the other can only be regarded as a possible cause. In other words, we can look for possible causes by checking which of the two events occurred first. (For checking this, we can check the tense etc. of the sentences)

For example, consider Q.2 of our sample problem. Here, event A has occurred today, and event B is due *next week*. This means that A occurs before B and hence only A can be a possible cause. B can't be a cause. This eliminates choices 1,3. Again, consider Q.3 of our sample problem. Here, event A is in present perfect tense: the event (fall in prices) has already happened. While event B is still happening. Hence, A has happened before B and hence B can't be a cause. This eliminates choices 1,3. For the same reasons, B can't be a cause in Q.4 of our sample problem and this eliminates choices 1 and 3.

10.5: Our strategy for solution

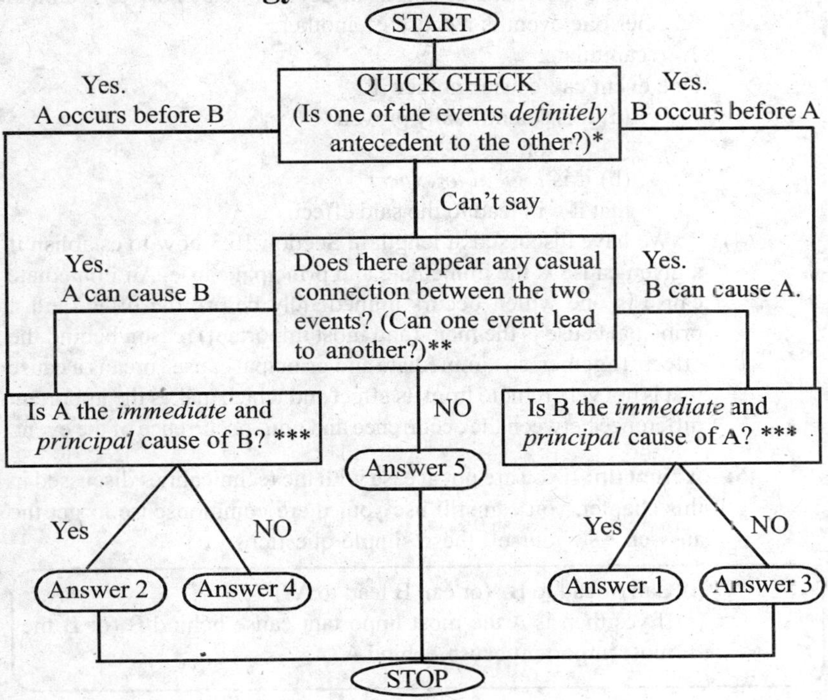

Note: (1) In the above flow chart, we assume that

Choice 5 means: "none of these"

Choice1 means: "A is effect and B is its immediate and principal cause"

Choice 2 means: "B is effect and A is its immediate and principal cause"

Choice 3 means: "A is effect but B is not its immediate and principal cause"

Choice 4 means: "B is effect but A is not its immediate and principal cause"

In the actual exams, there might be some variations in this. For example, in some exam choice 5 may stands for "A is effect and B is its immediate and principal cause" and choice 1 may stands for "none of these." The reader should keep this aspect in mind.

(2)*: We have already discussed in section 10.4 that cause is always antecedent to effect and by using this fact we can eliminate some choices. The fact of antecedence can be established by using our knowledge of "tense" and also of some key word such as "before," "next week," "now," "then," "today," "tomorrow," "ever since," etc.

(3)**: We have discussed at length in Section 10.3; how to establish whether one event is a cause of another,

To recapitulate:

One event can cause another if

(a) it is scientifically proven

or

(b) it is *logical to expect*

that it will lead to the said effect.

(4)***: We have discussed at length in Section 10.3 how to establish if a given cause is the immediate and principal cause. An immediate cause is one which occurs immediately before the effect and a principal cause is the main (and most important) reason behind the effect. Together, an "immediate and principal cause" means a cause that is not very remote from its effect and which makes the important difference between the occurrence and non- occurrence of the event.

(5) **A final tip:** If you are not at ease with the technicalities discussed in this chapter, you can still use your mere commonsense to get the answer. Ask yourself these simple questions:

(i) Can A lead to B? (or can B lead to A?)

(ii) If yes then is A the most important cause behind B (or B the most important cause behind A?)

Even if you ignore everything taught in this chapter and rely on these extremely simple questions, you will get the right answer with some commonsense and a bit of luck.

10.6: Complete solution to our sample problem

Q. 1. Quick check: Both events are in "present perfect" tense. So, it can't be definitely said which one is antecedent to which one.

Next, we check for any causal connections. We conclude that there doesn't seem to be any possible link between India winning prizes in designs and rise in prices of gold in the local market. Correct choice: 5

Q. 2: Quick check: Event A is in "present perfect" tense and event B is in "future" tense. So, A is antecedent to B. this means B can't be a cause of A and this eliminates choices 1and 3.

Next, we check for any causal connection. Apparently, A *can* cause B. Now, is A the immediate and principal cause? Yes. It is immediate because B follows A very soon and it is principal because had A not occurred, B would also not have followed. Correct choice: 2

Q. 3: Quick check: Event A is in "present perfect" and event B is in "present continuous". So, A occurs before B. This eliminates choices 1 and 3 and B can't be a cause.

Now, we check if A can be a cause. Apparently, A *can* cause B, in the sense that low prices may result in more purchases and more purchases may result in more computers per school and, therefore, it may result in more children showing interest. Obviously, it is a long chain and although A can be said to cause B somehow, A can't be said to be an *immediate* cause of B. Correct choice: 4

Q. 4: Quick check: Event A is in " present perfect" tense and B is present continuous. So, A occurs before B and hence B can't be a cause. This eliminates choices 1and 3.

Now, can A cause B? No. Bank M is celebrating its silver jubilee- (Remember. You are not to assume anything beyond this information)- and merely this does not provide any cause for getting more customers. Do you open an account in a bank only because the bank is celebrating its silver jubilee? Correct choice: 5

Q. 5. Quick check: Both A and B in present perfect tense. So, which is antecedent to which, can't be declared by mere glance.

Next, we check for any causal links. Apparently, B *can cause* A. In fact, B is the immediate and principal cause behind A because the opening of the flyover has a direct bearing on the traffic. Correct choice: 2

Appendix

(Rules of antecedence)

Rule: Past tense (antecedent to) Present perfect (antecedent to) present continuous (antecedent to) Future tense.

Ex: Past tense: I went/ I was going etc.
Present perfect: I have gone.
Perfect continuous: I am going.
Future tense: I will go.

Summary

- Cause is an event which leads to a said effect and this fact is either scientifically proven or logically expected.
- Technically, cause means a sufficient condition i.e. a collection of all necessary conditions in the presence of which the effect must take place.
- But, practically we mean cause to be the immediate and principal reason behind the effect.
- An immediate cause means a cause that immediately precedes the effect and a principal cause means a cause that was the most important reason behind the effect.
- Since cause must occur *before* the effect, we can merely look at the given two events first and by analysing the tense thus, we can declare which event *can't* be a cause.
- A complete solution strategy is given in the flow-chart.

Practice Exercises

Directions (Q. 1-45): Given below are pairs of events 'A' and 'B'. You have to read both the events 'A' and 'B' and decide their nature of relationship. You have to assume that the information given in 'A' and 'B' is true and you will not assume anything beyond the given information in deciding the answer. Mark answer

1) If 'A' is the effect and 'B' is its immediate and principal cause
2) If 'A' is the immediate and principal cause and 'B' is its effect
3) If 'A' is an effect but 'B' is not its immediate and principal cause
4) If 'B' is an effect but 'A' is not its immediate and principal cause
5) None of these

1. **Event A:** Madan died while on way to the hospital.
   Event B: A car dashed into the motorcycle Madan was driving.
2. **Event A:** Major Dayal was educated in one of the best educational institutions of India.
   Event B: Major Dayal has extremely fluent speaking power.
3. **Event A:** People of Taslimganj eat a lot of fruits and vegetables.
   Event B: It has been noticed that the people of Taslimganj have less hypertension and related problems than the rest of the Indians.

4. **Event A:** Madhumita has got a strange skin infection that seems incurable.
   Event B: Last week, Madhumita spent a week with the villagers of Sultanganj where water is not potable.
5. **Event A:** Manumita is suffering from scurvy.
   Event B: Manumita has had inadequate intake of Vitamin C.
6. **Event A:** Anumita is suffering from AIDS.
   Event B: Anumita is a prostitute.
7. **Event A:** Young people in the colleges watch a lot of MTV and rock videos.
   Event B: Drug addiction is a big problem with our college-going generation.
8. **Event A:** People in north Bihar take bath early in the morning even if it is very cold.
   Event B: In North Bihar, cleanliness is valued more than in the rest of the India.
9. **Event A:** Orissa has a lot of corruption.
   Event B: Orissa is one of the poorest states of our country.
10. **Event A:** The Second World War stopped after the US dropped two atomic bombs in Japan.
    Event B: Hitler never surrendered during or after the War.
11. **Event A:** The doctor has advised Sonu to take Vitamin C tablets.
    Event B: Sonu complained of cough and cold.
12. **Event A:** XYZ co. has recorded a 20% jump in its sales.
    Event B: XYZ co. has reduced the prices of its products considerably.
13. **Event A:** Burglars came and stole cash and jewellery from Sony Jewellers shop.
    Event B: The owner of Sony Jewellers shop went and registered a complaint of theft at the police station.
14. **Event A:** Romeo loved beauty and innocence.
    Event B: Juliet was beautiful and innocent.
15. **Event A:** The MP has announced that the Government will take measures to remove subsidies on diesel in a phased manner.
    Event B: Subsidies on diesel result in a lot of loss of revenue to the Government.
16. **Event A:** Monica Lewinsky is said to have had illicit relations with the US President.
    Event B: A lot of journalists are reporting interviews of Monica Lewinsky and giving her media attention.
17. **Event A:** XYZ co. has benefited immensely by the Finance ministry's decision to free naphtha from import duty.
    Event B: The turnover of XYZ co. has almost doubled in the last financial year.
18. **Event A:** A peace accord was signed between the Government and the ultras and a popular government was democratically established in Mizoram.
    Event B: Mizoram is peaceful now.

19. **Event A:** There is a lot of political uncertainty in the country.
Event B: The country faces its worst economic crisis of the decade.

20. **Event A:** The Indian Vikas Party promised to bring in a corruption-free government.
Event B: The Indian Vikas party won the elections with a thumping margin.

21. **Event A:** BHM Ltd. was plagued with a lot of labour problems in the year 1999-2000.
Event B: Production in BHM Ltd. dropped by nearly 19% in the said year.

22. **Event A:** Uttarkashi is very prone to earthquakes.
Event B: According to seismologists, there is a lot of tectonic activity going on in the belt below Uttarkashi.

23. **Event A:** Reliance Multiferrous Ltd. has come out with very good financial results this year.
Event B: Last year, Mr. Dhirubhai Lalwani, the CEO of Reliance, resigned.

24. **Event A:** The US crushed Iraq in the gulf war.
Event B: The US had almost total international support in the gulf war.

25. **Event A:** India won the world cup cricket in 1983 despite being the underdogs.
Event B: Kapil Dev and Roger Binny played very well in the 1983 world cup.

26. **Event A:** Cogentrix Power Project proposal has been rejected by the Govt. of India.
Event B: Moody's has downgraded India's credit rating.

27. **Event A:** ABCL Ltd. has rejected the proposal of Doordarshan in which Doordarshan offered to buy software from ABCL.
Event B: Prices quoted by Doordarshan were very high.

28. **Event A:** India's proposal to delink social issues such as labour from trade issues was turned down at the WTO meet.
Event B: Indian proposal would have hurt the interests of the developed nations.

29. **Event A:** Nobody speaks to or makes friends with Shobhraj Khatri.
Event B: Shobhraj Khatri is an accused in multiple murder cases.

30. **Event A:** The Revlon range of lipsticks is very costly, compared to other lipsticks of about the same quality.
Event B: The Revlon range has not been able to penetrate much in the market.

31. **Event A:** Kalyan Singh has been expelled from the Bhartiya Vikas Dal.
Event B: Kalyan Singh was the founder- member of Bhartiya Vikas Dal.

32. **Event A:** PT Usha has been awarded the Arjuna Award for excellence in Sports.
Event B: PT Usha is a very dedicated athlete.

33. **Event A:** Banking Services Chronicle offers the most comprehensive correspondence course for PO at a reasonable price.

Event B: Demand for Banking Services Chronicle courses is continuously increasing.

34. **Event A:** Pakistan's proposal for a third- party mediation in Kashmir has been rejected by India.
    Event B: India considers Kashmir to be a purely bilateral issue.
35. **Event A:** Ramesh succeeded.
    Event B: Ramesh worked hard.
36. **Event A:** Madan failed.
    Event B: Madan did not buy books of ABC Publication.
37. **Event A:** Gurubhajan Tohra has been expelled from the Party.
    Event B: Tohra has formed a new Party.
38. **Event A:** Prakash Bhagat has been expelled from the Party.
    Event B: Bhagat was planning to form a new party, it was heard some time back.
39. **Event A:** The boys pelted stones at the policemen.
    Event B: The policemen resorted to lathi-charge.
40. **Event A:** Modiguard brand of cosmetics does not sell much.
    Event B: Modiguard brand of cosmetics is poorly advertised.
41. **Event A:** There has been a communal riot in the city following rumours that an important Muslim leader has been killed.
    Event B: The magistrate has declared curfew in the city.
42. **Event A:** There is hardly any visible activity in the city and the shops are closed.
    Event B: Curfew has been declared in the city.
43. **Event A:** Annual production of leather goods (for which this city is famous) is going to drop.
    Event B: Curfew has been declared in the city.
44. **Event A:** Some of the goonda elements in the city have been enjoying political patronage for the last few years.
    Event B: Curfew has been declared in the city.
45. **Event A:** Farookh Engineer is doing research on "Imposition of curfew and its impact on macro-economics of the locality".
    Event B: Curfew has been imposed in the city.

Directions (Q.46-68): Below in each question are given two statements (A) and (B). These statements may be either independent causes or may be effects of independent causes or of a common cause. One of these statements may be the effect of the other statement. Read both the statements and decide which of the following answer choices correctly depicts the relationship between these two statements. Mark answer

1) if statement (A) is the cause and statement (B) is its effect.
2) if statement (B) is the cause and statement (A) is its effect.
3) if both the statements (A) and (B) are independent causes.

4) if both the statements (A) and (B) are effects of independent causes.
5) if both the statements (A) and (B) are effects of some common cause.

46. **A.** State Govt has ordered immediate ban on airing of certain movie channels on television.
    B. A few social activists have come together and demanded ban on telecasting 'Adult' movies on television.
47. **A.** Employment scenario in the country has remarkably improved recently.
    B. The number of prospective job-seekers going abroad has increased recently.
48. **A.** Government has tightened security checks at all important places and also at various public places.
    B. Incidences of terrorist attacks are increasing day by day.
49. **A.** The high court has fixed a time limit for repairing all the roads in the city.
    B. Road development authorities in the city are carrying out road repair work on an urgent basis.
50. **A.** There is an outbreak of several epidemics in the country.
    B. There was a worst flood situation ever experienced in the past in most parts of the country.
51. **A.** The government of India has allowed the private airline companies to operate on specified international routes.
    B. There has been a considerable increase in the flow of foreign tourists to India.
52. **A.** Many seats in the private engineering colleges in the state have remained vacant this year.
    B. The government engineering colleges in the state could not accommodate all the students who sought admission this year.
53. **A.** The banks have decided to give advances to the priority sector at the rate of interest at par with the corporate sector.
    B. The percentage of bad loans given by the banks to the priority sector is very low as compared to the corporate sector.
54. **A.** The state government has now decided to increase the stamp duty on house purchases with immediate effect.
    B. The real estate prices have decreased considerably during the last few months.
55. **A.** Most of the steel manufacturing companies in the country have made considerable profit during the last fiscal year.
    B. Many Asian countries have been importing huge quantities of steel from India.
56. **A.** The average day temperature of the city has increased by about 2 degrees in the current year over the average of past ten years.
    B. More people living in rural areas of the state have started migrating to the urban areas in comparison with the earlier year.

57. **A.** Most of the shopkeepers in the locality closed their shops for the second continuous day.
    B. Two groups of people living in the locality have been fighting with each other with bricks and stones, forcing people to stay indoors.
58. **A.** The Govt has decided to increase the prices of LPG cylinders with immediate effect.
    B. The Govt has decided to increase the prices of kerosene with immediate effect.
59. **A.** A cyclonic storm is expected to hit the coastline in the state during the next 48 hours.
    B. Warning has been issued that heavy rains are expected in the coastal region in the state during the next 48 hours.
60. **A.** Majority of the first year students of the engineering college failed in Mathematics in the semester examination.
    B. The college authority terminated the contract of the Professor who taught mathematics to the first-year students.
61. **A.** The Govt has marginally increased the procurement price of wheat for the current crop.
    B. The current wheat crop is expected to be twenty per cent more than the previous wheat crop.
62. **A.** The braking system of the tourist bus carrying 40 passengers failed while negotiating a stiff climb on a hilly road.
    B. The tourist bus fell into the gorge killing at least ten passengers and seriously injuring all the remaining.
63. **A.** The state govt has decided to boost English language education in all the schools from the next academic year.
    B. The level of English language of the school students of the State is comparatively lower than that of the neighbouring states.
64. **A.** The municipal authority demolished the tea stall located on the footpath on the busy road.
    B. A large number of people have been taking their evening tea at the tea stall located on the footpath on the main road, blocking pedestrian movement.
65. **A.** Majority of the students left the local school as the school building was in a dilapidated condition.
    B. The school authority decided to close down the school immediately and shift the remaining students to a make-shift school.
66. **A.** The government has decided to take strict action against the builder responsible for construction of the bridge for having used low-quality material, thereby risking several lives.
    B. The government has decided to build a vehicular bridge over the river

connecting the suburban area to the city in order to reduce the traffic load on the main road.

67. **A.** Many people prefer to shop at the big retail chains than the local grocery stores.

B. Retail chains offer a discount of more than 25% as compared to the local grocery shops.

68. **A.** More than two billion pounds of chemicals are spewed in the air everyday by industries and vehicles of some countries.

B. International Pollution Control Organisation is expected to penalise the countries which cross the maximum emission limits.

Answers and explanations

1. 1; Both sentences are in past tense; hence, quick check fails. But it is obvious that Madan died *because of* the accident.

2. 4; Event B is in present tense while A is in past tense. So, only A can be the cause. Now, if we analyse closely, Event A could be a cause but it is not the principal cause. Being educated in a good institution is not a *sufficient condition* to guarantee fluency in speaking. Had it been so, all persons passing from good schools would have been phenomenal speakers.

3. 4; Both sentences are in present tense, so quick check fails. But it is obvious that good health must be an effect (and not a cause) of eating good food. So, A is an effect. But we can't *definitely* say if B is its principal and main cause, because less hypertension may also accrue from some other causes, say for example, lower sodium intake.

4. 3; Event B in past tense, A in present. So, A must be the effect. But we can't *definitely* say if her skin infection is caused by the unpotable drinking water.

5. 1; It is a *scientifically proven fact* that vitamin C deficiency causes scurvy.

[Note: Compare the fine difference between Q4 and Q5]

6. 1; Being a prostitute is the most likely cause for AIDS.

7. 4; The cause-effect scheme suggested here is simple: cultural influence is cause, drug addiction is effect. But it is debatable if the said cultural influences are the main and immediate cause for the drug addiction. Can we surely say that if we stop all such broadcasts immediately, the problem will go away? We can't. It may diminish but it won't be wiped out. This is because drug addiction has several causes and cultural influence is only one (and not the principal one) of them.

8. 3; If cleanliness were more valued in North Bihar, still people would have cleaned themselves by an afternoon bath. Early morning bath must be more of a tradition. Yet B must be a cause of A, else people would not have bothered to take early morning baths. But B is not the principal cause: principal cause is societal tradition.

[**Note:** If you are tempted to argue that B is debatable as a true statement, remember that according to the directions you have to assume everything given as true.]

9.4; Corruption does lead to underdevelopment and hence poverty but corruption can't be the immediate and principal cause of poverty. Had it been so, all non-poor states must be non-corrupt; but this is very debatable.

10.5; The two statements have no correlation with each other.

11.1; The doctor must have given his advice *because of* Sonu's complaint.

12.1; Reduction in prices can be said to be logically expected to result in increased sales.

13.2; Obviously, A is the cause of B.

14.5; The two statements have no causal connection with each other.

15.1; Loss of revenue must be the main cause behind PM's decision to stop subsidies.

16.2; Obviously the media attention is (principally) caused by her alleged affair with a President of a very powerful nation. Had she had relations with a common man, she wouldn't have got so much attention.

17.2; The doubling of turnover is *caused* by a favourable policy.

18.2; A is in past tense, B is in present tense. So, B must be an effect. Obviously, B is caused by an *agreement* of peace (peace accord) and the *fair* (democratic) *execution* of the agreement.

19.4; This one is tough. Does political uncertainty cause economic crisis or is it vice versa? Sounds more like the classical dilemma: chicken first or egg? But if you think deeply you would agree that political uncertainty almost always causes economic crisis while on the other hand, economic crisis may or may not cause political uncertainty. Recent South East Asian crisis did not cause too much of a political uncertainty. However political uncertainty may not always be the *immediate* cause of economic crisis.

20.4; Winning the elections is the *effect*. One of the several causes could be the party's anti-corruption plank. But merely an anti-corruption plank is not a *sufficient condition* for victory: it is not the principal cause.

21.2; Labour problems is the immediate cause of the shortfall in production.

22.1; Tectonic activities underneath are the immediate and principal cause for the area being prone to earthquake.

23.5; One person resigning should normally have nothing to do with a company fairing very well. The only cause where it could be acceptable would be the assumption, that Mr. Dhirubhai was a very inefficient CEO. But that would be a long-drawn assumption. In the normal course, we should take the two events as unrelated unless the question itself gives hints about the CEO's inefficiency.

24. 3; Crushing of Iraq is an effect. One of the several causes could be the international support US got in the war. But this does not give a sufficient

condition for victory: it is not the principal cause. [The principal cause could be the US' technological supremacy and advanced weaponry.]

[**Note:** Compare Q2, Q20, Q24 and Q25. Do you now understand the concept of cause as a sufficient condition?]

25.3; India's victory is an effect but merely two persons' good performance does not give *sufficient condition* for victory. So, B does not constitute the principal cause. That *all* persons played very well may be taken as a sufficient condition and hence as the principal cause but not the performance of merely two players.

26.4; Moody's have downgraded India's credit rating *because* India must have faltered on many accounts. Cogentrix fiasco can be only one of them and hence not a sufficient condition.

27.5; This one was tricky. There is no reason why ABCL would reject proposals where it could get "too high" prices. So, there is no causative link between the two statements. [The answer would have been 1 if the prices quoted by Doordarshan were "very low" instead of "very high".]

28.1; B must be the cause of A. [If you are conversant with the current affairs, you know the answer.]

29.1; Since Shobhraj is accused in a heinous crime, he is being socially boycotted.

30.2; The high cost must be the immediate and principal cause of the failure of the product.

31.5; The two events have no causative link with each other.

32.3; The award is an effect. The cause of this effect is her success in various races. The cause of her success is her talent and her dedication. Therefore, her dedication is a cause of the award but it is not the *immediate cause*.

33.2; Good quality and reasonable price are sufficient to ensure good sales.

34.1; B is the cause of A. If you are conversant with current affairs, you know the answers.

[**Note:** Compare Q. 28 and Q. 34]

35.1; Normally, we take hard work to be a sufficient cause for success.

36.5; There is no link between the two statements. Unless we assure that books of ABC Publication are necessary for success; the two statements are uncorrelated. And there is nothing for us to make these assumptions.

37.2; Since he was expelled, he formed a new party.

38.1; Since he was planning to form a new party, he got expelled.

[**Note:** Compare the difference between Q37 and Q38. Getting expelled from the party is a cause in Q37 and an effect in Q38. Forming a new party is an effect in Q37 and cause in Q38.how do we differentiate? We can do so by our quick check. In Q38, event B is in past tense so it must be the cause, A is in present tense so it can only be on effect.]

39.2; Lathi-charge was a result of the pelting of stones.

40.3; Poor sales are caused by poor advertisement. But poor advertisement is not *sufficient* to guarantee poor sales. Had it been so, all poorly advertised products would necessarily have poor sales. But this is not always true. [Have you ever seen a Bata shoe ad on TV or in magazines? Yet they sell very well.]

41. 2; Curfew has been imposed *because* of the rumours.
42. 1; Activities have gone down *because* of the curfew.
43. 3; The chain of events goes like this: curfew- closure of shops and factories- drop in monthly production- drop in annual production. Obviously, curfew **is** a cause for the drop in annual production but it is not an immediate cause.

[**Note:** Compare Q. 32 with Q. 43]

44. 4; The chain of events goes like this: patronage to goonda elements- increased goonda activity- riot- curfew. Obviously, the said patronage is a cause for the curfew but it is not an immediate cause.

[**Note:** Compare Q. 32, Q. 43 and Q. 44]

45. 5; The two events have no causal links with each other.

[**Note:** Compare Q. 41 to Q. 44. In Q. 41 and Q. 44, imposition of curfew is an effect but the rumours give an immediate cause while patronage to goonda elements is a long-drawn cause. In Q. 42, 43, imposition of curfew is a cause but it is an immediate cause of the decrease in market activity while it is a long drawn cause of a drop in annual production.]

46. 2; The pressure of the social activists has led to the banning.
47. 4; The two are contradictory and must be the effects of independent causes.
48. 2; The large number of terrorist attacks has led to tightened security checks.
49. 1; The court order has led to the urgent work.
50. 2; The flood has led to epidemics.
51. 2.
52. 4
53. 2
54. 2
55. 2
56. 4; The 2 statements appear to have contrary causes.
57. 2; The fighting has led to the closure of the shops.
58. 5; It seems the price of petroleum has increased in general. Alternatively, subsidies may have been reduced, again a cause common to both the statements.
59. 1; The cyclone is expected to cause heavy rains.
60. 1; The poor performance of the students has led to the exit of the professor
61. 1; The govt initiative has led to greater wheat cultivation.
62. 1; Brake failure led to the accident.
63. 2; Since the level is lower, the govt has decided to boost English language education.

64. 2; Since pedestrian movement was get- ting blocked, the authority demolished the tea stall.
65. 1; The leaving of students led to the ur- gent action by the authority.
66. 4; (A) is the effect of the poor quality of the bridge. (B) is the effect of the traffic load on the main road.
67. 2; The offering of the discount leads to the preference for the big retail chains.
68. 1; The excessive emission has led to the framing of the penal rules.

Part II
Reasoning Based on Rules

Chapter Eleven

Syllogism

11.1: Introduction

Syllogism is originally a word given by the Greeks. It means 'inference' or 'deduction'. The problem of syllogism is supposed to be one of the very roots of logic and it has its history dating back to the times of Aristotle and Plato.

But ours is not a quest for the history of syllogism. We are interested in syllogism more because it appears in many competitive examinations and is important, therefore, from the examination point-of-view. Therefore, we now restrict ourselves to the problem of syllogism and, of course, the solution to it. Let us begin by looking at the format in which the problem appears in the competitive examinations.

11.2: Format of the Questions

A typical question of syllogism as asked in the competitive examination is being provided below.

Directions: In the following type of questions, two statements are being provided followed by two conclusions A and B. You have to study the two statements and then decide whether, from those two statements,

a) Only A follows
b) Only B follows
c) Both A and B follow
d) Either A or B follows
e) Neither A nor B follows.

1. **Statements:** All pine trees are coniferous.
All coniferous are beautiful.
Conclusions: **A.** All pine trees are beautiful.
B. Some beautiful are pine trees.

2. **Statements:** All smart are vociferous.
No vociferous is introvert.
Conclusions: **A.** Some smart are introvert.
B. Some vociferous are not smart.

11.3: Theoretical Background

The problem of syllogism can be solved mentally by using a little intelligence and common sense. But this amateur approach may be time-consuming and sometimes erroneous too. We need to have, therefore, a definite and well-defined method to tackle the problem.

In the next few pages, we shall be explaining at length a definite and well-defined method to solve the problems on syllogism. But before that we need to have adequate theoretical background of the topic. This section, therefore, is devoted to explaining the theoretical aspects required. After finishing that we shall be coming back to our original problem.

Let us begin with a few definitions:

Proposition

A proposition is a sentence that makes a statement and gives a relation between two terms. It consists of three parts: a) the subject, b) the predicate and c) the relation between the subject and the predicate.

Some examples of propositions are being given below:

i) All elephants are big.

ii) No schoolboy is disciplined.

iii) Some girls are pretty.

iv) Some wigs are not cute.

Subject and Predicate

A subject is that part of the proposition about which something is being said. A predicate, on the other hand, is that term of the proposition which is stated about or related to the subject.

Thus, for example, in the four propositions mentioned above, 'elephants', 'schoolboy', 'girl' and 'wigs' are subjects while 'big', 'disciplined', 'pretty' and 'cute' are predicates.

Categorical Propositions

A categorical proposition makes a direct assertion. It has no conditions attached with it. For example, "All S are P", "No S are P", "Some S are P" etc. are categorical propositions, but "If S, then P" is not a categorical proposition.

Note: There is another class of propositions known as 'disjunctive propositions'.

Types of categorical propositions

a) Universal proposition: Universal propositions either fully include the subject or fully exclude it. Examples are:

All boys are cute. No box is square-shaped.

Usually, universal propositions begin with "All", "Every", "Any" etc. or "No", "None of the", "Not a single" etc. A proposition of the form "All S are P" is called a *universal positive proposition* while a proposition of the form "No S is P" is called a *universal negative proposition.* Further, a universal positive proposition is usually denoted by the letter **'A'** while a universal negative proposition is usually denoted by the letter **'E'**

b) Particular proposition: Particular propositions either only partly include or only partly exclude the subject while making a statement. Examples are:

Some boys are cute.

Some bases are not circular.

Usually, particular propositions have relational clauses like "some", "many", "quite a few" etc. or" "some......not", "not many", "very little" etc.

A proposition of the form "Some S are P" is called a *particular positive proposition* while a proposition of the form "Some S are not P" is called a particular negative proposition. Further, a particular positive proposition is denoted by the letter **"I"** while a particular negative proposition is denoted by the letter **'O'.**

*The definition of the **A, E, I, O** propositions are very, very important and the student must have the ability to immediately recognise these types.* With this need in mind we are listing these four types of propositions in the following table:

Table 1: The four types of propositions

Type of Proposition	Universal	Particular
Positive	**A** Format: All are P.	**I** Format: Some S are P.
Negative	**E** Format: No S are P.	**O** Format: Some S are not P

The Euler's circles or Venn diagrams

There is a pictorial way of representing the propositions, formulated by Euler, an ancient mathematician. Suppose that the proposition is trying to relate the subject (S) with the predicate (P). Then there are four ways in which the relation could be made according to the four propositions:

Type-A

Fig. I
All S are P.

Type-E

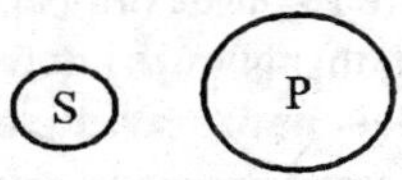

Fig. II
No S are P.

Type-I

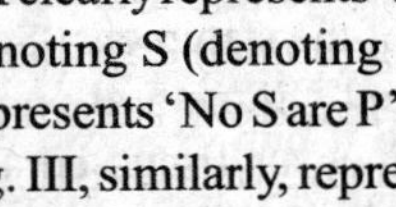

Fig. III
Some S are P.

Type-O

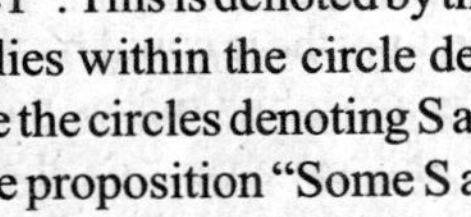

Fig. IV
Some S are not P.

Fig.I clearly represents 'All S are P'. This is denoted by the fact that the whole circle denoting S (denoting 'all S') lies within the circle denoting P. Similarly, Fig. II represents 'No S are P' because the circles denoting S and P do not intersect at all. Fig. III, similarly, represents the proposition "Some S are P" because some part of the circle denoting S as indicated by the shaded area of S (representing 'some S') lies within the circle denoting P. Slightly more attention-seeking is the representation for the **O** proposition "Some S are not P". For this, take a closer look at Fig. IV. The figure shows that some portion of the circle S has no intersection with the circle P, while the remaining portion of the circle S is left incomplete and it is uncertain whether this portion touches P or not. The verbal interpretation of this figure would be: "there are some S that are definitely not P while there may be some S that might be P or might not be P".

The case may be better understood by taking the following two sets.

Let S= {Green, Red, Blue, Madan, Mohan } and let P = {names}. Now, in this case, there are some S (Green, Red, Blue) that are not names and therefore not P. While there are some S (Madan, Mohan) that are names and are, therefore, P. Therefore, here, we have "Some S are not P" while "Some S are P". The correct pictorial representation for such a case would be like Fig. Ill, that is:

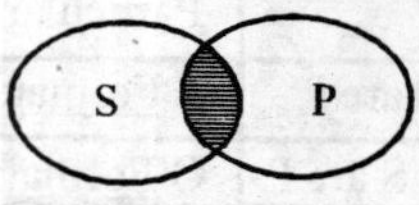

"Some S are not P".
["Some S are P".]

Fig. V

Now, consider another case.

Let, S = {even numbers}, that is, S - {2,4,6,8,.....}, and let P = {odd numbers}, that is, P = {1,3,5,7,....}. Now, here again, we may find "Some S", say {2,4,8} that are not odd numbers and, therefore, not P. Therefore, the proposition "Some S are not P" is true in this case as well. But on a closer scrutiny we find that there is no element in S which is an odd number or which is a P. In fact, here, we have "No S are P". The correct pictorial representation for such a case would be like figure II, that is,

"Some S are not P"
["No S are P"]

Fig. VI

Fig. IV is a general representation for the statement "Some S are not P". This proposition gives no clue whether the remaining S are there in P or not. The dotted portion of Fig. IV represents this lack of information only. If it is further known that the remaining S are in P then the dotted portion should be drawn to intersect with the circle P and it would take the shape of Fig. V, while if it is known, on the other hand, that the remaining S are not in P either, then the dotted portion too, should be outside the circle P and hence the representation would take the form of Fig. VI.

Quite similar to this, there could be the case of the statement "Some S are P". This statement is as ambiguous as the statement "Some S are not P". The reader may analyse this statement on the same lines as discussed above. He should be able to appreciate the fact that "Some S are P" may have two aspects. One, where the remaining S are not P, and two, where the remaining S are also P. Correspondingly, there could be two representations, viz:

"Some S are P".
["Some S are not P".]

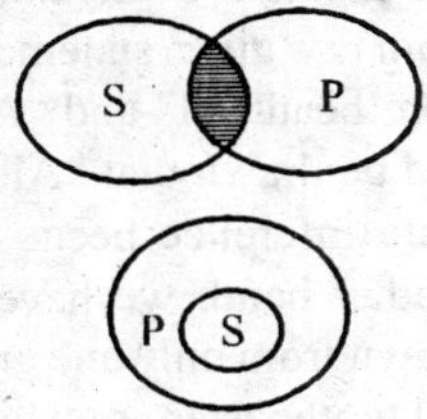

and
"Some S are P"
["All S are P".]

Fig. VII

Based on the discussions made so far, we tabulate the concepts developed in the following table.

Table 2: Euler's Circles and representation of the four propositions

If the Type of the given proposition is	Then its pictorial representation is
A All S are P	Always 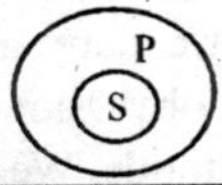
E No S are P	Always 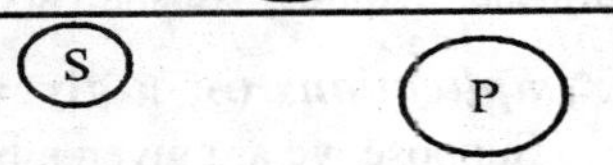
I Some S are P	Either  Some S are P. [Some S are not P]
	Or,  Some S are P [All S are P]
	Or, 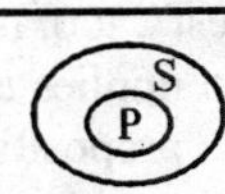 Some S are not P [All S are P]
O Some S are not P	Either 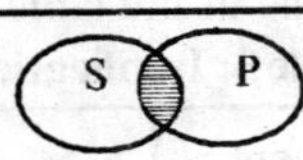 Some S are not P [Some S are P]
	Or, 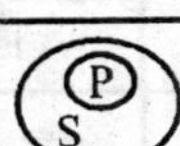 Some S are not P [All P are S]
	Or,  Some S are not P [No S are P]

Immediate inference

Syllogism is actually a problem of mediate inference. In mediate inference, conclusion is drawn from two given statements. For example, if two statements are given: "All birds are beautiful" and "All beautiful objects are precious", then a conclusion could be drawn that "All birds are precious". This is a case of syllogism or mediate inference because conclusion is drawn from two propositions. On the other hand, we have the case of immediate inference where conclusion is drawn from only one given proposition. For example, let a given statement be "All toothpastes are white". Then, based on this statement, a conclusion could be drawn that "Some white objects are toothpastes". This is a case of immediate inference.

We hope that the meaning of immediate inference is clear to the reader by now. The reader might be wondering whether this reference to immediate inference was needed at all, if our main aim is to seek the solution of syllogism, that is, mediate inference. The answer is, in fact, a strong and loud 'yes'. In order to be able to solve syllogism problems completely and speedily, we *do need to* have a thorough idea of immediate inference.

There are many aspects or methods of immediate inference. These include conversion, obversion, contraposition etc. We shall not study the less important of these methods. We shall see two important cases of immediate inference.

I. *Implications* (of a given proposition)

Suppose we are given a proposition "All birds have feathers". Then this proposition naturally implies that the conclusion "Some birds have feathers" must be true. It is very easy to comprehend because if "all" have feathers, then "some" ("some" is only a part of "all") must have feathers. This example only states that if a given proposition is **A**-type, then it also implies that the I-type conclusion must be true. As another example, take the statement "No businessmen are honest". If this statement is true then the conclusion "Some businessmen are not honest", too, must be true. This example illustrates that an E-type proposition also implies an **O**-type conclusion.

We are listing various propositions and their implicational relations with the other propositions in the table below.

Table 3: Implication from a given proposition

If the given statement is of type	then the conclusion of the type			
	A is	**E** is	**I** is	**O** is
A	—	False	True	False
E	False	—	False	True
I	Doubtful	False	—	Doubtful
O	False	Doubtful	Doubtful	—

[The reader should not have any difficulty in reading the table given above. For example, the table states that if a statement is of type 'O' then the type 'A' conclusion is definitely false while the type 'E' and type T conclusions are both doubtful, that is, they may or may not be true. Thus, if a statement is

Some boys are not meritorious. **(O)**

Then we have,

Conclusions:

All boys are meritorious (A) = false

No boys are meritorious (E) = doubtful (may or may not be true)

Some boys are meritorious (I) = doubtful (may or may not be true)

II. *Conversion*

The second important method of immediate inference is conversion. An example of conversion is given below:

Let a given statement be "All books are study materials". This is converted to give the conclusion "Some study materials are books".

How to convert a given proposition?

The following rules are to be employed in order to convert a given proposition:

Step 1: The subject becomes the predicate and the predicate becomes the subject.

Step 2: The type of the given proposition is changed according to the pattern given in Table 4.

Table 4: Rules of Conversion

A statement of the type	when converted becomes a statement of the type
A	**I**
E	**E**
I	**I**
O	**O**-type statement cannot be converted

[The reader should not have any difficulty in converting a statement. Suppose we have to convert the statement: "No book is readable". Then it is converted according to the two rules stated above. Table 4 says that E-type statement becomes E-type statement after conversion. Also, the subject becomes the predicate while the predicate becomes the subject. Therefore, the conclusion will be, "No readable thing is book".]

Learners' Exercise Set I

Number of Questions: 20 Limit:8 minutes

Directions: Classify the following propositions into their respective type of A, E, I or O.

1. All books are printed.

2. Some students use pencils.
3. All snakes are reptiles.
4. All mammals give birth to twins.
5. Chandrashekhar Azad was a revolutionary.
6. Some revolutionaries relied on terrorism.
7. Many of the books are oblong.
8. Not a single city in India is without pollution.
9. SSC conducts fair examinations.
10. Only steel is safe for furniture.
11. BSC is the short form of Banking Services Chronicle.
12. Quite a few of the soldiers are brave.
13. Very few writers research before they write.
14. Some authors do not expect authenticity.
15. Some scholars do not give value to originality.
16. Talent is God-gifted.
17. Many dark glasses are injurious to eyes.
18. Some toothbrushes are not smooth.
19. All toothpastes use cosmetic substances.
20. Only the students can save the country today.

Answers

1. A 2. I 3. A 4. A 5. A 6. I 7. I 8. A 9. A
10. A or E or I 11. A 12. I 13. I 14. O 15. O 16. A 17. I
18. O 19. A 20. A or E or I.

A (All (who can save the country today) are students.)
E (No non-student can save the country today.)
I (Some students can save the country today.)

How to determine the hidden proposition

The reader must have noticed that there are some sentences in the previous exercise that are on standard patterns as given in the Table 1. But some other sentences are not on the standard patterns. We should know, therefore, how to find out the hidden propositions in such sentences.

Some A-type propositions not beginning with 'All'

i) All positive propositions beginning with 'every', 'each', 'any', are A-type propositions.

Examples:

a) Every man makes sandwiches.
(All men make sandwiches.)

b) Each of them has a share of profit.
(All (of them) have a share of profit.)

c) Any one could kill a mosquito.
(All (men) can kill mosquitoes.)

ii) *A positive sentence with a particular person as its subject is always an **A**-type proposition.*

Examples:

a) He should be awarded a gold medal.

He (is a man) who should be awarded a (gold medal).

Subject Predicate.

b) Chandraswami is a controversial personality.

iii) *A positive sentence with a very definite exception is also of **A**-type.*

Example:

All students except Ram have failed.

(All except Ram (are the students) who have failed.)

Subject Predicate

Some E-type propositions not beginning with 'No'

i) *All negative sentences beginning with 'no one', 'none', 'not a single', etc. are **E**-type propositions.*

Examples:

a) None can escape from Tihar.

(No man is one who/can escape from Tihar).

Subject Predicate

b) Not a single student is present. (No student is present.)

ii) *A sentence with a particular person as its subject but a negative sense is an **E**-type proposition.*

Examples:

a) He does not deserve a gold medal.

(He (is not a man) who deserves a gold medal.)

Subject Predicate

b) Chandraswami is not a controversial personality.

iii) *A negative sentence with a very definite exception is also of **E**-type.*

Example:

No student except Ram has failed.

iv) *When an 'interrogative sentence is used to make an assertion, this could be reduced to an **E**-type proposition.*

Examples:

a) Is there any sanity left in the world?

(No sanity is left in the world.)

b) Is there any person who can cheat himself?

(None can cheat himself.)

Some I-type propositions not beginning with 'Some'

i) *Positive propositions beginning with words such as 'most', 'a few', 'mostly', 'generally', 'almost', 'frequently', 'often' are to be reduced to the **I**-type.*

Examples:

a) Girls are usually feminine.
(Some girls are feminine.)

b) Students are frequently short-tempered.
(Some students are short-tempered.)

c) Almost all the books have been sold.
(Some books have been sold.)

d) A few dollars are left in my pocket.
(Some dollars are left in my pocket.)

e) Most of the paper is handmade.
(Some (of the) paper is handmade.)

ii) *Negative propositions beginning with words such as 'few', 'seldom', 'hardly', 'scarcely', 'rarely', 'little' etc. are to be reduced to the **I**-type.*

Examples:

a) Few men are not corruptible.
(Some men are corruptible.)

b) Seldom are people not jealous.
(Some people are jealous.)

c) Rarely is a rich man not worried.
(Some rich (men) are worried.)

iii) *A positive sentence with an exception which is not definite, is reduced to **I**-type proposition.*

Examples:

a) All students except three have passed.
(Some students have passed.)

b) All students except a few are present.
(Some students are present.)

Some O-type propositions not beginning with "Some...not"

i) *All negative propositions beginning with words such as 'all', 'every', 'any', 'each' etc. are to be reduced to **O**-type propositions.*

Examples:

a) All men are not rich.
(Some men are not rich.)

b) Every one is not present.
(Some are not present.)

c) All that glitters is not gold.
(Some glittering objects are not gold.)

ii) *Negative propositions with words as 'most', 'a few', 'mostly', 'generally', 'almost', 'frequently' are to be reduced to the **O**-type.*

Examples:

a) Girls are usually not feminine.
(Some girls are not feminine.)

b) Students are not frequently short-tempered.
(Some students are not short-tempered.)

c) Almost all the books have not been sold.
(Some books have not been sold.)
d) Most of the paper is not handmade.
(Some (of the) paper is not handmade.)

iii) *Positive propositions with beginning words such as yew', 'seldom', 'hardly''scarcely', 'rarely', 'little'etc. are to be reduced to the* ***O****-type.*

Examples:

a) Few men are corruptible.
(Some men are not corruptible.)
b) Seldom are people jealous.
(Some people are not jealous.)
c) Rarely is a rich man worried.
(Some rich men are not worried.)

iv) *A negative sentence with an exception, which is not definite, is to be reduced to the* ***O****-type.*

Examples:

a) No-students except two have passed.
(Some students have not passed.)
b) No students except a few are absent.
(Some students are not absent.)

Exclusive Propositions

Propositions beginning with 'only', 'alone', 'none but', 'none else but' are called exclusive propositions. Such propositions can be reduced to **A** or **E** or **I** form. Consider, for example, the sentence:

"Only educated are IAS officers."

This sentence implies that "No uneducated is IAS officer" and therefore, "All IAS officers are educated". In general, an exclusive proposition is reduced in the following way:

Table 5: Reduction of an exclusive proposition

Let the given exclusive proposition be	then it is reduced to a proposition of the type		
	A	E	I
	in the following way		
Only S is P or S alone is P or None but S is P or No one else but S is P	All P are S	No non-S is P or No P is non-S	Some S are P

Learners' Exercise Set II

Number of questions: 20 Time limit: 4 minutes

Directions: Classify the following propositions into their respective types (A, E, I or O).

1. No businessman except Jhaverijee is honest.
2. No businessman is honest.
3. No businessman except a few is honest.
4. Only graduates are eligible.
5. Not a single merchant is from India.
6. Premchand was a great novelist.
7. He is going to Patna.
8. Politicians are not generally trustworthy.
9. Any book is not good.
10. Students are often carefree.
11. Anyone can answer this question.
12. None but God could help me.
13. None except Indians were killed.
14. He does not eat curry.
15. No student except Rahim is absent.
16. Can anyone kill his parents?
17. Few soldiers do not suffer from nostalgia.
18. Few soldiers suffer from nostalgia.
19. A few soldiers suffer from nostalgia.
20. A few soldiers do not suffer from nostalgia.

Answers

(Please try to write the given sentences in their reduced standard form, as well)

1. E	2. E	3. O	4.*	5.**E	6. A	7. A	8. O
9. O	10. I	11. A	12. *	13. *	14. E	15. E	16. E
17. I	18. O	19. I	20. O				

* (Exclusive proposition) can be reduced to either A or E or I. See Table 5.

Imp. Note: Usually, it is advisable to reduce an exclusive proposition "Only S is P" to A-form, i.e, "All P are S".

**No merchant is Indian. (E-form).

Learners' Exercise Set III

Number of questions: 10 Time: 5 minutes.

Directions: Draw Venn diagrams for the following propositions.

1. Not a single merchant is from India.
2. He does not eat curry.
3. All except Ram have failed.

4. All except a few have failed.
5. Can anyone kill his parents?
6. Premchand was a great novelist.
7. No businessman except Jhavereejee is smart.
8. Only graduates are IAS officers.
9. Things are rarely cheap.
10. Chandraswami is not a controversial personality.

Answers

1. 

M = Merchant I = Indians

2. 

H = He C = Curry eaters

3. 

S = All students except Ram

R = Ram

F = Those who failed

4. 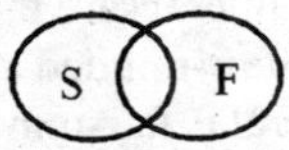

S = Students

F = Those who failed

5. 

P = People

K = Those who can kill their parents

6. 

P = Premchand

G = Great novelists

7. 

B = All businessmen except Jhavereejee

J = Jhavereejee

S = Those who are smart

8. 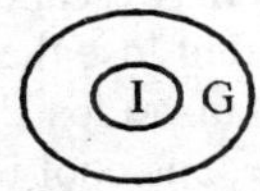

I = IAS officers

G = Graduates

9. 

T = Things

C = Cheap commodities

10. 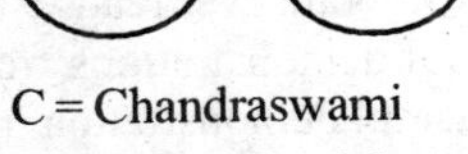

C = Chandraswami

P = Controversial personality

Learners' Exercise Set IV

Number of questions: 10 Time limit 10 minutes.

Directions: Assuming that the given statement is true, find out which of the four alternatives is definitely true or definitely false or uncertain.

1. All Indians eat curry.
a) Some Indians eat curry.
b) Some Europeans eat curry.
c) No non-Indian eats curry.
d) Curry is eaten by all and sundry:

2. All students are not genius.
a) Many students are not genius.
b) Every student is a non-genius,
c) Every non-student is a genius.
d) Many students are genius.

3. Only liberals are fair-minded.
a) All who are liberals are fair-minded.
b) All who are fair-minded are liberals.
c) No non-liberal is fair-minded.
d) No fair-minded is non-liberal.

4. Conservatives are never intolerant.
a) Whoever is conservative is intolerant.
b) Many conservatives are intolerant,
c) A few conservatives are tolerant.
d) All conservatives are tolerant.

5. Draft ledgers will be prosecuted.
a) At least one draft ledger will not be prosecuted.
b) Most draft ledgers will be prosecuted.
c) Few draft ledgers will be prosecuted.
d) Draft ledgers may escape prosecution.

6. Adults do not often lose their cool.
a) No one who fails to lose his cool is an adult.
b) Whoever loses his cool is other than an adult.
c) Few persons other than adults fail to lose their cool
d) Everyone who fails to lose his cool is a non-adult.

7. No book is read by an illiterate.
a) All books that are read are read by graduates.
b) Some books that are read are read by graduates.
c) Some books are not read by illiterates.
d) No illiterate ever reads a book.

8. Peaceful demonstrations frequently lead to violence
a) Peaceful demonstration may remain non-violent as well.
b) All peaceful demonstrations lead to violence.
c) No peaceful demonstration leads to violence.
d) Some peaceful demonstrations do not lead to violence.

9. No student except two have passed.
a) Some students have passed.
b) Some students have not passed.
c) All students have not failed.
d) Two students have passed.

10. Premchand was a great novelist.
a) Some novelists are great.
b) At least one novelist was great.
c) Premchand was not an ordinary writer.
d) Sometimes Premchand used to write great novels.

Answers

Question Number	Answer Choice			
	a	b	c	d
1.	T	U	U	U
2.	T	U	U	U
3.	U	T	T	T
4.	F	F	T	T
5.	F	T	F	F
6.	U	U	U	U
7.	U	U	T	T
8.	U	U	F	U
9.	T	T	T	T
10.	U	T	T	T
	T = Definitely true. U = Uncertain. F = Definitely false.			

Learners' Exercise Set V

Number of questions: 30 Time Limit: 15 minutes

Directions (Q. 1-5): In these questions, a statement is given followed by four inferences A, B, C and D. Which of these definitely follows from the given statements?

1. 'Soldiers serve their country.'
A) Those who serve their country are soldiers.
B) Women do no serve their country because they are not soldiers.
C) Men generally serve their country.
D) Some men who are soldiers serve their country.

2. Most of the students are of outstanding merit.
A) Some of the students are of outstanding merit.
B) There are no students who are not of outstanding merit.

C) There are some students who are below par.

D) All students are of outstanding merit.

3. 'Most of the pens in that shop are expensive.'

A) There are no cheap pens in that shop.

B) Some of the pens in that shop are expensive.

C) There are cheap pens also in that shop.

D) Camlin pens in that shop are expensive.

4. 'If a person is rich, he has a lot of influence.'

A) John has a lot of influence, so he is rich.

B) If a person is not rich, he does not have a lot of influence.

C) Kasim is rich and so he has a lot of influence.

D) Poor people cannot have influence.

5. 'Many smokers get cancer.'

A) Cancer-patients are smokers.

B) Smoking may lead to cancer.

C) Most smokers get cancer.

D) Smoking is injurious to health.

Directions (Q. 6-20): In each of the following questions proposition (a) is to be taken as true. Based on this information, determine the truth value of (b) as True, False, or Uncertain.

6. a) Few labour leaders fail to be sympathetic to the problem of unemployment.
   b) Labour leaders never fail to be sympathetic to the problem of unemployment.
7. a) Peaceful demonstrations frequently lead to violence.
   b) Peaceful demonstrations always lead to violence.
8. a) A few of the wise lack a formal education.
   b) Many of the wise do not lack a formal education.
9. a) Every dog has his day.
   b) Some dogs have their day.
10. a) Never have so few owed so little to so many.
    b) So few have frequently owed so little to so many.
11. a) All that sparkles is not a diamond.
    b) Only diamonds sparkle.
12. a) All that glitters is not gold.
    b) Some glittering objects are not gold.
13. a) Every dodo loves to run a caucus race.
    b) Few dodos love to run a caucus race.
14. a) Rabbits never carry watches in their pockets.
    b) A few rabbits carry watches in their pockets.
15. a) Anyone who falls down in a rabbit hole is dreaming.
    b) At least one person fell down in a rabbit hole who wasn't dreaming.

16. a) Many supporters of unilateral disarmament are communist sympathizers.
    b) Many supporters of unilateral disarmament are not communist sympathizers.
17. a) Babies cannot manage crocodiles.
    b) Few babies can manage crocodiles.
18. a) Some students are lazy
    b) All students are lazy.
19. a) A few logicians are logical.
    b) No logicians are logical.
20. a) No professors make mistakes.
    b) All professors make mistakes.

Directions (Q. 21-30): In the following questions a statement is given followed by an immediate conclusion. Decide the correctness of the conclusion by marking them as True, False or Uncertain.

21. **Statement:** The sight of beauty gives pleasure.
    Conclusion: The sight of misery creates pain.
22. **Statement:** Ignorance is good.
    Conclusion: Knowledge is bad.
23. **Statement:** No man is perfect.
    Conclusion: Some imperfect persons are men.
24. **Statement:** To be or not to be, that is the question.
    Conclusion: What is other than the question is not whether to be or not to be.
25. **Statement:** At least a few hardworking people will eventually become richer.
    Conclusion: At least a few hardworking people will not become richer.
26. **Statement:** All triangles are three-sided figures.
    Conclusion: All three-sided figures are triangles.
27. **Statement:** Agricultural labourers are hardworking.
    Conclusion: Some hardworking persons are agricultural labourers.
28. **Statement:** Women workers are not inferior to men workers.
    Conclusion: Some men workers are inferior to women workers.
29. **Statement:** Some students are not intelligent.
    Conclusion: Some intelligent persons are not students.
30. **Statement:** Every student of this university is employed.
    Conclusion: No student of this university is other than those who are employed.

Answers

1. D	2. A	3. B	4. C	5. C	6. U	7. U	8. T	9. T	10. F
11. F	12. T	13. F	14. F	15. F	16. U	17. T	18. U	19. U	20. F
21. U	22. U	23. T	24. F	25. U	26. U	27. T	28. U	29. U	30. T

Explanation of some selected questions

1. If A is true, I is true (Table 3).
6. If O is true, E is uncertain (Table 3).
7. If I is true, A is uncertain (Table 3). (Given statement is of I type. See **How to determine the bidden proposition.)**
23. No man is perfect → All men are imperfect → on conversion → Some imperfect are men.
28. 'Women are not inferior' does not imply that 'Women are necessarily superior'. It may also imply that 'Women are equally good' which leaves the given conclusion false.
29. Given statement is of type O. This may be depicted by the following three diagrams:

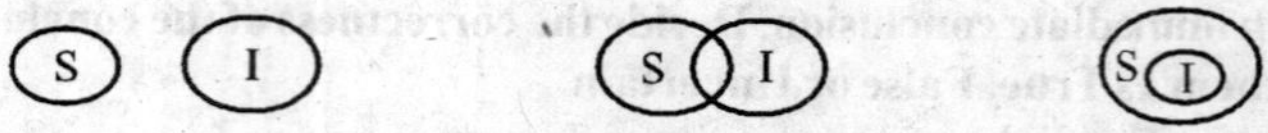

i ii iii

S = Students I = Intelligent

Now the given conclusion: "Some intelligent are not students" is true in case i and ii but false in case iii.

11.4: How to solve syllogism

1. The Analytical Method **2. The Method of Venn Diagrams**

11.4.1: The Analytical Method

There can be two methods of solving syllogism: the analytical method and the method of Venn diagrams. Let us first study the analytical method. The analytical method for solving syllogism consists of two extremely simple steps

Step I: Properly align the given sentences.

Step II: Use Table 6 to draw the conclusion.

Step I: Aligning the given sentences

The first step is to properly align the two sentences. **What do we mean by 'aligning' the given proposition?** You must have seen that a syllogism problem consists of two propositions and the conclusions. The two given propositions always have one common term. (This is a must otherwise no conclusion could be drawn.) The following four examples illustrate this fact:

Ex 1. Statements: **I.** All **boys** are goodlooking.
II. Some **boys** are Indian.

Ex 2. Statements : **I.** Some girls are **cute**.
II. Some Americans are **cute.**

Ex 3. Statements : **I.** No **table** is chair.
II. Some doors are **tables**.

Ex 4. Statements: **I.** Some books are **pants.**
II. No **pants** are worthy.

You see that all the four examples have two statements where one term is common to both the statements (depicted by bold letters). Thus, **boys, cute, table** and **pants** are the common terms in Examples 1, 2, 3 and 4 respectively.

Now, by a properly aligned pair of propositions we mean that the two propositions should be *written in such a way that the common term is the predicate of the first proposition and the subject of the second.*

To do this, we may take the statements in any order. The statements given in Ex 5 are properly aligned while those given in Ex 6 are not.

Ex 5. Statements: I. Some lamps are **books.**
II. No **book** is readable.

(The predicate of the first statement is the subject of the second. Hence, the statements are properly aligned).

Ex 6. Statements: I. Some **books** are crooks.
II. Some hooks are **books.**

(The predicate of the first statement is not the subject of the second. Hence, the sentences are not aligned.)

How do we align the sentences? If the statements are not already aligned then they can be aligned by

(i) changing the order of the sentences and/or
(ii) converting one of the sentences.

Ex: Align all the pair of statements given in Ex 1 to Ex 6 above.

Solution:

Ex 1. Statements: I. All **boys** are goodlooking.
II. Some **boys** are Indian.

We can align this by

(a) converting the first statement:
All boys are goodlooking $\xrightarrow{\text{conversion}}$ Some goodlooking are boys.
Hence, the aligned pair is: [Some goodlooking are boys.
Some boys are Indian.]

(b) converting the second statement and changing the order of the sentences.
The aligned pair will be:
[Some Indian are boys (converted form of second statement).
All boys are goodlooking.]

Ex 2. Statements: I. Some girls are **cute.**
II. Some Americans are **cute.**

We can align the pair by

(a) converting the first statement and changing the order of the statements.
The aligned pair will be:
[Some Americans are cute.
Some cute are girls (converted form of first statement).]

(b) converting the second statement, the aligned pair will be:
[Some girls are cute.
Some cute are Americans (converted form of second statement).]

Ex 3. Statements: I. No **table** is chair.

II. Some doors are **tables.**

We can align this pair by changing the order of the statements. The aligned pair will be: [Some doors are tables.

No table is a chair.]

Ex 4. Statements: I. Some books are **pants.**

II. No **pants** are worthy.

The sentences are already aligned.

Ex 5. (Proceed as in Ex 4 above.)

Ex 6. (Proceed as in Ex 3 above.)

An important note: You may Have seen that in order to align a sentence, conversion is necessary when the common term is either a subject in both die sentences or a predicate in both the sentences (see Ex 1 and Ex 2 in previous example). In such cases, we *have to* convert one of the sentences. A question may arise here as to which of the two statements to choose for conversion. *For this, remember the rule of IEA.* That is, given a pair of to-be-aligned sentences, the priority should be given, while converting, to I-type statement, to E-type statement and then to A-type statement, in that order. Hence, if in the given pair one sentence is of type I and the other of type A then the sentence of type I should be converted.

Step II: Use table 6 to draw conclusions

After step I (which involved aligning the two sentences) has been completed, we are left with the easy and self-explanatory table 6 which can be used to draw conclusions.

Table 6: To draw conclusions from a pair of aligned statements

If the first statement is of the type	and the second statement is of the type	then the conclusion will be
A	**A**	**A**
A	**E**	**E**
A	I	–
A	O	–
E	**A**	**O***
E	E	–
E	**I**	**O***
E	O	–
I	**A**	**I**
I	**E**	**O**
I	I	–
I	O	–
O	A or E or I or O	–

Note: The reader should note that

(i) There are only 6 cases where a conclusion can be drawn. These cases are highlighted in the table by bold letters and can be memorised in **short form** as:

A	+	A	=	A	
A	+	E	=	E	
E	+	A	=	O*	**Short form for table 6**
E	+	I	=	O*	
I	+	A	=	I	
I	+	E	=	O	

(ii) The '-' sign in the third column of table 6 means that no definite conclusion can be drawn.

(iii) *Table 6 gives correct results if and only if the two sentences have been properly aligned.*

(iv) **Format of the conclusion** (very important): The conclusion or the inference is itself a proposition whose subject is the subject of the first statement and whose predicate is the predicate of the second statement. The common term disappears.

(v) **The meaning of O*:** In the third column of table 6 we have written O* in place of O at two places. By O* we mean that the conclusion or inference is of type O but its format is exactly opposite the format mentioned in (iv). In this case, the subject of the inference is the predicate of the second sentence and the predicate of the inference is the subject of the first sentence.

An illustrative example

Draw inferences for the following pairs of statements:

(i) All books are hooks.
All books are crooks.

(ii) All tables are chairs.
All tables are glasses.

(iii) Some posters are goodlooking.
All posters are expensive.

(iv) Some pencils are torches.
No books are pencils.

(v) No bandit is kindhearted.
All bandits are blackmailers.

(vi) Some roses are red.
Some roses are good.

Solution:

(i) **Step I:** The sentences are already aligned.
Step II: By table 6 we see that A + A = A. Hence, the inference will be of

type A. Its subject will be the subject of the first sentence, i.e. *books,* and the predicate will be the predicate of the second sentence, i.e. *crooks.* Hence, inference: All books are crooks.

(ii) Step I: The common term 'tables' is a subject in both the sentences. Hence, we will have to convert in order to align. Since both the sentences are of the same type (A), we may convert any of them. We choose to convert the first. Consequently, the aligned pair of sentences is:
Some chairs are tables. (Converted form of All tables are chairs.)
All tables are glasses.

Step II: From table 6, I + A = I. Hence, the conclusion will be of type I, its subject being the subject of the first sentence (after aligning has - taken place), i.e. *'chairs',* and its predicate being the predicate of the second sentence, i.e. *'glasses'*. Hence, inference: Some chairs are glasses.

(iii) Step I: Again the common term 'posters' is a subject in both the sentences. By the rule of IEA we convert the I-type statement which is the first statement. Consequently, the aligned pair of sentences is:
Some goodlooking are posters (converted).
All posters are expensive.

Step II: I + A = A, hence inference is:
Some goodlooking are expensive.

(iv) Step I: The common term 'pencils' is a subject in one sentence and a predicate in the other. Hence, changing the order of the statements is sufficient to align the two sentences. Consequently, the aligned pair will be :
No books are pencils.
Some pencils are torches.

Step II: E + I = O*. As we know, O* means that the conclusion is of type O but the subject of the conclusion is the predicate of the second sentence and the predicate of the conclusion is the subject of the first sentence. Hence, inference is:
Some torches are not books.

(v) Step I: By the rule of IEA, we convert the E-type statement The aligned pair is:
No kindhearted is a bandit.
All bandits are blackmailers.

Step II: E + A=O*. Hence, inference is:
Some blackmailers are not kindhearted.

(vi) Step I: We convert the first sentence and obtain the following pair of aligned sentences:
Some red are roses.
Some roses are good.

Step II: I + I =_. This means that there can be no definite inference.

It is hoped that the examples given above are understood by the reader. We are giving one more set of examples but this time we are omitting the detailed explanations. The reader should verify that he is beginning to understand the underlying principles of mediate inference by being able to quickly gloss over the following set of examples without failing to understand it.

Ex: Draw the inferences from the following pairs of sentences :

(i) All bandits are pundits.
No pundit is decorloving.

(ii) Some crooks are hooks.
No hook is a book.

(iii) Some goods are expensive.
Some expensive objects are qualitative.

(iv) All posters are goodlooking.
Some posters are expensive.

(v) All expensive are posters.
Some goodlooking are posters.

(vi) Some hooks are crooks.
No hook is a book,

(vii) All boxes are dolls.
No boxes are baskets.

(viii) All dolls are boxes.
No baskets are boxes.

Solutions (Fast answers with as little explanation as possible):

(i) All bandits are pundits. No pundit is decorloving $\xrightarrow{A+E=E}$ No bandit is decorloving.

(ii) Some crooks are hooks. No hook is a book. $\xrightarrow{I+E=O}$ Some crooks are not books.

(iii) Some goods are expensive. Some expensive objects are qualitative. $\xrightarrow{I+I=}$ No conclusion.

(iv) All posters are goodlooking. Some posters are expensive. $\xrightarrow{\text{aligning by the IEA rule}}$ Some expensive are posters. All posters are goodlooking. $\xrightarrow{I+A=I}$ Some expensive are goodlooking.

(v) All expensive are posters. Some goodlooking are posters. $\xrightarrow{\text{aligning by the rule of IEA}}$ All expensive are posters. Some posters are goodlooking. $\xrightarrow{A+I=}$ No conclusion.

(vi) Some hooks are crooks. No hook is book. $\xrightarrow{\text{aligning by the rule of IEA}}$ Some crooks are hooks.
No hook is a book. $\xrightarrow{I+E=O}$ Some crooks are not books.

(vii) All boxes are dolls. No boxes are baskets. $\xrightarrow{\text{aligning by following the rule of IEA and changing order}}$ No baskets are boxes. All boxes are dolls. $\xrightarrow{E+A=O^*}$ Some dolls are not baskets.

(viii) All dolls are boxes. No baskets are boxes. $\xrightarrow{\text{aligning by the rule of IEA}}$ All dolls are boxes. No boxes are baskets. $\xrightarrow{\text{I+E=E}}$ No dolls are baskets.

Two very important additional steps

Step III: Check for any immediate inferences (implication or conversion)

Consider the following. Here, two statements are given, followed by two conclusions.

(i) Statements: All books are chairs.
All chairs are red.

Conclusions: (i) All books are red.
(ii) Some red (objects) are books.

Here, we have (the sentences ate already aligned) A + A = A. Hence, the conclusion should be: All books are red. But if we convert this conclusion, we obtain: Some red (objects) are books. Hence, both the conclusions given above should be taken as true.

(ii) Statements: Some buses are trucks.
Some trucks are cars.

Conclusions: (i) Some trucks are buses.
(ii) Some cars are trucks.

Here, we have (the sentences are already aligned) I + I =_, i.e., no conclusion. But if we convert the first statement 'Some buses are trucks.', we get 'Some trucks are buses'. Similarly, on converting the second statement, we get 'Some cars are trucks'.

Hence, we observe that although there is no conclusion or mediate inference using steps I and II, still on converting the given statements themselves we find that both the given conclusions are true.

(iii) Statements: All buses are trucks.
All trucks are cars.

Conclusions: (i) Some buses are trucks.
(ii) Some cars are buses.

Here, we have, A + A = A. Hence, the conclusion should be: "All buses are cars." But this answer choice is not given. But if we convert this statement we get "Some cars are buses" which is the second given conclusion. Also, an immediate implication of "All buses are trucks" is "Some buses are trucks". Hence, here again, both the conclusions are correct.

Hence, the above three examples show that while judging the given conclusions, *we should not only take the conclusion drawn from table 6 (if any) as correct, but the immediate inferences* (immediate implications and/or conversions) *of the given statements as well as of the conclusion drawn from table 6 should also be treated as correct inferences.*

Step IV: Check for complementary pair

Think over the following.

Conclusions: (i) Some pens are men.
(ii) Some pens are not men.

It is easy to understand that one of these conclusions must be true. That is, either some pens will be men or some pens will not be men. This is a typical case where the choice 'either (i) or (ii) follows' is true. Remember that this answer choice follows *even without looking at the statements. Such* pairs of statements are called **complementary pairs.** In a complementary pair, at least one of' the two statements is always true.

Which propositions make a complementary pair?

Two statements make a complementary pair if

(a) both of them have the same subject and the same predicate
and
(b) they are an I-O type pair or an A-O type pair or an I-E type pair.

Look at the following examples:

Ex:

Pair I: (i) All gardens are bulbs.
(ii) Some gardens are not bulbs.

Pair II: (i) Some gardens are bulbs.
(ii) Some gardens are not bulbs.

Pair III: (i) Some gardens are bulbs.
(ii) No gardens are bulbs.

Pair IV: (i) All gardens are bulbs.
(ii) No gardens are bulbs.

Pair V: (i) All gardens are bulbs.
(ii) Some bulbs are not gardens.

Comments: In the above example, pairs I, II and III make a complementary pair each while pairs' IV and V don't. In pair I, the first statement is of type A and the second is of type O. An A-O pair makes a complementary pair. In pair II, the first statement is of type I and the second is of type O. An I-O pair makes a complementary pair. In pair III, the first statement is of type I while the second is of type E. An I-E pair makes a complementary pair. In pair IV, the first statement is of type A while the second is of type E. An A-E pair does not make a complementary pair. In pair V, we have an A-O pair and an A-O pair does make a complementary pair, yet this pair will not be a complementary pair because the two sentences do not have the same subject and predicate.

Note: Step IV asks you to check for a complementary pair. If you do find a complementary pair you should choose "either of them follows". But remember that step IV is not needed if one of the inferences has already been found to be valid in steps II or III. **Step IV is applicable to only those conclusions which do not follow from steps II or III.**

Summary of the analytical method

Now, the discussion of the analytical method is complete. For the reader's benefit, I once again summarise the steps to do a syllogism problem.

Step I: Properly align the sentences.

Step II: Use table 6 to draw conclusion.

Step III: Check for immediate inferences.

Step IV: Check for complementary pairs if steps II and III fail.

Each of the steps given above has been elaborately and clearly explained before. The reader is advised to once again go through those details and then follow the examples given below:

Ex 1: Statements: All cats are bats.
All bats are tables.

Conclusions: (i) Some tables are bats.
(ii) Some tables are cats.

Solutions:

Step I: Sentences are already aligned.

Step II: A+A=A. All cats are tables.

Step III: (a) On converting "All bats are tables" we obtain 'some tables are bats'.

(b) On converting the conclusion obtained in step II, we get "Some tables are cats". From (a) and (b) we infer that *both the conclusions are true.*

Step IV: No need because a definite conclusion has already been obtained.

Ex 2. Statements: Some tables are watches. Some watches are lamps.

Conclusions: (i) Some tables are lamps.
(ii) Some tables are not lamps.

Solution: No conclusion is drawn by following step I to step III. Now, we see that the conclusions given are in the form of 'some' and 'some not'. Hence, we infer that *either I or II follows.*

Ex 3. Statements: No tables are watches.
Some watches are lamps.

Conclusions: (i) Some lamps are tables.
(ii) Some lamps are not tables.

Solution: Though the answer choice is in the form of 'some' and 'some not', we see that E+I=O* gives us "Some lamps are not tables". Hence, we obtain a definite conclusion that conclusion II is correct. Hence, step IV becomes unnecessary and we choose the answer choice *conclusion II follows.*

Learners' Exercise Set VI

Directions: In each question below are given two statements followed by two conclusions numbered I and II. You have to take the two given statements to be true even if they seem to be at variance with commonly known facts and then decide which of the given conclusions logically follows from the two given statements, disregarding commonly known facts. Give Answer:

A) if only conclusion I follows;
B) if only conclusion II follows;
C) if either I or II follows;
D) if neither I nor II follows; and
E) if both I and II follow.

1. **Statements:** Some rooms are stones.
All stones are radios.
Conclusions: I. Some rooms are radios.
II. Some stones are rooms.

2. **Statements:** All roads are poles.
No pole is a house.
Conclusions: I. Some roads are houses.
II. Some houses are poles.

3. **Statements:** All birds are trees.
Some trees are hens.
Conclusions: I. Some birds are hens.
II. Some hens are trees.

4. **Statements:** All tables are chalks.
All chalks are chairs.
Conclusions: I. All chairs are tables.
II. All tables are chairs.

5. **Statements:** Some girls are flowers.
Some flowers are books.
Conclusions: I. Some girls are books.
II. No book is a flower.

6. **Statements:** Some hens are cows.
All cows are horses.
Conclusions: I. Some horses are hens.
II. Some hens are horses.

7. **Statements:** Some dogs are bats.
Some bats are cats.
Conclusions: I. Some dogs are cats.
II. Some cats are dogs.

8. **Statements:** Some poets are goats.
Some goats are trees.
Conclusions: I. Some poets are trees.
II. Some trees are goats.

9. **Statements:** Some pens are tables.
No table is blue.
Conclusions: **I.** Some tables are pens.
II. No pen is blue.

10. **Statements:** All books are pencils.
All pencils are flowers.
Conclusions: **I.** All books are flowers.
II. Some pencils are not books.

11. **Statements:** Some crows are jackals.
No fox is a crow.
Conclusions: **I.** Some jackals are foxes.
II. Some jackals are not foxes.

12. **Statements:** Some crows are jackals.
Very few foxes are crows.
Conclusions: **I.** Some jackals are foxes.
II. Some jackals are not foxes.

13. **Statements:** All radios are electric goods.
All table-lamps are electric goods.
Conclusions: **I.** Some radios are table-lamps.
II. Some table-lamps are radios.

14. **Statements:** No man is a monkey.
John is a man.
Conclusions: **I.** John is not a monkey.
II. John may or may not be a monkey.

15. **Statements:** A graduate is a man.
This thief is a graduate.
Conclusions: **I.** This thief is a man.
II. Some men are thieves.

16. **Statements:** Only first divisioners are admitted.
Ram is a first divisioner.
Conclusions: **I.** Ram is admitted.
II. Only Ram is admitted.

17. **Statements:** Men are sinners.
Saints are men.
Conclusions: **I.** Saints are sinners.
II. Sinners are saints.

18. **Statements:** All businessmen except Bhimji are dishonest.
All dishonest people smoke.
Conclusions: **I.** All businessmen except Bhimji smoke.
II. Bhimji smokes.

19. **Statements:** Only cats are animals.
No historian is an animal.

Conclusions: **I.** Some cats are not historians.
II. Some historians are cats.

20. Statements: Few takers are givers.
No givers are almighty.
Conclusions: **I.** Some takers are almighty.
II. Some almighty are not takers.

Answers with Explanations

1. E; [I + A = I, Some rooms are radios.
Also, Some rooms are stones. $\xrightarrow{\text{conversion}}$ Some stones are rooms.]
2. D; [A + E = E, No roads are houses. But the given conclusions are different.]
3. B; [A + I= No conclusion. But, some trees are hens. $\xrightarrow{\text{conversion}}$ Some hens are trees.]
4. B; [A+A= A, All tables are chairs.]
5. D; [I + I= No conclusion.]
6. E; [I + A = I, Some hens are horses. $\xrightarrow{\text{conversion}}$ Some horses are hens]
7. D; [I + I = No conclusion.]
8. B; [I + I = No conclusion, but, Some goats are trees. $\xrightarrow{\text{conversion}}$ some trees are goats.]
9. A; [I + E = O, Some pens are not blue, but this conclusion is not given.
However, Some pens are tables. $\xrightarrow{\text{conversion}}$ Some tables are pens.].
10. A; [A + A = A; All books are flowers.]
11. B; [Change order of the statements to align. Now, No fox is a crow + Some crows are jackals = E + I = O*, Some jackals are not foxes.]
12. C; [Because of step IV which states that in case of one choice being 'some' and the other 'some not', at least one must be true.]
13. D; [Convert the first statement and change the order of the statements to align. Now, All table-lamps are electric goods + Some electric goods are radios = A + I = No conclusion]
14. A; [Change order to align. Now, John is a man + No man is a monkey = A + E = E, John is not a monkey.]
15. E; [Change order of the statements to align. Now, A + A = A, This thief is a man. $\xrightarrow{\text{conversion to}}$ Some men are thieves.]
16. D; [If you recall the definition of exclusive propositions, you must know that "only first divisioners are admitted" ≈ (is equivalent to) All admitted are first divisioners. This could be converted to : Some first divisioners are admitted. (A is converted to I-type.) Now, Ram is a first divisioner + Some first divisioners are admitted ⇒ A + I = No conclusion.

You may understand this slightly surprising result if you follow the logic that: Only first divisioners are admitted means that being a first divisioner is a necessary but not a sufficient criterion for being admitted.

Hence, Ram's being a first divisioner does not guarantee that he would be admitted.]

17. A; [Change order of statements to align. Now, A + A = A = (All) Saints are sinners.]

18. C; [This is the most tricky question on syllogism that you may have seen. If you recall some different types of A propositions (see **How to determine the hidden proposition),** you know that "All businessmen except Bhimji are dishonest" is an A-type proposition because it makes a definite exception. So, you may be tempted to infer that since A + A = A, hence "All businessmen except Bhimjee are dishonest + All dishonest people smoke = All businessmen except Bhimjee smoke". But this conclusion is erroneous. It may very definitely and correctly be inferred that "All businessmen smoke excluding Bhimji whose smoking habit is not known." Statement I has two dimensions: One that "All businessmen except Bhimji are dishonest," and two, which is a hidden meaning, that "Bhimji is honest". But it is never told whether honest people stroke or not. However, conclusion I, "All businessmen except Bhimji smoke", makes a definite assumption that Bhimji does not smoke. This actually may or may not be true. Hence, conclusion I is wrong.

However, since conclusion I has a hidden proposition that "Bhimji does not smoke" and since conclusion II states that "Bhimji smokes", one of the two conclusions must be true. Hence, choice C.

The above example is a sample of the many tricks that the bag of syllogism contains. They are commonly called **fallacies.** However, you may overcome these by a little bit of practice and intelligence.]

19. A; [Change order first. Now, No historian is an animal + Only cats are animals ≈ No historian is an animal + All animals are cats = E + A = O*, Some cats are not historians.]

20. C; [Few takers are givers ≈ Some takers are not givers. Now, O + E = no conclusion.] But conclusion I may be converted to "Some almighty are takers". Either this or conclusion II, "Some almighty are not takers", must be true. (Step IV)]

1.1.4.2: The Method of Venn diagrams

Step 1: Draw *standard* representations for both the statements separately as given below:

Note: By *standard* representation we mean a representation which is the most common and usually sufficient way to denote the statement.

For example, "Some X are Y" can be represented as:

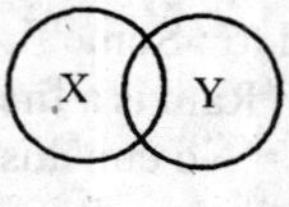

or

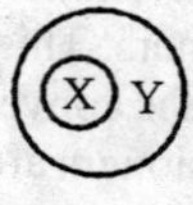

or

But, for all practical purposes the first of these representation suffices. And this is the standard representation for an **I**-type proposition.

Given below is a table of standard representation.

Table 11.4.2

Statement of Type	Standard representation
A (All X are Y)	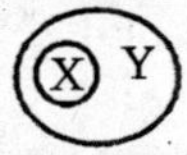
E (No X are Y)	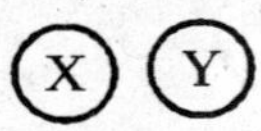
I (Some X are Y)	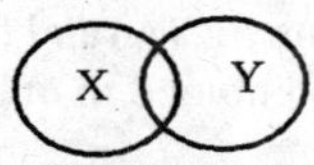
O (Some X are not Y)	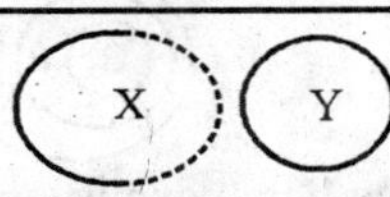

Step II: Now try to combine the representations (as drawn in step I) *in as many ways as possible.*

Note: When we say *as many ways as possible*, we mean that you should combine the representations in all possible ways. For example, if statement (1) is "All X are Y" and statement (2) is "Some Y are Z" then the standard representation are:

1. 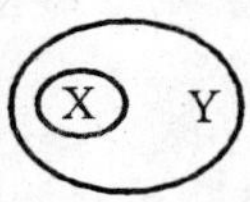

and

2. 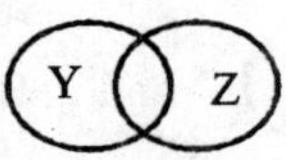

They can be combined in more than one ways the possible ways are:

Fig. (i) 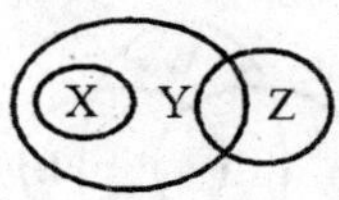

or Fig. (ii) 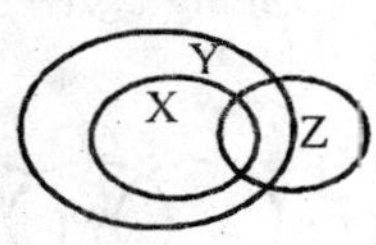

or, Fig. (iii) 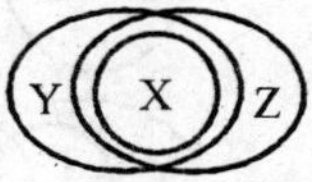

Therefore, step II asks you to draw all possible combinations.

Step III: Finally, make interpretations from the combined figures (obtained from step II) *Any given conclusion will be true if and only if it is supported by all the combined figures and no combined figure contradicts it.*

For example, in the illustration to step II, we see that a conclusion that

"Some X are Z" is supported by Fig. (ii) and (iii) but not by fig. (i). Since it is not supported by *all* the figures it does not follow.

Ex. 1: Statements: **A.** All cats are bats.
B. All bats are tables.
Conclusions: I. Some tables are bats.
II. Some tables are cats.

Solution:

Step I: Looking at table 11.4.2., we draw the standard representation for the two statements:

A) 

B) 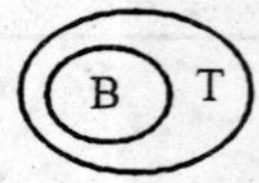

Let B = bats, C = cats, T = tables.

Step II: Now, combine fig. (A) and fig. (B) in all possible ways. Fig. (A) and fig. (B) can be combined in only one way. That is:

Step III: We see that both conclusions: *Some tables are bats and some tables are cats* are supported by the combined figure. Hence, both follow.

Ex. 2: Statements: **A.** Some tables are watches.
B. Some watches are lamps.
Conclusions: I. Some tables are lamps
II. Some tables are not lamps.

Solution:

Step I:

A) 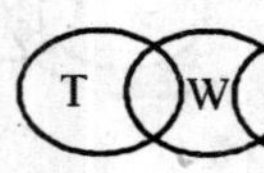

and B) 

Let T = tables, W = watches, L = lamps

Step II: Combining fig. (A) and fig. (B) in all possible ways.

C(i) 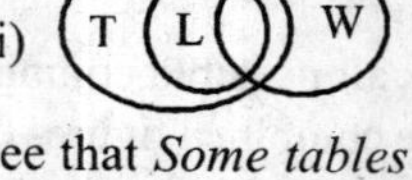

or 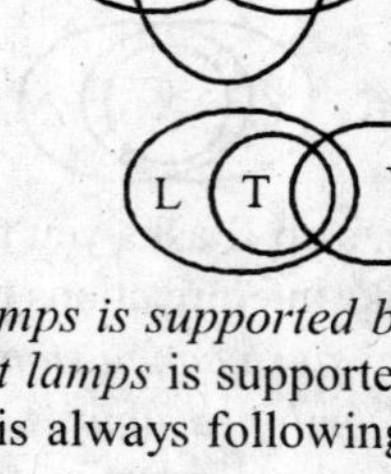

C (ii)

C (iii) 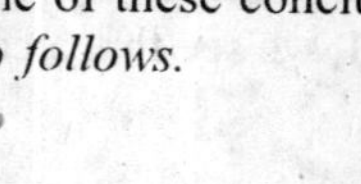

or 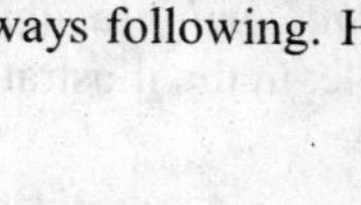

C (iv)

Step III: We see that *Some tables are lamps is supported by C (ii), C(iii) and C(iv) while Some tables are not lamps* is supported by C(i). Thus, at least one of these conclusions is always following. Hence, *either of the two follows.*

Ex. 3: Statements: **A.** No tables are watches.

B. Some watches are lamps.

Conclusions: **I.** Some lamps are not tables.

II. Some lamps are tables.

Solution:

Step I: We draw standard representation as drawn in table 11.4.2.

A) 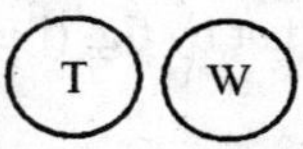

and B) 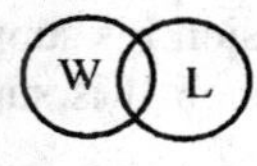

Let T = tables, W = watches, L = lamps

Step II: Now we combine the two figures in all possible ways. They are:

C(i) 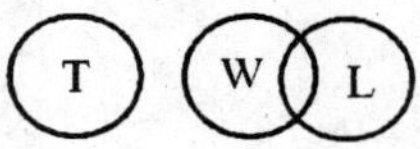

or 

C (ii)

or, C(iii) 

Step III: We see that the conclusion "Some lamps are not tables" is always supported by *all* the possible combinations. Hence, this conclusion is true.

Learners' Exercise VII

Directions: Solve questions from LEARNERS' EXERCISE SET VI by Venn-diagram method.

Answers with Explanations

[In the explanations below, we shall not draw the individual figures corresponding to each statement, i.e., we shall be jumping over step I. Also, we shall not draw all the possible combined figures since they may be too many in number. We shall, instead, draw only as many figures as will be sufficient to reach the answer.]

1. E; 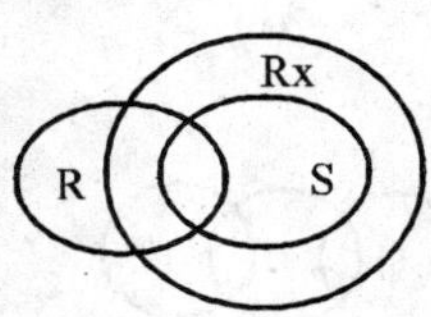

or 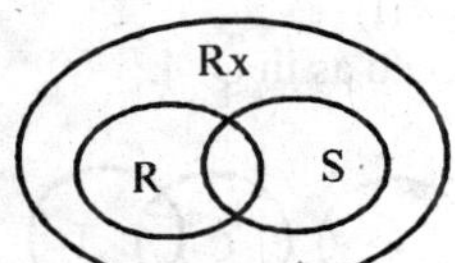

R = Room S = Stones Rx = Radios

2. D;

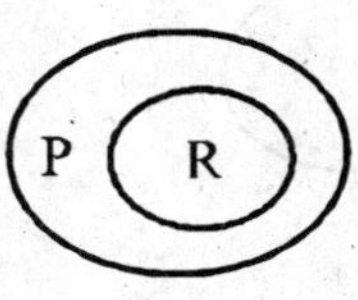

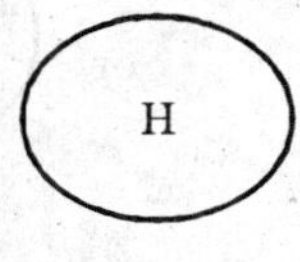

3. B;

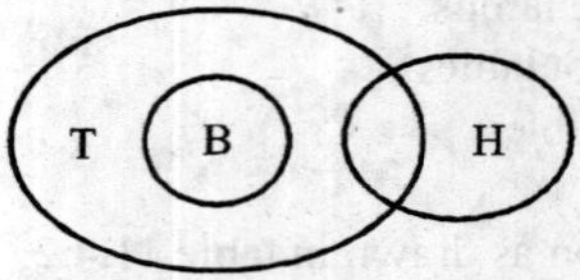

or

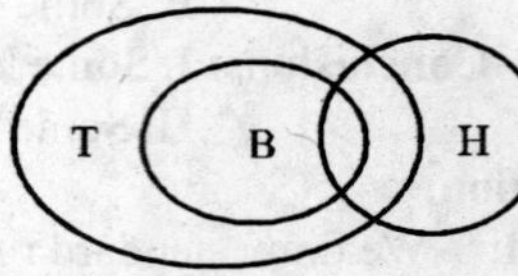

Conclusion I is supported by fig. (ii) but not by fig. (i).
Conclusion II is supported by both.

4. B;

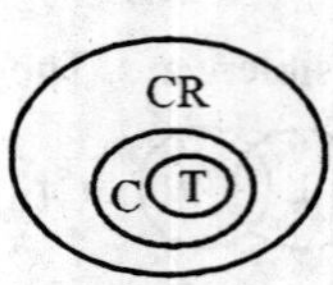

T = Tables C = Chalks CR = Chairs

5. D;

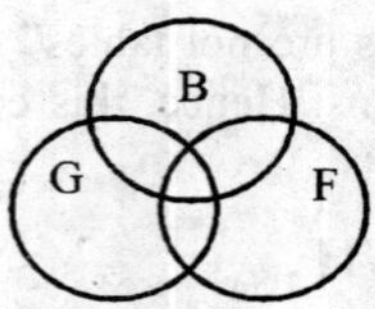

(i)

or

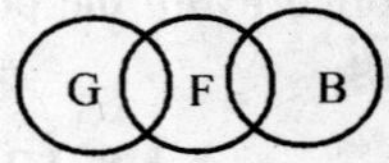

(ii)

Conclusion I is violated by fig. (ii) while conclusion II is violated by fig. (i).

6. E; Proceed as in Q. 1.
7. D; Proceed as in Q. 5.
8. B; Proceed as in Q. 7.
9. A;

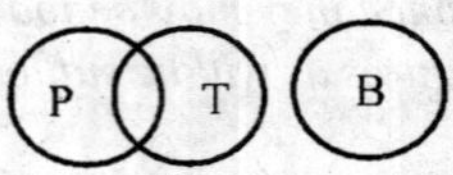

(i)

or

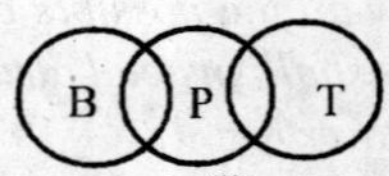

(ii)

10. A; Proceed as in Q. 4.
11. B;

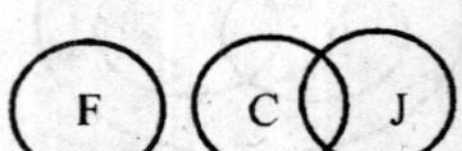

(i)

or

(ii)

or

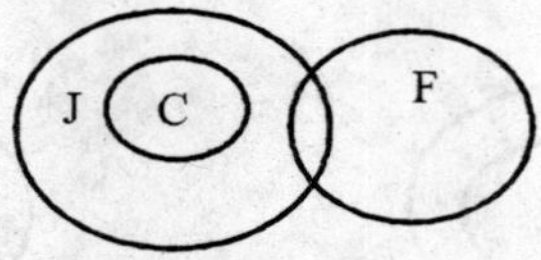

(iii)

12. C;

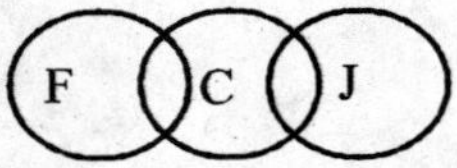

(i)

or

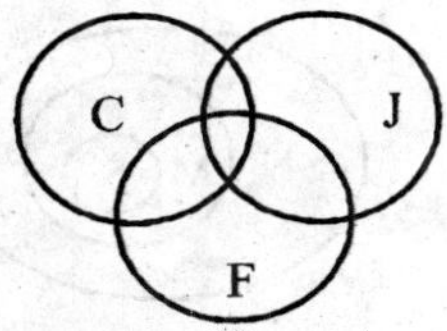

(ii)

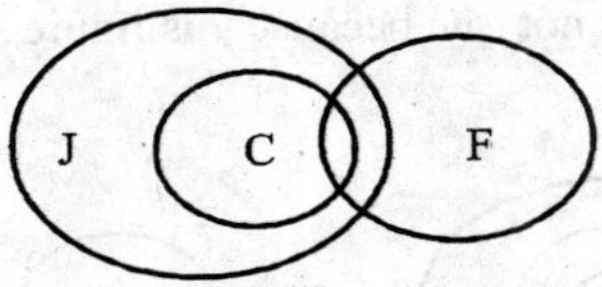

(iii)

13. D;

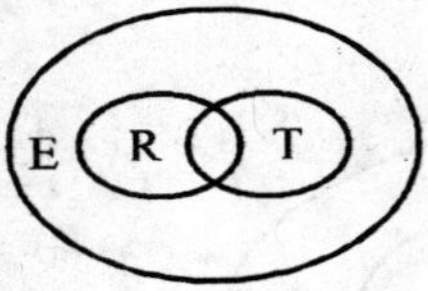

(i)

or

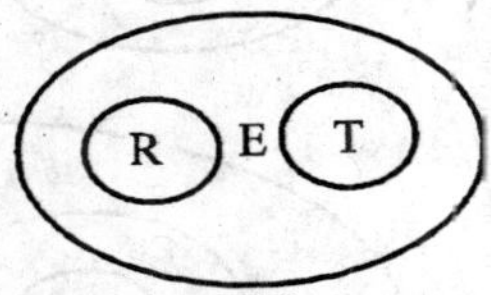

(ii)

14. A;

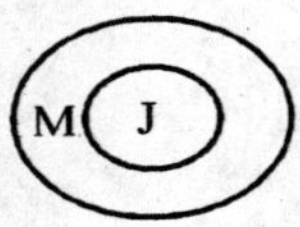

MK = Monkey

15. E;

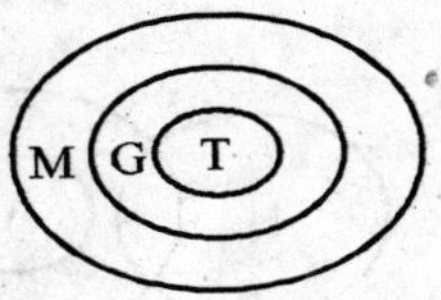

16. D;

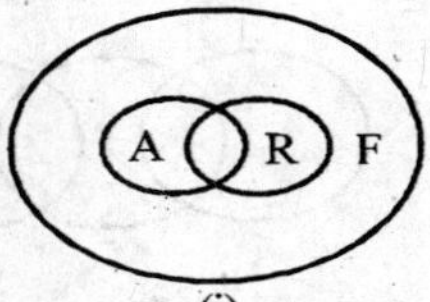

(i)

or

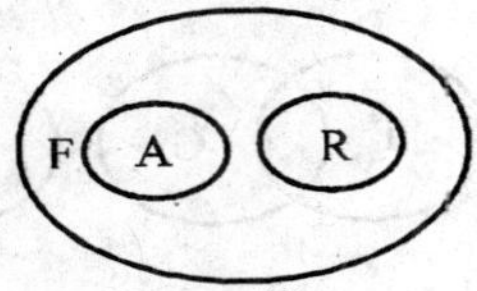

(ii)

A = Those who are admitted
F = First divisioners
R = Ram

[Fig (ii) violates conclusion (i) and (ii)]

17. A;

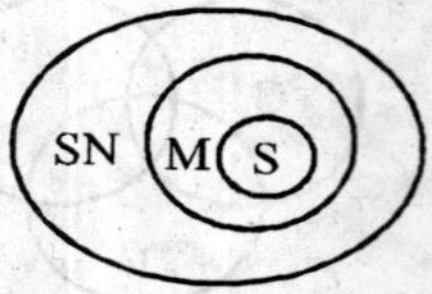

S = Saints SN = Sinners

Conclusion II is not true because this figure shows some sinners who are not saints.

18. C;

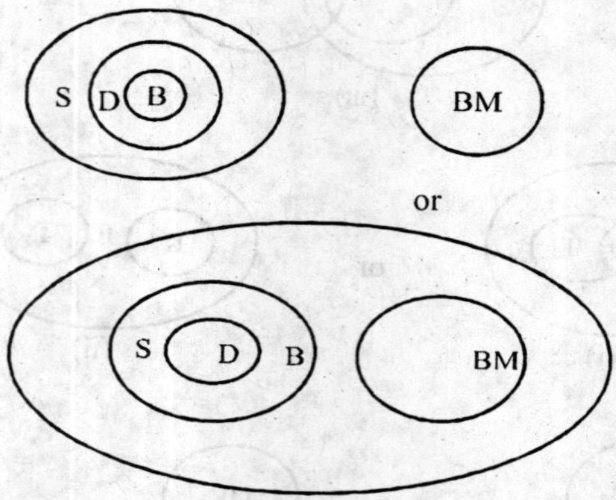

B = Businessmen except Bhimjee
BM = Bhimjee
D = Dishonest people
S = Smokers

19. A;

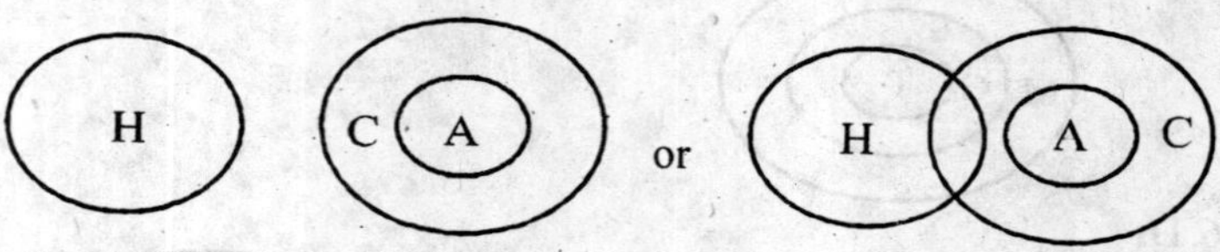

20. C;

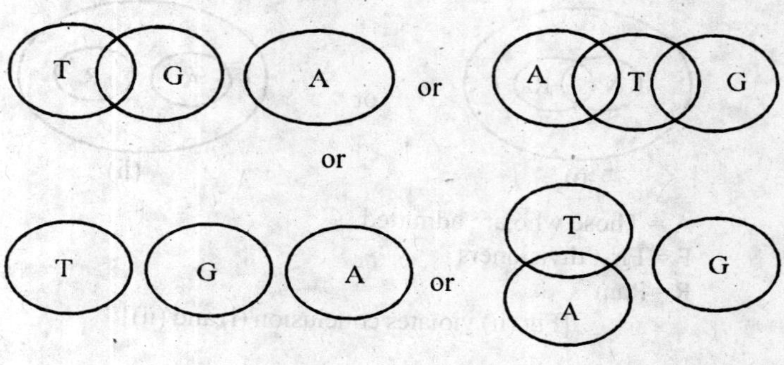

11.5: Three-Statement syllogism

Format of the problem

A typical three-statement syllogism problem reads like this:

Directions: Below are given three statements followed by several conclusions based on them. Examine the conclusions and decide whether they logically follow from the given statements. You have to take the given statements as true even if they appear to be at variance with commonly known facts.

Ex. 1: Statements: **(A)** All docks are boxes.
(B) Some cars are docks.
(C) No boxes are chocolates.

Conclusions: **I.** Some cars are boxes.
II. No chocolates are docks.
III. Some cars are chocolates.
IV. Some cars are not chocolates.

1) Only I and IV follow
2) Only I and II follow
3) Either III or IV, and I follow
4) I, IV and II follow
5) Either III or IV, and I and II follow

The Method

To begin with you must, first, convince yourself that a three-statement syllogism is certainly not more difficult than the usual two-statement syllogism. It may, of course, be a little more time-taking but it is not more difficult.

Step I:

The first step in solving a three-statement syllogism problem involves "carefully choosing the two relevant statements out of the three given statements". You should perform the first step in the following manner.

(i) Take a given conclusion.

(ii) See the subject and the predicate of this given conclusion.

(iii) Now see which of the two given statements has this subject and predicate.

(iv) **A.** If there is one term common between the two statements chosen in the previous part [(iii)], these two statements are your relevant statements.

B. If there is no term common between the two statements chosen in the previous part [(iii)], then all the three statements are your relevant statements. In this case you will have to apply a *chain-like formula.* [We will explain later what we mean by a "chain-like" formula. For the present you should just understand step I thoroughly.]

If you have any difficulty in understanding this first step, you will understand it at once after you go through the following solved example.

Performing Step I: An illustration

Consider Ex. 1. Here, we take all the four conclusions one by one.

Conclusion I. We first take conclusion I. Here, the subject is 'cars' and the predicate is 'boxes'. Now, we see that 'cars' is in statement B and 'boxes' is in statement A. Now, look at statements A and B. Do they have a common term? Yes, the common term is 'docks'. Therefore, A and B are our two relevant statements.

Conclusion II. Now, we take conclusion II. Here, the subject is 'chocolates' and the predicate 'docks'. Now, we see that 'chocolates' appears in statement 'C'. But 'docks' appears in both 'A' and 'B'. So, which of the two should we take? We should take 'A' because *(Note this)* there is a term common between A and C. We would not take B because there is no term common between B and C.

Conclusion III. Now, we take conclusion III. Here, the subject is 'cars' and the predicate 'chocolates'. We see that 'cars' appears in 'B' while 'chocolates' appears in 'C'. Now, is there any common term between 'B' and 'C'? We see that there is no term common between 'B' and 'C'. So, we will have to use a chain-like formula in this case because all the three statements are relevant here.

Conclusion IV. Same as in conclusion III.

Note: It is very important that you understand this first step. If necessary re-read the entire matter once again before going further.

Step II:

In syllogism, there are four types of statements, viz. A, E, I and O. **When two statements are given and they are arranged in such a way that the predicate of the first sentence and the subject of the second sentence is the same then the following six formulae are applicable.**

A + A = A	I + A = I	I + E = O
A + E = E	E + A = O*	E + I = O*

Note: O* means "O reversed." In this case, the predicate and the subject of the conclusion appear in reverse order. For example, "No bomb is comb" + "Some combs are bullets" is of the form E + I and it will give a conclusion "O reversed" i.e. "Some bullets are not bombs". It will not be "Some bombs are not bullets".

Thus, in the second step, you should apply the formulae to get conclusions. The second step should be performed in the following order.

(i) Take a given conclusion. See its subject and predicate. Now, by using the first step, find out how many and which statements are relevant for this conclusion.

(ii) I. If two statements are relevant for a given conclusion, write them in such an order that the predicate of the first sentence and the subject of the second sentence are the same.

II. If three statements are relevant for a given conclusion then write them as a chain. Arrange them in such a way that the predicate of the first sentence and the subject of the second sentence are the same, and the predicate of the second sentence and the subject of the third sentence are the same. For example,

A. No hook is a cook.
B. All books are docks.
C. Some docks are hooks.

These should be rearranged as a chain below.

All books are docks.

↔

Some docks are hooks.

↔

No hook is a cook.

(iii) Now, apply the formulae. Note that there are six formulae only. This means that there are only six types of cases in which a conclusion is possible. In any other type of cases, you may write "no conclusion". For example, A + I = no conclusion. Also, note that when three statements are simultaneously relevant, you have to write them in a chain and use the formula repeatedly. For example, if you get I + A + E, you should write it as $(I + A) + E \Rightarrow I + E\ (\because I + A = I) \Rightarrow O\ (\because I + E = O)$.

Thus, you get, I + A + E = O.

Similarly, you may see that A + E + I = (A + E) + I = (E) + I = O* or O reversed.

(iv) Now, compare the given conclusion with the result of the formula that you have applied. If they match, the given conclusion is true. If they do not match, it is false.

Step III:

In certain cases, a conclusion follows directly from one given statement only. This is called **immediate inference.** Also, in some cases, two given answer choices make a complementary pair, and in such cases "either of them follows" should be chosen. Therefore, in the third step you should do the following:

(i) **Check for immediate inference:** Take a given conclusion. If it has already been marked as a valid conclusion after step II then leave it. Otherwise, check if it is an immediate inference of any of the three given statements.

(ii) Check for complementary pair:

(a) Check if any two given conclusions have the same subject and the same predicate.

(b) If yes, then check that none of them has been marked as a valid conclusion after step II or as a case of immediate inference.

(c) If none of them has been marked as a valid conclusion then they will form a complementary pair if they are an A-O or an I-O or an I-E pair.

(d) If they do make a complementary pair then mark the choice "either of the two follows".

A summary of the method

The entire process of solving three-statement syllogism is performed in three simple steps. These three steps have been already described above. To make it clearer, we are giving below the gist of these three steps:

Take a given conclusion.

Perform step I. In other words, find out the relevant statements to test this conclusion.

Perform step II. In other words, use the formulae to test a given conclusion. [If more than two statements are relevant for a given conclusion, use the chain-like formulae].

If the given conclusion has been rejected in step II,

Perform step III: (i). In other words, check for immediate inference.

If the given conclusion has still not been accepted

Perform step III: (ii). In other words, check for complementary pair.

[**Note:** You not need to perform Step III (i), if a conclusion has already been accepted in step II. Again, you do not need to perform step III (ii), if a given conclusion has already been accepted in step III (i)].

Complete step-by-step solution of Ex 1

We hope that the method has become clear to you by now. If there are any doubts, see the detailed solution of Ex 1 that is given below. We have already given the details of step I for Ex 1. So, this solution will start from step II onwards.

Conclusion I: We have seen that for this conclusion, statements A and B are relevant. Now, we perform step II. For this, we first arrange A and B in such a way that the predicate of the first sentence is the subject of the second. This is done as:

Some cars are docks. (I)

All docks are boxes. (A)

Now, we have, I + A = I. So, the conclusion will be of type I; it will be "Some cars are boxes." Hence, conclusion I is valid.

(Now, we do not need to perform step III because the conclusion has been accepted in step II itself.)

Conclusion II: We have seen that statements A and C are relevant for this conclusion (step I). Now, we perform step II. For this, we write the sentences in such a way that the predicate of the first sentence is the subject of the second. This is done as:

All docks are boxes. (A)

No boxes are chocolates. (E)

Now, we have: A + E = E. Hence, the conclusion will be "No docks are chocolates". Now, the given conclusion is: "No chocolates are docks". But "No docks are chocolates" automatically implies "No chocolates are docks". Hence, this conclusion is also valid. [Again we do not need to perform step II because the conclusion has been accepted in step II itself]

Conclusion III: We have seen that all the three statements are relevant to this conclusion (step I). So, we should perform step II. For this we should write the three statements in such a way that the predicate of the first sentence is the subject of the second and the predicate of the second sentence is the subject of the first. This is done as:

Some cars are docks. (I)

All docks are boxes. (A)

No boxes are chocolates. (E)

Now, we have the chainlike formula:

I + A + E = (I + A) + E = (I) + E = O. Thus, a valid conclusion would be of type O; that is "Some cars are not chocolates". But this is conclusion IV. Hence, conclusion IV is valid. But conclusion III is not accepted in step II. So, we perform step III (i). We see that "Some cars are not chocolates" does not follow from any of the three given statements alone. So, this test fails. Now, we perform step III (ii). For this, we will have to first search any other conclusion that has the same subject and predicate. We see that conclusion IV fulfils this condition because the subject and the predicate of conclusions III and IV are the same: 'cars' and 'chocolates' respectively. Again, conclusion III is of type I and conclusion IV is of type O and we know that an I-O pair makes a complementary pair.

Still, we would not choose the choice "either of them follows" unless it is made sure that step II and step III (i) fail on conclusion IV too. But we see that conclusion IV is accepted in step II. So, despite the fact that conclusion III and IV make a complementary pair, we do not accept the choice "either of them follows" because conclusion IV is accepted in step II.

Conclusion IV: As already explained, it is a valid conclusion.

Answer: 4 (I, II and IV follow).

One more fully solved example

We are presenting a detailed solution of one more example so that you may understand the method fully.

Ex 2: Statements: **A.** Some bricks are dogs.
B. All kicks are sticks.
C. No sticks are bricks.

Conclusions: **I.** Some dogs are bricks.
II. Some dogs are not bricks.
III. Some dogs are kicks.
IV. Some dogs are not kicks.
V. Some kicks are dogs.
VI. No kicks are dogs.

1) Either I or II and either III or IV and either V or VI follow
2) Either I or II and IV and either V or VI follow
3) I, IV and either V or VI follow
4) I, IV and VI follow
5) Only IV and VI follow

Solution

Conclusions I and II

Step I: In both these conclusions, the subject and the predicate are 'dogs' and 'bricks' respectively. We see that 'bricks' and 'dogs' appear in one statement only is statement A. Hence, only statement (A) is relevant here.

Step II: Since only one statement is relevant, step II is not needed.

Step III: **(i)** We see that "Some dogs are bricks" follows from "Some bricks are dogs" as immediate inference. Hence, conclusion I is accepted. But conclusion II does not follow from "Some bricks are dogs".

(ii) Conclusion I and II make a complementary pair because both have the same subject and the same predicate and they are an I-O pair. But conclusion I has already been accepted; hence "either of them follows" is not a correct choice.

Conclusions III, IV, V, VI

Step I: In these conclusions, 'kicks' and 'dogs' appear as subject and predicate. Now, in the given statements, 'dogs' is in statement A while 'kicks' is in statement B. But there is no term common between A and B. This means that all the three statements are relevant to us.

Step II: We write the three statements in the following way:

All kicks are sticks. (A)

No sticks are bricks. (E)

Some bricks are dogs. (I)

Now, we have A + E + I = (A + E) + I = (E) + I = O reversed. Hence, a valid conclusion would be "Some dogs are not kicks." Hence, conclusion IV is valid.

Step III (i): Conclusion IV has been accepted. So, we need to perform the remaining steps on conclusions III, V and VI only. We see that none of these three conclusions directly follows from the three given statements alone. Hence, step III (i) fails.

Step III (ii): Conclusions III and IV make a complementary pair because one is of type I and the other of type O, and the subject and the predicate of both are the same. But conclusion IV has already been accepted. Hence, we cannot choose "either of these follows".

But conclusions V and VI also make a complementary pair (I-E pair; same subject and predicate) and none of these conclusions has been accepted. Hence, "either V or VI follows" would be a correct choice.

Answer: 3 (I, IV, and either V or VI follow).

One more example: Quicker approach

Till now, we have presented step-by-step, exhaustive solutions to the questions. This may give an indication that this method is very lengthy. But, actually it is not so. In fact, once you have solved ten such questions, the method will become very easy for you. First of all, **you should do step I *mentally*.** After a certain time you won't take more than a couple of seconds for this step. Similarly, after some practice, you will develop the ability of doing step II and step III mentally, too. Once you attain the skill you will be able to solve "5 questions of three-statement syllogism in less than 4 minutes. To convince you that this method is really fast, we are presenting another example. In this example, we are only writing the relevant steps and omitting unnecessary details.

Ex. 3: Statements: **A.** All birds are swans.
B. Some skirts are birds.
C. All swans are ducks.

Conclusions: **I.** Some ducks are birds.
II. Some skirts are ducks.
III. All birds are ducks.
IV. Some birds are not ducks.

1) Only I and II follow
2) Only II and III follow
3) Either III or IV follows
4) I, II and either III or IV follow
5) I, II and III follow

Solution

Conclusions I, III, IV: Subject and predicate are "ducks" and "birds". Hence, the relevant statements are A and C. Now, All birds are swans + All swans are ducks = A + A = A = All birds are ducks. Hence, III is valid. Again, "All birds are ducks" gives "Some ducks are birds". Hence, I is valid. III and IV make complementary pair but we do not choose "either III or IV follows" because III has already been accepted.

Conclusion II: Subject = 'skirts' and predicate = 'ducks'. 'Skirts' appears in B while 'ducks' appears in C. But there is no term common between B and C. Hence, all three statements are relevant. Now, rearrange the three statements. Some skirts are birds + All birds are swans + All swans are ducks = I + A + A = (I + A) + A = (I) + A = I = Some skirts are ducks. Hence, conclusion II is valid.

Answer: 5 (I, II, III follow).

11.6: Syllogism: Certain Controversies

Many books are available in the market and, surprisingly, each one of them offers different answers or explanations for the same syllogism problem. In such a scenario it is only to be expected that students feel dazed and confused. There are many controversies - many doubts that come into the minds of the students. Let us take a brief look at them:

Doubt I: *Who is correct?*

Explanation: This is a question that, we feel, does not deserve much attention. The answer is fairly simple: We *(Banking Services Chronicle)* are correct. (If any other magazine or book gives different answers, it is wrong. We are as sure of it as you can be of the sun rising in the east.)

Doubt II: *Some books and magazines (including one very popular magazine) assume that "Some S are P" automatically means "Some S are not P". Some other publications (including BSC) do not assume this. Which is correct?*

Explanation: The latter "Some S are P" does NOT automatically mean that "Some S are not P".

In most of the cases, "Some S are P" gives the impression that in the group of S, there are some members who are members of group P, while the remaining members of S are not the member of P. And hence the conclusion. This is true in most of the cases; but it is not *always* true. For illustration consider the statement: "Some Indians are Indians".

Do you agree with this statement? Of course, this statement is always true. Now, can we draw a conclusion from this statement that:

"Some Indians are not Indians"?

Of course, not. Thus, we see that there can be some cases where the statement "Some S are P" does not give rise to "Some S are not P".

For those, who prefer to understand the language of Venn's diagrams, the explanation is pictorially presented below. You can see that the statement 'Some S are P' can be represented by any of the three figures while the conclusion 'Some S are not P' is supported by fig I only.

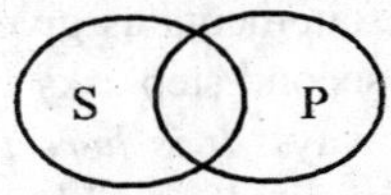

Some S are P.
[Some S are not P]
Fig. I

Some S are P.
[All S are P; All P are S]
Fig. II

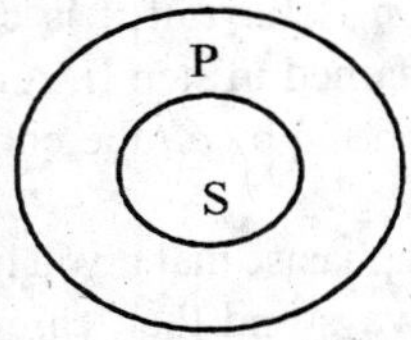

Some S are P
[All S are P; All P are not S]
Fig. III

Doubt III: *One of the books says that from a given statement of the form "All S are P" a conclusion of the form "Some P are S" cannot be derived. Many other publications (including* Banking Services Chronicle) *say that it can be derived. Which is correct?*

Explanation: The latter. Frankly, I have not seen any such book. But since one of our correspondence course students have written this doubt to me, I am forced to believe that some such books exist. The explanation is very simple: "All S are P" automatically implies "Some P are S". There is no question of any doubt here.

To those of our readers, who have seen a book saying that, my sincere advice to them is that they should stop reading this chapter, immediately find that book and throw it into the dustbin. The case, by the way, is explained by the following Venn's diagrams:

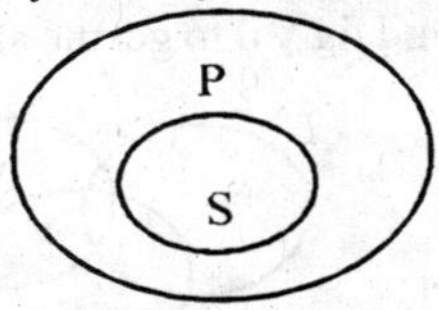

All S are P
[All P are not S]
Fig IV

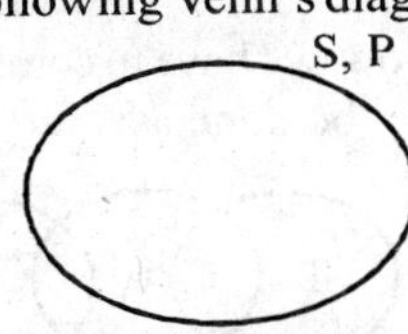

All S are P
[All P are S]
Fig V

You can clearly see that 'Some P are S' is true in both the cases.

Doubt IV: *Sometimes we fail to get the correct answer by the method of Venn's diagrams. Why?*

Explanation: Such a thing happens with some trickier questions. The strategy for solution using Venn diagrams is a simple three-step strategy as given in Section 11.4.2. In first step, you have to draw standard representation for both the statements as given in Table 11.4.2. Obviously, this is easy. The second step asks you to combine the two figures in *all* possible ways. *It is here that most students commit a mistake* by not drawing *all* possible combinations. Step III is merely a step of interpreting from your figures. Some students make a mistake in this step also. They should not forget that a conclusion is false if it is contradicted by even a single combination obtained in step II. A conclusion will be true if and only if it is supported by *all* the combination figures obtained in step II.

Hence, we re-emphasise that if you have combined the two figures in all possible ways and then carefully done the interpretation, there is no way you can get a wrong answer.

Ex. 1. Statements: Some tables are watches.
Some watches are fans.

Conclusions: Some tables are not fans.
Some fans are not tables.

Analysis: 'Some tables are watches' may be represented as:

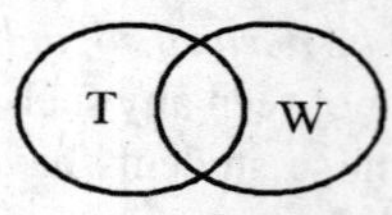

Fig. VI

'Some watches are fans, may be represented as:

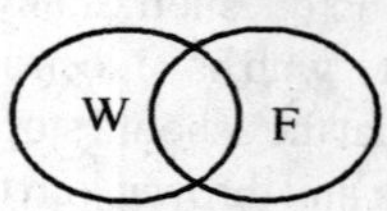

Fig. VII

Now, we have to combine fig VI and fig VII to get the answer figures. This can be done as:

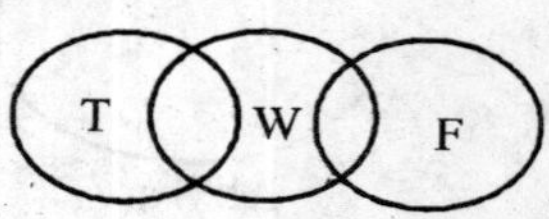

Fig. VIIIA

or

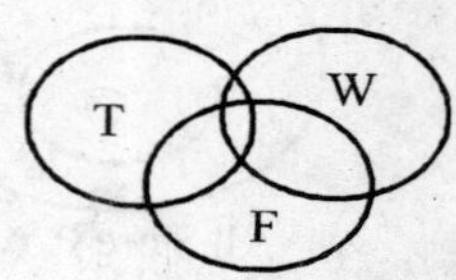

Fig. VIIIB

Interpreting these two figures, we infer that both the conclusions

('Some tables are not fans' and 'Some fans are not tables') are correct.

But a little deeper thought would indicate that again we have made a mistake. This time we have not considered all possible cases of combining the primary figures. Fig VII and Fig VI may also be combined as:

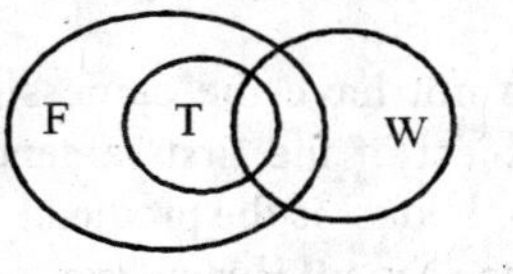

Fig VIII C

or

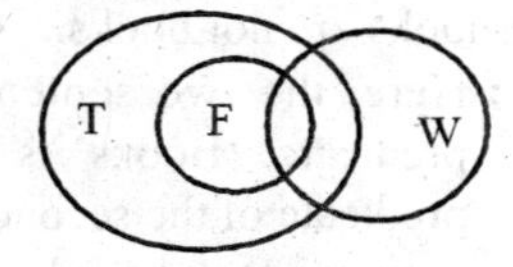

Fig VIII D

Now, we see that the conclusion 'Some tables are not fans' is violated by fig VIIIC while the conclusion 'Some fans are not tables' is violated by fig. VIII D. Thus, we conclude that both the conclusions are wrong.

A final tip: The best strategy to solve a question by Venn's diagrams is to try to prove the conclusion incorrect by all possible means. If a conclusion cannot be proved incorrect by all possible cases then it should be taken as correct.

Doubt V: *When is the choice 'either of the two follows' correct?*

Explanation: There are cases when, between the two given choices, at least one is certain to be correct. When one of them is true, the other is false, and when the other is true, the first is false. For example, consider the pair:' Some students are Indians' and' Some students are not Indians'. It is obvious that one of the two statements must be true. This is because when 'Some students are Indians' is false the other one is automatically true.

We call such a pair of sentences as **complementary pair.** Thus, a pair of sentences is called complementary pair if it is so that when one is false the other is true. Let us take some more examples of complementary pairs of statements:

Ex. 3. No student is a table.
Some students are tables.

Ex. 4. All beautiful are kind.
Some beautiful are not kind.

More generally, we can classify complementary pairs by the type of proposition. You may notice that in Ex 3, E and I type propositions made complementary pairs; in Ex 4, A and O type propositions made complementary pairs while in the earlier example, I and O type propositions ['Some students are Indians' and 'Some students are not Indians'] made complementary pairs.

On this basis, we can conclude that **two statements are complementary if they fall into any of these categories:**

(i) I and O
(ii) E and I

(iii) A and O

Please note that sometimes a pair of statements may be complementary although it may not appear so. For example, consider the example:

Ex. 5. Some books are hooks.

Some hooks are not books.

Explanation: Here, the two sentences do not have the same subject and predicate. 'Books' is the subject of the first sentence and the predicate of the second while 'hooks' is the predicate of the first sentence and the subject of the second. Hence, the sentences do not appear to be complementary. But if we convert the first sentence from 'Some books ate hooks' to 'Some hooks are books', the two sentences have the same subject and predicate now, and being ' an 'I and O' pair they are complementary.

With all these foregoing discussions in mind, let us come back to our original question, which is: "When is the answer choice 'either of the two follows' correct?".

You must be aware that usually there are the following five answer choices:

(i) Only A follows

(ii) Only B follows

(iii) Both A and B follow

(iv) None of them follows

(v) Either A or B follows

Now, when you read a question, you first read the statements and then the answer choices. You take the first choice A and check whether it is correct or not. Then you go to the second choice, B, and check it. Suppose none of the two choices come out to be correct. What should you do next? Do you then opt for the choice "None of them follows"? No, this is not the correct thing to do. After you have found that none of the two choices are correct, you should check whether the choice "Either of the two follows" is also incorrect, then you should move on to the last choice, viz. "None of them follows". This, finally, brings us to the answer of our original question:

The choice "Either of the two follows" should be chosen if

a. none of the given two choices are found to be correct, and

b. the two choices form a complementary pair.

The rule is explained by way of the following examples:

Ex. 6. Statements: Some stones are radios.

Some radios are chairs.

Conclusions: No stones are chairs.

Some chairs are stones.

Explanation: You may check that none of the given conclusions is correct. But the two answers form a complementary pair because they are E and F type. Hence, the choice 'either of them follows' is correct.

Ex. 7. Statements: Some stones are radios.
Some radios are chairs.

Conclusions: No stones are chairs.
Some chairs are not stones.

Explanation: You may check that none of the given conclusions is correct. The answer choices do not form a complementary pair [E-O pair is not complementary]. Hence, the choice 'none of them follows' is correct.

Ex. 8. Statements: Some stones are radios.
All radios are chairs.

Conclusions: Some stones are chairs.
Some stones are not chairs.

Explanation: We see that the answer choices form a complementary pair. But this does not mean that the choice "either of the two follows" is correct. This is because the conclusion 'Some stones are chairs' is correct.

I hope that this thorough and exhaustive analysis will be of immense help to the readers and they will never be confused for the choice "either of them follows".

[**Note:** Most generally, such answer choices are in the form 'Some S are P' and 'Some S are not P'; that is, I-O pair. So, one needs to be extra-conscious about this 'Some' and 'Some not' pair.]

Summary

- There are four types of propositions: A, E, I and O. Their Venn-diagrams are given in Table 2.
- Immediate inference means deriving conclusions from a single statement. There are two types of immediate inferences. These are explained in Table 3 and Table 4.
- In the analytical method for solving syllogism there are four steps. These are:

  Step I: Align (if needed).
  Step II: Use table 6.
  Step III: Check for immediate inferences.
  Step IV: Check for complementary pair

  In the Venn diagram method, there are three steps. These are:

  Step I: Draw all possible representations of both the statements separately.
  Step II: Combine the representations in all possible ways.
  Step III: If a given conclusion is not violated by any of the figure combination in step II, it is a valid conclusion, otherwise it is not.
- When more than two statements are given, you have to use the same rules. Only an additional step is needed. (See "Three-statement syllogism")
- There are certain controversies regarding syllogism. These have been separately discussed in the chapiter.

Practice Exercises

Type I: Exercise 11A

Directions : In each question below are given two statements followed by two conclusions numbered I and II. You have to take the two ' given statements to be true even if they seem to be at variance with the commonly known facts and then decide which of the given conclusions logically follows from the two given statements, disregarding commonly known facts.

Give answer (a) if only conclusion I follows; (b) if only conclusion II follows; (c) if either I or II follows; (d) if neither I nor II follows; and (e) if both I and II follow.

1. **Statements:** All cakes are ice-creams.
All ice-creams are toffees.
Conclusions: I. All cakes are toffees.
II. All toffees are ice-creams.
2. **Statements:** All tigers are ships.
Some ships are cupboards.
Conclusions: I. Some tigers are cupboards.
II. Some cupboards are tigers.
3. **Statements:** Some pearls are gems.
Some gems are ornaments.
Conclusions: I. Some gems are pearls.
II. Some ornaments are gems.
4. **Statements:** Some sticks are bolts.
Kite is a stick.
Conclusions: I. Some bolts are sticks.
II. Some kites are bolts.
5. **Statements:** Some teachers are adults.
Some adults are poets.
Conclusions: I. Some teachers are poets.
II. Some poets are teachers.
6. **Statements:** Lawyers marry only fair girls.
Shobha is very fair.
Conclusions: I. Shobha was married to a lawyer.
II. Shobha was not married to a lawyer.
7. **Statements:** All coats are bags.
Some bags are toys.
Conclusions: I. Some bags are coats.
II. Some toys are coats.
8. **Statements:** All pencils are bricks.
All bricks are bottles.
Conclusions: I. All pencils are bottles.
II. All bricks are pencils.

9. **Statements:** All men are prisoners.
No prisoners are educated.
Conclusions: I. All prisoners are educated.
II. No men are educated.

10. **Statements:** Some children are adults.
Some adults are old.
Conclusions: I. Some children are not old.
II. Some adults are not old.

11. **Statements:** All birds are trees.
Some trees are hens.
Conclusions: I. Some birds are hens.
II. Some hens are trees.

12. **Statements:** Some snakes are birds.
All cats are birds.
Conclusions: I. Some cats are snakes.
II. Some birds are snakes.

13. **Statements:** All shawls are carpets.
No carpet is a pullover.
Conclusions: I. No shawls are pullovers.
II. All carpets are shawls.

14. **Statements:** All pilots are brave men.
All astronauts are pilots.
Conclusions: I. All astronauts are brave men.
II. Some pilots are astronauts.

15. **Statements:** All teachers are good.
Some women are teachers.
Conclusions: I. All good teachers are women.
II. Some women are good.

16. **Statements:** Sohan is a good sportsman.
Sportsmen are healthy.
Conclusions: I. All healthy persons are sportsmen.
II. Sohan is healthy.

17. **Statements:** All students in my class are intelligent.
Rohit is not intelligent.
Conclusions: I. Rohit is not a student of my class.
II. Rohit must work hard.

18. **Statements:** All boys are honest.
Sachin is honest.
Conclusions: I. Sachin is a boy.
II. All honest persons are boys.

19. **Statements:** Many books are rocks.
All rocks are clips.

Conclusions: **I.** Some books are clips.
II. No rock is a book.

20. **Statements:** All locks are keys.
No key is a spoon.
Conclusions: **I.** No lock is a spoon
II. No spoon is a lock.

21. **Statements:** All young scientists are open-minded.
No open-minded men are superstitious.
Conclusions: **I.** No scientist is superstitious.
II. No young people are superstitious.

22. **Statements:** Some hats are pins.
All pins are watches.
Conclusions: **I.** No watch is a hat.
II. All pins are hats.

23. **Statements:** All politicians are intelligent.
Some women are politicians.
Conclusions: **I.** Some women are intelligent.
II. All those who are intelligent are women.

24. **Statements:** All bulbs are rods.
No rod is a gun.
Conclusions: **I.** All rods are bulbs.
II. No bulb is a gun.

25. **Statements:** Some ministers are clerks.
All clerks are businessmen.
Conclusions: **I.** Some ministers are businessmen.
II. All businessmen are clerks.

26. **Statements:** Some desks are caps.
No cap is red.
Conclusions: **I.** Some caps are desks.
II. No desk is red.

27. **Statements:** All lights are trucks.
Some trucks are jeeps.
Conclusions: **I.** All jeeps are lights.
II. Some lights are jeeps.

28. **Statements:** Some tables are glasses.
All trees are tables.
Conclusions: **I.** Some trees are glasses.
II. Some glasses are trees.

29. **Statements:** Most clocks are fans.
Some fans are walls.
Conclusions: **I.** Some walls are fans.
II. Some clocks are walls.

30. **Statements:** All cars are tables.
Some children are tables.
Conclusions: I. Some cars are children.
II. Some children are cars.

31. **Statements:** All horses are bullocks.
All bullocks are goats.
Conclusions: I. All horses are goats.
II. All goats are horses.

32. **Statements:** Some books are pencils.
Some pencils are pens.
Conclusions: I. Some books are pens.
II. Some pens are books.

33. **Statements:** All trays are erasers.
All pens are erasers.
Conclusions: I. All trays are pens.
II. Some pens are trays.

34. **Statements:** Some pastries are toffees.
All toffees are chocolates.
Conclusions: I. Some chocolates are toffees.
II. Some toffees are not pastries.

35. **Statements:** Some chalks are wires.
Some wires are frames.
Conclusions: I. Some chalks are frames.
II. Some frames are chalks.

36. **Statements:** All scientists are researchers.
Some researchers are teachers.
Conclusions: I. No scientist is a teacher.
II. Some teachers are scientists.

37. **Statements:** Some authors are teachers.
No teacher is a lady.
Conclusions: I. Some teachers are not ladies.
II. Some ladies are teachers.

38. **Statements:** No women can vote.
Some women are politicians.
Conclusions: I. Male politicians can vote.
II. Some politicians can vote.

39. **Statements:** All young girls are modern.
No modern men are superstitious.
Conclusions: I. No girl is superstitious.
II. No young man is superstitious.

40. **Statements:** All books are pens.
All pens are boxes.
Conclusions: I. All books are boxes.
II. All pens are books.

41. **Statements:** All readers are teachers.
All writers are teachers.
Conclusions: I. Some teachers are writers.
II. Some writers are readers.

42. **Statements:** All dogs are rats.
Some rats are lizards.
Conclusions: I. Some dogs are lizards.
II. Some lizards are dogs.

43. **Statements:** All lawyers are cheats.
Some women are lawyers.
Conclusions: I. Some women are cheats.
II. All cheats are women.

44. **Statements:** All plants are trees.
No tree is green.
Conclusions: I. Some plants are green.
II. Those plants which are not trees are green.

45. **Statements:** All hill-stations have a sunset point.
X is a hill-station.
Conclusions: I. X has a sunset point.
II. Places other than hill-stations do not have sunset points.

46. **Statements:** Some girls are flowers.
Some flowers are books.
Conclusions: I. Some girls are books.
II. No book is a girl.

47. **Statements:** Some parrots are crows.
No crow is green.
Conclusions: I. No parrot is green.
II. No crow is white.

48. **Statements:** All clerks are lazy.
Some men are clerks.
Conclusions: I. All lazy are men.
II. Some men are lazy.

49. **Statements:** All goats are wolves.
Some wolves are tigers.
Conclusions: I. Some goats are tigers.
II. Tigers which are wolves are not goats.

50. **Statements:** Some pots are belts.
No belt is white.
Conclusions: I. Some pots are white.
II. Some pots are not white.

51. **Statements:** Some aeroplanes are living beings.
Some non-living beings are ghosts.
Conclusions: I. Some aeroplanes are ghosts.
II. Some aeroplanes are not ghosts.

52. **Statements:** Some papers are needles.
All needles are sharp.
Conclusions: I. All papers are sharp.
II. All needles are papers.

53. **Statements:** All bags are cakes.
All lamps are cakes.
Conclusions: I. Some lamps are bags.
II. No lamp is a bag.

54. **Statements:** Some soldiers are famous.
Some soldiers are intelligent.
Conclusions: I. Some soldiers are either famous or intelligent.
II. Some soldiers are neither famous nor intelligent.

55. **Statements:** All radios are pencils.
Some pencils are files.
Conclusions: I. No radio is a file.
II. Some files are radios.

56. **Statements:** Some machines are racks.
All wheels are machines.
Conclusions: I. Some wheels are racks.
II. Some racks are wheels.

57. **Statements:** All roads are poles.
No pole is a house.
Conclusions: I. Some roads are houses.
II. Some houses are poles.

58. **Statements:** Some men are educated.
Educated persons prefer small families.
Conclusions: I. All small families are educated.
II. Some men prefer small families.

59. **Statements:** All players are tall.
Sohan is tall.
Conclusions: I. Sohan is a player.
II. Sohan is not a player.

60. **Statements:** All students are boys.
No boy is dull.
Conclusions: I. No student is dull.
II. There are no girls in the class.

61. **Statements:** Some mangoes are nuts.
Some nuts are fruits.
Conclusions: I. Some mangoes are fruits.
II. Some fruits are mangoes.

62. **Statements:** Some kites are horses.
All horses are dogs.
Conclusions: I. All dogs are horses.
II. Some dogs are horses.

63. **Statements:** All beds are towels.
Some towels are sheets.
Conclusions: I. Some towels are beds.
II. Some sheets are not towels.

64. **Statements:** No boy is a thief.
Some men are thieves.
Conclusions: I. Some men are not boys.
II. Some thieves are not boys.

65. **Statements:** All dresses are shoes.
No shoe is brown.
Conclusions: I. No dresses are brown.
II. Some shoes are dresses.

66. **Statements:** Some hens are cows.
All cows are horses.
Conclusions: I. Some horses are hens.
II. Some hens are horses.

67. **Statements:** Some chairs are stools.
Table is a chair.
Conclusions: I. Some stools are chairs.
II. Table is not a stool.

68. **Statements:** Some dogs bark.
All dogs bite.
Conclusions: I. Even those dogs who do not bark, bite.
II. Those dogs who do not bark, do not necessarily bite.

69. **Statements:** All poets are readers.
No reader is wise.
Conclusions: I. No poet is wise.
II. All readers are poets.

70. **Statements:** Some trees are houses.
Biscuit is a tree.
Conclusions: I. Biscuit is not a tree.
II. Some houses are trees.

71. **Statements:** All cows are Rambha.
Some buffaloes are Rambha.
Conclusions: I. All Rambhas are not cows.
II. Some Rambhas are not buffaloes.

72. **Statements:** Some rooms are stones.
All stones are radios.
Conclusions: I. Some rooms are radios.
II. Some stones are rooms.

73. **Statements:** Some gowns are shirts.
Some shirts are trousers.
Conclusions: I. Some gowns are trousers.
II. Some trousers are shirts.

74. **Statements:** Some books are cars.
Some cars are boxes.
Conclusions: I. Some books are boxes.
II. Some boxes are books.

75. **Statements:** Some dogs are horses.
No horse is black.
Conclusions: I. Some dogs are black.
II. Some horses are dogs.

76. **Statements:** All trucks fly.
Some scooters fly.
Conclusions: I. All trucks are scooters.
II. Some scooters do not fly.

77. **Statements:** All businessmen are hardworking.
No hardworking man is superstitious.
Conclusions: I. No businessman is superstitious.
II. All superstitious are not businessmen.

78. **Statements:** All educated people read newspapers.
Rahul does not read newspaper.
Conclusions: I. Rahul is not educated.
II. Reading newspaper is not essential to be educated.

79. **Statements:** All poets are authors.
All singers are authors.
Conclusions: I. All singers are poets.
II. Some authors are not singers.

80. **Statements:** Most crops are machines.
Some machines are fools.
Conclusions: I. Some fools are machines.
II. Some crops are fools.

81. **Statements:** Some clips are small.
All small are big.
Conclusions: I. All big are small.
II. All small are clips.

82. **Statements:** All windows are doors.
No door is a wall.
Conclusions: I. No window is a wall.
II. No wall is a door.

83. **Statements:** All stones are diamonds.
Some diamonds are pearls.
Conclusions: I. Some pearls are stones.
II. All diamonds are pearls.

84. **Statements:** All scholars are genius.
No woman is a scholar.
Conclusions: I. No woman is a genius.
II. All genius are men.

85. **Statements:** Some rivers are lakes.
All lakes are ponds.
Conclusions: I. All ponds are lakes.
II. Some rivers are ponds.

86. **Statements:** Some files are ants.
All insects are ants.
Conclusions: I. All files are ants.
II. Some ants are insects.

87. **Statements:** Some stones are cups.
Some cups are black.
Conclusions: I. Some blacks are not cups.
II. Some blacks are cups.

Type II: Exercise 11B

Directions: In each question below, there are two or three statements followed by four conclusions numbered I, II, III and IV. You have to take the given statements to be true even if they seem to be at variance with commonly known facts and then decide which of the given conclusions logically follow(s) from the given statements.

1. **Statements:** All hunters are punters.
Some punters are tigers.
Conclusions: I. Some hunters are tigers.
II. All tigers are punters.
III. Some punters are hunters.
IV. No punters are hunters.

1) I and II follow
2) II and III follow
3) I and III follow
4) II and IV follow
5) None of these

2. **Statements:** Some boxes are dogs.
All dogs are pens.
Conclusions: **I.** Some boxes are pens.
II. Some pens are boxes.
III. Some pens are dogs.
IV. All pens are dogs.
1) I, II and III follow
2) II, III and IV follow
3) I, III and IV follow
4) I, II and IV follow
5) All follow

3. **Statements:** Some diggers are jokers.
All jokers are cute.
Conclusions: **I.** Some diggers are cute.
II. No diggers are cute.
III. Some diggers are not cute.
IV. All diggers are cute.
1) I and III follow
2) Either II or IV follows
3) I and either III or IV follow
4) Either I or III follows
5) None of these

4. **Statements:** Some barbers are painters.
No painters are watches.
Conclusions: **I.** Some barbers are not watches.
II. Some barbers are watches.
III. Some watches are not barbers.
IV. Some watches are barbers.
1) I and III follow
2) Only I follows
3) Either I or II and III follow
4) Either III or IV and I follow
5) Either I or II and either III or IV follow

5. **Statements:** Some carts are darts.
No smart is cart.
Conclusions: **I.** Some darts are not smarts.
II. All darts are smarts.
III. Some smarts are not darts.
IV. All smarts are darts.
1) I and III follow
2) Only I follows
3) Only III follows
4) I and either III or IV follow
5) III and either I or II follow

6. **Statements:** Some boys are girls
All girls are cute.
Conclusions: I. Some boys are cute.
II. No boys are cute.
III. Some cute are girls.
IV. No cute are girls.
1) Only I follows
2) Only III follows
3) Either I or II follows
4) Either III or IV follows
5) I and III follow

7. **Statements:** Some copies are desks.
No desks are pens.
Conclusions: I. Some copies are pens.
II. Some copies are not pens.
III. Some pens are desks.
IV. Some pens are not desks.
1) Only II follows
2) II and III follow
3) Either I or II follows
4) II and IV follow
5) Either III or IV follows

8. **Statements:** All books are pens.
Some pens are pencils.
Conclusions: I. Some pens are books.
II. No pens are books.
III. Some books are pencils.
IV. No books are pencils.
1) I and III follow
2) Only I follows
3) Either I or II follows
4) Either III or IV and I follow
5) Either I or II and III follow

9. **Statements:** No systems are decks.
All decks are books.
Conclusions: I. Some systems are books.
II. Some systems are not books.
III. Some books are systems.
IV. Some books are not systems.
1) Only II follows
2) Only IV follows
3) II and IV follow
4) I and either HI or IV follow
5) Either I or II and IV follow

10. **Statements:** Some singers are rockers.
All rockers are westerners.
Conclusions: I. Some rockers are singers.
II. Some westerners are rockers.
III. Some singers are westerners.
IV. Some singers are not westerners.

1) I, II and III follow
2) I, II and IV follow
3) II, III and IV follow
4) I, III and IV follow
5) All follow

11. **Statements:** All cats are bulls.
Some bulls are dogs.
Conclusions: I. All bulls are cats.
II. Some cats are dogs.
III. No cats are dogs.
IV. Some bulls are cats.
1) Only IV follows
2) Only III follows
3) Only II follows
4) IV and II follow
5) IV and either II or III follow

12. **Statements:** All bars are coins.
Some bars are books.
Conclusions: I. Some books are bars.
II. Some books are coins.
III. Some books are not bars.
IV. Some books are not coins.
1) Only I follows
2) I and II follow
3) Either I or III follows
4) Either II or IV follows
5) I and either II or IV follow

13. **Statements:** Some stars are birds.
No birds are elephants.
Conclusions: I. Some stars are not elephants.
II. All stars are elephants.
III. Some elephants are not stars.
IV. All elephants are stars.
1) Either I or II and either III or IV follow
2) Only I follows
3) Either III or IV follows
4) I and III follow
5) I and either III or IV follow

14. **Statements:** No book is a hook.
All hooks are birds.
Conclusions: I. Some birds are not books.
II. Some birds are books.
III. Some books are not birds.
IV. Some books are birds.
1) Either I or II and either III or IV follow
2) Either I or II and III follow
3) Either III or IV and I follow
4) I and III follow
5) Only III follows

15. **Statements:** Some blankets are pillows.
All pillows are books.
Conclusions: I. Some books are blankets.
II. Some books are pillows.
III. No book is a pillow.
IV. Some blankets are not books.
1)1 and IV follow 2) I and II follow
3) I and either II or III follow 4) Either I or IV and II
5) Either I or IV or II or III follows

16. **Statements:** No girl is an Indian.
No American is an Indian
Conclusions: I. Some girls are Americans.
II. Some girls are not Americans.
III. All girls are Americans.
IV. No girls are Americans.
1) Only II follows 2) Only IV follows
3) Either I or II follows 4) Either III or IV follows
5) None of these

17. **Statements:** All classes are glasses.
All brasses are glasses.
Conclusions: I. Some classes are brasses.
II. Some brasses are glasses.
III. Some brasses are classes.
IV. Some classes are glasses.
1) Only I follows 2) Only II follows
3) I and II follow 4) II and IV follow
5) All follow

18. **Statements:** No Indian is an Asian.
Some Americans are Indians.
Conclusions: I. Some Indians are not Asians.
II. Some Asians are not Americans.
III. Some Americans are not Asians.
IV. All Americans are Asians.
1) Either III or IV follows 2) Either I or II follows
3) I and III follow 4) Either II or III follows
5) None of the above

19. **Statements:** Only red are blues.
All reds are yellows.
Conclusions: I. Some blues are yellows.
II. No blues are yellows.
III. Some yellows are reds.
IV. Some yellows are not reds.

1) Only I follows
2) Only III follows
3) Either I or II follows
4) Either III or IV fallows
5) I and III follows

20. **Statements:** Some songs are throngs.
Some throngs are longs.
Conclusions: I. Some songs are longs.
II. No songs are longs.
III. Only longs are songs.
IV. Only songs are longs.

1) Only I follows
2) Only III follows
3) Either I or II follows
4) Either III or IV follows
5) Either I or II and either III or IV follow

21. **Statements:** Some books are helmets.
Only copies are helmets.
Conclusions: I. Some books are copies.
II. All helmets are copies.
III. All copies are helmets.
IV. Some copies are not helmets.

1) I and II follow
2) II and III follow
3) I and III follow
4) I, II and either III or IV follow
5) None of the above

22. **Statements:** Some states are capitals.
No pens are capitals.
Conclusions: I. Some states are not pens.
II. All states are pens.
III. Some pens are not states.
IV. All pens are states.

1) Only I follows
2) Only III follows
3) Either I or II follows
4) Either III or IV and I follow
5) I and III follow

23. **Statements:** No pen is a pencil.
All pencils are streets.
Conclusions: I. No pen is a street.
II. No street is a pen.
III. Some streets are not pens.
IV. Some pens are not streets.

1) Only I follows
2) Only II follows
3) Only III follows
4) I, II and IV follow
5) I, II and III follow

24. **Statements:** All pigs are elephants.
No pig is baker.

Conclusions: I. Some bakers are not pigs.
II. Some pigs are not bakers.
III. Some elephants are not bakers.
IV. Some bakers are not elephants.

1) I, II and III follow
2) I, II and IV follow
3) I, III and IV follow
4) II, III and IV follow
5) All follow

25. **Statements:** All nibs are tips.
Many nibs are ribs.

Conclusions: I. Some nibs are tips.
II. Some tips are nibs.
III. All nibs are ribs.
IV. Some nibs are not ribs.

1) Only I follows
2) Only II follows
3) Either III or IV follows
4) I and II follow
5) I and II and either III or IV follow

26. **Statements:** Some charts are darts.
All darts are carts.
Some carts are smarts.

Conclusions: I. Some charts are carts.
II. Some carts are darts.
III. Some darts are smarts.
IV. Some smarts are charts.

1) Only I and III follow
2) Only II and III follow
3) I and II follow
4) I, III and IV follow
5) None of these

27. **Statements:** All boxes are tables.
No desk is table.
Some desks are curtains.

Conclusions: I. No boxes are desks.
II. Some boxes are desks.
III. Some curtains are not boxes.
IV. Some curtains are boxes.

1) III and either I or II follow
2) I and either III or IV follow
3) Either I or II and either III or IV follow
4) I and III follow
5) None of these

28. **Statements:** Some drops are cops.
All cops are docks.
No dock is a flop.

Conclusions: **I.** Some drops are not flops.
II. Some docks are drops.
III. No cop is a flop.
IV. Some flops are not cops.

1) I, II and III follow
2) II, III and IV follow
3) I, II and IV follow
4) I, III and IV follow
5) All follow

29. **Statements:** Some big are small.
No small is large.
Some large are tiny.

Conclusions: **I.** Some large are not big.
II. No big is large.
III. Some small are not tiny.
IV. Some big are not tiny.

1) Only I follows
2) Only II follows
3) Only III follows
4) Only IV follows
5) None follows

30. **Statements:** No student is decent.
Some decent are bags.
All bags are roses.

Conclusions: **I.** Some bags are not students.
II. All bags are students.
III. Some decents are roses.
IV. All roses are decent.

1) Only I follows
2) Either I or II follows
3) Only III follows
4) Either I or II, and III follow
5) I and III follow

31. **Statements:** Some birds are stones.
Some tigers are birds.
All stones are grapes.

Conclusions: **I.** Some stones are birds.
II. Some stones are not birds.
III. Some grapes are birds.
IV. Some tigers are stones.

1) I, II and III follow
2) I, III and IV follow
3) Either I or II and III follow
4) I and III follow
5) None of these

32. **Statements:** Some desks are tables.
All tables are icecreams.
Some icecreams are straps.

Conclusions: **I.** Some tables are icecreams.
II. Some desks are icecreams.
III. Some desks are straps.
IV. Some desks are not straps.

1) I, II and III follow
2) I, II and IV follow
3) II and III follow
4) II and either III or IV follow
5) I, II and either III or IV follow

33. **Statements:** No killer is a sweater.
No jacket is a sweater.
Some jackets are roses.

Conclusions: **I.** Some roses are sweaters.
II. Some roses are not sweaters.
III. No killer is a jacket.
IV. Some jackets are killers.

1) Either I or II and III follow
2) Either III or IV and II follow
3) Either II or III follows
4) Either I or II and either III or IV follow
5) None of the above is true

34. **Statements:** All blondes are beautiful.
All brunnettes are beautiful.
All brunnettes are cute.

Conclusions: **I.** Some cute are beautiful.
II. Some blondes are cute.
III. Some blondes are brunnettes.
IV. Some brunnettes are not cute.

1) Only I follows
2) Only II follows
3) Only III follows
4) Either II or III follows
5) I, II and III follow

35. **Statements:** Some boxes are chocolates.
Some tables are desks.
No box is a desk.

Conclusions: **I.** Some chocolates are desks.
II. Some chocolates are not desks.
III. Some tables are boxes.
IV. Some tables are not boxes.

1) Only I follows
2) Either I or II, and either III or IV follow
3) II and IV follow
4) Any three of the above follow.
5) None of the above is true.

36. **Statements:** Some drums are baskets.
All baskets are gaskets.

Conclusions: **I.** All gaskets are drums.
II. Some gaskets are drums.
III. Some gaskets are baskets.
IV. Some gaskets are not baskets.

1) Either II or IV follows
2) Either II or I follows
3) I and II follow
4) Only II follows
5) II and III follow

37. **Statements:** No paper is a graper.
All grapers are takers.

Conclusions: **I.** Some papers are not takers.
II. Some papers are takers.
III. Some takers are not papers.
IV. All takers are papers.

1) Either I or II follows
2) Only I follows
3) Either III or IV follows
4) Only III follows
5) Either I or II and III follow

38. **Statements:** Many bucks are ducks.
All trucks are ducks.

Conclusions: **I.** Some ducks are not bucks.
II. Some bucks are trucks.
III. Some ducks are trucks.
IV. All ducks are trucks.

1) Only I follows
2) II and III follow
3) Only III follows
4) Only IV follows
5) III and IV follow

39. **Statements:** All students are patriots.
All Indians are patriots.

Conclusions: **I.** Some students are Indians.
II. Some Indians are students.
III. All Indians are students.
IV. All students are Indians.

1) Only I and III follow
2) Only II and IV follow
3) Only I and II follow
4) I and II and either III or IV follow
5) None follows

40. **Statements:** Some tables are chairs.
All tables are lawns.

Conclusions: **I.** Some chairs are lawns.
II. Some chairs are not lawns.
III. Some tables are lawns.
IV. Some tables are not lawns.

1) Either I or II follows
2) Either I or II and III follow
3) Only II and III follow
4) II and either III or IV follow
5) None of these

41. **Statements:** Some turks are studs.
All studs are gritty.

Conclusions: I. All turks are gritty.
II. Some gritty are turks.
III. Some gritty are studs.
IV. All studs are turks.

1) Only I follows
2) Only I, II and III follow
3) All follow
4) Only II and III follow
5) None follows

42. **Statements:** All bricks are tricks.
Some tricks are bicks.

Conclusions: I. No brick is a bick.
II. Some bricks are bicks.
III. Some bicks are tricks.
IV. Some tricks are not bicks.

1) Only II follows
2) Only II and IV follow
3) Only II and III follow
4) Either I or II follows
5) Either I or II, and III follow

43. **Statements:** Some gardens are wardens.
All gardens are locks.

Conclusions: I. Some locks are not wardens.
II. Some locks are wardens.
III. No lock is a warden.
IV. Some locks are gardens.

1) Only I follows
2) Only II and IV follow
3) Either I or II follows
4) Either I or II and IV follow
5) Either I or II and III follow

44. **Statements:** Only books are readable.
Only eatables are books.

Conclusions: I. All readables are books.
II. Some readables are books.
III. All readables are eatables.
IV. All eatables are readables.

1) Only I and III follow
2) Only I and IV follow
3) Either I or II and III follow
4) Either I or II and IV follow
5) I, II and III follow

45. **Statements:** Some bags are packets.
Some packets are keys.
Conclusions: I. Some bags are keys.
II. Some packets are bags.
III. Some bags are not keys.
IV. Some packets are not bags.
1) I and II follow
2) Either I or III and II follow
3) I and either II or IV follow
4) Either I or III and either II or IV follow
5) None of the above

46. **Statements:** All grasses are brasses.
All brasses are wickets.
Conclusions: I. Some brasses are grasses.
II. Some wickets are grasses.
III. Some grasses are not wickets.
IV. All wickets are brasses.
1) Only I and II follow
2) Only II and III follow
3) Only I and III follow
4) Only I and IV follow
5) All follow

47. **Statements:** All teachers are students.
Some students are gypsies.
Conclusions: I. All teachers are gypsies.
II. Some gypsies are teachers.
III. Some gypsies are students.
IV. All students are teachers.
1) Only I follows
2) Only I, II and III follow
3) Only III follows
4) Only II and III follow
5) None of the above

48. **Statements:** Some trees are sharks.
Some sharks are balloons.
Conclusions: I. All balloons are sharks.
II. All balloons are trees.
III. Some trees are balloons.
IV. No tree is a balloon.
1) Only I follows
2) Only II and III follow
3) Only either I or III follows
4) Only either I or IV follows
5) Only either III or IV follows

49. **Statements:** Some snakes are cute.
All cute are wicked.

Conclusions: **I.** Some cute are snakes.
II. No cute is a snake.
III. Some wicked are snakes.
IV. All wicked are snakes.

1) Only I follows 2) Only either I or II follows
3) Only either III or IV follows 4) Only I and III follow
5) None of the above

50. **Statements:** Some bricks are not sockets.
No socket is a pouch.

Conclusions: **I.** No brick is a pouch.
II. Some bricks are not pouches.
III. Some sockets are bricks.
IV. No socket is a brick.

1) Only either III or IV follows 2) Only II and III follow
3) Only I and III follow 4) All follow
5) None follows

51. **Statements:** Some greens are teens.
All teens are cleans.

Conclusions: **I.** All greens are cleans.
II. Some greens are cleans.
III. Some cleans are teens.
IV. All teens are greens.

1) Only I follows 2) Only I, II and III follow
3) All follow 4) Only II and III follow
5) None of these

52. **Statements:** All girls are cute.
All cutes are westernised.

Conclusions: **I.** Some cutes are girls.
II. No cute is a girl.
III. Some westernised are girls.
IV. All westernised are girls.

1) Only I follows 2) Either I or II follows
3) Either III or IV follows 4) Only I and III follow
5) None of the above

53. **Statements:** Some biscuits are pens.
Some pens are pouches.

Conclusions: **I.** Some biscuits are pouches.
II. Some pouches are pens.
III. Some pouches are not pens.
IV. Some biscuits are not pouches.

1) Only II follows
2) I and II follow
3) Either II or III follow
4) Either I or IV follows
5) II and either I or IV follow

54. **Statements:** Some girls are brunettes.
No brunette is wicked.

Conclusions: I. Some brunettes are girls.
II. Some wickeds are girls.
III. Some girls are not wicked.
IV. All wickeds are girls.

1) Only I follows
2) Either II or III follows
3) Only I and III follow
4) Only I and II follow
5) Either III or IV follows

55. **Statements:** All tractors are scooters.
Some scooters are boys.

Conclusions: I. All boys are scooters.
II. All boys are tractors.
III. Some tractors are boys.
IV. No tractor is a boy.

1) Only I follows
2) Only II and III follows
3) Either II or III follows
4) Either I or IV follows
5) Either III or IV follows

Type III: Exercise 11C

Directions (Q. 1-25): Below are given three statements, a, b and c, followed by four conclusions. You have to take the given statements to be true even if they appear to be at variance with commonly known facts and then decide which of the conclusions logically follow(s) from the given statements. For each question, mark an appropriate answer choice that you think is correct.

1. **Statements: a.** All bulbs are radios.
b. All radios are fans.
c. No fans are tables.

Conclusions: I. Some fans are bulbs.
II. No table is a bulb.
III. Some radios are bulbs.
IV. Some tables are radios.

1) I, II and III follow
2) II, III and IV follow
3) Only I and II follow
4) Only I and III follow
5) II and IV follow

2. **Statements:** **a.** Some books are bulbs.
b. All biscuits are pens.
c. No bulb is a biscuit.

Conclusions: **I.** Some books are not biscuits.
II. Some bulbs are not pens.
III. Some books are not pens.
IV. Some pens are not bulbs.

1) I and IV follow 2) II and IV follow
3) I and III follow 4) II and III follow
5) I, II and IV follow

3. **Statements:** **a.** All books are notes.
b. Some notes are watches.
c. No watch is a pencil.

Conclusions: **I.** Some watches are books.
II. Some notes are pencils.
III. No watch is a book.
IV. Some notes are not pencils.

1) I and either II or IV follow 2) I, III and IV follow
3) I, II and III follow 4) Only I and IV follow
5) Either I or III and IV follow

4. **Statements:** **a.** Some blondes are Indians.
b. Some Asians are blondes.
c. No Asian is a brunette.

Conclusions: **I.** Some Indians are Asians.
II. Some blondes are brunettes.
III. Some brunettes are not blondes.
IV. Some blondes are not brunettes.

1) I and IV follow 2) II and III follow
3) Only III follows 4) Only IV follows
5) Either II or IV and III follow

5. **Statements:** **a.** All nips are tips.
b. No coin is a tip.
c. Some balls are nips.

Conclusions: **I.** Some balls are coins.
II. Some balls are tips.
III. Some coins are not balls.
IV. Some balls are not coins.

1) Only II and III follow 2) Only II and IV follow
3) Either I or IV follows 4) Only IV follows
5) Either I or IV, and III follow

6. **Statements:** **a.** All crooks are spooks.
b. All books are jokes.
c. Some books are crooks.

Conclusions: **I.** Some jokes are crooks.
II. Some spooks are jokes.
III. Some crooks are jokes.
IV. Some spooks are books.

1) I, II and III follow
2) II, III and IV follow
3) I, III and IV follow
4) I, II and IV follow
5) All follow

7. **Statements:** **a.** Some papers are nibs.
b. No file is a cutter.
c. Some files are papers.

Conclusions: **I.** Some files are nibs.
II. Some papers are cutters.
III. Some files are not nibs.
IV. Some papers are not cutters.

1) Either I or III, and II follow
2) Either I or III, and IV follow
3) Either II or IV, and I follow
4) Either II or IV, and III follow
5) Either II or IV, and either I or III follow

8. **Statements:** **a.** All gardens are boxes.
b. Some gardens are flowers.
c. No chocolate is a box.

Conclusions: **I.** Some flowers are chocolates.
II. No garden is a chocolate.
III. Some flowers are boxes.
IV. Some flowers are not chocolates.

1) II, III and IV follow
2) I, III and IV follow
3) Only II and III follow
4) Only III and either I or IV follow
5) Only II, III and either I or IV follow

9. **Statements:** **a.** Some bulbs are chocolates.
b. No fruit is a bulb.
c. Only Amul is a chocolate.

Conclusions: **I.** Some fruits are not chocolates.
II. Some chocolates are not fruits.
III. Some bulbs are Amuls.
IV. No bulb is an Amul.

1) Only II and III follow
2) Only II and IV follow
3) Either III or IV follows
4) Either III or IV and I follow
5) Only I and III follow

10. **Statements:** **a.** Some Indians are not Africans.
b. All Africans are Asians.
c. Some Asians are Americans.
Conclusions: **I.** Some Indians are not Asians.
II. Some Indians are not Americans.
III. All Africans are Americans.
IV. Some Americans are Indians.
1) Only I follows 2) Only II follows
3) Only III follows 4) Only IV follows
5) Either II or IV follows

11. **Statements:** **a.** Some cards are papers.
b. All papers are vans.
c. Some vans are trams.
Conclusions: **I.** Some cards are trams.
II. Some papers are trams.
III. Some trams are papers.
IV. Some vans are cards.
1) II and III follow 2) I and IV follow
3) Only IV follows 4) II, III and IV follow
5) I, II and III follow

12. **Statements:** **a.** No fruit is a mango.
b. No oranges is a potato.
c. All mangoes are oranges.
Conclusions: **I.** Some fruits are not oranges.
II. Some oranges are not fruits.
III. No mango is a potato.
IV. Some oranges are fruits.
1) Only III and I follow 2) Only II and IV follow
3) Either II or IV follow 4) Only II and III follow
5) Either II or IV and III follow

13. **Statements:** **a.** Some carts are docks.
b. All carts are clocks.
c. No frock is a clock.
Conclusions: **I.** All carts are clocks.
II. No frock is a cart.
III. Some docks are not frocks.
IV. Some docks are frocks.
1) Either III or IV follows 2) Only I and II follow.
3) I, II and III follow 4) I, II and either III or IV follow
5) I and either III or IV follow

14. **Statements:** **a.** Some tablets are capsules.
b. No capsule is a medicine.
c. All medicines are syrups.

Conclusions: **I.** Some tablets are not medicines.
II. Some medicines are not capsules.
III. Some syrups are medicines.
IV. Some syrups are not capsules.

1) I, II and III follow
2) I, III and IV follow
3) II, III and IV follow
4) I, II and IV follow
5) All follow

15. **Statements:** **a.** All coats are pants.
b. No pant is a shirt.
c. Some shirts are vests.

Conclusions: **I.** Some vests are shirts.
II. Some coats are shirts.
III. No coat is a shirt.
IV. Some vests are not coats.

1) I, II and III follow
2) I and IV follow
3) I and III follow
4) I, III and IV follow
5) I, IV and either II or III follow

16. **Statements:** **a.** All chalks are cheese.
b. No cheese is a ship.
c. Some herds are ships.

Conclusions: **I.** Some herds are not chalks.
II. Some herds are not cheese.
III. Some cheese are not herds.
IV. No chalk is a ship.

1) I, III and IV follow
2) II, III and IV follow
3) II and IV follow
4) III and II follow
5) I, II and IV follow

17. **Statements:** **a.** Some birds are peacocks.
b. No cock is a hen.
c. All hens are peacocks.

Conclusions: **I.** Some cocks are peacocks.
II. Some birds are hens.
III. No cock is a peacock.
IV. Some peacocks are not cocks.

1) Either I or IV follows
2) II and IV follow
3) Either I or III and IV follow
4) Either I or III, II and IV follow
5) Only II follows

18. **Statements:** **a.** Only stars are moons.
b. No cosmos is a star.
c. No planets are moons.
Conclusions: **I.** Some moons are not planets.
II. No moon is a cosmos.
III. No cosmos is a planet.
IV. No star is a planet.
1) I, II and IV follow 2) I, III and IV follow
3) II, III and IV follow 4) III and IV follow
5) I and II follow

19. **Statements:** **a.** Some bunkers are arms.
b. No gun is a dagger.
c. All arms are daggers.
Conclusions: **I.** No arm is a gun.
II. Some bunkers are not guns.
III. Some daggers are bunkers.
IV. Some daggers ate not bunkers.
1) Only I and II follow 2) I, II and III follow
3) Either III or IV follows 4) I, II and either III or IV follow
5) II and III follow

20. **Statements:** **a.** No minister is honest.
b. Some politicians are females.
c. All politicians are ministers.
Conclusions: **I.** Some honest are not females.
II. No honest person is a politician.
III. Some females are ministers.
IV. Some females are not honest.
1) I, II and III follow 2) II and III follow
3) I and II follow 4) II, III and IV follow
5) I and III follow

21. **Statements:** **a.** Some blondes are stupid.
b. Some trees are blondes.
c. All stupid are girls.
Conclusions: **I.** Some stupid are blondes.
II. Some stupid are not blondes.
III. Some girls are blondes.
IV. Some trees are stupid.
1) I, II and III follow 2) I, III and IV follow
3) Either I or II and III follow 4) I and III follow
5) None of these

22. **Statements:** **a.** Some doctors are treatments
b. All treatments are Indians.
c. Some Indians are stars.
Conclusions: **I.** Some treatments are Indians.
II. Some doctors are Indians.
III. Some doctors are stars.
IV. Some doctors are not stars.
1) I, II and III follow
2) I, II and IV follow
3) II and III follow
4) II and either III or IV follow
5) I, II and either III or IV follow

23. **Statements:** **a.** No kite is a slate.
b. No jug is a slate.
c. Some jugs are ropes.
Conclusions: **I.** Some ropes are slates.
II. Some ropes are not slates.
III. No kite is a jug.
IV. Some jugs are kites.
1) Either I or II and III follow
2) Either III or IV and II follow
3) Either II or III follows
4) Either I or II and either III or IV follow
5) None of these above is true

24. **Statements:** **a.** All blanks are beamers.
b. All bridges are beamers.
c. All bridges are cows.
Conclusions: **I.** Some cows are beamers.
II. Some blanks are cows.
III. Some blanks are bridges.
IV. Some bridges are not cows.
1) Only I follows
2) Only II follows
3) Only III follows
4) Either II or III follows
5) I, II and III follow

25. **Statements:** **a.** Some bags are charts.
b. Some trees are docks.
c. No bag is a dock.
Conclusions: **I.** Some charts are docks.
II. Some charts are not docks.
III. Some trees are bags.
IV. Some trees are not bags.
1) Only II follows
2) Either I or II and either III or IV follow
3) II and IV follow
4) Any three of I, II, III and IV are true
5) None of the above is true

Answers and Explanations

Exercise 11A

1. a; A + A = A. ∴ I follows.
2. d; A + I = No conclusion.
3. e; I + I = No conclusion. But both conclusions follow directly from the given statements.
4. a; 1st sentence = Kite is a stick (A)
   2nd sentence = Some sticks are bolts (I)
   Now, A + I = No conclusion.
   But Some sticks are bolts → on conversion → Some bolts are sticks.
   ∴ I follows.
5. d; I + I = No conclusion.
6. c; Change it to: Shobha is very fair (A) + Some fair girls are married to lawyers (I) = A + I
   = No conclusion.
   But, one of the choices must be true. Hence, either I or II follows.
7. a; A + I = No conclusion. But All coats are bags → on conversion → Some bags are coats.
   ∴ I follows.
8. a; A + A = A. ∴ I follows.
9. b; A + E = E. ∴ II follows.
10. d; I + I = No conclusion.
11. b; A + I = No conclusion. But, Some trees are hens → on conversion → Some hens are trees.
12. b; First, align. All cats are birds + Some birds are snakes (converted form of first sentence) = A + I = No conclusion. But II is nevertheless true.
13. a; A + E = E.
14. e; All astronauts are pilots + All pilots are brave men = A + A = A = All astronauts are brave. Also, All astronauts are pilots → on conversion → Some pilots are astronauts.
15. b; I + A = I. Hence, II follows.
16. b; A + A = A. Hence, II follows.
17. a; Change to: Rohit is non-intelligent + No student of my class is non-intelligent = A + E = E = Rohit is not a student of my class. Conclusion II has no logical deduction, even though it may look true.
18. d; Sachin is honest + Some honest are boys = A + I = No conclusion.
19. a; I + A = I. ∴ Some books are clips.
20. e; A + E = E. ∴ No lock is a spoon. Again, this may be converted to → No spoon is a lock.
21. d; This is a good tricky question. A + E = E.
    ∴ No young scientists are superstitious. But conclusion I does not talk of only 'young' scientists. It says 'scientists'. Hence, the conclusion

"No scientists are superstitious" is invalid. Similarly, "No young are superstitious" is also invalid.

22. d; I + A = I. ∴ Some hats are watches. But this conclusion is not given.
23. a; First align by changing the order. Some women are politicians + All politicians are intelligent = I + A = I = Some women are intelligent.
24. b; A + E = E
25. a; I + A = I
26. a; I + E = O. ∴ Some desks are not red. But this conclusion is not given. However, conclusion I is obvious.
27. d; A + I = No conclusion.
28. d; All trees are tables + Some tables are glasses = A + I = No conclusion.
29. a; I + I = No conclusion. But second sentence on conversion, gives: Some walls are fans.
30. d; First align by converting the second sentence to: Some tables are children. Then, A + I = No conclusion.
31. a; A + A = A
32. d; I + I = No conclusion.
33. d; All pens are erasers → on conversion → Some erasers are pens. Now, All trays are erasers + Some erasers are pens = A + I = No conclusion.
34. a; All toffees are chocolates → on conversion → Some chocolates are toffees.
35. d; I + I = No conclusion.
36. c; A + I = No conclusion. But if we convert conclusion I and take it along with conclusion II they make an I-E pair which is a complementary pair. So, either of them follows.
37. a; I + E = O. ∴ Some authors are not ladies. But this conclusion is not given. However, 'No teacher is a lady' means that 'Some teachers are not ladies' must always be correct. Hence, the answer choice is (a).
38. d; Align : Some politicians are women + No women can vote = I − E = O = Some politicians can not vote. But this conclusion is not given.
39. d; See Q. 21.
40. a; A + A = A
41. a; All writers are teachers → on conversion → Some teachers are writers. Now, All readers are teachers + Some teachers are writers = A + I = No conclusion. But I is valid, nevertheless.
42. d; A + I = no conclusion.
43. a; Align: (change order) Some women are lawyers + All lawyers are cheats = I + A = I = Some women are peats.
44. d; A + E = E = No plant is green. But this conclusion is not given.
45. a; X is a hill-station + All hill-stations have a sunset point = A + A = A = X has a sunset point.

46. c; I + I = No conclusion. But the choices make a complementary pair: at least one is always true.
47. d; I + E = O = Some parrots are not green. But this conclusion is not given.
48. b; Some men are clerks + All clerks are lazy = I + A = I = Some men are lazy.
49. d; A + I = No conclusion.
50. b; I + E = O
51. c; No conclusion can be derived as there are four terms instead of the usual three: aeroplanes, living beings, non-living beings and ghosts. However, one of the two facts, 'Some aeroplanes are ghosts' and 'Some aeroplanes are not ghosts' must be correct.
52. d; I + A = I. ∴ Some papers are sharp. But this conclusion is not given.
53. c; Choices make a complementary pair.
54. c; I + I = No conclusion. But, on second thought, any soldier must be either famous or intelligent or none of these. Hence, either of the choices follow.
55. c; A + I = No conclusion. But the choices make a complementary pair.
56. d; Align : All wheels are machines + Some machines are racks = A + I = No conclusion.
57. d; A + E = E. No roads are houses. But this conclusion is not given.
58. b; I + A = I.
59. c; Align : Sohan is tall + Some tall are players = A + I = No conclusion. But, Sohan should either be a player or a non-player. Hence, either of the two choices follows.
60. a; A + E = E.
61. d; I + I = No conclusion.
62. b; All horses are dogs → on conversion → Some dogs are horses.
63. a; All beds are towels → on conversion → Some towels are beds.
64. e; Align: Some men are thieves + No boy is a thief = Some men are thieves + No thief is a boy (converted) = I + E = O = Some men are not boys. Also, conclusion II follows from the first statement obviously.
65. e; A + E = E. ∴ No dresses are brown. Also, All dresses are shoes → on conversion → Some shoes are dresses.
66. e; I + A = I. ∴ Some hens are horses. Again, Some hens are horses → on conversion → Some horses are hens.
67. a; Some chairs are stools → on conversion → Some stools are chairs.
68. a; No conclusion can be derived from the two given statements. But conclusion I must be true nevertheless because *all dogs bite.*
69. a; A + E = E
70. b; Some trees are horses → on conversion → Some horses are trees.
71. d; All cows are rambhas + Some rambhas are buffaloes = A + I = No conclusion.
72. e; I + A = I. ∴ Some rooms are radios. Also, Some rooms are stones → on

conversion → Some stones are rooms.

73. b; I + I = No conclusion. But, Some shirts are trousers → on conversion → Some trousers are shirts.

74. d; I + I = No conclusion.

75. b; I + E = O. ∴ Some dogs are not black. This conclusion is not given. But, Some dogs are horses → on conversion → Some horses are dogs.

76. d; Try yourself.

77. e; A + E = E. ∴ No businessmen are superstitious. Further, No businessmen are superstitious → on conversion → No superstitious are businessmen. If it is true that no superstitious are businessmen then the O proposition 'All superstitious are not businessmen' also must be true.

78. a; Try yourself.

79. d; See Q. 41.

80. a; Some machines are fools → on conversion → Some fools are machines.

81. d; Try yourself.

82. e; A + E = E. Also, convert the second sentence.

83. d; A + I = No conclusion.

84. d; Align : No woman is scholar + All scholars are genius. Now, E + I = O = Some genius are not women. But this conclusion is not given.

85. b; I + A = I.

86. b; Try yourself.

87. b; Try yourself.

Exercise 11B

1. 5; A + I = No conclusion. But 'Some punters are hunters' follows from 'All hunters are punters'. So, only III follows.

2. 1; 'Some boxes are pens' follows by the rule I + A = I. This can be converted to 'Some pens are boxes'. 'Some pens are dogs' follows from 'All dogs are pens'.

3. 3; I + A = I. Hence, only 'Some diggers are cute' follows. But III and IV are complementary.

4. 4; I + E = O. Hence, conclusion I follows. Conclusions II and IV make a complementary pair.

5. 4; Rearrange as: "No smarts are carts + Some carts are darts" = E + I = O reversed. Hence, 'Some darts are not smarts' follows. Also, III and IV make a complementary pair.

6. 5; I + A = I. Hence, 'Some boys are cute' follows. III follows from 'All girls are cute'.

7. 4; I + E = O. Hence, 'Some copies are not pens' follows. Again, 'Some pens are not desks' is obvious from 'No desks are pens'.

8. 4; I follows directly from 'All books are pens'. III and IV are a complementary pair. [III does not follow *definitely* because of the rule: I + I = No conclusion.]

9. 5; E + A = O reversed. Hence, 'Some books are not systems' follows. Again, I and II are a complementary pair.

10. 1; I follows from 'Some singers are rockers' while II follows from 'All rockers are westerners' III follows from the rule: I + A = I.

11.5; We have: All cats are bulls + Some bulls are dogs = A + I = No conclusion. But, "Some bulls are cats" follows on conversion from "All cats are bulls". Again, II and III make a (I-E type) complementary pair.

12. 2; Rewrite the sentences in this order:
Some bars are books → on conversion → Some books are bars. Hence, I follows. Now, Some books are bars + All bars are coins = I + A = I = Some books are coins. Hence, II follows.

13. 5; Some stars are birds + No birds are elephants = I + E = O. Hence, "Some stars are not elephants" follows. Again, III and IV make a complementary pair [O-A type]. Hence, one of them must be true.

14. 3; No book is a hook + All hooks are birds = E + A = O reversed. Hence, "Some birds are not books" follows. Again, III and IV make a [I-O type] complementary pair; hence one of them must be true.

15. 2; Some blankets are pillows + All pillows are books = I + A = I. Hence, "Some blankets are books" follows. This may be converted to "Some books are blankets". Hence, I follows. Also, "All pillows are books" → on conversion → "Some books are pillows". Hence, II follows.

16. 3; E + E = No conclusion. Hence, no definite conclusion can be established between 'girl' and 'American'. But I and II form a complementary pair: one of them will always be true. Note that I, IV and II, III are also complementary but no such choice is given.

17. 4; All classes are glasses → on conversion → Some glasses are classes. Now, All brasses are glasses + All classes are glasses = All classes are glasses + Some glasses are brasses = A + I = No conclusion. Hence, no conclusion can be established between 'brasses' and 'classes'. But All classes are glasses → obviously → Some classes are glasses. Similarly, All brasses are glasses → Some brasses are glasses.

18. 3; Some Americans are Indians + No Indian is an Asian = I + E = O = Some Americans are not Asians. Hence, III follows. Again, No Indian is an Asian → obviously → Some Indians are not Asians.

19. 5; We know that, Only reds are blues → on conversion (on conversion an exclusive proposition becomes A-type) → All blues are reds. Hence, Only reds are blues + All reds are yellows = All blues are yellows (A + A = A) → obviously → Some blues are yellows. Hence, I follows. Again, All reds are yellows → on conversion → Some yellows are reds.

20. 3; I + I = No conclusion. Hence, no conclusion can be established between 'songs' and 'longs'. But we see that I and II form a complementary pair. One of them must be true. Hence, either of them follows.

21.4; We know that propositions beginning with 'Only' are called exclusive propositions and they can be converted to A-type propositions by interchanging the subject and the predicate. Thus, we have "Only copies are helmets" → "All helmets are copies." Now, some books are helmets + only copies are helmets = Some books are helmets + All helmets are copies = I + A = I = Some books are copies. Thus, I and II follow. Further, statements III and IV, being A-O pair, form a complementary pair and hence, at any time, one of them must be true. Hence, either III or IV also follows.

22. 4; Some states are capitals + No pens are capitals = Some states are capitals + No capitals are pens (on conversion) = I + E = O = Some states are not pens. Hence, I follows. II, III and IV do not follow by the given statements, but III and IV make a complementary pair.

23. 3; No pen is a pencil + All pencils are streets = E + A = O reversed = Some streets are not pens. Hence, III follows.

24. 1; No pigs are bakers. (If E is true, O obviously follows). Similarly, No pigs are bakers → on conversion → No bakers are pigs → (obviously) → Some bakers are not pigs. Thus, I and II shall follow. Again. All pigs are elephants + No pigs are bakers = I + E = O = Some elephants are not bakers. Thus, III follows.

25. 5; Many nibs are tips = Some nibs are tips → on conversion → Some tips are nibs. Hence, II follows. Also, III and IV, being an A-O pair, make a complementary pair and hence either of these must be true. I is obvious.

26. 3; Some charts are darts + All darts are carts = I + A = I = Some charts are carts. Hence, I follows. Again, All darts are carts → on conversion → Some carts are darts. Hence, II follows. All darts are carts + Some carts are smarts = A + I =No conclusion. Hence, III does not follow. On the same logic, you can see that IV does not follow.

27.4; All boxes are tables + No desks are tables = All boxes are tables + No tables are desks (converted form) = A + E = E = No boxes are desks. Hence, I follows. Again, No boxes are desks + Some desks are curtains = E + I = O reversed = Some curtains are not boxes.

28. 5; Some drops are cops + All cops are docks = I + A = I = Some drops are docks. → on conversion → Some docks are drops. Hence, II follows. Now, Some drops are docks + No dock is a flop = I + E = O = Some drops are not flops. Hence, I follows. Again, All cops are docks + No dock is a flop. = A + E = E = No cop is a flop. Hence, II follows. Finally, No cop is a flop → (obviously) → Some flops are not cops. Hence, IV also follows.

29. 5; Possible conclusions are: from first two statements, I + E = O, hence, 'Some big are not large'; and from second and third statements, E + I = O reversed, hence 'Some tiny are not small'. Thus, a possible conclusion relating 'big' and 'large' is 'Some big are not large', and since I and II are

different from this, both do not follow. Similarly, a possible conclusion between 'tiny' and 'small' is 'some tiny are not small' which is different from 'some small are not tiny'. Hence, III does not follow. To see the validity of the fourth conclusion, we need to find a conclusion relating 'big' and 'tiny'. Since 'big' is in the first statement and 'tiny' in the third statement, we have a chain of I + E + I = (I + E) + I = O + I = No conclusion. Hence, IV also does not follow.

30. 5; E + I = O reversed (∴ No student is decent + Some decent are bags = Some bags are not students). Hence, I follows. Again I + A = I, hence III follows.

31.4; Some birds are stones → on conversion → Some stones are birds. Hence I follows. Also, Some birds are stones + All stones are grapes = I + A = I = Some birds are grapes → on conversion → Some grapes are birds. Hence, III follows.

32. 5; Some desks are tables + All tables are icecreams = I + A = I = Some desks are icecreams. Hence, II follows. Also, All tables are icecreams → (obviously) → Some tables are icecreams. Hence, I follows. Ill and IV form a complementary pair, one of them has to be true. (See 'Controversy on syllogism') Hence, either III or IV follows.

33. 2; Some jackets are roses → on conversion → Some roses are jackets. Now, Some roses are jackers + No jacket is a sweater = I + E = O = Some roses are not sweaters. Hence, II follows. Also, III and IV form a complementary pair; at least one of them will always be true, hence either III or IV follows.

34. 1; All brunnettes are cute → on conversion → Some cute are brunnettes. Now, Some cute are brunnettes + All brunnettes are beautiful = I + A = I = Some cute are beautiful. Hence, I follows.

35.3; Some boxes are chocolates → on conversion → Some chocolates are boxes. Now, Some chocolates are boxes + No box is a desk = I + E = O = Some chocolates are not desks. Hence, II follows. Again, No box is a desk → on conversion → No desk is a box. Now, Some tables are desks + No desk is a box = I + E = O = Some tables are not boxes. Hence, IV follows.

36. 5; I + A = I. Hence, Some drums are gaskets follows. This gives, on conversion, Some gaskets are drums. Also, Some gaskets are baskets follows on converting All baskets are gaskets.

37. 5; E + A = O reversed. Hence, Some takers are not papers follows. Further, I and II are an I-O pair. They are complementary and either of them must be true.

38. 3; The sentences are not aligned because the common term 'ducks' is at the end in both the statements. To align them, we convert the second statement to 'Some ducks are trucks'. Hence, III follows. Now, I + I = No conclusion. Other conclusions don't follow.

39. 5; Similar explanation as in previous question.

40. 5; Only I and III follow.
41. 4; I + A = I. Hence, Some turks are gritty. This gives, on conversion, Some gritty are turks. Ill follows on converting All studs are gritty.
42. 5; I and II make a complementary pair (E-I); hence one must be true. III follows on converting Some tricks are kicks.
43. 2; Some gardens are wardens + All gardens are locks = Some wardens are gardens (converted) + All gardens are locks = I + A = I = Some wardens are locks. This, on conversion, gives II. IV follows after converting, All gardens are locks.
44. 5; **Note:** 'Only S are P' is an exclusive proposition. On conversion, this gives, 'All P are S'. Now, 'Only books are readables' gives All readables are books. Similarly, Only eatables are books gives All books are eatables. Now, All readables are books + All books are eatables = A + A = A = All readables are eatables. Conclusion II is obvious from conclusion I.
45. 2; I and III form a complementary pair. II follows after converting the first statement.
46. 1; Some brasses are grasses, follows from the conversion of All grasses are brasses. Further, All grasses are brasses + All brasses are wickets = A + A = A = All grasses are wickets → on conversion → Some wickets are grasses. Hence, II follows.
47. 3; A + I = No conclusion. Hence, no definite conclusion can be established between 'teachers' and 'gypsies'. This negates I and II. III follows because it is the converted form of Some students are gypsies. IV does not follow.
48. 5; I + I = No conclusion. Hence, no definite conclusion can be established between 'trees' and 'balloons'. This negates II, III and IV. But III and IV are an I-E pair or a complementary pair. So, one of them must be true. I does not follow in any way. Thus, a suitable choice is not given.
49. 4; I + A = I. Hence, Some snakes are wicked follows. This, on conversion, gives Some wicked are snakes. Further, Some snakes are cute gives, on conversion, Some cute are snakes.
50. 1; O + E = No conclusion. So, no conclusion can be established between 'bricks' and 'pouches'. But, looking at the answer choices, we see that III and IV are a complementary pair: one of them must be true.
51. 4; I + A = I. Hence, Some greens are cleans follows. Also, on converting "All teens are cleans" we obtain "Some cleans are teens".
52. 4; A + A = A. Hence, "All girls are westernised" follows. On conversion, this gives "Some westernised are girls." Hence, II follows. Also, on converting All girls are cute, Some cute girls follows.
53. 5; I + I = No conclusion. Hence, no conclusion can be established between 'biscuits' and 'pouches'. But the two given conclusions between

'biscuits' and 'pouches' are an I-O pair; hence they are complementary. Thus, either I or IV follows. Again, Some pens are pouches gives, on conversion, Some pouches are pens.

54. 3; I + E = O. Hence, Some girls are not wicked follows. Also, Some brunettes are girls follows from Some girls are brunettes on conversion.

55. 5; A + I = No conclusion. But, III and IV form an E-I (which is complementary) pair. So, one of them must be true.

Exercise 11C

1. 1; All bulbs are radios + All radios are fans = All bulbs are fans. [∴ A + A - A] → Some fans are bulbs [on conversion]. III follows on converting the first statement. Also, All bulbs are fan + No fans are tables = No bulbs are tables [∵ This gives, No tables are bulbs on conversion.]

2. 1; (a) + (c) gives I [∴ I + E = O]. (c) + (b) gives IV [∴ E + A = O reversed]. No other conclusion is possible.

3. 5; I and III have a conclusion between 'watches' and 'books'. For a conclusion between watches and books our relevant statements are (a) and (b). Now, (a) + (b) = A + I = No conclusion. But, I and III make an I-E pair, which is complementary. Hence, either of them follows. Also, (b) + (c) = I + E = O = Conclusion IV.

4. 4; (b) can be converted to "Some blondes are Asians". This plus (c) gives conclusion IV [∵ I + E = O]. No other conclusion is possible.

5. 2; (c) + (a) gives conclusion II [∴ I + A = I]. Conclusion II + converted form of (b), gives conclusion IV [∴ I + E = O]. (**Note:** converted form of (b) is : No tips are coins.)

6. 5; (c) + (a) gives Some books are spooks [∵ I + A = I], which may be converted to conclusion IV. Converted form of (c) [which is: Some crooks are books] + (b) gives conclusion III. From conclusion III, we get conclusion I, on conversion. Conclusion II automatically follows from conclusion IV + (b).

7. 2; (c) gives, on conversion, "Some papers are files". This plus (b) gives conclusion IV [∴ I + E = O]. No other conclusions are valid. But, I and III make a complementary pair [I-O pair].

8. 1; (a) + converted (c) = Conclusion II [∴ A + E = E]. Converted (b) + (a) = Conclusion III [∴ I + A = I]. Converted (b) + conclusion II = Conclusion IV [∴ I + E = O]. [**Note:** Converted (b) is: Some flowers are gardens. Converted (c) is: No boxes are chocolates]

9. 1; (a) + converted (c) = Conclusion III [∴ I + A = I], (b) + (a) = Conclusion II [∴ E + I = O reversed]. No other given conclusions are possible. [**Note:** (c) is an exclusive proposition. When converted it gives A-type proposition. Hence, converted (c) is: All chocolates are Amuls.]

10. 5; By the rules of syllogism, no conclusion can follow. But II and IV make a complementary pair because at any time at least one of them must be true. When II is false, IV would be true; when IV is false, II would be true. **[Note:** Converted (c) is: Some Indians are Americans. This and II make an I-E pair which is a complementary pair].

11. 3; (a) + (b) gives Some cards are vans, [∴ I + A = I]. This gives, on conversion: Some vans are cards. None of the other given conclusions can be proved.

12. 4; (a) + (c) gives conclusion II [∴ E + A = O reversed], (c) + (b) gives conclusion III [∵ A + E = E]. None of the other conclusions are possible.

13. 3; (b) and conclusion I are identical, (b) + converted (c) gives No carts are frocks. On conversion, this gives conclusion II. Now, conclusion II – (a) gives conclusion III [∴ E + I = O reversed].

14. 5; (a) + (b) gives conclusion I [∵ I + E = O]. (b) + (c) gives conclusion IV [E + A = O reversed]. Conclusion II follows immediately from (b). Conclusion III follows immediately from (c).

15. 4; (a) + (b) gives conclusion III [∴ A + E = E]. (c) gives conclusion I on conversion. Conclusion III + (c) gives conclusion IV [∴ E + I = O reversed].

16. 5; (a) + (b) gives conclusion IV [∴ A + E = E]. Conclusion IV + converted (c) gives conclusion I [∴ E + I = O reversed]. Again, (b) + converted (c) gives conclusion II [∴ E + I = O reversed].

17. 3; (b) + (c) gives conclusion IV [∴ E + A = O reversed]. I and III make a complementary pair (I-E pair), so either of them follows. II cannot follow by our rules.

18. 5; Conclusion I follows as an immediate implication of (c). Converted (a) + converted (b) read thus: All moons are stars + No star is a cosmos. This is A + E and gives E. Hence, we get conclusion II. Other given conclusions are not possible to be proved.

19. 2; (c) + converted (b) gives conclusion I [∴ A + E = E]. Again, (a) + conclusion I gives conclusion II [∴ I + E - O]. Finally, (a) + (c) gives : Some bunkers are daggers. On conversion, this gives conclusion III.

20. 4; Converted (b) is Some females are politicians. Now, converted (b) + (c) gives conclusion III [∴ I + A = I]. Now, conclusion III + (a) gives conclusion IV [∴ I + E = O]. Again, (c) + (a) gives No politician is honest [∴ A + E = E]. On conversion, this gives conclusion II.

21. 4; Conclusion I follows from (a), on conversion. Now, (a) + (c) gives Some blondes are girls [∴ I + A = I]. On conversion, this gives conclusion III. No other conclusion is possible.

22. 5; Conclusion I follows as an immediate implication of (b). (a) + (b) gives conclusion II [∴ I + A = I]. III and IV do not follow from the rules of syllogism but they make a complementary pair [I-O pair], so either of them follows.

23. 2; Converted (c) is : Some ropes are jugs. Now, converted (c) + (b) gives conclusion II [∴ I + E = O]. Further, III and IV make a complementary pair.

24. 1; Converted (b) is: Some beamers are bridges. Now, converted (b) + (c) gives: Some beamers are cows. On conversion, this gives conclusion I. No other conclusion follows from the rules.

25. 3; Converted (a) is: Some charts are bags. Now, converted (a) + (c) gives conclusion II [∵ I + E = O]. Again, converted (c) is: No docks are bags. Now, (b) + converted (c) gives conclusion IV. [∵ I + E = O]

Alternative solution:

Converted (c) is: No docks are bags. Now, converted (c) + (a) gives conclusion II [∵ E + I = O reversed]. Again, converted (b) is: Some docks are trees. Now, (c) + converted (b) gives conclusion IV [∵ E + I = O reversed].

Chapter Twelve

Analytical Decision-Making

12.1: Format of the problem (What is the problem like?)

Directions: Study the following information carefully and answer the questions based on it:

The following are the conditions for the recruitment of persons as faculty members in a computer education centre. The candidate must

(a) be in the range of 23 years to 28 years as on 1 Nov, 1993.

(b) have work experience — teaching experience or programming experience — of not less than two years.

(c) have a postgraduate degree in computer application, i.e., MCA, M.Tech. or M.Sc. (Computer Science), with at least 60% marks.

(d) obtain at least 25 marks in the interview out of a total of 50 marks.

In the case of a candidate who

(e) fulfils the above criteria, he or she shall be appointed as a senior faculty member.

(f) has a postgraduate degree in computer application with less than 60% marks but more than 50% marks, he or she shall be appointed as a junior faculty member.

(g) is of age more than 28 years but less than 32 years as on 1 Nov, 1993, the case may be referred to the director of the centre.

On the basis of the above conditions and the information provided about each of the candidates in the question below, you have to decide which of the following courses of action should be taken against each candidate. Please note that you do not assume anything regarding any candidate. The decision should be based only on the information provided. Mark answer

(1) if the candidate is to be selected as a junior faculty member.

(2) if the candidate is to be selected as a senior faculty member.

(3) if the case is to be referred to the director of the centre.

(4) if the data are inadequate.

(5) if the candidate is not to be selected.

Questions:

1. Manisha Punjabi is M.Sc. in Computer Science with 65% marks.Her date of birth is 31st July,1965. She has been working in an institution as a programmer for the last 4 years.
2. Kishore Garg is MCA with 61% marks. His date of birth is 14 August, 1970. He has worked as a computer teacher for 3 years. He has obtained 60% marks in the interview.

3. Babli Sarkar is M.Tech. with 58% marks. Her date of birth is 31 Dec, 1971. She has been working as a programmer for the last two-and-a-half years. She has obtained 40 marks in the interview.

4. Manish Kumar is M.Sc.(Comp. Science) with 52% marks. His date of birth is 10 July, 1968. He has been working as a computer teacher for 4 years. He has obtained 40% marks in the interview.

5. Sudha Ranjan is MCA with 56% marks. She has been working as a programmer for 3 years. Her date of birth is 12 February, 1969. She has obtained 55% marks in the interview.

12.2: An analysis of the problem

Perhaps you are familiar with such questions. They have become quite frequent in the competitive examinations, especially in the exams for Bank POs. If you look carefully, you can see that the question consists of the following simple steps:

I. Information about a candidate is provided.

II. There are some conditions (in the example above, there are four conditions) which a candidate has to fulfil in order to get selected for a particular job or post etc.

III. In case a candidate fulfils all the criteria except some (which are mentioned), some different course of action has to be taken for him.

Now, at this point, it would be worthwhile to define some of the conditions so that further reference to these could be easy.

A. Basic Conditions and Additional Conditions

In the problem above, there are four conditions - (a), (b), (c) and (d), which are the 'original' conditions. We shall call them, let us say, **"basic conditions"**.

Similarly, in the above problem, there are two more conditions - (f) and (g), which are to be looked into in case of exceptions. We shall call them **"additional conditions"**. (Please note that (e) is not an additional condition as it does not talk of exceptions. It is only a totality of the four basic conditions given earlier.)

B. Inadequacy of data

Because one of the answer choices mentions the inadequacy of data, it is important that we clearly define and understand what exactly should be called data's inadequacy. *If the details given about any candidate give no information as required by the basic conditions (or the additional conditions), then this case would be called* **inadequacy of data**. For example, take the 1st question in the example above. No information is given regarding Manisha Punjabi's marks in the interview. Hence, the data are indequate here.

12.3: Suggested method

Taking into account various aspects of this problem as also the practical hindrances, we are suggesting below a method which ought to prove very fast after some practice has been done. The experienced reader must be knowing that (i) rough work is allowed on the question-sheet (in fact, rough work is not allowed anywhere else) and (ii) enough space exists on the left of the questions so that some rough work could easily be done there. Using these facts, the following method should be adopted.

Step I

First of all, write the symbols (a, b, c, d) of the basic conditions to the top-left of where the actual questions start (see the arrangement below). Now, write the symbols of the additional conditions (f and g) below the symbol of that basic condition with which these might be related. For example, (f) is a condition about educational qualification and so it is an exception of (c). Hence (f) should be written below (c). Similarly, (g) should be written below (a). **To differentiate between the basic conditions and additional conditions, put the basic conditions without brackets and the additional conditions within brackets.**

After performing **step I**, your question-sheet will look like this:

a b c d

(g) (f)

1. Manisha Punjabi is M. Sc

....

....

....

5. Sudha Ranjan.....

Step II

Now, look carefully at the answer choices and decide which combination of the conditions leads to which conclusion. For the example given above, the following combinations can be prepared:

a + b + c + d ⇒ (2) (senior faculty member)

g + b + c + d ⇒ (3) (to be referred to director)

a + b + f + d ⇒ (1) (junior faculty member).

After you have decided the above three combinations, two answer- choices remain — (4) and (5). The answer-choice (5), which states that the candidate is not to be selected, should be chosen when any one or more of the given conditions is violated. The answer-choice (4), which states that the data are inadequate, should be chosen when no information is given about any one or more conditions.

12.3.1: Suggested method for examining data

In **Step III**, you will be asked to read carefully all the statements one by one. Take each question. Read carefully and then compare it with the conditions given. In the process of comparing, we suggest the following symbols to be used:

(i) If a basic condition is fulfilled, put a '√' mark below it.

(ii) If a basic condition is violated and there are no additional conditions attached to it put a '×' mark below it.

(iii) If a basic condition is violated but there exist additional conditions attached to it [(a) and (c) in the given example], then if the additional condition is also violated put a '(×)' mark below it, and if the additional condition is fulfilled put a '√' mark below it.

(iv) When no information is given about any condition put a '?' mark below it.

These symbols are to be carefully understood by the reader. As an illustration, we give the following example.

Ex:- I	II (V)	III (VI)	IV	Question No.
√	√	√	×	(1)
√	√	√	√	(2)
√	(√)	(√)	√	(3)
√	√	(×)	√	(4)
√	?	√	√	(5)

The above example illustrates that

(1) I, II, III and IV are four basic conditions. V and VI are two additional conditions. V is attached to II while VI is attached to III.

(2) In question (1), I, II, III are satisfied while IV is violated.

(3) In question (2), all the basic conditions I, II, III and IV are satisfied.

(4) In question (3), the basic conditions I and IV are satisfied and though the basic conditions II and III are violated, the additional conditions V and VI are satisfied.

(5) In question (4), the basic conditions I, II and IV are satisfied while both III and VI are violated.

(6) In question (5), basic conditions I, III and IV are satisfied but no information is given about II or V.

Step III

You have already performed step I and step II. In step I, you have written the basic and additional conditions at a suitable place. In step II you have prepared your answer-combinations. You have also become familiar with the necessary symbols to be used while examining the data. Now, in step III:

A. Read each question carefully and compare the facts given in it with the various conditions one by one.

B. Put the appropriate mark [√ or × or (√) or ?, as suitable] below each condition.

C. Whenever you obtain a × and a (×) sign, do not bother to examine the remaining conditions. Select the answer-choice "not to be selected" and move over to the next question. This is because if a condition as well as its additional condition (if any) are violated, it means that one necessary requirement is not being fulfilled. Which therefore implies that selection is not possible even if other conditions are fulfilled.

Step IV

Now, select your answer-choices on the following pattern:

A. If these is a cross [× or (×)] below any condition, select the answer-choice which states "not to be selected".

B. If there is no cross but a question mark below any condition, select the answer-choice "data are inadequate".

C. If there are neither any crosses nor any question-mark, then compare the combination with the three answer-combinations obtained in step II and accordingly select the answer-choice.

I can imagine that by now you have developed only an intuitive idea of this method, that there are many points which you have not very clearly understood, that you are doubtful if this method is really faster and better than the one you used to employ earlier. So, I find that two jobs are still due on me. First, that I make you understand the method clearly and second, that I convince you that the method is fast. I take up the first job, i.e., to explain the method clearly. For this, a complete solution of the above example is being provided.

An illustrative example

Ex: Solve completely the above example.

Solution:

a (g)	b	c (f)	d	
(√)	√	√	?	(1) Manisha Punjabi is M. Sc. in Comp. Sc. with 65% marks. Her date of birth is 31st July, 1965. She has been working as a programmer for 4 years.
√	√	√	√	(2) Kishore Garg is MCA with 61% marks. His date of birth is 14th August, 1970. He has worked as a computer teacher for 3 years and obtained 60% marks in the interview.
(×)		√		(3) Babli Sarkar is M.Tech. with 58% marks. Her date of birth is 31 Dec. 1971. She has been working as a programmer for two-and-a-half years. She obtained 40 marks in the interview.
√	√	(√)	×	(4) Manish Kumar is M.Sc. (Comp. Sc.) with 52%. He was born on 10.7.1968. He has been working as a computer teacher for 4 yrs. He obtained 40% in interview.
√	√ (√)		√	(5) Sudha Ranjan is M.C.A. with 56% marks. She has been working as a programmer for 3 years. Her date of birth is 12 Feb, 1969. She obtained 55% marks in the interview.

Step I

First of all, we read the question and find that there are four basic conditions (a, b, c, d) and two additional conditions (g,f). We also see that 'g' mentions an exception of 'a' and 'f' is an exception of c. Therefore, we write a, b, c, d at the top left of the first question. (Remember we are supposing that we are taking an actual examination and hence we are writing on the question sheet.) Then, we write 'g' below 'a' and 'f' below 'c'.

Step II

Next, we look at the answer-choices and accordingly prepare our answer-combinations. This will be:

$$a + b + c + d \Rightarrow 2$$
$$g + b + c + d \Rightarrow 3$$
$$a + b + f + d \Rightarrow 1$$

Step III

Now, we read each question carefully and compare the facts given in it with the various conditions.

A detailed analysis of each question is being presented below. I would advise the reader to take a pencil and follow this line by line.

(i) **Question 1:** Manisha is an M.Sc. (Comp Sc) with 65% marks. This fulfils condition **c**. Hence, we put a √ mark below **c**. Next, Manisha's date of birth is 31st Jul, 1965. We quickly do a mental calculation that on 31st Jul, 1993 she turned 28, so on 1st Nov, 1993 she is more than 28 years. Thus, **a** is violated. So, we look at the additional condition of **a** which is **g**. **g** is fulfilled, so we put a √ mark here. Lastly, Manisha is having a programming experience of more than 2 years. So, we put a √ mark below **b**. At this point, we see that the space below condition **d** is vacant. We refer to condition **d** in the question. We see that **d** is about marks in the interview. No information is given about Manisha's marks in the interview. So, we put a ? mark below **d**.

(ii) **Question 2:** Kishore Garg is an M.C.A. with 61% marks. This fulfils **c**, so we put a √ mark below **c**. His date of birth is 14 Aug, 1970; so on 1st Nov, 1993 he is slightly more than 23 years. This fulfils **a**, so we put a √ mark below **a**. He has worked as a computer teacher for 3 years. This fulfils **b**. Lastly, he has acquired 60% marks in the interview. This is more than the required 50% (25 out of 50), hence **d** is also fulfilled.

(iii) **Question 3:** Babli is an M.Tech. with 58% marks. This violates **c**. We see that an additional condition is attached to **c**, which is **f**. Referring to **f**, we see that **f** is fulfilled. So, we put a (√) mark over there. Her date of birth is sometime in 1971, so she is certainly below 23 yrs in 1993. This violates **a**. We see that there is an additional condition attached to **a**, which is **g**. We see that **g** is also violated. So, we put a (×) mark. Now, because a cross-mark has been obtained, we need not go any further (see Step III 'C'). So, we move on to the next question.

(iv) Question 4: Manish is an M.Sc. with 52% marks. This violates **c** but fulfils the attached additional condition **f.** We put a (√) mark. He is born in 1968, so he is roughly 25 years. Hence, **a** is fulfilled. We put a √ mark below **a**. He has worked as a computer teacher for 4 years. This fulfils **b**. He has obtained 40% in interview. This violates **d**. So, we put a × mark below **d.**

(v) Question 5: Sudha is an M.C.A. with 56% marks. This violates **c** but fulfils **f**. We put a (√) mark there. She has programming experience of 3 years. This fulfils **b**. She was born in 1969, so she is roughly 24 years. So, **a** is fulfilled. She has obtained more than 50% (25 out of 50) marks in the interview, so **d** is fulfilled.

Step IV

Now, let us select the answer choices.

(i) Question 1: No cross mark and a question mark.
Hence : data inadequate. Answer choice: 4

(ii) Question 2: $a + b + c + d \Rightarrow 2$. (step II)

(iii) Question 3: A cross-mark is there. Hence, "not to be selected." Answer choice: 5.

(iv) Question 4: Answer choice: 5 (For the same reason that a cross-mark exists).

(v) Question 5: $a + b + f + d \Rightarrow 1$. (step II)

For the readers' practice and full for understanding of the method we are giving one more example with solutions. But this time we are omitting the unnecessary details.

Example:

Directions: Study the following information to answer the given questions. The following are the criteria for registration in a Training Workshop. The participant must

(i) be more than 30 years of age.
(ii) be a graduate with 60% marks.
(iii) have at least four years of experience of working in industry.
(iv) be sponsored by his/her employer for the workshop.
(v) have sent one paper for presentation in the workshop.

However, if a person fulfils all these criteria except

(a) (iii) above, he or she should be registered as Trainee Participant.
(b) (ii) above, but is a post-graduate, he or she should be registered.
(c) (v) above, he or she should be referred to the Workshop Coordinator.

On the basis of these criteria and the information provided in each case, you have to make the decision regarding registration for the Workshop. Do not assume anything. If the information provided is not adequate to take the decision, the answer would be "data inadequate". Study each case and give answer

(1) If to be registered.
(2) If registered as a Trainee Participant.

(3) If referred to Workshop Coordinator.

(4) If data are inadequate.

(5) If NOT to be registered.

Questions:

1. 31-year-old Kavita Sinha has 66% marks in her post-graduation. She has 2 years' experience in industry and has been sponsored by her employer. She has also submitted the paper.

2. 31-year-old Anjanee Konar is a post-graduate in Economics. She has been sponsored by her employer and has submitted the paper. She has been working in the industry for 10 years.

3. Mohan Dule has been working in the industry for the last six years. He informed that he would not be submitting the paper. He has been sponsored by his employer. He is 29 years old and has got 64% marks in his graduation.

4. Vijay Madhav is 32 years old and has been working in the industry for the last seven years. He has been sponsored by his employer and has sent the paper.

5. Ram Vilavan is a graduate with 60% marks and has 3 years' experience in industry. He is 31 years old. He has submitted the paper.

6. Dipen Shah is a post-graduate with five years' experience in industry. He is 38 years old and has been sponsored by his employer. He will not present a paper in the Workshop.

7. Ashok Dongre is 35 years old. He has submitted a paper and has also been sponsored by his employer. He has three years' experience in industry. He has 59% marks in graduation.

8. Vinay Kelkar has been sponsored by his employer. He is 36 years old and will not present a paper. He is a post-graduate with four years' industry experience.

9. Madhu Sapre has got two years' experience in industry. She has submitted a paper. She is a post-graduate and has been sponsored by her employer.

10. 45-year-old Ragini Ratan has been sponsored by her employer. She has got 59% marks in her post-graduation and has six years' experience in industry. She has sent a paper for presentation.

Solution: We are omitting the various details as given in the previous example. The reader is asked to verify that after performing step I and step III his answer sheet looks like this:

i	ii	iii	iv	v	
	(b)	(a)		(c)	
√	? (√)	(√)	√	√	1. 31-year-old Kavita........
√	? (√)	√	√	√	2. 31-year-old Anjanee.......
×					3. Mohan Dule has .....

i	ii	iii	iv	v	
	(b)	(a)		(c)	
√	?	√	√	√	4. Vijay Madhav ....
√	√	(√)	?	√	5. Ram Vilavan........
√	? (√)	√	√	(√)	6. Dipen Shah.......
√	?	(√)	(√)	√	7. Ashok Dongre......
√	(√)	√	√	(√)	8. Vinay Kalkar........
?	(√)	(√)	√	√	9. Madhu Sapre.......
√	(√)	√	√	√	10. 45-year-old Ragini ......

Step II: Answer Combinations

i + ii + iii + iv + v

or i + (b) + iii + iv + v ⇒ (1)

i + ii + (a) + iv + v ⇒ (2)

i + ii + iii + iv + (c) ⇒ (3)

Important Note:- Please note that (a) and (c) are not conditions as such. They merely mention the negation of iii and v respectively: i.e., whenever iii is false (a) is true, and whenever v is false (c) is true. On the other hand, (b) does mention an alternate condition. However, it is still advisable to treat (a) and (c) also as additional conditions. In many questions, you will come across conditions like (a) and (c), where no alternate condition would be seen. You should still treat them as additional conditions.

Step IV

Comparing the arrangements for each question with the answer combinations, we reach at the following conclusions:

Question #	Answer Choice
1.	5; More than one basic condition violated: ii and iii.
2.	1; i + (b) + iii + iv + v.
3.	5
4.	4
5.	4
6.	5
7.	5
8.	5; Same reason as in Q. 1.
9.	5; Same reason as in Q. 7.
10.	1; Same reason as in Q. 2.

There are some points in the example above, where you might need some explanations. For example:

(1) In Q.1., Kavita Sinha is described as a post-graduate with 66% marks. But her marks in graduation is not known. Hence, a question-mark below ii.

(2) In Q. 6 and Q. 8, one may be tempted to select answer choice 3. But remember that, in both these questions, two basic conditions are violated: ii and iv. Whereas, the directions clearly state that an answer choice has to be chosen only if "a person fulfils *all these* criteria" except any single one (not more than one).

(3) In Q.7, Ashok Dongre has been described as a graduate with 59% marks. It has not been told whether he is a post-graduate or not. Hence, the question-mark. Still, the answer choice is 5 because it would be so even if he were a post-graduate.

12.4: How fast is this method?

Now remains my second job of convincing you that this suggested method is really fast. At the outset, let me tell you that the method mentioned above has no miraculous short-cuts.

The method mentioned above has no miraculous short-cuts. It only emphasises that for questions of such lengthy type, it would be better to have a well-defined, well-thought "order" in the method. The "order" or the "cleanliness" with which this method seeks to solve the problem is its highlight. And that is where it economises on unnecessary wastage of time. Also, by clearly laying down that whenever a basic condition (as well as its additional condition, if any) is violated, one should put a × [and (×) in case of additional condition] and move over to the next question, we save a lot of time. In fact, you can add further improvisations of your own. For example, you know that usually a definite answer choice is to be selected only if not more than one basic condition is violated. Using this fact, you could stop whenever you saw more than one basic condition being violated. [For illustration, in the previous example, it was not necessary to examine iv and v in Q. 1, Q. 7 and Q. 9). You can think over all this very carefully and make out a plan for yourself that suits you the best. What we have provided you with is only a set of guidelines.

However, coming back to the original question of the speed of this method, I could make a reasonable claim that, depending upon the mind that applies it, this method should solve 10 questions in 4 to 7 minutes after reasonable practice.

Practice Exercises

Exercise 11

Directions (Q. 1-10): Read the following information and answer the questions given below it.

The following are the criteria for the admission to the medical course in a college.

The student must:

(A) have passed XII Std. examination in Science with at least 50% marks,

(B) be at least 18 years old as on 1.4.1991,

(C) have scored at least 65% marks in the entrance examination,

(D) be able to pay the monthly tuition fee of Rs. 400, and

(E) be able to pay one-time deposit of Rs. 15,000.

(F) The case of a student who satisfies all other criteria but can pay the one-time deposit only upto Rs. 10,000, is to be referred to the Director of the Institute.

(G) The case of a candidate who satisfies all other criteria apart from the percentage of marks in XIIth Std. is to be referred to the Chairman, Admission.

(H) A student who has satisfied all other criteria but has not yet received the result of the final examination of XIIth standard may be provisionally admitted.

On the basis of the above criteria and the information given in each of the following questions you have to take decisions as regards admittance of the student. Please note you are not to assume anything in the case of any student. Mark answer:

1) if the student is not to be admitted.

2) if the student is to be admitted.

3) if the student is to be referred to the Director.

4) if the student is to be referred to the Chairman, Admission.

5) if the student is to be provisionally admitted.

1. Irene Fernandez has passed XIIth Std. exam in Science with 70% marks. She has secured 75% marks in the entrance exam and was 18 years old on 1.7.90. She can pay tuition fee of Rs. 400 per month but can pay one-time deposit of only Rs. 10,000.

2. Prabir Singhal secured 60% marks in the XIIth Std. exam with Science. He was 19 years old on 1.3.90 and has secured 80% marks in the entrance test. He can pay the stipulated one-time deposit of Rs. 15,000 and the monthly tuition fee of Rs. 400.

3. Sharad Joshi has passed his XIIth Std. exam with 52% marks and will be 20 years old, as on 8th December 1991. He has secured 70% marks in the entrance test. He is able to pay one-time deposit of Rs. 15,000 and the monthly tuition fee of Rs 400.

4. Utpal Ghosh has passed XIIth Std. in Science with first class and was 18 years old in Jan. 1991. He has secured 70% marks in the entrance test and can pay monthly tuition fee of Rs. 400 and one-time deposit of Rs. 15,000.

5. Deven Verma has passed XIIth Std. exam in Science with 48% marks and was born on 25th July, 1972. He has secured 80% marks in the entrance examination. He is able to pay one-time deposit of Rs. 15,000 and monthly tuition fee of Rs 400.

6. Prashant Kohli has passed XIIth Std. exam in Science with 45% marks. He was 19 years old as on 1.2.91. He has secured 70% marks in the entrance examination. He is able to pay the stipulated one-time deposit and monthly tuition fees.
7. Nitish Sharma has secured 72% marks in the entrance examination and was born on 17th September 1971. He is yet to receive his marksheet of his XIIth Std. final exam in Science stream. He is able to pay the one-time deposit of Rs. 15,000 and the monthly tuition fee of Rs 400.
8. Avinash Mundra passed XIIth Std. in Science with 55% marks and was born on 1.3.73. He has secured 65% marks in the entrance exam and can pay the monthly tuition fee of Rs. 400. He can pay one-time deposit of Rs. 9,000 only.
9. Jyoti Deshmukh has appeared for the final exam of XIIth Std. in Science stream. She was 19 years old on 20.3.91. She has secured 75% in the entrance examination. She is able to pay the one-time deposit of Rs. 15,000 and the monthly tuition fee of Rs. 400.
10. Prakash Sawant secured 50% and 65% marks in the XIIth Std. and entrance exam respectively. He will be 18 years and 6 months old on 1.6.91. He can pay the stipulated one-time deposit and monthly tuition fees.

Directions (Q. 11-20): Read the following information carefully and answer the questions given below it.

A student can be awarded free studentship by an institute if the following conditions are fulfilled:

a) Total family income of the student should not be more than Rs. 24,000 per annum.
b) A student should have secured not less than 60% marks in Higher Secondary and Graduation.
c) A student should not be more than 22 years old as on 30.6.92.
d) A student must not be availing any other scholarship.
e) If a student satisfies all these criteria except (a) above and has excelled in games or sports at the district level, he will be entitled for free studentship.
f) If a student has secured 90% marks in Graduation but has secured less than 60% marks in Higher Secondary, the student may be offered free studentship.
g) If the total family income of the student is less than Rs. 12,000 per annum, this is to be referred to the Principal for waiving condition (d) above.
h) If a student has secured at least 80% marks in both Higher Secondary and Graduation, the case may be referred to the Registrar to waive condition (c) above.

On the basis of the above conditions, decide about the course of action that should be taken in the case of each of the students given below. You are not to assume anything in the case of any student.

Mark answer

1) if the student can be given free studentship;

2) if the student cannot be given free studentship;

3) if the data provided are inadequate;

4) if the case is to be referred to the Principal; and

5) if the case is to be referred to the Registrar.

11. Vikram Dubey, who was born on 20th December 1973, has secured 90% marks in Higher Secondary and 50% marks in Graduation. He has not been awarded any other scholarship. The total income of the family is Rs. 1,500 per month.

12. Surekha Dwivedi was born on 10th October, 1974. She is the district badminton champion. She has secured 55% marks in both Higher Secondary and Graduation. She has not been awarded any other scholarship. The total income of her family is Rs. 20,000 per annum.

13. Pratibha Kapoor was 18 years old as on 27th October, 1989. She has secured 90% marks in Graduation and 55% marks in Higher Secondary. She has not been awarded any other scholarship.

14. Prakash Timle has secured 75% marks in both Higher Secondary and Graduation. He is a district tennis champion. His age, as on 15th February, 1992, was 22 years. The total income of his family is Rs. 1,800 per month.

15. Rajan Jain was 20 years old as on 20th July 1990. He has secured 85% marks in both Higher Secondary and Graduaton. The total income of his family is Rs. 15,000 per annum. He has not been awarded any other scholarship.

16. Nineteen years old as on 25.6.1992, Bhabani Das has secured 65% marks in both Higher Secondary and Graduation. The total income of his family is Rs. 20,000 per annum. He does not have any other scholarship.

17. Nalini Srivastava was born on 15th December, 1961. She has secured 95% marks in Graduation. The total annual family income is Rs. 22,000. She has not been awarded any other scholarship.

18. Samir Phadnis will be 24 years old as on 20th March, 1994. He has secured 65% marks in both Higher Secondary and Graduation. He has been awarded state level scholarship for higher studies. The total income of his family is Rs. 10,000 per annum.

19. Mohan Seth has secured 70% marks in both Graduation and Higher Secondary. He will be 23 years old as on 5th August, 1993. The total income of his family is Rs. 2,400 per month. He has not been awarded any other scholarship.

20. Subodh Kelkar has secured 85% marks in both Higher Secondary and Graduation. His date of birth is 15th March, 1960. He has not been awarded any other scholarship. The total income of his family is Rs 21,000 per annum.

Directions (Q. 21-30): Read the following information and answer the questions given below it.

The following are the conditions for selecting a "Management Trainee" for a reputed public sector company. The candidate must:

a) be a post-graduate in commerce with 60% marks or a C.A.

b) not be more than 25 years old and less than 20 years old as on 1.12.92.

c) have fluency in English and Hindi.

d) be in a position to pay Rs. 10,000/- as deposit to the company.

e) give an undertaking to work for at least 5 years for the company.

However,

(i) if a person satisfies all the conditions except (a) above, he should be referred to the Managing Director of the company.

(ii) if a person satisfies all the conditons except (d) and/or (e) above, he should be referred to the Chairman of the company.

On the basis of the above criteria and the information provided, you have to decide each case. You are not to assume anything which is beyond what is given in the questions. The alternative courses of decision and the method of indicating the same are as follows.

Mark answer:

1) if data provided is not complete in the case of any of the candidates.

2) if the candidate cannot be selected as a Management Trainee.

3) if the candidate can be selected as a Management Trainee.

4) if the candidate is to be referred to the Managing Director.

5) if the candidate is to be referred to the Chairman.

21. 22-year-old Raju is a Post-Graduate in commerce with 60% marks. He is fluent in Hindi only. He can pay the required deposit and is also ready to give 5 years' undertaking.

22. 21-year-old Vijay has obtained 63% marks in Post-Graduation with Commerce, is fluent in Hindi and English and can pay the required deposit. He is willing to give 5 years' undertaking.

23. 23-year-old Suresh is a C.A. with fluency in Hindi and English. He can pay Rs. 8,000 as deposit and will give 5 years' undertaking.

24. Amar is a Post Graduate with 59% marks in Commerce. He is fluent in Hindi and English and also willing to give an undertaking of 5 years. He can pay the required deposit.

25. Rajan is a Post-Graduate in Commerce with 70% marks. He is fluent in Hindi and English. He can pay the required deposit and is ready to give 5 years' undertaking. His date of birth is 01.11.1973.

26. Anil, whose date of birth is 01.09.1972, has obtained 70% marks in Post Graduation and has also completed his C.A. He can pay the required deposit, is fluent in Hindi and English and also has no objection to giving 5 years' undertaking to the company.

27. 24-year-old Saurabh is a Post Graduate in Commerce with 64% marks. He is fluent in Hindi and English. He can pay the required deposit and is willing to give 5 years' undertaking.

28. Neelam Garg, whose date of birth is 01.08.1973, has a C.A. degree. She is fluent in Hindi and English, can pay the deposit and also has no objection to giving 4 years' undertaking.

29. 24-year-old Madan has got 62% in Graduation with Commerce. He has fluency in Hindi and English. He can pay the required deposit and is also ready to give 5 years' undertaking.

30. Sujan Ray is a Post-Graduate with 65% marks, is fluent in Hindi and English, and has done C.A. also. He is 23 years old and willing to give an undertaking of 5 years.

Directions (Q. 31-40): The following are the criteria that a newspaper has made while considering the applications for the posts of editors:

I. The candidate must be at least 30 years old but not more than 45 years old as on 1-1-94.

II. The candidate must have post-graduate diploma in either Media Communications or Investigative Journalism or an equivalent qualification. [An M. Phil. or a Ph. D. is considered an equivalent qualification.]

III. The candidate must have at least five years' experience in a newspaper or a weekly magazine.

IV. The candidates must possess a certificate of good conduct (CGC) given to him by his previous employer, if any.

V. The candidate must obtain 60% marks in the interview, the full marks being 150.

If a person fulfils these criteria, he will be employed as an editor. However, if a person fulfils all these criteria except

a) I above, the case may be referred to the President of the newspaper's company.

b) II above, but is an Ll.B./C.A./M.B.A., he may yet be selected.

c) III above, the case may be referred to the GM, Printing and Execution.

On the basis of the above criteria decide about the course of action that has to be taken for each of the candidates. You are not to assume anything in the case of any candidate.

Mark Answer:

1) if the candidate has to be selected as editor.

2) if the case has to be to be referred to the President.

3) if the case has to be referred to the GM, Printing and Execution Deptt.

4) if the information given about the candidate is not sufficient to reach any answer.

5) if the candidate is not to be selected.

31. Ashish Gupta, an LL.B., was born on 25th of July, 1958. He possesses the CGC, has worked for seven years with *Anand Avinash*, a sports magazine published from Calcutta. He has obtained 120 marks in the interview.

32. Avinash Bokil previously worked with *Sandhya Express*, a newspaper, for more than a decade; he was fired over a small ego clash with his boss. However, the boss was human enough to give him the CGC. He has a postgraduate diploma in investigative journalism. He has obtained 95 marks in the interview. He is 43 years old.

33. Sandip Kurnam has a work experience of seven years with a weekly magazine. He has obtained 89 marks in the interview. He has a PG Dip. in Mass Communications. He was born in 1960 and has obtained the required CGC.

34. Pramil Dhanoa has obtained 65% marks in the interview. He was born on 25-11-1963. He has the certificate of good conduct. He is an MBA and has a work experience of four-and-a-half years with a newspaper.

35. Devendra Tomar is an M. Phil. in Industrial Psychology. He is 40 years old. He has a work experience of 15 years with a newspaper. He has obtained the CGC. He has got more marks in the interview than Sandeep Kurman. Nobody has got marks in fractions or decimals.

36. Amitabh Manu, an M. Phil. in Journalism, worked with *Career Express* - a weekly magazine - for six years. He is 40 years old. He has got 63 per cent marks in the interview. He has a track record of exceptionally good conduct throughout his career.

37. Pradeep Biswas is a Ph.D. He is 39 years old and has obtained 93 marks in the interview. He has a work experience of seven years in a monthly magazine. He has obtained the CGC.

38. Shanu Khurana has finished her Post-Graduate Diploma in Mass Media Communications. She used to work with a newspaper during the course of his study. The editor of the newspaper regards her as talented and sincere and, therefore, he readily gave the CGC when she asked for it. She worked for this newspaper for more than six years. She has obtained as many marks as Devendra Tomar has in the interview.

39. Kalpana Trehan is an M. Phil. in Social Anthropology. She has obtained 75 per cent marks in the interview. She used to work in the same newspaper in which Shanu Khurana worked. She has an experience of seven years and has got the CGC. She was born on the 1st of February, 1964.

40. Rashmi Pandey is an MBA and has obtained 120 marks in the interview. She is 36 years old. She has a work experience of four-and-a-half years with a newspaper. She has a CGC.

Directions (Q. 41-45) : The following are the directions to be followed for the selection of music directors for a recording company:

I. The candidate must be over 35 years of age as on 1.6.96.

II. The candidate must be at least a graduate in music.

III. The candidate must have at least one recorded cassette of his or her music.

IV. The candidate must have given music for at least two T.V. serials.

If a candidate fulfils all these criteria, he or she will be selected as a music director. However, if a candidate fulfils all these criteria except

(a) IV above, his or her case will be referred to the Producer.

(b) I above, his or her case will be referred to the Director.

(c) II above, but has given music for some films (feature film only), he or she will be selected as a Music Director.

On the basis of these conditions decide what course of action has to be taken in the case of the following candidates. Give answer

1) if the candidate is to be selected as a Music Director.

2) if the candidate is not to be selected as a Music Director.

3) if his or her case is to be referred to the Producer.

4) if his or her case is to be referred to the Director.

5) if the data given about the candidate are inadequate to give a definite course of action.

41. Partha Sah is 37 years old as on 1.1.95. He is a graduate in music. He has given music for several T.V. serials (three serials). He has given music in some feature films.

42. Manju Majumdar was born on 7.2.1960. She has given music in five T.V. serials. She has given music in two feature films and has seven cassettes of her music.

43. Manu Srivastava has several cassettes of his music. He has given music in four T.V. serials and three feature films. He is a graduate in music and he is older than Manju Majumdar.

44. Shravan Mohapatra has a graduate degree in music. He is 40 years old. He has not given music in either any T.V. serial or any film. He has recorded some cassettes of his music.

45. Mohit Saxena has given music in several T.V. serials. He was born on 7.8.1969. He is a graduate in music and has recorded ten casettes of his music. He has also given music in five documentary films.

Directions (Q. 46-55) : The following are the criteria laid down by a publishing house for the selection of Desk Officers:

I. The candidate must be between 25 and 30 years old as on 1.1.95.

II. The candidate must be a graduate from a recognised Indian University with at least 55% marks.

III. The candidate must possess a work experience of at least 3 years in some publishing house.

IV. The candidate must not be suffering from colour blindness.

If a candidate fulfils all these criteria, he may be selected as Desk Officer. However, if a candidate fulfils all these criteria except

(a) I above, but possesses a work experience of more than seven years in a publishing house, he or she may be selected.

(b) II above, but has done 10+2 (or Intermediate) followed by a computer education of at least two years, he or she may be selected as Desk Officer on Probation.

(c) III above, but is a post-graduate with at least 50% marks, his or her case may be referred to the Proprietor of the publishing house.

On the basis of the criteria as laid above, decide the course of action that should be taken in case of the candidates below. Give answer:

1) if the candidate is to be selected for the post of Desk Officer.

2) if the candidate is to be selected for the post of Desk Officer on Probation.

3) if the case of the candidate is to be referred to the Proprietor.

4) if the data are inadequate, i.e. if, on the basis of the given facts, it is not possible to decide the exact course of action that should be taken in the case of the candidate.

5) if the candidate is not to be selected.

Now, read the informations below and give appropriate answer.

46. Rajat Kapoor is a graduate with 60% marks. He was born on 1.7.1969. He has done a two years' computer course as well. He does not suffer from colour blindness.

47. Shalini Bandopadhyaya does not suffer from colour blindness. She has done her post-graduation with 52% marks. She has a work experience of about 40 months in a publishing house. She was born on 25th of July, 1967.

48. Abhigyan Mohanthi is a graduate with 62% marks. He is older than Rajat but younger than Shalini. He does not suffer from colour blindness. He has a work experience of 5 years.

49. Sudesh Bhonsle is a graduate with 73% marks. He was born on the 3rd of December, 1971. He has a work experience of about seven-and-a-half years and does not suffer from colour blindness.

50. Abhinav Chauthala was 16 years old on 1st Dec, 1982. He does not suffer from colour blindness. He has been working in a publishing hourse for the past five years. He is not a graduate but has done Advanced Diploma in Computer Applications.

51. Rajni Trivedee was 18 years old on 3rd January, 1985. She is a graduate from a recognised Indian University with 60% marks. She does not suffer from colour blindness. She has been working in another publishing house for the past six years.

52. Ashish Gairola has done post-graduation with 52% marks which is 8% less than his marks in graduation. He is 27 years old and does not suffer from colour blindness. He has been working in a publishing house for the past 28 months.

53. Virendramani Sakhlecha suffers from colour blindness. He has 76% marks in graduation. He is 26 years old and has a work experience of four years in a publishing house.

54. Rahul Sanskrityayan joined a 3-year computer course after passing his intermediate examination. At that time he was 19 years old. He immediately joined a publishing house, after finishing the computer course, and has been working there till now. He does not suffer from colour blindness. His work experience in the publishing house is of 49 months, as of now.

55. Pawan Mishra was 22 years old on 1.1.85. He has had a work experience of 8 years in a publishing house. He does not suffer from colour blindness. He is not a graduate but has done computer education of three years after 10+2.

Directions (Q. 56-60): The following are the criteria laid down by Ship Management Services Company Limited for the selection of Marine Engineers:

I. The candidate must be between 21 and 30 years of age as on 1.1.95.

II. The candidate must possess a passport.

III. The candidate must have an eyesight of ± 2.5 with no colour.

IV. The candidate must be a B.E. or a B. Tech. in Mechanical Engineering.

V. The candidate must possess a work experience of 3 years in an industry in the capacity of a Mechanical Engineer.

If a candidate fulfils all these criteria, he or she will be selected for the job. However, if a candidate fulfils all other criteria except :

a) II above, he or she may be provisionally selected.

b) I above, but is less than 35 years of age and has a working experience of at least 5 years as marine engineer, he or she may be selected.

c) V above, the case may be referred to the chairman of the company.

Read the information given about a candidate and decide the course of action that should be taken in his or her case. Give answer

1) if the candidate is to be selected.

2) if the candidate is to be selected provisionally.

3) if the candidate is to be referred to the Chairman.

4) if the date given about the candidate are inadequate to say which course of action would be taken.

5) if the candidate is not to be selected.

56. Ranjana Sabharwal has an eyesight of ±2.5 with no colour. She is a B.Tech. and has served as a Mechanical Engineer for five years. She was born on 7.1.1967.

57. Shantan Chhabaria was born on 2.1.1965. He has an eyesight of ±2.5 with no colour. He is a B.E. in Mechanical Engineering. He has worked as a mechanical engineer for four years and has a passport.

58. Ranjan Srinivasan has the eyesight as required by the company. He was born on 25.07.1964. He is a B. Tech. in Mechanical Engineering and he has a working experience of seven years as marine engineer. He has applied for a passport and is yet to get it.

59. Manu Srivastava is a diploma holder in Mechanical Engineering. His eyesight is within the limits stipulated by the company. He has a passport and has worked as a Mechanical Engineer for 4 years. On 1st January, 1990 he was 23 years old.

60. Sunita Vadhawar is a B. Tech. in Mechanical Engineering. She has a work experience of 28 months in the capacity of Mechanical Engineer. Born on 7 Aug, 1969, she has the eyesight within the stipulated limits and also a passport.

Directions (Q. 61-70): The following are the criteria laid down by a government agency to accept or reject a proposal for foreign investment by a foreign company:

I. The company should be willing to employ only Indians in its cadre except for the post of chairman.

II. The company must have a business proposal of at least $ 1 million (Rs 3.5 crore).

III. The company should have a global turnover of at least $ 100 million (Rs. 350 crore).

IV. The company's business offer must not cover the privileged category (bulk drugs, oil, defence and space research).

If a company fulfils all these criteria, the agency would clear the proposal. However, if a company fulfils all these criteria except

(a) I above, but is willing to export at least 80% of its production, its offer will be cleared.

(b) II above, the case will be referred to the finance ministry.

(c) III above, the case will be referred to the commerce ministry.

You have to read the details of all the proposals given below and then decide the course of action that would be taken by the agency.

Give answer :

1) if the proposal will be cleared.

2) if the proposal will be referred to the finance ministry.

3) if the proposal will be referred to the commerce ministry.
4) if the data are inadequate to come to a definite conclusion.
5) if the proposal will not be cleared.

Now read the information carefully and choose appropriate answers.

61. AIWA of S. Korea has proposed to manufacutre audio equipments in India. It has a global turnover of $ 2000 million and proposes to invest $ 20 million in India. It is willing to employ an all-Indian staff.

62. SOTIZA of Japan proposes to invest $ 100,000 in India for the production of terry-towels. This company has a global turnover of $ 120 million. It is willing to employ only Indians except for the post of Chairman.

63. PHILIPSIC of Holland has a global turnover of over $ 680 million. It proposes to invest $ 15 million in India. It is willing to employ only Indians in the company.

64. STERLING INC. of USA proposes to invest $ 160 million in India in a project of power generation. The company has given an undertaking to the effect that it will employ only Indians in its Indian subsidiary.

65. HAZARAT-UL-SULEMAN is willing to invest 150 million dollars in a project of space-research equipments. It proposes to employ an all-Indian staff. If has a global turnover of $ 1500 million.

66. SAM PETERPAN of Holland proposes to have an all-Indians staff in a project of terry-towel manufacturing. It has a global turnover of 180 million rupees and it proposes to invest 50 million rupees in India.

67. STANDARD ORGANIC of Australia proposes to manufacture car accessories in India. It does not agree to have Indian workers in the project. It has a global turnover of $ 120 million and its proposed investment outlay in India is of $ 800,000.

68. CIPLA of U.A.E. is not willing to have Indian workers in its proposed business of manufacturing synthetic dye in India. It has a global turnover of $ 1200 million and proposes to invest $ 80 million in India.

69. SOMU ELECTRONICS INC. of U.A.E. has a global turnover of S 160 million. It proposes to invest $ 300,000 in a project to manufacture ball-point pens and is willing to export 80% of its production. It does not disagree to the condition of having an all-Indian staff.

70. SECADA INC. of U.K. is not willing to employ Indian workers in a project to manufacture cigarettes. It proposes to invest $ 10 million in the project and is willing to export 100% of its production. The global turnover of the company is $ 1600 million.

Directions (Q.71-80) : The following are the criteria laid down by an organisation to select personnel in its Research Department:

I. The candidate must not be above 30 years of age as on 1st August, 1995.

II. The candidate must be an M.Sc. with at least 65 % marks.

III. The candidate must have submitted at least one paper on science during his academic career.

IV. The candidate's application must be accompanied by the recommendation of a professor of his institute.

V. The candidate should have obtained at least 60% marks in the interview that carries full marks of 150.

If a candidate fulfils all these criteria, he or she would be appointed as a Science Officer in the organisation. However, if a candidate fulfils all other criteria except

a) I above, his or her case may be referred to the M.D., Personnel.

b) II above, but has submitted more than two papers, he or she may be appointed as Assistant Science Officer.

c) III above, but has 75% or more marks in M.Sc., he or she may be appointed as Science Officer.

Now read the information presented about each of the candidates below, and decide what course of action would be taken in his or her case. Mark answer:

1) if the candidate should be appointed as Science Officer.

2) if the candidate should be appointed as Assistant Science Officer.

3) if the case needs to be referred to the M.D., Personnel.

4) if the data are inadequate, i.e., if it is not possible to decide, on the basis of the given data, the exact course of action that would be taken.

5) if the candidate is not to be selected.

Now read the information carefully and mark appropriate answers:

71. Shanten Dasgupta is 27 years old. He is an M.Sc. and obtained 67% marks in his Post-Graduation. He has obtained 90 marks in the interview. He has submitted a paper during his academic career.

72. Rajneesh Pandey is an M.Sc. with 70% marks. He was born on 1st September, 1972. He has obtained 62% marks in the interview. He has submitted two papers during his career. He has obtained the recommendation of his professor.

73. Abhinav Mathur has not obtained a recommendation of his professor but has submitted three papers during his career and has 79% marks in M.Sc. He is 27 years old. He obtained 65% in the interview.

74. Sarita Kid Lakshmi has obtained 89 in the interview. She is an M.Sc. with 80% marks. She has submitted a paper and has been recommended by a professor of her institute. She is 25.

75. Animesh Mohapatra has obtained the recommendation of his professor. He is an M.Sc. with 68% marks. He has not submitted any paper. He obtained 96 in the interview and is 27 years old.

76. Ranjan Manudhanaiah is 29 years old. He is an M.Sc. with 71% marks. He has obtained the required recommendation. He has submitted two papers during his career. The marks obtained by him in the interview are more than that obtained by Sarita Kid Lakshmi.

77. Anantha Padmanabhan is an M.Sc. with 63% marks in Post-Graduation. He has submitted three papers during his career. He has secured 93 in the interview and obtained the recommendation of his professor. He was born on 2nd July, 1968.

78. Vandana Dhadhel is an M.Sc. with 70% marks in Post-Graduation. She has more marks in the interview than Animesh. She has obtained her professor's recommendation. She has submitted two papers during her academic career.

79. Anita Sapru was born on 2nd July, 1965. She is a Post-Graduate in Science with more than 70% marks. She has submitted two papers during her academic career. She has obtained the recommendation of her professor. She obtained 62% in the interview.

80. Arvind Mishra is an M.Sc. with 79% marks but has not submitted any paper. He has obtained the recommendation of his Professor. He has 98 in the interview. He was born earlier than Ms. Sapru.

Directions (Q. 81-90): The following are the criteria laid down by the Law College, Univesity of Boston, for admission-seekers.

I. The student must not be less than 21 years of age and more than 33 years of age, as on 1st August, 1995.

II. The student must possess a passport and an educational visa.

III. The student must possess a TOEFL score of at least 550.

IV. The student must be prepared to make a statutory deposit of $ 25,000 towards expenses (equal to Rs 8 lakh).

V. The student must not have any criminal record or any fatal or infectious disease. A student who has obtained eligibility certificate from the Law College will be deemed to have fulfilled this criterion, otherwise he or she would need to show a character certificate and a health certificate.

If a candidate fulfils all these criteria, he or she would be granted admission into the college. However, if a candidate fulfils all these criteria except

(a) II above, he may be granted provisional admission into the college.

(b) I above, the case may be referred to the Dean of the college.

(c) IV above, but is sponsored by a Company having a minimum equity capital of $ 2 million (Rs 6 crore), he or she will be granted admission.

On the basis of the conditions mentioned above, decide upon the course of action that should be taken in the case of each of the candidates mentioned below. Mark answer:

1) if the candidate is to be granted admission.

2) if the candidate is not to be granted admission.

3) if the candidate is to be granted provisional admission.

4) if the case is to be referred to the Dean.

5) if the data are inadequate to predict what course of action needs to be taken.

81. Sudhir Kashyap was born on 1st July, 1969. He is sponsored by a company Voltech India Ltd. He possesses a passport, a visa and an eligibility certificate. He is prepared to make a statutory deposit of $ 25,000.

82. Anju Kulshreshtha possesses an eligibility certificate. She was born on 2nd August, 1974. She has a passport and a visa. She is willing to make the required statutory deposit.

83. Rakesh Yadav is a B. Tech. and possesses a character certificate as well as a health certificate. He is sponsored by O. A. P. India Ltd., a company having an equity base of 12.5 crore rupees. He has a TOEFL score of 720. He possesses a passport and a visa. He is 26 years old.

84. Pranab Dasgupta has a TOEFL score of 570. He is ready to make a statutory deposit of $ 25,000. He has a passport but not a visa. He does have the eligibility certificate and is 24 years old.

85. Shantanu Mukherjea is 27 years old. He cannot deposit $ 25,000 on his own; nor is he sponsored by any company. He has a TOEFL score of 600. He possesses a passport, visa and an eligibility certificate.

86. Rana Kumar Bhadra Singh is willing to make the required statutory deposit. His TOEFL score is 600. He was born on 2nd August, 1973. He possesses a passport but not a visa. Similarly, he has the required health certificate but not the character certificate.

87. Umesh Unnikrishnan was born on 2nd September, 1974. He has a TOEFL score of 660. He is not capable of making the required deposit, but is sponsored by a Company having an equity capital of Rs 10 crore. He has all the relevant certificates as required by the Law College.

88. Rakesh Mohapatra is a 27-year-old student sponsored by a company having an equity base of Rs 12 crore. He possesses all the relevant certificates as required. His TOEFL score is 546.

89. Madan Varshneya was born on 2nd September, 1963. He is willing to make the required statutory deposit. He possesses a passport and a visa. He is yet to receive any health certificate although he has a character certificate. He has a TOEFL score of 600.

90. Ranjan Madhusudan is 28 years old. He is willing to make a statutory deposit of upto Rs 9 lakh. He posseses a passport and a visa. He also has the required character certificate. His TOEFL score is 620.

Directions (Q.91-100) : Study the following information carefully and answer the questions given below it.

The following are the conditions to appoint a Distributor for petroleum gas throughout Delhi. The applicant should

1) be an Indian by nationality.

2) be in the age group of 21-50 years on 5th September, 1993.

3) be at least a Matriculate or recognised equivalent.

4) be a resident of Delhi for not less than 5 years immediately preceding the date of application.

5) have family income of not more than Rs. 50,000 annually.

6) not have any dealership in any oil company.

7) have no close relatives as a dealer / distributor of any oil company.

However,

8) restrictions relating to annual income would not be applicable to persons working in corporations owned or controlled by State government, but the case shall be referred to the Managing Director.

9) for unemployed graduates, conditions (6) and (7) may be waived.

10) if a person belongs to SC/ST but is not a resident of Delhi, the case may be referred to the Chairman.

On the basis of the above conditions and the informations provided against each applicant, decide which of the following courses of action should be taken. Mark answer

1) if the applicant is to be selected;

2) if the candidate is not to be selected;

3) if the data is inadequate;

4) if the case is to be referred to the Managing Director; and

5) if the case is to be referred to the Chairman.

91. Amandeep is an unemployed graduate who has been living in Delhi since 1983. He is a citizen of India and his date of birth 2nd February, 1970. His father is the only earner in the family drawing Rs 800 per month.

92. Raju Narayan is a matriculate who has been living in Delhi since August 1988. He was born on 7th November, 1953. His family income is less than Rs. 25,000 per annum and he has no close relatives as a dealer of any oil company.

93. Kishan Gopal born on 22nd January, 1963 is an Indian by nationality. He is a matriculate having dealership in Tamsha Oil Company. His family income is Rs 21,000 per annum and he is a resident of Delhi since 1974. He has no close relatives as dealer/distributor in any oil company.

94. Balvinder Singh working in the State Corporation is an Indian by nationality and is 23 years of age. He is a graduate and his family income is Rs. 60,000 per annum. He has been in Delhi for 7 years. He does not work himself or has any of his relatives working as distributor or dealer in any oil company.

95. Parvesh Kaur, an Indian, born in 1970, is an Intermediate staying in Delhi since 1979. He does not hold any dealership in any oil company and the income of his mother, the sole earner, is not more than Rs 500 per month.

96. Chalukam, an Indian resident of Bombay, is a matriculate with a family income of Rs 20,000 per annum. His date of birth is 15.3.1972. He does not have any dealership in any oil company nor has any close relative as dealer or distributor. He is an SC candidate.

97. A 27-year-old Indian, Naresh Saini is an unemployed graduate and a resident of Delhi since 1984. He has a family income of Rs 16,000 per annum.

98. Pran Chaturvedi working in Haryana State Corporation has been living in Delhi for 5 years and has passed Senior Secondary. He is a citizen of India born on 13th June, 1969. His family's annual income is Rs 75,000. Neither he nor any of his relatives has a dealership or distributorship of any oil company.

99. Maninder Vohra, aged 33 years, is an unemployed graduate and an Indian by nationality. His family income is Rs. 55,000 annually and he has been living in Delhi for 12 years now.

100. Prashant Kohli, an Indian citizen, has no dealership in any oil company nor has any close relatives doing the same job. His family income is Rs. 15,000 per month.

Directions (Q.101-110): Study the following information carefully and answer the questions given below it.

Given here are the conditions to become the members of a Resort Country Club. A person must:

1) be in the age group of 18-50 years as on August 3, 1993.
2) be drawing a minimum salary of Rs 1 lakh per annum.
3) own a house.
4) not have a family of more than four members including himself.
5) have exhibited excellence in any field of arts and sports.

However, if a person

6) satisfies all the conditions except (3) above, the case may be referred to the Club Secretary.
7) satisfies all the conditions except (4) above, but draws a salary of more than Rs. 2 lakh per annum, the case may be referred to the Club President.

On the basis of the above conditions and the information provided for each person in the questions given below, decide which of the following courses of action should be taken regarding each candidate. Mark answer

(1) if the person is eligible to be a member;
(2) if the person cannot be allowed the membership;
(3) if the data provided is inadequate;
(4) if the case is to be referred to the Club Secretary; and
(5) if the case is to be referred to the Club President.

101. Mr. Sanjeev Rana, an I.A.S. officer, draws a salary of Rs 6,500 per month. His date of birth is 19th June, 1964. He holds a certificate of being the best volleyball player in his college. He lives with his wife and a daughter. He stays in government accomodation.

102. Ms. Sangeeta Sethi, living with her mother and father, is a college professor earning Rs. 8,500 monthly. The house she lives in is on her name. She has a good record in the field of fine arts.

103. Mr. Ashok Taneja, a bachelor, lives in a private house owned by him with his parents and grandparents (all alive). He is a Senior Manager in a private firm drawing a salary of above Rs 2 lakh per annum. He has won the State Singles' Trophy in badminton. He is 25 years of age.

104. Ms. Radha Kapoor, living with her husband, is a senior official in a company receiving Rs 10,000 per month. She completed 10 years of service in the company on 9th January, 1992.

105. Mr. Kantinath completed 32 years in April 1991. He stays in his own house along with his wife and three sons. He works as a supervisor in a company and draws Rs 1,12,000 per annum. He has exhibited excellence in the field of arts.

106. Mr. Vipin Chandra, who is 35 years old, works as a superintendent in a fertiliser plant. He lives as a tenant with his wife and two sons. He draws a monthly salary of Rs 8,700. He holds a certificate of merit in modern arts.

107. Mr. Rajan Khanna was born in October 1958. He is the Chairman of a Company and draws Rs 1,05,000 per annum. He has been the captain of the Basketball team of his office and lives in his own house with his wife.

108. Mr. Vivek Chandrawal is 43 years old. He lives alone in his own house. He works as a supervisor in a textile mill and earns Rs. 9,000 every month.

109. Mr. Ajay Bhatnagar is a Branch Manager in a bank and draws a salary of Rs. 2,08,000 per annum. He lives in a flat owned by him, along with his parents, wife and a son. He holds a certificate of excellence in Tennis. His date of birth is 16th November, 1968.

110. Mr. Pankaj Mehta lives in his own house with his wife and a daughter. He gets a monthly salary of Rs. 7,500. He is a good painter and owns a gallery. He is 37 years of age.

Directions (Q. 111-115): Study the following information carefully and answer the questions given below it.

The following are the qualifications necessary for the recruitment of a Librarian in a State University.

The candidate must:

1) have a Master's degree in Library Science with at least 55% marks or its equivalent grade and a consistently good academic record.

2) have a one-year specialisation or Master's Degree in an area of Information Technology / Archives and Manuscript-keeping.

3) have at least ten years' experience as a Deputy Librarian in a University.

4) bear an evidence of innovative library service and organisation of published work.

In the case of a candidate who

5) has 15 years' experience as a College Librarian, the case may be referred to the Vice-Chancellor.

6) has obtained less than 55% marks in Library Science but has 13 years' experience as a Deputy Librarian in a University, the case may be referred to the Registrar of the University for his consideration.

7) has M.Phil./Ph.D. degree in Library Science/ Information Science/ Documentation/ Archives and Manuscript-keeping but has only ten years' experience as a College Librarian, the condition at (1) may be waived.

Based on the above conditions and the information provided against each of the candidates in the questions given below, decide which of the following courses of action should be taken in the case of each candidate. Mark answer

(1) if the candidate is to be selected;
(2) if the candidate is not to be selected;
(3) if the data are inadequate;
(4) if the case is to be referred to the Registrar; and
(5) if the case is to be referred to the Vice-Chancellor.

111. Amit Sharma, having Master's Degree in Library Science with 70% marks and a one-year specialisation in an area of Information Technology, joined as a Librarian in the Indian College on 22nd January, 1977. He also holds a certificate of innovative library service in the college.

112. Rahul Sehgal, an M. Phil. in Library Science, has been a Deputy Librarian in the Rohilkhand University since 27th August, 1980. He also has Master's Degree in Archives and Manuscript-keeping. He holds a evidence of innovative organisation of published work of the college students doing Ph.D.

113. Sanjay Verma has been a Deputy Librarian in the IMS University since 1973. He holds an evidence of contributing library service in the same institution. He has a Master's Degree in Library Science with 53% marks.

114. Ramesh Singhani, holding a Ph.D. in Library Science, has one year's specialisation in Archives and Manuscript-keeping. He has been a Deputy Librarian in the Assam University since 11th April, 1982. He also bears a certificate of innovative library service in a public library for three years.

115. Sunil Garewal has been a College Librarian since 15th December, 1975. He holds an M.Phil. Degree in Library Science.

Directions (Q. 116-120): Study the following information carefully and answer the questions given below:

Following are the conditions for selecting Senior Manager-Credit in a bank. The candidate must

i. be a graduate in any discipline with at least 60 per cent marks.
ii. have post-qualification work experience of at least ten years in the Advances Section of a bank.
iii. be at least 30 years and not more than 40 years as on 1.4.2010.
iv. have secured at least 40 per cent marks in the Group Discussion.

v. have secured at least 50 per cent marks in the Interview.

In the case of a candidate who satisfies all the conditions **EXCEPT**

A. at (i) above, but has secured at least 50 per cent marks in graduation and at least 60 percent marks in post-graduation in any discipline, the case is to be referred to the General Manager-Advances.

B. at (ii) above, but has total post-qualification work experience of at least seven years, out of which at least three years as Manager-Credit in a bank, the case is to be referred to the Executive Director.

In each question below details of one candidate are given. You have to take one of the following courses of action based on the information provided and the conditions and sub- conditions given above and mark the number of that course of action as your answer. You are not to assume anything other than the information provided in each question. All these cases are given to you as on 01- 04- 2010.

Give answer

1) if the case is to be referred to the Executive Director.

2) if the case is to be referred to the General Manager-Advances.

3) if the data are inadequate to take a decision.

4) if the candidate is not to be selected.

5) if the candidate is to be selected.

116. Shobha Gupta has secured 50 per cent marks in the Interview and 40 per cent marks in the Group Discussion. She has been working for the past eight years, out of which four years as Manager-Credit in a bank, after completing her BA degree with 60 per cent marks. She was born on 12th September 1978.

117. Rohan Maskare was born on 8th March 1974. He has been working in a bank for the past twelve years after completing his B Com degree with 70 per cent marks. He has secured 50 per cent marks in both the Group Discussion and the Interview.

118. Prakash Gokhale was born on 4th August 1977. He has secured 65 per cent marks in postgraduation and 58 per cent marks in graduation He has been working for the past ten years in the Advances Department of a bank after completing his postgraduation. He has secured 45 percent marks in the Group Discussion and 50 per cent marks in the Interview.

119. Sudha Mehrotra has been working in the Advances Department of a bank for the past twelve years after completing her B Com Degree with 60 per cent marks. She has secured 50 per cent marks in the Group Discussion and 40 per cent marks in the Interview. She was born on 15th February 1972.

120. Amit Narayan was born on 28th May 1974. He has been working in the Advances department of a bank for the past eleven years after completing his B Sc Degree with 65 per cent marks. He has secured 55 per cent marks in the Group discussion and 50 per cent marks in the interview.

Directions (Q. 121-130): Study the following information carefully and answer the questions given below:

Following are the conditions for selecting Chief Manager-Marketing in an organisation:

The candidate must

(i) be at least 35 years old as on 1-2-2010.

(ii) have secured at least 55 per cent marks in graduation.

(iii) have secured at least 60 per cent marks in post- graduate degree/diploma in Marketing Management.

(iv) have post-qualification work experience of at least 10 years in the Marketing Division of an organization.

(v) have secured at least 50 per cent marks in the selection process.

In the case of a candidate who satisfies all the above conditions EXCEPT

(A) at (iv) above, but has post-qualification work experience of at least six years as Manager- Marketing, the case is to be referred to Head-Marketing Division.

(B) at (ii) above, but has secured at least 65 per cent marks in post graduate degree/diploma in Marketing Management, the case is to be referred to GM- Marketing.

In each question below are given the details of one candidate. You have to take one of the following courses of action based on the information provided and the conditions and sub-conditions given above and mark the number of that course of action as your answer. You are not to assume anything other than the information provided in each question. All these cases are given to you as on 01-02-10.

Mark answer

1) if the candidate is to be selected.

2) if the case is to be referred to Head- Marketing Division.

3) if the case is to be referred to GM- Marketing.

4) if the candidate is not to be selected.

5) if the data provided are inadequate to take a decision.

121. Arnab Behera has secured 65 per cent marks in PG degree in Marketing Management and 58 per cent marks in graduation. He has been working in the Marketing Division of an organisation for the past eleven years after completing his postgraduate degree. He has secured 55 per cent marks in the selection process. He was born on 8th July 1970.

122. Neeta Ghosal was born on 4th May 1974. She has been working in the Marketing Division of an organization for the past twelve years after completing her postgraduate diploma in Management with 70 per cent marks. She has obtained 60 per cent marks in graduation and 50 per cent marks in the selection process.

123. Sudesh Sarkar was born on 15th June 1974. He has secured 55 per cent marks in the selection process and 50 per cent marks in graduation. He has been working in the Marketing Division of an organisation for the past twelve years after completing postgraduate degree in Marketing Management with 75 per cent marks.

124. Sudha Naik was born on 14th April 1973. She has been working in the Marketing Division of an organisation for the past fourteen years after completing her post- graduate diploma in Marketing Management with 70 per cent marks. She secured 50 per cent marks in the selection process and 52 per cent marks in graduation.

125. Sunita Jaiswal was born on 5th July 1976. She has secured 55 per cent marks in graduation and 58 per cent marks in the selection process. She has been working in the Marketing Division of an organisation for the past ten years after completing postgraduate degree in Marketing Management with 57 per cent marks.

126. Nayan Dastur was born on 8th October 1968. He has secured 55 per cent marks in both graduation and the selection process. He has been working in the Marketing Division of an organisation for the past ten years after completing postgraduate diploma in Marketing Management with 65 per cent marks.

127. Sunil Kamath has secured 58 per cent marks in graduation. He was born on 24th May 1974. He has been working in the Marketing Division of an organisation for the past seven years as Manager Marketing after completing postgraduate degree in Marketing Management with 65 per cent marks. He has secured 50 per cent marks in the selection process.

128. Md. Yusuf was born on 29th January 1975. He has secured 55 per cent marks in graduation and 52 per cent marks in the selection process. He has also secured 68 percent marks in postgraduate diploma in Marketing Management. He has been working for the past twelve years in the Marketing Division of an organisation.

129. Navind Ghosh was bom on 12th December 1973. He has been working in the Marketing Division of an organisation for the past ten years after completing his postgraduate degree in Marketing Management with 63 per cent marks. He has secured 54 per cent marks in graduation and 45 per cent marks in the selection process.

130. Avinash Sargota has been working for the past eight years, out of which for six years as Manager Marketing in an organisation after completing his post graduate degree in Marketing Management with 62 per cent marks. He has secured 58 per cent marks in graduation and 52 per cent marks in the selection process. He was born on 14th February 1972.

Directions (Q. 131-135): Study the following information carefully and answer the questions given below.

Following are the conditions for selecting Manager- HR in an organisation:
The candidate must

(i) be at least 30 years and not more than 35 years as on 1.3.2012.
(ii) have scored at least 60 per cent marks in graduation in any discipline.
(iii) have scored at least 65 per cent marks in the Postgraduate Degree/ Diploma in Personnel Management/HR.
(iv) have post-qualification work experience of at least five years in the Personnel/HR Department of an organisation.
(v) have scored at least 50 per cent marks in the selection process.

In the case of a candidate who satisfies all the above conditions except

(a) (ii), but has scored at least 55 per cent marks in graduation in any discipline and at least 70 per cent marks in Postgraduate Degree/Diploma in Personnel Management/HR, the case is to be referred to GM - HR.
(b) (iv), but has post-qualification work experience of at least four years, out of which at least two years as Deputy Manager - HR, the case is to be referred to President - HR.

In each question below are given details of one candidate. You have to take one of the following courses of actions based on the information provided and the conditions and sub-conditions given above and mark the number of that course of action as your answer. You are not to assume anything other than the information provided in each question. All these cases are given to you as on 1.3.2012.

Mark answer

1) if the candidate is not to be selected.
2) if the data provided are not adequate to take a decision.
3) if the case is to be referred to President-HR.
4) if the case is to be referred to GM-HR.
5) if the candidate is to be selected.

131. Rita Bhatt was born on 25th July 1978. She has scored 62 per cent marks in graduation and 65 per cent marks in Postgraduate Diploma in Management. She has been working for the past six years in the Personnel Department of an organisation after completing her Postgraduation. She has scored 55 per cent marks in the selection process.

132. Ashok Pradhan was born on 8th August 1980. He has been working in the Personnel Department of an Organisation for the past four years after completing his Postgraduate Degree in Personnel Management with 67 per cent. Out of his entire experience, he has been working for the past two years as Deputy Manager-HR. He has scored 62 per cent marks in graduation and 58 per cent marks in the selection process.

133. Alok Verma was born on 4th March 1976. He has been working in the Personnel Department of an organisation for the past six years after completing his Postgraduate Diploma in Personnel Management with 66 per cent marks. He has scored 57 per cent marks in the selection process and 63 per cent marks in graduation.

134. Swapan Ghosh has been working in the Personnel Department of an organisation for the past five years after completing his Postgraduate degree in HR with 72 per cent marks. He has scored 56 per cent marks in graduation. He was born on 12th May 1977. He has scored 58 per cent marks in the selection process.

135. Seema Behl has been working in the Personnel Department of an organisation for the past seven years after completing her Postgraduate Diploma in Personnel Management with 70 per cent marks. She was born on 5th July 1979. She has scored 65 per cent marks in graduation and 50 per cent marks in the selection process.

Directions (Q. 136-145): Study the following information carefully and answer the questions given below:

Following are the conditions for selecting Marketing Manager in an organization:

The candidate must

(i) be a graduate in any discipline with at least 55 per cent marks.

(ii) have a postgraduate degree/diploma in Marketing Management with at least 60 per cent marks.

(iii) have post-qualification work experience of at least five years in the marketing division of an organisation.

(iv) have secured at least 45 per cent marks in the selection examination.

(v) have secured at least 40 per cent marks in the selection interview.

In the case of a candidate who satisfies all the conditions **except**

(a) at (iii) above, but has post-qualification work experience of at least three years as Deputy Marketing Manager, the case is to be referred to GM-Marketing.

(b) at (v) above, but has secured at least 60 per cent marks in the selection examination, the case is to be referred to VP-Marketing.

In each question below, details of one candidate are given. You have to take one of the following courses of action based on the information provided and the conditions and sub-conditions given above and mark the number of that course of action as your answer. You are not to assume anything other than the information provided in each question. All these cases are given to you as on 01.05.2010.

Mark answer

1) if the candidate is to be selected.

2) if the candidate is not to be selected.

3) if the case is to be referred to GM-Marketing.

4) if the case is to be referred to VP- Marketing.

5) if the data provided are not adequate to take a decision.

136. Nidhi Agrawal has secured 60 per cent marks in the selection interview and 40 per cent marks in the selection examination. She has been working in the marketing division of an organisation for the past eight years after completing her postgraduate degree in Marketing Management with 65 per cent marks. She has secured 59 per cent marks in BSc.

137. Navin Desai has secured 56 per cent marks in BA. He has been working in the marketing division of an organisation for the past seven years after completing his postgraduate degree in Marketing with 62 per cent marks. He has secured 62 per cent marks in the selection examination and 38 per cent marks in the selection interview.

138. Sabina Handa has been working for the past four years as Deputy Marketing Manager in an organisation after completing her postgraduate diploma in Marketing Management with 65 per cent marks. She has secured 45 percent marks in both selection examination and selection interview. She has also secured 58 per cent marks in BCom.

139. Manoj Malhotra has secured 65 per cent marks in BSc and 60 per cent marks in postgraduate degree in Marketing Management. He has also secured 50 per cent marks in both selection examination and selection interview. He has been working in the marketing division of an organisation for the past six years after completing his postgraduation in Marketing.

140. Varsha Akolkar has secured 59 per cent marks in BA. She has secured 42 per cent marks in the selection interview and 48 per cent marks in the selection examination. She has been working in the marketing division of an organisation for the past seven years after completing her postgraduation in Marketing Management with 57 per cent marks.

141. Utpal Goswami has been working in the marketing division of an organisation for the past five years after completing his postgraduate diploma in Marketing Management with 65 per cent marks. He is a first-class Science graduate with 60 per cent marks. He has secured 45 per cent marks in the selection examination and 40 per cent marks in the selection interview.

142. Anindita Ghosh has been working for the past eight years in an organisation after completing her postgraduate degree in Marketing Management with 70 per cent marks. She has secured 56 per cent marks in BA. She has also secured 50 per cent marks in the selection examination and 45 per cent marks in the selection interview.

143. Samir Phukan has been working in the marketing division of an organisation for the past five years after completing his post graduate diploma in management with 65 per cent marks. He has secured 60 per cent marks in BCom. He has also secured 50 per cent marks in both selection examination and selection interview

144. Nimisha Patil has secured 59 per cent marks in BCom. She has also secured 50 per cent marks in both selection examination and the selection interview. She has been working as Deputy Marketing Manager in an organisation for the past three years after completing her postgraduate degree in Marketing Management with 63 per cent marks.

145. Sadashiv Ghatge has secured 60 per cent marks in BCom. He has been working for the past five years in the marketing division of an organisation after completing his post- graduate degree in Marketing Management with 68% marks. He has secured 35 per cent marks in the selection

Directions (Q. 146-155): Study the following information carefully and answer the questions given below:

Following are the conditions for selecting Assistant General Manager-HR in an organisation.

The candidate must

i. be at least 40 years and not more than 50 years old as on 01-05-2010.

ii. be postgraduate in Personnel Management/HR with at least 60 per cent marks.

iii. have post-qualification work experience of at least fifteen years out of which at least five years as Senior Manager-HR in an organisation.

v. have successfully implemented HR-System in his/ her organisation some time during the past three years.

v. have secured at least 45 per cent marks in the selection process.

In the case of a candidate who satisfies all the conditions

EXCEPT at

a. (ii) above but has secured at least 50 per cent marks in postgraduation and at least 65 per cent marks in the selection process, the case is to be referred to Executive Director.

b. (iii) above but has at least twelve years' post qualification work experience out of which at least eight years as Senior Manager-HR in an organisation, the case is to be referred to Chairman.

In each question below details of one candidate are given. You have to take one of the courses of action based on the information provided and the conditions and sub-conditions given above and mark the number of that course of action as your answer. You are not to assume anything other than the information provided in each question. All these cases are given to you as on 01-05-2010.

Mark answer

1) if the candidate is to be selected.

2) if the candidate is not to be selected.

3) if the data provided are not adequate to take a decision.

4) if the case is to be referred to Executive Director.

5) if the case is to be referred to Chairman.

146. Pranab Ghosh was born on 8th March 1968. He has been working for the past eighteen years in an organisation out of which last seven years as Senior Manager-HR after completing his postgraduation in HR with 68 per cent marks. He had successfully implemented HR-System last year in his organisation. He has secured 50 per cent marks in the selection process.

147. Sheetal Jha has been working in an organisation for the past twenty years out of which ten years as Senior Manager-HR after completing her postgraduation in Personnel Management with 70 per cent marks. She was born on 2nd December 1965. She has secured 45 per cent marks in the selection process.

148. Prabir Sengupta was born on 8th May 1963. He has secured 65 per cent marks in the selection process. He has been working for the past fifteen years in an organisation, out of which twelve years as Senior Manager HR, after completing his post graduation in HR with 55 per cent marks. He has successfully implemented HR-System in his organisation during the last two years.

49. Shailesh Kumar has been working in an organisation for the past thirteen years, out of which nine years as Senior Manager-HR after completing his postgraduation in HR with 68 per cent marks. He was born on 15th September 1968. He has secured 48 per cent marks in the selection process. He has successfully implemented HR-System in his organization two years back.

150. Navin Chopra was born on 12th June 1967. He has been working for the past sixteen years, out of which seven years as Senior Manager-HR after completing his post- graduation in Personnel Management with 75 per cent marks. He has secured 44 per cent marks in the selection process. He has successfully implemented HR-System in his organisation last year.

151. Meera Kulkarni has been working for the past seventeen years, out of which eight years as Senior Manager-HR, after completing her postgraduation in Personnel Management with 66 per cent marks. She has successfully implemented HR-System in her organisation during the last two years. She has secured 49 per cent marks in the selection process. She was born on 14th December 1971.

152. Akash Shastri was born on 12th April 1967. He has been working for the past sixteen years, out of which six years as Senior Manager-HR, in an organisation after completing his postgraduation in HR with 58 per cent marks. He has successfully implemented HR-System in his organization last year. He has secured 65 per cent marks in the selection process.

153. Shekhar Jena has been working for the past fifteen years, out of which last seven years as Senior Manager-HR, in an organisation after completing his postgraduation in HR with 68 per cent marks. He has secured 60 per cent marks in the selection process. He was born on 16th August 1965. He has successfully implemented HR- System in his organisation in past three years.

154. Sunetra Govil was born on 5th April 1964. She has been working for the past seventeen years, out of which nine years as Senior Manager-HR, in an organisation. She has secured 48 per cent marks in the selection process.She has also secured 69 per cent marks in her post-graduation in Personnel Management. She successfullyimplemented HR-System in her organisation last year.

155. Mohit Saxena was born on 27th July 1963. He has been working for the past thirteen years, out of which nine years as Senior Manager-HR, after completing his post- graduation in HR with 67 per cent marks. He has secured 49 per cent marks in the Selection process. He has successfully implemented HR-System in his organisation during the past three years.

Directions (Q. 156-165): Study the following information carefully and answer the questions which follow:

A Research Institute is recruiting a librarian to digitise its information resources among other duties. Candidates must possess the following criteria. The candidate must

I. be not less than 35 years and not exceed 40 years as on 01.11.2009.

II. have a Bachelor's Degree in Library and Information Science with 65 per cent marks.

III. have a PhD in Library Science.

IV. have post qualification experience of at least 4 years in a University Library.

However, if the candidate fulfils the above mentioned criteria except

A. II above, but has a UGC NET certification with all the other above criteria fulfilled, he/she may be referred to the Dean.

B. (IV), but all the eligibility criteria are met and the candidate has at least one year's experience in a research institute, he/she may be offered contractual appointment for a year.

Based on the above criteria, study carefully whether the following candidates are eligible for the recruitment process and mark your answer as follows. You are not to assume anything other than the information provided in each question. All cases are given to you as on 1.11.2009.

Mark answer

1) if he/she is to be shortlisted.
2) if he/she is not to be shortlisted.
3) if he/she should be referred to the Dean.
4) if he/she may be offered contractual appointment, if required.
5) if the data provided is inadequate to take a decision.

156. Anil Rath has a doctorate in Library Science from Karnataka University in 2003. Born on July 21, 1969, he graduated in Library and Information Science from Karnataka University, where he was Assistant Librarian for four years since 2005.

157. Dr Samir Bali has a PhD in Library Science and has been with the Institute of Fundamental Research as Assistant Librarian since October 2008. He graduated with a degree in Library and Information Science in 1994 at the age of 22. He obtained 70 per cent in his graduation.

158. Vaishali Shetty has been a librarian at STS University since 2007 when she qualified in the UGC NET examination. She has a degree in Library and Information Science with 60 per cent. Her first job was as junior librarian at TRP Institute of Development Research from October 2000 to December 2001.

159. Vivek Jha has a PhD in Library and Information Science. He graduated in Library and Information Science in 1992 with 65 per cent. He was born on 1.10.1974. Since July 2005, he has been working as Deputy Librarian at a deemed University.

160. A graduate in Library Science with 69 per cent, Dr M Puri has been working at Ranchi University for 4 years as Deputy Librarian. She earned her doctorate while working for the Labour Research Institute for 5 years as Assistant Librarian. She is 38 years old as on the required date.

161. Megha Vaidya has a graduate degree in Library Science from Punjab University where she has been a librarian for the past 5 years. In 2002 she obtained UGC NET qualification at the age of 29. She obtained 72 percent in graduation.

162. Anup Gupta is obtaining his PhD from YCM University, where he has been Junior Librarian since 2004. He qualified in the UGC NET exam in June 2000. He has degree in Library and Information Science with 62 per cent. His date of birth is 17. 10. 1973.

163. Kirti Shukla obtained her doctorate and Bachelor's degree from Patna University. She obtained 63 per cent at graduation. She obtained her UGC NET qualification in 1998 when she was 26.

164. Prakash Sinha has been a librarian for a government institution for three years. Prior to this, he was a University Librarian for 7 years after completing his PhD in Library Science. He graduated in 1991 with 68 per cent in Library Science. He is exactly 40 years of age on the specified date.

165. Rohan Sachdev obtained his UGC NET qualification after his graduation in 1998 when he began working. He has been Assistant Librarian for the past two years with a research institute. He obtained 65 per cent in his graduation in Library Science. He earned his PhD in Library Science in 2007. His date of birth is 22.10.1974

Answers and Explanations

Q.1-10: The table is constructed as follows:

A	B	C	D	E	Question Number
(G)				(F)	
[H]					
√	√	√	√	(√)	1
√	√	√	√	√	2
√	√	√	√	√	3
√	√	√	√	√	4
(√)	×				5
(√)	√	√	√	√	6
[√]	√	√	√	√	7
√	√	√	√	(×)	8
[√]	√	√	√	√	9
√	√	√	√	√	10

Answer combinations:

A + B + C + D + E ⇒ answer 2

A + B + C + D + (F) ⇒ answer 3

(G) + B + C + D + E ⇒ answer 4

[H] + B + C + D + E ⇒ answer 5

Otherwise ⇒ answer 1

Note: Please note that there are two additional conditions attached to A. Hence they are represented in two ways: condition G is written within brackets while H is written within box. If G is fulfilled, a √ mark would be placed within a brackets. If H is fulfilled a √ mark would be placed within a box.

Answers: Looking at the answer table and the answer combinations, we see that the following answers could be obtained:

1.3 2.2 3.2 4.2 5.1 6.4 7.5

8.1 9.5 10.2

Q. 11-20: The analysis table is constructed as follows:

a	b	c	d	Question Number
(e)	(f)	(h)	(g)	
	×	√		11
	×	√		12
?	(√)	√	√	13
√	√	(×)		14
√	√	(√)	√	15
√	√	√	√	16
√	? (√)	√	√	17
		(×)		18
(?)	√	√	√	19
√	√	(√)	√	20

Answer combinations

a + b + c + d
or a+(f)+c+d
or (e)+b+c+d ⇒ answer 1
a+b+c+(g) ⇒ answer 4
a+b+(h)+d ⇒ answer 5
not to be given ⇒ answer 2
data inadequate ⇒ answer 3

The following answers are obtained by looking at the analysis table and the answer combinations:

11.2 12.2 13.3 14.2 15.5

16.1 17.1 18.2 19.3 20.5

In question 19, the student may yet have won free studentship if he was a good sportsman at district level, but this information is got given.

Q.21-30:

Please note that (ii) in itself is a condition attached to both d and e. If either (or both) of the two is violated, (ii) becomes true. Therefore, for convenience we break (ii) into two parts (α) and (β).

a	b	c	d	e	Question Number
(i)			(α)	(β)	
√	√	×			21
√	√	√	√	√	22
√	√	√	(√)	√	23
(√)	?	√	√	√	24
√	×	√	√	√	25
√	√	√	√	√	26
√	√	√	√	√	27
	×				28
?	√	√	√	√	29
√	√	√	?	√	30

Answer combinations:

a+b+c+d+e ⇒ answer 3

(i)+b+c+d+e ⇒ answer 4

a+b+c+d+(β)

or a+b+c+(α)+e

or a+b+c+(α) + (β) ⇒ answer 5

not to be selected ⇒ answer 2

data inadequate ⇒ answer 1

Now the answer combinations are:

21. 2	22. 3	23. 5	24. 1	25. 2
26. 3	27. 3	28. 2	29. 1	30. 1

In Q. 29, the candidate may have done C.A., which is not mentioned. Hence data indequate. In Q. 24, no information is given about the age. Hence, data inadequate.

Q.31-40:

Note: We have named the additional conditions as 'a', 'b' and 'c'.

I	II	III	IV	V	Question Number
(a)	(b)	(c)			
√	(√)	(?)	√	√	31
√	√	√	√	√	32
		√		×	33
√	(√)	(√)	√	√	34
√	√	√	√	√	35
√	√	√	?	√	36
√	√	(√)	√	√	37
?	√	√	√	√	38
(√)	√	√	√	√	39
√	(√)	(√)	√	√	40

Answer combinations:

I+II+III+IV+V
or I+(b)+III+IV+V ⇒ answer choice 1
(a)+II+III+IV+V ⇒ answer choice 2
I+II+(c)+IV+V ⇒ answer choice 3
data inadequate ⇒ answer choice 4
not to be selected ⇒ answer choice 5

Note that Sandip Kurnam got 89 in the interview. Devendra Tomar has got more marks than Sandip which means that Devendra Tomar got 90 marks (fractional marks was not given, so a mark like 89.6 is not possible) or more. Hence, Devendra Tomar and Shanu Khurana fulfil condition V. Also note that it is not mentioned whether *Anand Avinash*, for which Asish Gupta worked, was a weekly magazine. Hence the ? mark.

Now, we see that the following should be the answers:

31. 4	32. 1	33. 5	34. 5	35. 1
36. 4	37. 3	38. 4	39. 2	40. 5

Note that Dhanoa and Rashmi Pandey violate more than one basic conditions simultaneously, hence they are not selected.

Note: We have provided detailed solutions to the questions till now by providing an analysis table etc. Now onwards, we will present brief explanations only for each of the questions, starting from Q. 41.

41. 5; Has the candidate any cassette recorded of his music? No such information.
42. 1; No information about condition II. But condition (C) is fulfilled nevertheless.
43. 1; All conditions fulfilled.
44. 3; All conditions except IV fulfilled.
45. 4; All conditions except I fulfilled. (The additional information about documentary films is irrelevant.)
46. 4; No information about working experience. The additional information about computer education is useless.
47. 4; No information about graduation. Information about post-graduation could be useful only if work-experience was lacking.
48. 4; No information about the nature of experience; was it or was it not in a publishing house?
49. 4; The same reason as in the previous case.
50. 4; No information about the nature of computer education: is it or is it not a course of at least 2 years?
51. 1; All conditions fulfilled.

52. 3 53. 5

54. 2; It is obvious that Rahul is not a graduate. But he satisfies that additional condition of having computer education of more than 2 years. Further, he does not suffer from colour blindness and has a work experience of 49 months, which is more than 3 years. Now, we come to his age. At the time of joining the computer course he was 19. Since his career is continuous, with no breaks, he must be (19 + 3) years + 49 months old now which is equal to 26 years and 1 month. So, conditions I, III, IV and (b) are satisfied. Correct choice: (2).
55. 5; He violates more than one basic condition at a time. He is over-aged and also a non-graduate. The additional conditions are not applicable to him since the directions clearly say that these conditions will work only if he satisfies *all other* criteria except any one.
56. 4; No information about passport.
57. 1; All conditions fulfilled.
58. 5; More than one basic condition is violated at the same time. He does not have a passport and he is more than 30 years old. The additional conditions are to be used (see directions) *only if all* other conditions are satisfied except one.

59. 5; He does not have a degree, B.E. or B. Tech.
60. 3; Condition V violated.
61. 1
62. 2; $100,000 < $ 1 million
63. 4; No information about the nature of business.
64. 4; No information about global turnover.
65. 5; Condition IV violated.
66. 1; 10 million rupees = 1 crore rupees.
67. 5; More than one basic condition violated: II and I.
68. 4; No information as to whether the company agrees to export 80% of its production, in case it does not agree to have Indian staff.
69. 1
70. 1; Although condition I is violated, condition (a) is fulfilled.
71. 4; No information about recommendation.
72. 1; All conditions satisfied.
73. 5; Condition IV not satisfied.
74. 5; Condition V violated.
75. 5; Condition III violated. Condition (c) also.
76. 4; Minimum marks required in the interview is: 60% of 150 = 90. Sarita has 89. He has more than Sarita. But it means he may have 89.5 or 91 as well. Hence, data are inadequate.
77. 2
78. 4; No information about age.
79. 3
80. 5; More than one basic condition violated.
81. 5; No information about TOEFL score.
82. 5; No information about TOEFL score.
83. 1 84. 3 85. 2
86. 2; More than one basic condition violated.
87. 2; More than one basic condition violated.
The directions state that if he fulfils *all other criteria* except one, then his case may still be considered. But he violates *two* conditions. So his application will be rejected.
88. 2; Condition III violated.
89. 2; Condition V violated.
90. 5; No information about character certificate.
91. 1; The candidate satisfies all conditions except (6) and (7). But he fulfils condition (9), so (6) and (7) are waived.
92. 3; Condition (1) is missing.
93. 2; Having dealership in an oil company, the candidate does not satisfy condition (6).
94. 4; Condition (8) is fulfilled instead of condition (5).

95. 3; Condition (7) is missing.
96. 5; Condition (10) is satisfied instead of condition (4).
97. 1; All conditions of eligibility and condition (9) instead of conditions (6) and (7) are satisfied.
98. 4; The candidate satisfies condition (8) instead of condition (5).
99. 2; Having a family income of more than Rs 50,000 despite not working in a State Corporation, the candidate does not satisfy condition (5).
100. 3; The age of the candidate is not mentioned.
101. 2; The candidate does not satisfy conditions (2) and (3) as he draws a salary of Rs 78,000 per annum and does not own a house.
102. 3; Condition (1) is missing.
103. 5; Condition (7) is fulfilled instead of condition (4) as the candidate has a family of five members including himself.
104. 3; Condition (1) is missing.
105. 2; Having a family of five members including himself, the candidate does not satisfy condition (4).
106. 4; Condition (6) is fulfilled, as the candidate does not own a house.
107. 1; All conditions of eligibility are satisfied.
108. 3; Condition (5) is missing.
109. 5; The candidate has a family of five members, but he draws a salary of more than Rs. 2 lakh per annum. So, he satisfies condition (7) instead of condition (2).
110. 2; Having a salary of Rs. 90,000 per annum, the candidate does not satisfy condition (2).
111. 5; Clearly, the candidate Amit Sharma fulfils conditions (1), (2) and (4). Further, being a College Librarian for 16 years, he satisfies conditions (5). So, the answer is (5).
112. 1; Rahul Sehgal, being an M. Phil, satisfies condition (7) so that condition (1) is waived. Then, he satisfies conditions (2), (3) and (4) evidently. So he is selected and the answer is (1).
113. 2; The candidate satisfies condition (4) evidently. Being a Deputy Librarian for the last 20 years, he satisfies condition (3). But having marks less than 55%, he violates condition (1) and so the answer is (2).
114. 1; The candidate, being a Ph.D., satisfies condition (7) so that condition (1) is waived. He satisfies conditions (2) and (4) evidently and, being a Deputy Librarian for eleven years, he satisfies condition (3). So the answer is (1).
115. 3; Here, information about the candidate regarding (2) and (4) is not mentioned. So, the answer is (3).

(116-120):

Q.No.	Candidate	(i)/(A)	(ii)/(B)	(iii)	(iv)	(v)	Ans
116.	Shobha	✓	(✓)	✓	✓	✓	1
117.	Rohan	✓	—	✓	✓	✓	3
118.	Prakash	(✓)	✓	✓	✓	✓	2
119.	Sudha	✓	✓	✓	✓	×	4
120.	Amit	✓	✓	✓	✓	✓	5

(121–130):

Q.No.	Name	(i)	(ii)/B	(iii)	(iv)/(A)	(v)	Ans
121.	Arnab	✓	✓	✓	✓	✓	1
122.	Neeta	✓	✓	—	✓	✓	5
123.	Sudesh	✓	(✓)	✓	✓	✓	3
124.	Sudha	✓	(✓)	✓	✓	✓	3
125.	Sunita	×	✓	×	✓	✓	4
126.	Nayan	✓	✓	✓	✓	✓	1
127.	Sunil	✓	✓	✓	(✓)	✓	2
128.	Yusuf	✓	✓	✓	—	✓	5
129.	Navind	✓	×	✓	✓	×	4
130.	Avinash	✓	✓	✓	(✓)	✓	2

(131-135):

Q.No.	Person	I	II/(a)	III	IV/(b)	V	Ans
131.	Rita Bhatt	√	√	√	√	√	5
132.	Ashok Pradhan	√	√	√	(√)	√	3
133.	Alok Verma	×	√	√	√	√	1
134.	Swapan Ghosh	√	(√)	√	√	√	4
135.	Seema Behl	√	√	√	√	√	5

136. 2; Does not satisfy (iv).
137. 4; Satisfies (b).
138. 3; Satisfies (a).
139. 1; Satisfies all conditions.
140. 2; Does not satisfy (ii).
141. 1; Satisfies all conditions.

142. 5; We don't know whether Anindita has been working in the marketing division.

143. 5; Was it Marketing Management?

144. 3; Satisfies (a).

145. 4; Satisfies (b).

(146-155):

Q.No.	Person	(i)	(ii)/(A)	(iii)/(B)	(iv)	(v)	Ans
146.	Pranab	√	√	√	√	√	1
147.	Sheetal	√	√	√	—	√	3
148.	Prabir	√	(√)	√	√	√	4
149.	Shailesh	√	√	(√)	√	√	5
150.	Navin	√	√	√	√	×	2
151.	Meera	×	√	√	√	√	2
152.	Akash	√	(√)	√	√	√	4
153.	Shekhar	√	√	√	√	√	1
154.	Sunetra	√	√	—	√	√	3
155.	Mohit	√	√	(√)	√	√	5

(156-165):

Q.No.	Candidate	I	II/(A)	III	IV/(B)	Ans
156.	Anil	×	–	✓	–	2
157.	Samir	✓	✓	✓	(✓)	4
158.	Vaishali	–	✓	–	×	2
159.	Vivek	✓	✓	✓	–	5
160.	M Puri	✓	✓	✓	–	5
161.	Megha	✓	✓	–	–	5
162.	Anup	✓	(✓)	×	–	2
163.	Kirti	✓	(✓)	–	–	5
164.	Prakash	✓	✓	✓	✓	1
165.	Rohan	✓	✓	✓	(✓)	4

Chapter Thirteen

Input-Output

(Introduction to basics)

13.1: Introduction

These are not really very new type of problems the BSRBs and some other examining bodies of management have been asking them for quite a few years by now. Substance-wise these problems are not very tough. But usually they take a good deal of time before they could be solved. In other words, they are time-consuming. And in today's competitive world time is what really matters.

In the discussion to follow, we are trying to give some really fast methods and time-saving tips. There are essentially four types of problems on input-output that are asked.

13.2 INPUT-OUTPUT: Four Basic Types of Problem

In input-output problems you are asked to imagine that there is some kind of computer or a word-processing machine and this machine performs some operation on a given input. These operations are performed repeatedly as per a pre-fixed pattern and subsequently we have different output in different steps.

Ex 1. For example, suppose an input of four words is given to a computer; as given below:

Input: sherry quart pint bar

Now, suppose that the machine operates on this input on a prefixed rule whereas the first two words are interchanged and the remaining two words are left untouched. (Let us call it **Operation One**). Then according to this rule, our output will be:

First output: quart sherry pint bar

Now, suppose that the machine doesn't stop here but goes on performing its operations. If it wants to perform an operation again, **this time last output will be the input.** Now, suppose that the machine is to perform another operation. Suppose that the rule this time is, to interchange the last two words and leaving the first two words interchanged. (Let us call it **Operation Two**) Then, according to this rule (our **input** will be the first output and) the output will be:

Second Output: quart sherry bar pint.

Now, suppose that the machine is programmed to perform Operation One and Operation Two, alternately. If the machine goes on then for the third output, the input will be the second output and the operation performed will be Operation One i.e. leaving the last two words unchanged and interchanging the first two. So, we have:

Third Output: sherry quart bar pint.

Obviously, the next step will be consisting of Operation Two and it will be performed on 3rd output. In this, as already mentioned, we will leave the first two words unchanged and interchange the last two words.

Fourth Output: sherry quart pint bar

If the machine went on, the sequence would be generated as shown below.

Input :	sherry	quart	pint	bar
Step I :	quart	sherry	pint	bar
Step II :	quart	sherry	bar	pint
Step III:	sherry	quart	bar	pint
Step IV:	sherry	quart	pint	bar
Step V :	quart	sherry	pint	bar
Step VI:	quart	sherry	bar	pint

Note that we perform operation One (interchanging only the first two words) and operation Two (interchanging only the last two words) alternately.

Ex 2: We will now look at a different type of operation performed by a different machine. Suppose the input is:

Input: sherry quart pint bar

Now, suppose that the machine does the following operation on this input: *it scans the words given, it then looks for the word that comes first in the dictionary and puts that word in the first place.* So, the 1st output is.

1st output. bar sherry quart pint

(**Note:** "bar" is alphabetically the first word, therefore it is put in the first place. Remaining words are pushed to the right *without* changing their order.)

If the machine went on with its logic, it is obvious that the second output will be as follows:

2nd Output: bar pint sherry quart

(**Explanation:** Since "pint" is alphabetically the second word found in the dictionary it comes to the second place. Remaining words are shifted to the right *without* any change in their order.)

And then the Third Output will be:

3rd Output: bar pint quart sherry

(**Explanation:** Since "quart" is the alphabetically the third word after bar and pint, it comes to the third place. The remaining word is sherry and it automatically occupies its due place that is fourth.

Note: Please note that here the 3rd Output is arranged in correct alphabetical order and **therefore this is the last step and the machine *stops* after this step.**

Ex 3: We will now have a look at yet another type of operation. Suppose we begin with our input:

Input: sherry quart pint bar

Now, suppose that the machine performs a set of random operations as given below.

(i) to get step I, the last two letters of the input are deleted. Then step I is.

Step I: sher qua pi b

(ii) to get step II, the last letter of the words of input are prefixed to it:

Step II: ysherry tquart tpint rbar

(iii) to get step III, all the vowels of the words of the input are deleted:

Step III: shrry qurt pnt br

And, so on ....

Ex 4: We will now have a look at yet another machine and see its output. Suppose our input is as follows:

Input: 12 14 5 18 13

And suppose our various outputs are:

1st step:	3	5	5	9	4
2nd step:	36	42	15	54	39
3rd step:	169	225	36	361	196
4th step:	24	28	10	36	26

Obviously, the various steps are obtained as per the following rules.

(i) the 1st step is obtained by adding the digits of the numbers of the input.

(ii) the 2nd step is obtained by multiplying the input by 3.

(iii) the 3rd step is obtained by adding 1 to the input numbers and then squaring it.

(iv) The fourth step is obtained by doubling the input.

For example consider the last number of the input. It is 13. In the 1st step, we add its two digits: We get, $1 + 3 = 4$. In the second step we multiply it by 3: $13 \times 3 = 39$. In the next step we add 1 and then square : $(13 + 1)^2 = (14)^2 = 196$. In the last step we multiply 13 by 2: $13 \times 2 = 26$.

The four basic types of operations

Having discussed the foregoing four examples, we are now in a position to discuss the four basic types of questions that are usually asked. They are:

(1) **SHIFTING:** In this type of questions, we usually *shift* the given words (or numbers) of the given input as per a fixed pattern.

In Ex 1, we have seen it already. In Ex 1, we had the first two words shifting their places in operation 1 and then the last two words shifting their places in operation Two. This was an example of shifting.

(2) **ARRANGING:** In this type of questions, the words or the numbers are arranged as per a fixed *order.* This order can be an alphabetical order in case of words; it can be an increasing or decreasing order in case of numbers. *Note that whereas shifting goes on endlessly; arranging ends as soon as the order intended is achieved.*

An example of arranging is Ex 2. In this we saw that the given input was arranged alphabetically in subsequent steps.

(3) **ARITHMETIC OPERATIONS:** In this type of questions, the input consists of some numbers. The subsequent steps are obtained by taking the numbers of the input and then performing different arithmetic operations.

An example of arithmetic operations was seen in Ex 4. If you recall, we had taken an input there and then subsequent steps were obtained by performing different arithmetic operations (like adding, multiplying, squaring etc.) on the numbers of the input.

(4) **MISCELLANEOUS:** As the name suggests, this covers miscellaneous cases. The input can be anything and the machine can perform a set of random operations on this. **We have given an illustration in Ex 3.** Normally, a case that does not fall under any of the first three categories falls under this category.

13.3: First Step: Identification of the type of problem

Till now, we have seen that the problems on input-output could be of any of the following four types: *shifting, arranging; arithmetical operations* or *miscellaneous*.

But it would not be mentioned in the questions itself that it is about shifting or arranging or something else.

Naturally, then, the first step towards your solution would be to identify the basic operations that are taking place. The moment you get a question on input-output you should first identify the basic type. This is an important first step and you should not take more than five seconds for this.

How to identify the basic operation

- *Check for arrangement first*

First of all, you should try to check if there is any arrangement. If arrangement is there, the words would be continuously arranged in an alphabetical order. If the input is consisting of numbers then the numbers would be continuously arranged in an increasing or decreasing order.

Just look at the first two-three steps. Do you see a word that comes alphabetically first (or last) in dictionary going to the first (or last) place, in the first step? Do you see a word that comes alphabetically second (or second last) going to the second (or second last) place, in the next step?... Alternately, if the input consists of numbers do you see the smallest (or largest) number going to the first (or last) place, in the first step? Do you see the second smallest (or largest) number going to the second (or second last) place in the second step?

If yes, it is a problem of arrangement.

- *Check for shifting, next*

If the chances of arrangement have been ruled out, then you should check if shifting is taking place.

Just look at the first two-three steps. *Do you see that words (or numbers) from a particular position are going to a fixed particular position? Is this being repeated*? If yes, then it is a problem of shifting.

- **Next check for "arithmetic operations"** (*only if input is of numbers*)

If the input consists of numbers and the chances of arrangement and shifting are ruled out then you should see if it is a case of "arithmetic operations".

For this, take the first two numbers of the input and the first two numbers of Step I and Step II. Now, *see the relation between the first number of input, first number of step I and first number of step II. Do we have the* ***same*** *relation between the second number of input, second number of step I and second number of step II*? If yes, then it is a case of arithmetic operations.

- If none of the above is applicable, it is of course a case of miscellaneous category. In that case, you will have to apply your mind a bit more carefully and discover the logic on which the machine works.

Learner's Exercise I

(Identification of pattern)

Directions (Q. 1 to 10): Ten word-processing machines when given an input line of words (or numbers) rearrange them following a particular rule, in each step. We are giving below ten sets of inputs and the various sequential outputs generated on them by the ten different machines. You are asked to find if the machine is working on a logic of shifting or arranging or arithmetical operations or miscellaneous (Time allotted: 10 seconds per questions)

(1)

Input:	gone	are	the	days	of	yore
Step I:	are	gone	the	days	of	yore
Step II:	are	days	the	gone	of	yore
Step III:	are	days	gone	the	of	yore
Step IV:	are	days	gone	of	the	yore

(2)

Input:	abi	cop	ktp	rjk	mon
Step I:	cop	abi	ktp	rjk	mon
Step II:	cop	abi	mon	ktp	rjk
Step III:	abi	cop	mon	ktp	rjk
Step IV:	abi	cop	rjk	mon	ktp

(3)

Input:	15	18	22	14	10	19
Step I:	6	9	4	5	1	10
Step II:	12	18	8	10	2	20
Step III:	36	81	16	25	1	100
Step IV:	20	26	34	18	10	28

(4)

Input:	rjb	bkp	str	qua	mon
Step I:	str	rjb	bkp	mon	qua
Step II:	bkp	str	rjb	qua	mon
Step III:	rjb	bkp	str	mon	qua
Step IV:	str	rjb	bkp	qua	mon

(5)	**Input:**	16	12	14	13	15
	Step I:	15	12	14	13	16
	Step II:	13	12	14	15	16
	Step III:	12	13	14	15	16
(6)	**Input:**	17	18	20	19	12
	Step I:	17	18	12	19	20
	Step II:	12	19	17	18	20
	Step III:	12	19	20	18	17
	Step IV:	20	18	12	19	17
(7)	**Input:**	I	was	looking	at	her
	Step I:	at	I	was	looking	her
	Step II:	at	her	I	was	looking
	Step III:	at	her	I	looking	was
(8)	**Input:**	I	was	looking	at	her
	Step I:	was	I	at	looking	her
	Step II:	was	at	I	her	looking
	Step III:	looking	was	at	I	her
	Step IV:	was	looking	I	at	her
	Step V:	was	I	looking	her	at
	Step VI:	at	was	I	looking	her
(9)	**Input:**	I	was	looking	at	her
	Step I:	I	looking	at	her	was
	Step II:	at	I	looking	her	was
	Step III:	at	I	her	looking	was
	Step IV:	at	her	I	looking	was
(10)	**Input:**	I	was	looking	at	her
	Step I:	I	aas	looking	aat	heer
	Step II:	I	sow	grikool	ta	reh
	Step III:	j	xbt	mppljoh	bu	ifs
	Step IV:	II	swas	glooking	tat	rher

Detailed solutions:

We are now presenting detailed solutions of all the above questions. Beforehand, we must tell that Q1, Q5, Q7 and Q9 are on *arrangement*; Q2, Q4, Q6, Q8 are on *shifting*; Q3 involves *arithmetic operations* and Q10 is of *miscellaneous* type. (If you have worked out this answer already, you are on the right track and you don't need to read the detailed solutions. However, if you have the slightest of doubts, please do go ahead and read the solutions. Ensure that you understand this.)

Q1, Q5, Q7, Q9 (arrangement)

1. Look at the first step. In this, *are* comes to the first place and *are* is alphabetically the first word. Now, look at the second step. In this, *days* comes to the second place and *days* is alphabetically the second word in the given sentence.

This means that the words are being *arranged* (in alphabetically increasing order).

5. Look at the first step. In this, 16 replaces 15 and goes to the last place. Also, 16 is the largest number. In the second step, 15 replaces 13 to go to the second last place and 15 is the second largest number.
   This means that the numbers are being arranged (in increasing order).
7. Look at the first place. In this, *at* (which is alphabetically the first word of the sentence) comes to the first place and all other words are "pushed" to its right. Similarly, in 2nd step, *her* (which is the second word after *at* in the dictionary) comes to the second place.
   Hence, this is also a case of arrangement.
9. In the first step, *was* goes to the last place and remaining letters are "pushed" to the left; in second step, *at* goes to the first place and remaining letters are "pushed" to its right, in the third step, *looking* goes to the second last step and remaining letters are "pushed" to its left and so on. Note that *was* and *looking* are alphabetically the last and the second-last words of the sentence while *at* is the first word of the sentence. This means that the sentence is basically being reorganised in alphabetically increasing order.

Note: Please note that arrangement can be done in many ways leading to the same result. We can pick the alphabetically first, second words and put them at the first, second place (as in Q1), or we can pick the largest and second largest... numbers and put them in the last, second last... place (as in Q5); or we can put the last word in the last place then put the first word in the first place then put the second last word in the second last place ... and so on (as in Ex 9). Specially note how the same objective of arranging in alphabetical order is achieved in Q7 and Q9 in two different ways

Q2, Q4, Q6, Q8 (Shifting):

2. In first step, first two words are interchanged and remaining words are unchanged. (Let us call it operation One). In second step, first two words remain unchanged, third word becomes fourth, fourth becomes fifth, fifth becomes third. (Let us call it Operation Two). Then Operation One and Operation Two follow alternately.
   So here, we have words being shifted from particular places to particular places according to a fixed rule; repeatedly.Therefore, it is shifting.
4. In first step, third word becomes first, first becomes second, second becomes third, and the fourth and fifth words interchange. (Let us call it Operation One.) The same process (of shifting on a fixed pattern) repeatedly goes on. Therefore, it is shifting.
6. In first step, third and fifth numbers interchange and remaining numbers remain unchanged. I (Let us Call it operation one). In second step, first and third words interchange, second and fourth words interchange while the fifth word remains unchanged. (Let us call it operation two). These two operations of shifting goes on repeatedly. Hence, it is a case of shifting.

8. In first step, first and second words and, third and fourth words interchange. (Call it operation one). In second step, second and third words and, fourth and fifth words interchange. (Call it operation two). In third step, last word becomes first and all other words shift to the right. (Call it operation three). In fourth, fifth and sixth steps; operation one, operation two and operation three are repeated respectively. Thus, we have three different shifting-plans operating here successively. Hence, it is a case of shifting.

Note: Please note that within the same machine more than one shifting-plans may operate alternately. Therefore, in Q4; we had a case of a single shifting-plan; in Q2 and Q6 we had two shifting-plans (two operations) and in Q8, we had three different shifting-plans (or three operations).

Q.3. **Arithmetical operations:** The first step is obtained by adding the digits of the input. The second step is obtained by doubling the numbers of step I, 3rd step is obtained by squaring the numbers of step I, 4th step is obtained by subtracting 5 from the numbers of the input and then doubling it.

Q. 10. Miscellaneous

In first step, all the vowels are repeated twice. In second step, words of the input are written in reverse fashion. In third step, all the letters in the words of the input are replaced by the next letter of the alphabet (i becomes j; w becomes x, a becomes b ... etc.) and in the last step, the last letter of each word of the input is prefixed to the word.

13.4: Short cuts for identification

By now, you must have become very familiar with the basic type of questions that are asked and how to identify them. You must also have realised that this identification is a relatively easy job and it should not take more than ten to fifteen seconds. Although we have given rather detailed explanations to our questions of the learner's exercise I; in practice. This identification is (and must be) mental and merely a glance should show it. Although I personally feel that this (identification) is a most elementary step and just a little practice would enable you to judge the type of problem by having a cursory glance at the given pattern; we are still giving some useful practical tips to come to a quick conclusion.

Tip 1: *If the input and the subsequent steps involve the same words (or numbers) then it is most likely to be a problem of either shifting or arrangement. Else if the words (or numbers) change in subsequent steps it is a problem of arithmetical operation or miscellaneous type.*

Explanation: Look at Q1, 2, 4, 5, 6, 7, 8 and 9. In all of them all the words (or numbers) in various steps are the same as those given in the input. Hence these are either arrangement problems or shifting problems.

On the other hand, look at Q3 and Q10. Here, the content of the input is different from the content of the various steps. For example, in Q3; step I has 6 which is not there at all in input; in Q10, step I has II which is not present in input. Hence, these must belong to arithmetical operations or miscellaneous category.

Tip 2: *If either the first or the last word (or number) of all the steps (excluding input) remains unchanged then it is (almost) certain that it is an arrangement problem.*

Explanation: Look at Q1, Q5, Q7, Q9. In Q1, the first word of Step I to Step IV is the same (i.e. are); in Q5, the last word of Step I to Step III is the same (i.e. 16); in Q7, the first word in Step I to Step III is the same (i.e. at); in Q9, the last word in Step I to Step IV is the same (i.e. was). Therefore, Q1, Q5, Q7, Q9 are (almost) certainly arrangement problems.

On the other hand, consider Q2, Q4, Q6, Q8. In Q2, the first word of Step I and Step II is different from the first word of step III, IV; similarly the last word of step I is different from Step II. Again, in Q4, the first and last words of step I change in the step II itself. Again, in Q6, the first word of step I changes in step II while the last number of step I and II changes in step III. Finally in Q8; the first word of step I and step II changes in step III and the last word of step I changes in step II.

This means that in Q2, Q4, Q6, Q8, neither the first nor the last word (or number) remains unchanged after step I. Therefore, none of these could be arrangement problems.

We are now in a position to draw a plan for lightning quick identification of the problem. The strategy can be shown by the following flowchart

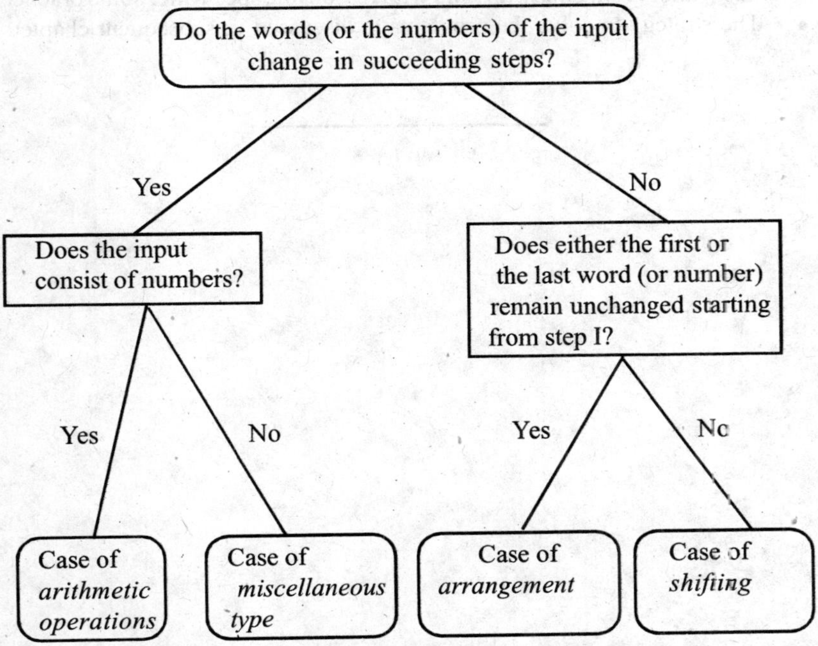

FLOWCHART: IDENTIFICATION OF PROBLEM

13.5: Remaining strategy

We have seen that input-output questions can have many types. In this chapter, we have merely given an introduction to these types. The solution strategy for each of these types is different and, therefore, we have decided to cover these in different chapters. For the present we have merely taught you to identify the problem-type quickly. The problem of how to actually solve it will be discussed in subsequent chapters.

Summary

- Input-output problems consist of an input fed to a machine that generates a series of outputs on a fixed pattern.
- There are four different ways in which the machine can generate the output. They are:
  - Shifting
  - Arranging
  - Arithmetical operations
  - Miscellaneous
- The two tips and the flowchart given in the chapter would help the student for quick identification of the type of problem. However, he can identify this without using these tips and with reasonable speed after some practice.
- The strategy to solve the problems is discussed in subsequent chapters.

Chapter Fourteen

Input-Output (...contd.): Shifting

14.1: Introduction

In the last chapter, we have seen the basic pattern of input-output problems. We have seen that the input when fed to a word-processing machine can generate output in many ways and one of which was shifting. If you recollect, *shifting* means an operation where the words (or numbers) of a given step are "shifted" from their place to a different place as per a pre-fixed plan or rule. If you look at the note following the solutions to Learner's exercise No. 1 of previous chapter; you will realise that sometimes within the same machine more than one shifting plans may be generated.

14.2: A Sample Problem (What's the problem like)

Ex. 1

Directions (Q. 1-5): A word arrangement machine, when given a particular input, rearranges it following a particular rule. The following is the illustration of the input and the steps of arrangement:

Input: I have long awaited for your reply
Step I: reply long have awaited for your I
Step II: long reply awaited have for I your
Step III: your awaited reply have for I long
Step IV: awaited your have reply for long I and so on till step VII.

1. Given the following
   Step IV: I know you will not reply back
   What step will be the following arrangement?
   Arrangement: You back I reply not will know
   1) X 2) XI 3) IX
   4) VIII 5) None of these
2. If step VI of a given input be 'have I done anything wrong with you', what would be the input?
   1) you done with have wrong I anything
   2) you done with have wrong anything I
   3) done you have with wrong anything I
   4) I have you with wrong anything done
   5) None of these
3. If step XII of a given input be 'it is impossible to do everything right' what is the 17 step of that input?
   1) is it everything right do impossible to
   2) It is right everything do to impossible

3) It is everything right do impossible to
4) to everything is right do impossible it
5) None of these

4. Given the input, what would be step V of the input?
Input: Only you can do all thing right.
1) you only right thing all do can
2) only you thing right all can do
3) only thing you right all do can
4) thing only you right all do can
5) None of these

5. If step IV of a given input be 'It is last serious warning to you', what is step I of that input?
1) you last is to serious it warning
2) last you is to warning it serious
3) serious last to it warning is you
4) warning to serious it is you last
5) None of these

14.3: Basic definition and illustration

For this, please refer to Ex. 1 of the last chapter. (Please dont proceed further without reading Ex. 1 of the last chapter).

14.4: Some additional elementary definitions

14.4.1: 1-Step, 2-Step and 3-Step shifting:

If you recall the note following the solutions to learner's exercise # 1 of last chapter, you have already seen that sometimes more than one shifting operations are performed alternately by the some machine. For example, in the above mentioned exercise of the last chapter, Q4 had only **one** shifting operation going on, Q6 and Q2 had **two** shifting operations while Q8 had **three** different shifting operations going on.

When we have a **single** operation going on repeatedly it is called **1-Step** shifting, when we have **two** operations it is called **two-step** shifting and when we have **three** operations going on, it is called **three-step** shifting.
For example, consider the following:

Ex. 2: (a) **Input:** Ram was here only
Step I: was Ram here only
Step II: Ram was here only
Step III: was Ram here only

(b) **Input:** Ram was here only
Step I: was Ram here only
Step II: was Ram only here
Step III: Ram was only here
Step IV: Ram was here only

(c) **Input:** Ram was here only
Step I: was Ram here only
Step II: was Ram only here
Step III: here Ram only was
Step IV: Ram here only was
Step V: Ram here was only
Step VI: only here was Ram

Explanations:

Ex.2: (a) is a case of 1-Step shifting. This is because in going from Input to Step I only the first two words are being interchanged. (Call it Operation One). And the same operation is being separated all the time.

(b) is a case of 2-Step shifting. This is because in going from Input to Step I only the first two words inter-change (Call it operation One) while, in going from Step I to Step II only the last two words interchange. (Call it Operation Two). These two operations are being performed alternately hence it is a two-step case.

(c) is a case of 3-Step shifting. This is because in going from Input to Step I only the first two letters interchange (Call it Operation One); in going from Step I to Step II the last two letters interchange (Call it Operation Two) and in going from Step II to Step III first and last words interchange (Call it Operation Three). Thus, three operations are being performed one after another and hence it is a 3-type case.

14.4.2: Identification of 1-Step/2-Step/3-Step types

When a problem is given to us it is extremely important that we identify if it is a 1-step or 2-step or 3-step type of shifting. Let us see how we can do it.

If you look at Ex.2 (a) you will notice that in a 1-step type shifting the same operation takes place over and over again. Thus, the change in going from Input to Step I is the same as the change in going from Step I to Step II and so on. But in case of a 2-Step type shifting [See Ex2(b)] two operations take place alternately. This means that the change in going from Input to Step I is different from the change in going from Step I to Step II. But the change from Input to Step I is the same as the change from Step II to Step III while the change from Step I to Step II is same as the change from Step III to Step IV. Similarly, in a 3-Step type shifting the change in going from Input to Step I is different from the change from Step I to Step II and from Step II to Step III. There, change from Input to Step I is same as the change from Step III to Step IV; change from Step I to Step II is same as the change from Step IV to Step V and the change from Step II to Step III is same as the change from Step V to Step VI.

On this basis, we can evolve the following strategy to identify the type of shifting:

Flow chart 1: Identification of 1-Step/2-Step/3-Step etc.

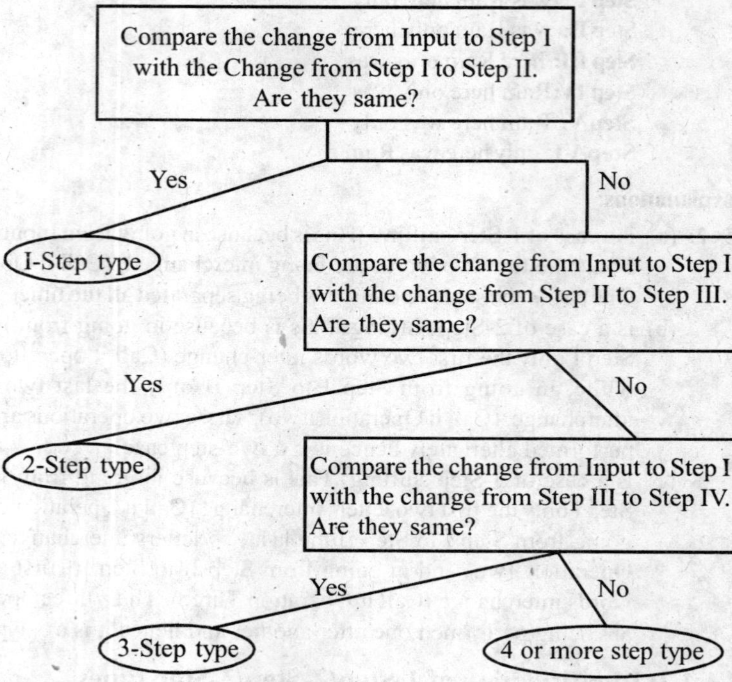

Time saving tip: When you use the above mentioned flowchart to judge if it is a 1-Step or 2-Step or 3-Step case; you need not take all the words or members of the given input. You can take only two or three words and see their movements to compare the various changes. See the following example to understand this.

Ex. 3: By using the flowchart 1 and the tip given above identify the type of shifting given in the examples of Ex 2.

Soln: To compare the changes we will monitor only the first two words (as told in the time saving tip above) and not the entire sentence.

(a) In Input to Step I; first word becomes second and second word becomes first. Again, in Step I to Step II; first word becomes second and second becomes first. Hence, by virtue of our flowchart (the two changes being similar) it is a 1-Step type shifting.

(b) In Input to Step I, first and second words interchange. In Step I to Step II; first and second words do not interchange. Hence, by virtue of our flowchart it is not a 1-Step type case. Again, watch the movement of the first two words from Step II to Step III. Here, the first two words interchange. Hence, by virtue of our flowchart it is a 2-Step type case.

(c) In Input to Step I, first and second words interchange. First and second words don't interchange in Step I to Step II or even in Step II to Step III. Hence, by virtue of our flowchart, it is a case of neither 1-Step nor 2-Step type. But, in Step III to Step IV, first and second words do interchange. Hence, by virtue of our flowchart, it is a 3-Step type case.

14.4.3: A terminology for convenience

(i) **Numerals for steps:** Sometimes, for convenience sake we shall use

0 in place of Input
1 in place of Step I
2 in place of Step II
3 in place of Step III and so on.

Again, sometimes we shall write a long phrase like "*the change in going from Input to Step I*"; in a shorter way as "**0** to **1**". For example, we can write "**2** to **3**" which will mean "the change in going from Step II to Step III."

Exercise 1 (A) Write the word-equivalent for

(i) **1** to **4** (ii) **4** to **0** (iii) **5** to **10**

(B) Write the following symbolically

(i) the change from Step I to Step V
(ii) the change from Step III to Input
(iii) the change from Step V to Step X

Ans: (A) (i) (**1** to **4** means) = the change from Step I to Step IV
(ii) the change from Step IV to Input
(iii) the change from Step V to Step X

(B) (i) **1** to **5** (ii) **3** to **0** (iii) **5** to **1**

Now, we have seen that sometimes similar kind of change is effected between a pair of steps. For example, in Ex 1; Input to Step I carries the same change as that from Step II to Step III. (In both of these; the change is characterised by interchanging the first and the last word and the second and the third word). We can write this in words as:

"*The change in going from Input to Step I is the same as the change in going from Step II to Step III.*"

OR, we can write it more concisely as

0 to **1** = **2** to **3**

Learner's Exercise 3:

(A) Write the meaning of the following into words:

(i) **0** to **4** = **6** to **10**
(ii) **2** to **1** = **6** to **5**

(B) Write the following symbolically:

(i) Similar changes are effected in going to Step III from Step I and in going from Step V to Step III.
(ii) The change in going from Input to Step IV is the same as the change in going from Step II to Step VI.

Ans. (A): (i) The change in going from input to Step IV is the same as the change in going from Step VI to Step X

(ii) The change in going from Step II to Step I is the same as the change in going from Step VI to Step V

(B) (i) **3** to **1** = **5** to **3**

(ii) **0** to **4** = **2** to **6**

Note that using this terminology our flowchart 1 takes the following elegant form:

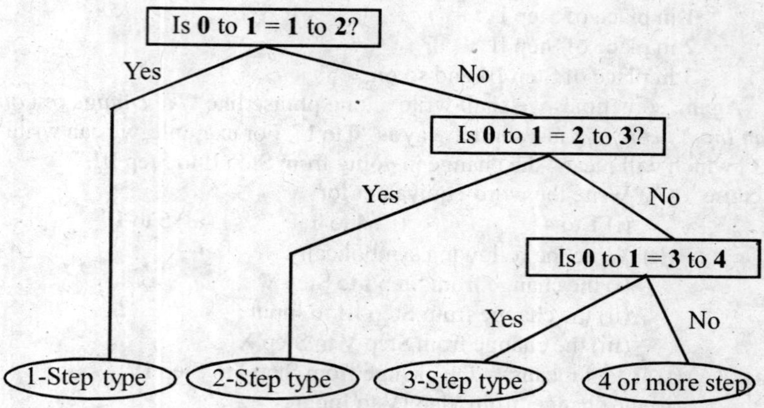

Flowchart 2 = Identification of 1-Step/2-Step etc.

14.5: Golden rule of reduction

Using our terminology, we can say that:

(i) In a 1-Step case:

0 to **1** = **1** to **2** = **2** to **3** .....

(ii) In a 2-Step case:

(a) **0** to **1** = **2** to **3** = **4** to **5** ..... and

(b) **1** to **2** = **3** to **4** = **5** to **6** .....

(iii) In a 3-Step case:

(a) **0** to **1** = **3** to **4** = **6** to **7** = ... and

(b) **1** to **2** = **4** to **5** = **7** to **8** = ... and

(c) **2** to **3** = **5** to **6** = **8** to **9** = ...

all these can be rewritten as:

(i) In a 1-step case:

0 to **1** = $(0 + 1 \times 1)$ to $(1 + 1 \times 1)$ = $(0 + 2 \times 1)$ to $(1 + 2 \times 1)$

(ii) In a 2-step case:

(a) **0** to **1** = $(0 + 1 \times 2)$ to $(1 + 2 \times 2)$ = $(0 + 2 \times 2)$ to $(1 + 2 \times 2)$

(b) **1** to **2** = $(1 + 2 \times 1)$ to $(2 + 2 \times 1)$ = $(1 + 2 \times 2)$ to $(2 + 2 \times 2)$

(iii) In a 3-step case:

(a) **0** to **1** = $(0 + 1 \times 3)$ to $(1 + 1 \times 3) = (0 + 2 \times 3)$ to $(1 + 2 \times 3)$

(b) **1** to **2** = $(1 + 1 \times 3)$ to $(2 + 1 \times 3) = (1 + 2 \times 3)$ to $(2 + 2 \times 3)$

(c) **2** to **3** = $(2 + 1 \times 3)$ to $(3 + 1 \times 3) = (2 + 2 \times 3)$ to $(3 + 2 \times 3)$

If we analyse the above, we find that:

(a) *In case of a 1-Step; the same change can be rewritten by adding or subtracting any multiple of 1.* Thus; if it is a 1-Step case, we can have;

Ex. 4: (a) **0** to **4** = $(0 + 1 \times 1)$ to $(4 + 1 \times 1)$ = **1** to **5** = $(0 + 2 \times 1)$ to $(4 + 2 \times 1)$ = **2** to **6** etc.

(b) **13** to **9** = $(13 - 9 \times 1)$ to $(9 - 9 \times 1)$ = **4** to **0** etc.

(b) *In case of a 2-Step, the change can be rewritten by adding or subtracting any multiple of 2.* Thus, if it is a 2-Step case, we can have

Ex. 5: (a) **0** to **4** = $(0 + 1 \times 2)$ to $(4 + 1 \times 2)$ = **2** to **6**
= $(0 + 2 \times 2)$ to $(4 + 2 \times 2)$ = **4** to **8**

(b) **13** to **9** = $(13 - 4 \times 2)$ to $(9 - 4 \times 2)$ = **5** to **1** etc.

(c) *In case of a 3-Step, the change can be rewritten by adding or subtracting any multiple of 3.* Thus, if it is a 3-Step case, we can have

Ex. 6: (a) **0** to **4** = $(0 + 1 \times 3)$ to $(4 + 1 \times 3)$ = **3** to **7**
= $(0 + 2 \times 3)$ to $(4 + 2 \times 3)$ = **6** to **10** .....

(b) **13** to **9** = $(13 - 3 \times 3)$ to $(9 - 3 \times 3)$ = **4** to **0** ..... etc.

The above mentioned rules given in italics are called golden rule of reduction. We can put that in words more concisely:

Golden rule of reduction:

The change between any two steps in a 1-Step (or 2-Step or 3-Step) case can be substituted by a change between two new steps that can be obtained by adding or subtracting any multiple of 1 (or 2 in a 2-Step case, or 3 in a 3-Step case) from the given steps.

Learner's Exercise 4

(A) Reduce the following to its minimum

(a) **4** to **6**

(b) **3** to **7**

(c) **14** to **18**

(d) **12** to **7**

(e) **9** to **6**

by assuming a 1-type, 2-type and a 3-type case for each, separately.

(B) In a question, the first five steps (Input to Step IV) generated by a word arrangement machine are given. On analysis it is found that Input to Step I and Step II to Step III are obtained by a similar change and; Step I to Step II and Step III to Step IV are obtained by a similar change. What type of a case is this? If you are given Step X how will you calculate Step XIII?

(C) In a word rearrangement problem, the question reads — "If Step VI of a given input is 'Have I done anything wrong with you', what would be the input?" Write this question symbolically.

(D) In a word rearrangement problem, Input to Step VI are given. You find that Input to Step I and Step III to Step IV are having same changes; Step I to Step II and Step IV to Step V are having same changes. Now, one other question reads — "If Step XIV is 'you are only mine' what will be Step X." How will you apply the golden rule of reduction to get the answer?

Soln: (A) I. **Assuming a 1-Step case**

(a) **4** to **6** = (4 - 1 × 4) to (6 - 1 × 4) = **0** to **2**

Note that we can't reduce it any further because less than **0** is not possible.

(b) **3** to **7** = (3 - 1 × 3) to (7 -1 × 3) = **0** to **4**

Similarly for the next three questions we can quickly write:

(c) **14** to **18** = **0** to **4** [Reduce 1 × 14 from both numbers]

(d) **12** to **7** = **5** to **0** [Reduce 1 × 7 from both numbers]

(e) **9** to **6** = **3** to **0** [Reduce 1 × 6 from both numbers]

II. **Assuming a 2-Step case**

(a) **4** to **6** = (4 - 2 × 2) to (6 - 2 × 2) = **0** to **2**

Note that any more reduction is not possible as less than **0** is not possible.

(b) **3** to **7** = (3 - 2) to (7 - 2) = **1** to **5**

Note that any more reduction is not possible because we can't subtract 2 from 1.

(c) **14** to **18** = (14 - 2 × 7) to (18 - 2 × 7) = **0** to **4**

Similarly, we can answer the next two questions quickly.

(d) **12** to **7** = **6** to **1** [Reduce 2 × 3 from both numbers]

(e) **9** to **6** = **3** to **0** [Reduce 2 × 3 from both numbers]

III. **Assuming a 3-Step case**

(a) **4** to **6** = (4 - 3) to (6 -3) = **1** to **3**.

Note that any more reduction is not possible as we can't subtract 3 from 1.

(b) **3** to **7** = **0** to **4** [Subtracting 3 from both numbers]

(c) **14** to **18** = (14 - 3 × 4) to (18 - 3 × 4) = **2** to **6**

Note that any more reduction is not possible as we can't subtract 3 from 2.

(d) **12** to **7** = **6** to **1** [Reduce 3 × 2 from both numbers]

(e) **9** to **6** = **3** to **0** [Reduce 3 × 2 from both numbers]

(B) The second line clearly indicates that the pattern is of two different types of operations repeating alternately. Hence, it is a 2-step case.

Now, if we are to find Step XII given Step X. We can write this symbolically as:

10 to 12

Now, by golden rule of reduction : **10** to **12** : **0** to **2.** [Reduce 2 × 5 from both numbers]

This means that Step XII will be obtained from Step X in the same way as Step II can be obtained from Input.

Therefore, we will assume the given Step X as if it was an input and we will find Step II for this assumed Input. The answer will be our required Step XII.

(C) Symbolically, we can write it as:

Find **6** to **0**; (given that **6**: "Have I done anything wrong with you")

(D) The arrangements have **3** different kinds of changes, so it is a **3 type** case:

Now, the question can be written symbolically as:

Find **14** to **10**, (given that **14**: "You are only mine").

Now, by golden rule of reduction, for a **3 type** case:

14 to **10** = (14 - 3 × 3) to (10 - 3 × 3) = **5** to **1**

Thus, *we will solve this case by taking "you are only mine" as Step V and finding Step I for this.*

Importance (use) of golden rule of reduction

Suppose that you are given a problem and in one of the questions you are given Step 20 and you have to find step 23. In our terminology you can write it as "find **20** to **23**". Suppose that you have already analysed the given pattern and using our flowchart found out that it is a 2-step type case Now, by using our golden rule you can write **20** to **23** = (20 - 10 × 2) to (23 - 10 × 2) = **0** to **3**. In words it means that step 20 to step 23 would involve the same changes as Input to step 3. *This means that you can treat the given Step 20 as input and find Step 3 for this input. Your finding would be nothing but the required Step 23.* This means that you don't need to go as far as finding step 23. Your job is done by going only as far as step 3.This saves a whopping amount of time. This makes our golden rule of reduction an extremely useful tool.

14.6: Suggested method for solution: method of reference charts

Almost everybody solves the input output problems (base on shifting) by drawing what is called a reference chart. This method consists of replacing the words (or numbers) given in the input by digits 1, 2, 3 ... etc. and then drawing a chart on the basis of their shiftings. Normally, this is the best way for solving. But the usual complaint is that it is a very time taking process to draw the reference - chart and the method is not suitable in today's rapidfire questionnaires. Keeping this complaint in mind, we are giving two methods to solve the problem. The first method is of course the usual method of reference charts. The second method is called a method of intelligent observation and I have introduced this method for the first time in this book. This method's beauty is that it is indeed very fast once it has been mastered but the problem is that it is a bit difficult to understand initially and a bit more difficult for students who are uncomfortable with mathematics. The student is advised to go through both these methods. The first one (reference chart method) will be easier to apply and understand but the second one (intelligent observation method) would save a lot of time.

We first give the method of reference charts.

14.6.1: To determine the largest step upto which the reference chart should be drawn

For this, we should have a cursory look at the questions given in the problem and see if any of them could be reduced using golden rule of reduction.

Ex 7: As an example consider Q1 to Q5 of our sample problem. In Q1, Step IV is given and we have to find which step is a given arrangement. (In such cases take the answer choice giving the largest range.) Q2, Q3, Q4 and Q5 can be written as **6** to **0**, **12** to **17**, **0** to **5** and **4** to **0**, respectively. Out of these, golden rule of reduction can be applied in (Q1), and (Q3). The whole scheme can be written down as:

Q. 1: 4 to **11*** = (4 - 2 × 2) to (11 - 2 × 2) = **0** to **7**
Q. 2: 6 to **0**
Q. 3: 12 to **17** = (12 - 6 × 2) - (17 - 6 × 2) = **0** to **5**
Q. 4: 0 to **5**
Q. 5: 4 to **0**

* We take 11 as (4 to 11) gives the largest range in the given answer choices.

Now, we see that in our reduced forms the largest step involved is **7** or step VII. Hence, we need to draw our reference chart upto Step 7.

14.6.2: Two types of questions in shifting

Consider the following:

Step III: Ram weds Sita tomorrow as

Here, III (or 3) is the number of the Step and let us define it as **Step Number.** Again, "Ram weds Sita tomorrow as "is the content of the Step III and let us define this as **Step Content**.

Now, in input-output problems on shifting there are essentially two types of problems. They are:

(i) *Given as Step Number and its content to find the content of another Step Number* (Look at our sample problem. Q2, Q3, Q4 and Q5 are examples of this type.)

(ii) *Given a step number and its content to find the step number for another given content* (look at our sample problem. Q1 is an example of this type.)

14.6.3 A step by step approach for solution using method of reference charts

Step-by-step approach

Step A: Determine whether it is 1-type or 2-type or 3-type case.

[**Note:** For quick determination take only two to three words and not all. To be still quicker follow this approach:

* If **0** to **1** = **1** to **2** it is 1-type
* If **0** to **1** ≠ **1** to **2** but **0** to **1** = **2** to **3** it is 2-type
* If **0** to **1** ≠ **1** to **2** and **0** to **1** ≠ **2** to **3** but **0** to **1** = **3** to **4** it is 3-type.]

Step B: Determine how many steps should be drawn in the reference chart. (Use golden rule of reduction. See Section 14.6.1, Ex 7)

Step C: Replace words of given input by 1,2,3... and draw a reference chart Complete the chart by following the movement of the words. Draw the chart for as many steps as determined in step B.

Step D: After completing Step A to Step C, go on to respective questions.

Step E: (i) In problems where you have to find the content of another step; given the content of one step-number

(a) first see if any reduction is possible using the golden rule

(b) after reducing (if possible) assume the given step to be its reduced step-number

(c) now, to the words of the given step, attribute the digits as they appear in the reference chart

(d) now, find the digit - pattern for the reduced step-number

(e) finally, replace the words in place of the digits

Quick method: You can save a lot of time by not taking the entire sentence of the given step but by taking only two-three words. Choose these two - three words in such a way that all of them do not appear at identical positions in more than one answer choices.

Step E: (ii) In problems where you have to find the step number of an step whose content is given; given the content of another step:

(a) first, select that step from the answer choices which coupled with the given step gives the biggest range. (See Ex 12)

(b) now, see if any reduction is possible using the golden rule

(c) after reducing (if possible) assume the given step to be its reduced step-number

(d) now, replace the words of the known step by the digits corresponding to the reduced step-number in the reference chart

(e) now, put these digits in place of the words in the given arrangement

(f) look at this digit pattern and decide which step it corresponds to, in the reference chart

(g) finally, add back as much to this step-number as you had substracted while reducing by golden rule. (important)

14.6.4: Detailed solution to our sample problem

We agree that the method given above in 14.6.3 is vague and you might not have understood much of it. But actually it is very easy. Once you read the following example (Ex. 8) and go through its solution carefully you would understand the method very well. I advise you to read the solution for each question (specially step E) and compare it with the method described in 14.6.3. See how the method is employed in practice.

Ex 8: Solve Ex 1 completely

Soln: Step A: We see that 0 to 1 # 1 to 2
and 0 to 1 = 2 to 3. Hence it is a two - step type shifting.

Step B: We need to draw upto 7 steps (See section 14.6.1, Ex 7).

Step C: For our problem, we replace the word of the input by 1, 2, 3, 4 ..... We have, I = 1, have = 2, long = 3, awaited = 4, for = 5, your = 6, reply = 7, Now, we draw a reference chart of *upto 7 steps*:

Input:	**1**	**2**	**3**	**4**	**5**	**6**	**7**
Step I:	**7**	**3**	**2**	**4**	**5**	**6**	**1**
Step II:	**3**	**7**	**4**	**2**	**5**	**1**	**6**
Step III:	**6**	**4**	**7**	**2**	**5**	**1**	**3**
Step IV:	**4**	**6**	**2**	**7**	**5**	**3**	**1**
Step V:	**1**	**2**	**6**	**7**	**5**	**3**	**4**
Step VI:	**2**	**1**	**7**	**6**	**5**	**4**	**3**
Step VII:	**3**	**7**	**1**	**6**	**5**	**4**	**2**

Explanation: The given problem itself gives us upto Step IV. Remaining steps are drawn by copying from appropriate changes. Since, it is a 2-Step type case 4 to 5 = 2 to 3. Hence, Step V is drawn from Step IV in same way as Step III is drawn from Step II. Similarly, Step VI is drawn from Step V in the same way as Step IV is drawn from Step III.

Step D: Once we complete Step A to Step C; in other words, once we complete our reference chart, we will move on to the questions.

Step E (i) and (ii): Now, there are two types of questions possible. In type one, you are given the content of a step and you have to find the content of another step. Q2, Q3, Q4 and Q5 are examples of this type of questions. In the second type of questions, you are given the content of one step and the content of another unknown step and you have to find this unknown step-number, Q1 is an example of it.

(i) Q2, 3, 4, 5: Now, we will follow the following strategy to solve these questions. In questions of the first type, we will first see if any reduction is possible by our golden rule. Then, we will take the given step and to its words we will assign the same digits as they appear for that step in the reference chart. Now, we will find out the sequence of these digits for the step of which we have to find the content. Finally, we resupply the words for the given digits.

Q. 2: For example, Q. 2 is:

6 to **0**, (given 6 = "Have I done anything wrong with you") Now, Step 6 in our reference chart is, 2 1 7 6 5 4 3. So, we assign: Have = 2, I = 1, done = 7, anything = 6, wrong = 5, with = 4, you = 3.

Now, Input in our reference chart is = 1 2 3 4 5 6 7. Resupplying the words, we get:

Input = I have you with wrong anything done. **Correct answer: 4**

Q. 3: Q. 3 is:

12 to **17**, (given, 12 = "It is impossible to do everything right") By golden rule of reduction **12** to **17** = **0** to **5**.

Now, **0** = 1, 2, 3, 4, 5, 6, 7. So we assign: If = 1, is = 2, impossible = 3, to = 4, do = 5, everything = 6, right = 7. Now, from our reference chart, Step V = 1 2 6 7 5 3 4. Resupplying the words, we get: It is everything right do impossible to. **Correct Answer: 1**

Q. 4: Q. 4 is:

0 to **5**, (given **0** = Only you can do all thing right)

From reference chart: 0 = 1 2 3 4 5 6 7. So, we assign:

only = 1, you = 2, can =3, do = 4, all = 5, things = 6, right = 7. Now, from reference chart : 5 = 1 2 6 7 5 3 4. Resupplying the words, we get Only you thing right all can do. **Correct answer: 2**

Q. 5: Q. 5 asks:

4 to **1**; (given, 4 = It is last serious warning to you)

From reference chart, **4** = 4 6 2 7 5 3 1. Hence we assign:

It = 4, is = 6, last = 2, serious = 7, warning = 5, to = 3, you = 1. Now, from reference chart: **1** = 7 3 2 4 5 6 1. Thus, the correct answer is serious to last it warning is you. **Correct answer : 5**

Quicker Method: A quicker method can be used by not taking all the words but taking only a few words. The best way is to look at the answer choices and select two or three words that are differently placed in the answer choices. To understand better, look at the quicker solutions below:

Q. 2: Q. 2 is:

6 to **0:** (given, 6 = 'Have I done anything wrong with you")

Now, if you look at the answer choices you can easily see that *have* and *I* are not placed at identical positions is any of the answer choices. For example, in choice (1) and choice (2), *I* is placed differently; in choice (2) and (3) *have* is placed differently,in choice (3) and (4) both *I* and have are placed differently. Thus, for our purposes it would suffice to consider only *I* and *have* instead of the whole sentence. For caution's sake we will also take *you*.

Now, from ref. chart step VI = 2 1 7 6 5 4 3. Thus, *have* = 2, *I* = 1, *you* = 3. Now, Input = 1 2 3 4 5 6 7. Which means that the Input should have 1 i.e. *I* in the first place; *have* i.e. 2 in the second place and *you* i.e. 3 in the third place and so on. We see that only choice **4** satisfies this condition. Hence, Answer: 4.

Q. 3: Q. 3 is:

12 to **17:** (given, **12** = "It is impossible to do everything right")

By golden rule of reduction; **12** to **17** = **0** to **5**.

If we look at the answer choices, we can see that if we take only *it*, *is* and *right* our purpose is served because these words don't appear at identical places in more than one answer choices.

Now, from ref. chart, step **0** = Input = 1 2 3 4 5 6 7. So, *it* = 1, *is* = 2, ... *right* = 7. Again by ref. chart, step V = **5** = 1 2 6 7 5 3 4. Thus, *it* (=1) should appear first, (*is* = 2) should appear second and *right* (= 7) should appear fourth from left. Only choice 3 satisfies this condition. Correct Answer: 3.

Q. 4: Q. 4 is:

0 to **5:** (given **0** = Only you can do all thing right).

Look at the answer choices. You can easily see that if we take only the two words *only* and *you* our purpose is served because these two words don't appear at identical places in more than one answer choices. For certainty's sake let us also take the last word: **right**. Now, use the method explained in the previous para. Correct answer = 2.

Q. 5: Q. 5 is:

4 to **1**: (given, **4** = "It is last serious warning to you")

Looking at the answer choices, it is obvious that we can take only *last* as sufficient because this word doesn't appear at identical places in more than one choice. For certainty's sake, we also take '*is*'.

Now, from ref. Chart, Step IV = 4 6 2 7 5 3 1. So, we have: is = 6, last = 2. From ref. chart, Step I = 7 3 2 4 5 6 1. So, 6 i.e. *is* goes to sixth place [This eliminates answer choices (1), (2) and (4)] and 2 i.e. *last* goes to third place [This eliminates choice (3)]. Hence, correct answer = 5

[**Note:** The quicker method suggested above is helpful only to eliminate the other answer choice which are definitely wrong. But it can't tell you the correct answer choice with 100% accuracy. In 90% of the cases, you will get the correct answer by this method but in 10% of the cases where the answer is 'None of these' you may get a wrong answer also. For ex., in Q5 above, if you try this short-cut method with *it*, *is* and *you* only; you won't be able to eliminate answer choice 4. Because these three words are correctly placed in the answer choice. But if we take *last* then we realise that the choice is not correct. It is a matter of bad luck if you didn't take *last* as your test-word but took other words. **However,** since the method would get you correct answers in 90% of the cases and since it saves you good deal of time, I would still advocate this method.]

Step E(ii): The second type of questions could be where we are given the content of one step and the content of another unknown step would be given. We will have to find this unknown step. Q. 1 is an example of such type.

For solving questions of this type, **we will take that step from the answer choices which, coupled with the given step, gives you the biggest range.** See the following illustration to understand this:

(Q1) Known step = **4.** Choices are: **10, 11, 9, 8**. We take **11** as this given largest range. Now, **4** to **11** = **0 to 7** by golden rule. So, we assume "I know you will not reply back" to be input rather than Step IV. Now, digit pattern for input is 1 2 3 4 5 6 7. So, we take I = 1, know = 2, you = 3, will = 4, not = 5, reply = 6, back = 7. Now, the given arrangement *you back I reply not will know* becomes 3 7 1 6 5 4 2. We see in the ref. chart that it corresponds to Step 7. This means that *you back I reply not will know* is step 7 *if I know you will not reply back* was input. But, *I known you will not reply back is* step 4 (0 +4). Hence, *you back .... not will know is 4 + 7 = step 11.*

TWO MORE FULLY SOLVED EXAMPLES

Ex. 9:

Directions (Q. 1-5): A word rearrangement machine when given an input line of words, rearranges them following a particular rule in each step. The following is an illustration of input and the steps of rearrangement:

Input: software scrips are red hot in bourses

Step I: software in are red hot scrips bourses

Step II: red are in software bourses scrips hot

Step III: in are red hot scrips bourses software

Step IV: in bourses red hot scrips are software

And so on.

As per the rule followed in the above steps, find out the appropriate step for the given input or vice versa in the following questions:

1. **Input:** the sudden need to alter policy stems

   Which of the following steps would be 'policy stems to alter sudden need the'?

   1) step I 2) step II 3) step III

   4) step IV 5) None of these

2. If step IV of an input is 'none of the players have turned India', what would be the 9th step?
   1) have players none the turned India of
   2) India players have turned the none of
   3) have the none players turned India of
   4) India have players none of the turned
   5) None of these
3. **Input:** most of the players were given approvals
   Which of the following will be the 4th step for this input?
   1) approvals were given the most players of
   2) the players of most were given approvals
   3) approvals given were the players most of
   4) given approvals players were of the most
   5) None of these
4. If step V of an input is 'none of this has happened at all', which of the following would definitely be the input?
   1) happened all at of none has this
   2) all at happened none of as this
   3) this has none of at all happened
   4) Can't be determined
   5) None of these
5. If step I of an input is 'in this form of trading by Amway', what would be Step VII of the input?
   1) Amway in trading by form of this
   2) in this trading by form of Amway
   3) Amway in trading by this of form
   4) Can't be determined
   5) None of these

Soln: Step A: Let us take first two words i.e. software and scrips

We see that,

0 to **1** # **1** to **2**

0 to **1** # **2** to **3**

0 to **1** = **3** to **4**

∴ It is a 3 - type case

Step B: In (Q1) the largest range is **0** to **4**.

In Q. 2, we have to find **4** to **9**. By golden rule: **4** to **9** = **1** to **6**. In Q. 3, we have to find **0** to **4** and it can't be reduced. In Q. 5, we have **5** to **0** and it can't be reduced. In Q. 6, we have **1** to **7** and it can't be reduced. The largest number in these five pairs (**0** to **4**, **1** to **6**, **0** to **4**, **5** to **6** and **1** to **7**) is 7 so we would draw our reference chart upto Step VII.

Step C: Let software = 1, Scrips = 2, are = 3 .... bourses = 7. Now, chart can be prepared as:

Input:	1	2	3	4	5	6	7
Step I:	1	6	3	4	5	2	7
Step II:	4	3	6	1	7	2	5
Step III:	6	3	4	5	2	7	1
Step IV:	6	7	4	5	2	3	1
Step V:	5	4	7	6	1	3	2
Step VI:	7	4	5	2	3	1	6
Step VII:	7	1	5	2	3	4	6

Step D: Now, we go to Questions.

Step E:

Q. 1: Given pattern is **input**. Largest choice = Step IV. But 0 to 4 can't be reduced. So, take Input as Input only. Let, the = 1, sudden = 2, need = 3 .... stems = 7. Now, "policy stems to alter sudden need the "is "6745231", Which from the ref. chart is Step IV. Hence, correct answer: 4.

Q. 2: We have to find **4** to **9**. By golden rule, **4** to **9** = **1** to **6**. So, let "none of the players have turned India" be Step I. By looking at reference chart, it means that none = 1, of = 6, the = 3, players = 4, have = 5, turned = 2, India = 7. And Step VI is 7 4 5 2 3 1 6 which will be "India players have turned the none of". Correct answer : 2.

Quicker method: 4 to 9 = 1 to 6. Let "none of the players... India " be Step I. Look at ref. chart. So, none = 1, of = 6, the = 3. Let us take only these three words. Now in Step VI, 1 is at 6th, 6 is at last and 3 is at 5 th position. So correct answer should have **none** at 6th, **of** at last and **the** at 5th place. Correct answer: 2.

Q. 3: We have to find **0** to **4**. Let given Input be 0. So, most = 1, of = 3 the = 3 ..... approvals = 7. Now in Step IV, we have 6 7 4 5 2 3 1. Putting back the words we get: "given approvals players were of the most." Correct answer: 4.

Q. 4: We have to find **5** to **0**. Step V from ref. chart is 5 4 7 6 1 3 2. So, let none = 5, of = 4, this = 7, has = 6, happened = 1, at = 3, all = 2. Now, Input is 1 2 3 4 5 6 7 which is reworded as "happened all at of none has this". Correct answer = 1.

Q. 5: We have to find **1** to **7**. But Step I = 1 6 3 4 5 2 7. So, we have : in = 1, this = 6, form = 3, ... Amway =7," Now, Step VII = 7 1 5 2 3 4 6 = Amway in trading by form of this. Correct answer = 1.

Ex. 10:

Directions (Q. 1-5): A word arrangement machine when given a particular input, rearranges them following a particular rule. The following is the illustration of the input and the steps of arrangement:

Input: cry an fire pull tee anes see

Step I: see an pull fire tee anes cry

Step II: an pull cry tee fire see anes
Step III: anes pull tee cry fire see an
Step IV: pull tee an fire cry anes see

And so on goes the machine. Study the logic and answer the questions that follow:

1. If Step XIII of a given input be 'blut ne fur sur say trep dawn', what is the 17th step of the input?
   1) sur say ne blut trep fur dawn 2) blut say sur ne dawn trep fur
   3) dawn ne trep sur fur say blut 4) sur ne dawn blut say fur trep
   5) None of these
2. If Step V of a given input be 'quir fe din list re puss kin', what would be the input?
   1) kin quir fe list re puss din 2) list fe kin din puss re quir
   3) re list din kin fe puss quir 4) list fe quir din re puss kin
   5) None of these
3. Given the following input, what would be Step VIII of the input?
   Input: From tree hins risea ful len je
   1) tree risea from ful len je hins 2) from risea je tree ful len hins
   3) je ful tree len risea from hins 4) hins from ful tree risea len je
   5) None of these
4. Given the following
   Input: crue be bel nel fare ros bik
   What number will be the following step?
   Step: fare bel nel crue be bik ros
   1) II 2) IV 3) V 4) VIII 5) VI
5. If Step VII of an input is 'go nol bole fula run quu bue', what is Step V of that input?
   1) quu bue nol run bole go fula 2) fula nol run quu bue bole go
   3) run nol quu bue go fula bole 4) bole quu run go fula bue nol
   5) None of these

Soln: Step A: Let us monitor the movement of the first two words in each line; i.e. *cry* and *an*

So, we have **0** to **1** ≠ **1** to **2,** but **0** to **1** = **2** to **3**.

Hence, it is a **2 type** case.

Step B: In Q(1), we have: **13** to **17** which reduces by our golden rule to = **1** to **5**.

In Q(2), we have: **5** to **0** and it can't be further reduced.

In Q(3), we have: **0** to **8** and it can't be further reduced.

In Q(4), biggest choice is step VIII and thus the biggest range is **0** to **8**.

In Q(5), we have: **7** to **5** and it can be reduced to **3** to **1**.

So, we have five pairs of (**1** to **5**), (**5** to **0**), (**0** to **8**) and (**7** to **5**). The largest number here is 8 and, therefore, our reference chart should be drawn upto Step VIII.

Step C: Let cry = 1, an = 2, fire = 3, pull = 4, tee = 5, ones = 6, see = 7. Now, our chart can be preapred as:

Input:	1	2	3	4	5	6	7
Step I:	7	2	4	3	5	6	1
Step II:	2	4	1	5	3	7	6
Step III:	6	4	5	1	3	7	2
Step IV:	4	5	2	3	1	6	7
Step V:	7	5	3	2	1	6	4
Step VI:	5	3	4	1	2	7	6
Step VII:	6	3	1	4	2	7	5
Step VIII:	3	1	5	2	4	6	7

Step D: Now we go to questions.

Step E: **Question 1:** We have **13** to **17** = **1** to **5**. So, let "blut ne fur sur say trep dawn" be Step I. Thus : blut = 7, ne = 2, fur = 4 etc. Now, Step V = 7 5 3 2 1 6 4. So here 7 is at first, 2 is at fourth place and 4 is at last place. Hence correct answer should have **blut** at first, **ne** at fourth and **fur** at last place. Correct answer: 2.

Question 2: We have **5** to **0**, Now, Step V = 7 5 3 2 1 6 4. Let quir = 7, fe = 5, din = 3 etc. Now, Input = 1 2 3 4 5 6 7 and here 7 is at last, 5 is at fifth and 3 is at third place. Hence, correct answer should have *quir* at last, *fe* at fifth and *din* at third place. Correct answer: 3.

Question 3: We have 0 to 8. Now, Input = 1 2 3 4 5 6 7. So, Step VIII is 3 1 5 2 4 6 7. Let from = 1, tree = 2, hins = 3 etc. So in Step VIII, **from** should be second, **tree** should be fourth and **hins** should be first. Correct answer : 4.

Question 4: Input = 1 2 3 4 5 6 7. So, let crue = 1, be = 2, bel = 3 etc. Now, in the given step crue = 1 is at fourth, be = 2 is at fifth and bel = 3 is at second position. This is obviously Step VI. (Because in Step VI, 5 3 4 1 2 7 6; 3 is second, 1 is fourth and 2 is fifth.)

Question 5: We have 7 to 5. Now, Step VII = 6314275. So, we have: go = 6, nol = 3, bole = 1 etc. Now, in Step V: 7532164; nol = 3 is third, bole = 1 is fifth and go = 6 is sixth. Correct answer: 1.

14.7: The method of intelligent observation

In the earlier part of this chapter, we have described the method of reference charts, the commonly used technique for solving input-output problems. This technique works very fine but the problem is that in creating a reference chart of upto 7 - 8 (or even more) steps a good deal of precious time is lost. Instead, we can solve these questions by just being smart and intelligent: the special BSC technique, just for you. In this method, if you do some practice, you will not need a pen to solve the questions (1) and yet you will reach your answers in super-quick time (2). Please go through this method, try to understand it by rereading it time and again, go through the solved examples and try to master the method. Just in case a student doesn't feel comfortable with this method, he always has the method of reference charts to go back to.

In order to make our method a bit clearer to explain, we shall first like to introduce some terminology and definitions:

14.7.1: Some basic definitions

Before we begin to describe this method we will be giving some definitions.

(i) Operation: In every subsequent step, the machine performs a pre-fixed shifting. We may call it on **operation**. In a 1-step shifting we always have the some operation, in a 2-step shifting we have two-operations taking place alternately, in 3-step shifting we have three operations taking place alternately. (We have seen this in greater detail already. Please refer to section 14.4.1.)

(ii) P_1, P_2, P_3,.... etc.

In Ex. 1, you can see that there are 7 words and they are being jumbled in every step. In the Input ("I have long awaited for your reply"), **I** is at first place, **have** is at second place, **long** is at third place and so on. Finally, reply is at seventh place. For convenience sake we can say that

P_1 = I
P_2 = have
P_3 = long
P_7 = reply,

This is just another way of saying the some thing. Thus, **P_1 means the word at 1st position, P_2 means the word at 2nd position, P_3 means the word at 3rd position and so on.**

(iii) Shift or (→)

When the machine operates upon one sequence and produces another sequence, it basically shifts a word from one position to another. For example, in Ex 1 from Input to Step I; *the first word becomes the last word.* Instead of saying this in as many words, we can write it concisely as:

$$P_1 \rightarrow P_7$$

This statement ($P_1 \rightarrow P_7$) means that the **word at 1st position shifts to the 7th position**.

Ex. 11: As another example, consider **reply** in step III to Step IV in Ex 1. In step III, **reply** is at 3rd position and in step IV it is at 5th position. We can show this by the following diagram:

$$P_3 \rightarrow P_5$$

(iv) Denoting an operation in this new terminology

Consider Input and Step I of Ex 1. They are:

Input: I have long awaited for your reply

Step I: reply long have awaited for your I

What kind of on operation has the machine performed here? If you analyse closely, you can easily say that

(A) In going from Input to Step I

(B) *"first word becomes seventh, second becomes third, third becomes second, seventh becomes first while fourth, fifth and sixth words don't change places".*

Now, in our concise terminology we will replace them by

(A) $0 \rightarrow 1$ (It means that "in going from Input to Step I")

and

(B) $P_1 \rightarrow P_7$, $P_2 \rightarrow P_3$, $P_3 \rightarrow P_2$, $P_7 \rightarrow P_1$, $P_4 = P_4$, $P_5 = P_5$, $P_6 = P_6$

Thus, we can denote the entire operation performed from Input to Step I as:

$(P_1 \rightarrow P_7, P_2 \rightarrow P_3, P_3 \rightarrow P_2, P_7 \rightarrow P_1)$ in $0 \rightarrow 1$

$P_4 = P_4, P_5 = P_5, P_6 = P_6$

Ex. 12: As another example consider Step I and Step II. They are:

Step I: reply long have awaited for your I

Step II: long reply awaited have for I Your

Here, the changes can be written as:

(A) In going from Step I to Step II

OR

$1 \rightarrow 2$

and (B) "1st word becomes second, 2nd word becomes 1st, 3rd word becomes 4th and 4th becomes third, sixth word becomes 7th and 7th becomes sixth,"

OR

$(P_1 \rightarrow P_2, P_2 \rightarrow P_1, P_3 \rightarrow P_4, P_4 \rightarrow P_3, P_6 \rightarrow P_7, P_7 \rightarrow P_6)$

In short, the complete change from Step I to Step II can be written as:

$1 \rightarrow 2$: $((P_1 \rightarrow P_2, P_2 \rightarrow P_1, P_3 \rightarrow P_4, P_4 \rightarrow P_3, P_5 = P_5, P_6 \rightarrow P_7, P_7 \rightarrow P_6)$

14.7.2: The method: basic ideas

14.7.2.1: Chain-splitting

When we go from one step (say, step I) to another (say, step V); it is basically a chain of various steps. Instead of saying that we went directly from step I to step V, we could also say that we went from step I to (say) step III and then, from step III to step V. It is the same as saying that we went from Bhopal to Agra and from Agra to Delhi instead of saying that we directly went from Bhopal to Delhi.

This concept and its fantastic uses will be explained by giving the following pictorial example:

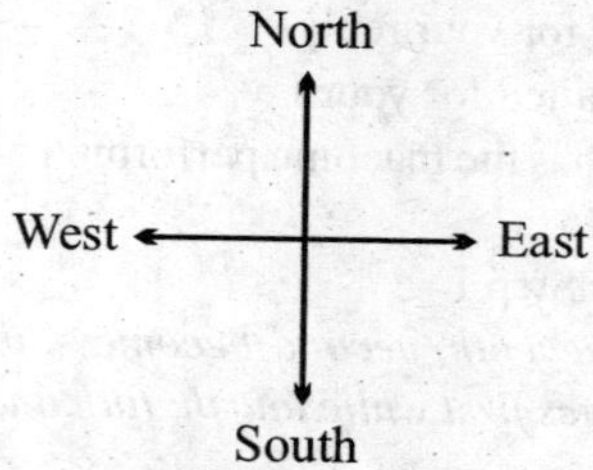

Imagine that a man is standing at a place. Let the name of this place be O. Imagine that he starts from O, moves 1 km East and reaches 1, then he turns left and moves 1 km North and reaches 2, then he turns right and moves 1 km East and reaches 3 and so on .... Thus he is making two kinds of movements. He is moving 1 km east (call it **operation 1**) and then, he is moving 1 km North (call it **operation 2**). These two operations go on alternately.

Since two operations are going on alternately, it is very much like our example of 2-step shifting.

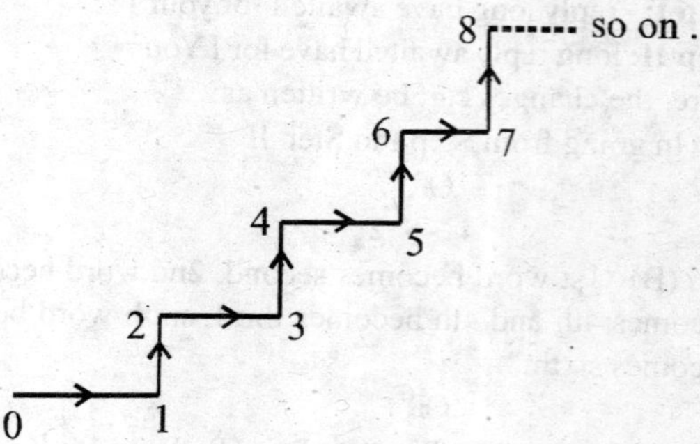

Fig. I

Chain-splitting: Now, in the figure above, imagine that a person went from 2 to 7. We can, for convenience sake, write it as:

2 to 7.

But another person can say that the person went from 2 to 4 and then from 4 to 7. This also is, of course, correct, and this can be written as:

2 to 4, 4 to 7.

Another person can insist that the journey be defined as 2 to 5 and 5 to 7. This can be described as:

2 to 5, 5 to 7.

This means that instead of writing one full sequence, we can split it (at our convenience) at a convenient point and write a chain of sequences. Thus, in the above illustration, we have:

2 to 7 = 2 to 4, 4 to 7 = 2 to 5, 5 to 7 = ...

14.7.2.2: Application of golden rule:

Since our figure I behaves like a 2-step case (because two operations go on alternately); we can expect that the golden rule will also work on this. For example, consider 5 to 7. We see that the journey from 5 to 7 involve two steps: one, going 1 km North and then, two; going 1 km East. This can be illustrated by the following figures:

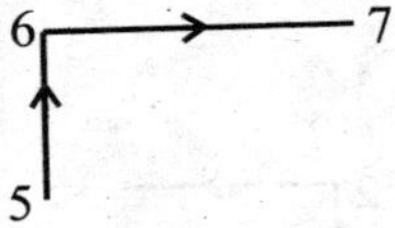

Fig II A

But we see that, 3 to 5 also has similar changes and 1 to 3 also has similar change.

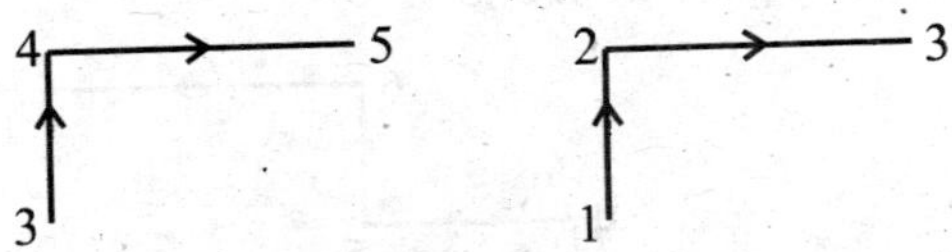

Fig IIB

Therefore, we can say that *the change in going from 5 to 7* is same as the change in going from 3 to 5 which, in turn is the same as the *change in going from 1 to 3*. Symbolically, this can be written as:

5 to **7** = **3** to **5** = **1** to **3**

So, we see that

5 to **7** = **(5 - 2)** to **(7 - 2)** = **(5 - 2 × 2)** to **(7 - 2 × 2)**

Therefore, in this case, a multiple of 2 can be to or subtracted from both the step numbers and the result denotes the some change. In other words, *golden rule of reduction is being obeyed here.*

14.7.2.3: Base-changing:

Earlier we have seen that **2** to **7** can be written as **2** to **5**, **5** to **7**. Again, we have seen that golden rule can be applied to conclude that **5** to **7** = **1** to **3**. Using both of these, we can conclude that **2** to **7** = **2** to **5**, **1** to **3**. What is the meaning of this? The meaning is that if we went from 2 to 5 and then assumed that we had reached **1** (not **5**) and went from this (assumed) **1** to **3**; we would actually be reaching **2** to **7**. This can be explained by the following explanatory stages:

a) We go from **2** to **5**

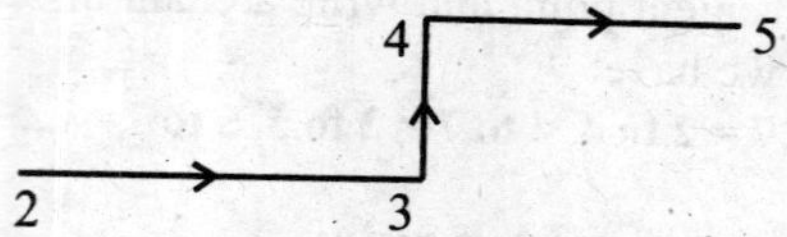

b) We assume that we have reached **1** not **5**.

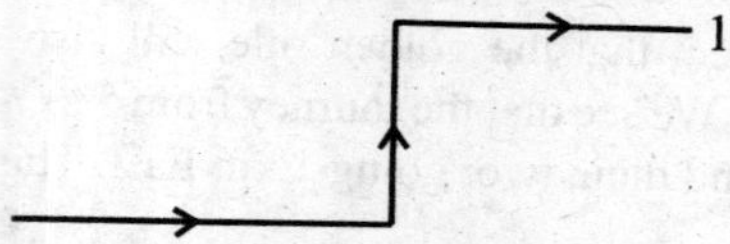

c) From this **1,** we go to **3**

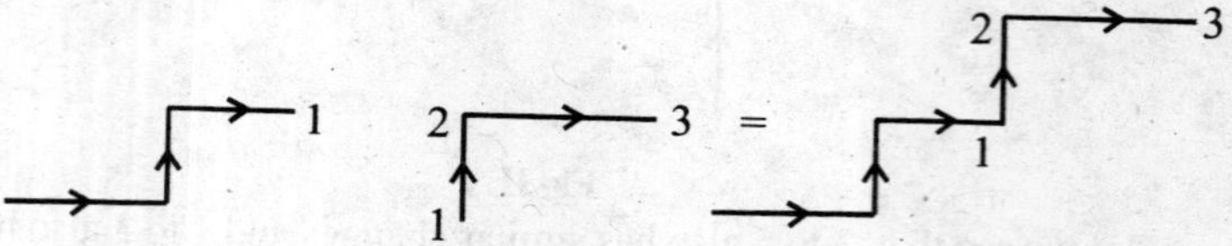

d) We have actually gone from **2** to **7**.

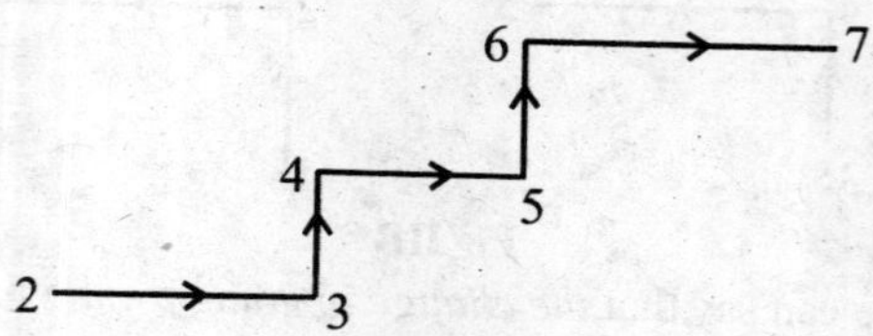

Fig III

Thus, what we actually did in the above operation was that we chain-split the sequence from **2** to **7** to **2** to **5**, **5** to **7** then we applied golden rule to the later sequence (of **5** to **7** = **1** to **3**) and accordingly changed our base from **5** to **1**. Then we applied the reduced change **1** to **3**.

What is the use of this process? Imagine that our original figure had given us only five steps. In other words, it ended at 5, as shown in the following figure:

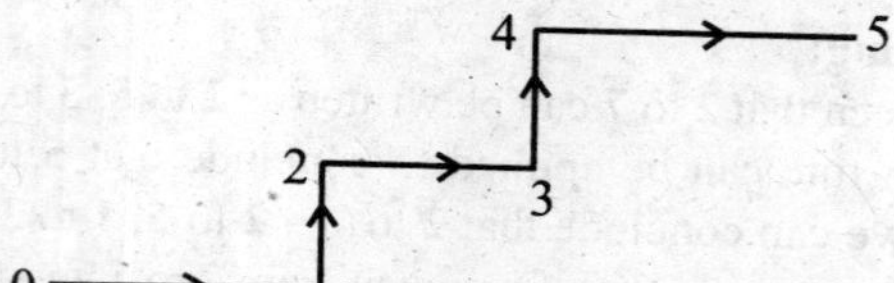

(and so on)

Now, suppose we were asked to find **2** to **7**. But our figure didn't show us anything after **5**. So, in such cases we could break **2** to **7** as **2** to **5**, **5** to **7**; then reduce **5** to **7** as **1** to **3**. Then, we could find **2** to **5**, assume this **5** to be **1** (base changing) and then find **1** to **3**. Since, both **2** to **5** and **1** to **3** are given in our diagram; we won't have any difficulty finding both of these. Thus, the benefit of our method lies in the fact that we don't need to draw extra steps and we can find our answers with the given diagram itself.

14.7.2.4: Use of above mentioned concepts in shifting problems

Suppose that we have a problem, which reads like this:

Input: I am going to Patna
Step I: am I going Patna to
Step II: am going I Patna to
Step III: going am I to Patna
Step IV: going I am to Patna
Step V: I going am Patna to

Here, we see that it is a 2-step shifting because in **0** to **1** ($P_1 \rightarrow P_2$, $P_2 \rightarrow P_1$, $P_3 = P_3$, $P_4 \rightarrow P_5$, $P_5 \rightarrow P_4$) and in **1** to **2** ($P_1 = P_1$, $P_2 \rightarrow P_3$; $P_3 \rightarrow P_2$, $P_4 = P_4$, $P_5 = P_5$) and **0** to **1** = **2** to **3** ... etc.

Now, suppose we were asked to find **2** to **7**. That is, suppose a question read:

Q. If step II is "She was playing with him" what will step VII be?

Then, to solve this question, if we used the method of reference-charts; we would need to draw a chart for step VI and step VII. But we can instead chain-split **2** to **7** as **2** to **5**, **5** to **7**. That is, we can first find step V for the given step II. This is easy because upto step V is given in our question itself. Once we have found our step V, we can assume that it was not step V it was step I. Then we can find **1** to **3** for this assumed step I. Thus, in the net analysis, we have found **2** to **5**, **1** to **3** but **1** to **3** = **5** to **7**. So, we have found (**2** to **5**, **5** to **7**) which is **2** to **7**.

Let us work out the above. We see that in the given diagram:

2 = step II = am going I Patna to.

5 = step V = I going am Patna to.

So, in **2** to **5**; P_1 (am) $\rightarrow P_3$, P_2 (going) $= P_2$, P_3(I) $\rightarrow P_1$, P_4 (Patna) $= P_4$, P_5 (to) $= P_5$.

So, in **2** $\rightarrow$ **5** we have $P_1 \rightarrow P_3$, $P_2 = P_2$, $P_3 \rightarrow P_1$, $P_4 = P_4$, $P_5 = P_5$.

Now, we assume the step V so arrived to be step I and find its step III. We see that in the given question.

Step I: am I going Patna to
Step III: going am I to Patna.

Thus, we see that in **1** to **3:** ($P_1 \rightarrow P_2$, $P_2 \rightarrow P_3$, $P_3 \rightarrow P_1$, $P_4 \rightarrow P_5$, $P_5 \rightarrow P_4$).

Now, if we compare **2 to 5** and **1 to 3**, we see that P_1 of step II becomes P_3 in **2** to **5** and P_3 becomes P_1 in **1** to **3**. So, $P_1 \rightarrow P_3 \rightarrow P_1$ in 2 to 5, 1 to 3. Similarly, we have: $P_2 = P_2 \rightarrow P_3$, $P_3 \rightarrow P_1 \rightarrow P_2$, $P_4 = P_4 \rightarrow P_5$, $P_5 = P_5 \rightarrow P_4$ in **2** to **5**, **1** to **3**. If we drop the middle terms (for example, P_3 in $P_1 \rightarrow P_3 \rightarrow P_1$) we get $P_1 \rightarrow P_1$, $P_2 \rightarrow P_3$, $P_3 \rightarrow P_2$, $P_4 \rightarrow P_5$, $P_5 \rightarrow P_4$ in **2 to 5, 1 to 3**. But **1 to 3** = **5** to 7. Hence, **2 to 5** = **2 to 5, 5 to 7** = **2 to 7**.

Now, in our given question She = P_1, was = P_2, playing = P_3, with = P_4, him = P_5. So, step VII will be *She playing was him with* because we have seen that in **2 to 7** = $P_1 \rightarrow P_1$, $P_2 \rightarrow P_3$, $P_3 \rightarrow P_2$, $P_4 \rightarrow P_5$, $P_5 \rightarrow P_4$

Therefore, we have seen that we have solved the problem using the combined technique of chain-splitting, reducing by golden rule and base-changing. What we did actually is analogous to our Fig. III in the following manner:

a) We find step V from step II i.e. **2** to **5**.
b) We assume that we have reached **1** not **5**.
c) From this **1**, we find **3**.
d) We thus reach **2** to **7**.
(Compare with Fig III)

The advantage of this method lies two fold:

a) you don't have to draw any reference-charts, only the steps given in the question suffice
b) you don't have to replace given words by digits 1, 2, 3, ... etc.

These two facts make this method fast reliable and efficient. You may have a feeling that it is a very complex method. Relax. In fact it is not. It looks complicated because we have tried to explain each and every step. In reality, the problems can be solved with much less effort and not all the steps would be necessary. Now that you have a vague idea about the method, you are advised to go through the actual technique alongwith some short-cut techniques advised in the next few sections. Rereading in case of confusions and good deal of practice would make you a master of this technique.

14.7.3: The method

We hope that the definitions and terminology used in the previous sections are clear to you. We are now in a position to tell you the special BSC method of intelligent observation. Suppose that you are given a step number and its content and you are asked to find the content of a subsequent step number.For example, suppose you are told that step III is "gone are the days" and you are asked to find Step VII. Since **7** is **after** (or **subsequent** to) **3**, this qualifies for our discussion. Let us see how to solve such questions.

Step A: First, find out if it is a 1-step or 2-step or a 3-step case.

Note: The method of determining this has already been discussed in great detail. Please see section 14.4.1 again if you have any doubt. (Also see flowchart 2).

Step B: Next, use the golden rule of reduction and simplify the question if possible.

Ex 13: For example, consider Q3 of Ex 1. Here you are asked to find Step 17, given Step 12. Thus you have:

12 → 17

Since it is a 2-Step case, we can subtract a multiple of 2 (i.e. 12) from both sides by our golden rule of reduction and it becomes:

$$(12 - 12) \rightarrow (17 - 12) = 0 \rightarrow 5$$

In other words, we can assume that "it is impossible to do everything right" was input and we were asked to find Step 5.

Step C: Next, break the reduced operation into steps and apply the golden rule of reduction to the **later** steps. (Break the operation into constituent steps as many times as you wish and see that ultimately you have only those step numbers that are already given in the question.)

Note: The above is a very important step and it is this step that is the core of our method. Therefore, it is very important that you understood not only this step but also the idea behind this step. We are giving some illustration below:

Ex 14: Consider Q. 3 of Ex 1. Here, we have: **12 → 17**. We have already seen (in Ex 13) that we can reduce it as **0 → 5**. Now, we notice that **5** is not there in the question because the question mentions only upto **4** (Step IV). [**Imp.** Please note]

Therefore, we break **0 → 5** as (**0 → 4, 4 → 5**). Now, we apply golden rule of reduction to **4 → 5** (the **later** part) and we get **(4 - 4) → (5 - 4)** i.e. **0 → 1**,

So, we have: **0 → 5 = (0 → 4; 0 → 1)**.

> *This means that (1) if we assumed 'It is impossible to do everything right" as input and found Step IV for it, and (2) then again, if we assumed the Step IV thus found to be input and found Step I for it, we will actually be finding Step V.* [**Imp.** You must understand this part.]

Consider another example.

Ex 15: Suppose you have information exactly similar to the one mentioned in Ex 9. Suppose, you are told that Step 14 is "I go to school before Rom does" and you are asked to find Step 21.

Explanation: By Step A, we find that it is a 3-step case. By step B, we reduce **14 → 21** by subtracting a multiple of 3. So, we have [(**14 - 12) → [(21 - 12)] = 2 → 9**. Thus, if we assume "I go to school before Rom does" as step 2 and find step 9 (for this step 2); we will be getting our answer. Now, let us come to step C. We see that in Ex 9, the question gives us info. only till Step IV i.e. **4**. Therefore, any step number after that must be reduced. Hence, we break, **2 → 9** as **(2 → 4, 4 → 9)**. Now, we reduce the later part **4 → 9** and we get **4 → 9 = (4 - 3) → (9 - 3) = 1 → 6**. We again see that 6 is beyond our tolerance limit (of step 4). So we again break **1 → 6** as **(1 → 4, 4 → 6)**. We again break **4 → 6** as **(4 - 3) → (6 - 3)** i.e. **(1 → 3)**.

Hence, we have broken and reduced $2 \rightarrow 9$ as ($2 \rightarrow 4$, $1 \rightarrow 4$, $1 \rightarrow 3$).
** *This means that, (1) if we assumed "I go to school before Ram Does" as Step 2 and found Step 4 for it; and, (2) then, if we assumed the Step 4 thus found to be Step 1 and found Step 4 for it, and, (3) then, if we assumed the Step 4 thus found to be step 1 and found Step 3 for it; we will be getting our required answer.*

**** Note:** (i) Please ensure that you understand the sentences marked with the stars. It is important that you understand the idea.

(ii) Ex 15 in particular was a bit more difficult than what you would actually get in the examination. We have deliberately given a tough illustration so that you have a smooth sailing later.

(iii) If you have not understood **anything** of Step C till now, go back right now and reread it. But if you have developed a vague but not crystal clear idea of the subject, don't worry and go ahead. Later examples would make everything very clear.

Step D: *Now take the given content and find its new form by referring to the series of operations obtained in step C. Use the chart given in the question itself for the purpose.*

Quicker method: Note that Step D asks you to "take the given content". Now, if you take the entire content of 5-6 or even 7 words and follow the movement of all of them, it would be time taking. **To save time, look at the answer choices and pick out that word which is at different positions in different choices. This will help you eliminate some choices.** Again, take another word, (if needed) and repeat the process. This way, you can eliminate all the incorrect choices by following only two or three words. Look at the illustrations below to understand Step D.

Ex 16: Solve Q3 of Ex 1.

Soln: By Step A, we find it is a 2-step case. By step B, we reduce **$12 \rightarrow 17$** to **$0 \rightarrow 5$** and by step C, we break it as **($0 \rightarrow 4$, $0 \rightarrow 1$)**.

Now, look at the answer choices. We see that 'it' is at three different places in the four choices. So, it is consider 'it'. (See, quicker method for step D.)

We see that *it* is P_1 in step 12. But we are taking step 12 as **0**, So, *it* is P_1 in **0**. Now, we have **($0 \rightarrow 4$, $0 \rightarrow 1$)**. Where does P_1 of **0** go in 4? Look at the chart in the question. P_1 of **0** (input) i.e. '*I*' goes to P_7 in **4** (step IV). So, *it* will be P_7 in step IV. Now, we will assume step 4 to be input and try to find **$0 \rightarrow 1$**. So, *it* in P_7 is **0**. We see that P_7 of **0** (input) i.e. **reply** becomes P_1 in step 1.

$\therefore$ Net result is: P_1 remains P_1. This eliminates choices (1) and (4).

Now, we are left with choices (2) and (3). We notice that the word **right** is at different places in these choices. So, we pick **right** for our analysis.

We see that **right** is P_7 in our step 12. But step 12 is assumed step 0. So,

right is P_7 of input. Where does P_7 of input go in Step IV? Look at the chart given with the question. It goes to P_4. So, **right** is P_4 in Step IV. Now, we assume this step IV to be 0 (input) and find **0 → 1** i.e. step I. Where does P_4 of input go in **step I**? It remains P_4. So, net result is: **right** should be at P_4. This eliminates choice (2).
Hence, choice (3) is the answer.

Ex 17: Solve Q. 2 of Ex. 9.

Soln: **Step A:** It is a 3-Step case.
Step B: 4 → 9 = (4 -3) → (9 - 3) = 1 → 6
Step C: 1 → 6 = (1 → 4, 4 → 6)
= (1 → 4, (4 - 3) → (6 - 3)
= (1 → 4, 1 → 3).

Step D: We see that the word "*the*" is at four different places in the four choices. So, we take "*the*" for our analysis. Now, *the* is P_3 in step 4. But step 4 is step 1 for us. Now, we first track **1 → 4**. Where does P_3 of step 1 go in step 4? (See "are" in the given chart). It goest to P_6. So, *the* is P_6 in our step 4. Again, we assume this step 4 to be step 1 and track **1→ 3**. Where does P_6 of step 1 go in step 3. (See *scrips* in the given chart.) It goes to P_5.
∴ *the* must be P_5 in our answer. This eliminates choice 1, 3 and 4. Hence, 2 is our answer.
[**Warning:** You must note that we generally use the quicker method in step D wherein we take only one or two words and using them we eliminate the incorrect choices. But this does not guarantee that the remaining choice is the correct answer. There is a likelihood that "None of these" could also be correct. If you want to eliminate this likelihood you should track *all* the words. Then you will get a certain answer but lose considerable time. And if you, after all the efforts, find out that the choice that you had reached by tracking only one word was indeed the correct choice, you may feel very frustrated over the wasted time. My personal advice would be that you always follow the quicker method: experience has it, that in these questions "none of these" is not a frequent answer. Sometimes you may also to take an extra word and test your answer already arrived at.]

14.7.3.1: An important note: 3 type of questions

Please refer to and reread section 14.6.2 once again. There we have mentioned that there are two major types of questions:

- One, where you have to find the content of a known step number where you are given the content of another step number.
- Two, where you have to find the step number of a known contet, where you are given the content of another step number.

Now, for convenience, we will divide the first type of questions in two subtypes.

For example, in the first case you may have to find the content of a step number that comes (a) after or (b) before the step number whose content is given. To summarise, we have the following three types of possible questions:

Question Type I: *Given a step number and its content, to find the content of a* ***subsequent*** *step number.*

Ex. 18: (i) If the IIIrd step of a machine is "long live our cherished freedom", what is the 5th step?

(ii) If input is "so long buddy", what is step IV?

Explanations: (i) Here, we have to find **5** given **3**. Since **5** comes *after* **3**; it is question type 1.

(ii) Here, we have to find **4** given **0**. Since, **4** comes *after* **0**, it is question type I.

Question Type II: Given a step number and its content, to find the content of a **previous** step number.

Ex. 19: (i) If the IIIrd step of a machine is "long live our cherished freedom", what is input?

(ii) If step IV is "buddy long so", what is step I?

Explanations: (i) Here, we have to find **0** given **3**. Since, 0 comes **before 3**, it is question type II.

(ii) Here, we have to find **1** given **4**. Since, **1** comes **before 4** it is question type II.

Question Type III: Given a step number and its content, to find the step number for a given content.

Ex. 20: (i) If step III is "long live our cherished freedom"; "live our long freedom cherished" is

1) step IV 2) step V 3) step VI
4) step VII 5) None of these

(ii) If Step VII is "buddy long so", what step is "long buddy so"?

1) step II 2) step IV 3) step VIII
4) step IX 5) None of these

Explanations: In both (i) and (ii), we have to find the step number for a content when a step number and its content are already given. So, it is question type III.

14.7.3.2: Method to solve questions of Type II and Type III

In section 14.7.3, we have given a method which tells you have to find the content of a *subsequent* step number. So, it covered Question Type I only. With some modifications we can apply this method for question type II and III also, as shown below.

For Question Type II: In such questions, look at the answer choices and pick a word that is at different places in different choices. Now, use the logic given in Step A,B,C and D of section 14.7.3; *but this time, follow a backward route rather than a forward route.*

The following illustrations would explain this:

Ex 21: Solve Q. 2 of Ex. 1.

Soln: Here, given Step 6 we have to find input i.e. step 0.

Step A: It is a 2-step case.

Step B: 6 → 0 (can't be reduced)

Step C: 6 → 0 = (6 → 2, 2 → 0)
= [(6 - 2) → (2 - 2), 2 → 0]
= [4 → 0, 2 → 0].

These, (a) if we assume "Have I done anything wrong with you" as step 4 and find its input and, (b) if we again assume the input thus found as step 2 and find its input; we will get our answer.

Step D: We see that word *you* is at 3 different places in four choices. So, we track it. Now, *you* is P_7 to start with. Assume, *you* is P_7 in step 4. Where does P_7 of step 4 go in input? Refer to chart. It goes to P_1. Now, we assume *you* to be P_1 of step 2. Where does P_1 of step 2 go in input? It goes to P_3.

∴ *You* must be at P_3. This eliminates choice 1, 2 and 3. Hence, (4) must be the (likely) answer.

Ex 22: Solve Q4 of Ex 9.

Soln: **Step A:** It is a 3-step case

Step B: 5 → 0 (Can't be reduced)

Step C: 5 → 0 = (5 → 3, 3 → 0) = [(5 - 3) → (3 - 3), 3 → 0] = (2 → 0, 3 → 0).

Thus, if we assume "none of this has happened at all" as step 2 and find its input and again, assume the input thus found as step 3 and find its input, we will get the answer.

Step D: We see that the word "*all*" is at three different places in three choices. So, we take it for tracking. Now, *all* is our P_7 in step 5. But we assume step 5 to be step 2. So, let *all* be P_7 of step 2. Where does P_7 of step 2 go in input? It goes to P_5. Now, assume *all* is P_5 of step 3. Where does P_5 of step 3 go in input? It goes to P_2,

So, *all* must be P_2 in the answer. This eliminates choice (2) and (3). So, (1) must be our (likely) answer.

It is immaterial how you break the operation into steps in step C.

You need not be nervous over how to break into steps as asked by step C. Any which way you choose to do it you will get the same answer. For example, consider Ex 22. There we broke **5 → 0** as **(5 → 3, 3 → 0)**. Suppose, you choose to break it as **(5 → 4, 4 → 0)**. (Note that if you break it as **(5 → 2, 2 → 0)** it would be useless because **(5 → 2)** can't be reduced as 2 is smaller than 3 and it is a 3-step case). Now, we may reduce it as **[(5 - 3) → (4 - 3), 4 → 0]** or (2 → 1, 4 → 0).

This means that we will need to assume "none of this has happened at all" as step 2 and find its step 1; and then assume the step 1 thus found to be step 4 and find its input.

Now, suppose we pick all for our tracing. So, all is our P_7 of step 2. We see that P_7 of step 2 goes to P_5 in step 1. So, now all is P_5 of our step 1. We assume it to be step 4 now. We see that P_5 of step 4 goes to P_2 in input. ∴ So, all must be P_2 in the answer. Thus, we get the same answer, although we get a different route.

Ex 23: In Ex 21, break **6 → 0** as **(6 → 4, 4 → 0)** and then check that you find the same answer. Then break **6 → 0** as **(6 → 3, 3 → 0)** and check that you find the same answer.

Soln: Do it yourself.

For Question Type III: For such questions, take the given step and pair it with each of the steps given in choices. Then perform, step A,B,C, as usual. Now, take one of the words in the given step and see where it has shifted in the unknown step. Check, using the technique of step D, which choice obeys this rule. (If all wrong choices are not eliminated, you may need to consider more than one word.) The following illustrations will make this process clear.

Ex 24: Solve Q1 of Ex 1?

Soln: Let us take P_1 i.e. I of given step 4. We see that it becomes P_3 in the unknown step. Therefore, the problem can be stated like this: "In which step does P_1 of step 4 becomes P_3?"

Now, look at the choices. They are: step 8, step 9, step 10, step 11. Hence, by step B, we can reduce them as.

(Choice 4) **4 → 8** = (4 - 2 × 2) → (8 - 2 × 2) = **0 → 4**

(Choice 3) **4 → 9 = 0 → 5**

(Choice 1) **4 → 10 = 0 → 6**

(Choice 2) **4 → 11 = 0 → 7**

This means that our problem can be retranslated as: "In which step does P_1 of *input become* P_3?" If the answer to this question is step 4, or step 5 or step 6 or step 7; our actual answers would be choice 4, choice 3, choice 1 or choice 2; respectively. We see by the chart given with the question, that P_1 of input becomes P_7 in step 4. (This means that choice 4 is not correct). Now, the remaining choices are step 5, step 6 and step 7.

By step C, we can break them as

0 → 5 = (0 → 4, 4 → 5) = [0 → 4, (4 - 4) → (5 - 4)]
= (0 → 4, 0 → 1);

0 → 6 = (0 → 4, 0 → 2)

0 → 7 = (0 → 4, 0 → 3).

This means that if we consider an input and found step 4 and then again assume this step 4 as input; then if we find step 1 we would actually be finding step 5, if we find step 2, we would actually be finding step 6 and if step 3, we would be finding step 7.

Now, we see that P_1 of input becomes P_7 in step 4. Now, assume step 4 as input again. In which step does the P_7. Of input become P_3? It is step

3. So, our answer is: **(0 → 4, 0 → 3)** or **(0 → 7)** or **(0 + 4 → 7 + 4)** or **(4 → 11)**. Hence, choice (2) is the (likely) answer.

Ex 28: Solve Q.1 of Ex. 9.

Soln: Here, the choices make a range of **0 → 1, 0 → 2, 0 → 3, 0 → 4**. This cannot be reduced and there is no need to go for step B or step C.
A very simple question. Look at P_1 of the given step. It is *the*. It becomes P_7 in the unknown step. Now, in which of the steps P_1 of input becomes P_7? Look at the chart. We see that P_1 of input is P_7 in both step III and step IV. Now, we need to eliminate one from step III and IV. We choose P_7 of input because we see that P_7 of input occupies dissimilar positions [see "bourses"] in step III and IV. In the question, P_7 (stems) becomes P_2. We see that P_7 of input becomes P_2 in Step IV.
So, Step 4, choice (4) is the answer

14.8: Some Final Tips

Tip 1: In questions on shifting, **"Can't be determined" is almost never the correct answer. (Very Imp.)**

Tip 2: Try to practise the method of intelligent observation of section 14.7. After some practice you should develope the ability to solve questions without needing a pen!

Tip 3: Before anything else, make sure that the input-output question is about shifting. (See the previous chapter, section 13.4, flowchart).

Tip 4: Be confident.

Practice Exercises

Directions (Q. 1-5): A word arrangement machine, when given an input line of words, rearranges them following a particular rule in each step. The following is the illustration of the input and the steps of arrangement:

Input: man's mood varies with time and environment
Step I: varies with man's mood environment and time
Step II: and time environment mood man's varies with
Step III: environment time and varies with mood man's
Step IV: and varies environment time man's mood with

And so on for subsequent steps. You have to find out the logic and answer the questions given below.

1. If **Step V** reads "bees are sucking juice from colourful flowers", what would **Step III** read?
   1) sucking are bees colourful flowers juice from
   2) colourful juice from bees sucking flowers are
   3) colourful flowers from juice sucking bees are
   4) from juice colourful flowers are bees sucking
   5) None of these

2. If **Step III** reads "old streets of Calcutta attract me lots", what would be the arrangement for **Step VII**?
   1) me of old attract lots streets Calcutta
   2) lots attract me of Calcutta streets old
   3) streets old Calcutta of me lots attract
   4) Calcutta of streets old attract lots me
   5) None of these
3. If **Step IV** reads "everyone were aware about their intimate friendship", what will be the middle three words of **Step II**?
   1) their intimate aware 2) aware intimate their
   3) everyone were friendship 4) aware were intimate
   5) None of these
4. If the given input is "he has learnt a lot from Krishna", what will be **Step VI**?
   1) he a has from learnt lot Krishna 2) has from he a Krishna lot learnt
   3) lot learnt Krishna a he has from 4) Krishna a lot learnt from has he
   5) None of these
5. **Input:** he is member of the dancing club
   For the above input, which step will be the following arrangement?
   Arrangement: is of he the club dancing member
   1) Step IV 2) Step V 3) Step VI
   4) Step III 5) None of these

Directions (Q. 6-10): A word arrangement machine, when given an input line of words, rearranges them following a particular rule in each step. The following is the illustration of the input and the steps of arrangement:

Input: one cannot but feel sorry for him
Step I: but cannot one sorry feel him for
Step II: cannot but feel sorry one for him
Step III: but cannot sorry feel him for one
Step IV: sorry cannot but him feel one for

And so on for subsequent steps. You have to find out the logic and answer the questions given below.

6. If **Step V** read "weeks of tepid slothful and weak performance", what would **Step IV** read?
   1) performance weeks and tepid of weak slothful
   2) of weeks and slothful tepid performance weak
   3) of tepid slothful performance weak and weeks
   4) performance and tepid weeks of weak slothful
   5) None of these

7. If **Step II** reads "it was the name bestowed upon series", what would be the arrangement for **Step VII**?
   1) bestowed it was the name upon series
   2) series it name bestowed the was upon
   3) it was series the name bestowed upon
   4) upon the series was it bestowed name
   5) None of these
8. If **Step VI** reads "scientists must take a stand against working", what will be the last word of **Step III**?
   1) scientists　　2) must　　3) take
   4) a　　5) None of these
9. If **Step III** reads "the best way of promoting our nation", what will be the arrangement of the input?
   1) best the nation way of our promoting
   2) our promoting the best nation way of
   3) nation best the of way our promoting
   4) of our best the way nation promoting
   5) None of these
10. If the given input is "this is a good approach with caution", what will be **Step IV**?
    1) with approach this is a good caution
    2) approach is a caution good this with
    3) a good approach this is with caution
    4) caution with a good approach is this
    5) None of these

Directions (Q. 11-15): A word arrangement machine, when given an input line of words, rearranges them following a particular rule in each step. The following is the illustration of the input and the steps of arrangement:

Input: designers often come up with ideas
Step I: designers up come often with ideas
Step II: with up ideas often designers come
Step IV: come designers often ideas up with
Step V: come ideas often designers up with

And so on in subsequent steps. Study the logic and answer the questions that follow:

11. If **Step VI** reads "mercury up power down water out", which of the following will be the last three words of **Step II**?
    1) up water out　　2) power down up　　3) water down power
    4) power up water　　5) None of these

12. If **Step V** reads "Delhi was caught in power crisis", which step would read "in caught Delhi power crisis was"?
    1) Step I 2) Step II 3) Step III
    4) Step IV 5) None of these
13. If **Step IV** reads "the load-shedding to be carried out", what would be the arrangement in **Step VII**?
    1) be to the out carried load-shedding
    2) load-shedding be carried out the to
    3) carried be out load-shedding the to
    4) be out carried to the load-shedding
    5) None of these
14. If the **input** reads "the problem had arisen from over-drawal", what would **Step III** read?
    1) the arisen had problem from overdrawal
    2) from arisen had problem the overdrawal
    3) from arisen overdrawal problem the had
    4) had the problem overdrawal arisen from
    5) None of these
15. If **Step IV** reads "to restrict the use of airconditioners", which of the following will **definitely** be the input?
    1) use to of the airconditioners restrict
    2) restrict the to of airconditioners use
    3) the airconditioners of restrict use to
    4) Can't be determined
    5) None of these

Directions (Q. 16-22): Read the following information carefully and answer the questions given below:

A famous museum issues entry passes to all its visitors for security reasons. Visitors are allowed in batches after every one hour. In a day, there are six batches. A code is printed on entry pass which keeps on changing for every batch. Following is an illustration of pass-codes issued for each batch.

Batch I: clothes neat and clean liked are all by

Batch II: by clothes neat all are and clean liked

Batch III: liked by clothes clean and neat all are and so on...

16. If pass-code for the third batch is 'night succeed day and hard work to for', what will be the pass-code for the sixth batch?
    1) work hard to for succeed night and day
    2) hard work for and succeed night to day
    3) work hard for to succeed night and day
    4) hard work for to succeed night and day
    5) None of these

17. If 'visit in zoo should the we time day' is the pass-code for the fifth batch, 'zoo we the should visit day time in' will be the pass-code for which of the following batches?
    1) II 2) IV 3) I 4) III 5) VI
18. Sanjay visited the museum in the fourth batch and was issued a pass-code 'to fast rush avoid not do very run'. What would have been the pass-code for him had he visited the museum in the second batch?
    1) rush do not avoid to run very fast
    2) rush not do avoid to run very fast
    3) avoid rush not do to run very fast
    4) Date inadequate
    5) None of these
19. Subodh went to visit the museum in the second batch. He was issued a pass-code 'length the day equal of an night are'. However, he could not visit the museum in the second batch as he was a little late. He then prefered to visit in the fifth batch. What will be the new pass-code issued to him?
    1) and of are night the length equal day
    2) and are of night the length equal day
    3) and of are night the equal day length
    4) and of are the night length day equal
    5) None of these
20. If pass-code for the second batch is 'to confidence hard you leads work and success', what will be the pass-code for the fourth batch?
    1) leads success to you hard confidence and work
    2) leads success you to hard confidence and work
    3) leads success to you hard confidence work and
    4) leads to success you hard confidence and work
    5) None of these
21. If the pass-code issued for the last (sixth) batch is 'and pencil by all boys used are pen', what will be the pass-code for the first batch?
    1) pencil and pen are used by all boys
    2) pen and pencil used are by all boys
    3) pen and pencil are used by all boys
    4) pencil and pen are used all by boys
    5) None of these
22. If the pass-code for the sixth batch is 'not go the way to of out do', what will be the pass-code for the third batch?
    1) of do to out go not way the
    2) of to do out not go way the
    3) of to go out do not way the
    4) Data inadequate
    5) None of these

Directions (Q. 23-27): Study the following information to answer the given questions:

A word rearrangement machine, when given an input line of words, rearranges them following a particular rule in each step. The following is an illustration of input and the steps of rearrangement:

Input: Over you pat me crow easy to.

Steps: (I) pat over you crow easy to me

(II) crow pat over you to me easy

(III) over crow pat to me easy you

(IV) to over crow pat easy you me and so on.

As per the rule followed in the above steps, find out the appropriate step for the given input in the following questions:

23. If **Step II** of an input is 'ge su but he for game free', what would be **step VI**?
 1) ge for but free he game su 2) for free ge game su he but
 3) free ge for but game su he 4) he ge su but game free for
 5) None of these
24. If **step IV** of an input is 'blue navy kit lime se get out', which of the following would definitely be the input?
 1) navy get lime out kit se blue 2) lime navy get kit se blue out
 3) lime blue navy kit get out se 4) kit blue navy se get out lime
 5) None of these
25. **Input:** but calm free are so not eat.
 Which of the following will be the **3rd step** for this input?
 1) so free but calm eat are not 2) but calm are free not so eat
 3) are but calm free not eat so 4) but so free eat are not calm
 5) None of these
26. If **step V** of an input is 'put down col in as much sa', what would be the 8th **step**?
 1) down in put much sa as col 2) in put down col much sa as
 3) much in put down sa as col 4) col put down as much sa in
 5) None of these
27. **Input:** rim bye eat klin fe to low
 Which of the following steps would be 'fe low rim to bye klin eat'?
 1) VIth 2) Vth 3) IVth
 4) IIIrd 5) None of these

Directions (Q. 28-32): A word arrangement machine, when given a particular input, rearranges it following a particular rule. The following is the illustration of the input and the steps of arrangement:

Input: Put pocket hand watch he for them

Step I: Put for he watch hand pocket them

Step II: Put he for watch pocket hand them

Step III: Put hand pocket watch for he them

Step IV: Put pocket hand watch he for them

And so on goes the machine. Study the logic and answer the questions that follow:

28. If **Step III** of a given input be 'fly sky birds my su fur say', what is the **seventh step** of the input?
1) fly sky birds my su fur say
2) fly birds sky my fur su say
3) fly fur su my birds sky say
4) fly su fur my sky birds say
5) None of these

29. If **Step VII** of an input is 'slow ran dhurwa pat hak dig vi', what is step V of that input?
1) slow dig hak pat dhurwa ran vi
2) slow hak dig pat ran dhurwa vi
3) slow dhurwa ran pat dig hak vi
4) slow ran dhurwa pat hak dig vi
5) None of these

30. Given the following
Input: Ana dhir raj ran san rah aji
What step will be the following arrangement?
Arrangement: Ana san rah ran dhir raj aji
1) IV 2) V 3) VI 4) VIII 5) None of these

31. If **Step VI** of a given input be 'la pe cho bal chu bi pin', what would be the input?
1) la pe cho bal chu bi pin
2) la cho pe bal bi chu pin
3) la bi chu bal cho pe pin
4) la chu bi bal pe cho pin
5) None of these

32. Given the following input, what would be step VIII of the input?
Input: Raj gan ind son pri neh moh
1) Raj ind gan son neh pri moh
2) Raj gan ind son pri neh moh
3) Raj neh pri son ind gan moh
4) Raj pri neh son gan ind moh
5) None of these

Directions (Q. 33-37): A word arrangement machine, when given a particular input, rearranges it following a particular input. The following is the illustration of the input and the steps of arrangement:

Input: cri end yam stu the

Step I: yam che cri end stu

Step II: yam che stu end cri

Step III: stu cri yam che end

Step IV: stu cri end che yam

And so on goes the machine. Study the logic and answer the questions that follow:

33. If **Step VII** of an input is 'over the pre new bone', what is **step IV** of that input?
1) bone the pre over new
2) the pre bone new over
3) the bone pre over new
4) pre bone the over new
5) None of these

34. Given the following
Input: 'sym reach lad photo cal'
What step will be the following arrangement?
Arrangement: reach lad photo sym cal
1) VI 2) V 3) IV 4) III 5) None of these

35. If **Step VI** of a given input be 'map ind pak rus eng', what would be the input?
1) ind map pak rus eng
2) ind map eng rus pak
3) eng rus ind pak map
4) rus map ind eng pak
5) None of these

36. Given the following input, what would be **step VIII** of the input?
Input: bank cris attract with prize
1) prize win cris attract bank
2) cris bank prize win attract
3) prize win bank attract cris
4) cris bank attract win prize
5) None of these

37. In which **step** will we get the same arrangement as the **input**?
1) VIII 2) IX 3) X 4) XI 5) Not possible

Directions (Q. 38-42): Read the following information and answer the questions given below:

In an exhibition the timings for entry are 10 AM to 3 PM and 4 PM to 9 PM. There are 5 batches in each session of one-hour duration. The tickets issued for entry are coded of seven words, which gets rearranged for different batches following a definite rule. Which is described below:

Batch 1 (10 AM - 11 AM): you all are welcomed in this exhibition
Batch 2 (11 AM - 12 AM): are all this welcomed exhibition in you
Batch 3 (12 AM - 1 PM): this all in welcomed you exhibition are
And so on till the last batch.

38. If the code on the ticket of sixth batch is 'enjoy your life equally after the marriage', which of the following would be the code on the ticket of the third batch?
1) the your equally after marriage enjoy life
2) the your after equally enjoy marriage life
3) your after equally marriage life the enjoy
4) the after equally life marriage enjoy your
5) None of these

39. If the code of ticket of the batch between 8 and 9 PM in the evening is 'Anand Roop Chaudhary is my best friend', which of the following would be the code on the ticket of the batch between 10 and 11 Am in the morning session?

1) best Roop Choudhary is my friend Anand
2) Choudhary Roop best is my Anand friend
3) Choudhary Roop best is friend my Anand
4) my Roop friend is Choudhary Anand best
5) None of these

40. If the code of ticket of the last batch is 'Vijay Prakash Singh likes beautiful red roses' then what will be the code of the ticket issued in the first batch in morning session?
1) Singh Prakash red likes beautiful roses Vijay.
2) roses Prakash red likes Vijay Singh beautiful.
3) red Prakash Singh likes Vijay beautiful roses.
4) Singh Prakash red likes roses beautiful Vijay.
5) None of these

41. If the code of ticket issued during 1 pm to 2 pm batch is 'Digvijay Pathak hates beautiful birds during exam' then the code on ticket 'During Pathak birds beautiful Digvijay exam hates' will represent which of the following batches?
1) 1st batch 2) 2nd batch 3) 3rd batch
4) 4th batch 5) None of these

42. If the code of ticket issued during the eighth batch is 'Pranab Sinha is not tall as Ashok', what will be the code of ticket issued during 2 to 3 PM?
1) tall Sinha as not Ashok is Pranab
2) as Sinha tall not Pranab Ashok is
3) as Sinha Pranab not tall is Ashok
4) Ashok Sinha as not Pranab tall is
5) None of these

Directions (Q. 43-47): A word arrangement machine, when given a particular input, rearranges it following a particular rule. The following is the illustration of the input and the steps of arrangement:

Input: you do things to help others in difficulty.
Step I: do you others to help things difficulty in.
Step II: do others you help to difficulty things in.
Step III: do others help you difficulty to things in.
Step IV: others do help difficulty you to in things.

And so on goes the machine. Study the logic and answer the questions that follow:

43. If **step II** of a given input be 'why are you not in contact with me', what is the **seventh step** of the input?
1) why in you with are not contact me
2) why you in are with not contact me
3) why in you are with contact not me
4) you why in with are not contact me
5) None of these

44. If **step VI** of an input is 'above is the massage to you from me', what is the **step III** of that input?
1) above from the massage to you is me
2) above the from massage to is you me
3) above the massage from to you is me
4) the above from massage you to is me
5) None of these

45. Given the following
Input: I am talking about you Digvijay Pranav Ashok
What **step** will be the following arrangement?
Arrangement: about am I talking Digvijay Ashok Pranav you
1) VI 2) VII 3) VIII 4) V 5) None of these

46. If **step VII** of a given input be 'I am serious about the conversation to you', what would be the input?
1) the I serious to am conversation you about
2) the I to serious conversation am you about
3) serious am the I you to about conversation
4) serious I the am to about you conversation
5) None of these

47. Given the **input**, what would be the **step VIII** of the input?
Input: I am waiting for your reply in future
1) for am I waiting reply future in your
2) for am waiting reply I future in your
3) reply am your I future in waiting for
4) am reply your I future for waiting in
5) None of these

Directions (Q. 48-52): Study the following information to answer the given questions:

A word arrangement machine when given an input line of words, rearranges them following a particular rule in each step. The following is an illustration of input and steps of rearrangement.

Input: gale pa tu is wind law
Step I: is law gale pa tu wind
II: is law wind tu pa gale
III: tu gale is law wind pa
IV: tu gale pa wind law is
and so on .....

As per the rules followed in the above steps, find out in the given questions the appropriate steps for the given input.

48. If **step III** of an input is 'low fat say by gain over', what would be the **input**?
1) low fat over gain by say
2) say by fat over low gain
3) over gain say by fat low
4) fat over low say gain by
5) None of these

49. If **step V** of an input is 'are me top cake fu cho', which of the following **steps** would read as 'me cho are top fu cake'?
1) II 2) I 3) IV 4) VI 5) None of these

50. If **step VII** of an input is 'rye se key no win for', which of the following **steps** would read as 'se for no win key rye'?
1) VIII 2) VI 3) II 4) I 5) None of these

51. If **step VI** of an input is 'rat bow tin if you fly', which of the following will be the **step II**?
1) you if fly bow rat tin 2) if fly rat bow tin you 3) bow tin rat fly if you
4) fly you bow tin rat if 4) None of these

52. **Input:** crow lime put to my set.
Which of the following would be the step III for this input?
1) to set my put lime crow 2) put crow to set my lime
3) to set crow lime put my 4) put crow lime my set to
5) None of these

Directions (Q. 53-57): A word and number arrangement machine when given an input line of words and numbers rearranges them following a particular rule in each step. The following is an illustration of an input and rearrangement.

Input: 17 put show on 39 27 85 gold
Step I: show 17 put on 39 27 85 gold
Step II: show 85 17 put on 39 27 gold
Step III: show 85 put 17 on 39 27 gold
Step IV: show 85 put 39 17 on 27 gold
Step V: show 85 put 39 on 17 27 gold
Step VI: show 85 put 39 on 27 17 gold
StepVII: show 85 put 39 on 27 gold 17

and Step VII is the last step of the rearrangement of the above input.

As per the rules followed in the above steps, find out in each of the following questions the appropriate step for the given input.

53. **Input:** glass full 15 37 water now 85 67
Which of the following will be step VI of the above input?
1) water 85 now 67 full glass 15 37
2) water 85 now 67 glass full 15 37
3) water 85 now 67 glass 37 full 15
4) There will be no such step.
5) None of these

54. Step II of an input is : ultra 73 12 16 mail sort 39 kite Which of the following steps will be the last but one?
1) VIII 2) IX 3) VII
4) VI 5) None of these

55. Step III of an input is: win 75 voice 15 39 store gap 26 Which of the following is definitely the input?
1) voice 15 win 75 39 store gap 26
2) voice win 75 15 39 store gap 26
3) 15 75 win voice store gap 26
4) Cannot be determined
5) None of these

56. Step II of an input is : tube 83 49 34 garden flower rat 56 How many steps will be required to complete the rearrangement?
1) Four 2) Five 3) Six
4) Three 5) None of these

57. **Input:** hunt for 94 37 good 29 48 book
How many steps will be required to complete the rearrangement?
1) Four 2) Five 3) Six
4) Seven 5) None of these

Directions (Q. 58-61): Study the following information carefully and answer the given questions:

A word and number arrangement machine when given an input line of words and numbers rearranges them following a particular rule in each step. The following is an illustration of input and rearrangement. (All the numbers are two-digit numbers.)

Input: tall 48 13 rise alt 99 76 32 wise jar high 28 56 barn
Step I: 13 tall 48 rise 99 76 32 wise jar high 28 56 barn alt
Step II: 28 13 tall 48 rise 99 76 32 wise jar high 56 alt barn
Step III: 32 28 13 tall 48 rise 99 76 wise jar 56 alt barn high
Step IV: 48 32 28 13 tall rise 99 76 wise 56 alt barn high jar
Step V: 56 48 32 28 13 tall 99 76 wise alt barn high jar rise
Step VI: 76 56 48 32 28 13 99 wise alt barn high jar rise tall
Step VII: 99 76 56 48 32 28 13 alt barn high jar rise tall wise

And Step VII is the last step of the above input, as the desired arrangement is obtained.

As per the rules followed in the above steps, find out in each of the following questions the appropriate step for the given input.

Input: 84 why sit 14 32 not best ink feet 51 27 vain 68 92
(All the numbers are two-digit numbers.)

58. Which step number is the following output?
32 27 14 84 why sit not 51 vain 92 68 feet best ink
1) Step V 2) Step VI 3) Step IV
4) Step III 5) There is no such step.

59. Which word/number would be at 5th position from the right in Step V?
1) 14 2) 92 3) feet
4) best 5) why

60. How many elements (words or numbers) are there between 'feet' and '32' as they appear in the last step of the output?
1) One 2) Three 3) Four
4) Five 5) Seven

61. Which of the following represents the position of 'why' in the fourth step?
1) Eighth from the left 2) Fifth from the right
3) Sixth from the left 4) Fifth from the left
5) Seventh from the left

Answers and Explanations

1. Solutions by method of reference chart

Q. 1-5: Let us find out the logic: In Step I, the last three words get reversed while the first and third, and second and fourth interchange their positions. In Step II, the middle three words get reversed and the alternate words interchange among themselves in the remaining four. In Step III, the three-word group is at the beginning and changes take place accordingly. From Step III to Step IV, changes are similar to those from Input to Step I. And so on.

Now, if we mark the words in the input by digits 1 to 7 respectively the digital arrangement will be:

Input:	1	2	3	4	5	6	7
Step I:	3	4	1	2	7	6	5
Step II:	6	5	7	2	1	3	4
Step III:	7	5	6	3	4	2	1
Step IV:	6	3	7	5	1	2	4
Step V:	2	4	1	5	7	6	3
Step VI:	1	4	2	6	3	5	7
Step VII:	2	6	1	4	7	5	3

1. 4; Let us write down the words given in step V along with its code from the above table.

Step V:	bees	are	sucking	juice	from	colourful	flowers
Code:	2	4	1	5	7	6	3

Thus, we have each word being assigned a digit. Now, what would step III be? The table says: 7563421. We know that 7 stands for *from*, 5 stands for *juice*, and so on.

2. 5; **Step III:** old streets of Calcutta attract me lots

Code:	7	5	6	3	4	2	1
Step VII:	2	6	1	4	7	5	3

me of lots attract old streets Calcutta

3. 2 4. 1 5. 2

(6-10): Let us find out the logic. In Step I, the first three words get reversed while the words inside each of the remaining two pairs interchange their positions. In step II, the three-word group becomes the middle one and changes take place accordingly. In step III, the three-word group is at the end. Here, the series gets completed.

From Step III to Step IV, changes are similar to those from Input to Step I. And so on.

Now, if we mark the words in the Input by digits 1 to 7 respectively, the digital arrangement will be:

Input:	1	2	3	4	5	6	7
Step I:	3	2	1	5	4	7	6
Step II:	2	3	4	5	1	6	7
Step III:	3	2	5	4	7	6	1
Step IV:	5	2	3	7	4	1	6
Step V:	2	5	4	7	3	6	1
Step VI:	5	2	7	4	1	6	3
Step VII:	7	2	5	1	4	3	6

6. 2; Let us write down the words given in step V along with its code from the above table.

Step V:	weeks	of	tepid	slothful	and	weak	performance.
Code:	2	5	4	7	3	6	1

Thus we have each word being assigned a digit. Now, what would step IV be? The table says: 5237416. We know that 5 stands for *of*, 2 for *weeks*, and so on.

7. 2 8. 5; stand 9. 3 10. 2

(11-15): Let us try to understand the logic of the arrangement. In step I, the second and the fourth words interchange their positions. In step II, the first and the fifth words interchange their positions. In step III, the thrid and the sixth words interchange their positions. In step IV, the entire arrangement is written in a reverse order. And here as if the series gets completed. Hereafter, the series is repeated.

Now, if we denote each of the words by digits, it would be easy for us to have a stepwise digital arrangement. Let us take the order as it is in the input: **designers - 1; often - 2; come - 3; up - 4; with - 5; ideas - 6.** The arrangement then becomes:

Input:	1	2	3	4	5	6
Step I:	1	4	3	2	5	6
Step II:	5	4	3	2	1	6
Step III:	5	4	6	2	1	3
Step IV:	3	1	2	6	4	5

Step V: 3 6 2 1 4 5
Step VI: 4 6 2 1 3 5
Step VII: 4 6 5 1 3 2

Note: Why did we go till step VII? Because this is the highest- numbered step among the given questions.

11. 2; **Step VI:** mercury up power down water out
Code: 4 6 2 1 3 5
Now, the last three words of step II are 2 and 6. In other words, "power down up". [**Note:** For codes, refer to the digital arrangement given above.]

12. 5; **Step V:** Delhi was caught in power crisis
Code: 3 6 2 1 4 5
Now, let us write the step in question and the corresponding digits (which can be found from the above line) to find out the code.
in caught Delhi power crisis was
1 2 3 4 5 6
Now, if you see the table, this is the code for the input itself.

13. 3; **Step IV:** the load-shedding to be carried out
Code: 3 1 2 6 4 5
For step VII, we arrange the words as 465132.

14. 3; **Input:** the problem had arisen from overdrawal
Code: 1 2 3 4 5 6
Step III (code): 5 4 6 2 1 3
Step III: from arisen overdrawal problem the had

15. 2

(16-22): Here the rule followed is.
The last word of the previous batch becomes first and the first and second words shift rightwards i.e. becomes second and third respectively. Now, the second-last and the third-last words of the previous batch become fourth and fifth respectively and the third, fourth and fifth become sixth, seventh and eight respectively.
For convenience,we assign numeric value to these words as: clothes-1, neat-2, and-3, clean-4, liked-5, are-6, all-7, by-8

Batch I:	1	2	3	4	5	6	7	8
Batch II:	8	1	2	7	6	3	4	5
Batch III:	5	8	1	4	3	2	7	6
Batch IV:	6	5	8	7	2	1	4	3
Batch V:	3	6	5	4	1	8	7	2
Batch VI:	2	3	6	7	8	5	4	1

16. 3; **Batch III:** night succeed day and hard work to for
5 8 1 4 3 2 7 6
Batch VI: 2 3 6 7 8 5 4 1
work hard for to succeed night and day

17. 4; **Batch V:** visit in zoo should the we time day
3 6 5 4 1 8 7 2

Batch III: zoo we the should visit day time in
5 8 1 4 3 2 7 6

18. 1; **Batch IV:** to fast rush avoid not do very run
6 5 8 7 2 1 4 3

Batch II: 8 1 2 7 6 3 4 5
rush do not avoid to run very fast

19. 1 20. 1 21. 3 22. 5

(23-27): For the sake of convenience, assign numbers to each word of the input.

Input: over you pat me crow easy to
1 2 3 4 5 6 7

Now, in **Step I,** the third word comes at the beginning and the first and second words are pushed rightwards. Also the fourth word goes at the end and the remaining words are pushed leftwards.

In **Step II,** the fourth word from the first step comes at the beginning and the first, second and third words of Step I are pushed rightwards. Also, the fifth word of Step II goes at the end and the remaining words are pushed leftwards.

These steps are repeated thereafter.

For convenience, we plot the movement of each word in each step by the numbers assigned to them in the input.

Input:	1	2	3	4	5	6	7
Step I:	3	1	2	5	6	7	4
Step II:	5	3	1	2	7	4	6
Step III:	1	5	3	7	4	6	2
Step IV:	7	1	5	3	6	2	4
Step V:	5	7	1	6	2	4	3
Step VI:	6	5	7	1	4	3	2
Step VII:	7	6	5	4	3	2	1
Step VIII:	4	7	6	5	2	1	3

23. 3; From the table, the numbers in **Step II** are
5 3 1 2 7 4 6
ge su but he for game free

In **Step VI**, we have the numbers arranged as
6 5 7 1 4 3 2
free ge for but game su he

24. 1

25. 4

26. 5; The answer is ‘much down in put as col sa’.

27. 2

(28-32): From Input to Step I: The second and sixth words are interchanged; and so are third and fifth.

From Step I to Step II: The second and third words are interchanged; and so are fifth and sixth.

These steps are repeated thereafter. For convenience, we plot the movement of each word in each step by the numbers assigned to them in the input; put-1, pocket-2, hand-3, watch-4, he-5, for- 6, them-7.

Input:	1	2	3	4	5	6	7
Step I:	1	6	5	4	3	2	7
Step II:	1	5	6	4	2	3	7
Step III:	1	3	2	4	6	5	7
Step IV:	1	2	3	4	5	6	7

Since **step IV** is the same as input, **step V** would be the same as **step I**, and so on. Thus the arrangement gets repeated every four steps.

28. 1; Since the arrangement is repeated every four steps, **step VII** would be the same as **step III**.

29. 2; **Step VII** would be the same as **step III**. Hence,

slow ran dhurwa pat hak dig vi

1 3 2 4 6 5 7

Now, **step V** would be the same as step I, i.e. 1654327.

30. 3 31. 4 32. 2

(33-37): From input to step I: The third and fifth words come in place of first and second respectively and the rest get shifted rightward.

From step I to step II: The third and fifth words are interchanged.

These steps are repeated thereafter.

For convenience, we plot the movement of each word in each step by the numbers assigned to them in the input, i.e. cri-1, end-2, yam-3, stu-4, che-5.

Input:	1	2	3	4	5
Step I:	3	5	1	2	4
Step II:	3	5	4	2	1
Step III:	4	1	3	5	2
Step IV:	4	1	2	5	3
Step V:	2	3	4	1	5
Step VI:	2	3	5	1	4
Step VII:	5	4	2	3	1
Step VIII:	5	4	1	3	2
Step IX:	1	2	5	4	3
Step X:	1	2	3	4	5

33. 3; From the table, the numbers in step VII are

5 4 2 3 1

over the pre new bone

In step IV, we have numbers rearranged as

4 1 2 5 3

the bone pre over new

34. 2; From the table, the numbers in Input are

1 2 3 4 5

sym reach lad photo cal

Now, the given arrangement is

reach lad photo sym cal

2 3 4 1 5

Which is step V.

35. 4 36. 3

37. 3; See the table

(38-42): The order of words changes from one batch to the next as follows: the first word becomes the last; the second remains the same; the third becomes the first; the fourth remains the same; the fifth becomes the sixth; the sixth becomes the third; while the seventh becomes the fifth. For convenience, we plot the movement of each word in each step by the numbers assigned to them in the first batch:

you-1, *all*-3, *welcomed*-4, *in*-5, *this*-6, *exhibition*-7

Batch 1 (10 am - 11 am):	1	2	3	4	5	6	7
Batch 2 (11 am - 12 am):	3	2	6	4	7	5	1
Batch 3 (12 am - 1 pm):	6	2	5	4	1	7	3
Batch 4 (1 pm - 2 pm):	5	2	7	4	3	1	6
Batch 5 (2 pm - 3 pm):	7	2	1	4	6	3	5
Batch 6 (4 pm - 5 pm):	1	2	3	4	5	6	7

Since Batch 6 is the same as Batch 1, Batch 7 would be the same as Batch 2, and so on. Thus, the arrangement gets repeated.

38. 2; Since Batch 6 is the same as the first batch, thus

enjoy your life equally after the marriage

1 2 3 4 5 6 7

Now, to get the code on the ticket of Batch 3, arrange the words as 6254173

39. 3 40. 4 41. 1 42. 2

(43-47):

From input to step I: The first and the second words are interchanged: so are the seventh and eighth; and so are the third and sixth.

From step I to step II: The second and the third are interchanged: so are the fourth and the fifth and the sixth and the seventh.

From step II to step III: The third and the fourth are interchanged and so are the the fifth and the sixth.

From step III to step IV: The first and the second word are interchanged and so are the seventh and the eighth. Similarly, the fourth and the fifth words are interchanged.

From step IV to step V: Same as from input to step I. These steps are repeated thereafter. For convenience, we plot the movement of each word in each step by the numbers assigned to them in the input: you-1, do-2, things-3, to-4, help-5, others-6, in-7, difficulty-8.

Input:	1	2	3	4	5	6	7	8
Step I:	2	1	6	4	5	3	8	7
Step II:	2	6	1	5	4	8	3	7
Step III:	2	6	5	1	8	4	3	7
Step IV:	6	2	5	8	1	4	7	3
Step V:	2	6	4	8	1	5	3	7
Step VI:	2	4	6	1	8	3	5	7
Step VII:	2	4	1	6	3	8	5	7
Step VIII:	4	2	1	3	6	8	7	5

43. 3 44. 2 45. 3 46. 4 47. 1

48-52: For convenience, we plot the movement of each word in each step by the numbers assigned to them in the input; gale-1, pa-2, tu-3, is-4, wind-5, law-6.

Input:	1	2	3	4	5	6
Step I:	4	6	1	2	3	5
Step II:	4	6	5	3	2	1
Step III:	3	1	4	6	5	2
Step IV:	3	1	2	5	6	4
Step V:	5	4	3	1	2	6
Step VI:	5	4	6	2	1	3
Step VII:	2	3	5	4	6	1
Step VIII:	2	3	1	6	4	5

There are two movements i.e. input to step I and step I to step II. Which are repeated thereafter.

48. 4; **Step III:** low fat say by gain over
3 1 4 6 5 2
Input: 1 2 3 4 5 6
fat over low say gain by

49. 1; **Step V:** are me tip cake fu cho
5 4 3 1 2 6
Hence, me cho are top fu cake
4 6 5 3 2 1
Which is step II.

50. 5 51. 3 52. 2

Important Note

In all these solutions we have not applied the golden rule of reduction. This has been done with the intention of giving the easiest (although lengthier solution first. We shall now see what difference does golden rule make in these questions.

Q. 1-5: Q. 4 asks for **0 - 6**. It can't be reduced further. So, as chart will have to have upto step VI Q. 2 wants us to find **3 → 7** which can be reduced to **(3 - 3) → (7 - 3)** [∴ V is a 3-step case]. So, we could have saved drawing of step VII here.

Q. 6-10: It is a 3-step case again. Q7 wants us to give **2 → 7** and it can't be reduced. So, we must draw our chart upto step VII.

Q. 11-15: It is a 4-step case. Q.3 wants us to give **4 → 7** and they can be reduced to **0 → 3**, Q. 12 wants **6 → 2** and it can't be reduced. So, we could have found our answer by drawing upto step VI only. Step VII was not necessary.

Q. 16-22: It is a 1-step case. Here too, we must find all 6 batches as Q21 wants us to give **6 → 1** and it cant be reduced.

Q. 23-27: It is a 2-step case. Here, Q26 wants us to give **5 → 8** which can be reduced to **1 → 4**.
Similarly, Q23 can be reduced from **2 → 6** to **0 → 4**. So, we can get our answers by drawing upto step IV only. We don't need to draw step V, Step VI, Step VII and Step VIII to solve Q23 to Q26.

Q. 28-32: It is a 2-step case. Q32 wants **0 → 8** and it can't be reduced. So we must draw our chart upto step VIII.

Q. 33-37: It is a 2-step case. Q36 wants **0 → 8**. It can't be reduced. So we must draw upto step VIII.

Q. 38-42: Here, pattern is repeated in Batch 6 itself. So, in any case, we don't need to repeat after Batch 6.

Q.43-47: It is a 4-step case. Because of 47, we must draw upto step VIII.

Q. 48-52: It is a 2-step case. Because of Q50, we must draw upto step VII.

Solution using the second method

(Method of intelligent observation)

(Q1-5): In **0 → 1**, $P_1 \rightarrow P_3$, $P_7 \rightarrow P_5$ and in 1 → 2; $P_1 \rightarrow P_6$, $\rightarrow P_7 \rightarrow P_2$, 2 → 3, $P_1 \rightarrow P_3$, $P_7 \rightarrow P_5$ and in 3 → 4, $P_1 \rightarrow P_3$, $P_7 \rightarrow P_5$.
Hence, by taking a sample of P_1 and P_7 and watching their movements we many conclude that: **0 → 1 ≠ 1 → 2 ≠ 2 → 3** but **0 → 1 = 3 → 4**.
∴ By the logic given in flowchart 2; it is a 3-step type case.
Now, let us go to the questions one by one.

1.4; We have to find **5 → 3**. By golden rule, **5 → 3 = (5 - 3) → (3 - 3) = 2 → 0**.
So, assume that *"bees are sucking juice from colourful flowers"* is step II. What is the input?
In the given table, we see that in **2 → 0**; P_1 (*and*) → P_6 and P_2 (time) → P_5. So P_1 = *bees* should be at P_6 and P_2 = are should be at P_5. Hence, choice 4 is likely. On verification, it is indeed correct.

2. 5; We have to find **3 → 7**. By golden rule, **3 → 7 = 0 → 4**. So, assume *old streets ... me lots* is input. What is step IV for this input. Clearly, none of these. (Refer to the given chart.)

3. 2; We have to find **4 → 2**. In table, we see that in **2 → 4**; middle three words i.e. P_3 (*environment*), P_4 (*mood*) and P_5 (*man's*) go to P_3, P_6 and P_5 respectively. In other words, P_3, P_4 and P_5 of step II must come from P_3, P_6 and P_5 respectively. In our *"everyone was .... friendship"* P_3, P_6 and P_5 are as given in choice 2.

4. 1; We have to find **0 → 6**. Break it as, **(0 → 4, 4 → 6)** and then again **[0 → 4, (4 - 3) → (6 - 3)]** i.e. **(0 → 4, 1 → 3)**. So, we treat *"he has ... Krishna"* as input, find its step IV; then we will again treat the step IV thus found as step I and find its step III.
We see that in **0 → 4**, $P_1 \rightarrow P_5$, $P_2 \rightarrow P_6$. So, in step IV P_1 and P_2 become P_5 and P_6. Now, we assume that this is our step I we see that in 1 → 3, $P_5 \rightarrow P_7$, $P_6 \rightarrow P_6$. So, in our final answer; we must have $P_1 \rightarrow P_7$, $P_2 \rightarrow P_6$. That is, *he* must be P_7, *has* must be P_6.

5. 5; In input to given step, we see that P_1 (he) → P_3. But in **0 → 3** and in **0 → 4**; $P_1 \rightarrow P_7$ and $P_1 \rightarrow P_5$ respectively. So, step III and step IV are ruled out. Now, let us consider **0 → 5** and **0 → 6**. We can break them as **(0 → 3, 3 → 5)** and **(0 → 3, 3 → 6)** and reduce again as **(0 → 3, 0 → 2)** and **(0 → 3, 0 → 3)**. Therefore, we can find step V and step VI for *"he is .. club"* by assuming it as input and finding step III; again assuming step III so obtained as input and finding step II (to find step V) or step III (to find step VI). We take P_1 and P_2 (*he* and *is*). In **0 → 3**, P_1 and P_2 become P_7 and P_3, respectively. Now, again P_7 and P_3 become P_3 and P_6 in 0 → 2 and become P_1 and P_5 respectively in 0 → 3. So, we must have $P_1 \rightarrow P_3$, $P_2 \rightarrow P_6$ in 0 → 5 and $P_1 \rightarrow P_1$, $P_2 \rightarrow P_5$ in 0 → 6. But looking our P_1 (*he*) and P_2 (*is*) we realise that none of these is true.

Q. 6-10: We see that in **0 → 1**, $P_1 \rightarrow P_3$, $P_7 \rightarrow P_6$; in **1 → 2**, $P_1 \rightarrow P_2$, $P_7 \rightarrow P_6$, in **2 → 3**, $P_1 \rightarrow P_2$, $P_7 \rightarrow P_5$, in **3 → 4**, $P_1 \rightarrow P_3$, $P_7 \rightarrow P_6$. So, **0 → 1 = 3 → 4**. By flowchart 2, we have a **3-step** case

6. 2; We have to find 5 → 4. By golden rule, 5 → 4 = (5 - 3) → (4 - 3) = 2 → 1. So, assume *"weeks of .... performance"* as step II and find its step I. We see by our chart that in 2 → 1, P_1 (*cannot*) → P_2, P_7 (*him*) → P_6. So, in our answer P_1 (*weeks*) and P_7 (*performance*) must be at P_2 and P_6. So, choice 2 is likely.

7. 2; We have to find **2 → 6**. Break it as **2 → 4, 4 → 6**. Reduce **4 → 6** as **(4 - 3) → (6 - 3) = 1 →** 3. So, **2 → 6** becomes **2 → 4, 1 → 3**. So, we assume *"it was ... series"* as step II, find step IV assume that step IV as step I and find step III. Let us take P_2.
From table we see that $P_2 \rightarrow P_2$ in 2 → 4 and $P_2 \rightarrow P_2$ in 1 → 3. So, $P_2 \rightarrow P_2$ in 2 → 6. Correct choice: 2.

8. 5; We have to find P_7 for **6 → 3**. By golden rule **6 → 3 = 3 → 0**. So, we assume *"Scientists... against working"* as step III and find its input. We see that in **0 → 3**, $P_7 \rightarrow P_5$. In other words , in **3 → 0**, $P_5 \rightarrow P_7$. So, last word of input must be P_5 of step III. That word is *stand*.

9. 3. We have to find **3 → 0**. We see that in the choices P_1 is different in all the choices. So, we try P_1 of input we see from table that in 0 → 3, $P_1 \rightarrow P_7$. So, in 3 → 0, $P_7 \rightarrow P_1$. So, *nation* must be P_1 in our answer.

10. 2; We have to find **0 → 4**. Look at the table itself to find it.

Q. 11-15 We see that in 0 → 1, $P_1 \rightarrow P_1$, $P_7 \rightarrow P_7$; in 1 → 2, $P_1 \rightarrow P_6$, $P_7 \rightarrow P_7$; in 2 → 3, $P_1 \rightarrow P_1$, $P_7 \rightarrow P_3$; in 3 → 4, $P_1 \rightarrow P_7$, $P_7 \rightarrow P_1$ and in 4 → 5, $P_1 \rightarrow P \rightarrow P_1$, $P_7 \rightarrow P_7$. So, **0 → 1 = 4 → 5**. Hence, it is a **4-step** arrangement.

11. 2; We have to find last three words of Step II in 6 → 2. But, we see that in the choices, the *last* word is different in all the choices. So, we will limit ourselves with the P_7 of step II. Now, **2 → 6** can be written as **2 → 4, 4 → 6**. But, **4 → 6** can be reduced as (by golden rule) **(4 - 4) → (6 - 4)** i.e. **0 → 2**. So, **2 → 6** can be broken as **(2 → 4, 0 → 2)**. Now, P_7 becomes P_5 in **2 → 4** and P_5 becomes P_2 in **0 → 2**. So, $P_7 \rightarrow P_2$ in **(2 → 4, 0 → 2)** i.e. 2 → 6. Hence, $P_2 \rightarrow P_7$ in 6 → 2. So, *up* is P_7 in step II.

12. 5; Look at the table itself.

13. 5. We have to find **4 → 7**. By golden rule, **4 → 7 = (4 - 4) → (7 - 4) = 0 → 3**. So, we can assume *"Delhi was .... crisis"* as input and find its step 11. Look at the table and do it yourself. (*Hint*: Just watch the movement of P_7 in 0 → 3 because in our case, given P_7 (*out*) is at different places in all the different choices. We see that in 0 → 3, P_7 is P_3. So, in correct choice, *out* is P_3).

14. 3; We have to find **0 → 3**. Look at the table itself. (*Hint:* Just watch movement of *the* i.e. P_1. P_1 is P_6 in 0 → 3. So, *the* is P_6 in our answer).

15. 2; We have to find 4 → 0. Look at the table to find it. (*Hint:* Just watch the movement of *to* i.e. P_1. In 4 → 0, $P_1 \rightarrow P_3$; from the table. So, *to* must be P_1 in correct choice.

Q. 16-22: We see that in **0 → 1**, $P_1 \rightarrow P_2$, $P_8 \rightarrow P_1$ and in **1 → 2**, $P_1 \rightarrow P_2$, $P_8 \rightarrow P_1$. So, **0 → 1 = 1 → 2**. So, it is a 1-step case.

16. 3; We have to find **3 → 6**. By golden rule, **3 → 6** = 3 - 3 → 6 - 3 = **0 → 3**. So, assume *night succeed day ... for* to be input and find step III. (**Hint:** Watch movements of to and hard i.e. P_5 and P_7. These two words are at different pairs of places in different choices.

17. 4; **5 → 2 = (5 - 1 × 1) → (2 - 1 × 1) = 4 → 1**. So, we may assume **5 → 2 = 4 → 1**. Similarly, **5 → 3 = 3 → 1, 5 → 4 = 2 → 1, 5 → 6 = 1 → 2**. Now, we see that from *"visit ... day"* to *"zoo ... in"* $P_1 \rightarrow P_5$. From table, we see that $P_1 \rightarrow P_5$ is in 3 → 1 but 3 → 1 = 5 → 3.

18\. 1; We have to find, **4 → 2**. But **4 → 2 = 3 → 1**. So, assume *"to fast ... run"* as step III and find step I.

19\. 1; We have to find **2 → 5**. Break it as **2 → 3, 3 → 5**. Reduce by golden rule, **3 → 5 = (3 - 1 × 2) → (5 - 1 × 2) = 1 → 3**. So, **2 → 5** becomes **(2 → 3, 1 → 3)**. Now, let us choose *of* and *day* for our quick elimination. *of* is P_5 and *day* is P_3 in given Step II. Now, in **2 → 3** (from table), $P_5 \rightarrow P_8$, $P_3 \rightarrow P_6$ and $P_8 \rightarrow P_2$, $P_6 \rightarrow P_8$ in **1 → 3**. So, *of* is P_2 and *day* is P_8 in our answer.

20\. 1; We have to find **2 → 4**. but **2 → 4 = 1 → 3**. Now, see the table and solve.

21\. 3; We have to find **6 → 1**. But **6 → 1 = 6 → 4, 4 → 2, 2 → 1**. But, **6 → 4 = 3 → 1** and **4 → 2 = 3 → 1**. So, **6 → 1 = (3 → 1, 3 → 1, 2 →1)**. So, assume *"and pencil ... are pen"* as step III. Find its step I; assume this step I again as step III, find step I; assume this step I again as step II and find its step I. Looking at the answer choices, we realise that we need to study movements of *success*, to and *work* to eliminate our wrong choices. Now, in given step II, *success* is P_8, *to* is P_1, *work* is P_6.
Now, in **3 → 1**, $P_8 \rightarrow P_6$, $P_1 \rightarrow P_5$, $P_6 \rightarrow P_2$. So, in our step I, P_8, P_1 and P_6 are P_6, P_5 and P_2 respectively. We treat them as step III again. Now, in 3 → 1, $P_6 \rightarrow P_2$, $P_5 \rightarrow P_3$, $P_2 \rightarrow P_8$. So, the new step I has P_6, P_5 and P_2 as P_2, P_3 and P_8 respectively. Now, we treat this step I as step II and find step I. We see that in 2 → 1, $P_6 \rightarrow P_3$, $P_3 \rightarrow P_2$ and $P_8 \rightarrow P_5$ respectively.
So, correct answer must have *success, to* and *work* as P_3, P_2 and P_5 respectively.

22\. 5; We see that in the given answer choices, P_3 is different in all three choices. (P_3 = *to* in choice 1, P_3 = *do* in choice 2 and P_3 = *go* in choice 3).
Therefore, if we merely restrict ourselves to P_3 of step III and find its position in step VI; we can find our answer.
Now, **3 → 6 = 1 → 4** by golden rule. **1→ 4 = (1 → 3, 3 → 4)**; but **3 → 4 = (3 -2) → (4 - 2) = 1 → 2**. So, **1 → 4 = 1 → 3, 1 → 2**. Hence, we first find position of P_3 in **1 → 3**. Now, in **1 → 3**, $P_3 \rightarrow P_5$ (as seen from given table.). Now, we assume step III as step I and find its step II. So, $P_5 \rightarrow P_8$ in step II. Net result = $P_3 \rightarrow P_8$ in 1 → 4. But, 1 → 4 = 3 → 6. So, $P_3 \rightarrow P_8$ in 3 → 6. That is, $P_8 \rightarrow P_3$ in 6 → 3. Thus, P_8 or do should be P_3. This eliminates choices 1 and 3.
But even choice 2 is wrong, if you also consider one more word: not

23 → 27: We see that in 0 → 1, $P_1 \rightarrow P_2$, $P_4 \rightarrow P_7$, $P_7 \rightarrow P_6$; in 1 → 2, $P_1 \rightarrow P_2$, $P_4 \rightarrow P_1$, $P_7 \rightarrow P_6$ in 2 → 3, $P_1 \rightarrow P_2$, $P_4 \rightarrow P_7$, $P_7 \rightarrow P_6$. So, 0 → 1 = 2 → 3. Hence, it is a 2-step case.

23\. 3; We have to find **2 → 6**. By golden rule, **2 → 6 = (2 - 2) → (6 - 2) = 0 to 4**. Hence, we can assume *"ge su ... free"* as input and its step IV would be our answer.

24\. 1; We have to find 4 → 0. Look at the table and solve it yourself. **(Hint:**

From given table, we see that in **4 → 0**, $P_1 \rightarrow P_7$. So, *blue* must be P_7 *in* correct answer).

25. 4; We have to find **0 → 3**. Look at the table and do it yourself. (**Hint:** From given table, we see that $P_2 \rightarrow P_7$ in 0 → 3. So, *Calm* must be P_7 in correct choice)

26. 5; We have to find **5 → 8**. By golden rule, a multiple of 2 (as it is a 2-step case) can be reduced from both sides, so we reduce 2 × 2 = 4, Hence, **5 → 8 = (5 - 4) → (8 - 4) = 1 → 4**.

Hence, assume that *"put down... much sa"* is step I and find its step IV from table.

27. 2; From *"rim bye .... low"* to *"fe low .... eat"* we see that P_1 (*rim*) becomes P_3, P_2 (*bye*) becomes P_5 and so on. In the given table, we see that $P_1 \rightarrow P_3$ only in **0 → 2** which eliminates step III or step IV but $P_2 \nrightarrow P_5$ in **0 → 2**.

That means, step II or step III or step IV is not a correct answer. So, let us try step V or Step VI. Now, **0 → 5 = 0 → 4, 4 → 5** but **4 → 5 = 4 - 4 → 5 - 4 = 0 → 1**. So, 0 → 5 = 0 → 4, 0 → 1. Similarly, 0 → 6 = 0 → 4, 0 → 2. Now, $P_1 \rightarrow P_2$, $P_2 \rightarrow P_6$ in **0 → 4**. Assuming this new position (P_2 and P_6) of step IV to be input again and finding step I and step II; we see that in **0 → 1**, $P_2 \rightarrow P_3$, $P_6 \rightarrow P_5$ and in **0 → 2**, $P_2 \rightarrow P_4$, $P_6 \rightarrow P_7$. Hence, **0 → 5** means $P_1 \rightarrow P_3$, $P_2 \rightarrow P_5$ while **0 → 6**, means $P_1 \rightarrow P_4$, $P_2 \rightarrow P_7$. Obviously, **0 → 5** is correct answer.

Q. 28-32: We see that in **0 → 1**, $P_2 \rightarrow P_6$, $P_3 \rightarrow P_5$; in **1 → 2**, $P_2 \rightarrow P_3$, $P_3 \rightarrow P_2$, in **2 → 3**, $P_2 \rightarrow P_6$, $P_3 \rightarrow P_5$. So, **0 → 1 = 2 → 3**. Hence, it is a 2-step case.

28. 1; We have to find 3 → 7. But **3 → 7 = 3 → 4, 4 → 7** and by golden rule **4 → 7 = (4 - 4) → (7 - 4) = 0 → 3**. So, **3 → 7 = 3 → 4, 0 → 3**. Hence, we assume *"fly sky ... fur say"* as step III. We see that, 3 → 4 has $P_3 \rightarrow P_2$. So, *birds* should be P_2 in step IV. Again, assume it as input and find step III. We see that in 0 → 3, $P_2 \rightarrow P_3$. So, *birds* should be P_3 in correct choice. (**Note:** We take *birds* for our analysis because we have *birds* at different places in all the choices.)

29. 2; We have to find 7 → 5. By golden rule, 7 → 5 = 3 → 1. So, assume *"slowran .... dig vi"* as step III. Its step I can easily be found from the given table.

30. 3; We note that from *"Ana dhir ... aji" to "Ana san ... aji"*; $P_2 \rightarrow P_5$, $P_3 \rightarrow P_6$ ... and so on.

We know that **0 → 5 = 0 → 4, 4 → 5 = 0 → 4, (4 - 4) → (5 - 4) = 0 → 4, 0 → 1**. Similarly, **0 → 6 = 0 → 4, 0 → 2** and **0 → 7 = 0 → 4, 0 → 3**. This means that step V, step VI and step VII can be found by finding step IV from input, assuming this step IV to be input again and finding step I, step II and step III, respectively.

Now, in **0 → 4**; $P_2 \rightarrow P_2$, $P_3 \rightarrow P_3$. And then, $P_2 \rightarrow P_6$, $P_3 \rightarrow P_5$ in 0 → 1;

$P_2 \to P_5, P_3 \to P_6$ in $0 \to 2$; $P_2 \to P_3, P_3 \to P_2$ in $0 \to 3$. So, $0 \to 4, 0 \to 2$ is our answer. But, $0 \to 4, 0 \to 2 = 0 \to 6$. Hence, step VI is correct.

31. 4; We see that out of the four given choices, 2nd place is occupied by different words every time. So, let us consider P_2 of input.
Now, $\mathbf{0 \to 6 = 0 \to 4, 4 \to 6 = 0 \to 4, 0 \to 2}$.
Now, $P_2 \to P_2$ in $\mathbf{0 \to 4}$ and $P_2 \to P_5$ in $\mathbf{0 \to 2}$.
So, $P_2 \to P_5$ in $\mathbf{(0 \to 4, 0 \to 2)}$ or, $P_2 \to P_5$ in $\mathbf{0 \to 6}$.
In other words, $P_5 \to P_2$ in $6 \to 0$. So, P_5 = *chu* should be P_2 in step II.

32. 2; We have to find $0 \to 8$. We see that *gan* occupies different places in all choices and *gan* is P_2 of input. So, let us concentrate only on P_2.
Now, $\mathbf{0 \to 8 = 0 \to 4, 4 \to 8 = 0 \to 4, 0 \to 4}$. Now, $P_2 \to P_2$ in $\mathbf{0 \to 4}$ and $P_2 \to P_2$ in $\mathbf{0 \to 4}$. So, $P_2 \to P_2$ in $\mathbf{(0 \to 4, 0 \to 4)}$ or $P_2 \to P_2$ in $0 \to 8$.
Hence, *gan* must be P_2 incorrect answer.

Q. 33-37: We see that in $\mathbf{0 \to 1}$, $P_1 \to P_3$, $P_3 \to P_1$; in $1 \to 2$, $P_1 \to 1$, $P_3 \to P_5$ and in $\mathbf{2 \to 3}$, $P_1 \to P_3$, $P_3 \to P_2$. So, $\mathbf{0 \to 1 = 2 \to 3}$. Hence, it is a 2-step case.

33. 3; We have to find $\mathbf{7 \to 4}$. But, $\mathbf{7 \to 4 = (7 - 2 \times 2) \to (4 - 2 \times 2) = 3 \to 0}$.
So, we assume *over the ... new bone* as step IV and find its input.

34. 2; We see that from *"Sym reach ... cal"* to *"reach lad ... cal"* $P_1 \to P_4$, $P_5 \to P_5$. But, $P_1 \to P_4$ in $\mathbf{0 \to 3}$ or $\mathbf{0 \to 4}$. So, step III and step IV are not correct. Now, let us try step V and step VI.
Now, $\mathbf{0 \to 5 = 0 \to 4, 4 \to 5 = 0 \to 4, 0 \to 1}$ and $\mathbf{0 \to 6 = 0 \to 4, 0 \to 2}$.
Thus, we can find step IV from input, treat this step IV as input again, find its step I (to find step V) or find step II (to find step VI). Now, in $\mathbf{0 \to 4}$, $P_1 \to P_2$, and $P_5 \to P_4$. Again, $P_2 \to P_4$, $P_4 \to P_5$ in $\mathbf{0 \to 1}$ while $P_1 \to P_4$, $P_4 \to P_3$ in $0 \to 2$. So, we have, $P_1 \to P_4$, $P_5 \to P_5$ in $0 \to 4, 0 \to 1$ i.e. $0 \to 5$, while $P_1 \to P_4$, $P_5 \to P_3$ in $0 \to 4, 0 \to 2$ i.e. $0 \to 6$.

35. 4; We have to find $\mathbf{6 \to 0}$. But $\mathbf{6 \to 0 = 6 \to 4, 4 \to 0}$. But $\mathbf{6 \to 4 = (6 - 2) \to (4 - 2) = 4 \to 2}$.
So, let us assume "map ind ... eng" as step IV.
Now, from table: $P_1 \to P_3$, $P_2 \to P_5$ in $4 \to 2$.
Again, assume the new step to be step IV and find its input. From table, $P_3 \to P_2$, $P_5 \to P_3$ in $4 \to 0$.
So, $P_1 \to P_2$, $P_2 \to P_3$ in $\mathbf{4 \to 2, 4 \to 0}$, i.e. $\mathbf{6 \to 0}$. So, correct answer must have *map* at P_2 and *ind* at P_3.

36. 3; We have to find $\mathbf{0 \to 8}$. But, $\mathbf{0 \to 8 = 0 \to 4, 4 \to 8}$. But, $\mathbf{4 \to 8 = (4 - 4) \to (8 - 4) = 0 \to 4}$. So, $\mathbf{0 \to 8 = 0 \to 4, 0 \to 4}$.
Now, consider P_1 and P_2 (*bank* and *cris*). In, $0 \to 4$, from table, $P_1 \to P_2$, $P_2 \to P_3$. So, *bank* and *cris* should be P_2 and P_3 in step IV. We again treat this as input and find step IV. We see that $P_2 \to P_3$ and $P_3 \to P_5$ in $\mathbf{0 \to 4}$.
This means that *bank* is P_3 and *cris* is P_5 in our final answer.

37. 3; **Since it is a 2-step case, complete reappearance of input will occur only at a step that is a multiple of 2. (Imp.)**
This eliminates choices 2 and 4. Consider, step VIII. **0 → 8 = 0 → 4, 0 → 4.**
$P_1 \rightarrow P_2$ in **0 → 4** and $P_2 \rightarrow P_3$ in **0 → 4.**
Hence, $P_1 \rightarrow P_3$ in **0 → 8.**
So, step VIII is ruled out. Now, consider step X. **0 → 10 = 0 → 8, 8 → 10** but **8 → 10 = (8 - 2 × 4) → (10 - 2 × 4) = 0 → 2**. So, **0 → 10 = 0 → 8, 0 → 2**. Now, $P_1 \rightarrow P_3$ in **0 → 8**. Also, $P_3 \rightarrow P_1$ in **0 → 2.**
So, $P_1 \rightarrow P_1$ in **0 → 8, 0 → 2** or **0 → 10**.
[On further verification we find that it is indeed a correct answer.]

Q. 38-42: We see that $P_1 \rightarrow P_7$, $P_7 \rightarrow P_5$, $P_3 \rightarrow P_1$ in **0 → 1, 1 → 2**. So, **0 → 1 = 1 → 2**. Hence, it is a 1-step case.

38. 2; We have to find **6 → 3. 6 → 3 = (6 - 2) → (3 - 2) = 4 → 1.**
But, **4 → 1 = 4 → 3, 3 → 1** or **(4 - 1) → (3 - 1), 3 → 1** or, **3 → 2, 3 → 1.**
So, assume "*enjoy your life* .... to be step III. Find step II; assume this step II to be step III and find its step I.
Let us consider *enjoy* (P_1) as it is at different positions in different choices. Now, in **3 → 2**, $P_1 \rightarrow P_3$. So, *enjoy* is P_3 in step II. We assume it to be step III and find step I. Now, in 3 → 1, $P_3 \rightarrow P_5$. So, *enjoy* in P_5 in our final answer.

39. 3; 8 to 9 PM is the 10th batch of the evening and 10 to 11 AM is the 1st batch of next morning. We can also take 10 to 11 AM as (10 + 1) = 11th batch because it comes after 10th batch. So, we have to find **10 → 11**. Now, by golden rule: **10 → 11 = (10 - 9 × 1) → (11 - 9 × 1) = 1 → 2**. So, we can assume that "Anand Roop ...." is batch I and find its batch II.

40. 4; Same as Q. 39.

41. 1; 1 PM to 2 PM is batch 4. Now, Batch 4 has Digvijay as P_1. So, batch 3 will have *Digvijay* as P_3. [Since **4 → 3 = (4 - 1) → (3 - 1) = 3 → 2** . And $P_1 \rightarrow P_3$ in **3 → 2**, from table.]
Now, $P_3 \rightarrow P_5$ in 3 → 1, and $P_3 \rightarrow P_6$ in **3 → 2**. So, *Digvijay* will be P_5 in step I and P_2 in step II.

42. 2; Between 2 to 3 PM, the 5th batch is issued. So, we have to find **8 → 5**. But, **8 → 5 = 4 → 1**. As seen in Q. 41, correct choice can be found out.

Q. 43-47: We see that in **0 → 1**, $P_1 \rightarrow P_2$, $P_8 \rightarrow P_7$, $P_5 \rightarrow P_5$, in **1 → 2**, $P_1 \rightarrow P_1$, $P_8 \rightarrow P_8$, $P_5 \rightarrow P_4$, in **2 → 3**, $P_1 \rightarrow P_1$, $P_8 \rightarrow P_8$, $P_5 \rightarrow P_6$, in **3 → 4**, $P_1 \rightarrow P_2$, $P_8 \rightarrow P_7$, $P_5 \rightarrow P_4$, in **4 → 5**, $P_1 \rightarrow P_2$, $P_8 \rightarrow P_7$, $P_5 \rightarrow P_5$. So, **0 → 1 = 4 → 5**. Hence, it is a 4-step case.

43. 3; We have to find 2 → 7. Let us consider *are* (P_2) and *you* (P_3) as these two are at different pairs of places in different choices.
We have, 2 → 7 = 2 → 5, 5 → 7. But 5 → 7 = 5 - 4 → 7 - 4 = 1 → 3.
So, 2 → 7 = 2 → 5, 1 → 3. Now, in 2 → 5 $P_2 \rightarrow P_2$, $P_3 \rightarrow P_5$

So, *are* and *you* are P_2 and P_5 in step V. Assume it as step I. Now, in $1 \to 3, P_1 \to P_4, P_5 \to P_3$. So, *are* and *you* are P_4 and P_3 in $\mathbf{2 \to 5, 1 \to 3}$ i.e. $2 \to 7$.

44.2; We have to find $\mathbf{6 \to 3}$. Let us consider *the* (P_3) and *from* (P_7) because these two are at different pairs of places in different choices. Now, $\mathbf{6 \to 3 = 6 \to 5, 5 \to 3}$. But $\mathbf{6 \to 5 = (6-4) \to (5-4) = 2 \to 1}$. So, $\mathbf{6 \to 3 = 2 \to 1, 5 \to 3}$. Now, in $\mathbf{2 \to 1}, P_3 \to P_2, P_7 \to P_6$. Again, in $5 \to 3, P_2 \to P_2, P_6 \to P_3$. So, $P_3 \to P_2$, $P_7 \to P_3$ in $\mathbf{2 \to 1, 5 \to 3}$ i.e. $\mathbf{6 \to 3}$. So, *the* and *from* should be P_2 and P_3 is correct answer.

45.3; $\mathbf{0 \to 6 = 0 \to 4, 4 \to 6 = 0 \to 4, 4-4 \to 6-4}$ or $\mathbf{0 \to 4, 0 \to 2}$. Similarly, $\mathbf{0 \to 7 = 0 \to 4, 0 \to 3}$ and $\mathbf{0 \to 8 = 0 \to 4, 0 \to 4}$. Hence, step VI, step VII, step VIII can be found out by first finding step IV, then assuming this step IV as input and then finding step II (to find step VI) or step III (to find step VII) or step IV (to find step VIII), respectively.
Rest, please do yourself.

46.4; We see that in the given four choices, P_6 is different in all of them. So, let us find $P_6 = ?$ in $\mathbf{0 \to 7}$. Now, $\mathbf{0 \to 7 = 0 \to 5, 5 \to 7 = 0 \to 5, (5-4) \to (7-4) = 0 \to 5, 1 \to 3}$. Now, in $\mathbf{0 \to 5}, P_6 \to P_2$. Let us assume this P_2 to be in step I now. Now, in $\mathbf{1 \to 3}, P_2 \to P_4$. So, we conclude that in $\mathbf{0 \to 5, 1 \to 3}; P_6 \to P_4$. Or, in $\mathbf{0 \to 7}, P_6 \to P_4$. In other words, in $\mathbf{7 \to 0}, P_4 \to P_6$. So, P_6 must be *about*.

47.1; We have to find $\mathbf{0 \to 8}$. $\mathbf{0 \to 8 = 0 \to 4, 4 \to 8}$. But $\mathbf{4 \to 8 = (4-4) \to (8-4) = 0 \to 4}$. Hence, $\mathbf{0 \to 8 = 0 \to 4, 0 \to 4}$.
Let us take *I* (P_1) and *am* (P_2). Now, in $\mathbf{0 \to 4}, P_1 \to P_5, P_2 \to P_2$. So, in step IV *I* and *am* become P_5 and P_2. Assume it again to be input. Again, in $\mathbf{0 \to 4}, P_5 \to P_3, P_2 \to P_2$. Hence, in $\mathbf{(0 \to 4, 0 \to 4)}$. *I* becomes P_3 and *am* becomes P_2.

Q. 48-52: We see that in $\mathbf{0 \to 1}, P_1 \to P_3, P_2 \to P_4$ in $\mathbf{1 \to 2}, P_1 \to P_1, P_2 \to P_2$, in $\mathbf{2 \to 3}, P_1 \to P_3, P_2 \to P_4$. So, $\mathbf{0 \to 1 = 2 \to 3}$. Hence, it is a 2-step case.

48.4; We have to find $\mathbf{3 \to 0}$. Look at the table and do it yourself. (**Hints:** We see that in the given table P_1 (i.e. *tu*) of step III becomes P_3 in input. So, here *low* must be P_3.)

49.1; If the answer was step II or step IV or step VI; then the basic operation would have been $\mathbf{5 \to 2}$ or $\mathbf{5 \to 4}$ or $\mathbf{5 \to 6}$ and by golden rule, they could be reduced as $\mathbf{3 \to 0, 3 \to 2, 3 \to 4}$. So, assume *"are me ...."* to be step III. We see that in *"are me ..." to "me cho ...."*, $P_1 \to P_3$. We see from our table that P_1 (*tu*) becomes P_3 in $\mathbf{3 \to 0}$. So, correct choice is $\mathbf{3 \to 0}$ or $\mathbf{5 \to 2}$. So, step II is the correct answer.

50.5; We see that in *"rye se ...."* to *"se for ...."* $P_1 \to P_6, P_2 \to P_1$. Let us consider each choice one by one.
Choice 1: $\mathbf{7 \to 8 = (7-6) \to (8-6) = 1 \to 2}$.
Now, in $\mathbf{1 \to 2}, P_1 = P_1$ and $P_1 \neq P_6$.
Choice 2: $7 \to 6 = 1 \to 0$. Now, in $1 \to 0, P_1 \to P_4$ and $P_1 = P_6$

Choice 3: 7 **→ 2 = 7 → 4, 4 → 2** = **(7 - 4) → (4 - 4), 4 → 2 = 3 → 0, 4 → 2**. Now, P_1 → P_3 in 3 → 0 and P_3 → P_2 in 4 → 2. So, P_1 → P_2 in 3 → 0, 4 → 2 i.e. in 7 → 2. Here too, $P_1 = P_6$.

Choice 4: 7 → 1 = 7 → 4, 4 → 1 = 3 → 0, 4 → 1. Now, P_1 → P_3 in 3 → 0 and P_3 → P_2 in 4 → 1. So, P_1 → P_4 in 3 → 0, 4 → 1 i.e. in 7 → 1. Here too, $P_1 = P_6$.

51\. 3; We have to find **6 → 2. 6 → 2 = 4 → 0**. Now, do it yourself.

52\. 2; We have to find **0 → 3**. Look at the table given and do it yourself.

Important note:

1. In most of the questions above, we have found the result of operations like **0 → 2, 2 → 5, 5 → 1** etc by only taking one or two words ie. by merely taking, say, P_1 or P_2 ... etc. This helps us eliminate wrong choices. But please note that this does not guarantee that you have reached the correct choice. To be sure you will need to take all i.e. P_1, P_2 ... P_6, P_7 etc. But that will be too time consuming. Experience shows that if you pick the element (see, solution to Q. 46. We picked P_6 there. Why?) with a little bit of foresight, then analysing merely one or two of them would give you more than 95 per cent chance of reaching the correct answer.
2. For those who are still at a loss about this method we briefly enumerate its steps once again.
   - (i) Find out if it is 1-step, 2-step, 3-step .... case? (Use flowchart 1 or 2).
   - (ii) Write the basic desired operation symbolically. (Example: **0 → 2, 4 → 1** ... etc)
   - (iii) Reduce by golden rule if necessary (See Ex. 14).
   - (iv) (a) Select one or two elements (see Q. 46, we chose P_6 there, Q. 32, we chose P_2. Why?)

     (b) **Now, use the table given in the question to find its new position.** (For example see Q. 24. Here, we see that in the given table to is P_1 in step IV and it becomes P_7 in input. So, we say that P_1 → P_7 in **4 → 0**. Now, *blue* is P_1 in given step IV. So, it must be P_7 in input. Therefore please note that whenever we write things like P_1 → P_2 in 0 → 3 or P_3 → P_5 in 4 → 1; don't get flummexed that we are doing some covert trick. *We are using the table that is already given to draw these conclusions.*)
   - (v) In case, the range of an operation is much bigger, it can be broken. For example, **8 → 1** can be broken as **8 → 4, 4 → 1**. Then on one part golden rule can be applied.

Ex: Supposing a 2-step case, **8 → 4** becomes **(8 - 2 × 2) → (4 - 2 × 2) = 4 → 0**. So, **8 → 1** becomes **(4 → 0, 4 → 1)**.

The above means that if you have chosen (say) P_1 and P_4, you should first find from the given table the new positions of P_1 and P_4 in **4 → 0**. Suppose, P_1 → P_2, P_4 → P_6 in **4 → 0**. So, new positions are P_1 and P_6. Then, we assume that these new positions are in Step IV. And we find new position of P_2 and P_6 in **4 → 1**.

What we now get is our final position of P_1 and P_4 in **8 → 1**.

(53-57): In step I, the word that comes last in the alphabetical order comes to the first place, pushing the rest of the line rightward. In Step II, the largest number comes at the second place, pushing the line rightward. Thus, words and numbers get arranged alternately till all the words are in reverse alphabetical order and numbers in descending order.

53. 4; **Input:** glass full 15 37 water now 85 67
Step I: water glass full 15 37 now 85 67
Step II: water 85 glass full 15 37 now 67
Step III: water 85 now glass full 15 37 67
Step IV: water 85 now 67 glass full 15 37
Step V: water 85 now 67 glass 37 full 15
Since the arrangement has been done, there will be no step VI.

54. 4; **Step II:** ultra 73 12 16 mail sort 39 kite
Step III: ultra 73 sort 12 16 mail 39 kite
Step IV: ultra 73 sort 39 12 16 mail kite
Step V: ultra 73 sort 39 mail 12 16 kite
Step VI: ultra 73 sort 39 mail 16 12 kite
Step VII: ultra 73 sort 39 mail 16 kite 12
Hence, Step VI will be the last but one.

55. 4; We can't work backward in an arrangement type.

56. 3; **Step II:** tube 83 49 34 garden flower rat 56
Step III: tube 83 rat 49 34 garden flower 56
Step IV: tube 83 rat 56 49 34 garden flower
Step V: tube 83 rat 56 garden 49 34 flower
Step VI: tube 83 rate 56 garden 49 flower 34

57. 1; **Input:** hunt for 94 37 good 29 48 book
Step I: hunt 94 for 37 good 29 48 book
Step II: hunt 94 good for 37 29 48 book
Step III: hunt 94 good 48 for 37 29 book
Step IV: hunt 94 good 48 for 37 book 29

(58-61): The machine rearranges words and numbers in such a way that numbers are arranged from left side with the smallest number coming first and move subsequently so that in the last step numbers are arranged in descending order. While the words are arranged from right side as they appear in English alphabetical order.

Input: 84 why sit 14 32 not best ink feet 51 27 vain 68 92
Step I: 14 84 why sit 32 not ink feet 51 27 vain 68 92 best
Step II: 27 14 84 why sit 32 not ink 51 vain 68 92 best feet
Step III: 32 27 14 84 why sit not 51 vain 68 92 best feet ink
Step IV: 51 32 27 14 84 why sit vain 68 92 best feet ink not
Step V: 68 51 32 27 14 84 why vain 92 best feet ink not sit

Step VI: 84 68 51 32 27 14 why 92 best feet ink not sit vain

Step VII: 92 68 84 51 32 27 14 best feet ink not sit vain why

58. 5

59. 4

60. 2; 27, 14 and best

61. 3; **Step IV:** 51 32 27 14 84 why sit vain 68 92 best feet ink not.

The position of 'why' in this step is sixth from the left end.

Chapter Fifteen

Input-Output (...contd.): Arranagement

15.1: Introduction

In chapter 13, we have given an introduction to questions that are basically based on arrangement. We have also given a flowchart for quick identification of this type of problems.

If you recall, arrangement essentially means putting or arranging things as per a certain "order". Words can be arranged alphabetically while numbers can be arranged in increasing or decreasing order.

Let us first have a look at a sample problem.

15.2: A sample problem

Directions (Q. 1-5): A word arrangement machine, when given an input line of words, rearranges them following a particular rule in each step. The following is the illustration of the input and the steps of arrangement:

Input: gone was the excitement of Friday polls

Step I: excitement was the gone of Friday polls

Step II: excitement Friday the gone of was polls

Step III: excitement Friday gone the of was polls

Step IV: excitement Friday gone of the was polls

Step V: excitement Friday gone of polls was the

Step VI: excitement Friday gone of polls the was

Since the words are already arranged, the machine stops after this step. Otherwise the machine may carry on its logic until the words get fully arranged. Study the logic and answer the questions that follow.

1. What will be the Step III for the following input?

   Input: it had swept the four seats last year

   1) four had it last seats swept the year
   2) four had it last swept seats the year
   3) four had it the swept seats last year
   4) four had swept the it seats last year
   5) None of these

2. **Input:** for some this loss is a message

   For the above input, which step will the following arrangement be?

   Arrangement: a for is loss message some this

   1) Step IV   2) Step V   3) Step VI
   4) Can't say   5) None of these

3. **Input:** we were over with counting at noon
Which of the following will be the penultimate step for the above input?
1) Step IV   2) Step V   3) Step VI
4) Can't say   5) None of these

4. **Input:** how much can we check and prune
What will be the fifth step for the above input?
1) and much can we check how prune
2) and can check how much we prune
3) and can check how much prune we
4) and can much we check how prune
5) None of these

5. What will be the second step for the following input?
Input: he has been seen wearing a loose shirt
1) a has been seen wearing he loose shirt
2) a been has seen wearing he loose shirt
3) a been has he wearing seen loose shirt
4) a been has he loose seen wearing shirt
5) None of these

Ex. 2: Study the following information to answer the given questions:

A word arrangement machine, when given an input line of words, rearranges them following a particular rule in each step. The following is an illustration of input and the steps of rearrangement:

Input: as if it on an zoo figure of in at
Step I: an as if it on zoo figure of in at
Step II: an as at if it on zoo figure of in
Step III: an as at figure if it on zoo of in
Step IV: an as at figure if in it on zoo of
Step V: an as at figure if in it of on zoo

(and Step V is the last step for this Input.)

As per the rules followed in the above steps, find out in the given questions the appropriate step for the given input.

1. Which of the following will be step II for the given input?
Input: am ace all if is
1) ace all am is if   2) all am ace if is   3) is if am ace all
4) ace all am if is   5) None of these

2. **Input:** you are at fault on this
Which of the following steps would be — are at fault on you this?
1) I   2) II   3) III   4) IV   5) V

3. **Input:** him and his either or her
Which step will be the last step for this input?
1) I   2) II   3) III   4) IV   5) V

4. Step IV was like this — an apple at cot was red on one side
Which of the following will definitely be the input?

1) was cot red an on at one apple side
2) cot an at apple was red on one side
3) apple at an cot was red on one side
4) Cannot be determined
5) None of these

15.3: A discussion

15.3.1: Identification

In the previous chapters, we have already discussed how to identify problems of this type. A sureshot rule for identifying problems of this type is to check if either the first or the last word from Step I onwards remains unchanged till the very end. (Look at the flowchart in chapter 13.)

15.3.2: Arrangements: Possible ways

In order to master and quickly solve questions of this type, we need to know what are the possible ways in which arrangement can be done. The cases are:

a) Words or numbers

Arrangement can be of words or it can be of numbers. Words are arranged alphabetically while numbers are arranged in their increasing or decreasing order of magnitude. For example consider — star players don't abandon. Now, if this was to be arranged alphabetically then the word starting with a should come first because that word comes first in the dictionary. Therefore, step I would be — abandon star players don't. This is an example of arrangement of words. As another example consider 15, 9, 8, 5. Now, if this was to be arranged in increasing order we will put 5 in the first place as it is the smallest number. So, step I would be — 5, 15, 9, 8. This is an example of arrangement with numbers.

b) Left-side only

If we are arranging in increasing order, we can bring the first word of the dictionary in the first place. This would be step I. After that, in step II, we would bring second word of dictionary in the second place. And so on. In this way, in succeeding steps, the first, second, third places from left are filled by alphabetically first, second, third words.

Ex. 3: Input: star players don't abandon
Step I: abandon star players don't
Step II: abandon don't star players
... and so on

c) Right-side only

Sometimes the same task of arranging (in say, increasing order) can be achieved by putting the last word of the dictionary in the last place. This would be step I. Then we can put the second-last word of the dictionary at the second place from **right**. And so on. In this way, in succeeding steps, the first, second, third steps from right, are filled by alphabetically last, second last, third last word.

Ex. 4: Input: star players don't abandon
Step I: players don't abandon star
Step II: don't abandon players star
... and so on

d) Left-right alternate

Sometimes, the same task of arranging (in say, increasing order) can be achieved by putting the first word at first place, then alphabetically last word at last place, then alphabetically second word at second place from left... and so on. In other words, words are positioned from the left and from the right alternately. See the following two examples.

Ex. 5: Input: star players don't abandon
Step I: abandon star players don't
Step II: abandon players don't star
Step III: abandon don't players star

Ex. 6: Input: star players don't abandon
Step I: players don't abandon star
Step II: abandon players don't star
Step III: abandon don't players star

e) Increasing or decreasing order

Since *a* comes before *b* which comes before *c* in the dictionary, a word starting with *a* would come before a word starting with *b* which would come before a word starting with *c*. Thus, if you have three words: *cat*, *ass*, and *bat*; *cat* is alphabetically the third, *ass* is first, while *bat* is alphabetically the second word in the dictionary. Therefore, if we have (*ass*, *bat*, *cat*), this is an alphabetically increasing sequence while (*cat*, *bat*, *ass*) is alphabetically decreasing sequence. Similarly, (5, 7, 9) is an increasing sequence while (9, 7, 5) is a decreasing sequence. Now, we can have a machine that arranges in an increasing sequence or we can have one that arranges in a decreasing sequence.

Ex. 7: Input: star players don't abandon
Step I: abandon star players don't
Step II: abandon don't star players
... and so on.

The above is an example of arranging in an increasing sequence.

Ex. 8: Input: don't players star abandon
Step I: star don't players abandon
Step II: star players don't abandon

[This is an example of decreasing sequence because alphabetically last word has occupied first place while abandon (which is alphabetically first) occupied last place.]

Ex. 9: Input: 15 19 11 17
Step I: 11 15 19 17
Step II: 11 15 17 19

(Above is an example of arranging in an increasing order.)

Ex. 10: Input: 15 19 11 17
Step I: 19 15 11 17
Step II: 19 17 15 11
(Above is an example of arranging in a decreasing order.)

f) Interchange vs push

In each successive step, the machine does same ordering. This is done by putting one word (or number) in its rightful place, at a time. When a word is put at its rightful place, what happens to the word that was previously occupying that place? There are two answers. The earlier word either quietly shifts (see Ex. 11, 12) or it interchanges position with its replacing word (Ex. 13). In the former case, it looks as if the new word has simply jumped from its place, occupied its new and due place and given the remaining words a push. In the second case, it is a case of interchange.

Ex. 11: Input: star players don't abandon
Step I: abandon star players don't
Step II: abandon don't star players

[*abandon* is alphabetically first word so it comes to first place. Other words are *pushed* to the right. Then *don't* comes to second place and the remaining two players are *pushed* to the right.]

Ex. 12: Input: star players don't abandon
Step I: players don't abandon star
Step II: don't abandon players star

[Arrangement is in increasing order, fillings are "right-only". So, alphabetically last word *star* comes to last place other words are shifted to the left. Again, *players* comes to the second last place and remaining words are shifted to the left.]

Ex. 13: Input: star players don't abandon
Step I: abandon players don't star
Step II: abandon don't players star

[*abandon* is brought to the first place, and the word that was previously at first place *interchanges* positions with *abandon*. In the next step, we bring *don't* at the second place. Earlier, *players* was at second place. So, *don't* and *players* **interchange** places.]

Note: Student must check and realise that Ex. 1 is based on interchange while Ex. 2 is based on push.

15.3.3: Checkpoint

Having discussed the various types of possible arrangements we now give a summary.

Whenever you come across an arrangement problem please try to understand the logic on which the machine works. For this, ask yourself the following questions:

1. Increasing or decreasing order?
2. Fillings from left only or right only or left-right alternately?
3. Fillings by interchange or by push?

Once you have been able to answer these questions, you have understood the reasoning and that means you can solve the questions easily.

15.4: Strategy for solution

15.4.1: Some tips for quick answers

We will first give some tips for reaching answers quickly or at least, for eliminating the incorrect answer. They include,

Rule 1: *In an arrangement scheme, in step number x(say)* ***at least*** *x words (or numbers) must have occupied their due positions.*

The explanation is simple. In step I, at least one word would find its due position. In step II, another word would find its due place. Thus, after 2nd step, 2 words would have found their due places, and so on.

For example, consider Ex. 13. In step I, *abandon* comes at first place. In step II, *don't* comes at second place. So, after step II, *at least* two words have found their correct places.

Use of Rule 1: We can use this rule to eliminate some incorrect answers. Suppose we are asked to find the content of step IV. Now, by rule 1; Step IV should have at least 4 words at their due places. If fillings are from left-only, this means that at least first four words should be alphabetically the first four. Look at the following example.

Ex. 14: Consider Q. 4 of Ex. 1. Here, we have to find fifth step. So, in fifth step, at least first five words should have come to the first five places. Now, in *How much can be check and prune*, alphabetically first five words are *and*, *can*, *check*, *how* and *much* and, therefore, they should occupy the first five places. Using this rule, we can eliminate answer choice 1 and 4.

Rule 2: *In arrangement problems, the contents of an* ***earlier*** *step can never be determined with certainty.*

Ex. 15: Consider Q. 4 of Ex. 2. Here, you are asked to find input, given step IV. Hence, you are asked to find the content of an earlier step. Don't lose your sleep: nor your precious time. It can't be determined. Correct choice: 4.

Rule 3: *If there are n words (or numbers) then the machine will take at most (n - 1) steps to arrange the words totally.*

Ex. 16: Consider Q. 3 of Ex. 1. Here, there are 7 words in *we were over with counting at noon*. So, it will take at most 7 - 1 = 6 steps to arrange it totally. So, penultimate step would be either step V or less. This eliminates choices 3 and 4.

Rule 4: *(For push type only) To find the content of step x for a given input mentally lift the first x alphabetical words and just put them before the remaining words [in increasing order sequence]. In case of decreasing* order sequence, we will have to lift the last *x* words.

Ex. 17: Consider Q. 1 of Ex. 2.

Here, input is *am ace all if is*. Since you have to find step II, lift first two words. Alphabetically, first two words are: *ace* and *all*. When we mentally lift them the remaining sequence is: *am if is*. So, we put *ace* and *all* before *am if is* and *get ace all am if is*. Correct choice is: 4.

Rule 5: (For push type only): *To find the total number of steps needed to arrange a sequene attach digits 1, 2, 3... etc. to words as per their alphabetical rank. Now, ask yourself this question: how many of these digits should I mentally remove so that the remaining digits will be in order? The answer to your question will be your required answer.*

Ex. 18: Consider Q. 3 of Ex. 2.

Alphabetically, *and* is 1st, *either* is 2nd, *her* is 3rd, *him* is 4th, *his* is 5th, *or* is 6th. So, we replace

him	and	his	either	or	her
4	1	5	2	6	3

If we mentally remove 1, we get 45263. This is not in order.

If we mentally remove 1 and 2, we get 4563. This is not in order. If we mentally remove 1, 2, 3, we get 456. This is in order. So, we need to mentally remove 3 words to get the remaining words in order. So, our correct answer is 3 steps. Choice: (c) or (3).

Note: *Note that rule 4 or 5 are not applicable for problems of arrangement based on interchange. It is applicable only when we have cases of push [See 15.3.2.(f)].* Hence, Ex. 1 cannot utilise Rule 4 or 5.

15.4.2: General Strategy

There is no special strategy for solving these questions. These problems are very easy once you have understood the basic reasoning. Then you only have to do some paperwork. You can always use Rule 1, 2 and 3 for reaching quick answers. In case of Rule 4 and 5, you can use them only in case of *push* problems.

15.5: Complete Solutions to Ex. 1, Ex. 2

Ex. 19: Complete solution of Ex. 1

Soln: Looking at the problem, we understand that the logic of arrangement is following:

- increasing order
- left-side only
- interchange

(*Increasing* order because words are being arranged in alphabetically increasing order. *Left-side only* because fillings are done only from left. *Interchange* because replacements are done by interchanging positions. For example, in step I, *excitement* comes at first place by interchanging positions with gone. In second step, *Friday* comes at second place and interchanges places with *was*.)

Now, let us come to the questions:

1. **In step I:** *four* interchanges places with *it*. In step II, *had* is already at 2nd place, so it replaces *swept* to come to third place. In 3rd step, last replaces *the* to come to 4th place. Correct choice: 2.
2. We have the following logic:
for some this loss is a message
Step I: a some this loss is for message
Step II: a for this loss is some message
Step III: a for is loss this some message
Step IV: a for is loss message some this

[**Note:** In step III, loss is alphabetically 4th and it has already occupied 4th place. Therefore, in step IV, we put message (which is alphabetically the fifth) at fifth place.]

3. **Correct choice:** Try yourself as in Q. 2.
4. **Quick Method:** By rule 1, Step V should have at least first five words in place which are *and*, *can*, *check*, *how* and *much*. This eliminates choices 1 and 4. Now, *prune* must be in the end because this place is not touched in any of the previous operations. Correct choice: 2.
5. **Quick Method:** By rule 1, at least first two words should be alphabetically the first two i.e. *a* and *been*. This eliminates choice 1. Now, a interchanges with *he* in step I and in second step, this scheme is not disturbed. So, *he* should be where *a* was originally i.e. at 6th place. Correct choice: 2.

Ex. 20: Complete solution to Ex. 2.

Soln: You can yourself analyse that the logic is:

- increasing order
- left only
- push

[*Increasing* order, because the words are being arranged in increasing order. *Left only* because fillings are only from left side. Push because a word fills its due position not by interchanging with any other word, it sort of flies to its new place and pushes the remaining sequence to the right. For example, in step I, *an* takes the first place and the entire remaining sequence is pushed to the right, in step II, *At* takes the third place and entire remaining sequence is pushed to the right. In step II, *as* is already at second place so *at* is placed at third place here.)

1. Correct choice: 4. (See Ex. 17)
2. **Input** is *you are at fault on this*. Now, in *are at fault on you this*, **four** words (*are*, *at*, *fault* and *on*) are taken off one by one and placed before *you*. Correct choice: 4.
3. Correct choice: 3. (See Ex. 18)
4. Correct choice: (d) or (4) (see Rule 2).

Practice Exercises

Directions (Q. 1-5): Study the following information and answer the questions given below it:

An electronic device when fed with the numbers, rearranges them in a particular order following certain rules. The following is a step-by-step process of rearrangement for the given input of numbers.

Input:	85	16	36	04	19	97	63	09
Step I:	97	85	16	36	04	19	63	09
Step II:	97	85	63	16	36	04	19	09
Step III:	97	85	63	36	16	04	19	09
Step IV:	97	85	63	36	19	16	04	09
Step V:	97	85	63	36	19	16	09	04

(For the given input, step V is the last step.)

1. Which of the following will be Step V for the given input?
   Input: 25 08 35 11 88 67 23
   1) 88 67 35 25 23 11 08 2) 88 67 35 25 08 11 23
   3) 08 11 23 25 35 67 88 4) 88 67 35 25 23 08 11
   5) None of these
2. Which of the following will be step III for the given input?
   Input: 09 25 16 30 32 18 17 06
   1) 32 09 25 16 30 18 17 06 2) 32 30 09 25 16 19 17 06
   3) 32 30 25 09 16 19 17 06 4) 32 25 09 16 30 19 17 06
   5) None of these
3. Which of the following will be the last step for the given input?
   Input: 16 09 25 27 06 05
   1) I 2) II 3) III 4) IV 5) None of these
4. Which of the following will be the last step for the given input?
   Input: 03 31 43 22 11 09
   1) IV 2) V 3) VI
   4) Cannot be determined 5) None of these
5. If the step IV is as given below, which of the following was the input?
   Step IV: 92 86 71 69 15 19 06 63 58
   1) 86 92 69 71 15 19 06 63 58 2) 15 86 19 92 06 69 63 58 71
   3) 15 19 06 63 58 86 92 69 71 4) Cannot be determined
   5) None of these

Directions (Q. 6-10): Study the following information and answer the given questions:

A word arrangement machine, when given an input line of words, rearranges them following a particular rule in each step. The following is an illustration of input and the steps of rearrangement.

Input: Go for to Though By easy to Access at
Step I: Access Go for to Though By easy To at

Step II: Access at Go for to Though By easy To
Step III: Access at By Go for to Though easy To
Step IV: Access at By easy Go for to Though To
Step V: Access at By easy for Go to Though To
Step VI: Access at By easy for Go Though to To
Step VII: Access at By easy for Go Though To to
(and Step VII is the last step for this input)

As per the rules followed in the above steps, find out in the given questions the appropriate step for the given input.

6. **Input:** story For around on was He at
Which of the following will be Step IV for the given input?
1) around at For He on was story 2) around at For He on story was
3) around at For He story on was 4) around at He For story on was
5) None of these

7. **Input:** every and peer to an for
Which of the following steps would be 'an and every for peer to'?
1) II 2) III 3) IV 4) V 5) None of these

8. **Input:** Together over series on feast the so
Which of the following steps will be the last but one?
1) II 2) III 3) IV 4) V 5) None of these

9. **Input:** Over Go For through at one
Which step number will be the last step of the above input?
1) III 2) V 3) VI 4) VII 5) None of these

10. The step II of an input is as follows:
and Do pet to on that
Which of the following would definitely be the input?
1) Do on pet to and that 2) Do pet to and that on
3) Do and pet to on that 4) Cannot be determined
5) None of these

Directions (Q. 11-16): A word arrangement machine, when given a particular input, rearranges it following a particular rule. The following is the illustration of the input and the steps of arrangement:

Input: there was no light in the room
Step I: was there no light in the room
Step II: was there the no light in room
Step III: was there the room no light in

Since the words are already arranged, the machine stops after this step. Otherwise the machine may carry on its logic until the words get fully arranged. Study the logic and answer the questions that follow:

11. Which of the following will be the Step II for the input given below?
Input: a poet knows the meaning of night
1) the poet a knows meaning of night
2) the a poet knows meaning of night

3) the poet of a knows meaning night
4) the poet of knows meaning a night
5) None of these

12. **Input:** Indians perform good at night compared to Australians
For the above input, which step will be the following arrangement?
Arrangement: to perform night Indians good compared at Australians
1) Step III 2) Step IV 3) Step V 4) Step VI 5) None of these

13. If following is the second step for an input, what will be the fifth step?
Step II: with satisfied he is his room partner
1) with satisfied room partner is his he
2) with satisfied room he is his partner
3) with satisfied room partner is he his
4) with satisfied room partner he is his
5) None of these

14. Which of the following is the last step for the following input?
Input: he has no experience of dancing and jumping.
1) of no jumping he has experience dancing and
2) of no jumping has he dancing experience and
3) of jumping no has he experience dancing and
4) of no jumping has he experience dancing and
5) None of these

15. If following is the fourth step for an input, what will be the input?
Step IV: yalk put ox nice lamb and bull
1) and bull ox put yalk lamb nice 2) bill ox and put lamb yalk nice
3) nice bull and ox put lamb yalk 4) Can't be determined
5) None of these

16. How many steps will be required to get the final output of the following input?
Input: celebrating picnic in winter is good for health
1) 4 2) 5 3) 6 4) 7 5) None of these

Directions (Q. 17-21): An arrangement machine when given an input line of words, rearranges them following a particular rule in each step. The following is the illustration of the input and the steps of arrangement.

Input: the government will favour higher average tariff
Step I: average government will favour higher the tariff
Step II: average favour will government higher the tariff
Step III: average favour government will higher the tariff
Step IV: average favour government higher will the tariff
Step V: average favour government higher tariff the will

Since the words are already arranged, the machine stops after this step. Otherwise the machine may carry on its logic until the words get fully arranged. Study the logic and answer the questions that follow:

17. **Input:** this was to prepare the domestic industry
    Which of the following will be the Step III for the given input?
    1) domestic was to prepare the this industry
    2) domestic industry prepare this was to the
    3) domestic industry to prepare the this was
    4) domestic industry prepare to the this was
    5) None of these
18. **Input:** there were several other areas for the country
    For the above input, which step will be the following arrangement?
    Arrangement: areas country for other there several the were
    1) Step IV 2) Step V 3) Step II 4) Step III 5) None of these
19. **Input:** reviewing commitments already made by previous governments
    Which of the following will be the last step for the above input?
    1) Step V 2) Step IV 3) Step III 4) Step II 5) None of these
20. Which of the folowing will be the penultimate step for arranging the following input?
    Input: the products include milk powder grape wheat
    1) Step I 2) Step II 3) Step III 4) Step IV 5) None of these
21. Which of the following will be the step IV for the following input?
    Input: Samsung proposal to hike stake in the Indian venture
    1) hike proposal to Samsung stake in the Indian venture
    2) hike in Indian proposal stake Samsung the to venture
    3) hike in Indian Samsung stake proposal the to venture
    4) hike in to Samsung stake proposal the Indian venture
    5) None of these

Directions (Q. 22-26): An arrangement machine, when given an input line of numbers, rearranges them following a particular rule in each step. The following is the illustration of the input and the steps of arrangement:

Input: 37, 29, 17, 51, 46, 22, 71, 33
Step I: 71, 29, 17, 51, 46, 22, 37, 33
Step II: 71, 37, 17, 51, 46, 22, 29, 33
Step III: 71, 37, 29, 51, 46, 22, 17, 33
Step IV: 71, 37, 29, 46, 51, 22, 17, 33
Step V: 71, 37, 29, 46, 51, 17, 22, 33
Step VI: 71, 37, 29, 46, 51, 17, 33, 22

Since the numbers are already arranged, the machine stops after this step. Otherwise the machine may carry on its logic until the numbers get fully arranged. Study the logic and answer the questions that follow:

22. **Input:** 19, 59, 23, 36, 60, 75, 71
    What will be the 3rd step?
    1) 71, 59, 23, 36, 60, 75, 19 2) 71, 59, 60, 36, 23, 75, 19

3) 71, 59, 75, 36, 60, 23, 19 4) 71, 59, 60, 75, 23, 36, 19
5) None of these

23. **Input:** 81, 89, 72, 43, 69, 28, 90
Which of the following will be the last step?
1) 89, 90, 43, 72, 81, 69, 28 2) 90, 89, 72, 81, 43, 69, 28
3) 90, 89, 81, 72, 69, 43, 28 4) 89, 69, 43, 90, 81, 72, 28
5) None of these

24. **Input:** 28, 63, 65, 58, 57, 42, 40
How many steps will it take to arrange the above input?
1) Two 2) Three 3) Four
4) Five 5) None of these

25. The step two of an input is as follows:
54, 27, 45, 36, 63, 17
Which of the following would definitely be the first step?
1) 27, 45, 54, 36, 63, 17 2) 17, 63, 45, 36, 27, 54
3) 45, 54, 17, 36, 63, 27 4) Can't be determined
5) None of these

26. **Input:** 7, 17, 27, 37, 47, 57, 67
Which of the following will be the last two terms of step IV?
1) 57, 7 2) 27, 7 3) 17, 7 4) 57, 7 5) None of these

Directions (Q. 27-32): An arrangement machine when given an input line of numbers, rearranges them following a particular rule in each step. The following is the illustration of the input and the steps of arrangement:

Input: 40, 72, 89, 4, 25, 48, 15, 59
Step I: 4, 72, 89, 40, 25, 48, 15, 59
Step II: 4, 72, 89, 40, 25, 48, 59, 15
Step III: 4, 25, 89, 40, 72, 48, 59, 15
Step IV: 4, 25, 89, 59, 72, 48, 40, 15
Step V: 4, 25, 48, 59, 72, 89, 40, 15
Step VI: 4, 25, 48, 89, 72, 59, 40, 15
Step VII: 4, 25, 48, 72, 89, 59, 40, 15

Since the numbers are already arranged, the machine stops after this step. Otherwise the machine may carry on its logic till the numbers get fully arranged. Study the logic and answer the questions that follow:

27. Which of the following will be the penultimate step of the following input?
Input: 76, 43, 29, 81, 5, 96, 17
1) 5, 29, 43, 81, 76, 96, 17 2) 5, 29, 96, 81, 76, 43, 17
3) 5, 29, 76, 81, 96, 43, 17 4) 5, 29, 76, 96, 81, 43, 17
5) None of these

28. Which of the following will be step III of the given input?
Input: 48, 31, 17, 67, 29, 89, 26, 101
1) 17, 31, 48, 67, 29, 89, 26, 101 2) 17, 29, 48, 67, 31, 89, 101, 26
3) 17, 31, 48, 67, 29, 89, 101, 26 4) 17, 29, 48, 67, 101, 89, 31, 26
5) None of these

29. Which of the following will be the second step for the given input?
Input: 21, 6, 72, 67, 39, 54, 17
1) 6, 21, 72, 67, 39, 54, 17 2) 6, 17, 72, 67, 39, 54, 21
3) 6, 17, 72, 67, 54, 39, 21 4) 6, 21, 54, 67, 72, 39, 17
5) None of these

30. In how many steps will be following input be fully arranged?
Input: 21, 5, 37, 69, 28, 76, 54
1) Step V 2) Step IV 3) Step III 4) Step II 5) None of these

31. Which of the following will be Step IV for the given input?
Input: 4, 47, 97, 9, 50, 102, 11, 60
1) 4, 47, 97, 60, 50, 102, 11, 9 2) 4, 11, 97, 60, 50, 102, 47, 9
3) 4, 11, 50, 102, 97, 60, 47, 9 4) 4, 11, 50, 60, 97, 102, 47, 9
5) None of these

32. Which of the following will be the last step for the given input?
Input: 79, 57, 81, 6, 5, 94
1) 5, 57, 81, 79, 94, 6 2) 5, 57, 81, 6, 79, 94
3) 5, 57, 81, 94, 79, 6 4) 5, 57, 94, 81, 79, 6
5) None of these

Directions (Q. 33-37): A word arrangement machine arranges the given input of words in a particular manner to generate codes for the disposal of manufactured goods in a factory in different lots. Following is an illustration of arrangement of words for different lots:

1st lot: fam mus tan san vic dev ith
2nd lot: dev fam mus tan san vic ith
3rd lot: dev fam ith mus tan san vic
4th lot: dev fam ith mus san tan vic

And so on till the words are fully arranged. When the words are fully arranged, as above, the machine comes to a halt.

33. If the code for the third lot is "cen fro hum gin tur nin tee", what would be the code for the fifth lot?
1) cen fro gin hum nin tur tee 2) cen fro gin hum nin tee tur
3) cen fro gin nin hum tee tur 4) cen fro gin hum tur nin tee
5) None of these

34. If the code for the second lot is "amb dek dah poi con sem ned", what would be the code for the sixth lot?
1) amb con dah dek poi sem ned 2) amb con dek dah poi sem ned
3) amb con dah dek ned poi sem 4) There would be no sixth lot.
5) None of these

35. Which of the following could be the code for the first lot if the code for the fourth lot reads "clo ele mex reh tem tru"?
1) clo reh ele tem tru mex 2) reh tru clo ele tem mex
3) reh ele tem tru clo mex 4) Can't be determined
5) None of these

36. If the code for the third lot is "ato fir har waj neh rus mot", which of the following lot code would read as "ato fir har mot neh waj rus"?
1) fifth 2) third 3) sixth 4) fourth 5) None of these

37. If the code for the first lot is "tod tex til ide nol lux ros", what would be the code for the fourth lot?
1) ide tod tex til nol lux ros 2) ide lux tod tex til nol ros
3) ide lux nol ros tod tex til 4) ide lux nol ros tex tod til
5) None of these

Directions (Q. 38-43): A word arrangement machine, when given a particular input, rearranges it following a particular rule. The following is the illustration of the input and the steps of arrangement:

Input:	87	321	293	47	176	409	215
Step I:	47	321	293	87	176	409	215
Step II:	47	321	293	87	176	215	409
Step III:	47	87	293	321	176	215	409
Step IV:	47	87	293	215	176	321	409
Step V:	47	87	176	215	293	321	409

This is the final arrangement and step V is the last step for this input.

38. How many steps will be required to get the final output from the following input?
Input: 182 317 67 249 417 91 293
1) 3 2) 4 3) 5 4) 6 5) None of these

39. What will be the fourth step for the following input?
Input: 76 172 372 43 243 361 165
1) 43 76 165 172 243 361 372 2) 43 172 165 76 243 361 372
3) 43 172 372 76 243 361 165 4) Can't be determined
5) None of these

40. If following is the second step for an input, what will be the fourth step?
Step II: 46 122 343 48 56 212 415
1) 46 122 212 48 56 343 415 2) 46 48 212 122 56 343 415
3) 46 48 343 122 56 212 415 4) 46 48 212 122 56 343 415
5) None of these

41. Which of the following is the last step for the following input?
Input: 26 12 68 36 46 87 9
1) 9 12 26 36 68 46 87 2) 9 12 36 26 46 68 87
3) 9 12 26 36 46 68 87 4) 9 12 26 46 36 68 87
5) None of these

42. Following is the step III for an input. What will be the second step for the input?

Step III: 45 47 342 121 55 211 414

1) 45 121 342 47 55 211 414 2) 45 55 342 121 47 211 414
3) 45 211 342 121 55 47 414 4) Can't be determined
5) None of these

43. If 23, 142, 348, 96, 400, 200, 410 is the second step of an input, which of the following steps will be
23, 96, 142, 348, 200, 400, 410?

1) Third 2) Fourth 3) Fifth
4) Can't be determined 5) None of these

Directions (Q. 44-48): Study the following information carefully and answer the given questions.

A word and number arrangement machine, when given an input line of words and numbers, rearranges them following a particular rule in each step. The following is an illustration of input and rearrangement.

Input: gone over 35 69 test 72 park 27
Step I: 27 gone over 35 69 test 72 park
Step II: 27 test gone over 35 69 72 park
Step III: 27 test 35 gone over 69 72 park
Step IV: 27 test 35 park gone over 69 72
Step V: 27 test 35 park 69 gone over 72
Step VI: 27 test 35 park 69 over gone 72
Step VII: 27 test 35 park 69 over 72 gone

Step VII is the last step of the rearrangement.

As per the rules followed in the above steps, find out in each of the following questions the appropriate step for the given input.

44. **Input:** 86 open shut door 31 49 always 45
How many steps will be required to complete the rearrangement?

1) Five 2) Six
3) Seven 4) Four 5) None of these

45. Step III of an input: 25 yes 37 enemy joy defeat 52 46 Which of the following is definitely the input?

1) enemy 25 joy defeat yes 52 37 46
2) 37 enemy 25 joy yes defeat 52 46
3) enemy joy defeat 25 52 yes 46 37
4) Cannot be determined
5) None of these

46. Step II of an Input: 18 win 71 34 now if victory 61.
How many more steps will be required to complete the rearrangement?

1) Three 2) Four 3) Five
4) Six 5) More than six

47. **Input:** where 47 59 12 are they going 39
Which of the following steps will be the last but one?
1) VII 2) IV 3) V
4) VIII 5) None of these

48. Step II of an input: 33 store 81 75 full of goods 52 Which of the following will be step VI?
1) 33 store 52 of 75 81 full goods
2) 33 store 52 of 75 full 81 goods
3) 33 store 52 of 75 goods 81 full
4) There will be no such step.
5) None of these

Directions (Q. 49-53): Study the following information to answer the given questions:

A word arrangement machine when given an input line of words rearranges them following a particular rule. The following is an illustration of input and rearrangement.

Input: age road own wire tire ink pen uni dice eat
Step I: uni age road own wire tire ink pen eat dice
Step II: uni own age road wire tire ink eat pen dice
Step III: uni own ink age wire tire eat road pen dice
Step IV: uni own ink eat age wire tire road pen dice

And step four is the last step of the rearrangement.

As per the rules followed in the above steps, find out in each of the following questions the appropriate step for the given input.

Input for the questions

Input: gem stat ace cast omit fan rate uncut era input

49. Which of the following would be the final arrangement?
1) cast gem fan rate stat uncut omit input era ace
2) uncut omit input era ace cast fan gem rate stat
3) uncut omit input era ace stat rate gem fan cast
4) uncut omit input era ace stat fan gem rate cast
5) None of these

50. In step III, which of the following words would be at 6th position from the left?
1) rate 2) ace 3) stat
4) gem 5) None of these

51. Which step number would be the following output?
uncut omit gem stat ace rate era input fan cast
1) II 2) III 3) V
4) IV 5) None of these

52. In step IV of the rearrangement, if **omit** is related to **era** and **rate** is related to **fan** in a certain way, which of the following would **ace** be related to, following the same pattern?

1) rate 2) input 3) stat
4) gem 5) None of these

53. Which of the following would be step VII?
1) uncut omit input era ace stat rate gem fan cast
2) uncut omit input era ace rate stat fan gem cast
3) uncut omit input era ace cast fan gem rate stat
4) uncut omit input era stat ace rate gem fan cast
5) There will be no such step as the input gets rearranged before step VII.

Answers and Explanations

Note: Below we are giving concise but straight solutions to all the problems. Later on, we have given some short-cut solutions to some selected problems.

Q. 1-5: Clearly, in the given arrangement, the numbers have been arranged in descending order in a sequence, altering the position of only one number in each step.

1. 1;

Input:	25	08	35	11	88	67	23
Step I:	88	25	08	35	11	67	23
Step II:	88	67	25	08	35	11	23
Step III:	88	67	35	25	08	11	23
Step IV:	88	67	35	25	23	08	11
Step V:	88	67	35	25	23	11	08

2. 3;

Input:	09	25	16	30	32	19	17	06
Step I:	32	09	25	16	30	19	17	06
Step II:	32	30	09	25	16	19	17	06
Step III:	32	30	25	09	16	19	17	06

3. 2;

Input:	16	09	25	27	06	05
Step I:	27	16	09	25	06	05
Step II:	27	25	16	09	06	05

Since all the numbers in the given input have been arranged in descending order uptil Step II, so it is the last step.

4. 2;

Input:	03	31	43	22	11	09
Step I:	43	03	31	22	11	09
Step II:	43	31	03	22	11	09
Step III:	43	31	22	03	11	09
Step IV:	43	31	22	11	03	09
Step V:	43	31	22	11	09	03

5. 4; Can't say (See Rule 2)

Q. 6-10: In the given arrangement, the words have been arranged alphabetically in a sequence, altering the position of only one word in each step.

6. 3; **Input:** story For around on was He at
Step I: around story For on was He at
Step II: around at story For on was He
Step III: around at For story on was He
Step IV: around at For He story on was

7. 2; **Input:** every and peer to an for
Step I: an every and peer to for
Step II: an and every peer to for
Step III: an and every for peer to

8. 4; **Input:** Together over series on feast the so
Step I: feast Together over series on the so
Step II: feast on Together over series the so
Step III: feast on over Together series the so
Step IV: feast on over series Together the so
Step V: feast on over series so Together the
Step VI: feast on over series so the Together
Clearly, Step VI is the last step and V is the last but one (second last).

9. 5; **Input:** Over Go For through at one
Step I: at Over Go For through one
Step II: at For Over Go through one
Step III: at For Go Over through one
Step IV: at For Go one Over through
Since all the words in the given input have been arranged alphabetically uptil Step IV, so it is the last step.

10. 4; See Rule 2.

Q. 11-16: The arrangement is simple: all you have to do is to follow the reverse alphabetical order.

11. 1; **Input:** a poet knows the meaning of night
Step I: the a poet knows meaning of night
Step II: the poet a knows meaning of night

12. 2

13. 3; **Step II:** with satisfied he is his room partner
Step III: with satisfied room he is his partner
Step IV: with satisfied room partner he is his
Step V: with satisfied room partner is he his

14. 1; **Input:** he has no experience of dancing and jumping
Last step: of no jumping he has experience dancing and
Note: Last step can be written directly.

15. 4; Previous steps can't be determined in these types.

16. 4

Q. 17-21: The logic is: the words get arranged in alphabetical order by interchanging places. That is, when *average* goes to the first place, the word in the first place takes the position that *average* vacates.

17. 4; **Input:** this was to prepare the domestic industry
Step I: domestic was to prepare the this industry
Step II: domestic industry to prepare the this was
Step III: domestic industry prepare to the this was

18. 4; **Input:** there were several other areas for the country
Step I: areas were several other there for the country
Step II: areas country several other there for the were
Step III: areas country for other there several the were

19. 1; **Input:** reviewing commitments already made by previous governments
Step I: already commitments reviewing made by previous governments
Step II: already by reviewing made commitments previous governments
Step III: already by commitments made reviewing previous governments
Step IV: already by commitments governments reviewing previous made
Step V: already by commitments governments made previous reviewing

20. 3; **Input:** the products include milk powder grape wheat
Step I: grape products include milk powder the wheat
Step II: grape include products milk powder the wheat
Step III: grape include milk products powder the wheat
Step IV: grape include milk powder products the wheat
Hence, Step III will be penultimate.

21. 2; **Input:** Samsung proposal to hike stake in the Indian venture
Step I: hike proposal to Samsung stake in the Indian venture
Step II: hike in to Samsung stake proposal the Indian venture
Step III: hike in Indian Samsung stake proposal the to venture
Step IV: hike in Indian proposal stake Samsung the to venture

Q. 22-26: Study the changes very carefully. What happens? Clearly, it is not a case of simple arrangement in ascending or descending order. Look at the way 51 and 17 are brought together, so also 33 and 22. Multiples of 17 and then multiples of 11. So the clue: *something to do with multiples.*

What really happens is the following: in case of a composite number, the largest factor (other than the number itself) is taken into account. In the case of a prime number, the number itself is considered. In case there are two multiples, the larger multiple is arranged first.

Thus $37 = \underline{37} \times 1, 29 = \underline{29} \times 1, 17 = \underline{17} \times 1, 51 = \underline{17} \times 3, 46 = \underline{23} \times 2, 22 = \underline{11} \times 2, 71 = \underline{71} \times 1, 33 = \underline{11} \times 3$. Now, the underlined parts are our **key numbers** and these are arranged in a descending order. That is why 46 comes after 29 because the key number for 46 is 23, which is less than 29.

Also, when a number is arranged, it *interchanges* its position with the wrongly-placed number.

22. 4; **Input:** 19, 59, 23, 36, 60, 75, 71
Step I: 71, 59, 23, 36, 50, 75, 19
Step II: 71, 59, 60, 36, 23, 75, 19 (59 was already arranged)
Step III: 71, 59, 60, 75, 23, 36, 19

23. 1; The last step will be a fully arranged one. hence, all we have to see is whether the order is correct. Note the key numbers: 89, 90 (= 45 × 2), 43, 72 (= 36 × 2), 81 = (27 × 3), 69 (= 23 × 3), 28 (= 14 × 2)

24. 3; **Input:** 28, 63, 65, 58, 57, 42, 40
Step I: 58, 63, 65, 28, 57, 42, 40
Step II: 58, 63, 42, 28, 57, 65, 40
Step III: 58, 63, 42, 40, 57, 65, 28
Step IV: 58, 63, 42, 40, 57, 28, 65

25. 4; A backward calculation is not possible. [**See Rule 2.**]

26. 2; **Input:** 7, 17, 27, 37, 47, 57, 67
Step I: 67, 17, 27, 37, 47, 57, 7
Step II: 67, 47, 27, 37, 17, 57, 7
Step III: 67, 47, 37, 27, 17, 57, 7
Step IV: 67, 47, 37, 57, 17, 27, 7

Q. 27-32:

Step I: The smallest number goes to the left, interchanging its place with the leftmost number.

Step II: The second smallest number interchanges its position with the rightmost number.

Step III: The third smallest number interchanges its position with that in the second-from-left position.

Step IV: The fourth smallest number interchanges its position with that in the second from right position.

And so on. Till the final arrangement of 1, 2, 3, 4, 5, 6, 7, 8, 9 for example, looks like the following.

1, 3, 5, 7, 9, 8, 6, 4, 2

27, 3; **Input:** 76, 43, 29, 81, 5, 96, 17
Step I: 5, 43, 29, 81, 76, 96, 17
Step II: 5, 29, 43, 81, 76, 96, 17
[**Note:** 17 was already arranged]
Step III: 5, 29, 96, 81, 76, 43, 17
Step IV: 5, 29, 76, 81, 96, 43, 17
Step V: 5, 29, 76, 96, 81, 43, 17

28. 2 29. 5 30. 1 31. 3

32. 3; **Note:** Don't solve it step by step. Just bear the particular type of ascending order in mind.

Q. 33-37: The logic is very simple: alphabetical arrangement

33. 1; **3rd lot:** cen fro hum gin tur nin tee
4th lot: cen fro gin hum tur nin tee
5th lot: cen fro gin hu nin tur tee

34. 4; **2nd lot:** amb dek dah poi con sem ned
3rd lot: amb con dek dah poi sem ned
4th lot: amb con dah dek poi sem ned
35. 4; You can't work backward. [See Rule 2]
36. 1; **3rd lot:** ato fir har waj neh rus mot
4th lot: ato fir har mot waj neh rus
5th lot: ato fir har mot neh waj rus
37. 5; **1st lot:** tod tex til ide nol lux ros
2nd lot: ide tod tex til nol lux ros
3rd lot: ide lux tod tex til nol ros
4th lot: ide lux nol tod tex til ros

Q. 38-43: Here, the rule followed is: numbers are getting arranged in ascending order. The smallest no. interchanges with the first position. Then the largest no. interchanges with the last position. Next, the second smallest no. interchanges with the second position. And so on.

38. 1; **Input:** 182 317 67 249 417 91 293
Step I: 67 317 182 249 417 91 293
Step II: 67 317 182 249 293 91 417
Step III: 67 91 182 249 293 317 417
39. 4; **Input:** 76 172 372 43 243 361 165
Step I: 43 172 372 76 243 361 165
Step II: 43 172 165 76 243 361 372
Step III: 43 76 165 172 243 361 372
[Machine will stop after step III.]
40. 2; **Step II:** 46 122 343 48 56 212 415
Step III: 46 48 343 122 56 212 415
Step IV: 46 48 212 122 56 343 415
41. 3; In such types of questions, we do not require to go in detail considering all steps. The last step will be definitely in strictly ascending order.
42. 4; In such types of settings, previous step can't be determined. [**See Rule 2.**]
43. 3; **Step II:** 23 142 348 96 400 200 410
Step III: 23 96 348 142 400 200 410
Step IV: 23 96 348 142 200 400 410
Step V: 23 96 142 348 200 400 410

Quicker solutions to selected problems

Q. 1-5: Decreasing order. Push type (because 97 *pushes* 85 to its right in step I). Left side only.

1. Step V must have at least 5 numbers at their due places (Rule 1). So, first five biggest numbers must have occupied. So, either (a) or (d) is correct. But in pushing, 08 must be *before* 11 upto step V because it is *before* 11 in input.
(**Hint:** Try solving the same using Rule 4. See Ex. 17.)

2. 3; Use Rule 4. Lift largest 3 numbers from input. Remaining input is: 09 16 19 17 06.
Before it, put 32, 30, 25.

3. 2; Use Rule 5. We see that in the input if we mentally life 27 and 25 (2 numbers) remaining are already in order. So, *two* words are needed to be lifted, so, step II is our answer.

4. 2; Use Rule 5.

5. 4; Use Rule 2.

Q. 6-10: Increasing order. Push type. Left side only.

6. 3; Use Rule 4. (To find step IV, we lift alphabetically first four words from input. What remains is: *story on was*. So, we must have *around at for the* followed by *story on was*.

7. 2; *an and* and *for*: these 3 words have moved in the given input.

10. 4; Use rule 2.

Q. 11-16: Alphabetically decreasing order. Left side only. Push type. (because *was* pushes *there* in step I).

11. 1; Use rule 4. (See solution to Q. 6.)

14. 1; Last step must have words arranged totally in decreasing sequence.

15. 4; Use rule 5.

Q. 17-21: Alphabetically increasing sequence. Left side only. Interchange type (because, *average* interchanges place with *the*, it doesn't *push the*) Looking at the problems, we see that there is not much we can do for short-cuts in these five questions.

Q. 22-26: This has an altogether different basis of arranging and we have already discussed it in solutions.

Q. 27-32: This too has peculiar arrangement and it has already been discussed.

Q. 33-37: Increasing order, push (because *dev* pushes *fam* and does not "interchange places") type and left- side only.

35. 4; See Rule 2.

37. 3; Use Rule 4. To find fourth lot, we lift alphabetically first four words. They are: *ide, lux, nol, ros*. Remaining three words are: *tod, tex, til.* So, we put *ide, lux, nol, ros,* before *tod, tex, til*.

Q. 38-43: Increasing order, interchange type, left-right alternate. (Left-right alternate, because 47 is filled from left in step I and 409 is filled from right in step II.)

42. 4; [See Rule 2.]

(44-48): The machine rearranges numbers in ascending order and word in reverse alphabetical order alternately.

44. 2; **Input:** 86 open shut door 31 49 always 45
Step I: 31 86 open shut door 49 always 45
Step II: 31 shut 86 open door 49 always 45
Step III: 31 shut 45 86 open door 49 always

Step IV: 31 shut 45 open 86 door 49 always
Step V: 31 shut 45 open 49 86 door always
Step VI: 31 shut 45 open 49 door 86 always

45. 4 Can't proceed backward.

46. 2; **Step II:** 18 win 71 34 now if victory 61
Step III: 18 win 34 71 now if victory 61
Step IV: 18 win 34 victory 71 now if 61
Step V: 18 win 34 victory 61 71 now if
Step VI: 18 win 34 victory 61 now 71 if
Four more steps are needed to complete the rearrangement.

47. 5; **Input:** where 47 59 12 are they going 39
Step I: 12 where 47 59 are they going 39
Step II: 12 where 39 47 59 are they going
Step III: 12 where 39 they 47 59 are going
Step IV: 12 where 39 they 47 going 59 are

48. 3; **Step II:** 33 store 81 75 full of goods 52
Step III: 33 store 52 81 75 full of goods
Step IV: 33 store 52 of 81 75 full goods
Step V: 33 store 52 of 75 81 full goods
Step VI: 33 store 52 of 75 goods 81 full

(49-53): In each step, one word gets arranged from the left and one from the right. Note that words starting with vowels get arranged from the left and those starting with consonants get arranged from the right. This goes on in such a manner that finally we have vowel-starting words arranged in reverse alphabetical order followed by consonant-starting words arranged in reverse alphabetical order.

Input: gem stat ace cast omit fan rate uncut era input
Step I: uncut gem stat ace omit fan rate era input cast
Step II: uncut omit gem stat ace rate era input fan cast
Step III: uncut omit input stat ace rate era gem fan cast
Step IV: uncut omit input era stat ace rate gem fan cast
Step V: uncut omit input era ace stat rate gem fan cast

49. 3
50. 1
51. 1
52. 4
53. 5

Chapter Sixteen

Input-Output (...contd.): Miscellaneous

16.1: Introduction

We have seen that most of the problems on input-output involve planned shifting or planned ordering (arrangement) of given words. However, there can always be a logic; different from these two. In this chapter, we shall be covering some of these cases.

16.2: A sample problem

As we are covering problems of miscellaneous types in this chapter, *one* sample won't suffice. Therefore, in this chapter, we will be giving some sample examples only, followed by practice exercises.

16.3: Some Possible Cases

16.3.1: Arithmetical Operations

In this type, the input consists of numbers and some arithmetic operations are performed upon them. For example, in Ex. 1 below, the numbers in the input are doubled and then two is added.

Ex. 1: Input: 3 4 1 5 6 7

Step I: 8 10 4 12 14 16

(Note: $8 = 3 \times 2 + 2$, $10 = 4 \times 2 + 2$, ... and so on)

Possible arithmetic operations

We give below a list of some possible and frequent operations:

(a) **multiplying by a number and then adding or subtracting a number**

Ex. 2: (Multiply by 3, subtract 4)

Input: 5 6 8 9 18

Step I: 11 14 20 23 50

(b) **adding or subtracting a number and then multiplying**

Ex. 3: (Add 2 and then multiply by 4)

Input: 5 6 9 4 5

Step I: 28 32 44 24 28

Ex. 4: (Subtract 3 and then multiply by 5)

Input: 2 3 5 9 6

Step I: 5 0 10 30 15

(c) **Dividing by a number and omitting the fractional part**

Ex. 5: (Divide by 3 and omit the fractional part)

Input: 4 5 10 15 29

Step I: 1 1 3 5 9

Explanation: $4 \div 3 = 1.33$. Omit fractional part, we get 1. $29 \div 3 = 9.66$. Omit fractional part, we get 9.

(d) **Taking digit-sum**

Ex. 6: Taking digit-sum of given numbers

Input: 83 47 25 17 68

Step I: 11 11 7 8 14

Explanation: 83 gives $8 + 3 = 11$, 68 gives $6 + 8 = 14$ and so on.

Ex. 7: Taking digit-sum repeatedly

Input: 83 47 25 17 68

Step I: 2 2 7 8 5

Explanation: 83 gives $8 + 3 = 11$, 11 gives $1 + 1 = 2$, ... and so on.

(e) **Squaring or cubing the digit-sum (... and may be adding or subtracting a number too)**

Ex. 8: Squaring digit-sum

Input: 83 47 25 17 68

Step I: 121 121 49 64 196

Explanation: 83 gives $8 + 3 = 11$, $11^2 = 121$, ...

Ex. 9: Cubing digit-sum and adding 50

Input: 19 4 18 29 6

Step I: 1050 114 779 1381 266

Explanation: 19 gives $1 + 9 = 10$, $10^3 = 1000$, $1000 + 50 = 1050$, 29 gives $2 + 9 = 11$, $11^3 = 1331$, $1331 + 50 = 1381$ ...

(f) **adding or subtracting the square or cubes of natural numbers**

Ex. 10: Adding squares (1^2, 2^2, 3^2 ...) of natural numbers to the given numbers

Input: 14 17 12 10 9

Step I: 15 21 21 26 34

Explanation: $14 + 1^2, 17 + 2^2, 12 + 3^2$ ...

Ex. 11: Subtracting cubes of natural numbers from given numbers

Input: 171 69 481 95 168

Step I: 170 61 454 31 43

Explanation: ($171 - 1^3, 69 - 2^3, 481 - 3^3$ ...)

Note: There can be many more cases. The above is just an indicative list. The reader is advised to apply himself while solving the problem.

16.3.2: Arranging on the basis of size

Sometimes words can be arranged on the basis of their sizes. For example, in Ex. 12 below, successive steps lead to an arrangement so that a two-letter word comes first, three-letter words come second and third while a four-letter word occupies last place.

Ex. 12: Input: wait and see me

Step I: me wait and see

Step II: me and wait see

Step III: me and see wait

Explanation: In step I, two-letter word "me" occupies first place. Then three-letter word *and* occupies second place in step II: In step III, *see* comes to third place while *wait* which is four-lettered-goes to fourth place. Note that both *and* and *see* are three-lettered and therefore *and* which is alphabetically prior to *see*, gets priority.

16.3.3: Other possibilities

In addition to the above mentioned two cases which are more frequent, we can have infinitely many possibilities. It is not possible for us to cover all such cases. But we are going to give a large number of examples so that you have ample practice.

16.4: Method to tackle these problems

There is no great trick in tackling these problems. The only thing that stops you from reaching your solution is your failure to understand the logic. Once you have understood the logic on which the sequence progresses it is easy to answer questions. Go through section 16.3 again just to reappraise yourself with various possibilities. And if you find something new in the question, think carefully and apply your mind. A bit of practice would go a long way in enabling you to catch the logic.

16.5: A solved example

Ex. 13:

Directions (Q. 1-5): A number arrangement machine, when given an input line of number rearranges them following a particular rule in each step. The following is the illustration of the input and the steps of arrangement:

Input:	23,	56,	28,	15,	17,	20,	13
Step I:	5,	11,	10,	6,	8,	2,	4
Step II:	31,	64,	36,	23,	25,	28,	21
Step III:	16,	49,	21,	8,	10,	13,	6
Step IV:	169,	2116,	324,	25,	49,	100,	9
Step V:	36,	102,	46,	20,	24,	30,	16
Step VI:	70,	169,	85,	46,	52,	61,	40

1. What will be the sixth step of the following input?
   Input: 8, 11, 25, 18, 21, 6, 32
   1) 23, 32, 74, 55, 62, 20, 98 2) 25, 34, 76, 55, 64, 19, 97
   3) 24, 31, 75, 54, 63, 20, 98 4) 25, 34, 76, 54, 63, 20, 98
   5) None of these
2. If the fifth step of a given input is 8, 14, 42, 28, 34, 4, 56 what will be the input?
   1) 9, 12, 26, 19, 22, 7, 33 2) 10, 12, 19, 26, 7, 23, 34
   3) 11, 18, 12, 9, 21, 23, 41 4) 7, 10, 26, 22, 19, 32, 47
   5) None of these

3. In how many steps would the following arrangement be yielded by the given input?
   Input: 8, 10, 23, 21, 52, 31, 19
   Arrangement: 1, 3, 16, 14, 45, 24, 12
   1) VI   2) V   3) IV   4) III   5) None of these
4. The first step of the given input is 7, 12, 11, 8, 6, 2, 4. What will be step VI for the input?
   1) 61, 30, 92, 44, 15, 11, 13   2) 52, 21, 83, 51, 15, 11, 13
   3) 61, 30, 56, 17, 15, 20, 13   4) Can't be determined
   5) None of these
5. What would be step IV for the following input?
   10, 11, 12, 13, 14, 15, 16
   1) 5, 9, 4, 16, 22, 23, 38   2) 4, 0, 9, 16, 22, 25, 36
   3) 0, 1, 4, 9, 16, 25, 36   4) 0, 4, 9, 16, 28, 25, 37
   5) None of these

Soln: Here, the rule followed is:

Step I: Digit-sum of input.
Step II: Add 8 to each number of the input.
Step III: Subtract 7 from each number of the input.
Step IV: Subtract 10 from each number of the input and square it.
Step V: Multiply each number of the input by 2 and subtract 10 from it.
Step VI: Multiply each number of the input by 3 and add 1 to each.

1. 2   2. 1   3. 4   4. 5   5. 3

Note: We have given the rule already. Please try to check yourself that the answers given above match with your answers.

Practice Exercises

Directions (Q. 1-5): A number arrangement machine, when given a particular input, rearranges it following a particular rule. The following is the illustration of the input and the steps of arrangement:

Input:	44	38	24	55	16	14	85
Step I:	8	2	6	1	7	5	4
Step II:	60	0	32	-3	45	21	12
Step III:	6	0	5	-3	9	3	3
Step IV:	7	4	14	13	34	39	52
Step V:	15	12	22	21	42	47	60
Step VI:	6	3	4	3	6	2	6

1. What will be the 4th step of the following input?
   Input: 23, 61, 15, 35, 54, 75, 85
   1) 4, 13, 14, 22, 30, 41, 52   2) 4, 12, 14, 20, 30, 41, 52
   3) 3, 13, 14, 20, 30, 41, 52   4) 4, 13, 15, 22, 32, 41, 52
   5) None of these

2. The second step of a given input is 45, 60, 21, 77, 0, -3, 32. What will be step V for the input?
   1) 10, 18, 20, 28, 33, 41, 52   2) 18, 10, 20, 28, 33, 41, 52
   3) 18, 18, 20, 29, 33, 41, 62   4) 18, 18, 29, 20, 33, 41, 52
   5) None of these
3. In how many steps would the following arrangement be yielded by the given input?
   Input: 43, 37, 42, 64, 25, 23, 76
   Arrangement: 10, 1, 14, 13, 34, 39, 52
   1) IV   2) V   3) III   4) II   5) None of these
4. What would be the **5th step** of the input?
   Input: 35, 56, 33, 46, 16, 32, 94
   1) 12, 15, 21, 22, 42, 47, 60   2) 15, 12, 22, 21, 42, 47, 60
   3) 7, 4, 14, 13, 34, 39, 52   4) 6, 3, 4, 6, 3, 2, 6
   5) None of these
5. What will be the input for the following **5th step**?
   Step V: 14, 11, 23, 27, 34, 56, 62
   1) 57, 42, 68, 17, 14, 81, 29   2) 62, 41, 17, 81, 14, 68, 29
   3) 81, 42, 71, 17, 15, 23, 61   4) Can't be determined
   5) None of these

Directions (Q. 6-12): A number arrangement machine, when given a particular input, rearranges it following a particular rule. The following is the illustration of the input and the steps of arrangement:

Input: 245, 316, 436, 519, 868, 710, 689
Step I: 710, 316, 436, 519, 868, 245, 689
Step II: 710, 316, 245, 519, 868, 436, 689
Step III: 710, 316, 245, 436, 868, 519, 689
Step IV: 710, 316, 245, 436, 519, 868, 689
Step IV is the last step for the given input.

6. If 655, 436, 764, 799, 977, 572, 333 is the input, which of the following steps will be '333, 436, 572, 655, 977, 764, 799'?
   1) Second   2) Third   3) Fourth   4) First   5) None of these
7. How many steps will be required to get the final output from the following input?
   Input: 544, 653, 325, 688, 461, 231, 857
   1) 5   2) 4   3) 3   4) 6   5) None of these
8. For the given input, which of the following will be the third step?
   Input: 236, 522, 824, 765, 622, 463, 358
   1) 522, 236, 765, 824, 622, 463, 358   2) 522, 622, 236, 824, 765, 463, 358
   3) 522, 622, 236, 765, 824, 463, 358   4) 522, 622, 236, 463, 824, 765, 358
   5) None of these

9. If following is the second step for an input, what will be the fourth step?
Step II: 620, 415, 344, 537, 787, 634, 977
1) 620, 415, 344, 537, 634, 787, 977
2) 620, 415, 344, 634, 537, 787, 977
3) 620, 415, 344, 634, 787, 537, 977
4) Can't be determined
5) None of these

10. Following is the step III for an input. What will be the first step for the input?
Step III: 432, 433, 542, 666, 734, 355, 574
1) 666, 542, 432, 734, 433, 574, 355
2) 542, 666, 734, 432, 4333, 574, 355
3) 355, 574, 433, 432, 734, 666, 542
4) Can't be determined
5) None of these

11. Which of the following is the last step for the following input?
Input: 473, 442, 735, 542, 367, 234, 549
1) 234, 442, 542, 473, 735, 367, 549 2) 234, 442, 542, 735, 473, 367, 549
3) 234, 442, 542, 473, 367, 735, 549 4) 234, 442, 542, 735, 367, 473, 549
5) None of these

12. What will be the third step for the following input?
Input: 653, 963, 754, 345, 364, 861, 541
1) 541, 345, 754, 963, 364, 816, 653 2) 541, 345, 364, 653, 963, 754, 861
3) 541, 345, 364, 963, 754, 861, 653 4) 541, 345, 364, 653, 861, 754, 963
5) None of these

Directions (Q. 13-17): Study the following information to answer the given questions.

A word arrangement machine when given an input line of words, rearranges them following a particular rule in each step. The following is an illustration of the input and the steps of rearrangement.

Input: going but for crept te light sir
Step I: crept going but for te light sir
Step II: crept going light but for te sir
Step III: crept going light but for sir te
(Step III is the last step for this input)

As per the rules followed in the above steps, find out in the given questions the appropriate step for the given input.

13. **Input:** the in car as he may me
Which of the following will be the third step for this input?
1) car the in as he may me 2) car may the as in he me
3) car as may he the in me 4) car may the in as he me
5) None of these

14. If the second step of an input is 'clever remand window sales batch tiger never', which of the following will be its sixth step?
    1) clever remand window batch sales tiger never
    2) window remand clever sales batch tiger never
    3) batch never sales tiger clever remand window
    4) clever remand window tiger batch sales never
    5) It cannot have sixth step.
15. If the input is 'true se veto be nuke my like', which of the following will be the IV step?
    1) like nuke true veto be se my 2) be my like se true veto nuke
    3) be my se like true veto nuke 4) veto true nuke like so be my
    5) Cannot be determined
16. **Input:** 'more fight cats cough sough acts idea'
    Which of the following steps would be the last step for this input?
    1) III 2) IV 3) V 4) VI 5) VII
17. If the V step of an input is 'more pure soft cat not so sir at', what will be the II step?
    1) at so more pure cat not soft sir 2) more pure soft so sir cat at not
    3) more pure soft cat so sir at not 4) more so sir soft pure cat at not
    5) Cannot be determined

Directions (Q. 18-23): A number arrangement machine, when given a particular input, rearranges it following a particular rule. The following is the illustration of the input and the steps of arrangement:

Input: 75, 133, 37, 15, 79, 113, 63, 29
Step I: 29, 133, 37, 15, 79, 113, 63, 75
Step II: 29, 63, 37, 15, 79, 113, 133, 75
Step III: 29, 63, 113, 15, 79, 37, 133, 75
Step IV: 29, 63, 113, 79, 15, 37, 133, 75
Step V: 121, 81, 25, 256, 36, 100, 49, 144
Step VI: 119, 77, 19, 248, 26, 88, 35, 128
Step VII: 128, 77, 19, 248, 26, 88, 35, 119
Step VIII: 128, 35, 19, 248, 26, 88, 77, 119
and so on.

18. Which of the following will be **Step III** of the following input?
    Input: 87, 58, 49, 92, 21, 27
    1) Can't be determined 2) 81, 9, 121, 169, 169, 289
    3) 27, 21, 49, 92, 58, 87 4) 27, 21, 92, 49, 58, 87
    5) None of these
19. If following is the Step IV of the input, what will be the input?
    Step IV: 121, 169, 81, 144, 100, 49
    1) 74, 85, 54, 66, 37, 25 2) 25, 37, 66, 54, 85, 74
    3) 49, 100, 144, 81, 169, 121 4) Cannot be determined
    5) None of these

20. For the following input, some steps are given below (not necessarily in the same order). One of them may be wrong. You have to find out that as answer. If all steps are found correct then choose 'no error', i.e. option '5'.
Input: 82, 74, 53, 22, 40, 64
1) 98, 12, 10, 56, 111, 88 2) 100, 16, 16, 64, 121, 100
3) 64, 40, 53, 22, 74, 82 4) 88, 12, 10, 56, 111, 98
5) No error

21. In how many steps will the following input be fully arranged?
Input: 15, 38, 24, 26, 42, 68, 53, 85
1) IXth step 2) Xth step 3) VIIIth step
4) Can't be determined 5) None of these

22. If following is the step IV of the input then what will be Step II of that input?
Step IV: 17, 22, 41, 34, 48, 73, 62, 58
1) 17, 22, 73, 48, 34, 41, 62, 58 2) 17, 62, 73, 48, 34, 41, 22, 58
3) 58, 62, 73, 48, 34, 41, 22, 17 4) Can't be determined
5) None of these

23. Which number will not appear for the given input in any step up to step VII, during arrangement process by the machine?
Input: 73, 84, 62, 52, 29, 63, 14, 40
1) 121 2) 113 3) 64 4) 52 5) All appear

Directions (Q. 24-30): Study the following information to answer the given questions.

A number arrangement machine when given an input of numbers, rearranges them following a particular rule in each step. The following is an illustration of input and steps of arrangement.

Input: 46, 185, 310, 436, 96, 217, 39
Step I: 436, 46, 185, 310, 96, 217, 39
Step II: 436, 39, 46, 185, 310, 96, 217
Step III: 436, 39, 310, 46, 185, 96, 217
Step IV: 436, 39, 310, 46, 217, 185, 96
Step V: 436, 39, 310, 46, 217, 96, 185

This is the final arrangement and Step V is the last step for this input.

24. If 631, 29, 520, 474, 48, 312, 502, 36, 68 is the third step of an input, which of the following steps will be 631, 29, 520, 36, 502, 48, 474, 312, 68?
1) Sixth 2) Fifth 3) Seventh
4) Cannot be determined 5) None of these

25. Which of the following is the last step for the following input?
Input: 47, 432, 127, 52, 309, 87, 28, 116
1) 432, 28, 309, 52, 127, 47, 116, 87 2) 432, 28, 309, 47, 52, 127, 116, 87
3) 432, 28, 309, 47, 127, 52, 116, 87 4) 432, 28, 309, 47, 127, 116, 52, 87
5) None of these

26. Following is the step IV for an input. What will be the first step for the input?
Step IV: 726, 19, 537, 33, 412, 315, 115, 47, 81
1) 115, 47, 726, 19, 537, 33, 412, 315, 81
2) 537, 19, 726, 412, 33, 315, 115, 47, 81
3) 33, 412, 315, 726, 19, 537, 115, 47, 81
4) Cannot be determined
5) None of these

27. How many steps will be required to get the final output from the following input?
Input: 20, 105, 17, 37, 76, 121, 123, 41
1) 5 2) 6 3) 7 4) 8 5) None of these

28. If following is the second step for an input, what will be the fourth step?
Step II: 317, 9, 217, 20, 226, 16, 115
1) 317, 9, 226, 20, 217, 16, 115
2) 317, 9, 226, 16, 217, 20, 115
3) 317, 9, 217, 20, 226, 16, 115
4) 317, 9, 226, 16, 115, 20, 217
5) None of these

29. What will be the third step for the following input?
Input: 17, 85, 102, 9, 119, 311, 13
1) 311, 9, 119, 17, 85, 102, 13
2) 311, 9, 119, 17, 102, 85, 13
3) 311, 9, 102, 17, 119, 85, 13
4) 311, 9, 102, 13, 119, 17, 85
5) None of these

30. What will be the second step for the following input?
Input: 727, 17, 548, 19, 348, 27, 402, 43
1) 727, 19, 548, 17, 348, 27, 402, 43
2) 727, 17, 348, 548, 19, 27, 402, 43
3) 727, 348, 17, 19, 548, 27, 402, 43
4) Cannot be determined
5) None of these

Directions (Q. 31-35): Study the following information carefully and then answer the questions given below. A spying organisation receives messages from its spies via a computerised fax machine which generates different rearrangements of words to maintain secrecy of the transmitted messages. The following is an illustration of input and steps of rearrangement.

Input: Anis goes to the bar after dinner everyday
Step I: After Anis goes to the bar dinner everyday
Step II. Anis after goes to the bar dinner everyday
Step III: everyday Anis after goes to the bar dinner

Step IV: bar everyday Anis after goes to the bar dinner
Step V: dinner bar everyday Anis after goes to the
Step VI: goes dinner bar everyday Anis after to the
And so on.

31. What will be the seventh step of the rearrangement process?
 1) the goes dinner bar everyday Anis after to
 2) Anis dinner everyday bar to goes after
 3) everyday bar dinner Anis goes the after to
 4) goes Anis the to bar dinner everyday after
 5) None of these
32. **Input:** the men will arrive on Monday
 Which of the following would be the fifth step for the above input?
 1) arrive on the men will Monday
 2) on Monday men arrive the will
 3) men the will Monday arrive on
 4) Monday will the on arrive men
 5) None of these
33. If the fourth step of an input is 'him gateway at intercept we will the', what is the sixth step of that input?
 1) we intercept the him will gateway
 2) at intercept we will him the gateway
 3) the intecept we will him gateway at
 4) we gateway will him the at intercept
 5) we the him gateway at intercept will
34. If the third step of an input is 'money be after the will paid sunset', then what is the middle word of the sixth step?
 1) the 2) paid 3) will 4) be 5) money
35. **Input:** 'during off lights were put the murder'. What would be the second and the last words of step V of this input?
 1) lights, put 2) during, off 3) murder, the
 4) during, put 5) None of these

Directions (Q. 36-40): A word arrangement machine when given an input line of words, rearranges them following a particular rule in each step. The following is the illustration of the input and the steps of arrangement:

Input: she was shot dead at her residence
Step I: at was shot dead she her residence
Step II: at her shot dead she was residence
Step III: at her she dead shot was residence
Step IV: at her she was shot dead residence
Step V: at her she was dead shot residence

Since the words are fully arranged, the machine stops. Otherwise it may go on till the words get fully arranged. Study the logic and answer the questions that follow:

36. In how many steps will the following input be fully arranged?
Input: India has always been a critical factor
1) One 2) Three 3) Five
4) Six 5) None of these
37. What would be the Step III for the following input?
Input: this is one thing on which I caution
1) I is one thing on which this caution
2) I is on one this which thing caution
3) I is on thing one which this caution
4) I is on one thing which this caution
5) None of these
38. If Step II of an input reads "by he out the efforts made spells us", which of the following would be the last step?
1) Step III 2) Step IV 3) Step V
4) Step VI 5) None of these
39. What would be the penultimate step for the following input?
Input: you hardly see any motorised vehicles
1) Step I 2) Step II 3) Step III
4) Step IV 5) None of these
40. What would be the Step IV for the following input?
Input: the foliage along road can deceive you
1) can foliage along road the deceive you
2) can the you road along deceive foliage
3) can the you road foliage deceive along
4) can the along road foliage deceive you
5) None of these

Directions (41-46): Study the following information carefully and answer the given questions:

A word and number arrangement machine when given an input line of words and numbers rearranges them following a particular rule in each step. The following is an illustration of input and rearrangement.

Input: gone 93 over 46 84 now for 31
Step I: 31 gone 93 over 46 84 now for
Step II: 31 over gone 93 46 84 now for
Step III: 31 over 46 gone 93 84 now for
Step IV: 31 over 46 now gone 93 84 for
Step V: 31 over 46 now 84 gone 93 for
and Step V is the last step of the rearrangement of the above input.

As per the rules followed in the above steps, find out in each of the following questions the appropriate step for the given input.

41. **Step III of an Input:** 15 window 29 93 86 sail tower buy Which of the following will be step VI?

1) 15 window 29 tower 86 sail 93 buy
2) 15 window 29 tower 86 93 sail buy
3) 15 window 29 tower 93 86 sail buy
4) There will be no such step
5) None of these

42. **Input:** station hurry 39 67 all men 86 59
How many steps will be required to complete the rearrangement?
1) Four 2) Five 3)Six
4) Three 5) None of these

43. **Step II of an input is:** 49 zone car battery 56 87 71 down
Which of the following is definitely the input?
1) car 49 battery zone 56 87 71 down
2) zone 49 car battery 56 87 71 down
3) battery car 49 zone 56 87 71 down
4) Cannot be determined
5) None of these

44. **Input:** news 79 53 glory for 46 29 task Which of the following will be step IV?
1) 29 task 46 news 53 glory 79 for 2) 29 task 46 news 53 79 glory for
3) 29 task 46 news 79 53 glory for 4) 29 news 79 53 glory for 46 lask
5) None of these

45. **Step III of an input is:** 27 tube 34 gas chamber row 74 53 Which of the following steps will be the last but one?
1) VI 2) VII 3) VIII
4) V 5) None of these

46. **Step II of an Input:** 19 year 85 74 near gone 26 store How many more steps will be required to complete the rearrangement?
1) Three 2) Four 3) Two
4) Five 5) None of these

Directions (Q. 47-51): Study the following information carefully and answer the given questions:

A word and number arrangement machine when given an input line of words and numbers rearranges them following a particular rule in each step. The following is an illustration of input and rearrangement:

Input: gain 96 63 forest 38 78 deep house
Step I: deep gain 96 63 forest 38 78 house
Step II: deep 38 gain 96 63 forest 78 house
Step III: deep 38 forest gain 96 63 78 house
Step IV: deep 38 forest 63 gain 96 78 house
Step V: deep 38 forest 63 gain 78 96 house
Step VI: deep 38 forest 63 gain 78 house 96

and Step VI is the last step of the rearrangement of the above input.

As per the rules followed in the above steps, find out in each of the following questions the appropriate step for the given input.

47. **Input:** train 59 47 25 over burden 63 sky
Which of the following steps will be the last but one?
1) VI 2) V 3) IV
4) VII 5) None of these

48. **Input:** service 46 58 96 of there desk 15
Which of the following will be step VI?
1) desk 15 over service 46 58 96 there
2) desk 15 over 46 service there 58 96
2) desk 15 over 46 service 58 there 96
6) desk 15 over 46 service 58 96 there
7) There will be no such step.

49. Step II of an input is: below 12 93 house floor 69 57 task Which of the following will definitely be the input?
1) 93 house 89 57 below task floor 12
2) 93 house below 69 57 task floor 12
3) 93 house floor 69 57 task below 12
4) Cannot be determined
5) None of these

50. Step III of an input is: art 24 day 83 71 54 star power Which of the following steps will be the last?
1) V 2) VIII 3) IX
4) VII 5) None of these

51. Step II of an input is: cold 17 wave 69 never desk 52 43 How many more steps will be required to complete the rearrangement?
1) Six 2) Five 3) Four
4) Three 5) None of these

Directions (52-57): Study the following information carefully and answer the given questions:

A word and number arrangement machine when given an input line of words and numbers rearranges them following a particular rule in each step. The following is an illustration of input and rearrangement.

Input: sale data 18 23 for 95 then 38
Step I: data sale 18 23 for 95 then 38
Step II: data 95 sale 18 23 for then 38
Step III: data 95 for sale 18 23 then 38
Step IV: data 95 for 38 sale 18 23 then
Step V: data 95 for 38 sale 23 18 then
Step VI: data 95 for 38 sale 23 then 18

and step VI is the last step of the rearrangement of the above input.

As per the rules followed in the above steps, find out in each of the following questions the appropriate step for the given input.

52. **Input:** year 39 stake 47 house full 94 55
    How many steps will be required to complete the rearrangement?
    1) Five 2)Six 3) Four
    4) Seven 5) None of these
53. Step II of an input is: car 83 lost ever 32 46 74 now
    How many more steps will be required to complete the rearrangement?
    1) Three 2) Four 3) Five
    4)Six 5) None of these
54. Step III of an input is: and 79 code 27 18 new goal 34 Which of the following will definitely be the input?
    1) code and 79 27 18 new goal 34 2) code 27 18 new goal 34 and 79
    3) code 27 and 18 79 new goal 34 4) Cannot be determined
    5) None of these
55. **Input:** water full never 35 78 16 height 28 Which of the following steps will be the last?
    1)VI 2) VII 3) VIII
    4) IX 5) None of these
56. Step II of an input is: high 69 store pay 36 43 15 there
    Which of the following will be step VI?
    1) high 69 pay 43 store 36 there 15 2) high 69 pay 43 store 36 15 there
    3) high 69 pay 36 43 store 15 there 4) There will be no such step
    5) None of these
57. **Input:** train more 29 53 fast gear 37 84
    Which of the following steps will be the last but one?
    1) IX 2) VIII 3) VII
    4) VI 5) None of these

Directions (Q. 58-62): Study the following information, carefully to answer the given questions.

A word and number arrangement machine when given an input line of words and numbers rearranges them following a particular rule. The following is an illustration of input and rearrangement steps:

Input: why is 25 bigger than 14 but smaller than 32
Step I: than 14 why is 25 bigger but smaller than 32
Step II: than 14 is 25 why bigger but smaller than 32
Step III: than 14 is 25 than 32 why bigger but smaller
Step IV: than 14 is 25 than 32 why smaller bigger but
Step V: than 14 is 25 than 32 why smaller but bigger

And Step V is the last step of the rearrangement of the above input as the intended rearrangement is obtained.

As per the rules followed in the above steps, indicate the answer in each of the following questions with respect to the appropriate step for the given input;

Input for the questions:

Input: any number less than 30 and more than 20 does not equal 40

58. Which step number would be the following output?
than 20 any number less than 30 and more does not equal 40
1) III 2) IV 3) V
4) VI 5) None of these

59. How many steps would be needed to complete the arrangement?
1) X 2) VIII 3) IX
4) VII 5) None of these

60. Which of the following would be Step IV?
1) than 20 than 30 equal 40 any number less and more does not
2) than 20 any number less than 30 and more does not equal 40
3) 20 30 40 than equal number any less and more does not
4) 20 than 30 than 40 equal number any less and more does not
5) None of these

61. Which of the following would be Step II?
1) 20 than 30 than any number less and more does not equal 40
2) than 20 than 30 equal 40 any numberless and more does not
3) than 20 than 30 any number less and more does not equal 40
4) than 20 than 30 any number less and more does not 40 equal
5) None of these

62. Which word/number would be on the 8th position from left side in Step V?
1) any 2) not 3) 40
4) number 5) None of these

Directions (Q. 63-67): Study the following information to answer the given questions:

A word and number arrangement machine when given an input line of words and numbers rearranges them following a particular rule. The following is an illustration of input and rearrangement.

(All numbers in these questions are two-digit numbers.)

Input: 16 today 32 waiting 21 are 11 people 46 bus 66 long
Step I: 16 today 32 waiting 21 11 people 46 bus 66 long are
Step II: 16 today 32 waiting 21 people 46 bus 66 long 11 are
Step III: 16 today 32 waiting 21 people 46 66 long bus 11 are
Step IV: today 32 waiting 21 people 46 66 long 16 bus 11 are
Step V: today 32 waiting people 46 66 21 long 16 bus 11 are
Step VI: today 32 waiting 46 66 people 21 long 16 bus 11 are
StepVII: today waiting 46 66 32 people 21 long 16 bus 11 are
StepVIII: waiting 46 66 today 32 people 21 long 16 bus 11 are

Step IX: waiting 66 46 today 32 people 21 long 16 bus 11 are

Step X: 66 waiting 46 today 32 people 21 long 16 bus 11 are

Step X is the last Step of the arrangement of the above input as the intended arrangement is obtained.

Now, answer the questions based on the following input:

Input: 23 you 13 wake 81 me 43 before 72 go 34 up

63. Which of these words/numbers would be fourth (from left side) in Step IV for the input?
1) me 2) 43 3) 81
4) wake 5) None of these

64. The following stands for which step of the rearrangement?
you wake 81 43 72 34 up me 23 go 13 before
1) Step IX 2) Step IV 3) Step VI
4) Step V 5) None of these

65. Which of the following would be Step II for the above Input?
1) 23 you wake 81 me 43 72 34 up go 13 before
2) 23 you 13 wake 81 me 43 72 go 34 up before
3) 23 you wake 81 me 43 72 go 34 up before 31
4) 23 you wake 81 me 43 72 go 34 up 13 before
5) None of these

66. How many Steps would be needed to complete the arrangement for the above input?
1) X 2) XI 3) VIII
4) VII 5) None of these

67. Which of the following would be the **last but one step** for the input?
1) you 81 72 wake up 43 34 me 23 go 13 before
2) you 81 72 wake 43 up 34 me 23 go 13 before
3) you wake 81 72 43 up 34 me 23 go 13 before
4) 81 you 72 wake 43 up 34 me 23 go 13 before
5) None of these %

Directions (Q. 68-72): Study the following information to answer the given questions:

A word and number arrangement machine when given an input line of words and numbers rearranges them following a particular rule. The following is an illustration of input and rearrangement.

Input: sum 28 have 19 96 48 luck nice 78 rope

Step I: have sum 28 19 48 luck nice 78 rope 96

Step II: luck have sum 28 19 48 nice rope 96 78

Step III: nice luck have sum 28 19 rope 96 78 48

Step IV: rope nice luck have sum 19 96 78 48 28

Step V: sum rope nice luck have 96 78 48 28 19

And step V is the last step of the rearrangement.

As per the rules followed in the above steps, find out in each of the following questions the appropriate step for the input given below:

Input: 49 last zen 16 82 yet can vast 33 aim 87 54

68. How many steps will be needed to complete the arrangement?
1) IV 2) V 3) VI
4) VII 5) None of these

69. vast last can aim zen 16 yet 33 87 82 54 49
1) III 2) II 3) VII
4) IV 5) There will be no such step

70. Which of the following would be step I?
1) aim 49 can zen 16 yet vast 33 54 87 82 last
2) vast last can aim zen 16 yet 33 87 82 54 49
3) zen 49 last 16 82 yet can vast 33 aim 54 87
4) aim 49 last zen 82 yet can vast 33 87 54 16
5) None of these

71. In step V, which of the following words numbers would be at 6th position from the right?
1) 87 2) 16 3) 33
4) zen 5) aim

72. Which of the following would be the final arrangement?
1) zen yet vast last can aim 16 33 49 54 82 87
2) aim can last vast yet zen 16 33 49 54 82 87
3) aim can last vast yet zen 87 82 54 49 33 16
4) zen yet vast last can aim 87 82 54 49 33 16
5) None of these

Directions (Q. 73-77): Study the following information carefully and answer the given questions.

A word and number arrangement machine when given an input line of words and numbers rearranges them following a particular rule in each step. The following is an illustration of input and rearrangement.

Input: say dry 42 96 get 39 kite 67
Step I: 96 say dry 42 get 39 kite 67
Step II: 96 dry say 42 get 39 kite 67
Step III: 96 dry 39 say 42 get kite 67
Step IV: 96 dry 39 say 67 42 get kite
Step V: 96 dry 39 say 67 get 42 kite

Step V is the last step of the rearrangement.

You have to answer the questions by following the same rules as illustrated above.

73. If the second step of an input is "76 from 48 super itself 56 18 went", how many more steps will be required to complete the arrangement?

1) Five 2) Six 3) Four
4) Three 5) None of these

74. Which step will be the last step of an input for which the third step is "91 go 28 mock pet 43 lead 37" ?
1) Eighth 2) Seventh 3) Sixth
4) Fifth 5) None of these

75. What will be the third step if the input is "thirty days from now 32 56 87 24"?
1) 87 thirty days from now 32 56 24 2) 87 days thirty from now 32 56 24
3) 87 days 24 thirty from now 32 56 4) 87 thirty 24 days 32 from now 56
5) None of these

76. If the third step of an input is "65 daily 12 tie 42 23 foreign urgent", what will definitely be the input?
1) foreign 65 tie urgent 12 42 23 daily
2) foreign 65 urgent tie 42 daily 23 12
3) foreign 65 12 urgent tie 42 daily 23
4) Cannot be determined
5) None of these

77. If the second step of an input is "52 at deep follow 41 16 road 32", what will be the fifth step?
1) 52 at 16 road 32 deep follow 41 2) 52 at 16 road 41 deep follow 32
3) 52 at 16 road 32 follow 41 deep 4) There will be no such step.
5) None of these

Directions (Q. 78-86): Study the following information and answer the questions given:

When a word arrangement machine is given an input line of words, it arranges them following a particular rule. The following is an illustration of input and rearrangement:

Input: deep snow built offer zinc note find answer can
Step I: answer deep snow built offer zinc note find can
Step II: answer built deep snow offer zinc note find can
Step III: answer built can deep snow offer zinc note find
Step IV: answer built can deep find snow offer zinc note
Step V: answer built can deep find note snow offer zinc
Step VI: answer built can deep find note offer snow zinc

Step VI is the last step of the above arrangement as the intended arrangement is obtained.

As per the rules followed in the above steps, find out in each of the following questions the appropriate steps for the given input.

Input: held nature yeast rich win alter infer lost so done

78. Which of the following is second to the right of the one that is seventh from the right end of step IV?

1) infer 2) lost 3) yeast
4) nature 5) None of these

79. Which of the following will be step VI for the given input?
1) alter done held infer lost nature rich so win yeast
2) alter done held infer nature lost rich so win yeast
3) alter done held infer lost nature rich so yeast win
4) alter done held infer lost nature so rich yeast win
5) None of these

80. What will be the position of 'infer' in step III?
1) Fifth from the left end 2) Eighth from the right end
3) Fourth from the right end 4) Eighth from the left end
5) None of these

81. How many steps will be required to complete the arrangement?
1) VII 2) VIII 3) IX
4) VI 5) None of these

82. Which of the following is the third word from the right of step IV?
1) win 2) rich 3) yeast
4) lost 5) None of these

Directions (Q. 83-86): Following are steps of an input. Rearrange them and answer the questions:

A. ancient cones dish vault rope yell hint
B. ancient cones vault dish rope yell hint
C. ancient cones dish hint rope vault yell
D. ancient vault dish rope cones yell hint
E. ancient cones dish hint vault rope yell

83. Which of the following is step V?
1) D 2) A 3) E
4) B 5) C

84. Which of the following is step III?
1) E 2) B 3) D
4) C 5) A

85. Which of the following is step IV?
1) A 2) B 3) C
4) D 5) E

86. Which of the following is step II?
1) A 2) C 3) B
4) E 5) D

Directions (Q. 87-91): Study the following information and answer the questions given:

A word and number arrangement machine when given an input line of words and numbers rearranges them following a particular rule. The following is an illustration of input and rearrangement. (All the numbers are two-digit numbers.)

Input: sine 88 71 cos theta 14 56 gamma delta 26
Step I: cos sine 71 theta 14 56 gamma delta 26 88
Step II: delta cos sine theta 14 56 gamma 26 88 71
Step III: gamma delta cos sine theta 14 26 88 71 56
Step IV: sine gamma delta cos theta 14 88 71 56 26
Step V: theta sine gamma delta cos 88 71 56 26 14

Step V is the last step of the rearrangement.

As per the rules followed in the above steps, find out in each of the following questions the appropriate steps for the given input.

Input for the questions:

Input: for 52 all 96 25 jam road 15 hut 73 bus stop 38 46

(All the numbers given in the arrangement are two-digit numbers.)

87. Which word/number would be at 8th position from the right in step IV?
1) 15 2) road 3) hut
4) jam 5) stop

88. Which step number would be the following output? bus all for 52 25 jam road 15 hut stop 38 46 96 73
1) There will be no such step. 2) III
3) II 4)V
5) VI

89. Which of the following would be step VII?
1) stop road jam hut for bus all 15 96 73 5246 38 25
2) road jam hut for bus all stop 15 25 38 46 52 73 96
3) stop road jam hut for bus all 96 73 52 46 38 25 15
4) jam hut for bus all 25 road stop 15 96 73 52 46 38
5) There will be no such step.

90. Which word/number would be at 6th position from the left in step V?
1) 25 2) stop 3) jam
4) all 5) road

91. Which of the following would be step III?
1) hut for bus all 25 jam road 15 stop 38 96 73 52 46
2) for bus all 25 jam road 15 hut 38 stop 96 46 73 52
3) hut for bus all jam road 15 stop 38 96 73 52 46 25
4) for bus all 25 jam road 15 hut stop 38 46 96 73 52
5) None of these

Answers and Explanations

1-5: Step I: is the digit-sum of the numbers in the input.

Step II: is obtained by squaring the numbers in step 1 and than subtracting '4' (some numbers could be negative.)

Step III: is the digit-sum of the numbers in step 2.

Step IV: the squares of natural nos. is added to the nos. in step 3. [ie $+1^2, +2^2, +3^2$ ...]

Step V: We add 8 to the nos. in step 4.

Step VI: is the digit sum of numbers in step 5.

1. 1; **Input:** 23 61 15 35 54 75 85
Step I: 5 7 6 8 9 3 4
Step II: 21 45 32 60 77 5 12
Step III: 3 9 5 6 5 5 3
Step IV: 4 13 14 22 30 41 52

2. 3 3. 1

4. 2; **Input:** 35 56 33 46 16 32 94
Step I: 8 2 6 1 7 5 4
As step I is same as given in example. Hence, step V will be same.

5. 4; As step I and III are determined by digit-sum, previous step can't be determined.

6-12: Here, the rule followed is: the sum of the digits is calculated. Then in step I, the number with lowest sum of its digits interchanges with the first number. [If the first number has already the lowest sum of its digits then the number with second lowest sum of its digit interchanges with the second number.] The process continues until the numbers get arranged in ascending order on the basis of their sum of digits.

6. 2

7. 1; **Input:** 544, 653, 325, 688, 461, 231, 857
(13) (14) (10) (22) (11) (6) (20)
Step I: 6 14 10 22 11 13 20
Step II: 6 10 14 22 11 13 20
Step III: 6 10 11 22 14 13 20
Step IV: 6 10 11 13 14 22 20
Step V: 6 10 11 13 14 20 22
Hence, 231, 325, 461, 544, 653, 857, 688

[**Note:** It is easy to proceed with the help of sum of their digits and substitute when required.]

8. 3 9. 2

10. 4; In these types, where arrangement or ordering is involved, previous steps can't be determined. [See previous chapter.]

11. 1 12. 3

13-17: The words are arranged according to the number of letters they have, one at a time. The word with the maximum number of letters is put first. If two words have the same number of letters, we go for alphabetical arrangement.

13. 2; **Input:** the in car as he may me
Step I: car the in as he may me
Step II: car may the in as he me
Step III: car may the as in he me

14. 5; **Step II:** clever remand window sales batch tiger never
Step III: clever remand window batch sales tiger never
Step IV: clever remand window batch never sales tiger
Now, step IV would be the last step.

15. 1; **Input:** true se veto be nuke my like
Step I: like true se veto be nuke my
Step II: like nuke true se veto be my
Step III: like nuke true veto se be my
Step IV: like nuke true veto be se my

16. 4; **Input:** more fight cats cough sough acts idea
Step I: cough more fight cats sough acts idea
Step II: cough fight more cats sough acts idea
Step III: cough fight sough more cats acts idea
Step IV: cough fight sough acts more cats idea
Step V: cough fight sough acts cats more idea
Step VI: cough fight sough acts cats idea more

17. 5; We can't move backward

18-23: Here, rule followed is: The first and the last numbers are interchanged in first step and so are the second and the second-last in second step and so on in each step, until the series is arranged in reverse order.
Now, the sum of digits is calculated and square of that sum is substituted in the next step.
The next step is arrived at by deducting 2, 4, 6, 8 ... (depends on no. of terms in the input) from the number in the previous step respectively.
Hereafter, the same process is repeated.

18. 1; **Input:** 87, 58, 49, 92, 21, 27
Step I: 27, 58, 49, 92, 21, 87
Step II: 27, 21, 49, 92, 58, 87
Step III: 27, 21, 92, 49, 58, 87

19. 4; As there are only 6 nos. for arrangement so when we start from input, in Step III, the nos. get arranged in reverse order. Now, step IV will be the squares of sum of the digits of each no.
Hence, when we start from step IV towards input, because of the numerous possibilities of sum of digits of nos., we can't determine the previous step.

20. 5 21. 4; Process never ends. 22. 1

23. 5; 29 $\Rightarrow$ (2 + 9 =) $11^2 = 121$
121 - 8 = 113 [as the nos. are reversed in step IV];
62 $\Rightarrow 8^2 = 64$; 64 - 12 = 52

24-30: Here, the rule followed is: The numbers are getting arranged in alternate series; one in descending order and the other in ascending order.

Step I: The largest of the given numbers comes to the place of first number and the rest shift rightward.

Step II: The smallest of the given numbers comes to the place of second number and the rest shift rightward.

Step III: The second largest of the given numbers comes to the place of third number and the rest shift rightward.

Step IV: The second smallest of the given numbers comes to the place of fourth number and the rest shift rightward and so on until the alternate series is formed.

24. 1; **Step III:** 631, 29, 520, 474, 48, 312, 502, 36, 68
Step IV: 631, 29, 520, 36, 474, 48, 312, 502, 68
Step V: 631, 29, 520, 36, 502, 474, 48, 312, 68
Step VI: 631, 29, 520, 36, 502, 48, 474, 312, 68

25. 3; **Input:** 47, 432, 127, 52, 309, 87, 28, 116
In such case, the final step can be written directly.
432, 28, 309, 47, 127, 52, 116, 87

26. 4; Previous step can't be determined.

27. 5; **Input:** 20, 105, 17, 37, 76, 121, 123, 41
Step I: 123, 20, 105, 17, 37, 76, 121, 41
Step II: 123, 17, 20, 105, 37, 76, 121, 41
Step III: 123, 17, 121, 20, 105, 37, 76, 41

28. 2 29. 1

30. 4; Since the input is finally set, hence further step can't be determined.

31-35: Rule: Rearrange the input by first bringing words which begin with a vowel. Then bring the words which begin with a consonant. If there is more than one word beginning with a vowel/consonant, then follow the alphabetical order in bringing them first. Do not replace words, meaning once a word has been brought at the beginning, it is not changed in the next step.

31. 1 32. 2

33. 5; The input is 'we will intercept him at the gateway'.

34. 5; The input is 'The money will be paid after sunset'. The middle word is the fourth word from either side.

35. 3; Step V is 'put murder light during off were the'.

36-40: The logic of arrangement here is: The word with the least number of letters (*at* has only two letters) gets arranged first. If the number of words with the same number of letters is more than one, alphabetical preference is given. Also, arrangement is done through interchange of words. For example, since *at* has to occupy the first position, the position vacated by *at* is filled with the earlier first-position word, i.e., *she*.

36. 5; **Input:** India has always been a critical factor
Step I: a has always been India critical factor
Step II: a has been always India critical factor
Step III: a has been India always critical factor
Step IV: a has been India always factor critical

Note: *has* automatically got arranged in Step I. Similarly, *always* got automatically arranged in Step III.

37. 4; **Input:** this is one thing on which I caution
Step I: I is one thing on which this caution
Step II: I is on thing one which this caution
Step III: I is on one thing which this caution

38. 3; **Step II:** by he out the efforts made spells us
Step III: by he us the efforts made spells out
Step IV: by he us out efforts made spells the
Step V: by he us out the made spells efforts

39. 3

40. 2

(41-46): In the first step, the smallest number comes to the leftmost position, pushing the rest of the line rightward. In the next step, the word that comes last in the alphabetical order comes to second from left, pushing the rest of the line rightward. Thus, the numbers and words get arranged alternately till the numbers are in ascending order and the words in reverse alphabetical order.

41. 1; **Step III:** 15 window 29 93 86 sail tower buy
Step IV: 15 window 29 tower 93 86 sail buy
Step V: 15 window 29 tower 86 93 sail buy
Step VI: 15 window 29 tower 86 sail 93 buy

42. 2; **Input:** station hurry 39 67 all men 86 59
Step I: 39 station hurry 67 all men 86 59
Step II: 39 station 59 hurry 67 all men 86
Step III: 39 station 59 men hurry 67 all 56
Step IV: 39 station 59 men 67 hurry all 86
Step V: 39 station 59 men 67 hurry 86 all

43. 4; We can't proceed backward.

44. 2; **Input:** news 79 53 glory for 46 29 task
Step I: 29 news 79 53 glory for 46 task
Step II: 29 task news 79 53 glory for 46
Step III: 29 task 46 news 79 53 glory for
Step IV: 29 task 46 news 53 79 glory for

45. 4; **Step III:** 27 tube 34 gas chamber row 74 53
Step IV: 27 tube 34 row gas chamber 74 53

Step V: 27 tube 34 row 53 gas chamber 74
Step VI: 27 tube 34 row 53 gas 74 chamber
Hence step V will be the last but one.

46. 2; **Step II:** 19 year 85 74 near gone 26 store
Step III: 19 year 26 85 74 near gone store
Step IV: 19 year 26 store 85 74 near gone
Step V: 19 year 26 store 74 85 near gone
Step VI: 19 year 26 store 74 near 85 gone
Hence 6 - 2 = 4 more steps will be required

(47-51): In step I the word that comes first in the alphabetical order comes to the leftmost position, pushing the rest of the line rightward. In step II the smallest number comes to the second position, pushing the rest of the line rightward. Thus the words and numbers get arranged alternately until the former make an alphabetical order and the latter an ascending one.

47. 2; **Input:** train 59 47 25 over burden 63 sky
Step I: burden train 59 47 25 over 63 sky
Step II: burden 25 train 59 47 over 63 sky
Step III: burden 25 over train 59 47 63 sky
Step IV: burden 25 over 47 train 59 63 sky
Step V: burden 25 over 47 sky train 59 63
Step VI: burden 25 over 47 sky 59 train 63
Hence step V is the last but one.

48. 5; **Input:** service 46 58 96 over there desk 15
Step I: desk service 46 58 96 over there 15
Step II: desk 15 service 46 58 96 over there
Step III: desk 15 over service 46 58 96 there
Step IV: desk 15 over 46 service 58 96 there
Step V: desk 15 over 46 service 58 there 96
Since the input is already arranged, there will be no step VI.

49. 4; We can't proceed backward.

50. 4; **Step III:** art 24 day 83 71 54 star power
Step IV: art 24 day 54 83 71 star power
Step V: art 24 day 54 power 83 71 star
Step VI: art 24 day 54 power 71 83 star
Step VII: art 24 day 54 power 71 star 83

51. 3; **Step II:** cold 17 wave 69 never desk 52 43
Step III: cold 17 desk wave 69 never 52 43
Step IV: cold 17 desk 43 wave 69 never 52
Step V: cold 17 desk 43 never wave 69 52
Step VI: cold 17 desk 43 never 52 wave 69
Hence 6 - 2 = 4 more steps will be required

(52-57): In step I the word that comes first in the alphabetical order comes to the first po- sition, pushing the rest of the line rightward. In the next step the largest number comes to the second position, pushing the rest of the line rightward. This goes on alternately till the words get arranged in an alphabetical or- der and the numbers in a descending order at alternate positions.

52. 2; **Input:** year 39 stake 47 house full 94 55
Step I: full year 39 stake 47 house 94 55
Step II: full 94 year 39 stake 47 house 55
Step III: full 94 house year 39 stake 47 55
Step IV: full 94 house 55 year 39 stake 47
Step V: full 94 house 55 stake year 39 47
Step VI: full 94 house 55 stake 47 year 39

53. 2; **Step II:** car 83 lost ever 32 46 74 now
Step III: car 83 ever lost 32 46 74 now
Step IV: car 83 ever 74 lost 32 46 now
Step V: car 83 ever 74 lost 46 32 now
Step VI: car 83 ever 74 lost 46 now 32
Hence 6 - 2 = 4 more steps will be required.

54. 4; We can't proceed backward.

55. 1; **Input:** water full never 35 78 16 height 28
Step I: full water never 35 78 16 height 28
Step II: full 78 water never 35 16 height 28
Step III: full 78 height water never 35 16 28
Step IV: full 78 height 35 water never 16 28
Step V: full 78 height 35 never water 16 28
Step VI: full 78 height 35 never 28 water 16

56. 4; **Step II:** high 69 store pay 36 43 15 there
Step III: high 69 pay store 36 43 15 there
Step IV: high 69 pay 43 store 36 15 there
Step V: high 69 pay 43 store 36 there 15
Since the input is already arranged, there will
Since the input is already arranged, there will be no further steps.

57. 5; **Input:** train more 29 53 fast gear 37 84
Step I: fast train more 29 53 gear 37 84
Step II: fast 84 train more 29 53 gear 37
Step III: fast 84 gear train more 29 53 37
Step IV: fast 84 gear 53 train more 29 37
Step V: fast 84 gear 53 more train 29 37
Step VI: fast 84 gear 53 more 37 train 29
Hence step V will be the last but one

(58-62): After a long time, some fresh air in the Input-Output question! Look at what is happening here. The numbers are not independent but have a word attached with them. Thus the entities are (is 25), (than 14) and (than 32). Now, first the numbers(along with their word attachments) get arranged, one at a time, in the ascending order. The remaining words then get arranged in reverse alphabetical order.

Input: any number less (than 30) and more (than 20) does not (equal 40)
Step I: (than 20) any number less (than 30) and more does not (equal 40)
Step II: (than 20) (than 30) any number less and more does not (equal 40
Step III: (than 20) (than 30) (equal 40) any number less and more does not
Step IV: (than 20) (than 30) (equal 40 number any less and more does not
Step V: (than 20) (than 30) (equal 40) number not any less and more does
Step VI: (than 20) (than 30) (equal 40) number not more any less and does
Step VII: (than 20) (than 30) (equal 40) number not more less any and does
Step VIII: (than 20) (than 30) (equal 40) number not more less does any and

58. 5; Step I
59. 2
60. 5; than 20 than 30 equal 40 number any less and more does not
61. 3
62. 2

(63-67): Look at the last step. Obviously, in the final step, the words are in reverse alphabetical order and numbers in descending order. But we start the arrangement from the right and begin with words. Thus, in the first step, the word that comes first in alphabetical order goes at the right most position. Next, the smallest number goes at second from right. And so on.

Input: 23 you 13 wake 81 me 43 before 72 go 34 up
Step I: 23 you 13 wake 81 me 43 72 go 34 up before
Step II: 23 you wake 81 me 43 72 go 34 up 13 before
Step III: 23 you wake 81 me 43 72 34 up go 13 before
Step IV: you wake 81 me 43 72 34 up 23 go 13 before
Step V: you wake 81 43 72 34 up me 23 go 13 before
Step VI: you wake 81 43 72 up 34 me 23 go 13 before
Step VII: you wake 81 72 43 up 34 me 23 go 13 before

Step VIII: you 81 72 wake 43 up 34 me 23 go 13 before
Step IX: 81 you 72 wake 43 up 34 me 23 go 13 before

63. 1
64. 4
65. 4
66. 5, Nine
67. 2

(68-72): In the given word and number arrangement machine, in step I the word coming first alphabetically is shifted at the 1st place and the greatest number is shifted to the end. In step II the word coming second alphabetically is shifted at the first place and the second greatest number is shifted to the end. Same pattern is followed in the next steps till all the words and numbers are arranged as in step V.

Input: 49 last zen 16 82 yet can vast 33 aim 87 54
Step I: aim 49 last zen 16 82 yet can vast 33 54 87
Step II: can aim 49 last zen 16 yet vast 33 54 87 82
Step III: last can aim 49 zen 16 yet vast 33 87 82 54
Step IV: vast last can aim zen 16 yet 33 87 82 54 49
Step V: yet vast last can aim zen 16 87 82 54 49 33
Step VI: zen yet vast last can aim 87 82 54 49 33 16

68. 3
69. 4
70. 5; aim 49 last zen 16 82 yet can vast 33 54 87
71. 2
72. 4

(73-77): In the given word and number arrangement machine, numbers are arranged alternately with words. Among numbers, first the largest number is taken to the leftmost side, then the smallest and so on. Among words, the first word as per the alphabetical order is taken to the leftmost side, then the word coming last as per the alphabetical order, and so on.

73. 3; **Step II.** 76 from 48 super itself 56 18 went
Step III. 76 from 18 48 super itself 56 went
Step IV. 76 from 18 went 48 super itself 56
Step V. 76 from 18 went 56 48 super itself
Step VI. 76 from 18 went 56 itself 48 super
Step VI is the last step, so four more steps are required to complete the arrangement.

74. 2; **Step III:** 91 go 28 mock pet 43 lead 37
Step IV: 91 go 28 pet mock 43 lead 37
Step V: 91 go 28 pet 43 mock lead 37
Step VI: 91 go 28 pet 43 lead mock 37
Step VII: 91 go 28 pet 43 lead 37 mock

75. 3; **Input:** thirty days from now 32 56 87 24
Step I: 87 thirty days from now 32 56 24
Step II: 87 days thirty from now 32 56 24
Step III: 87 days 24 thirty from now 32 56

76. 4

77. 2; **Step II:** 52 at deep follow 41 16 road 32
Step III: 52 at 16 deep follow 41 road 32
Step IV: 52 at 16 road deep follow 41 32
Step V: 52 at 16 road 41 deep follow 32

(78-86): In the given word arrangement machine, words are shifted to the left in alphabetical order one by one.

(78-82): Input: held nature yeast rich win alter infer lost so done
Step I: alter held nature yeast rich win infer lost so done
Step II: alter done held nature yeast rich win infer lost so
Step III: alter done held infer nature yeast rich win lost so
Step IV: alter done held infer lost nature yeast rich win
Step V: alter done held infer lost nature rich yeast win so
Step VI: alter done held infer lost nature rich so yeast win
Step VII: alter done held infer lost nature rich so win yeast

78. 4

79. 3

80. 5; fourth from the left end or seventh from the right end.

81. 1

82. 2

(83-86): Step I: D
Step II: B
Step III: A
Step IV: E
Step V: C

83. 5

84. 5

85. 5

86. 3

(87-91): Input: for 52 all 96 25 jam road 15 hut 73 bus stop 38 46
Step I: all for 52 25 jam road 15 hut 73 bus stop 38 46 96
Step II: bus all for 52 25 jam road 15 hut stop 38 46 96 73
Step III: for bus all 25 jam road 15 hut stop 38 46 96 73 52
Step IV: hut for bus all 25 jam road 15 stop 38 96 73 52 46
Step V: jam hut for bus all 25 road 15 stop 96 73 52 46 38
Step VI: road jam hut for bus all 15 stop 96 73 52 46 38 25
Step VII: stop road jam hut for bus all 96 73 52 46 38 25 15

87. 2; **Step IV:** hut for bus all 25 jam **road** 15 stop 38 96 73 52 46
Eighth from the right – road.

88 3

89. 3

90. 1; **Step V:** Jam hut for bus all **25** road 15 stop 96 73 52 46 38
Sixth from the left is 25

91. 4

Chapter Seventeen

Introduction to Coding and Decoding

(LET'S GO BANANA s)

17.1: Introduction

All of us are familiar with the concept of coding even though we may not have studied it consciously. Many of us might have come across occasions since our childhood days, where we use a separate set of words or symbols to denote or express a familiar word. For example it is a common situation where children use some code-words like "are you doing the home work now?" to discuss their favourite video games when their parents are around and listening to the conversation and "are you doing the home work now?" might actually mean "are you playing the game now?"

To understand the concept of coding we should just refresh our understanding about what we mean by *language*. Let us say that we hear a word called "banana". Now the word banana means an edible fruit that's long and sweet to eat when it's ripe. All of us understand what the meaning of a banana is. We also know that this fruit is expressed by six symbols which are B, A, N, A, N, A and these 6 symbols have to be arranged in that order. Only then does it mean that these 6 letters that is B, A, N, A, N, A means a banana; the fruit. It is a rule that humans who understand and speak and write the language English have agreed upon. So in English language: the six letters arranged in that particular order mean the fruit banana. So, in a simplistic way, it can be said that

1. Language is assigning of symbols to mean known things.

Just as some human beings can agree that henceforth B, A, N, A, N, A means a banana some other humans can also agree that henceforth A, B, A, N, A, N would mean the yellow ripe fruit that is otherwise called banana. So this would be a new language and in this ABANAN would mean the same sweet fruit. And nothing is wrong with that. Just as we can make a rule that B, A, N, A, N, A would mean a banana we can also make a rule that A, B, A, N, A,N would mean the same sweet fruit. So, here we have created a new set of symbols to mean the same thing. And since the new set of symbols have come from the old set of the same six letters, it's called coding.

2. Coding is rearranging the old symbols (as per some rule) to mean the same known things.

since the use of symbols to associate with meanings is the specialty of only the human beings which are more intelligent animals than any other on the planet ; therefore it is only natural that for intelligence tests or test of reasoning; most of the examiners give a good emphasis on our capacity to play with symbols. Coding and decoding; the use of language etc. is the distinguishing feature of human intelligence. Therefore test of coding and decoding is a very good test of Intelligence and a favourite in most of the examinations.

In this chapter we are going to have just a basic idea about coding and decoding, what are the common ways in which words can be coded and we will look at some of the standard types in a brief manner. We will solve and have a practice of some exercises. This will be a brief introduction because in the next few chapters after this chapter; we are going to take a deeper dive into the interesting world of coding and how they can be used to assess our intelligence and our capabilities of reasoning.

Let's go back to our BANANA.

1. **POSITION –SHIFTING:** In cases of positional shifting each letter of the original word is retained, only its position is shifted one or two places (or even maybe 3) towards the right OR towards the left. Original letters are not, only the arrangement of the letters is changed. Let us look at the following examples:

1.1 POSITION - SHIFTING: (1 SPACE TO LEFT)

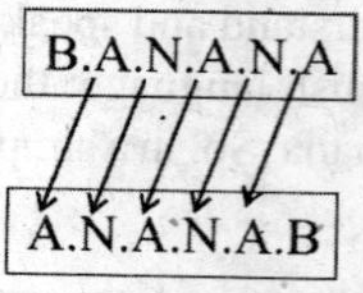

1.2 SHIFTING: (2 SPACE TO LEFT)

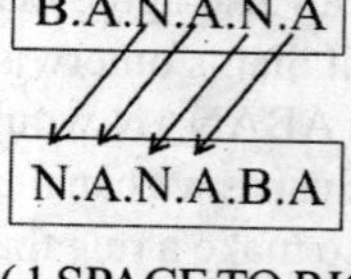

1.3 SHIFTING: (1 SPACE TO RIGHT)

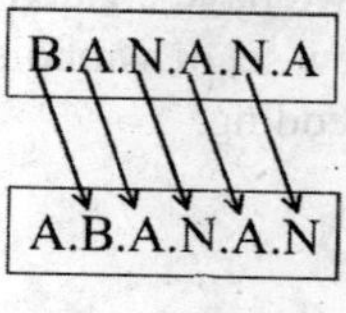

1.4 SHIFTING: (2 SPACES TO RIGHT)

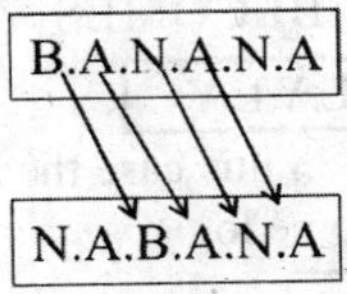

2. **SUBSTITUITION:** In cases of substitution, each of the original letters are replaced by a new letter and this replacement is based on certain logic. Those logics can be different.

For example, we may have a case of

2.1 Alphabetical shifting: Where each original letter is replaced by another letter that is 1 or 2 or 3 letters towards its right or r towards its left or two letters towards its left in the original alphabet.

2.1.1 Alphabetical shifting: 1 SPACE TO RIGHT

Old letter	A	B	C	D	E	F	G	H	I
New letter	B	C	D	E	F	G	H	I	J

ORIGINAL WORD: B.A.N.A.N.A

CODED WORD: (B BECOMES C, A BECOMES B, N BECOMES O,) C.B.O.B.O.B

2.1.2 Alphabetical shifting: 2 SPACES TO RIGHT

Old letter	A	B	C	D	E	F	G	H	I
New letter	C	D	E	F	G	H	I	J	K

ORIGINAL WORD: B.A.N.A.N.A

CODED WORD: (B BECOMES D, A BECOMES C, N BECOMES P) D.C.P.C.P.C

2.1.3 Alphabetical shifting: 1 SPACES TO LEFT

Old letter	A	B	C	D	E	F	G	H	I
New letter	Z	A	B	C	D	E	F	G	H

ORIGINAL WORD: B.A.N.A.N.A

CODED WORD: (B BECOMES A, A BECOMES Z, N BECOMES M) A.Z.M.Z.M.Z

2.1.4 Alphabetical shifting: 2 SPACES TO LEFT

Old letter	A	B	C	D	E	F	G	H	I
New letter	Y	Z	A	B	C	D	E	F	G

ORIGINAL WORD: B.A.N.A.N.A

CODED WORD: (B BECOMES Z, A BECOMES Y, N BECOMES L) Z.Y.L.Y.L.Y

2.2 **Numerical substitution:** in this case the letter is substituted by some number based on some logic.

Ex 2.2.1 : B.A.N.A.N.A

Is now coded as 2.1.14.1.14.1

Here each letter is substituted by its position in alphabet. So N is substituted by 14 as its position is 14th in the alphabet (A is 1st letter, B is 2nd ….M is 13th)

Ex 2.2.2: B.A.N.A.N.A

Is now coded as 1.0.13.0.131

Here each letter is substituted by its position in alphabet and then 1 is subtracted. So N is substituted by 13 as its position is 14th in the alphabet so code for N is 14 minus one = 13.A is 1st letter so code for A is 1 - 1=0

2.3 **R and om substitution: here there can be preassigned pairs where any given letter is always coded as its preassigned pair.** So if NAB is coded as RFG, code for BANANA will be GFRGFR. Here the preassigned pairs are N-R, A-F, B-G.

So, B.A.N.A.N.A

↓ ↓ ↓ ↓ ↓

Is coded as G F. R. G F. R

3. **MATRIX CODING**: In such cases each letter maybe assigned 2 numbers, 1st one may be equal to its row – value and the second may be equal to its column value. This may be explained by the following example:

Directions: In each of the following questions, a word is represented by only one set of numbers as given in any one of the alternatives. The sets of numbers given in the alternatives are represented by two classes of alphabets as in the two given matrices. The columns and rows of matrix I are numbered from 0 to 4 and that of matrix II from 5 to 9. A letter from these matrices can be represented first by its row and next by column number in the matrices for question 1, A can be represented by 13, 23 etc. T can be represented by 58, 65 etc. Similarly, you have to identify the set for the word given in each question.

MATRIX 1

	0	1	2	3	4
0	D	K	A	E	C
1	C	D	K	A	E
2	K	C	E	A	D
3	K	C	D	E	A
4	E	D	A	K	C

MATRIX 2

	5	6	7	8	9
5	P	L	0	T	N
6	T	P	N	L	0
7	P	N	T	0	L
8	0	N	T	P	L
9	L	0	P	N	T

Ex 3: Find the code for COLD?

1) 44, 96, 95, 22 2) 31, 99, 77, 22
3) 30, 66, 86, 43 4) 10, 85, 79, 24

Soln: From matrix 1, C can be coded as 04, 10, 21, 31 or 44.
From matrix 2, O can be coded as 57, 69, 78, 85 or 96.
From matrix 2, L can be coded as 56, 68, 79, 89 or 95.
From matrix1, D can be coded as 00, 11, 24, 32 or 41.
Clearly, only (4) contains all correct codes.

4. **NUMBER TO LETTER CODING:** As we have seen earlier in one example, how B.A.N.A.N.A became 2.1.14.1.14.1 on substitution. The ***number to letter substitution*** is exactly the opposite of this process. In this case instead of letter being substituted by a number the opposite happens ; so now a number is replaced by a letter.

Ex 4: Directions (Q. 1-2): The number in each question below is to be codified in the following code:

Digit	7	2	1	5	3	9	8	6	4
Letter	W	L	M	S	I	N	D	J	B

4.1. 184632

1) MDJBSI 2) MDJBIL 3) MDJBWL
4) MDBJIL 5) None of these

Soln: The correct answer is (4). As given, 1 is coded as m, 8 as D, 4 as B, 6 as J, 3 as I and 2 as L . So 184632 is coded as MDBJIL.

4.2. 879341

1) DWNIBS 2) DWNBIM 3) DWNIBM
4) NDWBIM 5) None of these

Soln: The correct answer is (3). As given 8 is coded as D, 7 as W, 9 as N, 3 as I, 4 as B and 1 as M. So 879341 is coded as DWNIBM.

5. **NUMBER TO WORD CODING:** Sometimes, a number my not just mean a letter. Instead it might mean an entire word. In a certain code.

Ex 5 : '786' means 'study very hard', '958' means 'hard work pays' and '645' means 'study and work'. Which of the following is the code for 'very'?

Soln: In the first and second statements, the common word is 'hard' and the common code digit is '8'. So, '8' means 'hard'.

In the first and third statements, the common word is 'study' and the common coded digit is '6'. So, '6' means 'study'.

Thus, in the first statement '7' means 'very'.

6. Coding by Combinations of Letters, Numbers or Symbols

Ex 6: Directions: In each questions below is given a group of digits followed by four combinations of letters or symbols numbered 1, 2, 3 and 4. You have to find out which of the combinations correctly represents the group of digits based on the coding system and the conditions given below and mark the number of that combination as your answer. If none of the combinations correctly represents the group of digits, mark 5, i.e., None of these as your answer.

Digit	5	1	3	4	9	6	8	2	7
symbol	P	A	K	%	R	@	d	©	M

Conditions:

(i) If the first digit is odd and the last digit is even, the codes for the first and last digits are to be interchanged.

(ii) If both the first and the last digits are even, both are to be coded as

(iii) If both the first and the last digits are odd, both are-to be coded as $.

Example 6.1: What is the code of 215349?

1) RAPK%© 2) APK%$ 3) $APK%$

4) © PAK%R 5) None of these

Solution. (5); Since 2 is coded as © and 1 has to be coded as A, first 2 codes must be ©A.

Example 6.2: What is the code of 794821?

1) MR%D©A 2) AR%D©M 3) M%RD©R

4) $R%D©$ 5) None of these

Solution. (4); Code for 794821, as per the table would be MR%d© A. But here both first and last digits are odd, so condition iii is applied . hence first and last digits will be coded as $. Hence MR%d© A becomes $R%dC$.

Useful Quick Reference Table For Coding

Position of Alphabets from Left to Right (Forward Order)

A	B	C	D	E	F	G	H	I	J	K	L	M
1	2	3	4	5	6	7	8	9	10	11	12	13
N	O	P	Q	R	S	T	U	V	W	X	Y	Z
14	15	16	17	18	19	20	21	22	23	24	25	26

Table 1

Position of Alphabets from Right to Left (Backward Order)

Z	Y	X	W	V	U	T	S	R	Q	P	O	N
1	2	3	4	5	6	7	8	9	10	11	12	13
M	L	K	J	I	H	G	F	E	D	C	B	A
14	15	16	17	18	19	20	21	22	23	24	25	26

Table 2

Opposite Alphabets

A	B	C	D	E	F	G	H	I	J	K	L	M
Z	Y	X	W	V	U	T	S	R	Q	P	O	N

Table 3

Practice Exercises

1. If in a certain language, MADRAS is coded as NBESBT, how is BOMBAY coded in that code
   1) CPNCBX 2) CPNCBZ 3) CPOCBZ
   4) CQOCBZ 5) None of the above
2. In a certain code, TRIPPLE is written as SQHOOKD. How is DISPOSE written in that code?
   1) CHRONRD 2) DSOESPI 3) ESJTPTF
   4) ESOPSID 5) None of these
3. In certain code, TOGETHER is written as RQEGRJCT. In the same code PAROLE will be written as
   1) NCPQJG 2) NCQPJG 3) RCPQJK
   4) RCTQNG 5) None of these
4. In certain language, CHAMPION is coded as HCMAIPNO, how is NEGATIVE coded in that code?

1) ENAGITEV 2) NEAGVEIT 3) MGAETVIE
4) EGAITEVN 5) NEGATIEV

5. If in a certain language, GAMBLE is coded as FBLCKF, how is FLOWER coded in that code?
1) GKPVFQ 2) EMNXDS 3) GMPVDS
4) HNQYGT 5) EKNVDQ

6. If in a certain language, NATURE is coded as MASUQE, how is FAMINE coded in that code?
1) FBMJND 2) FZMHND 3) GANIOE
4) EALIME 5) FZNJME

7. If in a certain code, TEACHER is written as VGCEJGT, how would DULLARD be written in the same code?
1) FWMNCTF 2) FWNNBTE 3) FWNNCSF
4) FWNNCTF 5) None of these

8. If in a certain language FASHION is coded as FOIHSAN. How is PROBLEM coded in that code?
1) ROBLEMP 2) PELBORM 3) PRBOELM
4) RPBOELM 5) PELBRON

9. If in a certain language KINDLE is coded as ELDNIK, how is EXOTIC coded in that code?
1) EXOTLC 2) CXOTIE 3) COXITE
4) CITOXE 5) EOXITC

10. If VICTORY is coded as YLFWRUB. How can SUCCESS be coded?
1) VXEEIW 2) VXFFHW 3) VYEEHW
4) VYEFIW 5) None of these

11. In a code language, DISTANCE is written as IDTUBECN and DOCUMENT is written as ODDVNTNE. How is THURSDAY written in that language?
1) DTVSTEYA 2) HTTQRYAD 3) HTVSTYDA
4) HTVSYADS 5) HTVSTYAD

12. In a certain language, CHAMPION is coded as HCMAIPNO, how is NEGATIVE coded in that code?
1) ENAGITEV 2) NEAGVEIT 3) MGAETVIE
4) EGAITEVN 5) NECATIEV

13. If PEOPLE is coded as PLPOEE, how is TREND coded?
1) TREDN 2) DNERT 3) NDETR
4) TRDNE 5) TNERD

14. In a certain code, MUNICIPALITY is written as INMUAPCIYTLI. How is JUDICIAL written in that code?
1) UJDILACI 2) IDUJLACI 3) IDJULAIC
4) IDJULACI 5) None of these

15. If CIGARETTE is coded as GICERAETT, then DIRECTION will be coded as

1) RIDTCENOI 2) NORTECDII 3) NOIETCRID
4) IRDCTIONE 5) None of these

16. If in a certain language, UTENSIL is coded as WVGPUKN, which word would be coded as DMSFXG?
1) BKQEVE 2) BKQDWE 3) BKQDWF
4) BKQDVF 5) BKQDVE

17. If in a certain code, SWITCH is written as TVJSDG, which word would be written as CQFZE?
1) BARED 2) BRAED 3) BREAD
4) BRADE 5) BRDAE

18. In a certain code, REFRIGERATOR is coded as ROTAREGIRFER. Which word would be coded as NOITINUMMA?
1) ANMOMIUTNI 2) AMNTOMUIIN 3) AMMUNITION
4) NMMUNITIOA 5) None of these

19. If in a certain language, REMOTE is coded as ROTEME, which word would be coded as PNIICC?
1) NPIICC 2) PICCIN 3) PINCIC
4) PICNIC 5) PICINC

20. If FULFNHW is the code for CRICKET, then EULGH is the code for which word?
1) PRIDE 2) BRIDE 3) BLADE
4) BLIND 5) None of these

21. If in a certain language, SHIFT is coded as RFFBO, which word would be coded asLKUMB?
1) MMXQG 2) MLVNC 3) KJVLA
4) MJVLC 5) KJTLA

22. If LBAEHC is the code for BLEACH, then which of the following is coded as NBOLZKMH?
1) OBNKZLHM 2) LOBNHMKZ 3) OCPMALNI
4) MANKYJLG 5) BNLOKZHM

23. In a code, CORNER is written as GSVRI. How can CENTRAL be written in that code?
1) DFOUSBM 2) GIRXVEP 3) GJRYVEP
4) GNFJKER 5) None of these

24. If DELHI is coded as CCIDD, how would you encode BOMBAY?
1) AJMTVT 2) AMJXVS 3) MJXVSU
4) WXYZAX 5) None of these

25. If in a certain language, POPULAR is coded as QPQVMBS, which word would be coded as GBNPVT?
1) FAMOSU 2) FAMOUS 3) FASOUM
4) FOSAUM 5) FAMSUO

26. If ROBUST is coded as QNATRS in a certain language, which word would be coded as ZXCMP?
1) BKQEVE 2) BKQDWE 3) BKQDWF
4) AYDNQ 5) BZEOR
27. If in a certain code, ALMIRAH is written as BNPMWGO, which word would be written as DNRWLUA?
1) COSGOLT 2) TOGSOLC 3) TOGCLOS
4) CLOSGOT 5) COLSTOG
28. If in a certain language, MACHINE is coded as LBBIHOD, which word would be coded as SLTMFNB?
1) RKSLEMA 2) TKULGMC 3) RMSNEOA
4) TMTNGOC 5) TMUNGMC
29. If NARGRUED is the code for GRANDEUR, which word is coded as SERPEVRE?
1) PERSEVER 2) PRESEVER 3) PERSERVE
4) PREVERSE 5) PRESERVE
30. In a certain code language 24685 is written as 33776. How is 35791 written in that code?
1) 44826 2) 44880
3) 46682 4) 44682
31. In a certain code language 35796 is written as 44887. How is 46823 written in that code?
1) 57914 2) 55914
3) 55934 4) 55714
32. If MINJUR is coded as 312547 and TADA as 6898, how can MADURAI be coded?
1) 3498178 2) 3894871
3) 3849781 4) 3894781
33. If PALAM could be given the code number 43, what code number can be given to SANTACRUZ?
1) 75 2) 85
3) 120 4) 123
34. If Z = 52 and ACT = 48, then BAT will be equal to
1) 39 2) 41
3) 44 4) 46
35. If REASON is coded as 5 and BELIEVED as 7, what is the code number for GOVERNMENT?'
1) 6 2) 8
3) 9 4) 10
36. If GO = 32, SHE = 49, then SOME will be equal to
1) 56 2) 58
3) 62 4) 64

37. If XT = 20, BAT=40, then CAT will be equal to
1) 30 2) 50
3) 60 4) 70
38. In a certain code, 15789 is written as XTZAL and 2346 is written as NPSU. How is 23549 written in that code?
1) NPTUL 2) PNTSL 3) NPTSL
4) NBTSL 5) None of these
39. In a certain code, 33946 is coded as PPOAL and 1987 is coded as ROSE. How is 94678 coded in that code?
1) ROSEP 2) OALES 3) POALE
4) OSEPL 5) REAPS
40. If in a certain language, 943 is coded as BED and 12448 is coded as SWEET, how is 492311 coded in that language?
1) EDSWBS 2) TSWBDD 3) DSWTEE
4) EBDSWE 5) EBWDSS
41. If *water* is called *food, food is* called *tree,* free is called *sky, sky* is called *wall,* on which of the following grows a fruit?
1) Water 2) Food 3) Sky
4) Tree 5) Wall
42. If *water* is called *blue, blue* is called red, *red* is called *white, white* is called *sky, sky* is called *rain, rain* is called *green* and *green* is called *air*, which of the following is the colour of milk?
1) Air 2) Green 3) White
4) Rain 5) Sky
43. If *paper* is called *wood, wood* is called *straw, straw* is called *grass, grass* is called *rubber* and *rubber* is called cloth, what is the furniture made up of?
1) Paper 2) Wood 3) Straw
4) Grass 5) Cloth
44. If *pen* is *table, table* is *fan, fan* is *chair* and *chair* is *roof,* on which of the following will a person sit?
1) Fan 2) Chair 3) Roof
4) Table 5) Pen
45. If *bat* is *racket, racket* is *football, football* is *shuttle, shuttle* is *Zudo* and *Zudo* is *carrom*, what is cricket played with?
1) Racket 2) Football 3) Bat
4) Shuttle 5) Carrom
46. If *banana* is *apple, apple* is *grapes, grapes* is *mango, mango* is *nuts, nuts* is *guava,* which of the following is a yellow fruit?
1) Mango 2) Guava 3) Apple
4) Nuts 5) Grapes

47. If air is called *green, green* is called *blue, blue* is called *sky, sky* is called *yellow, yellow* is called *water* and *water* is called *pink*, then what is the colour of clear sky?

1) Blue 2) Sky 3) Yellow
4) Water 5) Pink

48. If *cushion* is called *pillow, pillow* is called *scraf, scraf* is called *bedsheet* and *bedsheet* is called *cover*, which will be spread on the floor?

1) Cover 2) Bedsheet 3) Mat
4) Pillow 5) None of these

49. If *wall* is called *window, window* is called *door, door* is called *floor, floor* is called *roof* and *roof* is called *ventilator*, what will a person stand on?

1) Window 2) Wall 3) Floor
4) Roof 5) Ventilator

50. In a certain code language, *'Tom Kun Sud'* means *'Dogs are barking'*, *'Kun Jo Mop'* means '*Dogs and horses*' and *'Mut Tom Ko'* means '*Donkeys are mad*'. Which word in that language means '*barking*'?

1) Sud 2) Kun 3) Jo
4) Tom 5) Ko

51. In a certain code language, *'put tir fin'* means *'delicious juicy fruit'*, *'tied ip sig'* means *'beautiful white lily'* and *'sig Ion fin'* means *'lily and fruit'*. Which of the following stand for *'and'* in that language?

1) Ion 2) sig
3) fin 4) None of these

52. If *'nit cosco tingo'* stands for '*softer than flower*'; *'tingo rho mst'* stands for *'sweet flower fragrance'* and *'mst scot mp'* stands for '*sweet than smile*' what would *'fragrance'* stand for?

1) rho 2) mst
3) tmp 4) sco

53. In a certain code language, *'dom pul ta'* means *'bring hot food'*; *'pul tir sop'* means *'food is good'* and *'tak da sop'* means *'good bright boy'*. Which of the following does mean *'hot'* in that language?

1) dom 2) pul
3) ta 4) Can't be determined
5) None of these

54. In a certain language, *'pre nat bis'* means '*smoking is harmful*', *vog dor nat'* means *'avoid harmful habit'* and *'dorb is ye'* means *'please avoid smoking'*. Which of the following means *'habit'* in that language?

1) vog 2) nat 3) dor
4) bis 5) None of these

55. If *'gnr tag zog qmp'* stands for *'Seoul Olympic Organis ing Committee'*; *'hyto gnr emf'* stands for *'summer Olympic games'* and *'esm sdr hyto'* stands for *'modern games history'* what would be the code for *'summer'*?

1) hyto 2) gnr
3) emf 4) zog

56. If in a certain language, *'oka peru'* means *'fine cloth'*; *'meta lisa'* means *'clear water'* and *'donal is aperu'* means *'fine clear weather'*. Which word in that language means *'weather'*?
1) peru 2) oka
3) meta 4) dona

57. In a code language, *'mok dan si'* means *'nice big house'*; *'fit kon dan'* means *'house is good'* and *'warm tir fit'* means *'cost is high'*. Which word stands for *'good'* in that language?
1) rpok 2) dan
3) fit 4) kon

58. In a certain code language, *'Mink Yang Pe'* means *'Fruits are ripe'*; *'Pe Lao May Mink'* means *'Oranges are not ripe'* and *'May Pe Nue Mink'* means *'Mangoes are not ripe'*. Which word in that language means *'Mangoes'?*
1) May 2) Pe
3) Nue 4) Mink

Directions (Q. 59-60): In a certain code language,
(A) *'mxy das zci'* means *'good little frock'*;
(B) *'jmx cos zci'* means *'girl behaves good'*;
(C) *'nvg drs cos'* means *'girl makes mischief'*;
(D) *'das ajp cos'* means *'little girl fell'*.

59. Which word in that language stands for *'frock'?*
1) zci 2) das 3) nvgi
4) cyp 5) None of these

60. Which of the given statements is superfluous?
1) A 2) B 3) C
4) D 5) None of these

Directions (Q. 61-63): In a certain code language,
(A) *'pod na joe'* means *'very bright boy'*;
(B) *'ta mnu pod'* means *'the boy comes'*;
(C) *'nu per ton'* means *'keep the doll'*;
(D) *'joc ton su'* means *'very good doll'*.

61. Which of the following means *'bright'* in that language?
1) joc 2) pod 3) ton
4) na 5) None of these

62. Which of the following statements can be dispensed with for answering the above question?
1) A only 2) C only 3) C or D only
4) D only 5) None of these

63. To find the answer to the above question, which of the given statements is not necessary?
1) A 2) B 3) C
4) D 5) None of these

64. In a certain code language, *'nee muk pic'* means *'grave and concern'*; *'ill die so'* means *'every body else'*; and *'tur muk so'* means *'body and soul'*. Which of the following would mean *'every concern'*?
1) die pic 2) ill nee
3) pic nee 4) Can't be determined
5) None of these

65. In a certain code language, *'Ka Bi Pu Ya'* means *'You are very intelligent'*; *'Ya La Ka Wo'* means *'They seem very intelligent'*; *'La Pu Le'* means *'You can see'* and *'Sun Pun Yun Ya'* means *'How intelligent she is'*. In that language, which of the following words means *'are'*?
1) Ka 2) Bi 3) Le
4) Pu 5) Ya

66. If in a certain code, *'bir le nac'* means *'green and tasty'*; *'pic nac hor'* means *'tomato is green'* and *'coc bir hor'* means *food is tasty'*. Which of the following means *'tomato is tasty'* in that code?
1) bir le hor 2) pic hor nac
3) hor bir pic 4) None of these

67. In a certain code, '2 5 6' means *'red colour chalk'*, '5 8 9' means *green colour flower'* and '2 4 5' means *'white colour chalk'*. Which digit in that code means *'white'?*
1) 2 2) 4
3) 5 4) Can't be determined
5) None of these

68. In a certain code language, '5 2 6' means *'sky is blue'*; '2 4' means *'blue colour'* and '4 3 6' means *'colour is fun'*. Which digit in that language means *'fun'?*
1) 5 2) 4 3) 3
4) 2 5) None of these

69. In a certain code language, '3 8 1' means *'Hari is honest'*, '1 6 2' means *'Shashi is intelligent'* and '9 4 8' means *'Har is houldgo'*. Which digit in that language means *'honest'?*
1) 3 2) 8 3) 1
4) 9 5) None of these

70. In a certain code, '2 5 3' means *'books are old'*, '5 4 6' means *'man is old'* and '3 7 8' means *'buy good books'*. What stands for *'are'* in that code?
1) 2 2) 4 3) 5
4) 6 5) 9

71. In a certain code, '9 7 5' means *'Throw away garbage'*; '5 2 8' means *'Give away smoking'* and '2 1 3' means *'Smoking is harmful'*. Which digit in that code means *'Give'?*

1) 5 2) 2 3) 8
4) 3 5) None of these

Directions (Q. 72-73): In a certain code language,

(A) '1 3 4' means *'you are well',*
(B) '7 5 8' means *'they go home',*
(C) '8 3 9' means *'we are home'.*

72. Which of the following represents *'they'* in that code language?

1) 5 2) 7 3) 3
4) 8 5) Data inadequate

73. Which of the statements can be dispensed with while answering the above question?

1) A only 2) B only 3) A or C only
4) B and C only 5) None of these

Directions (Q. 74-78): According to a code language, words in column I are given in column II. Decode the language and choose the correct code for each of the words given in the following questions. The Utters in column II need not appear in the same order as they do in column I.

Column I	Column II	Column I	Column II
(1) CHIEF	(A) knqwy	(9) BASED	(I) gstnd
(2) NIGHT	(B) akwjh	(10) PSYCO	(J) qutzb
(3) THIRD	(C) kvhwg	(11) TOWEL	(K) nzche
(4) MONEY	(D) njumz	(12) FALSE	(L) ynest
(5) WOMAN	(E) zcjms	(13) DOWRY	(M) cvguz
(6) WORKS	(F) ctvzo	(14) STOCK	(N) toqhz
(7) BASIC	(G) dtwsq	(15) TRAIN	(O) swhvj
(8) HENRY	(H) jvunk		

74. AUGUST

1) hhatdb 2) llstah
3) altpss 4) nstddz

75. BOARD

1) wtvgz 2) ctdzg
3) sdwqzI 4) gzdvs

76. JUNIOR

1) jlwzvf 2) clogwj
3) flogvz 4) ljfzco

77. DIGEST

1) kwghqv 2) angwht
3) aknthj 4) gonqwt

78. DEAF
1) tgnz
2) knty
3) ygns
4) wgsd

Directions (Q. 79-80):

MATRIX 1

	0	1	2	3	4
0	D	K	A	E	C
1	C	D	K	A	E
2	K	C	E	A	D
3	K	C	D	E	A
4	E	D	A	K	C

MATRIX 2

	5	6	7	8	9
5	P	L	O	T	N
6	T	P	N	L	O
7	P	N	T	O	L
8	O	N	T	P	L
9	L	O	P	N	T

79. Find for POND?
1) 88, 99, 76, 22
2) 57, 78, 59, 32
3) 66, 96, 76, 11
4) 57, 68, 89, 42

80. Find for DONE?
1) 00, 57, 76, 41
2) 11, 78, 71, 41
3) 10, 57, 76, 37
4) 78, 11, 20, 41

Directions (Q. 81-84):

MATRIX 1

	0	1	2	3	4
0	F	A	N	O	I
1	I	O	F	A	N
2	A	N	O	I	F
3	O	F	I	N	A
4	N	I	A	F	O

MATRIX 2

	5	6	7	8	9
5	S	E	H	B	T
6	H	S	E	T	B
7	B	T	S	E	H
8	E	H	T	B	S
9	T	S	E	H	B

81. Find for NEST?
1) 33, 85, 88, 86
2) 21, 76, 77, 76
3) 14, 67, 66, 67
4) 02, 56, 55, 59

82. Find for FAITH?
1) 43, 42, 41, 78, 89
2) 31, 34, 23, 76, 79
3) 24, 31, 10, 59, 57
4) 12, 20, 40, 68, 65

83. Find for FINE?
1) 31, 32, 33, 82
2) 24, 19, 21, 78
3) 12, 10, 13, 67
4) 00, 04, 02, 56

Answers and Explanations

1. 2; Each letter in the word is moved one step forward to obtain the corresponding letter of the code.
2. 1; Each letter in the word is moved one step backward to obtain the corresponding letter of the code.
3. 1; The letters at odd positions are each moved two steps backward and those at even positions are each moved two steps forward to obtain the corresponding letters of the code.
4. 1; The letters of the word are reversed in order, taking two at a time, to obtain the code.
5. 2; The first, third and fifth letters are each moved one step backward, while the second, fourth and sixth letters are each moved one step forward to obtain the corresponding letters of the code.
6. 4; The second, fourth and sixth letters of the words remain unchanged, while the first, third and fifth letters are each moved one step backward to obtain the corresponding letters of the code.
7. 4; Each letter of the word is moved two steps forward to obtain the code.
8. 2; The first and the last letters of the word remain as such and the remaining letters are written in a reverse order to obtain the code.
9. 4; The letters of the word are written in a reverse order to obtain the code.
10. 2; Each letter of the word is moved three steps forward to obtain the code.
11. 5; The places of the first two letters and the sixth and eighth letters of the word are interchanged, while the third, fourth and fifth letters are each moved one step forward, to obtain the code.
12. 1; The letters of the word are reversed in order, taking two at a time, to obtain the code.
13. 5; The first and the last letters of the word remain unchanged, while the second and second last, third and third last letters and so on are interchanged, to obtain the code.
14. 4; The code formation can be shown as under:

Word	MUNI	CIPA	LITY
Code	INMU	APCI	YTU

15. 1; The word is divided into groups of three letters each and then the letters in each group are written in a reverse order to obtain the code.
16. 5; Each letter of the word is two steps behind of the corresponding letter of the code.
17. 3; Each letter at odd place in the word is one step behind and each letter at even place in the word is one step ahead of the corresponding letter of the code.

18. 3; The order of letters of the word is reversed in the code. So, reverse the letters in the code to get the word.

19. 4; The groups of second and third letters and fourth and fifth letters in the word interchange places in the code.

20. 2; Each letter of the word is three steps behind the corresponding letter of the code.

21. 1; The first, second, third, fourth and fifth letter in the word are respectively one, two, three, four and five steps ahead of the corresponding letter of the code.

22. 5; The word is formed into pairs of letters and the letters in each pair are reversed.

23. 2; each letter of the word moved four steps forward to obtain the code.

24. 2; The first, second, third, ... Letters of the word are respectively moved one, two, three, ... steps to backward to obtain the corresponding letters of the code.

25. 2; Each letter of the word is one step behind the corresponding letter of the code.

26. 4; Each letter of the word is one step ahead of the corresponding letter of the code.

27. 4; In the code, the first letter is one step ahead, the second letter is two steps ahead and so on than the corresponding letter in the word

28. 2; In the code, we have alternately one letter one step behind and the other one step ahead of the corresponding letter in the word.

29. 5; In the code, the first four and the last four letters of the word are separately interchanged.

30. 1; Clearly, in the code the letters at odd places arc one place ahead and those at even places are one place before the corresponding letter in the word.

So, in 35791, 3 is written as 4, 5 as 4, 7 as 8, 9 as 8 and 1 as 0 i.e. the code comes 44880.

31. 2; The same pattern as in Q. 30 is followed i.e. 4 will be written as 5, 6 as 5, 8 as 9, 2 as 1 and 3 as 4. So, the code becomes 55914.

32. 4; The alphabets are coded as shown below :

M	I	N	J	U	R	T	A	D	A
3	1	2	5	4	7	6	8	9	8

i.e. M is coded as 3, A as 8, D as 9, U as 4, R as 7 and I as 1. So, MADURAI is coded as 3894781.

33. 4; In the given code. A = 1, B = 2, C = 3, Z = 26.

So, PALAM = 16 + 1 + 12 + 1 + 13 = 43

Similarly, SANTACRUZ = 19 + 1 + 14 + 20 + 1 + 3 + 18 + 21 + 26 = 123.

34. 4; In the given code. A = 2, B = 4, C = 6, Z = 52.
So, ACT = 2 + 6 + 40 = 48 and BAT = 4+ 2 + 40 = 46.

35. 3; Code for the given word = (Number of letters in the word) – 1.
So, code for GOVERNMENT = 10 – 1 = 9.

36. 1; In the given code. Z = 1, Y =2, X = 3, C = 24, B = 25, A = 26.
So, GO = 20 + 12 = 32 and SHE = 8 + 19 + 22 = 49.
Similarly, SOME = 8+1 2 + 14 + 22 = 56.

37. 3; Taking A = 1, B = 2, ... T = 20, Z = 26, we have,
AT = A × T = 1 × 20 = 20; BAT = B × A × T = 2 ×1 × 2 0 = 40.
Similarly, CAT = C × A × T= 3 × 1 × 20 = 60.

38. 3

39. 2

40. 5

41. 3; The fruits grow on a 'tree' and 'tree' is called 'sky'. So, the fruits grow on the 'sky'.

42. 5; The colour of milk is 'white' and as given 'White' is called 'sky'. So, the colour of milk is 'sky'.

43. 3; The furniture is made up of"wood' and as given 'wood' is called 'straw'. So, the sky is made up of 'straw'.

44. 3; A person will sit on the 'chair' but a 'chair' is called 'roof'. So, the person will sit on the roof.

45. 1; Cricket if played with a 'bat' and a 'bat' is called a 'racket'. So, cricket is played with a 'racket'.

46. 4; Clearly, 'mango' is the yellow fruit but 'mango' is called "nuts'. So, 'nuts is the yellow fruit.

47. A; The colour of clear sky is 'blue' and as given, "blue' is called 'sky'. So, the colour of clear sky is 'sky'.

48. 2; 'Mat' will be spread on the floor. But 'mat' is called 'bedsheet'. So, a 'bedsheet' will be spread on the floor.

49. 4; A person will stand on the floor and 'floor' is called 'roof'. So, a person will stand on the 'roof'.

50. 1; In the first and second statements, the common code word is *'Kun'* and the common word is *'Dogs'*. So, *'Kun'* means *'Dogs'*.
In the first and third statements, the common code word is *'Tom'* and the common word ia *'are'*. So, *'Tom'* means *'are'*.
Thus, in the first statement, *'Sud'* means *'barking'*.

51. 1; In the first and third statements, the common code word is *fin'* and the common word is *'fruit'* So, *'fin'* stands for *fruit'*.
In the second and third statements, the common code word is *'sig'* and the common word is *lily'. So, 'sig'* stands for *'lily'*.
Thus, in the third statement, *'Ion'* means *'and'*.

52. 1; In the first and second statements, the common code word is *'tingo'* and the common word is *'flower'*. So, *'tingo* stands for *'flower'*.
In the second and third statements, the common code word is *'mst'* and the common word is *'sweet'*. So, *'mst'* stands for *'sweet'*.
Thus, in the second statement, *'rho'* stands for *'fragrance'*.

53. 4; We can find the code for *food'* from the first and second statements Now, to find the code for *'hot',* we need the code for *'bring'* which cannot be determined from the given information.

54. 1; In the first and second statements, the common code word is *'nat'* and the common word is *'harmful'*. So, *'nat'* stands for *'harmful'*.
In the second and third statements, the common code word is *'dor'* and the common word is *'avoid'*. So, *'dor'* stands for *'avoid'*.
Thus, in the second statement, *'vog'* means *'habit'*.

55. 3; In the first and second statements, the common code word ia *'gnr'* and the common word is *Olympic'*. So, *'gnr'* means *'Olympic'*.
In the second and third statements, the common code is *'hyto'* and the common word is *'games'*. So, *'hyto'* means *'games'*.
Thus, in the second statement, *'emf'* means *'summer'*.

56. 4; In the first and third statements, the common code word is *'peru'* and the common word is *'fine'*. So, *'peru'* means *'fine'*.
In the second and third statements, the common code word is *'lisa'* and the common word is *'clear'*. So, *'lisa'* means *'clear'*.
Thus, in the third statement, *'dona'* means *'weather'*.

57. 4; In the first and second statements, the common code word is *'dan'* and the common word is *'house'*. So, *'dan'* stands for *'house'*.
In the second and third statements, the common code word is *'fit'*. So, *'fit'* stands for *'is'*.
Thus, in the second statement, *'kon'* stands for *'good'*.

58. 3; In the second and third statements, the common code words are *'Pe'*, *'Mink'* and *'May'* and the common words are *'are'*, *'not'* and *'ripe'*.
So, in the third statement, *'Nue'* stands for *'mangoes'*.

59. 5; In statements A and B. the common code word is *'zci'* and the common word is *'good'*. So, *'zci'* stands for *'good'*.
In statements A and D, the common code word is *'das'* and the common word is *'little'*. So, *'das'* stands for *little'*. So, in (A), *'mxy'* means *'frock'*.

60. 3; Clearly, statement (C) is not required.

61. 4; In statements (A) and (B), the common code word is *'pod'* and the common word is *'boy'*. So, *'pod'* stands for *'boy'*. In statements (A) and (D). the common code word is *'joc'* and the common word is *'very'*. So, *'joc'* stands for *'ta'*. So, in (A), *'na'* stands for *'bright'*.

62. 2; Clearly, statement (C) is not required and can be dispensed with.

63. 1; Clearly, statement (A) is not required.

64. 4; Proceeding as in above questions, the code for *'every'* is either *'ill'* or *'die'* and the code for *'concern'* is either *'nee'* or *'pic'*.

65. 2; In the first and second statements, the common code words are *'Ka'* and *'Ya'* and the common words are *'very'* and *'intelligent'*. So, *'Ka'* and *'Ya'* are the codes for *'very'* and *'intelligent'*. In the first and third statements, the common code word is *'Pu'* and the common word is *'You'* So, *'Pu'* stands for You'.
Thus, in the first statement, '*Bi'* stands for *'are'*.

66. 3; In the first and second statements, the common code word is *'nac'* and the common word is *'green'*. So, *'nac'* stands for *'green'*.
In the second and third statements, the common code word is *'La'* and the common word is *'is'*. So, *'hor'* stands for *'is'*.
So, in the second statement, *'pic'* means *'tomato'*. In the first and third statements, the common code word is *'bir'* and the common word is *tasty'*. So, *'bir'* stands for *tasty'*.

67. 2; In the second and third statements, the common code digit is '5' and the common word is *'colour'*. So, '5' means *'colour'*.
In the first and third statements, '5' means *'colour'*. The other common code digit is '2' and the common word is *'chalk'*. So, '2' means *'chalk'*.
Thus, in the third statement, '4' means *'white'*.

68. 3; In the First and third statements, the common code digit is '6' and the common word is '6'. So, '6' means '$'. In the second and third statements, the common code digit is '4' and the common word is *'colour'*. So, '4' means *'colour'*.
Thus, in the third statement. '3' means *'fun'*.

69. 1; In the first and second statements, the common code digit is T and the common word is *'is'*. So, T means *'is'*.
In the first and third statements, the common code digit is '8' and the common word is *'Hari'*. So, '8' stands for *'Hari'*.
Thus, in the first statement, '3' means *'honest'*.

70. 1; In the first and second statements, the common code digit is '5' and the common word is *'old'*. So, '5' means *'old'*. In the first and third statements, the common code digit is '3' and the common word is *'books'*. So, '3' means *'books'*.
Thus, in the first statement, '2' means *'are'*.

71. 3; In the first and second statements, the common code digit is '5' and the common word is *'away'*. So, '5' means *'away'*.
In the second and third statements, the common code digit is '2' and the common word is *'smoking'*. So, '2' means *'smoking'*.
Thus, in the second statement, '3' means *'Give'*.

(72-73): We can find the code for 'home' from the second and third statements. For finding the code for 'they', we need the code for 'go' which cannot be determined from the given data.

72. 5; Data inadequate

73. 1; Clearly, statement A is not necessary.

(74-78): In CHIEF and PSYCO, the common code letter is q and the common letter is C. So, q stands for C.

In CHIEF and MONEY, the common code letter n stands for E. In CHIEF and HENRY, the common code letter n stands for E. So, the other common code letter k stands for H.

In CHIEF and BASIC, the common code letter q stands for C. So, the other common code letter w stands for 1.

Thus, in CHIEF, the remaining code letter y stands for F.

In NIGHT and MONEY, the common code letter j stands for N. In NIGHT and TOWEL, the common code letter h stands for T. Thus, in NIGHT, the remaining code letter a stands for G.

In THIRD and BASED, the common code letter g stands for D. Thus, in THIRD, the remaining code letter v stands for R.

In MONEY and WORKS, the common code letter z stands for O. In MONEY and PSYCO, the common code letter z stands for O.

So, the other common code letter u stands for Y. In MONEY and WOMAN, the common code letter % stands for O and j stands for N. So, the remaining code letter m stands for M. In WORKS and TOWEL, the common code letter z stands for O.

So, the remaining common code letter c stands for W.

In WORKS and BASIC, the common code letter is t and the common letter is 8. So, t stands for S. Thus, in WORKS, the remaining code letter o stands for K.

In BASIC and FALSE, the common code letter t stands for 8. So, the other common code letter 8 stands for A.

In BASIC and BASED, the common code letters s and t stand for A and 8 respectively.

So, the remaining code letter d stands for B. In PSYCO, the remaining code letter b stands for P.

The information can he summarised as follows:

Code	q	n	k	w	y	j	h	a	k	v	z	u	m	c	t	o	s	d	b	i
Letter	C	E	H	I	F	N	T	G	D	R	O	Y	M	W	S	K	A	B	P	1

74. 2; The code for A is s, for G is a, for S is t and for T is h.

So, the code contains the letters, sath which are contained in llstah only.

75. 4; The code for B is d, for O is z, for A is s, for R is v and for D is g. BOARD is coded as dzsvg or gzdvs.

76. 1; The code for U as in Q. 36 is I, for N is j, for I is w, for O is z and for R is v.
So, the code for JUNIOR contains jwzv.

77. 2; The code for D is g. for I is wf for G is a, for E is n, for S is t and for T is h.
So, the code for DIGEST is gwanth or angwht.

78. 3; The code for D is g for E is n, for A is s and for F is y.
So, the code for DEAF is gnsy or ygns.

79. 3; From matrix 2, P can be coded as 55, 66, 75, 88 or 97.
From matrix 2, O can be coded as 57, 69, 78, 85 or 96.
From matrix 2, N can be coded as 59, 67, 76, 86 or 98.
From matrix 1, D can be coded as 00, 11, 24, 32 or 41.
Clearly, only (3) contains all correct codes.

80. 1; From matrix 1, D can be coded as 00, 11, 24, 32 or 41.
From matrix 2, O can be coded as 57, 69, 78, 85 or 96.
From matrix 2, N can be coded as 59, 67, 76, 86 or 98.
From matrix 1, E can be coded as 03, 14, 22, 33 or 40.
Clearly, only (1) contains all correct codes.

81. 4; From matrix 1, N can be coded as 02, 14, 21, 33 or 40.
From matrix 2, E can be coded as 56, 67, 78, 85 or 97.
From matrix 2, Scan be coded as 55, 66, 77, 89 or 96.
From matrix 2, T can be coded as 59, 68, 76, 87 or 95.
Clearly, only (4) contains all correct codes.

82. 2; From matrix 1, F can be coded as 00, 12, 24, 31 or 43.
From matrix 1, A can be coded as 01, 13, 20, 34 or 42.
From matrix 1, I can be coded as 04, 10, 23, 32 or 41.
From matrix 2, T can be coded as 59, 68, 76, 87 or 95.
From matrix 2, H can be coded as 57, 65, 79, 86 or 98.
Clearly, only(b) contains all correct codes.

83. 4; From matrix 1, F can be coded as 00, 12, 24, 31 or 43.
From matrix 1, I can be coded as 04, 10, 23, 32 or 41.
From matrix 1, N can be coded as02, 14, 21, 33 or 40.
From matrix 2, E can be coded as 56, 67, 78, 85 or 97.
Clearly, only (4) contains all correct codes.

Chapter Eighteen

Coded Relationships

18.1: Introduction

This type of problems is also a relatively new feature but nowadays it is appearing quite frequently. The problem involves interpreting a given relationship-string which is coded in a particular fashion and then matching it with the relationship mentioned in the question. The process of decoding each and every relation and then interpreting from the given relationship-string the final relationship is a cumbersome process and doing all of it for all the choices makes it very time taking. However, some clever short-cut techniques may make the solution miraculously quick. Let us see how. But before that, let us have a look at a sample problem.

18.2: A sample problem

Directions (Q. 1-5): Read the following information to answer the questions:

A + B means A is the father of B

A – B means A is the sister of B

A × B means A is the husband of B

A ÷ B means A is the wife of B

1. Which of the following means 'T is the nephew of Q'?

   1) Q × R - S + T 2) Q + R ÷ S + T 3) Q - R ÷ S + T

   4) Q ÷ R + S - T 5) None of these

2. Which of the following means 'S has a blood-relationship with T'?

   1) S ÷ R + T × Q 2) S ÷ Q + R × T 3) S - R × T - Q

   4) S × Q - R - T 5) None of these

18.3: Our standard code

In order to explain many of the points that I am going to make later in the chapter, I will be referring to some of these codes again and again. In order to avoid confusion and also to avoid repetition, I am going to follow one standard set of codes for the rest of this chapter. (Later, of course, when we face the actual problems we will follow the coding pattern as given in *that* problem.) So, our standard coding system for the rest of the chapter will be as follows:

Type I (Forward type)

A + B means A is the father of B

A – B means A is the mother of B

A × B means A is the brother of B

A ÷ B means A is the sister of B

A @ B means A is the husband of B

A Δ B means A is the wife of B

A α B means A is the son of B

A β B means A is the daughter of B

Type II (Backward type)

A ^ B means B is the father of A

A ~ B means B is the mother of A

A # B means B is the brother of A

A $ B means B is the sister of A

A γ B means B is the husband of A

A δ B means B is the wife of A

$A > B$ means B is the son of A

$A < B$ means B is the daughter of A

Note: Difference between Forward type and Backward type codes

The difference is obvious by its very appearance. In the forward type codes, the first person is the given relation of the second person. For example, in A + B, the relationship is of *father*. Now, in A + B, A appears first and B later. So, A is the father of B means it is a forward-type code. But in the backward type code, the second person is the given relation of the first person. For example, in A ^ B, the relationship is again that of *father. But, here, the second man is the father*. So, here, the meaning is that *B is the father of A* and hence it is a backward-type coding.

As another example compare, A - B and A ~ B. In both these cases, the relationship is that of *mother*. But in first case, A is the mother of B and in the second, B is the mother of A. Therefore, the first is a forward-type code while the second is a backward-type code.

18.4: Some Quick Techniques for Eliminating Wrong Answers

We will now discuss some quick methods to eliminate the wrong answers:

Rule I: Check sex:

Sometimes the person under consideration must be a male (or a female) if the given answer choice were to be true. But the choices start with informations that the person is a mother- sister .. (or a father, brother.) etc, which means that this choice can be easily eliminated.

Consider the following examples to understand this.

Ex. 1: Which of the following means that "A is the grandmother of B"?

1) $A + B \times C - D \div F$ 2) $A \times C - D + B \times F$

3) $A - B - C + D + E$ 4) $A - C \times B + D \div F$

5) None of these

Here, in this question, since A is to be the grandmother of B. A must be a female. But the very first words in (1) and (2) mean that A is a male. Because in (1), A + B means A is the father (a male) of B and in (2), A × C means A is the brother (a male) of C. Therefore, in these two choices we don't need to look any further and straightaway eliminate them.

Ex. 2: Which of the following means that "X is the grandson of Y"?

1) X ÷ A + B - C × Y 2) X ÷ A α B α C ÷ Y

3) X α A ÷ B ÷ C α Y 4) X β A β B × C × Y

5) None of these

Here, in this question, if X is to be the grandson of Y, X must be a male. But the very first words in choices (1), (2) and (4) make X out to be a female. For example, in (1), X ÷ A means X is a sister (hence a female) of A. Same is true of (2). In (4), X β A means X is a daughter (hence a female) of A. Therefore, we can straightaway eliminate choices (1), (2) and (4).

Ex. 3: Which of the following means that "B is the grandfather of E"?

1) A > B > C # D > E 2) A < B < C # D > E

3) A $ B $ C # D $ E 4) A $ B $ C > D # E

5) None of these

Here, in this question, since B is to be the grandfather of E; B must be a male. But choice (2), (3) and (4) are quickly rejected as these B turns out to be a female in the first glance. For example, in (2): A < B means B is the daughter (hence, a female) of A; in (3) A $ B means B is the sister (hence a female) of A and same in (4). Hence, (2), (3), (4) are quickly eliminated.

Note: Note that Ex. 3 was a case where the relationships were coded in the *backward type* format. And in this case we rejected the wrong choices (2), (3) and (4) because there the code that indicated the wrong sex of B appeared **before** B.

[See, A < B in (2), A $ B in (3) and (4)]. On the other hand, in Ex. 1 and Ex. 2, the relationships were coded in the *forward type* format. And in that case we rejected the wrong choices because there the codes that indicated the wrong sex of A and X appeared *after* A and X.

For example, [See, A + B in (1) and A × C in (2) of Ex. 1, X ÷ A in (1) and (2) and X β A in (4) of Ex. 2].

This gives us our brief and quick short-cut technique.

In forward-type coding, reject an answer choice if the symbol immediately *after* the person in question indicates the wrong sex. Conversely, reject the choice if the symbol immediately *before* the person in question indicates the wrong sex, in case of backward-type coding.

To understand the above rule consider Ex. 1, Ex. 2, Ex. 3 once again:

Ex. 1: Person in question is A (because the question wants us to find if A is the grandmother). All codings are forward-type. Now, immediately **after** A, we have + and × signs in choices (1) and (2) respectively and these indicate the wrong sex because + and × mean father and brother respectively which is a male-sex. So, (1) and (2) are eliminated.

Ex. 2: Person in question is X (because the question wants us to find if X is a grandson). Codings are forward-type. Now, immediately **after** X, we have ÷ in (1) and (2) and β in (4). They indicate wrong (female) sex as + stands for sister and β stands for daughter. So, choices 1, 2 and 4 are quickly eliminated.

Ex. 3: Person in question is B (because the question wants us to find if B is a grandfather). Here, the codings are backward-type and hence we analyse the symbols immediately *before* B. The symbols immediately before B are <, $ and $ in choice 2, 3 and 4. They indicate the wrong sex (famale) as < stands for daughter and $ stands for sister. So, 2, 3 and 4 are quickly eliminated.

Rule II: Check Generation-gap

It may be time-consuming to actually draw the family-tree (using the method I am going to describe later) and see if A is indeed a, say, grandfather of say, B. But we can easily and quickly check by giving mere cursory glances that A is indeed two generations over B. So, all choices that are possibly correct must have a generation gap of 2 between A and B. *Using this tip we can eliminate all the choices that don't have this neessary generation gap.*

Consider the following statements, for example:

1) A + B + C   2) A × B × C

3) A × B + C   4) A - B Δ C α D

In (1), we have, A is the father of B and B is the father of C. Clearly, A is the grandfather of C. The generation gap is *two*, between A and C. The gap between A and B is 1 (because A is father of B). Similarly, gap between B and C is 1. So, gap between A and C is 1 + 1 = 2.

In (2), we have A is brother of B who is brother of C. Clearly, A is brother of C. So, there is no i.e. zero generation-gap. The gap between A and B is 0 (as A and B are of the same generation, i.e. brothers) and that between B and C is 0. So, gap between A and C is 0 + 0 = 0.

In (3), we have A is brother of B who is father of C. Clearly, A is uncle of C. So, there is a gap of one generation between A and C. Here, gap between A and B is zero (as A and B are brothers and, therefore, of the same generation) and that between B and C is 1 (as B is father of C). So, gap between A and C is 0 + 1 = 1.

In 4, we have: A is mother of B, who is wife of C who is son of D. Clearly, A is the *Samdhan* of D and the generation-gap between them is zero. Here, gap between A and B is 1 (because A is a mother of B), that between B and C is zero (as they are husband and wife and hence, no generation gap), that between C and D is **minus one** or **-1*** (as C is a son of D). So, the total gap between A and D is 1 + 0 + (-1) = 0.

- Since a son is a generation below the father's generation, we take the gap as negative. So, in cases of sons or daughters, the generation gap is taken as 1. By the foregoing analysis it is clear that:

> for father/mother: gap is taken as +1
> for brother/sister/husband/wife: gap is taken as 0
> for son/daughter: gap is taken as -1

Now for each choice, calculate the generation-gap between two persons. If it is proper we don't reject the choice but if it is not we reject it. For example if A is to be the grandfather of B, the gap between A and B must be 2. Similarly if X is to be the grandniece of Y, the gap between X and Y must be -2.

How to calculate the generation-gap between two persons

We give below an easy, step-by-step approach to calculate the generation gap:

- Take one of the persons under consideration
- Move rightwards. For each father/mother relation put a +1, for each brother/sister/husband/wife relation put a 0, for each son/daughter relation put a -1.
- Do the sum total

Note: The above is applicable **only for forward-type** coding. *In the backward-type coding, the process remains the same but there is one minor change.* **Here, instead of moving to the right, we start from the right side and move to the left.** Rest of the method remains the same.

Ex. 4: Consider the following: A - B × C β D α E Δ F × G

Find the generation gap between

(i) A and C (ii) C and E (iii) E and B (iv) G and A

Soln: (i) A and C

Since A is on left we start from A and move towards C. – means mother so we write +1, × means brother so we write 0.

gap: +1 + 0 = +1.

[**Conclusion:** A is of C's father's generation]

(ii) C and E

Since C is to the left of E, we start from C and move righwards to E. We have a β and an α between C and E. Since both are son/daughter relations we write -1 for both.

gap: (-1) + (-1) = -2

[**Conclusion:** C is of E's grandson's generation]

(iii) E and B

Since E is to the right of B, we don't start from E. We start from left i.e. we start from B and move right. × means brother so we write 0, β means daughter so we write -1 and α means son so we write -1.

gap: 0 + (-1) + (-1) = -2

[**Conclusion:** B is E's grandson's generation]

Note: If gap between B and E is -2, gap between E and B is +2. In other words, E is B's grandfather's generation.

(iv) G and A

We start from A as A is on the left of G. – means mother so we write +1, for × we write 0, for β we write -1, for α we write -1, for Δ we write 0, for × we write 0.

gap: +1 + 0 + (-1) + (-1) + 0 + 0 = -1

[**Conclusion:** A is G's son's generation]

Note: If gap between A and G is -1, gap between G and A is +1. In other words, G is A's father's generation.

Ex. 5: Consider the following:

S # R δ Q > P < O # N ^ M

Find the generation gap between

(i) S and Q (ii) R and O (iii) O and Q (iv) M and S

Soln: (i) S and Q

This is a backward-coding case. So, we will always take the right letter and move to the left.

Here, we take Q and move to the left. δ means wife so we write 0, # means brother so we write 0.

gap: 0 + 0 = 0

[**Conclusion:** S and Q are of the same generation.]

(ii) R and O

We take O and proceed to the left. < means daughter so we write -1, > means son so we write -1, δ means wife so we write 0.

gap: (-1) + (-1) + 0 = -2

[**Conclusion:** O is R's grandson's generation].

Note: If gap between O and R is -2, gap between R and O is +2. In other words, R is O's grandfather's generation.

(iii) O and Q

We take O and proceed to the left. For < we write –1 and for > we write -1.

gap: (-1) + (-1) = -2.

[**Conclusion:** O is Q's grandson's generation]

(iv) M and S

We take M and proceed to the left. For ^ we write +1; for #, 0, for <, -1, for >, -1, for δ, 0, for # 0.

gap: +1 + 0 + (–1) + (–1) + 0 + 0 = –1

[**Conclusion:** M is S's son's generation]

Tip: In our examples, we are considering more than six relations in a single expression. We are also considering backward-type coding. *In the examinations, you'll generally get only forward- type coding* and there too, not more than three-four relations in a single expression. In that case, finding generation-gap is still easier and fast. *Just take the two persons under consideration and consider the symbols between them. Ignore all brother/sister/husband/wife/relations, put +1 for mother-father and -1 for son-daughter and; add. Usually we have forward-coding, so start from left to right.*

18.5: Drawing a family tree

The tips given in 18.4 are techniques for quicly eliminating the obviously wrong answers. But even after employing that technique, we may not be able to eliminate *all* the wrong choices. In that case, two or more choices may still be left for consideration. If that be the case, we will have to actually analyse each of these remaining choices and see which one is correct.

The best way to draw quick conclusions about relationships in these type of questions is by drawing a family tree. [Detailed method of drawing a family tree is given in chapter 12. See Ex. 10, Ex. 11, Chapter 12] Here we give a brief method:

Drawing a family tree

(a) Vertical or diagonal lines should be used to represent parent-child relationships.

(b) A double horizontal line (like ⇔) should be used to represent marriages.

(c) a dashed line should be used to represent brother or sister relationships.

[**Note:** Apart from dashed lines, brother or sister relationships are also easily established if two persons have the same root (i.e. parents depicted by vertical or diagonal lines).]

(d) Put a + sign before someone who is a male and a - sign before someone who is a female.

(e) Whenever something is not known put a ? mark or some such symbol (x, y, z etc., for example) before it.

For example, consider the following diagram:

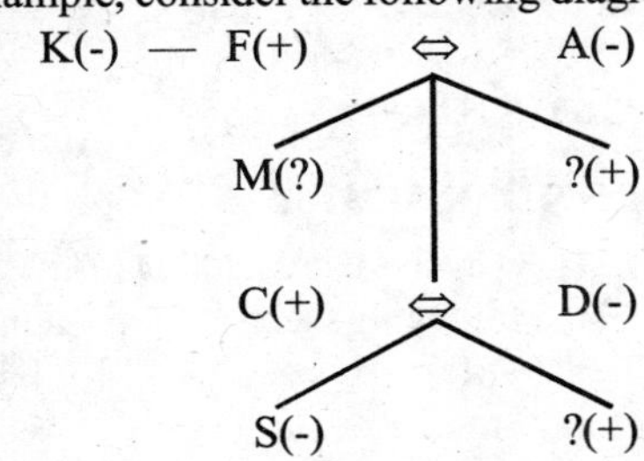

The above diagram tells us that:

(i) F and A are a couple; F is the husband while A is the wife.
(ii) F has a sister K.
(iii) The couple, F and A, has three children: M, C and another son, whose name is not known. C is also a son while the sex of M is not known.
(iv) M and the other unknown son are unmarried while C is married to D.
(v) The couple, C and D, has a daughter S and a son whose name is not known.

18.6: Suggested method for solution

We are now in a position to lay down our integrated approach towards our solution. That is:

Step I: Eliminate all wrong choices by the quick method discussed in S 18.4 i.e.
(a) **check sex**, and (b) **check generation-gap**
Step II: Draw family-tree for the remaining choices and pick the correct answer.

18.7: Complete solution to our sample problem

Quick methods

1. **Check sex:** If T is to be a nephew, T must be a male. But in all the choices sex of T is uncertain. So, eliminate all choices. Hence, correct answer is 5.
2. If S has to have a blood relationship with T and nothing else, we don't need to check either the sex of S or the gap between S and T. We straightaway draw the family trees:

1) S(-) ⇔ R(+)
|
T(+) ⇔ Q(-)

Clearly, S is mother of T.

A relationship of mother-son is clearly a blood-relation and we have found our answer. Correct choice is 1.

But let us have a look at the other options, merely for academic interest:

2) S(-) ⇔ Q(+) (S is mother-in-law of T)
|
R(+) ⇔ T(-)

3) S(-) — R(+) ⇔ T(-) — Q(?) (S is sister-in-law of T)

4) S(+) ⇔ Q(-) — R(-) — T(-) (S is brother- in-law of T)

18.8: Some more solved problems

Ex. 6: P × Q means P is the sister of Q; P + Q means P is the father of Q; P - Q means P is the mother of Q. Which of the following means S is the aunt of T?

1) T × M + S 2) S + T × M 3) S × M + T
4) S × M + R - T 5) None of these

Soln: If S is to be the aunt of T, S must be a female and S must be one generation over T.

Check sex: Immediately *after* S, we should not have a + sign because + stands for father which is a male relation.

This means choice (1) [because here sex of S is uncertain] and (2) are eliminated.

Check generation-gap: In choice (4), we have a generation gap of 2. [Start from S to T, we get an ×, a + and a - sign which stand for sister, father and a mother, respectively. So, put a 0 for ×, 1 for + and 1 for -. So, total gap is $0 + 1 + 1 = 2$]. Hence, choice 4 is eliminated.

Now we are left with only choice (3) or none of these (choice 5). Let us draw a family tree for choice (3) and check:

```
S(-) — M(+)
         |
        T(?)
```

∴ S is aunt of T

∴ Correct choice: (3)

Ex. 7: If $A + B$ means A is the son of B, $A - B$ means A is the husband of B, $A \times B$ means A is the sister of B, then which of the following shows the relation that Q is the maternal uncle of P?

1) $P + B - R \times Q$ 2) $P - B + R \times Q$ 3) $P + B \times R - Q$
4) $P \times B - R + Q$ 5) None of these

Soln: If Q is to be maternal uncle of P; Q must be a male and Q must be one generation over P. Now:

Check sex: (By our rule, there must not be a × sign immediately after Q as × stands for a sister i.e. a female. There must instead be a + or - sign immediately after Q as + or - stand for 'son' and 'husband' respectively, which are male relations). But in all four choices there are no signs *after* Q: this means sex of Q is *uncertain*. But Q must certainly be a male in order to be a maternal uncle. Correct choice: (5).

Ex. 8: If $A + B$ means A is the mother of B; $A \div B$ means A is the brother of B; $A \times B$ means A is the son of B and $A - B$ means A is the daughter of B, which of the following means C is the niece of D?

1) $D - C$ 2) $D \times P - C$ 3) $C - P \div D$
4) $P + D \div C$ 5) $D - P \div C$

Soln: If C is to be a niece of D; C must be a female and C must be one generation below D. Now,

Check sex: (By our rule, immediately after C there must be a + (mother) or - (daughter) signs.) This eliminates choices (1), (2), (4) and (5).

The only choice left is (3). Correct choice: (3).

Ex. 9: If X o Y means X is the wife of Y; X * Y means X is the son of Y and X □ Y means X is the sister of Y, which of the following would mean that A is the daughter of B?

1) A * C □ D o B 2) A o C * D □ B 3) A □ C o D * B
4) A □ C * D o B 5) None of these

Soln: If A is to be the daughter of B, A must be a female and A must be one generation below B. Now:

Check sex: (By our rule, there must be a o or a □ *after* A as these are female relations). This eliminates choice (1).

Check generation gap: (By our rule, we will start from A to B and put a zero for o, -1 for * and zero for □). By this rule, generation gap between A and B is -1 in all the remaining choices 2, 3 and 4.

So, we draw a family tree for these choices, one by one:

Choice 2:

```
        D(-) — B(?)
          |
A(-) ⇔ C(+)
```

∴ A is niece of B

Choice 3:

```
         B(?)
           |
A(-) — C(-) ⇔ D(+)
```

∴ A is daughter-in-law of B.

Choice 4:

```
B(+) ⇔ D(-)
          |
  A(-) — C(+)
```

∴ A is daughter of B.

Correct choice: 4.

Directions (Ex. 10-11): Answer the questions on the basis of the direction given below:

Ex. 10: If (A) P + Q means P is the brother of Q,
(B) P × Q means P is the father of Q,
(C) P - Q means P is the sister of Q,

which of the following represents S is the niece of T?

1) T × M + S - K 2) K - S × M + T 3) T + M × S - K
4) T × S + M - K 5) None of these

Ex. 11: To find out the answer to the above question, which of the statements can be dispensed with?

1) A only 2) B only 3) C only
4) B or C only 5) All are necessary

Soln:

Ex. 10: If S is to be a niece of T, S must be a female and S must be one generation below T.

Check sex: There must be a - sign after S. This eliminates choices (2) and (4).

Check generation gap: Since T is on the left (and the coding is forward-type) we will proceed from T to S. If S must be one generation *below* T, T (in other words) must be one generation *over* S. That is, generation gap between T and S must be +1.

By our rule, we will move from T to S and assign a +1 for × and 0 for + or –. This eliminates neither choice (1) nor (3).

Choice (1): Proceed from T to S. We get a × sign. It means a 'father', so put a +1. Then we get a + sign. It means a 'brother', so put a 0. Net gap: 1 + 0 = 1

Choice (3): Start from T to S. We get a + sign which means 'brother'. So we put a 0. Then we get a × sign which means 'father'. So, we put a +1. Net gap = 0 + 1 = 1.

So, we draw a family tree for choices (1) and (3).

Choice (1):

```
T(+)
|                                   ∴ S is daughter of T.
 M(+) — S(-) — Q(?)
```

Choice 3:

```
T(+) — M(+)
        |                ∴ S is niece of T.
       S(-) — K(?)
```

Correct choice: 3.

Ex. 11: We have found our answer (3) in the previous question by making use of all the three given signs. So, all are necessary. Correct choice: 5.

Directions (Ex. 12-14): Read the following information and answer the questions given below it:

A + B means A is the daughter of B; A × B means A is the son of B and A - B means A is the wife of B.

12. If P × Q - S, which of the following is true?
    1) S is wife of Q 2) S is father of P 3) P is daughter of Q
    4) Q is father of P 5) None of these
13. If T - S × B - M, which of the following is not true?
    1) B is mother of S 2) M is husband of B 3) T is wife of S
    4) S is daughter of B 5) S is son of B
14. If Z × T - S × U + P, what is U to Z ?
    1) Mother 2) Grandmother 3) Father
    4) Can't be determined 5) None of these

Soln: In these questions, we do not have to find out the correct coded relationship for a given relation. Instead, here the coded relation is given and we merely have to decode it. Hence, the first steps of check sex and generation gap are not needed here. We only have to draw the family tree to decode the given relation.

Ex. 12: Q(-) ⇔ S(+)
|
P(+)

∴ S is father of P.

Correct choice: 2.

Ex. 13: M(+) ⇔ B(-)
|
T(-) ⇔ S(+)

∴ (i) B is mother of S
(ii) M is husband of B
(iii) T is wife of S
(iv) S is son of B
Correct choice: 4

Quicker method: Consider choice (4) and (5). S can be either a son or a daughter of B. So, one of these choices must be false. But in the given statement, immediately after S we have a × sign (which is a *male* sign as × stands for 'son'). So, by our rule in section 18.4; × must be a male. Hence, choice 4 must be false.

∴ Correct answer: 4.

Ex. 14: P(?)
|
U(-)
|
T(-) ⇔ S(+)
|
Z(+)

∴ U is grandmother of Z.

Correct choice: 2.

Practice Exercises

Directions (Q. 1-4): Read the following information carefully and answer the questions given below it:

P ÷ Q means P is the father of Q
P + Q means P is the mother of Q
P - Q means P is the brother of Q
P × Q means P is the sister of Q

1. If A + B ÷ C - D, then A is D's
1) sister 2) grandfather 3) grandmother
4) father 5) None of these
2. If A × B ÷ C - D + E, then A is E's
1) great-aunt 2) brother 3) maternal uncle
4) mother 5) None of these

3. Which of the following shows that A is the aunt of E?

1) A - B + C ÷ D × E   2) A × B ÷ C × D - E   3) A ÷ B × C + D - E

4) A + B - C × D ÷ E   5) None of these

4. P - Q means Q is son of P and P × Q means P is brother of Q, P ÷ Q means Q is sister of P, and P + Q means P is mother of Q. Which of the following is definitely TRUE about N × K - M ÷ L?

1) K is father of L and M.

2) L is the daughter of K and is the niece of her uncle N.

3) K is the father of M and L - his son and daughter respectively.

4) M is the uncle of K's brother N.

5) None of these

Directions (Q. 5-6): Read the following inforamtion to answer these questions.

(i) A Δ B means A is mother of B.

(ii) A © B means A is sister of B.

(iii) A * B means A is father of B.

(iv) A β B means A is brother of B.

5. Which of the following means X is uncle of Y?

1) X β Z © K Δ J © γ   2) X © N Δ A β γ   3) γ © N * L © X

4) X © C Δ K * γ   5) None of these

6. Which of the following means R is grandfather of Q?

1) QΔF*E*R   2) R*S©TΔQ   3) RβLβM*Q

4) R*G*HΔQ   5) None of these

Directions (Q. 7-12): Read the following information carefully and then answer the questions given below.

i) A Δ B means A is mother of B.

ii) A ● B means A is sister of B.

iii) A * B means A is father of B

iv) A β B means A is brother of B.

7. Which of the following means R is uncle of T?

1) R*PβSΔQ●T   2) S*PβR*UβT   3) P*RβQ●S*T

4) P*R●Q●S*T   5) None of these

8. Which of the following means L is paternal grandfather of O?

1) L*R●Mβ KβO   2) R*LΔPβK● O   3) L*MΔR*KβO

4) L*RβM*KβO   5) None of these

9. Which of the following means X is mother of U?

1) XΔYβZ * K●U   2) PβXΔOβU   3) XΔZ ●KβY*U

4) P*XΔY*OβU   5) None of these

10. Which of the following means R is daughter of P?
1) P*LβKβR 2) XΔP*R ●O 3) XΔY● PΔKβ L●R
4) XΔP*RβO 5) None of these

11. Which of the following means C is cousin of E?
1) CΔMβN*E 2) PΔCβMβE 3) OβCβN*MβE
4) EβM*N●C 5) None of these

12. If '×' means 'is father of', '+' means 'is sister of', '-' means 'is brother of', and '÷' means 'is mother of' then which of the statements means 'S' is granddaughter of 'P'?
1) P × T + R ÷ S 2) P ÷ Q - R ÷ S - T 3) P × R - T × S
4) P ÷ Q - R × S + T 5) None of these

Directions (Q. 13-14): Read the following information to answer the questions.

i) A Δ B means A is mother of B.
ii) A●B means A is sister of B.
iii) A * B means A is father of B.
iv) A β B means A is brother of B.

13. Which of the following means 'Q is grandfather of P'?
1) P Δ N * M * Q 2) Q * N ● M Δ P 3) Q β M β N * P
4) Q * M ● N Δ P 5) None of these

14. Which of the following means N is uncle of M?
1) NβP ● LΔE ●M 2) N●YΔAβM 3) M●Y*P ●N
4) NβCΔF*M 5) None of these

15. P + Q means P is the brother of Q, P - Q means P is the mother of Q and P × Q means P is the sister of Q. Which of the following means M is the maternal uncle of R?
1) M + K + R 2) M - R + K 3) M + K - R
4) M + K × R 5) None of these

16. If A + B means A is the brother of B. A ÷ B means A is the father of B and A × B means A is the sister of B, which of the following means M is the uncle of P?
1) N × P ÷ M 2) M + S ÷ R ÷ P 3) M ÷ N × P
4) M + K ÷ T × P 5) None of these

Directions (Q. 17-19): Study the following information given below and answer the questions that follow:

A + B means A is the daughter of B.
A - B means A is the husband of B.
A × B means A is the brother of B.

17. If P + Q - R, which of the following is true?
1) R is the mother of P. 2) R is the sister-in-law of P.
3) R is the aunt of P. 4) R is the mother-in-law of P.
5) None of these

18. If $P \times Q + R$, which of the following is true?
    1) P is the brother of R.
    2) P is the uncle of R.
    3) P is the son of R.
    4) P is the father of R.
    5) None of these
19. If $P + Q \times R$, which of the following is true?
    1) P is the niece of R.
    2) P is the daughter of R.
    3) P is the cousin of R.
    4) P is the daughter-in-law of R.
    5) None of these
20. If $P + Q$ means P is the husband of Q; $P \div Q$ means P is the sister of Q and $P \times Q$ means P is the son of Q, which of the following shows A is the daughter of B?
    1) $C \times B \div A$
    2) $B + C \times A$
    3) $D \times B + C \div A$
    4) $A \div D \times B$
    5) None of these
21. X - Z means X is the mother of Z; $X \times Z$ means X is the father of Z and $X + Z$ means X is the daughter of Z. Now, if $M - N \times T + Q$, then which of the following is not true?
    1) T is N's daughter
    2) N is wife of Q
    3) M is mother-in-law of Q
    4) Q is wife of N
    5) T is granddaughter of M

Directions (Q. 22-24): Read the following information to answer the questions:

$A + B$ means A is father of B.

$A - B$ means A is sister of B.

$A \times B$ means A is husband of B

$A \div B$ means A is wife of B.

22. Which of the following means S is granddaughter of R?
    1) $R + P \div Q + S$
    2) $K \div R + P \times Q - L + S$
    3) $K \div R + P \div Q + S - L$
    4) Can't be determined
    5) None of these
23. Which of the following means P has a blood-relationship with Q?
    1) $R \div P + K \times L - M + Q$
    2) $R \div P + K \div L + Q - M$
    3) $R \div P + K - L \times M - N + Q$
    4) $R \div P + K \times L - Q$
    5) None of these
24. Which of the following means P is grandmother of Q?
    1) $P \div R + S \times T - U \times Q$
    2) $P \div R + S + T \div Q$
    3) $P \div R + S + B + K \times L - Q$
    4) $P \div R + S - T + Q \times U$
    5) None of these

Directions (Q. 25-27): Read the following information to answer the questions.

(i) P # Q means Q is father of P.
(ii) P * Q means Q is mother of P.
(iii) P £ Q means Q is brother of P.
(iv) P $ Q means Q is sister of P.

25. Which of the following means X is grandmother of Y?
1) Z $ X * K # L £ Y 2) Y £ L # K * X $ Z 3) X * K # L £ Y
4) Can't be determined 5) None of these

26. Which of the following means A is nephew of D?
1) D £ C # B £ A 2) A £ B # D £ C 3) C £ D # B £ A
4) Can't be determined 5) None of these

27. Which of the following means C is aunt of F?
1) E £ F # D # C * B 2) F £ E # D $ C * B 3) B * C $ D # E £ F
4) Can't be determined 5) None of these

Directions (Q. 28-29): Read the following information carefully and answer the questions given below it.

A - B means A is the sister of B.
A × B means A is the husband of B.
A ÷ B means B is the brother of A.
A + B means B is the mother of A.

28. If P + Q - R ÷ S × T, then R is T's
1) Brother-in-law
2) Sister-in-law
3) Either brother-in-law or sister-in-law
4) Can't be determined
5) None of these

29. Which of the following shows N is the mother-in-law of K?
1) K ÷ L × M + N 2) K × L - M + N 3) K - L + M × N
4) K ÷ L + M × N 5) None of these

Directions (Q. 30-31): Read the following information carefully and answer the questions given below it.

A + B means A is the brother of B.
A - B means A is the sister of B.
A × B means A is the father of B.
A ÷ B means A is the mother of B.

30. If P ÷ Q - R × S, then P is S's
1) grandmother 2) maternal grandmother
3) maternal aunt 4) sister
5) None of these

31. Which of the following shows that T is the grandmother of W?
1) T × U + V ÷ W 2) T × U - V ÷ W 3) T + U ÷ V × W
4) T ÷ U × V - W 5) None of these

Directions (Q. 32-34): Read the following information carefully and answer the questions given below it:

A + B means A is the sister of B.

A - B means A is the father of B.

A × B means A is the brother of B.

A ÷ B means A is the mother of B.

32. If K ÷ L + M × N, then K is N's

1) aunt 2) uncle 3) great-aunt

4) grandmother 5) None of these

33. If K + L - M × N ÷ P, then K is P's

1) great-aunt 2) grandmother 3) mother

4) sister 5) None of these

34. Which of the following shows that C is the maternal grandfather of F?

1) C + D - E ÷ F 2) C × D - E + F 3) C × D + E - F

4) C - D ÷ E × F 5) None of these

35. If A + B means A is the sister of B; A - B means A is the brother of B; A × B means A is the daughter of B, which of the following shows the relation that E is the maternal uncle of D?

1) D + F × E 2) D - F × E 3) D × F + E

4) D × F - E 5) None of these

Directions (Q. 36-37): Study the following information carefully and answer the questions given below:

(i) 'P × Q' means' P is sister of Q'

(ii) 'P + Q' means 'P is mother of Q'.

(iii) 'P - Q' means 'P is father of Q'.

(iv) 'P ÷ Q' means 'P is brother of Q'.

36. Which of the following represents 'W is grandfather of H'?

1) W + T - H 2) W ÷ T - H 3) W × T + H

4) W ÷ T + H 5) None of these

37. Which of the following represents 'M is nephew of R'?

1) M ÷ T - R 2) R ÷ T - M 3) R × T + M × J

4) R ÷ T - M ÷ J 5) None of these

Directions (Q. 38-39): Read the following information carefully and answer the questions which follow:

If 'A × B' means 'A is son of B'.

If 'A + B' means A is daughter of B'.

If 'A ÷ B' means 'A is wife of B'.

If 'A – B' means 'A is father of B'.

38. What will come in place of the question mark, to establish that Q is mother of N in the following expression? 'N + O – P ? Q'

1) + 2) × 3) –

4) ÷ 5) Either (1) or (2)

39. Which of the following relations are true based upon the relations given in the equation:
'$S \div T \times V - W + Y$' ?
1) T is brother of Y.
2) S is daughter-in-law of W.
3) S is daughter-in-law of Y.
4) Y is daughter of V.
5) None is true

Answers and Explanations

1. 3; Choice 2 and 4 are wrong as A + B means A is a mother, hence a female. Generation gap between A and D is (+1) + (+1) + (0) = 2. So, A must be a grandmother.

2. 1; A × B so A is a sister, hence a female. Generation gap: (0) + (+1) + (0) + (+1) = +2.
So, A is E's grandmother's generation.
Correct choice

```
A(-) — B(+)
        |
       C(+) — D(-)
               |
               E
```

3. 2; In choice 1, generation gap is: 0 + 1 + +1 + 0 = 2. So, A is E's grandma's generation. In choice 2, gap is: 0 + 1 + 0 + 0 = 1.
In choice 3, gap is: 1 + 0 + 1 + 0 = 2. So, A is E's grandma's generation.
So, Choices 1, 3 and 4 are eliminated.
Correct choice: 2.

```
A(-) — B(+)
        |
       C(-) — D(+) — E
```

4. 2; N × K means N(+) — K(?)
K - M means K(?)

```
|
M(+)
```

M ÷ L means M(+) — L(-)
combining, N × K - M ÷ L means:

```
N(+) — K(?)
        |
       M(+) — L(-)
```

So, choice (2) is correct. Note that sex of K is not known.

5. 1; Choice 2 and 4 are wrong as they indicate that X is a female because X is followed by ©. Generation gap between X and Y in choice 1 is: 0 + 0 + 1 + 0 = 1. So, (1) could be correct. Drawing its family tree, we get:

```
X(+) — Z(-) — K(-)
               |
              J(-) — Y   Indeed, X is uncle of Y here.
```

6. 2; Choice 1 is wrong as R must appear before Q. Choice 2 has a generation gap of 1 + 0 + 1 = 2. Let us draw the family tree:

```
R(+)
|
S(-) — T(-)
        |
        Q
```

Indeed 2 is correct. Note that R is maternal grandfather of Q.

7. 3; Choice 4 is wrong as R is followed by a female sign. In choice 1, generation gap between R and T is 1 + 0 + 1 + 0 = 2. So, 1 is wrong. In choice 3, gap between R and T is 0 + 0 + 1 = 1. So, 3 could be correct. Let us draw its tree:

```
P(+)
|
R(+) — Q(-) — S(*)
               |
               T      Indeed R is an uncle of T here.
```

8. 4; Choice 2 is wrong as L is followed by a female sign. In choice 1, gap between L and O is 1 + 0 + 0 + 0 = 1. So, it is wrong. In choice 3, gap between L and O is 1 + 1 + 1 + 0 = 3; so it is wrong. In choice 4, gap is: 1 + 0 + 1 + 0 = 2. So, it could be correct. Let us try its tree:

```
L(+)
|
R(+) — M(+)
        |
       K(+) — O        Indeed L is paternal grandfather of O.
```

9. 2; Gap between X and U in choice 1 is: 1 + 0 + 1 + 0 =2, in choice 2 is = 1 + 0 = 1, in choice 3, it is: 1 + 0 + 0 + 1 =2 and in choice 4 it is 1 + 1 + 0 = 2. So, choices 1, 3 and 4 are definitely wrong. Let us try tree for choice 2:

```
P(+) — X(-)
        |
       O(+) — U        Indeed X is mother of U.
```

10. 2; In choice 1, 3; sex of R is not known while in choice 4, R is a brother as it is followed by a male sign β. So, choice 1, 3 and 4 are eliminated. Let us try tree for choice 2:

```
X(-)
|
P(+)
|
R(-) — B               Indeed R is daughter of P.
```

11. 5; If C and E are to be cousins the generation gap between C and E must be zero. But the gap is 1 + 0 + 1 = 2 in choice 1, 0 + 0 + 0 = 0 in choice 2, 0 + 1 + 0 = 1 in choice 3, 0 + 1 + 0 =1 in choice 4. So, choice 1, 3 and 4 are definitely wrong. Even, 2 is wrong as C β M β E means that C is brother of E and not cousin.

12. 4; In choice 1, 3 sex of S is not known as S is not followed by any sign that could tell its sex. Choice 2 is wrong as S is a brother and hence a male. We have only one choice remaining. Let us try its tree:

```
P(-)
 |
Q(+) — R(+)
         |
        S(-) — T
```

Indeed S is granddaughter of P.

13. 5; Choice 1 is wrong as Q appears after P which means P is of earlier generation here. *Note that choice 2 and 4 are exactly similar, only M and N are interchanged. So, if Q was grandfather of P in choice 2 it would also be so in choice 4. So, both must be wrong as both cant be correct.* So, we are left with choice 3.

But here the gap between Q and P is 0 + 0 + 1 = 1. Which means Q is P's father's generation. Hence, choice 4 is also wrong.

14. 1; Choice 2 is wrong as here N is followed by ● which means N is a female. Choice 3 is wrong as there is no sign after N indicating that sex of N is unknown. In choice 1, gap between N and M is 0 + 0 + 1 + 0 = 1.

Let us draw its tree:

```
N(+) — P(-) — L(-)
               |
              E(-) — M
```

Indeed N is uncle of M. (A maternal uncle)

15. 3; Choice 2 is wrong as here M is a mother and hence a female. In choice 1, 3 and 4, the gap between M and R is 0 + 0 = 0, 0 + 1 = 1 and 0 + 0 = 0 respectively. So, choice 1 and 4 are wrong. Let us try the tree for choice 3. We have:

```
M(+) — K(-)
         |
         R
```

Indeed M is material uncle of R here.

16. 4; Choice 1 is wrong as sex of M is unknown. Gap between M and P is 0 + 1 + 1 = 2 in choice 2, 0 + 1 = 1 in choice 3, 0 + 1 + 0 = 1 in choice 4. So, choice 3 and 4 could be possibly correct. But, common sense tells us that if M was to be an uncle of P, M must be a brother of somebody who is a father of P. Since choice 3 does not give us whether M is a brother, we settle for choice 4. Drawing its family tree we see that it indeed is a correct choice.

M(+) — K(+)
|
T(-) — P

17. 1; Q(+) ⇔ R(-)
|
P (-) R is mother of P

18. 3; R
|
P(+) — Q(-) P is son of R

19. 1; Q(+) — R P is niece of R
|
P(-)

20. 4; Try yourself

21. 4; Try yourself

22. 3; Choice 1, 2 is not correct as sex of S is not known. Let us try the tree for choice 3:

K(-) ⇔ R(+)
|
P(-) ⇔ Q(+)
|
S(-) — L Indeed S is granddaughter of R

23. 4; Try yourself

24. 4; If P is to be grandmother of Q, P and Q should have a generation gap of 2 between them. Now, out of the given four relationships only one i.e. + (father) has a relationship that has some gap. So, a correct answer must have exactly 2 + sign between P and Q. This eliminates choice 1.
Again, if Q was to be a grandchild; the path between P and Q should have continuous blood-relations **(Very Important note)**. But in choice (2), Q and T are not blood related; in choice 3, S and B are not blood-related. This leaves choice 4 only. Let us try its tree:

P(-) ⇔ R(+)
|
S(-) — T(+)
|
Q(-) ⇔ U(+)

25. 2; Note that here we have backward coding so if X is to be grandmother of Y, X must come after Y in the sequence. So, choice 1 and 3 are wrong. Draw family tree for 2:

```
Z(-) — X(-)
        |
       K(+)
        |
       L(+) — Y
```

26. 5; Choice 2 is wrong as sex of A is not known. **(In backward coding, if there is no sign before A, it means its sex is unknown.)**
Choice 1 and 3 are wrong as A must be before D. *(In backward coding, a man of later generation must come earlier in the sequence.)*

27. 2; Choice 1 is wrong as C is a male here (C is father of D). Choice 3 is wrong as C comes before F here. *(In backward coding, if C comes before F, C must be of a later generation.)*
We are left with choice 2. We verify that it is indeed a correct answer.

28. 3;

```
Q(-) — R(-) — S(+) ⇔ T
 |
 P
```

29. 2; Try yourself

30. 1;

```
P(-)
 |
Q(-) — R(+)
        |
        S
```

31. 4; Choice 1, 2, 3 are wrong as they indicate wrong sex of T. Choice 4 is correct, on verification.

32. 5; (mother)

```
K(-)
 |
L(-) — M(+) — N
```

33. 1;

```
K(-) — L(+)
        |
       M(+) — N(-)
               |
               P
```

34. 4; **Quick method:** *C must be a maternal grandfather. So, between C and F there should be at least one mother (÷) sign.*

35. 5; All choices are wrong as sex of E is not known in any of them.

36. 5; 2, 3 and 4 are rejected because in them W is only one generation away from H. 1 is rejected because W is a female.

37. 4; 2 is rejected because we don't know the sex of M.
3 is rejected because M is a female. Check 1 and 4.

(1) ⇒ M(+) – T(+)
|
R

Hence M is uncle of R.

(4) ⇒ R(+) – T(+)
|
M(+) – J

Hence M is nephew of R.

38. 5;

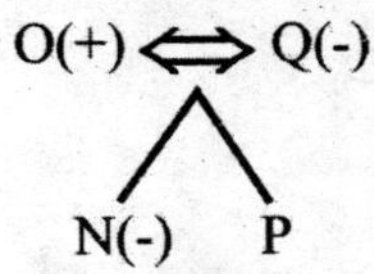

Hence P is either son or daughter of Q.

39. 3;

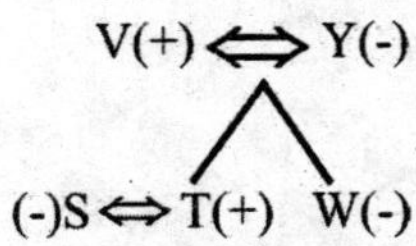

Chapter Nineteen

Coded Binary Numbers

19.1: Introduction

These days questions of this type have been appearing quite frequently and leave almost all the students flummoxed. About 90% of students don't know anything about binary numbers and therefore when they read questions of this type they don't know what has hit them. Many leave these five questions unattempted and thus lose precious edge.

The truth is that these questions are, in fact, very easy and once you have read this chapter, you won't have to leave such questions unattempted any more.

19.2: Format of the problem

Directions (Q. 1-5): Study the following information and answer the questions given below:

In a certain code, the symbol for 0 (zero) is @ and for 1 is $. There are no other symbols for all other numbers. greater than one. The numbers greater than 1 are to be written only by using the two symbols given above. The value of the symbol for 1 doubles itself every time it shifts one place to the left. Study the following examples:

'0' is written as @   '1' is written as $

'2' is written as $ @   '3' is written as $ $

'4' is written as $@@ and so on

1. Which of the following will represent 11?
   1) $ @ $ $ 2) @ $ $ @   3) $ $ @ @
   4) $ @ $ @ @   5) None of these
2. Which of the following will represent 8?
   1) $ $ @ @   2) @ $ $ @   3) $ $ @ @
   4) @ @ $ $ 5) None of these
3. Which of the following numbers will be represented by $ $ @ $?
   1) 8   2) 11   3) 13
   4) 12   5) None of these
4. Which of the following will represent the value of the product 3 × 3 + 1?
   1) $ $ @ $ 2) $ @ $ @   3) $ @ @ $ $
   4) $ $ $ 5) None of these
5. Which of the following numbers will be represented by $ @ @ @ $?
   1) 22   2) 31   3) 14
   4) 17   5) None of these

19.3: Binary numbers: A discussion

In order to understand what a binary number is, we should first understand what a decimal number is.

Decimal numbers

(i) In our everyday life, we represent numbers by using ten digits (which are: 0, 1, 2, 3, 4, 5, 6, 7, 8, 9) and, therefore, these numbers are called **decimal numbers** (*deci* means *ten* in Latin).

(ii) Any number can be represented using these ten digits.

(iii) Consider, for example, a sequence of digits 197. Here, we have three digits 1, 9 and 7 written in that order. All of us know that when 1, 9 and 7 are written in that order this sequence of digits is equal to the number: "One hundred and ninety-seven". How do we arrive at this value for the given sequence? We do it in the following manner:

$$197 = 1 \times 10^2 + 9 \times 10^1 + 7 \times 10^0 = 100 + 90 + 7 = 197$$

[**Note:** $10^0 = 1$. In fact, the value is always equal to 1 if *any* number is raised to the power zero.]

This means that **to get the value of any decimal number we follow the following rules:**

The 1st digit from the right is multiplied by 10^0.

The 2nd digit from right is multiplied by 10^1.

The 3rd digit from right is multiplied by 10^2.

" " " "

" " " "

The nth digit from right is multiplied by 10^{n-1}.

And finally, all these are added.

Ex. 1: What is the value if 3, 5, 7 and 9 are written in this order: 5793.

Soln: $5793 = 5 \times 10^3 + 7 \times 10^2 + 9 \times 10^1 + 3 \times 10^0$

$= 5 \times 1000 + 7 \times 100 + 9 \times 10 + 3 \times 1 = 5793$

(Five thousand seven hundred and ninety-three)

(iv) We get the value of numbers in these cases by multiplying every digit by powers of **10**. Here, this **10** is called the **base** or the **radix**. *Therefore, under a decimal system our base is* **10** *and we use a total of* **ten** *digits to represent any number.*

Binary numbers

(i) Just as we use ten digits to represent a decimal number, we may as well use only *two digits* (which are: 0, 1) to represent any number. This will be called a *binary* system as *bi* means *two* in Latin.

(ii) *Any* number can be represented using these two digits: 0 and 1.

(iii) Consider, for example, a sequence of the digits: 1010. Here, we have a sequence of digits: 1, 0, 1 and 0, in that order. What is the value of this number? We get the value in the following manner:

$$1010 = 1 \times 2^3 + 0 \times 2^2 + 1 \times 2^1 + 0 \times 2^0$$
$$= 1 \times 8 + 0 \times 4 + 1 \times 2 + 0 \times 1$$
$$= 8 + 0 + 2 + 0 = 10 \text{ (ten)}.$$

Therefore, 1010 in the binary system represents the number: *ten*. (Which is represented as 10 in our usual decimal system.)

This means that to get the value of any binary number we follow the following rules:

The 1st digit from right is multiplied by 2^0 (= 1).
The 2nd digit from right is multiplied by 2^1 (= 2).
The 3rd digit from right is multiplied by 2^2 (= 4).
" " " "
The nth digit from right is multiplied by 2^{n-1}.
Finally, all these are added.

Ex. 2: What is the value if 1, 0, 1, 1 are written in this sequence: 1101?

Soln: $1101 = 1 \times 2^3 + 1 \times 2^2 + 0 \times 2^1 + 1 \times 2^0$

$= 8 + 4 + 0 + 1 = 13$. (Thirteen)

Thus, the binary number 1101 represents thirteen. Which is represented as 13 in the decimal system.

(iv) **Obviously, here the base or radix is 2.**

Conclusion: Thus, we see that binary system is a system of representing numbers just as decimal system is a system of representing numbers. The difference is that in case of decimal system we represent numbers by ten digits (0, 1, 2, 3, 4, 5, 6, 7, 8 and 9) and the value of the number is obtained by multiplying different digits of the sequence by powers of 10 and adding; while in case of binary system we represent numbers by two digits (0 and 1) and the value of the number is obtained by multiplying different digits of the sequence by powers of 2 and adding.

19.3.1 Converting binary numbers to decimal numbers

We have already seen how to do it. A binary number is converted to a decimal number by

(1) multiplying the nth digit from right by 2^{n-1}, where n = 1, 2, ...
(2) adding all these.

Ex. 3: Convert the following binary numbers into decimal numbers:

(a) 1010 (b) 1111 (c) 100
(d) 10000 (e) 1110010

Soln: (a) $1010 = 1 \times 2^3 + 0 \times 2^2 + 1 \times 2^1 + 0 \times 2^0$

$= 8 + 0 + 2 + 0 = 10$ (Ten)

(b) $1111 = 1 \times 2^3 + 1 \times 2^2 + 1 \times 2^1 + 1 \times 2^0$

$= 8 + 4 + 2 + 1 = 15$ (Fifteen)

(c) $100 = 1 \times 2^2 + 0 \times 2^1 + 0 \times 2^0$

$= 4 + 0 + 0 = 4$ (Four)

(d) $10000 = 1 \times 2^4 + 0 \times 2^3 + 0 \times 2^2 + 0 \times 2^1 + 0 \times 2^0$

$= 16 + 0 + 0 + 0 + 0 = 16$ (Sixteen)

(e) $1110010 = 1 \times 2^6 + 1 \times 2^5 + 1 \times 2^4 + 0 \times 2^3 + 0 \times 2^2 + 1 \times 2^1 + 0 \times 2^0$

$= 64 + 32 + 16 + 0 + 0 + 2 + 0 = 114$ (Hundred Fourteen)

Table 1: List of powers of 2

Power	Value		Power	Value
2^0	1		2^5	32=2×2×2×2×2
2^1	2=2		2^6	64=2×2×2×2×2×2
2^2	4=2×2		2^7	128=2×2... 7 times
2^3	8=2×2×2		2^8	256=2×2... 8 times
2^4	16=2×2×2×2		2^9	512=2×2... 9 times

For a quicker conversion of binary numbers to decimal numbers we must remember the above-mentioned table by heart. Thus, we can save time by directly writing the value to be multiplied (for example instead of writing 1×2^3 we can directly write 1×8). Now, since anything multiplied by 1 gives the same number and since anything multiplied by 0 gives zero, we can further save time by writing (i) only the value of the power of 2 wherever it has to be multiplied by 1, and (ii) zero, wherever it has to be multiplied by zero. Thus, in Ex 2, to convert 1010 we may directly write as $1\times 2^3 + 1\times 2^1$ or $8 + 2$ (because other terms will be multiplied by 0 and give 0 in any case). Thus, we can develop the following quicker method for conversion of binary into decimal numbers:

Quicker method for converting binary numbers to decimal

Step I: Starting from the rightmost digit of the given binary number, write 1, 2, 4, 8, 16, 32... and so on below each digit as you proceed towards the left.

Step II: Ignore the numbers below the 0s (zeroes). Add all the remaining numbers below the 1s.

Ex. 4: Solve Ex. 3 by quicker method.

Soln: (a) 1010

Step I: Starting from right we write 1, 2, 4 and 8 below the digits. We get

1	0	1	0
8	4	2	1

Step II: 4 and 1 fall below the zeroes. We ignore them and add the remaining. We get $8 + 2 = 10$ (Ten).

(b) 1111

Step I: Starting from right, we write 1, 2, 4, and 8 below the digits. We get

1	1	1	1
8	4	2	1

Step II: All numbers fall below 1s. So, we add all of them to get 8 + 4 + 2 + 1 = 15 (fifteen)

(c) 100.

Step I: Starting from right, we write 1, 2 and 4 below the digits. We get:

1	0	0
4	2	1

Step II: 1 and 2 fall below the zeroes, we ignore them. This leaves 4 (four).

(d) 10000.

Step I: Starting from right, we write 1, 2, 4, 8, and 16 below the digits. We get

1	0	0	0	0
16	8	4	2	1

Step II: 1, 2, 4, 8 fall below the zeroes. Ignore them. That leaves 16. (Sixteen)

(e) 1110010

Step I: Starting from right, we write 1, 2, 4, 8, 16, 32 and 64 below the digits. We get

1	1	1	0	0	1	0
64	32	16	8	4	2	1

Step II: We ignore 8, 4 and 1 as they fall below the zeroes. Adding the rest. 64 + 32 + 16 + 2 we get 114 (One hundred and fourteen)

19.3.2: Converting decimal numbers into binary

A decimal number is converted into binary by the method of successive divisions. **Each time the dividend is divided by 2. The remainder is noted and the quotient becomes the next dividend, which is again divided by 2. This process is repeated until no more division is possible**.

We will explain it by the following example.

Ex. 5: Convert 17 into a binary number:

Soln: Step I: We divide 17 by 2. The remainder is 1 and the dividend is 8. (See below)

17	
8	1

Step II: In the previous step, the dividend was 8. That is, our new quotient. We divide it again by 2. Now, the remainder is 0 and dividend is 4. (See below)

17	
8	1
4	0

Step III: Last step's dividend is our new quotient. If we divide it again by 2, our dividend is 2 and remainder 0. (See below)

17	1
8	0
4	0
2	

Step IV: Last step's dividend is now our quotient, i.e. 2. If we divide it by 2, our dividend is 1 and remainder 0. (See below)

17	1
8	0
4	0
2	0
1	

Note that any more divisions are not possible because 1 is not divisible by 2. Now, we write all our remainders from left to right in the order shown below by the arrows

17	1
8	0
4	0
2	0
1	

∴ Our binary number for 17 is 10001.

Ex. 6: Convert **(a)** 11 and **(b)** 14 into binary:

Soln: (a)

11	1
5	1
2	0
1	

∴ 11 = 1011 in binary

(b)

14	0
7	1
3	1
1	

∴ 14 = 1110 in binary

[**Note:** We can use the method of 19.3.1 to check if our answer is right.

For example, $1011 = 1 \times 2^3 + 0 \times 2^2 + 1 \times 2^1 + 1 \times 2^0$

$= 8 + 2 + 1 = 11$ (Eleven).

$1110 = 1 \times 2^3 + 1 \times 2^2 + 1 \times 2^1 + 0 \times 2^0$

$= 8 + 4 + 2 = 14$ (Fourteen)]

Table 2: Some decimal numbers and their binary representation

(The following table could be used for ready reference in case you require a quick solution. You may also like to memorise the binary representation of first 16 numbers: it will save you a lot of time.)

Decimal number	Binary form	Decimal number	Binary form	Decimal number	Binary form
1	1	12	1100	23	10111
2	10	13	1101	24	11000
3	11	14	1110	25	11001
4	100	15	1111	26	11010
5	101	16	10000	27	11011
6	110	17	10001	28	11100
7	111	18	10010	29	11101
8	1000	19	10011	30	11110
9	1001	20	10100	31	11111
10	1010	21	10101	32	100000
11	1011	22	10110	—	—

19.4: Our strategy for solution

We have armed ourselves with adequate theoretical input and we are now ready to look at the questions and tackle them.

If you look closely at the directions in our sample problem of Section 19.2.2, you will realise that the question is essentially about binary representation of decimal numbers. The only difference is that instead of the usual 0 and 1 to represent the binary numbers, you have @ and $. Thus, 0 is @, 1 is $, 2 is not 10 but $ @, and so on.

It is, therefore, pretty obvious that your solution strategy should consist of the following steps:

Step I: In questions where you have to give the symbols for a (decimal) number,
(a) first convert that decimal number to binary (use concepts of Section 19. 3. 2 and Table 2).
(b) and then, replace 0 and 1 by appropriate symbols.

Step II: In questions where symbols are given and you have to give their decimal value,
(a) first replace symbols by 0 and 1 to get the binary form.
(b) and then, convert the binary numbers to decimal (use concepts of Section 19. 3. 1 and Table 2).

19.5: Some Tips for quick answers

Tip 1: **(A)** *The binary form of an odd number will always have a 1 in the end and the binary form of an even number will always have a 0 in the end.*
(B) *Conversely, if the binary form has a 0 in the end, it must be an even number and if it has a 1 in the end, it must be an odd number*

Tip 2: **(A)** *The binary form of 4, 5, 6 and 7 has three digits; that of 8, 9, ..., 15; has four digits and that of 16, 17, ..., 31 has five digits.*
(B) *Conversely, if the binary form has three digits, it must be one of 4, 5, 6 or 7; if it has four digits, it must be one of 8, 9, ..., 15; if it has five digits, it must be one of 16, 17..., 31.*

Tip 3: *Just as a zero at the leftmost place has no value for a decimal number, it has no value for a binary number also. (For example, 010 is the same as 10 in binary system and it equals 2 in the decimal. So, effectively, 010 is not a 3- digit number but a 2- digit number.)*

19.6: Complete solution for our sample problem

Ex 7: Solve the sample problem of Section 19.2.

Soln: Q. 1: To get the binary equivalent of 11, we use the method of successive divisions by 2.

11	1
5	1
2	0
1	

Hence, the binary form is 1011. Replacing 1 by $ and 0 by @ we have: $ @ $ $. Correct choice: (1)

Quicker method: (4) is not correct as, by Tip 2 (A), 11 can't have five digits in decimal form. (3) is not correct as 11 is an odd number, so it can't have, by Tip 1 (A), a 0, i.e. a @ in the end. (2) can't be correct as it is essentially a three-digit number because the leftmost digit is 0 (i.e. @) (see Tip 3). That leaves only answer choice 1. [Unless, choice *None of these* is correct, our quicker method gives correct answer. Therefore, note that our quicker method essentially helps you eliminate the wrong answers but doesn't help you get the right one.]

Q. 2: For 8, we have:

8	0
4	0
2	0
1	

i.e. 1000 or \$ @ @ @. Correct choice: 5.

Q. 3: \$ \$ @ \$ $= 1101 = 1 \times 8 + 1 \times 4 + 1 \times 1 = 13$.

Correct choice: 3

Q. 4: $3 \times 3 + 1 = 10$. For 10, the binary form is:

10	0
5	1
2	0
1	

or, 1010 or, \$@\$@. Correct choice: (2).

Quicker method: Choices (1), (3) and (5) all have a \$, i.e. a 1, in the rightmost place. By Tip 1 (A), it is not possible as 10 is an even number. This leaves only choices (2) and (5). Trying out (2), we see that it is indeed a right answer.

Q. 5: \$ @ @ @ \$ = 10001

$$= 1 \times 2^4 + 0 \times 2^3 + 0 \times 2^2 + 0 \times 2^1 + 1 \times 2^0$$
$$= 16 + 1 = 17$$

Correct choice: 4

Quicker method: We write 1, 2, 4, 8, and 16 below the digits and add only those that fall below the 1s.

1	0	0	0	1
16	8	4	2	1

$\therefore 16 + 1 = 17$.

19.7: Some additional points

(i) Sometimes a number may cause confusion if we don't explicitly mention which system it belongs to. For example, 100 equals Hundred in decimal system and Eight in binary system. It may create confusion. Further, if we write:

$$100 = 8$$

It looks ridiculous. To avoid this confusion, the ideal way is to always put a number in a bracket and write the base as the subscript. Thus, the correct non-confusing way of writing the above is

$$(100)_2 = (8)_{10}$$

The above means that 100 in binary form is equal to 8 in decimal form.

Similarly, $(10)_2 = (2)_{10}$

$(1010)_2 = (10)_{10}$

$(1111)_2 = (15)_{10}$

mean that 10, 1010 and 1111 in the binary form mean 2, 10 and 15 respectively in the usual decimal system.

[This point is merely for your academic clarity and is not directly important for your questions.]

(ii) Just as we have a binary system with base 2, a decimal system with base 10, we may have a tertiary system with a base 3, an octal system with base 8, etc. In fact, we can have *any* system for *any* given base. For example, a tertiary system with base 3 will have three digits to represent all numbers: 0, 1 and 2. In this case, numbers will be converted to decimal by multiplying with appropriate powers of 3.

For ex:

$(12012)_3 = 1 \times 3^4 + 2 \times 3^3 + 0 \times 3^2 + 1 \times 3^1 + 2 \times 3^0$

$= 81 + 18 + 0 + 3 + 2 = (104)\ 10$ etc

[Again, this point is also made for your academic interest and has no direct relevance for your exam.]

Practice Exercises

Directions (Q. 1-5): Study the following information and answer the questions given below:

In a certain code, the symbol for 0 (zero) is * and that for 1 is Δ. There are no other symbols for all other numbers greater than one. The numbers greater than 1 are to be written only by using the two symbols given above. The value of the symbol for 1 doubles itself every time it shifts one place to the left. Study the following examples:

'0' is written as * 'l' is written as Δ

'2' is written as Δ* '3' is written as Δ Δ

'4' is written as Δ* * and so on.

1. Which of the following numbers will be represented by ΔΔΔ *Δ?
   1) 31 2) 27 3) 29 4) 23 5) None of these
2. Which of the following will represent the multiplication of Δ*Δ and ΔΔΔ?
   1) Δ***ΔΔ 2) Δ Δ* *ΔΔ 3) ΔΔΔ * ΔΔ
   4) Δ****Δ 5) None of these
3. Which of the following will represent $13 \times 8 \div 2 + 3$?
   1) Δ**ΔΔΔ 2) ΔΔ*ΔΔΔ 3) ΔΔΔ*ΔΔ
   4) ΔΔΔ* *Δ 5) None of these
4. Which of the following will represent the HCF of 10, 20 and 15?
   1) Δ*Δ 2) ΔΔΔ 3) Δ* *
   4) Δ**Δ 5) None of these

5. Which of the following will represent the LCM of 10, 20 and 15?
   1) ΔΔΔ* *Δ 2) ΔΔ* *ΔΔ 3) ΔΔ*Δ*Δ
   4) ΔΔ ΔΔ* * 5) None of these

Directions (Q. 6- 10): Study the following information and answer the questions given below:

In a certain code, the symbol for 0 (zero) is α and for 1 is β. There are no other symbols for all other numbers greater than one. The numbers greater than 1 are to be written only by using the two symbols given above. The value of the symbol for 1 doubles itself every time it shifts one place to the left. Study the following examples:

'0' is written as α 'l' is written as β
'2' is written as β α '3' is written as β β
'4' is written as β α α and so on.

6. Which of the following will represent the LCM of 10, 15 and 18?
   1) β α β β β α α 2) β α β β α β α 3) β β βαα βα
   4) β ααββαβ 5) None of these
7. Which of the following will be represented by β β α β β?
   1) 30 2) 25 3) 27 4) 23 5) None of these
8. Which of the following will represent the value of 2 + 10 ÷ 2?
   1) β αα 2) β αβ 3) β ββ
   4) β ααβ 5) None of these
9. Which of the following will represent the HCF of 10, 15 and 18?
   1) β 2) α 3) β β
   4) Can't be determined 5) None of these
10. Which of the following will represent the average of βαβαα and βαβα?
    1) β ααβ 2) β ααα 3) β βββ
    4) β βαα 5) None of these

Directions (Q 11-15): These questions are based on the same directions and rules as given in Q 1 to Q 5.

11. Which of the following is represented by ΔΔ**Δ?
    1) 25 2) 23 3) 22 4) 18 5) None of these
12. Which of the following is the HCF of Δ**, ΔΔ* and Δ*Δ*?
    1) ΔΔ 2) ** 3) Δ*
    4) Δ** 5) None of these
13. What is the value of ΔΔΔΔ divided by ΔΔ?
    1) ΔΔΔ 2) Δ** 3) Δ*Δ
    4) ΔΔ* 5) None of these
14. How does one write 14 + 2 - 7 in this code?
    1) Δ*Δ* 2) Δ*ΔΔ 3) ΔΔΔΔ
    4) Δ*Δ 5) None of these
15. What is the value of 4 × 5 + 23 – 6 × 6 + 4?
    1) Δ**Δ 2) Δ*ΔΔ 3) ΔΔΔ*
    4) Δ*** 5) None of these

Direction (Q. 16-20): The following questions use the same rule and directions as used in Q 6-Q 10:

16. Which of the following represents 30?
 1) β β β α α 2) β α β α α 3) β α α β α
 4) β β β β α 5) None of these
17. Which of the following is the value of β β β β β?
 1) 15 2) 17 3) 19 4) 21 5) None of these
18. Which of the following is the HCF of β β β β, β α β α β and β β α α α?
 1) 2 2) 3 3) 4 4) 5 5) None of these
19. Which of the following is the average of β α β α and β β β β α?
 1) β α α α α 2) β α β β α 3) β α β β β
 4) β β β α α 5) None of these
20. Which of the following is the average of β α β α α and 14?
 1) β α α α α 2) β α α α β 3) β β β α β
 4) β β β β 5) None of these

Directions (Q. 21-25): The following questions use the same directions as used in the sample problem in section 19.2 of the chapter:

21. Which of the following represents 14?
 1) $@@@ 2) $$$@ 3) $$@@ 4) $$@$ 5) None of these
22. Which of the following numbers is represented by $$@@$$?
 1) 47 2) 48 3) 49 4) 51 5) None of these
23. What is the average of $$$@@ and $$@@?
 1) $@@@@ 2) $$$$@ 3) $@$@@
 4) $@@$@ 5) None of these
24. What is the value of [($@) + ($@) ÷ ($@)]^$@?
 1) $@@$@ 2) $@$@$ 3) $$$ × $$ − $@
 4) ($$)^$@ 5) None of these
25. What is the value of [(8 + 16) ÷ (4 × 3)] 3?
 1) $@@$ 2) $$@@ 3) $$$@
 4) $@@@ 5) None of these

Solutions

1. 3; 11101 =

1	1	1	0	1
16	8	4	2	1

Adding all the numbers below the 1s, we get: 29.

2. 1; We have to multiply 101 and 111.

Now,

1	0	1
4	2	1

and

1	1	1
4	2	1

Adding the numbers below the 1s, 101 = 4 + 1 = 5, 111 = 4 + 2 + 1 = 7.

The product is 35. Now dividing 35 by 2 successively,

35	1
17	1
8	0
4	0
2	0
1	

$\therefore$ 35 = 100011 = Δ***ΔΔ

3. 2; 13 × 8 ÷ 2 + 3 = 13 × 4 + 3 = 55. To convert 55 into binary we divide successively by 2.

55	1
27	1
13	1
6	0
3	1
1	

$\therefore$ 55 = 110111 = ΔΔ*ΔΔΔ

4. 1; HCF of 10, 20 and 15 is obviously 5. 5 is represented as:

5	1
2	0
1	

$\therefore$ 101 = Δ*Δ

5. 4; LCM of 10, 20 and 15 is obviously 60. 60 is represented as:

60	0
30	0
15	1
7	1
3	1
1	

$\therefore$ 111100 = ΔΔΔΔ**

6. 2; LCM of 10, 15, 18 is 90. 90 is represented as:

90	0
45	0
22	1
11	0
5	1
2	1
1	0

$\therefore$ 1011010 = β α β β α β α

7. 3; β β α β β =

1	1	0	1	1
16	8	4	2	1

Adding all numbers below the 1s, we get 16 + 8 + 2 + 1 = 27

8. 3; 2 + 10 ÷ 2 = 2 + 5 = 7.

Now,

7	1
3	1
1	

$\therefore$ 111 = β β β

9. 1; HCF of 10, 15 and 18 is one.

10. 3; Average of 10100 and 1010.

1	0	1	0	0
16	8	4	2	1

and

1	0	1	0
8	4	2	1

Adding only the numbers below the 1s, we get 16 + 4 = 20 and 8 + 2 = 10. Average of 20 and 10 is 15. Now, 15 is represented as:

15	1
7	1
3	1
1	

$\therefore$ 1111 = β β β β

11. 1;

1	1	0	0	1
16	8	4	2	1

Adding the numbers below the 1s only, we get 16 + 8 + 1 = 25.

12. 3; HCF of Δ**, ΔΔ* and Δ*Δ* means HCF of 100, 110 and 1010. We can convert them into decimal using our usual method. They are: 4, 6, and 10. HCF of 4, 6 and 10 is 2. 2 is represented in binary representation as 10 or Δ*.

13. 3; ΔΔΔΔ and ΔΔ, i.e. 1111 and 11 can be converted into decimal easily. They are 15 and 3. Now, $15 \div 3 = 5$. And 5 can be converted to binary as 101.

14. 5; $14+2-7=9$. We write 9 as 1001. (Use method of successive divisions by 2)

15. 2; $4 \times 5+23 - 6 \times 6+4=20+23-36+4=11$. Now, 11 can be converted into binary.

11	1
5	1
2	0
1	

∴ 1011 = Δ*ΔΔ

16. 4; To find binary code for 30:

30	0
15	1
7	1
3	1
1	

∴ 11110 = β β β β α

17. 5; Value of β β β β β or 11111:

1	1	1	1	1
16	8	4	2	1

Adding all numbers below the 1s, we get $16+8+4+2+1=31$.

18. 2; HCF of 1111, 10101, 11000. These numbers can be easily converted into decimal. They are: 15, 21, and 24. HCF is 3.

19. 1; Average of 1010 and 11110. They are converted into decimal easily. They are 10 and 30. Average is 20. 20 is converted into binary as : 10100.

20	0
10	0
5	1
2	0
1	

20. 2; β α β α α or 10100 is converted into decimal as 20. Average of 20 and 14 is 17. 17 is converted as

17	1
8	0
4	0
2	0
1	

∴ 10001 = β α α α β

21. 2;

14	0
7	1
3	1
1	

∴ 1110 = $$$@

22. 4;

1	1	0	0	1	1
32	16	8	4	2	1

Add the numbers below the 1s. We get: $32 + 16 + 2 + 1 = 51$.

23. 3; Average of 11100 and 1100. We convert them into decimal as: 28 and 12. Average is 20. 20 is represented in binary as 10100.

24. 4; 10 is equal to 2 in decimal. $2 + 2 \div 2 = 2 + 1 = 3$.
$\therefore (2 + 2 \div 2)^2 = 3^2 = 9$. Choice 3 is $(11)^{10}$. Now, 11 is equal to 3 in decimal. Choice 3 is $3^2 = 9$.

25. 4; $(8 + 16) \div (4 \times 3) = 24 \div 12 = 2$
$\therefore [(8 + 16) \div (4 \times 3)]^3 = 2^3 = 8$.
8 is converted into binary as 1000.

Chapter Twenty

Coded Inequalities

20.1: Introduction

These type of questions are asked in some of the middle-level competitive exams such as PO, AAO, CPO etc. However, sometimes they are also included in MBA entrance tests such as CAT, XLRI, etc. These are extremely easy problems for people who are even slightly comfortable with elementary mathematics. However, those who are not at ease with Maths may find it a bit flummoxing. Moreover, the fact that the inequalities are coded makes the solution a bit more cumbersome and time-consuming.

This chapter would give you the basic concepts of inequalities to enable you to understand the basic concepts. Further we will also be giving you some tips on how to quickly solve the problems in the form as they appear in the examinations.

20.2: Format of the problem

Ex. 1:

Directions (Q. 1-5): In the following questions, the symbols α, β, γ, δ, and η are used with following meaning:

P α Q means P is greater than Q.

P β Q means P is either greater than or equal to Q.

P γ Q means P is equal to Q.

P δ Q means P is smaller than Q.

P η Q means P is either smaller than or equal to Q.

Now in each of the following questions, assuming the given statements to be true, find which of the two conclusions I and II given below them is / are definitely true. Give answer

1) if only conclusion I is true;
2) if only conclusion II is true;
3) if either I or II is true;
4) if neither I nor II is true; and
5) if both I and II are true.

1. **Statements:** M α N, L γ M, O δ N, L η K
   Conclusions: I. M δ K **II.** L α N
2. **Statements:** E γ F, C δ D, F β G, D α E
   Conclusions: I. E α G **II.** C γ E
3. **Statements:** L β M, O γ N, L δ H, M γ O
   Conclusions: I. L γ N **II.** L α N

4. **Statements:** $Z\eta Y, K\gamma L, Y\delta X, Z\alpha K$
Conclusions: **I.** $Y\alpha L$ **II.** $Y\gamma L$
5. **Statements:** $R\delta I, S\gamma C, S\beta I, C\alpha O$
Conclusions: **I.** $C\delta I$ **II.** $S\alpha R$

20.3: An analysis of the problem

It is extremely clear that the problem involves essentially a combination of two elementary problems:

(i) Inequalities (ii) Coding

Another thing that is equally clear is that the coding part is not a big challenge here because the coding scheme is told entirely in advance. Therefore, to decode the inequalities in a given problem would not mean any more headache than a couple of extra seconds. *Essentially, it is a problem of inequalities* and it is this aspect that should be mastered. Hence, before we proceed further and learn a technique to solve such problems: we will first learn the basics of inequalities.

20.4: Inequalities: A Theoretical Discussion

To understand an *inequality* you should first understand what is meant by an *equality*. We know that 3 × 2 = 6. In other words, the result of a multiplication between 3 and 2, and; the number 6; are *equal. Since they are* ***equal*** *it is an* ***equality***. In the same way, 3 × 3 ≠ 6. Here, the product of 3 and 3 is **not equal** to the number 9. And since they are **not equal** it is an **inequality**. Now, once we know that one thing is not equal to another; there can be only two possibilities. Either it is **greater than** or it is **less than** the other thing. To denote this mathematically, we use '>' to denote 'greater than' and '<' to denote less than. Thus, 3 × 3 > 6. And 3 × 1 < 6. In words it means that the product of 3 and 3 is greater than 6 and product of 3 and 1 is less than 6.

20.4.1: The signs of "greater than or equal to" and "less than or equal to"

Sometimes we are faced with two numbers where we don't know the exact state of inequality between them. For example, we may have two numbers x and y and all that we know is that "y is not less than x". In this case, x can be *either equal to or greater than y.* Such situations can be represented as '≥' sign. Thus, we have '≥' meaning 'greater than or equal to' and '≤' meaning 'less than or equal to'.

So, $x \geq y$ means x is either greater than or equal to y

$a \leq b$ means a is either less than or equal to b.

Ex. 2. (i) Rama went to a market with 20 rupees in her pocket. There she spent some money to buy a toothbrush. But she does not remember how much she spent on the toothbrush. But one thing is for sure. Since she had only 20 rupees with her: her expenditure on toothbrush can be either less than or at most equal to 20 rupees. Suppose that she spent x rupees on the toothbrush. Then, mathematically;

$$x \leq 20$$

(ii) After purchasing the toothbrush, Rama goes to a Bank where she had deposited 500 rupees two weeks ago. She is not sure whether the Bank will give her any interest for an account which is merely 2 weeks old. But one thing is for sure. The amount that she has in her account can be either greater than (if interest is given) or at least equal to (if no interest given) to 500 rupees. Suppose that she had y rupees in her account. Then, mathematically:

$$y \geq 500$$

20.4.2: Chain of Inequalities (Inequalities with more than two terms)

Sometimes we may combine two or more inequalities to create a single inequality with three or more terms. For Example 25 > 20 and 20 > 18 can be combined as 25 > 20 > 18. Similarly, 14 < 18; 18 < 32 and 32 < 39 may be combined as 14 < 18 < 32 < 39.

If you look at our sample problem closely enough, you will realise that **our task primarily is to be able to combine two or more inequalities into one**.

20.4.3: When can we combine TWO inequalities into ONE?

Sometimes we CAN combine two inequalities into one and sometimes we can not. In the discussion to follow we will see when is this possible and when not.

Ex 3. Try to combine the following pair of inequalities into one, if possible.

(i) 15 > 14, 14 > 12
(ii) 18 < 20, 20 < 22
(iii) 15 > 14, 13 > 12
(iv) 15 < 18, 19 < 20
(v) 15 > 14, 18 > 14
(vi) 12 < 18, 13 < 18

Soln: (i) 15 > 14, 14 > 12 can be easily combined as 15 > 14 > 12.
(ii) 18 < 20, 20 < 22 can be easily combined as 18 < 20 < 22.
(iii) 15 > 14, 13 > 12 cannot be combined.
(iv) 15 < 18, 19 < 20 cannot be combined.
(v) 15 > 14, 18 > 14 cannot be combined.
(vi) 12 < 18, 13 < 18 cannot be combined.

Now, let us ask ourselves this question: **What went wrong with (iii), (iv), (v) and (vi) above?** For this, there must be something right with (i) and (ii) and that thing must be absent from (iii), (iv), (v) and (vi).

If you look closely, you will find that there are two conditions that (iii), (iv), (v) and (vi) don't fulfil. These are:

A. In (iii) and (iv), the two inequalities don't have a common term. **Two inequalities can not be combined if they don't have a common term.** For example in (i), 14 is a common term and in (ii), 20 is a common term.

B. In (v) and in (vi), we do have a common term. (In (v), 14 is a common term and in (vi), 18 is a common term). But here, the common term is either less than both the other numbers (in (v), 14 is less than both 15 and 18) or is greater than both the other numbers (in (vi), 18 is greater than both 12 and 13). **Two inequalities can not be combined if the common term is greater than both the other numbers or less than both the other numbers.** They can be combined only if the common term is greater than one number and less than the other number. (For example, in (i); the common term is 14 which is greater than 12 but less than 15. Again in(ii), the common term is 20 which is greater than 18 but less than 22. Therefore, these two inequalities could easily be combined.)

[Note: In the foregoing discussion we have restricted ourselves to the '>' sign and the'<'sign. But whatever holds true there, also holds true for '≥' and '≤' signs.]

Now, based on the foregoing note and the discussion in para (A) and (B) above, we can devise our own "golden rules" for combination of inequalities.

Two Golden rules (for combining two inequalities)

(1) **Two inequalities can be combined if and only if they have a common term**

(2) **Two inequalities can be combined if and only if the common term is greater than (or 'greater than or equal to') one and less than (or 'less than or equal to') the other.** (And the combined inequality will have the common term in the middle with the greater and the smaller terms on the two extremes.) **[Note: Also see, visual method in Tip 3, Section 20.7.]**

Learner's Exercise I

Ex. 4: State which of the following inequalities can be combined and which not? Write the combined form, if possible.

i) $A > B, B > C$ ii) $A \geq B, C < B$

iii) $B < A, B \geq C$ iv) $A > B, C > B$

v) $A \geq B, B < C$ vi) $B \geq A, C \geq B$

vii) $A \geq B, B \leq C$ viii) $B \leq A, B \geq C$

ix) $A > B, C > D$ x) $A \leq B, M \geq N$

Soln: By first golden rule, no combination is possible in case of (ix) and (x) because they have four terms each. [(ix) has A, B, C and D while (x) has A, B, M and N]. Thus, they do not have a common term.

First golden rule rejects (ix) and (x) but it does not reject (i), (ii) ....up to (viii) because all these pairs of inequalities have three terms with a common term B.

To see if they can indeed be combined let us apply our second golden rule to each of them;

(i) $A > B, B > C$. Here, common term B is greater than one term C and less than the other, A. So, a combination is possible:
Combined inequality: $A > B > C$

(ii) $A \geq B, C < B$. Here, common term B is less than (or equal to) one term, A, and greater than the other term, C: Hence, combination is possible:
Combined inequality: $A \geq B > C$ or $C < B \leq A$

(iii) $B < A, B \geq C$. Here, common term B is less than one term, A; and greater than (or equal to) the other term, C. Hence, combination is possible.
Combined inequality: $A > B \geq C$ or $C \leq B < A$

(iv) $A > B, C > B$. Here, common term is less than both the other terms, A and C. So, a combination is not possible.

(v) $A \geq B, B < C$. Here, common term B is less than (or equal to) both terms.
No combination possible.

(vi) $B \geq A, C \geq B$. Here, common term B is greater than (or equal to) one term, A, and less than (or equal to) another term, C. Hence, **combination is possible**.
Combined inequality: $A \leq B \leq C$ or $C \geq B \geq A$.

(vii) $A \geq B, B \leq C$. Here, common term B is less than (or equal to) both A and C combination is not possible.

(viii) $B \leq A, B \geq C$. Here, common term B is less than (or equal to) one term A; and greater than (or equal to) other term, C. Combination is possible.
Combined inequality: $A \geq B \geq C$ or $C \leq B \leq A$.

20.4.4: Deriving conclusions from a combined inequality

Suppose you are told that Ram is older than Shyam and then again that, Shyam is older than Madan. You can combine these two statements into one as, Ram is older than Shyam who is older than Madan. And then by virtue of it you can *conclude* that Ram is older than Madan.

Mathematically, the above can be written as:

Ram > Shyam, Shyam > Madan

Now, these two are combined as:

Ram > Shyam > Madan

And finally, we reach a conclusion:

Ram > Madan

How do we reach the conclusion? By simply letting the middle term of the combined inequality (which is the common term of the two given inequalities) disappear.

Thus, the simple rule to derive a conclusion from a combined inequalities is: *make the common term disappear.*

Ex. 5: Derive a conclusion from the following combined inequalities:

(i) $x>y>z$ (ii) $x<y<z$

Soln: (i) $x>z$ (ii) $x<z$

Ex. 6: However, when we have '≥' signs in the combined inequalities, then the process is a bit more thought-provoking. For example, consider the following combined inequality:

$$x \geq y > z$$

Here, x is either greater than y or equal to y. Therefore, the minimum value for x is equal to y.

But y is always greater than z. Therefore, x is always greater than z (because even when x attains its least value it is equal to y and y is always greater than z. Therefore, x will always be greater than z). Hence, the inequality as conclusion is:

$$x > z$$

Ex. 7: Now, consider the combined inequality

$$x > y \geq z$$

Here, x is always greater than y and y is either greater than z or equal to it. When y is greater than z; x will obviously be greater than z. Even when y is equal to z; x will be greater z because x is always greater than y. Hence, in all cases, our conclusion is:

$$x > z.$$

Ex. 8: Now, consider the combined inequality

$$x \geq y \geq z.$$

Here, x is either greater than y or equal to y. When x is greater than y; we have: $x > y \geq z$ which gives the conclusion $x > z$ ... (a) [see Ex. 7]

When x is equal to y; we have:

$x = y \geq z$ which gives the conclusion $x \geq z$ ... (b)

Combining conclusion (a) and (b); we have

$$x \geq z$$

What lessons do we learn from Ex 5, 6, 7 and 8? It is pretty obvious. The lesson we learn is our *Golden Rule # 3.*

Third Golden rule (for deriving a conclusion from a combined inequality)

The conclusion-inequality will have an '≥' sign (or a '≤' sign) if and only if *both* the signs in the combined inequality were '≥' (or '≤'; as the case maybe).

To understand this golden rule, look at examples 5, 6, 7, and 8 again. They are rewritten below:

Ex. 5: $x>y>z$

Ex. 6: $x \geq y > z$

Ex. 7: $x > y \geq z$

Ex. 8: $x \geq y \geq z$

Here, in *only* Ex 8, *both* the signs of the combined inequality are '≥'. Therefore, the conclusion- inequality will have a '≥' sign only in this case and a '>' sign in all other cases. As we have already seen; the conclusion- inequality does obey this rule and we have:

Ex. 5: $x > y > z$ (conclusion: $x > z$)

Ex. 6: $x \geq y > z$ (conclusion: $x > z$)

Ex. 7: $x > y \geq z$ (conclusion: $x > z$)

Ex. 8: $x \geq y \geq z$ (conclusion: $x \geq z$)

Ex. 9: Draw a conclusion-inequality using the golden-rule in the following cases.

i) $a < b < c$ ii) $a \leq b < c$

iii) $a < b \leq c$ iv) $a \leq b \leq c$

Soln: We have a '≤' sign *twice* only in (iv). So, only (iv) will have a '≤' sign in conclusion, all other will have a '<' sign. So, we have:

i) $a < c$ (ii) $a < c$

iii) $a < c$ (iv) $a \leq c$

20.4.5: Combining two inequalities (if possible) and deriving a conclusion from them (very Important)

In 15.4.3, we have seen how to combine two inequalities, if it was possible. There are two golden rules to be followed for this. Then, in 15. 4. 4, we have seen how to write the conclusions inequality from the combined inequality. For this, we have the third golden rule. Combining them, we have our three steps to quickly, almost magically combine two inequalities into one and then write the conclusion. Let us rewrite them once again.

(First golden rule) First see, if the two inequalities have a common term. (Go to step II and III only if they have, otherwise don't waste your time).

(Second golden rule). Now see, if the common term is greater than (or equal to) one term and less than (or equal to) the other one. (If it is greater than (or equal to) both or less than (or equal to) both, a combination is not possible.)

(Third golden rule). Combine the two inequalities and draw a conclusion by letting the middle term disappear. The conclusion will normally have a '>' (or a '<') sign strictly, unless the '≥' sign (or '≤') appears twice in the combined inequality.

Learner's Exercise II

Given below are ten pairs of inequalities. Combine them if possible and write the conclusion-inequality.

(i) $A > B, C > D$ (ii) $A < B, C \leq M$

(iii) $A > B, C < B$ (iv) $A > B, B \leq C$

(v) $A \leq B, C \leq B$ (vi) $A < B, C > B$

(vii) $A \geq B, B \leq C$ (viii) $A \leq B, C \geq B$

(ix) $A \geq B, B \geq C$ (x) $A \leq B, B < C$

Soln:

Step I: We see that (i) and (ii) have four terms each and hence there is no common term. Therefore, a combination is not possible for these as they fail in step I itself. For all others, there are three terms in all the pairs and the common term is B. So, we apply step II to all of these.

Step II: (iii) B less than one term A, greater than another one C, combination possible.

Combined inequality: $A > B > C$ or $C < B < A$

(iv) B less than (or equal to) C, and B less than A, combination not possible.

(v) B greater than (or equal to) both A and C, combination not possible.

(vi) B less than one term C, greater than another term A, combination possible.

Combined inequality: $A < B < C$ or $C > B > A$

(vii) B less than (or equal to) both terms, combination not possible.

(viii) B greater than (or equal to) one term A and less than (or equal to) other term C, combination possible.

Combined inequality: $C \geq B \geq A$ or $A \leq B \leq C$

(ix) B less than (or equal to) one term A and greater than (or equal to) other term C, combination possible.

Combined inequality: $A \geq B \geq C$ or $C \leq B \leq A$

(x) B less than one term C and greater than (or equal to) other term A, combination possible.

Combined inequality: $A \leq B < C$ or $C > B \geq A$.

Step III: (iv), (v), (vii) were rejected in step II.

Now, let us apply third golden rule to the combined inequality obtained in case of (iii), (vi), (viii), (ix) and (x).

(iii) **Combined inequality:** $A > B > C$

Conclusion: $A > C$

(Because '≥' sign does not appear twice in the combined inequality, it does not appear in the conclusion.)

(vi) **Combined inequality:** $A < B < C$

Conclusion: $A < C$

(Because '≤' sign does not appear twice in the combined inequality, it does not appear in the conclusion.)

(viii) **Combined inequality:** $C \geq B \geq A$

Conclusion: $C \geq A$

(Because '≥' sign appears twice in the combined inequality, it does appear in the conclusion.)

(ix) **Combined inequality:** $A \geq B \geq C$

Conclusion: $A \geq C$

(Because '≥' sign appears twice in the combined inequality, it does appear in the conclusion.)

(x) **Combined inequality:** $A \leq B < C$

Conclusion: $A < C$

(Because '≤' sign does not appear twice; it appears only once, it does not appear in the conclusion.)

Thus, our solution is:

(i) no combination possible.
(ii) -do-
(iii) $A > B > C$. **Conclusion:** $A > C$
(iv) no combination possible.
(v) -do-
(vi) $A < B < C$. **Conclusion:** $A < C$
(vii) no combination possible.
(viii) $C \geq B \geq A$. **Conclusion:** $C \geq A$
(ix) $A \geq B \geq C$. **Conclusion:** $A \geq C$
(x) $A \leq B < C$. **Conclusion:** $A < C$

20.5: The Strategy for Solution

We have had enough theoretical background by now to tackle the problem in a quick, neat and efficient fashion. Without wasting much space, I straight, away come to the various steps needed to solve the problem.

First Step: *Neatly decode.*

The question itself tells you which code stands for which arithmetical operation. For example, in our sample problem as given in 20. 2 we have given that P α Q means P > Q. Therefore replace 'α' by '>' wherever you see them. Then, replace 'β' by '≥', 'γ' by '=', 'δ' by '<' and 'η' by '≤'. *You should take one code at a time and replace it by its original mathematical symbol in* ***all the five questions*** *before going to the next code. And you should do it quickly:*

Second step: Take one conclusion at a time and decide which statements are relevant for evaluating the conclusion.

Now, this needs some thinking. What do we mean by relevant statements? By a relevant statement we mean the statement that is not useless for deriving a conclusion. If there is a conclusion, say, x > y then a statement like b > c is useless because this statement has neither x nor y. Therefore, any analysis of this statement can't tell us anything about the conclusion: x > y. For any conclusion, the relevant statements are those that can be combined to prove or disprove that conclusion. How do we find the relevant statements?

It is simple....

To decide which statements are relevant for a conclusion; *take the two terms of a given conclusion and see if each of them separately appears with a single common term in the given statements in the question.* These statements will be our "relevant statements".

To understand the above let us take conclusion I; (M δ K). This conclusion has two terms M and K. Now, we look at the given statements (M α N, L γ M, O δ N and L η K) and find that M and K appear separately with a common term L in the following two statements:

L γ M, L η K.

Hence, the above two statements are the relevant statements for us, for evaluating our conclusion.

Learner's Exercise III

In our sample problem given in section 20.2; find out the relevant statements for conclusions in Q 1, Q 2, and Q 3.

Soln: (1) Q. 1: Given Statements: M α N, L γ M, O δ N, L η K

(i) **Conclusion I:** M δ K.

It has two terms M and K. Now, out of the four statements given: M and K appear separately with a common term L in these two statements:

L γ M, L η K.

Hence, these are our relevant statements.

(ii) **Conclusion II:** L α N

It has two terms L and N. Now, L and N appear separately with a common term M in the following statements:

M α N, L γ M.

Hence, these two are our relevant statements.

(2) Q. 2: Given Statements: E γ F, C δ D, F β G, D α E

(i) **Conclusion I:** E α G.

It has two terms E and G. Now, E and G appear separately with a common term F in the following statements:

E γ F, F β G.

Hence, these two are our relevant statements.

(ii) **Conclusion II:** C γ E

It has two terms C and E. Now, C and E appear separately with a common term D in the following statements:

C δ D, D α E.

Hence, these two are our relevant statements.

(3) Q. 3: Given Statements: L β M, O γ N, L δ H, M γ O

(i) **Conclusion I:** L γ N

It has two terms L and N. Here, we see that L and N do not appear with a common term in any pair of statements. This means that in this case more than two statements may be relevant for us. Here, we see that N appears only once (with O) in O γ N. Now, O appears with M (in M γ O) and M appears with L (in L β M). Hence, in this case we have:

O γ N, M γ O, L β M

as our relevant statements.

(ii) **Conclusion II:** L α N.

Relevant statements are O γ N, M γ O, L β M.

(For explanation see explanation for conclusion I).

Third step: *Use the golden rules to derive a conclusion from the relevant steps chosen in second step.* (And check if it matches with the conclusion under consideration.)

Ex. 10: For example, consider Q 1 of Ex 1

Soln: Given Statements: M α N, L γ M, O δ N, L η K

Conclusions: I. M δ K **II.** L α N

We first decode these: (**First step**)

Given Statements: M > N, L = M, O > N, L ≤ K

Conclusions: I. M < K **II.** L > N

Now, take conclusion I. For this, we find that the relevant statements are (**second step**):

M = L, L ≤ K.

We combine them and get M ≤ K. (**Third step**)

Now, M ≤ K does not imply that M < K because M ≤ K allows for M to be even equal to K which is not true in case of M < K. Hence, conclusion I does not follow. Now, take conclusion II. For this, the relevant statements are:

M > N, L = M.

Combining, we get L > N. Hence conclusion II follows.

Correct answer: 2 (Only conclusion II follows).

We are now fully conversant with our method. There are some minor details that we need to look into. We will do this now and after that we will go over to our complete solution-strategy.

20.5.1: Some additional points to keep in mind

Check 1: *Check if the conclusion directly follows from only single given statement.*

Sometimes, a statement may be in the form of A ≥ B and one conclusion may be in the form of B ≤ A. Obviously, both these are completely identical but sometimes we are prone to ignoring such minor tricks of the examiner.

Ex. 11: For example, consider the following:

(Let a mean >, β mean ≥, γ mean =, δ mean <, η mean ≤)

Let, given statement: E γ F, C δ D, F β G, D β F

Conclusion: I. G η F.

Here, conclusion I is G η F or $G \leq F$ and it is identical to F β G or $F \geq G$. Hence, it directly follows from one single statement. (Also see, Q 46, 47 Practice Exercises)

Check 2: *The conclusion you reach after the Third Step (Section 20.5) may be identical to the given conclusion although it may not look so in the first glance.* Check.

For Example, if you arrive at a conclusion- inequality: $A \leq B$ then a given conclusion $B \geq A$ is obviously true.

Check 3: *If after the third step you get a conclusion that has a '≥' (or a '≤') sign and the two given conclusions have a '>' (or a '<') sign and a '=' sign between the same terms; the choice either I or II follows is correct.* **(Very Imp.)**

For example, suppose you reach $A \geq B$ after performing the Third step. Now, suppose the given conclusions are: I. $A > B$ and II. $A = B$. Then, the choice "either I or II follows" is correct and correct answer: 3. Similarly, if you conclude that $M \leq N$ and the given conclusions are I. $M < N$ and II. $M = N$ then again the same answer follows.

(**Note:** See Q 4, 11, 13 etc. of Practice Exercise)

Check 4: *If the two given conclusions have a*

(i) '≤' and '>' signs, or

(ii) '' and '≥' signs, or

(iii) '>' and '≤' signs, or

(iv) '≥' and '<' signs

between the same terms; and if neither of the conclusion has been accepted in any of the steps above; the choice "either of the two follows" is correct. *(Important)*

[**Note:** Also see, Q 50, Practice Exercise]

For example, suppose in a given question the given conclusions are:

I. $A \geq B$ **II.** $A < B$.

And suppose that neither of them have been proved to be true by virtue of any of the preceding steps.

Then, since they have the same pair (A and B) and the sign are '≥' and '<'; the choice "either follows" is correct. Correct choice is: 3.

A note on Check 3 and Check 4:

Check 3: Check 3 merely tells you that if you have concluded that [$A \geq B$] you can as well write it as [$A > B$ or $A = B$].

Again, if you have concluded that [$A \leq B$] you can as well write it as [either $A < B$ or $A = B$].

Check 4: Check 4 merely tells you that one number can only have three positions vis-a-vis another number. It can be either less than or equal to or greater than the other.

This is true **universally** of any two numbers. That is, [$A \leq B$ **or** $A > B$] is a universally correct statement, because A can be either (less than or equal to) or (greater than) B.

Thus, for any two numbers A and B the following are *always* correct:

i) $(A \leq B)$ or $(A > B)$

ii) $(A < B)$ or $(A \geq B)$

iii) $(A > B)$ or $(A \leq B)$

iv) $(A \geq B)$ or $(A > B)$

We can call these four pairs of statements as our **complementary pairs**. Obviously, since one out of the two statements will always be true in such cases, we chooses "either follows" as our answer. But remember, we choose this as our answer *only if* neither of the two statements have been otherwise proved in any previous step. This is because if we have already proved that $A < B$ is definitely true it is ridiculous to still settle for the rather uncertain-looking answer that " either $A < B$ is true or $A \geq B$ is true". To understand this point better, consider Ex 12 and Ex 13 below.

Ex. 12: Given Statements: $A \geq B, B = D, D \leq C, C \leq B$

Conclusions: I. $A \geq C$ **II.** $A < C$

Soln: Here, both conclusions are between A and C here. We see that A and C appear with a common term B in

$$A \geq B \text{ and } C \leq B.$$

So, these are our relevant statements. They can be combined because they have a common term and because the common term B is less than (or equal to) one term A and greater than (or equal to) another term B.

Combining we get: $A \geq C$.

So, conclusion I follows. Correct Answer:1

Ex 13: Given Statements: $A \geq B, B = D, D \leq C, B \leq C$

Conclusions: I. $A \geq C$ **II.** $A < C$

Soln: By the same analysis as in Ex 12; our relevant statements are: $A \geq B$, $B \leq C$.

Now, these two can not be combined because the common term B is less than (or equal to) both A and C. Hence, no conclusion is possible.

But the two conclusions I and II from a complementary pair. And hence either of them must follow. Correct Answer: 3.

Note that we had the same complementary pair as our answer- choices in both Ex 12 and Ex 13. Yet we did not choose "either follows" in Ex 12 because there conclusion I was definitely established. But in Ex 13 no conclusion was definitely established and, therefore, we choose "either follows" as our answer.]

Complete Strategy For Solution: A Recap

Let us recapitulate our complete strategy for solving these problems. The strategy is:

First step: Neatly and quickly decode the symbols

Second Step: Take one conclusion at a time and decide which statements are relevant for evaluating it. (See Learner's Exercise V to understand it)

Third Step: Use the three golden rules to combine the relevant statements and derive a conclusion from it.

Those three golden rules are:

Rule 1: There must be a common term.

Rule 2: The common term must be less than (or equal to) one term and greater than (or equal to) another .

Rule 3: The conclusion-inequality is obtained by letting the common-term disappear and it has a '≥' or a '≤' sign if and only if the both the inequalities in second step had a '≥' or a '≤' sign. In all other cases, there will be a '>' or a '<' sign in the conclusion.

After performing these three steps, if a conclusion is established and verified; well and good. If not, then perform the following four checks:

Check 1: Check if the given conclusion directly follows from any one single statement.

Check 2: Check if the conclusion- inequality you reach is essentially the same as the given conclusion but written differently.

Check 3: If your derived conclusion (or a given statement) is of the type $A \geq B$ (or $A \leq B$) then check if the two given conclusions are $A > B$ and $A = B$ (or, $A < B$ and $A = B$). If yes, choice "either follows" is true.

Check 4: If neither of the conclusions has been proved correct till now, check if the given conclusions from a complementary pair. (They form a complementary pair in the following four cases:

(i) $A \geq B$ and $A < B$ (ii) $A > B$ and $A \leq B$

(iii) $A \leq B$ and $A > B$ (iv) $A < B$ and $A \geq B$

In such a case, the choice "either follows" is correct.

A complete and detailed solution to our sample problem

We will now demonstrate how to utilise the method above to quickly solve problems of this type.

Ex. 14: Solve Ex. 1 completely.

Soln: In first step, we quickly decode the symbols. Thus, we have:

1. **Statements:** $M > N$, $L = M$, $O < N$, $L \leq K$
   Conclusions: I. $M < K$ **II.** $L > N$
2. **Statements:** $E = F$, $C < D$, $F \geq G$, $D > E$
   Conclusions: I. $E > G$ **II.** $C = E$
3. **Statements:** $L \geq M$, $O = N$, $L < H$, $M = O$
   Conclusions: I. $L = N$ **II.** $L > N$

4. **Statements:** Z ≤ Y, K = L, Y < X, Z > K
   Conclusions: I. Y > L **II.** Y = L
5. **Statements:** R < I, S = C, S ≥ I, C > O
   Conclusions: I. C < I **II.** S > R

Now, we will take each of the questions separately and perform step II and III for each of the conclusions.

1. (i) **Conclusion I:** See Learner's Exercise V. Relevant statements are: L = M, L ≤ K.
   Combining, we get: M ≤ K. This does not match with the given conclusion; M < K.
   (ii) **Conclusion II:** See Learner's Exercise V. Relevant statements are: M > N, L = M.
   Combining, we get L > N. Hence, only conclusion II follows correct answer: 2
2. (i) **Conclusion I:** See Learner's Exercise V. Relevant statements are: E = F, F ≥ G.
   Combining, we get E ≥ G. This does not match with the conclusion given: E > G.
   (ii) **Conclusion II:** See Learner's Exercise V. Relevant statements are: C < D, D > E.
   Combining we get, C < E. This does not match with C = E. Hence both conclusions are rejected. Check 1, 2, 3, 4; as mentioned in section 20.5.2 are also futile. Correct answer: 4
3. (i) **Conclusion I:** See Learner's Exercise V. Relevant statements are: O = N, M = O, L ≥ M.
   Combining the first two, we get M = N. Combining this with L ≥ M, we get: L ≥ N. This means that conclusion I does not follow.
   (ii) **Conclusion II:** we have already seen that L ≥ N follows. This is different from L > N so conclusion II does not follow. But, by virtue of Check 3, choice 3 is correct.
4. (i) **Conclusion I:** Conclusion I is Y? L. Now, from the given statements, Y and l do not appear separately with a single common term. Y appears with Z, Z with K and K with L. Hence, we will have to take these three as our relevant statements. They are:

   Z ≤ Y, Z > K, K = L

   Combining Z ≤ Y and Z > K (see golden rule III, question (x), learner's exercise III) we get: Y > K. Now, combining it with K = L; we get Y > L. So, conclusion I follows.
   (ii) **Conclusion II:** Conclusion II is Y = L. Which is not true as Y > L has been proved.

Correct answer: 1

5. (i) **Conclusion I:** Conclusion I is C < I. C and I appear separately with S in S = C and S ≥ I. So, these two are our relevant statements. Combining, we get: C ≥ I. This means conclusion I is not true.

   (ii) **Conclusion II:** Conclusion II is S > R. Now, S and R appear separately with a common term I; in R < I and S ≥ I. So, these two are our relevant statements and combining them we get: R < S. By Check 2, it is the same as S > R. Hence, conclusion II follows. Correct answer: 2

20.6: Quick method: some final time saving tips

We have already discussed a complete and elaborate strategy for solution. Initially, the method may look long and cumbersome to you. But after a sufficient amount of practice, you may see how easy and quick it actually is. Below we are giving you some additional time saving tips for each of the steps.

Tip 1: First step of decoding should be done on the question-sheet itself. Usually, you have enough space in the Question-sheet to put an additional sign. So, if a stood for 'greater than' then for A α B you should write a small '>' above 'α', So that it looks like A $\overset{>}{\alpha}$ B. You should not do the foolishness of copying the entire questions and then choices and substituting the decoded signs.

Tip 2: Second step of finding out the relevant statements is very important from the point of view of speed. You should (1) understand this procedure clearly and there should be no doubt: if needed, go through Learner's Exercise V again and again; and (2) be able to perform second step mentally and write it in a few seconds. This is very important and please give a lot of practice to this.

Tip 3: In the third step, you first combine the two statements. For this, you first see if a combination is possible using the first and second golden rule. The second golden rule says that a combination is possible only if the common term is greater than (or equal to) one term and less than (or equal to) another term.

You can check this more quickly by following a *visual-rule*. If the common term is greater than (or equal to) one term and less than (or equal to) another term; then the pointed side of the '>' sign (or a '≥' sign) will be *towards* the common term in one case and away from the common term in the other. So, a combination is possible in only such cases. In all other cases, the pointed side of the '>' sign (or a '≥' sign) will be *towards* the common term in *both* the cases or *away from* the common terms in *both* the cases.

Ex. 15: When is combination possible in Ex 4. Tell by the visual method described above.

Soln: (i) A > B, B > C. Combination possible as the tip of '>' sign points towards the common term in the first case and away from it in B > C.

(ii) A ≥ B, C < B. Combination possible as the tip points towards B in A ≥ B and away from B in C < B.

(iii) B < A, B ≥ C. Combination possible as the tip points towards B in B < A and away from B in B ≥ C.

(iv) A > B, C > B. Combination not possible as the tip points towards B in *both* cases.

(v) A ≥ B, B < C. Combination not possible as the tip points towards B in *both* cases.

(vi) B ≥ A, C ≥ B. Combination possible as the tip points away from B in B ≥ A and towards B in C ≥ B.

(vii) A ≥ B, B ≤ C. Combination not possible as the tip points towards B in both cases.

(viii) B ≤ A, B ≥ C. Combination possible as the tip points towards B in B ≤ A and away from B in B ≥ C.

Tip 4: When combining inequalities with '≥' or '≤' sign never forget the third golden rule. (See Ex 5, 6, 7, 8, and 9)

Tip 5: Check 1 and check 2 should not be taken as additional steps. They should be obvious to you if they are needed. (See solution to Q 5, Ex 1; conclusion II).

Tips: **Check 3 and check 4 are required only if both the conclusions have the same pair of terms**. Thus, if conclusion I is A > B and conclusion II is A ≤ C then we need not go for check 3 or 4 because one conclusion has a different pair (A and B) from the other (A and C).

Tip 7: Two terms can never be equal if in the original statements these two terms don't appear in separate equalities. (Very Imp.)

That is, unless there are two (or more) separate equalities with A in one and B in another, a conclusion of the type A = B is definitely false.

In other words, if the original statement had statements like A = X... B = Y then it fulfils the criterion that both a and B have equalities in the original statements. In such a case, the conclusion A = B may not be false. But if there are no separate equalities involving A and B; such a conclusion is definitely false.

Ex 16: Consider:

Statements: M = N, P ≥ Q, M < P, N = R

Conclusions: I. N = P ....etc.

In this case, the conclusion N = P must be false because there are no equalities involving P in the original four statements. In other words, P is not equal to any other term in the original four statements, so N = P must be false.

Tip 8: (i) If a term was not less than (or, "less than or equal to") any other term in the given statements, then it can't be less than (or less than or equal to") any term in a conclusion. (Such a conclusion is definitely false.)

(ii) If a term was not greater than (or, "greater than or equal to") any other term in the given statements, then it can't be greater than (or, "greater than or equal to") any term in a conclusion. (Such a conclusion is definitely false.) (Very Imp.)

Ex. 17: Consider Ex 16 above. Let us consider the conclusions:

I. P < R **II.** M > Q

Soln: (I) Here, P < R must be false because in the original four statements P has never been less than any term. It has appeared twice in P ≥ Q, M > P and on both occasions it has not been the lesser term. So, by virtue of Tip 8 (i); this conclusion must be false.

(II) Here, M > Q must be false because in the original four statements M was never greater than any term. It appeared twice in M = N and M < P and on no occasion it has been the greater term. So, by virtue of Tip 8 (ii), this conclusion must be false.

[Note: Tip 7 and 8 give you the power to reject a conclusion straight away without going into any steps. Be sure you understand them. See the next fully solved example to further grasp these time-saving tips.]

20.7: One more fully solved example

Before we move on to exercises, we will give one more fully solved example. This time we will also incorporate the timesaving tips given. But this time we wont be explaining each and every step in detail.

Ex. 18:

Directions (Q. 1-5): In the following questions, the symbol ⊗, ©̲, =, @ and @̲ are used with the following meaning:

P ⊗ Q means P is greater than Q.

P ©̲ Q means P is either greater than or equal to Q.

P = Q means P is equal to Q.

P @ Q means P is smaller than Q.

P @̲ Q means P is either smaller than or equal to Q.

Now, in each of the following questions assuming the given statements to be true, find which of the two conclusions I and II given below them is /are definitely true. Give answer

1) if only conclusion I is true;
2) if only conclusion II is true;
3) if either I or II is true;
4) if neither I nor II is true; and
5) if both I and II are true.

1. **Statements:** A ©̲ N, J @ U, S ⊗ A, J = N

Conclusions: I. J @ S **II.** U ⊗ N

2. **Statements:** T = M, U @ A, T ⊗ U, G ©̲ A
   Conclusions: I. A = M **II.** G ⊗ U
3. **Statements:** N ⊗ A, H @ C, A = H, N @̲ D
   Conclusions: I. D ⊗ N **II.** D = N
4. **Statements:** M = R, N ⊗ A, R @ T, M @̲ A
   Conclusions: I. M @ N **II.** T = M
5. **Statements:** Y ⊗ N, T @ N, A = Y, J ©̲ A
   Conclusions: I. J = Y **II.** Y @ T

SOLUTION:

Step I: We first decode entire questionnaire. We have

1. **Statements:** $A \geq N, J < U, S > A, J = N$
   Conclusions: I. $J < S$ **II.** $U > N$
2. **Statements:** $T = M, U < A, T > U, G \geq A$
   Conclusions: I. $A = M$ **II.** $G > U$
3. **Statements:** $N > A, H < C, A = H, N \leq D$
   Conclusions: I. $D > N$ **II.** $D = N$
4. **Statements:** $M = R, N > A, R < T, M \leq A$
   Conclusions: I. $M < N$ **II.** $T = M$
5. **Statements:** $Y > N, T < N, A = Y, J \geq A$
   Conclusions: I. $J = Y$ **II.** $Y < T$

Rest of the steps

1. (i) **Conclusion I:** given conclusion $J < S$. Relevant statements $J = N$, $A \geq N$, $S > A$. Combining first two: $A \geq J$. Now, combining $A \geq J$ and $S > A$ we have $S > J$. By check 2, conclusion I is true.
   (ii) **Conclusion II:** $U > N$. Relevant statements are $J < U$ and $J = N$. Combining, $N < U$. By check 2, conclusion II is true. Correct answer is 5.
2. (i) **Conclusion I:** $A = M$. But by Tip 7, it can't be true because A is not equal to any term in the four given statements. [Note that by virtue of Tip 7, we saved the time in doing step II, III etc...]
   (ii) **Conclusion II:** $G > U$. Relevant statements are: $G \geq A, U < A$. (Combination possible because tip points towards common term A in $G \geq A$ and away from it in $U < A$). Combining, we have $G \geq A > U$ which gives $G > U$. So, II follows.
   Correct answer: 2
3. (i) **Conclusion I:** $D > N$.
   (ii) **Conclusion II:** $D = N$.
   By check 3; either of them must follow from $N \leq D$ which is already given.
   Correct answer: 3
4. (i) **Conclusion I:** $M < N$. Relevant statements are: $M \leq A, N > A$. Combining, $M \leq A < N$. Conclusion is $M < N$. So, conclusion I follows.
   (ii) **Conclusion II:** $T = M$. Not possible because T is not equal to any other term in the four given statements (by virtue of Tip 7).
   Correct answer: 1

5. (i) **Conclusion I:** J = Y. Not possible because J is not equal to any other term in the four given statements (Tip 7).
   (ii) **Conclusion II:** Y < T. Not possible because Y is not less than any other term in any of the four given statements. (So, it can't be less than T.) This follows from Tip 8. (Note that by virtue of Tip 8, you save the time in doing Step II, III etc.). **Correct answer: 4**

Appendix I

Table: Various possible pairs of inequalities and their conclusions (if possible)
(**Note:** For clarity's sake we take y as a common term)

First Inequality	Second Inequality	Combined Inequality if) possible)	Conclusion Inequality
$x > y$ $x < a$	$y > a$ $y < z$	Not possible because 4 terms. No common term (Golden rule 1 violated)	— None —
$x > y$ $x > y$ $x \geq y$ $x \geq y$	$y < z$ $y \leq z$ $y < z$ $y \leq z$	Not possible because the tip of the inequality sign is pointed *towards* the common term y in *both* inequalities. (Tip 3. Golden rule 2 violated)	— None —
$x < y$ $x \leq y$ $x \leq y$ $x < y$	$y > z$ $y > z$ $y \geq z$ $y \geq z$	Not possible because the tip is pointed *away* from the common term y in *both* cases. (Tip 3. Golden rule 2 violated)	— None —
$x > y$ $x > y$ $x \geq y$ $x \geq y$	$y > z$ $y \geq z$ $y > z$ $y \geq z$	$x > y > z$ $x > y \geq z$ $x \geq y > z$ $x \geq y \geq z$	$x > z$ $x > z$ $x > z$ $x \geq z$*
$x < y$ $x < y$ $x \leq y$ $x \leq y$	$y < z$ $y \leq z$ $y < z$ $y \leq z$	$x < y < z$ $x < y \leq z$ $x \leq y < z$ $x \leq y \leq z$	$x < z$ $x < z$ $x < z$ $x \leq z$*

* The conclusion has a ≥ (or a ≤) sign if and only if both the parent inequalities have ≥ (or ≤) signs.

Practice Exercises

Directions (Q. 1- 60): In all the questions that follow different symbols have been used with different meanings. For each set of questions, you have to assume given statements to be true and then decide which of the two given conclusions is/ are definitely true. Give answer:

1) if only I is true
2) if only conclusion II is true
3) if either conclusion I or II is true
4) if neither I nor II is true
5) if both are true

Directions (Q. 1- 5): In the following questions, the symbols @, $\underline{@}$, =, ©, $\underline{\text{©}}$ are used with the following meaning:

P @ Q means P is greater than Q.
P $\underline{@}$ Q means P is either greater than or equal to Q.
P = Q means P is equal to Q.
P © Q means P is smaller than Q.
P $\underline{\text{©}}$ Q means P is either smaller than or equal to Q.

1. **Statements:** A @ B, B $\underline{\text{©}}$ C, C $\underline{\text{©}}$ D
   Conclusions: **I.** A @ D **II.** C = D
2. **Statements:** L $\underline{\text{©}}$ K, M © N, K = M
   Conclusions: **I.** N @ L **II.** K $\underline{\text{©}}$ N
3. **Statements:** X @ Y, Z $\underline{\text{©}}$ R, Y = Z
   Conclusions: **I.** X @ R **II.** Y = R
4. **Statements:** G $\underline{@}$ F, D $\underline{\text{©}}$ E, E = F
   Conclusions: **I.** E © G **II.** E = G
5. **Statements:** I $\underline{\text{©}}$ J, K = J $\underline{\text{©}}$ L, H $\underline{@}$ J
   Conclusions: **I.** J = L **II.** I $\underline{\text{©}}$ H

Directions (Q. 6-10): In the following questions, the symbols ⊕, $\underline{\text{©}}$, =, @ and $\underline{@}$ are used with the following meaning:

P ⊕ Q means P is greater than Q.
P $\underline{\text{©}}$ Q means P is either greater than or equal to Q.
P = Q means P is equal to Q.
P @ Q means P is smaller than Q.
P $\underline{@}$ Q means P is either smaller than or equal to Q.

6. **Statements:** N @ W, L ⊕ N, K = L, W = D
   Conclusions: **I.** L = W **II.** D ⊕ N
7. **Statements:** L $\underline{\text{©}}$ A, S @ E, A = S, G ⊕ L
   Conclusions: **I.** A @ E **II.** G ⊕ A

8. **Statements:** M = I, A ⊕ M, T $\underline{@}$ I, T = K
   Conclusions: I. M = K **II.** K @ M
9. **Statements: I.** $\underline{@}$ R, D @ I, E = C, R ⊕ E
   Conclusions: I. R ⊕ C **II.** I = R
10. **Statements:** U ⊕ N, S © O, N @ D, O = U
   Conclusions: I. N @ S **II.** U = D

Directions (Q. 11-15): In the following questions, the symbol ⊕, ©, =, @ and $\underline{@}$ are used with the following meaning:

P ⊕ Q means P is greater than Q.

P © Q means P is either greater than or equal to Q.

P = Q means P is equal to Q.

P @ Q means P is smaller than Q.

P $\underline{@}$ Q means P is either smaller than or equal to Q.

11. **Statements:** M @ L, O ⊕ P, M = N, O $\underline{@}$ N
   Conclusions: I. M ⊕ O **II.** M = O
12. **Statements:** W @ N, S = Q, R © N, S @ R
   Conclusions: I. W @ R **II.** N = Q
13. **Statements:** A @ B, D $\underline{@}$ E, C = D, C © B
   Conclusions: I. E ⊕ B **II.** B = E
14. **Statements:** W ⊕ U, Y = X, Z @ Y, X © W
   Conclusions: I. Z = W **II.** X ⊕ Z
15. **Statements:** R © A, U ⊕ L, A = H, H © U
   Conclusions: I. H = L **II.** L @ H

Directions (Q. 16-20): In the following questions the symbols $, @, *, ** and # are used with the following meaning:

A $ B means A is greater than B.

A @ B means A is either greater than or equal to B.

A * B means A is equal to B.

A ** B means A is smaller than B.

A # B means A is either smaller than or equal to B.

16. **Statements:** P @ Q, M # N, N ** Q
   Conclusions: I. P $ M **II.** N # P
17. **Statements:** D ** X, F @ Y, D $ F
   Conclusions: I. X @ Y **II.** Y # D
18. **Statements:** M ** P, S $ T, M @ T
   Conclusions: I. S * M **II.** T ** P
19. **Statements:** U * V, X $ W, U ** W
   Conclusions: I. W $ V **II.** U ** X
20. **Statements:** G $ H, J # K, H * K
   Conclusions: I. H $ J **II.** J * H

Directions (Q. 21-25): In the following questions, the symbols ⊕, $\underline{©}$, =, @ and $\underline{@}$ are used with the following meanings:

P ⊕ Q means P is greater than Q.
P $\underline{©}$ Q means P is either greater than or equal to Q.
P = Q means P is equal to Q.
P @ Q means P is smaller than Q.
P $\underline{@}$ Q means P is either smaller than or equal to Q.

21. **Statements:** H $\underline{@}$ V, A = Z, H $\underline{©}$ Z, F ⊕ V
    Conclusions: I. A = H **II.** H ⊕ A
22. **Statements:** Q @ R, C ⊕ D, F $\underline{©}$ R, D = F
    Conclusions: I. Q @ C **II.** C ⊕ F
23. **Statements:** M = X, L @ O, N ⊕ M, L $\underline{@}$ X
    Conclusions: I. N ⊕ L **II.** X @ O
24. **Statements:** I ⊕ O, R $\underline{©}$ I, Z = R, J @ Z
    Conclusions: I. Z = I **II.** Z ⊕ I
25. **Statements:** S $\underline{@}$ F, K @ S, B = K, R ⊕ B
    Conclusions: I. F ⊕ K **II.** K @ R

Directions (Q. 26-30): In the following questions, the symbols α, β, γ, δ and η are used with the following meaning:

P α Q means P is greater than Q.
P β Q means P is either greater than or equal to Q.
P γ Q means P is equal to Q.
P δ Q means P is smaller than Q.
P η Q means P is either smaller than or equal to Q.

26. **Statements:** M β I, T γ B, M δ A, I α T
    Conclusions: I. M γ T **II.** A α I
27. **Statements:** H γ A, N δ A, C α H, N η D
    Conclusions: I. C α N **II.** A γ D
28. **Statements:** D β I, J δ V, G η I, V γ G
    Conclusion: I. G δ D **II.** D γ G
29. **Statements:** P γ O, R α T, S η P, R δ O
    Conclusions: I. S γ O **II.** P δ T
30. **Statements:** O α K, S β H, S δ A, H γ O
    Conclusions: I. S α O **II.** A α K

Directions (Q. 31-35): In the questions given below, certain symbols are used with the following meaning:

A @ B means A is greater than B.
A + B means A is either greater than or equal to B.
A † B means A is smaller than B.
A ⊗ B means A is either smaller than or equal to B.
A $ B means A is equal to B.

31. **Statements:** T $ G, K @ P, M † T, P + M
    Conclusions: I. K @ T **II.** G $ P

32. **Statements:** R + N, S ⊗ B, A @ α, B $ A
Conclusions: I. S $ N **II.** A @ N
33. **Statements:** G $ K, F @ J, K + Q, Q + F
Conclusions: I. K $ F **II.** F † K
34. **Statements:** W @ S, K ⊗ Z, U + W, S $ K
Conclusions: I. U @ K **II.** Z @ S
35. **Statements:** G $ E, D † K, E † S, K ⊗ G
Conclusions: I. S @ D **II.** D † E

Directions (Q. 36-40): In the following questions, the symbols @, +, ©, ⊗, and $ are used with the following meanings:

A @ B means A is greater than B.
A + B means A is greater than or equal to B.
A $ B means A is equal to B.
A © B means A is smaller than B.
A ⊗ B means A is smaller than or equal to B.

36. **Statements:** W @ K, S ⊗ Z, X + W, S $ K
Conclusions: I. K $ Z **II.** X @ K
37. **Statements:** L + R, N $ M, L © M, N ⊗ P
Conclusions: I. M @ R **II.** R @ P
38. **Statements:** P © Q, W + N, P + N, T @ W
Conclusions: I. P $ W **II.** Q © W
39. **Statements:** D ⊗ S, N @ V, D $ R, R @ V
Conclusions: I. S @ V **II.** D @ N
40. **Statements:** K $ P, M © J, C © P, K ⊗ M
Conclusions: I. M @ P **II.** M $ P

Directions (Q. 41-45): In the following questions, the symbols @, +, ©, ⊗, and $ are used with the following meanings:

A @ B means A is greater than B.
A + B means A is greater than or equal to B.
A $ B means A is equal to B.
A © B means B means A is smaller than B.
A ⊗ B means A is smaller than or equal to B.

41. **Statements:** T ⊗ G, L © T, C $ L, S @ C
Conclusions: I. G @ L **II.** L © S
42. **Statements:** J @ P, S + J, A $ S, K © A
Conclusions: I. A $ J **II.** A @ J
43. **Statements:** N $ Y, M © P, O @ N, M ⊗ Y
Conclusions: I. O @ M **II.** Y © P
44. **Statements:** R © S, D @ E, G + S, E $ G
Conclusions: I. R © D **II.** D @ G
45. **Statements:** I. ⊗ W, B $ A, I + A, G @ W.
Conclusions: I. B $ I **II.** I @ B

Directions (Q. 46- 50): In the following questions, the symbols Δ, □, $, @ and £ are used with the following meanings:

A Δ B means A is greater than B.

A □ B means A is greater than or equal to B.

A $ B means A is equal to B.

A @ B means A is lesser than B.

A £ B means A is lesser than or equal to B.

46. **Statements:** P □ R, S @ T, U @ V
Conclusions: **I.** V Δ U **II.** S □ R

47. **Statements:** C Δ D, D $ E, D Δ F
Conclusions: **I.** D @ C **II.** C $ E

48. **Statements:** L Δ M, N □ O, N @ P
Conclusions: **I.** N @ M **II.** O @ M

49. **Statements:** G @ H, I Δ J, H @ J
Conclusions: **I.** J Δ G **II.** I $ H

50. **Statements:** S £ T, L @ P, P □ S
Conclusions: **I.** T @ P **II.** P £ T

Directions (Q. 51- 55): In the following questions, the symbols +, ±, =, @, and $\underline{@}$ are used with the following meanings:

A + B means A is greater than B.

A ± B means A is greater than or equal to B.

A = B means A is equal to B.

A @ B means A is smaller than B.

A $\underline{@}$ B means A is smaller than or equal to B.

51. **Statements:** J @ K, J @ L, L + M
Conclusions: **I.** J @ M **II.** L = J

52. **Statements:** G $\underline{@}$ H, H $\underline{@}$ J, L @ G
Conclusions: **I.** L @ H **II.** H + L

53. **Statements:** M + N, M + P, O = N
Conclusions: **I.** N + M **II.** O @ M

54. **Statements:** T = U, U = V, V @ W
Conclusions: **I.** W + T **II.** W = U

55. **Statements:** A @ B, C $\underline{@}$ A, C + D
Conclusions: **I.** C @ B **II.** B + D

Directions (Q. 56-60): In the following questions, the symbols @, $\underline{@}$, =, © and $\underline{©}$ are used with the following meaning:

P @ Q means P is greater than Q.

P $\underline{@}$ Q means P is either greater than or equal to Q.

P = Q means P is equal to Q.

P © Q means P is smaller than Q.

P $\underline{©}$ Q means P is either smaller than or equal to Q.

56. **Statements:** B @ V, K © C, C $\underline{©}$ B
Conclusions: **I.** V @ C **II.** B @ K

57. **Statements:** K @ T, S = K, T $\underline{\copyright}$ R

Conclusions: **I.** S @ R **II.** T = R

58. **Statements:** U = M, P $\underline{@}$ U, M $\underline{@}$ B

Conclusions: **I.** P = B **II.** P @ B

59. **Statements:** L $\underline{@}$ N, J $\underline{\copyright}$ P, P $\underline{@}$ L

Conclusions: **I.** J = L **II.** P = N

60. **Statements:** H $\underline{@}$ G, D @ E, H = E

Conclusions: **I.** D @ H **II.** G © D

Directions (Q. 61-65): In the following questions, the symbols @, $, , # and δ are used with the following meaning as illustrated below:

'P $ Q' means 'P is not smaller than Q'.

'P @ Q' means 'P is neither smaller than nor equal to Q'.

'P # Q' means 'P is neither greater than nor equal to Q'.

'P δ Q' means 'P is neither greater than nor smaller than Q'.

'P Q' means 'P is not greater than Q'.

Now in each of the following questions assuming the given statements to be true, find which of the four conclusions I, II, III and IV given below them is/are **definitely true** and give your answer accordingly.

61. **Statements:** H @ T, T # F, F δ E, E V

Conclusions: **I.** V $ F **II.** E @ T

III. H @ V **IV.** T # V

1) Only I, II and III are true 2) Only I, II and IV are true

3) Only II, III and IV are true 4) Only I, III and IV are true

5) All I, II, III and IV are true

62. **Statements:** D # R, R K, K @ F, F $ J

Conclusions: **I.** J # R **II.** J # K

III. R # F **IV.** K @ D

1) Only I, II and III are true 2) Only II, III and IV are true

3) Only I, III and IV are true 4) All I, II, III and IV are true

5) None of these

63. **Statements:** N δ B, B $ W, W # H, H M

Conclusions: **I.** M @ W **II.** H @ N

III. W δ N **IV.** W # N

1) Only I is true 2) Only III is true

3) Only IV is true 4) Only either III or IV is true

5) Only either III or IV and I are true

64. **Statements:** R D, D $ J, J # M, M @ K

Conclusions: **I.** K # J **II.** D @ M

III. R # M **IV.** D @ K

1) None is true 2) Only I is true

3) Only II is true 4) Only III is true

5) Only IV is true

65. **Statements:** M $ K, K @ N, N R, R # W

Conclusions: I. W @ K **II.** M $ R

III. K @ W **IV.** M @ N

1) Only I and II are true
2) Only I, II and III are true
3) Only III and IV are true
4) Only II, III and IV are true
5) None of these

Directions (Q. 66-70): In the following questions, the symbols @, ©, %, $ and are used with the following meanings illustrated.

‘P © Q’ means ‘P is not greater than Q’.

‘P Q’ means ‘P is not smaller than Q’.

‘P % Q’ means ‘P is neither greater than nor equal to Q’.

‘P $ Q’ means ‘P is neither smaller than nor equal to Q’.

‘P @ Q’ means ‘P is neither greater than nor smaller than Q’.

In each of the following questions, assuming the given statements to be true, find out which of the three conclusions I, II and III given below them is/are **definitely true**.

66. **Statements:** J $ D, D © K, K % R

Conclusions: I. R $ J **II.** R $ D

III. K $ J

1) None is true
2) Only I is true
3) Only II is true
4) Only III is true
5) Only II and III are true

67. **Statements:** M K, K @ R, R % N

Conclusions: I. R % M **II.** R @ M

III. N $ K

1) Only I is true
2) Only II is true
3) Only III is true
4) Only either I or II is true
5) Only either I or II and III are true

68. **Statements:** B % H, H $ J, J M

Conclusions: I. B % J **II.** M % B

III. H $ M

1) None is true
2) Only I is true
3) Only II is true
4) Only III is true
5) Only II and III are true

69. **Statements:** Z © K, K % E, E @ R

Conclusions: I. R $ K **II.** Z % E

III. R $ Z

1) Only I is true
2) Only I and II are true
3) Only I and III are true
4) Only II and III are true
5) All I, II and III are true

70. **Statements:** W @ M, M © R, R $ F
Conclusions: I. F % M **II.** R W
III. W % F
1) None is true 2) Only I is true
3) Only II is true 4) Only III is true
5) Only I and II are true

Directions (Q. 71-75): In the following questions, the symbols @, $, #, © and % are used with the following meaning as illustrated below.

'P $ Q' means 'P is not smaller than Q'.
'P © Q' means 'P is neither greater than nor equal to Q'.
'P # Q' means 'P is neither smaller than nor equal to Q'.
'P % Q' means 'P is not greater than Q'.
'P @ Q' means 'P is neither greater than nor smaller than Q'.

Now, in each of the following questions, assuming the given statements to be true, find which of the four conclusions I, II, III and IV given below them is/are definitely true and give your answer accordingly.

71. **Statements:** R # J, J $ D, D @ K, K % T
Conclusions: I. T # D **II.** T @ D
III. R # K **IV.** J $ T
1) Only either I or II is true
2) Only III is true
3) Only III and IV are true
4) Only either I or II and III are true
5) None of these

72. **Statements:** T % R, R $ M, M @ D, D © H
Conclusions: I. D % R **II.** H # R
III. T © M **IV.** T % D
1) Only I is true 2) Only I and IV are true
3) Only I and III are true 4) Only II and IV are true
5) None of these

73. **Statements:** M @ B, B # N, N $ R, R © K
Conclusions: I. K # B **II.** R © B
III. M $ R **IV.** N © M
1) Only I and III are true 2) Only I and II are true
3) Only II and IV are true 4) Only II, III and IV are true
5) None of these

74. **Statements:** F # H, H @ M, M © E, E $ J
Conclusions: I. J © M **II.** E # H
III. M © F **IV.** F # E
1) Only I and II are true 2) Only II and III are true
3) Only I, II and III are true 4) Only II, III and IV are true
5) None of these

75. **Statements:** D % A, A @ B, B © K, K % M
Conclusions: **I.** B $ D **II.** K # A
III. M # B **IV.** A © M
1) Only I, II and IV are true
2) Only I, II and III are true
3) Only II, III and IV are true
4) Only I, III and IV are true
5) All I, II, III and IV are true

Directions (Q. 76-80): In the following questions, the symbols @, #, %, $ and © are used with the following meaning as illustrated below:

'P # Q' means 'P is neither greater than nor equal to Q'.
'P © Q' means 'P is neither equal to nor smaller than Q'.
'P % Q' means 'P is neither smaller than nor greater than Q'.
'P $ Q' means 'P is not smaller than Q'.
'P @ Q' means 'P is not greater than Q'.

Now in each of the following questions, assuming the given statements to be true, find which of the three conclusions I, II and III given below them is/are definitely true and give your answer accordingly.

76. **Statements:** R @ D, D © W, B $ W
Conclusions: **I.** W # R **II.** B © D
III. W $ R
1) None is true 2) Only I is true
3) Only III is true 4) Only either I or III is true
5) All are true

77. **Statements:** H $ V, V % M, K © M
Conclusions: **I.** K © V **II.** M @ H
III. H © K
1) Only I and III are true 2) Only II and III are true
3) Only I and II are true 4) All are true
5) None of these

78. **Statements:** K # T, T $ B, B @ F
Conclusions: **I.** F $ T **II.** K # B
III. T $ F
1) None is true 2) Only I is true
3) Only I and II are true 4) Only II and III are true
5) All are true

79. **Statements:** Z # F, R @ F, D © R
Conclusions: **I.** Z # R **II.** F # D
III. D © Z
1) None is true 2) Only I is true
3) Only III is true 4) Only either I or III is true
5) All are true

80. **Statements:** M © R, R % D, D @ N
Conclusions: **I.** M © N **II.** N $ R
III. M © D
1) Only I and II are true 2) Only II and III are true
3) Only I and III are true 4) All are true
5) None of these

Directions (Q. 81-86): In the following questions, the symbols @, ©, %, and $ are used with the following meaning as illustrated below:

'P © Q' means 'P is not greater than Q'.
'P $ Q' means 'P is not smaller than Q'.
'P @ Q' means 'P is neither smaller than nor greater than Q.
'P   Q' means 'P is neither equal to nor greater than Q'.
'P % Q' means 'P is neither smaller than nor equal to Q'.

Now in each of the following questions, assuming the given statements to be true, find which of the three conclusions I, II and III given below them is/are definitely true and give your answer accordingly.

81. **Statements:** D @ M, M $ B, B   R, R % T
Conclusions: **I.** B   D **II.** B @ D
III. T   M
1) None is true 2) Only I is true
3) Only II is true 4) Only III is true
5) Only either I or II is true

82. **Statements:** W © F, F @ D, D   K, K $ J
Conclusions: **I.** K % W **II.** D $ W
III. F   K
1) Only I and II are true 2) Only I and III are true
3) Only II and III are true 4) All I, II and III are true
5) None of these

83. **Statements:** R   K, K © M, M % T, T $ J
Conclusions: **I.** J   M **II.** R   M
III. K © J
1) Only I is true 2) Only II is true
3) Only I and II are true 4) All I, II and III are true
5) None of these

84. **Statements:** R @ K, T © K, T $ M, M   W
Conclusions: **I.** W % K **II.** M © R
III. T © R
1) Only I is true
2) Only II is true
3) Only III is true
4) All I, II and III are true
5) None of these

85. **Statements:** T $ N,, N % B, B @ W, K © W

Conclusions: I. K $ B **II.** K $ T

III. T % B

1) Only I and II are true
2) Only I and III are true
3) Only II and III are true
4) All I, II and III are true
5) None of these

86. **Statements:** Z % V, V J, J © M, M @ R

Conclusions: I. R % V **II.** M % V

III. Z % M

1) Only I and II are true 2) Only I and III are true
3) Only II and III are true 4) All I, II and III are true
5) None of these

Directions (Q. 87-91): In the following questions, the symbols , δ, %, @ and © are used with the following meaning as illustrated below:

'P % Q' means 'P is not smaller than Q'.

'P © Q' means 'P is neither smaller than nor equal to Q',

'P Q' means 'P is neither greater than nor equal to Q'.

'P δ Q' means 'P is not greater than Q'.

'P @ Q' means 'P is neither greater than nor smaller than Q'.

Now, in each of the following questions, assuming the given statements to be true, find which of the three conclusions I, II and III given below them is/are definitely true and give your answer accordingly.

87. **Statement:** R δ K, K M, M @ J

Conclusions: I. J © K **II.** M © R

III. R J

1) Only I and II are true 2) Only II and III are true
3) Only I and III are true 4) All I, II and III are true
5) None of these

88. **Statements:** Z @ M, M © K, K F

Conclusions: I. F © Z **II.** K Z

III. F © M

1) None is true 2) Only I is true
3) Only II is true 4) Only III is true
5) Only II and III are true

89. **Statements:** B J, J % W, W © M

Conclusions: I. M J **II.** W B

III. B © M

1) None is true 2) Only I is true
3) Only II is true 4) Only III is true
5) Only I and III are true

90. **Statements:** V % H, H @ F, F δ E

Conclusions: I. F @ V **II.** F V

III. E % H

1) Only either I or II is true 2) Only III is true

3) Only I and II are true 4) All I, II and III are true

5) Only either I or II and III are true

91. **Statements:** W © T, T δ N, N % D

Conclusions: I. D T **II.** W © N

III. D @ T

1) None is true 2) Only I is true 3) Only II is true

4) Only III is true 5) Only I and II are true

Directions (Q. 92-97): In the following questions, the symbols @, ©, $, % and # are used with the following meaning as illustrated below:

'P $ Q' means 'P is not greater than Q'.

'P @ Q' means 'P is neither smaller than nor equal to Q'.

'P # Q' means' P is not smaller than Q'.

'P © Q' means 'P is neither greater than nor equal to Q'.

'P % Q' means 'P is neither smaller than nor greater than Q'.

Now in each of the following questions assuming the given statements to be true, find which of the three conclusions I, II and III given below them is/are **definitely true** and give your answer accordingly.

92. **Statements:** D # K, K @ T, T $ M, M % J

Conclusions: I. J @ T **II.** J % T

III. D @ T

1) Only I is true 2) Only II is true

3) Only either I or II is true 4) Only IV is true

5) Only either I or II and III are true

93. **Statements:** R @ N, N © D, D $ J, J # B

Conclusions: I. R @ J **II.** J @ N

III. B @ D

1) None is true 2) Only I is true

3) Only II is true 4) Only III is true

5) Only I and III are true

94. **Statements:** W © B, B % V, V $ R, R @ K

Conclusions: I. K © B **II.** R # B

III. V @ W

1) Only I and II are true 2) Only I and III are true

3) Only II and III are true 4) All I, II and III are true

5) None of these

95. **Statements:** H $ M, M # T, T @ D, D © R

Conclusions: I. D © M **II.** R @ M

III. H $ T

1) None is true
2) Only I is true
3) Only II is true
4) Only III is true
5) Only I and II are true

96. **Statements:** B % J, J @ K, K © T, T $ F
Conclusions: I. F @ K **II.** B @ K
III. B @ F
1) Only I and II are true
2) Only I and III are true
3) Only II and III are true
4) All I, II and III are true
5) None of these

97. **Statements:** F # B, B $ M, M @ K, K © N
Conclusions: I. N @ M **II.** F $ M
III. K © B
1) Only I is true
2) Only II is true
3) Only III is true
4) Only II and III are true
5) None is true

Directions (Q. 98-102): In the following questions, the symbols @, ©, #, $ and % are used with the following meanings:
d
'P © Q' means 'P is either smaller than or equal to Q'.
'P % Q' means 'P is neither smaller than nor equal to Q'.
'P @ Q' means 'P is either greater than or equal to Q'.
'P $ Q' means 'P is neither greater than nor equal to Q'.
'P # Q' means 'P is neither greater than nor smaller than Q'.

Now in each of the following questions, assuming the given statements to be true, find which of the two conclusions I and II given below them is/are definitely true. Give answer
1) if only conclusion I is true.
2) if only conclusion II is true.
3) if either conclusion I or II is true.
4) if neither conclusion I nor II is true.
5) if both conclusions I and II are true.

98. **Statements:** M © D, D # F, F @ B
Conclusions: I. B © D **II.** F # M

99. **Statements:** W$K, K©H, H@R
Conclusions: I. R$K **II.** H%W

100. **Statements:** K @ R, R % T, T # J
Conclusions: I. J $ R **II.** T$K

101. **Statements:** H $ T, T%W, W@K
Conclusions: I. W $ H **II.** W@H

102. **Statements:** B % E, E @ F, F © M
Conclusions: I. M % E **II.** B@F

Answers and Explanations

1. 4; **Statements:** $A > B, B \leq C, C \leq D$

Conclusions: I. $A > D$ **II.** $C = D$

For conclusion I, all statements are relevant. Combining $B \leq C$ and $C \leq D$. We get $B \leq C \leq D$ which means $B \leq D$. But we can't combine this with $A > B$ because in both of them B is the smaller number (tip points to B in both cases). Conclusion II is obviously false because C and D are not *equal* to any thing in the given question. (tips 7: **quick method**)

2. 4; **Statements:** $L \leq K, M < N, K = M$

Conclusions: I. $N > L$ **II.** $K \leq N$

For I, all statements are relevant. Combining $M < N$ and $K = M$ we get $K < N$. This means II is wrong. But $K < N$ and $L \leq K$ together give $L \leq K < N$ which means $L \leq N$. But $L \leq N$ is not the same as $L < N$. So, I is also wrong.

3. 4; **Statements:** $X > Y, Z \leq R, Y = Z$

Conclusions: I. $X > R$ **II.** $Y = R$

Combining $X > Y$ and $Y = Z$, we get $X > Z$. Combining this to $Z \leq R$, is not possible as the tip is pointed toward Z in both cases: so no conclusion about X and R. II is of course wrong as R is not equal to any other term in the given statements (Tip 7).

4. 3; **Statements:** $G \geq F, D \leq E, E = F$

Conclusions: I. $E < G$ **II.** $E = G$

From $G \geq F$ and $E = F$, we get $G \geq E$ which means that either $E < G$ or $E = G$.

5. 2; **Statements:** $I \leq J, K = J \leq L, H \geq J$

Conclusions: I. $J = L$ **II.** $I \leq H$

There are no equalities involving L in the given statements; so there can't be any equality involving L in any conclusion (Tip 7): So, I is wrong. For II, $I \leq J$ and $H \geq J$ are relevant. Combining them we get $I \leq J \leq H$ which gives $I \leq H$.

6. 2; **Statements:** $N < W, L > N, K = L, W = D$

Conclusions: I. $L = W$ **II.** $D > N$

For I, $N < W$ and $L > N$ are relevant but they can't be combined as the tip is pointed towards N in both cases. So, I is uncertain. II is true; it follow from $D = W > N$.

7. 5; **Statements:** $L \geq A, S < E, A = S, G > L$

Conclusions: I. $A < E$ **II.** $G > A$

For I, $S < E$ and $A = S$ are relevant. Combining them we get $A < E$. So, I is true. For II, $G > L$ and $L \geq A$ are relevant. Combining, We get $G > L \geq A$ which gives $G > A$.

8. 3; **Statements:** $M = I, A > M, T \leq I, T = K$

Conclusions: I. $M = K$ **II.** $K < M$

We have T = K and M = I. So, replacing T by K and I by M in $T \le I$ we get $K \le M$ which means that either K = M or K < M. (Check 3)

9. 1; **tatements:** $I \le R, D < I, E = C, R > E$

Conclusions: I. $R > C$ **II.** $I = R$

I follows from $R > E$ and $E = C$. II can't be true as there are no equalities involving I or R in given statements **(Tip 7: quick method)**.

10. 1; **Statements:** $U > N, S \ge O, N < D, O = U$

Conclusions: I. $N < S$ **II.** $U = D$

For I, combine $U > N$ with $O = U$ to get $O > N$. Now, combine this with $S \ge O$ to get $S \ge O > N$. Now, this gives $S > N$. So, I is true. II can't be true as there are no equalities involving D in the given statements.

11. 3; **Statements:** $M < L, O > P, M = N, O \le N$

Conclusions: I. $M > O$ **II.** $M = O$

Combining $M = N$ and $O \le N$; we have $O \le M$. This gives $M > O$ or $M = O$. (Check 3)

12. 1; **Statements:** $W < N, S = Q, R \ge N, S < R$

Conclusions: I. $W < R$ **II.** $N = Q$

Combining $W < N$ and $R \ge N$ we have $W < N \le R$ which gives $W < R$. So, I is true. II must be false as there are no equalities involving N in the given statements **(Tip 7: quick method)**

13. 3; **Statements:** $A < B, D \le E, C = D, C \ge B$

Conclusions: I. $E > B$ **II.** $B = E$

Combining $D \le E$ and $C = D$ we get $C \le E$. This, combined with $C \ge B$, gives $B \le C \le E$ which gives $B \le E$. So, either $B < E$ or $B = E$. (Check 3)

14. 2; **Statements:** $W > U, Y = X, Z < Y, X \ge W$

Conclusions: I. $Z = W$ **II.** $X > Z$

I is wrong as there are no equalities involving Z or W in the given statements. For II, relevant statements are: $Y = X$, $Z < Y$. They give: $Z < X$. So, II is true.

15. 2; **Statements:** $R \ge A, U > L, A = H, H \ge U$

Conclusions: I. $H = L$ **II.** $L < H$

To get a conclusion between L and H; relevant statements are $U > L$ and $H \ge U$. Combining, we get $H \ge U > L$ which gives $H > L$. So, only II is correct.

16. 1; **Statements:** $P \ge Q, M \le N, N < Q$

Conclusions: I. $P > M$ **II.** $N \le P$

Combining $P \ge Q$ and $N < Q$, we get $P \ge Q > N$ so $P > N$ follows. But $P > N$ is different from $P \ge N$ (or $N \le P$.) So, II does not follow. Now, combine $P > N$ with $M \le N$ to get $P > N \ge M$, so $P > M$ follows.

17. 1; **Statements:** $D < X, F \ge Y, D > F$

Conclusions: I. $X \ge Y$ **II.** $Y \le D$

Combining $F \ge Y$ and $D > F$ we get $D > F \ge Y$ so that $D > Y$ follows. So, II does not follow. Now, D > Y and D < X give X > D > Y so that X > Y follows but it is not the same as X ≥ Y. So, I does not follow.

18.2; **Statements:** M < P, S > T, M ≥ T
Conclusions: I. S = M **II.** T < P
I is wrong (**see Tip 7: quick method**). II is obtained by combining M < P and M ≥ T to get T ≤ M < P so that T < P follows.

19.5; **Statements:** U = V, X > W, U < W
Conclusions: I. W > V **II.** U < X
From U = V and U < W; I follows. From U < W and X > W; we get U < W < X so that II follows.

20.3; **Statements:** G > H, J ≤ K, H = K
Conclusions: I. H > J **II.** J = H
From J ≤ K and H = K; we get J ≤ H or H ≥ J. Now by check 3, either I or II follows.

21.3; **Statements:** H ≤ V, A = Z, H ≥ Z, F > V
Conclusions: I. A = H **II.** H > A
From A = Z and H ≥ Z we get H ≥ A. By check 3, I or II follows.

22.5; **Statements:** Q < R, C > D, F ≥ R, D = F
Conclusions: I. Q < C **II.** C > F
For I, all elements are relevant and need to be used, combine Q < R with F ≥ R to get Q < R ≤ F to give Q < F. So, we eliminate R and get a conclusion between Q and F. Now, let us put D = F in Q < F to get Q < D. So, we eliminate F this time and get a conclusion between Q and D. Now, Q < D and C > D give Q < D < C to give Q < C. So, I follows. II follows from C > D and D = F.

23. 1; **Statements:** M = X, L < O, N > M, L ≤ X
Conclusions: I. N > L **II.** X < O
Combining N > M and M = X; we get N > X. Now, N > X and L ≤ X gives; N > X ≥ L to give N > L. Conclusion II must be wrong because X is not less than any term in the given statements but conclusion II says X is less than O. [**Quick method, Tip 8(i)**]

24.3; **Statements:** I > O, R ≥ I, Z = R, J < Z
Conclusions: I. Z = I **II.** Z > I
For a conclusion between Z and I; R ≥ I and Z = R are relevant statements. They give: Z ≥ I. By check 3; either follows.

25. 5; **Statements:** S ≤ F, K < S, B = K, R > B
Conclusions: I. F > K **II.** K < R
From S ≤ F and K < S we get K < S ≤ F to get K < F. So, I follows. Now, From B = K and R > B; II follows.

26. 2; **Statements:** M ≥ I, T = B, M < A, I > T
Conclusions: I. M = T **II.** A > I
I is wrong as M does not appear in any equality in the statements. (**Tip 7: quick method**). For II, M < A and M ≥ I are relevant statements.

They give $A > M \geq I$ to give $A > I$.

27. 1; **Statements:** $H = A, N < A, C > H, N \leq D$
Conclusions: I. $C > N$ **II.** $A = D$
From, $C > H$ and $H = A$ we get $C > A$. Now, $C > A$ and $N < A$ gives $C > A > N$ to give $C > N$. $A = D$ is false as there are no equalities with D in the given statements. **(Tip 7: quick method)**

28. 3; **Statements:** $D \geq I, J < V, G \leq I, V = G$
Conclusions: I. $G < D$ **II.** $D = G$
From $D \geq I$ and $G \leq I$ we get $D \geq I \geq G$ to get $D \geq G$. By check 3; either follows.

29. 4; **Statements:** $P = O, R > T, S \leq P, R < O$
Conclusions: I. $S = O$ **II.** $P < T$
I is wrong **(Tip 7: quick method)** as given statements contain no equalities having S. II must be wrong as T is not greater than any term in the given inequalities. **(Tip 8(ii): quick method)**

30. 2; **Statements:** $O > K, S \geq H, S < A, H = O$
Conclusions: I. $S > O$ **II.** $A > K$
From $S \geq H$ and $H = O$; we get $S \geq O$ but it is different from $S > O$. So, I does not follow. Also, O is not *less than anything in the given statements, so it shouldn't be less than* anything in a conclusion. So, **(Tip 8(i): Quick method)** I doesn't follow. To verify II, first combine: $S < A$ and $S \geq H$ to get $H \leq S < A$ to get $H < A$. Combine $H < A$ with $H = O$ to get $O < A$. Combine $O < A$ with $O > K$ to get $K < O < A$ to get $K < A$. So, II follows.

31. 4; **Statements:** $T = G, K > P, M < T, P \geq M$
Conclusions: I. $K > T$ **II.** $G = P$
I is wrong as T is not less than any term in any of the statements. **(Tip 8(i): quick method)**. II is wrong as P is not equal to any term in any statement. **(Tip 7: quick method)**

32. 4; **Statements:** $R \geq N, S \leq \beta, A > \alpha, B = A$
Conclusions: I. $S = N$ **II.** $A > N$
I is wrong as there are no equalities involving S or N in the given statements. II can't be established as there are no relevant statements that can be linked to get a conclusion between A and N.

33. 3; **Statements:** $G = K, F > J, K \geq Q, Q \geq F$
Conclusions: I. $K = F$ **II.** $F < K$
From $K \geq Q$ and $Q \geq F$; we get $K \geq Q \geq F$ to get $K \geq F$.
From check 3, either I or II follows.

34. 1; **Statements:** $W > S, K \leq Z, U \geq W, S = K$
Conclusions: I. $U > K$ **II.** $Z > S$
Combining $U \geq W$ and $W > S$ we get $U \geq W > S$ which gives $U > S$. Now, $S = K$ gives $U > K$. So, I follows. From, $K \leq Z$ and $S = K$, we get $S \leq Z$ which is different from $Z > S$.

35. 5; **Statements:** $G = E, D < K, E < S, K \leq G$

Conclusions: I. $S > D$ **II.** $D < E$

From, $G = E$ and $K \leq G$ we have $K \leq E$. With $K \leq E$ and $D < K$, we get $D < K \leq E$ to get $D < E$. So, II follows. Now, $D < E$ and $E < S$ give $D < E < S$ to give $D < S$. So, I follows.

36. 2; **Statements:** $W > K, S \leq Z, X \geq W, S = K$

Conclusions: I. $K = Z$ **II.** $X > K$

I is not true as there are no equalities with Z in the given statements. (**Tip 7: quick method**). II follows from $X \geq W$ and $W > K$.

37. 1; **Statements:** $L \geq R, N = M, L < M, N \leq P$

Conclusions: I. $M > R$ **II.** $R > P$

From $L < M$ and $L \geq R$; I follows. II must be wrong as P is not smaller than any quantity in the given statements. (**Tip 8(i): quick method**).

38. 4; **Statements:** $P < Q, W \geq N, P \geq N, T > W$

Conclusions: I. $P = W$ **II.** $Q < W$

I must be wrong as there are no equalities in the given statements. (**Tip 7: quick method**). II must be wrong as Q is not less than any number in the given statements. (**Tip 8(i): quick method**).

39. 1; **Statements:** $D \leq S, N > V, D = R, R > V$

Conclusions: I. $S > V$ **II.** $D > N$

Combining $D \leq S$ and $D = R$ we get $R \leq S$. Now, combining $R \leq S$ and $R > V$ we get $V < R \leq S$ to get $V < S$. II must be wrong because (**Tip 8(ii): Quick method**) D is not *greater than* anything int he given statements.

40. 3; **Statements:** $K = P, M < J, C < P, K \leq M$

Conclusions: I. $M > P$ **II.** $M = P$

From $K = P$ and $K \leq M$ we have $P \leq M$. By **check 3**, either I or II follows.

41. 5; **Statements:** $T \leq G, L < T, C = L, S > C$

Conclusions: I. $G > L$ **II.** $L < S$

From, $T \leq G$ and $L < T$; I follows. II follows from $C = L$ and $S > C$.

42. 3; **Statements:** $J > P, S \geq J, A = S, K < A$

Conclusions: I. $A = J$ **II.** $A > J$

From $A = S$ and $S \geq J$; we have $A \geq J$. By **check 3**, either I or II follows.

43. 1; **Statements:** $N = Y, M < P, O > N, M \leq Y$

Conclusions: I. $O > M$ **II.** $Y < P$

From $O > N$ and $N = Y$ we have $O > Y$. This combines with $M \leq Y$ to give $O > Y \geq M$ to give $O > M$. For II, a relevant pair is $M < P$ and $M \leq Y$ but they can't be combined because M is the lesser term in both the cases here and this violates **golden rule 2** (or **tip 3: quick method**).

44. 5; **Statements:** $R < S, D > E, G \geq S, E = G$

Conclusions: I. $R < D$ **II.** $D > G$

From $D > E$ and $E = G$; we get $D > G$. $D > G$ and $G \geq S$ give $D > G \geq S$ to give $D > S$. Now, $D > S$ and $R < S$ give $D > S > R$ to give $R < D$.

45. 3; **Statements:** $I \leq W, B = A, I \geq A, G > W$

Conclusions: I. $B = I$ **II.** $I > B$

From $I \geq A$ and $B = A$; we get $I \geq B$. By **check 3**, either I or II follows.

46. 1; **Statements:** $P \geq R, S < T, U < V$

Conclusions: I. $V > U$ **II.** $S \geq R$

From $U < V$, $V > U$ follows. (**Check 1**). II can't be established as there are no links (common terms) to link S with R.

47. 1; **Statements:** $C > D, D = E, D > F$

Conclusions: I. $D < C$ **II.** $C = E$

I follows from $C > D$. (Check 1). II must be wrong as there are no equalities with C in the given statements. **(Tip 7: quick method)**

48. 4; **Statements:** $L > M, N \geq O, N < P$

Conclusions: I. $N < M$ **II.** $O < M$

(**Tip 8: quick method**). Both must be wrong as M is not greater than any quantity in any of the given statements.

49. 1; **Statements:** $G < H, I > J, H < J$

Conclusions: I. $J > G$ **II.** $I = H$

From $G < H$ and $H < J$; I follows. II must be wrong as there are no inequalities in the given statements. (**Tip 7: quick method**).

50. 3; **Statements:** $S \leq T, L < P, P \geq S$

Conclusions: I. $T < P$ **II.** $P \leq T$

I can't be established because T is not a lesser number in any of the statements. II can't be established as P is not a lesser number in any of the statements. But by **Check 4** either I or II follows.

51. 4; **Statements:** $J < K, J < L, L > M$

Conclusions: I. $J < M$ **II.** $L = J$

I must be wrong because of **Tip 8(ii): quick method**. II must be wrong because of **Tip 7: quick method.**

52. 5; **Statements:** $G \leq H,\ H \leq J,\ L < G$

Conclusions: I. $L < H$ **II.** $H > L$

From $L < G$ and $G \leq H$; I follows.

53. 4; **Statements:** $M > N, M > P, O = N$

Conclusions: I. $N > M$ **II.** $O < M$

I is wrong as it is opposite of $M > N$. II does not follow from anything. **Quick method:** I is wrong because N is not *greater than* anything in the given statements, so **Tip 8(ii)** applies. II is wrong because O is not *less than* anything in the given statements, so **Tip 8(i)** applies.

54. 1; **Statements:** $T = U, U = V, V < W$

Conclusions: I. $W > T$ **II.** $W = U$

From $V = U$ and $V < W$; we get $U < W$, so II does not follow. $U < W$ and $T = U$ makes I follow. (**Note:** By **Tip 7: Quick Method**, II can be rejected as W is not equal to anything in the given statements.)

55. 5; **Statements:** $A < B, C \le A, C > D$
Conclusions: I. $C < B$ **II.** $B > D$
I follows from $C \le A$ and $A < B$. Combining this conclusion with $C > D$, conclusion II follows.

56. 2; **Statements:** $B > V, K < C, C \le B$
Conclusions: I. $V > C$ **II.** $B > K$
I must be wrong as V is not greater than any number in the given statements. (Tip 8: quick method). From $K < C$ and $C \le B$; II follows.

57. 4; **Statements:** $K > T, S = K, T \le R$
Conclusions: I. $S > R$ **II.** $T = R$
I is wrong as R is not less than any number in the given statements (**Tip 8: quick method**). II is wrong by virtue of **Tip 7: quick method**.

58. 3; **Statements:** $U = M, P \ge U, M \ge B$
Conclusions: I. $P = B$ **II.** $P > B$
From $U = M$ and $P \ge U$; we get $P \ge M$. From $P \ge M$ and $M \ge B$; we get $P \ge B$. By check 3; either I or II follows.

59. 4; **Statements:** $L \ge N, J \le P, P \ge L$
Conclusions: I. $J = L$ **II.** $P = N$
By **tip 7: quick method** both must be wrong.

60. 5; **Statements:** $H \ge G, D > E, H = E$
Conclusions: I. $D > H$ **II.** $G < D$
I follows from $D > E$ and $H = E$. Combining conclusion I with $H \ge G$; II follows.

61. 2; $H > T$ ...(i); $T < F$ ...(ii); $F = E$ ...(iii); $E \le V$ ...(iv)
Combining (ii), (iii) and (iv), we get
$T < F = E \le V$ ...(v)
Hence $V \ge F$ and I is true.
Also, $E > T$ and II is true.
Again, $T < V$ and IV is true.
From (i) and IV, H and V can't be compared. Hence III is not true.

62. 5; $D < R$ ...(i); $R \le K$ ...(ii); $K > F$ ...(iii); $F \ge J$ ...(iv)
Combining these, we get $D < R \le K > F \ge J$.
Now, J and R can't be compared. Hence I does not follow.
$J < K$ and II follows.
R and F can't be compared. Hence III does not follow.
$K > D$ and IV follows.

63. 5; $N = B$ ...(i); $B \ge W$ ...(ii); $W < H$ ...(iii); $H \le M$ ...(iv)
Combining these, we get $N = B \ge W < H \le M$.
Hence $M > W$ and I is true.
H and N can't be compared. Hence II does not follow.
Again, $W \le N$. Which means either III ($W = N$) or IV ($W < N$) is true.

64\. 1; $R \leq D$ ...(i); $D \geq J$ ...(ii); $J < M$ ...(iii); $M > K$ ...(iv)
None of these given quantities can be compared.

65\. 5; $M \geq K$ ...(i); $K > N$ ...(ii); $N \leq R$ ...(iii); $R < W$ ...(iv)
From (i) and (ii), $M \geq K > N$ or $M > N$ ...(v)
From (iii) and (iv), $N \leq R < W$ or $N < W$ ...(vi)
Now, from (ii) and (vi), W and K can't be compared. Hence I is not true.
From (iii) and (v), M and R can't be compared. Hence II is not true.
From (ii) and (vi), K and W can't be compared. Hence III is not true.
IV is definitely true from from (v).

66\. 3; $J > D$ ...(i); $D \leq K$ ...(ii); $K < R$ ...(iii)
Combining these, we get $J > D \leq K < R$
Hence R and J can't be compared and I does not follow. $R > D$ and hence II is true.
But J and K can't be compared and hence III does not follow.

67\. 5; $M \geq K$ ...(i); $K = R$ ...(ii); $R < N$ ...(iii)
Combining these, we get $M \geq K = R < N$
Hence $M \geq R$ or $R \leq M$. Which means either I ($R < M$) or II ($R = M$) is true.
Also, $N > K$ and hence III is true.

6\. 4; $B < H$ ...(i); $H > J$ ...(ii); $J \geq M$ ...(iii)
Combining these, we get $B < H > J \geq M$
Hence B and J, or B and M can't be compared. Which implies I and II are not true.
But, $H > M$ and hence III is true.

69\. 5; $Z \leq K$ ...(i); $K < E$ ...(ii); $E = R$ ...(iii)
Combining these, we get $Z \leq K < E = R$.
Hence $R > K$ and I is true.
Again, $Z < E$ and II is true.
Also, $R > Z$ and III is true.

70\. 3; $W = M$ ...(i); $M \leq R$ ...(ii);
$R > F$ ...(iii).
Combining these, we get $W = M \leq R > F$.
Hence F and M, or F and W can't be compared. So, I and III are not true.
But $R \geq W$ and hence II is true.

(71-75):

 # → >, $ → ≥, © → <, % → ≤ , @ → =

71\. 4; $R > J \geq D = K \leq T$
Hence, $T \geq D$. Which means either I ($T > D$) or II ($T = D$) is true.
Again, $R > K$. Hence III is true.
But J and T can't be compared. Hence IV is not true.

72\. 1; $T \leq R \leq M = D < H$
Hence I ($D \leq R$) is true.

92. 5; $D \geq K$ ...(i); $K > T$ ...(ii); $T \leq M$ ...(iii); $M = J$ ...(iv)
Combining these, we get $D \geq K > T \leq M = J$.
Hence $J \geq T$. Which means either I ($J > T$) or II ($J = T$) is true.
Again, $D > T$ and hence III is true.

93. 3; $R > N$ ...(i); $N < D$ ...(ii); $D \leq J$ ...(iii); $J \geq B$ ...(iv)
Combining these, we get $R > N < D \leq J \geq B$.
Clearly, R and J can't be compared. Hence I does not follow.
$J > N$ and hence II follows.
Again, B and D can't be compared and hence III does not follow.

94. 3; $W < B$ ...(i); $B = V$ ...(ii); $V \leq R$ ...(iii); $R > K$ ...(iv)
Combining these, we get $W < B = V \leq R > K$
Obviously, K and B can't be compared and hence I does not follow.
$R \geq B$ and hence II is true.
$V > W$ and hence III is true.

95. 2; $H \leq M$ ...(i); $M \geq T$ ...(ii); $T > D$ ...(iii); $D < R$ ...(iv)
Combining these, we get $H \leq M \geq T > D < R$
Hence $D < M$ and I is true.
But R and M can't be compared and hence II does not follow.
Again, H and T can't be compared and hence III does not follow.

96. 1; $B = J$ ...(i); $J > K$ ...(ii); $K < T$ ...(iii);
$T \leq F$ ...(iv)
combining these, we get $B = J > K < T \leq F$
Hence $F > K$ and I is true.
Also, $B > K$ and II is true.
But B and F can't be compared and hence III is not true.

97. 5; $F \geq B$ ...(i); $B \leq M$ ...(ii); $M > K$ ...(iii); $K < N$ ...(iv)
No comparisons can be made.

98. 1; $M \leq D = F \geq B$
I. $B \leq D$ follows **II.** $F = M$ does not follow

99. 2; $W < K \leq H \geq R$
I. $R < K$ does not follow **II.** $H > W$ follows

100. 5; $K \geq R > T = J$
I. $J < R$ follows **II.** $T < K$ follows

101. 3; $H < T > W \geq K$
I. $W < H$ **II.** $W \geq H$
Either conclusion I or conclusion II is true.

102. 4; $B > E \geq F \leq M$
I. $M > E$ does not follow **II.** $B \geq F$ does not follow
Neither conclusion I nor II is true.

Chapter Twenty One

Conditional Coding & Artificial Language

21.1 : Introduction

We have studied the technique of coding in the previous chapters. We have seen a chapter in which the basics of coding and decoding was introduced. After that we have seen some chapters in which the technique of coding and decoding was used directly or indirectly such as the topic of coded inputs, coded relationships and coded inequalities. Recently, a new type of question is being introduced (rather reintroduced because such questions used to be asked in the early 90s also) in which the logic of coding follows a particular rule but the rule itself changes if some additional conditions are met. Because these type of questions are being asked very frequently and because many of my readers have requested to dedicate a separate chapter and explain the technique to solve these questions, I am discussing this type of questions in a separate brief chapter.

In this chapter we are also discussing a type of question which can be best described as artificial language. In this type of questions known words are replaced by meaningless combination of letters but one combination stands for a particular fixed word as if it was some new language. They are not very difficult type of questions and as a matter of fact we have already dealt with them in the previous chapter called introduction to coding. And therefore this will be discussed very briefly in this chapter. Let us first begin by looking at what type of questions are asked.

21.2 : Format of the problem

Ex. 1. Conditional Coding

Directions (Q. 1-4): In each question below is given a group of letters followed by four combinations of digits/symbols numbered 1), 2), 3) and 4). You have to find out which of the four combinations correctly represents the group of letters based on the following coding system and the conditions that follow and mark the number of that combination as your answer. If none of the combinations correctly represents the group of letters, mark 5), ie 'None of these' as your answer.

Letter :	B	A	D	E	F	H	J	K	M	I	U	O	W	F	P
Digit/Symbol Code :	6	$	7	8	#	1	2		%	3	©	4	9	@	5

Chapter Twenty One

Conditional Coding & Artificial Language

21.1 Introduction

21.2 Format of the problem

Conditional Coding

Thus , if *ans brd tyh* stands for *he looks good* it does not mean that the first word of the artificial language (ans) stands for the first word of the given sentence (he).

The best way to solve such questions is the following :

Step 1 : LOOK FOR LONELY WORDS

Check if any sentence has a word that is NOT there in any other sentence. Then the code that is there in that sentence but not in any other sentence must be the code for that lonely word. **(very important trick)**

Step 2: LOOK FOR COMMON WORDS

Check if any pair of sentences has a common word. If yes, that common word will correspond to a common code. : Now continue the same logic in remaining sentences.

With this background that is now go back to the example and try to solve the questions using the two steps given above.

Solution to Ex 2 :

Step 1: Lonely words

A. 'name in spark list' has a unique word ***in*** that is not there in any other sentence. And in its code '*nam yan gon kem* ;the word *gon* is not there in any other code. So *gon* must be the code for **in**.

B. 'his game has spark' has a unique word **game** that is not there in any other sentence. And in its code '*fon lam bun nam* ';the word *fon* is not there in any other code. So *fon* must be the code for **game**.

C. 'spark list has been displayed' has a unique word **been** that is not there in any other sentence. And in its code *'jon kem lam sin nam'*;the word *jon* is not there in any other code. So *jon* must be the code for **been.**

D. 'his name displayed there' has a unique word **there** that is not there in any other sentence. And in its code '*yan sin bun zom* ';the word *zom* is not there in any other code. So *zom* must be the code for **there.**

Step 2: Common words

A. *his game has spark* and *his name displayed here* ; here , *his* is a common word.the corresponding codes *fon lam bun nam* and *yan sin bun zom* have a common word *bun.* so , code for **his** must be *bun.*

B. *his game has spark* and *name in spark list* ; here , *spark* is a common word.the corresponding codes *fon lam bun nam* and 'nam yan gon kem have a common word *nam*. So, code for **spark** must be *nam*.

C. *his name displayed there* and *name in spark list* ; here , *name* is a common word.the corresponding codes *yan sin bun zom'* and *'nam yan gon kem'* have a common word *yan*. so, code for **name** must be *yan*.

D. spark list has been displayed' and his name displayed there'; here , displayed is a common word. The corresponding codes *'jon kem lam sin nam'* and *'yan sin bun zom'* have a common word *sin*. so , code for **displayed** must be *sin*.

E. Now compare codes for his game has spark and spark list has been displayed'. They have two common words : has and spark. And common codes are *lam* and *nam*. But we already know that code for spark is *nam*. So code for **has** must be *lam*.

F. Now we have got codes for all words except **list** which must be kem.

SO , the answers will look like the following.

HIS	BUN
GAME	FON
HAS	LAM
SPARK	NAM
LIST	KEM
BEEN	JON
DISPLAYED	SIN
NAME	YAN
THERE	ZOM
IN	GON

Answers:

Q1. 5

Q2. 2

Q3. 2

Q4. 1

Practice Exercises

Directions (Q. 1-6): In each question below is given a group of letters followed by four combinations of digits/symbols numbered 1), 2), 3) and 4). You have to find out which of the four combinations correctly represents the group of letters based on the following coding system and the conditions that follow and mark the number of that combination as your answer. If none of the combinations correctly represents the group of letters, mark 5), ie 'None of these' as your answer.

Letter	: B	A	D	E	F	H	J	K	M	I	U	O	W	F	P
Digit/Symbol Code	: 6	$	7	8	#	1	2		%	3	©	4	9	@	5

Conditions:

(i) If the first letter is a vowel and the last letter is a consonant, their codes are to be interchanged.

16. 54# @6

1) PBURIT 2) PBRUIP 3) TBRUIP
4) TBRUIT 5) None of these

17. $63©94

1) NTMAEN 2) BTMAEB 3) ZTMAEB
4) NTMAEB 5) None of these

Directions (Q. 18-22): In each of the following questions, a group of letters is to be coded by number/symbol codes as per the codes given below and the conditions that follow. In each question, a group of letters is given followed by groups of number/symbol code numbered 1), 2), 3) and 4). The correct combination of codes is your answer. If none of the four combinations is correct, your answer is (5), ie 'None of these'.

Letter	:	P	D	A	F	L	H	M	R	K	T	B	E	U
Number/Symbol Code	:	3	6	#	8	$	4	2	7	@	9	5	1	%

Conditions:

(i) If the first letter is a vowel and the last letter is a consonant, both are to be coded as '0'.

(ii) If the first letter is a consonant and the last letter is a vowel, both are to be coded as '©'.

(iii) If the first as well as the last letter are vowels, both are to be coded as the code for the first letter.

18. KEDURT

1) @16%7@ 2) 916%7@ 3) 916%79
4) @16$79 5) None of these

19. EDRTMP

1) 167923 2) 167921 3) 067920
4) 067923 5) None of these

20. FHRAMU

1) 847#28 2) %47#28 3) 847#2%
4) ©47#2© 5) None of these

21. ULTPHE

1) %$934% 2) 1$9341 3) %$9341
4) 1$934% 5) None of these

22. HKEDLB

1) 5@16$4 2) 4@16$5 3) ©@16$4
4) 0@16$5 5) None of these

Directions (Q. 23-27): Study the following information to answer the given questions:

In a certain code '**a friend of mine**' is written as '4 9 1 6', '**mine lots of metal**' is written as '3 1 0 9' and '**a piece of metal**' is written as '7 1 6 3'.

236. What is the code for 'piece'?
1) 3 2) 6 3) 1
4) 7 5) Cannot be determined

24. What does '9' stand for?
1) of 2) mine 3) friend
4) lots 5) metal

25. Which of the following may represent 'a pleasure of mine'?
1) 6 3 0 9 2) 5 2 16 3) 9 2 1 6
4) 3 6 9 4 5) 5 0 4 1

26. What does '0' stand for?
1) mine 2) metal 3) of
4) lots 5) a

27. '8 7 3' would mean
1) a metal piece 2) metal for friend 3) piece of advise
4) friend of mine 5) large metal piece

Directions (Q. 28-33): Study the following information to answer the given questions.

In a certain code, **'her idea has merit'** is written as 'fo la bu na', **'merit list has been displayed'** is written as 'jo ke la si na', **'her name displayed there'** is written as 'ya si bu zo' and **'name in merit list'** is written as 'na ya go ke'.

28. What does 'ke' stand for?
1) been 2) has 3) merit
4) name 5) list

29. What is the code for 'idea'?
1) fo 2) la 3) bu
4) na 5) Either bu or na

30. Which of the following represents 'name has been displayed'?
1) ya la ke si 2) jo si ya la 3) si jo ke na
4) bu ya ke la 5) ya si jo zo

31. What does 'zo' stand for?
1) there 2) displayed 3) name
4) her 5) Cannot be determined

32. Which of the following may represent 'her name is there'?
1) zo ya go wo 2) bu ya zo go 3) zo ya bu ke
4) ya zo wo bu 5) wo go zo ya

33. What is the code for 'in'?
1) na 2) ya 3) go
4) ke 5) Cannot be determined

Directions (Q. 34-39): Study the following information to answer the given questions:

In a certain code 'for profit order now' is written as 'ho ja ye ga', 'right now

54. "riy rtv roi" could be a code for which of the following?
1) rise above challenge
2) rise health challenge
3) day rise challenge
4) with rise challenge
5) challenge every rise

55. Which of the following is the code for 'facing'?
1) nop
2) rtv
3) ngi
4) snk
5) sa

56. "riy snk mlp" could be a code for which of the following?
1) problem every day
2) challenge with health
3) with health day
4) every challenge facing
5) challenge facing with

57. Which of the following is the code for 'day'?
1) riy
2) nop
3) ngi
4) hus
5) Cannot be determined

Answers and Explanations

1. 2; Condition (i) applies.
2. 1; Condition (ii) applies.
3. 3; Condition (iii) applies.
4. 4; Condition (ii) applies.
5. 1; No condition applies.
6. 5; No condition applies and we get © 57%3.
7. 1; Condition (iii) applies.
8. 2; No condition applies.
9. 3; Condition (i) applies.
10. 5; No condition applies and we get δ @ 4 6 % $.
11. 4; Condition (ii) applies.
12. 4; Condition (iii) applies.
13. 1; Condition (ii) applies.
14. 3; Condition (iv) applies.
15. 2; No condition applies.
16. 5; No condition applies and we get PBR UIT.
17. 2; Condition (i) applies.
18. 5; No condition applies and we get @16%79.
19. 3; Condition (i) applies.
20. 4; Condition (ii) applies.
21. 1; Condition (iii) applies.
22. 2; No condition applies.

(23-27): a friend of mine = 4 9 1 6 ...(i)
mine lots of metal = 3 1 0 9 ...(ii)
a piece of metal = 7 1 6 3 ...(iii)
From (i), (ii) and (iii), of = 1 ...(iv)

From (i), (iii) and (iv), a = 6 ...(v)
From (i), (ii) and (iv), mine = 9 ...(vi)
From (i), (iv), (v) and (vi), friend = 4 ...(vii)
From (ii), (iii) and (iv), metal = 3 ...(viii)
From (ii), (iv), (vi) and (viii), lots = 0 ...(ix)
From (iii), (iv), (v) and (viii), piece = 7 ...(x)

23. 4 24. 2 25. 3 26. 4 27. 5

(28-33): Using the given four statements, the codes are

her ⇒ bu been ⇒ jo
idea ⇒ fo displayed ⇒ si
has ⇒ la name ⇒ ya
merit ⇒ na there ⇒ zo
list ⇒ ke in ⇒ go

28. 5 29. 1 30. 2 31. 1

32. 4; Code for 'is' is not known but out of the given five options only 'ya zo wo bu' may be the coding.

33. 3; go

(34-39): for profit order now → ho ja ye ga ...(1)
right now for him → ga ve ja se ...(2)
place order for profit → ga bi ho ye ...(3)
only in right order → ve du ye zo ...(4)
Using (3) and (4), order → ye
Using (2) and (3), for → ga
Using the just found codes and equations,
profit → ho
place → bi
right → ve
him → se
only in → du zo
now → ja

34. 4 35. 3 36. 1
37. 5 38. 3 39. 1

(40-46): school — ni
is — to
far — ba
from — ga
here — di
come — mo
late — fa
the bus — ru zi

40. 1 41. 2 42. 1 43. 4 44. 3
45. 4 46. 5

(47-52): 'always create new ideas' → 'ba ri sha gi' ...(1)
'ideas and new thoughts' → 'fa gi ma ri' ...(2)
'create thoughts and insights' → 'ma jo ba fa' ...(3)
'new and better solutions' → 'ki ri to fa' ...(4)
Using (1) and (4),
new → ri
Using (1), (2) and (4),
ideas → gi
and → fa
thoughts → ma
Using (1) and (3),
create → ba
always → sha
insights → jo
better solutions → ki to

47. 3 48. 4 49. 2
50. 2 51. 4 52. 1

(53-57): facing problems with health → mlp hlt ngi snk ...(i)
health problems on rise → hlt sa rtv mlp ...(ii)
rise with every challenge → snk rtv lne riy ...(iii)
facing challenge each day → ngi riy nop hus ...(iv)
From (i) and (iv), facing → ngi ...(v)
From (i) and (iii), with → snk ...(vi)
From (ii) and (iiii), rise → rtv ...(vii)
From (iii) and (iv), challenge → riy ...(viii)
From (iii), (vi), (vii) and (viii), every → lne ...(ix)
From (i) and (ii), health → mlp or hlt
problems → mlp or hlt ...(x)
From (iv), (v) and (viii), each → nop or hus
day → nop or hus ...(xi)
From (ii), (vii) and (x), on → sa ...(xii)

facing	with	rise	challenge	every	on	each	day	health	problems
ngi	snk	rtv	riy	lne	sa	nop or hus	nop or hus	mlp or hlt	mlp or hlt

53. 3
54. 1; roi: given new code for 'above'.
55. 3 56. 2 57. 5

Chapter Twenty Two

Problem-Solving

22.1: Introduction

This lesson will acquaint you with a typical problem wherein you would be given a series of interlinked information or data and you would be expected to have the ability to quantitatively analyse the data in order to reach certain conclusions. Such questions are mostly asked in Bank PO, LIC, AAO, MBA entrance examinations. They are also asked in Income Tax, Asstt Grade etc, albeit in a simpler form.

Let us begin straightaway by first looking at the format of the problem. We are enclosing two sample questions in order to enable you to develop an acquaintance with the problem.

22.2: Format of the problem (What is the problem like?)

Ex.1: Read the following information carefully and answer the questions that follow.

There are six cities A, B, C, D, E and F.

A is not a hill-station.

B and E are not historical places.

D is not an industrial city.

A and D are not historical cities.

A and B are not alike.

1. Which two cities are industrial centres ?

(a) A and B (b) E and F (c) C and D

(d) B and F (e) A and D

2. Which two cities are historical places ?

(a) A and C (b) B and F (c) C and F

(d) B and E (e) A and D

3. Which two cities are hill stations ?

(a) A and B (b) C and A (c) B and D

(d) A and F (e) None of the above

4. Which city is a hill station and an industrial centre but not a historical place?

(a) E (b) F (c) A

(d) B (e) C

5. Which two cities are neither historical places nor industrial centres ?

(a) A and B (b) D and E (c) F and C

(d) B and D (e) None of the above

Ex 2: Read the following information carefully and answer the questions given below.

Six persons A, B, C, D, E and F are sitting in two rows, three in each.

E is not at the end of any row.

D is second to the left of F.

C, the neighbour of E, is sitting diagonally opposite to D.

B is the neighbour of F.

1. Which of the following are sitting diagonally opposite to each other ?
   (a) F and C (b) D and A (c) A and C
   (d) A and F (e) A and B
2. Who is facing B ?
   (a) A (b) C (c) D
   (d) E (e) F
3. Which of the following are in the same row ?
   (a) A and E (b) E and D (c) C and B
   (d) A and B (e) C and F
4. Which of the following are in one of the two rows ?
   (a) FBC (b) CEB (c) DBF
   (d) AEF (e) ABF
5. After interchanging seat with F, who will be the neighbours of D in the new positions ?
   (a) C and A (b) E and B (c) Only B
   (d) Only A (e) Only C

22.3. An analysis

From practical experience and the general trends, it can be asserted that problems of this type can be generally classified into the following:

(1) Simple problems of categorisation
(2) Arrangement problems
(3) Comparison problems
(4) Blood relations
(5) Blood relations and professions
(6) Conditional selection
(7) Miscellaneous problems.

In this lesson, you shall be given fast-working and efficient methods for all the types of problems above. Before that, however, let us see what is the pattern of each of these types. But to begin with, we will give you some general tips and rules that should be applied by you for all the types mentioned above. These rules can be considered as the preliminary steps that should be taken before you really begin solving the problem.

Some preliminary steps

I. First of all, take a quick glance at the question. This would need not more than a couple of seconds. After performing this step you would develop a general idea as to what the general theme of the problem is.

II. Next, determine the usefulness of each of the informations and classify them accordingly into 'actual information' or 'useful secondary information' or 'negative information' as the case may be. This can be done in the following way :

A. **USEFUL SECONDARY INFORMATION:** Usually the first couple of sentences of the given data are such that they give you some basic information that is essential to give you the general idea of the situation. These can be classified as *useful secondary information*. For example, in the sample problem above the following sentence makes up 'useful secondary information':

Ex.2: "Six persons A, B, C, D, E and F ....three in each".

B. **ACTUAL INFORMATION:** Whatever remains after putting aside the useful secondary information can be categorised as *actual information*. In the two sample passages above, the data minus the useful secondary information can be declared as actual information. *While trying to solve a problem, one should begin with the actual information while the useful secondary information should be borne in mind.*

C. **NEGATIVE INFORMATION:** A part of the actual information may consist of negative sentences or negative information. A *negative information* does not inform us anything exactly but it gives a chance to eliminate a possibility. Sentences like "B is not the mother of A" or " H is not a hill-station" are called negative information.

As we shall see, negative information, like useful secondary information, does not help us directly in reaching an answer. Usually we have to analyse the (non-negative) actual information. The negative information and the useful secondary information are supplementary data and they are used to reach a definite conclusion.

To conclude, we can say that step II consists of categorising the data information in three groups, viz. Actual information, Useful secondary information and Negative information, and then separating the actual information so that they could be scrutinised more deeply while bearing the useful information and the negative information in mind.

For example, if we perform step II on the sample problem Ex 2 above, we would (i) decide that our scrutiny should begin with the last three sentences while (ii) we would keep this in mind that there are six persons sitting in two rows of three each and E is not at the end of any row.

Types of problems

22.4. Simple problems of categorisation

The most simple type of problems in this lesson falls under this category wherein you would be supposed to analyse the given data and simply place different items in different categories according to the given information. **Such problems can be easily and quickly solved by constructing a table** as per the given information. The following examples illustrate the type of such problems and the way to solve them:

Q. Refer to sample example 1 given above.

Detailed solution: The data can be analysed by preparing a table in the following manner :

	A	B	C	D	E	F
Historical						
Industrial						
Hill-station						

We see that the first and the last sentences are useful secondary information (U.S.I., in short) while all the remaining are negative information. Reading the second, third, fourth and fifth sentences we put a '×' mark wherever applicable. As a result, the table looks like the one below :

	A	B	C	D	E	F
Historical	×	×		×	×	
Industrial				×		
Hill-station	×					

We see that the above table gives definite information about A and D. A is neither a historical city nor a hill-station. So it must be an industrial city. Similarly, D is neither historical nor industrial, so it must be a hill-station. Consequently we put a '√' mark at the appropriate places. The table then becomes like the one below:

	A	B	C	D	E	F
Historical	×	×		×	×	
Industrial	√			×		
Hill-station	×			√		

Now, we make use of the U.S.I. which says that A and B are not alike. This means that B is not an industrial city. Also, B is not a historical place either. So, it must be a hill-station.

Lastly, since the informations are all negative, a lack of negative information about a city would mean that the city does have the qualities whose absence is not mentioned. For example, there is no negative information about C. Hence, we can assume that C is a hill-station as well as a historical place and an industrial city. Combining all these aspects, we can prepare the final table as shown below:

	A	B	C	D	E	F
Historical	×	×	√	×	×	√
Industrial	√	×	√	×	√	√
Hill-station	×	√	√	√	√	√

Now, please analyse the questions yourself and see that you get the following answer:

Q. 1. (b) Q. 2. (c) Q. 3. (c) Q. 4. (a) Q. 5. (d)

As another example consider the following question.

Ex 3: Directions (Questions 1 to 5): Read the following information carefully and answer the questions given below it :

On a shelf are placed six volumes side by side labelled A, B, C, D. E and F. Three volumes B, C and E have green covers while the other volumes have yellow covers. A, D and B are new volumes while the rest are old volumes. A, C and B are law reports, while the rest are Gazetteers.

Questions:

1. Which volume is new, yellow-covered and a Gazetteer ?
   (a) B (b) D (c) C (d) F (e) None of these
2. Which two volumes are old Gazetteers and have green covers ?
   (a) B, C (b) B, E (c) B, F (d) E, F (e) None of these
3. Which is green-covered, old and a law report volume ?
   (a) A (b) B (c) C (d) D (e) E
4. Which is the yellow-covered new law report volume ?
   (a) E (b) D (c) B (d) C (e) A
5. Which of the following is the old volume of a Gazetteer ?
   (a) C (b) D (c) E (d) B (e) None of these

Detailed solution : After performing the first preliminary step (i.e., a quick reading) we can easily see that three properties of the volumes are mentioned, viz. whether *green* - or *yellow- covered*, whether *old or new*, and *whether law report or gazetteers*. So we prepare the structure of a table in the following way:

	A	B	C	D	E	F
Y/G						
L/Gaz						
O/N						

Y = Yellow, G = Green, L = Law report, Gaz = Gazetteer, O = Old, N = New.

Now, we read the information and see that all of them are non- negative actual information and easy to tabulate. Hence, in a matter of seconds, we fill up the entries in the table as shown below :

	A	B	C	D	E	F
Y/G	Y	G	G	Y	G	Y
L/Gaz	L	L	L	Gaz	Gaz	Gaz
O/N	N	N	O	N	O	O

Now, please analyse the data yourself and see that you get the following answers:

Q. 1. (b) Q. 2. (e) Q. 3. (c) Q. 4. (e) Q. 5. (c)

Note: By the way of the two examples illustrated above you must have noticed that solving this types of problem (on categorisation) is very easy. But when you read the other types and finish the lesson, a doubt may emerge in your mind as to how to recognise whether a given question is of this type or not. But this doubt will be easily dispelled if you note that the identification mark of such problems is their 'flatness'. The data in such questions look like plain 'Yes/No'-type facts. You will be able to appreciate this difference in a still better way when you have finished the lesson.

22.5. Arrangement problems

In this type of questions, the problem is essentially of arranging a group of people, objects etc. according to the given specifications. They may have to be arranged in a row or in a circle, etc. The following problems come under this category of problems:

Ex 4. Refer to sample problem 2.

Ex 5.

Directions (Q. 1 to 5): Study the following informations carefully and answer the questions given below it :

Five friends A,B,C,D and E are sitting on a bench.

(1) A is sitting next to B.

(2) C is sitting next to D.
(3) D is not sitting with E.
(4) E is on the left end of the bench.
(5) C is on the second position from the right.
(6) A is on the right of B and E.
(7) A and C are sitting togetter.

Questions:

1. Where is A sitting ?
(a) Between B and D (b) Between D and C (c) Between E and D
(d) Between C and E (e) Between B and C
2. Who is sitting in the centre ?
(a) A (b) B (c) C (d) D (e) E
3. C is sitting between
(a) B and D (b) A and E (c) D and E (d) A and D (e) A and B
4. What is the position of D ?
(a) Extreme left (b) Extreme right (c) Third from left
(d) Second from left (e) None of these
5. What is the position of B ?
(a) Second from right (b) Centre (c) Extreme left
(d) Second from left (e) None of these

Ex 6.

Directions (Q. 1 to 5): Read the following information carefully and answer the questions given below it:

In a car exhibition, seven different companies, viz. Cardilac, Ambassador, Fiat, Maruti, Mercedes, Bedford and Fargo, were displayed in a row, facing east such that:

(1) Cardilac car was to the immediate right of Fargo.
(2) Fargo was fourth to the right of Fiat.
(3) Maruti car was between Ambassador and Bedford.
(4) Fiat, which was third to the left of Ambassador car, was at one of the ends.

Questions:

1. Which of the following was the correct position of the Mercedes ?
(a) Immediate left of Cardilac (b) Immediate left of Bedford
(c) Between Bedford and Fargo (d) Fourth to the right of Maruti
(e) None of these
2. Which of the following is definitely true ?
(a) Fargo car is between Ambassador and Fiat.
(b) Cardilac car is to the immediate left of Mercedes.
(c) Fargo is to the immediate right of Cardilac.
(d) Maruti is fourth to the right of Mercedes.
(e) None of these

3. Which cars are on the immediate either sides of the Cardilac car ?
   (a) Ambassador and Maruti (b) Maruti and Fiat
   (c) Fiat and Mercedes (d) Ambassador and Fargo
   (e) None of these
4. Which of the following is definitely true ?
   (a) Maruti is to the immediate left of Ambassador.
   (b) Bedford is to the immediate left of Fiat.
   (c) Bedford is at one of the ends.
   (d) Fiat is second to the right of Maruti.
   (e) None of these
5. Which of the following groups of cars is to the right of the Ambassador car?
   (a) Cardilac, Fargo & Maruti (b) Maruti, Bedford and Fiat
   (c) Mercedes, Cardilac and Fargo (d) Bedford, Cardilac and Fargo
   (e) None of these

Suggested method

First of all you should keep aside the *U.S.I.* and the *negative information* and focus your attention on the *actual information*. Now, in arrangement problems, even the *actual information* can be classified into two categories. These are:

(i) Definite information: When the place of any man or object is *definitely mentioned*, we say that it is definite information.

(ii) Comparative information : When the place of any object or man is not mentioned definitely *but only a comparative position (in comparison to another object or man)* is mentioned, we say that it is comparative information.

For example, in Ex 5, the sentences "E is on the left end of the bench" and "C is on second position from right" are *definite information* because here the positions of E and C are clearly mentioned. But sentences like "A is sitting next to B" and "A and C are sitting together" are *comparative information* because here the places of A and B or of A and C are not definitely known; we know only their comparative positions.

Now, we lay down the following steps in order to solve such problems:

(i) Make a diagram of empty places.
(ii) Using all the definite information, fill up as many empty places as possible.
(iii) Now, move on to the comparative information. Taking these comparative information into account (and also the U.S.I. or negative information, if any) consider all possibilities and choose the possiblity which does not violate any condition.

Note: After step (ii), you are required to move over to comparative information. There may be many sentences comprising the comparative information. Which of these sentences should be chosen first? Think. This is an important point because it may save you an extra second or minute.

Well, you should select that sentence which gives the comparative information about an object or person *whose position has already been established* because of the definite information. For example, in Ex 5, the 4th and 5th sentences give definite information about E and C. Information about E and C is also given in 2nd, 6th and 7th sentences; hence, they should be considered first, before 1st sentence. (3rd sentence is negative information, hence it is of secondary use only.)

Now, let us see the detailed solution of Ex 4, 5 and 6 by the application of the rules discussed so far:

Solution to Ex 4:

We see that there are no definite informations and there are only comparative informations or negative informations. But on a close observation we see that the second and third sentences are definite information in a hidden way. E is not at the end of any row; it implies that E must be in the middle of the row. [In a row of only three, one is either at one of the ends or at the middle.] Also *D is second to the left of F means that D is at the left corner of any row and F is at the right corner of the row. [Again the reason is that the row is of only three people.]* We proceed with this definite information:

---------- ---------- ----------

D ---------- F

(E can be in the middle of either of the rows.)

Now, we go the the last two sentences. One of these says that C is diagonally opposite to D. It means that C is at the upper right corner. The same sentence also says that C is the neighbour of E. This means that E is in the middle of the *upper* row. Now, the last sentence. It says that B is the neighbour of F. This implies that B is in the middle of the *lower* row. Hence, the positions of B, C, D, E and F are determined. The only position remaining must belong to A. The complete diagram would be as given below:

A E C

D B F

Now, read the questions and check that you get the following answers:

Q. 1. (d) Q. 2. (d) Q. 3.(a) Q. 4. (c) Q. 5.(a)

Solution to Ex 5:

First of all, we see that the 4th and the 5th sentences constitute definite information; 1st, 2nd, 6th and 7th constitute comparative information while the 3rd is a negative information.

Starting with the definite information, you can immediately draw the following arrangement:

E__ __ C __

Now, let us look for the comparative informations that tell about E and C. These are the 2nd, 6th and 7th sentences. Take the 7th sentence and the 1st sentence. If A and C are together and also B and A are together, then A must be between B and C. This leads to:

E B A C __

Now, by virtue of the 2nd sentence :

E B A C D

Now, read the questions and check that you get the following answers:

Q. 1. (e) Q. 2. (a) Q. 3. (d) Q. 4. (b) Q. 5. (d)

Solution to Ex 6:

The last sentence gives a definite information about the positions of Fiat and Ambassador. If Fiat is at one of the ends and it is to the left of the Ambassador, it must be at the left end. Hence :

Fi ____ ____ Am ____ ____ ____

Now, we go to the second sentence since it gives comparative information about Fiat and Fargo. Hence :

Fi ____ ____ Am Fa ____ ____

Now, by virtue of the 1st sentence,

Fi ____ ____ Am Fa Ca ____

Now, the third sentence. Maruti must be to the left of Ambassador since the right place is filled. Hence, Bedford and Maruti would come to the immediate left of Ambassador. The rightmost place would then go to the only car remaining, viz. Mercedes. Hence, the final configuration would look like:

Fi Be Ma Am Fa Ca Me.

Now, try the questions and check that you get the following answers:

Q. 1. (d) Q. 2. (b) Q. 3. (e) Q. 4. (a) Q. 5. (c)

22.6. Problems on comparison

In these questions, a comparison of different objects or persons has to be made and conclusions have to be arrived at on the basis of this comparison. The following are some of the many possibilities on the basis of which a comparison can be made:

(i) Comparison of heights

(ii) Comparison of marks

(iii) Comparison of age

The following examples would give you an idea of these types of questions:

Ex 7:

Directions: Read the following informations and answer the questions given below it :

(1) Seven students P, Q, R, S, T, U and V take a series of tests.
(2) No two students get the same marks.
(3) V always scores more than P.
(4) P always scores more than Q.
(5) Each time either R scores the highest and T gets the least, or alternatively S scores the highest and U or Q scores the least.

Questions:

1. If S is ranked sixth and Q is ranked fifth, which of the following can be true?
   (a) V is ranked first or fourth. (b) R is ranked second or third.
   (c) P is ranked second or fifth. (d) U is ranked third or fourth.
   (e) T is ranked fourth or fifth.
2. If R gets most, V should be ranked not lower than
   (a) Second (b) Third (c) Fourth (d) Fifth (e) Sixth
3. If R is ranked second and Q is ranked fifth, which of the following must be true?
   (a) S is ranked third (b) T is ranked sixth (c) P is ranked sixth
   (d) V is ranked fourth (e) U is ranked sixth
4. If S is ranked second, which of the following can be true ?
   (a) U gets more than V (b) V gets more than S (c) P gets more than R
   (c) P gets more than V (e) T gets more than Q
5. If V is ranked fifth, which of the following must be true ?
   (a) S scores the highest (b) R is ranked second (c) T is ranked third
   (d) Q is ranked fourth (e) U scores the least

Suggested method: Same as that for arrangement problems.

[**Note:** Comparing is very much like arranging. For example, while comparing the heights you may assign the leftmost place to the shortest man and the rightmost place to the tallest man. Similarly, while comparing marks you can assign the leftmost place to the student getting the minimum marks and the rightmost place to the student getting the maximum marks. Thus, the rules for solving comparison problems would remain the same as those for solving problems on arrangement].

Now, we present the solution to Ex 7.

Solution to Ex 7:

We see that there is no definite information. Sentence (5) gives a definite information but is conditional. Still, we draw all the possibilities based on this sentence:

(a) R _ _ _ _ _ T
or (b) S _ _ _ _ _ U
or (c) S _ _ _ _ _ Q

We see that the two additional informations (3) and (4) are inadequate to reach a definite conclusion. Hence, keeping these in mind, we move on to the questions.

Q. 1. S is ranked sixth and Q is fifth. This means possibilities (b) and (c) are violated. Hence (a) must be true. Hence, we have :

R __ __ __ Q S T

Also, by virtue of (3) and (4) we can have only one arrangement for V, P and Q which is V P Q. Accordingly, there are two possibilities:

R V P U Q S T

or R U V P Q S T

Correct answer: (d)

Q. 2. Look at the analysis of Q.1.

Correct answer : (c)

Q. 3. R is ranked second means possibility (a) is false. Hence, the possibilities (b) and (c) remain. Now, Q is ranked fifth means possibility (c) is false. Hence, possibility (b) remains:

S R __ __ Q __ U

Now, by virtue of (3) and (4), we must have V and P before Q in that order. Consequently the sixth place would go to the only letter remaining, viz. T. Hence,

S R V P Q T U

Correct answer: (b)

Q. 4. S is ranked second means possibilities (b) and (c) are false. Hence possibility (a) is true. Now, look at the analysis of Q.1.

Correct answer: (a)

Q. 5. If V is ranked fifth we can not definitely say which among the three possibilities (a), (b) and (c) are true or false. But sentences (3) and (4) definitely imply that the position of P will be sixth and that of Q seventh. Now, if Q is seventh, it means that possibility (c) is true. And consequently we have

S ? ? ? V P Q

Correct answer: (a)

22.7. Problems on blood relations

Problems of this type involve analysis of certain blood relations and then inferring on the basis of the given informations. Some examples of such questions are:

Ex 8. Pointing to a man in a photograph, a woman said, 'His brother's father is the only son of my grandfather.' How is the woman related to the man in the photograph?

(a) Mother (b) Aunt (c) Sister

(d) Daughter (e) Grandmother

Ex 9. Manoj said to Vij, 'That boy playing with football is the younger of the two brothers of the daughter of my father's wife'. How is the boy playing football related to Manoj?

Ex. 10.

Directions: Read the following information carefully and answer the questions given below:

All the six members of a family A, B, C, D, E and F are travelling together. B is the son of C but C is not the mother of B. A and C are a married couple. E is the brother of C. D is the daughter of A. F is the brother of B.

1. How many male members are there in the family?
   (a) 1 (b) 3 (c) 2 (d) 4 (e) 5
2. Who is the mother of B?
   (a) D (b) F (c) E (d) A (e) None of these
3. How many children does A have?
   (a) One (b) Two (c) Three (d) Four (e) None of these
4. Who is the wife of E?
   (a) A (b) F (c) B
   (d) Can't be determined (e) None of these
5. Which of the following is a pair of females?
   (a) AE (b) BD (c) DF (d) AD (e) None of these
6. How is E related to D?
   (a) Father (b) Brother (c) Uncle
   (d) Can't be determined (e) None of these

Ex 11.

Directions (Q. 1 to 4): Read the following information carefully and answer the questions that follow:

In a family, there are six members – A, B, C, D, E and F. A and B are a married couple, A being the male member. D is the only son of C, who is the brother of A. E is the sister of D. B is the daughter-in-law of F, whose husband has died.

1. How is F related to A?
   (a) Mother (b) Sister-in-law (c) Sister
   (d) Mother-in-law (e) None of these
2. How is E related to C?
   (a) Sister (b) Daughter (c) Cousin
   (d) Aunt (e) Mother
3. Who is C to B?
   (a) Brother (b) Brother-in-law (c) Son-in- law
   (d) Nephew (e) None of these
4. How many male members are there in the family?
   (a) Two (b) Three (c) Four
   (d) Five (e) One

Chart of Useful Relations

The following chart would prove immensely beneficial to you for solving such questions:

Mother's or Father's son: **Brother**
Mother's or Father's daughter: **Sister**
Mother's or Father's brother: **Uncle**
Mother's or Father's sister: **Aunt**
Mother's or Father's mother: **Grandmother**
Mother's or Father's father: **Grandfather**
Son's wife: **Daughter-in-law**
Daughter's husband: **Son-in-law**
Husband's or wife's sister: **Sister-in-law**
Husband's or wife's brother: **Brother-in-law**
Brother's son: **Nephew**
Brother's daughter: **Niece**
Uncle or aunt's son or daughter: **Cousin**
Sister's husband: **Brother-in-law**
Brother's wife: **Sister-in-law**
Grandfather's only son: **Father**
Grandmother's only son: **Father**
Grandfather's son: **Father or uncle**
Grandmother's son: **Father or uncle**
Grandfather's only daughter-in-law: **Mother**
Grandmother's only daughter-in-law: **Mother**

Suggested method for questions like Ex 8, Ex 9

Backtracking: For questions like Ex 8 and Ex 9 it is best to 'backtrack', i.e., start with the last information and proceed backwards. For example, if it is given that he is the son of the mother of my grandfather's daughter, then we proceed with the last information: 'grandfather's daughter'. Grandfather's daughter means aunt (sister of father). Now, 'mother of my grandfather's daughter' becomes 'mother of my aunt'. Mother of my aunt is my grandmother. Hence, he is the son of the mother of my grandfather's daughter becomes 'son of my grandmother' which is father or uncle.

Soln to Ex 8: His brother's fathers is *only son of my grandfather* ⇒ His brother's father is my father (Since only son of my grandfather = my father)
Now, is brother's father is my father
⇒ His brother is my brother
⇒ He is my brother.
Answer: (c)

Soln to Ex 9: Younger of the two brothers of the daughter of *my father's wife*
(Since my father's wife = my mother)
⇒ Younger of the two brothers of the *daughter of my mother*.
(Since daughter of my mother = my sister)
⇒ Younger of the two brothers of my sister
⇒ my younger brother.

Suggested method for questions like Ex 10, Ex 11

(I) In questions of this type, one is required to establish the relationships within a whole family and not between only two persons. For this, *one should have the ability to draw a family-tree* which is essential in order to easily solve such problems. Here, we suggest a convenient method of drawing family-trees.

Drawing a family tree

(a) Vertical or diagonal lines should be used to represent parent-child relationships.

(b) A double horizontal line (like ⇔) should be used to represent marriages.

(c) a dashed line should be used to represent brother or sister relationships.

[Note: Apart from dash-lines, brother or sister relationships are also easily established if two persons have the same root (i.e. parents depicted by vertical or diagonal lines).]

(d) Put a + sign before someone who is a male and a - sign before someone who is a female.

(e) Whenever something is not known put a ? mark or some such symbol (x, y, z etc., for example) before it.

For example, consider the following diagram :

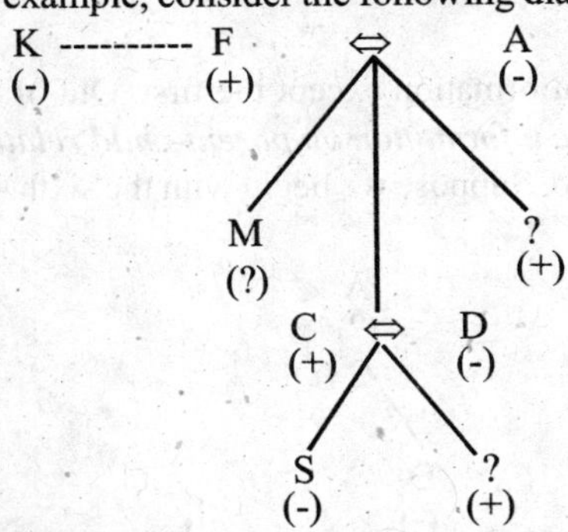

The above diagram tells us that:

(i) F and A are a couple; F is the husband while A is the wife.

(ii) F has a sister K.

(iii) The couple, F and A, has three children: M, C and another son, whose name is not known. C is also a son while the sex of M is not known.

(iv) M and the other unknown son are unmarried while C is married to D.

(v) The couple, C and D, has a daughter S and a son whose name is not known.

(II) Now that you have learnt the methods of drawing the family tree, let us see the actual method of solving problems such as Ex 10 and Ex 11.

To solve such problems:

i) Read the data quickly. This would give you a 'feel' of the problem.

ii) Separate the actual information, the USI or the negative information.

iii) Each of the actual informations would give you some information that can be used to draw a part of the family tree. **It is advisable to begin with a sentence that gives information about parent-child relationship. Grandfather-grandson relationships and brother-sister relationships should be touched later. (Very Imp)**

iv) Go on reading the actual information, one by one, and make diagrams for each of these informations. These diagrams would be like parts or components of the final family tree. Simultaneously, try your best that you do not draw a new diagram for every new information that you read. Instead, try to 'add' to the existing diagram on reading a new information. The USI and the negative informations would be of immense use in this regard.

v) Finally, with the help of all the given information etc. combine all these components into a family tree and answer the questions.

We are presenting the solution to Ex 10 and Ex 11 so that you understand the methods:

Solution to Ex 10:

All the sentences are actual information except the first. Out of these *the second and the fifth sentences give information on parent-child relationships.* We can begin with either of the two. Suppose we begin with the sixth sentence. The diagram is:

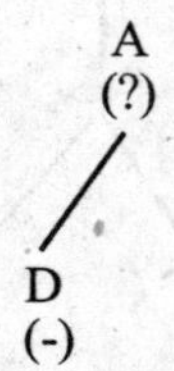

Since we do not want to make many diagrams and instead we would prefer to only add to the existing diagrams, therefore, we should look for sentences that talk of A or D. The third sentence talks about A. Hence, we add this information, that A and C are married couple, in our diagram.

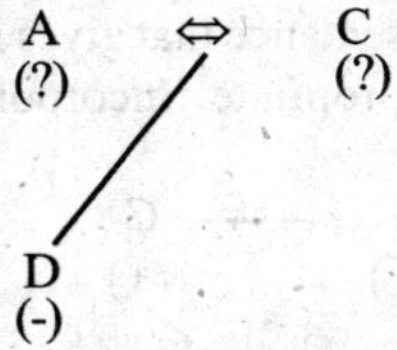

Now, the second sentence talks sbout C. It says that B is the son of C but C is not the mother of B. Obviously, C must be the father of B. This means C is a male and hence A must be a female. Hence :

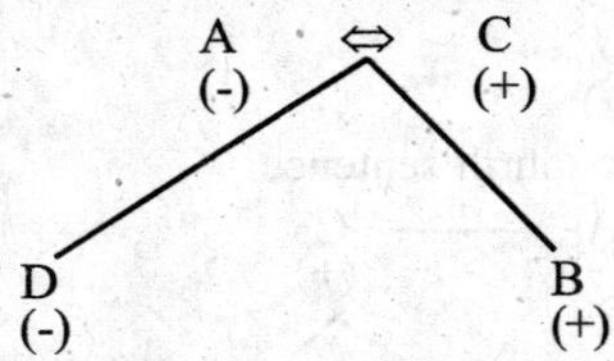

Now, we add the two sentences 'E is the brother of C' and 'F is the brother of B' and we get:

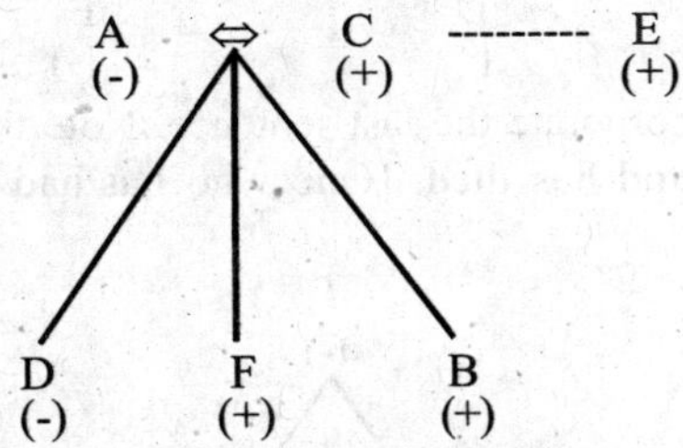

Now, read the questions and check your answers.

Q. 1. (d) Q. 2. (d) Q. 3. (c)
Q. 4. (d) Q. 5. (d) Q. 6.(c)

Solution to Ex 11:

The first sentence is U.S.I. while all others are actual information. We start with the 3rd sentence since it gives a parent-child relationship. The diagram is:

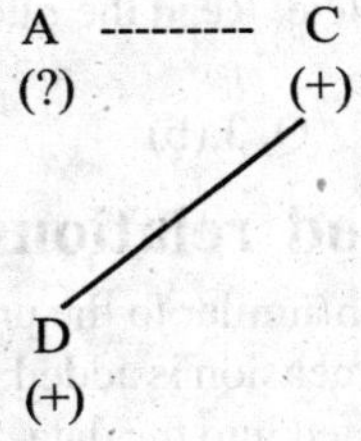

[D is the only son of C who is the brother of A.]

Now, we should look for a sentence that gives information about A or C or D. The second sentence is appropriate. Incorporating it into the diagram, we have

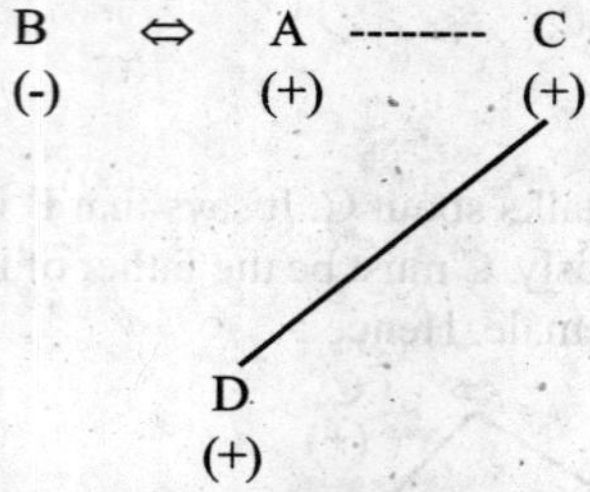

[A and B are married couple, A being the male member.]

Now, we incorporate the fourth sentence:

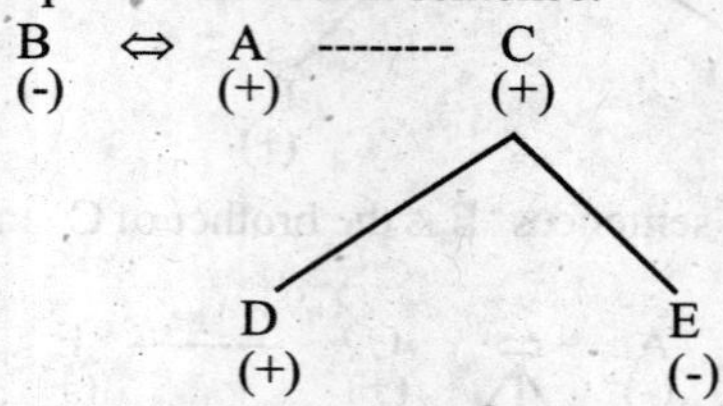

[E is the sister of D]

Finally, we incorporate the last sentence. Note that F must be a female because her husband has died. [One who has/had a husband must be a female.]

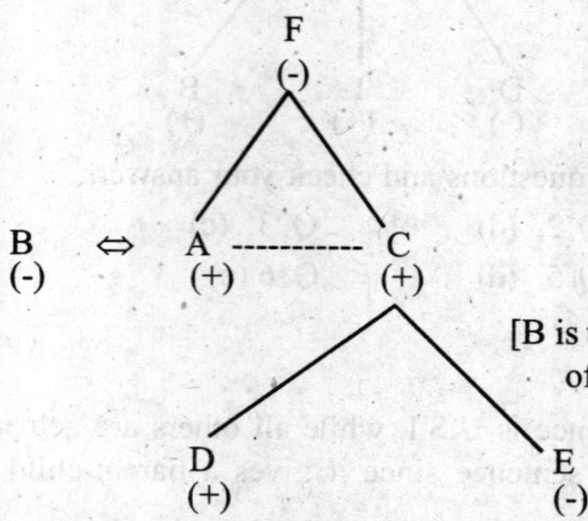

[B is the daughter-in-law of F, whose husband has died]

Now, the family tree is complete. Read the questions now and check you answer:

Q. 1. (a) Q. 2.(b) Q. 3.(b) Q. 4. (b)

22.8. Problems on blood relations and professions

These problems are very much similar to the problems on blood relations. Only in these questions another dimension is added. The professions of various family members are also incorporated into the data. Some sample questions are provided below:

Ex 12.

Directions: Read the following information carefully and answer the questions given below it:

1) There is a group of six persons A, B, C, D, E and F in a family. They are Psychologist, Manager, Lawyer, Jeweller, Doctor and Engineer.
2) The doctor is the grandfather of F who is a Psychologist.
3) The Manager D is married to A.
4) C, the Jeweller, is married to the Lawyer.
5) B is the mother of F and E.
6) There are two married couples in the family.

Questions

1. What is the profession of E?
   (a) Doctor (b) Jeweller (c) Manager
   (d) Psychologist (e) None of these
2. How is A related to E?
   (a) Brother (b) Uncle (c) Father
   (d) Grandfather (e) None of these
3. How many male members are there in the family?
   (a) One (b) Three (c) Four
   (d) Two (e) Can't be determined
4. What is the profession of A?
   (a) Doctor (b) Lawyer (c) Jeweller
   (d) Manager (e) None of these
5. Which of the following is one of the pairs of couples in the family?
   (a) AB (b) AC (c) AD
   (d) Can't be determined (e) None of these

Ex 13.

Directions: Read the following information carefully and answer the questions given below it :

P, Q, R, S, T and X are members of a family. There are two married couples. Q is an engineer and the father of T. X is the grandfather of R and is a lawyer. S is the grandmother of T and is a housewife. There is one engineer, one lawyer, one teacher, one housewife and two students in the family.

Questions:

1. Who is the husband of P?
   (a) R (b) X (c) Q (d) S (e) T
2. Which of the following are two married couples ?
   (a) XS, QP (b) XS, QT (c) XS, RP (d) TS, RX (e) None of these
3. Which of the following is definitely a group of male members ?
   (a) Q, X, T (b) X, T (c) Q, X, P (d) Q, X (e) None of these

4. Who is the sister of T ?
   (a) R (b) S (c) P
   (d) Data inadequate (e) None of these
5. Which of the following can be P's profession?
   (a) Housewife (b) Engineer (c) Teacher
   (d) Engineer or Teacher (e) Housewife or Teacher

Suggested method: *Same as that for solving problems on blood relations.*

[Note: These problems are, in spirit and in application, very similar to the problems on blood relations. Only, this time the professions are taken into account. Hence, *while making the tree, the professions of each individual should also be incorporated below their names*, in addition to their sex. For example,

D
(+, doc) means D is male and doctor. While,

E
(-, ?) means that E is a female whose profession is unknown.]

We now present the solution to Ex 12 and Ex 13.

Solution to Ex 12:

The 1st sentence and the 6th sentence are U.S.I. Let us begin with the 5th sentence because it has a parent-child relationship. The diagram is:

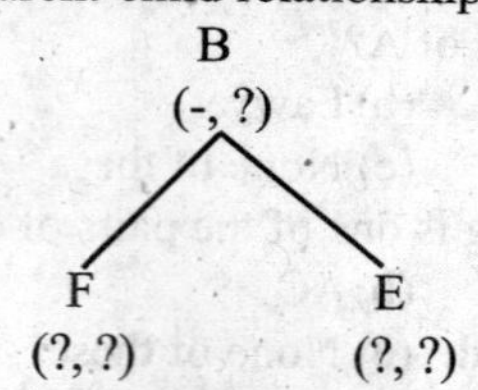

[B is the mother of F and E]

Now, we should look for another sentence that involves B or F or E. We see that the only such sentence is the 2nd which gives some information about F. Please note that if the doctor is the grandfather of F and if B is the mother of F, then B must be the daughter-in-law of the doctor. The diagram becomes:

[The doctor is the grandfather of F, who is a psychologist]

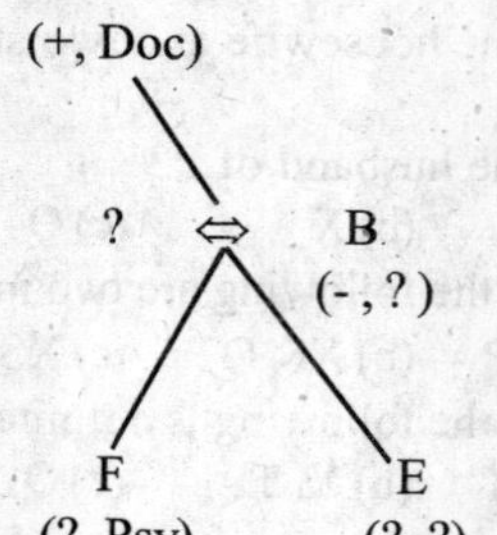

Now, the only two sentences remaining are 3rd and 4th. Their diagrams are:

D ⇔ A [The manager D is married to A]
(? , Man.) (? ,?)

C ⇔ ? [C, the jeweller, is married to the lawyer]
(?, Jew) (?, Law)

We see that we have made three components or three different diagrams. How do we combine these informations into one? Since all the actual informations are exhausted, we turn to the only information remaining. It is the last sentence that says that there are two married couples in the family. It means (look at the first diagram) that the doctor's wife is alive. She must be the manager D and the doctor must be A because the professions of the other couple are jeweller and lawyer and not doctor. Now, C, the only one remaining, must be the husband of B, and hence B must be the lawyer. Hence, we have :

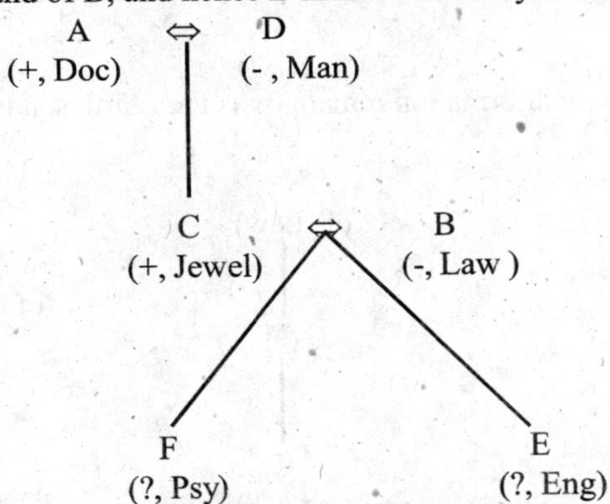

Note that the sex of F and E can't be determined. But the profession of E must be Engineer, thanks to the U.S.I. (1st sentence). Now read the questions and check you answers:

Q. 1. (e) Q. 2. (d) Q. 3. (e) Q. 4. (a) Q. 5. (c)

Solution to Ex 13:

The first two sentences are U.S.I. So is the last sentence. The third, fourth and fifth sentences make up the actual information. We begin with the 3rd sentence because it mentions a parent-child relationship. The diagram is:

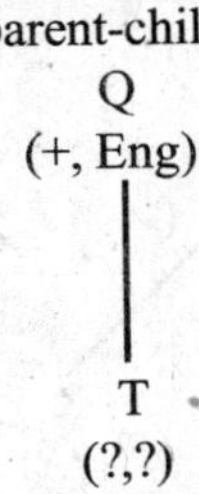

[Q is an engineer and the father of T.]

Now, we should look for another sentence that involves either Q or T. The fifth sentence gives some information about T. It says that S is the grandmother of T. Note that if S is the grandmother of T, then the son of S must be T's father and hence Q is the son of S. Hence:

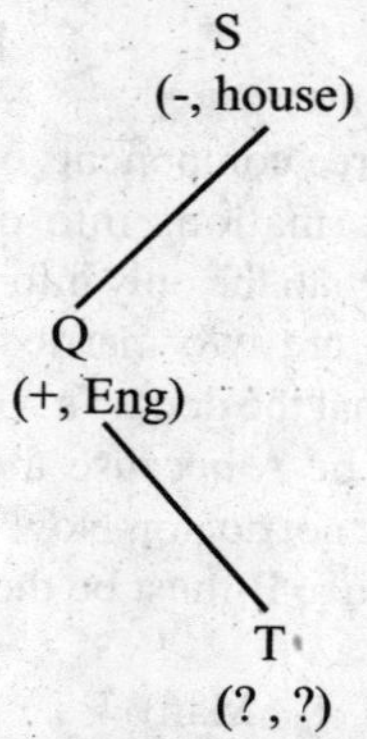

[S is grandmother of T and is a housewife.]

Now, the only information remaining is the fourth sentence. The diagram for it is:

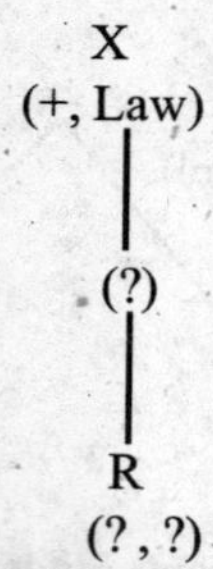

[X is grandfather of R and is a lawyer.]

Now, we see that we have ended up with two different components. To resolve this deadlock we make use of the U.S.I.: "There are two married couples in the family". Obviously, the two possible pairs are of grandfather, grandmother and father, mother. Hence, we combine the two diagrams into the following way:

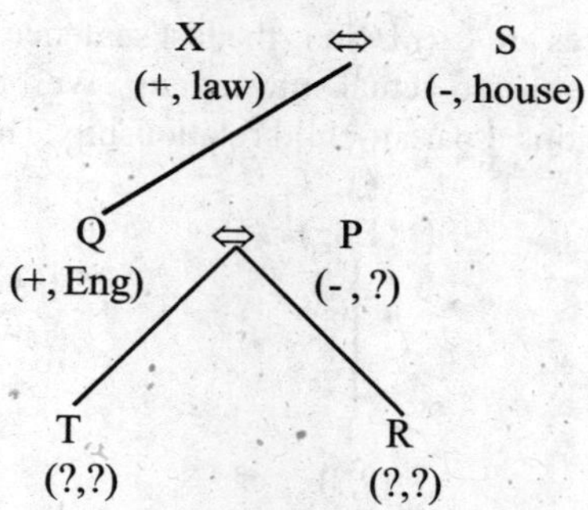

The above is the logically explicable diagram for the problem. Note that the professions of P, T and R are yet unknown. However, with reasonable justification, we may assume that the mother (P) should be the teacher and the two children T and R should be students. But this conclusion can be challenged and not without reason. Also, the sexes of T and R can't be determined.

Now, read the questions and check your answers:

Q. 1. (c) Q. 2. (a) Q. 3. (d) Q. 4. (d) Q. 5. (c)

22.9. Problems on conditional selection

In this type of questions, a group of objects or persons has to be selected from a given larger group, according to some given restrictions. The following sample problem would give you an idea of such questions:

Ex 14.

Directions: Study the following information carefully and answer the questions given below it:

From amongst six boys A, B, C, D, E and F and five girls P, Q, R, S and T, a team of six is to be selected under the following conditions :

(1) A and D have to be together.
(2) C cannot go with S.
(3) S and T have to be together.
(4) B cannot be teamed with E.
(5) D cannot go with P.
(6) B and R have to be together.
(7) C and Q have to be together.

Questions:

1. If there be five boys in the team, the only girl member is
   (a) P (b) Q (c) R (d) S
2. If, including P, the team has three girls, the members other than P are
   (a) BCFQR (b) ADEST (c) ADBST (d) BFRST
3. If the team including C consists of four boys, the members of the team other than C are
   (a) ADEPQ (b) ABDQR (c) DEFAQ (d) BEFRQ
4. If four members including E have to be boys, the members other than E are
   (a) ABCQR (b) ADFST (c) BCFQR (d) ACDFQ
5. If four members have to be girls, the members of the team are
   (a) BCPQRS (b) BFPRST (c) BCQRST (d) BCPQRT

Suggested method:

Solving such problems is very easy. Group all the pairs that have to be together on one side and the pairs that must not be together on the other side. *Next read each of the questions and treat that as an additional information.* Now, analyse the possiblilities and select the possibility that satisfies all the conditions.

We present below the solution to Ex 14 so that you understand the method.

Solution to Ex 14:

We can summarise the conditions in the following way:-

The 'must be together' groups -	A, D	;	S, T		
	(+) (+)		(-) (-)		
	B, R	;	C, Q		
	(+) (-)		(+) (-)		
The 'never be together' groups -	C, S	;	B, E	;	D, P
	(+) (-)		(+) (+)		(+) (-)

Now, let us read the questions one by one.

Q. 1. There are five boys. We see that B and E can never be together. Hence, there are only two ways of selecting five boys, viz. ABCDF and AECDF. But the first possibility is not possible because if B would go then R should also go, and if C goes then Q should also go. Hence, AECDF is the only possibility in which case C's friend Q would be the lone girl member. Correct answer : (b).

Q. 2. There are three girls including P. P is there, so D must not be there. If D is not there, A would not be there. So, two boys A and D are eliminated. Since the team should have only six members, hence there should be three boys. Two boys A and D are eliminated. Hence, the possibilities of selecting three boys are: BCE, BCF, BEF, CEF. But B and E can't be together. Hence, the remaining possibilities are BCF, CEF. Now, B must be with R while C must be with Q. Hence, we have BRCQF and CQEF. Hence, including P, the two possibilities are PBRCQF and PCQEF. To the second possibility we need to add a girl. We can't add R since R can't go without B. We can't add T since T can't go without S. Conversely, we can't add S either. Hence this possibility is also eliminated. Hence, the only possible choice is PBRCQF. Correct answer: (a).

Short-cut method:

Start with the answer choices. Choice (b) and choice (c) have D in them. D can't go because P is there. Choice (d) is not correct because it has more than three girls including P. Hence, the correct choice must be (a). (On verifying we see that (a) is indeed the correct choice as it does not violate any restriction.)

Q. 3. There are four boys including C. So, there must be two girls. Now, if C is present, S can't go and if S can't go, T won't go. Hence three girls remain: P, Q and R. Out of these, two can be selected in the following ways : PQ, PR, QR. Now if P is selected, D can't go and if D can't go, A won't go. In that case, the team would have to include B and E because four boys have to be selected. But B and E can't be together. This means that P should not be selected. Hence, the only possibility of selecting two girls is QR. But R means the necessary inclusion of B, which in turn means necessary exclusion of E. Hence, the possible team is CBQR. To this we should add two boys out of A, D and F. The only possibility is adding A and D because neither of these would go without the other. Hence, the team is ADCBQR. Correct answer : (b).

Short-cut method:

Choice (a) is incorrect because it has D and P together. Choice (c) is incorrect because it has only one girl. Choice (d) is incorrect because it has B and E together. Hence, choice (b) must be correct.

Q. 4. Inclusion of E ⇒ exclusion of B ⇒ exclusion of R. Four boys ⇒ there should be two girls. How can we select two girls out of P, Q, S and T if S and T have always to be together? The only two possible ways are : P,Q and S,T. If we select P we can't select D, and hence we can't select A either. This means the exclusion of A and D in addition to that of B. Since this is not possible, in order to have four boys, we must not select P. Hence, we select S,T. Now, selecting S means excluding C. Hence, B and C are excluded. The team would be : ADEFST. Correct answer : (b)

Short-cut method:

Choices (a) and (c) are incorrect because they include B which is impossible if E is included. Choice (d) is incorrect since it has only one girl. Hence, (b) must be correct.

Q. 5. Four members have to be girls provided S and T are always together. The possibilities are : PQST, PRST, QRST. Now, when S is included C must be excluded, which means that Q should also be excluded. Hence, the first and the last possibilities are eliminated. The only remaining possibility is PRST. With R, B must be present. Now, we have to add one more boy. We can't add E because B is there; we can't add C because S is there; we can't add A or D because they won't go without each other; hence we have to add F. The team would be : BFPRST. Correct answer: (b).

Short-cut method:

Choices (a) and (c) are incorrect because they have C and S together. Choice (d) is incorrect because it does not have S and T together. Hence, correct answer must be (b).

22.10. Miscellaneous

Till now we have covered an exhaustive pattern and types of problems in our study of problem-solving. But all the problems are not as typical and as purely standardised as we have made them out to be. Many a time the questions are a mix of the various categories studied till now. For example, we may have profession-problems outside a family, we may have blood relations and arrangement problems mixed into each other. In fact, there are numerous ways of giving you puzzles and the examiner is always with surprises up his sleeves. We are giving you some additional examples so that you understand the miscellaneous types of problems that may be asked:

Ex 15.

Directions: Study the following information and answer the questions given below it:

There are five persons P, Q, R, S and T. One is a football player, one is a chess player and one is a hockey player. P and S are unmarried ladies and do not participate in any game. None of the ladies plays chess or football. There is a married couple in which T is the husband. Q is the brother of R and is neither a chess player nor a hockey player.

Questions:

1. Who is the football player?
   (a) P (b) Q (c) R
   (d) S (e) T
2. Who is the hockey player?
   (a) T (b) S (c) R
   (d) Q (e) P
3. Who is the chess player?
   (a) S (b) P (c) T
   (d) R (e) Q
4. Who is the wife of T?
   (a) P (b) Q (c) R
   (d) S (e) Data inadequate
5. The three ladies are
   (a) P, Q and R (b) Q, R and S (c) P, Q and S
   (d) P, R and S (e) None of these

Ex 16.

Directions: Study the following information carefully and answer the questions given below it:

All the roads of a city are either perpendicular or parallel to one another. The roads are all straight. Roads A, B, C, D and E are parallel to one another. Roads G, H, I, J, K, L and M are parallel to one another.

(1) Road A is 1 km east of road B.
(2) Road B is 1/2 km west of road C.
(3) Road D is 1 km west of road E.
(4) Road G is 1/2 km south of road H.
(5) Road I is 1 km north of road J.
(6) Road K is 1/2 km north of road L.
(7) Road K is 1 km south of road M.

Questions:

1. Which is necessarily true?
   (a) E and B intersect. (b) D is 2 km west of B.
   (c) D is at least 2 km west of A. (d) M is 1.5 km north of L.
   (e) I is 1 km north of L.

2. If E is between B and C, which of the following is false?
(a) D is 2 km west of A.
(b) C is less than 1.5 km from D.
(c) Distance from E to B added to distance from E to C is 1/2 km.
(d) E is less than 1 km from A.
(e) D is less than 1 km from B.
3. If road E is between B and C then the distance between A and D is
(a) 1/2 km (b) 1 km (c) 1.5 km
(d) 1.5-2 km (e) 2-2.5 km
4. Which of the following possibilities would make two roads coincide?
(a) L is 1/2 km north of I.
(b) C is 1 km west of D.
(c) I is 1/2 km north of K.
(d) D is 1/2 km east of A.
(e) E and B are 1/2 km apart.
5. If X is parallel to I and X is 1/2 km south of J and 1 km north of G, which two roads would be 1/2 km apart?
(a) I and X (b) J and G (c) I and G
(d) J and H (e) X and J

Ex 17.

Directions: Read the following information and answer the questions that follow:

A, B, C, D and E are five towns out of which two are hill-stations and the rest are in the plain. Two towns, which are in the plain, are harbours. Four towns out of five are capitals and two are industrial towns. The population of two towns is less than 5 lakh. It is 20 lakh of one town and more than 50 lakh of two towns. Two towns are on the same latitudes and other two are on the same longitudes. Latitudes and longitudes of both harbours are different and out of these one is an industrial town. The population of both industrial towns is more than 50 lakh. The longitudes of one hill-station and one of the industrial towns are the same. The latitudes and longitudes of the other hill-station and other harbour are different. One industrial town is neither a hill-station nor a harbour. None of the hill-stations, is an industrial town. The hill-station of which the longitudes are the same as that of a harbour, is a capital. B is a hill-station while the longitudes of A and E are the same. E is a harbour. The latitudes of D and C are the same and the population of D is 20 lakh. Both the harbours are capitals and one of them is an industrial town.

Questions:

1. Which of the following two towns are those whose population is less than 5 lakh?
(a) D and A (b) B and C (c) A and B
(d) A and C (e) None of these

2. Which of the following towns is not a capital?
   (a) A (b) C (c) D
   (d) E (e) B
3. Which of the following is the harbour, capital and industrial town?
   (a) A (b) B (c) C
   (d) E (e) D
4. Which of the following towns have population more than 50 lakh?
   (a) A and D (b) B and E (c) C and E
   (d) C and D (e) A and C
5. Which one of following towns is a hill-station as well as a capital?
   (a) B (b) C (C) E
   (d) D (e) A

You can see that although the problems given above are similar to some of the problems earlier discussed, they are slightly different in their own subtle way. We now present their solutions so that you understand the way to solve them.

Solution to Ex 15:

We see that there are many dimensions attached to each individual in this problem. These dimensions are sex, marital status and favourite sport. Let us take them one by one.

Sex: P and S are females. T is a husband, so he must be a male. Q is a brother and so he must be a male. The one remaining is R. Since T is a husband and since the two ladies P and S are unmarried, R must be the wife of T. Hence R is a female.

Marital status: P and S are unmarried. R and T are married to each other. Whether Q is married or not is not known.

Favourite sport: P and S don't play anything. Out of the remaining three, one plays football, another chess and another hockey. R is a lady and no lady plays football or chess. Hence, R plays hockey. Q plays neither chess nor hockey. Hence, Q must be playing football. Hence, T plays the only remaining sport, chess.

Now, read the questions and check the answers:

Q. 1. (b) Q. 2. (c) Q. 3. (c) Q. 4. (c) Q. 5. (d)

Solution to Ex 16 :

From statements 1, 2 and 3 the following figures follow :

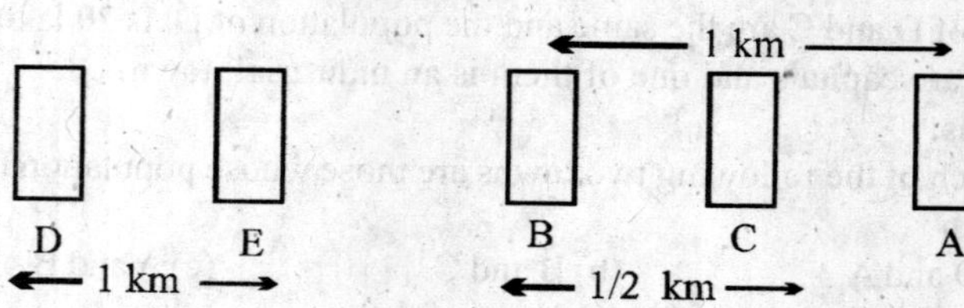

From statements 4, 5, 6 and 7 the following figures follow:

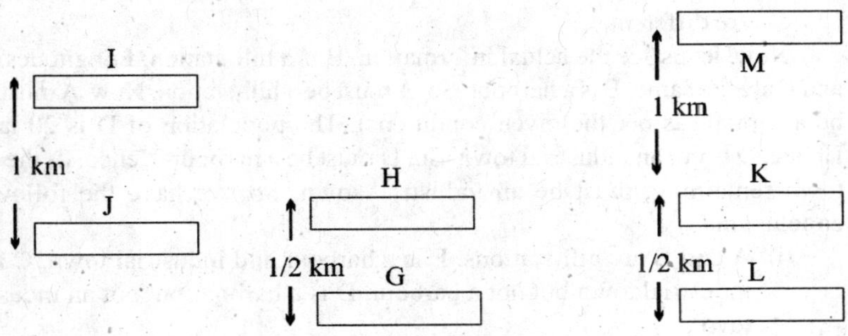

We now read the questions one by one and check the answers.

Q. 1. (d) Q. 2. (a) Q. 3. (d) Q. 4. (e) Q. 5. (e)

Solution to Ex 17:

Let us begin with the facts about the type of towns, i.e., hill-stations, harbours etc. The relevant informations are:

(i) 2 hill-stations, 2 harbours in plain, 1 in plain.

(ii) 2 industrial towns.

(iii) 4 capitals.

(iv) 1 harbour is an industrial town.

(v) No hill-station is an industrial town.

(vi) One industrial town is neither a hill station nor a harbour.

(vii) Both harbours are capitals.

The above can be summarised as:

(i) 2 hill-stations, 1 harbour and industrial town, 1 harbour but not industrial town, 1 industrial town but not harbour.

(ii) 4 capitals.

(iii) both harbours are capitals.

To these we now add the population criteria. The data then becomes:

(i) 2 hill-stations, 1 harbour and industrial town with population more than 50 lakh, 1 harbour but not industrial town, 1 industrial town but not harbour with population more than 50 lakh.

(ii) the population of others are less than 5 lakh, less than 5 lakh and 20 lakh.

(iii) 4 capitals.

(iv) 2 harbours are capitals.

To these we now add the latitude-longitude criteria which are:

(i) 2 towns have the same latitudes, 2 other towns have the same longitudes.

(ii) 2 harbours have different latitudes and longitudes.

(iii) Longitudes of one hill-station and one industrial town are the same.

(iv) Longitudes and latitudes of the other hill-station and other harbour are different.

Now, let us see the actual information. B is a hill-station. Longitudes of A and E are the same. E is a harbour. So, A must be a hill-station. Now, A must also be a capital (as per the given conditions). The population of D is 20 lakhs. Hence, D is not an industrial town. So, D must be a harbour. Hence, C, the only town remaining, must be an industrial town. So, we have the following conclusions:

(i) A and B are hill-stations. E is a harbour and industrial town. C is an industrial town but not a harbour. D is a harbour but not an industrial town.

(ii) Populations of A and B: less than 5 lakh; populations of C and E: more than 50 lakh; population of D: 20 lakh.

(iii) C, A, E and D are capitals.

Now, read the questions and check your answers.

Q. 1. (c) Q. 2. (e) Q. 3. (d) Q. 4. (c) Q. 5. (e)

Practice Exercises

Exercise 22 A

1. Amit said, 'This girl is the wife of the grandson of my mother.' What is Amit to the girl?
   a) Father b) Grandfather c) Husband
   d) Father-in-law e) None of these

2. Pointing to a man in a photograph, a woman said, 'His brother's father is the only son of my grandfather.' How is the woman related to the man in the photograph?
   a) Mother b) Aunt c) Sister
   d) Daughter e) Grandmother

3. Showing the man receiving the prize, Seema said, 'He is the brother of my uncle's daughter'. What is the man to Seema?
   a) Son b) Brother-in-law c) Nephew
   d) Uncle e) Cousin

4. Pointing to a person, a man said to a woman, 'His mother is the only daughter of your father.' How was the woman related to the person?
   a) Aunt b) Mother c) Wife
   d) Daughter e) None of these

5. Pointing to a lady, a girl said, 'She is the daughter-in-law of the grandmother of my father's only son.' How is the lady related to the girl?
   a) Sister-in-law b) Mother c) Aunt
   d) Mother-in-law e) Cousin

6. Rita told Mani, 'The girl I met yesterday at the beach was the youngest daughter of the brother-in-law of my friend's mother.' How is the girl related to Rita's friend?
a) Cousin b) Daughter c) Niece
d) Friend e) Aunt
7. If B says that his mother is the only daughter of A's mother, how is A related to B?
a) Son b) Father c) Brother
d) Grandfather e) Uncle
8. Ramesh told Ashish, 'Yesterday I defeated the only brother of the daughter of my grandmother.' Whom did Ramesh defeat?
a) Son b) Father c) Brother
d) Father-in-law e) Cousin
9. When Amir saw Manjeet, he recalled 'He is the son of the father of the mother of my daughter.' What is Manjeet to Amir?
a) Brother-in-law b) Brother c) Cousin
d) Uncle e) Nephew
10. Introducing a man, a woman said, 'He is the only son of my mother's mother.' How is the woman related to the man?
a) Mother b) Aunt c) Sister
d) Niece e) None of these
11. Introducing a girl, Vipin said, "Her mother is the only daughter of my mother-in-law." How is Vipin related to the girl?
a) Uncle b) Husband c) Brother
d) Father e) None of these
12. Pointing to a lady, a man said, "The son of her only brother is the brother of my wife." How is the lady related to the man?
a) Mother's sister b) Grandmother c) Mother-in-law
d) Sister of father-in-law e) Maternal aunt
13. Pointing to an old man, Kailash said, 'His son is my son's uncle.' How is the old man related to Kailash?
a) Brother b) Uncle c) Father
d) Grandfather e) None of these
14. Pointing to a man in a photograph, Asha said, 'His mother's only daughter is my mother.' How is Asha related to that man?
a) Nephew b) Sister c) Wife
d) Niece e) Grand-daughter
15. Showing the lady in the park, Vineet said, 'She is the daughter of my grandfather's only son.' How is Vineet related to that lady?
a) Brother b) Cousin c) Father
d) Uncle e) None of these

16. Introducing a man, a woman said, 'His wife is the only daughter of my father.' How was that man related to the woman?
a) Brother b) Father-in-law c) Maternal uncle
d) Husband e) None of these

17. Deepak said to Nitin, 'That boy playing with football is the younger of the two brothers of the daughter of my father's wife'. How is the boy playing football related to Deepak?
a) Son b) Brother c) Cousin
d) Nephew e) Brother-in-law

18. Pointing to a photograph, a person tells his friend, 'She is the granddaughter of the elder brother of my father.' How is the girl in the photograph related to this man?
a) Niece b) Sister c) Aunt
d) Sister-in-law e) Maternal aunt

19. A woman introduces a man as the son of the brother of her mother. How is the man related to the woman?
a) Nephew b) Son c) Cousin
d) Uncle e) Grandson

20. While walking with his friend, Mahesh meets another man whose mother is the wife of Mahesh's father's only son. How is the man related to Mahesh?
a) Son b) Nephew c) Cousin
d) Uncle e) Father

21. A man said to a lady, 'Your mother's husband's sister is my aunt.' How is the lady related to the man?
a) Daughter b) Granddaughter c) Mother
d) Sister e) Aunt

22. A girl introduced a boy as the son of the daughter of the father of her uncle. The boy is the girl's
a) Brother b) Son c) Uncle
d) Son-in-law e) Nephew

23. If X is the brother of the son of Y's son, how is X related to Y?
a) Son b) Brother c) Cousin
d) Grandson e) Uncle

24. Neelam, who is Deepak's daughter, says to Deepika, 'Your mother Rekha is the younger sister of my father, who is the third child of Ramlal.' How is Ramlal related to Deepika?
a) Uncle b) Father c) Grandfather
d) Father-in-law e) None of these

25. P is the brother of D. X is the sister of P. A is the brother of F. F is the daughter of D. M is the father of X. Who is the uncle of A?
a) X b) P c) F
d) M e) None of these

26. P is the brother of Q and R. S is R's mother. T is P's father. Which of the following statements cannot be definitely true?
a) T is Q's father b) S is P's mother c) P is S's son
d) T is S's husband e) Q is T's son

27. K is the brother of N and X. Y is the mother of N, and Z is the father of K. Which of the following statements is not definitely true?
a) K is the son of Z b) Y is the wife of Z c) K is the son of Y
d) K is the father of X e) N is the brother of X

28. E is the son of A. D is the son of B. E is married to C. C is B's daughter. How is D related to E?
a) Brother b) Uncle c) Father-in-law
d) Brother-in-law e) None of these

29. A and B are both children of C. If C is the mother of A, A is the son of C but B is not the daughter of C. How are A and B mutually related?
a) A is the brother of B b) A is the sister of B c) A is the cousin of B
d) A is the nephew of B e) None of these

30. C is the brother of A. B is the daughter of A. E is the sister of C. D is the brother of B. Who is the uncle of D?
a) A b) B c) C
d) E e) None of these

31. Q is the brother of R. P is the sister of Q. T is the brother of S. S is the daughter of R. Who are the cousins of Q?
A) R and P b) P and T c) Q and T
d) S and T e) None of these

32. Lakshmi and Meena are Rohan's wives. Shalini is Meena's stepdaughter. How is Lakshmi related to Shalini?
a) Sister b) Mother-in-law c) Mother
d) Stepmother e) None of these

33. C is A's father's nephew. D is A's cousin but not the brother of C. How is D related to C?
a) Father b) Sister c) Mother
d) Aunt e) None of these

34. A party consists of grandmother, father, mother, four sons and their wives and one son and two daughters of each of the sons. How many females are there in all?
a) 14 b) 16 c) 18
d) 24 e) None of these

Exercise 22 B

Directions (Q. 1-5): Read the following set of informations and then answer the questions that follow:

(i) There is a group of six persons living in a four-storeyed building. The persons are A, B, C, D, E and F. Each storey of the building has two flats; thus there are eight flats in all, two of them being empty.

(ii) The heaviest of the group lives on top floor while the lightest lives on the ground floor.

(iii) C is heavier than B, who, in turn, is heavier than F.

(iv) E is lighter than D.

(v) One of the flats on the first floor is vacant while one on the second floor is also vacant.

(vi) A is neither the heaviest nor the lightest.

(vii) There are only two people heavier than C; A is not one of them.

(viii) B shares the floor with the heaviest of the group while C shares it with the lightest.

1. Who among the folowing is the heaviest of the group?
   1) D 2) C 3) A
   4) Can't say 5) None of these
2. Who does C share the floor with?
   1) F 2) E 3) A
   4) Can't say 5) None of these
3. On which floor does A live?
   1) Ground floor 2) First floor 3) Second floor
   4) Top floor 5) Can't say
4. E and A live ______.
   1) on the same floor
   2) on two continuous floors
   3) with one floor between their floors
   4) with two floors between their floors
   5) Can't say
5. Starting from the heaviest of the group, what is the rank of A in order of weight?
   1) fourth 2) fifth 3) sixth
   4) fourth or fifth 5) fifth or sixth

Questions (6-11): J, L, M, N, O and P are members of a spy network. For security reasons, only certain spies are able to contact other spies. The only contacts allowed are:

J can contact both L and N.

O can be contacted by L, M and P.

N can contact M.

O can contact both L and N.

P can be contacted by M.

A spy can receive a message from any spy who can contact him and, in turn, relay the message to any spy he is able to contact.

6. Which of the following spies can not be contacted by any other spy in the network?

1) J 2) M 3) N
4) O 5) P

7. N can get a message from which of the folowing spies by using exactly one intermediate contact?

I. O II. L III. P

1) I only 2) III only 3) I and III only
4) II and III only 4) I, II and III

8. How can O send a message to M?

1) O can contact M directly.
2) O can send a message to M via J.
3) O can send a message to M via L.
4) O can send a message to M via N.
5) O can send a message to M via P.

9. If, for security reasons, O cannot be contacted, which of the following messages can be sent, either directly or with an intermediary?

1) J to P 2) L to M 3) L to N
4) M to L 5) M to N

10. If the following messages were sent using the smallest possible number of intermediaries, which message would require the greatest number of intermediaries?

1) J to P 2) L to O 3) M to N
4) N to O 5) O to M

11. If, for security reasons, N cannot be contacted, which of the following message can not be sent, either directly or through an intermediary?

1) J to O 2) J to P 3) M to L
4) M to O 5) P to L

Directions (Q. 12-19): Read the set of informations given below carefully, and then answer the subsequent questions:

I. There is a group of seven persons in a family, A, B, C, D, E, F and G. They all appeared in an I. Q. test to test their intelligence.

II. There are two married couples in the family and three females in total.

III. G, a female, is the most intelligent.

IV. B, the father of E, is more intelligent than his son.

V. C has one son and one daughter. She is more intelligent than her husband.

VI. The father of B is more intelligent than B himself.

VII. E, the grandson of F, is the least inteligent. F, the grandfather, is the second most intelligent in the family.

VIII. The mother of B is less intelligent than B.

IX. None among the married topped the I.Q. test.

X. The grandmother of G has two sons, one of whom is D, who is more intelligent than his brother but less intelligent than his wife.

XI. Nobody is a widow or a widower in the family.

12. Who among them is a married couple?
1) AF 2) AE 3) AC
4) AD 5) None of these

13. How is G related to D?
1) cousin 2) daughter 3) daughter-in-law
4) niece 5) None of these

14. Who is the third most intelligent in the family?
1) C 2) D 3) A
4) B 5) Can't say

15. How are C and A related?
1) daughter-in-law and mother-in-law
2) daughter-in-law and father-in-law
3) sisters-in-law
4) mother and daughter
5) Can't say

16. Who among the following is not of the same generation as others?
1) D 2) B 3) C
4) A 5) Can't say

17. The one who is the most intelligent is not a
1) granddaughter 2) daughter 3) niece
4) sister 5) None of these

18. Who is less intelligent than all but E?
1) A 2) B 3) C
4) D 5) Can't say

19. Who is B married to?
1) A 2) D 3) C
4) Can't say 5) None of these

Questions (20-26): During a trial, an attorney is planning to call to the stand to testify six different witnesses - *T, V, W, X, Y* and Z. She will call each witness exactly one time and the order in which she calls them is subject to the following conditions:

The fourth witness must be *T*.
W and *Y* must both be called before *V*.
X must be called before *W*.

20. Which of the following could be the order in which the attorney calls the six witnesses?
1) *W, X, Y, T, Z, V* 2) *X, W, V, T, Y, Z* 3) *X, Y, W, T, Z, V*
4) *Z, T, X, W, Y, V* 5) *Z, X, W, T, V, Y*

21. Which of the following must be true of the order in which the attorney calls the witnesses?
1) She calls *V* before *T*. 2) She calls *X* before *V*.
3) She calls *Y* before *W*. 4) She calls *Y* before *X*.
5) She calls *Z* before *T*.

22. Which of the following could be true of the order in which the witnesses are called?
1) *T* is called sixth. 2) *V* is called fourth.
3) *W* is called first. 4) *X* is called fifth.
5) *Y* is called first.

23. If the attorney calls Z last, which witness must be called fifth?
1) *T* 2) *V* 3) *W* 4) *X* 5) *Y*

24. If the attorney calls *X* immediately after *Y* and immediately before *Z*, she must call *V*
1) first 2) second 3) third 4) fifth 5) sixth

25. The attorney could call any of the following witnesses immediately before *T*, EXCEPT
1) *V* 2) *W* 3) *X* 4) *Y* 5) *Z*

26. If the attorney calls *Z* first, which of the following could be her fifth and sixth witnesses respectively?
1) *T* and *X* 2) *V* and *W* 3) *X* and *V* 4) *Y* and *V* 5) *Y* and *X*

Directions (Q. 27-31): Study the following information carefully and answer the questions given below:

(i) A, B, C, D, E and F are six members in a family in which there are two married couples.
(ii) D is the brother of F. Both D and F are lighter than B.
(iii) B is the mother of D and lighter than E.
(iv) C, a lady, is neither the heaviest nor the lightest in the family.
(v) E is lighter than C.
(vi) The grandfather is the heaviest in the family.

27. How many male members are there in the family?
1) Data inadequate 2) 2 3) 4
4) 3 5) None of these

28. How is E related of F?
1) Grandmother 2) Brother 3) Father
4) Data inadequate 5) None of these

29. How is C related to D?
 1) Sister 2) Grandmother 3) Mother
 4) Cousin 5) None of these
30. Which of the following is a pair of married couples?
 1) AD 2) BC 3) AB
 4) BE 5) None of these
31. Who among the following will be in the second place if all the members in the family are arranged in the descending order of their weight?
 1) D 2) A 3) C
 4) Data inadequate 5) None of these

Questions (32-38): Five males - B, C, D, E, and F - and four females - J, K, L, and M - are to be divided into three debating teams of three persons each. The teams are designated as the Blue Team, the Red team, and the Green Team.

D, E, and F must be the captains of their respective teams.
B and C cannot be on the same team.
J and F cannot be on the same team.
L must be on a team with either B or E or both.
L must be on the Blue Team.

32. Which of the pairs of students could be on the same team as John?
 1) B and E 2) E and F 3) E and M
 4) K and L 5) K and M
33. Any of the following pairs of students could be on the Blue Team EXCEPT
 1) B and F 2) D and E 3) E and J
 4) E and M 5) M and F
34. If B and J are on the Red Team, then which of the following must be true?
 1) C is on the Blue Team.
 2) D is on the Green Team.
 3) D is on the Red Team.
 4) K is on the Blue Team.
 5) M is on the Green Team.
35. If F is the only male on his team, which of the following pairs could be the other members of his team?
 1) K and J 2) L and M 3) L and K
 4) M and J 5) M and K
36. If B and F are on the Red Team, then which of the following is NOT an acceptable assignment of students for the other two teams?

	Blue Team	Green Team
1)	C, E, L	D, J, M
2)	E, J, L	C, D, M
3)	L, E, K	C, D, J
4)	L, M, E	J, C, D
5)	K, L, E	M, D, C

37. Which of the following must be true?
1) B is on the Blue Team.
2) E is on the Blue Team.
3) Either B or E is not on the Green Team.
4) Either B or C is on the same team as J.
5) One team will consist of a male and two females.

38. If D, M, and K are on the Red Team then which of the following must be the constituents of the Green Team?

1) B, E, J B) B, F, J 3) C, F, J
D) E, C, F 5) J, C, E

Directions (Q. 39-43): Read the following set of informations correctly and then answer the questions that follow:

(i) There is a group of six persons, A, B, C, D, E and F, seated around a circular table.
(ii) There are two females and four males in this group.
(iii) Both the females are married to two males of the same group. The remaining two males are bachelors.
(iv) A, a female, is sitting opposite one of the bachelors, F. Her husband is not on either of her sides.
(v) Another female is sitting opposite her husband D.
(vi) The two females are not sitting adjacently.
(vii) On the immediate right of both the females is sitting a bachelor.
(viii) C has the same marital status as F while B is a father of two sons.

39. Who is the other female in the group?
1) E 2) C 3) D
4) Can't say 5) None of these

40. How many females are sitting between the two husbands?
1) 1 2) None 3) 2
4) Can't say 5) None of these

41. Moving clockwise, how many bachelors are there between A and her husband, if one starts from the husband?
1) Zero 2) 1 3) 2
4) Can't say 5) None of these

42. Which of the following depicts the correct couples?
1) ED, AB 2) EB, AD 3) EC, AB
4) ED, Can't say 5) Can't say

43. If the two bachelors were to exchange their seats via the shorter route, how many females would they cross?
1) Zero 2) One 3) Two
4) Can't say 5) None of these

Directions (Q. 44-50): A candidate for public office plans to visit each of the six cities *J, K, L, M, N* and *O* exactly once during her campaign. Her aides are setting up the candidate's schedule according to the following restrictions:

The candidate can visit M only after she has visited both *L* and *N*.

The candidate cannot visit *N* before *J*.

The second city visited by the candidate must be *K*.

44. Which of the following could be the order in which the candidate visits the six cities?

1) *J,K,N,L,O,M* 2) *K,J,L,N,M,O* 3) *O,K,M,L,J,N*
4) *L,K,O,N,M,J* 5) *M,K,N,J,L,O*

45. Which of the following must be true of the candiate's campaign schedule?

1) She visit *J* before *L*. 2) She visit *K* before *M*.
3) She visit *K* before *O*. 4) She visit *M* before *J*.
5) She visit *N* before *L*.

46. If the candidate visits *O* first, which city could she visit third?

I. *J* II. *L* III. *M*
1) I only 2) III only 3) I and II only
4) II and III only 5) I, II and III

47. If the candidate visit *J* immediately after *O* and immediately before *N*, then she must visit *L*

1) first 3) third 3) fourth
4) fifth 5) sixth

48. Which of the following could be true of the candidate's schedule?

1) She visit *J* first. 2) She visit *K* first. 3) She visit *L* sixth.
4) She visit *M* fourth. 5) She visit *N* sixth.

49. The candidate could visit any of the following immediately after *K*, EXCEPT

1) *J* 2) *L* 3) *M* 4) *N* 5) *O*

50. If the candidate visit *O* last, which of the following could be the first and third cities on her schedule, respectively?

1) *J* and *L* 2) *J* and *O* 3) *L* and *N* 4) *L* and *O* 5) *N* and *J*

Directions (Q. 51-55): Read the information below and answer the questions that follow:

(1) There is a group of seven persons seated around a table.

(2) Their professions are: Housewife, Doctor, Engineer, Teacher, Chemist, Manager, Professor respectively.

(3) There are three females including the housewife. The Engineer is not a female.

(4) Two of them are husband-wife. The profession of the wife is teaching. Her husband is the oldest of the seven.

(5) The youngest of the group is a female. She does not teach and she is not a housewife.

(6) The individual ages of the Professor, the Doctor and the Manager are more than the average age of the whole group.

(7) If the Professor is not counted then the average age of the group decreases.

Now, answer the following questions:

51. Who among the following is the married couple?
1) Teacher-Professor 2) Teacher-Chemist
3) Teacher-Manager 4) Can't be said
5) None of these

52. Who among the following is only younger than the oldest?
1) Manager 2) Doctor 3) Manager or Doctor
4) Can't be said 5) None of these

53. Who among the following is not a female?
1) Teacher 2) Housewife 3) Chemist
4) Can't be said 5) None of these

54. What are the sexes of the doctor and the manager?
1) male and male 2) male and female 3) female and female
4) female and male 5) Can't be said

55. Who is the youngest of the group?
1) Chemist 2) Doctor 3) Engineer
4) Can't be said 5) None of the above

Directions (Q. 56-61): Read the following information carefully and then answer the questions given below.

The President of the Residents Welfare Association (RWA) of *XYZ Vihar* lives in the C block of the neighbourhood. There are seven houses in the C block, including the president's — the president's house being located at the centre. The other houses are located in the same row as the president's house. These houses are occupied by other officebearers of the RWA. The seven residents in the C block are P, Q, R, S, T, U and V. The closer a resident's house is to the president's house, the higher is his rank in the RWA, with a person on the president's left outranking one equidistant from the president's right.

1) T is four places to the left of the secretary.
2) V's neighbous are P and the secretary.
3) S is two places to the left of U.
4) The Convenor, the Organiser and the Cashier are seated together, in that order, from left to right.
5) The secretary is two places to the right of Q.
6) The remaining functionaries of the RWA are the Treasurer and the officer.

56. The cashier of the RWA is
1) P 2) T 3) R 4) Q 5) U

57. The president of the RWA is
1) R 2) U 3) T 4) V 5) P

58. The fourth-ranking person in the RWA is
1) V 2) P 3) S 4) U 5) Q

59. The officer in the RWA
I. outranks the Secretary
II. outranks the Convenor
III. is outranked by the Organiser
IV. is outranked by the Cashier
1) I and IV 2) III and I 3) I and II 4) II and IV 5) None of these

60. If R is ordered to vacate his house and move to the house occupied by a person two places lower to him, which of the following is true?
1) The officer has to vacate his house for R.
2) The organiser and the convenor exchange houses.
3) The cashier and U exchange houses.
4) V has to vacate his house for R.
5) All of these

61. How many of the RWA outrank the convenor?
1) 2 2) 4 3) 6 4) None 5) 5

Directions (Q. 62-71): Read the information given below and answer the questions that follow:

(i) There is a group of seven persons A, B, C, D, E, F and G.
(ii) There are four males, three females, two married couples and three unmarried persons in the group.
(iii) The seven persons are seated in a row on the bench.
(iv) Their professions are: engineer, teacher, doctor, psychologist, businessman, architect and student.
(v) B is not married and another person, the psychologist, is the most intelligent.
(vi) The engineer is married to the teacher, who is the least intelligent of the group.
(vii) D is an architect. He is sitting on the leftmost corner.
(viii) The student is sitting on the rightmost corner of the bench.
(ix) The doctor is married to C. C is the second most intelligent of the group followed by her husband.
(x) The least intelligent of the group is sitting on the immediate right of D, followed by the most intelligent.
(xi) There are as many more intelligent persons than the engineer as there are less intelligent.
(xii) On the bench, followed by D there are three females sitting in succession.
(xiii) The psychologist is a female.

(xiv) The student is more intelligent than the architect, who is more intelligent than only one person, F.

(xv) Neither A nor G is a female.

62. Who is sitting on the immediate right of D?
1) F 2) E 3) C
4) Can't say 5) None of these

63. What is the profession of A?
1) Engineer 2) Doctor 3) Teacher
4) Can't say 5) None of these

64. What is the profession of G?
1) Doctor 2) Engineer 3) Teacher
4) Can't say 5) None of these

65. Which two are sitting together?
1) D and E 2) E and A 3) Teacher and businessman
4) Engineer and doctor 5) Can't say

66. The engineer is not more intelligent than
1) Student 2) Architect 3) Teacher
4) Businessman 5) Can't say

67. Which is the married couple?
1) A-F 2) B-F 3) G-F
4) Can't say 5) None of these

68. Which of these cannot be a married couple?
1) A-F 2) A-C 3) G-F
4) G-C 5) None of these

69. Who is the student?
1) A 2) C 3) D
4) B 5) Can't say

70. Which of these represents the correct order of intelligence (in the decreasing sequence)?
1) EBF 2) CDF 3) ECB
4) BCF 5) None of these

71. Which of the given statements in the question is definitely superfluous?
1) iv 2) iii 3) vi
4) xiii 5) xv

Directions (Q. 72-78): Read the information given below and then answer the questions that follow:

A lawyer must schedule appointments with eight clients *F*, *G*, *H*, *I*, *J*, *K*, *L* and *M* during one week, Monday through Friday. She must schedule two appointments for Monday, Tuesday and Wednesday and one each for Thursday and Friday.

i) She must see *H* on Thursday.

ii) She must see *G* on a day before the day on which she sees *I*.

iii) She must see *J* on a day before the day on which she sees *L*.
iv) She must see *F* on a day before the day on which she sees *L*.
v) She must see *K* and *F* on the same day.

72. Which of the following is an acceptable schedule for the week's appointments?

	Mon.	Tues.	Wed.	Thurs.	Fri.
1)	*G, M*	*I, L*	*K, F*	*H*	*J*
2)	*G, M*	*I, J*	*K, F*	*H*	*L*
3)	*G, I*	*M, L*	*J*	*H*	*K, F*
4)	*L, G*	*I, J*	*K, M*	*H*	*F*
5)	*G, L*	*M, K*	*F*	*H, J*	*I*

73. Which of the following cannot be true?
1) She sees *M* on Monday. 3) She sees *K* on Tuesday.
3) She sees *L* on Tuesday. 4) She sees *I* on Wednesday.
5) She sees *M* on Friday.

74. Which of the following is a complete and accurate listing of the clients the lawyer could see on Friday?
1) *I, J* 2) *I, M* 3) *L, M*
4) *I, L, M* 5) *M, L, G*

75. If the lawyer sees *I* on Tuesday, then which of the following must be true?
1) She sees *J* on Monday. 2) She sees *M* on Tuesday.
3) She sees *K* on Tuesday. 4) She sees *M* on Friday.
5) She sees *L* on Friday.

76. If the lawyer sees *K* on Wednesday, which of the following must be true?
I. She sees *I* on Tuesday.
II. She sees *M* on Monday.
III. She sees *L* on Friday.
1) I only 2) III only 3) I and III only
4) II and III only 5) I, II and III

77. If the lawyer sees *I* and *L* on the same day, which of the following is a complete and accurate listing of the days on which she could see them?
1) Monday 2) Tuesday 3) Wednesday
4) Monday and Wednesday 5) Tuesday and Wednesday

78. Which of the following, if true, provides sufficient additional information to determine on which day each client will have his appointment?
1) *M*'s appointment is scheduled for Monday.
2) *G*'s appointment is scheduled for Monday.
3) *G*'s appointment is scheduled for Tuesday.
4) *K*'s appointment is two days before *G*'s.
5) *G*'s appointment is two days before *I*'s.

Directions (Q. 79-83): Read the information given below and then answer the questions that follow:

I. There is a group of six persons in a family: A, B, C, D, E and F.
II. There are two married couples in the family.
III. A is the most talkative in the family while D talks less than E or C.
IV. F is more talkative than D or B.
V. The least talkative in the family is married to the second most talkative in the family.
VI. There are three females and three males.
VII. Nobody is a widow or a widower.
VIII. D is an unmarried male; B is a female.
IX. A is of the same sex as the unmarried person other than D.
X. E is married and is not of the same sex as A or married to A.
XI. The marital status of the most talkative and the least talkative of the family are the same.

79. Who is the least talkative member of the family?
1) B 2) D 3) B or D 4) Can't say 5) None of these

80. Which of the following represents a correct couple?
1) ED 2) EB 3) AB 4) AC 5) Can't say

81. Who is the third most talkative in the family?
1) E 2) F 3) C D) Can't say 5) None of these

82. The marital status of F and C are
1) Unmarried, Married 2) Married, Unmarried 3) Married, Married
4) Unmarried, Unmarried 5) Can't say

83. Which set of statements is sufficient to find out the least talkative person of the family?
1) III, IV, VIII 2) III, V, VIII 3) I, II, III, IV, V VI, VIII
4) III, IV, V, VIII 5) II, III, IV, V, VI, VII, VIII

Directions (Q. 84-90): A student planning his curriculum for the upcoming semester must enrol in three courses. The available courses fall into one of the five general areas: Maths, English, Social Studies, Science and Fine Arts.

(i) The student must take courses from at least two different areas.
(ii) If a student takes an English course, he cannot take a Fine Arts course; and if he takes a Fine Arts course, he cannot take an English course.
(iii) If he takes a Science course, he must take a Maths course; and if he takes a Maths course, he must take a Science course.
(iv) He can take a Social Studies course only if he takes a Fine Arts course.

84. Which of the following is an acceptable schedule of courses?
1) One Science course, one English course and one Fine Arts course
2) One Maths course, one Science course and one Social Studies course
3) One Maths course, one Social Studies and one Fine Arts course
4) One English course, one Social Studies course and one Fine Arts course
5) One Maths course, one Science course and one Fine Arts course

85. Which of the following is NOT an acceptable schedule?
 1) Two Maths and one Science course
 2) Two Science courses and one Maths course
 3) Two Fine Arts courses and one Maths course
 4) Two Social Studies courses and one Fine Arts course
 5) One Social Studies course and two Fine Arts courses

86. Which of the following courses, when taken with one course in Social Studies, is an acceptable schedule?
 1) One course in Maths and one course in Science
 2) One course in Fine Arts and one course in English
 3) Two courses in Fine Arts
 4) Two courses in Maths
 5) Two courses in English

87. If the student wishes to take a course in Maths and a course in English, then he must select his third course in the area of
 1) English 2) Fine Arts 3) Maths
 4) Science 5) Social Studies

88. Which of the following pairs of courses CANNOT be combined in an acceptable schedule?
 1) A course in Maths and a course in Fine Arts
 2) A course in Science and a course in Fine Arts
 3) A course in Maths and a course in English
 4) A course in Social Studies and a course in Science
 5) A course in Science and a course in English

89. If the student wished to take a course in Science, then which of the following pairs of courses would complete an acceptable schedule?
 1) Two Maths courses
 2) Two Science courses
 3) Two English courses
 4) One Science course and one English course
 5) One Maths course and one Social Studies course

90. An acceptable schedule CANNOT include two courses in
 1) English 2) Fine Arts 3) Maths
 4) Science 5) Social Studies

Directions (Q. 91-95): Read the information given below and answer the questions that follow:

(i) There are six friends — A, B, C, D, E and F. Together they start a business by investing Rs. 60,000 in total.

(ii) A invested twice as much as B while D invested half as much as C. E invested as much as F.

(iii) B is not the tallest while F is not the shortest among them.

(iv) The one who invested most stands second in order of height. (He is the second tallest person.) The man who invested the least stands fourth.

(v) B invested more than E; D invested less than F.

(vi) A stands third in order of height.

91. How much did B invest?
1) Rs. 7500 2) Rs. 6500 3) Rs. 4500
4) Can't say 5) None of these

92. Who invested the most?
1) D 2) A 3) C
4) Can't say 5) None of these

93. Who is the tallest?
1) E 2) F 3) C
4) Can't say 5) None of these

94. What is the rank of F in terms of height?
1) 1st 2) 4th 3) 3rd
4) 1st or 5th 5) Can't say

95. What is the rank of B in order of investment?
1) First 2) Second 3) Third
4) Fourth 5) Can't say

Directions (Q. 96-100): Read the following information and then answer the questions.

A certain musical scale consists of exactly six notes: *F*, *G*, *H*, *I*, *J* and *K*. The notes are arranged from the lowest (the first note of the scale) to the highest (the sixth note of the scale). Each note appears once and only once in the scale, and the intervals between the notes are all equal.

i) *J* is lower than *K*.
ii) *G* is higher than *F*.
iii) *I* is somewhere between *F* and *G*.
iv) *H* is the highest note of scale.

96. Which of the following CANNOT be true of the scale?
1) *G* is the second note. 2) *G* is the third note.
3) *I* is the second note. 4) *I* is the third note.
5) *I* is the fourth note.

97. If *J* is the fourth note of the scale, which of the following must be true?
1) *F* is the third note. 2) *F* is the fifth note.
3) *I* is the fourth note. 4) *I* is the second note.
5) *G* is the first note.

98. If exactly two notes separate *F* and *I*, then which of the following must be true?
1) *F* is the lowest note. 2) *K* is the fifth note.
3) *K* is higher than *I*. 4) *J* is somewhere between *G* and *I*.
5) *K* and *J* are separated by exactly one note.

99. If *J* is the second note, then *G* and *I* could be which of the following respectively?
I. 4 and 3 II. 5 and 3 III. 5 and 4
1) I only 2) III only 3) I and II only
4) II and III only 5) I, II and III

100. If *F* and *I* are separated by exactly one note, which of the following must be true?
1) *G* is note 4. 2) *K* is note 5. 3) *J* is lower than *I*.
4) *I* is lower than *K*. 5) *J* is between *F* and *I*.

Exercise 22 C

Directions (Q. 1-2): Read the information given below and answer the questions that follow:

In a question paper, there are 12 questions in all, out of which only six are to be answered. Six questions have one alternative each. Each question has four parts, only three of which are to be answered.

1. How many questions (including parts) are there in the question papers?
1) 24 2) 48 3) 72
4) 96 5) 36

2. Of these, how many are to be answered?
1) 6 2) 12 3) 15
4) 18 5) 24

3. In a queue, Sohan is 9th from the back. Ramesh's place is 8th from the front. Radhey is standing between the two. What could be the minimum number of boys standing in the queue?
1) 20 2) 18 3) 19
4) 12 5) 14

4. Suresh is older than Ramesh and Mohan is younger than Surender. Murari is younger than Mohan but older than Suresh. Who is the youngest?
1) Suresh 2) Ramesh 3) Murari
4) Mohan 5) Surender

5. Seven boys are sitting in a row. Satyendra is on the left of Khalid and Madhukar is on the left of Balan and right of Khalid. Rehman is between Satyendra and Ahmed and Kutty is at the extreme right. Who is in the middle?
1) Rehman 2) Satyendra 3) Khalid
4) Madhukar 5) Balan

Questions (6-12): A researcher studying organic compounds has found that five different molecules — *T, W, X, Y* and *Z* — form chains according to the following rules:

i) A chain consists of three or more molecules, though the molecules in the chain are not necessarily different.

ii) *T* is never found on either end of a chain.

iii) If *W* appears in a chain, it appears more than once.

iv) *X* is never found next to *Y* in a chain.

v) *W* is never found on the end of a chain unless *Z* is found somewhere in the chain.

vi) If *Y* appears in a chain, *Z* appears also.

6. Which of the following is a possible chain of molecules?
   1) *TXYZ* 2) *YTXX* 3) *WZTY*
   4) *WWXZ* 5) *ZYXW*

7. Which of the following is NOT a possible chain of molecules?
   1) *XXTZ* 2) *ZXWWZ* 3) *WXZYW*
   4) *WWWZXW* 5) *YWTZXX*

8. In the chain _*WWZ*, which of the following would be substituted for the dash to make a chain?
   I. *Z* II. *W* III. *T*
   1) I only 2) II only 3) I and II only
   4) I and III only 5) I, II and III

9. The chain — *WWTYZX* can be changed into another chain by carrying out any one of the following EXCEPT
   1) Replacing the *T* molecule with a *W* molecule
   2) Replacing the *Y* molecule with an *X* molecule
   3) Replacing the *X* molecule with a *T* molecule
   4) Interchanging the *T* and the *Z* molecules
   5) Interchanging the *Y* and the *X* molecules

10. Which of the following is not a chain but could be converted into a chain by changing the order of the molecules?
    1) *XYTX* 2) *WXTY* 3) *TXXY*
    4) *WTTW* 5) *WXXW*

11. Which of the following could be converted into a chain by replacing the dash with a molecule?
    1) *WW_YTX* 2) WXTY_Y 3) *X_XYTY*
    4) _*XXTWY* 5) _*XXTWT*

12. Which of the following sequences can be converted into a chain by adding Z and rearranging the molecules?
    I. *XYXT* II. *WTTZ* III. *XXYW*
    1) I only 2) II only 3) III only
    4) I and III only 5) I, II and III

Directions (Q.13-17): Read the information given below and answer the questions that follow:

There are five villages, viz. A, B, C, D and E. Two of these have post offices, three have schools and three are accessible by road. Two have population of more than 5000 each, two have population between 2000 and 5000 each, and one has a population of less than 2000. Two of these villages have electricity in addition to certain other facilities such as school and accessibility by road. One village with a population of less than 2000 also has a school but neither has a post office nor is accessible by road while each of the villages with a population of more than 5000 has a school. Of the two villages having population between 2000 and 5000, only one has a post office and is accessible by road. A is accessible by road. B has a population of more than 5000, D has a school and is accessible by road but does not have a post office, while E has a school but is not accessible by road.

13. Which village has a school and also a post office?
    1) A 2) B 3) C 4) D 5) E
14. Which village does not have any of the facilities available to other villages?
    1) A 2) B 3) C 4) D 5) E
15. Which two villages have electricity?
    1) A, B 2) B, C 3) B, D 4) C, D 5) None of these
16. Which three villages are accessible by road?
    1) A, B, D 2) A, B, E 3) A, D, E 4) B, D, E 5) A, B, C
17. Which village has a population of less than 2000?
    1) B 2) C 3) D 4) E 5) A

Directions (Q.18-24): An information processing system consists of seven stations - *M*, *N*, *P*, *Q*, *R*, *S* and *T*. Every request is classified as either normal or priority. Requests for information are processed in the following ways:

(i) All normal requests are received by either *M* or *N*, and all priority requests are received by *M* or *Q*.
(ii) All requests processed by *M* are then sent to *T*.
(iii) All requests processed by *N* are then sent to *S*.
(iv) Normal requests processed by *T* are then sent to *P*; priority requests processed by *T* are then sent to *Q*.
(v) All requests processed by *S* are then sent to either *T* or *P*.
(vi) Normal requests processed by *P* are then sent to *Q*, and priority requests processed by *P* are then sent to *R*.
(vii) All requests processed by *Q* are then sent to either *P* or *R*.
(viii) *R* is the station which issues a final response.

18. Any of the following can be true EXCEPT
    1) *M* sends a request to *T*. 2) *S* sends a request to *T*.
    3) *S* sends a request to *P*. 4) *S* sends a request to *Q*.
    5) *Q* sends a request to *P*.

19. A priority request could reach *R* via which of the following sequences?
1) *M* to *Q* to *R*. 2) *N* to *Q* to *R*. 3) *N* to *S* to *R*.
4) *Q* to *P* to *R*. 5) *P* to *Q* to *R*.

20. Any request that is first received by *M* and is finally received by *R* must also have previously been processed by
I. *T* II. *Q* III. *P*
1) I only 2) III only 3) I and II only
4) I and III only 5) I, II and III

21. What is the minimum number of stations that must have processed a normal request *before* the request is sent to *R*?
1) 1 2) 2 3) 3
4) 4 5) 5

22. If a request is processed more than once by the same station, then that station must be
I. *P* II. *Q* III. *T*
1) I only 2) II only 3) III only
4) I and II only 5) I, II and III

23. If a request is finally processed by *R*, it is possible that which of the following stations did NOT process the request?
I. *P* II. *Q* III. *M*
1) I only 2) III only 3) I and II only
4) I and III only 5) II and III only

24. If a normal request reaches *R*, what is the maximum number of stations through which that request could have passed before reaching *R*?
1) 2 2) 3 3) 4 4) 5 5) 6

Directions (Q. 25-29): Read the information given below and find out the correct answers to the questions that follow:

(i) There are six members in a club: A, B, C, D, E and F.
(ii) A is not the heaviest while E is not the most intelligent.
(iii) The lightest of the group is the most intelligent of the group.
(iv) B is more intelligent than D, who is more intelligent than F.
(v) A is less intelligent than D but is heavier than D.
(vi) B is heavier than C but lighter than F.
(vii) F is more intelligent than A while D is heavier than F.

25. Who is the heaviest of the group?
1) A 2) E 3) B
4) Can't be determined 5) None of these

26. What is the rank of B in the decreasing order of weight?
1) Third 2) Fourth 3) Fifth
4) Can't say 5) None of these

27. Who is the most intelligent?
   1) B   2) E   3) C
   4) D   5) Can't say
28. What is the rank of E in decreasing order of intelligence?
   1) Second   2) Third   3) Fourth
   4) Can't say   5) None of these
29. What is the rank of D in decreasing order of intelligence?
   1) Fourth   2) Fifth   3) Can't say
   4) Sixth   5) None of these

Directions (Q. 30-36): Six people, Prem, Ram, Som, Tinu, Viju and Om, were all born on the same day of the year, but each was born in a different year during a single six-year period.

i) Prem is older than Som.
ii) Ram is older than both Tinu and Viju.
iii) Om is two years older than Tinu.
iv) Prem was born either in 1962 or in 1963.
v) The oldest member of the group was born in 1960.

30. Which of the following could be a correct listing of the group from the youngest to the oldest?
   1) Som, Prem, Ram, Tinu, Viju, Om   2) Som, Viju, Prem, Tinu, Om, Ram
   3) Som, Viju, Prem, Om, Tinu, Ram   4) Som, Viju, Tinu, Prem, Om, Ram
   5) Viju, Ram, Prem, Tinu, Som, Om
31. If Prem was born in 1962, then which of the following must also be true?
   1) Ram was born in 1960.   2) Om was born in 1961.
   3) Som was born in 1963.   4) Viju was born in 1963.
   5) Viju was born in 1965.
32. If Om is the oldest of the group, then which of the following must be true?
   1) Ram was born in 1961.   2) Tinu was born in 1961.
   3) Prem was born in 1962.   4) Som was born in 1964.
   5) Viju was born in 1965.
33. If Om was born in 1962, then which of the following must be true?
   1) Viju was born in 1960.   2) Ram was born in 1961.
   3) Tinu was born in 1964.   4) Som was born in 1964.
   5) Tinu was born in 1965.
34. If Prem is younger than Tinu, all of the following must be true EXCEPT
   1) Om was born in 1960.   2) Ram was born in 1961.
   3) Tinu was born in 1962.   4) Prem was born in 1963.
   5) Viju was born in 1964.

35. If Viju is older than Tinu, which of the following must be true?
I. Ram was born in 1960.
II. Viju was born in 1961.
III. Prem was born in 1963.
1) I only 2) II only 3) I and II only
4) I and III only 5) I, II and III

36. If Prem is older than Om then in how many different orders could the six people have been born?
1) 1 2) 2 3) 3
4) 4 5) 5

Directions (Q. 37-43): A jazz group plans to play six pieces - *J, K, L, M, N* and *O* - during a set. Each piece will be played exactly thrice. The order in which the pieces are to be played is subject to the following conditions:

N must be played before *J* and before *O*.
M must be played later than *J*.
K must be the third piece.

37. Which of the following could be the order in which the pieces are played?
1) *K, L, N, O, M, J* 2) *K, O, N, J, M, L* 3) *M, J, K, O, L, N*
4) *N, L, K, J, O, M* 5) *N, O, J, M, K, L*

38. Which of the following must be true of the order in which the pieces are played?
1) *L* is played after *K*. 2) *M* is played after *N*. 3) *N* is played after *K*.
4) *O* is played after *M*. 5) *O* is played after *J*.

39. Which of the following could be true of the order in which the pieces are played?
2) *J* is played sixth. 2) *K* is played first. 3) *M* is played second.
4) *N* is played third. 5) *O* is played sixth.

40. If the group plays *L* first, which piece must be played second?
1) *J* 2) *K* 3) *M*
4) *N* 5) *O*

41. If the group plays *M* immediately after *L* and immediately before *O* then *J* must be played
1) First 2) Second 3) Fourth
4) Fifth 5) Sixth

42. If the group plays *L* sixth, which of the following could be the first and second pieces of the set, respectively?
I. *N* and *J* II. *N* and *O* III. *J* and *O*
1) I only 2) II only 3) I and II only
4) I and III only 5) I, II and III

43. All of the following could be played immediately after *K*, EXCEPT
1) *J* 2) *L* 3) *M*
4) *N* 5) *O*

Directions (Q. 44-49): The President of a club is appointing nine officials - *J, K, L, M, N, O, P, Q* and *R* - to serve on three committees to study three different aspects of activities at the club. There will be a Games Committee, a Food Service Committee and an Entertainment Committee. Her appointments must respect the following:

i) Each committee must have exactly three members.
ii) No person can serve on more than one committee.
iii) *Q* must serve on the Entertainment Committee.
iv) *L* and *M* must serve on the same committee.
v) *J* and *K* cannot serve on the same committee.
vi) *N* cannot serve on the same committee as *R*.
vii) *O* must serve on the same committee as *K* or *Q* or both *K* and *Q*.

44. Which of the following groups could consititute the Games Committee?
1) *J, K, N* 2) *J, M, P* 3) *L, Q, N*
4) *J, O, P* 5) *O, R, K*

45. If *R* is on the Entertainment Committee and *K* is on the Food Service Committee then which of the following must be true?
1) *O* is on the Entertainment Committee.
2) *L* is on the Games Committee.
3) *P* is on the Food Service Committee.
4) *O* is on the Games Committee.
5) *P* is on the Games Committee.

46. Any of the following could serve on the same committee as *L*, EXCEPT
1) *J* 2) *K* 3) *O*
4) *P* 5) *Q*

47. If *K* and *P* serve on the Games Committee, which of the following must serve on the Food Service Committee?
1) *J* 2) *M* 3) *N*
4) *O* 5) *R*

48. If *O* serves on the Food service Committee and *L* serves on the same committee as *Q* then which of the following must serve on the Games Committee?
I. *J* II. *P* III. *R*
1) I only 2) III only 3) I and II only
3) II and III only 5) I, II and III

49. If *J* is assigned to the Food Service Committee and *L* is appointed to the Entertainment Committee then which of the following must be true?
I. *P* is appointed to the Food Service Committee.
II. *N* is appointed to the Games Committee.
III. *R* is appointed to the Entertainment Committee.
1) I only 2) III only 3) I and III only
4) II and III only 5) I, II and III

Directions (Q. 50-54): Study the following information and answer the questions below:

There is a family of six persons, viz. A, B, C, D, E and F. They are Lawyer, Doctor, Teacher, Salesman, Engineer and Accountant. There are two married couples in the family. D, the Salesman, is married to the Lady Teacher. The Doctor is married to the lawyer. F, the Accountant, is the son of B and brother of E. C, the Lawyer, is the daughter-in-law of A. E is the unmarried Engineer. A is the grandmother of F.

50. How is E related to F?
1) Brother 2) Sister 3) Cousin
4) Can't be determined 5) None of these

51. What is the profession of B?
1) Teacher 2) Doctor 3) Lawyer
4) Can't be determined 5) None of these

52. What is the profession of A?
1) Lawyer 2) Teacher 3) Doctor
4) Can't be determined 5) None of these

53. Which of the following is one of the couples?
1) F and D 2) D and B 3) E and A
4) A and C 5) None of these

54. How is D related to F?
1) Grandfather 2) Father 3) Uncle
4) Brother 5) None of these

Directions (Q. 55-59): Read the following information carefully and answer the questions below:

A family consists of six members, viz. P, Q, R, S, T and U. There are two married couples. Q is a doctor and the father of T. U is the grandfather of R and is a contractor. S is the grandmother of T and is a housewife. There is one doctor, one contractor, one nurse, one housewife and two students in the family.

55. Who is the husband of P?
1) R 2) U 3) Q
4) S 5) T.

56. Who is the sister of T?
1) R 2) U 3) T
4) Information insufficient 5) None of these

57. What is the profession of P?
1) Doctor 2) Nurse 3) Doctor or Nurse
4) Housewife 5) None of these

58. Which of the following are two married couples?
1) US, QT 2) US, QP 3) TS, RU
4) US, RP 5) None of these

59. Which of the following is definitely a group of male members?
1) QU 2) QUT 3) QUP
4) UT 5) None of these

Directions (Q. 60-64): Read the following information carefully and answer the questions given below:

i) Six persons A, B, C, D, E and F are sitting in two rows, three in each.
ii) E is not at the end of any row.
iii) D is second to the left of F.
iv) C, the neighbour of E, is sitting diagonally opposite D.
v) B is the neighbour of F.

60. Which of the following are sitting diagonally opposite to each other?
1) F and C 2) D and A 3) A and C
4) A and F 5) A and B

61. Who is facing B?
1) A 2) C 3) D
4) E 5) F

62. Which of the following are in the same row?
1) A and E 2) E and D 3) C and B
4) A and B 5) C and E

63. Which of the following are in the same row?
1) FBC 2) CEB 3) DBF
4) AEF 5) ABF

64. After interchanging seat with F, who will be the neighbour of D in the new position?
1) C and A 2) E and B 3) Only B
4) Only A 5) Only C

Directions (Q. 65-69): Read the following information carefully and answer the questions given below:

i) There are five friends - Shailendra, Keshav, Madhav, Ashish and Rakesh.
ii) Shailendra is shorter than Keshav but taller than Rakesh.
iii) Madhav is the tallest.
iv) Ashish is a little shorter than Keshav and a little taller than Shailendra.

65. Who is the shortest?
1) Rakesh 2) Shailendra 3) Ashish
4) Keshav 5) None of these

66. If they stand in order of their heights, who will be in the middle?
1) Keshav 2) Rakesh 3) Shailendra
4) Ashish 5) None of these

67. If they stand in order of increasing heights, who will be the second?
1) Ashish 2) Shailendra 3) Rakesh
2) Keshav 5) None of these

68. Who is the second tallest?
   1) Shailendra 2) Keshav 3) Ashish
   4) Rakesh 5) None of these
69. Who is taller than Ashish but shorter than Madhav?
   1) Madhav 2) Keshav 3) Rakesh
   4) Ashish 5) Shailendra

Directions (Q. 70-73): Read the following information carefully and answer the questions given below it:

K is the brother of X. Z is the son of X. P, the daughter of K, is married to N. G and X are sisters.

70. How is P related to G?
   1) Niece 2) Daughter 3) Daughter-in-law
   4) Cousin 5) Sister
71. How is Z related to P?
   1) Maternal uncle 2) Uncle 3) Cousin
   4) Brother-in-law 5) None of these
72. How is N related to K?
   1) Son 2) Nephew 3) Father-in-law
   4) Son-in-law 5) None of these
73. How is G related to Z?
   1) Sister 2) Wife 3) Aunt
   4) Mother-in-law 5) Mother

Directions (Q. 74-77): Read the following information carefully and answer the questions given below it.

In a car exhibition, seven cars of seven different companies, viz. Cardilac, Ambassador, Fiat, Maruti, Mercedes, Bedford and Fargo were displayed in a row, facing east such that:

1) Cardilac car was on the immediate right of Fargo.
2) Fargo was fourth to the right of Fiat.
3) Maruti car was between Ambassador and Bedford.
4) Fiat, which was third to the left of Ambassador car, was at one of the ends.

74. Which of the following was the correct position of the Mercedes?
   1) Immediate left of Cardilac 2) Immediate left of Bedford
   3) Between Bedford and Fargo 4) Fourth to the right of Maruti
   5) None of these
75. Which of the following is definitely true?
   1) Fargo car is between Ambassador and Fiat.
   2) Cardilac car is on the immediate left of Mercedes.
   3) Fargo is on the immediate right of Cardilac.
   4) Maruti is fourth to the right of Mercedes.
   5) None of these

76. Which cars are on the immediate either sides of the Cardilac car?

1) Ambassador and Maruti
2) Maruti and Fiat
3) Fiat and Mercedes
4) Ambassador and Fargo
5) None of these

77. Which of the following is definitely true?

1) Maruti is to the immediate left of Ambassador.
2) Bedford is to the immediate left of Fiat.
3) Bedford is at one of the ends.
4) Fiat is second to the right of Maruti.
5) None of these

Directions (Q. 78-82): Study the following information carefully and answer the questions given below it:

A sales representative plans to visit each of the six companies M, N, P, Q, R and S exactly once during the course of one day. She is setting up her schedule for the day according to the following conditions:

1) She must visit M before N and R.
2) She must visit N before Q.
3) The third company she visit must be P.

78. Which of the following must be true of the sales representative's schedule?

1) She visits M before Q
2) She visits N before R
3) She visits P before M
4) She visits P before S
5) She visits Q before R

79. If the sales representative visits S first, which company must she visit second?

1) M
2) N
3) P
4) Q
5) R

80. The sales representative could visit any of the followig companies immediately after P except

1) S
2) R
3) Q
4) N
5) M

81. If the sales representative visits Q immediately before R and immediately after S, she must visit Q

1) First
2) Second
3) Fourth
4) Fifth
5) Sixth

82. Which of the following could be the order in which the sales representative visits the six companies?

1) M, S, P, N, R, Q
2) Q, N, P, R, S, M
3) M, R, N, Q, P, S
4) P, S, M, R, Q, N
5) P, R, M, N, Q, S

Directions (Q. 83-87): Read the following information carefully and answer the questions given below it:

1) There is a group of six persons A, B, C, D, E and F in a family. They are Psychologist, Manager, Lawyer, Jeweller, Doctor and Engineer.
2) The doctor is the grandfather of F, who is a Psychologist.
3) The Manager D is married to A.
4) C, the Jeweller, is married to the Lawyer.
5) B is the mother of F and E.
6) There are two married couples in the family.

83. What is the profession of E?
1) Doctor 2) Jeweller 3) Manager
4) Psychologist 5) None of these

84. How is A related to E?
1) Brother 2) Uncle 3) Father
4) Grandfather 5) None of these

85. How many male members are there in the family?
1) One 2) Three 3) Four
4) Two 5) Can't be determined

86. What is the profession of A?
1) Doctor 2) Lawyer 3) Jeweller
4) Manager 5) None of these

87. Which of the following is one of the pairs of couples in the family?
1) AB 2) AC 3) AD
4) Can't be determined 5) None of these

Directions (Q. 88-92): Study the following information carefully and answer the questions given below it:

In a group of five persons A, B, C, D and E,
1) B and C are intelligent in Mathematics and Geography.
2) A and C are intelligent in Mathematics and History.
3) B and D are intelligent in Political Science and Geography.
4) D and E are intelligent in Political Science and Biology.
5) E is intelligent in Biology, History and Political Science.

88. Who is intelligent in Political Science, Geography and Biology?
1) E 2) D 3) C 4) B 5) A

89. Who is intelligent in Mathematics, Political Science and Geography?
1) A 2) B 3) C 4) D 5) E

90. Who is intelligent in Mathematics and History but not in Geography?
1) C 2) E 3) A 4) B 5) D

91. Who is intelligent in Mathematics, Geography and History?
1) E 2) A 3) D 4) C 5) B

92. Who is intelligent in Political Science, History and Biology?
1) A 2) B 3) C 4) D 5) E

Directions (Q. 93-97): Study the following information carefully and answer the questions given below it:

From amongst six boys A, B, C, D, E and F, and five girls P, Q, R, S and T, a team of six is to be selected under the following conditions:

1) A and D have to be together.
2) C cannot go with S.
3) S and T have to be together.
4) B cannot be teamed with E.
5) D cannot go with P.
6) B and R have to be together.
7) C and Q have to be together.

93. If there be five boys in the team, the lone girl member is
1) P 2) Q 3) R 4) S 5) None of these

94. If including P, the team has three girls, the members are
1) BCFQR 2) ADEST 3) ADBST 4) BFRST 5) None of these

95. If the team including C consists of four boys, the members of the team other than C are
1) ADEPQ 2) ABDQR 3) DEFAQ 4) BEFRQ 5) None of these

96. If four members including E have to be boys, the members other than E are
1) ABCQR 2) ADFST 3) BCFQR 4) ACDFQ 5) None of these

97. If four members have to be girls, the members of the team are
1) BCPQRS 2) BFPRST 3) BCQRST 4) BCPQRT 5) None of these

Directions (Q. 98-102): Read the following information carefully and answer the questions given below it:

There are six persons A, B, C, D, E and F in a school. Each of the teachers teaches two subjects, one compulsory subject and the other optional subject. D's optional subject was History while three others have it as compulsory subject. E and F have Physics as one of their subjects. F's compulsory subject is Mathematics which is an optional subject of both C and E. History and English are A's subjects but in terms of compulsory and optional subjects, they are just reverse of those of D's. Chemistry is an optional subject of only one of them. The only female teacher in the school has English as her compulsory subject.

98. What is C's compulsory subject?
1) History 2) Physics 3) Chemistry
4) English 5) Mathematics

99. Who is a female member in the group?
1) A 2) B 3) C 4) D 5) E

100. Which of the following has the same compulsory and optional subjects as those of F's?
1) D 2) B 3) A 4) C 5) None of these

101. Disregarding which is the compulsory and which is the optional subject, who has the same two-subject combination as F?

1) A 2) B 3) E

4) D 5) None of these

102. Which of the following groups has History as the compulsory subject?

1) A, C and D 2) B, C and D 3) C and D

4) A, B and C 5) A and D

Directions (Q. 103-107): Read the following information and answer the questions given below it:

Six plays — A, B, C, D, E and F — are to be staged one on each day from Monday to Saturday. The schedule of the plays is to be in accordance with the following:

1) A must not be staged a day before E.
2) C must not be staged on Tuesday.
3) B must be staged on the day following the day on which F is staged.
4) D must be staged on Friday only and should not be immediately preceded by B.
5) E must not be staged on the last day of the schedule.

103. Which of the following plays immediately follows B?

1) A 2) C 3) D 4) E 5) F

104. Which of the following plays is on Monday?

1) E 2) F 3) C 4) B 5) A

105. Play D is between which of the following pairs of plays?

1) B and E 2) E and F 3) A and E 4) C and E 5) C and F

106. Which of the following is the schedule of plays, the order of their staging being from Monday?

1) E, A, B, F, D, C 2) A, F, B, E, D, C 3) A, F, B, C, D, E

4) F, A, B, E, D, C 5) None of these

107. Play C cannot definitely be staged on which of the following days in addition to Tuesday?

1) Monday 2) Wednesday 3) Friday

4) Thursday 5) Saturday

Directions (Q. 108-110): Read the following information and answer the questions given below it:

1) Six friends A, B, C, D, E and F are sitting in a closed circle facing the centre.
2) E is to the left of D.
3) C is between A and B.
4) F is between E and A.

108. Who is on the left of B?

1) A 2) C 3) D

4) E 5) None of these

109. Who is on the right of C?

1) A   2) B   3) D
4) E   5) F

110. Which of the above given statements is superfluous?

1) 1   2) 2   3) 3
4) 4   5) None of these

Directions (Q. 111-115): Study the following information carefully and answer the questions given below it:

There are six persons A, B, C, D, E and F in a family. C is the sister of F. B is the brother of E's husband. D is the father of A and grandfather of F. There are 2 fathers, 3 brothers and a mother in the group.

111. Which of the following is a group of brothers?

1) ABC   2) ABD   3) ABF
4) BDF   5) BFC

112. Who is E's husband?

1) B   2) C   3) D
4) F   5) None of these

113. Who is the mother?

1) A   2) B   3) E
4) D   5) None of these

114. How many male members are there in the group?

1) Two   2) Four   3) One
4) Three   5) Five

115. How is F related to E?

1) Son   2) Daughter   3) Husband
4) Uncle   5) Father-in-law

Directions (Q. 116-121): Study the following information and answer the questions given below it:

A blacksmith has five iron articles A, B, C, D, and E, each having a different weight.

1) A weighs twice as much as B.
2) B weighs four-and-a-half times as much as C.
3) C weighs half as much as D.
4) D weighs half as much as E.
5) E weighs less than A but more than C.

116. Which of the following is the lightest in weight?

1) A   2) B   3) C
4) D   5) E

117. E is lighter in weight than which of the other two articles?

1) A, B 2) D, C 3) A, C
4) D, B 5) B, E

118. Which of the above given statements is not necessary to determine the correct order of articles according to their weights?

1) 1 2) 2 3) 3
4) 4 5) None of these

119. E is heavier than which of the following two articles?

1) D, B 2) D, C 3) A, C
4) A, B 5) None of these

120. Which of the following articles is the heaviest in weight?

1) A 2) B 3) C
4) D 5) E

121. Which of the following represents the descending order of weights of the articles?

1) A, B, E, D, C 2) B, D, E, A, C 3) E, C, D, A, B
4) C, A, D, B, E 5) A, B, D, E, C

Directions (Q. 122-126): Read the following information and answer the questions given below it:

Five persons are sitting in a row. One of the two persons at the extreme ends is intelligent and the other one is fair. A fat person is sitting on the right of a weak person. A tall person is on the left of the fair person and the weak person is sitting between the intelligent and the fat persons.

122. The tall person is at which place, counting from right?

1) First 2) Second 3) Third
4) Fourth 5) None of these

123. Which of the following describes the person on the left of the weak person?

1) Intelligent 2) Fat 3) Fair
4) Tall 5) Cannot be determined

124. Which of the following persons is sitting at the centre?

1) Fair 2) Weak 3) Intelligent
4) Tall 5) Fat

125. On whose left is the fat person sitting?

1) Fair 2) Intelligent 3) Tall
4) Weak 5) Cannot be determined

126. If the fair person and the fat person exchange their positions, and so also do the tall and the weak ones then who will be sitting on the left of the weak person?

1) Tall 2) Fair 3) Fat
4) Intelligent 5) Cannot be determined

Directions (Q. 127-131): Study the following information and answer the questions given below it:

A training college has to conduct a refresher course for teachers of seven different subjects - Mechanics, Psychology, Philosophy, Sociology, Economics, Science and Engineering - from 22nd July to 29th July.

1) The course should start with Psychology.
2) 23rd July, being Sunday, should be a holiday.
3) Science should be on the previous day of Engineering.
4) The course should end with Mechanics.
5) Philosophy should be immediately after the holiday.
6) There should be a gap of one day between Economics and Engineering.

127. The refresher course will start with which one of the following subjects?
1) Psychology 2) Mechanics 3) Philosophy
4) Economics 5) None of these

128. Which subject will be on Tuesday?
1) Mechanics 2) Engineering 3) Economics
4) Psychology 5) None of these

129. Which subject precedes Mechanics?
1) Economics 2) Engineering 3) Philosophy
4) Psychology 5) None of these

130. How many days' gap is there between Science and Philosophy?
1) One 2) Two 3) Three
4) No gap 5) None of these

131. Which subject is followed by Science?
1) Engineering 2) Psychology 3) Philosophy
4) Economics 5) None of these

Directions (Q. 132-135): Study the following information carefully and answer the questions given below it:

Prashant Arora has three children - Sangeeta, Vimal and Ashish. Ashish married Monika, the eldest daughter of Mr and Mrs Roy. The Roys married their youngest daughter to the eldest son of Mr and Mrs Sharma, and they have two children named Amit and Shashi. The Roys have two more children, Roshan and Vandana, both older than Veena. Sameer and Ajay are the sons of Ashish and Monika. Rashmi is the daugher of Amit.

132. What is the surname of Rashmi?
1) Sharma 2) Roy 3) Arora
4) Can't be determined 5) None of these

133. How is Sameer related to the father of Monika?
1) Grandson 2) Son 3) Cousin
4) Son-in-law 5) None of these

134. What is the surname of Sameer?

1) Roy 2) Sharma 3) Arora
4) Can't be determined 5) None of these

135. How is Mrs Roy related to Ashish?

1) Aunt 2) Mother-in-law 3) Mother
4) Sister-in-law 5) None of these

Directions (Q. 136-137): Study the following information and answer the questions given below it:

1) Kailash, Govind and Harinder are intelligent.
2) Kailash, Rajesh and Jitendra are hardworking.
3) Rajesh, Harinder and Jitendra are honest.
4) Kailash, Govind and Jitendra are ambitious.

136. Which of the following persons is neither hardworking nor ambitious?

1) Kailash 2) Govind 3) Harinder
4) Rajesh 5) None of these

137. Which of the following persons is neither honest nor hardworking but is ambitious?

1) Kailash 2) Govind 3) Rajesh
4) Harinder 5) None of these

138. The cricket ball is lighter than the hockey ball and the volleyball is lighter than the football. The hockey ball is lighter than the football but heavier than the tennis ball. Which of the following is the heaviest?

1) Hockey ball 2) Cricket ball 3) Football
4) Volleyball 5) None of these

139. Five children are sitting in a row. S is sitting next to P but not T. K is sitting next to R, who is sitting on the extreme left and T is not sitting next to K. Who are sitting adjacent to S?

1) K and P 2) R and P 3) Only P
4) P and T 5) Insufficient information

Directions (Q. 140-144): Read the following statements and answer the questions that follow:

Of the six men of literature — A, B, C, D, E and F — being considered here, two belonged to the 17th century, three to the 19th and one to the 20th. Four were recognised as great poets, three as great novelists and three as great dramatists. One contributed to Bengali literature, two to Hindi, two to Marathi and one to Tamil. The 20th-century writer wrote poetry only and contributed to Marathi literature and the other Marathi writer contributed to poetry, novel and drama. One Hindi writer and the only Tamil writer belonged to the 19th century. The former contributed to poetry and novel while the latter to novel and drama. The Bengali writer belonged to the 17th century and contributed to poetry only. A belonged to the 20th century, B wrote drama only, C contributed to Marathi literature, D was a Hindi poet and novelist and belonged to the 19th century. E also belonged to the 19th century, and F contributed to poetry only.

140. To which language did B contribute?
1) Bengali 2) Hindi 3) Marathi
4) Tamil 5) None of these

141. Among these, who was the Tamil writer?
1) A 2) B 3) E
4) F 5) None of these

142. To which branch of literature did A contribute?
1) Poetry 2) Novel 3) Drama
4) All the three 5) None of these

143. Among these, who was the Bengali writer?
1) A 2) B 3) E
4) F 5) None of these

144. To which branch of literature did C contribute?
1) Poetry 2) Drama 3) Novel
5) All the three 5) None of these

Directions (Q. 145-149): Read the following information carefully and answer the questions that follow:

(i) There is a group of five persons A, B, C, D and E.
(ii) One of them is a horticulturist, one is a physicist, one is a journalist, one is an industrialist and one is an advocate.
(iii) Three of them, A, C and the advocate, prefer tea to coffee and two of them, B and the journalist, prefer coffee to tea.
(iv) The industrialist and D and A are friends to one another but two of them prefer coffee to tea.
(v) The horticulturist is C's brother.

145. Who is a horticulturist?
1) A 2) B 3) C
4) D 5) E

146. Who is an industrialist?
1) E 2) C 3) B
5) D 5) A

147. Which of the following groups includes a person who likes tea but is not\ an advocate?
1) ACE 2) DE 3) BCE
4) BD 5) None of these

148. Who is a physicist?
1) A 2) E 3) D
4) C 5) B

149. Which of the statements above is superfluous?
1) (iii) 2) (iv) 3) (ii)
4) (v) 5) None

Directions (Q. 150-154): Study the following information carefully and answer the questions given below:

A, B, C, D, E, F, G and H are eight employees of an organization working in three departments, viz Personnel, Administration and Marketing with not more than three of them in any department. Each of them has a different choice of sports from football, cricket, volleyball, badminton, lawn tennis, basketball, hockey and table tennis, not necessarily in the same order.

D works in Administration and does not like either football or cricket. F works in Personnel with only A, who likes table tennis. E and H do not work in the same department as D. C likes hockey and does not work in Marketing. G does not work in Administration and does not like either cricket or badminton. One of those who work in Administration likes football. The one who likes volleyball works in Personnel. None of those who work in Administration likes either badminton or lawn tennis. H does not like cricket.

150. Which of the following groups of employees work in Administration department?
1) EGH 2) AF 3) BCD
4) BGD 5) Data inadequate

151. In which department does E work?
1) Personnel 2) Marketing 3) Administration
4) Data inadequate 5) None of these

152. Which of the following combinations of employee-department-favourite sport is correct?
1) E - Administration - Cricket 2) F - Personnel - Lawn Tennis
3) H - Marketing - Lawn Tennis 4) B - Administration - Table Tennis
5) None of these

153. What is E's favourite sport?
1) Cricket 2) Badminton 3) Basketball
4) Lawn Tennis 5) None of these

154. What is G's favourite sport?
1) Cricket 2) Badminton 3) Basketball
4) Lawn Tennis 5) None of these

Directions (Q. 155-159): In each question below is given a group of letters followed by four combinations of digits/symbols numbered 1), 2), 3) and 4). You have to find out which of the combinations correctly represents the group of letters based on the following coding system and the conditions that follow and mark the number of that combination as your answer. If none of the combinations correctly represents the group of letters, mark 5), ie 'None of these' as your answer.

Letter	:	W	P	J	Q	E	T	I	A	Ú	F	D	B	V	M	H
Digit/Symbol code	:	5	6	9	1	2	3	@	4	©	8	%		7	#	$

Conditions:

(i) If the first letter is a consonant and the fourth letter is a vowel, both are to be coded as the code for the vowel.

(ii) If the second letter is a vowel and the last letter is a consonant, both are to be coded as 8.

(iii) If both the first and the last letters are consonants, both their codes are to be interchanged.

155. MBUVWE
   1) # ©#52   2) 7 ©#52   3) #© 752
   4) #8©75S   5) None of these

156. AJBMFU
   1) 49 48©   2) #9 #8©   3) 49 #8©
   4) ©9 #84   5) None of these

157. AEIMVH
   1) 42@#7$ 2) 42@47$ 3) #2@47$
   4) 4δ@#7δ   5) None of these

158. THAFIQ
   1) 3$48@3   2) 1$48@3   3) 1$48@1
   4) 3$48@1   5) None of these

159. WMEIJU
   1) @#2@9©   2) 5#2@9©   3) @#259©
   4) 5#259©   5) None of these

36-40 PRA4

Directions (Q. 160-164): Study the following information carefully and answer the questions given below:

A, B, C, D, E, F, G and H are sitting around a circle facing the centre. B is second to the right of D, who is third to the right of F. C is second to the left of A, who is second to the left of F. G is third to the right of E.

160. In which of the following combinations is the first person sitting between the second and the third persons?
   1) GCD   2) FGH   3) EFH
   4) ABE   5) None of these

161. Who is third to the right of H?
   1) G   2) D   3) C
   4) Data inadequate   5) None of these

162. Who is on the immediate right of A?
   1) B   2) E   3) F
   4) Data inadequate   5) None of these

163. What is H's position with respect to B ?
1) Fifth to the right 2) Third to the left 3) Fifth to the left
4) Third to the right 5) Fourth to the left

164. Who is on the immediate left of G ?
1) H 2) F 3) D
4) Data inadequate 5) None of these

Derection (Q. 165-169): Study the following information carefully and answer the questions given below :

A, B, C, D, E, F, G and H are eight friends travelling in three different cars, viz X, Y and Z, with at least two in one car to three different places, viz. Delhi, Chandigarh and Agra.

There is at least one female member in each car. D is travelling with G to Delhi but not in car Y. A is travelling with only H in car Z but not to Chandigarh. C is not travelling with either D or E. F and D are studying in the same only girls' college. H, B and G are studying in the same only boys' college.

165. Which of the following represents the group of females?
1) F, C, A 2) F, G, A 3) D, C, A
4) Data inadequate 5) None of these

166. Which of the following combinations is correct?
1) Delhi – X – C 2) Chandigarh – X – F S) Agra – Z – E
4) Delhi – Y – E 5) None of these

167. Which of the following cars is carrying four people?
1) Either X or Z 2) Y 3) Either X or Y
4) Z 5) None of these

168. In which of the following cars is C travelling?
1) X 2) Y 3) Z
4) Either X or Y 5) Data inadequate

169. Which of the following cars is carrying people to Chandigarh?
1) Y 2) X 3) Either X or Y
4) Data inadequate 5) None of these

Directions (Q. 170-176): Study the following information carefully and answer the given questions

A, B, C, D, E, F, G and H are sitting around a circle facing the centre but not necessarily in the same order.

B sits second to the left of H's husband. No female is an immediate neighbour of B.

D's daughter sits second to the right of F. F is the sister of G. F is not an immediate neighbour of H's husband.

Only one person sits between A and F. A is father of G. H's brother D sits on the immediate left of H's mother. Only one person sits between H's mother and E.

Only one person sits between H and G. G is the mother of C. G is not an immediate neighbour of E.

170. What is the position of A with respect to his mother-in-law?
1) Immediate left 2) Third to the right 3) Third to the left
4) Second to the right 5) Fourth to the left

171. Who amongst the following is D's daughter?
1) B 2) C 3) E
4) G 5) H

172. What is the position of A with respect to his grandchild?
1) Immediate right 2) Third to the right 3) Third to the left
4) Second to the left 5) Fourth to the left

173. How many people sit between G and her uncle?
1) One 2) Two 3) Three
4) Four 5) More than four

174. Four of the following five are alike in a certain way based on the given information and so form a group. Which is the one that does not belong to that group?
1) F 2) C 3) E
4) H 5) G

175. Which of the following is true with respect to the given seating arrangement?
1) C is cousin of E.
2) H and H's husband are immediate neighbours of each other.
3) No female is an immediate neighbour of C.
4) H sits third to the left of her daughter.
5) B is mother of H.

176. Who sits on the immediate left of C?
1) F's grandmother 2) G's son 3) D's mother-in-law
4) A 5) G

Directions (Q. 177-179): Study the following information carefully to answer the given questions:

Each of the six friends – A, B, C, D, E and F – scored different marks in an examination. C scored more than only A and E. D scored less than only B. E did not score the least. The one who scored the third highest marks scored 81 marks. E scored 62 marks.

177. Which of the following could possibly be C's score?
1) 70 2) 94 3) 86
4) 61 5) 81

178. Which of the following is true with respect to the given information?
1) D's score was definitely less than 60.
2) F scored the maximum marks.
3) Only two people scored more than C.

4) There is a possibility that B scored 79 marks.
5) None is true

179. The person who scored the maximum, scored 13 marks more than F's marks. Which of the following can be D's score?

1) 94 2) 60 3) 89
4) 78 5) 81

Directions (Q. 180-187): Study the following information carefully to answer the given questions

Eight persons from different banks, viz UCO Bank. Syndicate Bank, Canara Bank, PNB, Dena Bank, Oriental Bank of Commerce, Indian Bank and Bank of Maharashtra, are sitting in two parallel rows containing four people each, in such a way that there is an equal distance between adjacent persons. In row 1 A, B, C and D are seated and all of them are facing south. In row 2, P, Q, R and S are seated and all of them are facing north. Therefore, in the given seating arrangement each member seated in a row faces another member of the other row. (All the information given above does not necessarily represent the order of seating as in the final arrangement.)

C sits second to right of the person from Bank of Maharashtra. R is an immediate neighbour of the person who faces the person from Bank of Maharashtra.

Only one person sits between R and the person from PNB. The immediate neighbour of the person from PNB faces the person from Canara Bank.

The person from UCO bank faces the person from Oriental Bank of Commerce. R is not from Oriental Bank of Commerce. P is not from PNB. P does not face the person from Bank of Maharashtra.

Q faces the person from Dena Bank. The one who faces S sits to the immediate left of A.

B does not sit at any of the extreme ends of the line. The person from Bank of Maharashtra does not face the person from Syndicate Bank.

180. Which of the following is true regarding A?

1) The person from UCO Bank faces A.
2) The person from Bank of Maharashtra is an immediate neighbour of A.
3) A faces the person who sits second to the right of R.
4) A is from Oriental Bank of Commerce.
5) A sits at one of the extreme ends of the line.

181. Who is seated between R and the person from PNB?

1) The person from Oriental Bank of Commerce
2) P
3) Q
4) The person from Syndicate Bank
5) S

182. Who amongst the following sit at extreme ends of the rows?
   1) D and the person from PNB
   2) The persons from Indian Bank and UCO Bank
   3) The persons from Dena Bank and P
   4) The persons from Syndicate Bank and D
   5) C, Q
183. Who amongst the following faces the person from Bank of Maharashtra?
   1) The person from Indian Bank 2) P
   3) R 4) The person from Syndicate Bank
   5) The person from Canara Bank
184. P is related to Dena Bank in the same way as B is related to PNB based on the given arrangement. Who amongst the following is D related to, following the same pattern?
   1) Syndicate Bank 2) Canara Bank
   3) Bank of Maharashtra 4) Indian Bank
   5) Oriental Bank of Commerce
185. Four of the following five are alike in a certain way based on the given seating arrangement and thus form a group. Which is the one that does not belong to that group?
   1) Canara Bank 2) R 3) Syndicate Bank
   4) Q 5) Oriental Bank of Commerce
186. Who amongst the following is from Syndicate Bank?
   1) C 2) R 3) P
   4) D 5) A
187. C is from which of the following banks?
   1) Dena Bank 2) Oriental Bank of Commerce
   3) UCO Bank 4) Syndicate Bank
   5) Canara Bank

Directions (Q. 188-193): Study the information given below and answer the given questions.

Eight friends A, B, C, D, E, F, G and H are sitting in a circle, but not necessarily in the same order. Four of them are facing outside and four of them are facing the centre.

E faces outside. Both the immediate neighbours of E face the centre. H sits second to the right of E. B sits third to the left of E.

D faces the centre. Both the immediate neighbours of D face outside.

G sits second to the left of A. B sits third to the right of H.

F is an immediate neighbour of D. C is an immediate neighbour of G.

D is not an immediate neighbour of B.

188. Who amongst the following sits on the immediate right of H?
   1) A 2) D 3) C
   4) G 5) None of these

189. Who amongst the following sits third to the right of A?
1) D 2) E 3) F
4) A 5) None of these

190. Four of the following five are alike in a certain way, based on the information given above and so form a group. Which is the one that does not belong to that group?
1) HA 2) FH 3) GC
4) DA 5) AE

191. If all the people are made to sit in an alphabetical order, in clockwise direction, starting from A, the position of whom amongst the following remains the same (excluding A)?
1) E 2) F 3) C
4) G 5) None of these

192. How many people are seated between A and C (counting clockwise from A)?
1) Two 2) Four 3) None
4) One 5) Three

193. Who amongst the following sits exactly between F and C (and is also their neighbour)?
1) E 2) B 3) G
4) A 5) None of these

Directions (Q. 194-202): Study the information given below and answer the given questions.

Nine people, A, B, C, D, E, F, G, H and J stay in a building, but not necessarily in the same order. The building has nine floors and only one person stays on one floor. All of them own one car each, and each car is of a different colour, ie blue, grey, white, black, yellow, green, red, orange and pink, but not necessarily in the same order. The ground floor is numbered 1, the floor above it is numbered 2, and so on, and the topmost floor is numbered 9.

H owns a black-coloured car and stays on an even-numbered floor. A stays on any even-numbered floor below the floor on which H stays. The one who owns an orange-coloured car stays on the fourth floor. E stays on the second floor and owns a white-coloured car. The one who owns a pink-coloured car stays on the third floor. A does not own a green-coloured car. There are two floors between the floors on which the people owning the red and the black-coloured cars stay. C owns a grey-coloured car. There are three floors between the floors on which C and G stay. D stays on a floor immediately above J's floor. There is one floor between the floors on which F and G stay. F does not own the pink-coloured car. The one who owns the blue car stays on the topmost floor. F does not stay on the ground floor.

194. Who amongst the following owns the green-coloured car
1) D 2) J 3) G
4) F 5) None of these

195. Who amongst the following stays on the topmost floor?
1) F 2) G 3) D
4) C 5) None of these

196. A owns a car of which of the following colours?
1) Orange 2) Pink 3) Yellow
4) Blue 5) None of these

197. Who stays on the floor which is exactly between the floor on which H stays and the floor on which A stays?
1) B 2) G 3) C
4) F 5) None of these

198. How many floors are there between the floor on which J stays and the floor on which C stays?
1) One 2) Two 3) None
4) Three 5) More than three

199. Which of the following is true as per the given information?
1) B stays on a floor immediately below the floor on which H stays.
2) G stays on a floor immediately above the floor on which A stays,
3) F stays on the eighth floor.
4) D owns the orange-coloured car.
5) None is true

200. On which of the following floors does G stay?
1) 1st 2) 6th 3) 5th
4) 7th 5) None of these

201. B is related to C in the same way as H is related to E as per the given information. Following the same pattern, F is related to which of the following?
1) J 2) D 3) A
4) G 5) None of these

202. What is the colour of the car of the person who stays on the ground floor?
1) Red 2) Green 3) Yellow
4) Grey 5) None of these

Directions (Q. 203-207): Study the following information carefully and answer the questions given below:

P, Q, R, S, T, V, W and Z are sitting round a circle facing the centre. T is second to the right of R, who is third to the right of P. S is second to the left of P and fourth to the right of Q. Z is third to the right of V, who is not an immediate neighbour of P.

203. In which of the following combinations is the first person sitting between the second and the third persons?
1) VTS 2) TZS 3) QRV
4) PWQ 5) VRT

204. Who is second to the right of T?
1) S 2) Z 3) P
4) R 5) None of these

205. What is P's position with respect to S?
1) Fourth to the left 2) Fourth to the right 3) Fifth to the left
4) Sixth to the left 5) Third to the right

206. Who is on the immediate left of Z?
1) T 2) P 3) S
4) V 5) None of these

207. Who is second to the right of W?
1) R 2) Q 3) Z
4) S 5) None of these

Directions (Q. 208-212): Study the following information carefully and answer the questions given below:

P, Q, R, S, T, U, V and W are sitting around a circle facing the centre. T is second to the left of P and third to the right of V. S is second to the right of W, who is on the immediate right of T. Q is third to the right of U.

208. In which of the following pairs is the third person sitting in between the first and the second persons?
1) USP 2) VRU 3) TQW
4) WPS 5) None of these

209. Who is on the immediate left of T?
1) Q 2) W 3) R
4) Data inadequate 5) None of these

210. Who is second to the right of P?
1) S 2) V 3) U
4) Q 5) Date inadequate

211. What is R's position with respect to W?
1) Third to the left 2) Fourth to the left 3) Sixth to the right
4) Fifth to the left 5) None of these

212. Who is fourth to the left of R?
1) U 2) P 3) S
4) W 5) None of these

Directions (Q. 213-217): Study the following information carefully and answer the questions given below:

A, B, C, D, E, F, G and H are sitting around a circle facing the centre. F is second to the right of A and third to the left of C. B is second to the left of C and fourth to the right of H. D is second to the right of G

213. Who is to the immediate left of D?

1) H 2) C 3) G
4) Data inadequate 5) None of these

214. Who is second to the right of E?

1) B 2) G 3) H
4) Data inadequate 5) None of these

215. Who is third to the left of B ?

1) E 2) H 3) F
4) Data inadequate 5) None of these

216. What is the position of G with respect to A?

1) Third to the left 2) Third to the right 3) Fifth to the left
4) Fourth to the right 5) Fifth to the right

217. In which of the following combinations is the third person sitting in between the first and the second persons?

1) BGC 2) EFB 3) DAH
4) AEF 5) GCD

Directions (Q. 218-222): Study the following information to answer the given questions:

(a) Six plays are to be organised from Monday to Sunday—one play each day with one day when there is no play. 'No play' day is not Monday or Sunday.

(b) The plays are held in sets of 3 plays each in such a way that 3 plays are held without any break, ie 3 plays are held in such a way that there is no 'No play' day between them but immediately before this set or immediately after this set it is 'No play' day.

(c) Play Z was held on 26th and play X was held on 31 st of the same month.

(d) Play B was not held immediately after play A (but was held after A, not necessarily immediately) and play M was held immediately before Q.

(e) All the six plays were held in the same month.

218. Which play was organised on Monday?

1) Z 2) M
3) Q 4) Cannot be determined
5) None of these

219. Which day was play Z organised?

1) Tuesday 2) Monday
3) Wednesday 4) Cannot be determined
5) None of these

220. Which date was a 'No play' day?

1) 26th 2) 28th
3) 29th 4) Cannot be determined
5) None of these

221. Which of the following is true?
   1) Play B is held immediately before play M.
   2) Play Z is held after play B.
   3) There was a gap after 2 plays and then 4 plays were organised.
   4) First play was organised on the 25th.
   5) Play B was held on Friday.

222. Which day was play Q organised?
   1) Friday
   2) Wednesday
   3) Saturday
   4) Cannot be determined
   5) None of these

Directions (Q. 223-227): Study the following information to answer the given questions:

(i) In a family of 6 persons, there are two couples.
(ii) The Lawyer is the head of the family and has only two sons — Mukesh and Rakesh—both Teachers.
(iii) Mrs. Reena and her mother-in-law both are Lawyers.
(iv) Mukesh's wife is a Doctor and they have a son, Ajay.

223. Which of the following is definitely a couple?
   1) Lawyer-Teacher
   2) Doctor-Lawyer
   3) Teacher-Teacher
   4) Cannot be determined
   5) None of these

224. What is the profession of Rakesh's wife ?
   1) Teacher
   2) Doctor
   3) Lawyer
   4) Cannot be determined
   5) None of these

225. How many male members are there in the family?
   1) Two
   2) Three
   3) Four
   4) Cannot be determined
   5) None of these

226. What is/was Ajay's Grandfather's occupation?
   1) Teacher
   2) Lawyer
   3) Doctor
   4) Cannot be determined
   5) None of these

227. What is the profession of Ajay?
   1) Teacher
   2) Lawyer
   3) Doctor
   4) Cannot be determined
   5) None of these

Directions (Q. 228-232): Study the following information to answer the given questions:

I. A, B, C, D, E and F are six members of a family.
II. One couple has parents and their children in the family.

III. A is the son of C and E is the daughter of A.

IV. D is the daughter of F who is the mother of E.

228. Who are the male members in the family?

1) A and C
2) C and F
3) A, B and D
4) Cannot be determined
5) None of these

229. Which of the following pairs is the parents of the children?

1) BC
2) CF
3) BF
4) Cannot be determined
5) None of these

230. Which of the following pairs is the parents of the couple?

1) AB
2) BC
3) AF
4) CF
5) None of these

231. How many female members are there in the family?

1) Two
2) Three
3) Four
4) Can't be determined
5) None of these

232. What relationship do D and E bear to each other?

1) Sister and Brother
2) Mother and Son
3) Grandmother and Grand daughter
4) Sister
5) None of these

Directions (Q. 233-236): Study the following information to answer the given questions:

(i) In a family of six persons A, B, C, D, E and F, there are two married couples.

(ii) D is grandmother of A and mother of B.

(iii) C is wife of B and mother of F.

(iv) F is the grand daughter of E.

233. What is C to A?

1) Daughter
2) Grandmother
3) Mother
4) Cannot be determined
5) None of these

234. How many male members are there in the family?

1) Two
2) Three
3) Four
4) Cannot be determined
5) None of these

235. Which of the following is true?

1) A is brother of F.
2) A is sister of F.
3) D has two grandsons.
4) B has two daughters.
5) None of these

236. Who among the following is one of the couples?

1) CD 2) DE
3) EB 4) Cannot be determined
5) None of these

Directions (Q. 237-241): Study the following information to answer the given questions:

There are six persons A, B, C, D, E and F. C is the sister of F. B is the brother of E's husband. D is the father of A and grandfather of F. There are two fathers, three brothers and a mother in the group.

237. Who is the mother?
1) A 2) B 3) D
4) E 5) None of these

238. Who is E's husband?
1) B 2) C 3) A
4) F 5) None of these

239. How many male members are there in the group?
1) One 2) Two 3) Three
4) Four 5) None of these

240. How is F related to E?
1) Uncle 2) Husband 3) Son
4) Daughter 5) None of these

241. Which of the following is a group of brothers?
1) ABF 2) ABD 3) BFC
4) BDF 5) None of these

Directions (Q. 242-244): Study the following information to answer the given questions:

In a village of Bastar district in Madhya Pradesh, only two types of people live who belong to a tribal class. The first type is known as class A, while the other is known as class B. In that village, there is no other type of person except these two. The activities of both types of people are governed by perfectly patterned norms of social behaviour. Each person of the tribe has to obey the norms. They are rigid about this.

As far as marriage is concerned, the following norms are to be followed:

(A) The people of class A cannot marry any other member of their own class, though they can marry members of class B.

(B) After being married, each male member ceases to be a member of that class in which he was born but automatically, he becomes the member of the other class to which his wife belongs.

(C) As far as females are concerned, they remain the members of their own class after being married.

(D) On his birth, the child automatically becomes the member of his mother's class.

(E) When any male member becomes widower or divorcee, then he again belongs to the group in which he was born.

(F) Nobody can marry more than one person according to social laws.

242. Any class B female can have

(P) Grandfather born in class A

(Q) Grandmother born in class A

1) Only (P) can be true 2) Only (Q) can be true

3) Either (P) or (Q) can be true 4) Neither (P) and (Q) can be true

5) Both (P) and (Q) can be true

243. One boy, who was born in class B (boy and his wife both can have married and unmarried brothers),

1) can have his daughter in class B

2) can have a son-in-law born in class A

3) can have his uncle from any class

4) can have a divorced son in class B

5) can have a daughter-in-law born in class A.

244. Which of the following marriages is not permissible according to the social laws?

1) Any girl of class B marries his mother's brother.

2) Any widower marries his wife's sister.

3) Any boy of class B marries his father's sister.

4) Any widower born in class A marries his brother's widow.

5) Any widow marries the former divorced husband of her daughter.

Directions (Q. 245-249): Study the following information to answer the given questions:

In a school, there were five teachers. A and B were teaching Hindi and English. C and B were teaching English and Geography. D and A were teaching Mathematics and Hindi. E and B were teaching History and French.

245. Who among the teachers was teaching maximum number of subjects?

1) A 2) B 3) C

4) D 5) E

246. Which of the following pairs was teaching both Geography and Hind i?

1) A and B 2) B and C 3) C and A

4) D and B 5) None of these

247. More than two teachers were teaching which subject?

1) History 2) Hindi 3) French

4) Geography 5) Mathematics

248. D, B and A were teaching which of the following subjects?

1) English only 2) Hindi and English

3) Hindi only 4) English and Geography

5) Mathematics and Hind i

249. Who among the teachers was teaching less than two subjects?

1) A 2) B
3) D 4) Data inadequate
5) There is no such teacher

Directions (Q. 250-254): Study the following information to answer the given questions:

Madhu and Shobha are good in Dramatics and Computer Science. Anjali and Madhu are good in Computer Science and Physics. Anjali, Poonam and Nisha are good in Physics and History. Nisha and Anjali are good in Physics and Mathematics. Poonam and Shobha are good in History and Dramatics.

250. Who is good in Computer Science, History and Dramatics?

1) Anjali 2) Madhu 3) Shobha
4) Nisha 5) None of these

251. Who is good in Physics, Dramatics and Computer Science?

1) Shobha 2) Poonam 3) Madhu
4) Anjali 5) None of these

252. Who is good in Physics, History and Dramatic s?

1) Poonam 2) Shobha 3) Madhu
4) Anjali 5) None of these

253. Who is good in History, Physics, Computer Science and Mathematics?

1) Poonam 2) Nisha 3) Madhu
4) Anjali 5) None of these

254. Who is good in Physics, History and Mathematics but not in Computer Science?

1) Madhu 2) Poonam 3) Nisha
4) Anjali 5) None of these

Directions (Q. 255-259): Study the following information to answer the given questions:

(i) P, Q, R, S, T and U are six students procuring their Master's degree in six different subjects — English, History, Philosophy, Physics, Statistics and Mathematics.
(ii) Two of them stay in hostel, two stay as paying guest (PG) and the remaining two stay at their home.
(iii) R does not stay as PG and studies Philosophy.
(iv) The students studying Statistics and History do not stay as PG.
(v) T studies Mathematics and S studies Physics.
(vi) U and S stay in hostel. T stays as PG and Q stays at home.

255. Who studies English?

1) R 2) S 3) T
4) U 5) None of these

256. Which of the following combinations of subject and place of stay is not correct?
1) English — Hostel 2) Mathematics — PG
3) Philosophy — Home 4) Physics — Hostel
5) None of these

257. Which of the following pairs of students stay one each at hostel and at home?
1) QR 2) SR 3) US
4) Data inadequate 5) None of these

258. Which subject does Q study?
1) History 2) Statistics 3) History or Statistics
4) Data inadequate 5) None of these

259. Which of the following pairs of students stay at home?
1) PQ 2) QR 3) RS
4) ST 5) None of these

Directions (Q. 260-264): Study the following information to answer the given questions:

Seven friends Kamla, Manish, Rohit, Amit, Gaurav, Pritam and Priya are sitting in a circle. Kamla, Manish, Rohit, Amit, Pritam and Priya are sitting at equal distances from each other. Rohit is sitting two places right of Pritam, who is sitting one place right of Amit. Kamla forms an angle of 90 degrees from Gaurav and an angle of 120 degrees from Manish. Manish is just opposite Priya and is sitting on the left of Gaurav.

260. Who is the only person sitting between Rohit and Manish?
1) Pritam 2) Amit 3) Gaurav
4) Kamla 5) None of these

261. Gaurav is not sitting at equal distances from
1) Rohit and Pritam 2) Amit and Kamla 3) Manish and Pritam
4) All of the above 5) None of these

262. Gaurav is sitting of Priya.
1) to the left 2) to the right 3) two places right
4) cant say 5) None of these

263. The angle between Gaurav and Manish in the clockwise direction is
1) 150° 2) 180° 3) 210°
4) 90° 5) None of these

264. Which of the following statements is not correct?
1) Pritam is between Manish and Kamla.
2) Manish is two places away from Priya.
3) Gaurav is sitting opposite Pritam.
4) All of the above
5) None of these

Directions (Q. 265-269): Study the following information to answer the given questions:

(i) A, B, C, D, E and F are six students in a class.
(ii) B and C are shorter than F but heavier than A.
(iii) D is heavier than B and taller than C.
(iv) E is shorter than D but taller than F.
(v) F is heavier than D.
(vi) A is shorter than E but taller than F.

265. Who among them is the tallest?
1) A 2) B 3) D
4) E 5) None of these

266. Who is third from the top when they are arranged in descending order of height?
1) A 2) B 3) C
4) E 5) None of these

267. Which of the following groups of friends is shorter than A?
1) B, C only 2) D, B, C only 3) E, B, C only
4) F, B, C, only 5) None of these

268. Who among them is the lightest?
1) A 2) B 3) C
4) B or C 5) Data inadequate

269. Which of the following statements is true for F as regards height and weight?
1) He is lighter than E and taller than E.
2) He is heavier than B and taller than E.
3) He is heavier than B and C but shorter than D.
4) He is lighter than E and also shorter than E.
5) He is lighter than B and C but taller than D.

Directions (Q. 270-274): Study the following information to answer the given questions:

Six lectures A, B, C, D, E and F are to be organised in a span of seven days—from Sunday to Saturday, only one lecture on each day in accordance wit h the following rules:

(i) A should not be organised on Thursday.
(ii) C should be organised immediately after F.
(iii) There should be a gap of two days between E and D.
(iv) One day there will be no lecture (Friday is not that day), just before that day D will be organised.
(v) B should be organised on Tuesday and should not be followed by D.

270. On which day, there is no lecture?
1) Monday 2) Friday 3) Sunday
4) Cannot say 5) None of these

271. How many lectures are organised between C and D?
1) None 2) One 3) Two
4) Three 5) None of these

272. Which day will the lecture F be organised?
1) Thursday 2) Friday 3) Saturday
4) Sunday 5) None of these

273. Which of the following is the last lecture in the series?
1) A 2) B
3) C 4) Cannot be determined
5) None of these

274. Which of the following informations is not required in finding the complete sequence of organisation of lectures?
1) (i) only 2) (ii) only 3) (i) and (ii) only
4) (v) only 5) All are required

Directions (Q. 275-279): Study the following information to answer the given questions:

The Director of the Institute has announced that six guest lectures on different areas like Leadership, Decision Making, Quality Circles, Motivation, Assessment Centre and Group Discussion are to be organised only one on each day from Monday to Sunday.

(i) Motivation should be organised immediately after Assessment Centre.
(ii) Quality Circle should be organised on Wednesday and should not be followed by Group Discussion.
(iii) Decision Making should be organised on Friday and there should be a gap of two days between Leadership and Group Discussion.
(iv) One day there will be no lecture (Saturday is not that day), just before that day Group Discussion will be organised.

275. Which of the pairs of lectures were organised on first and last day?
1) Quality Circle & Motivation
2) Group Discussion & Quality Circle
3) Group Discussion & Decision Making
4) Leadership & Assessment Centre
5) None of these

276. How many lectures are organised between Motivation and Quality Circle?
1) One 2) Two 3) Three
4) Four 5) None of these

277. Which day will the lecture on Leadership be organised?
1) Tuesday 2) Wednesday 3) Friday
4) Saturday 5) None of these

278. On which day there is no lecture?
1) Sunday 2) Monday 3) Tuesday
4) Wednesday 5) None of these

279. Which of the following informations is not required for the above lecture arrangements?

1) Only (i) 2) Only (ii) 3) Only (iii)
4) Only (iv) 5) All are required

Directions (Q. 280-284): Study the following information to answer the given questions:

A team of five is to be selected from amongst five boys A, B, C, D and E and four girls P, Q, R and S. Some criteria for selection are:

A and S have to be together.

P cannot be put wit h R.

D and Q cannot go together. C and E have to be together.

R cannot be put wit h B.

Unless otherwise stated, these criteria are applicable to all the questions below:

280. If two of the members have to be boys, the team will consist of:

1) ABSP Q 2) ADSQR 3) BDSRQ
4) CESPQ 5) None of these

281. If R be one of the members, the other members of the team are:

1) PSAD 2) QSAD 3) QSCE
4) SACE 5) None of these

282. If two of the members are girls and D is one of the members, the members of the team other tna n D are:

1) PQBC 2) PQCE 3) PSAB
4) PSCE 5) None of these

283. If A and C are members, the other members of the team cannot be:

1) BES 2) DES 3) ESP
4) PQE 5) None of these

284. If including P at least three members are girls, the members of the team other than P are:

1) QSAB 2) QSBD 3) QSCE
4) RSAD 5) None of these

Directions (Q. 285-289): Study the following information to answer the given questions:

(i) P, Q, R, S, T and U are six members in a family in which there are two married couples.

(ii) T, a teacher is married to the doctor who is mother of R and U.

(iii) Q, the lawyer is married to P.

(iv) P has one son and one grandson.

(v) Of the two married ladies one is a housewife.

(vi) There is also one student and one male engineer in the family.

285. How is P related to R?
1) Grandfather 2) Mother 3) sister
4) Grandmother 5) None of these

286. Who among the following is the housewife?
1) P 2) Q 3) S
4) T 5) None of these

287. How is R related to U?
1) Brother 2) Sister 3) Brother or Sister
4) Data inadequate 5) None of these

288. Which of the following represents the group of females in the family?
1) PSR 2) PS U 3) QT R
4) Data inadequate 5) None of these

289. Which of the following is true about the grand-daughter in the family?
1) She is a lawyer. 2) She is a student. 3) She is an engineer.
4) Data inadequate 5) None of these

Directions (Q. 290 -294): Study the following information to answer the given questions:

(i) There is a family of six members A, B, C, D, E and F.
(ii) There are two married couples in the family and the family members represent three generations.
(iii) Each member has a distinct choice of a colour amongst green, yellow, black, red, white and pink.
(iv) No lady member likes either green or white,
(v) C, who likes black colour is the daughter-in-law of E.
(vi) B is brother of F and son of D and likes pink.
(vii) A is grandmother of F and F does not like red.
(viii) The husband has a choice of green colour, his wife likes yellow.

290. Which of the following is the colour preference of A?
1) Red 2) Yellow
3) Either Red or Yellow 4) Cannot be determined
5) None of these

291. How many male members are there in the family?
1) Two 2) Three
3) Four 4) Cannot be determined
5) None of these

292. Which of the following is true about F?
1) Brother of B 2) Sister of B
3) Daughter of C 4) Either sister or brother of B
5) None of these

293. Which of the following is the colour combination of one of the couples?
1) Red-Yellow 2) Yellow-Red 3) Green-Black
4) Yellow-Green 5) None of these

294. Which of the following is one of the married couples?
1) AC 2) CD
3) DA 4) Cannot be determined
5) None of these

Directions (Q. 295-299): Study the following information to answer the given questions:

A, B, C, D and E are five towns out of which two are hill stations and the rest are in plain. Two towns, which are in plain, are harbours. Four towns out of five are capitals and two are industrial towns. Population of two towns is less than 5 lacs. It is 20 lacs of one town and more than 50 lacs of two towns. Two towns are on the same latitudes and other two are on the same longitudes. Latitudes and longitudes of both harbours are different and out of these one is an industrial town. The population of both industrial towns is more than 50 lacs. The longitudes of one hill station and one of the industrial towns are same. The latitudes and longitudes of the other hill station and other harbour are different. One industrial town is neither a hill station nor a harbour. None of the hill stations is an industrial town. The hill station of which longitudes are same as that of a harbour, is a capital. B is a hill station while the longitudes of A and E are same. E is a harbour. The latitudes of D and C are same and the population of D is 20 lacs. Both the harbours are capitals and one of them is an industrial town.

295. Which of the following two towns are those whose population is less than 5 lacs?
1) D and A 2) B and C 3) A and B
4) A and C 5) None of these

296. Which of the following towns is not a capital?
1) A 2) C 3) D
4) E 5) B

297. Which of the following is harbour, capital and industrial town?
1) A 2) B 3) C
4) E 5) D

298. Which of the following towns have population more than 50 lacs?
1) A and D 2) B and E 3) C and E
4) C and D 5) A and C

299. Which one of the following towns is hill station as well as capital?
1) B 2) C 3) E
4) D 5) A

Directions (Q. 300-304): Study the following information to answer the given questions:

Of the five boys A, B, C, D and E two are good, one is poor and two are average in studies. Two of them study in post-graduate classes and three in under-graduate classes. One comes from a rich family, two from middle-class families and two from poor families. One of them is interested in music, two in acting and one in sports. Of those studying in under-graduate classes, two are average and one is poor in studies. Of the two boys interested in acting, one is a post-graduate student. The one interested in music comes from a middle-class family. Both the boys interested in acting are not industrious. The two boys coming from middle-class families are average in studies and one of them is interested in acting. The boy interested in sports comes from a poor family, while the one interested in music is industrious. E is industrious, good in studies, comes from a poor family and is not interested in acting, music or sports. C is poor in studies inspite of being industrious. A comes from a rich family and is not industrious but good in studies. B is industrious and comes from a middle-class family.

300. Name the boy interested in music.
 1) A 2) B 3) C
 4) D 5) Cannot say

301. Name the boy interested in music.
 1) A 2) B 3) C
 4) D 5) Cannot say

302. Name the middle-class family boy interested in acting.
 1) A 2) B 3) C
 4) D 5) Cannot say

303. Name the boys studying in post-graduate classes.
 1) A, D 2) A, E 3) B, C
 4) D, E 5) Cannot say

304. Name the boy who is not industrious and is average in studies:
 1) A 2) B 3) C
 4) D 5) Cannot say

Answers with explanations

Exercise 22 A

1. d; Mother's grandson $\Rightarrow$ son; Son's wife $\Rightarrow$ daughter-in-law.
2. c; Only son of woman's grandfather $\Rightarrow$ woman's father; Man's brother's father $\Rightarrow$ Man's father. So, the woman is man's sister.
3. e; Brother of uncle's daughter $\Rightarrow$ Uncle's son $\Rightarrow$ Cousin; man is Seema's cousin.
4. a; Daughter of your father $\Rightarrow$ your sister; the person's mother is the woman's sister. Woman is person's aunt.
5. b; My father's only son $\Rightarrow$ My brother; Grandmother of my brother $\Rightarrow$ My grandmother; Daughter-in-law of my grandmother $\Rightarrow$ My mother. So, the lady is girl's mother.
6. a; Daughter of brother-in-law is niece. Mother's niece $\Rightarrow$ Cousin. So, the girl is the cousin of Rita's friend.
7. e; Let B's mother be X. Then X is the only daughter of A's mother means A is the brother of X. So, A is B's maternal uncle.
8. b; Daughter of grandmother $\Rightarrow$ aunt; Aunt's only brother $\Rightarrow$ father.
9. a; My daughter's mother $\Rightarrow$ my wife; My wife's father $\Rightarrow$ my father-in-law; My father-in-law's son $\Rightarrow$ my brother-in-law. So, Manjeet is Amir's brother-in-law.
10. d; My mother's mother $\Rightarrow$ my grandmother; My grandmother's only son $\Rightarrow$ my maternal uncle. So the woman is his niece.
11. d; Only daughter of mother-in-law $\Rightarrow$ wife; Girl's mother is Vipin's wife. So, Vipin is girl's father.
12. d; Brother of my wife $\Rightarrow$ my brother-in-law; Son of lady's brother is the brother-in-law of the man. So, lady's brother is man's father-in-law, i.e., Lady is the sister of man's father-in- law..
13. c; Kailash's son's uncle $\Rightarrow$ Kailash's brother; Old man's son is Kailash's brother. So, old man is Kailash's father.
14. d; Asha's mother's mother $\Rightarrow$ man's mother, i.e., Asha's mother $\Rightarrow$ man's sister, i.e., Asha is man's niece.
15. a; Grandfather's only son $\Rightarrow$ father; Daughter of father $\Rightarrow$ sister. So, Vineet is lady's brother.
16. d; Only daughter of my father $\Rightarrow$ myself. So, man is woman's husband.
17. b; Father's wife $\Rightarrow$ mother; Mother's daughter $\Rightarrow$ sister; Sister's younger brother $\Rightarrow$ my younger brother. So, the boy is Deepak's brother.
18. a; Brother of father $\Rightarrow$ uncle; Uncle's granddaughter $\Rightarrow$ daughter of uncle's son $\Rightarrow$ daughter of cousin $\Rightarrow$ niece.

19. c; Brother of mother ⇒ uncle; Uncle's son ⇒ Cousin.
20. a; Mahesh's father's only son ⇒ Mahesh; Mahesh's wife is the mother of his son. So, the man is Mahesh's son.
21. d; Your mother's husband ⇒ your father; Your father's sister ⇒ your aunt. So, lady's aunt is man's aunt and therefore lady is man's sister.
22. a; Daughter of uncle's father ⇒ uncle's sister ⇒ mother; Mother's son ⇒ brother.
23. d; Son of Y's son ⇒ Y's grandson; brother of Y's grandson ⇒ Y's grandson.
24. c; Neelam's father is Deepak. Deepika's mother is Rekha. Deepak is the third child of Ramlal. So, Deepak's younger sister Rekha is the daughter of Ramlal. So, Ramlal is the father of Rekha and grandfather of her daughter Deepika.
25. b; A is the brother of F, who is the daughter of D. So, A is the son of D. P is the brother of D. So, P is the uncle of A.
26. e; P, Q and R are children of the same parents. So, S, who is R's mother, and T, who is P's father, will be the mother and the father of all the three. However, it is not mentioned whether Q is a male or female. So, (e) cannot be definitely true.
27. e; K is the brother of N and X. So, Y, who is the mother of N, and Z, who is the father of K, will be the mother and father of all the three. However, it is not mentioned whether N is a male or female. So, the statement (e) cannot be definitely true.
28. d; C is B's daughter and D is B's son. So, D is the brother of C. E is a male married to C. So, E is the husband of C, whose brother is D. So, D is the brother-in-law of E.
29. a; B is the child of C but not daughter, means B is the son of C. Also, A is the son of C. So, A is the brother of B.
30. c; D is the brother of B, who is the daughter of A. So, D is the son of A. C is the brother of A. Thus, C is the uncle of D.
31. d; Q is the brother of R. T is the brother of S, who is the daughter of R. So, T and S are cousins of Q.
32. c; Shalini is Meena's stepdaughter, means she is the daughter of the other wife of Rohan. So, Shalini is the daughter of Lakshmi, or Lakshmi is the mother of Shalini.
33. b; C is A's father's nephew, means C is the son of A's father's brother, i.e., C is the cousin of A. D is also A's cousin. So, D must be a sibling of C. But D is not brother of C. So, D must be the sister of C.
34. a; Grandmother is one female, mother is another, wives of four sons are the four females and two daughters of all four sons are eight females. So, in all there are $1 + 1 + 4 + 8 = 14$ females.

Exercise 22 B

Q. 1-5:

We have from (iii) and (iv):

C > B > F

and D > E [in increasing order of weights]

Now, A is neither the heaviest nor the lightest. Also, C is lighter than only two people and A is not one of them.

But B and F are already lighter than C. And A is not heavier than C. Hence, the remaining two, viz. D and E, must be heavier than C. Thus, we may combine the two series as:

D > E > C > B > F.

In the above, A must come after C but before F [after C because C is lighter than only two, before F because A is not the lightest.]

Hence, there are two possibilities:

D > E > C > A > B > F

or

D > E > C > B > A > F

Now, the heaviest is on the top floor along with B and the lightest is on the ground floor along with C. Thus, D (the heaviest) and B are on the top floor while F (the lightest) and C are on the ground floor. Since the two middle floors have one flat vacant each, E and A occupy the middle two floors, one each of one floor. The two possible ways are:

			or	
D	B	Top Floor	D	B
E	—	2nd Floor	A	
A	—	1st Floor	E	
C	F	G. Floor	C	F

Now check your answers:

1. 1 2. 1 3. 5; [IInd or IIIrd fllor] 4. 2 5. 4

Q. 6-11:

Begin with the first condition.

J can contact both L and N:

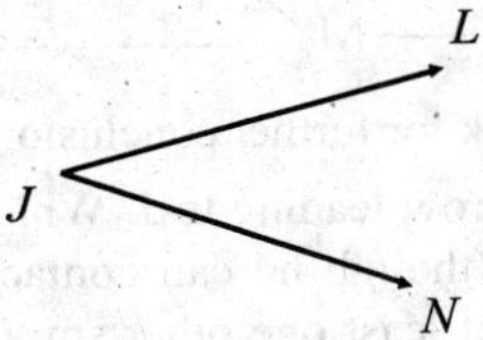

Next, O can be contacted by L, M and P:

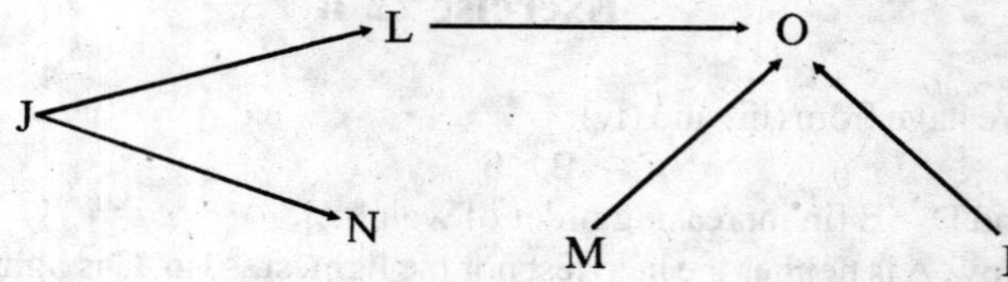

Next, N can contact M:

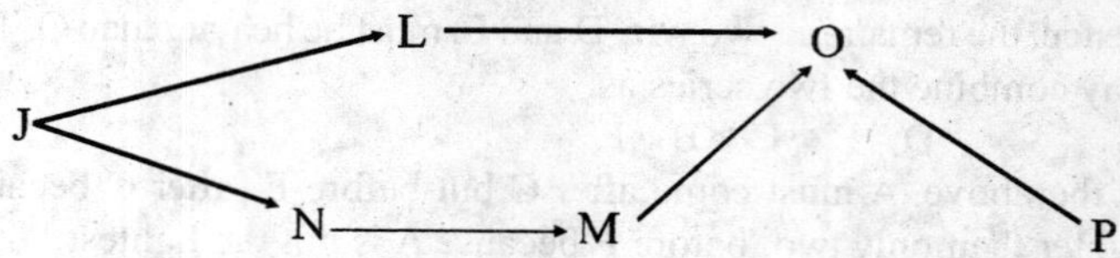

Then, O can contact both L and N:

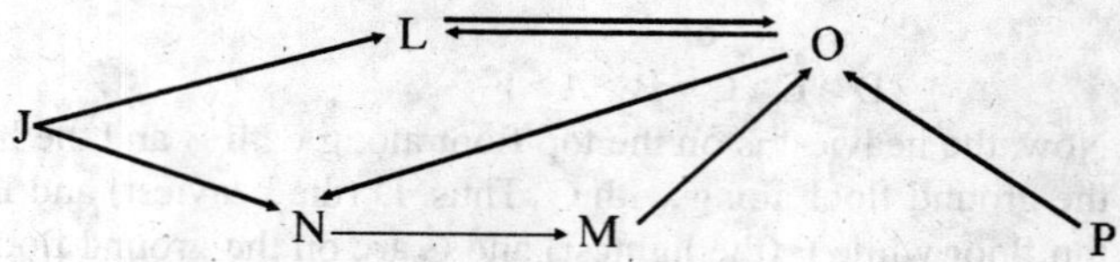

Finally, P can be contacted by M:

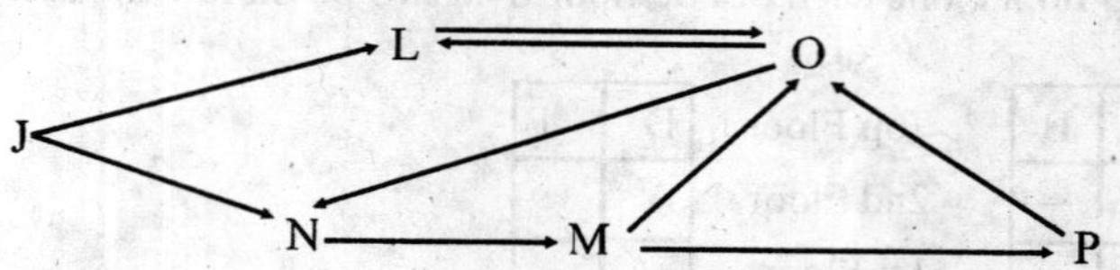

With a "network" set, any further conclusions that you might need to draw are already implicit in the diagram. For Example, J can have N relay a message to M, who in turn can relay the message to O:

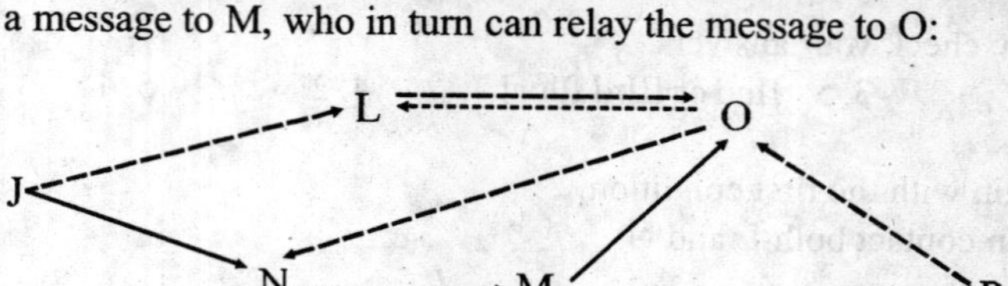

So, there is no need to look for further conclusions. Go to the questions.

6. 1; The diagram shows no arrow leading to J. Which means that J cannot be contacted by anyone (though he can contact others). Every other spy can be contacted by at least one other spy.

7. 3; The diagram shows that N can contact M, who in turn can contact P and O.

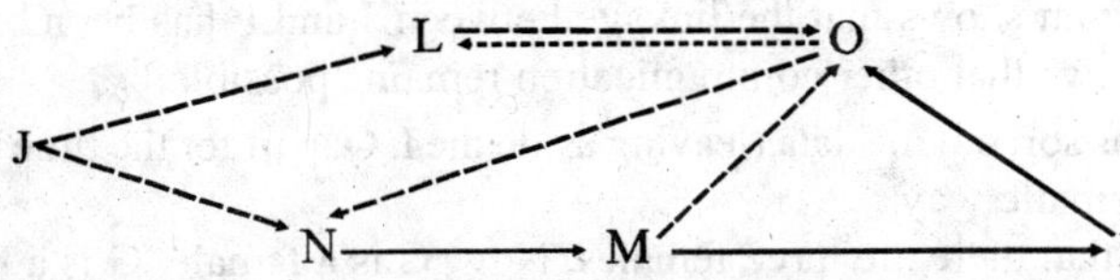

So, using just one intermediate contact, N can contact those two spies.

8. 4; O can contact only L and N, and N is the only one who can contact M:

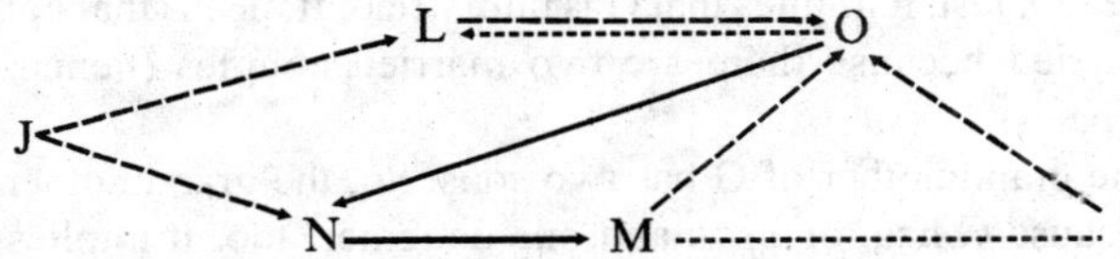

9. 1; The modified diagram looks like this:

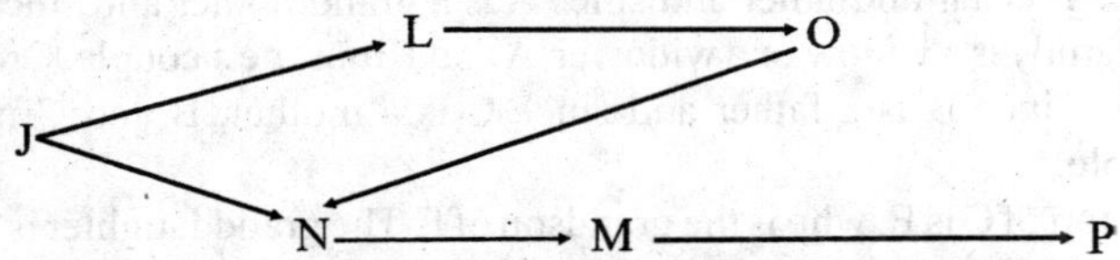

On the actual test, you would block out O in your mind's eye. Our modified diagram shows that J is still able to get a message to P:

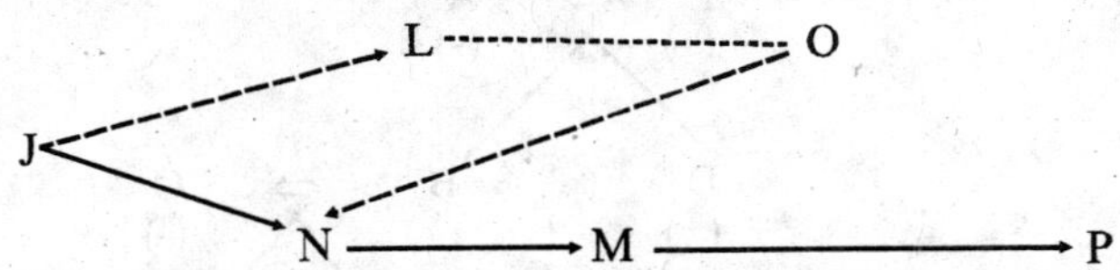

The diagram shows that none of the other communications is possible.

10. 1; Trace with your finger the various possibilities:

(a) J (to N to M) to P (Two intermediaries)

(b) L to O (No intermediaries)

(c) M (to O) to N (One intermediary)

(d) N (to M) to O (One intermediary)

(e) O (to N) to M (One intermediary)

Note: A communication from M to N could theoretically take two intermediaries, P and O, but the question stipulates that the message takes the shortest route. Thus, (3) is incorrect.

11. 2; The modified diagram looks like this:

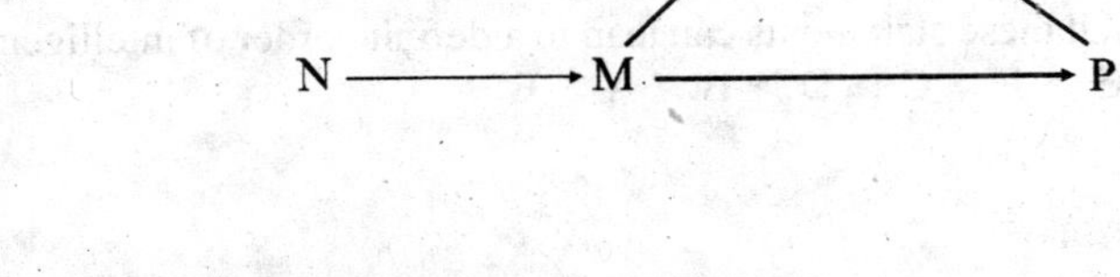

The diagram shows that the linkage between J and P has been broken, and it shows that other communication remains possible.

Q. 12-19: Let us sort out the data (leaving aside the I. Q. part for the time being) in a systematic way:

I. We note that there are three females. Now, C is a female, G is a female while B, F, E and D are all males. It implies that the third female is A.

II. Now, since G is the most intelligent and since none of the married topped the I.Q. test, it implies that G is unmarried. It means that both A and C are married because there are two married couples (hence two married females).

III. The grandmother of G has two sons. So, the grandmother cannot be C because C has 'one son and one daughter' too. It implies that A is the grandmother.

IV. Since F is a grandfather and since A is a grandmother and since none in the family is a widow or a widower, A and F must be a couple. On the same logic, since B is a father and since C is a mother, B and C must be a couple.

V. The son of C is E, who is the grandson of F. The granddaughter is G, whose grandmother A has two sons: one, her own father B and the other, D. The family-tree can now be easily constructed as shown below:

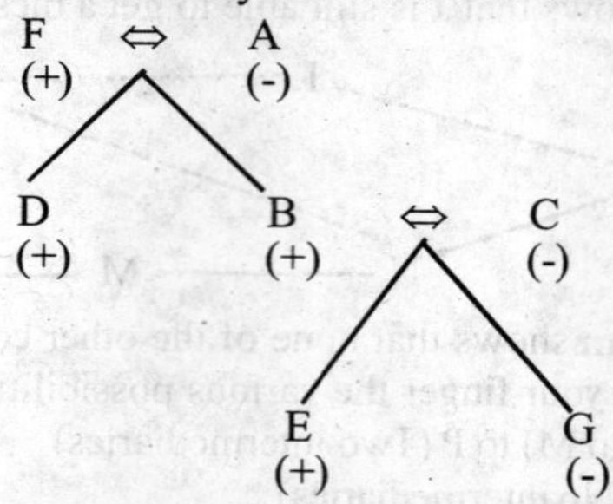

+ means male
– means female

Also, let us pick the relevant information regarding the I.Q. test. These are:

(i) G is the most intelligent.
(ii) B is more intelligent than his son.
(iii) C is more intelligent than her husband.
(iv) The father of B is more intelligent than B.
(v) E is the least intelligent.
(vi) F is the second most intelligent.
(vii) The mother of B is less intelligent than B.
(viii) D is more intelligent than his brother but less intelligent than his wife.

All these statements can lead to a definite order of intelligence as shown:
G > F > C > D > B > A > E

Now, the question can easily be answered as:

12. 1 13. 4 14. 1 15. 1 16. 4

17. 5; [G is the granddaughter of F, daughter of B, niece of D, sister of E.]

18. 1 19. 3

Q. 20-26:

Begin by summarising the information: T = 4

$(W + Y) < V$

$X < W$

Note: The "<" is used to indicate *before* because the number of the witness called earlier will be lower than that of a witness called later; e.g. , if X is called first and W is called third, $X < W$ because $1 < 3$. The initial conditions do not determine any particular order, except that T must be fourth.

There is one further conclusion: since $W < V$ and $X < W$, $X < V$. This further conclusion is the basis for the correct answer to Question 21. If you miss this further conclusion, when you get to Question 21, the fact that you don't find a correct answer will prompt you to return to the initial conditions to look for it and this will consume some precious extra minutes.

20. 3; This question does not provide any additional information. Attack it by applying each of the initial conditions to the choices, eliminating impermissible orders until you are left with just one answer choice. That will be the correct choice.

The first condition specifies that T must be fourth and you can eliminate (4) on this score.

The second condition specifies that W and Y must both be called before V is called, and you can eliminate (2) and (5) on this basis.

The third condition specifies that X must be called before W, and you can eliminate (1).

You are left with choice (3), which must be correct. (3) does describe a possible order because it does not contradict any of the initial conditions.

21. 2; This question does not supply any additional information, so it is answerable using just the information given in the initial conditions. As noted above, however, you must combine the second and third conditions to produce a further conclusion. If you missed this insight in your first look at the initial conditions, the fact that you would not be able to answer this question would prompt you to take another, closer look at them. Since X must be called before W, and W before V, X must be called before V.

As for the other choices, the following possible order demonstrates that they are not necessarily true:

1	2	3	4	5	6
X	W	Y	T	V	Z

22. 5; Test each of the choices to determine whether or not it describes a legitimate possibility.

(1) No. T must be called fourth, not sixth.
(2) No. T, not V, must be called fourth.
(3) No. X must come before W, so W cannot be first.
(4) No. X must be called before W and so before V, so X cannot be called fifth. (X can be called no later than third.)
(5) Yes. The only restriction on Y is that Y precede V, so Y can apparently be first.

At this point, we should raise a question about test strategy. Our analysis of (5) suggests that (5) is correct simply because it does not constitute an obvious violation of the initial conditions. We did not, however, construct a scenario in which Y is actually first. We could have done so, for example:

1	2	3	4	5	6
Y	X	W	I	V	Z

If you do this, you will confirm that it is possible to call Y first; but, of course, working out a possible order takes time. Once you have eliminated (1) through (4), you need not bother to work out a complete order to prove that (5) is possible.

23. 2; Set up a rough diagram to keep track of the additional information and your further deductions:

1	2	3	4	5	6
			T		Z

Above we learned that X as well as W and Y must be called before V. This means that X, W and Y must be first, second and third (though not necessarily in that order) and that V must be fifth.

1	2	3	4	5	6
			T	V	Z

24. 5; The question stem stipulates an order for X, Y, and Z: Y-X-Z. There is only one place for three consecutive letters:

1	2	3	4	5	6
Y	X	Z	T		

Next, we reason that W and V must be called fifth and sixth and that W must come before V:

1	2	3	4	5	6
Y	X	Z	T	W	V

25. 1; V must be called later than W and Y and X. So (since T is called fourth), V can be called no earlier than fifth. That the other four witnesses could be called third (immediately before T) is demonstrated by the following diagrams:

1	2	3	4	5	6
X	Y	W	T	V	Z
Y	Z	X	T	W	V
X	W	Y	T	V	Z
X	W	Z	T	Y	V

Remember, however, to save time you want to avoid working out these possibilities. Once you have explained to yourself why V cannot be called third, mark (1) and go to the next item.

26. 4; Enter the additional information on a diagram:

1	2	3	4	5	6
Z			T		

Now, look for further conclusions. We know that W, X and Y must be called before V, so V must be sixth:

1	2	3	4	5	6
Z			T		V

Since X must be called before W, there are three possible orders:

1	2	3	4	5	6
Z	X	W	T	Y	V
Z	X	Y	T	W	V
Z	Y	X	T	W	V

So, the fifth and sixth witnesses can only be Y and V or W and V, in that order.

Q. 27-31 :

Let us contruct the family tree on the one hand and the line (in ascending order) of weight on the other. Let us take all the informations about weights.

These informations are:

(i) Both D and F are lighter than B.
(ii) B is lighter than E.
(iii) C is neither the heaviest nor the lightest.
(iv) E is lighter than C.
(v) The grandfather is the heaviest.

The corresponding accomodations can be made pictorially as:

(i) D, F < B
(ii) B < E
(iii) ....C.... (C is not at any extreme)
(iv) E < C
(v) all < grandfather.

This can be accomodated in one diagram as,

D, F < B < E < C < grandfather.

Obviously, the grandfather must be A. Hence,

D, F < B < E < C < A(grandfather).

Now, we take the family tree. The relevant informations are:

(i) There are two married couples.

(ii) D is the brother of F.

(iii) B is the mother of D.

(iv) C is a female.

Let us start with (iii). It can be represented as:

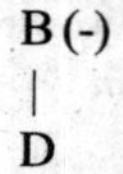

- means female.

To this we accomodate (ii). Now, it becomes:

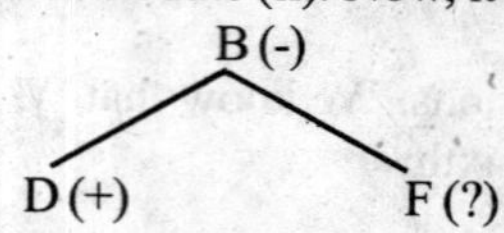

Now, to complete this tree, we have only three additional informations. One, that A is the grandfather; two, that there are two married couples; and three, that C is a female. This, obviously, is insufficient to complete the family tree. A could either be married to B or C. Or, he may as well be married to E, whose sex is unknown. Thus we see that as far as relations are concerned, we find 'data inadequate' for all the questions. Hence, our answers are:

27. 1 28. 4 29. 5 30. 5 31. 3

Q. 32-38: Begin by summarising the information:

Capts = D, E, F

B ≠ C

J ≠ F

L = B or E or (B + E)

L = Blue

There don't appear to be any further useful conclusions to be drawn, so go to the questions.

32. 3; This question provides no additional information, so just measure each answer choice by the initial conditions. The first condition requires that D, E, and F be captains. Using this condition, you can eliminate (4) and (5), for a team of J, K, and L or a team of J, K, and M would lack a captain. Then, the second condition requires that B and C be separated. The remaining choices, however, all respect this condition, so it isn't possible to eliminate any more choices on this ground. Next, the third condition requires that F and J be separated, and we eliminate (2) for this reason. Finally, the fourth condition requires that L be on a team with either B or E (or both). This eliminates (1). A team of J, B and E is not possible because L would be placed on a team without either B or E.

33. 2; This question is similar to Question 32, but here we have a thought-reverser (EXCEPT). This means that four of the five choices will describe possible teams. The correct choice is the one that violates one or more of the initial conditions. The correct choice is (2). We are told in the initial conditions that L must be on the Blue Team. A team consisting of L, D and E would violate the condition that D and E be the captains of their respective teams.

34. 3; Use a diagram to keep track of the new information and any further conclusions you reach:

Blue Team	Green Team	Red Team
L		B, J

L must be on a team with either B or E. Since B is already assigned to the Red Team, we can deduce that E is assigned to the Blue Team:

Blue Team	Green Team	Red Team
L, E		B, J

Next, F cannot be on the Red Team (because J is on that team), and she cannot be on the Blue Team (because E is already captain of that team). So F is on the Green Team:

Blue Team	Green Team	Red Team
L, E	F	B, J

This means that the captain of the Red Team must be D:

Blue Team	Green Team	Red Team
L, E	F	B, J, D

Have we overlooked something? Perhaps. But at this point we will look at the answer choices that are available. If we find one and only one seemingly correct response, we know we have solved the problem:

(1) This is possibly, though not necessarily, true.
(2) This is necessarily false.
(3) This is necessarily true.
(4) This is possibly, though not necessarily, true.
(5) This is possibly, though not necessarily, true.

We have only one choice that is necessarily true, so this indicates that we have solved the problem correctly.

35. 5; Test each choice against the initial conditions:

(1) F, K and J. (No. F and J cannot be on the same team.)
(2) F, L and M. (No. L must be on a team with either B or E, or both.)
(3) F, L and K. (No. L must be on a team with either B or E, or both.)
(4) F, M and J. (No. F and J cannot be on the same team.)
(5) F, M and K. (Yes. This combination does not violate any of the initial conditions.)

36. 5; You may have noticed that the questions are growing more difficult. This question contains a thought-reverser. You can attack it by testing each of the combinations given for the Blue Team and the Green Team. You will reach the following conclusions:

In each choice, the Blue Team and the Green Team have exactly one captain.

In no choice are B and C together on either the Blue or the Green Team.

In each choice, L is on the Blue Team with E.

This suggests that all are possible assignments, but we know that one of them must violate some restriction. What have we failed to consider? The effect of the assignments to the Blue and Green Teams on the third member of the Red Team! The person not assigned to either the Blue Team or the Green Team must be assigned to the Red Team:

(1) K (OK)

(2) K (OK)

(3) M (OK)

(4) K (OK)

(5) J (No! John cannot be assigned to the Red Team because F is assigned to that team.)

37. 5; This question calls your attention to a constraint on the overall distribution of individuals. First, as a matter of test-taking strategy, given the extreme flexibility of the situation here, neither (1) nor (2) is likely to be the correct choice. I would not study them too seriously. As for (3), this too seems unlikely. Make sure you don't make the mistake of assuming that just because either B or E must be on the Blue Team (with L), neither can be on a team other than the Blue Team.

(4) and (5) seem more promising, and here is where you should concentrate your attack. You can test (4) by trying to find a possible distribution in which J is not on a team with either B or C:

Red Team	Blue Team	Green Team
J	L, B	C

Distribute the rest of the individuals:

Red Team	Blue Team	Green Team
J, E, K	L, B, F	C, D, M

This counter-example proves that (4) is not necessarily true.

Finally, we turn to (5). There are three teams with a total of nine positions to be filled. We know that each team has at least one male — its captain. This leaves only two other males, B and C, who cannot both be assigned to the same team. So, B will be assigned to one team and C to another. Their teams will be completed by two of the females, which means that the other two females will be assigned to the remaining team. So one team will consist of a male (its captain) and two females.

38. 5; This question seems to be fairly difficult (as we might expect). The Blue Team and the Green Team will both need a captain, so E and F must be assigned, one to one of those teams and the other to the other team:

Blue	**Green**
F/E	F/E

Since J cannot be assigned to the same team as F, he must be assigned to E's team:

Blue	**Green**
F/(E+J)	F/(E + J)
L	

B and C must be on different teams:

Blue	**Green**
F/(E+J)	F/(E+J)
L	
B/C	B/C

We can now see that E and J cannot be on the Blue Team, for that team would then consist of E, J, L and either B or C — four people. So, E and J must be assigned to the Green Team.

Blue	**Green**
F	E
L	J

And B must be assigned to L's team:

Blue	**Green**
F	E
L	J
B	C

Q. 39-43: Let us draw a diagram for the statements (iv), (v), (vi) and (vii). Let us start with (iv).

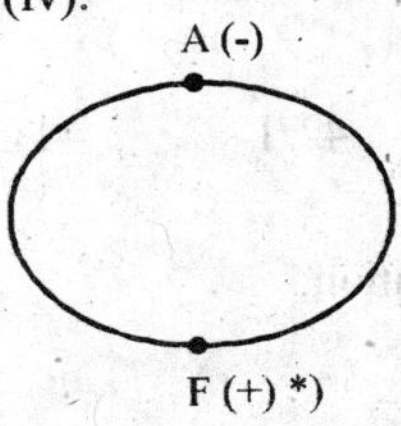

- means female
+ means male.
* means unmarried

Since the two females are not sitting adjacently, hence both persons around A must be males. Hence,

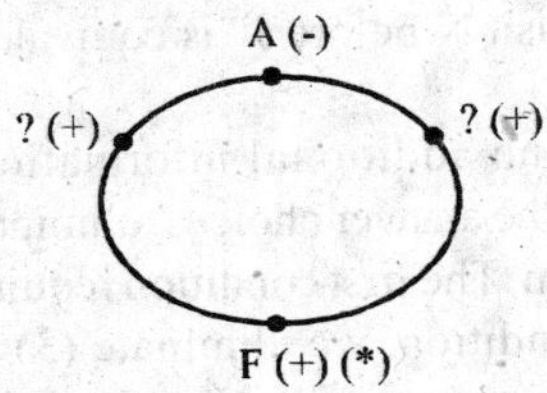

Now, the other female could be between F and either of the question marks. But since, on the immediate right of both the females is a bachelor, the position of the other female will be as shown:

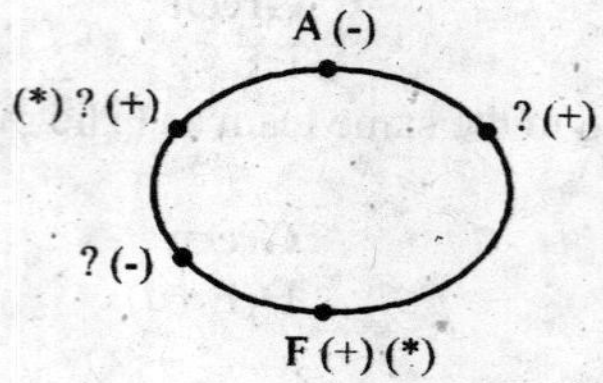

Now, D, the husband of the other female, sits opposite her. Hence,

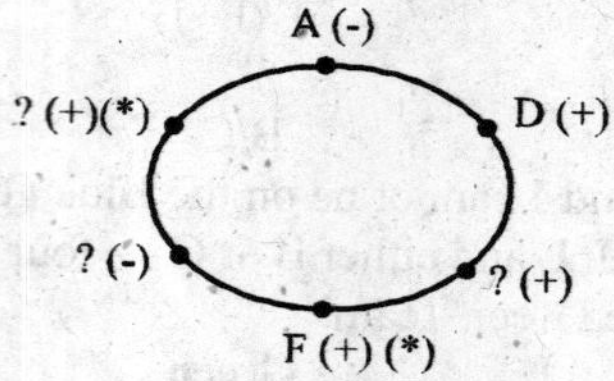

Now, let us consider statement (viii). It implies that C is a bachelor and B is a male. This completes the picture:

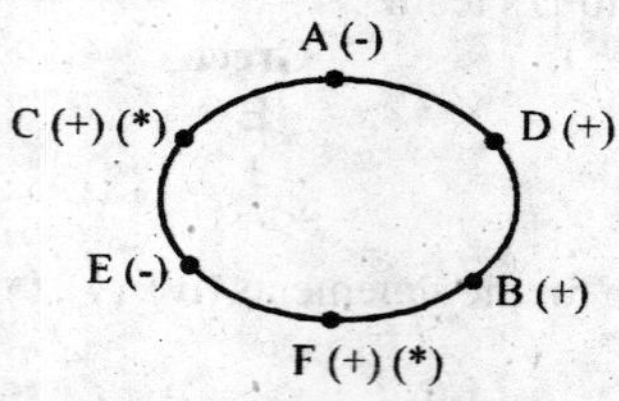

Now, check your answers:

39. 1 40. 2 41. 3 42. 1 43. 2

Q. 44-50:

Begin by summarising the information:

(L + N) < M

J < N

K = 2

Note: Since the candidate cannot visit two cities simultaneously, the condition "The candidate cannot visit N before J" is equivalent to "She must visit J before N."

44. 1; This question supplies no additional information, so just take each condition and apply it to the answer choices, eliminating those that fail to comply with any condition. The first condition requires that L and N come before M. Using this condition, we eliminate (3) and (5). The second condition states that J must come before N, and we eliminate (4). The third condition requires that K be the second city, so we eliminate (2). This leaves us with (1); and (1), with respect to all three conditions, is a possible order.

45. 2; M must be visited after both L and N, so given that K is visited second, M could not possibly be visited earlier than fourth, which means that K comes before M. So, (2) is correct. In fact, given that J comes before N, and N comes before M, M must also come later than J. So, M cannot be visited until L, N, J and K have been visited, which means M is either fifth or sixth. As just noted, J must come before M, so (4) is necessarily false. The other three responses describe possible schedules only:

1	2	3	4	5	6
J	K	N	L	M	O

which shows that (1), (3) and (5) are possible. But:

1	2	3	4	5	6
O	K	L	J	N	M

shows that (1), (3) and (5) are not necessarily true.

46. 3; Begin by entering the additional information on a diagram:

1	2	3	4	5	6
O	K				

Next, we reason that J, N and L must all come before M, which means that M comes last:

1	2	3	4	5	6
O	K				M

The only condition left to take care of is the one that requires J before N, but this still leaves three possibilities:

1	2	3	4	5	6
O	K	J	N	L	M
O	K	J	L	N	M
O	K	L	J	N	M

So, either J or L could be third.

47. 1; This question stipulates an order for three of the cities: O, J, N. Given that J and N must come before M, this means that the order must be:

1	2	3	4	5	6
	K	O	J	N	M

Which means that L must be visited first:

1	2	3	4	5	6
L	K	O	J	N	M

48. 1; This question is a good occasion to talk about test-taking strategy. A question of this form has this peculiarity: a choice like (1) may not contradict any single initial condition and may still be wrong because of the way the initial conditions work together. The only way to exclude this possibility is to devise a complete order, part of which is the segment you want to test - a time-consuming process. What should you do?

The solution to the dilemma is this: Make a first run through the choices, testing them by each single initial statement. If you can eliminate all but one, then you have your correct answer. If more than one choice remains, then the key to the question is some interaction among the initial conditions, e.g., a further inference that you have overlooked. Then, and only then, try working up an entire order to test the remaining choices.

Here, we are fortunate because we can find the correct choice quickly:

1) Doesn't contradict any single condition, so go to the next choice.

2) No. (K must be second.)

3) No. (L must come before M.)

4) No. (M must come after J, L and N, and therefore K as well. So M cannot be visited earlier than fifth.)

5) No. (N must come before M, so N cannot be last.)

Thus, (1) must be the correct choice, so we don't have to try to construct the entire order using (1).

Just for reasons of completeness of explanation, however, here is a schedule in which J is the first city:

1 2 3 4 5 6
J K L N M O

49. 3; As just noted, M cannot be earlier than fifth, so M could not immediately follow K. That the others could follow K, is shown by the following schedules:

1 2 3 4 5 6
(1) O K J L N M
(2) J K L N M O
(4) J K N L M O
(5) J K O N L M

50. 1; Start by entering the additional information on a diargam:

1 2 3 4 5 6
K O (K under 2, O under 6)

Next, we have already determined that M cannot be earlier than fifth:

1 2 3 4 5 6
K M O (K under 2, M under 5, O under 6)

Next, since J must precede N, there are three possibilities:

1 2 3 4 5 6
J K N L M O
J K L N M O
L K J N M O

(1) describes the second of these possibilities. The other choices do not describe one of the three possible schedules.

51. 1 52. 4 53. 5 54. 1 55. 1

Q. 56-61: Statements (1) to (6) can be summarised as below

T___ Sec .... (1)
PV Sec or Sec VP .... (2)
S U .... (3)

Convenor Organiser Cashier .... (4)
Q _ Sec .... (5)
(1) and (5) ⇔ T _ Q _ Sec .... (a)
Looking at (a), we understand that the first case in (2) is untenable as then P would have to occupy the same place as Q. So the second case in (2) is correct. Incorporating it in (a) we have
T _ Q _ Sec VP .... (b)
The two vacant places can be filled up by (3).
Adding (3) to (b), we get
T S Q U Sec VP .... (c)
Then R must be the Secretary and U the President.
Adding (4) to (c) we know that
T → Convenor
S → Organiser
Q → Cashier
From (6), we are however not sure as to who among V or P is the Treasurer or the Officer.
Now, answer the questions

56. 4 57. 2 58. 1
59. 5; Actually it should be III and IV.
60. 4
61. 5; The President is also included.

Q. 62-71 : Let us make an intelligence-wise, a profession-wise and a seating-wise analysis of the given facts. Start with intelligence because the most direct statements are made about intelligence only.

We have:

a) The psychologist is the most intelligent.
b) The teacher is the least intelligent.
c) C is the second most intelligent.
d) The doctor (husband of C) is the third most intelligent.
e) The engineer is the fourth most intelligent.
f) The student is the fifth most intelligent while D (the architect) is the sixth most intelligent.

Explanation of (e): See statement (ix). There are as many more intelligent persons than the engineer as there are less. It means that the engineer is the fourth most intelligent, i.e., there are three persons more intelligent and three less intelligent than him.

Explanation of (f) : Statement (xii) says that the student is more intelligent than the architect and the architect is more intelligent than just one person F. It means that **F must be the least intelligent**, the architect must be the sixth most intelligent and the student, the fifth most intelligent.

Now, the intelligence-tree could be drawn as shown below:

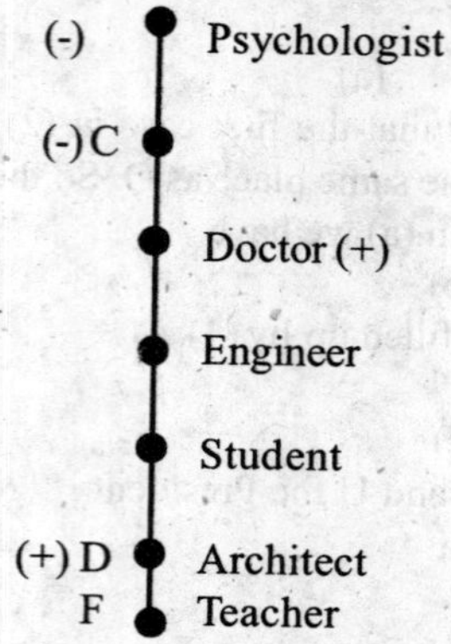

Fig 1

Note: (a) The negative sign before C and the positive sign before doctor means female and male respectively. This follows from the fact that the doctor is the husband of C.

(b) Look at statement (v). Here, 'he' and not 'she' is used for D, the architect. So he must be a male.

Hence, a positive sign before D. Also, it is given that the psychologist is a female.

Let us now make a seating-wise analysis. We have:

a) D is sitting on the leftmost corner.

b) The student is on the rightmost corner.

c) D is followed by the least intelligent (it is F, the teacher) who is followed by the most intelligent (it is the psychologist.)

Further, see (x) - there are three females followed by D on the bench. It means, that F, the psychologist, and then C are followed by him because C is the only female in addition to F and the psychologist. Hence, we obtain the following seating-outline:

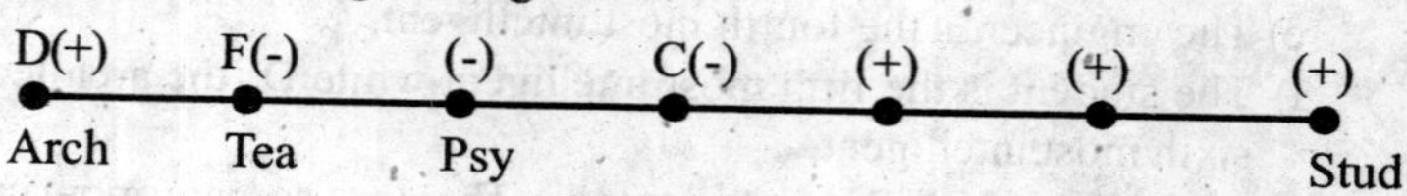

Fig 2

Note: a) The student must be a male and so are others because there are only three females in the group.

b) Look at Fig 1. It is obvious that **C must be the businessman** because it is the only profession left.

c) There are only two couples. We know that Engineer-teacher and C (businessman)-doctor are two couples. This means that all others are unmarried. Hence, the architect (D), the psychologist and the student are unmarried. Further, B is unmarried. So B could either be the student or the psychologist. But statement (v) clearly says that the psychologist is 'another person'. Hence, **B must be the student.**

Now, who is the psychologist? The psychologist can't be D, F, C or B because their professions are known. It leaves A, E and G. But A and G are not females - see statement (xiii) - and the psychologist is a female. Hence, E must be the psychologist.

d) Who is the doctor? And who is the engineer? We can see that we have exhausted all information and nothing more could be established. Either A or G are the doctor and the engineer; both are males. This is all that can be known.

Thus we have fig 1 and fig 2 redrawn as:

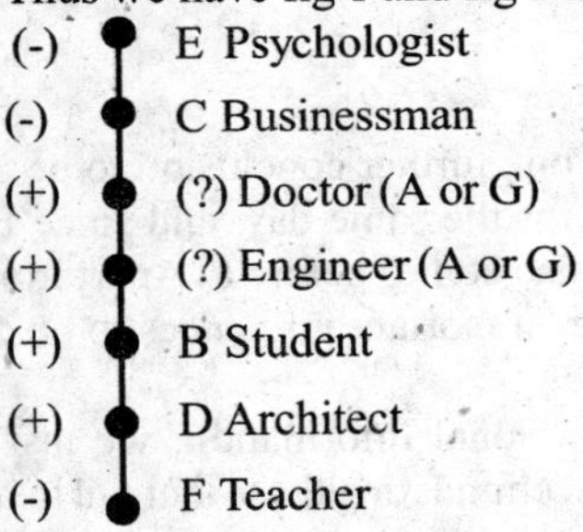

Fig. 1: Intelligence tree

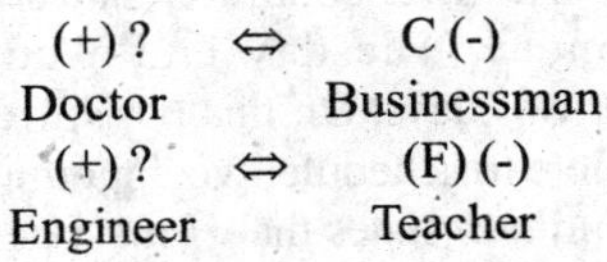

Fig 2: Two couples

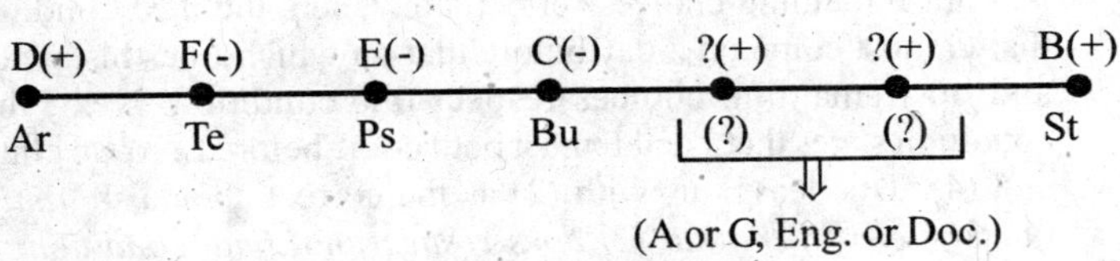

Fig 3: Seating arrangement

Now, read the questions and check your answers:

62. 1 63. 4 64. 4 65. 4

66. 1 67. 4

68. 5; [None of the choices is impossible.]

69. 4 70. 1

71. 4; It is not needed to state that the psychologist is a female. This can be inferred with the help of (v), (x), and (xii). (v) tells us that the psychologist is the most intelligent. (x) tells us that the most intelligent (and hence the psychologist) is sitting third from the left, beginning with D. (xiii) tells us

that the three persons after D are females. Hence, the psychologist must be a female. Hence, statement (xiii) was not needed.

All other statements are needed. For example, (iv) is needed because otherwise we could not have known that C is a businessman. (iii) is needed because we must know whether there is one row or two rows or a circular seating arrangement. (vi) is needed because otherwise we could not find out who the two couples are. (xv) is needed because otherwise we could not have found that E is a female (and hence the psychologist).

Q. (72-78): *Here, more than one individual can be placed in a given position (more than one appointment can be scheduled for certain days).*

Start by summarizing the information:

$$H = Th.$$
$$G < I$$
$$(J + F) < L$$
$$K = F$$

You might notice that there is one further conclusion to be drawn. Since K and F must be scheduled for the same day, and since F must come before L, we can infer that K also comes before L. Apart from that, there do not appear to be any further important inferences to be drawn, so we go to the questions.

72. 2; Since the question supplies no additional information, we just apply each condition to the answer choices, eliminating those that fail to respect one or more conditions. The first condition states that there are two appointments for Monday, Tuesday and Wednesday and one appointment on the other two days. On this basis, we eliminate (3) and (5) because it is not possible to schedule two appointments on Thursday or Friday. The second condition states that H must be seen on Thursday, and our remaining choices reflect that. Then, the next condition states that G must come on a day before that on which I has his appointment, and our remaining choices respect this condition. Next, the fourth condition states that J and F must both come before L, so we eliminate (1) and (4). This leaves us with (2) as the correct choice. *You might want quickly to confirm that (2) does respect that final condition: K and F are both scheduled for the same day.*

73. 3; This question allows us to talk about strategy. One way of proving that a particular partial order is possible is to construct an example of a permissible order using that part. Thus, the following example proves that (1) is a possible order (and, therefore, not the correct answer to this question):

M	TU	W	TH	F
M	*K*	*L*	*H*	*I*
J	*F*	*G*		

The difficulty with this approach is that constructing an example for each choice is time-consuming. Instead of trying to construct an entire order for each choice, a better strategy is to look for an answer choice that is not possible for a specific reason, e.g., because X cannot follow Y or because Z must come before W. Here is how this strategy would apply to this question.

(1) is not likely to be correct because M is not under any specific restriction, thus M could go almost anywhere. As for (2), though K is under a certain restriction, the import of that restriction is that K come earlier in the week — as (2) suggests. So (2) is probably not the correct choice. Now look at (3). L is under the restriction that he be scheduled later than both J and F and (as we learned above) later than K as well. This "pushes" L towards the latter part of the week. This choice, however, has L early in the week. So, this choice merits some study.

The way to determine whether it is possible for L to have an appointment on Tuesday is to assume that he can and see whether that assumption is consistent with the initial conditions. If L is scheduled for Tuesday, then both J and F must be scheduled for Monday. But that can't be, as K would also have to be scheduled for Monday. This demonstrates that (3) cannot be true.

As for (4) and (5), you can construct schedules that show that they are possible.

74. 4; One way of attacking this question would be to try to construct all of the possibilities for Friday. For example, you would reason that K cannot be seen on Friday because K must be seen on the same day as F (and only one appointment is available on Friday). The difficulty with this "direct" approach is that you must do a lot of "grinding". Here, I would use an "indirect" approach. I would *go to the choices*.

Since one of the choices is correct, I know that the test writer has already done the "grinding" to find all of the possibilities for Friday. I just need to find the one choice that contains all the ones that are workable schedules.

I eliminate (1) because I know J cannot be seen on Friday. As for (2), it seems to me that I and M could be seen on Friday, because they are very flexible. (M is under no restriction, and I is under a restriction that forces him to a day later in the week.) As for (3), L is under a restriction, but that restriction pushes L to a later day, so L too seems a possibility for Friday. As for (4), this contains I, L, and M, so it begins to look like a correct choice. As for (5), I know that G cannot be scheduled for Friday because G comes before I.

At this point, I must make a decision. My intuition is that (4) is the correct choice. I can either mark (4) as correct and move on to another item, or I can work out examples that prove that I, L and M can be scheduled for Friday. Which of these I choose to do will depend on how much time I have left. (For the reader, it is not difficult to verify that (4) indeed is a correct choice.)

75. 5; Start by entering the additional information on a diagram:

M TU W TH F
I *H*

G must come before I:

M TU W TH F
G *I* *H*

K and F must be scheduled for the same day, which must now be Wednesday:

M TU W TH F
G *I* *KF* *H*

L must be later in the week than F, however:

M TU W TH F
G *I* *KF* *H* *L*

So, J and M must have appointments on Monday and Tuesday, though not necessarily in that order. Our diagram shows that (5) is necessarily true; that (1) and (2) are possibly, though not necessarily true; and that (3) and (4) are false.

76. 3; Enter the additional information on a diagram:

M TU W TH F
K *H*

This means that F is also scheduled for Wednesday:

M TU W TH F
KF *H*

L must be seen sometime after F:

M TU W TH F
KF *H* *L*

Then, G must be seen before I.

M TU W TH F
G *I* *KF* *H* *L*

M and J will be seen on Monday and Tuesday, though not necessarily in that order:

M TU W TH F
GJ *IM* *KF* *H* *L*
or *GM* *IJ* *KF* *H* *L*

Our diagram confirms that statements I and III are true. Statement II, however, is only possibly true and, therefore, not part of the correct choice.

77. 3; **There are two ways to approach this question.** *You can use a direct approach, in which you work with the initial conditions to track down all of the possibilities.* The problem with the direct approach is that you will always worry that you haven't got all the possibilities. *The alternative approach is to work backwards from the answer choices. Here's how this approach works.* (Note it carefully)

Does (1) contain all and only the possible days? No. I must follow G; therefore, I cannot be seen on Monday, and we eliminate (1). What about (2)? As for Tuesday, L must follow later in the week than J, F and K, so L cannot be seen on Tuesday—and we eliminate (2). At this point, we should eliminate both (4) and (5), for (4) contains "Monday" and (5) contains "Tuesday." The only day on which both I and L could have appointments is Wednesday. For example:

M	TU	W	TH	F
JG	*KF*	*IL*	*H*	*M*

78. 4; Here, one way or another, you are going to have to test each choice. That makes this a difficult question, but that is to be expected since it is the last one. To make the question manageable, you have to think abstractly about the individuals who are most likely to determine a certain order. As for (1), as we have noted, M is not under any particular restriction, so he is not likely to precipitate a fixed order. As for (2) and (3), G and I are under a certain restriction, but this works primarily only between the two of them. (5) is a bit better than either (2) or (3), because it establishes that G and I are scheduled for either Monday and Wednesday or Wednesday and Friday.

(4), however, offers even more promise. It affects not only G and I, but K and therefore F and L as well. Start with (4). If K has his appointment two days before G, then (given that H is already scheduled for Thursday) they must be scheduled either for Monday and Wednesday, or Wednesday and Friday. Here, since G must come before I, K and G must be scheduled for Monday and Wednesday:

M	TU	W	TH	F
K		*G*	*H*	

This means that F is scheduled for Monday and I for Friday:

M	TU	W	TH	F
KF		*G*	*H*	*I*

However, L cannot be scheduled before Wednesday:

M	TU	W	TH	F
KF		*GL*	*H*	*I*

That means that J and M must be scheduled for Tuesday:

M	TU	W	TH	F
KF	*JM*	*GL*	*H*	*I*

Q. 79-83: There are two married couples, three females and three males. It means, there are two married males and females each and one unmarried male and female each. Now, statements III and IV make it obvious that A or E or C or F are not the least talkative. This leaves D or B. But statement V says that the least talkative person is married while statement VIII says that D is unmarried. **It is, therefore, obvious that B is the least talkative**

person. She is a married female. Now, D is a male and hence the other unmarried person must be a female and thus, by virtue of IX, A is a female. Again, A is the most talkative person and by virtue of XI, A is a married female. Now, E is a married male, so he must be married to either A or B (because there are only two married females); but X says that E is not married to A, hence **E must be married to B.**

It is not possible to exactly find the sex, marital status and relative rank (in talkativeness) of F and C because sufficient data is not given. Now check your answers:

79. 2   80. 2   81. 4   82. 5

83. 4; [See the third to sixth sentences of the explanation given above.]

Q. 84-90:

84. 5; Just test each choice by the initial conditions. First, the student must select from at least two different areas, and all of the choices pass muster on this score. Next, he cannot take course in both English and Fine Arts, and we eliminate (1) and (4). Next, if he takes a Science course, he must take a Maths course, and vice versa, so we eliminate (3). Finally, if he takes a Social Studies course, he must take a course in Fine Arts, and we eliminate (2). By the process of elimination, (5) is the correct choice.

Note: Don't misread that last condition. It states only that a course in Social Studies must be accompanied by a course in Fine Arts. It is possible to take a Fine Arts course without taking a Social Studies course.

85. 3; This question is the mirror image of the first. Just test each choice by the initial conditions. All are acceptable on the basis of the first condition (that he take courses in at least two different areas) and the second condition (English and Fine Arts cannot be taken together). (3), however, runs afoul of the third condition, for there we have a Maths course without an accompanying Science course. (You can check the other choices and see that they do respect the final condition.)

86. 3; If the student takes Social Studies then he must take a course in Fine Arts. With a course in Fine Arts, he cannot take a course in English; and with two courses already scheduled (Social Studies and Fine Arts), he cannot take either Maths or Science (for those must go together). His only choice, therefore, is to take another Fine Arts course (as (3) suggests) or another Social Studies course.

87. 4; If the student takes a course in Maths, he must also take a course in Science, so his third course must be Science.

88. 4; If you simply screen choices here by the initial conditions, it seems that all of the pairs taken in isolation are acceptable. This means that the trick for the question must be what happens to the third course. As for (1) and (2), Maths requires Science and vice versa, and a schedule of Maths, Science, and Fine Arts is acceptable. As for (3) and (5), Maths requires

Science, and a schedule of Maths, Science, and English is acceptable. (4), however, is not acceptable. Social Studies requires Fine Arts, and Science requires Maths, but there is not room on the schedule for both Fine Arts and Science.

89. 1; Test each of the choices:
   1) Science, two Maths (OK.)
   2) Three Science (No. Must schedule two different areas.)
   3) Science, two English (No. Maths must accompany Science.)
   4) Two Science, one English (No. Maths must accompany Science.)
   5) Science, Maths, Social Studies (No. Fine Arts must accompany Social Studies.)

90. 1; Test each choice. As for (1), it is not possible to take two English courses. With two English courses, the student cannot take either Maths or Science (each requires the other), nor Fine Arts, nor Social Studies (because Social Studies requires Fine Arts). It is possible to take two courses in the other areas:
   2) Two Fine Arts plus one Social Studies
   3) Two Maths plus one Science
   4) Two Science plus one Maths
   5) Two Social Studies plus one Fine Arts

Q. 91-95: Let us separate the statements regarding investments on one side and the statements regarding height on the other.

Investment:

Statement (ii) implies : $A = 2B, C = 2D, E = F$.

Statement (v) implies : $B > E$, $F > D$.

These can be combined into one as:

$A > B > E = F > D$

also $C = 2D$, $\therefore$ $C > D$

Looking at the above it is obvious that D invested the least. The exact status of C is not known. Now let us consider the aspect of height.

Height:

From the above it is obvious that either A or C is the biggest investor. Hence, at second position either A or C should stand. [Look at statement (iv).]

Also, D invested the least, so he stands fourth.

Again, it is given that A stands third. It means that at second position C stands. Now, B is not the tallest while F is not the shortest. Taking these considerations into account the following are established:

E or F
C
A
D
B or E or F
B or E

Now, since C stands second, he must be the biggest investor. So, the order of investment is:

C > A > B > E = F > D

Now, check your answers;

91. 4 92. 3 93. 3 94. 4 95. 3

Q. 96-100:

Begin by summarising the information:

J < K

F < G (G is higher than F ⇒ F is lower than G.)

F - I - G or G - I - F

H = 6

There is one further conclusion you should probably note. Since G is higher than F, and since I is between F and G, the order for those three notes is: F < I < G.

96. 1; Test each choice to learn which are possible and which are not. As for (1), G cannot be the second note on the scale because G must be higher than both F and I. You can grasp that the other choices are possible if you think in the following way. Imagine that FIG are consecutive notes (they may be, though they don't have to be). If they are, then they could be 1, 2, and 3; or 2, 3 and 4; or even 3, 4, and 5. This will not affect the placement of J and K since in each of those arrangements there will be two spaces left on the scale and K can be higher than J.

97. 4; Enter the additional information on a diagram:

6 H
5
4 J
3
2
1

Since J is lower than K:

6 H
5 K
4 J
3
2
1

Further, G, I, F must be notes 3, 2 and 1:

6 H
5 K
4 J
3 G
2 I
1 F

98. 1; If exactly two notes separate F and I, then they must be placed as follows:

6 H
5 G
4 I
3
2
1 F

J and K are entered as follows:

6 H
5 G
4 I
3 K
2 J
1 F

The diagram shows that (1) is necessarily true, while the other choices are necessarily false.

99. 5; Enter the new information:

6 H
5
4
3
2 J
1

If J is second, then K must be either third, fourth or fifth:

6	H	H	H
5	K		
4		K	
3			K
2	J	J	J
1			

For G to be higher than I, and I higher than F, they must be entered as follows:

6	H	H	H
5	K	G	G
4	G	K	I
3	I	I	K
2	J	J	J
1	F	F	F

There are three possibilities. G and I are 4 and 3, or 5 and 3, or 5 and 4. Thus, I, II and III are all possible.

100. 3; Start by assuming that F is the lowest note on the scale and that I is therefore the third. On that assumption there are two positions for G:

6	H	H
5	G	
4		G
3	I	I
2		
1	F	F

J and K must be placed in the other two positions, with K higher than J:

6	H	H
5	G	K
4	K	G
3	I	I
2	J	J
1	F	F

Now, assume that F is the second note on the scale and that I is, therefore, the fourth:

6	H
5	
4	I
3	
2	F
1	

G must be higher than I:

6	H
5	G
4	I
3	
2	F
1	

K and J must be entered as follows:

6	H
5	G
4	I
3	K
2	F
1	J

Now, try assuming that F is the third note on the scale, which would mean that I is the fifth. That is not possible, however, for G would then have to be higher than the fifth. Thus, we have accounted for all the possibilities:

6	H	H	H
5	G	G	K
4	I	K	G
3	K	I	I
2	F	J	J
1	J	F	F

Only (3) is necessarily true. The other choices are only possibly true.

Exercise 22 C

1. 3; Out of 12 questions, 6 have one alternative each. It means 6 × 2 = 12 questions for these. The remaining 6 have no alternative. Thus, a total of 12 + 6 = 18 questions. Each question has 4 parts. So a total of 18 × 4 = 72 questions.

2. 4; 6 questions have to be answered with 3 parts from each. It means 6 × 3 = 18 questions.

3. 5; The queue will have a minimum number of boys if Sohan is ahead of Ramesh (from the front).

The possible arrangement is:

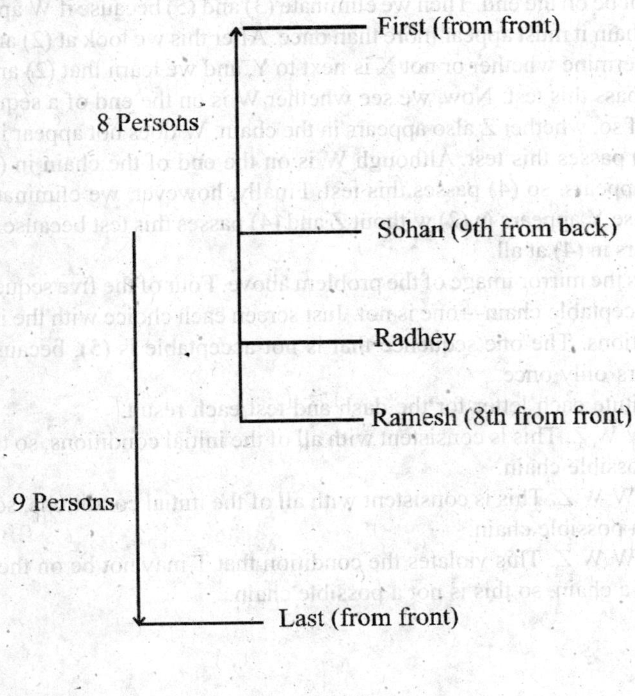

4. 2; Suresh is older than Ramesh, so Suresh can't be the youngest. Mohan is younger than Surender, so Surender can't be the youngest. Murari is younger than Mohan, so Mohan can't be the youngest. Murari is older than Suresh, so Murari can't be the youngest. This leaves only Ramesh, so Ramesh must be the youngest.

5. 2; Let us arrange the facts.
(i) Satyendra is to the left of Khalid ⇒ Sa — Kh
(ii) Madhukar is to the left of Balan and to the right of Khalid
⇒ Kh — Ma — Ba
(iii) Rehman is between Satyendra and Ahmed ⇒ (a) Sa — Re — Ah or
(b) Ah — Re — Sa
(iv) Kutty is on the extreme right.
Now, the configuration "Sa — Re — Ah" in (iii) is rejected because it shows Rehman on the right of Satyendra, whereas Khalid is on the right of Satyendra [from (i)]. Thus, we will combine (i), (ii), (iii)(b), (iv) and the arrangement is:
Ku — Ah — Re —Sa —Kh —Ma — Ba.

Correct answer: Satyendra.

Q. 6-12:

6. 4; Screen each choice using the initial conditions. First, all of the sequences meet the minimum-length requirement. Next, we eliminate (1) because T cannot be on the end. Then we eliminate (3) and (5) because if W appears in a chain it must appear more than once. After this we look at (2) and (4) to determine whether or not X is next to Y, and we learn that (2) and (4) both pass this test. Now, we see whether W is on the end of a sequence and, if so, whether Z also appears in the chain. W does not appear in (2), so (2) passes this test. Although W is on the end of the chain in (4), Z also appears, so (4) passes this test. Finally, however, we eliminate (2) because Y appears in (2) without Z and (4) passes this test because no Y appears in (4) at all.

7. 5; This is the mirror image of the problem above. Four of the five sequences are acceptable chain—one is not. Just screen each choice with the initial conditions. The one sequence that is not acceptable is (5), because W appears only once.

8. 3; Substitute each letter for the dash and test each result.
I. Z W W Z. This is consistent with all of the initial conditions, so this is a possible chain.
II. W W W Z. This is consistent with all of the initial conditions, so this is a possible chain.
III. T W W Z. This violates the condition that T may not be on the end of a chain, so this is not a possible chain.

9. 3; Again, test each of the resulting chain.
   1) W W W Y Z X This sequence is a possible chain.
   2) W W T X Z X This sequence is a possible chain.
   3) W W T Y Z T This is not a chain, because T is on one end.
   4) W W Z Y T X This sequence is a possible chain.
   5) W W T X Z Y This sequence is a possible chain.

10. 5; You first have to determine what is wrong with the sequence and then whether or not you can correct it by reordering the letters.
   1) There are two difficulties here. One, X is next to Y; two, Y appears with Z. Reordering alone will not provide a Z, so this cannot be changed into a chain just by reordering.
   2) Here there are three difficulties: 1) W appears without another W; 2) W is on the end without a Z in the sequence; 3) Y appears without Z. In short, you cannot supply the missing letters just by reordering.
   3) There are three problems with this sequence: 1) you have T on the end; 2) X and Y are together; and 3) Y appears without Z. The third cannot be corrected just by reordering.
   4) The problem here is that you have W on the end without a Z in the sequence. If you try to correct this by reordering the letters, e.g., putting the Ws inside the sequence, you wind up with Ts on the ends.
   5) This sequence is not a chain because W appears on the end without a Z order: X W W X. This sequence is a chain.

11. 1; Again, analyse the defect in each sequence.
   1) Here, we have a W on the end of the sequence without a Z; and we have a Y without a Z. Placing a Z in the space where there is a dash solves both problems, and the resulting sequence —W W Z Y T X— is a chain.
   2) Here, a W appears without another W; W appears on the end without Z and Y appears without Z. So we need both W and Z to turn this sequence into a chain, but we have only one missing link.
   3) Regardless of what is substituted for the dash in this sequence, the resulting sequence will have an X next to a Y, so it cannot be a chain.
   4) Here, we need both a W (for the one W) and a Z (for the Y) to turn this into a chain, but we have only one dash, so this sequence cannot be salvaged.
   5) Regardless of what is substituted for the dash, T will still be on the end of the sequence, so this sequence cannot be a chain.

12. 1;Test of three statements.
   I. Adding a Z to this sequence will correct the problem of having a Y without a Z. Then, reordering can move T from the end into the interior of the sequence and separate the X and Y:

      X Z Y T X

   This is a chain.

II. This sequence has a W without a second W and the addition of a Z will not cure that defect.

III. This sequence also has a W without a second W and the addition of a Z will not cure the defect.

Q. 13-17:

Let us prepare a chart for the given data. A '+' sign would mean 'yes' and a '×' sign would mean a 'No'.

Town	Post Office (?)	School (?)	Accessible by road (?)	Electricity (?)	Population		
					> 5000	2000 to 5000	< 2000
A			+				
B					+		
C							
D	×	+	+				
E		+	×				
Total	2	3	3	2	2	2	1

Now, read the information one by one and fill up a column wherever possible. The chart given above stores the first-hand information of the problem. They are:

(i) There are 2 villages having post offices, 3 having schools, 3 accessibility to road, 2 having electricity, 2 having a population greater than 5000, 2 having population between 2000 and 5000 and 1 having a population less than 2000.

(ii) D does not have a post office, has a school and is accessible by road. E has a school and is not accessible by road. A is accessible by road while the population of B is more than 5000.

Now, let us apply other conditions of the question to the chart. Let us take them one by one.

(iii) Each village with population greater than 5000 has a school. *It means that B must have a school.* Put a '+' mark in the school column before B. Now, since there are only 3 schools and three '+' marks have been obtained in the school column, it means that the other two villages A and C do not have schools. Now, there is one more village having population more than 5000, and this too has a school. Apart from it, there is only one village which has a school. This has a population of less than 2000 but it neither has a post office nor is accessible by road. But we see that D has a school and is accessible by road. *So, the only other village having a school, i.e., E should be the one which has a population of less than 2000, has a school but neither has a post- office nor is accessible by road.* (Put × marks and + marks, wherever applicable, in the row of E.) It then automatically means that D has a population of more than 5000. By now, our table changes to the following configuration:

Town	Post Office (?)	School (?)	Accessible by road (?)	Electricity (?)	Population		
					> 5000	2000 to 5000	< 2000
A		×	+		×	+	×
B		+			+	×	×
C		×			×	+	×
D	×	+	+		+	×	×
E	×	+	×		×	×	+
Total	2	3	3	2	2	2	1

(iv) Now, A and C have population between 2000 and 5000. Of them, only one has a post office and is accessible by road. But A is accessible by road. So, it must also have a post office. C does not have a post office. So, the post office must be in B. Also, C is not accessible by road. [Remember, between A and C, *only one* has a post office and is accessible by road.] So, it is B which must be accessible by road.

Also, there are only two villages, B and D respectively, that have school and accessibility to road. So, the additional facility of electricity must be there in these two villages. This completes our table as shown below:

Town	Post Office (?)	School (?)	Accessible by road (?)	Electricity (?)	Population		
					> 5000	2000 to 5000	< 2000
A	+		+			+	
B	+	+	+	+	+		
C						+	
D		+	+	+	+		
E		+					+
Total	2	3	3	2	2	2	1

Note : The '×' marks have been removed.

Now, check your answer:

13. 2 14. 3 15. 3 16. 1 17. 4

Q. 18-24 :

This is a "network" set. Begin by drawing the diagram:

All normal requests are received by either M or N, and all priority requests are received by M or Q:

NORMAL M
N

PRIORITY M
Q

All requests processed by M are then sent to T:

NORMAL M → T
N

PRIORITY M → T
Q

All requests processed by N are sent to S:

NORMAL M → T
N → S

PRIORITY M → T
Q

Normal requests processed by T are then sent to P; priority requests processed by T are then sent to Q:

NORMAL M → T → P
N → S

PRIORITY M → T
Q ↙ (from T)

Normal requests processed by S are then sent either to T or P:

NORMAL M → T → P
↑ ↗ (from S)
N → S

PRIORITY M → T
Q ↙ (from T)

Normal requests processed by P are then sent to Q and priority requests processed by P are then sent to R:

NORMAL M → T → P → Q
↑ ↗ (from S)
N → S

PRIORITY M → T R
Q ↙ (from T) ↑
P

All requests processed by Q are then sent to either P or R:

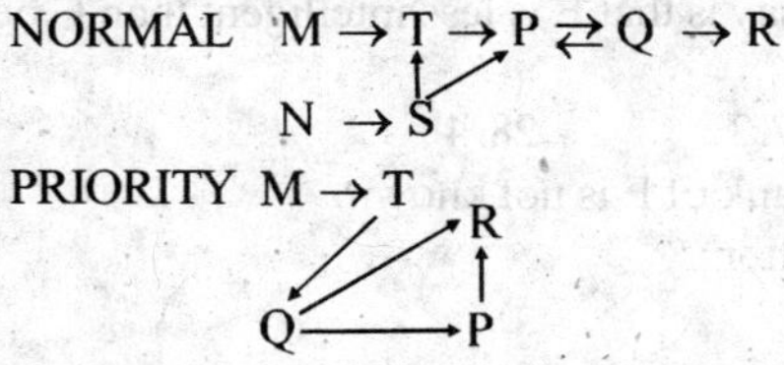

18. 4; The diagram shows that S cannot send a request to Q, though he can send one to P, who in turn can send one to Q.

19. 4; The diagram shows that Q can forward a request to P, who in turn can forward it to R.

20. 3; A normal request received by M must be processed by T, P and Q before it goes to R. A priority request received by M must go to both T and Q but need not go to P before it is passed to R. Q can forward a priority request directly to R.

21. 4; The two shortest routes to R for normal requests are: M T P Q R and N S P Q R. In each case, a minimum of four stations must handle the request before it gets to R.

22. 4; A normal request can be shuffled back and forth between P and Q any number of times. T, however, is not within such a loop.

23. 4; Everything R receives must at some point have passed through station Q, so II is not part of the correct answer. There are certain requests, however, that P does not handle, namely those priority requests forwarded by Q directly to R. Also, there are certain requests that M does not handle, namely those normal requests that begin with N and those priority requests that begin with Q.

24. 4; A normal request that enters at N and passes to S, at which point it could pass to T, then to P, and then to Q (or five stations) before reaching R.

Q. 25-29:

From (iv): B > D > F (intelligence)
From (v): D > A (intelligence), A > D (weight)
From (vi): F > B > C (weight)
From (vii): F > A (intelligence), D > F (weight)
These can be combined as:
B > D > F > A (intelligence)
A > D > F > B > C (weight)
Now, A is not the heaviest. But A is heavier than all except F. So, E must be the heaviest. Hence, we have:
E > A > D > F > B > C (weight)
Now, the lightest of the group is the most intelligent. So, C must be the most intelligent. So we have:
C > B > D > F > A (intelligence).

Note: The exact position of E in terms of intelligence cannot be found using the given data. All that we can say is that E is less intelligent than C because C is the most intelligent.

25. 2 26. 3 27. 3 28. 4

29. 3; Rank of D is not known if rank of E is not known.

Q. 30-36: Summarise the information:

P > S

R > T and R > V

O = T + 2

P = 62 or 63

30. 4; Using the first condition (P is older than S), we eliminate (5). Using the second condition (R is older than both T and V), we eliminate (1). Using the third condition (O is two years older than T), we eliminate (2) and (3). We are left with (4), which must be the one correct listing.

31. 1; Here, you will probably want to use a diagram:

60	61	62	63	64	65
		P			

Since P was born in 1962, there are only two possible places on the diagram for O and T:

60	61	62	63	64	65
	O	P	T		
		P	O		T

As for the first possibility, R (who is older than T) was born in 1960, with V and S born in 1964 and 1965, though not necessarily respectively:

60	61	62	63	64	65
R	O	P	T	S/V	S/V

As for the second possibility, S (who is younger than P) was born in 1964, and R and V were born in 1960 and 1961, respectively:

60	61	62	63	64	65
R	V	P	O	S	T

Under either scenario, Ram was born in 1960.

32. 1; Use a diagram to keep track of the logic:

60	61	62	63	64	65
O					

Then T was born in 1962 and P in 1963:

60	61	62	63	64	65
O		T	P		

This means that R, who is older than T and V, was born in 1961:

60	61	62	63	64	65
O	R	T	P		

S and V were born in 1964 and 1965, though not necessarily respectively. So, only (1) is necessarily true.

33. 3; Again, you will need a diagram:

60 61 62 63 64 65
O

This means that P was born in 1963 and T in 1964:

60 61 62 63 64 65
O P T

Since P is older than S:

60 61 62 63 64 65
O P T S

Also, since R is older than V:

60 61 62 63 64 65
R V O P T S

Only (3) is true.

34. 5; If P is younger than T then (since R and O are both older than T) R, O and T are all older than P. So P must have been born in 1963. O, T and R are related as follows:

60 61 62 63 64 65
O R T P

It is not possible to determine, however, in which order V and S were born. This is sufficient, however, to answer the questions. (1) through (4) are necessarily true, while (5) is only possibly true.

35. 3; If V is older than T, then R, V and O are all older than T, which means that T could not have been born before 1963. T could only have been born in 1964 or 1965:

60 61 62 63 64 65
O T
O T

We add P and S to the diagram:

60 61 62 63 64 65
O P T S
P O S T

Then since R is older than V:

60 61 62 63 64 65
R V O P T S
R V P O S T

Thus, statements I and II are necessarily true, while III is only possibly true.

36. 1; If P is older than O then P is also older than T:

60 61 62 63 64 65
P O T

Since P is older than S, and since R is older than V:

60 61 62 63 64 65
R V P O S T

So, if P is older than O, there is only one possible order in which the group could have been born.

Q. 37-43: Begin by summarising the information: $N < (J + O)$
$J < M$
$K = 3$

There is one further conclusion that can be drawn. Since N is to be played before J and J before M, N must be played before M.

37. 4; Using the first condition that N be played before both J and O, we eliminate (2) and (3). Using the second condition, that J come before M, we eliminate (1). Finally, using the third condition that K be played third, we eliminate (5). So, the one choice that fits all of the conditions is (4).

38. 2; At the outset, we deduced one further conclusion: that N must come before M. That the other choices are not logically necessary can be demonstrated by the following possible order:

1 2 3 4 5 6
N L K O J M

39. 5; As for (1), J cannot be played last because J is played before M. As for (2), K must be played third, not first. As for (3), M cannot be played second, because (as we learned above) both J and N must be played before M. As for (4), it is K that must be played third<197>not N. (5), however, is a possibility, as shown by the diagram:

1 2 3 4 5 6
N J K L M O

40. 4; Enter the additional information in a diagram:

1 2 3 4 5 6
L K

N must be played before J and O and also M. And this means that N must be played second:

1 2 3 4 5 6
L N K

Then the order of the other three pieces is not fixed, but these further conclusions are sufficient to answer the question asked.

41. 2; With K as the third piece, there is only one place to accommodate a series of three pieces:

1 2 3 4 5 6
K L M O

Then, since N comes before J, the order must be:

1 2 3 4 5 6
N J K L M O

So, J must be played second.

42. 3; Enter the additional information on a diagram:

1	2	3	4	5	6
		K			L

Since N must be played before J, O, and M, N must be first:

1	2	3	4	5	6
N		K			L

Now, given that J must precede M, there are only three possibilities:

1	2	3	4	5	6
N	J	K	M	O	L
N	J	K	O	M	L
N	O	K	J	M	L

So, the first and second pieces could be N and J, or N and O.

43. 4; N must be played before three other pieces (J, O and M), so (given that K is played third) N cannot be played later than second. So, N cannot be played after K. It is possible, however, to play the others immediately after K:

	1	2	3	4	5	6
	N	L	K	J	M	O
or	N	J	K	L	M	O
or	N	J	K	M	L	O
or	N		K	O	M	L

Q. 44-49:

Here is another selection set. Begin by summarising the information:

Q = Entertainment

L = M

J ≠ K

N ≠ R

O = K or Q or both

44. 5; Using the first condition, that Q serves on the Entertainment Committee, we eliminate (3). Using the second condition, that L and M must serve together, we eliminate (2). Using the third condition, that J and K cannot serve together on a committee, we eliminate (1). Finally, using that last condition, that O must serve with either K or Q (or both), we eliminate (4). By the process of elimination, therefore, the only acceptable committee listed is (5).

45. 2; You may want to diagram this:

FS	E	G
K	*QR*	

Next, try placing L and M together. If you put L and M on the Food Services Committee then O must be on the Entertainment Committee (to respect the last condition), which places both N and R on the Games Committee—in violation of the fourth condition. Since L and M cannot go to the Entertainment Committee, they must go to the Games Committee:

FS E G
K QR LM

Now, it doesn't seem possible to assign the other members to a specific committee. O could go either with K or with Q, and J and K and N and R could go to any committee—so long as we separate them. Is this enough to answer the question, however? Yes. Our diagram confirms that (2) is necessarily true.

46. 3; If L is on a committee then M is also on that committee. This means that two members of the committee have already been assigned. O cannot be assigned to this committee because O must be assigned to one with either K or Q or both.

47. 2; This one you may want to diagram:

E FS G
Q KP

L and M must be appointed either to the Entertainment Committee or to the Food Services Committee. Take the first alternative:

E FS G
QLM KP

So, O must be assigned to the Games Committee:

E FS G
QLM KPO

But now we cannot separate N and R. So we try the second alternative:

E FS G
Q LM KPO

N and R cannot serve on the same committee:

E FS G
Q N/R LM N/R KPO

So, J must be assigned to the Entertainment Committee:

E FS G
QJ N/R LM N/R KPO

48. 3; Again, we will use a diagram:

E FS G
QL O

Of course, M must serve with L, which means that K must serve with O:

E FS G
QLM OK

This means J must serve on the Games Committee; N and R must be appointed one to the Food services Committee and one to the Games Committee; and P is appointed to the Games Committee:

E FS G
QLM OK JP
N/R N/R

So, statements I and II are necessarily true, while III is only possibly true.

49. 1; Enter the information on a diagram:

E	FS	G
QL	*J*	

So, M must also be appointed to Entertainment (filling up that committee), and K must be appointed to Games (J and K cannot be together):

E	FS	G
QLM	*J*	*K*

So, O must be appointed to Games (to be with K), and N and R must be appointed one to Games and the other to Food Services, with P being appointed to Food Services:

E	FS	G
QLM	*JP*	*KO*
	N/R	*N/R*

So, only statement I is necessarily true.

Q. 50-54: E is the unmarried Engineer. C is the daughter-in-law of A, who is the grandmother of F, means C is the mother of F. But F is the son of B. So, B is C's husband. But C, the Lawyer, is married to the Doctor, Thus, C, the Lawyer, is the wife of B, the Doctor. F, the Accountant, will be the son of B and C. E is the unmarried Engineer. So, the other married couple can be that of grandmother of F, i.e. A, and D. But D, the Salesman, is married to the Lady Teacher. So, D, the salesman, is the grandfather of F, father of B and husband of A, the Lady Teacher.

50. 4; Clearly, from the given data the relation between E and F cannot be determined.

51. 2; Clearly, B is the doctor.

52. 2; A is the Lady Teacher.

53. 5; The two couples are C and B, and D and A, none of which is among the choices.

54. 1; D is the grandfather of F.

Q. 55-59: Q, the Doctor, is the father of T. S, the Housewife, is the grandmother of T and hence the mother of Q. Since there are only two married couples — one being that of Q —, the grandfather of R, i.e. U, must be married to S. Thus, R and T will be both children of Q and these must be the students. So, P, who remains, shall be the wife of Q and she alone can be the nurse. Thus, U must be the Contractor.

55. 3; The husband of P will be Q.

56. 1; Clearly, R and T are children of the same parents. So, R will be the sister of T.

57. 2; P is the nurse.

58. 2; The two married couples are Q, P and U, S.

59. 1; Clearly, for certain the males are Q, the father, and U, the grandfather.

Q. 60-64: (See study material Ex 2.)

Q. 65-69: Let us denote the friends by the first letter of each name, namely S, K, M, A and R. Then,

$R < S < K < M$ and $S < A < K$; $\therefore$ $R < S < A < K < M$

65. 1; Rakesh is the shortest.
66. 4; Ashish is in the middle.
67. 2; In the order of increasing heights, i.e. shortest to tallest, Shailendra is the second.
68. 2; Keshav is the second tallest.
69. 2; Keshav is taller than Ashish but shorter than Madhav.

Q. 70-73:

70. 1; P is the daughter of K and K is the brother of G. So, P is the niece of G.
71. 3; P is the daughter of K and K is the brother of X. So, P is the niece of X. Z is the son of X. Thus, Z is the cousin of P.
72. 4; The daughter of K is married to N. So, N is the son-in-law of K.
73. 3; Z is the son of X and G is the sister of X. So, G is the aunt of Z.

Q. 74-77: Refer to study material. See Ex 6.

Q. 78-82:

78. 1; Clearly, she visits M before N and N before Q. So, she must visit M before Q.
79. 1; Of the six companies, if S is the first, P is the third and the orders M N Q and M R are followed, then M must be visited second.
80. 5; Since P is at the third place and orders M, N, Q and M, R are to be followed, so immediately after P she can visit any company except M, which may occupy first or second place, because Q, R and N cannot precede it.
81. 4; If Q is visited just before R and immediately after S, the order followed will be M N S Q R. Since P must be in the 3rd place, so we have M N P S Q R, i.e. Q will be visited fifth.
82. 1; According to the information, P must be in the third place and the order M N Q must not be violated. This is followed only in the arrangement M S P N R Q.

Q. 83-87: F is a Psychologist. B is the mother of F & E means E is the brother or sister of F. There are only two married couples in the family. Since D is married to A, so C, the Jeweller who is married to a Lawyer, will be married to B. Again, the Manager D is married to A, means A is the Doctor and grandfather of F & E. Also, no one else is an Engineer. So, E must be an Engineer.

83. 5; Clearly, E is an Engineer. So, the answer is 'None of these'.
84. 4; Clearly, A is the grandfather of F, and E is the brother or sister of F. So, A is the grandfather of E.
85. 5; Since nothing is mentioned about E and F, so the number of males cannot be determined.
86. 1; Clearly, A, who is the grandfather of F, is the Doctor.
87. 3; Clearly D, the Manager, is married to A. So, AD is one of the couples.

Q. 88-92: We prepare a table from the given data as under:

	Maths	Geography	History	Political Science	Biology
A	✓	×	✓	✓	×
B	✓	✓	×	✓	×
C	✓	✓	✓	×	×
D	×	✓	×	✓	✓
E	×	×	✓	✓	✓

88. 2; Clearly, from the table D is intelligent in Political Sc., Geography and Biology.
89. 2; B is intelligent in Mathematics, Political Sc. and Geography.
90. 3; A is intelligent in Mathematics and History but not in Geography.
91. 4; C is intelligent in Mathematics, History and Geography.
92. 5; E is intelligent in Political Sc., History and Biology.

Q. 93-97: Try yourself. See Ex 14, study material.

Q. 98-102:

The given information can be analysed as follows.
Let 'O' denote optional and 'C' denote compulsory.

	A	B	C	D	E	F
History	C	C	C	O	–	–
Physics	–	–	–	–	C	O
Maths	–	–	O	–	O	C
English	O	–	–	C	–	–
Chemistry	–	O	–	–	–	–

One compulsory subject of F is Mathematics. F has Physics as one of the subjects. So, Physics is the compulsory subject of E. A and D have the same subjects, History and English. D has History as optional subject and so English is the compulsory subject of D. The subjects of A and D are reverse in regard of being optional and compulsory.
So, A has History as compulsory subject and English as optional.
Chemistry is the optional subject of only one teacher. So it is the optional of B, who is the only one that remains. We know that History is the compulsory subject of three teachers. So, it is compulsory for A, B and C.
Now, read the questions and verify your answers;

98. 1
99. 4; D is the teacher whose compulsory subject is English. Hence D is a female.

100. 5 101. 3 102. 4

Q. 103-107:

Clearly, D must be staged on Friday. A must be staged before E, i.e., the order A E must be followed. But E cannot be staged on the last day. Also, B must be staged immediately after F, i.e., the order F B must be followed. But B cannot precede D. So, F and B can be staged on Monday and Tuesday, and A and E on Wednesday and Thursday. C, which cannot be staged on Tuesday, shall be staged on Saturday. Thus, the order followed will be:

Monday	Tuesday	Wednesday	Thursday	Friday	Saturday
F	B	A	E	D	C

103. 1; Clearly, A immediately follows B.
104. 2; F will be played on Monday.
105. 4; Play D is between E and C.
106. 5; Clearly, the order of staging is as given above and none from amongst the choices.
107. 3; C cannot be staged on Friday as well because D has to be staged on that day.

Q. 108-110: Clearly, in the circle the arrangement is as shown.

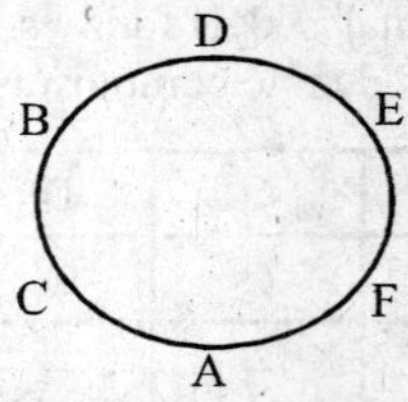

108. 3; Clearly, D is to the left of B.
109. 1; Clearly, A is to the right of C.
110. 5; Since all the statements are necessary to determine the arrangement, none of them is superfluous.

Q. 111-115: Try yourself.

Q. 116-121: Let C's weight be x. Then D's weight is 2x, E's weight is 4x, B's weight is 4.5x and A's weight is 9x.
So, the order of weights can be A > B > E > D > C.

116. 3; C is the lightest in weight.
117. 1; E is lighter in weight than A and B.
118. 5; Clearly, statement (5) is not required to determine the order of weights.
119. 2; E is heavier than D and C.
120. 1; Clearly, A is the heaviest in weight.
121. 1; Clearly, the descending order of weights is A, B, E, D, C.

Q. 122-126: Let the fair person sit on the extreme right because it is given that a tall person is on his left. This means that the order Tall, Fair is followed. Also, then the intelligent person will be on the extreme left. A fat person is on the right of a weak person, i.e. the order Weak, Fat is followed. The weak person in sitting between the intelligent and the fat persons means the order Intelligent, Weak, Fat is followed. Combining the informations, we have Intelligent, Weak, Fat, Tall, Fair.

122. 2; The tall person is second from the right.

123. 1; The person on the left of the weak person is intelligent.

124. 5; The fat person is sitting at the centre.

125. 3; The fat person is on the left of the tall person.

126. 2; If positions are exchanged as given, the new arrangement will be Intelligent, Tall, Fair, Weak, Fat.
So, the fair person will be on the left of the weak person.

Q. 127-131: The course starts with Psychology. So, Psychology will be on the 22nd. 23rd, being a Sunday, will be a holiday. Science will be before Engineering and Economics will have a one-day gap with Engineering, means the order followed can be Eco, Sc. and Engg. Mechanics will be the last, i.e., on the 29th. So, Sociology will fill the gap on the 28th. Thus, we have

22nd	23rd	24th	25th	26th	27th	28th	29th
Psychology	Sunday	Philosophy	Economics	Science	Engineering	Sociology	Mechanics

127. 1; The course will start with Psychology.

128. 3; Economics will be on Tuesday the 25th.

129. 5; Sociology precedes Mechanics.

130. 1; There is only one day gap between Philosophy and Science.

131. 4; Economics is followed by Science.

Q. 132-135:

132. 1; Rashmi is the daughter of Amit, who is the eldest son of the Sharmas and is married to Veena, the youngest daughter of the Roys. So, the surname of Rashmi will be Sharma.

133. 1; Sameer is the son of Ashish, who is the son of Prashant Arora. So, Sameer will be the grandson of Monika's father.

134. 3; Sameer is the son of Ashish, who is the son of Prashant Arora. So, the surname of Sameer is Arora.

135. 2; Ashish is married to Monika, who is the daughter of Mrs Roy. So, Mrs @SP30 = Roy will be the mother-in-law of Ashish.

Q. 136-137: The given information can be summarised as follows:

	Kailash	Govind	Harinder	Rajesh	Jitendra
Intelligent	✓	✓	✓	–	–
Hardworking	✓	–	–	✓	✓
Honest	–	–	✓	✓	✓
Ambitious	✓	✓	–	–	✓

136. 3; Harinder is neither hardworking nor ambitious.

137. 2; Govind is neither hardworking nor honest.

138. 3; Cricket ball is lighter than Hockey ball. So, the order C, H will be followed. Volleyball is lighter than Football. So, the order V, F will follow. Hockey ball is lighter than Football but heavier than Tennis ball. So, the order T, H, F is followed.
Thus, from the three arrangements, it follows that Football is the heaviest.

139. 4; S is sitting next to P. So, the order S, P or P, S is followed. K is sitting next to R. So, the order R, K is followed because R is on the extreme left. T is not next to P or K. So, the arrangement will be R, K, P, S, T. Clearly, P and T are sitting adjacent to S.

Q. 140-144: Clearly, there is one belonging to the 20th century. So, A, who belongs to the 20th century, contributes to Marathi poetry. Also, D is a Hindi poet and novelist who belongs to the 19th century.
There are only two Marathis. So, C, who is a Marathi, will contribute to poetry, novel and drama.
Clearly, there are only four poets. So, F, who is a poet, will be the Bengali belonging to the 17th century. There is now no other Bengali, no other Marathi and no other poet. B, who wrote drama only, cannot be Tamil and does not belong to the 19th century. So, B belongs to the 17th century and is a Hindi dramatist. Thus, E, belonging to the 19th century, is a Tamil novelist and dramatist. C belongs to the 19th century.

140. 2; B contributes to Hindi.
141. 3; E is the Tamil writer.
142. 1; A contributes to poetry alone.
143. 4; F is the Bengali writer.
144. 4; C contributes to all the three— poetry, novel and drama.

Q. 145-149: The information can be summarised as follows:
A cannot be an advocate and prefers tea.
C cannot be an advocate and prefers tea.
An advocate prefers tea.
B cannot be a journalist and prefers coffee.
The journalist prefers coffee.
A cannot be an industrialist but prefers tea.
So, the industrialist prefers coffee.
D, who cannot be an industrialist, prefers coffee.
Since the journalist prefers coffee, so D, who cannot be an industrialist and prefers coffee, is the journalist.
Also, the industrialist prefers coffee. So, B, who cannot be a journalist, will be the industrialist. Now, A and C will be the horticulturist or the physicist but C cannot be the horticulturist. So, A will be the horticulturist and C will be the physicist. Thus, the remaining person, E, will be the advocate.

145. 1; A is the horticulturist.
146. 3; B is the industrialist.
147. 5; Clearly, A and C are the persons who like tea but are not advocates.
148. 4; C is the physicist.
149. 5; Since all the statements are required to analyse the given data, none of them is superfluous.

(150-154):

Employee	Department	Sport
A	Pers	TT
B	Admin	Football
C	Admin	Hockey
D	Admin	Basketball
E	Mktg	Cricket
F	Pers	Volleyball
G	Mktg	LT
H	Mktg	Badminton

150. 3 151. 2 152. 5 153. 1 154. 4

155. 5; No conditions applies and we get # ©752.
156. 3; No condition applies.
157. 4; Condition (ii) applies.
158. 2; Condition (iii) applies.
159. 1; Condition (i) applies.

(160-164):

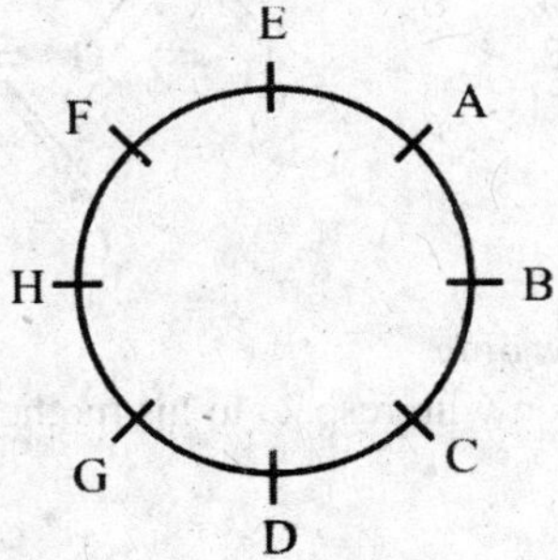

160. 4 161. 3 162. 2 163. 5 164. 1

(165-169):

X (Delhi)	Y (Chandigarh)	Z (Agra)
D (-) G (+) E	C F (-) B (+)	A (-) H (+)

165. 4 166. 5 167. 5 168. 2 169. 1

(170-176):

(+) male, (–) female

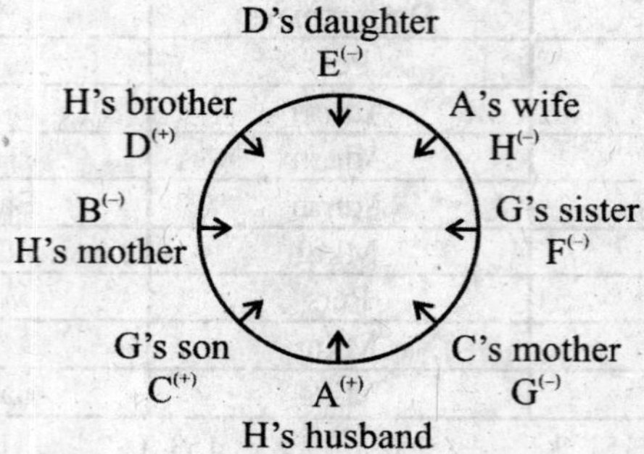

Family Trees

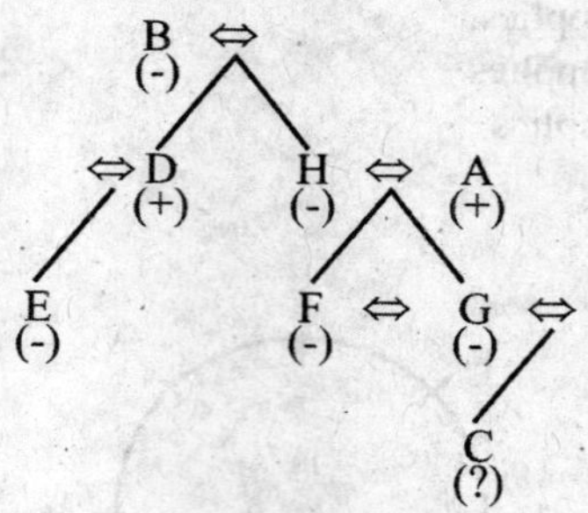

170. 4; B is mother-in-law of A.
Hence, A's position with respect to his mother-in-law is second to the right.

171. 3

172. 1; C is grandchild of A.
Thus, A's position with respect to his grand child is immediate right.

173. 3; D is uncle of G.

174. 2; Except C, all are females.

175. 5

176. 1

(177-179):

From given information,

_ > _ > _ > _ C > A, E ...(i)

B > D > _ > _ > _ > _ ...(ii)

Since E did not score the least, we get

B > D > F > C > E > A

(81) (62)

177. 1; C is most likely to score 70 marks as he is between F, who scored 81 marks and E, who scored 62 marks.

178. 5

179. 3; B's score is maximum according to above sequence.
F has scored 81 marks. Then B's score = 81 + 13 = 94 marks and D is between B and F.
D is most likely to score 89 marks.

(180-187):

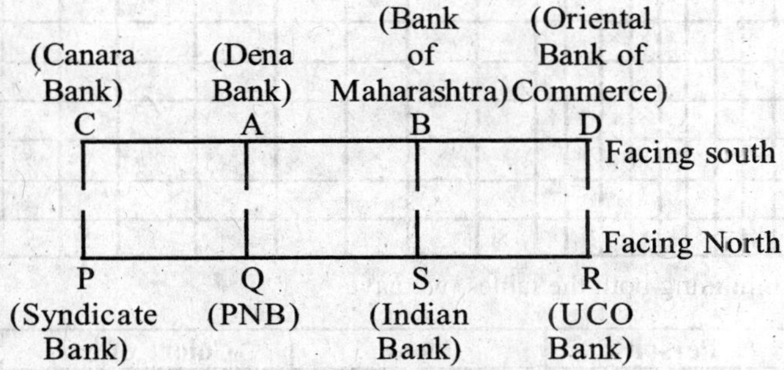

180. 2 181. 5 182. 4 183. 1 184. 4

185. 4; Except Q, all are at the end of a row.

186. 3

187. 5

(188-193):

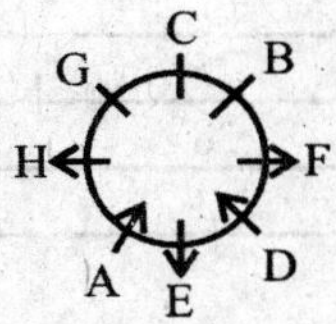

188. 4 189. 3 190. 3

191. 2;

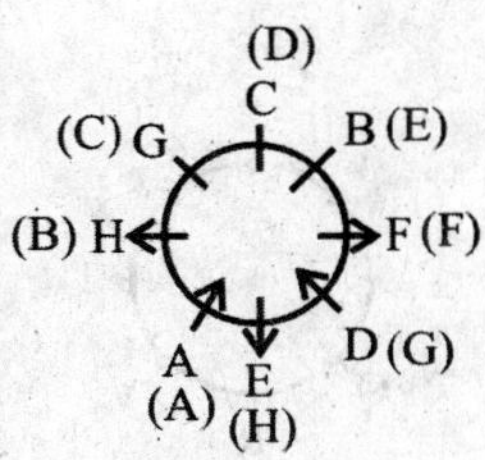

192. 1 193. 2

(194-202): You are suggested to put the information in the following table. Put a (√) if you get positive information, and a cross (×) if you get negative information.

Person	(Table 1) Floor									(Table 2) Colour of car								
	1	2	3	4	5	6	7	8	9	Blue	Black	Grey	White	Yellow	Green	Red	Pink	Orange
A	×	×	×	×	×	√	×	×	×	×	×	×	×	√	×	×	×	×
B	×	×	×	×	×	×	×	×	√	√	×	×	×	×	×	×	×	×
C	√	×	×	×	×	×	×	×	×	×	×	√	×	×	×	×	×	×
D	×	×	×	√	×	×	×	×	×	×	×	×	×	×	×	×	×	√
E	×	√	×	×	×	×	×	×	×	×	×	×	√	×	×	×	×	×
F	×	×	×	×	×	×	√	×	×	×	×	×	×	×	√	×	×	×
G	×	×	×	×	√	×	×	×	×	×	×	×	×	×	×	√	×	×
H	×	×	×	×	×	×	×	√	×	×	√	×	×	×	×	×	×	×
J	×	×	√	×	×	×	×	×	×	×	×	×	×	×	×	×	√	×

Combining both the tables, we have

Person	Floor	Colour of car
A	6	Yellow
B	9	Blue
C	1	Grey
D	4	Orange
E	2	White
F	7	Green
G	5	Red
H	8	Black
J	3	Pink

194. 4
195. 5; B
196. 3 197. 4 198. 1 199. 4 200. 3
201. 1 202. 4

(203-207):

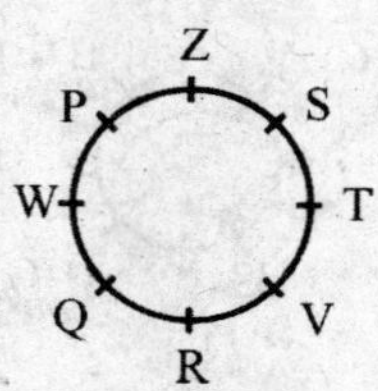

203. 5 204. 2 205. 4 206. 3 207. 1

(208-212):

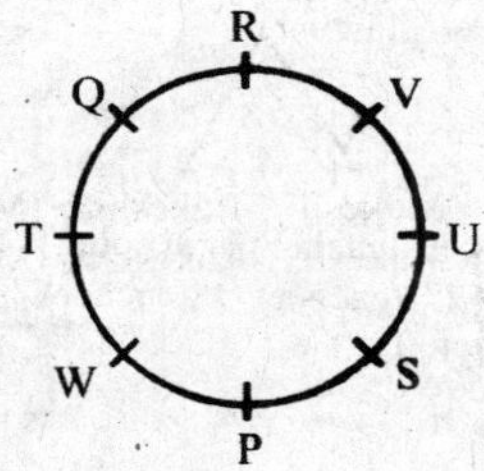

208. 5 209. 1 210. 3 211. 1 212. 2

(213-217):

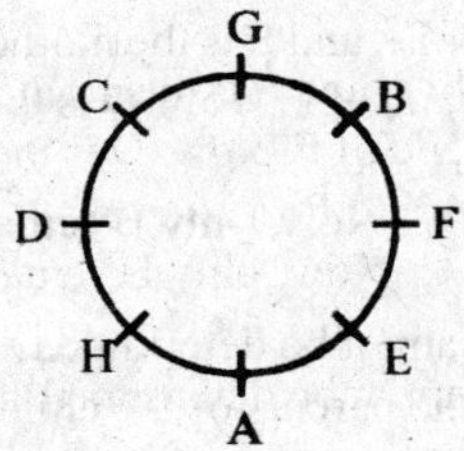

213. 2 214. 1

215. 5; A

216. 4 217. 3

(218-222):

Date	Day	Play
25	Monday	A
26	Tuesday	Z
27	Wednesday	B
28	Thursday	No play
29	Friday	M
30	Saturday	Q
31	Sunday	X

218. 5; A

219. 1 220. 2 221. 4 222. 3

(223-227):

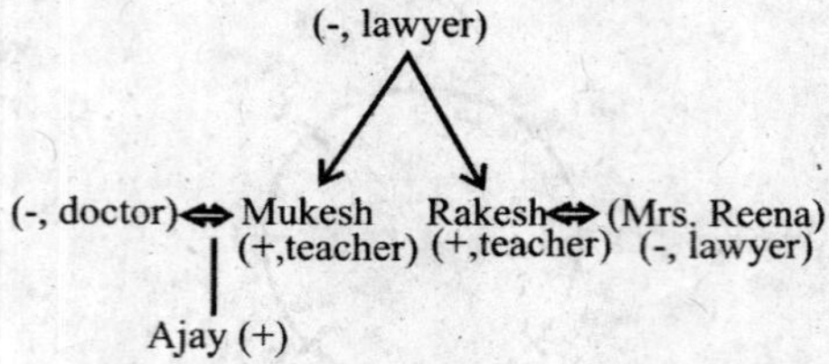

223. 1
224. 3
225. 2; Rakesh, Mukesh and Ajay
226. 4; The family doesn't have Ajay's grandfather.
227. 4

(228-232): E is the daughter of A and F is the mother of E. So, A is the father of E and hcnce the husband of F. Now. D is the daughter of F So, D and E are the daughters of A and P.

Also, A is the son of C. Now, only B remains. Thus. B and C are the parents of A.

228. 4; The sex of B and C cannot be determined.
229. 5; Clearly, A and F are the parents of the children D and E.
230. 2; Clearly, B and C are the parents of the couple.
231. 3; Clearly, the females in the family are : either B or C, F, D and E.
232. 4; Clearly, D and E are sisters.
233. 3; C is the wife of B and D is mother of B. So, C is the grandmother of A. So, C is the mother of A.
234. 4; Clearly, the sex of A cannot be determined.
235. 5; The sex of A is not Known. So. neither (a) nor (b) is definitely true Clearly. D in the grandmother of A and F.
236. 2; C is wife of B. So. one couple is BC. Now. D is grandmother of A B is the son of D and his wife C is the mother of F So, D is also the grandmother of F But F is the granddaughter of E. So, E is the grandfather of F and the husband of D. Thus, DE is another couple.

(237- 241): D is father of A and grandfather of P. So. A is father of F. Thus. D and A are the two fathers. C is the sister of F. So. C is the daughter of A. Since there is only one mother, it is evident that E is the wife of A and hence the mother of C and F. So, B is brother of A. There are three brothers. So, F is the brother of C.

237. 4; Clearly, E is the mother.
238. 3; Clearly, A is E's husband.
239. 4; A, the father, is male B. the brother, is male. C. the sister, is female. D, the grand- father, is male. E. the mother, is female. F, the brother, is male So, there are four males.

240. 3; Clearly, F is the son of A.
241. 1; Clearly. B and A are brothers. F is the brother of C. So, three brothers are A, B, F.
242. 2; The mother of class B female belongs to class B. So. her father was born in class A. Thus, her fathers mother belonged to class A, and fathers father was born in class B. So, the Grandfather belongs to class B and Grandmother belongs to class A
243. 3; The boy born in class B will marry a girl of class A. So. the daughter will belong to class A. Thus, (1) is false.
Since the boy's daughter will belong to class A, she would marry a boy of class B and so the son-in-law would be from class B So, (2) is false.
The boy, born in class B. wil l have mother born in class B and father born in class A. So, his uncle (i.e. mothers brother or father's brother) can be from class A or B. So, (3) is true.
244. 1; A girl of class B wil l have mother born in class B and so the mother's brother will also belong to class B. Since people of any class cannot marry the members of their own class, so the condition in (1) is not permissible.

(245-249):

	English	Hindi	Mathematics	Geography	History	French
A	√	√	√			
B	√	√		√	√	√
C	√			√		
D		√	√			
E					√	√

245. 2; B teaches maximum number of subjects i.e. 5.
246. 5; Only B teaches both Hindi and Geography.
247. 3; Three teachers were teaching Hindi - A , B and D.
248. 3; D. B and A were teaching Hindi.
249. 5; None of the teachers was teaching less than two subjects.

(250-254):

	Dramatics	Computer Sc.	Physics	History	Mathematics
Madhu	√	√	√		
Shobha	√	√		√	
Anjali		√	√	√	√
Poonam	√		√	√	
Nisha			√	√	√

250. 3; Shobha is good in Computer Science. History and Dramatics.
251. 3; Madhu is good in Physics. Dramatics and Computer Science.
252. 1; Poonam is good in Physics. History and Dramatics.
253. 4; Anjali is good in History, Physics, Computer Science and Mathematics.
254. 3; Nisha is good in Physics, History and Mathematics but not in Computer Science.

(255-259):

(I) T stays as PG; S stays in hostel.
U stays in hostel and Q stays at home.
Now, R does not stay as PG. So, P stays as PG. Clearly. R stays at home.

(II) S studies Physics; R studies Philosophy and T studies Mathematics.
Now. P who stays as PG does not study Statistics or History. So, P studies English

	Place of stay	Subject
P	PG	English
Q	Home	Statistics or History
R	Home	Philosophy
S	Hostel	Physics
T	PG	Mathematics
U	Hostel	Statistics or History

255. 5; P studies English.
256. 1; Clearly the incorrect combination is English–Hostel
257. 2; S stays in hostel and R stays at home.
258. 3; Q studies History or Statistics.
259. 2; Q and R stay at home.

(260-264): Clearly in a circle the arrangement is as shown

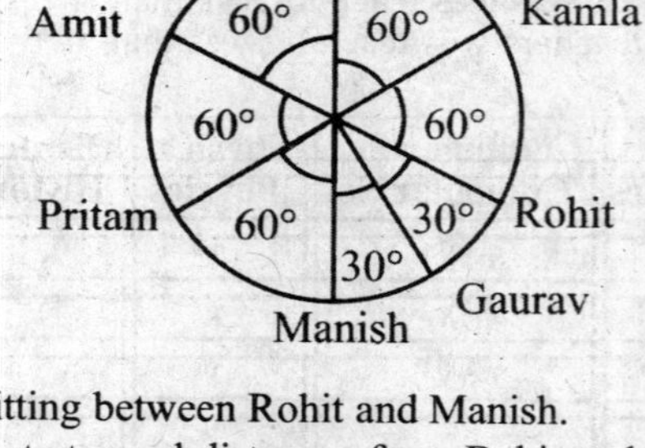

260. 3; Gaurav is sitting between Rohit and Manish.
261. 4; Gaurav is not at equal distances from Bohit and Pritazn or Amit and Kamla or Manish and Pritam.

262. 4; Gaurav is three places left or four places right of Priya.
263. 4; The angle between Gaurav and Manish in clockwise direction is 30°.
264. 4; Clearly, all the statements follow from the diagram above.

(265-269):

In terms of height, we have :
$B < F, C < F, C < D, E < D. F < E. A < E, F < A.$
So, $C < F < E < D, B < F, F < A < E$
Thus, the sequence becomes :
$B < C < F < A < E < D$
or, $C < B < F < A < E < D.$
In terms of weight, we have :
$A < B, A < C, B < D, D < F.$
So, $A < B < D < F, A < C.$
Thus, the sequence becomes :
$A < C < B < D < F$
or, $A < B < C < D < F$
or, $A < B < D < C < F$

265. 3; Clearly, D is the tallest
266. 1; The descending order of height is:
$D > E > A > F > B > C$
or, $D > E > A > F > C > B.$
Clearly. A is third from the top.
267. 4; Clearly, F, B and C are shorter than A.
268. 5; Data is inadequate as no clue regarding E's weight is given.
269. 3; Clearly, F is heavier than B and C but shorter than D.

(270- 274): B is organised on Tuesday. Now. D is followed by the day with no lecture. D cannot be organised on Friday because then E will be on Tuesday (there is a gap of two days between D and E). It cannot be organised on Thursday (because then, there will be no lecture on Friday). B cannot be followed by D. So. D will be organised on Sunday and E on Wednesday. No lecture will be organised on Monday. A cannot be organised on Thursday. So. A wil l be organised on Saturday. F and C wil l be organised on Thursday and Friday respectively.
So, the correct order is:

Sunday	Monday	Tuesday	Wednesday	Thursday	Friday	Saturday
D	X	B	E	F	C	A

270. 1; There is no lecture on Monday.
271. 3; Three lectures are organised between C and D — B, E and F.
272. 1; F is organised on Thursday.
273. 1; A is the last lecture.
274. 5; All the given statements are required.

(275-279): It can be solved like the previous question.

Monday	Tuesday	Wednesday	Thursday	Friday	Saturday	Sunday
Group Discussion	X	Quality Circle	Leadership	Decision Making	Assessment Centre	Motivation

275. 5; The first lecture is on Group Discussion and the last one is on Motivation.

276. 3; Three lectures are organised between Motivation and Quality Circle — Assessment' Centre, Decision Making and Leadership.

277. 5; The lecture on Leadership is on Thursday.

278. 3; There is no lecture on Tuesday.

279. 5; Al l the given informations are required.

(280-284):

280. 1; If A is selected, S has to be selected.
If B is selected, R cannot be selected
If D is selected, Q cannot be selected.
So. A D S Q R and B D S R Q are wrong. C E S P Q is not possible because S has to be accompanied with A

281. 4; If R is selected, P cannot be selected. So, P S A D is wrong.
D and Q cannot go together. So Q S A D is wrong. S and A hav e to be together. So, Q S C E is wrong.

282. 3; If D is selected. Q cannot be selected. So, P Q B C and P Q C E are not correct.
S and A hav e to be together. So, P S C E is also wrong.

283. 4; If A and C are members, S and E have also to be selected. So, P Q E is not the correct combination.

284. 1; P and R cannot be together. So. R S A D is wrong.
S and A have to be together. So, Q S B D and Q S C E are incorrect.

(285-289):

One couple is QP.
Now, R and U are the children of T. So. the other couple is TS.
T ia a teacher
S is a female doctor.
Q is a lawyer
Clearly. P is a housewife and hence a female.
S is the mother of R and U.
P has one son and one grandson.
Clearly, T is the son of P and R or U is the grandson.
The grandson is a male engineer and the grand-daughter is a student.

285. 4; P is the grandmother of R.

286. 5; P is the housewife.
287. 3; R may be the brother or sister of U.
288. 4; Since the sex of R and U is not given, so the set of three females cannot be determined.
289. 2; The grand-daughter is a student.

(290-294):

B and F are children of D.

A is grandmother of F. So. B and F represent third generation.

Now, C is the daughter-in-law of E. So, A and E form a couple and represent first generation. A, being grandmother, is a female and so E is a male.

C is the daughter-in-law of E and so D is E's son. Thus, CD is the other couple and represents second generation.

C likes black, B likes pink. Green and yellow are the preferences of a couple. So, A likes yellow and E likes green. Now, F does not like red. So. F likes white and D likes red.

Now. F likes white and so cannot be a lady. B is the son of D and hence a male.

290. 2; A prefers yellow colour.
291. 3; There are four male members — E, D, B, F.
292. 1; Both F and B are males and both are children of D. So, F is the brother of B.
293. 4; Yellow-Green is the colour combination of the couple AE.
294. 2; AE and CD are two couples.

(295-299): Analysis of given facts can be done as follows:

Two are hill stations.

Three are plains of which two are harbours.

Four towns are capitals. Two towns are industrial.

Two towns have population less than 5 lacs. One town has population 20 lacs.

Two towns have population more than 50 lacs. Two towns are on same latitudes.

B is a hill station. E is a harbour. Clearly, A which has the same longitude as E, cannot be a harbour and clearly, D having population 20 lacs cannot be an industrial town. So, it is a harbour. Thus, E and D are harbours.

Clearly, one harbour is industrial town but D is not. So. E is an industrial town with population more than 50 lacs.

Clearly, longitudes of a hill station and industrial town are same. So, A having same longitude as E, is a hill station.

Latitudes of D and C are same and D is a harbour. So, C cannot be a hill station. So, B is the other hill station

Thus, three plains are C, D, E. One industrial town is neither a hill station nor a harbour. So, C is an industrial town with population more than 50 lacs. Clearly, both harbours are capitals. So. E and D are capitals. The hill station A, having same longitude as a harbour, is also a capital. Population of D is 20 lacs. So, population of A and B is less than 5 lacs. Clearly, only one hill station is capital. So, C is the other capital.

295. 3; Clearly, population of A and B is less than 5 lacs.

296. 5; Clearly, B is not a capital.

297. 4; Harbours are E an«. D, capitals are A, C, D and E and industrial towns are C and E. So, E is harbour, capital and industrial town.

298. 3; Clearly, the industrial towns C and E have a population of more than 50 lacs.

299. 5; The capitals are A, C, D and E. The hill stations are A and B. So, A is a hill station as well as a capital.

(300-304): Analysis of given facts can be done as follows:

Point 1: A and E are good in studies; C is poor in studies. The remaining two i.e. B and D are average in studies.

Point 2: A comes from a rich family; E belongs to a poor family. Now. B and D are average in studies. So, B and D come from middle-class families. Now, C remains. So, C belongs to a poor family (because two boys come from poor families).

Point 3: The students who are poor and average in studies are in under-graduate classes i.e. B, C and D.

Point 4: The remaining two i.e. A and E study post-graduate classes.

Point 5: B, C and E are industrious. A is not industrious. Now, two boys are not industrious. So, D is also not industrious.

Point 6: Two boys interested in acting are not industrious So, A and D are interested in acting. The boy interested in music comes from middle-class family. B and D come from middle-class families. But D is interested in acting. So, B is interested in music. E is not interested in any activity. Clearly, C is interested in sports.

300. 3; C is interested in sports.

301. 2; B is interested in music.

302. 4; D is the middle-class family boy interested in acting.

303. 2; A and E study in post-graduate classes.

304. 4; D is not industrious and is average in studies.